T0191642

# Lecture Notes in Computer Science　　9028

*Commenced Publication in 1973*
Founding and Former Series Editors:
Gerhard Goos, Juris Hartmanis, and Jan van Leeuwen

More information about this series at http://www.springer.com/series/7407

Antonio M. Mora
Giovanni Squillero et al. (Eds.)

# Applications of Evolutionary Computation

18th European Conference, EvoApplications 2015
Copenhagen, Denmark, April 8–10, 2015
Proceedings

 Springer

*Editors*

see next page

ISSN 0302-9743 ISSN 1611-3349 (electronic)
Lecture Notes in Computer Science
ISBN 978-3-319-16548-6 ISBN 978-3-319-16549-3 (eBook)
DOI 10.1007/978-3-319-16549-3

Library of Congress Control Number: 2015933503

LNCS Sublibrary: SL1 – Theoretical Computer Science and General Issues

Springer Cham Heidelberg New York Dordrecht London

Cover illustration: Designed by Mauro Castelli, ISEGI, Universidade Nova de Lisboa, Portugal

Printed on acid-free paper

Springer International Publishing AG Switzerland is part of Springer Science+Business Media
(www.springer.com)

# Volume Editors

Antonio M. Mora
Universidad de Granada, Spain
amorag@geneura.ugr.es

Giovanni Squillero
Politecnico di Torino, Italy
giovanni.squillero@polito.it

Alexandros Agapitos
University College Dublin, Ireland
alexandros.agapitos@ucd.ie

Paolo Burelli
Aalborg University Copenhagen, Denmark
pabu@create.aau.dk

William S. Bush
Case Western Reserve, USA
wsb36@case.edu

Stefano Cagnoni
University of Parma, Italy
cagnoni@ce.unipr.it

Carlos Cotta
Universidad de Málaga, Spain
ccottap@lcc.uma.es

Ivanoe De Falco
ICAR/CNR, Italy
ivanoe.defalco@na.icar.cnr.it

Antonio Della Cioppa
University of Salerno, Italy
adellacioppa@unisa.it

Federico Divina
Universidad Pablo de Olavide, Sevilla, Spain
fdivina@upo.es

A.E. Eiben
VU University Amsterdam, The Netherlands
a.e.eiben@vu.nl

Anna I. Esparcia-Alcázar
S2 Grupo, Spain
aesparcia@s2grupo.es

Francisco Fernández de Vega
University of Extremadura, Spain
fcofdez@unex.es

Kyrre Glette
University of Oslo, Norway
kyrrehg@ifi.uio.no

Evert Haasdijk
VU University Amsterdam, The Netherlands
e.haasdijk@vu.nl

J. Ignacio Hidalgo
Universidad Complutense de Madrid, Spain
hidalgo@ucm.es

Michael Kampouridis
University of Kent, UK
m.kampouridis@kent.ac.uk

Paul Kaufmann
University of Paderborn, Germany
paul.kaufmann@gmail.com

Michalis Mavrovouniotis
De Monfort University, UK
Mmavrovouniotis@dmu.ac.uk

Trung Thanh Nguyen
Liverpool John Moores University, UK
T.T.Nguyen@ljmu.ac.uk

Robert Schaefer
AGH University of Science and Technology, Poland
schaefer@agh.edu.pl

Kevin Sim
Edinburgh Napier University, UK
k.sim@napier.ac.uk

Ernesto Tarantino
ICAR/CNR, Italy
ernesto.tarantino@na.icar.cnr.it

Neil Urquhart
Edinburgh Napier University, UK
n.urquhart@napier.ac.uk

Mengjie Zhang
Victoria University of Wellington, New Zealand
mengjie.zhang@ecs.vuw.ac.nz

# Preface

Evolutionary Computation (EC) is composed of a set of metaheuristics inspired by Darwin's Theory of natural evolution. These methods apply mechanisms based on the principles of genetics and selection, in order to solve, mainly, search, optimization, and machine learning problems. It is a very active research field, with several branches and subfields, and in which an increasing number of researchers and professionals are working.

This book presents a careful selection of state-of-the-art papers, sharing the application of EC approaches to several different problems. Its aim is to inspire other researchers to design and develop their own methods for problem solving.

All the papers in this volume were presented during EvoApplications 2015, which includes a set of different and complementary tracks on application-oriented aspects of EC. This conference was initially baptized as EvoWorkshops in 1998, and during these 18 years it has provided an excellent opportunity for EC researchers to meet and discuss different ways of application of EC to a variety of domains.

EvoApplications is a part of Evo* (EvoSTAR), Europe's premier colocated event in the field of evolutionary computing. Evo* 2015 was held during April 8–10 in the beautiful city of Copenhagen, Denmark. This event included, in addition to EvoApplications: EuroGP, the main European event dedicated to genetic programming; EvoCOP, the main European conference on evolutionary computation in combinatorial optimization and EvoMUSART, the main International Conference on Evolutionary and Biologically Inspired Music, Sound, Art, and Design.

The proceedings for all of these events in their 2015 (and previous) editions are also available in the LNCS series.

EvoApplications 2015 consisted of the following individual tracks:

- *EvoBIO*, track on EC and related techniques in bioinformatics and computational biology, which brings together experts across multiple fields, who draw inspiration from biological systems in order to produce solutions to complex biological problems.
- *EvoCOMNET*, track on nature-inspired techniques for telecommunication networks and other parallel and distributed systems. It addresses the application of EC techniques to problems in distributed and connected systems such as telecommunication and computer networks, distribution and logistics networks, interpersonal and interorganizational networks, etc. To address the challenges of these systems, this track promotes the study and the application of strategies inspired by the observation of biological and evolutionary processes that usually show the highly desirable characteristics of being distributed, adaptive, scalable, and robust.
- *EvoCOMPLEX*, track on evolutionary algorithms and complex systems. It covers all aspects of the interaction of evolutionary algorithms (and metaheuristics in general) with complex systems. Complex systems are ubiquitous in physics, economics, sociology, biology, computer science, and many other scientific areas. Typically, a

complex system is composed of smaller aggregated components, whose interaction and interconnectedness are nontrivial. This leads to emergent properties of the system, not anticipated by its isolated components. Furthermore, when the system behavior is studied from a temporal perspective, self-organization patterns typically arise.

- *EvoENERGY*, track on EC in energy applications, which is intended as a platform for new, innovative computational intelligence, and nature-inspired techniques in the domain of energy-related optimization research. It seeks for contributions ranging from new control concepts for decentralized generation, strategies for their coordination in the network to the morphological optimization of distributed generators.
- *EvoFIN*, track on evolutionary and natural computation in finance and economics. This is the only European event specifically dedicated to the applications of EC, and related natural computing methodologies, to finance and economics. Financial environments are typically hard, being dynamic, high-dimensional, noisy, and coevolutionary. These environments serve as an interesting test bed for novel evolutionary methodologies.
- *EvoGAMES*, track on bio-inspired algorithms in games. It aims to focus the scientific developments in computational intelligence techniques that may be of practical value for utilization in existing or future games. Recently, games, and especially video games, have become an important commercial factor within the software industry, providing an excellent test bed for application of a wide range of computational intelligence methods.
- *EvoIASP*, track on EC in image analysis signal processing and pattern recognition. This is the longest-running of all EvoApplication tracks which celebrates its 16th edition this year. It has been the first international event solely dedicated to the applications of EC to image analysis and signal processing in complex domains of high industrial and social relevance.
- *EvoINDUSTRY*, track on nature-inspired techniques in industrial settings, i.e., it seeks contributions from researchers, developers, and industrialists who have utilized EC within an industrial context.
- *EvoNUM*, track on bio-inspired algorithms for continuous parameter optimization. It aims at applications of bio-inspired algorithms, and cross-fertilization between these and more classical numerical optimization algorithms, to continuous optimization problems. It deals with applications where continuous parameters or functions have to be optimized, in fields such as control, chemistry, agriculture, electricity, building and construction, energy, aerospace engineering, and design optimization.
- *EvoPAR*, track on parallel implementation of evolutionary algorithms. It covers all aspects of the application of parallel and distributed systems to EC as well as the application of evolutionary algorithms for improving parallel architectures and distributed computing infrastructures. EvoPAR focuses on the application and improvement of distributed infrastructures, such as grid and cloud computing, peer-to-peer (P2P) system, as well as parallel architectures, GPUs, manycores, etc., in cooperation with evolutionary algorithms.
- *EvoRISK*, track on computational intelligence for risk management, security, and defense applications. This track focuses on challenging problems in risk management, security, and defense, and covers both theoretical developments and

applications of computational intelligence to subjects such as cyber crime, IT security, resilient and self-healing systems, risk management, critical infrastructure protection (CIP), military, counter terrorism and other defense-related aspects, disaster relief, and humanitarian logistics.

- *EvoROBOT*, track on EC in robotics. It focuses on evolutionary robotics: the application of evolutionary computation techniques to automatically design the controllers and/or hardware of autonomous robots, real or simulated, which is a multifaceted field that combines approaches from other fields such as neuro-evolution, evolutionary design, artificial life, or robotics.
- *EvoSTOC*, track on evolutionary algorithms in stochastic and dynamic environments. It addresses the application of EC in stochastic and dynamic environments. This includes optimization problems with changing, noisy, and/or approximated fitness functions and optimization problems that require robust solutions, providing the first platform to present and discuss the latest research in this field.
- And finally, a General track including those papers dealing with applications not covered by any of the established tracks.

EvoApplications 2015 had 125 submissions, with 52 papers accepted for oral presentation and 21 for poster presentation, but having both types of contributions the same length in the proceedings. These figures correspond to a low acceptance rate of 58.4 %, which is an indicator of the high quality of the articles presented at the conference.

Many people helped to make EvoApplications 2015 a success. We would like to thank first the authors for submitting their work, to the members of the Program Committees for devoting their energy to reviewing those papers, and to the audience for their participation.

We would also like to thank the Institute for Informatics and Digital Innovation at Edinburgh Napier University, UK, for their coordination efforts, especially to Jennifer Willies for her invaluable work and support to organize the Evo* event along these years.

We are sincerely grateful to Marc Schoenauer of Inria, France, for his great assistance in providing, hosting, and managing the submission, reviewing, and selecting system, MyReview.

We would like to thank the Local Organizers: Paolo Burelli (Aalborg University Copenhagen) and Sebastian Risi (IT University of Copenhagen), and to the National Museum of Denmark at Copenhagen as the venue.

We thank Pablo García Sánchez from Universidad de Granada, Spain for creating and maintaining the official Evo* 2015 website, and Mauro Castelli from Universidade Nova de Lisboa, Portugal for handling Evo* 2015 publicity.

Finally, we would also like to express our sincerest gratitude to our invited speakers, who gave the inspiring keynote talks: Pierre-Yves Oudeyer, Research Director at Inria Paris, and Paulien Hogeweg of Utrecht University at The Netherlands.

April 2015                                                                Antonio M. Mora
                                                                      Giovanni Squillero

# Organization

## EvoApplications Chair

Antonio M. Mora        Universidad de Granada, Spain

## Proceedings Chair

Giovanni Squillero        Politecnico di Torino, Italy

## Local Chairs

Paolo Burelli        Aalborg University Copenhagen, Denmark
Sebastian Risi        IT University of Copenhagen, Denmark

## Website and Publicity

Mauro Castelli        ISEGI, Universidade Nova de Lisboa, Portugal
Pablo García Sánchez        Universidad de Granada, Spain

## EvoBIO Chairs

William S. Bush        Case Western Reserve, USA
Federico Divina        Universidad Pablo de Olavide, Spain

## EvoCOMNET Chairs

Ivanoe De Falco        ICAR/CNR, Italy
Antonio Della Cioppa        University of Salerno, Italy
Ernesto Tarantino        ICAR/CNR, Italy

## EvoCOMPLEX Chairs

Carlos Cotta        Universidad de Málaga, Spain
Robert Schaefer        AGH University of Science and Technology, Poland

## EvoENERGY Chairs

Paul Kaufmann        University of Paderborn, UK
Kyrre Glette        University of Oslo, Norway

## EvoFIN Chairs

Alexandros Agapitos                    University College Dublin, Ireland
Michael Kampouridis                    University of Kent, UK

## EvoGAMES Chairs

Paolo Burelli                          Aalborg University Copenhagen, Denmark
Antonio M. Mora                        Universidad de Granada, Spain

## EvoIASP Chairs

Stefano Cagnoni                        University of Parma, Italy
Mengjie Zhang                          Victoria University of Wellington, New Zealand

## EvoINDUSTRY Chairs

Neil Urquhart                          Edinburgh Napier University, UK
Kevin Sim                              Edinburgh Napier University, UK

## EvoNUM Chair

Anna I Esparcia-Alcázar                S2 Grupo, Spain

## EvoPAR Chairs

Francisco Fernández de Vega            Universidad de Extremadura, Spain
J. Ignacio Hidalgo                     Universidad Complutense de Madrid, Spain

## EvoRISK Chair

Anna I Esparcia-Alcázar                S2 Grupo, Spain

## EvoROBOT Chairs

Evert Haasdijk                         VU University Amsterdam, The Netherlands
A.E. Eiben                             VU University Amsterdam, The Netherlands

## EvoSTOC Chairs

Trung Thanh Nguyen                     Liverpool John Moores University, UK
Michalis Mavrovouniotis                De Monfort University, UK

## Sponsoring Organizations

Institute for Informatics and Digital Innovation at Edinburgh Napier University, UK
National Museum of Denmark at Copenhagen
The World Federation on Soft Computing

## Invited Speakers

| | |
|---|---|
| Paulien Hogeweg | Utrecht University, The Netherlands |
| Pierre-Yves Oudeyer | Inria Paris, France |

## MyReview Conference Management System

| | |
|---|---|
| Marc Schoenauer | Inria Saclay - Île-de-France, France |

## Program Committees

### EvoBIO

| | |
|---|---|
| Jitesh Dundas | Edencore Technologies, Indian Institue of Technology, Mumbai, India |
| Florentino Fernández | University of Vigo, Spain |
| Alex Freitas | University of Kent, UK |
| Mario Giacobini | Universitá di Torino, Italy |
| Rosalba Giugno | University of Catania, Italy |
| Casey Greene | Dartmouth College, USA |
| Jin-Kao Hao | University of Angers, France |
| Timothy J. Hohman | Vanderbilt University, USA |
| Ting Hu | Dartmouth College, USA |
| Penousal Machado | University of Coimbra, Portugal |
| Vincent Moulton | University of East Anglia, UK |
| Carlotta Orsenigo | Politecnico di Milano, Italy |
| Michael Raymer | Wright State University, USA |
| Stephen Turner | University of Virginia, USA |
| Leonardo Vanneschi | Universidade Nova de Lisboa, Portugal |

### EvoCOMNET

| | |
|---|---|
| Mehmet E. Aydin | University of Bedfordshire, UK |
| Luca Gambardella | IDSIA, Switzerland |
| Rolf Hoffmann | Technical University Darmstadt, Germany |
| Graham Kendall | University of Nottingham, UK |
| Farrukh Aslam Khan | National University of Computer & Emerging Sciences, Pakistan |
| Kenji Leibnitz | National Institute of Information and Communications Technology, Japan |

| Manuel Lozano Márquez | University of Granada, Spain |
| Domenico Maisto | ICAR-CNR, Italy |
| Davide Marocco | University of Plymouth, UK |
| Roberto Montemanni | IDSIA, Switzerland |
| Enrico Natalizio | Université de Technologie de Compiègne, France |
| Chien-Chung Shen | University of Delaware, USA |
| Robert Schaefer | University of Science and Technology, Poland |
| Sevil Sen | Hacettepe University, Turkey |
| Georgios Sirakoulis | Democritus University of Thrace, Greece |
| Pawel Topa | AGH University of Science and Technology, Poland |
| Umut Tosun | Baskent University, Turkey |
| Jaroslaw Was | AGH University of Science and Technology, Poland |
| Lidia Yamamoto | University of Strasbourg, France |
| Nur Zincir-Heywood | Dalhousie University, Canada |

## EvoCOMPLEX

| Jhon Edgar Amaya | Universidad Nacional Experimental del Táchira, Venezuela |
| Anca Andreica | Universitatea Babes-Bolyai, Romania |
| Tiago Baptista | Universidade de Coimbra, Portugal |
| Antonio Córdoba | Universidad de Sevilla, Spain |
| Carlos Fernandes | Technical University of Lisbon, Portugal |
| José Enrique Gallardo | Universidad de Málaga, Spain |
| Carlos Gersherson | Universidad Nacional Autónoma de México, Mexico |
| Evert Haasdijk | Vrije Universiteit Amsterdam, The Netherlands |
| Juan Luis Jiménez Laredo | Université du Havre, France |
| Iwona Karcz-Duleba | Wrocław University of Technology, Poland |
| Raúl Lara Cabrera | Universidad de Málaga, Spain |
| Gabriel Luque | Universidad de Málaga, Spain |
| Juan Julián Merelo | Universidad de Granada, Spain |
| Antonio Nebro | Universidad de Málaga, Spain |
| Maciej Smolka | AGH University of Science and Technology, Poland |
| Giovanni Squillero | Politecnico di Torino, Italy |
| Marco Tomassini | Université de Lausanne, Switzerland |
| Alberto Tonda | Inria, France |

## EvoENERGY

| Konrad Diwold | Siemens, Vienna, Austria |
| Ralph Evins | Laboratory of Building Science and Technology, Empa, Switzerland |
| Oliver Kramer | University of Oldenburg, Germany |

Chenjie Ma                          Fraunhofer Institute for Wind and Energy System
                                    Technology, Kassel, Germany
Ingo Mauser                         FZI Karlsruhe, Germany
Martin Middendorf                   University of Leipzig, Germany
Maizura Mokhtar                     University of Sheffield, UK
Sanaz Mostaghim                     University of Magdeburg, Germany
Frank Neumann                       University of Adelaide, Australia
Peter Palensky                      Technical University of Delft, The Netherlands
Cong Shen                           University of Kassel, Germany
Bernhard Sick                       University of Kassel, Germany
Andy Tyrrell                        University of York, UK
Markus Wagner                       University of Adelaide, Australia

## EvoFIN

Alex Agapitos                       University College Dublin, Ireland
Eva Alfaro                          Technical University of Valencia, Spain
Anthony Brabazon                    University College Dublin, Ireland
Shu-Heng Chen                       National Chengchi University, Taiwan
Wei Cui                             University College Dublin, Ireland
Malcolm Heywood                     Dalhousie University, Canada
Ronald Hochreiter                   University of Vienna, Austria
Michael Kampouridis                 University of Kent, UK
Ahmed Kattan                        Umm Al-Qura University, Saudi Arabia
Piotr Lipinski                      University of Wroclaw, Poland
Michael Mayo                        University of Waikato, New Zealand
Krzysztof Michalak                  University of Economics, Wroclaw, Poland
Michael O'Neill                     University College Dublin, Ireland
Andrea Tettamanzi                   University of Nice Sophia Antipolis, France
Ruppa Thulasiram                    University of Manitoba, Canada

## EvoGAMES

David Camacho                       Universidad Autónoma de Madrid, Spain
Francisco Luis Gutiérrez Vela       Universidad de Granada, Spain
Antonio J. Fernández Leiva          Universidad de Málaga, Spain
Pablo García Sánchez                Universidad de Granada, Spain
Federico Liberatore                 Invited Researcher at Universidad de Granada,
                                    Spain
Juan Julián Merelo Guervós          Universidad de Granada, Spain
Krzysztof Krawiec                   Poznan University of Technology, Poland
Patricia Paderewski Rodríguez       Universidad de Granada, Spain
Simon Lucas                         University of Essex, UK
Antonio J. Fernández-Ares           Universidad de Granada, Spain
Erin Hastings                       University of Central Florida, USA
Moshe Sipper                        Ben-Gurion University, Israel
Georgios N. Yannakakis              University of Malta, Malta

| Philip Hingston | Edith Cowan University, Australia |
| Antonio González Pardo | Universidad Autonóma de Madrid, Spain |
| Penousal Machado | Universidade de Coimbra, Portugal |
| Rodica Ioana Lung | Universitatea Babes-Bolyai, Romania |
| Julian Togelius | IT-Universitetet i København, Denmark |
| Tommaso Urli | NICTA's Canberra Research Lab, Australia |
| Mike Preuss | University of Münster, Germany |
| Noor Shaker | IT-Universitetet i København, Denmark |
| Antonios Liapis | University of Malta, Malta |
| Hector P. Martínez | University of Malta, Malta |
| Johan Hagelbäck | Blekinge Tekniska Högskola, Sweden |
| Tobias Mahlmann | IT-Universitetet i København, Denmark |
| Francisco Fernández de Vega | Universidad de Extremadura, Spain |

## EvoIASP

| Lucia Ballerini | University of Dundee, UK |
| Vitoantonio Bevilacqua | Politecnico di Bari, Italy |
| Leonardo Bocchi | University of Florence, Italy |
| Sergio Damas | European Center for Soft Computing, Spain |
| Fabio Daolio | Shinshu University, Japan |
| Ivanoe De Falco | ICAR - CNR, Italy |
| Antonio Della Cioppa | University of Salerno, Italy |
| Laura Dipietro | Cambridge, USA |
| Marc Ebner | Ernst Moritz Arndt University, Greifswald, Germany |
| Francesco Fontanella | University of Cassino, Italy |
| Mario Koeppen | Kyushu Institute of Technology, Japan |
| Josep Llados | Universitat Autonoma de Barcelona, Spain |
| Jean Louchet | Inria, France |
| Evelyne Lutton | Inria, France |
| Simone Marinai | University of Florence, Italy |
| Pablo Mesejo Santiago | Inria, France |
| Youssef Nashed | Argonne National Laboratory, USA |
| Ferrante Neri | De Monfort University, UK |
| Gustavo Olague | CICESE, Mexico |
| Riccardo Poli | University of Essex, UK |
| Sara Silva | INESC-ID Lisbon, Portugal |
| Stephen Smith | University of York, UK |
| Giovanni Squillero | Politecnico di Torino, Italy |
| Roberto Ugolotti | Henesis srl, Italy |
| Leonardo Vanneschi | Universidade Nova de Lisboa, Portugal |

## EvoINDUSTRY

| Nelishia Pillay | University of KwaZulu-Natal, South Africa |
| Shengxiang Yang | De Monfort University, UK |

| | |
|---|---|
| Sanja Petrovic | University of Nottingham, UK |
| Ender Ozcan | University of Nottingham, UK |
| Sanem Sariel | Istanbul Technical University, Turkey |
| Emma Hart | Edinburgh Napier University, UK |
| Graham Kendall | University of Nottingham, UK |
| Jason Atkin | University of Nottingham, UK |
| Nysret Musliu | Vienna University of Technology, Austria |
| Bahriye Basturk Akay | Erciyes University, Turkey |
| María Arsuaga-Ríos | CERN, Switzerland |
| Nadarajen Veerapen | University of Stirling, UK |
| Ben Paechter | Edinburgh Napier University, UK |

## EvoNUM

| | |
|---|---|
| Anne Auger | Inria, France |
| Hans-Georg Beyer | Vorarlberg University of Applied Sciences, Austria |
| Ying-ping Chen | National Chiao Tung University, Taiwan |
| Salma Mesmoudi | Institut des Systèmes Complexes, France |
| Boris Naujoks | Cologne University of Applied Sciences, Germany |
| Petr Pošík | Czech Technical University in Prague, Czech Republic |
| Mike Preuss | University of Münster, Germany |
| Ivo Fabian Sbalzarini | Max Planck Institute of Molecular Cell Biology and Genetics, Germany |
| Guenter Rudolph | University of Dortmund, Germany |
| Marc Schoenauer | Inria, France |
| Olivier Teytaud | Inria, France |
| Ke Tang | University of Science and Technology of China, China |

## EvoPAR

| | |
|---|---|
| Ignacio Arnaldo | Massachusetts Institute of Technology, USA |
| Gianluigi Folino | L'ICAR-CNR, Cosenza, Italy |
| José Carlos Ribeiro | Politechnique Institute of Leiria, Portugal |
| Garnett Wilson | Afinin Labs Inc., Canada |
| Malcolm Heywood | Dalhousie University, Canada |
| Juan Luís Jiménez Laredo | Université du Havre, France |
| William B. Langdon | University College London, UK |
| Francisco Luna | Universidad de Extremadura, Spain |
| Marco Tomassini | University of Lausanne, Switzerland |
| Jose Manuel Colmenar | Universidad Complutense de Madrid, Spain |

## EvoRISK

| | |
|---|---|
| Robert K. Abercrombie | Oak Ridge National Laboratory, USA |
| Rami Abielmona | University of Ottawa, Canada |
| Nabendu Chaki | University of Calcutta, India |

| | |
|---|---|
| Mario Cococcioni | NATO Undersea Research Centre, Italy |
| Josep Domingo-Ferrer | Rovira i Virgili University, Spain |
| Stenio Fernandes | Federal University of Pernambuco (UFPE), Brazil |
| Frank W. Moore | University of Alaska Anchorage, USA |
| Javier Montero | Universidad Complutense de Madrid, Spain |
| Pamela Nolz | Austrian Institute of Technology (AIT), Austria |
| Kay Chen Tan | National University of Singapore, Singapore |
| Vicenç Torra | University of Skövde, Sweden |
| Antonio Villalón | S2 Grupo, Spain |
| Nur Zincir-Heywood | Dalhousie University, Canada |

## EvoROBOT

| | |
|---|---|
| Nicolas Bredeche | Institut des Systèmes Intelligents et de Robotique, France |
| Anders Christensen | University Institute of Lisbon, ISCTE-IUL, Portugal |
| Stéphane Doncieux | Institut des Systèmes Intelligents et de Robotique, France |
| Marco Dorigo | Université Libre de Bruxelles, Belgium |
| Gusz Eiben | Vrije Universiteit Amsterdam, The Netherlands |
| Evert Haasdijk | Vrije Universiteit Amsterdam, The Netherlands |
| Heiko Hamann | University of Paderborn, Germany |
| Jacqueline Heinerman | Vrije Universiteit Amsterdam, The Netherlands |
| Joost Huizinga | University of Wyoming, USA |
| Giorgos Karafotias | Vrije Universiteit Amsterdam, The Netherlands |
| Jean-Marc Montanier | Barcelona Supercomputing Center, Spain |
| Jean-Baptiste Mouret | Institut des Systèmes Intelligents et de Robotique, France |
| Stefano Nolfi | Institute of Cognitive Sciences and Technologies, Italy |
| Abraham Prieto | Universidade da Coruña, Spain |
| Claudio Rossi | Universidad Politécnica de Madrid, Spain |
| Sanem Sariel | İstanbul Teknik Üniversitesi, Turkey |
| Thomas Schmickl | Karl-Franzens-Universität Graz, Austria |
| Luís Simoẽs | Vrije Universiteit Amsterdam, The Netherlands |
| Kasper Stoy | IT University of Copenhagen, Denmark |
| Jürgen Stradner | Karl-Franzens-Universität Graz, Austria |
| Jon Timmis | University of York, UK |
| Andy Tyrrell | University of York, UK |
| Alan Winfield | University of the West of England, UK |

## EvoSTOC

| | |
|---|---|
| Peter A.N. Bosman | Centre for Mathematics and Computer Science, The Netherlands |
| Juergen Branke | University of Warwick, UK |

# Contents

**EvoBIO**

Heat Map Based Feature Selection: A Case Study for Ovarian Cancer . . . . .    3
   *Carlos Huertas and Reyes Juárez-Ramírez*

A Novel Multi-objectivisation Approach for Optimising the Protein Inverse
Folding Problem . . . . . . . . . . . . . . . . . . . . . . . . . . . . . . . . . . .   14
   *Sune S. Nielsen, Grégoire Danoy, Wiktor Jurkowski,*
   *Juan Luis Jiménez Laredo, Reinhard Schneider, El-Ghazali Talbi,*
   *and Pascal Bouvry*

**EvoCOMNET**

Black Holes and Revelations: Using Evolutionary Algorithms
to Uncover Vulnerabilities in Disruption-Tolerant Networks . . . . . . . . . . . .   29
   *Doina Bucur, Giovanni Iacca, Giovanni Squillero, and Alberto Tonda*

A Novel Grouping Genetic Algorithm for Assigning Resources to Users
in WCDMA Networks . . . . . . . . . . . . . . . . . . . . . . . . . . . . . . . .   42
   *L. Cuadra, S. Salcedo-Sanz, A.D. Carnicer, M.A. Del Arco,*
   *and J.A. Portilla-Figueras*

Combining Ensemble of Classifiers by Using Genetic Programming
for Cyber Security Applications . . . . . . . . . . . . . . . . . . . . . . . . . . .   54
   *Gianluigi Folino and Francesco Sergio Pisani*

A Fast FPGA-Based Classification of Application Protocols Optimized
Using Cartesian GP . . . . . . . . . . . . . . . . . . . . . . . . . . . . . . . . .   67
   *David Grochol, Lukas Sekanina, Martin Zadnik, and Jan Korenek*

Parallel Extremal Optimization with Guided State Changes
Applied to Load Balancing . . . . . . . . . . . . . . . . . . . . . . . . . . . . . .   79
   *Ivanoe De Falco, Eryk Laskowski, Richard Olejnik, Umberto Scafuri,*
   *Ernesto Tarantino, and Marek Tudruj*

A Swarm Intelligence Approach to 3D Distance-Based Indoor
UWB Localization . . . . . . . . . . . . . . . . . . . . . . . . . . . . . . . . . .   91
   *Stefania Monica and Gianluigi Ferrari*

Studying the Geographical Cluster Paging with Delay Constraint
in Registration Areas with the Algorithm NSGAII . . . . . . . . . . . . . . . . . .  103
   *Víctor Berrocal-Plaza, Miguel A. Vega-Rodríguez, and Juan M. Sánchez-Pérez*

A Multiobjective Evolutionary Algorithm for Personalized Tours
in Street Networks . . . . . . . . . . . . . . . . . . . . . . . . . . . . . . . . . . . . . . .    115
  *Ivanoe De Falco, Umberto Scafuri, and Ernesto Tarantino*

Planning the Deployment of Indoor Wireless Sensor Networks
Through Multiobjective Evolutionary Techniques . . . . . . . . . . . . . . . . . . . .    128
  *Jose M. Lanza-Gutierrez, Juan A. Gomez-Pulido, S. Priem-Mendes,
  M. Ferreira, and J.S. Pereira*


**EvoCOMPLEX**

Hierarchic Genetic Search with α-Stable Mutation . . . . . . . . . . . . . . . . . . .    143
  *Adam K. Obuchowicz, Maciej Smołka, and Robert Schaefer*

Emergence of Cooperation in the Prisoner's Dilemma Driven by Conformity . . . .    155
  *Marco Alberto Javarone, Antonio Emanuele Atzeni, and Serge Galam*

An Experimental Evaluation of Multi-objective Evolutionary Algorithms
for Detecting Critical Nodes in Complex Networks . . . . . . . . . . . . . . . . . . .    164
  *Mario Ventresca, Kyle Robert Harrison, and Beatrice M. Ombuki-Berman*

Self-Balancing Multimemetic Algorithms in Dynamic Scale-Free Networks . . .    177
  *Rafael Nogueras and Carlos Cotta*

Investigating Fitness Measures for the Automatic Construction
of Graph Models. . . . . . . . . . . . . . . . . . . . . . . . . . . . . . . . . . . . . . . . .    189
  *Kyle Robert Harrison, Mario Ventresca, and Beatrice M. Ombuki-Berman*

Object Detection in Natural Images Using the Brain Programming Paradigm
with a Multi-objective Approach . . . . . . . . . . . . . . . . . . . . . . . . . . . . . . .    201
  *Eddie Clemente, Gustavo Olague, Daniel Hernández, José L. Briseño,
  and José Mercado*

Fair Resource Allocation Using Multi-population Evolutionary Algorithm . . .    214
  *Tohid Erfani and Rasool Erfani*


**EvoENERGY**

Multiobjective Methodology for Assessing the Location of Distributed
Electric Energy Storage . . . . . . . . . . . . . . . . . . . . . . . . . . . . . . . . . . . . .    227
  *José Gonçalves, Luís Neves, and António Gomes Martins*

Evolutionary Optimization of Smart Buildings with Interdependent Devices . . .    239
  *Ingo Mauser, Julian Feder, Jan Müller, and Hartmut Schmeck*

An Energy Management System Aggregator Based on an Integrated
Evolutionary and Differential Evolution Approach. . . . . . . . . . . . . . . . . . .   252
    *Andreia M. Carreiro, Carlos Oliveira, Carlos Henggeler Antunes,
    and Humberto M. Jorge*

## EvoFIN

Generating Directional Change Based Trading Strategies
with Genetic Programming. . . . . . . . . . . . . . . . . . . . . . . . . . . . . . . . . . . .   267
    *Jeremie Gypteau, Fernando E.B. Otero, and Michael Kampouridis*

An Evolutionary Optimization Approach to Risk Parity Portfolio Selection. . . .   279
    *Ronald Hochreiter*

Training Financial Decision Support Systems with Thousands of Decision
Rules Using Differential Evolution with Embedded
Dimensionality Reduction  . . . . . . . . . . . . . . . . . . . . . . . . . . . . . . . . . . . .   289
    *Piotr Lipinski*

## EvoGAMES

A Procedural Method for Automatic Generation of Spelunky Levels . . . . . . .   305
    *Walaa Baghdadi, Fawzya Shams Eddin, Rawan Al-Omari,
    Zeina Alhalawani, Mohammad Shaker, and Noor Shaker*

Evolving Random Forest for Preference Learning . . . . . . . . . . . . . . . . . . .   318
    *Mohamed Abou-Zleikha and Noor Shaker*

Procedural Personas as Critics for Dungeon Generation . . . . . . . . . . . . . . .   331
    *Antonios Liapis, Christoffer Holmgård, Georgios N. Yannakakis,
    and Julian Togelius*

Evolving Diverse Strategies Through Combined Phenotypic Novelty
and Objective Function Search . . . . . . . . . . . . . . . . . . . . . . . . . . . . . . . . .   344
    *Davy Smith, Laurissa Tokarchuk, and Chrisantha Fernando*

It's Time to Stop: A Comparison of Termination Conditions in the Evolution
of Game Bots. . . . . . . . . . . . . . . . . . . . . . . . . . . . . . . . . . . . . . . . . . . . . .   355
    *A. Fernández-Ares, P. García-Sánchez, Antonio M. Mora,
    Pedro A. Castillo, J.J. Merelo, María Isabel G. Arenas,
    and Gustavo Romero*

General Video Game Evaluation Using Relative Algorithm
Performance Profiles . . . . . . . . . . . . . . . . . . . . . . . . . . . . . . . . . . . . . . . .   369
    *Thorbjørn S. Nielsen, Gabriella A.B. Barros, Julian Togelius,
    and Mark J. Nelson*

A Progressive Approach to Content Generation. . . . . . . . . . . . . . . . . . . . .     381
*Mohammad Shaker, Noor Shaker, Julian Togelius,*
*and Mohamed Abou-Zleikha*

The Role of Behavioral Diversity and Difficulty of Opponents
in Coevolving Game-Playing Agents. . . . . . . . . . . . . . . . . . . . . . . . . . . .     394
*Marcin Szubert, Wojciech Jaśkowski, Paweł Liskowski,*
*and Krzysztof Krawiec*

PowerSurge: A Serious Game on Power Transmission Networks. . . . . . . . . .     406
*Sebastian von Mammen, Fabian Hertwig, Patrick Lehner,*
*and Florian Obermayer*

Collaborative Diffusion on the GPU for Path-Finding in Games . . . . . . . . . .     418
*Craig McMillan, Emma Hart, and Kevin Chalmers*

A Projection-Based Approach for Real-Time Assessment and Playability
Check for Physics-Based Games. . . . . . . . . . . . . . . . . . . . . . . . . . . . . . .     430
*Mohammad Shaker, Noor Shaker, Mohamed Abou-Zleikha,*
*and Julian Togelius*

How the World Was MADE: Parametrization of Evolved Agent-Based
Models for Backstory Generation . . . . . . . . . . . . . . . . . . . . . . . . . . . . .     443
*Rubén H. García-Ortega, Pablo García-Sánchez, J.J. Merelo,*
*María Isabel G. Arenas, Pedro A. Castillo, and Antonio M. Mora*

A Benchmark for Virtual Camera Control . . . . . . . . . . . . . . . . . . . . . . . .     455
*Paolo Burelli and Georgios N. Yannakakis*

## EvoIASP

Alternating Optimization of Unsupervised Regression
with Evolutionary Embeddings. . . . . . . . . . . . . . . . . . . . . . . . . . . . . . . .     471
*Daniel Lückehe and Oliver Kramer*

Hybrid Manifold Clustering with Evolutionary Tuning. . . . . . . . . . . . . . . . .     481
*Oliver Kramer*

A Supervised Figure-Ground Segmentation Method
Using Genetic Programming. . . . . . . . . . . . . . . . . . . . . . . . . . . . . . . . . .     491
*Yuyu Liang, Mengjie Zhang, and Will N. Browne*

A Multi-objective Evolutionary Algorithm for Interaction Systems
Based on Laser Pointers. . . . . . . . . . . . . . . . . . . . . . . . . . . . . . . . . . . . .     504
*Francisco Chávez, Eddie Clemente, Daniel E. Hernández,*
*Francisco Fernández de Vega, and Gustavo Olague*

Topology-Preserving Ordering of the RGB Space
with an Evolutionary Algorithm ............................... 517
  Francisco Flórez-Revuelta

Planar Surfaces Recognition in 3D Point Cloud Using a Real-Coded
Multistage Genetic Algorithm................................ 529
  Mosab Bazargani, Luís Mateus, and Maria Amélia R. Loja

Gaussian Transformation Based Representation in Particle Swarm
Optimisation for Feature Selection............................ 541
  Hoai Bach Nguyen, Bing Xue, Ivy Liu, Peter Andreae, and Mengjie Zhang

Genetic Programming with Alternative Search Drivers for Detection of
Retinal Blood Vessels ...................................... 554
  Krzysztof Krawiec and Mikołaj Pawlak

Analysis of Diversity Methods for Evolutionary Multi-objective
Ensemble Classifiers ....................................... 567
  Stefan Oehmcke, Justin Heinermann, and Oliver Kramer

Applying Non-dominated Sorting Genetic Algorithm II
to Multi-objective Optimization of a Weighted Multi-metric Distance
for Performing Data Mining Tasks ............................ 579
  Muhammad Marwan Muhammad Fuad

## EvoINDUSTRY

Many-Objective Optimization of a Hybrid Car Controller............... 593
  Tobias Rodemann, Kaname Narukawa, Michael Fischer,
  and Mohammed Awada

Optimising the Scheduling and Planning of Urban Milk Deliveries ........ 604
  Neil Urquhart

Multi-Noisy-Hard-Objective Robust Design of Balanced Surface Acoustic
Wave Filters Based on Prediction of Worst-Case Performance ........... 616
  Kiyoharu Tagawa and Shoichi Harada

Clustering Local Tourism Systems by Threshold Acceptance ............ 629
  Joseph Andria and Giacomo di Tollo

## EvoNUM

Seed Disperser Ant Algorithm: An Evolutionary Approach
for Optimization .......................................... 643
  Wen Liang Chang, Jeevan Kanesan, and Anand Jayant Kulkarni

Neuro-evolutionary Topology Optimization with Adaptive
Improvement Threshold . . . . . . . . . . . . . . . . . . . . . . . . . . . . . . . . . . . .     655
   *Nikola Aulig and Markus Olhofer*

Evaluating Reward Definitions for Parameter Control . . . . . . . . . . . . . . . .     667
   *Giorgos Karafotias, Mark Hoogendoorn, and A.E. Eiben*

Chromatic Selection – An Oversimplified Approach
to Multi-objective Optimization. . . . . . . . . . . . . . . . . . . . . . . . . . . . . . . .     681
   *Giovanni Squillero*

## EvoPAR

Parallel Cooperation for Large-Scale Multiobjective Optimization
on Feature Selection Problems . . . . . . . . . . . . . . . . . . . . . . . . . . . . . . . . .     693
   *Dragi Kimovski, Julio Ortega, Andrés Ortiz, and Raúl Baños*

Automatic Evolution of Parallel Sorting Programs on Multi-cores . . . . . . . . .     706
   *Gopinath Chennupati, R. Muhammad Atif Azad, and Conor Ryan*

## EvoRISK

Heuristics for the Design of Safe Humanitarian Aid Distribution
Itineraries. . . . . . . . . . . . . . . . . . . . . . . . . . . . . . . . . . . . . . . . . . . . . . . . .     721
   *José M. Ferrer, M. Teresa Ortuño, Gregorio Tirado,*
   *and Begoña Vitoriano*

Improving Maritime Awareness with Semantic Genetic Programming
and Linear Scaling: Prediction of Vessels Position Based on AIS Data . . . . .     732
   *Leonardo Vanneschi, Mauro Castelli, Ernesto Costa, Alessandro Re,*
   *Henrique Vaz, Victor Lobo, and Paulo Urbano*

Automatic Generation of Mobile Malwares Using Genetic Programming . . . .     745
   *Emre Aydogan and Sevil Sen*

## EvoROBOT

On the Tradeoff Between Hardware Protection and Optimization Success:
A Case Study in Onboard Evolutionary Robotics for Autonomous
Parallel Parking . . . . . . . . . . . . . . . . . . . . . . . . . . . . . . . . . . . . . . . . . . .     759
   *Mostafa Wahby and Heiko Hamann*

Real-World Reproduction of Evolved Robot Morphologies: Automated
Categorization and Evaluation. . . . . . . . . . . . . . . . . . . . . . . . . . . . . . . . . .     771
   *Eivind Samuelsen and Kyrre Glette*

Evolving Generalised Maze Solvers............................ 783
David Shorten and Geoff Nitschke

Evolving Robot Controllers for Structured Environments Through
Environment Decomposition................................. 795
Rodrigo Moreno, Andres Faiña, and Kasper Støy

Autonomous Learning of Procedural Knowledge in an Evolutionary
Cognitive Architecture for Robots........................... 807
Rodrigo Salgado, Francisco Bellas, and Richard J. Duro

Evolutionary Training of Robotised Architectural Elements ............ 819
Claudio Rossi, Pablo Gil, and William Coral

Evolving Controllers for Programmable Robots to Influence
Non-programmable Lifeforms: A Casy Study ...................... 831
Payam Zahadat and Thomas Schmickl

## EvoSTOC

Applying Ant Colony Optimization to Dynamic Binary-Encoded Problems ... 845
Michalis Mavrovouniotis and Shengxiang Yang

An Experimental Study of Combining Evolutionary Algorithms
with KD-Tree to Solving Dynamic Optimisation Problems.............. 857
Trung Thanh Nguyen, Ian Jenkinson, and Zaili Yang

Coevolutionary Intransitivity in Games: A Landscape Analysis........... 869
Hendrik Richter

Making IDEA-ARIMA Efficient in Dynamic Constrained
Optimization Problems.................................... 882
Patryk Filipiak and Piotr Lipinski

## General

A Concept for Real-Valued Multi-objective Landscape Analysis
Characterizing Two Biochemical Optimization Problems .............. 897
Susanne Rosenthal and Markus Borschbach

**Author Index** ...................................... 911

# EvoBIO

# Heat Map Based Feature Selection:
# A Case Study for Ovarian Cancer

Carlos Huertas[(✉)] and Reyes Juárez-Ramírez

Department of Computer Science, University of Baja California, Tijuana, Mexico
{chuertas, reyesjua}@uabc.edu.mx

**Abstract.** Public health is a critical issue, therefore we can find a great research interest to find faster and more accurate methods to detect diseases. In the particular case of cancer, the use of mass spectrometry data has become very popular but some problems arise due to that the number of mass-to-charge ratios exceed by a huge margin the number of patients in the samples. In order to deal with the high dimensionality of the data, most works agree with the necessity to use pre-processing. In this work we propose an algorithm called Heat Map Based Feature Selection (HmbFS) that can work with huge data without the need of pre-processing, thanks to a built-in compression mechanism based on color quantization. Results shows that our proposal is very competitive against some of the most popular algorithms and succeeds where other methodologies may fail due to the high dimensionality of the data.

**Keywords:** Mass spectrometry · Feature selection · Algorithm · High dimensionality · Ovarian cancer · Color theory

## 1 Introduction

Diseases that are detected at an advanced stage, usually lead to high death rate, hence early detection of conditions such as cancer are critical for public health [1]. With the development of new technologies for data analysis such as microarrays and mass spectrometry (MS) it has been possible to understand diseases much better than before [2]. For several diseases, but in the particular case of cancer, the use of MS to profile high resolution complex protein and compare the results of cancer vs normal samples has become very popular and early diagnosis has been made possible [3, 4]. The main idea is to find measurable indicators for a biological condition, these indicators are known as biomarkers and help in a considerable way for the early detection of diseases [5].

To gather MS data a mass spectrometer device is required, and the most common current techniques are [2]: (1) Matrix-Assisted Laser Desorption and Ionization Time-Of-Flight, known as MALDI-TOF which allows the analysis of biomolecules (such as DNA, proteins, peptides and sugars) and (2) Surface-Enhanced Laser Desorption and Ionization Time-Of-Flight, known as SELDI-TOF that it is used mainly for the analysis of protein mixtures in tissues samples such as blood, urine and other clinical samples [6].

In this research we have used data that was collected using SELDI approach. Using this technology is possible to generate protein features information that has been successfully used in the detection of several diseases using serum and other complex

© Springer International Publishing Switzerland 2015
A.M. Mora and G. Squillero (Eds.): EvoApplications 2015, LNCS 9028, pp. 3–13, 2015.
DOI: 10.1007/978-3-319-16549-3_1

biological specimens [7, 8]. When analyzing the MS data, the value (height) for each feature represents the ion abundance at a specific mass-to-charge (m/z) interval. The combination of multiple m/z values produces a pattern that represents a condition or state, such representation is known as the fingerprint for such condition. Hence if we have different fingerprints for some conditions, e.g. for cancer and non-cancer samples, it would be possible to identify the disease presence or absence.

The use of high resolution MS data to search proteins that help to detect the presence of a particular disease has greatly accelerated the biomarkers discovery phase [9], however it has been found that very few biomarkers reappear in new test data, which leads to the conclusion that there is a classifier overfitting problem caused by learning from very few samples with lots of variables [10]. When dealing with a large number of variables, techniques such as Support Vector Machines (SVM) are used as they can work with very high dimensional data, however even with such approaches, it has been found that improvement is possible after variable reduction [11, 12].

The task of selecting just a part of the spectra, i.e. a subset of features, is a complex process that can be divided in two main approaches [13, 14]: (1) Feature extraction: where the key idea is to transform the high dimensional features into a whole new space of lower dimensionality e.g. Principal Component Analysis (PCA) [15], and (2) Feature selection: which main goal is to find the smallest number of features that still describes the data in a reasonable way [16]. This is the approach used in this work.

When dealing with MS data, feature selection (FS) becomes a very fundamental part of the learning process as the number-of-features to number-of-samples ratio is quite unbalanced. In our particular research we used the high-resolution ovarian dataset provided by the National Cancer Institute (NCI): Center for Cancer Research [17] which has 370,575 features for each sample and includes a total of 216 patients; such amount of data gives us a matrix size of over 80,000,000 that most works prefer to avoid due to the complexity it represents.

As part of this research we have developed an algorithm called Heat Map Based Feature Selection (HmbFS) which is domain independent (i.e. not specifically designed for MS data) and it is able to compute a large amount of data with limited memory resources. Experiments were carried out using an on-line machine learning framework known as ML Comp that allows objectively algorithm comparison and provides external researchers with the ability to reproduce all our experiments, something that is usually hard to achieve on most works of this kind [18].

The remaining of this paper is structured as follows: In Sect. 2, some related works are presented. In Sect. 3 we present the formal proposal and algorithm description. In Sect. 4 we describe our experiments and results. In Sect. 5 we present the final conclusions and discuss future work.

## 2 Related Works

In the past decade we have seen many works dealing with MS data and trying to reduce its inherent high dimensionality by several different techniques, in this section we present some of the works that are more closely related with ours.

In 2005, Yu, et al. [1] used a Bayesian neural networks to identify ovarian cancer from the high-resolution NCI dataset. Using binning as pre-processing it was possible to removed almost 97 % of the data, leaving only 11,301 features (m/z ratios). According to their results they managed to get an overall accuracy of 98.49 % using a leave-one-out cross validation approach.

In 2006, Susmita et al. [2] used the NCI ovarian cancer dataset but in low-resolution form (15,154 features). The FS methods Bonferroni [19] and Westfall and Young [20] were employed to reduce the original data to 1700 (11.21 %) and 1912 (12.61 %) respectively. Best result in their experiments is achieved by a combination of Westfall and Young with SVM with an accuracy of 96.5 %.

In 2009, Liu [21] proposes a new application of wavelet feature selection extraction that in conjunction with SVM was used to do classification on the same ovarian cancer dataset that we are using. A pre-processing step to resample the data was employed, resulting dataset was almost 96 % smaller and using SVM they got a classification accuracy of 98 % although using an unknown dataset partition.

In 2010, Jiqing et al. [22], used NCI low-resolution ovarian dataset and proposed a sparse representation based FS for MS data. Authors managed to remove around 68 % of the data by limiting the m/z range from 1,500 to 10,000; this decision is based on the rationale that points lower than 1,500 are distorted by those of energy-absorbing molecules (EAM). Further reduction is achieved by baseline correction using local linear regression [23] and normalization. Using a wrapper FS approach guided by SVM, authors achieved an accuracy of 98.3 %.

In 2013, Soha et al. [24], presented a genetic programming (GP) approach for FS in MS data. The data was pre-processed reducing it from the 370,575 features to 15,000. The key idea in this work is to combine two well known FS algorithms Information-Gain (IG) [25] and Relief-F [26] and use their outputs as terminals for the GP method. However the process is very exhaustive as the GP method is designed in a wrapper approach. When using a SVM approach for classification they got an accuracy of 93.15 %.

As a summary, we can see a common pattern in all related works, due to constrains such as computer resources and algorithms complexity, dealing with raw MS data is reported as unmanageable. In this work we present an efficient algorithm that is capable of dealing with huge number of features with limited resources.

## 3 Formal Proposal

The context of this work is focused on supervised machine learning, in order to formally express the place that FS takes in the learning process, we first must define the supervised learning process itself.

In order to build a model to solve a problem, for supervised learning it is required to have a set of data known as training set, this data is composed by a set of labeled (e.g. cancer vs normal) instances which are features vectors containing the information that is required to learn.

An instance is therefore formalized as an assignment of values $V = (v_1, ..., v_n)$ to a set of features $F = (f_1, ..., f_n)$, where each instance is labeled with at least one of the possible $c_1, ..., c_n$ classes of C. In the case of MS data, each possible value in the m/z spectrum is a feature, and the specific m/z concentration is the value assigned to that feature; later each instance is labeled with the condition they represent.

Since the training set is the input to build a classifier, it is clear that its performance is inherently dependent of the values of such features. And as pointed out by Yu [27], in theory, the more features we have, the more power to discriminate between classes we would have, however, in practice with a limited number of instances (as is the case of MS data) the excessive number of features not only causes the learning process to be slow but there is a high risk of overfitting the data, as irrelevant or noisy features may confuse the learning algorithm. To handle this problem is where FS takes place.

To formalize the concept of FS, let $R$ be a reduced (subset) version of $F$ and $V_R$ the value vector for $R$. So in general, FS can be defined [28] as finding the minimum subset $R$ such as $P(C \mid R = V_R)$ is equal or close to $P(C \mid F = V)$, or in other words, if the probability distribution of different classes given the reduced subset is equal or close to the original distribution for the whole features in $F$.

Since our goal is to reduce the original space, it is required to identify such features that are relevant to the learning process and discard the rest. John et al. [29] propose a relevance categorization that is shown below.

Let $F$ be the full set of features, $F_i$ a particular feature and $S_i = F - \{F_i\}$. Now we can identify three types of features, strongly relevant, weakly relevant and irrelevant given the following conditions:

A feature $F_i$ is strongly relevant iff: $P(C \mid F_i, S_i) \neq P(C \mid S_i)$

A feature $F_i$ is weakly relevant iff: $P(C \mid Fi, Si) = P(C \mid Si)$ and $\exists\, S'_i \subset S_i$ such as $P(C \mid F_i, S'_i) \neq P(C \mid S'_i)$.

A feature $F_i$ is irrelevant iff: $\forall\, S'_i \subseteq S_i, P(C \mid F_i, S'_i) = P(C \mid S'_i)$

Given these definitions, we have that a feature is strongly relevant if it is always required in order to keep (or improve) the original conditional class distribution, while a weakly relevant feature may or may not be required to keep the probability. Then an irrelevant feature is simply not required and its removal causes very minimal or not impact at all in class probability.

Our proposal hence consist in finding such relevant features in an automatic way employing our algorithm called Heat Map Based Feature Selection (HmbFS) which has been designed to work with very high dimensional datasets (such as MS data) with very low memory footprint thanks to a data compression mechanism. The FS process is divided in two stages: (1) Compression and (2) Selection, which are described below.

**Stage 1 - Compression:** in order to handle the analysis of hundred thousands of features with efficiency, a key factor that takes our proposal apart from others is that we do not perform single feature analysis but instead we join features in "*groups*", hence reducing the number of required iterations to compare the usefulness of features. Therefore our relevance definition had a slight change as we do not analyze $F_i$ anymore but instead a group $G_i$ that is defined as $G_i = \{F_r, F_g, F_b\}$, these features stands for $Feature_{Red}$, $Feature_{Green}$ and $Feature_{Blue}$ and their corresponding values represent color intensities, but together (i.e., as a group) the relation between them creates a true color.

In order to produce these groups $G$, we employ a lossy compression technique that builds a graphical representation of the data, the result of such transformation is known as *Heatmap*. The first step for compression is the normalization of each isolated feature at a time, i.e. each feature is treated independently, to formalize this, let $I$ be the full set of instances (e.g. samples in MS data) and $I_x$ a particular sample for the whole dataset $D$, each value for $F_i$ that belongs to a instance $I_x$ ($I_xF_i$) is then normalized to a 0–255 interval as shown:

$$\forall I_xF_i \in D: \widehat{I_xF_i} = \left( \frac{I_xF_i - min(IF_i)}{max(IF_i) - min(IF_i)} \right) * 255 \tag{1}$$

Where $min(IF_i)$ and $max(IF_i)$ represents the minimum and maximum value respectively that a feature gets across all the instances of the dataset. This process is repeated for every feature $F_i$ across all instances $I_x$. Once the features have been normalized, each of the packages containing $F_r$, $F_g$ and $F_b$ can be mapped to a true color expressed in red/green/blue (RGB) format, together the three features can represent up to 16,777,216 different colors or patterns. However, since the idea is to build a generalization of the original data, we apply a technique called *Color Quantization* that allows the mapping of a true color to a lower depth color scale, in this case we have reduced to a 4-Bit 16-Colors. The idea is to discard small data variations or uniqueness, and produce a new set of data which is more general and consistent, the process of quantization is performed by finding the minimum euclidean distance between the true color and the 16 reference colors, ranging from $R_{j=1}$ to $R_{j=16}$, the RGB values for each of those colors are the standard values defined in the HTML 4.01 specification.

To formalize the information quantization, let $G$ be the set of all the built groups and $G_i$ a particular group (which is composed by $F_r$, $F_g$ and $F_b$) that belongs to a instance $I_x$, each of those $I_xG_i$ combinations are then compared against all the reference colors $R_j$ in set $R$ to produce the new single-value compressed feature $F_i$ that will represent the old 3-feature as shown below:

$$\forall I_xG_i \in D \text{ and } \forall j \in \{1, \ldots, 16\}$$
$$new\ I_xF_i = min\left( \sqrt{ \begin{array}{c} (I_xG_iF_r - R_jF_r)^2 + (I_xG_iF_g - R_jF_g)^2 \\ + (I_xG_iF_b - R_jF_b)^2 \end{array} } \right) \tag{2}$$

Once all the distances between true color and reference color have been calculated, we select the reference color $R_j$ with the minimum euclidean distance, and this process gives origin to a new dataset that is purely built in reference colors, or in other words, it is a compressed lossy version of the original. Dataset reduction is possible due to the fact that the reference color is represented by a single value (e.g.: red, which is composed by RGB values of 255,0,0) instead of three different features, this compression makes possible to reduce the original 370,575 feature dataset to only 123,525. It is important to notice that such reduction is only performed for selection, the original data is untouched.

**Stage 2 - Feature Selection:** after compression is completed (Stage 1), selecting relevant features is based on the rationale that different classes should look different, hence their associated quantized colors should look different as well. Since FS occurs in the new compressed dataset, the process see regular features $F_i$ although we know they represent a group in the original space. The *mode* is calculated for each feature-class (FC) relation i.e. a *mode* for feature 1 and class 1 ($F_1C_1$) and another *mode* for $F_1C_2$, and so on.

The conditional probability that a given value for *mode* belongs to a class or another is compared and if such probability exceeds other classes then we define the feature as useful. A threshold $Th$ can be applied to produce more strict comparisons. In order to formalize the criteria, let $P(C_j|Mo(F_i))$ be the probability that a given mode in $F_i$ be associated to a class $C_j$, then the feature $F_i$ usefulness is defined as follows:

$$Useful(F_i) iff:$$
$$\exists \{C_j, C_k\} \subset C | P(C_j | Mo(F_i)) > [P(C_k|Mo(F_i)) * Th] \qquad (3)$$

After all useful features have been identified, we need to restore the original data, however such process is very efficient as each group is mapped to exactly 3 features, e.g. if FS process selected (compressed groups) $F_i = \{2\}, \{5\}, \{7\}$ and $\{10\}$, we know they are mapped to the original space to $F_i = \{4, 5, 6\}, \{13, 14, 15\}, \{19, 20, 21\}$ and $\{28, 29, 30\}$. Below we present the algorithm's pseudo-code:

```
01|  From Feature 1 to N do:
02|    From Sample 1 to N do:
03|      Normalize Feature to 0-255
04|  Build Feature-Groups F
05|  From Feature-Group Fᵢ to N do:
06|    From Class Cⱼ to N do:
07|      From Class Cₖ to N do:
08|       If Pr.Mode(Cⱼ,Fᵢ) > [ Pr.Mode(Cₖ,Fᵢ)*Th ]:
09|         Tag as useful feature Fᵢ
10|  For each useful feature do:
11|    Map to original data and save
```

As it can be seen from pseudo-code, our proposal is very programming friendly. The compression stage allows to reduce problem complexity and evaluate features in a smaller space without losing the original data because, at the end of the process we map our results to it. Figure 1 summarizes the whole process:

In the next section we present our experiments setup and results obtained after processing the NCI High-resolution MS Ovarian Cancer dataset, which is commonly used as we reviewed in related works.

## 4   Experiments and Results

As correctly pointed out by Zhang [18], reproduce experiments in works such as this one is sometimes hard to achieve, in our approach we want to fill that gap by allowing

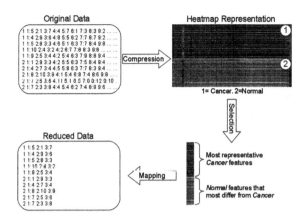

**Fig. 1.** HmbFS algorithm process overview

readers to easily replicate our experiments and open the possibility to objectively compare any future work with ours. In order to achieve our goal we have performed our experiments in the Machine Learning (ML) Comp framework which can be accessed on-line for free in order to review our experiments or create new ones, this allows researchers to work in the same conditions than we did, with the exact same data, train/test partitions and hardware resources.

To test HmbFS we selected the NCI High-resolution ovarian cancer dataset as several works can be found using this dataset. Unlike most works, we wanted to deal with raw MS-data in order to push the limits of FS algorithms. In Table 1 we present our dataset setup compared with related works.

**Table 1.** NCI ovarian cancer dataset characteristics comparison

| Authors | Resolution | Original features | Features after pre-processing | Reference |
|---------|-----------|-------------------|------------------------------|-----------|
| Yu et al. | High | 373,401 | 11,301 | [1] |
| Susmita et al. | Low | 15,154 | No pre-processing. 15,154 | [2] |
| Liu | High | 368,750 | 15,000 | [21] |
| Jiqing et al. | Low | 15,154 | 10,000 | [22] |
| Soha et al. | High | 370,575 | 15,000 | [24] |
| This work | High | 370,575 | No pre-processing. 370,575 | |

As it can be seen from Table 1, we performed all experiments with raw MS-data, no pre-processing of any kind was performed, the only modification to the data was a transformation to the SVM-light format that ML Comp requires. The summary of performed experiments is reviewed below:

**Exp. 1 – Learning without FS:** Our first goal was to find out how important FS can be when dealing with such big amount of data, for that task, we selected 5 well known multi-class algorithms and run the learning process without any FS aid.

**Exp. 2 – FS in high-dimensional space:** In a previous work [12] we evaluate the top 10 feature selection algorithms. In this work we used the top performers, Chi2 [30], Fcbf [31] and Relief-F [32] and coupled them with top classification algorithms to evaluate results.

**Exp. 3 – Learning from HmbFS reduced datasets:** Since experiments 1 & 2 proved that most current techniques are not efficient enough to handle such amount of data with limited resources, we decided that in order to have a reference point to compare HmbFS we had to reduce the datasets to allow other FS algorithms to handle the problem. However, HmbFS handled the full 370,575 features without any issue as can be seen in http://mlcomp.org/runs/36467.

The summary of classification error for our experiments is presented in Table 2, multiple partitions of data using stratified random subsampling can be found on MLComp as well as the experiments ID (reported in parenthesis) to validate our results. Two main threshold values are evaluated, using Th = 2, the number of selected features was 86,010 but for more aggressive reduction a Th = 12 was used to reduce the original data to only 2,802, over 99.4 % reduction compared with original data. The first 4 rows represent experiment 1, rows 5–8 are for experiment 2, and last 4 for experiment 3.

**Table 2.** Classification test error for multiple FS and classification algorithms

| Classifier/Feature selection | Selected features | Bonzai Boost | SVM with SMO | Logistic regression | Adagrad with SGD | MIRA |
|---|---|---|---|---|---|---|
| None | 370,575 | OOM$_{(36388)}$ | OOM$_{(36396)}$ | OOM$_{(36399)}$ | 0.077$_{(36402)}$ | OOM$_{(37004)}$ |
| Fcbf (FS cause OOM) | – | OOM$_{(36941)}$ | OOM | OOM | OOM | OOM |
| Relief-F (FS cause OOM) | – | OOM$_{(36391)}$ | OOM | OOM | OOM | OOM |
| Chi2 (FS cause OOM) | – | OOM$_{(36390)}$ | OOM | OOM | OOM | OOM |
| HmbFS Threshold=2 (Two) | 86,010 | OOM$_{(36946)}$ | OOM$_{(36396)}$ | 0.046$_{(36945)}$ | 0.077$_{(37007)}$ | 0.154$_{(37008)}$ |
| HmbFS Th=2 + Fcbf | 286 | 0.123$_{(36600)}$ | 0.154$_{(37003)}$ | 0.062$_{(37045)}$ | 0.108$_{(37006)}$ | 0.108$_{(37005)}$ |
| HmbFS Th=2 + Relief-F | 60,202 | 0.123$_{(36599)}$ | 0.077$_{(37011)}$ | 0.046$_{(37047)}$ | 0.062$_{(37012)}$ | 0.123$_{(37013)}$ |
| HmbFS Th=2 + Chi2 | 34,265 | 0.077$_{(36598)}$ | 0.123$_{(37015)}$ | 0.046$_{(37046)}$ | 0.108$_{(37017)}$ | 0.154$_{(37016)}$ |
| HmbFS Threshold=12 (Twelve) | 2,802 | 0.077$_{(36499)}$ | 0.092$_{(36507)}$ | 0.108$_{(36511)}$ | 0.108$_{(36509)}$ | 0.092$_{(37018)}$ |
| HmbFS Th=12 + Fcbf | 31 | 0.108$_{(36518)}$ | 0.154$_{(37020)}$ | 0.123$_{(37042)}$ | 0.138$_{(37022)}$ | 0.123$_{(37019)}$ |
| HmbFS Th=12 + Relief-F | 2,685 | 0.092$_{(36503)}$ | 0.092$_{(37026)}$ | 0.092$_{(37044)}$ | 0.108$_{(37023)}$ | 0.092$_{(37024)}$ |
| HmbFS Th=12 + Chi2 | 2,695 | 0.031$_{(36502)}$ | 0.092$_{(37028)}$ | 0.092$_{(37043)}$ | 0.123$_{(37030)}$ | 0.108$_{(37029)}$ |

From Table 2, we can clearly see the problem under investigation by reviewing the first 4 rows, where most of the values are Out-Of-Memory (OOM). Current FS algorithms cannot easily handle the amount of data that raw MS represents, learning algorithms suffer from similar problems, since only Adagrad was able to process the entire dataset without any FS aid. Our proposal, HmbFS was the only FS algorithm capable of reducing the entire dataset, but in order to have a reference for comparison, we reduce the data in $\sim 23$ % (using $_{Th=2}$) to make feasible the FS for competing algorithms. Best result was obtained by a combination of $HmbFS_{Th=12}$ and Chi2, together they achieved an accuracy of 96.9 % with only $\sim 0.7$ % of the original data.

## 5  Conclusions and Future Work

From the related works we reviewed, the ones that used the high resolution NCI ovarian cancer dataset had to use different techniques for pre-processing, our experiments confirmed the necessity for such approach, as dealing with the raw MS data its very complex because at least two reasons: (1) There is a lot of noise and (2) Complexity to process such big data. After pre-processing the data however, we can notice a FS step is still performed, hence reducing the data even more. Since a FS algorithm main goal is to remove useless data (e.g. noise) and produce a small subset of feature that inherently reduce processing complexity, it would be ideal to employ a FS on MS data without the need for pre-processing, however it is hard to find FS algorithms capable to reduce such big datasets, in our experiments, none of the reviewed top algorithms was able to handle the data, all of their tests failed due to OOM errors.

Our proposal, HmbFS aims to be memory efficient in order to manage very high dimensional datasets. Experiments proves that our algorithm was able to process the almost 56 million elements (370,575 features by 151 train samples) where others failed, we were forced to help competing algorithms with a pre-filtering by HmbFS in order to have a reference point to compare with. Based on the way our algorithm works (grouping features), it can be used as a first-pass followed by a second-pass filtering by a classical FS algorithm that evaluates individual features, however this may not necessary lead to better results as shown in Table 2.

Our best result overall was achieved by using $Hmbfs_{Th=12}$ and Chi2 as a second-pass FS, with an accuracy of 96.9 % (run id 36502), such result however was achieved without any pre-processing, that excludes any alignment of the MS data as well, comparing with other works, we believe HmbFS can lead to very competitive results as very similar accuracies were obtained, even without pre-processing the data. Another remarkable detail of our experiments, is that all of them can be (1) replicated and (2) objectively compared, thanks to the ML Comp framework.

As far a future work it can be divided in three sections right now:

(1)  General dataset comparison: we want to perform more experiments of HmbFS with very different datasets in order to prove its usefulness in other areas other than MS data.
(2)  Automatic threshold: right now we need to set a manual threshold *Th* in order to decide "how much we want to reduce", while the *Th* is the only required

parameter and its quite intuitive, it is interesting to get rid of it by an automatic approach.

(3) Human interaction in feature selection: since the theory behind HmbFS involves color generation, we would like to experiment with human-in-the-loop (HITL) to find patterns in such colors that may lead to improved selection.

# References

1. Yu, J., Chen, X.: Bayesian neural network approaches to ovarian cancer identification from high-resolution mass spectrometry data. Bioinformatics **21**, i487–i494 (2005)
2. Datta, S., DePadilla, L.M.: Feature selection and machine learning with mass spectrometry data for distinguishing cancer and non-cancer samples. Stat. Methodol. **3**(1), 79–92 (2006). ISSN 1572-3127
3. Liotta, L.A., Ferrari, M., Petricoin, E.: Clinical proteomics: written in blood. Nature **425**, 905 (2003)
4. Wulfkuhle, J.D., Loitta, L.A., Petricoin, E.F.: Proteomic applications for the early dectection of cancer. Nature **3**, 267–275 (2003)
5. Srinivas, P.R., Verma, M., Zhao, Y., Srivastava, S.: Proteomics for cancer biomarker discovery. Clin. Chem. **48**, 1160–1169 (2002)
6. Tang, N., Tornatore, P., Weinberger, S.R.: Current developments in SELDI affinity technology. Mass Spectrom. Rev. **23**, 34–44 (2004)
7. Herrmann, P.C., Liotta, L.A., Petricoin, E.F.: Cancer proteomics: the state of the art. Dis. Markers **17**, 49–57 (2001)
8. Vlahou, A., Schellhammer, P.E., Mendrinos, S., Patel, K., Kondylis, F.L., Gong, L., Nazim, S., Wright, G.L., Jr.: Development of a novel proteomic approach for the detection of transitional cell carcinoma of the bladder in urine. Am. J. Pathol. **158**, 1491–1520 (2001)
9. Kuschner, K., Malyarenko, D., Cooke, W., Cazares, L., Semmes, O., Tracy, E.: A Bayesian network approach to feature selection in mass spectrometry data. BMC Bioinform. **11**, 177 (2010)
10. Malyarenko, D., Cooke, W.E., Adam, B.L., Malik, G., Chen, H., Tracy, E.R., Trosset, M.W., Sasinowski, M., Semmes, O.J., Manos, D.M.: Enhancement of sensitivity and resolution of surface-enhanced laser desorption/ionization time-of-flight mass spectrometric records for serum peptides using time-series analysis techniques. Clin. Chem. **51**, 65–74 (2005)
11. Guyon, I., Weston, J., Barnhill, S., Vapnik, V.: Gene selection for cancer classification using support vector machines. Mach. Learn. **46**(1), 389–422 (2002)
12. Huertas, C., Juarez-Ramirez, R.: Filter feature selection performance comparison in high-dimensional data: a theoretical and empirical analysis of most popular algorithms. In: 17th Information Fusion (FUSION) Conference (2014)
13. Dittmann, B., Nitz, S.: Strategies for the development of reliable QA/QC methods when working with mass spectrometry-based chemosensory systems. Sens. Actuators, B **69**, 253–257 (2000)
14. Depczynski, U., Frost, V., Molt, K.: Genetic algorithms applied to the selection of factors in principal component regression. Anal. Chim. Acta **420**, 217–227 (2000)
15. Suganthy, M., Ramamoorthy, P.: Principal component analysis based feature extraction, morphological edge detection and localization for fast iris recognition. J. Comput. Sci. **8**, 1428–1433 (2012)
16. Dash, M., Liu, H.: Feature selection for classification. Intell. Data Anal. **1**, 131–156 (1997)

17. Petricoin, E., Ardekani, A.M., Hitt, B.A., Levine, P.J., Fusaro, V.A., Steinberg, S.M., Mills, G.B., Simone, C., Fishman, D.A., Kohn, E.C., Liotta, L.A.: Use of proteomic patterns in serum to identify ovarian cancer. Lancet **359**, 572–577 (2002)
18. Zhang, X., Lu, X., Shi, Q., Xu, X., Leung, H., Harris, L., Iglehart, J., Miron, A., Liu, J., Wong, W.: Recursive SVM feature selection and sample classification for mass-spectrometry and microarray data. BMC Bioinform. **7**(1), 197 (2006)
19. Bonferroni, C.E.: Il calcolo delle assicurazioni su gruppi di teste. In: Studi in Onore del Professore Salvatore Ortu Carboni, Rome, pp. 13–60 (1935)
20. Westfall, P., Young, S.: Resampling-Based Multiple Testing, Examples and Methods For p-Value Adjustment. Wiley, New York (1993)
21. Liu, Y.: Feature extraction and dimensionality reduction for mass spectrometry data. Comput. Biol. Med. **39**(9), 818–823 (2009)
22. Jiqing, K., Lei, Z., Bin, H., Qi, D., Yaojia, W., Lihua, L., Shenhua, X., Hanzhou, M., Zhiguo, Z.: Sparse representation based feature selection for mass spectrometry data. In: Bioinformatics and Biomedicine Workshops (BIBMW), pp. 57–62 (2010)
23. Wu, B., Abbott, T., Fishman, D., McMurray, W., Mor, G., Stone, K., Ward, D., Williams, K., Zhao, H.: Comparison of statistical methods for classification of ovarian cancer using mass spectrometry data. Bioinformatics **19**(13), 1636 (2003)
24. Ahmed, S., Zhang, M., Peng, L.: Feature selection and classification of high dimensional mass spectrometry data: a genetic programming approach. In: Vanneschi, L., Bush, W.S., Giacobini, M. (eds.) EvoBIO 2013. LNCS, vol. 7833, pp. 43–55. Springer, Heidelberg (2013)
25. Sebastiani, F., Ricerche, C.N.D.: Machine learning in automated text categorization. ACM Comput. Surv. **34**, 1–47 (2002)
26. Sun, Y., Wu, D.: A relief based feature extraction algorithm. In: SDM, pp. 188–195 (2008)
27. Yu, L., Liu, H.: Efficient feature selection via analysis of relevance and redundancy. J. Mach. Learn. Res. **5**, 1205–1224 (2004)
28. Koller, D., Sahami, M.: Toward optimal feature selection. In: Proceedings of the Thirteenth International Conference on Machine Learning, pp. 284–292 (1996)
29. John, G., Kohavi, R., Pfleger, K.: Irrelevant feature and the subset selection problem. In: Proceedings of the Eleventh International Conference on Machine Learning, pp. 121–129 (1994)
30. Liu, H., Setiono, R.: Chi2: feature selection and discretization of numeric attributes. In: Proceedings of the Seventh IEEE International Conference on Tools with Artificial Intelligence, pp. 388–391. IEEE Computer Society (1995)
31. Yu, L., Liu, H.: Feature selection for high-dimensional data: a fast correlation-based filter solution. In: Proceedings of the 20th International Conference on Machine Learning (ICML 2003), pp. 856–863 (2003)
32. Kira, K., Rendell, L.: A practical approach to feature selection. In: Proceedings of the Ninth International Conference on Machine Learning (ICML 1992), pp. 249–256 (1992)

# A Novel Multi-objectivisation Approach for Optimising the Protein Inverse Folding Problem

Sune S. Nielsen[1]([✉]), Grégoire Danoy[1], Wiktor Jurkowski[3],
Juan Luis Jiménez Laredo[4], Reinhard Schneider[2],
El-Ghazali Talbi[5], and Pascal Bouvry[1]

[1] FSTC, University of Luxembourg, Walferdange, Luxembourg
{sune.nielsen,gregoire.danoy,pascal.bouvry}@uni.lu
[2] LCSB, University of Luxembourg, Walferdange, Luxembourg
reinhard.schneider@uni.lu
[3] TGAC, Norwich Research Park, Norwich, UK
wiktor.jurkowski@tgac.ac.uk
[4] LITIS, Université du Havre, Le Havre, France
jimenezj@univ-lehavre.fr
[5] INRIA Lille, Nord Europe Research Centre, Lille, France
el-ghazali.talbi@inria.fr

**Abstract.** In biology, the subject of protein structure prediction is of continued interest, not only to chart the molecular map of the living cell, but also to design proteins of new functions. The Inverse Folding Problem (IFP) is in itself an important research problem, but also at the heart of most rational protein design approaches. In brief, the IFP consists in finding sequences that will fold into a given structure, rather than determining the structure for a given sequence - as in conventional structure prediction. In this work we present a Multi Objective Genetic Algorithm (MOGA) using the diversity-as-objective (DAO) variant of multi-objectivisation, to optimise secondary structure similarity and sequence diversity at the same time, hence pushing the search farther into wide-spread areas of the sequence solution-space. To control the high diversity generated by the DAO approach, we add a novel Quantile Constraint (QC) mechanism to discard an adjustable worst quantile of the population. This DAO-QC approach can efficiently emphasise exploitation rather than exploration to a selectable degree achieving a trade-off producing both better and more diverse sequences than the standard Genetic Algorithm (GA). To validate the final results, a subset of the best sequences was selected for tertiary structure prediction. The super-positioning with the original protein structure demonstrated that meaningful sequences are generated underlining the potential of this work.

**Keywords:** Inverse Folding Problem · Protein design · Genetic Algorithm · Multi-objectivisation

© Springer International Publishing Switzerland 2015
A.M. Mora and G. Squillero (Eds.): EvoApplications 2015, LNCS 9028, pp. 14–25, 2015.
DOI: 10.1007/978-3-319-16549-3_2

# 1   Introduction

Protein engineering in general aims at designing molecules with desired properties and a method that allows to successfully design such molecules would find applications in a number of areas. For example, it could allow to design improved enzymes for biotechnology applications (e.g., waste-water treatment or biomass production), or new antibodies more specific towards already known targets (e.g., antibodies targeting a given pathogen like HIV, by binding to its envelope spikes to neutralize the virus [11]).

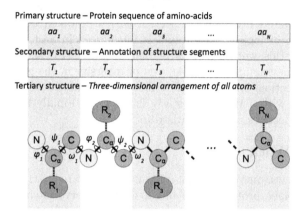

**Fig. 1.** Three levels of protein structure

The structure of a protein is typically represented by different levels of structures (see Fig. 1). The primary structure is the protein sequence of $N$ amino acids (also referred to as residues) $\{aa_i\}$ where $1 \leq i \leq N$ is the residue position. The secondary structure defines the organisation of *helices*, *sheets*, *turns* and *coils* of the tertiary structure and can be expressed by a type $\{T_i\} \in \{H, S, T, C\}$ for each position $i$ in the protein. The tertiary structure completely describes the arrangement of all atoms in the three-dimensional space. A simplified example is presented in Fig. 1 with only $N$ and $C$ atoms and $R_i$ residue side-chains.

With this hierarchical definition in mind, the Inverse Folding Problem (IFP), first mentioned by Pabo in [16] can be defined as follows: given a primary structure (protein sequences) and its corresponding tertiary structure, find alternative primary structures that will result in the same tertiary structure. This makes the solution of the IFP a key part of any protein design-process, where a specific tertiary structure is targeted while keeping a certain degree of freedom in the choice of protein sequence. Furthermore, the IFP is of general scientific interest to study the size, shape and characteristics of the sequence space that matches a given target structure, and how far from the original sequence solutions can be found. In this work, the fact that matching secondary structures is a necessary, but not a sufficient condition for proteins to have the same tertiary structures is exploited to reduce the IFP to its simplest formulation: given a protein's secondary structure and its corresponding protein sequence, find a set of highly dis-similar protein sequences that could result in the most similar secondary structure. With a fast estimate of the sequence's secondary structure as objective function, the computational time can be dramatically diminished, allowing a larger part of the feasible sequence space to be explored than existing exact methods.

The resulting optimisation problem is highly *multi-modal*. Therefore the algorithm proposed in this work addresses this aspect by using a diversity measure as objective through multi-objectivisation. Additionally, the algorithm incorporates a novel constraint method that allows controlling of the high diversity induced by the multi-objectivisation approach.

The remainder of this article is organised as follows. First the current work is situated in related literature in Sect. 2, then a detailed description of the problem and the biological background is introduced in Sect. 3. In Sect. 4 the contributions of this work in terms of modeling the IFP as an optimisation problem and achieving an adjustable level of diversity in the genetic algorithm are presented. Sections 5.1 and 5.2 describe the experiments conducted and the results obtained with a validation study in Sect. 5.3. Finally the contribution, results and perspectives are summarised in Sect. 6.

## 2   Related Work

This section reviews some of the most relevant works related to the two main areas covered in this paper: protein design and diversity preservation in metaheuristics.

### 2.1   Protein Design

Since the first design of a peptide by Gutte *et al.* [8] using secondary structure rules, numerous works have described different approaches to the IFP problem. Ponder and Richards [17] used a systematic exhaustive approach of enumerating a selected subset of residue positions while Bowie *et al.* [2] introduce a 3D to 1D score at each residue position in the protein sequence. The first reported use of a Genetic Algorithm (GA) for sequence design is by Jones [9] where simplified energy and amino-acid composition terms are optimised. Until the present day the leading methods are largely based on branch-and-bound algorithms or Monte Carlo enumeration techniques, changing a limited number of residue positions [12,15,21]. Common for these methods is that they rely on evolutionary information of existing structures and use energy potential and atomic scale force-field approximations to different degrees of detail. In some works the flexibility inherent in the tertiary structure of proteins is taken into account, referred to with terms such as rotamer conformations and backbone flexibility. The complexity and exhaustive nature of most methods effectively limits the size of the sequence or decision space that can be sampled, and the final output consists of a single or few sequences close to the original sequence.

### 2.2   Multi-modal Optimisation and Niching

In metaheuristics, the subject of exploration vs. exploitation characteristics has been thoroughly studied. For population based optimisation algorithms it is well-known that a higher level of population diversity results in more exploration at the expense of exploitation. An elevated population diversity is especially desirable for *multi-modal*, *deceptive* and/or *dynamic* problems. In general, if diversity tends towards zero it indicates that the algorithm has converged towards a single solution, which might be an undesired behavior if it occurs too early. A number of works have sought to maintain and control diversity, e.g. crowding methods by DeJong [3], fitness sharing by Goldberg and Richardson [7], cellular algorithms by Alba and Dorronsoro [1], diversity preserving selection strategies based on hamming distance Shimodaira [20] and on altruism by Laredo *et al.* [13]. Another approach consists in designing new objectives through multi-objectivisation and thereby extending the problem to a bi- or multi-objective one. Extending problems with an objective designed specifically for diversity preservation has been proposed by Toffolo and Benini [22], Wessing *et al.* [24], as well as Deb *et al.* [5]. In these works, objectives have been designed based on the hamming distance to the closest neighbor, the distance to the nearest better and the number of individuals in the neighborhood. In this work, the diversity preserving objective is based on the average distance of each individual to all others which directly targets the global diversity measure stated by the problem, contrary to the pairwise local view of existing works. Given the discrete nature, complexity and multi-modality of the problem, an effective diversity limiting mechanism is required. The proposed approach achieves this with the added value of making the population diversity highly variable depending on a single algorithm setting.

## 3    Problem Description

With the focus on finding diverse solutions to the Inverse Folding Problem (IFP), we tackle a simplified model developed to matching solely the reference secondary structure - a requirement for the tertiary structure. A single solution is represented as a sequence $A = \{aa_i\}$ to consist of $N$ residue positions, where $1 \leq i \leq N$ and $aa_i \in \{1, 2, ...20\}$ corresponds to the set of 20 possible amino-acids. As the solution space consists of a total of $20^N$ different combinations, considering that $N$ is around 50–200 for typical design targets, it is clear that alternatives to exhaustive exploration are required.

### 3.1    Secondary Structure Estimation

The primary goal of this estimate is to obtain sequences that match the reference secondary structure. Secondary structure refers to the annotation of segmentation of the sequence into structural components, here only *helices* and *sheets* are considered. These segments are the result of the protein naturally folding so that different parts of the 3D structure connect through bonds between amino-acids on separated residue positions in the sequence. *Helices* are characterised by a corkscrew shape, *sheets* are parallel connected segments, and *loops* are everything else. Using the tool PROFphd, updated to ReProf [18], the likely secondary structure type $T_{pred}(i)$ can be predicted per amino acid $aa_i$ in $A$ with a reliability, $R_{pred}(i) \in \{1...10\}$ by means of posterior neural network training.

With $T_{ref}(i)$ the actual type found at position $i$ of the reference secondary structure, the estimated similarity score $F_{sec}(A)$ is calculated as a sum of reliability weighted (mis)matches:

$$F_{sec}(A) = \frac{\Sigma_{max} - \sum_{i=1}^{N} M_i}{\Sigma_{max}}, \tag{1}$$

where

$$M_i = \begin{cases} 0 & \text{if } T_{pred}(i), T_{ref}(i) \notin \{helix, sheet\} \\ R_{pred}(i) & \text{if } T_{pred}(i) = T_{ref}(i) \\ -R_{pred}(i) & \text{if } T_{pred}(i) \neq T_{ref}(i) \end{cases}$$

and

$$\Sigma_{max} = \max R_{pred} \cdot |\{i | T_{ref}(i) \in \{H, E\}\}|$$

The reference types $T_{ref}(i)$ are extracted from the reference structure $S_{ref}$, per residue position $i$ using the standard 'Define Secondary Structure of Proteins' (DSSP) algorithm [10]. As seen from Eq. 1, the calculation is only concerned with *helix* and *sheet* structures. A position $i$ only contributes to the score if one of these are found at either $T_{ref}(i)$ or $T_{pred}(i)$ and the contribution magnitude is equal to the reliability of the prediction $R_{pred}(i)$ where match or mis-match determines the sign.

### 3.2   Diversity Measure

As a requirement stated in the problem description, the algorithm should not only find a single very good solution, but rather a number of good solutions as different as possible. An effective and simple measure of distance between two sequences is the Hamming-distance, defined as the number of permutations necessary to convert one into the other. Not taking gaps or varying sequence lengths into account, for two sequences $A = \{aa_i\}$ and $A' = \{aa_i'\}$ where $1 \leq i \leq N$, the Hamming distance between them is defined as:

$$d_{Hamm}(A, A') = \sum_{i=1}^{N} d_i, \ d_i = \begin{cases} 0 \text{ if } aa_i = aa_i' \\ 1 \text{ otherwise} \end{cases}. \tag{2}$$

Equation 2 states that $d_{Hamm}(A, A')$ is essentially the amount of positions one needs to change to transform $A$ into $A'$. To obtain a non-negative objective value for minimisation, the average Hamming distance to all other $M - 1$ individuals in the current population, minus the sequence length $N$ is computed:

$$F_{div}(A) = N - \frac{1}{M-1} \sum_{i=1}^{M-1} d_{Hamm}(A, A_i). \tag{3}$$

## 4   Methodology

With the two functions, $F_{sec}(A)$ and $F_{div}(A)$ defined for integer encoded solutions $A = \{aa_i\}$, a novel multi-objective GA based on NSGA-II [4] was applied.

---

**Algorithm 1.** DAO-QC NSGA-II

---

1: $Initialise(P_0)$                  // randomly generated individuals
2: $t \leftarrow 0$
3: **while** $t < t_{max}$ **do**
4:     $Q_t \leftarrow makeNewPop(P_t)$        // selection, mutation, re-combination
5:     $R_t \leftarrow P_t \cup Q_t$
6:     $mutateDoubles(R_t)$           // eliminate doubles by mutation
7:     $F \leftarrow fastNonDominatedSort(R_t)$
8:     $P_t \leftarrow truncate(F)$             // based on domination and crowding
9:     $setQuantileConstraint(P_t)$      // to penalise worst quantile
10: **end while**

---

To achieve better performance, two modifications were done which are discussed in the following and highlighted in Algorithm 1.

In the context of diversity preservation it is clear that having two or more identical individuals in the population is undesired. Hence doubles are removed by mutating them with a probability of $\frac{5}{chrom\_length}$ in Step 6, rather than eliminating them. A consequence of the nature of the objectives $F_{sec}(A)$ and $F_{div}(A)$ is that the latter is much easier to optimise, hence the population quickly consists of very diversified individuals with poor fitness according to $F_{sec}(A)$. To counter this effect the Quantile Constraint (QC) is introduced in Step 9 which prevents a precisely defined worst quantile of the population from being selected during the next generation starting in Step 4. The selection pressure can then be selectively adjusted by changing the size of the quantile $C_q$, which has been tested using $C_q \in \{0\,\%, 5\,\%, 25\,\%\}$.

# 5 Experiments

To study the performance of the proposed modified NSGA-II, with diversity objective and quantile constraint, a number of experiments have been conducted. For baseline comparison, the performance results have been compared to a standard Genetic Algorithm (GA). As final validation of the results is only really possible in the lab, an altsernative is running a top ranked protein structure prediction framework, like I-TASSER [19], on selected sequences.

## 5.1 Experimental Setup

Table 1 summarises the settings of the standard generational GA and the GA extended by multi-objectivisation into a Multi Objective Genetic Algorithm (MOGA) with DAO and QC. The DAO-QC MOGA version applies NSGA-II with standard selection and crossover operators: Binary tournament selection, 1-point crossover and uniform mutation. For the single objective version, a standard GA was applied using the same crossover and mutation operators. The total number of function evaluations is limited to 20000 and every experiment was repeated 30 times. As target samples, two proteins of different structural classes were chosen as reference: 256b (E. Coli Cytochrome B562) and 1b3a

**Table 1.** Algorithm settings

| Setting | Value |
|---|---|
| Population size | 100 |
| Algorithm | NSGA-II and std GA |
| Termination condition | 20000 function evaluations |
| Selection | Binary tournament (BT) |
| Crossover operator | 1-point, $p_c = 1.0$ |
| Mutation operator | Uniform, $p_m = \frac{1}{N}$ |
| Quantile constraint | $C_q \in \{0\%, 5\%, 25\%\}$ |

(human C-C motif chemokine 5, RANTES). *256b* consists of $N = 106$ amino-acids packed into 4 main helices whereas *1b3a* consists of $N = 67$ amino-acids packed into 1 helix, and 3 beta-sheets as well as a long unstructured coil region.

## 5.2   Algorithm Results

In the following we present and compare the results observed in terms of population fitness and diversity averaged over the 30 individual runs. Figure 2 shows the convergence of the population average fitness and population diversity. Table 2(a) and (b) present the average final fitness values in numbers by pair-wise cross-comparing the three $C_q$ settings with the GA. The Wilcoxon test indicator [25] with a 5 % significance level provides statistical confidence in comparing the sets with symbols '▲', '▽' and '-' indicating superior, inferior and no difference. The symbols refer to the column value, which is the second in each cell.

**Table 2.** Summary of final fitness averages

(a) 256b

| | QC 0% | QC 5% | QC 25% | GA |
|---|---|---|---|---|
| QC 0% | / | 0.498 - 0.095 ▲ | 0.498 - 0.066 ▲ | 0.498 - 0.093 ▲ |
| QC 5% | | / | 0.095 - 0.066 ▲ | 0.095 - 0.093 ▲ |
| QC 25% | | | / | 0.066 - 0.093 ▽ |
| GA | | | | / |

(b) 1b3a

| | QC 0% | QC 5% | QC 25% | GA |
|---|---|---|---|---|
| QC 0% | / | 0.613 - 0.136 ▲ | 0.613 - 0.098 ▲ | 0.613 - 0.143 ▲ |
| QC 5% | | / | 0.136 - 0.098 ▲ | 0.136 - 0.143 ▽ |
| QC 25% | | | / | 0.098 - 0.143 ▽ |
| GA | | | | / |

Clearly, the higher diversity comes at the expense of lower average fitness due to the exploration/exploitation trade-off. However the average fitness plots show that the DAO approach has better final characteristics: The $C_q = 5\%$ quantile

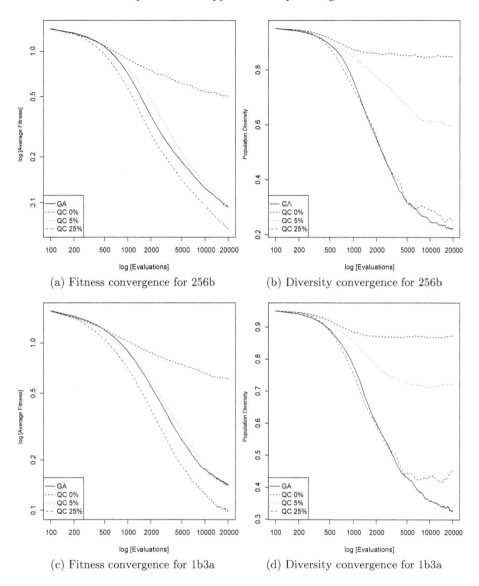

(a) Fitness convergence for 256b

(b) Diversity convergence for 256b

(c) Fitness convergence for 1b3a

(d) Diversity convergence for 1b3a

**Fig. 2.** Algorithm convergence

DAO-QC NSGA-II overtakes the standard GA for the *1b3a* sample scoring a significantly better final average of 0.136 vs. 0.143 with statistical confidence. For both samples with $C_q \in \{5\,\%, 25\,\%\}$ the final slope is steeper than the GA, indicating better performance given enough evaluation budget. With $C_q = 25\,\%$ the algorithm clearly outperforms the GA with statistical confidence for both samples with values 0.066 vs. 0.093 and 0.098 vs. 0.143 respectively. The steeper final slopes can be partially explained by the constantly high diversity seen in

Fig. 2. From the figure it is also evident that the size of the quantile has a direct impact on the population diversity, providing an effective tool to achieve the diversity preferred.

## 5.3  Validation Results

Ten generated sequences have been randomly selected between different runs per each sample (*256b* and *1b3a*) for prediction by I-TASSER [19] with the goal of assessing the meaningfulness of the generated sequences. Table 3(a) and (b) summarise super-positioning results of the predicted structures. The first column contains the standard sequence identity score [14] based on alignment with gaps. The remaining columns are well-known quality assessment metrics computed with the tertiary structure alignment tool LGA detailed in [26] with default Global Distance Test (GDT) and Longest Continuous Segments (LCS) analysis settings. The second column contains the length of the longest continuous segment $N'$ that can be fitted below a 5A threshold after super-positioning the two structures. With $S^a = \{s_1^a, s_2^a, ...s_N^a\}$ and $S^b = \{s_1^b, s_2^b, ...s_N^b\}$ denoting the 3D positions of every residue in the two structures to compare, root-mean-square deviation (RMSD) is defined in Eq. 4, assuming the structures are optimally aligned.

$$RMSD(S^a, S^b) = \sqrt{\frac{1}{N'} \sum_i |s_i^a - s_i^b|^2}, \ i \in \{i| \ |s_i^a - s_i^b| < 5A\} \qquad (4)$$

The Global Distance Test (GDT) Total Score (TS) is a measure indicating the total average of the average percentage of residues that can be fitted below each of the thresholds $\{0.5A, 1.0A, 1.5A, ...10.0A\}$. The final column is a quality estimate where values below 2.0 indicates a rather weak alignment (for further details please refer to [26]). Figure 3(a) and (b) show a graphical super-positioning of the best scoring generated sequences of Table 3 with PyMol [6]. Overall the sequences generated for the first sample *256b* do better than the *1b3a* sample, which can also be seen visually. This can largely be explained by the fact that only secondary structure prediction has been used, and that the

**Table 3.** Summary of alignment scores of selected sequences

| (a) 256b | | | | | (b) 1b3a | | | | |
|---|---|---|---|---|---|---|---|---|---|
| ID[%] | $N' < 5A$ | RMSD | GDT_TS | LGA_Q | ID[%] | $N' < 5A$ | RMSD | GDT_TS | LGA_Q |
| 8.65 | 92 | 2.82 | 60.142 | 3.148 | 10.94 | 36 | 3.04 | 39.552 | 1.148 |
| 12.38 | 98 | 2.19 | 69.811 | 4.276 | 6.35 | 47 | 3.18 | 54.104 | 1.432 |
| 11.43 | 106 | 3.09 | 61.557 | 3.325 | 10.94 | 36 | 3.22 | 40.299 | 1.083 |
| 14.42 | 104 | 2.21 | 75.943 | 4.506 | 16.92 | 41 | 3.71 | 44.776 | 1.076 |
| 8.57 | 53 | 3.53 | 37.264 | 1.458 | 12.70 | 37 | 3.1 | 38.806 | 1.157 |
| 10.48 | 94 | 3.36 | 55.425 | 2.72 | 7.94 | 49 | 2.96 | 54.478 | 1.603 |
| 17.14 | 104 | 2.65 | 70.283 | 3.776 | 9.23 | 34 | 3.12 | 35.821 | 1.055 |
| 10.48 | 39 | 2.62 | 32.783 | 1.432 | 14.06 | 56 | 2.63 | 67.91 | 2.05 |
| 14.42 | 47 | 2.15 | 38.208 | 2.089 | 15.00 | 32 | 3.39 | 38.433 | 0.916 |
| 11.54 | 64 | 3.08 | 46.934 | 2.014 | 12.70 | 49 | 2.94 | 51.493 | 1.614 |

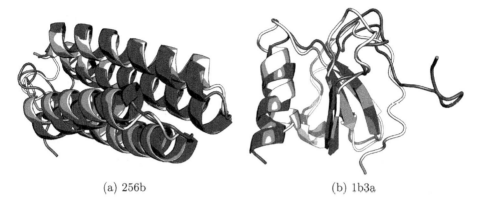

(a) 256b                              (b) 1b3a

**Fig. 3.** Predicted (lighter) and reference (darker) structures superpositioned

latter sample contains less structured elements and mainly beta-sheet segments. The differences are mostly in coil regions and due to slight mispositioning of the main structure elements. For the highly structured *256b*, the best prediction gave a global score (GDT_TS) of almost 76 % with most residues within 5A. The non-structured coil of *1b3a* diverts away from the target, giving a best GDT_TS of less than 68 %, but a low RMSD of 2.63 of the 56 residues that fit below 5A. Overall about half of the generated sequences were predicted with a total score above 50 % and an RMSD below or close to 3A, which is reasonable considering that only secondary structure was optimised and that the main part have sequence identity below 15 % with a minimum of 6.35 % - much lower than existing approaches where values below 25 % are rare.

## 6   Conclusion

In this paper we have presented a novel approach to find a large amount of protein sequences that may result in a given reference 3D structure. This problem, referred to as the Inverse Folding Problem (IFP), has received a lot of attention in theoretical chemistry and biophysics over the last 30 years, mostly for its potential application in protein design. It is also of interest to study the extent of the sequence space that may produce similar tertiary structures, and how far from the original reference sequence such solutions can be found.

By defining the task as finding highly diverse sequences with most similar secondary structures, an optimisation problem was modeled to find many well-scoring sequences in a few hours, which is fast compared to state-of-the-art methods. To achieve high diversity we have adapted the requirement as an additional objective and extended the problem through *multi-objectivisation* to become Multi-Objective with Diversity-As-Objective (DAO). Combining the novel Quantile Constraint (QC) with the DAO approach allows to shift focus arbitrarily between diversity or fitness, and final results found are comparable or better than the standard GA on average, while the diversity of found sequences remains higher at the same time. In addition, the algorithm convergence was observed as being steeper than the standard GA which promises very good solutions given an evaluation budget beyond the computational limitations set in this work.

Selected sequences of the highly diverse sets generated were inspected further by predicting their structure with I-TASSER (a top ranked structure prediction software). Final validation was done by comparing the predicted structures to their respective reference by tertiary structure super-position. For both samples *256b* and *1b3a* meaningful predictions were generated with close to 76 % and 68 % GDT_TS scores respectively and RMSD well below 3A. As could be expected, the method works better for the sample with more defined secondary structure, and less well in coil regions which are not captured by the objective function.

Future and ongoing works will address the identification of those sequences that actually fold into the reference structure by designing new objectives and constraints also addressing coil regions. Independent of this, sequences found could already be used as starting points for other exact protein design methods and possibly generate successful designs with a very low sequence identity comparing to the reference.

**Acknowledgments.** Work funded by the National Research Fund of Luxembourg (FNR) as part of the EVOPERF project at the University of Luxembourg with the AFR contract no. 1356145. Experiments were carried out using the HPC facility of the University of Luxembourg [23]

# References

1. Alba, E., Dorronsoro, B.: The exploration/exploitation tradeoff in dynamic cellular genetic algorithms. IEEE Trans. Evol. Comput. **9**(2), 126–142 (2005)
2. Bowie, J.U., Lüthy, R., Eisenberg, D.: A method to identify protein sequences that fold into a known three-dimensional structure. Science (New York, N.Y.) **253**(5016), 164–170 (1991)
3. De Jong, K.A.: Analysis of the behavior of a class of genetic adaptive systems. Ph.D. thesis, University of Michigan Ann Arbor, MI, USA (1975)
4. Deb, K., Agrawal, S., Pratap, A., Meyarivan, T.: A fast elitist non-dominated sorting genetic algorithm for multi-objective optimization: NSGA-II. Lect. Notes Comput. Sci. **849–858**, 2000 (1917)
5. Deb, K., Saha, A.: Finding multiple solutions for multimodal optimization problems using a multi-objective evolutionary approach. In: Proceedings of the 12th Annual Conference on Genetic and Evolutionary Computation, pp. 447–454. ACM (2010)
6. DeLano, W.L.: The pymol molecular graphics system, delano scientific, San Carlos, CA, USA (2002). There is no corresponding record for this reference (2002)
7. Goldberg, D.E., Richardson, J.: Genetic algorithms with sharing for multimodal function optimization. In: Genetic Algorithms and Their Applications: Proceedings of the Second International Conference on Genetic Algorithms, pp. 41–49 (1987)
8. Gutte, B., Däumigen, M., Wittschieber, E.A.: Design, synthesis and characterisation of a 34-residue polypeptide that interacts with nucleic acids. Nature **281**(5733), 650–655 (1979)

9. Jones, D.T.: De novo protein design using pairwise potentials and a genetic algorithm. Protein Sci. **3**, 567–574 (1994)
10. Kabsch, W., Sander, C.: Dictionary of protein secondary structure: pattern recognition of hydrogen-bonded and geometrical features. Biopolymers **22**(12), 2577–2637 (1983)
11. Klein, F., Mouquet, H., Dosenovic, P., Scheid, J.F., Scharf, L., Nussenzweig, M.C.: Antibodies in HIV-1 vaccine development and therapy. Science (New York, N.Y.) **341**(6151), 1199–1204 (2013)
12. Klepeis, J.L., Floudas, C.A., Morikis, D., Tsokos, C.G., Lambris, J.D.: Design of peptide analogues with improved activity using a novel de novo protein design approach. Ind. Eng. Chem. Res. **43**(14), 3817–3826 (2004)
13. Jiménez Laredo, J.L., Nielsen, S.S., Danoy, G., Bouvry, P., Fernandes, C.M.: Cooperative selection: improving tournament selection via altruism. In: Blum, C., Ochoa, G. (eds.) EvoCOP 2014. LNCS, vol. 8600, pp. 85–96. Springer, Heidelberg (2014)
14. Larkin, M.A., Blackshields, G., Brown, N.P., Chenna, R., McGettigan, P.A., McWilliam, H., Valentin, F., Wallace, I.M., Wilm, A., Lopez, R., Thompson, J.D., Gibson, T.J., Higgins, D.G.: Clustal w and clustal x version 2.0. Bioinformatics **23**(21), 2947–2948 (2007)
15. Mitra, P., Shultis, D., Brender, J.R., Czajka, J., Marsh, D., Gray, F., Cierpicki, T., Zhang, Y.: An evolution-based approach to de novo protein design and case study on Mycobacterium tuberculosis. PLoS Comput. Biol. **9**(10), e1003298 (2013)
16. Pabo, C.: Molecular technology: designing proteins and peptides. Nature **301**(5897), 200 (1983)
17. Ponder, J.W., Richards, F.M.: Tertiary templates for proteins: use of packing criteria in the enumeration of allowed sequences for different structural classes. J. Mol. Biol. **193**(4), 775–791 (1987)
18. Rost, B., Sander, C.: Combining evolutionary information and neural networks to predict protein secondary structure. Proteins **19**(1), 55–72 (1994)
19. Roy, A., Kucukural, A., Zhang, Y.: I-TASSER: a unified platform for automated protein structure and function prediction. Nat. Protoc. **5**(4), 725–738 (2010)
20. Shimodaira, H.: Dcga: a diversity control oriented genetic algorithm. In: ICTAI, pp. 367–374 (1997)
21. Smadbeck, J., Peterson, M.B., Khoury, G.A., Taylor, M.S., Floudas, C.A.: Protein wisdom: a workbench for in silico de novo design of biomolecules. J. Vis. Exp. **77**, e50476 (2013)
22. Toffolo, A., Benini, E.: Genetic diversity as an objective in multi-objective evolutionary algorithms. Evol. Comput. **11**(2), 151–167 (2003)
23. Varrette, S., Bouvry, P., Cartiaux, H., Georgatos, F.: Management of an academic HPC cluster: the UL experience. In: Proceedings of the 2014 International Conference on High Performance Computing & Simulation (HPCS 2014), Bologna, Italy. IEEE, July 2014
24. Wessing, S., Preuss, M., Rudolph, G.: Niching by multiobjectivization with neighbor information: trade-offs and benefits. In: 2013 IEEE Congress on Evolutionary Computation (CEC), pp. 103–110. IEEE (2013)
25. Wilcoxon, F.: Individual comparisons by ranking methods. Biometrics Bull. **1**(6), 80–83 (1945)
26. Zemla, A.: LGA: a method for finding 3D similarities in protein structures. Nucleic Acids Res. **31**(13), 3370–3374 (2003)

# EvoCOMNET

# Black Holes and Revelations: Using Evolutionary Algorithms to Uncover Vulnerabilities in Disruption-Tolerant Networks

Doina Bucur[1], Giovanni Iacca[2]([⊠]), Giovanni Squillero[3], and Alberto Tonda[4]

[1] Johann Bernoulli Institute, University of Groningen,
Nijenborgh 9, 9747 AG Groningen, The Netherlands
d.bucur@rug.nl
[2] INCAS[3],
Dr. Nassaulaan 9, 9401 HJ Assen, The Netherlands
giovanniiacca@incas3.eu
[3] Politecnico di Torino,
Corso Duca degli Abruzzi 24, 10129 Torino, Italy
giovanni.squillero@polito.it
[4] INRA UMR 782 GMPA,
1 Avenue Lucien Brétignières, 78850 Thiverval-Grignon, France
alberto.tonda@grignon.inra.fr

**Abstract.** A challenging aspect in open ad hoc networks is their resilience against malicious agents. This is especially true in complex, urban-scale scenarios where numerous moving agents carry mobile devices that create a peer-to-peer network without authentication. A requirement for the proper functioning of such networks is that all the peers act legitimately, forwarding the needed messages, and concurring to the maintenance of the network connectivity. However, few malicious agents may easily exploit the movement patterns in the network to dramatically reduce its performance. We propose a methodology where an evolutionary algorithm evolves the parameters of different malicious agents, determining their types and mobility patterns in order to minimize the data delivery rate and maximize the latency of communication in the network. As a case study, we consider a fine-grained simulation of a large-scale disruption-tolerant network in the city of Venice. By evolving malicious agents, we uncover situations where even a single attacker can hamper the network performance, and we correlate the performance decay to the number of malicious agents.

**Keywords:** Disruption-tolerant network · Routing · Evolutionary algorithm

## 1 Introduction

In a complex, open environment such as a city, pedestrians and motorized vehicles are heavily mobile agents, and their movement is constrained to well-defined paths and streets. Mobile communication devices carried by these agents are the

© Springer International Publishing Switzerland 2015
A.M. Mora and G. Squillero (Eds.): EvoApplications 2015, LNCS 9028, pp. 29–41, 2015.
DOI: 10.1007/978-3-319-16549-3_3

nodes in such an *urban network*. The nodes' communication range and bandwidth are limited by their hardware platform and energy supply. Consider an *ad hoc message-routing protocol* for these agents which, unlike the cellular network, uses no centralized communication infrastructure. This protocol should achieve both a good *data delivery rate* and a low *latency* of data messages sent by any node to any other node, while only using as communication primitive the peer-to-peer transmission of data between any two nodes (when these agents are within communication range and can connect reliably). This class of data-routing protocols form (Delay- or) Disruption-Tolerant Networks (DTNs) [1,2].

As a complete source-to-destination path may not always exist in a DTN, intermediate nodes are required to *store* the data and *wait* for an opportunity to *forward* the message to another node towards its final destination, thus creating a *space-time* communication path. Originally developed for solving routing problems in space missions [3], DTNs have been applied, over the years, also to terrestrial applications. Nowadays, DTNs are mostly used as a communication service in open urban environments [4] and several different DTN routing protocols have been designed.

While much research has been devoted to optimizing the data delivery rate and latency of DTNs, the *security* of DTN protocols is still an open problem. This is a particularly serious issue, since urban DTNs must often remain *open* to all willing participants (i.e., DTNs do not perform agent authentication). In such scenarios, security attacks typically consist in one or more agents in the network having malicious behavior; examples are *black holes*, i.e., agents which route no messages to any other agents, and *data flooders*, i.e., agents which inject an unusually large number of messages into the network. To assess the vulnerabilities of DTN protocols to such attacks, one must first determine how "badly" an attacker can affect realistic DTNs. However, the problem of determining the optimal attack method for a fixed DTN environment (i.e., the city map and the movement pattern of all honest agents) was proven NP-hard [4].

We propose an alternative solution: for a realistic urban DTN, we design a *DTN testing framework* based on evolutionary algorithms (EAs), which can highlight the vulnerabilities of any DTN protocol more effectively than existing methods. As a case study, we focus on the classic First Contact (FC) protocol for routing messages in a DTN [1]. FC adopts a simple logic in which an agent forwards a message to the first agent with which a data connection is formed. In FC, a single copy of each message in the network exists at a time, and it is forwarded until the message reaches its destination. The results of our testing on FC clearly demonstrate the potential of the approach: we found scenarios where even a single attacker, purposely "evolved" by the testing framework to exploit the movement patterns in a large network, can reduce the global data delivery in the network to *half* that of the network with no attackers.

The rest of the paper is organized as follows: the next section summarizes the main results from related literature and positions our work with respect to them. Then, Sect. 3 describes our evolutionary-based methodology; Sect. 4 illustrates the experimental setup and presents the numerical results. Finally, Sect. 5 concludes this work.

## 2   Related Work

Existing studies [5,6] propose a defense against data-flooding attackers, which consists of embedding into the routing protocol heuristic rules such that agents refuse to forward messages injected by flooders. On the other hand, an effective defense against black holes is more difficult to design, and would require each agent to maintain long-term trust relationships with other agents, thus complicating the protocol logic.

On the other hand, very few studies focused on a thorough empirical analysis of the vulnerabilities in existing DTN protocols. The most relevant work was done by John Burgess et al. [7], who quantified the damages caused by a set of attackers in a given application scenario. In their study, they model the town of Amherst (US) with a sparse bus-and-pedestrian open DTN of 71 nodes. The set of attackers is calculated either randomly or by using a greedy heuristic: attackers are added to the network such that they minimize the number of data connections that can be formed. Then, simulation repetitions are used to obtain an average data delivery rate of the network with attackers present.

The greedy heuristic for node selection was found much more effective than random selection at reducing the data delivery rate. For a protocol similar to FC, the effects of any type of attack were found to be minor: compared to a baseline of 33 % delivery rate without any attackers, only by turning malicious *half* of all the nodes in the network did the network's delivery rate fall to half of the baseline, i.e., a rate of message delivery of 17 %.

From the results, the work understandably draws a very favorable conclusion about the robustness of DTN routing to attacks; however, authors do admit that other DTN scenarios may exist which "cause the DTN to perform extremely poorly even with a small number of attackers. For instance, if node mobility is extremely low, and one node forms a nexus for all routing paths, the DTN will fail to deliver packets after corrupting that node. Similarly, if one attacker can corrupt all nodes by flooding an area with RF noise, the DTN will also fail" [7].

Our results show the exact contrary: even with the ideal conditions of high node mobility and no single-node bottlenecks, a small number of well-located, "strong" attackers executing an unsophisticated attacker logic will lower the delivery rate well under the thresholds found in [7].

## 3   Proposed Approach

The core idea of this work is to use an evolutionary algorithm to *optimize* the parameters and movement of attackers, with the final goal to disclose vulnerabilities in the DTN. To validate the proposed evolutionary testing framework, we simulate an urban environment composed of a map and a set of moving agents (the network nodes). Depending on their type, agents are constrained to different paths, and have different speeds. The building blocks of their movement patterns are the *points of interest* (POIs) located on the map: agent $i$ randomly chooses a destination $p$ from a set of points of interest $P_i$; travels to $p$ at a realistic speed on the shortest path; takes a break. Then, it repeats the whole process.

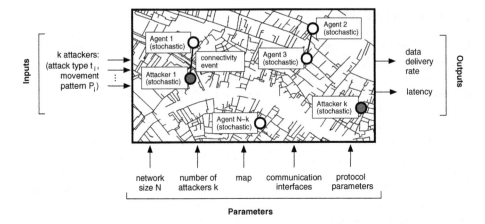

**Fig. 1.** Representation of the problem: given a set of scenario parameters, calculate the attackers (input) which will produce the most extreme situation in the DTN (output).

We assume two fixed groups of agents: "honest" and "malicious". For any honest agent $i$, the predetermined set $P_i$ of points of interest includes all the points on the map layer (see also the individual structure description in the next section). For added realism, a small number of these points may be given a higher probability of being selected as next destination. For any malicious agent $i$, the optimal set $P_i$ of points of interest (i.e. the parameters that would lead to a maximum damage in the network) is instead free to evolve. All honest nodes execute the FC routing protocol, while malicious nodes can act either as data flooders or black holes.

The evolutionary optimization process can then be summarized as follows: given a DTN of $N$ total nodes, a fixed number of malicious nodes $k < N$, and any parameters of the urban environment, find the attacker movement patterns $P_i$, $i = 1 \ldots k$ which would lower the data delivery rate (DDR) of the DTN the most, while maximizing also its average latency. A graphical representation of this problem is shown in Fig. 1, which visually describes how our testing framework finds those optimal inputs (attackers' parameters) which trigger the most "interesting" (i.e., bad) DTN performance in the outputs, namely lower DDR and higher latency, prioritized in this order.

**Evolutionary Framework.** We adopt a general-purpose evolutionary framework developed at Politecnico di Torino [8], $\mu GP^1$, a toolkit that has been successfully applied to a number of research projects, including the analysis of protocols used in wireless sensor networks [9,10]. Three interesting properties influenced our choice: first, the design of this framework is based on the notion of an *external evaluator*, which simplifies the integration with an external network simulator; secondly, the algorithm available in $\mu GP$ features a built-in support for multiple fitness functions, that can be evaluated both in a

---

[1] $\mu GP$ is available from http://ugp3.sourceforge.net.

lexicographical order and in a multi-objective approach; and finally, the evolutionary engine available in $\mu$GP makes use of self-adaptation techniques, greatly limiting the number of parameters that require to be set. The structure of the proposed framework is reported in Fig. 2.

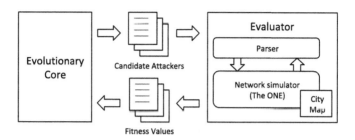

**Fig. 2.** Our DTN testing framework.

**Individual Structure.** In the problem under study, an individual represents one or more malicious individuals trying to attack a DTN network. Each attacker (as in Fig. 3) is defined by its type (here, pedestrian or boat) and a set of POIs which effectively define a set of paths on the map.

It is important to notice that the same POIs have different meanings depending on the type of attacker: even if a boat and a pedestrian pass close to the same coordinates, they may reach them using different paths, causing different network disruptions along the way. Also, since most of the POIs are accessible by certain types of attackers only (e.g., a point in open water cannot be reached by a pedestrian, nor one on land by a boat), for each type we overlap a *grid* layer onto the city map layer, and define the path of an attacker of that type as

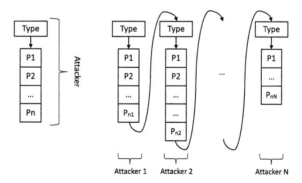

**Fig. 3.** Individual structure for (left) single and (right) multiple attackers. Multiple attackers are concatenated into a single individual. Each attacker is characterized by a variable number of points of interest and a type (pedestrian, boat) which points to that agent's map layer. The initial numbers of points of interest are drawn from a Gaussian distribution $\mathcal{N}(70, 60^2)$.

a set of grid squares inside that grid. During the simulation, we then map each grid square to the map point *closest* to the square; if a square contains more than one map point, the attacker visits them all.

**Fitness Functions.** As shown in Fig. 1, the outputs of each simulation (i.e., the fitness functions, in the evolutionary jargon), are:

- $(f_1)$ the data delivery rate, calculated as the percentage of messages originated *only* from honest nodes, and which are delivered successfully;
- $(f_2)$ similarly, the average latency of message deliveries (in seconds).

They are evaluated in lexicographic order: $f_1$ is minimized, and $f_2$ is maximized.

**Evolutionary Operators.** The genetic operators employed by the evolutionary framework include two crossover operators which are able to cross over individuals at the level of their corresponding paths, namely `onePointCrossover` and `twoPointCrossover`, and four mutation operators, namely `insertionMutation`, `removalMutation` and `replacementMutation`, that respectively add, remove or change a single POI in a path, and `singleParameterAlterationMutation`, that changes either a single coordinate in a POI, or the type of attacker.

## 4    Experimental Evaluation

The approach is validated by coupling $\mu$GP with the ad hoc network simulator *The ONE* [11]. As a case study, we consider a DTN with $N = 200$ mobile agents "operating" in the dense, $5\,\mathrm{km}^2$ core of the city of Venice, Italy. For this city, an agent is limited to either of two types: pedestrian, whose movements are confined to the map layer containing only foot paths; boat, whose movements are constrained to the map layer containing only waterways (see Fig. 4, left). Both types of nodes can be either honest or malicious. The number of pedestrians and boats is set, respectively, equal to 150 and 50. In each simulation, a small subset of $k < N$ nodes (of any combination of types, i.e. $n$ pedestrians and $k - n$ boats, $n = 0, \ldots, k$) is turned malicious and evolved by the evolutionary algorithm. The number of malicious nodes is fixed for the duration of the experiment, and all malicious agents perform the same kind of attack. Furthermore, each attacker's type is fixed, as shown by the genetic structure in Fig. 3.

Honest nodes are initially placed randomly on their map layer. The next point of interest visited by each node is then selected randomly from those available on that layer; a small number of map points (3 pedestrian, and 2 waterway locations) situated at main commercial or touristic spots in the city, have a higher probability of selection, at $10\,\%$ per map point. Then, the node travels to this next point on the shortest valid path on its map layer. Finally, once the target point of interest is reached, the node randomly selects a new one, and the execution proceeds from that point. This movement model based on shortest-path calculation quickly distributes the nodes non-uniformly on the map. As seen in the snapshot of a sample simulation (Fig. 4, right), preferred paths "emerge" on the map, as in real life. Unlike the honest nodes, attackers select their next destination *only* from their own list of points of interest, which is generated by the evolutionary framework, as described in the previous section.

Each network is simulated for 12 h (simulated time), starting after a warm-up simulated period of 1000 s. The warm-up helps to remove the transient effects due to the initial random node placement, and allows the movement patterns natural to this large-scale scenario to emerge. Also, to smoothen the fitness landscape and reduce the effect of the random seed on the simulation, we replicate each network simulation 10 times, initialized with different random seeds, and average the measured DDR and latency over the repetitions.

**Fig. 4.** (**left**) Map of Venice, Italy: a pedestrian layer $L_P$ (drawn in black), and a waterways layer $L_W$ (drawn in blue); the layers only overlap at bridges and boat stops. (**right**) A snapshot of a simulation of shortest-path movement of 200 nodes at a simulation time of 6 h: node identifiers (prefixed by P for pedestrians and W for boats) are drawn in blue, and their communication range in green (Color figure online).

During each simulation, a new data message of size 10 kB is created every 30 s by a random honest node in the network, with another random honest node as destination. All honest nodes have a message buffer of 5 MB, and execute the FC protocol [1], while attackers behave in one of two ways:

– A *black hole* attacker executes another, "passive" protocol logic in which the node offers to route data messages for other nodes, but in effect does nothing, effectively ending the communication path of all messages that reach it.
– A *data flooding* attacker executes the correct FC protocol, but creates new data messages of much larger size, aiming to overload the message buffers of honest nodes. These malicious messages are generated every 3 s, their size is set to 100 kB (a ten-fold increase with respect to a honest message) and the size of the message buffer for honest nodes is decreased five-fold to 1 MB.

These choices ensure that the flooding attack is sufficiently "heavy" to create an interesting fitness landscape for the problem.

**Table 1.** Simulation settings for all nodes in the DTNs under test

| Map settings | Map: | Figure 4 (left), size 2210 m × 2340 m |
|---|---|---|
| | Map layers: | $L_P$ (pedestrian paths), $L_W$ (waterways) |
| | No. of line segments: | 4993 in $L_P$, 362 in $L_W$ |
| | No. of map points: | 6910 in $L_P$, 1354 in $L_W$ |
| Simulation settings | Simulation time: | 12 h |
| | Types of nodes: | 150 pedestrians (constrained to $L_P$), 50 boats (constrained to $L_W$) |
| Movement model | Next point: | Chosen randomly from a map layer |
| | Path choice: | Shortest path to the next map point |
| | Pedestrian speed: | $[0.5 \ldots 1.5]$ mps |
| | Boat speed: | $[1.0 \ldots 5.0]$ mps |
| | Wait time: | $[0 \ldots 120]$ s at each destination point |
| Communication interfaces | Bluetooth: | Range 15 m, speed 250 kBps |
| | High-speed: | Range 100 m, speed 10 MBps |
| | Pedestrians use: | Bluetooth |
| | Boats use: | Bluetooth and High-speed |
| Data settings | Message created: | Every 30 s (honest node), 3 s (data flooder) |
| | Message size: | 10 kB (honest node), 100 kB (data flooder) |
| | Message buffer: | 5 MB (default), 1 MB (under flooding) |
| | Message TTL: | 5 h |

A summary of the simulation configuration parameters is reported in Table 1, while Table 2 shows the values for the parameters of the evolutionary algorithm. The latter were chosen according to simple recommendations from [8].

**Results.** The proposed DTN testing framework (from Fig. 2) chaining the evolutionary framework with the DTN simulator is run in separate evolutionary experiments for a fixed number of attackers $k$ ranging between 1 and 4, for

**Table 2.** $\mu$GP settings used during the experiments.

| Parameter | Description | Value |
|---|---|---|
| $\mu$ | Population size | 30 |
| $\lambda$ | Number of genetic operators applied at every step | 5 |
| $\tau$ | Size of the tournament selection | 2 |
| § | Stagnation condition (generation) | 50 |

**Table 3.** The best experiments obtained in this study. The number of evaluations and wall-clock time vary, respectively, because of the stagnation stop condition and due to different load on our computing facility ($[16 \div 24]$ available cores).

| Fitness functions max. (↑) or min. (↓) | Attacker type | No. of attackers | No. of evaluations | Wall-clock time | Best fitnesses |
|---|---|---|---|---|---|
| DDR ↓, Latency ↑ | black holes | 1 | 4645 | ~29 h | 26.17 %, 5142 |
| | | 2 | 9074 | ~63 h | 16.66 %, 3499 |
| | | 3 | 9418 | ~130 h | 12.73 %, 2794 |
| | | 4 | 10285 | ~94 h | 10.72 %, 2494 |
| DDR ↓, Latency ↑ | data flooder | 1 | 5739 | ~ 98h | 21.89 %, 2866 |
| | | 2 | 5813 | ~95 h | 18.43 %, 3752 |
| | | 3 | 3743 | ~47 h | 13.66 %, 3058 |
| | | 4 | 7859 | ~93 h | 12.11 %, 2804 |

each attack methodology (black hole or data flooding). Each of the 8 resulting experiments is run twice, with different random seeds. We summarize the configurations and best fitness of each experiment in Table 3 and Fig. 5. In the figure, we also show the comparison of the best $f_1$ obtained for each of the 8 experimental settings ($k \times$ attack method) with two baseline scenarios:

- A scenario in which all 200 nodes are honest (i.e., $k = 0$). In this case, given a sample of 30 simulations, the average $f_1$ (the delivery rate for the First Contact protocol) is 47.57 % with a standard deviation of 1.15 %.
- A scenario in which $k$ *random* attackers of the same attack method exist in the network. Their lists of points of interest are generated randomly. This baseline is calculated as the average and standard deviation of $f_1$ over 30 simulations (with different random seeds).

With reference to Fig. 5, it can be seen that, in each case, the evolutionary experiment found that single attackers (of either type) exist which lower the delivery rate to half that of the $k = 0$ baseline; also, there exist pairs of two attackers (also of either type) which lower the delivery rate to a third of the $k = 0$ baseline. The evolution of groups of attackers performs efficiently, lowering by approximately 10 % the delivery rate with respect to the baseline of $k$ random attackers with the same characteristics.

The progress of the evolutionary process for two of our experiments (with $k = 1$ and different types of attackers) is shown in Fig. 6. Each experiment is shown from the initial, random population until the stagnation condition is met. For each generation in the sequence, both fitnesses are plotted: both the best and worst data delivery rate ($f_1$), which is minimized first, and the best message latency ($f_2$), which is then maximized. It is the data delivery rate which has the most interesting evolution here: its smooth progress is likely sign of a generally smooth landscape for $f_1$. Also, we can observe that in both cases the latency positively correlates to the minimization of DDR, despite evolutionary attempts

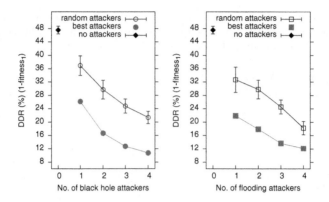

**Fig. 5.** Baseline values for $f_1$ (avg. ± std.dev.) and best values for $f_1$ obtained using our DTN testing framework for each number of attackers $k$ and method of attack: black hole (**left**), and data flooding (**right**). $k = 0$ corresponds to the baseline scenario with no attackers.

to maximize it. This can be explained as follows. In the black hole case, the latency of the few messages that are not intercepted by the attacker (and can reach their destination) is not affected. On the other hand, in the flooding case, the large number of messages injected by the flooder (sent to random honest nodes) creates a network congestion which lets very few messages reach their destination, likely only those destined to close neighbors; this explains why the average latency of delivered messages is significantly lower with a single flooder than with a single black hole attacker.

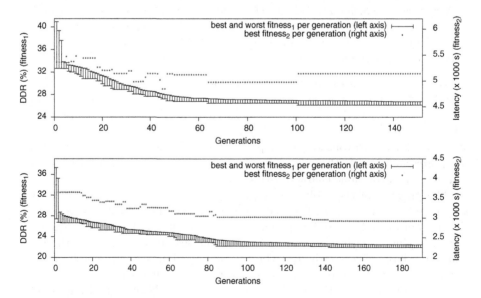

**Fig. 6.** Evolving a single black hole attacker (**top**) and data flooder (**bottom**): the progress of the two fitness functions through generations.

**Discussion of Results: Significance and Limitations.** The numerical test results (summarized in Fig. 5) clearly show that evolved attackers are *more efficient* than random attackers. Also, the drop in delivery rate experienced in that network which includes the optimized attackers is unexpectedly large, considering that only few nodes are malicious out of a large network of 200 nodes.

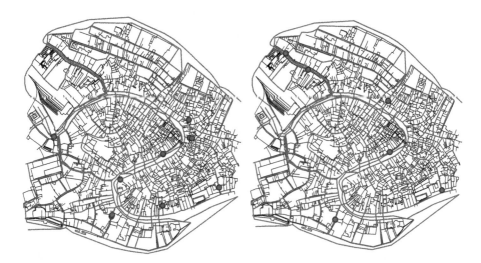

**Fig. 7.** (**left**) The best single black hole attacker. (**right**) The best single data flooding attacker. Both attackers are *boats* and move among the respective points of interest shown here on the waterways map layer.

We briefly present insights obtained from analyzing the movement patterns of the best attackers obtained by our tests; further analysis is left for future work. Figure 7 (left) depicts the best black hole attacker found. This attacker is a boat which only travels on the shortest path between any two of the points shown, and thus "covers" only the southern half of the main canal, and a small number of the lesser canals. For the result to be explained, these points should be seen in the context of the general mobility patterns of honest nodes (Fig. 4, right): many lead to map areas where either honest pedestrians or honest boats have their preferred routes. In contrast, the best data flooder (Fig. 7, right), which is also a boat, also travels among crowded areas, yet maintains a much wider territory. Interestingly, while the best attackers found are generally boats, the best group of four attackers was found to be mixed, composed of one pedestrian and three boats.

## 5  Conclusions

We introduced an evolutionary-driven testing framework for Disruption Tolerant Networks. The proposed framework uses an evolutionary algorithm to evolve the most disruptive paths that attackers should take to reduce the network performance (expressed in terms of data delivery rate and latency) the most. We showed the applicability of the approach with realistic *in silico* experiments which simulated the movement of a large number of agents of different types and networking behavior ("malicious" vs "honest", black holes vs flooders) in a complex urban environment. The evolution led us to discover the most malicious movement patterns that attackers should follow. We quantified the damage inflicted by groups of up to four attackers, and compared the resulting network performance with baseline values obtained in absence of attackers and with randomly generated attackers.

The study shows that single attackers can disrupt the network equally as much as (in the related work, Sect. 2) turning half of the entire network into attackers. This is partly caused by the fact that the scenarios (city map, movement model, network size) considered there are different than ours. Even so, our evolutionary testing method is more effective, and more generally applicable to testing complex networked systems than the previous methods based on heuristics: it requires no *prior* knowledge as to what an attacker type and location have as effect upon the overall network. Thus, it is likely to uncover *new* knowledge as to the cause-and-effect of security attacks.

Importantly, our methodology can be easily applied to assess the vulnerabilities of virtually any ad hoc network, allowing network experts to identify the weaknesses of protocols in large networks and, possibly, pro-actively find countermeasures. In future works, we plan to extend this approach, scaling up to larger networks and larger groups of attackers, studying alternative routing protocols, and more advanced evolutionary schemes such as cooperative evolution.

# References

1. Jain, S., Fall, K., Patra, R.: Routing in a delay tolerant network. In: Proceedings of the 2004 Conference on Applications, Technologies, Architectures, and Protocols for Computer Communications, SIGCOMM 2004, pp. 145–158. ACM, New York (2004)
2. Borrel, V., Ammar, M.H., Zegura, E.W.: Understanding the wireless and mobile network space: a routing-centered classification. In: Proceedings of the Second ACM Workshop on Challenged Networks, CHANTS 2007, pp. 11–18. ACM, New York (2007)
3. Jenkins, A., Kuzminsky, S., Gifford, K., Pitts, R., Nichols, K.: Delay/disruption-tolerant networking: flight test results from the international space station. In: Aerospace Conference, 2010 IEEE, pp. 1–8, March 2010
4. Burgess, J., Gallagher, B., Jensen, D., Levine, B.: Maxprop: routing for vehicle-based disruption-tolerant networks. In: INFOCOM 2006, 25th IEEE International Conference on Computer Communications, pp. 1–11, April 2006
5. Li, F., Wu, J., Srinivasan, A.: Thwarting blackhole attacks in disruption-tolerant networks using encounter tickets. In: INFOCOM 2009, IEEE, pp. 2428–2436, April 2009
6. Li, Q., Gao, W., Zhu, S., Cao, G.: To lie or to comply: defending against flood attacks in disruption tolerant networks. IEEE Trans. Dependable Secure Comput. **10**(3), 168–182 (2013)

7. Burgess, J., Bissias, G.D., Corner, M.D., Levine, B.N.: Surviving attacks on disruption-tolerant networks without authentication. In: Proceedings of the 8th ACM International Symposium on Mobile Ad Hoc Networking and Computing, MobiHoc 2007, pp. 61–70. ACM, New York (2007)
8. Sanchez, E., Schillaci, M., Squillero, G.: Evolutionary Optimization: The $\mu$GP Toolkit, 1st edn. Springer, New York (2011)
9. Bucur, D., Iacca, G., Squillero, G., Tonda, A.: The impact of topology on energy consumption for collection tree protocols: an experimental assessment through evolutionary computation. Appl. Soft Comput. **16**, 210–222 (2014)
10. Bucur, D., Iacca, G., Squillero, G., Tonda, A.: The tradeoffs between data delivery ratio and energy costs in wireless sensor networks: a multi-objective evolutionary framework for protocol analysis. In: Proceedings of the Sixtienth Annual Conference on Genetic and Evolutionary Computation Conference, GECCO 2014. ACM, New York (2014)
11. Keränen, A., Ott, J., Kärkkäinen, T.: The ONE simulator for DTN protocol evaluation. In: SIMUTools 2009, Proceedings of the 2nd International Conference on Simulation Tools and Techniques, New York, NY, USA, ICST (2009)

# A Novel Grouping Genetic Algorithm for Assigning Resources to Users in WCDMA Networks

L. Cuadra, S. Salcedo-Sanz[✉], A.D. Carnicer, M.A. Del Arco,
and J.A. Portilla-Figueras

Department of Signal Processing and Communications, University of Alcalá,
28871 Alcalá de Henares, Madrid, Spain
{lucas.cuadra,sancho.salcedo,miguelangel.arco,antonio.portilla}@uah.es,
antonio.carnicer@gmail.com

**Abstract.** In this work we explore the feasibility of applying a novel grouping genetic algorithm (GGA) to the problem of assigning resources to mobile terminals or users in Wideband Code Division Multiple Access (WCDMA) mobile networks. In particular, we propose: (1) A novel cost function (to be minimized) that contains, in addition to the common load factors, other utilization ratios for aggregate capacity, codes, power, and users without service. (2) A novel encoding scheme, and modifications for the crossover and mutation operators, tailored for resource assignment in WCDMA networks. The experimental work points out that our GGA approach exhibits a superior performance than that of the conventional method (which minimizes only the load factors), since all users receive the demanded service along with a minimum use of the assigned resources (aggregate capacity, power, and codes).

**Keywords:** Grouping genetic algorithm · WCDMA mobile networks · Telecommunication

## 1 Introduction

Electromagnetic spectrum is an extremely valuable resource for mobile telecommunication companies because of its scarcity and the need for expense licenses to use it. Thus, making an ever increasing more efficient use of the available spectrum has been an ongoing concern since the very beginning of mobile communications. In particular, among other technological advances, great efforts have been made in the field of the so-called multiple access techniques, which aim at enabling a number of devices to transmit over the same medium (the air interface, in this case), sharing its capacity. Key examples in mobile networks are TDMA (Time Division Multiple Access), WCDMA (Wide-band Code Division Multiple Access), and OFDMA (Orthogonal Frequency Division Multiple Access), which, respectively, are used in 2G (Second Generation) networks, 3G (Third Generation) networks, and in the in-deployment 4G mobile networks [1].

© Springer International Publishing Switzerland 2015
A.M. Mora and G. Squillero (Eds.): EvoApplications 2015, LNCS 9028, pp. 42–53, 2015.
DOI: 10.1007/978-3-319-16549-3_4

This evolution does not remove previous techniques but, on the contrary, results in forming a mobile access "ecosystem" to provide the best customer service.

Currently, HSPA (High Speed Packet Access), based on WCDMA, is the most widely used deployed mobile *broadband* technology in the world. In fact, HSPA is not an unique technology but a set of technologies that allow mobile operators to easily upgrade their already deployed WCDMA networks to support a very efficient provision of speech services and mobile broadband data services (high speed Internet access, music-on-demand, and TV and video streaming, to name just a few). This illustrates the importance of properly dimensioning WCDMA networks.

With this context in mind, the question arising here is how to optimally assign the limited WCDMA resources to mobile terminals (user equipments (UEs), or simply, users). In WCDMA cellular networks, a number of users are allowed to utilize simultaneously the same frequency. To separate the communications, the network assigns a "code" to each communication so that only the corresponding receiver is able to extract the information that has been sent to it. Then, the remaining communications using the same frequency become an interference signal. This is illustrated in Fig. 1 where the dashed sector $S_k$ of the base station (BS) or node-B (in WCDMA terminology) provides services to a number of users $n_u^{S_k}$. $p_{r,BS}(j)$ is the power received at the base station (BS) emitted by user $j$. Interferences appear both in the downlink (DL) −signals moving from the BS to the users− and in the uplink (UL) −from the users to the BS−. In this respect, the conventional approach to assigning resources to users is based on minimizing the total interference [1].

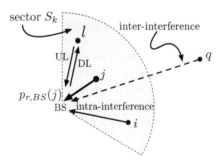

**Fig. 1.** Simplified representation of the basic concepts involved. $i$, $j$ and $l$ label users in sector $S_k$. See the main text for details.

However, the current rising demand of higher speeds reveals that there are other resources that should be taken into account. One of the most evident is based on the fact that the aggregation of higher data rates is leading to a bottleneck in the aggregation interface at the BSs in the sense that the aggregated rates could be higher than the available backhaul capacity for both UL and DL. Another limiting resources are the number of codes and the available power.

In this regard, the purpose of this paper is to explore the feasibility of a novel Grouping Genetic Algorithm (GGA) to assign resources (aggregate capacity, power, codes) to users in WCDMA networks.

The structure of the rest of this paper is as follows. Section 2 reviews the related work, while Sect. 3 focuses on describing the problem within the framework of WCDMA networks, and on modeling the resources to be assigned. Section 4 describes the GGA we propose to tackle the aforementioned problem of assigning resources to users. Finally, Sect. 5 shows the experimental work we have carried out, and Sect. 6 discusses the main findings.

## 2    Related Work

There is a number of recent works that study the problem of assigning users and base stations, although without using the GGA approach. In this respect, some solutions to optimize both the radio interface and the backhaul capacity have been recently explored [2,3]. There are also some works that focus on the jointly assignment of mobile users to base stations and power [4,5], and to base stations and beamforming schemes [6,7].

As mentioned before, the purpose of this paper is to assign resources (codes, power, capacity) to users by using a GGA-based approach that minimizes not only the interference but also the use of codes, capacity, power, and the number of user without service. The GGA, developed by Falkenauer *et al.* in a series of publications in the last 90's [8–10], was applied thereafter to a number of specific telecommunication applications such as mobile communication network design [11–13], or OFDMA-based multicast wireless systems [14], obtaining subgroups of users within the same multicast group so that OFDMA subcarriers are then assigned to each subgroup to maximize the aggregate data rate. In a more general context, it has been applied to assignment [15] or fuzzy partitioning problems [16], to name just a few. Following the proven good performance of the GGA, alternative meta-heuristic optimization engines for grouping problems have been subsequently developed during the last few years, mainly the Grouping Harmony Search (GHS) [17], the Grouping Particle Swarm Optimization algorithm (GPS) [18], and the Grouping Evolutionary Strategy approach [19].

Despite of the huge application of these techniques, and to the best of our knowledge, the feasibility of the GGA has not been yet explored in WCDMA networks to assign resources to users aiming at minimizing not only the interference but also the use of codes, backhaul capacity, power, and the number of users without service. Next section describes the problem along with the resources that our GGA will assign to users.

## 3    Problem Statement

The problem consists in optimally assigning $N$ active users to the $M$ sectors of a WCDMA network, by minimizing a novel cost function that will be described in detail in Subsect. 3.4. For the sake of clarity, we use the following notation: $S_k$

represents the $k$ sector in the network (with $k = 1, \cdots, M$), while $n_u^{S_k}$ stands for the number of users that our GGA will assign to sector $S_k$ in each generation.

Although it will be discussed deeply in Subsect. 4.1, it is worth introducing here the encoding our GGA will use because it will assist us in better describing the mathematical formulation of the problem. In this respect, a chromosome $\mathbf{c}_i$ encoding a trial solution to be explored will be of the form

$$\mathbf{c}_i = [u_1^{S_h}, \ldots, u_j^{S_k}, \ldots, u_N^{S_w} \mid n_u^{ws}, n_u^{S_1}, \ldots, \underline{n_u^{S_k}}, \ldots, n_u^{S_M}], \tag{1}$$

where, for the sake of clarity, we have underlined two elements: $u_j^{S_k}$ and $n_u^{S_k}$. $u_j^{S_k}$ encodes that user $j$ is assigned to sector $S_k$, while $n_u^{S_k}$ quantify the number of users in sector $S_k$. Note that the example chromosome in Expression (1) contains a "different" element labeled $n_u^{ws}$. It stands for the number of users *without service* (no sector has been assigned), and its discussion will be postponed to Sect. 4, where it will be better understood, within the context of the novel grouping encoding we propose.

### 3.1 Background

In a WCDMA network, the users (mobile devices or "user equipments") are allowed to use simultaneously the same electromagnetic carrier. To separate the communications on the same carrier frequency, $f_c$, the network has a number of (ideally) orthogonal *codes*, and automatically assigns a different code to each communication so that *only* the corresponding receiver is able to extract the information that specifically will be sent to it. This is done by multiplying the user data by a code or sequence of bits (called "chips"), whose rate ("chip rate", $W$) is much higher than that of the user bit rate.

The problem is that the remaining communications that use the same frequency become an *interference* signal. The effect of interference in the dimensioning of WCDMA celular networks is usually modeled by means of a concept called "load factor" [1]. It is a parameter that allows to quantify to what extent the active users are affecting or "loading" the system with interference.

### 3.2 Load Factor

Figure 1 will assist us in explain it. For simplicity, it shows only one of the 3 sectors the node-B has. The sector labeled $S_k$ has $n_u^{S_k}$ active users. $p_{r,BS}(j)$ represents the signal power received (subscript "$r$") *at* the BS, emitted by user $j$. Note that $p_{r,BS}(j)$ is corrupted by the interference produced by those signal coming from other users with the same frequency. The load factor in all the up-links of sector $S_k$, defined as the ratio between the interference and the *total* noise (thermal + interference) [1], can be estimated as

$$\eta_{UL}(\mathbf{c}_i) \approx (1 + \xi_{S_k}) \cdot \sum_{j=1}^{n_u^{S_k}} \frac{1}{1 + \frac{1}{(e_b/n_0)_s} \cdot \frac{W}{R_{b,s}^u(j) \cdot \nu_s^u}} \tag{2}$$

where:

- $\mathbf{c}_i = [u_1^{S_h}, \ldots, u_j^{S_k}, \ldots, u_N^{S_w} \mid n_u^{ws}, n_u^{S_1}, \ldots, n_u^{S_k}, \ldots, n_u^{S_M}]$ contains the whole required information: the sector to which any user is assigned ($u_j^{S_k}$), and ($n_u^{S_k}$). We have explicitly written $\eta_{UL} \equiv \eta_{UL}(\mathbf{c}_i)$ in the effort of emphasizing that the encoding chromosome $\mathbf{c}_i$ is related to the parameters that will be used to construct the cost function. This consideration also applies to the other parameters that will be stated below, so that we will not mention this again.
- $\xi_{S_k}$ is the ratio between the inter-interference (coming from users in other sectors, $S_l$, $l \neq k$) and intra-interference (produced by the $n_u^{S_k}$ users within the same sector $S_k$).
- $(e_b/n_0)_s$ is the value for the ratio between the mean bit energy and the noise power density (including thermal noise and interference) required to achieve a given quality for service $s$, for instance, in terms of block error rate (BLER). For the purpose of this paper, $(e_b/n_0)_s$ is an input parameter provided by the service requirements [1].
- $R_{b,s}^u(j)$ is the bit rate of service $s$ in the $j$ uplink within sector $S_k$. It is an input value stated by the service requirements. Throughout this paper, uppercases "$u$" and "$d$" will be used for labeling, respectively, uplink and downlink parameters.
- $\nu_s^u$ is an utilization factor, which is 1 for data service, and $0 < \nu_s < 1$ for voice services [1].

In a similar way, the downlink load factor in sector $S_k$ is [1]

$$\eta_{DL}(\mathbf{c}_i) \approx \left[(1 - \overline{\alpha}) + \overline{\xi}\,\right] \sum_{j=1}^{n_u^{S_k}} \frac{(e_b/n_0)_s}{\frac{W}{R_{b,s}^d(j)\cdot\nu_s^d}} \tag{3}$$

where $\overline{\alpha}$ is an average orthogonality factor in the sector, and $\overline{\xi}$ is an average (across the sector) of $\xi_{S_k}(j)$, since in the DL, the ratio of other-sectors to own-sector interference depends on the user location and is thus different for each user $j$ [1].

The conventional method, whose details will be explain in Sect. 6 for comparative purposes, is based on minimizing the total load factor in the network, $\eta = \eta_{UL} + \eta_{DL}$. Furthermore, in addition to the load factor, we consider a novel cost function that contains other five ratios or parameters that are not used in the conventional approach, and that we define in the next section.

### 3.3   Including More Parameters in the Problem

Each of these parameters aims to quantify the efficiency with which an available resource $\mathcal{R}$ is used, that is: $\Delta_\mathcal{R} = \mathcal{R}_{used}/\mathcal{R}_{available}$.

The first telecommunication resource whose use would be optimized is the available capacity for aggregating UL bit rates: $C_a^u$. In any sector $S_k$, the UL bit rates of any user $u_j$ for a service $s$, $R_{b,s}^u(j)$, must be aggregated for ulterior backhauling. The corresponding aggregated capacity ratio in each sector $S_k$ is defined ($\doteq$) as

$$\Delta_{C_a}^{u}(\mathbf{c}_i) = \Delta_{C_a}^{u}(n_u^{S_k}) \doteq \frac{1}{C_a^u} \sum_{j=1}^{n_u^{S_k}} R_{b,s}^{u}(j), \tag{4}$$

where lowercase "a" stands for "aggregated". Note in (5) that we have written explicitly that $\mathbf{c}_i$ contains the necessary information ($n_u^{S_k}$, the number of users to be assigned) to computed the ratio in Sector $S_k$. In the definitions that follow we will not use yet this notation in an explicit form for the sake of simplicity.

Similarly, its counterpart for DL is defined as

$$\Delta_{C_a}^{d}(\mathbf{c}_i) \doteq \frac{1}{C_a^d} \sum_{j=1}^{n_u^{\partial_k}} R_{b,s}^{d}(j) \tag{5}$$

Another important resource is the maximum power per sector that the BS has in order to serve the active users. We model the efficiency in its use as

$$\Delta_{P_{BS}}^{d}(\mathbf{c}_i) \doteq \frac{1}{p_{Max,BS}(k)} \sum_{j=1}^{n_u^{S_k}} p_{BS}^{d}(j) \tag{6}$$

where $p_{Max,BS}(k)$ is the available BS power in sector $S_k$, and $p_{BS}^{d}(j)$ is the power for serving user $j$.

The fraction on channelization codes used for service $s$ in DL in sector $S_k$ is

$$\Delta_{\mathcal{C}_s}^{d}(\mathbf{c}_i) \doteq \frac{n_u^{S_k}}{N_{\mathcal{C}_s}^{d}}, \tag{7}$$

$N_{\mathcal{C}_s}^{d}$ being the total amount of codes for service $s$.

Finally, the fraction of users *without* service is

$$\Delta_{n_u}^{ws}(\mathbf{c}_i) \doteq \frac{n_u^{ws}}{N} \tag{8}$$

where $n_u^{ws}$, the number of users without service defined in (1), will be discussed deeply in Sect. 4.1.

These ratios along with the load factors will allow us to propose a novel cost function.

## 3.4 Novel Cost Function: Complete Mathematical Formulation

Given a WCDMA network with $M$ sectors and $N$ active users, the problem consists in assigning (for each sector $S_k$, $k = 1, 2, \cdots, M$) the available resources (power, capacity and codes) to its potentially assigned $n_u^{S_k}$ users by minimizing the novel cost function

$$\mathcal{C}(\mathbf{c}_i) = \sum_{k=1}^{M} \sum_{l=1}^{n_u^{S_k}} [\eta_{UL}(\mathbf{c}_i) + \eta_{DL}(\mathbf{c}_i) + \Delta_{C_a}^{u}(\mathbf{c}_i)$$
$$+ \Delta_{C_a}^{d}(\mathbf{c}_i) + \Delta_{P_{BS}}^{d}(\mathbf{c}_i) + \Delta_{C_s}^{d}(\mathbf{c}_i) + \Delta_{n_u}^{ws}(\mathbf{c}_i)], \tag{9}$$

constrained to the conditions that all the ratios (2)–(8) are real numbers ranging from 0 to 1. Note that a further refinement of the cost function (9) could consist in using weighted sums of the ratios (2)–(8), constrained to the mentioned conditions. The values of these weights should depend on the relative importance that each ratio has in a particular design.

## 4    Proposed Grouping Genetic Algorithm

### 4.1    Problem Encoding

Our example chromosome in Expression (1) is a variation with respect to the classical grouping encoding proposed initially by Falkenauer [8,9], which is a variable-length encoding scheme. In this classical approach, the encoding is based on separating each chromosome $\mathbf{c}$ into two parts: $\mathbf{c} = [\mathbf{l}|\mathbf{g}]$, the first one being the *element* section, while the second part, the *group* section. Since the number of sectors in our network is constant $(M)$, we have used the following variations of the classical grouping encoding: (1) The group section is an $(M + 1)$ length vector, whose elements (labeled $n_u^{S_j}$) represent the number of users in the $j$-th sector $(S_j)$. Subscript $j$ ranges from $-1$ to $M$, $j = -1$ being used to represent those users that are *not* connected to any node, that is, those in an "imaginary" or virtual sector that we have labelled "Sector $-1$". (2) The element part is an $N$-length vector whose elements $(u_i^{S_j})$ mean that user $u_i$ has been assigned to sector $S_j$. As an example, following our notation, in a solution with $N$ elements (users) and $M$ groups (sectors), a candidate individual $\mathbf{c}_i$ could be $[u_1^{S_h}, u_2^{S_p}, \dots, u_i^{S_j}, \dots, u_N^{S_w} \mid n_u^{S_{-1}}, n_u^{S_1}, n_u^{S_2}, \dots, n_u^{S_j}, \dots, n_u^{S_M}]$, where $n_u^{S_{-1}}$ is the number of users in sector $S_{-1}$, that is, those without service: $n_u^{S_{-1}} = n_u^{ws}$ in (1), those that have not been assigned to resources and thus do not have service.

Note that $\sum_{k=-1}^{M} n_u^{S_k} = N$, which simply states that the total number of active users in the network are distributed among the $M$ sectors, although $n_u^{S_{-1}} = n_u^{ws}$ have not been received resources.

### 4.2    Fitness Function

With this in mind, a possible fitness function to describe to what extent candidate chromosome $\mathbf{c}_i$ encodes a trial solution of the problem described in Sect. 3.4 could be

$$f_i = 1 - \mathcal{C}_N(\mathbf{c}_i), \tag{10}$$

where $\mathcal{C}_N$ is the cost function defined by Expression (9) normalized between 0 and 1.

## 4.3   Selection Operator

Our selection operator is inspired by a rank-based wheel selection mechanism. In a first step, individuals are sorted in a list based on their quality. The position of the individuals in the list is called *rank of the individual*, and labeled $R_i$, $i = 1, \ldots, \mathcal{P}_{size}$, $\mathcal{P}_{size}$ being the population size. We consider a rank in which the best individual $x$ is assigned $R_x = \mathcal{P}_{size}$, the second best $y$, $R_y = \mathcal{P}_{size} - 1$, and so on. A *fitness* value associated to each individual is then defined as

$$f_i = \frac{2 \cdot R_i}{\mathcal{P}_{size} \cdot (\mathcal{P}_{size} + 1)} \tag{11}$$

Note that these values are normalized between 0 and 1, depending on the position of the individual in the ranking list. It is worth emphasizing that this rank-based selection mechanism is static, in the sense that probabilities of survival (given by $f_i$) do not depend on the generation, but on the position of the individual in the list.

The process carried out by our algorithm consists in selecting the parents for crossover using this selection mechanism. This process is performed with replacement, i.e., a given individual can be selected several times as one of the parents, however, individuals in the crossover operator must be different.

## 4.4   Crossover Operator

It works as follows:

1. Select randomly two individuals (father and mother), and two crossing points in their corresponding group part.
2. Insert the elements belonging to the selected groups of the first individual into the offspring.
3. Insert the elements belonging to the selected groups of the second individual into the offspring, if they have not been assigned by the first individual.
4. Randomly complete the elements not yet assigned with elements from the current groups.
5. Remove empty clusters, if any.
6. Modify the labels of the current groups in the offspring in order to numerate them from 1 to $M$, including the one labeled "$-1$" corresponding to users without the required Quality of Service (QoS).

## 4.5   Mutation Operator

The mutation operator used consists in splitting a randomly selected group into two different ones. The samples belonging to the original group are assigned to the new groups with equal probability. Note that one of the new generated groups will keep its label in the group section of the individual, whereas the other will be assigned a new label.

## 5   Experiments

They have been carried out with real data (Espoo, Finland) [1]: 19 B-nodes, tree-sector each ($M = 19 \times 3 = 57$ sectors), $\overline{\alpha} = 0.65$, $\overline{\xi} = 0.55$, $W = 3.84$ Mchip/s, $P_{Max,BS} = 12$ W/sector, $C_a^u = C_a^d = 1536$ kbps, and $N = 450$ users with 3 different services, labeled $s_i =$ "1", "2", and "3" in Table 1. The values of the GGA parameters are: crossover probability $\mathcal{P}_c = 0.8$, mutation probability $\mathcal{P}_m = 0.05$, and population size $\mathcal{P}_{size} = 100$ individuals.

**Table 1.** Values of the services parameters. ARM means adaptive multi-rate.

| Service, $s_i$ | $(E_b/N_0)_i$ (dB) | $R_{b,i}^u$ (kbps) | $R_{b,i}^d$ (kbps) | $\nu_i^u = \nu_i^d$ | $N_{C_i}^d$ (codes) |
|---|---|---|---|---|---|
| "1" (ARM voice) | 5 | 12.2 | 12.2 | 0.58 | 256 |
| "2" (data) | 1.5 | 64 | 64 | 1 | 32 |
| "3" (data) | 1 | 64 | 384 | 1 | 4 |

In any of the experiments, the $N$ users are distributed randomly (uniform distribution). We have carried out 100 experiments, with 300 generations each. Figure 2 represents the fitness function as a function of the number of generations.

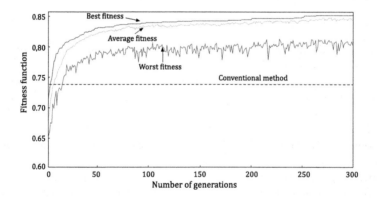

**Fig. 2.** Fitness values as a function of the number of generations.

The average fitness has been computed over the 100 experiments. The dashed line in Fig. 2 represents the fitness value computed by minimizing the load factor ("conventional method"). Note that the proposed GGA exhibits an average performance ($\overline{f} \approx 0.84$), which is superior to that of the conventional method ($f \approx 0.74$). Figures 3, 4, and 5 will assist us in completing the discussion by representing, respectively, $\eta = \eta_{UL} + \eta_{DL}$, $\Delta_{C_a} = \Delta_{C_a}^u + \Delta_{C_a}^d$, $\Delta_{P_{BS}}^d$, $\Delta_{C_s}^d$, and $\Delta n_u^{ws}$ as a function of the number of generations.

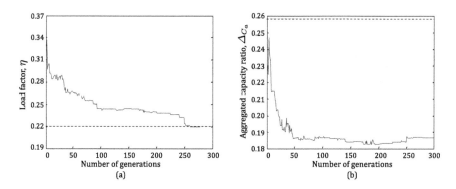

**Fig. 3.** (a) Load factor as a function of the number of generations. (b) Aggregated capacity ratio $\Delta_{C_a}$ as a function of the number of generations.

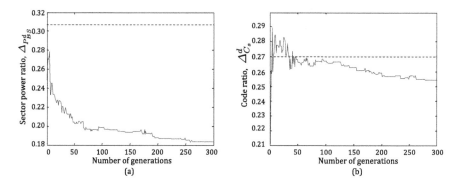

**Fig. 4.** (a) Sector power ratio $\Delta_{P_{BS}^d}$ as a function of the number of generations. (b) Code ratio $\Delta_{C_s}^d$ as a function of the number of generations.

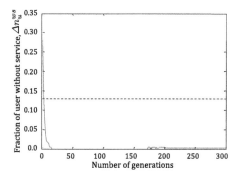

**Fig. 5.** Fraction of user without service $\Delta_{n_u}^{ws}$ as a function of the number of generations.

Dashed lines in Figs. 2, 3, 4, and 5 represent the defined ratios computed after using the solution found by the *conventional* method. As shown in Fig. 5, the GGA solution is better in the sense that the GGA assigns resources to *all* users —there is *no* user without service ($\Delta_{n_u}^{ws} = 0$), unlike the conventional one, in which about 13 % of users remain without service— along with a *more efficient use* (lower utilization) of $\Delta_{C_a}$, $\Delta_{P_{BS}}^d$, $\Delta_{C_s}^d$ (Figs. 3 and 4). In particular, $\Delta_{C_a}$ and $\Delta_{P_{BS}}^d$ are used *much more efficiently*: the fraction of aggregated capacity used $\Delta_{C_a}$ reduces from 25.8 % to 18.5 % (Fig. 3(b)), while the power consumption ratio $\Delta_{P_{BS}}^d$ decreases from 30.9 % to 18.5 % (Fig. 4(a)).

## 6  Summary and Conclusions

In this work we have proposed a novel GGA that aims at assigning resources (capacity, codes and power) to users in WCDMA networks. The first contribution is the definition of a novel cost function that contains, in addition to the common load factors, other utilization ratios for capacity, codes, power, and users without service. The second block of contributions is related to the GGA approach in itself: a novel encoding scheme, and modifications for the crossover and mutation operators, suited for assignment in WCDMA networks. The experimental work points out that our GGA approach exhibits a superior performance than that of the conventional method (which minimizes only the load factors). In particular, the proposed GGA assigns resources to *all* users (unlike the conventional one, in which about 13 % of users remain without service), along with a minimization of the used resources. In this respect, a representative results is the one corresponding to the fraction of aggregated capacity used, which reduces from 25.8 % (conventional method) to 18.5 %, while the power consumption ratio decreases from 30.9 % to 18.5 %.

**Acknowledgments.** This work has been partially supported by Comunidad de Madrid, under projects S2013/ICE-2933 ("PRICAM: Programa de redes eléctricas inteligentes en la Comunidad de Madrid"), and CCG2013/EXP-062 ("CROMN: Algoritmos meta-heurísticos para la optimización del coste de despliegue en redes de telecomunicación móvil").

## References

1. Holma, H., Toskala, A.: WCDMA for UMTS: HSPA Evolution and LTE. Wiley, Hoboken (2010)
2. Olmos, J., Ferrus, R., Galeana-Zapien, H.: Analytical modeling and performance evaluation of cell selection algorithms for mobile networks with backhaul capacity constraints. IEEE Trans. Wirel. Commun. **99**, 1–13 (2013)
3. Galeana-Zapien, H., Ferrus, R.: Design and evaluation of a backhaul-aware base station assignment algorithm for OFDMA-based cellular networks. IEEE Trans. Wirel. Commun. **9**(10), 3226–3237 (2010)

4. Ganti, A., Klein, T.E.: Base station assignment and power control algorithms for data users in a wireless multiaccess framework. IEEE Trans. Wirel. Commun. **5**(9), 2493–2503 (2006)
5. Dosaranian-Moghadam, M., Bakhshi, H., Dadashzadeh G., Godarzvand-Chegini, M.: Joint base station assignment, power control error, and adaptive beamforming for DS-CDMA cellular systems in multipath fading channels. In: Proceeding on 2010 IEEE Global Mobile Congress (GMC), pp. 1–7. IEEE (2010)
6. Dartmann, G.; Afzal, W.; Xitao Gong; Ascheid, G.: Joint optimization of beamforming, user scheduling, and multiple base station assignment in a multicell network. In: 2011 Proceeding on IEEE Wireless Communications and Networking Conference (WCNC), pp. 209–214. IEEE (2011)
7. Sanjabi, M., Razaviyayn, M., Zhi-Quan, L.: Optimal joint base station assignment and beamforming for heterogeneous networks. IEEE Trans. Sig. Process. **02**(8), 1950–1961 (2014)
8. Falkenauer, E.: The grouping genetic algorithm-widening the scope of the GAs. Proc. Belg. J. Oper. Res. Stat. Comput. Sci. **33**, 79–102 (1992)
9. Falkenauer, E.: Genetic Algorithms for Grouping Problems. Wiley, New York (1998)
10. De Lit, P., Falkenauer, E., Delchambre, A.: Grouping genetic algorithms: an efficient method to solve the cell formation problem. Math. Comput. Simul. **51**(3), 257–271 (2000)
11. Brown, E.C., Vroblefski, M.: A grouping genetic algorithm for the microcell sectorization problem. Eng. Appl. Artif. Intell. **17**(6), 589–598 (2004)
12. James, T., Vroblefski, M., Nottingham, Q.: A hybrid grouping genetic algorithm for the registration area planning problem. Comput. Commun. **30**(10), 2180–2190 (2007)
13. Agustín-Blas, L.E., Salcedo-Sanz, S., Vidales, P., Urueta, G., Portilla-Figueras, J.A.: Near optimal citywide WiFi network deployment using a hybrid grouping genetic algorithm. Expert Syst. Appl. **38**(8), 9543–9556 (2011)
14. Tan, C.K., Chuah, T.C., Tan, S.W., Sim, M.L.: Efficient clustering scheme for OFDMA-based multicast wireless systems using grouping genetic algorithm. Electron. Lett. **48**(3), 184–186 (2012)
15. Agustín-Blas, L.E., Salcedo-Sanz, S., Ortiz-García, E.G., Portilla-Figueras, A., Pérez-Bellido, A.M.: A hybrid grouping genetic algorithm for assigning students to preferred laboratory groups. Expert Syst. Appl. **36**, 7234–7241 (2009)
16. Salcedo-Sanz, S., Del Ser, J., Geem Z.W.: An island grouping genetic algorithm for fuzzy partitioning problems. Sci. World J. **2014**, Article ID 916371 (2014)
17. Landa-Torres, I., Salcedo-Sanz, S., Gil-López, S., Del Ser, J., Portilla-Figueras, J.A.: A novel grouping harmony search algorithm for the multiple-type access node location problem. Expert Syst. Appl. **39**(5), 5262–5270 (2012)
18. Kashan, A.H., Kashan, M.H., Karimiyan, S.: A particle swarm optimizer for grouping problems. Inf. Sci. **252**, 81–95 (2013)
19. Kashan, A.H., Rezaee, B., Karimiyan, S.: An efficient approach for unsupervised fuzzy clustering based on grouping evolution strategies. Pattern Recogn. **46**(5), 1240–1254 (2013)

# Combining Ensemble of Classifiers by Using Genetic Programming for Cyber Security Applications

Gianluigi Folino$^{(\boxtimes)}$ and Francesco Sergio Pisani

Institute of High Performance Computing and Networking (ICAR-CNR),
Rende, Italy
{folino,fspisani}@icar.cnr.it

**Abstract.** Classification is a relevant task in the cyber security domain, but it must be able to cope with unbalanced and/or incomplete datasets and must also react in real-time to changes in the data. Ensemble of classifiers are a useful tool for classification in hard domains as they combine different classifiers that together provide complementary information. However, most of the ensemble-based algorithms require an extensive training phase and need to be re-trained in case of changes in the data.

This work proposes a Genetic Programming-based framework to generate a function for combining an ensemble, having some interesting properties: the models composing the ensemble are trained only on a portion of the training set, and then, they can be combined and used without any extra phase of training; furthermore, in case of changes in the data, the function can be recomputed in an incrementally way, with a moderate computational effort.

Experiments conducted on unbalanced datasets and on a well-known cyber-security dataset assess the goodness of the approach.

## 1 Introduction

In the last few years, the interest in cyber security problems is really increasing, as cyber crime seriously threatens national governments and the economy of many industries [1]. In this domain, computer and network technologies have intrinsic security weaknesses, i.e., protocol, operating system weaknesses, etc. In addition, computer network activities, human actions, etc. generate large amounts of data. Potential threats to the network need to be identified, and the related vulnerabilities need to be addressed to minimize the risk of the threat.

Therefore, data mining techniques could be used to efficiently fight, alleviate the effect or to prevent the action of the cybercriminals. In particular, classification can be efficiently used for many cyber security application, i.e. in intrusion detection systems, in the analysis of the user behavior, risk and attack analysis, etc. However, in this particular domain, datasets often have different number of features and each attribute could have different importance and costs. Furthermore, the entire system must also works if some datasets are not present. Therefore, it would be really unlikely a single classification algorithm will perform well

© Springer International Publishing Switzerland 2015
A.M. Mora and G. Squillero (Eds.): EvoApplications 2015, LNCS 9028, pp. 54–66, 2015.
DOI: 10.1007/978-3-319-16549-3_5

for all the datasets, especially in presence of changes and with constraints of real time and scalability.

Ensemble [2,3] is a learning paradigm where multiple component learners are trained for the same task by a learning algorithm, and the predictions of the component learners are combined for dealing with new unseen instances. Among the advantages in using ensemble of classifiers, we would like to remind that they help to reduce the variance of the error, the bias, and the dependence from a single dataset; furthermore, they can be build in an incremental way and they are apt to distributed implementations. They are also particularly suitable for distributed intrusion detection, because they permit to build a network profile by combining different classifiers that together provide complementary information. However, the phase of building of the ensemble could be computationally expensive as when new data arrives, it is necessary to restart the training phase.

To this aim, we propose a more flexible approach, and design a distributed Genetic Programming (GP) framework, based on the distributed CellulAr GEnetic programming (CAGE) environment [4], named CAGE-Combiner, to evolve a function for combining the classifiers composing the ensemble, having some attractive characteristics. First, the models composing the ensemble can be trained only on a portion of the training set, and then they can be combined and used without any extra phase of training; furthermore, in case of changes in the data, the function can be recomputed in an incrementally way, with a moderate computational effort. In addition, all the phases of the algorithm are distributed and can exploits the advantages of running on parallel/distributed architectures to cope with real time constraints.

The rest of the paper is structured as follows. Section 2 presents some related works. In Sect. 3, the strategy to combine the ensemble and the distributed GP framework are illustrated. Section 4 shows some experiments conducted to verify the effectiveness of the approach and to compare it with other similar approaches. Finally, Sect. 5 concludes the work.

## 2   Related Works

Evolutionary algorithms have been used mainly to evolve and select the base classifiers composing the ensemble [5,6] or adopting some time-expensive algorithms to combine the ensemble [7]; however a limited number of papers concerns the evolution of the combining function of the ensemble by using GP, which we illustrate in the following.

Chawla et al. [8] propose an evolutionary algorithm to combine the ensemble, based on a weighted linear combination of classifiers predictions, using many well-known data mining algorithm as base classifiers, i.e. J48, NBTree, JRip, etc. In [9], the authors extend their work in order to cope with unbalanced datasets. In practice, they increase the total number of base classifiers and adopt an oversampling technique. In [10], the authors consider also the case of homogenous ensemble and show the impact of a cut-off level on the total number of classifiers used in the generated model. Our approach also uses heterogeneous classifiers, but we combine functions of different types, also considering weights derived by the performance of the classifiers on the training set; we take also into account the effect of unbalanced datasets and, in addition, our method is apt to operate with incomplete datasets, without using oversampling techniques.

Yan Wang et al. [11] use multiple ensembles to classify incomplete datasets. Their strategy consists in partitioning the incomplete datasets in multiple complete sets and to train the different classifier on each sample. Then, the predictions of all the classifiers could be combined according to the ratio between the number of features in this subsample and the total features of the original dataset. A similar approach could be included in our system.

In [12], the authors develop a GP-based framework to evolve the fusion function of the ensemble both for heterogenous and homogeneous ensemble. The approach is compared with other ensemble-based algorithms and the generalization properties of the approach are analyzed together with the frequency and the type of the classifiers presents in the solutions. The main aim of the paper is to improve the accuracy of the generated ensemble, while distributed implementations and the problems concerning incomplete and unbalanced datasets are not explored. In addition, differently form our approach, the authors do not consider weights depending from the performance of the classifiers on the datasets.

In [13], Brameier and Banzhaf use linear genetic programming to evolve teams of ensemble. A team consists of a predefined number of heterogeneous classifiers. The aim of genetic algorithm is to find the best team, i.e. the team having the best accuracy on the given datasets. The prediction of the team is the combination of individual predictions and it is based on the average or the majority voting strategy, also considering predefined weights. The errors of the individual members of the team are incorporated into the fitness function, so that the evolution process can find the team with the best combination of classifiers. Differently from our approach, the recombination of the team members is not completely free, but only a maximum pre-defined percentage of the models can be changed. In our approach, GP generates tree-based models and the number of base classifiers in the tree is not predefined; therefore, it will be the evolution process to select the best combination of the base classifiers.

## 3    Combining Ensemble of Classifiers

In this section, we show a general schema for combining an ensemble of classifiers and introduce the concept of "non-trainable functions", that can be used in order to combine an ensemble of classifiers without the need of a further phase of training. Then, we illustrated the distributed GP framework used to evolve the combining function of the ensemble.

### 3.1    Background: Ensemble of Classifiers and Non-trainable Functions

Ensemble permits to combine multiple (heterogenous or homogenous) models in order to classify new unseen instances. In practice, after a number of classifiers are built usually using part of the dataset, the predictions of the different classifiers are combined and a common decision is taken. Different schemas can be considered to generate the classifiers and to combine the ensemble, i.e. the same learning algorithm can be trained on different datasets or/and different algorithms can be trained on the same dataset. In this work, we follow the general approach shown in Fig. 1, in which different algorithms are used on the same dataset in order to build the different classifiers/models.

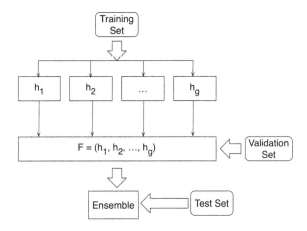

**Fig. 1.** A general schema for combining ensemble of classifiers

Let $S = \{(x_i, y_i) | i = 1, \ldots, N\}$ be a training set where $x_i$, called example or tuple or instance, is an attribute vector with $m$ attributes and $y_i$ is the class label associated with $x_i$. A predictor (classifier), given a new example, has the task to predict the class label for it.

Ensemble techniques build $g$ predictors, each on a different training set, then combine them together to classify the test set. As an alternative, the $g$ predictors could be built using different algorithms on the same/different training set.

The largely used boosting algorithm, introduced by Schapire [14] and Freund [15], follows a different schema; in order to boost the performance of any "weak" learning algorithm, i.e. an algorithm that "generates classifiers which need only be a little bit better than random guessing" [15], the method adaptively changes the distribution of the training set depending on how difficult each example is to classify.

This approach was successfully applied to a large number and types of datasets; however, it has the drawback of needing to repeat the training phase for a number of rounds and that could be really time-consuming for large datasets. The applications and the datasets in hard domains, as cyber security, have real-time requirements, which do not permit to re-train again the base models. On the contrary, ensemble strategies following the schema shown in Fig. 1 do not need any further phase of training, whether the functions used can be combined without using the original training set. The majority vote is a classical example of this kind of combiner function. Some types of combiner has no extra parameters that need to be trained and consequently, the ensemble is ready for operation as soon as the base classifiers are trained. These are named non-trainable combiners [16] and could be used as functions in a genetic programming tree.

Before describing the GP framework used, here, we introduce some definitions useful to understand how the algorithm works.

Let $x \in R^N$ be a feature vector and $\Omega = \{\omega_1, \omega_2 ..., \omega_c\}$ be the set of the possible class labels. Each classifier $h_i$ in the ensemble outputs $c$ degrees of support, i.e., for each class, it will give the probability that the tuple belong to that class. Without loss of generality, we can assume that all the $c$ degrees are in the interval $[0, 1]$, that is, $h_i : R^N \rightarrow [0, 1]^c$. Denote by $H_{i,j}(x)$ the support that classifier $h_i$ gives to the hypothesis that $x$ comes from class $\omega_j$. The larger the support, the more likely the class label $\omega_j$. A non-trainable combiner calculates the support for a class combining the support values of all the classifiers. For each tuple $x$ of the training set, and considering $g$ classifiers and $c$ classes, a Decision Profile matrix DP can be build as follow:

$$DP(x) = \begin{bmatrix} H_{1,1}(x) ... H_{1,j}(x) ... H_{1,c}(x) \\ H_{i,1}(x) ... H_{i,j}(x) ... H_{i,c}(x) \\ H_{g,1}(x) ... H_{g,j}(x) ... H_{g,c}(x) \end{bmatrix}$$

where the element $H_{i,j}(x)$ is the support for j-th class of i-th classifier.

The functions used in our approach simply combine the values of a single column to compute the support for $j - th$ class and can be defined as follow:

$$\mu_j(x) = F[H_{1,j}(x), H_{2,j}(x), ..., H_{g,j}(x)]$$

For instance, the most simple function we can consider is the average, which can be computed as: $\mu_j(x) = \frac{1}{g}\sum_{i=1}^{g} H_{i,j}(x)$.

The class label of $x$ is the class with maximum support $\mu$.

## 3.2   Functions, Terminals and Fitness Evaluation

In this subsection, we describe the model that our GP system use in order to combine the predictions of multiple base classifiers.

Differently from classical models in which the GP tool is used to evolve the models, in our approach, the classifiers (with an associated weight previously computed on the training set) are the leaves of the tree, while the combiner functions are placed on the nodes. In particular, the functions chosen to better combine the classifiers composing the ensemble are non-trainable functions and are listed in the following: average, weighted average, multiplication, maximum and median. They can be applied to a different number of classifiers, i.e. each function is replicated with a different arity, typically from 2 to 5. More details are supplied in the following.

The **average** function, used with an arity of 2, 3 and 5, is defined as: $\mu_j(x) = \frac{1}{g}\sum_{i=1}^{g} H_{i,j}(x)$.

The **multiplication** function (arity 2, 3 and 5) is defined as: $\mu_j(x) = \prod_{i=1}^{g} H_{i,j}(x)$.

The **maximum** function returns the maximum support for 2, 3 and 5 classifiers and can be computed as: $\mu_j(x) = \max_i \{H_{i,j}(x)\}$.

The **median** function (arity 3 and 5) can be computed as: $\mu_j(x) = median_i \{H_{i,j}(x)\}$.

Finally, the **weighted** version of the **average** function uses the weights computed during the training phase to give a different importance to the models on the basis of the performance on the training set, and can be computed as: $\mu_j(x) = \frac{1}{\sum_{i=1}^{g} w_{i,j}} \sum_{i=1}^{g} w_{i,j} * H_{i,j}(x)$. For this function the values of 2, 3 and 5 are chosen for the arity.

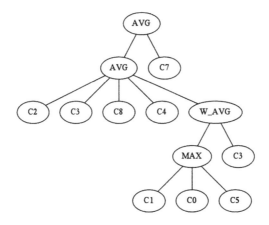

**Fig. 2.** An example of GP tree generated from the tool.

In order to better clarify, how the tree is built, in Fig. 2, an example of tree generated from the tool is illustrated. As for the fitness function, it is simply computed as the error of the ensemble on the validation set, i.e. the ratio between the tuples not correctly classified and the total number of tuples.

## 3.3   A Distributed Tool to Evolve Combiner Functions

The tool used to evolve the combining function is a distributed/parallel GP implementation, named CellulAr GEnetic programming (CAGE) [4], running both on distributed-memory parallel computers and on distributed environments. The tool is based on the fine-grained cellular model. The overall population of the GP algorithm is partitioned into subpopulations of the same size. Each subpopulation can be assigned to one processor and a standard (panmictic) GP algorithm is executed on it. Occasionally, migration process between subpopulations is carried out after a fixed number of generations. For example, the n best individuals from one subpopulation are copied into the other subpopulations, thus allowing the exchange of genetic information between populations.

The model is hybrid and modifies the island model by substituting the standard GP algorithm with a cellular GP (cGP) algorithm. In the cellular model each individual has a spatial location, a small neighborhood and interacts only within its neighborhood. The main difference in a cellular GP, with respect to a panmictic algorithm, is its decentralized selection mechanism and the genetic operators (crossover, mutation) adopted.

This tool is used to evolve the combiner functions and obtain an overall combiner function, which the ensemble will adopt to classify new tuples. Implicitly, the function selects the classifiers/models more apt to the particular datasets considered.

To summarize, if we consider a dataset partitioned in training, validation and test set, the approach works using the following steps.

1. The base classifiers are trained on the training set; then, a weight, proportional to the error on the training set, is associated to each classifier together with the support for each class, i.e. the decision support matrix is built. This phase could be computationally expensive, but it is performed in parallel, as the different algorithms are independent from each other.
2. The combiner function is evolved by using the distributed GP tool, CAGE, on the validation set. No extra computation on the data is necessary, as validation is only used to verify the correct class is assigned and consequently to compute the fitness function.
3. The final function is used to combine the base classifiers and classify new data (test set). This phase can be performed in parallel, by partitioning the test set among different nodes and applying the function to each partition.

## 4    Experimental Section

In this section, in order to assess the goodness of the proposed framework, using the parameters and the datasets described in the next subsection, we analyzed the size of the model and the accuracy obtained by CAGE-Combiner, with different configurations and compared our approach with different state-of-the-art combination strategies (Subsect. 4.2). Then, the performance of our approach was analyzed on a really unbalanced and hard intrusion detection dataset (Subsect. 4.3).

### 4.1    Datasets and Parameter Settings

All the experiments were performed on a Linux cluster with 16 Itanium2 1.4GHz nodes, each having 2 GBytes of main memory and connected by a Myrinet high performance network. No tuning phase has been conducted for the GP algorithm, but the same parameters used in the original paper [4] were used, listed in the following: a probability of crossover equal to 0.7 and of mutation equal to 0.1, a maximum depth equal to 7, and a population of 132 individuals per node. The algorithm was run on 4 nodes, using 1000 generations and the original training set was partitioned among the 4 nodes. The parsimony factor is varied using the values of 0, 0.01 and 0.1 in order to generate classifiers of different size and to study the effect of the size of classifiers on the classification error and on the generalization of the algorithm. All the results were obtained by averaging 30 runs.

In Table 1, the size, the number of features and of classes and the percentage of the minority class of the datasets used in the experiments is shown. The datasets present different characteristics in terms of number of attributes and classes; in addition, most of them have a distribution of the tuples belonging to one or more classes really unbalanced, as it is evident from the percentage of the minority class.

**Table 1.** Description of datasets ordered by decreasing percentage of minority class.

| Dataset | Number of examples | Number of features | Number of class | Minority class |
|---------|-------------------|-------------------|-----------------|----------------|
| Satimage | 6,435 | 36 | 6 | 0.0972 |
| DNA/Splice | 3,190 | 61 | 3 | 0.2404 |
| Phoneme | 5,404 | 5 | 2 | 0.2938 |
| Pendigit | 10,992 | 16 | 10 | 0.0959 |
| KDDCup | 494,020 | 41 | 5 | $1.052\text{E-}4$ |

The different classifiers composing the ensemble are trained on the same training set. In practice, each dataset is partitioned in three subsamples: the 70 % of original dataset is used to train the base classifiers, the remaining 30 % is equally partitioned in two parts: validation and test set. The validation part is used by the evolutionary algorithm to build the combination function, while the error rate of the best tree is calculated on the test partition. The learning algorithms are implemented in WEKA platform and the models are built using standard parameters.

The algorithms used as base classifiers in the experiments are based on the WEKA implementation[1] and are listed in the following: J48 (decision trees), JRIP rule learner (Ripper rule learning algorithm), NBTree (Naive Bayes tree), Naive Bayes, 1R classifier, logistic model trees, logistic regression, decision stumps and 1BK (k-nearest neighbor algorithm).

In Table 2, it is shown the error rate of each base classifier respectively on the training, validation and test set and this helps to understand the improvement obtained in terms of accuracy using an ensemble, how shown in the next subsection.

## 4.2 Comparing with Other Evolutionary Strategies and Meta-Ensemble Techniques

As stated in the previous subsection, the GP framework is executed without any tuning of the parameters. The only exception is that we want to analyze (Table 3)

---

[1] http://www.cs.waikato.ac.nz/ml/weka.

**Table 2.** Error rate of the base classifiers used to build the ensemble

| Dataset | Type | J48 | Jrip | NBTree | Naive Bayes | OneR | LMT | Logistic | Stump Stump | Ibk |
|---|---|---|---|---|---|---|---|---|---|---|
| Satimage | Training | 2.60 | 7.90 | 17.30 | 19.90 | 39.10 | 8.80 | 12.00 | 55.80 | 0.00 |
| | Validation | 15.00 | 13.20 | 19.10 | 20.40 | 43.40 | 13.20 | 14.50 | 58.30 | 9.30 |
| | Test | 15.30 | 14.20 | 20.60 | 22.90 | 41.30 | 13.60 | 15.80 | 56.60 | 10.10 |
| Phoneme | Training | 8.40 | 11.30 | 10.80 | 23.10 | 18.20 | 9.00 | 24.60 | 24.30 | 0.00 |
| | Validation | 14.40 | 14.90 | 13.90 | 22.90 | 25.60 | 12.80 | 25.40 | 24.80 | 9.40 |
| | Test | 14.80 | 16.60 | 14.30 | 25.20 | 23.20 | 15.20 | 26.00 | 25.40 | 11.30 |
| Pendigit | Training | 0.70 | 1.20 | 0.20 | 13.50 | 59.40 | 0.30 | 3.70 | 79.70 | 0.00 |
| | Validation | 4.10 | 4.50 | 4.90 | 14.90 | 63.50 | 1.70 | 4.40 | 79.20 | 1.00 |
| | Test | 3.90 | 3.30 | 5.20 | 14.90 | 60.50 | 1.90 | 4.80 | 79.80 | 0.50 |
| Dna | Training | 4.00 | 4.20 | 0.00 | 3.30 | 0.00 | 0.00 | 0.00 | 37.00 | 0.00 |
| | Validation | 5.50 | 4.80 | 8.30 | 5.00 | 71.40 | 3.50 | 11.30 | 40.90 | 27.80 |
| | Test | 4.50 | 4.30 | 5.50 | 4.30 | 73.70 | 3.80 | 11.00 | 37.80 | 24.10 |

**Table 3.** The error rate for different values of parsimony (0, 0.1 and 0.01), along with the average number of classifiers and functions used in the best tree.

| Dataset | Parsimony | Error train | Error test | Distinct classifiers | Total classifiers | Functions |
|---|---|---|---|---|---|---|
| Satimage | 0 | 7.77 ± 0.60 | 9.08 ± 0.56 | 8.64 ± 0.79 | 78.44 ± 42.03 | 30.56 ± 15.01 |
| | 0.01 | 7.46 ± 0.62 | 9.25 ± 0.58 | 7.26 ± 1.34 | 25.70 ± 11.49 | 11.10 ± 4.16 |
| | 0.1 | 7.48 ± 0.41 | 9.09 ± 0.51 | 6.57 ± 1.54 | 14.46 ± 4.61 | 6.76 ± 2.45 |
| Phoneme | 0 | **8.27 ± 0.43** | **11.63 ± 1.30** | 8.70 ± 0.55 | 99.95 ± 74.63 | 38.85 ± 30.36 |
| | 0.01 | 7.62 ± 0.65 | 11.14 ± 0.44 | 6.61 ± 1.41 | 26.15 ± 18.37 | 11.96 ± 6.98 |
| | 0.1 | 7.80 ± 0.46 | 10.91 ± 0.51 | 5.53 ± 1.33 | 13.73 ± 5.47 | 7.00 ± 2.75 |
| Pendigit | 0 | 0.66 ± 0.22 | 0.74 ± 0.22 | 8.86 ± 0.33 | 71.30 ± 37.16 | 27.95 ± 14.82 |
| | 0.01 | 0.60 ± 0.12 | 0.68 ± 0.12 | 6.13 ± 1.50 | 14.48 ± 7.84 | 6.10 ± 3.30 |
| | 0.1 | 0.64 ± 0.10 | 0.67 ± 0.12 | 6.13 ± 1.08 | 10.40 ± 3.20 | 5.16 ± 2.35 |
| Dna | 0 | **2.46 ± 0.85** | **3.71 ± 1.05** | 8.48 ± 0.89 | 88.31 ± 92.59 | 33.86 ± 36.10 |
| | 0.01 | 1.86 ± 0.15 | 3.48 ± 0.28 | 6.53 ± 0.92 | 11.70 ± 2.53 | *4.50 ± 1.25* |
| | 0.1 | 1.82 ± 0.13 | 3.53 ± 0.22 | 6.26 ± 0.81 | 9.20 ± 1.75 | *4.30 ± 1.29* |

the effect of the size of the combiner function on the accuracy, varying the value of the parsimony factor. In order to balance the accuracy against the size of tree, in GP algorithms, the fitness is augmented with an optional parameter, the *parsimony*, which measures the complexity of the individuals. Higher is the parsimony, simpler is the tree, but accuracy diminishes.

In order to statistically validate the comparison results, we performed the two-tailed t-test($\sigma = 0.05$) over the 30 runs. The values in bold highlight, for each value of parsimony, the results that, according to the t-test, are significantly differently from the other values. As for the last three columns, most of the values present statistically significant differences, so, for this case, the values are not significantly different are represented in italic. From the table, it is evident that most of the differences in accuracy is not significantly different with the exception of the DNA and Phoneme datasets for the case of using parsimony vs. not using parsimony, while there is no difference between the case of 0.1 and 0.01. On the contrary, the size of the trees and the distinct classifiers selected by the algorithm are affected by the parsimony factor. For this reason, we choose a parsimony factor of 0.1 for the other experiments conducted.

**Table 4.** Error rate for different strategies for the 4 datasets used in the experiments.

|                          | Satimage | Phoneme | Pendigit | DNA  |
|--------------------------|----------|---------|----------|------|
| CAGE-Combiner            | 9.09     | 10.92   | 0.68     | 3.53 |
| EVEN                     | 8.91     | 11.68   | 0.68     | 4.20 |
| EVEN (cut-off = 0.8)     | 8.69     | 11.06   | 0.66     | 4.34 |
| Majority Vote            | 10.52    | 15.85   | 0.98     | 4.20 |
| Weighted Vote            | 10.40    | 15.04   | 0.93     | 4.32 |
| Best classifier          | 10.60    | 12.59   | 0.89     | 4.82 |
| Stacking NB              | 10.75    | 14.93   | 0.81     | 4.55 |
| Stacking LR              | 9.72     | 11.12   | 0.82     | 5.03 |

In Table 4, CAGE-Combiner is compared with the EVEN algorithm, described in the related work section [10] and also with the meta-algorithms used in the same paper. Note that EVEN uses a population size of 120 (the number of classifiers) for 1000 generations. The results show that CAGE-Combiner obtain better or comparable accuracy for all the datasets; however, we would like to remark that the number of classifiers used is sensibly minor than the 120 used by the EVEN algorithm. However, in the latter, a cut-off threshold is introduced and only those classifiers whose weights are above this threshold are allowed to participate to the ensemble. The maximum value of cut-off used in the paper (0.8) and shown in the table permits to reduce the number of classifiers to about 25 % of the original size, while our approach (see Table 3) using the parsimony value of 0.1, obtains a better reduction of the number of classifiers (about 10 %), without any relevant reduction in the accuracy.

### 4.3   A Dataset in the Cyber Security Domain: KDD Cup 99

To evaluate the system proposed on a real-world dataset in the field of cyber security, we performed the same experiments as the previous subsection, using one of the most used dataset for the task of classification of intrusions: KDD Cup 1999[2]. This dataset contains 494,020 records, representing normal connections and 24 different attack types. Each attack is clustered into four main categories, so each connection belongs to the following classes: normal (normal, i.e., no

---

[2] http://www.sigkdd.org/kdd-cup-1999-computer-network-intrusion-detection.

attack), DoS (Denial of Service connections), R2L (Remote to User, remote attacks addressed to gain local access), U2R (User to Root, exploits used to gain root access) or Probe (probing attack to discover known vulnerabilities).

**Table 5.** The error rate for different values of parsimony (0, 0.1 and 0.01), along with the average number of classifiers and functions used in the best tree: KDD Cup 99.

| Pars. | Error | Distinct Cls | Total Cls | Functions | DoS | Normal | Probe | R2L | U2R |
|---|---|---|---|---|---|---|---|---|---|
| 0 | 0.0106 ± 0.0015 | 7.60 ± 0.71 | 65.23 ± 50.46 | 26.53 ± 19.03 | 0.0000 | 0.0003 | 0.0114 | 0.0506 | 0.2000 |
| 0.01 | 0.0105 ± 0.0012 | 6.20 ± 1.01 | 13.30 ± 6.76 | 5.80 ± 2.65 | 0.0000 | 0.0003 | 0.0109 | 0.0510 | 0.2333 |
| 0.1 | 0.0121 ± 0.0016 | 5.37 ± 0.80 | 9.03 ± 3.01 | 3.80 ± 1.45 | 0.0000 | 0.0003 | 0.0106 | 0.0490 | 0.2667 |

In Table 5, it is evident that the size of the trees and the distinct classifiers selected by the algorithm strongly depends on the parsimony factor, while for the accuracy the differences are minimal and the best results are obtained with the parsimony value of 0.01.

However, we are more interested to the behavior of our approach for the unbalanced datasets and in particular for the minority classes of the KDD Cup dataset, i.e., Probe, R2L and U2R.

To this aim, we consider the work in [17], which describes a boosting approach, named Greedy-Boost, to build an ensemble of classifier based on a linear combination of models, specifically designed to operate for the intrusion detection domain. The main idea is to extend the boosting process maintaining the models that behave better on the examples badly predicted in the previous round of the boosting algorithm (while the classical algorithm adjust only the weights and not the models).

In Table 6, CAGE-Combiner is compared with the Greedy-Boost algorithm on the KDDCup 99 datasets and the precision and the recall values are reported for all the classes. It is evident that our approach performs better both for the precision and the recall measure, especially in the case of the minority classes R2L and U2R.

**Table 6.** Precision and Recall for different strategies for the KDD Cup dataset. In the first column, it is reported the class distribution for the test set.

| | | Precision | | Recall | |
|---|---|---|---|---|---|
| | Class distribution | Greedy-Boost | CAGE-Combiner | Greedy-Boost | CAGE-Combiner |
| DoS | 0.7960 | 100.0 | 100.0 | 100.0 | 100.0 |
| Normal | 0.1936 | 99.1 | 99.9 | 100.0 | 100.0 |
| Probe | 0.0079 | 99.0 | 99.6 | 97.1 | 98.9 |
| R2L | 0.0023 | 93.2 | 98.5 | 71.9 | 94.9 |
| U2R | 4.85E-5 | 88.5 | 93.1 | 44.2 | 76.7 |

# 5    Conclusions and Future Work

A distributed framework for classifying unbalanced dataset, based on the ensemble model, is presented. The system evolves a combiner function, which does not need additional phases of training, after the heterogeneous classifiers composing the ensemble are trained. Preliminary experiments showed that the proposed system improves or is comparable to the performance of state-of-the-art approaches for combining ensemble, by using a smaller number of models. In future, we intend to investigate the ability of the algorithm to handle incomplete datasets and changes in data and to test the scalability of the algorithms on distributed machines mainly for large real-world datasets in the cyber security domain.

**Acknowledgment.** This work has been partially supported by MIUR-PON under project PON03PE_00032_2 within the framework of the Technological District on Cyber Security.

# References

1. CERT Australia: Cyber crime and security survey report. Technical report (2012)
2. Breiman, L.: Bagging predictors. Mach. Learn. **24**, 123–140 (1996)
3. Freund, Y., Shapire, R.: Experiments with a new boosting algorithm. In: Machine Learning: Proceedings of the Thirteenth International Conference (ICML 1996), pp. 148–156. Morgan Kaufmann (1996)
4. Folino, G., Pizzuti, C., Spezzano, G.: A scalable cellular implementation of parallel genetic programming. IEEE Trans. Evol. Comput. **7**, 37–53 (2003)
5. de Oliveira, D.F., Canuto, A.M.P., de Souto, M.C.P.: Use of multi-objective genetic algorithms to investigate the diversity/accuracy dilemma in heterogeneous ensembles. In: International Joint Conference on Neural Networks, pp. 2339–2346. IEEE (2009)
6. Folino, G., Pizzuti, C., Spezzano, G.: Training distributed GP ensemble with a selective algorithm based on clustering and pruning for pattern classification. IEEE Trans. Evol. Comput. **12**, 458–468 (2008)
7. Stefano, C.D., Folino, G., Fontanella, F., di Freca, A.S.: Using bayesian networks for selecting classifiers in GP ensembles. Inf. Sci. **258**, 200–216 (2014)
8. Sylvester, J., Chawla, N.V.: Evolutionary ensembles: combining learning agents using genetic algorithms. In: AAAI Workshop on Multiagent Learning, pp. 46–51 (2005)
9. Chawla, N.V., Sylvester, J.: Exploiting diversity in ensembles: improving the performance on unbalanced datasets. In: Haindl, M., Kittler, J., Roli, F. (eds.) MCS 2007. LNCS, vol. 4472, pp. 397–406. Springer, Heidelberg (2007)
10. Sylvester, J., Chawla, N.V.: Evolutionary ensemble creation and thinning. In: Proceedings of the International Joint Conference on Neural Networks, IJCNN 2006, pp. 5148–5155. IEEE (2006)
11. Wang, Y., Gao, Y., Shen, R., Yang, F.: Selective ensemble approach for classification of datasets with incomplete values. In: Wang, Y., Li, T. (eds.) ISKE2011. AISC, vol. 122, pp. 281–286. Springer, Heidelberg (2011)
12. Acosta-Mendoza, N., Morales-Reyes, A., Escalante, H.J., Gago-Alonso, A.: Learning to assemble classifiers via genetic programming. IJPRAI **28** (2014)

13. Brameier, M., Banzhaf, W.: Evolving teams of predictors with linear genetic programming. Genet. Program Evolvable Mach. **2**, 381–407 (2001)
14. Schapire, R.E.: The strength of weak learnability. Mach. Learn. **5**, 197–227 (1990)
15. Schapire, R.E.: Boosting a weak learning by majority. Inf. Comput. **121**, 256–285 (1995)
16. Kuncheva, L.: Combining Pattern Classifiers: Methods and Algorithms. Wiley-Interscience, Chichester (2004)
17. Bahri, E., Harbi, N., Huu, H.N.: Approach based ensemble methods for better and faster intrusion detection. In: Herrero, A., Corchado, E. (eds.) CISIS 2011. LNCS, vol. 6694, pp. 17–24. Springer, Heidelberg (2011)

# A Fast FPGA-Based Classification of Application Protocols Optimized Using Cartesian GP

David Grochol, Lukas Sekanina[(✉)], Martin Zadnik, and Jan Korenek

Faculty of Information Technology, IT4Innovations Centre of Excellence,
Brno University of Technology, Božetěchova 2, 612 66 Brno, Czech Republic
{igrochol,sekanina,izadnik,korenek}@fit.vutbr.cz

**Abstract.** This paper deals with design of an application protocol classifier intended for high speed networks operating at 100 Gbps. Because
a very low latency is the main design constraint, the classifier is constructed as a combinational circuit in a field programmable gate array.
The classification is performed using the first packet carrying the application payload. In order to further reduce the latency, the circuit is optimized by Cartesian genetic programming. Using a real network data, we
demonstrated viability of our approach in task of a very fast classification
of three application protocols (HTTP, SMTP, SSH).

## 1 Introduction

An abstract yet detailed network traffic visibility is a key prerequisite to network
management including tasks such as traffic engineering, application performance
monitoring and network security monitoring. In the recent years the diversity and
complexity of network applications and network threats have grown significantly.
This trend has rendered monitoring of network and transport layer insufficient
and it has become important to extend the visibility into application layer,
primarily to identify the application (or the application protocol) the traffic
belongs to. The port numbers are no longer reliable application differentiator
due to various applications evading the firewalls by hiding behind well-known
port numbers or utilizing unallocated port range [1].

The research in the area of application identification has come up with distinct approaches to identify applications carried in the traffic. These approaches
differ in the level of detail that is utilized in the identification method. The most
abstract one is behavioral analysis [2,3]. Its idea is to observe just port number
and destination of the connections per each host and then to deduce the application running on the host by its typical connection signature. If more details
per connection are available, statistical fingerprinting [4] comes into play. In this
case, a feature set is collected per each flow and the assumption is that the values of the feature set vary across applications and hence they leave a unique
fingerprint. Behavioral and statistical fingerprinting generally classifies traffic
to application classes rather than to the particular applications. The reason is

© Springer International Publishing Switzerland 2015
A.M. Mora and G. Squillero (Eds.): EvoApplications 2015, LNCS 9028, pp. 67–78, 2015.
DOI: 10.1007/978-3-319-16549-3_6

that different applications performing the same task exhibit similar behavior. For instance, application protocols such as Oscar (ICQ), MSN, XMPP (Jabber) transport interactive chat communications and hence have a similar behavior, which makes it very hard to differentiate between them. The inability to distinguish applications within the same class might be seen as a drawback in some situations when, for example, it is necessary to block a particular application while allowing others in the same class. The approach utilizing the greatest level of detail is a deep packet inspection. It identifies applications based on the packet payload. The payload is matched with known patterns (e.g. regular expressions) derived for each application [5].

The application identification poses several on-going challenges. The identification process is bound to keep pace with ever increasing link speeds. E.g. the time to process each packet is less than 7 ns in case of 100 Gbps link. Another challenge is represented by the growing number of protocols, i.e., the application identification must address the trends such as new emerging mobile applications or applications moving into network cloud [6]. Some deployments also require prompt (near real-time) identification to enable implementation of traffic engineering or application blocking [7].

Hardware acceleration (e.g. utilizing a field programmable gate array (FPGA)) is often employed to speed up network processing [8,9] including the application identification directly on the network card. FPGA renders it possible to utilize various pattern matching algorithms to identify applications. However, pattern matching may exhibit several constraints, that is, the high cost to process wide data inputs (which is the case for high throughput buses in FPGA) and the high complexity and overhead of pattern matching algorithm which consumes valuable hardware resources or constraints the achievable frequency.

These drawbacks are addressed by alternative methods which look for constants and fixed-length strings (for brevity we call them signatures) rather than regular expressions, e.g. [10]. We build upon this approach and we envision hardware-software codesign approach in which a simple circuit labels the traffic belonging to applications of interest with some probability of false positives while software can subsequently handle and check the labeled traffic with more complex algorithm effectively. This approach is supported by the software defined monitoring concept (SDM, [11]). Software defined monitoring employs sophisticated processes running in software to subsequently install rules in the hardware (network card). While it is not possible (or at the very high cost) to process all the traffic in software we offload the application identification into the hardware. The offload not only reduces the host memory and cpu load but it also increases the expressive strength of the SDM rules.

Within this scope, our work focuses on a design of a proprietary circuit, operating as an application protocol classifier, which is synthesizable into FPGA. The goal of our work is to identify application protocols as fast as possible over the whole traffic but at the same time with low resource utilization. We demonstrate viability of our approach on three protocols (HTTP, SMTP, SSH) we deem most crucial from perspective of network security. The proposed circuit, in fact, implements a deterministic parallel combinational signature matching algorithm.

The main contribution of this paper is showing that this circuit classifier can be optimized by means of Cartesian Genetic Programming (CGP) in order to significantly reduce its latency and resources requirements. CGP, which is a form of genetic programming suitable for evolutionary circuit design and optimization, is employed to minimize the number of gates in selected components of the whole classifier [12]. The improvements in latency and area obtained by CGP are validated using a professional FPGA design tool. The quality of classification is evaluated by means of real network data.

The rest of the paper is organized as follows. Section 2 introduces the proposed classifier, network data used for its evaluation and the principles of circuit optimization by means of CGP. Section 3 describes the implementation steps and the results in terms of area and delay in the FPGA. Section 3.2 deals with the experiments conducted using CGP. Finally, the quality of classification is assessed in terms of precision and recall. Conclusions are given in Sect. 4.

## 2 FPGA-Based Application Protocol Classifier

In order to design, implement and evaluate the FPGA-based application protocol classifier, we have considered the following issues. As this is the first version of the classifier, only 3 application protocols (HTTP, SMTP, SSH) will be supported; remaining protocols will be classified as unknown. Only the key component of the classifier (9 coders with a comparator) will be synthesized and optimized for FPGA. This will provide us with a sufficiently precise estimate of the latency and area of the whole classifier. Because the primary goal is achieving a very low latency, only the signatures of the first packet carrying the application payload are utilized. The classifier is intended for SDM system which transfers the data via a 512 bit bus. The application payload may start at nearly arbitrary offset on the bus and the application must be identified each clock cycle to keep pace even with the shortest incoming packets of 64 Bytes. The following subsections describe the whole design process and methods utilized.

### 2.1 Network Data

The data which has to be classified are common network data (available in the pcap format). In order to design a good solution, it is important to understand the data and to prepare relevant training and test sets. In our case, we utilized two complete network data sets with anonymized IP addresses, collected on CESACO link (connecting CESNET and ACONET networks) and CESPIO link (connecting CESNET and PIONIER networks), see Table 1. For example, the available record from CESPIO contains 43 M packets, where percentages are 78.72 % for TCP, 20.58 % for UDP, 0.18 % for ICMP and 0.53 % others. One can observe that only TCP and UDP are relevant for our purposes; ICMP is used for network monitoring and error reporting which is irrelevant. The packet traces were analyzed using Scapy. Because HTTP, SMTP and SSH operate over TCP, we consider the first packet containing the application payload, usually the third or the fourth packet of the TCP connection. The L7 filter [13] was utilized as a reference classifier to anotate each connection in the data set. Unfortunately, implementing the L7 filter, based on regular expressions, in hardware would lead to a high latency as well as resource utilization which is not acceptable in our case. Other packets were labeled as unknown.

**Table 1.** Network data sets

| Line | Speed [Gb/s] | Record duration | Size [Gb] | Date |
|------|--------------|-----------------|-----------|------|
| CESACO | 10 | 9 s | 1 | 26.9.2013 10:52:02 |
| CESPIO | 10 | 8 min | 35 | 26.2.2014 11:38:56 |

The resulting data set, which can be used for evaluation purposes, is available in the JSON format. Each record contains the source IP and port, the destination IP and port, the transport protocol number, and the whole packet encoded using base64 (see Fig. 1). Table 2 gives the mix of considered protocols in our data set.

**Table 2.** The flows corresponding to the application protocols in data sets CESACO and CESPIO

| Data set | CESACO | | CESPIO | |
|----------|--------|--|--------|--|
| Protocol | Count flows | Count flows [%] | Count flows | Count flows [%] |
| HTTP | 1914 | 38.12 | 15060 | 52.29 |
| SMTP | 4 | 0.08 | 34 | 0.12 |
| SSH | 1 | 0.02 | 0 | 0.00 |
| Others | 3102 | 61.78 | 13705 | 47.59 |
| All | 5021 | 100.00 | 28799 | 100.00 |

## 2.2 Deterministic Classifier

Because the classification utilizes only the start of the payload, we decided to analyze several initial bytes of various commonly used application protocols and find the characters which are unique for particular protocols. Table 3 shows the unique character *signatures* that were identified for considered protocols (the longest sequence is 9 bytes). The classifier can then be constructed as a combinational circuit by means of a decoder. However, it has to correctly manage the cases in which the signatures appear at various offsets within the frame due to preceding protocol headers, which is a natural situation in real network traffic data.

{
"dIP": "192.168.0.2",
"dPort": 80,
"data": "R0VUIC9zaXRlcy9kZWZhdWx0L3RoZW1lcy9mcmFtZWR5bmFtaWMv...
"id": "(' 192.168.0.1', '192.168.0.2', 52217, 80)",
"trProto": 6,
"protocol": "HTTP",
"sIP": " 192.168.0.1",
"sPort": 52217
},

**Fig. 1.** Example record in data set.

**Table 3.** Unique signatures in considered application protocols.

| Protocol | Unique pattern |
|----------|----------------|
| HTTP | "GET /" |
| | "PUT /" |
| | "POST /" |
| | "HEAD /" |
| | "TRACE /" |
| | "DELETE /" |
| | "OPTIONS /" |
| SSH | "SSH-" |
| SMTP | "220" |
| | "220-" |

## 2.3   Classifier in Hardware

The SDM system transfers frames over 512 bit bus. Each frame starts with the headers of low-level protocols such as Ethernet, IPv4 or IPv6, TCP or UDP. As a result, the start of the application payload may appear with certain offsets on the bus, namely 2 bytes from the position 0 or with $2 + 4k$ bytes, where $k = 1 \ldots 16$. Figure 2 shows that the proposed circuit implementation of the classifier consists of three levels of combinational logic.

In the first level, one coder is connected to each byte of the word (64 coders, in total). There are four types of the coders (c1, c2, c3, c4) because of the 4-byte offsets. Each coder implements a mapping from the set of characters allowed for the given position to a set of 8-bit values in which just 2 bits are not zeros. The mapping functions of the coders are given in Table 4. This remapping implemented by coders allows for a fast signature detection in the subsequent level of comparators. All possible occurrences of the application data within the buffer are thus processed in parallel.

The second level consists of comparators. Each of them compares the outputs of nine coders (note that the longest signature contains 9 characters) with the

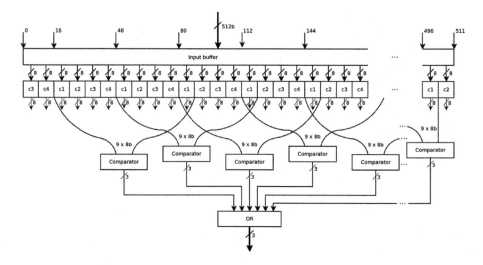

**Fig. 2.** Proposed classifier as a combinational circuit

unique patterns identified for the considered application protocols. If a particular application protocol is detected then its 3-bit code is visible at the output of the comparator (001 - HTTP, 010 - SMTP, 100 - SSH, 000 - unknown).

Finally, at the third level, all 3-bit codes are fed to an OR gate which indicates a presence of one of the expected application protocols or unknown protocol (000).

## 2.4   Circuit Optimization Using CGP

Based on our previous experience, we assumed that parameters of the circuit optimized by a professional FPGA design software can be improved if an evolutionary optimization is employed. As the whole classifier is a relatively complex circuit to be optimized, we propose to optimize its components - the 64 (combinational) coders. Each of the coder types c1, c2, c3 and c4 will be optimized by CGP. We will utilize a standard CGP as defined in [12]. Advanced techniques, such as circuit decomposition [14] or functional level evolution [15] are not needed in this case.

In CGP, a candidate circuit is modeled as a directed acyclic graph and represented in a 2D array of $n_c \times n_r$ processing nodes. Each node is capable of performing one of the functions specified in $\Gamma$ set. The setting of $n_c$, $n_r$ and $\Gamma$ significantly influences the performance of CGP. Current FPGAs utilize 6-input LUTs as building blocks of all circuits. However, employing CGP with 6-input nodes (each of them encoded using 64 bits in the chromosome) would lead to long chromosomes, complex search spaces and so inefficient search procedures. We propose to optimize the coders at the level of 2-input nodes (encoded using up to 4 bits) and let the professional circuit synthesis software implement the resulting optimized circuits using 6-input LUTs in the FPGA.

**Table 4.** Mapping functions in the coders. The * symbol means: "not utilized in a particular coder"

| coder 1 | coder 2 | coder 3 | coder 4 | output |
|---------|---------|---------|---------|--------|
| Space | Space | Space | Space | 00000011 |
| / | / | / | / | 00000101 |
| T | E | S | T | 00000110 |
| E | N | T | D | 00001001 |
| O | O | A | E | 00001010 |
| G | U | L | C | 00001100 |
| P | R | 0 | I | 00010001 |
| H | P | H | - | 00010010 |
| D | 2 | G | R | 00010100 |
| 2 | S | V | * | 00011000 |
| R | Y | E | * | 00100001 |
| S | A | N | * | 00100010 |
| B | C | R | * | 00100100 |
| C | T | K | * | 00101000 |
| A | L | * | * | 00110000 |
| I | * | * | * | 01000001 |
| Otherwise | Otherwise | Otherwise | Otherwise | 00000000 |

The remaining parameters of CGP are the number of primary inputs ($n_i$), the number of primary outputs ($n_o$), and the level-back parameter ($L$) specifying which nodes can be used as the inputs for a given gate. The primary inputs and the outputs of the nodes are labeled $0 \ldots n_c \cdot n_r + n_i - 1$ and considered as addresses which links can be connected to. In the chromosome, each node is then encoded using three integers (an address for the first input; an address for the second input; a node function). Finally, for each primary output, the chromosome contains one integer specifying the connection address. Figure 3 shows an example and a corresponding chromosome.

CGP utilizes a search method known as $1 + \lambda$, where $\lambda$ is the population size [12]. The initial population is randomly generated. New population consisting of $\lambda$ individuals is generated by applying the mutation operator on the best individual of the previous population. The mutation operator randomly modifies $h$ integers of the chromosome. The evolution is terminated after producing a given number of generations.

The fitness function consists of two steps. First, the fitness value is determined as the number of bits correctly calculated for all possible assignments to the inputs. If a fully functional circuit is discovered (in the case of 8-input/8-output coders, this fitness value is $8 \cdot 2^8$) then, in the second step, the fitness function is modified because the goal is to minimize the number of gates. The fitness is then

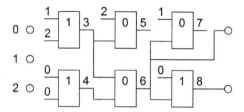

**Fig. 3.** Example of a 3-input circuit. CGP parameters are as follows: $n_i = 3$, $n_o = 2$, $l = 3$, $n_c = 3$, $n_r = 2$, $\Gamma = \{$AND (0), OR (1)$\}$. Gates 5 and 7 are not utilized. Chromosome: 1,2,1; 0,0,1; 2,3,0; 3,4,0; 1,6,0; 0,6,1; 6, 8. The last two integers indicate the outputs of the circuit.

reflecting the functionality and the number of used gates. Delay is not explicitly optimized; however, its maximum value is implicitly determined by $n_c$.

## 3  Results

The experimental evaluation consists of the following steps: (1) conventional implementation of the proposed classifier; (2) CGP-based optimization of selected subcomponents of the circuit; (3) resynthesis of the classifier with optimized subcomponents; (4) verification of the quality of classification. As mentioned earlier, we will implement and optimize in the FPGA only the key component of the classifier – the 9 coders with a comparator (9CC circuit, in short).

### 3.1  Circuit Design and Implementation

The 9CC circuit was behaviorally described in VHDL and synthesized into the Xilinx Virtex-7 XC7VH580T FPGA using Xilinx ISE Project navigator 14.4 tool. The target FPGA contains 6-input LUTs whose latency is 0.043 ns. We set the circuit delay as the main optimization target for the synthesis tool. The resulting circuit contains 188 LUTs and exhibits a delay of 4.621 ns.

### 3.2  Optimization by CGP

There are 4 types of coders in the classifier circuit; each of them with 8 inputs and 8 outputs (Fig. 2). These coders are optimized by CGP operating at the gate level. CGP is used with the following parameters: $n_i = 8$, $n_o = 8$, $n_c = 50$, $n_r = 12$, $L = n_c$, $\lambda = 4$, $h = 5$. In order to obtain basic statistics, each run consisting of 5 million generations was repeated 10 times. This setting of the parameters was recognized as useful after some experimenting with CGP in this task. Because of the limited space, experimental results are given, as an example of our methodology, only for one parameter – the function set. We compared CGP utilizing all logic functions over two inputs (except logic constants) in the function set ($\Gamma$) against and a reduced set ($\Gamma_r$ which includes in1, and, or,

**Table 5.** The number of gates obtained by CGP using $\Gamma_r$ and $\Gamma$ (see *)

|      | coder 1 | coder 2 | coder 3 | coder 4 | coder 1* | coder 2* |
|------|---------|---------|---------|---------|----------|----------|
| Min  | 58      | 60      | 59      | 39      | 60       | 61       |
| Max  | 83      | 84      | 83      | 56      | 94       | 100      |
| Mean | 72.25   | 70.33   | 69.04   | 44.81   | 70.25    | 69.23    |

xor, not_in1, not_in2, in1 and not_in2, nand, nor) in the case of coder 1 and 2. Table 5 gives the minimum, maximum and mean number of gates obtained for each coder. One can observe that while the mean values are lower for $\Gamma$, the minimum values are lower for $\Gamma_r$. Hence $\Gamma_r$ was used in further experiments.

### 3.3  Classifier Resynthesis Using Optimized Coders

The most compact implementations of coders obtained from CGP were translated to VHDL and utilized in the VHDL code of the whole 9CC circuit of the original components. The modified 9CC circuit was synthesized with the same setting as reported in Sect. 3.1. The results of synthesis are given in Table 6. One can observe that both crucial circuit parameters were improved. The area was reduced from 188 to 160 LUTs. The original as well as optimized latency is safely within the requested limit of 7 ns. However, the optimized implementation allowed us to increase the spare latency (to $7.0 - 4.156 = 2.844$ ns, see Table 6) which can be used to connect the 9CC circuit with the OR logic and subsequent components of the whole application.

### 3.4  Quality of Classification

The quality of classification was evaluated offline, utilizing a software model that we have developed for the proposed classifier. The evaluation was performed using both data sets, but we considered two scenarios for classification: (1) thinned traces containing first payload packets only and (2) complete traces containing all packets (i.e. the classifier's objective was to analyze every incoming packet in this case). The output of the proposed classifier was verified against

**Table 6.** Results of synthesis of the 9CC circuit for the Xilinx Virtex-7 XC7VH580T FPGA.

| Parameter       | Optimized by CGP | Original description |
|-----------------|------------------|----------------------|
| LUTs            | 160              | 188                  |
| Delay logic [ns]| 0.344            | 0.430                |
| Delay net [ns]  | 3.812            | 4.191                |
| Delay [ns]      | 4.156            | 4.621                |
| LUT levels      | 8                | 10                   |

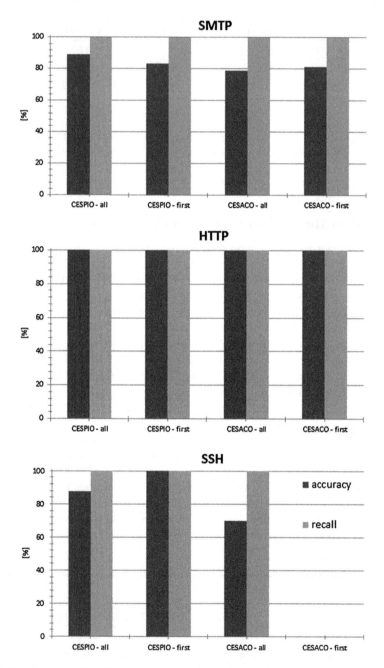

**Fig. 4.** Precision and Recall percentages for three classified protocols. Test data consists of first packets only (first) and complete network records (all).

the L7 filter which provides 100 % correct results for considered protocols. We calculated Precision and Recall metrics:

$$Precision = \frac{TruePositive}{TruePositive + FalsePositive} \tag{1}$$

$$Recall = \frac{TruePositive}{TruePositive + FalseNegative} \tag{2}$$

Precision informs us how many packets assigned to a given class are really correctly assigned. Figure 4 shows that HTTP, whose representation is rich in our data sets, is classified perfectly. The reason for lower percentages of Precision in the case of other protocols is the fact that their unique patterns are relatively short and can easily appear inside of other protocol packets. As the subsequent packet processing is done in software precisely the incorrectly classified protocols will be recognized anyway. The software task is simpler than that of the original one. Software must only verify the labelled traffic and dismiss false positives.

Considering the whole SDM, which the proposed classifier is targeted for, the Recall is even a more important metrics. High Recall values indicate that if a given application protocol is present in the traffic data, it is detected with almost 100 % probability and thus no information is lost.

Figure 4 does not give any data for SSH in CESACO (first packet) data set. The reason is that there is no record with SSH in this data set.

## 4   Conclusions

In this paper we presented a new application of the evolutionary design and optimization – the optimization of circuit implementation of the application protocol classifier intended for high speed networks. The proposed solution exploited the fact that results of conventional FPGA synthesis tools can further be improved when selected circuit components are optimized by CGP and the optimized versions replace the original ones in the target circuit. The whole classifier is composed of 9CC circuits working in parallel. By optimizing just the 9CC circuit we obtained a very good estimate of the total area of the classifier (16 instances of 9CC will be needed) and the total delay (which is the delay of 9CC plus a small delay of the OR network as seen in Fig. 2).

The proposed solution is capable of fast detection of key application protocols using a single packet only. It exhibits excellent Recall values (no monitored application protocols are missed). It is planned that further and detailed packet processing, which can improve the precision parameter of the hardware classifier, will be handled in software by the SDM framework. Our future work will consist in including other application protocols into the proposed hardware solution.

**Acknowledgments.** This work was supported by the Czech science foundation project 14-04197S, Brno University of Technology project FIT-S-14-2297 and the IT4 Innovations Centre of Excellence CZ.1.05/1.1.00/02.0070.

# References

1. Karagiannis, T., Broido, A., Brownlee, N., Claffy, K., Faloutsos, M.: Is P2P dying or just hiding? In: Global Internet and Next Generation Networks, Dallas, Texas, Globecom 2004, December 2004
2. Karagiannis, T., Papagiannaki, K., Faloutsos, M.: BLINC: multilevel traffic classification in the dark. SIGCOMM Comput. Commun. Rev. **35**(4), 229–240 (2005)
3. Yoon, S.-H., Park, J.-W., Park, J.-S., Oh, Y.-S., Kim, M.-S.: Internet application traffic classification using fixed IP-Port. In: Hong, C.S., Tonouchi, T., Ma, Y., Chao, C.-S. (eds.) APNOMS 2009. LNCS, vol. 5787, pp. 21–30. Springer, Heidelberg (2009)
4. Moore, A.W., Zuev, D.: Internet traffic classification using bayesian analysis techniques. In: Proceedings of the 2005 ACM SIGMETRICS International Conference on Measurement and Modeling of Computer Systems, SIGMETRICS 2005, pp. 50–60. ACM (2005)
5. Sen, S., Spatscheck, O., Wang, D.: Accurate, scalable in-network identification of P2P traffic using application signatures. In: Proceedings of the 13th International Conference on World Wide Web, pp. 512–521. ACM (2004)
6. Tongaonkar, A., Keralapura, R., Nucci, A.: Challenges in network application identification. In: Presented as part of the 5th USENIX Workshop on Large-Scale Exploits and Emergent Threats, Berkeley, CA, USENIX (2012)
7. Bernaille, L., Teixeira, R., Salamatian, K.: Early application identification. In: Proceedings of the 2006 ACM CoNEXT Conference, pp. 6:1–6:12. ACM, New York (2006)
8. Zilberman, N., Audzevich, Y., Covington, G., Moore, A.: NetFPGA sume: toward 100 Gbps as research commodity. Micro, IEEE **34**(5), 32–41 (2014)
9. Friedl, S., Pus, V., Matousek, J., Spinler, M.: Designing a card for 100 Gb/s network monitoring. Technical report, CESNET (2013)
10. Park, B.C., Won, Y., Kim, M.S., Hong, J.: Towards automated application signature generation for traffic identification. In: Network Operations and Management Symposium, 2008, NOMS 2008, pp. 160–167. IEEE, April 2008
11. Kekely, L., Pus, V., Korenek, J.: Software defined monitoring of application protocols. In: Proceedings of the IEEE INFOCOM 2014 - IEEE Conference on Computer Communications, pp. 1725–1733 (2014)
12. Miller, J.F.: Cartesian Genetic Programming. Springer, Heidelberg (2011)
13. L7filter: Application layer packet classifier for linux (l7-filter) (2009)
14. Stomeo, E., Kalganova, T., Lambert, C.: Generalized disjunction decomposition for evolvable hardware. IEEE Trans. Syst. Man Cybern. Part B **36**(5), 1024–1043 (2006)
15. Shanthi, A.P., Parthasarathi, R.: Practical and scalable evolution of digital circuits. Appl. Soft Comput. **9**(2), 618–624 (2009)

# Parallel Extremal Optimization with Guided State Changes Applied to Load Balancing

Ivanoe De Falco[1], Eryk Laskowski[2]([✉]), Richard Olejnik[3], Umberto Scafuri[1], Ernesto Tarantino[1], and Marek Tudruj[2,4]

[1] Institute of High Performance Computing and Networking, CNR, Naples, Italy
{ivanoe.defalco,umberto.scafuri,ernesto.tarantino}@na.icar.cnr.it
[2] Institute of Computer Science, Polish Academy of Sciences, Warsaw, Poland
{laskowsk,tudruj}@ipipan.waw.pl
[3] Computer Science Laboratory, University of Science and Technology of Lille,
Villeneuve-d'Ascq, France
richard.olejnik@lifl.fr
[4] Polish-Japanese Institute of Information Technology, Warsaw, Poland

**Abstract.** The paper concerns parallel methods for Extremal Optimization (EO) applied for processor load balancing for distributed programs. In these methods the EO approach is used which is parallelized and extended by a guided search of next solution state. EO detects the best strategy of tasks migration leading to a reduction in program execution time. We assume a parallel improvement of the EO algorithm with guided state changes which provides a parallel search for a solution based on two step stochastic selection during the solution improvement based on two fitness functions. The load balancing improvements based on EO aim at better convergence of the algorithm and better quality of program execution in terms of the execution time. The proposed load balancing algorithm is evaluated by experiments with simulated parallelized load balancing of distributed program graphs.

**Keywords:** Distributed program design · Extremal optimization · Load balancing · Parallel computing

## 1 Introduction

Many papers exist in literature dealing with dynamic load balancing in parallel and distributed systems [1,2]. However, they do not profit from Extremal Optimization (EO) [3] which is a technique following the approach of self-organized criticality [4]. The algorithms presented in this paper are parallelized versions of the EO–based load balancing algorithms [5,6], in which EO has been used for load balancing of processors in execution of distributed programs. In the previous paper, we have modified the EO algorithm to replace the fully random processor selection by the stochastic selection in which the probability used in the selection mechanism is guided by some knowledge of the problem (the EO-GS algorithm). The guidance is based on a formula which examines how a migrated

© Springer International Publishing Switzerland 2015
A.M. Mora and G. Squillero (Eds.): EvoApplications 2015, LNCS 9028, pp. 79–90, 2015.
DOI: 10.1007/978-3-319-16549-3_7

task fits a given processor in terms of the global computational balance in the system and the processor communication load. The algorithm was evaluated by simulation experiments in the DEVS (Discrete Event Simulation) model [7]. The experiments have assessed the new algorithm against different parameters of the application program graphs and the load balancing algorithm. The application speedups have been positively verified against those obtained with the standard EO-based version and in genetic algorithms.

An interesting aspect of Extremal Optimization is parallelization of the involved approach. Parallelization of Extremal Optimization can be considered in two ways. The first way is to intensify the actions aiming at a possibly stronger improvement of the current EO solution, frequently with the intro-duction of a population-based representation or a multipoint strategy during solution improvement. It can be done using a really parallel system or a sequen-tial system in which the components of an EO solution are identified based on the multipoint selection and improved in a possibly concurrent way. The second way consists in using a population-based approach for solutions with parallel component improvement. Both approaches have accumulated already some bib-liography. In [8] the authors propose an extended EO model in which a single EO solution is replaced by a set of EO solutions which are processed using the general EO strategy. These solutions are subject to selection and mutation to provide a set of solution vectors to be next processed in parallel.

In [9–11] the authors propose a rich set of EO improvements used for opti-mization of problems in molecular biology. The MEO (Modified EO) concept consists in random generation of a neighbour solution in component improve-ment but the best solution is selected among multiple thus formed new solutions in respect to the fitness function used in the component selection. The PMEO is a Population-based Modified EO in which a combination of a population-based approach to solution generation with the MEO approach to the selection of the best solution for further improvements. The generated solutions copy a substruc-ture of the solution which behaves well in the solution improvement. The third approach identified in the papers is the Distributed Modified EO (DMEO) which is a combination of the PMEO approach and the distributed genetic algorithms methodology. The DMEO is based on distribution of a population of solutions into islands. The islands evolve using the PMEO method. There are transfers of best solutions between the islands with back transfers of the replaced ones. Each island improves a set of solutions to find a best island solution which are next compared to find a globally best solution.

In this paper we propose an EO-based parallel approach for solving a proces-sor load balancing problem in execution of programs represented as layered graphs of tasks. In this approach, we first identify a load imbalance in the func-tioning of the executive system. Then, we apply a parallel EO-GS algorithm to select tasks which are to be migrated among processors to improve the general balance of processor loads. The EO-GS algorithm is performed in the background of the application program execution to execute a given number of EO cycles which find a number of best logical migrations of tasks. When the EO iterations are over, the physical migrations worked out by the EO take place. In the parallel EO-GS, a method similar to PMEO is applied but with an additional fitness function which is a base for the stochastic selection of the best solution state in the neighbourhood of the one chosen for improvement.

The paper is organized as follows. In Sect. 2 the Extremal Optimization principles including the guided state changes are presented. Section 3 presents the way of using EO for processor load balancing. Section 4 describes the proposed parallel version of the algorithm. Section 5 presents the experimental results which evaluate the proposed approach.

## 2  Extremal Optimization with Guided State Changes

In Extremal Optimization we use iterative updates of a single solution $S$ built of a number of components $s_i$, which are variables of the problem. For each component, a local fitness value $\phi_i$ is evaluated to select the worst variable $s_w$ in the solution. In a generic EO, $S$ is modified at each iteration step, by randomly updating the worst variable. As a result, a solution $S'$ is created which belongs to the neighbourhood $Neigh(S, s_w)$ of $S$. For $S'$ the global fitness function $\Phi(S)$ is evaluated which assess the quality of $S'$. The new solution $S'$ replaces $S$ if its global fitness is better than that of $S$. We can avoid staying in a local optimum in such EO, by using a probabilistic version $\tau$–EO, [3]. It is based on a user-defined parameter $\tau$, used in stochastic selection of the updated component. In a minimization problem solved by $\tau$–EO, the solution components are first assigned ranks k, $1 \leq k \leq n$, where $n$ is the number of the components, consistently with the increasing order of their local fitness values. It is done by a permutation $\pi$ of the component labels $i$ such that: $\phi_\pi(1) \leq \phi_\pi(2) \leq \ldots \phi_\pi(n)$. The worst component $s_i$ is of rank 1, while the best one is of rank $n$. Then, the component selection probability over the ranks $k$ is defined as follows: $p_k \sim k^{-\tau}$, for a given value of the parameter $\tau$. At each iteration, a component rank $k$ is selected in the current solution $S$ according to $p_k$. Next, the respective component $s_j$ with $j = \pi(k)$ randomly changes its state and $S$ moves to a neighboring solution, $S' \in Neigh(S, s_j)$, unconditionally. The parameters of the $\tau$–EO are: the total number of iterations $\mathcal{N}_{\text{iter}}$ and the probabilistic selection parameter $\tau$.

$\tau$–EO with guided state changes (EO–GS) has been proposed to improve the convergence speed of EO optimization. For this, some knowledge of the problem properties is used for next solution selection in consecutive EO iterations with the help of an additional local target function $\omega_s$. This function is evaluated for all neighbour solutions existing in $Neigh(S, s_{\pi(k)})$ for the selected rank $k$. Then, the neighbour solutions are sorted and assigned GS-ranks $g$ with the use of the function $\omega_s$. The new state $S' \in Neigh(S, s_{\pi(k)})$ is selected in a stochastic way using the exponential distribution with the selection probability $p \sim \text{Exp}(g, \lambda) = \lambda e^{-\lambda g}$. Due to this, better neighbour solutions are more probable to be selected. The bias to better neighbours is controlled by the $\lambda$ parameter. The general scheme of the EO–GS is shown as Algorithm 1.

**Algorithm 1.** EO algorithm with Guided State Changes (EO–GS)

---

initialize configuration $S$ at will
$S_{\text{best}} \leftarrow S$
**while** total number of iterations $\mathcal{N}_{\text{iter}}$ not reached **do**
    evaluate $\phi_i$ for each variable $s_i$ of the current solution $S$
    rank the variables $s_i$ based on their local fitness $\phi_i$
    choose the rank $k$ according to $k^{-\tau}$ so that the variable $s_j$ with $j = \pi(k)$ is selected
    evaluate $\omega_s$ for each neighbour $S_v \in Neigh(S, s_j)$, generated by $s_j$ change of the
    current solution $S$
    rank neighbours $S_v \in Neigh(S, s_j)$ based on the target function $\omega_s$
    choose $S' \in Neigh(S, s_j)$ according to the exponential distribution
    accept $S \leftarrow S'$ unconditionally
    **if** $\Phi(S) < \Phi(S_{\text{best}})$ **then**
        $S_{\text{best}} \leftarrow S$
    **end if**
**end while**
**return** $S_{\text{best}}$ and $\Phi(S_{\text{best}})$

---

## 3    EO-Based Load Balancing Foundations

In this section we will recall basic theoretical foundations for the proposed EO-based load balancing. The proposed load balancing method is meant for a clusters of multicore processors interconnected by a message passing network. Load balancing actions for a program are controlled at the level of indivisible tasks which are process threads. We assume that the load balancing algorithms dynamically control assignment of program tasks $t_k$, $k \in \{1 \dots |T|\}$ to processors (computing nodes) $n$, $n \in [0, |N| - 1]$, where $T$ and $N$ are the sets of all the tasks and the computing nodes, respectively. The goal is the minimal total program execution time, achieved by task migration between processors. The load balancing method is based on a series of steps in which detection and correction of processor load imbalance is done, Fig. 2. The imbalance detection relies on some run-time infrastructure which observes the state of the executive computer system and the execution states of application programs. Processors (computing nodes) periodically report their current loads to the load balancing control which monitors the current system load imbalance. When load imbalance is discovered, processor load correction actions are launched. For them an EO-based algorithm is executed, which identifies the tasks which need migration and the migration target processor nodes. Following this, the required physical task migrations are performed with the return to the load imbalance detection.

To evaluate the load of the system two indicators are used. The first is the computing power of a node $n$: $Ind_{power}(n)$, which is the sum of potential computing powers of all the active cores on the node. The second is the percentage of the CPU power available for application threads on the node $n$: $Time_{\text{CPU}}^{\%}(n)$, periodically estimated on computing nodes. The percentage of the CPU power available for a single thread is computed as a quotient of the time during which the CPU was allocated to a probe thread against the time interval of the measurement. $Time^{\%}_{\text{CPU}}(n)$ value is the sum of the percentage of CPU power available for the number of probe threads equal to the number of cores on the node.

System load imbalance $LI$ is a boolean defined based on the difference of the CPU availability between the currently most heavily and the least heavily loaded computing nodes:

$$LI = \max_{n \in N}(Time^{\%}_{\text{CPU}}(n)) - \min_{n \in N}(Time^{\%}_{\text{CPU}}(n)) \geq \alpha$$

The load imbalance equal true requires a load correction. The value of $\alpha$ is set using an experimental approach (during experiments we set it between 25 % and 75 %).

An application is characterized by two programmer-supplied parameters, based on the volume of computations and communications tasks: $\text{COM}(t_s, t_d)$ is the communication metrics between tasks $t_s$ and $t_d$, $\text{WP}(t)$ is the load weight metrics introduced by a task $t$. $\text{COM}(t_s, t_d)$ and $\text{WP}(t)$ metrics can provide exact values, e.g. for well-defined tasks sizes and inter-task communication in regular parallel applications, or only some predictions e.g. when the execution time depends on the processed data.

A task mapping solution $S$ is represented by a vector $\mu = (\mu_1, \ldots, \mu_{|T|})$ of $|T|$ integers ranging in the interval $[0, |N| - 1]$. $\mu_i = j$ means that the solution $S$ under consideration maps the $i$-th task $t_i$ onto the computing node $j$.

The global fitness function $\Phi(S)$ is defined as follows.

$$\Phi(S) = attrExtTotal(S) * \Delta_1 + migration(S) * \Delta_2 \tag{1}$$
$$+ imbalance(S) * [1 - (\Delta_1 + \Delta_2)]$$

where $1 > \Delta_1 \geq 0$, $1 > \Delta_2 \geq 0$ and $\Delta_1 + \Delta_2 < 1$ hold.

The function $attrExtTotal(S)$ represents the impact of the total external communication between tasks on the quality of a given mapping $S$. By "external" we mean the communication between tasks placed on different nodes. This function is normalized in the range $[0, 1]$. In executive systems with homogeneous communication links it is a quotient of an absolute value of the total external communication volume and the total communication volume of all communications (when all tasks are placed on the same node $attrExtTotal(S) = 0$, when tasks are placed in the way that all communication is external $attrExtTotal(S) = 1$); in heterogeneous executive systems equivalent measures of the communication time are used:

$$attrExtTotal(S) = totalExt(S)/\overline{\text{COM}}$$

where: $\overline{\text{COM}} = \sum_{s,d \in T} \text{COM}(s, d)$ and $totalExt(S) = \sum_{s,d \in T: \mu_s \neq \mu_d} \text{COM}(s, d)$.

The function $migration(S)$ is a migration costs metrics. The value of this function is in the range $[0, 1]$, i.e. it is equal to 0 when there is no migration, when all tasks have to be migrated $migration(S) = 1$, otherwise $0 \leq migration(S) \leq 1$:

$$migration(S) = |\{t \in T : \mu^S_t \neq \mu^{S*}_t\}|/|T|$$

where: $S$ is the currently considered solution and $S*$ is the previous solution (or the initial solution in the algorithm).

The function $imbalance(S)$ represents the numerical load imbalance metrics in the solution $S$. It is equal to 1 when in $S$ there exists at least one unloaded (empty) computing node, otherwise it is equal to the normalized average absolute load deviation of tasks in $S$, determined in the definition below:

$$imbalance(S) = \begin{cases} 1 & \text{exists at least one unloaded node} \\ D^*(S)/2 * N * \overline{WP} & \text{otherwise} \end{cases}$$

where: $D^*(S) = \sum_{n \in [0,N-1]} |NWP(S,n)/Ind_{power}(n) - \overline{WP}|$, $\overline{WP} = \sum_{t \in T} WP(t)/\sum_{n \in [0,N-1]} Ind_{power}(n)$, $NWP(S,n) = \sum_{t \in T : \mu_t = n} WP(t)$.

In the applied EO the local fitness function of a task $\phi(t)$ is designed in such a way that it forces moving tasks away from overloaded nodes, at the same time preserving low external (inter-node) communication. The $\gamma$ parameter $(0 < \gamma < 1)$ allows tuning the weight of load metrics.

$$\phi(t) = \gamma * load(\mu_t) + (1 - \gamma) * rank(t) \tag{2}$$

The function $load(n)$ indicates how much the load of node $n$, which executes $t$, exceeds the average load of all nodes. It is normalized versus the heaviest load among all the nodes. The $rank(t)$ function governs the selection of best candidates for migration. The chance for migration have tasks, which show low communication with their current node (attraction) and low load deviation from the average load:

$$rank(t) = 1 - (\beta * attr(t) + (1 - \beta) * ldev(t))$$

where: $\beta$ is a real number between 0 and $1$ – a parameter indicating the importance of the weight of attraction metrics. The attraction of the task $t$ to its executive computing node $attr(t)$ is defined as the amount of communication between task $t$ and other tasks on the same node, normalized versus the maximal communication inside the node. The load deviation compared to the average load $ldev(t)$ is defined as the absolute value of the difference between the load metrics of the task $t$ and the minimum load on the node, normalized versus the highest such difference for all tasks on the node.

We use the EO-GS algorithm to perform task and target node selection for migration. Target node selection is based on additional "biased" stochastic approach, to favour some solutions over others. In our case, the valid solution state neighbourhood includes the use of all system nodes. Therefore, at each update of rank $k$, all nodes $n \in N$ are sorted using the $\omega(n1, n2)$ function, $n1, n2 \in N$, with the assignment of GS-ranks $g$ to them. Then, one of the nodes is selected using the exponential distribution $Exp(g, \lambda) = \lambda e^{-\lambda g}$.

We propose the following definition of $\omega(n1, n2)$ for the sorting algorithm based on a pairwise ordering of the computing nodes $n1, n2$ as targets for migration of task $j$ in the load balancing algorithm. It takes into account the normalized load deviation of the nodes $n1, n2$ and the attraction of the task $j$ to the each of these nodes.

$$\omega(n1, n2) = \begin{cases} sgn(relload(n1) - relload(n2)) & \text{when } relload(n1) \neq relload(n2) \\ sgn(attrext^{\%}(j, n2) - attrext^{\%}(j, n1)) & \text{otherwise.} \end{cases}$$

where:

$$relload(n) = \frac{loaddev(n) - \min_{m \in [0,N-1]} loaddev(m)}{\max_{m \in [0,N-1]} loaddev(m) - \min_{m \in [0,N-1]} loaddev(m)}$$

$$loaddev(n) = \frac{\text{NWP}(S,n)}{Ind_{power}(n)} - \overline{\text{WP}}$$

$$attrext^{\%}(j,n) = \frac{attrext(j,n)}{\max_{e \in N}(attrext(j,e))}$$

$$attrext(j,n) = \sum_{e \in T(n)} (\text{COM}(e,j) + \text{COM}(j,e))$$

and $T(n) = \{t \in T : \mu_t = n\}$ — the set of threads, placed on computing node $n$.

## 4 Parallel Extremal Optimization Applied to Load Balancing

The general scheme of the parallel version of the EO algorithm applied in this paper to load balancing of distributed programs is presented in Fig. 1. This algorithm is a parallelized version of the Algorithm 1 in Sect. 2. In this scheme, after the setting of an initial solution $S$, the local fitness function $\phi(s_j)$ values are evaluated for all the components of $S$ and the ranking of the components

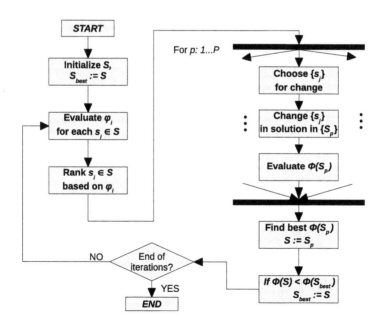

**Fig. 1.** The general scheme of the parallel version of the EO algorithm.

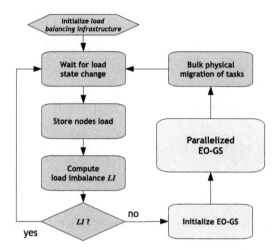

**Fig. 2.** The general scheme of load balancing based on parallel EO with guided state changes.

$S$ based on $\phi(s_j)$ is constructed. Next, a parallel EO part of the algorithm starts. The population-type parallel EO algorithm is applied, which replaces the single improvement of the EO solution by a parallel search for improvements performed on a population of $P$ EO solutions $S_p$. They are generated by a parallel selection of the solution components and, next, an improvement of the worst components stochastically selected based on the local fitness function with the highest probability of the worst components. During selection of components for solution improvement a single point or multipoint selection of components in the same basic solution can be performed. The set of components is improved using a parallelized random selection or a parallelized approach of guided state changes explained in Sect. 3. For each improved solution, the global fitness function $\Phi(S)$ is evaluated. The improved solution with the global fitness better than the current best value is selected as the base for next parallel EO iterations. The local and global fitness function definitions are explained in Sect. 3.

The general scheme of the load balancing algorithm based on the parallel EO-GS is shown in Fig. 2. The scheme is composed of two co-operating iterative parts represented in the left and right parts of Fig. 2. Both parts can be executed in a parallel way. In the left part, we first identify a sufficiently big load imbalance in the functioning of the executive system following the model explained in Sect. 3. When a sufficiently big processor load imbalance is noticed in program execution, then we apply a parallel version of EO-GS to select tasks which are to be migrated among processors to improve the general balance of processor loads (the right hand side of Fig. 2). The parallel EO-GS algorithm performs a given number of parallel iterations. EO-GS finds a number of best "logical" migrations of tasks, which are registered to be performed when the EO-GS iterations are over. Then, the physical migrations worked out by the EO-GS take place. The parallel EO-GS and the load imbalance detection are executed in the background of the application program. The online overhead introduced in the application execution time is due to task migration. The overhead is strongly dependent on whether only data or task codes are migrated.

## 5   Experimental Results

The experiments were performed using simulated execution of application programs in a distributed system. Applications were run in a simulated distributed memory cluster of 32 multi–core processors. Communication was based on message-passing. The DEVS-based system simulator [7] and parallel EO algorithms were run in a cluster of Intel i7-based, 8–core workstations.

During the experiments we used a set of 5 synthetic exemplary programs, which were randomly generated. The exemplary programs were composed of layers of parallel tasks. Tasks from the same layer could communicate. At the boundaries between layers there was a global exchange of data.The number of tasks in an application varied from 272 to 576. The communication/computation ratio for applications was in the range $[0.10, 0.20]$. The first exemplary program is an irregular application in which the execution time of tasks depends on the processed data. Thus, it exhibits unpredictable execution time of tasks and the communication scheme and load imbalance can occur in computing nodes. The next four programs are regular applications that have fixed tasks' execution times. In regular applications load imbalance can appear due to a non–optimized task placement of tasks or runtime conditions change.

During experiments, we have compared parallel EO and EO–GS to classic (sequential) EO and EO–GS which use the same local and global fitness functions. The following parameters for load balancing control were used: $\alpha = 0.5, \beta = 0.5, \gamma = 0.75, \Delta_1 = 0.13, \Delta_2 = 0.17, \tau = 1.5$, and for EO–GS $\lambda = 0.5$. Other settings of control parameters are not discussed here since we have presented them in [5,6]. Each experiment was repeated 5 times, for each run 4 different methods of initial task placements (random, round-robin, METIS, packed) were tested. Thus, 20 runs were executed in total for each experiment to produce an averaged result. Experiments were repeated for the number of iterations of EO and EO–GS set to 30, 60, 120 and 250.

In the first experiment, we tested the performance of standard EO parallelized by concurrent random mutation. Figure 3(a) and 3(b) show the average improvements over classic EO for the number of parallel candidate solutions in the range $[1, 8]$ (columns) and the different iteration count (rows). The reference was the speedup for the lowest number of iterations (30) and non-parallelized, classic EO. The speedup improvement is in the range $[0\%, 5\%]$, where better speedup is obtained when the number of iterations or parallel candidate solutions is higher. It means that we can substitute the number of iterations with widening the search area. The change of migrations number for different numbers of parallel candidate solutions and the iteration count, Fig. 3(b), reveals that a smaller number of migrations is obtained for parallelized version of EO.

In the second experiment, we investigated the performance of EO–GS parallelized with concurrent mutation guided by the search of the best solution state change as explained in Sect. 3, Fig. 4(a) and (b). Similarly as in the first experiment, the reference was speedup for 30 iterations and non-parallelized, classic EO. The speedup improvement was in the range [10 %, 12 %], substantially higher than that for the parallelized standard EO. On the other side, the speedup improvement less depends on the number of iterations of EO and the number of parallel candidate solutions. It confirms that EO–GS is able to find load balance solutions of high quality, thus eliminating the need for further intensive search of the solution space.

We analyzed also the impact of the regularity of applications on the obtained results. For irregular applications the speedup strongly depends on load balancing. Figure 5 shows the speedup improvement of irregular applications for parallelized EO and parallelized EO with Guided Search (EO–GS). The speedup improvement depends on the number of candidates and is noticeably better than the average values for all kinds of applications. For irregular applications it is more profitable to extend the search area by parallelizing EO than to increase the number of iterations of EO. For regular applications speedup was not sensitive to the number of candidate solutions.

|     | 1 | 2 | 4 | 8 |
|-----|-------|-------|-------|-------|
| 30  | 0,00% | 1,64% | 2,03% | 1,09% |
| 60  | 1,84% | 2,82% | 3,50% | 0,97% |
| 120 | 2,56% | 3,18% | 4,32% | 3,42% |
| 250 | 2,41% | 3,60% | 3,91% | 4,11% |

(a)

|     | 1 | 2 | 4 | 8 |
|-----|---------|---------|---------|---------|
| 30  | 100,00% | 118,15% | 127,34% | 133,53% |
| 60  | 136,45% | 141,01% | 139,68% | 145,25% |
| 120 | 148,15% | 152,45% | 156,10% | 152,93% |
| 250 | 168,66% | 169,05% | 156,03% | 154,68% |

(b)

**Fig. 3.** Average speedup improvement (a) and migrations number change (b) of parallelized EO against classic EO for different numbers of parallel candidate solutions (columns) and the iteration counts (rows).

|     | 1 | 2 | 4 | 8 |
|-----|--------|--------|--------|--------|
| 30  | 10,51% | 11,10% | 11,29% | 11,35% |
| 60  | 11,32% | 10,95% | 11,42% | 10,85% |
| 120 | 11,45% | 10,79% | 11,19% | 11,11% |
| 250 | 10,67% | 10,48% | 11,51% | 11,91% |

(a)

|     | 1 | 2 | 4 | 8 |
|-----|---------|---------|---------|---------|
| 30  | 150,44% | 155,86% | 161,70% | 160,06% |
| 60  | 166,01% | 170,26% | 163,01% | 174,60% |
| 120 | 172,26% | 173,54% | 171,80% | 174,75% |
| 250 | 184,19% | 182,71% | 173,66% | 174,16% |

(b)

**Fig. 4.** Average speedup improvement (a) and migrations number change (b) of parallelized EO with Guided Search (EO–GS) against classic EO for different numbers of parallel candidate solutions (columns) and the iteration counts (rows).

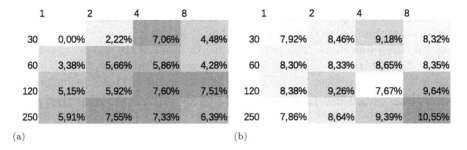

|     | 1 | 2 | 4 | 8 |     | 1 | 2 | 4 | 8 |
|-----|---|---|---|---|-----|---|---|---|---|
| 30  | 0,00% | 2,22% | 7,06% | 4,48% | 30  | 7,92% | 8,46% | 9,18% | 8,32% |
| 60  | 3,38% | 5,66% | 5,86% | 4,28% | 60  | 8,30% | 8,33% | 8,65% | 8,35% |
| 120 | 5,15% | 5,92% | 7,60% | 7,51% | 120 | 8,38% | 9,26% | 7,67% | 9,64% |
| 250 | 5,91% | 7,55% | 7,33% | 6,39% | 250 | 7,86% | 8,64% | 9,39% | 10,55% |

(a)                                              (b)

**Fig. 5.** Average speedup improvement of irregular applications for parallelized EO (a) and parallelized EO–GS (b) against classic EO for different numbers of parallel candidate solutions (columns) and the iteration counts (rows).

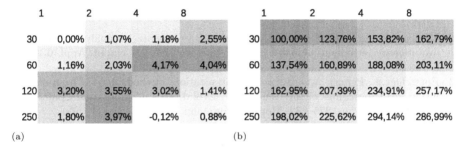

|     | 1 | 2 | 4 | 8 |     | 1 | 2 | 4 | 8 |
|-----|---|---|---|---|-----|---|---|---|---|
| 30  | 0,00% | 1,07% | 1,18% | 2,55% | 30  | 100,00% | 123,76% | 153,82% | 162,79% |
| 60  | 1,16% | 2,03% | 4,17% | 4,04% | 60  | 137,54% | 160,89% | 188,08% | 203,11% |
| 120 | 3,20% | 3,55% | 3,02% | 1,41% | 120 | 162,95% | 207,39% | 234,91% | 257,17% |
| 250 | 1,80% | 3,97% | -0,12% | 0,88% | 250 | 198,02% | 225,62% | 294,14% | 286,99% |

(a)                                              (b)

**Fig. 6.** Average speedup improvement (a) and migrations number change (b) in irregular application for EO parallelized according to island model against classic EO for different numbers of parallel candidate solutions (columns) and the iteration counts (rows).

In the last experiment we tested the EO parallelized using a "population model" but without solutions exchange, Fig. 6(a) and (b). In general, this kind of parallelization of EO did not provide satisfying speedup improvement. Only for irregular applications we got speedup improvement. The limiting factor was here the inadequate solution exchange between parallel EO instances.

The general conclusion coming from our experiments is that the extension of the solution search space in EO through parallel mutations of several candidate solutions even in its basic form provides satisfactory results. We were able to obtain better (or at least the same) quality of load balancing without increasing the number of iterations of EO but using computing power of multicore CPUs. Additional profit of using many parallel state changes in EO is a reduction in the number of task migrations needed to balance the system.

## 6   Conclusions

The paper has presented a parallel algorithm for dynamic processor load balancing in execution of distributed programs. The algorithm is based on internal use of an improved parallel EO method – EO-GS. The purpose of the parallel EO-GS algorithm was to determine candidates for task migrations in the overall load balancing procedure. The improvement consisted in the use of a guidance of an additional state quality function which corresponded to a better use of the knowledge of the problem. The experiments with simulated load balancing following the proposed algorithm have shown that the support by this guidance was successful. Application of the parallel EO-GS enabled obtaining better quality of load balancing compared to other tested methods.

# References

1. Khan, R.Z., Ali, J.: Classification of task partitioning and load balancing strategies in distributed parallel computing systems. Int. J. Comput. Appl. **60**(17), 48–53 (2012)
2. Mishra, M., Agarwal, S., Mishra, P., Singh, S.: Comparative analysis of various evolutionary techniques of load balancing: a review. Int. J. Comput. Appl. **63**(15), 8–13 (2013)
3. Boettcher, S., Percus, A.G.: Extremal optimization: methods derived from coevolution. In: Proceedings of the Genetic and Evolutionary Computation Conference (GECCO 1999), pp. 825–832. Morgan Kaufmann, San Francisco (1999)
4. Sneppen, K., et al.: Evolution as a self-organized critical phenomenon. Proc. Natl. Acad. Sci. **92**, 5209–5213 (1995)
5. De Falco, I., Laskowski, E., Olejnik, R., Scafuri, U., Tarantino, E., Tudruj, M.: Load balancing in distributed applications based on extremal optimization. In: Esparcia-Alcázar, A.I. (ed.) EvoApplications 2013. LNCS, vol. 7835, pp. 52–61. Springer, Heidelberg (2013)
6. De Falco, I., Laskowski, E., Olejnik, R., Scafuri, U., Tarantino, E., Tudruj, M.: Improving extremal optimization in load balancing by local search. In: Esparcia-Alcázar, A.I., Mora, A.M. (eds.) EvoApplications 2014. LNCS, vol. 8602, pp. 51–62. Springer, Heidelberg (2014)
7. Zeigler, B.: Hierarchical, modular discrete-event modelling in an object-oriented environment. Simulation **49**(5), 219–230 (1987)
8. Randall, M., Lewis, A.: An extended extremal optimisation model for parallel architectures. In: 2nd IEEE International Conference on e-Science and Grid Computing, e-Science 2006, p. 114 (2006)
9. Tamura, K., Kitakami, H., Nakada, A.: Reducing crossovers in reconciliation graphs with extremal optimization (in japanese). Trans. Inf. Process. Soc. Japan **49**(4(TOM 20)), 105–116 (2008)
10. Tamura, K., Kitakami, H., Nakada, A.: Distributed extremal optimization using island model for reducing crossovers in reconciliation graph. In: Proceedings of the International MultiConference of Engineers and Computer Scientists 2013, Hong-Kong, March 2013, pp. 1–6 (2013)
11. Tamura, K., Kitakami, H., Nakada, A.: Distributed modified extremal optimization using Island model for reducing crossovers in reconciliation graph. Eng. Lett. **21**(2), EL_21_2_05 (2013)

# A Swarm Intelligence Approach to 3D Distance-Based Indoor UWB Localization

Stefania Monica$^{(\boxtimes)}$ and Gianluigi Ferrari

Wireless Ad-hoc and Sensor Networks Laboratory,
Department of Information Engineering, University of Parma, 43124 Parma, Italy
stefania.monica@studenti.unipr.it, gianluigi.ferrari@unipr.it
http://wasnlab.tlc.unipr.it/

**Abstract.** In this paper, we focus on the application of Ultra Wide Band (UWB) technology to the problem of locating static nodes in three-dimensional indoor environments, assuming to know the positions of a few nodes, denoted as "beacons." The localization algorithms which are considered throughout the paper are based on the Time Of Arrival (TOA) of signals traveling between pairs of nodes. In particular, we propose to apply the Particle Swarm Optimization (PSO) algorithm to solve the localization problem and we compare its performance with that of the Two-Stage Maximum-Likelihood (TSML) algorithm. Simulation results show that the former allows achieving accurate position estimates even in scenarios where, because of ill-conditioning problems associated with the network topology, TSML fails.

**Keywords:** Wireless Sensor Networks · Localization · Time Of Arrival (TOA) · Maximum-Likelihood · Particle Swarm Optimization

## 1 Introduction

In the last years, the interest on Wireless Sensor Networks (WSNs) has become more and more evident, as they promise to be a scalable and low-cost technology which can be used to solve many practical challenges. They consist of a number of wirelessly connected nodes, each of which has one or more sensors to measure some physical quantities such as temperature, pressure, acceleration, etc. Typical applications of WSNs include home security, military surveillance, environmental monitoring, assistance for old people and patients in hospitals, and industrial process control [1].

Among the wide variety of fields in which WSNs are involved, in this paper we focus on accurate target localization, through wireless communications, in indoor environments. This is a challenging and, at the same time, very interesting problem: the use of WSNs is an attractive option to address it, as they combine low-to-medium rate communications and low power consumption with positioning capabilities. As a matter of fact, it is possible to estimate the distances between pairs of nodes by extracting some physical quantities—such as

© Springer International Publishing Switzerland 2015
A.M. Mora and G. Squillero (Eds.): EvoApplications 2015, LNCS 9028, pp. 91–102, 2015.
DOI: 10.1007/978-3-319-16549-3_8

the Time Of Flight (TOF), the Received Signal Strength (RSS), or the Angle Of Arrival (AOA), from the signals travelling between them.

Many localization estimate techniques have been proposed in the litera-ture, such as: iterative methods based on Taylor series expansion [2] or the steepest-descent algorithm [3], which guarantee fast convergence only for an ini-tial estimate value close to the true solution (often difficult to obtain in real applications); closed-form methods, such as the Circumference Intersection (CI) algorithms [4], the Plane Intersection (PI) algorithm [5,6], and the Two-Stage Maximum-Likelihood (TSML) algorithm [7,8]. These "geometrical" methods typically involve linear or non-linear systems of equations, which can become ill-conditioned (for instance, if the considered beacons lay on the same line or plane) and, thus, lead to wrong position estimates. In [9,10], it is shown that the initial system of equations of the TSML algorithm can be reformulated in terms of an optimization problem and solved through the use of Particle Swarm Optimization (PSO). Even if the TSML algorithm is particuarly interesting, as it can attain the Cramer-Rao lower bound [11], in [9,10] the PSO algorithm is shown to outperform the TSML algorithm. In [12], the use of the PSO algorithm is investigated to estimate the positions, with the use of a few "beacons" and considering Time Difference Of Arrival (TDOA) approaches, of nodes laying on a plane. We remark that the use of the PSO algorithm for localization purposes is not novel [13].

In this paper, we extend [12] by considering three dimensional node position estimation. In order to keep the derivation more tractable, we investigate Time Of Arrival (TOA) localization strategies. In particular, under the assumption of knowing the positions of a few nodes, denoted as beacons, the positions of other nodes, placed in three dimensional scenarios, are estimated. As already observed in two-dimensional scenarios, the PSO algorithm outperforms the TSML algo-rithm. The impact of the swarm size on the performance of the PSO-based localization strategy is investigated.

This paper is organized as follows. In Sect. 2, the considered scenario is described. In Sect. 3, the considered localization algorithms are described. In Sect. 4, the simulation-based performance results are presented. Section 5 con-cludes the paper.

## 2    Scenario

Assume to have $M$ beacons and denote their coordinates are $\underline{s}_i = [x_i, y_i, z_i]^T, \forall i \in \{1, \ldots, M\}$—we remark that the condition $M \geq 4$ needs to be satisfied in order to apply the localization algorithms described later. We indicate as $K_i$ the square of the Euclidean norm of the vector which identifies the position of the $i$−th node, namely:

$$K_i = x_i^2 + y_i^2 + z_i^2 \qquad i \in \{1, \ldots, M\}. \tag{1}$$

We denote as $\underline{u} = [x, y, z]^T$ the true position, unknown and to be estimated, of a generic node and as $\underline{\hat{u}} = [\hat{x}, \hat{y}, \hat{z}]^T$ its estimated position. Then, the true and estimated distances between the $i$-th beacon ($i \in \{1, \ldots, M\}$) and the currently considered node are, respectively:

$$r_i = \sqrt{(\underline{u} - \underline{s}_i)^T (\underline{u} - \underline{s}_i)} \qquad \hat{r}_i = \sqrt{(\underline{\hat{u}} - \underline{s}_i)^T (\underline{\hat{u}} - \underline{s}_i)}. \qquad (2)$$

In order to provide a statistical model for the errors on the estimated distance, the wireless communication protocol comes into the picture. Since we consider indoor environments, where the main sources of errors are non-line-of-sight propagation, multipath, and multiple access interference, we propose to use Ultra Wide Band (UWB) signaling, which can theoretically reduce the impact of these phenomena. As a matter of fact, UWB signals' large bandwidth allows penetrating through obstacles and resolving multipath components. Moreover, the high time resolution typical of UWB signals improves the ranging capability [14]. According to [15], the estimated distances can be modeled as

$$\hat{r}_i \simeq r_i + \nu_i \qquad i \in \{1, \ldots, M\} \qquad (3)$$

where:

$$\nu_i = \varepsilon_i + b$$

$\varepsilon_i \sim \mathcal{N}(0, \sigma_i^2)$; $\varepsilon_i$ is independent from $\varepsilon_j$ if $i \neq j$, $j \in \{1, \ldots, M\}$; and $b$ is a synchronization bias. Moreover, the standard deviation $\sigma_i$ of the position error estimate between two UWB nodes can be approximated as a linear function of the distance between them, namely $\sigma_i \simeq \sigma_0 r_i + \beta$. In the following, the values $\sigma_0 = 0.01$ m and $\beta = 0.08$ m are considered. These values are obtained in [15] by considering Channel Model 3 described in [16] and the energy detection receiver presented in [17], which is composed by a band-pass filter followed by a square-law device and an integrator, with integration interval set to $T_s = 1$ s. The results presented in the following hold under these channel and receiver assumptions.

## 3    Localization Algorithms

In this section, we first describe the TOA-based TSML algorithm. Then, we formulate the PSO algorithm applied to the minimization problem obtained by properly reinterpreting the TOA equations of the TSML algorithm.

### 3.1    Two-Stage Maximum-Likelihood Algorithm

Each measurement of the distance between a given beacon and a node provides the equation of the circumference, centered at the beacon, on which the node may lay. Therefore, considering all measurements of the distances between the node of interest and the beacons, the following quadratic system can be obtained:

$$\begin{cases} (x - x_1)^2 + (y - y_1)^2 + (z - z_1)^2 = \hat{r}_1^2 \\ \ldots \\ (x - x_M)^2 + (y - y_M)^2 + (z - z_M)^2 = \hat{r}_M^2. \end{cases} \qquad (4)$$

Defining a new variable as $\hat{n} \triangleq ||\hat{u}||^2$ (where $|| \cdot ||$ is the Euclidean norm), the system (4) can be written in matrix notation as

$$\underline{\underline{G}}\,\hat{\underline{w}} = \hat{\underline{h}} \tag{5}$$

where

$$\underline{\underline{G}} \triangleq -2 \begin{pmatrix} x_1 & y_1 & z_1 & -0.5 \\ x_2 & y_2 & z_2 & -0.5 \\ \vdots & \vdots & \vdots & \vdots \\ x_M & y_M & z_M & -0.5 \end{pmatrix} \qquad \hat{\underline{w}} \triangleq \begin{pmatrix} \hat{x} \\ \hat{y} \\ \hat{z} \\ \hat{n} \end{pmatrix} \qquad \hat{\underline{h}} \triangleq \begin{pmatrix} \hat{r}_1^2 - K_1 \\ \hat{r}_2^2 - K_2 \\ \vdots \\ \hat{r}_M^2 - K_M \end{pmatrix}. \tag{6}$$

The solution of (5) can be found in two steps and we refer the interested reader to [8] for all details. The idea behind the solution is that (5) can be interpreted as a linear system (which is not the case since $\hat{n} = \hat{x}^2 + \hat{y}^2 + \hat{z}^2$, i.e., the last component of the solution vector depends on the first three ones) and, then, be solved by using a Maximum Likelihood (ML) appraoch, obtaining [8]:

$$\hat{\underline{w}} = (\underline{\underline{G}}^T \underline{\underline{\Psi}}^{-1} \underline{\underline{G}})^{-1} \underline{\underline{G}}^T \underline{\underline{\Psi}}^{-1} \hat{\underline{h}} \tag{7}$$

where $\underline{\underline{\Psi}} \triangleq 4\underline{\underline{B}}\,\underline{\underline{Q}}\,\underline{\underline{B}}$, $\underline{\underline{B}} = \mathrm{diag}(r_1, \ldots, r_M)$, and $\underline{\underline{Q}} = \mathrm{diag}(\sigma_1^2, \ldots, \sigma_M^2)$.

Then, in order to take into account the fact that the elements of $\hat{\underline{w}}$ are not independent, a second step is necessary, and corresponds to solving the following system:

$$\underline{\underline{G}}' \, \hat{\underline{w}}' = \hat{\underline{h}}'$$

where

$$\underline{\underline{G}}' \triangleq \begin{pmatrix} 1 & 0 & 0 \\ 0 & 1 & 0 \\ 0 & 0 & 1 \\ 1 & 1 & 1 \end{pmatrix} \qquad \hat{\underline{h}}' \triangleq \begin{pmatrix} \hat{w}_1^2 \\ \hat{w}_2^2 \\ \hat{w}_3^2 \\ \hat{w}_4 \end{pmatrix} \qquad \hat{\underline{w}}' \triangleq \begin{pmatrix} \hat{x}^2 \\ \hat{y}^2 \\ \hat{z}^2 \end{pmatrix}.$$

The ML estimate of $\hat{\underline{w}}'$ ca be finally written as [8]

$$\hat{\underline{w}}' = (\underline{\underline{G}}^T \underline{\underline{\Phi}}^{-1} \underline{\underline{G}})^{-1} \underline{\underline{G}}^T \underline{\underline{\Phi}}^{-1} \hat{\underline{h}}' \tag{8}$$

where $\underline{\underline{\Phi}} \triangleq 4\underline{\underline{B}}'(\underline{\underline{G}}^T \underline{\underline{\Psi}}^{-1} \underline{\underline{G}})^{-1} \underline{\underline{B}}'$ and $\underline{\underline{B}}' \triangleq \mathrm{diag}(\hat{w}_1, \hat{w}_2, \hat{w}_3, 0.5)$. Finally, the position estimate is found to be [8]

$$\hat{\underline{u}} = \underline{\underline{U}} \left[ \sqrt{\hat{w}_1'}, \sqrt{\hat{w}_2'}, \sqrt{\hat{w}_3'} \right]^T$$

where $\underline{\underline{U}} = \mathrm{diag}(\mathrm{sgn}(\hat{\underline{w}}))$.

## 3.2  Particle Swarm Optimization

The system (4) can be written, in matrix notation, as

$$I_1 \hat{\underline{u}}^T \hat{\underline{u}} + \underline{\underline{A}}\,\hat{\underline{u}} = \hat{\underline{k}} \tag{9}$$

where: $\underline{I}_1$ is a $M \times 1$ vector with all elements equal to 1; $\underline{\underline{A}}$ is a $M \times 3$ matrix whose columns are the first three columns of the matrix $\underline{\underline{G}}$ in (5); and the $i$−th element of $\underline{\hat{k}}$ is $\hat{r}_i^2 - K_i$. Instead of solving the quadratic system (9), we re-interpret it as the following minimization problem:

$$\underline{\hat{u}} = \text{argmin}_{\underline{u}} F(\underline{u}) \tag{10}$$

where $F(\underline{u})$ is the fitness function defined as follows:

$$F(\underline{u}) \triangleq ||\underline{\hat{k}} - (\underline{I}_1 \underline{\hat{u}}^T \underline{\hat{u}} + \underline{\underline{A}}\, \underline{\hat{u}})||.$$

The PSO algorithm, introduced in [18], is an iterative method which can be used to solve optimization problems such as the one in (10). The set of potential solutions of the considered problem is modeled as a swarm of $S$ particles. At any given instant $t$, each particle $i \in \{1, \ldots, S\}$ in the swarm, is associated with a position $\underline{x}^{(i)}(t)$ in the region of interest and with a velocity $\underline{v}^{(i)}(t)$, which are both randomly initialized, at the beginning, with values $\underline{x}^{(i)}(0)$ and $\underline{v}^{(i)}(0)$. The particles are "guided" towards the optimal solution. In fact, the updating rules for the position and the velocity of each particle are meant to simulate "social" interactions between individuals [19]. More precisely, according to the most general formulation of the PSO algorithm, the velocity of particle $i$ is updated, at each iteration, according to the following rule [20]:

$$\underline{v}^{(i)}(t+1) = \omega(t)\underline{v}^{(i)}(t) + c_1 R_1(t)(\underline{y}^{(i)}(t) - \underline{x}^{(i)}(t))$$
$$+ c_2 R_2(t)(\underline{y}(t) - \underline{x}^{(i)}(t)) \qquad i \in \{1, \ldots, S\} \tag{11}$$

where: $\omega(t)$ is denoted as *inertial factor*; $c_1$ and $c_2$ are positive real parameters denoted as *cognition* and *social* parameters, respectively; and $R_1(t)$ and $R_2(t)$ are random variables uniformly distributed in $(0, 1)$. Finally, $\underline{y}^{(i)}(t)$ and $\underline{y}(t)$ are the positions of the $i$−th particle with the best fitness function and the position of the particle with the best (among all particles) fitness function reached until instant $t$ [19].

The idea behind the updating rule (11) for the velocities is to add to the previous velocity of each particle in the swarm (weighted by means of a multiplicative factor $\omega(t)$) a stochastic combination of the direction to its best position (corresponding to the second addend in (11)) and to the global best position (third addend in (11)). The position of each particle is then updated at each step by adding to the previous position the velocity obtained according to (11):

$$\underline{x}^{(i)}(t+1) = \underline{x}^{(i)}(t) + \underline{v}^{(i)}(t) \qquad i \in \{1, \ldots, S\}. \tag{12}$$

Possible stopping conditions for the PSO algorithm can be the achievement of a sufficiently low value of the fitness function or a given (maximum) number of iterations. At the end of the algorithm, the solution is the position of the particle which best suits the optimization requirements in the last iteration.

In the simulation-based performance analysis in Sect. 4, the stopping condition will be the reach of 50 iterations. The population size $S$ is set, in most of

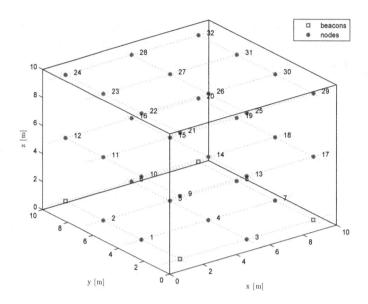

**Fig. 1.** The beacons (*red squares*) and the nodes with unknown positions (*blue dots*) are shown in a (three-dimensional) cubic region (Colour figure online).

the presented results, to 200 and the position of each particle is randomly initialized in the three dimensional cube region, with side equal to 10 m where the nodes are placed—this is the natural choice under the assumption of unknown node's positions. Finally, the parameters $c_1$ and $c_2$ in (11) are both set to 2, so that the weights for social and cognition parts to are, on average, equal to 1 and the inertial factor is $\omega(t) = 0.5 - 0.01t$ (i.e., it starts from 0.5 when $t = 0$ and decreases to 0 in the last iteration, i.e., when $t = 50$).

## 4    Simulation-Based Performance Analysis

In this section, we compare, through simulations, the performances of the two localization algorithms described in Sect. 3. Both TSML and PSO algorithms are implemented in a Matlab simulator. First, we consider the node configuration shown in Fig. 1, where the nodes are placed on regular spatial grid such that the coordinates of a generic point can be expressed as $(x_k, y_k, z_k)$, $k \in \{1, \ldots, 36\}$ with: $x_k \in \{1\,\text{m}, 5\,\text{m}, 9\,\text{m}\}$, $y_k \in \{0.5\,\text{m}, 3.5\,\text{m}, 6.5\,\text{m}, 9.5\,\text{m}\}$, and $z_k \in \{0.5\,\text{m}, 5\,\text{m}, 9.5\,\text{m}\}$. In Fig. 1, the four vertices in the bottom plane are the positions where beacons are placed. Then, we consider the node configuration in Fig. 2, where the positions of the 36 nodes are obtained by "perturbating" the positions of the nodes in Fig. 1. More precisely, the coordinates of the nodes can be expressed as: $(X_k, Y_k, Z_k)$, $k \in \{1, \ldots, 36\}$, where $X_k = x_k + \theta_k^{(x)}$, $Y_k = y_k + \theta_k^{(y)}$, and $Z_k = z_k + \theta_k^{(z)}$, with $\theta_k^{(x)}, \theta_k^{(y)}, \theta_k^{(z)} \sim \mathcal{N}(0\,\text{m}, 1\,\text{m})$ an independent of each other.

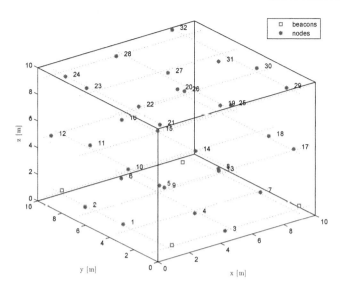

**Fig. 2.** The beacons (*red squares*) and the nodes with unknown positions (*blue dots*) are shown in a (three-dimensional) cubic region (Colour figure online).

For each node whose position needs to be estimated, we assume to make 100 independent estimates of the distance between the node and each beacon, assuming that the measurement error follows the statistical characterization in (3). Finally, each distance $\hat{r}_i$, $i \in \{1, \ldots, M\}$, used in the considered localization algorithms, is obtained by averaging over the 100 estimates, i.e.,

$$\hat{r}_i = \frac{\sum_{j=1}^{100} \hat{r}_i^{(j)}}{100}$$

where $\hat{r}_i^{(j)}$ is the $j$-th estimate of the $i$-th distance. We remark that this approach is different from the one followed in [10], where the localization algorithms were applied to each set of range measurements $\{r_i\}_{i=1}^{M}$ and the final position estimates were obtained by averaging the 100 position estimates. In each scenario, we assume that the number of beacons is $M = 4$, i.e., the minimum number which allows applying the localization techniques described in Sect. 3.

In Fig. 3, we investigate the performance of the scenario shown in Fig. 1, i.e., four beacons (red squares) laying on the same plane are considered. In this case, the matrix $\underline{G}$ involved in the TSML algorithm is not full rank, making this method inapplicable. At the opposite, the PSO algorithm guarantees accurate position estimates for all the nodes, as shown in Fig. 3.

In Fig. 4, the performance in the scenario of Fig. 2 is investigated. Since, in this case, the nodes do not lie exactly on parallel planes, as in Fig. 1, even though the matrix $\underline{G}$ of the TSML algorithm is full rank, it is ill-conditioned, leading to wrong position estimates of some nodes. In particular, the "critical" nodes are 3, 4, 7, 8, in correspondence to which the position estimation error is significantly

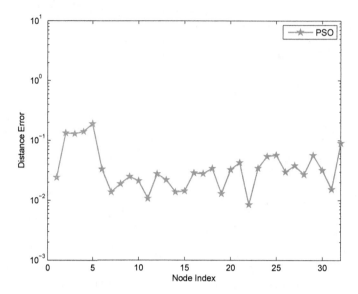

**Fig. 3.** The distance error, using the PSO algorithm, is shown as a function of the node index.

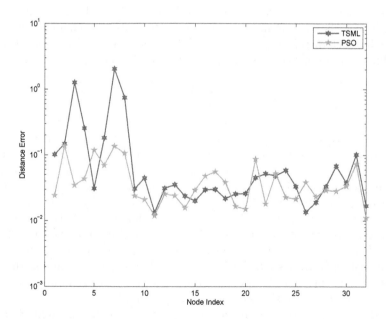

**Fig. 4.** The distance error on the position estimate of each node when using the TSML algorithm (*magenta hexagrams*) and the PSO algorithm (*green stars*) are shown (Colour figure online).

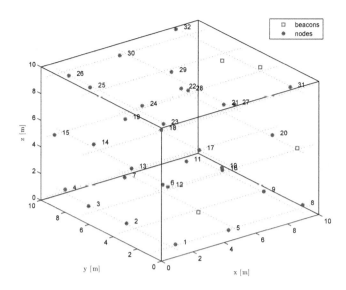

**Fig. 5.** The beacons (*red squares*) and the nodes with unknown positions (*blue dots*) are shown in a (three-dimensional) cubic region (Colour figure online).

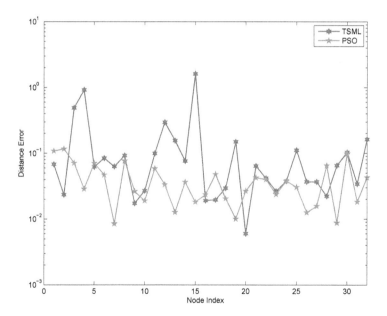

**Fig. 6.** The distance error on the position estimate of each node when using the TSML algorithm (*magenta hexagrams*) and the PSO algorithm (*green stars*) are shown (Colour figure online).

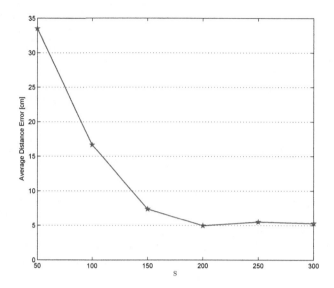

**Fig. 7.** Average distance error as a function of the swarm size $S$.

higher than with the PSO algorithm. Overall, the PSO algorithm allows locating all the nodes with a satisfying accuracy.

In Fig. 5, we consider once again the scenario described in Fig. 2, but with a more general configuration of the beacons, which are now randomly placed. Once again, the corresponding performance results, shown in Fig. 6, show that the PSO algorithm leads to sufficiently accurate position estimates for all nodes, while the TSML algorithm leads to inaccurate estimates of the positions of some nodes. Therefore, it can be concluded that the performance of the PSO algorithm is better not only in particular cases, i.e., when the beacons (almost) lay on the same plane, but also with generic positions of the beacons.

Considering the same scenario of Fig. 5, we now investigate the impact of the swarm size $S$ on the localization accuracy. More precisely, we are interested in evaluating the average distance errors, averaged over the 32 nodes with unknown positions, for different values of the swarm size $S$. Once again, the stopping condition for the PSO algorithm corresponds to reaching 50 iterations. In Fig. 7, the average distance error is shown as a function of the swarm size $S$. When considering values of the swarm size between 50 and 200, the average distance error is a decreasing function of $S$. This is an expected behaviour, since the higher is the swarm size, the faster is the convergence. At the opposite, when considering values of $S$ higher than 200, the average distance error is almost constant, showing that increasing the population size above 200 individuals does not improve the localization performance. Observe that the fact that the average distance error does not attain zero is due to the fact that we are using the estimated distances (and not the true ones) as an input for the PSO algorithm. Finally, one can conclude that setting $S$ equal to 200 is a good choice, as it is the lowest value of the population size which allows to obtain an accuracy around 5 cm—this, in particular, has motivated the choice of $S = 200$ in the previous performance results.

## 5   Conclusion

In this paper, we have proposed a swarm intelligent approach to UWB-signaling-based position estimation of nodes in a static three dimensional indoor scenario. Besides solving the non-linear system of the localization equations by means of the TSML algorithm, which is a "geometric" algorithm, the original problem has been re-written in terms of an optimization one, which is then solved by means of the PSO algorithm. Our results show that, while the accuracy of the TSML algorithm depends on the topology of the network and on relative positions of beacons and nodes, the approach based on the PSO algorithm allows to achieve a good accuracy in the position estimate, regardless of the configuration of nodes and beacons.

## References

1. Monica, S., Ferrari, G.: Accurate indoor localization with UWB wireless sensor networks. In: Proceedings of the 23rd IEEE International Conference on Enabling Technologies: Infrastructure for Collaborative Enterprises (WETICE 2014), Track on Capacity-Driven Processes and Services for the Cyber-Physical Society (CPS), Parma, Italy, pp. 287–289 (2014)
2. Foy, W.H.: Position-location solutions by Taylor-series estimation. IEEE Trans. Aerosp. Electron. Syst. **12**(2), 187–194 (1976)
3. Mensing, C., Plass, S.: Positioning algorithms for cellular networks using TDOA. In: Proceedings of the IEEE International Conference on Acoustics, Speech and Signal Processing (ICASSP 2006), Toulouse, France, pp. 513–516 (2006)
4. Monica, S., Ferrari, G.: An experimental model for UWB distance measurements and its application to localization problems. In: Proceedings of the IEEE International Conference on Ultra Wide Band (ICUWB 2014), Paris, France, pp. 297–302 (2014)
5. Schmidt, R.O.: A new approach to geometry of range difference location. IEEE Trans. Aerosp. Electron. Syst. **8**(6), 821–835 (1972)
6. Monica, S., Ferrari, G.: Optimized anchors placement: An analytical approach in UWB-based TDOA localization. In: Proceedings of the 9th International Wireless Communications & Mobile Computing Conference (IWCMC 2013), Cagliari, Italy, pp. 982–987 (2013)
7. Chan, Y., Ho, K.C.: A simple and efficient estimator for hyperbolic location. IEEE Trans. Signal Process. **42**(8), 1905–1915 (1994)
8. Shen, G., Zetik, R., Thomä, R.S.: Performance comparison of TOA and TDOA based location estimation algorithms in LOS environment. In: Proceedings of the 5th Workshop on Positioning, Navigation and Communication (WPNC 2008), Hannover, Germany, pp. 71–78 (2008)

9. Monica, S., Ferrari, G.: Particle swarm optimization for auto-localization of nodes in wireless sensor networks. In: Tomassini, M., Antonioni, A., Daolio, F., Buesser, P. (eds.) ICANNGA 2013. LNCS, vol. 7824, pp. 456–465. Springer, Heidelberg (2013)
10. Monica, S., Ferrari, G.: Impact of the number of beacons in PSO-based auto-localization in UWB networks. In: Esparcia-Alcázar, A.I. (ed.) EvoApplications 2013. LNCS, vol. 7835, pp. 42–51. Springer, Heidelberg (2013)
11. Monica, S., Ferrari, G.: UWB-based localization in large indoor scenarios: optimized placement of anchor nodes. IEEE Trans. Aerosp. Electron. Syst. (2015, to appear)
12. Monica, S., Ferrari, G.: Swarm intelligent approaches to auto-localization of nodes in static UWB networks. Appl. Soft Comput. **25**, 426–434 (2014)
13. Okamoto, E., Horiba, M., Nakashima, K., Shinohara, T., Matsumura, K.: Particle swarm optimization-based low-complexity three-dimensional UWB localization scheme. In: Proceedings of the International Conference on Ubiquitous and Future Networks, pp. 120–124 (2014)
14. Zhang, J., Orlik, P.V., Sahinoglu, Z., Molisch, A.F., Kinney, P.: UWB systems for wireless sensor networks. Proc. IEEE **97**(2), 313–331 (2009)
15. Busanelli, S., Ferrari, G.: Improved ultra wideband-based tracking of twin-receiver automated guided vehicles. J. Integr. Comput. Aided Eng. **19**(1), 3–22 (2012)
16. Molisch, A.F., Cassioli, D., Chong, C.C., Emami, S., Fort, A., Kannan, B., Karedal, J., Kunisch, J., Schantz, H.G., Siwiak, K., Win, M.Z.: A comprehensive standardized model for ultrawideband propagation channels. IEEE Trans. Antennas Propag. **54**(11), 3151–3166 (2006)
17. Dardari, D., Chong, C.C., Win, M.Z.: Threshold-based time-of-arrival estimators in UWB dense multipath channels. IEEE Trans. Commun. **56**(8), 1366–1378 (2008)
18. Kennedy, J., Eberhart, R.: Particle swarm optimization. In: Proceedings of the IEEE International Conference on Neural Networks (ICNN), Perth, Australia, pp. 1942–1948 (1995)
19. Poli, R., Kennedy, J., Blackwell, T.: Particle swarm optimization. Swarm Intell. J. **1**(1), 33–57 (2007)
20. Shi, Y., Eberhart, R.: A modified particle swarm optimizer. In: Proceedings of the IEEE International Conference on Evolutionary Computation (ICEC), Washington, DC, pp. 69–73 (1999)

# Studying the Geographical Cluster Paging with Delay Constraint in Registration Areas with the Algorithm NSGAII

Víctor Berrocal-Plaza[✉], Miguel A. Vega-Rodríguez,
and Juan M. Sánchez-Pérez

Department of Computers and Communications Technologies,
University of Extremadura Escuela Politécnica, Campus Universitario S/N,
10003 Cáceres, Spain
{vicberpla,mavega,sanperez}@unex.es

**Abstract.** The mobility management strategy based on registration areas is one of the most popular strategies to manage the subscribers' mobility in current Public Land Mobile Networks. For it, the network cells are arranged in continuous and non-overlapped sets in order to partially track the subscribers' movement. In this way, the network knows the location of its subscribers at a registration area level and the paging should only be performed in the cells within the last updated registration area. The paging scheme studied in this work is the geographical cluster paging, a probabilistic paging in which it is assumed that the probability of finding a mobile station (i.e. the subscriber's terminal) decreases as we move away from the last updated network cell following a normal distribution. The main appeal of this paging scheme is that we can considerably reduce the signaling traffic (with respect to the simultaneous paging) without including new elements in the network. Furthermore, we analyze it for different probability thresholds and considering delay constraints. On the other hand, we use our implementation of the Non-dominated Sorting Genetic Algorithm II (NSGAII) with the aim of finding the best possible sets of non-dominated solutions. Results show that each probability threshold has its own non-dominated region in the objective space, and that the signaling traffic can be reduced by about 30 % (with respect to the simultaneous paging).

**Keywords:** Geographical cluster paging · Registration areas · Multiobjective optimization · Non-dominated Sorting Genetic Algorithm II

## 1 Introduction

Public Land Mobile Networks (PLMNs) are widely used throughout the world. In fact, the GSM Association estimates that there will be approximately 3.9 billion of mobile subscribers in 2017 [1]. That is, approximately half of the world's population will use mobile communications. In these networks and in order to cope with such huge demand, the coverage area is divided into several smaller

© Springer International Publishing Switzerland 2015
A.M. Mora and G. Squillero (Eds.): EvoApplications 2015, LNCS 9028, pp. 103–114, 2015.
DOI: 10.1007/978-3-319-16549-3_9

land areas (known as network cells) among which the radio-electric resources are distributed and reused [2]. Nonetheless, an access network based on cells has an important issue related to the subscribers' movement because a mobile station (i.e. the subscriber's terminal) can be in any cell and receive a call at any time. Therefore, every PLMN must have a method to properly redirect the incoming calls (i.e. determine the exact cell in which the callee's terminal is located).

In the literature, we can find several mobility management strategies, most of them consist of two main procedures: the subscriber's location update and the paging [3]. The subscriber's location update is the procedure whereby a mobile station reports (to the network) that its location should be updated. There are several strategies of location update: never update (a mobile station never updates its location), always update (a mobile station updates its location whenever it moves from one network cell to another), cell-based (a mobile station updates its location whenever it moves to a specific type of network cell), and area-based (a mobile station updates its location whenever it moves from one registration area to another, where a registration area is a continuous and non-overlapped set of network cells). On the other hand, the network uses the paging to determine the exact cell in which the callee's terminal is located. For it, the network sends broadcast paging messages around the last updated location (for the mobile station in question). The different paging schemes can be classified into two main groups: simultaneous paging and sequential paging. In the simultaneous paging, all the network cells that have to be paged are polled simultaneously; and in the sequential paging, all the cells that have to be paged are arranged into paging areas that are sequentially polled (all the cells within a paging area are polled simultaneously). In this work, we study the mobility management strategy based on registration areas (because it is widely used in current PLMNs [4]) with the geographical cluster paging (a sequential paging in which it is assumed that the probability of finding a mobile station decreases following a normal distribution) in a multiobjective way. We analyze this paging scheme because it allows us to reduce the signaling traffic associated with the mobility management task (which could be more than 33 % of the total signaling traffic [4]) without including new elements in the network.

The optimization problem addressed in this manuscript is called the Registration Areas Planning Problem (RAPP), an optimization problem in where the main challenge consists in finding the configurations of registration areas than minimize simultaneously the number of location updates and the number of paging messages. It is important to empathize that this problem is a multiobjective optimization problem which was classified as an NP-hard problem in the literature [5]. This is the reason why our research is focused on the use of multiobjective optimization techniques applied to different mobility management strategies in PLMNs. In this work and with the aim of finding the best possible set of non-dominated solutions, we use our implementation of the Non-dominated Sorting Genetic Algorithm II (NSGAII, a well-known multiobjective evolutionary algorithm [6]).

The rest of the paper is organized as follows. Section 2 presents the related work. The optimization problem addressed in this manuscript is defined in

Sect. 3. Our implementation of NSGAII is briefly explained in Sect. 4. The performance of the geographical cluster paging is analyzed in Sect. 5. Finally, our conclusions and future work are discussed in Sect. 6.

## 2   Related Work

In the literature, we can find several manuscripts that tackle the Registration Areas Planning Problem (RAPP). Please, take into account the fact that the name of the registration area depends on the underlying mobile technology (e.g. location area in GSM (Global System for Mobile communications), routing area in GPRS (General Packet Radio Service), UTRAN registration area in UMTS (Universal Mobile Telecommunications System), or tracking area in LTE (Long Term Evolution)). P. R. L. Gondim was one of the first authors in using a Genetic Algorithm (GA) for finding quasi-optimal configurations of registration areas [5]. In that work, it was also shown that RAPP is an NP-hard combinatorial optimization problem. P. Demestichas et al. analyzed this optimization problem in different environments and with different metaheuristics (Simulated Annealing (SA), Tabu Search (TS), and GA) [7]. I. Demirkol et al. implemented a metaheuristic based on SA in where one of the two objective functions was considered as a constraint [8]. J. Taheri and A. Y. Zomaya analyzed the feasibility of different metaheuristics to optimize registration areas (Hopfield Neural Network (HNN) [9], SA [10], GA [11], and different combinations of HNN with GA (HNN-GA) [12]). S. M. Almeida-Luz et al. proposed other two optimization techniques based on Differential Evolution (DE) [13] and Scatter Search (SS) [14].

The main weakness of this related work is the fact that, although RAPP is in essence a multiobjective optimization problem (as we show in Sect. 3), this problem was tackled with single-objective optimization techniques (by considering one of the two objective functions as a constraint [8], or by using the linear aggregation of the objective functions [5,7,9–14]. Furthermore, these works only consider the simultaneous paging (i.e. the traditional paging scheme).

In our previous work, we have already analyzed the feasibility of different multiobjective evolutionary algorithms for optimizing registration areas [15], and the effect of increasing the number of paging cycles of the geographical cluster paging in the SUMATRA test network (a test network which was well-validated against real data measured in the San Francisco Bay) [16]. The main contribution of this manuscript is that, for a given number of paging cycles (i.e. considering delay constraints), we analyze the effect of varying the sizes of the paging areas in the geographical cluster paging. Furthermore, we study other set of mobile networks sited in four world capital cities. On the other hand and with the aim of finding the best possible set of non-dominated solutions, we use our implementation of the Non-dominated Sorting Genetic Algorithm II (NSGAII, a well-known multiobjective evolutionary algorithm) [6]. We have chosen NSGAII because it is the algorithm with which we obtain our better results in our previous work [15,16].

# 3    Registration Areas Planning

In a location update strategy based on registration areas (RAs), the network cells are arranged in continuous and non-overlapped sets in order to partially track the subscribers' movement [17]. In this way, a mobile station only initiates a location update procedure when moving from one registration area to another. Therefore, the network knows the location of its subscribers at a registration area level, and consequently, the paging should only be performed in the network cells within the last updated registration area (for the callee's terminal in question). It is noteworthy that a mobile station knows the cell in which it is currently located because every base station (i.e. the network entity that provides access to the mobile stations) periodically broadcasts its *cell global identification packet*, which contains the following information: cell identity, registration area identity, registration area code, mobile network code, and mobile country code [18].

The main challenge of the Registration Areas Planning Problem consists in finding the configurations of registration areas that minimize the number of location updates (or location update cost, $LU_{cost}$) and the number of paging messages (or paging cost, $PA_{cost}$) simultaneously. For a given configuration of registration areas (every cell has assigned an RA, that is, for a given combination of decision variables), these two costs can be calculated as follows:

$$\mathbf{f_1} = \min \left\{ LU_{cost} = \sum_{t=T_{ini}}^{T_{fin}} \sum_{i=1}^{N_{user}} \gamma_{t,i} \right\}, \tag{1}$$

$$\mathbf{f_2} = \min \left\{ PA_{cost} = \sum_{t=T_{ini}}^{T_{fin}} \sum_{i=1}^{N_{user}} \rho_{t,i} \cdot \varphi_{t,i} \right\}, \tag{2}$$

where $[T_{ini}, T_{fin}]$ is the time interval of the mobile activity trace. $N_{user}$ is the number of mobile stations. $\gamma_{t,i}$ is a binary variable which is equal to 1 when the mobile station $i$ crosses the boundary between two registration areas in the time $t$. $\rho_{t,i}$ is a binary variable which is equal to 1 when the mobile station $i$ has an incoming call in the time $t$. Finally, $\varphi_{t,i}$ is the number of network cells that have to be polled in order to locate the mobile station $i$ in the time $t$. It should be noticed that these two objective functions are conflicting, and therefore, this optimization problem can be classified as a multiobjective optimization problem. Suppose first that we want to reduce to its minimum the location update cost. For it, all the network cells must belong to the same registration area, because in this case a mobile station never updates its location ($\gamma_{t,i} = 0 \; \forall t,i$). However, the paging cost is maximum in this configuration because every mobile station should be searched in the whole network whenever it has an incoming call (please, note that in this case the network has not previous information about the location of its subscribers). On the other hand, if we want to minimize the paging cost, each network cell must be in a different registration area ($\varphi_{t,i} = 1 \; \forall t,i$). In this case, the network knows the location of its subscribers at a cell level, which leads to a maximum location update cost because a mobile station will initiate a location update whenever it moves from one network cell to another.

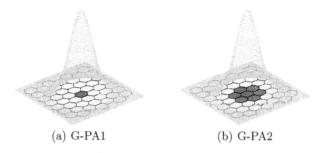

(a) G-PA1                    (b) G-PA2

**Fig. 1.** Geographical cluster paging with two paging cycles

## 3.1 Geographical Cluster Paging with Delay Constraint

The geographical cluster paging is a sequential paging scheme in which it is assumed that the probability of finding a mobile station decreases (following a normal distribution) as we move away from the last updated cell [19]. In this way, the paging procedure is performed in concentric rings starting from the last updated network cell until finding the mobile station in question. As a result, the network cells within the last updated registration area ($RA_{t,i}$) are arranged in different paging areas ($A_{t,i,j}$), where each paging area is composed by one or more concentric rings. This last can be mathematically expressed as:

$$RA_{t,i} = A_{t,i,1} \cup A_{t,i,2} \cup \cdots \cup A_{t,i,m}, \tag{3}$$

$$A_{t,i,j} \cap A_{t,i,k} = \emptyset, \forall j \neq k, j \leq m, k \leq m, \tag{4}$$

$$\alpha_{t,i,j\text{-}1} \geq \alpha_{t,i,j}, 2 \leq j \leq m, \tag{5}$$

$$\varphi_{t,i} = \sum_{j=1}^{m} \alpha_{t,i,j} \cdot \mid A_{t,i,j} \mid, \tag{6}$$

where $m$ is the number of paging cycles. $\alpha_{t,i,j}$ is a binary variable which is equal to 1 when the mobile station $i$ is located in a cell of the paging area $j$ in the time $t$. Finally, $\mid A_{t,i,j} \mid$ is the number of network cells within the paging area $A_{t,i,j}$. In real world applications, the paging procedure must be performed within a fixed time constraint known as *maximum paging delay*. This imposes limits on the number of paging cycles. In this work and in contrast to our previous work, we analyze the effect of increasing the size of the first paging area ($A_{t,i,1}$) in a geographical cluster paging with two paging cycles (i.e. $m = 2$), which is considered to be acceptable in practical implementations [19]. In the following, G-PA$n$ makes reference to each probability threshold studied in this manuscript, where $n$ represents the number of concentric rings inside the first paging area ($A_{t,i,1}$). Figure 1 presents an example for the probability thresholds $n = 1$ ($A_{t,i,1}$ is composed by the last updated network cell) and $n = 2$ ($A_{t,i,1}$ is composed by the last updated network cell and its neighboring cells), where $A_{t,i,1}$ is represented in red color (or dark gray in a B/W printed version).

# 4   Non-dominated Sorting Genetic Algorithm II

As stated in Sect. 3, RAPP is a multiobjective optimization problem. In this kind of problems, the challenge consists in finding the best possible set of non-dominated solutions, where each non-dominated solution is related to a specific trade-off among objectives [20]. For definition and assuming a minimization bi-objective optimization problem, a solution $\mathbf{x}^i$ is said to dominate another solution $\mathbf{x}^j$ (represented as $\mathbf{x}^i \prec \mathbf{x}^j$) if and only if $\forall k \in [1,2], \mathbf{z}_k^i = f_k(\mathbf{x}^i) \leq \mathbf{z}_k^j = f_k(\mathbf{x}^j) \wedge \exists k \in [1,2] : \mathbf{z}_k^i < \mathbf{z}_k^j$, where $\mathbf{z}^i = [\mathbf{z}_1^i, \mathbf{z}_2^i]$ is the objective vector of the solution $i$, and the graphical representation of the non-dominated objective vectors is known as Pareto front. In this work, every individual (i.e. an encoded solution of the problem) is a vector in which we store the registration area associated with each network cell, see Fig. 2.

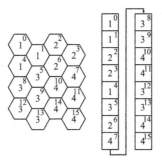

**Fig. 2.** Chromosome representation

With the aim of finding the best possible set of non-dominated solutions, we use our implementation of the Non-dominated Sorting Genetic Algorithm II (NSGAII), a well-known multiobjective evolutionary algorithm proposed by K. Deb et al. in [6]. NSGAII is an elitist genetic algorithm with a fitness function used to estimate the quality of a solution in the multiobjective context. This fitness function arranges the solutions in fronts according to the non-dominance concept. After that, the crowding distance is applied in order to discriminate among solutions within the same front. For further information about this fitness function, please consult [6]. In our implementation of NSGAII, we have used a multi-point crossover in where the maximum number of crossover points is equal to 4. Furthermore, we have defined two mutation operations specific to the problem. In the first one, we merge a randomly selected border cell (i.e. a network cell which is border among two or more registration areas) with its smallest neighboring registration area. On the other hand, in the second mutation operation, the smallest registration area is merged with its smallest neighboring registration area. For a detailed explanation of our implementation of NSGAII, please consult our previous work [15,16].

# 5    Results

In this section, we present the study accomplished to evaluate (in a multiobjective way) the performance of the geographical cluster paging with two paging cycles ($m = 2$) in a location update strategy based on registration areas. To the best of our knowledge, this analysis is a novel contribution of our research. As stated in Sect. 3.1, this paging scheme is analyzed for different probability thresholds (i.e. for different sizes of the first paging area, $n \in \{1, 2, 3, 4\}$). An analysis for higher values of $n$ is not presented because we did not notice a significant improvement in the results.

This study is performed over a set of mobile networks sited in four world capital cities: Rome (a mobile network with 218 cells), Hong Kong (a mobile network with 220 cells), London (a mobile network with 276 cells), and Paris (a mobile network with 345 cells). The mobile activity traces for these networks can be downloaded from http://arco.unex.es/vicberpla/MAT.html.

It is noteworthy that NSGAII is a stochastic optimization technique, and therefore, it is necessary a statistical study in order to determine whether the differences among the experiments are statistically significant. The first step consists in applying the Shapiro-Wilk test to know whether the samples follow a normal distribution. After that and whenever the Shapiro-Wilk test is positive, the Levene test is used to check the homogeneity of the variances. Finally and whenever the Levene test is positive, the ANOVA analysis is applied in order to determine whether the differences among the means of the experiments are statistically significant. Otherwise, the Mann-Whitney U test is applied to determine whether the differences among the medians of the experiments are statistically significant. All of these tests have been configured with a confidence level equal to 95 %.

After a parametric study, we have chosen the configuration of NSGAII that maximizes the Hypervolume indicator: $N_{POP} = 300$ (population size), $N_G = 3000$ (number of generations), $P_C = 0.90$ (crossover probability), and $P_M = 0.25$ (mutation probability). The Hypervolume ($I_H$) is a multiobjective indicator that associates the quality of a Pareto front with the area of the objective space that is dominated by these non-dominated solutions, and is bounded by the reference points [20]. According to this metric, a set of non-dominated solutions $A$ is said to be better than another set $B$ if and only if $I_H(A) > I_H(B)$.

Table 1 gathers statistical data of the Hypervolume (median $\tilde{I}_H$ and interquartile range (iqr)) of 31 independent runs per each experiment (probability threshold). Due to the fact that each probability threshold has its own maximum paging cost, we have used the reference points associated with the simultaneous paging ($m = 1$, also known as Blanket Polling (BP)). In this table, we can observe that, with some intelligence in the paging procedure, we can increase considerably the Hypervolume, which leads to a reduction in the signaling load. Furthermore, we notice that the Hypervolume gradually decreases as we increase the size of the first paging area, i.e. we can deduce that, in general, G-PA1 is the best probability threshold. Nonetheless, a different conclusion can be drawn if we combine the Pareto fronts of each probability threshold and we

**Table 1.** Statistics of Hypervolume ($\widetilde{I}_H \pm$ iqr)

|          | Rome | Hong Kong | London | Paris |
|----------|------|-----------|--------|-------|
| Referece | [1381003, 23341478] | [1822841, 23728980] | [2303888, 37283184] | [3475953, 58455420] |
| Points   | [0, 107071] | [0, 107859] | [0, 135084] | [0, 169436] |
| BP       | $94.15\pm_{0.124}$ $\ominus$ ◁ ▷ ◇ | $95.69\pm_{0.100}$ $\ominus$ ◁ ▷ ◇ | $96.34\pm_{4.94e-2}$ $\ominus$ ◁ ▷ ◇ | $96.84\pm_{2.67e-2}$ $\ominus$ ◁ ▷ ◇ |
| G-PA1    | $97.72\pm_{4.84e-2}$ • ◁ ▷ ◇ | $98.24\pm_{1.79e-2}$ • ◁ ▷ ◇ | $98.51\pm_{1.57e-2}$ • ◁ ▷ ◇ | $98.70\pm_{1.98e-2}$ • ◁ ▷ ◇ |
| G-PA2    | $97.59\pm_{5.78e-2}$ • $\ominus$ ▷ ◇ | $98.17\pm_{3.56e-2}$ • $\ominus$ ▷ ◇ | $98.46\pm_{1.29e-2}$ • $\ominus$ ▷ ◇ | $98.65\pm_{1.64e-2}$ • $\ominus$ ▷ ◇ |
| G-PA3    | $97.32\pm_{5.21e-2}$ • $\ominus$ ◁ ◇ | $97.97\pm_{2.30e-2}$ • $\ominus$ ◁ ◇ | $98.30\pm_{1.31e-2}$ • $\ominus$ ◁ ◇ | $98.48\pm_{1.58e-2}$ • $\ominus$ ◁ ◇ |
| G-PA4    | $96.95\pm_{3.14e-2}$ • $\ominus$ ◁ ▷ | $97.79\pm_{1.66e-2}$ • $\ominus$ ◁ ▷ | $98.18\pm_{1.83e-2}$ • $\ominus$ ◁ ▷ | $98.34\pm_{1.46e-2}$ • $\ominus$ ◁ ▷ |

• means that the difference with respect to BP is statistically significant
$\ominus$ means that the difference with respect to G-PA1 is statistically significant
◁ means that the difference with respect to G-PA2 is statistically significant
▷ means that the difference with respect to G-PA3 is statistically significant
◇ means that the difference with respect to G-PA4 is statistically significant

obtain the non-dominated solutions of this combined set, see Fig. 3, in where we present the Pareto fronts associated with the median Hypervolume ($\widetilde{I}_H$). As we can observe in this figure, every probability threshold has its own non-dominated region in the objective space. Thus, the network operator could choose a different probability threshold depending on the selected configuration of registration areas. It is also important to note that this feature of the geographical cluster paging would not have been detected without a multiobjective analysis. On the other hand, Fig. 4(a) presents a comparison between the simultaneous paging and the geographical cluster paging in the mobile network sited in Paris (similar comparisons were obtained with the other networks). As stated before, we can notice that the geographical cluster paging covers more area of the objective space than the simultaneous paging, and hence, we obtain more efficient configurations of registration areas. For example and assuming an LTE (Long Term Evolution) network with one Mobility Management Entity, if we select the non-dominated solution that minimize the total signaling load (see Fig. 4(b)), we can notice that the signaling load can be reduced by about 30 % (BP: 7,642,638 signaling messages per working day (4,787,136 messages due to location updates and 2,855,502 messages due to the paging procedure), G-PA: 5,363,228 signaling messages per working day (2,798,766 messages due to location updates and 2,564,462 messages due to the paging procedure)). It is also noteworthy that the use of a more efficient paging procedure allows configurations with higher registration areas, which leads to a reduction in the location update cost.

## 5.1   Comparison with Other Works

In this section, we compare our implementation of NSGAII with other optimization techniques published in the literature [9–14]. It should be noted that all of these optimization techniques are single-objective algorithms. Therefore and in order to compare with these previous manuscripts, we must select in our Pareto fronts the non-dominated solution that best optimizes the objective function used by these single-objective metaheuristics (i.e. $\mathbf{f}^{SO} = 10 \cdot \mathbf{f_1} + \mathbf{f_2}$). With the

Mobile network: Rome

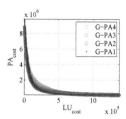

(a) Paret front per threshold

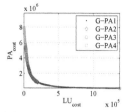

(b) Non-dominated solutions per threshold

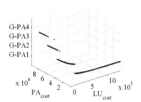

(c) Non-dominated solutions per threshold. 3D view

Mobile network: HongKong

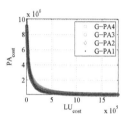

(d) Pareto front per threshold

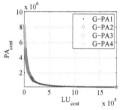

(e) Non-dominated solutions per threshold

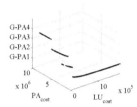

(f) Non-dominated solutions per threshold. 3D view

Mobile network: London

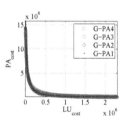

(g) Pareto front per threshold

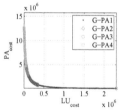

(h) Non-dominated solutions per threshold

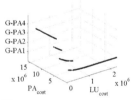

(i) Non-dominated solutions per threshold. 3D view

Mobile network: Paris

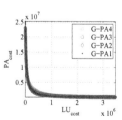

(j) Pareto front per threshold

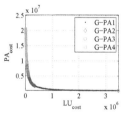

(k) Non-dominated solutions per threshold

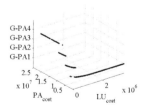

(l) Non-dominated solutions per threshold. 3D view

**Fig. 3.** Analysis of the obtained Pareto fronts

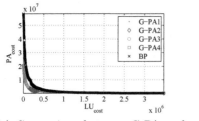

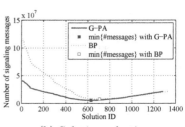

(a) Comparison between G-PA and BP

(b) Solution selection

**Fig. 4.** (a) Comparison with simultaneous paging. (b) Selection of the non-dominated solution (mobile network of Paris).

**Table 2.** Comparison with other works published in the literature [9–14]: $\mathbf{f}^{SO}$

|      | NSGAII | HNN [9] | SA [10] | GA [11] | GA-HNN1 [12] | GA-HNN2 [12] | GA-HNN3 [12] | DE [13] | SS [14] |
|------|--------|---------|---------|---------|--------------|--------------|--------------|---------|---------|
| LA25 | 26,990 | 27,249  | 26,990  | 28,299  | 26,990       | 26,990       | 26,990       | 26,990  | 26,990  |
| LA35 | 39,832 | 39,832  | 42,750  | 40,085  | 40,117       | 39,832       | 39,832       | 39,859  | 39,832  |
| LA49 | 60,685 | 63,516  | 60,694  | 61,938  | 62,916       | 62,253       | 60,696       | 61,037  | 60,685  |
| LA63 | 89,085 | 92,493  | 90,506  | 90,318  | 92,659       | 91,916       | 91,819       | 89,973  | 89,085  |

aim of performing a fair comparison, we have configured our implementation of NSGAII with the same population size ($N_{POP} = 300$) and the same number of generations ($N_G = 5000$) as in these previous works [9–14]. Furthermore, we use the same paging procedure (simultaneous paging) and the same test networks (LA$l$, where $l$ is the number of network cells). The results of this comparative study are gathered in Table 2, in where we present the minimum value found of $\mathbf{f}^{SO}$. Regrettably, an in-depth statistical study cannot be conducted because the experimental data of these previous works are not available. Furthermore, the authors of [9–12] only provide the minimum value found of $\mathbf{f}^{SO}$. This table reveals that our implementation of NSGAII is also able to equal or even improve the results obtained with single-objective metaheuristics. This last is far from trivial because a single-objective metaheuristic is specialized in finding only one solution (i.e. the one that best optimizes its objective function), and our implementation of NSGAII is specialized in finding a wide range of non-dominated solutions.

## 6  Conclusion and Future Work

This manuscript presents a multiobjective analysis of the geographical cluster paging in a location update strategy based on registration areas, a mobility management strategy that defines a multiobjective optimization problem with two objective functions. To the best of our knowledge, this is a novel contribution of our research. This paging scheme is studied considering delay constraints and for different probability thresholds. With the aim of finding the best possible set of non-dominated solutions, we have used our implementation of the

Non-dominated Sorting Genetic Algorithm II (a multiobjective evolutionary algorithm by means of which we have obtained our better results in our previous work). After an experimental study, we have noticed that the signaling traffic associated with the mobility management can be reduced by about 30 % with some intelligence in the paging procedure. Furthermore and after a multiobjective analysis, we have shown that each probability threshold has its own non-dominated region in the objective space. In this way, the network operator could choose a different probability threshold depending on the selected configuration of registration areas.

As a future work, it would be interesting to analyze the performance of other paging schemes and other location update strategies in a multiobjective way, as well as to compare them with the mobility management strategy studied in this manuscript. Concretely, the multiobjective analysis of paging schemes and dynamic location update strategies based on Markov chains could be a good challenge.

**Acknowledgments.** This work was partially funded by the Spanish Ministry of Economy and Competitiveness and the ERDF (European Regional Development Fund), under the contract TIN2012-30685 (BIO project). The work of Víctor Berrocal-Plaza has been developed under the Grant FPU-AP2010-5841 from the Spanish Government.

# References

1. GSM Association (GSMA): The Mobile Economy (2013)
2. Agrawal, D., Zeng, Q.: Introduction to Wireless and Mobile Systems. Cengage Learning, Stamford (2010)
3. Mukherjee, A., Bandyopadhyay, S., Saha, D.: Location Management and Routing in Mobile Wireless Networks. Artech House mobile communications series. Artech House, Boston (2003)
4. Nowoswiat, D., Milliken, G.: Managing LTE Core Network Signaling Traffic. Alcatel-Lucent, Techzine (2013)
5. Gondim, P.R.L.: Genetic algorithms and the location area partitioning problem in cellular networks. In: Procedings of the IEEE 46th Vehicular Technology Conference on Mobile Technology for the Human Race, vol. 3, pp. 1835–1838 (1996)
6. Deb, K., Pratap, A., Agarwal, S., Meyarivan, T.: A fast and elitist multiobjective genetic algorithm: NSGA-II. IEEE Trans. Evol. Comput. **6**(2), 182–197 (2002)
7. Demestichas, P., Georgantas, N., Tzifa, E., Demesticha, V., Striki, M., Kilanioti, M., Theologou, M.E.: Computationally efficient algorithms for location area planning in future cellular systems. Comput. Commun. **23**(13), 1263–1280 (2000)
8. Demirkol, I., Ersoy, C., Çaglayan, M.U., Deliç, H.: Location area planning and cell-to-switch assignment in cellular networks. IEEE Trans. Wireless Commun. **3**(3), 880–890 (2004)
9. Taheri, J., Zomaya, A.Y.: The use of a hopfield neural network in solving the mobility management problem. In: Proceedings of The IEEE/ACS International Conference on Pervasive Services, pp. 141–150 (2004)
10. Taheri, J., Zomaya, A.Y.: A simulated annealing approach for mobile location management. In: Proceedings of the 19th IEEE International Parallel and Distributed Processing Symposium, pp. 194–194 (2005)

11. Taheri, J., Zomaya, A.Y.: A genetic algorithm for finding optimal location area configurations for mobility management. In: Proceedings of the IEEE Conference on Local Computer Networks 30th Anniversary, pp. 568–577 (2005)
12. Taheri, J., Zomaya, A.Y.: A combined genetic-neural algorithm for mobility management. J. Math. Model. Algorithms **6**(3), 481–507 (2007)
13. Almeida-Luz, S.M., Vega-Rodríguez, M.A., Gómez-Púlido, J.A., Sánchez-Pérez, J.M.: Differential evolution for solving the mobile location management. Appl. Soft Comput. **11**(1), 410–427 (2011)
14. Almeida-Luz, S.M., Vega-Rodríguez, M.A., Gómez-Pulido, J.A., Sánchez-Pérez, J.M.: Applying scatter search to the location areas problem. In: Corchado, E., Yin, H. (eds.) IDEAL 2009. LNCS, vol. 5788, pp. 791–798. Springer, Heidelberg (2009)
15. Berrocal-Plaza, V., Vega-Rodríguez, M.A., Sánchez-Pérez, J.M.: On the use of multiobjective optimization for solving the location areas strategy with different paging procedures in a realistic mobile network. Appl. Soft Comput. **18**, 146–157 (2014)
16. Berrocal-Plaza, V., Vega-Rodríguez, M.A., Sánchez-Pérez, J.M.: Solving the location areas management problem with multi-objective evolutionary strategies. Wireless Netw. **20**(7), 1909–1924 (2014)
17. Kyamakya, K., Jobmann, K.: Location management in cellular networks: classification of the most important paradigms, realistic simulation framework, and relative performance analysis. IEEE Trans. Veh. Technol. **54**(2), 687–708 (2005)
18. Garg, V.: Wireless Communications & Networking, 1st edn. Morgan Kaufmann Publishers Inc., San Francisco (2007)
19. Krishnamachari, B., Gau, R.H., Wicker, S.B., Haas, Z.J.: Optimal sequential paging in cellular wireless networks. Wireless Netw. **10**(2), 121–131 (2004)
20. Coello, C.A.C., Lamont, G.B., Veldhuizen, D.A.V.: Evolutionary Algorithms for Solving Multi-Objective Problems (Genetic and Evolutionary Computation). Springer-Verlag New York Inc., Secaucus (2006)

# A Multiobjective Evolutionary Algorithm for Personalized Tours in Street Networks

Ivanoe De Falco, Umberto Scafuri, and Ernesto Tarantino[✉]

ICAR-CNR, Via P. Castellino 111, 80131 Naples, Italy
{ivanoe.defalco,umberto.scafuri,ernesto.tarantino}@na.icar.cnr.it

**Abstract.** The paper presents a novel optimizer to plan multiple–day walking itineraries, tailored to tourists' personal interests, in a street network modeled as a graph. The tour is automatically designed by maximizing the number of the Points of Interest (*POI*s) to visit as a function of both tourists' preferences and requirements, and constraints such as opening hours, visiting times and accessibility of the *POI*s, and weather forecasting. Since this itineray planning is classified as an NP–complete combinatorial optimization problem, a multiobjective evolutionary optimizer is here proposed. Such an optimizer is proven to be effective in designing personalized multiple–day tourist routes.

**Keywords:** Multiple–day orienteering problem with time windows · Personalized tour · Tourism · Multiobjective evolutionary algorithm

## 1 Introduction

A street network, namely a system of interconnecting lines and points that represent a system of streets or roads for a given area, provides the foundation for network analysis; for example, finding the best route. One of the most remarkable Operational Research (OR) problems related to a street network is that faced by a tourist who has to visit an area of a city in a limited amount of time. In this case the aim is that of selecting the most interesting places to visit on the basis of their personal interests, and of creating the shortest suitable route connecting them. In OR such a problem is usually modeled as a graph.

To plan a feasible tour the tourist has to collect information from different sources (websites, magazines or guidebooks) about the different Points of Interest (*POI*s), make a selection among these *POI*s and plan an itinerary connecting the selected points, considering the available time, the opening hours and visiting times of the different *POI*s, the weather forecasting and other different kinds of constraints [1]. Given the complexity of the problem, the building of the tour by combining all the preferences and constraints presents considerable difficulties.

In the last years several Personalized Electronic Tourist Guides (PETGs) relying on mobile computing have been developed to better perform the task fulfilled by the local tourist organizations.

© Springer International Publishing Switzerland 2015
A.M. Mora and G. Squillero (Eds.): EvoApplications 2015, LNCS 9028, pp. 115–127, 2015.
DOI: 10.1007/978-3-319-16549-3_10

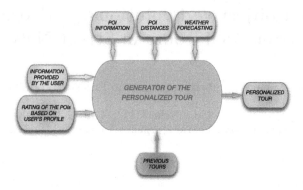

**Fig. 1.** The architecture of the PETG.

Within this paper the design of a personalized multiple–day walking tour in old city centres, which takes into account a set of *POIs* with a score, a set of waiting and visiting times, and a set of daily opening hours of these *POIs*, is investigated. Combined with the tourist's trip constraints and environmental contexts, these sets allow defining a problem which is an extension of the well–known Team Orienteering Problem with Time Windows (TOPTW) where the number of team members is replaced by the number of days available for the tourist to stay, the start and the arrival positions are not necessarily coincident in each day of the tour, and can change from day to day [2,3].

Since TOPTW is a highly–constrained combinatorial optimization problem [4] that cannot be solved in polynomial time [5,6], a multiobjective evolutionary optimizer is proposed to find in a reasonable computational time near–optimal solutions to the planning of a multiple–day route. Such an optimizer is innovative as it considers a higher number of objectives and of features with respect to some recent tools for building walking–only itineraries [2,7,8].

The paper is organized as follows: Sect. 2 presents a description of the optimizer used to deal with the problem under investigation. Section 3 describes the multiobjective evolutionary algorithm employed to find multiple–day tours. In Sect. 4 the findings of the proposed approach are shown and discussed. Finally, the last section contains conclusion remarks and future works.

## 2    The Generator of the Personalized Tour

The core of the hypothesized PETG, schematized as in Fig. 1, is our optimizer, i.e., the generator of the personalized tour. Such an optimizer is supposed to interact with several input modules to gather information about the tourist's interests and requirements, and environmental constraints, and with an output module to endow the tourist with the planned multiple–day itinerary.

Our optimizer needs the following input information:

– *Information provided by the user:* the user identifier, the average moving speed (young, old, family with children, etc.), the wheelchair or disabled access, the day of tour beginning, the number of days available for the tour, number and identification codes of the *POI*s that the user requests to be included in the visit. Moreover, for each day the optimizer needs the start/arrival positions and the start and finish times of programmed pauses.

The start and arrival positions, represented by the GPS coordinates, i.e., longitude and latitude, are selected by the user either from the map, or from the list of tourist attractions or from a set of locations ('access doors') corresponding to the public transportation stations/stops close to the area.

– *Rating of the POIs.* The evolutionary optimizer hypothesizes a recommender system which assigns the 'score' or 'rating' to each *POI* on the basis of the personal preferences of the tourist. The rating, which measures the *POI* attractiveness for that specific user, is supposed to be estimated by a profiling phase previously effected either through the data extracted from the social media or from a questionnaire which the same user is invited to fill during the preliminary connection phase.

– *POI information.* The information related to each *POI*, to the distance and routes between *POI*s, and to the context is stored in suitable databases. Specifically, the data supposed to be known for each *POI* are the *POI* identifier, the name of the *POI*, the position in terms of GPS coordinates, the average waiting and visiting times, the opening hours for each day of the tour, the accessibility for disabled people, a flag as outdoor or indoor site.

– *POI distances.* The *POI* distances are represented by a real–valued triangular matrix with a dimension equal to the number of *POI*s. The value of each cell $(i, j)$ of the matrix indicates the distance between the *POI*s $i$ and $j$ measured on the basis of the shortest route connecting them. This means that it is not the Euclidean or Manhattan distance evaluated on the basis of the GPS coordinates of the two *POI*s, rather it accounts for the actual structure of the streets in the area containing the *POI*s.

– *Weather table.* A weather table is used to propose, as far as possible, itineraries which take into account the weather conditions. The hourly forecasting is extremely complex, so a granularity equal to three hours (one hour before or after the time interval indicated) is considered As a consequence, for each day of the tour this table contains the weather forecasting subdivided in a number of items equal to that of the three–hour time slots in which the tour falls.

– *Previous tours.* Particularly useful is the data file which keeps track of the previous tours effected by the tourists in case of either a multiple–day tour or a tour requested by a user who previously visited the same area. In both cases the knowledge of previous tours avoids proposing an itinerary including already visited *POI*s, unless the user explicitly requires to visit again some such *POI*s. Each record of this file is related to a tour made by a single user and reports the user identifier, the day(s) of the tour, the number and the identifiers of the visited *POI*s.

## 2.1 Output of the Optimizer

The output of our evolutionary optimizer is the personalized tour automatically saved in a .csv file, named *tour.csv*, that is processed by an API devised to visualize the corresponding optimized tour on a map directly on the user's mobile device. The data stored in *tour.csv* are:

- The start time.
- For each *POI*: the identifier of the *POI*, the walking time between the current position and the *POI*, the arrival time at the *POI*, the waiting time and the finish time of the visit.
- For each pause: the start and finish times.
- The walking time to the final destination and the related arrival time.

Moreover a summary of the more relevant information related to the proposed tour is reported in terms of the total number of visited *POI*s specifically requested by the user, the total number of visited *POI*s, the total time employed for the tour including waiting, visiting and transfer times, the total covered distance and the score of the complete tour measured as the average of the score of the single *POI*s included in the tour.

## 2.2  Problem Statement

To generate personalized multiple–day itineraries respecting predefined time windows, the problem is modeled as a graph consisting of a set of locations and a set of the paths between each pair of these locations. A non–negative score representing the rating of the tourist for that location and a set of time windows is associated with each vertex. A positive weight corresponding to the walking time is associated with each path.

**The Objectives.** The goal of our optimizer in building a personalized multiple-day itinerary is to optimize five contrasting objectives, namely,

- maximize the score of the proposed *POI*s;
- visit as many *POI*s as possible among those explicitly requested by the user;
- visit as many *POI*s as possible among the recommended ones in addition to those specifically included by the user;
- complete the tour within the time limit fixed by the user respecting the following commitments: opening and closing hours of the *POI*s, average visit duration and pause times (rest, lunch, shopping, ... ) required by the user;
- minimize the covered distance;
- respect other constraints such as: accessibility to the *POI*s for people with disabilities and usability of the outdoor *POI*s in case of rain, high wind, etc.

Differently from the opening times of the *POI*s, which are hard constraints, the pause times requested by the user are handled as being soft temporal constraints, whose satisfaction can happen in suitable neighborhoods of the times requested by the user if this flexibility allows better encountering her/his preferences in terms of the accessibility and of the number of visited *POI*s. A detailed description of all the objectives is reported in the following items.

– *Rating of the tour by the tourist side.* As each generic *POI* $i$ is characterized by a real value $a(i)$ which represents its attractiveness for a specific user, the rating $\Phi_1$ of the complete route *tour* is equal to:

$$\Phi_1(tour) = \frac{1}{POI\_in\_tour} \sum_{i=1}^{POI\_in\_tour} a(i)$$

that is the average of the scores of the single *POIs*. *POI_in_tour* represents the number of *POIs* comprised in the proposed tour. This objective is to be maximized.

– *Number of the POIs explicitly required by the user and actually present in the proposed tour.* Denoting with *POI_req* the number of the *POIs* that the user requires to be comprised in the tour, an ideal tour will be one which includes all the *POI_req*. Nevertheless, due to the constraints, the tours proposed by the optimizer could include an actual number of required *POIs*, named *POI_act*, lower or equal to *POI_req*. In formula:

$$\Phi_2(tour) = POI\_req - POI\_act$$

This objective is to be minimized.

– *Number of total POIs included in the tour.* The user is naturally interested in visiting as many *POIs* as possible in the time available for her/his tour. Therefore the optimizer, in addition to the *POI_act*, has to propose a tour able at the same time to assure the greatest rating and to contain the highest number of *POIs* encountering at best user's preferences. So we can define the following objective:

$$\Phi_3(tour) = POI\_in\_tour$$

This objective is to be maximized and must respect all the constraints in terms of time, tour length, presence of all the desired *POIs* and so on.

– *Total duration of the tour.* It is supposed that the user desires to spend as much time as possible for the visit of the attractions, saving time for pauses (rest, lunch, shopping). To evaluate a generic tour the proposed optimizer takes into account the following variables:

  • $t\_tran(i,j)$ indicates the time needed to transfer from a *POI* $i$ to $j$ where $j$ represents the *POI* successive to $i$ in the tour under examination (in the case of the first *POI* it represents the time to reach the first *POI* from the start point chosen by the user);
  • $t\_wait(j)$ represents the waiting time to access *POI* $j$, due to queues, or other constraints;
  • $t\_vis(j)$ denotes the visiting time of the *POI* $j$;
  • $t\_tot\_vis(j)$ accounts for the total of the three above–mentioned times;
  • $t\_arr$ represents the time to reach the finish point chosen by the user from the last *POI* in the proposed tour;
  • $t\_pau(k)$ represents the duration of the generic pause $k$ required by the user (let *Tot_pau* be the total number of these pauses);

- *max_time_tour* denotes the time limit declared by the user to complete the tour.

This premised, the total time of the tour $\Phi_4$ is given by:

$$\Phi_4(tour) = t\_arr + \sum_{j=1}^{POI\_in\_tour} t\_tot\_vis(j) + \sum_{k=1}^{Tot\_pau} t\_pau(k)$$

This quantity is to be maximized while respecting the constraint $\Phi_4(tour) \leqslant max\_time\_tour$.

- *Total length of the tour.* Another important side to consider is the total covered distance of the tour which must be not excessively long in particular for some categories of potential users, as for example elderly people, families with children, or disabled people. It is to note that the classical Traveling Salesman Problem (TSP) which considers only the distances in order to find an itinerary cannot be used in this case. In fact, for a PETG, in addition to the spatial coordinates, also the temporal side is to be taken into account, as for example the opening and closing hours of the *POIs*. However, it is important also to account for a spatial objective with the aim to minimize the length of the tour proposed. Such a length is evaluated as:

$$\Phi_5(tour) = d\_init + \sum_{i=1}^{POI\_in\_tour} d(i, i+1) + d\_fin$$

where $d(i, i+1)$ is the distance between a generic *POI* $i$ and the next *POI* $(i+1)$ in the considered tour, $d\_init$ is the distance between the start position declared by the user and the first *POI* in the tour under examination, $d\_fin$ is the distance between the last *POI* in the tour and the finish point declared by the user.

- *Other constraints.* The generated solutions must respect these further constraints: in case of rain or high wind outdoor *POIs* are to be excluded from the itineraries, unless explicitly requested by the user, and in case of tours required by disabled people the *POIs* with limited access are to be discarded.

## 3   The Multiobjective Evolutionary Optimizer

To find near–optimal personalized multiple–day tours a multiobjective evolutionary algorithm, able to satisfy all the contrasting objectives reported in Sect. 2.2, is proposed.

### 3.1   Multiobjective Optimization Notions

To deal with the five contrasting objectives mentioned above, a multiobjective evolutionary algorithm based on the concept of the so–called *Pareto optimal set* is designed and implemented. To make this paper self–contained we report some fundamentals of the multiobjective optimization. This technique relies on the notion of *dominance*: as an example, for a problem with two objectives to optimize, each represented by a fitness function $\Phi_i$, representing the quality of the solution with respect to the objective, a solution $\boldsymbol{X}_1$ is said to dominate in the Pareto sense (P–dominate) another solution $\boldsymbol{X}_2$ if and only if, for any objective, the related $\Phi_i(\boldsymbol{X}_1)$ is not worse than $\Phi_i(\boldsymbol{X}_2)$ and is better for at least one of the objectives. A solution $\boldsymbol{S}^*$ is said Pareto–optimal if it belongs to Pareto optimal set. The Pareto–optimal set and the Pareto–optimal front are the sets of Pareto–optimal solutions in design variables and objective function domains, respectively. By doing so, at each generation a set of "optimal" solutions, namely the current Pareto front, emerges where none of them can be considered to be better than any other in the same set. As the number of generations increases the current Pareto front will shift, and will hopefully approach the Pareto–optimal front. Usually, at the end of the execution of the evolutionary algorithm the final Pareto front will be proposed to the user that, among the solutions contained therein, will choose the one which best suits his needs.

### 3.2   The Methodology

An evolutionary algorithm (EA) is a population–based optimization algorithm which uses mechanisms inspired by biological evolution to find approximate solutions for complex problems [9,10]. As in each EA, once initialized, a population of $NPOP$ solutions, called individuals, is let free to evolve from a generation $g$ to the next one by means of the operators of selection, recombination, and replacement. The components of the EA within this paper are standard with the exception of the mutation operator that is specific for the faced problem, and of the selection which is typical of this multiobjective version. In our case the basic steps of the algorithm can be described as follows:

- Initialization: an initial population of individuals is randomly generated.
- Selection: the choice of the individuals which undergo recombination takes place by a random uniform selection among the non dominated solutions. At the end of each generation, it is important to sort the solutions to individuate those belonging to the Pareto front (non–dominated solutions).
- Recombination: given two elements selected among the non–dominated solutions, we apply as evolutionary operators the uniform crossover [11,12] and the mutation to recombine the solutions. As mutation the classical exchange [13,14] and 2–opt variants [13,15] are employed. As a result one offspring is obtained.
- Evaluation: being the problem structured as having the five objectives described in Sect. 2.2, the fitness of each solution will be evaluated on each of those five optimization criteria. Considered that this implies the resolution of a multiobjective problem we will make reference to the notion of *dominance* reported in the above Sect. 3.1.
- Replacement: the $i$–th offspring obtained by the recombination is compared with the $i$–th individual in the current population and the already present individual is replaced only if it is dominated by the new generated one.

The four last steps are repeated for each individual so that a new population is obtained. This procedure is repeated for a maximum number of generations $g_{max}$, with the aim to individuate the best Pareto front solution to be presented as the output of the optimizer. We consider this solution as the one with the lowest distance from the theoretically optimal solution, i.e., the one which perfectly satisfies all the five objectives. This "best" solution is generally located in the intermediate region of the front and is the one which yields a better balance in satisfying all the objectives.

**Encoding.** Each individual in the population represents a potential multiple–day tour and is encoded by a vector of integer values with dimension equal to the number of *POI*s. This dimension is denoted with NPOI. Each integer denotes a *POI* and is present only once in each solution. For example a solution with NPOI=10 is shown in Fig. 2.

**Fig. 2.** Example of a tour encoding.

This solution, starting from the position chosen by the user (not explicitly contained in such an encoding), proposes to reach the *POI* in the first cell at the left side of the vector (9 in the figure) and then proceed forward visiting the *POI* in the second cell (1 in the figure) and so on. Differently from the TSP in which all the points are visited in the order indicated by the solution, in our PETG it is highly probable that not all the *POI*s are effectively visited. This can happen for several reasons:

– remaining available time: the tour must terminate when the residual available time is only sufficient to reach the final point from the *POI* in which the user currently is;
– closing: the tour can lead the user to a *POI* during its closing time;
– previous tours: the *POI* has already been visited in a previous tour and thus it will be not considered if not expressly required again;
– multiple–day tour: if the user has required a tour programmed in several days, the *POI* will be discarded if already included in the tour of one of the previous days.

If a *POI* is actually visited in the tour, a flag will be set for it. This allows the management of a multiple–day tour. In fact, for the second day the examination of the solution restarts from the leftmost position in the vector as for the first day and all the *POI*s already visited in the first day are now skipped. Analogously, for each further day, the vector which represents the solution will be examined again, always starting from its leftmost position.

# 4   Experiments

The algorithm has been coded in Java language and all the tests have been performed on a MacBookPro4.1 Intel Core Duo 2.4 GHz, 2 GB RAM. After a preliminary tuning phase, the population size $NPOP$ has been set equal to 500, while the number of generations $g_{max}$ has been set equal to 100. The crossover probability $CR$ has been set equal to 0.4. For the mutation, the exchange probability $EM$ has been fixed to 0.8 while the parameter $FV$ for the 2-opt mutation has been set equal to 1.0. Since evolutionary algorithms are nondeterministic, to individuate the best tour for any given problem 10 runs are performed. The execution time for all the 10 runs is about 13 s.

The algorithm is able to provide multiple–day walking tours in any area once the needed information are made available. Within this paper its ability has been tested for the area of the old city centre of Naples, Italy, by considering 20 $POIs$. These $POIs$ are listed in Table 1 together with some of the relevant information used for the building of the personalized tours. The list of the used information is not exhaustive. The waiting and visiting times are expressed in minutes. The possible start and finish points of the daily tours, outlined in Table 2, surround the selected area of interest and represent the 'access doors' to the old city centre through the local transportation means.

In the following, an example of a personalized tour generated as a function of the input information provided by the user is shown. The rating is quantified within the range [0, 100]. The value 100 is assigned to each $POI$ that the user expressly requires as belonging to the proposed tour. Moreover, beside the waiting and visiting times, also the walking and the total tour times are reported in minutes, while the walking and the total covered distances are measured in meters. Lastly, the weather is considered sunny during the whole visit.

In the example the case is considered that the user wishes to perform a two–day tour and requires to visit five $POIs$ as well.

The input information provided by the user is the following:

- Day of tour beginning: 01/05/2014
- average moving speed: 0.5 m/s
- disabled access request: no
- number of days available for the tour: 2
- number of $POIs$ that the user declares to be included in the visit: 5
- identification codes of these $POIs$: 3 6 9 12 15
- For the first day of the tour:
  - start and arrival times: 9.00 am - 7.00 pm
  - start and arrival positions: Dante (M1) - Università (M1)
  - number of programmed rests: 3
  - For each pause:
    - start and finish times of pause 1: 10.45 am - 11.15 am
    - start and finish times of pause 2: 1.00 pm - 2.30 pm
    - start and finish times of pause 3: 5.00 pm - 5.30 pm
- For the second day of the tour:

**Table 1.** The *POI*s for the old city centre of Naples.

| Identifier | Name of the *POI* | Waiting time | Visiting time | Opening hours | Indoor | Disabled access |
|---|---|---|---|---|---|---|
| 1 | Basilica of San Lorenzo Maggiore | 0 | 40 | 9.30 am - 5.30 pm | Y | Y |
| 2 | National Archaeological Museum | 10 | 120 | 9.00 pm - 7.30 pm | Y | Y |
| 3 | Church of Santa Chiara | 10 | 60 | 7.00 am - 1.00 pm<br>4.30 pm ÷ 8.00 pm | Y | Y |
| 4 | Capuano Castle | 0 | 30 | 8.00 am - 8.00 pm | Y | Y |
| 5 | Sant'Antoniello | 0 | 30 | 9.00 am - 6.00 pm | Y | Y |
| 6 | Sansevero Chapel Museum | 5 | 30 | 9.30 am - 6.30 pm | Y | Y |
| 7 | The Cathedral (Duomo) | 0 | 40 | 8.30 am - 1.30 pm<br>2.30 pm - 8.00 pm | Y | Y |
| 8 | San Marcellino | 0 | 20 | 8.00 am - 8.00 pm | N | Y |
| 9 | Roman Theater | 15 | 60 | 10.00 am - 6.00 pm | Y | N |
| 10 | Church of San Gregorio Armeno | 0 | 30 | 9.30 am - 5.00 pm | Y | Y |
| 11 | Church of Girolamini | 5 | 50 | 9.30 am - 5.00 pm | Y | Y |
| 12 | Church of Santa Maria Donnaregina | 0 | 40 | 9.30 am - 16.30 am | Y | Y |
| 13 | Basilica of San Paolo Maggiore | 0 | 30 | 10.00 am - 6.00 pm | Y | Y |
| 14 | Diomede Carafa Palace | 0 | 60 | 10.00 am - 1.30 pm | Y | Y |
| 15 | Filangieri Museum | 10 | 90 | 9.00 am - 1.00 pm | Y | Y |
| 16 | Conservatory of San Pietro a Majella | 0 | 45 | 10.00 am - 6.00 pm | Y | Y |
| 17 | Church of Gesù Nuovo | 0 | 40 | 6.30 am - 1.00 pm<br>4.00 pm - 8.00 pm | Y | Y |
| 18 | Venezia Palace | 0 | 60 | 9.00 am - 5.00 pm | Y | Y |
| 19 | Church of San Domenico Maggiore | 0 | 35 | 9.30 am - 12.00 pm<br>4.30 pm - 7.00 pm | Y | Y |
| 20 | God Nile Statue | 0 | 10 | 12.00 am - 12.00 am | N | Y |

- start and arrival times: 9.30 am - 4.30 pm
- start and arrival positions: Duomo (M1) - Museo (M1/M2)
- number of programmed rests: 2
- For each pause:
  * start and finish times of pause 1: 11.00 am - 11:30 am
  * start and finish times of pause 2: 1.30 pm - 2.30 pm

The best tour determined in all the runs in accordance to the user information and the rating of the *POI*s derived from the user's profile is:

( 17 18 3 2 15 6 7 9 12 11 5 4 16 1 13 18 20 19 10 4 )

The tour provided by the algorithm for each day is shown in Table 3. The two-day tour associated to this output file is also graphically reported in Fig. 3 over a

**Table 2.** The access points for the old city centre of Naples.

| Museo (M1/M2) |
| --- |
| Dante (M1) |
| Montesanto (Cumana/Funicular of Montesanto/M2) |
| Toledo (M1) |
| Piazzetta Augusteo (Central Funicular) |
| Municipio (M1/M6/Port/Car Parking) |
| Università (M1) |
| Duomo (M1) |
| Garibaldi (M1/M2/Circumvesuviana/Car Parking) |

**Table 3.** The output of the optimizer.

| The tour proposed for the first day | | | | | | | | | | |
| --- | --- | --- | --- | --- | --- | --- | --- | --- | --- | --- |
| POI (Pause) | Start time | Walking time | Waiting time | Visiting time | Visit end | Pause begin | Pause end | Distance | Total distance | Score |
| Start | 9.00 am | | | | | | | 0 | 0 | |
| 17 | | 7 | 0 | 40 | 9.47 am | | | 239 | 239 | 61 |
| 18 | | 5 | 0 | 60 | 10.52 am | | | 175 | 414 | 22 |
| (Pause 1) | | | 30 | | | 10.52 am | 11.22 am | | | |
| 3 | | 7 | 10 | 60 | 12.39 pm | | | 219 | 633 | 100 |
| (Pause 2) | | | 90 | | | 12.39 pm | 2.09 pm | | | |
| 2 | | 30 | 10 | 120 | 4.49 pm | | | 923 | 1556 | 80 |
| (Pause 3) | | | 30 | | | 4.49 pm | 5.19 pm | | | |
| 6 | | 23 | 5 | 30 | 6.17 pm | | | 698 | 2254 | 100 |
| 20 | | 5 | 0 | 10 | 6.32 pm | | | 158 | 2412 | 19 |
| Arrival | | 15 | | | 6.47 pm | | | 453 | 2865 | |
| The tour proposed for the second day | | | | | | | | | | |
| POI (Pause) | Start time | Arrival time | Waiting time | Visiting time | Visit end | Pause begin | Pause end | Distance | Total distance | Score |
| Start | 9.30 am | | | | | | | 0 | 0 | |
| 15 | | 5 | 10 | 90 | 11.15 am | | | 158 | 158 | 100 |
| (Pause 1) | | | 30 | | | 11.15 am | 11.45 am | | | |
| 7 | | 14 | 0 | 40 | 12.39 pm | | | 430 | 588 | 89 |
| (Pause 2) | | | 60 | | | 12.39 pm | 1.39 pm | | | |
| 9 | | 9 | 15 | 60 | 3.03 pm | | | 278 | 866 | 100 |
| 12 | | 20 | 0 | 40 | 4.03 pm | | | 622 | 1488 | 100 |
| Arrival | | 8 | | | 4.11 pm | | | 266 | 1754 | |
| Summary | | | | | | | | | | |
| Required POIs | | | 5 | out of | 5 | | | | | |
| Visited POIs | | | 10 | out of | 20 | | | | | |
| Total tour time | | | 988 | out of | 1020 | | | | | |
| Total covered distance | | | 4619 | | | | | | | |
| Total score | | | 77 | out of | 100 | | | | | |

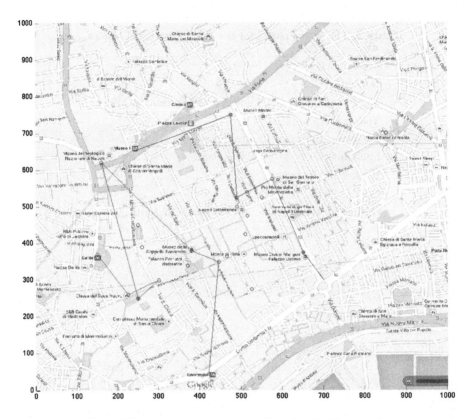

**Fig. 3.** The two-day tour proposed for the fourth example.

map of the area representing the old city centre of Naples. This figure evidences each day tour with a different color, namely the first day is reported in red whereas the second one is in blue. As it is simple to verify from Table 3, the tour proposed allows visiting all the POIs expressly required by the user. Moreover, the visualization reported in Fig. 3 demonstrates even more the effectiveness of our evolutionary optimizer. In fact, the proposed two-day tour carries out an "intelligent" optimization by automatically subdividing the area of the old city into two distinct zones, each visited in a different day. It is worth noting that on the first day the planned visit to *POI* 3 (Church of Santa Chiara) ends at 12.39 pm, i.e., in good time before this *POI* closes at 1 pm for lunch pause.

## 5    Conclusions and Future Works

Within this paper a multiobjective evolutionary optimizer for solving a TOPTW, characterized by multiple and contrasting objectives, is proposed. Such an optimizer is innovative as regards the number of both optimization criteria and features considered. Its ability to generate personalized multiple–day walking tours in a street network modeled as a graph, respecting user's interests and limitations, and environmental constraints, has been successfully tested for the old city centre of Naples. This optimizer will constitute the core of a PETG that will be distributed as a free app for use in the above mentioned area.

As future works, we aim to endow our optimizer with a higher flexibility by providing a route planning capable of adapting to new circumstances in real–time to assure an on–the–fly tour updating.

**Acknowledgements.** This work has been supported by the project "Organization of Cultural Heritage for Smart Tourism and Real–Time Accessibility (OR.C.HE.S.T.R.A.)" (PON04a2_D) financed within the 2012 "Smart Cities and Communities" call of the Italian Ministry for University and Research.

# References

1. Brown, B., Chalmers, M.: Tourism and mobile technology. In: Proceedings of the 8th European Conference on Computer Supported Cooperative Work, pp. 335–354 (2003)
2. Vansteenwegen, P., Souffriau, W., Vanden Berghe, G., Oudheusden, D.V.: The city planner: an expert system for tourists. Expert Syst. Appl. **38**, 6540–6546 (2011)
3. Rodríguez, B., Molina, J., Pérez, F., Caballero, R.: Interactive design of personalised tourism routes. Tourism Manage. **33**, 926–940 (2012)
4. Vansteenwegen, P., Van Oudheusden, D.: The mobile tourist guide: an OR opportunity. OR Insight **20**, 21–27 (2007)
5. Souffiau, W., Vansteenwegen, P., Vertommen, J., Berghe, G.V., Van Oudheusden, D.: A personalised tour trip design algorithm for mobile tourist guides. Appl. Artif. Intell. **22**, 964–985 (2008)
6. Vansteenwegen, P., Souffriau, W., Oudheusden, D.V.: The orienteering problem: a survey. Eur. J. Oper. Res. **209**, 1–10 (2011)
7. Cotfas, L.A., Diosteanu, A., Dumitrescu, S.D., Smeureanu, A.: Semantic search itinerary recommender systems. Int. J. Comput. **5**, 370–377 (2011)
8. Gavalas, D., Kenteris, M., Konstantopoulos, C., Pantziou, G.: Web application for recommending personalised mobile tourist routes. IET Softw. **6**, 313–322 (2012)
9. Bäck, T., Fogel, D.B., Michalewicz, Z. (eds.): Handbook of Evolutionary Computation. Oxford University Press, Oxford (1997)
10. Goldberg, D.E.: Genetic algorithms in search, optimization, and machine learning. Addison-Wesley Professional, New York (1989)
11. Syswerda, G.: Uniform crossover in genetic algorithms. In: Proceedings of the 3rd International Conference on Genetic Algorithms, pp. 2–9 (1989)
12. Spears, W.M., De Jong, K.A.: An analysis of multipoint crossover. In: Proceedings of the Workshop of the Foundations of Genetic Algorithms, pp. 301–315 (1991)
13. Banzhaf, W.: The molecular traveling salesman. Biol. Cybern. **14**, 7–14 (1990)
14. Deep, K., Mebrahtu, H.: Combined mutation operators of genetic algorithms for the travelling salesman problem. Int. J. Comb. Optim. Probl. Inform. **2**, 1–23 (2011)
15. Chiang, C.W., Lee, W.P., Heh, J.S.: A 2-opt based differential evolution for global optimization. Appl. Soft. Comput. **10**, 1200–1207 (2010)

# Planning the Deployment of Indoor Wireless Sensor Networks Through Multiobjective Evolutionary Techniques

Jose M. Lanza-Gutierrez[1,2]([✉]), Juan A. Gomez-Pulido[1], S. Priem-Mendes[2,3],
M. Ferreira[2,3], and J.S. Pereira[2,3,4]

[1] Department of Computers and Communications Technologies,
Polytechnic School, University of Extremadura, Caceres, Spain
{jmlanza,jangomez}@unex.es
[2] Center for Research in Informatics and Communications,
Polytechnic Institute of Leiria, Leiria, Portugal
{smendes,marco.ferreira,joao.pereira}@ipleiria.pt
[3] School of Technology and Management,
Polytechnic Institute of Leiria, Leiria, Portugal
[4] Instituto de Telecomunicações, Leiria Branch, Leiria, Portugal

**Abstract.** This work deals with how to efficiently deploy an indoor wireless sensor network, assuming a novel approach in which we try to leverage existing infrastructure. Thus, given a set of low-cost sensors, which can be plugged into the grid or powered by batteries, a collector node, and a building plan, including walls and plugs, the purpose is to deploy the sensors optimising three conflicting objectives: average coverage, average energy cost, and average reliability. Two MultiObjective (MO) genetic algorithms are assumed to solve this issue, NSGA-II and SPEA2. These metaheuristics are applied to solve the problem using a freely available data set. The results obtained are analysed considering two MO quality metrics: hypervolume and set coverage. After applying a statistical methodology widely accepted, we conclude that SPEA2 provides the best performance on average considering such data set.

**Keywords:** Coverage · Deployment · Energy · Indoor · Multiobjective · NSGA-II · SPEA2 · Reliability · Wireless sensor network

## 1 Introduction and Related Work

Nowadays, Wireless Sensor Networks (WSNs) are widely applied in many fields, such as intensive agriculture, robotics and home automation [1]. A traditional WSN is composed of a set of sensors capturing information about the environment and a sink node, also called collector node, which collects all the information captured by the sensors. The sensors have some features, encouraging the use of WSNs. For example, they are small, cheap, wireless, and power-autonomous. These features, among others, allow considering WSNs in environments where the deployment of other technologies would be really expensive or impossible.

© Springer International Publishing Switzerland 2015
A.M. Mora and G. Squillero (Eds.): EvoApplications 2015, LNCS 9028, pp. 128–139, 2015.
DOI: 10.1007/978-3-319-16549-3_11

WSNs also have shortcomings, e.g. energy efficiency and reliability, affecting critical features, such as quality of service and maintenance costs. Traditionally, the sensors are powered by batteries to reduce deployment costs and to assume cheap devices. All the information captured by the sensors is sent to the collector node, involving an energy cost. If the WSN assumes a star topology, the energy distribution is similar for all the sensors. However, if a habitual multihop topology is assumed, where the sensors forward data, the energy distribution could be unbalanced. Involving the existence of bottlenecks, i.e. sensors subject to higher energy cost than others. With the aim of alleviating this situation, a new type of device called router or relay node is added to traditional WSNs, having greater energy capacity than the sensors. This device relays all the information received to the sink node, so reducing the workload of the sensors [2].

The efficient deployment of WSNs is defined in the literature as an NP-hard optimisation problem [3,4]. Consequently, this type of problem cannot be solved through exact techniques, but non-conventional ones, such as Evolutionary Computation (EC) [5] and heuristics. Most papers in the literature about WSN deployment assume outdoor scenarios, or instead ideal scenarios, where obstacles are not considered. However, WSNs are widely assumed in indoor-scenarios, e.g. climate monitoring [6] and localization systems for mobile devices where GPS signal is insufficient or its accuracy is inadequate [7].

We find many works studying localization techniques for indoor WSNs. However, there are a few papers studying the deployment of such networks, including two main lines: authors studying how to deploy traditional WSNs and works adding relay nodes to traditional WSNs, the so-called Relay Node Placement Problem (RNPP). Taking the first line, we may cite some relevant papers assuming heuristics. Guangming Song et al. [8] proposed a self-deployment algorithm for mobile sensor networks to be used in scenarios inaccessible to humans, optimising coverage area, coverage rate, and deployment time. Lin and King [9] studied how to deploy WSNs for indoor robot navigation, with the aim of reducing deployment cost by considering target models. Another author considered EC to this end. Joon-Hong Seok et al. [10] assumed a Differential Evolution (DE) algorithm to deploy WSNs with full coverage for mobile positioning systems.

The deployment of WSN with many sensors has an important shortcoming. Being as the sensors are powered by batteries and the number of relayed packets is high, adding redundant sensors is common to enhance the performance of the network, implying additional costs. The efficient addition of relay nodes to traditional WSNs is presented in the literature as a way to solve this issue. Thus, taking the second line, some authors considered heuristics. Tarng et al. [11] proposed an algorithm to reduce the number of routers for bridging all disconnected sensors of a randomly deployed WSN. Yu et al. [12] implemented a method to deploy as few additional relay nodes as possible, ensuring each sensor was linked to the sink node. We did not find papers assuming EC to this end.

Our work is between both research lines. In this paper, we propose a novel approach of the indoor RNPP. We study how to deploy a low-cost indoor WSN optimising three conflicting objectives: average energy cost, average coverage

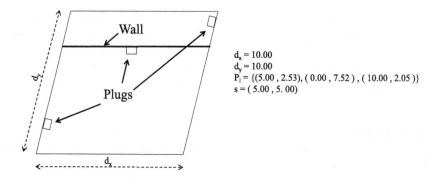

$d_x = 10.00$
$d_y = 10.00$
$P_l = \{(5.00, 2.53), (0.00, 7.52), (10.00, 2.05)\}$
$s = (5.00, 5.00)$

**Fig. 1.** Example of the WSN model assumed.

provided by the network, and average reliability. The WSN model assumed is composed of two types of devices: a set of sensors, which can be powered by batteries or plugged into the grid, and a collector node. The sensors plugged into the grid acts as relay nodes. To solve this issue, we consider two MultiObjective (MO) genetic algorithms from EC: NSGA-II [13] and SPEA2 [14]. Our proposal differs from the papers described before in the following: (i) We deploy sensors and relay nodes at the same time, trying to leverage existing infrastructure. (ii) We define an MO optimisation problem considering three relevant factors for the industry: energy, coverage, and reliability. In [8], they optimised three criteria. However, all of them were related to coverage. Thus, this is a more realistic approach. (iii) We consider two MO metaheuristics to solve the problem. It is well known that MO metaheuristics provide a trade-off between the objective functions. This way, the network designer has several possibilities to deploy the network. This is not the case for heuristics, providing a unique solution. In [10], the authors assumed a metaheuristic, but following a singleobjective approach. On the other hand, in previous works [15,16], we studied the RNPP for outdoor environments through several MO algorithms. As discussed previously, in this work we assume an indoor RNPP. Hence, this is a different approach.

The remainder of this paper is structured as follows. Next section defines the optimisation problem. Section 3 describes the MO metaheuristics considered to solve the problem. Section 4 discusses both the experimental methodology followed and the results obtained. Finally, conclusions are left for Sect. 5.

## 2    A New Approach for the Deployment of Indoor WSNs

The WSN model assumes a sink node and $N$ sensors, which are placed on a 2D-surface of size $d_x \times d_y$, including coordinates of red brick walls ($W_r$) and plugs ($P_l$) (see Fig. 1), that is

$$\forall c \in W_r \cup P_l, \ c = (x, y) \ / \ x \in [0, d_x] \ and \ y \in [0, d_y]. \tag{1}$$

The sensors capture information about the environment on a regular basis. This data is sent to the sink node, assuming a multi-hop routing protocol provided by Dijkstra's algorithm [17] for minimum path length among the devices. Being the sink node the only connection point of the network to the outside.

The sink node is plugged into the grid and the sensors are powered by batteries or plugged into the grid, according if they are close to a power source or not. The radio hardware of all the devices is based on the commercial device MICAz, considering the CC2420 chip [18]. This mote uses IEEE 802.15.4 protocol (ZigBee), transmitting information in the 2.4 GHz band with a maximum data rate of 250 kbits/s and maximum radio power setting of 1 mW (0 dBm). Thus, let $s$, $S_b(t)$, and $S_p(t)$ be the sink node, the set of sensors powered by batteries with an energy charge greater than 0 at time $t > 0$, and the set of sensors plugged into the grid, respectively. Being the devices in $S_b(t)$ and $S_p(t)$ accessible to the sink node at this time in one or more hops. Then, two any devices $i, j \in s + \{S_b(t) \cup S_p(t)\}/i \neq j$ can be linked if the transmission power needed $tpw_{i,j}$ is lower or equal than 1 mW. This value is expressed as

$$tpw_{i,j} = \frac{CST}{||i - j||^2} \cdot 10^{-wlost_{i,j} \cdot 10^{-1}}, \tag{2}$$

where $CST$ is a transmission constant, $||.||$ is the Euclidean distance between any two devices, and $wlost_{i,j}$ is the signal attenuation due to walls between both devices, where a red brick attenuates 4.4349 dBm [19].

As stated before, both the sink node and the sensors plugged into the grid have an unlimited power supply. Hence, the energy expenditure of these devices does not affect the behaviour of the WSN. This is not the case for the sensors powered by batteries. With the purpose of simulating this energy cost, we assume the energy model proposed by A. Konstantinidis et al. [20]. Thus, the energy expenditure suffered by a sensor $i \in S_b(t)$ at time $t > 0$ is given by

$$Ee_i(t) = (1 + P_i(t)) \cdot \beta \cdot amp \cdot k \cdot ||i - w_i^s(t)||^\alpha, \tag{3}$$

where $P_i(t)$ is the number of packets that $i$ forwards at $t$, the $+1$ term is because $i$ generates an information packet at this time, $amp$ is the energy cost per bit of the power amplifier, $k$ is the information packet size, $\alpha$ is the path loss exponent, $\beta$ is the transmission quality parameter, and $w_i^s(t)$ is the next device in the minimum path between $i$ and the sink node at $t$, $w_i^s(t) \in \{S_b(t) \cup S_p(t)\} + s - i$. According to this definition, we assume that the radio hardware is able to dynamically adjust the transmission power to reach the next device. This way, if the energy charge of a sensor equals 0, it cannot capture more data nor be linked again.

An important concept in WSNs is the network lifetime. It is the number of time unit over which a WSN is able to provide useful information, without performing maintenance tasks. To this end, a coverage threshold $co_{th}$ is often used, i.e. if the coverage provided by the WSN is lower than $co_{th}$, we consider that the amount of information is not enough. Thus, let $A(t)$ be the percentage of the surface covered by the sensors (both types) at time $t$, the network lifetime is given by

$$n_{lf} = |\{t > 0 \in \mathbb{N} \ / \ A(t) > co_{th}\}|, \tag{4}$$

where $|.|$ is the cardinal of a set. The coverage value does not include sensors which cannot be linked to the collector node nor walls. The coverage provided by a sensor is calculated by analysing its signal range, assuming the maximum radio power setting of $1\,mW$.

Let $f_1$ be the Average Energy Consumption (AEC) of the sensors powered by batteries over the network lifetime, that is given by

$$f_1 = \frac{\sum_{t=1}^{n_{lf}} \left( \sum_{i \in S_b(t)} \frac{Ee_i(t)}{|S_b(t)|} \right)}{n_{lf}} \qquad f_1 \in \mathbb{R}^+. \tag{5}$$

Let $f_2$ be the Average Coverage (AC) provided by the sensors, which is given by

$$f_2 = \frac{\sum_{t=1}^{n_{lf}} A(t)}{n_{lf}} \qquad f_2 \in [0,1]. \tag{6}$$

And let $f_3$ be the Average Network Reliability (ANR), denoting the probability that the sensors successfully send data to the collector node, that is defined as

$$f_3 = \frac{\sum_{t=1}^{n_{lf}} \left( \sum_{i \in S_b(t) \cup S_p(t)} \frac{re_i}{|S_b(t) \cup S_p(t)|} \right)}{n_{lf}} \qquad f_3 \in [0,1], \tag{7}$$

where $re_i$ is the reliability of the sensor $i$ defined in [21] as

$$re_i = 1 - \prod_{l=1}^{dp_i^s} \left( 1 - (1 - err)^{h_l^i} \right), \tag{8}$$

where $dp_i^s$ is the number of disjoint paths between $i$ and the collector node provided by Suurballe's Algorithm [22], $h_l^i$ is the number of hops in the $l$-th disjoint path between both devices, and $err$ is the local channel error.

This way, we define an MO optimisation problem, where given a scenario including walls and plugs, the objective is to place $N$ sensors to

$$min(f_1), max(f_2), and\ max(f_3), \tag{9}$$

subject to

$$\forall d \in S_b(t) \cup S_p(t),\ d = (x,y)\ /\ x \in [0, d_x]\ y \in [0, d_y],\ and\ d \notin W_r, \tag{10}$$

$$\forall d \in S_p(t), d \in P_l\ and\ \forall d \in S_b(t), d \notin P_l, \tag{11}$$

$$|S_b(t) \cup S_p(t)| = N\ for\ t = 0. \tag{12}$$

Note that, for $t = 0$, $S_b(t)$ and $S_p(t)$ show the initial deployment of the network, without considering energy cost nor connectivity.

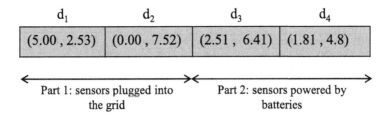

Fig. 2. Chromosome definition.

# 3   Multiobjective Metaheuristics: NSGA-II and SPEA2

As stated before, we consider two MO genetic algorithms. This type of algorithm is characterized by encoding their individuals as chromosomes, being an individual a possible solution to the optimisation problem. We assume that a chromosome is composed of two parts, each one consists of $S_b(t)$ and $S_p(t)$ genes, for $t = 0$. As Fig. 2 details, a gene shows the 2D-coordinate of a device.

NSGA-II assumes two populations $P_g$ and $Q_g$ of the same size $PS$. $P_g$ saves the parents of the generation $g$ and $Q_g$ contains the offspring generated through the individuals in $P_g$. Initially, $P_g$ is set randomly and $Q_g$ is empty. So long as the stop condition is not reached, both $P_g$ and $Q_g$ are combined in a new set $R_g$ of size $2 \cdot PS$. Then, the best $PS$ solutions of $R_g$ are added to $P_{g+1}$, considering both crossover and rank measures. Next, a new offspring population $Q_{g+1}$ is generated through $P_{g+1}$. With this purpose and so long as $Q_{g+1}$ is not filled, a pair of individuals is selected from $P_{g+1}$ by binary tournament. Then, a new individual is generated and inserted into $Q_{g+1}$ based on these two previously selected solutions, assuming crossover and mutation operators.

SPEA2 considers two populations $P_g$ and $\overline{P_g}$ with sizes $PS$ and $\overline{PS}$, respectively. $P_g$ is a regular population and $\overline{P_g}$ is an auxiliary population, saving the best solutions obtained over generations. Initially, $P_g$ is generated randomly and $\overline{P_g}$ is empty. So long as the stop criterion is not reached, each individual in $P_g \cup \overline{P_g}$ is assigned a fitness value based on the Pareto dominance and density information. Then, according to this fitness function, the best solutions are added to the new $\overline{P_{g+1}}$. Next, a new $P_{g+1}$ is generated through $\overline{P_{g+1}}$ as discussed for NSGA-II, assuming binary tournament and crossover and mutation operators.

As crossover operator, we consider the habitual one-point crossover, but assuming some considerations. Thus, let $i$ and $j$ be two individuals, having $|S_b(t)_i \cup S_p(t)_i|$ and $|S_b(t)_j \cup S_p(t)_j|$ sensors, we will generate a new individual $k$ through $i$ and $j$. Firstly, we define the number of sensors plugged in $k$ by generating a random number in the interval $[\max(0, N - (|S_b(t)_i \cup S_b(t)_j|), \min(N, |S_p(t)_i \cup S_p(t)_j|)]$, where $\max(.)$ and $\min(.)$ provide the maximum and minimum value between two numbers, respectively. Then, we perform a one-point crossover between the first part of each chromosome, getting the number of sensors plugged previously obtained. Next, we perform another one-point crossover between the second part of each chromosome, selecting the number of devices

**Table 1.** Description of the data set considered.

| Instance | $|P_i|$ | Test cases | Hyp. reference points (ideal, nadir) | | | General parameters | |
|---|---|---|---|---|---|---|---|
| $(d_x \times d_y)$ | | $(N)$ | $f_1$ | $f_2$ | $f_3$ | $\alpha = 2$ | $\beta = 1$ |
| 21.40x10.14 | 8 | 2,3,4 | (0.00000,0.00006) | (1.00,0.50) | (1.00,0.80) | $amp = 100pJ/bit/m^2$ $co_{th} = 0.70$ | |
| 32.80x17.60 | 16 | 2,3,...,8 | (0.00000,0.00025) | (1.00,0.15) | (1.00,0.70) | $err = 0.10$ $iec = 0.005J$ | |
| | | | | | | $k = 10Kb$ $CST = 100$ | |

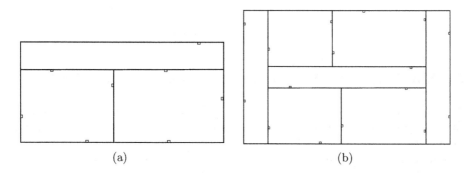

(a)                              (b)

**Fig. 3.** Walls and plugs in the scenarios. (a) $21.40 \times 10.14$. (b) $32.80 \times 17.60$.

needed to reach $N$ sensors. As usual, this operator considers a *crossover parameter*, showing the probability that the operator crosses the two individuals, or otherwise, it returns the best individual of the incoming pair.

The mutation operator generates random changes in the chromosomes. Given the individual $k$ previously generated, the operator tries to modify each gene attending to the *mutation parameter*, showing the probability that a gene is mutated. This way, the operator could modify the number and coordinates of the sensors powered by batteries and plugged into the grid.

## 4    Experimental Methodology and Results Obtained

This section studies the performance of the algorithms solving the problem. Being as we did not find any public testbed fitting this problem definition, we consider the freely available data set proposed by ourselves in [23]. As Table 1 details, the data set is composed of two different scenarios with sizes $216.99 \, \mathrm{m}^2$ and $577.28 \, \mathrm{m}^2$, having 8 and 16 plugs, respectively. Figure 3 shows the position of both walls and plugs in the scenarios, being the collector node placed on the middle of the surface. The network parameters assumed are detailed in the *General parameters* section of Table 1, being based on other works [20,21,24,25]. This data set is optimised by adding sensors. Being as the addition of these devices involves an economic cost, we study several test cases for each scenario to get a trade-off, three for the $21.40 \times 10.14$ and seven for the $32.80 \times 17.60$.

Each test case is optimised by the metaheuristics. To this end, we perform 31 independent runs, assuming several stop conditions based on the number of evaluations to study the convergence of the algorithms: 100 000, 200 000, 300 000,

**Table 2.** Parametric sweep.

| NSGA-II | | | SPEA2 | | |
|---|---|---|---|---|---|
| Parameter | Selected | Range | Parameter | Selected | Range |
| mutation | 0.25 | [0.05,0.10,...,0.95] | mutation | 0.30 | [0.05,0.10,...,0.95] |
| crossover | 0.35 | [0.05,0.10,...,0.95] | crossover | 0.15 | [0.05,0.10,...,0.95] |
| PS | 125 | [25,50,...,400] | PS | 325 | [25,50,...,400] |

and 400 000 evaluations. Being 30 runs a widely accepted value to reach statistical conclusions. The results obtained are analysed through both hypervolume [26] and set coverage [5] metrics. The reference points assumed to calculate the hypervolume appear in Table 1, where *ideal* and *nadir* are the best and the worst value of a fitness function. These values were obtained experimentally. The set coverage metric is calculated considering the median Pareto fronts, from the distribution of 31 samples for each test case, stop condition, and algorithm. Thus, the set coverage of an algorithm A regarding another B, SC(A,B), it is the percentage of solutions from B which are weakly dominated by A.

Before performing the experiments, the algorithms were configured through a parametric sweep. To this end, and starting from default values, a parameter of the algorithm is selected to be tuned. Next, 31 independent runs are performed for each value of the parameter, assuming a reduced stop criterion (50 000 evaluations). Then, the configuration providing the best performance on average is selected, according to the hypervolume metric. This procedure is repeated so long as all the parameters are fixed. Table 2 shows the configurations selected and the range of values assumed for each algorithm.

Table 3 shows average hypervolume ($\overline{Hyp}$) and InterQuartile Range (IQR) for each test case, stop condition, and algorithm, where higher hypervolumes are shaded. Analysing this table, we may note that SPEA2 seems to provide better performance than NSGA-II. However, we do not know if the differences are significant. To check this, we consider a widely accepted statistical methodology.

Firstly, we study if data follow a normal distribution through Shapiro Wilk's and Kolmogrov Smirnov Lilliefors's tests, assuming the hypothesis: $H_0$ if data follow a normal distribution and $H_1$ otherwise. P-values lower than 0.05 were obtained for all the cases. Hence, we cannot assume that data follow a Gaussian distribution and we must consider the median as average value.

Next, we study if there are significant differences between the algorithms through Wilcoxon Mann Whitney's test, being as samples do not come from a normal distribution and data are independent. To this end, we consider the hypothesis: $H_0$ if $\overline{Hyp}_i <= \overline{Hyp}_j$ and $H_1$ if $\overline{Hyp}_i > \overline{Hyp}_j$, with $i =$ SPEA2 and $j =$ NSGA-II. The p-values obtained are shown in Table 4, where values lower than 0.05 are shaded, because differences are significant. Analysing this table, we check as SPEA2 provides better performance than NSGA-II for all the cases.

Table 5 details the set coverage metric between the algorithms for each test case and stop condition, where higher set coverage values are shaded. Analysing this table, we reach similar conclusions as for hypervolume. SPEA2 provides the best coverage relation for all the cases.

**Table 3.** Average hypervolumes obtained.

| NSGA-II($\overline{Hyp}\%, IQR$) | | | | |
|---|---|---|---|---|
| Test case | Evaluations (Stop condition) | | | |
| Instance(N) | 100 000 | 200 000 | 300 000 | 400 000 |
| **21.40 × 10.14(2)** | 81.98 %, 0.0001 | 82.01 %, 0.0001 | 82.02 %, 0.0001 | 82.03 %, 0.0001 |
| **21.40 × 10.14(3)** | 95.93 %, 0.0023 | 96.17 %, 0.0028 | 96.29 %, 0.0027 | 96.34 %, 0.0031 |
| **21.40 × 10.14(4)** | 98.94 %, 0.0012 | 99.05 %, 0.0009 | 99.10 %, 0.0008 | 99.14 %, 0.0006 |
| **32.80 × 17.60(2)** | 28.16 %, 0.0010 | 28.18 %, 0.0036 | 28.40 %, 0.0043 | 28.54 %, 0.0050 |
| **32.80 × 17.60(3)** | 44.69 %, 0.0110 | 45.06 %, 0.0112 | 45.37 %, 0.0111 | 45.58 %, 0.0095 |
| **32.80 × 17.60(4)** | 57.98 %, 0.0136 | 58.81 %, 0.0091 | 59.07 %, 0.0096 | 59.16 %, 0.0072 |
| **32.80 × 17.60(5)** | 65.22 %, 0.0367 | 66.93 %, 0.0334 | 67.94 %, 0.0290 | 68.64 %, 0.0218 |
| **32.80 × 17.60(6)** | 75.45 %, 0.0165 | 76.27 %, 0.0111 | 76.81 %, 0.0087 | 77.15 %, 0.0060 |
| **32.80 × 17.60(7)** | 80.95 %, 0.0173 | 81.46 %, 0.0141 | 82.33 %, 0.0159 | 82.61 %, 0.0215 |
| **32.80 × 17.60(8)** | 85.37 %, 0.0286 | 86.39 %, 0.0145 | 87.01 %, 0.0104 | 87.02 %, 0.0103 |
| **SPEA2($\overline{Hyp}\%, IQR$)** | | | | |
| **21.40 × 10.14(2)** | **82.00 %, 0.0002** | **82.02 %, 0.0001** | **82.04 %, 0.0024** | **82.05 %, 0.0034** |
| **21.40 × 10.14(3)** | **96.70 %, 0.0009** | **96.83 %, 0.0005** | **96.88 %, 0.0007** | **96.91 %, 0.0006** |
| **21.40 × 10.14(4)** | **99.31 %, 0.0005** | **99.35 %, 0.0005** | **99.37 %, 0.0003** | **99.38 %, 0.0003** |
| **32.80 × 17.60(2)** | **28.54 %, 0.0020** | **28.63 %, 0.0028** | **28.72 %, 0.0024** | **28.76 %, 0.0021** |
| **32.80 × 17.60(3)** | **45.41 %, 0.0043** | **45.68 %, 0.0038** | **46.10 %, 0.0070** | **46.33 %, 0.0066** |
| **32.80 × 17.60(4)** | **59.41 %, 0.0141** | **59.96 %, 0.0135** | **60.12 %, 0.0138** | **60.25 %, 0.0119** |
| **32.80 × 17.60(5)** | **68.49 %, 0.0095** | **69.09 %, 0.0120** | **69.53 %, 0.0106** | **69.54 %, 0.0105** |
| **32.80 × 17.60(6)** | **76.44 %, 0.0122** | **77.08 %, 0.0083** | **77.28 %, 0.0080** | **77.57 %, 0.0079** |
| **32.80 × 17.60(7)** | **81.52 %, 0.0085** | **82.73 %, 0.0144** | **83.15 %, 0.0139** | **83.64 %, 0.0147** |
| **32.80 × 17.60(8)** | **86.34 %, 0.0196** | **88.18 %, 0.0189** | **89.09 %, 0.0172** | **89.38 %, 0.0186** |

**Table 4.** P-values obtained comparing hypervolumes.

| | SPEA2 vs NSGA-II | | | |
|---|---|---|---|---|
| **Test case** | **Evaluations (Stop condition)** | | | |
| **Instance(N)** | **100 000** | **200 000** | **300 000** | **400 000** |
| **21.40x10.14(2)** | 0.0020 | 0.0000 | 0.0000 | 0.0000 |
| **21.40x10.14(3)** | 0.0000 | 0.0000 | 0.0000 | 0.0000 |
| **21.40x10.14(4)** | 0.0000 | 0.0000 | 0.0000 | 0.0000 |
| **32.80x17.60(2)** | 0.0000 | 0.0000 | 0.0000 | 0.0001 |
| **32.80x17.60(3)** | 0.0001 | 0.0012 | 0.0000 | 0.0000 |
| **32.80x17.60(4)** | 0.0000 | 0.0000 | 0.0000 | 0.0000 |
| **32.80x17.60(5)** | 0.0000 | 0.0000 | 0.0000 | 0.0000 |
| **32.80x17.60(6)** | 0.0001 | 0.0001 | 0.0003 | 0.0006 |
| **32.80x17.60(7)** | 0.0097 | 0.0000 | 0.0000 | 0.0003 |
| **32.80x17.60(8)** | 0.0010 | 0.0000 | 0.0000 | 0.0000 |

Finally, with the purpose of analysing this behaviour graphically, in Fig. 4 we compare the median Pareto fronts obtained for 400 000 evaluations by solving some representative test cases.

**Table 5.** Set coverage metric between the algorithms.

| Test case | SC(NSGA-II,SPEA2) | | | | SC(SPEA2,NSGA-II) | | | |
|---|---|---|---|---|---|---|---|---|
| Instance(N) | 100 000 | 200 000 | 300 000 | 400 000 | 100 000 | 200 000 | 300 000 | 400 000 |
| **21.40 × 10.14(2)** | 44.44 % | 42.27 % | 50.00 % | 43.81 % | 51.22 % | 59.43 % | 48.94 % | 55.77 % |
| **21.40 × 10.14(3)** | 21.53 % | 18.72 % | 12.50 % | 20.00 % | 72.50 % | 94.32 % | 83.33 % | 68.38 % |
| **21.40 × 10.14(4)** | 29.41 % | 17.16 % | 19.84 % | 15.02 % | 94.09 % | 91.86 % | 92.70 % | 92.89 % |
| **Average** | 31.79 % | 26.05 % | 27.45 % | 26.28 % | **72.60 %** | **81.87 %** | **74.99 %** | **72.34 %** |
| **32.80 × 17.60(2)** | 30.23 % | 53.49 % | 8.33 % | 51.16 % | 74.47 % | 54.84 % | 87.50 % | 58.70 % |
| **32.80 × 17.60(3)** | 19.75 % | 29.73 % | 17.78 % | 20.73 % | 71.25 % | 53.60 % | 71.67 % | 72.62 % |
| **32.80 × 17.60(4)** | 24.25 % | 20.86 % | 32.58 % | 26.22 % | 70.71 % | 66.67 % | 64.68 % | 65.02 % |
| **32.80 × 17.60(5)** | 30.93 % | 23.01 % | 24.92 % | 25.71 % | 94.44 % | 94.29 % | 89.34 % | 85.97 % |
| **32.80 × 17.60(6)** | 11.26 % | 19.61 % | 14.75 % | 14.06 % | 67.96 % | 70.25 % | 71.63 % | 88.40 % |
| **32.80 × 17.60(7)** | 27.45 % | 13.35 % | 8.51 % | 8.57 % | 55.41 % | 78.53 % | 84.35 % | 86.27 % |
| **32.80 × 17.60(8)** | 3.48 % | 7.04 % | 2.22 % | 2.50 % | 84.56 % | 80.45 % | 93.58 % | 62.55 % |
| **Average** | 21.05 % | 23.87 % | 15.58 % | 21.28 % | **74.12 %** | **71.23 %** | **80.39 %** | **74.22 %** |

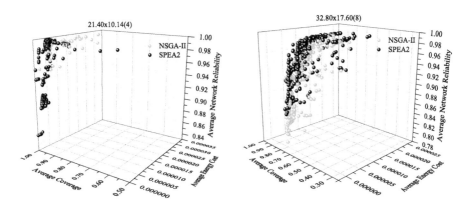

**Fig. 4.** Median Pareto fronts obtained solving some representative test cases.

## 5    Final Remarks

In this paper, we study how to deploy indoor WSNs trying to leverage existing infrastructure, with the purpose of optimising three relevant factors: average energy cost, average coverage, and average network reliability. This is an NP-hard optimisation problem. This type of problem cannot be solved assuming exact techniques, but non-conventional ones, such as evolutionary algorithms. To this end, we consider two MO genetic algorithms, NSGAI-II and SPEA2. These metaheuristics are applied to solve a freely available data set. The results obtained are analysed assuming two standard MO metrics, hypervolume and set coverage, concluding that SPEA2 provides the best performance on average for all the cases, solving the data set.

As future lines of research, it would be interesting to consider other meta-heuristics and a bigger data set. Conducting real-world experiments would be also a good extension of this work.

**Acknowledgements.** This work was partially funded by the Spanish Ministry of Economy and Competitiveness and the ERDF (European Regional Development Fund), under the contract TIN2012-30685 (BIO project), and by the Government of Extremadura, with the aid GR10025 to the group TIC015.

# References

1. Mukherjee, J.Y.B., Ghosal, D.: Wireless sensor network survey. Comput. Netw. **52**, 2292–2330 (2008)
2. Akyildiz, I., Su, W., Sankarasubramaniam, Y., Cayirci, E.: A survey on sensor networks. IEEE Commun. Mag. **40**, 102–114 (2002)
3. Cheng, X., Narahari, B., Simha, R., Cheng, M., Liu, D.: Strong minimum energy topology in wireless sensor networks: Np-completeness and heuristics. IEEE Trans. Mob. Comput. **2**, 248–256 (2003)
4. Chang, J.H., Tassiulas, L.: Maximum lifetime routing in wireless sensor networks. IEEE/ACM Trans. Netw. **12**, 609–619 (2004)
5. Zitzler, E.: Evolutionary algorithms for multiobjective optimization: methods and applications. (Doctoral dissertation). Swiss Federal Institute of Technology (ETH) (1999)
6. Yun, J., Kim, J.: Deployment support for sensor networks in indoor climate monitoring. Int. J. Distrib. Sens. Netw., 1–10 (2013)
7. Zhang, Z., Zhu, J., Ruan, J., Song, G.: Distance measurement for the indoor WSN nodes using WTR method. Int. J. Distrib. Sens. Netw. **2014**, 1–13 (2014)
8. Song, G., Zhuang, W., Song, A.: Self-deployment of mobile sensor networks in complex indoor environments. In: IEEE Conference WCICA, pp. 4543–4546 (2006)
9. Lin, C.H., King, C.T.: Sensor-deployment strategies for indoor robot navigation. IEEE Trans. Syst. Man Cybern. B Cybern. - Part A: Syst. Hum. **40**, 388–398 (2010)
10. Seok, J.-H., Lee, J.-Y., Oh, C., Lee, J.-J., Lee, H.J.: Rfid sensor deployment using differential evolution for indoor mobile robot localization. In: IEEE Conference IROS, pp. 3719–3724 (2010)
11. Tarng, J.H., Chuang, B.W., Liu, P.C.: A relay node deployment method for disconnected wireless sensor networks: Applied in indoor environments. J. Netw. Comput. Appl. **32**, 652–659 (2009)
12. Yu, M., Song, J.K., Mah, P.: RNIndoor: A relay node deployment method for disconnected wireless sensor networks in indoor environments. In: ICUFN Conference, pp. 19–24 (2011)
13. Deb, K., Pratap, A., Agarwal, S., Meyarivan, T.: A fast elitist multi-objective genetic algorithm: NSGA-II. IEEE Trans. Evol. Comput. **6**, 182–197 (2000)
14. Zitzler, E., Laumanns, M., Thiele, L.: Spea 2: Improving the strength pareto evolutionary algorithm. Technical report, Computer Engineering and Networks Laboratory (TIK), ETH Zurich (2001)
15. Lanza-Gutiérrez, J.M., Gómez-Pulido, J.A., Vega-Rodríguez, M.A.: A trajectory-based heuristic to solve a three-objective optimization problemfor wireless sensor network deployment. In: Esparcia-Alcázar, A.I., Mora, A.M. (eds.) EvoApplications 2014. LNCS, vol. 8602, pp. 27–38. Springer, Heidelberg (2014)

16. Lanza-Gutierrez, J.M., Gomez-Pulido, J.A., Vega-Rodriguez, M.A.: Intelligent relay node placement in heterogeneous wireless sensor networks for energy efficiency. Int. J. Robot. Autom. **29**, 1–13 (2014)
17. Cormen, T.H., Leiserson, C.E., Rivest, R.L., Stein, C. (eds.): Introduction to Algorithms, 3rd edn. The MIT Press, Cambridge (2009)
18. Chipcom, A.S.: Smartrf cc2420 preliminary datasheet (2004). http://inst.eecs.berkeley.edu/cs150/Documents/CC2420.pdf
19. Wilson, R.: Propagation losses through common building materials: 2.4 ghz vs 5 ghz. reflection and transmission losses through common building materials. Technical Report E10589, Magis Networks, Inc. (2002)
20. Konstantinidis, A., Yang, K.: Multi-objective k-connected deployment and power assignment in wsns using a problem-specific constrained evolutionary algorithm based on decomposition. Comput. Commun. **34**, 83–98 (2011)
21. Deb, B., Bhatnagar, S., Nath, B.: Reliable information forwarding using multiple paths in sensor networks. In: Proceedings of IEEE LCN, pp. 406–415 (2003)
22. Suurballe, J.W.: Disjoint paths in a network. Networks **4**, 125–145 (1974)
23. Lanza-Gutierrez, J.M., Gomez-Pulido, J.A.: Instance sets for indoor optimization in wireless sensor networks (2014). http://arco.unex.es/wsnopt
24. Mahboubi, H., Moezzi, K., Aghdam, A., Sayrafian-Pour, K., Marbukh, V.: Distributed deployment algorithms for improved coverage in a network of wireless mobile sensors. IEEE Trans. Industr. Inf. **10**, 163–174 (2014)
25. Martins, F., Carrano, E., Wanner, E., Takahashi, R., Mateus, G.: A hybrid multi-objective evolutionary approach for improving the performance of wireless sensor networks. IEEE Sens. J. **11**, 545–554 (2011)
26. Zitzler, E., Thiele, L.: Multiobjective evolutionary algorithms: a comparative case study and the strength pareto approach. IEEE Trans. Evol. Comput. **3**, 257–271 (1999)

# EvoCOMPLEX

# Hierarchic Genetic Search with $\alpha$-Stable Mutation

Adam K. Obuchowicz, Maciej Smołka$^{(\boxtimes)}$, and Robert Schaefer

AGH University of Science and Technology,
Al. Mickiewicza 30, 30-059 Kraków, Poland
freem@student.agh.edu.pl, {smolka,schaefer}@agh.edu.pl

**Abstract.** The paper analyzes the performance improvement imposed by the application of $\alpha$-stable probability distributions to the mutation operator of the Hierarchic Genetic Strategy (HGS), in solving ill-conditioned, multimodal global optimization problems in continuous domains. The performed experiments range from standard benchmarks (Rastrigin and multi-peak Gaussian) to an advanced inverse parametric problem of the logging measurement inversion, associated with the oil and gas resource investigation. The obtained results show that the application of $\alpha$-stable mutation can first of all decrease the total computational cost. The second advantage over the HGS with the standard, normal mutation consists in finding much more well-fitted individuals at the highest-accuracy HGS level located in attraction basins of local and global fitness minimizers. It might allow us to find more minimizers by performing local convex searches started from that points. It also delivers more information about the attraction basins of the minimizers, which can be helpful in their stability analysis.

**Keywords:** Multi-deme genetic search · $\alpha$-stable mutation · Hierarchic genetic strategy · Inverse problems

## 1 Motivation

A simplified and general definition of a class of parametric inverse problems for Partial Differential Equations (PDEs) can be formulated as follows.

Find parameter vector $\hat{\omega} \in \mathcal{D} \subset \mathbb{R}^n, n \geq 1$, being a solution to a global optimization problem

$$\arg \min_{\omega \in \mathcal{D}} \{ f(u_o, u(\omega)) : A(u(\omega)) = 0 \}, \tag{1}$$

where $A$ is a *forward problem operator*, $u(\omega) \in U$ is the forward solution corresponding to $\omega$, $u_o \in \mathcal{O}$ is an observation (typically a measured quantity related somehow to the forward solution) and $f(\mathcal{O}, U) \longrightarrow \mathbb{R}_+$ is *a misfit functional*.

The work presented in this paper has been partially supported by Polish National Science Center grants no. DEC-2011/03/B/ST6/01393.

© Springer International Publishing Switzerland 2015
A.M. Mora and G. Squillero (Eds.): EvoApplications 2015, LNCS 9028, pp. 143–154, 2015.
DOI: 10.1007/978-3-319-16549-3_12

Typically, $U$ is a Sobolev space and $A : U \longrightarrow U'$ is a differential operator between $U$ and its conjugate space (see for details *e.g.* [1] and references therein).

Solving inverse parametric problems plays a crucial role in many branches of science and technology, such as the Structural Health Monitoring [2,3], the oil and gas resource investigation [4], the tumor diagnosis [5], etc.

Problems (1) are usually ill-conditioned: unstable (small changes in parameters or observations result in huge misfit variations) or otherwise almost insensitive in some parameters, multimodal with a misfit valleys or plateaus or/and non-smooth in some subdomains. One of possible ways to overcome this obstacles is the misfit regularization (see *e.g.* [6]) typically making the problem smooth, unimodal and globally convex. This approach is often very effective, but its usefulness decreases when the misfit is inherently multimodal (see *e.g.* [7]) and has vast, almost flat regions (plateaus). In such cases the careless regularization may result in locating artifacts instead of true solutions.

Another, more advanced way is to find all "essential" minimizers to (1) and to evaluate roughly their stability. Such results give more information to the experts in the area allowing them to make right further decisions. Among methods of this type you can find stochastic [8] or multi-start [9] ones. Unfortunately, standard approaches of this kind exhibit unacceptable computational cost, mainly because of the high complexity of the forward problem numerical solution necessary for each misfit evaluation. All the above argument is a motivation to look for new, exceptionally economical strategies, skilfully joining the exhaustive exploration of large domains with the detailed investigation of the central parts of local minimizer attraction basins.

Such a combination is a fundamental idea of the *Hierarchic Genetic Strategy* (HGS). The strategy develops dynamically a tree of demes (sub-populations), among which the root deme performs the most broad, superficial search, while the demes located deeper in the tree search more locally and more accurately (see [10,11] for details). The strategy is further extended in $hp$-HGS and $hp$-HMS (see [4,7,12–15] and references therein) which combine hierarchic evolutionary search with the $hp$-adaptive Finite Element Method ($hp$-FEM) [16] for the misfit evaluation. They offer the advantageous, additional computational cost reduction, by the common scaling of $hp$-FEM error according to the accuracy of the inverse search at various branches of the deme tree.

A crucial role in each genetic strategy is played by the mutation operator, that influences greatly the structure of offspring populations. The heart of the operator is a selected probability distribution used to sample new individuals. A common choice for real number encoded individuals is the normal (Gaussian) distribution. However, it has recently been criticized because of its strong non-isotropy (dependence on the coordinate system setting), a pathological behavior near the parental individual (the "wall effect") as well as the lack of flexibility in density configuration in large domains (see e.g. [17]). An advantageous alternative for the normal mutation is the *stable mutation*, which uses various types of stable probability distributions [18] for an offspring sampling. The first study of applying stable distributions in genetic computations was performed by Rudolph [19]. An extended concept of applying $\alpha$-stable distributions, their isotropic and non-isotropic instances and the flexible adaptation to the necessary exploration/exploitation ratio was studied by A. Obuchowicz (see *e.g.* [17,20]).

The authors apply the α-stable distributions in the HGS strategy as the mutation and sprouting operators. We show the additional speedup obtained by the improved mutation at the various levels of the deme tree. Benchmark tests were used to study the influence of α-stable distribution configuration on the HGS performance. A computational example of DC logging measurement inversion by *hp*-HGS shows the impact of the α-stable mutation in solving a real-life engineering inverse problem.

## 2   Hierarchic Genetic Strategy with Adaptive Misfit Evaluation

The Hierarchic Genetic Strategy (HGS) was introduced by Kołodziej and Schaefer in [10]. It produces a tree-structured set of concurrently evolving demes (see Fig. 1). The structure of the tree may be dynamically changed, while its depth is bounded by $m < +\infty$. First, the *root deme* is created which performs a chaotic search with low accuracy. Demes at consecutive levels search with higher and higher accuracy. The maximum, target accuracy is used by leaves. After $K$ genetic epochs (a *metaepoch*), each non-leaf deme selects its best fitted individual and *sprouts* a child-deme in the neighboring region of this individual in the admissible domain $\mathcal{D}$. Sprouting new demes is repeated concurrently after each metaepoch. Two important mechanisms are applied in order to avoid the search redundancy: *conditional sprouting* and *branch reduction*. Roughly saying, they both prevent multiple demes from exploring the same region (see [14] for details).

We use the real-number encoding version of HGS [11], in which a genotype is a vector of floating point numbers. In order to introduce a sequence of increasing genetic spaces for subsequent orders of branches, we use scaling coefficients $+\infty > \eta_1 \geq \eta_2 \geq \ldots \geq \eta_m = 1$, so that the genetic space at $i$-th level is defined as $\prod_{i=1}^{N}[0, \frac{b_i-a_i}{\eta_i}] \subset \mathbb{R}^N$, where $a_i, b_i$; $a_i < b_i$ are the lower and upper bounds for $i$-th decision variable. The genetic space for leaves is of the same size as the admissible domain $\mathcal{D} = \prod_{i=1}^{N}[a_i, b_i] \subset \mathbb{R}^N$ allowing for most accurate search.

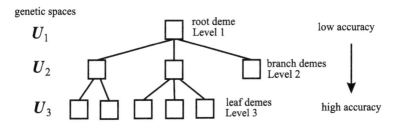

**Fig. 1.** HGS evolutionary population tree

If a search accuracy in leaves equals $\delta_m$, then the accuracy in higher order demes will be reduced to $\delta_j = \eta_j \, \delta_m$, for $j = 1, \ldots, m - 1$.

The evolution in demes (except for the root) is stopped when the search progress in unsatisfactory (mean misfit does not decrease). The whole strategy is stopped when the satisfactory number of well fitted individuals has already been found by HGS leaves.

Asymptotic analysis of HGS was studied in [10]. In particular, the asymptotic guarantee of success was proved as well as the cost decrement ratio with respect to the single population algorithm with the finest encoding, represented in HGS leaves. Analogous features of $hp$-HGS were studied in [21].

## 3   Stable Phenotypic Mutation

A random variable $X$ has stable distribution [22], if it satisfies the following condition:

$$\forall a, b > 0 \quad \exists c > 0 \quad \exists d \in \mathbb{R} \qquad aX_1 + bX_2 \overset{d}{=} cX + d, \tag{2}$$

where $X_1$ and $X_2$ are independent copies of $X$ and $\overset{d}{=}$ means that the random variables on both sides are identically distributed. We will use later a more convenient observation on characteristic functions of stable random variables (see *e.g.* [22]).

$$\varphi(k) = \begin{cases} \exp\left(-\sigma^\alpha |k|^\alpha \left\{1 - i\beta \mathrm{sign}(k) \tan\left(-\frac{\pi\alpha}{2}\right)\right\} + i\mu k\right), & \alpha \neq 1, \\ \exp\left(-\sigma |k| \left\{1 + i\frac{2}{\pi}\beta \mathrm{sign}(k) \ln|k|\right\} + i\mu k\right), & \alpha = 1. \end{cases} \tag{3}$$

Parameter $\alpha \in (0, 2]$, called the *stability index*, defines the distribution concentration and influences the existence of moments in the following way [22]:

$$E(X) < +\infty \text{ for } \alpha > 1 \text{ and } Var(X) = +\infty \text{ for } 0 < \alpha < 2. \tag{4}$$

$\mu \in \mathbb{R}$ is the shift parameter, whereas $\beta$, called the skewness parameter, is a measure of the distribution's asymmetry. We will denote by $S_\alpha(\sigma, \beta, \mu)$ the probability distribution with the characteristic function (3). Unfortunately, the density function of $S_\alpha(\sigma, \beta, \mu)$ is not explicitly given except for three cases: Gaussian ($\alpha = 2, \beta = 0$), Cauchy ($\alpha = 1, \beta = 0$), and Lévy ($\alpha = \frac{1}{2}, \beta = 1$) distributions. Nevertheless, there is a possibility to simulate $\alpha$-stable distribution using algorithms described in e.g. [20].

The mutation operation in floating-point phenotypic Evolutionary Algorithms (EAs) is performed by the addition of a random vector to current attributes of an individual. In order to define the mutation with a stable distribution we may replace the multivariate normally-distributed random vector $\mathcal{N}(\mathbf{0}, \sigma^2 \mathbf{I}_n)$ with the following random vector:

$$\mathbf{X} = [X_i \sim S_\alpha(\sigma, 0, 0) | i = 1, 2, \ldots, n]^T. \tag{5}$$

A big disadvantage of the obtained multivariate distribution is the lack of the spherical symmetry in case $\alpha < 2$ [22]. New individuals prefer directions along axes of Cartesian coordinate system, which is highly undesired. To avoid it, we may use sub-Gaussian stable random vector defined in [22]. In that paper it was also proved that this vector has multivariate isotropic stable distribution

$$\boldsymbol{X} = A^{1/2}\boldsymbol{G} \tag{6}$$

where $A \sim S_{\alpha/2}((cos(\frac{\pi\alpha}{4}))^{2/\alpha}, 1, 0)$ and $\boldsymbol{G} \sim \mathcal{N}(\boldsymbol{0}, \sigma^2\boldsymbol{I}_n)$ are independent.

The lack of moments' existence is of great significance in evolutionary process. If we take into consideration a numerical representation of real numbers, the normal mutation ($\alpha = 2$) has strict boundaries, where the mutated successor may be generated. Obviously this fact imposes a restriction on the explored area. For $\alpha \leq 1$ distribution $S_\alpha(\sigma, 0, 0)$ does not have the expected value. As a consequence one can observe a significant rise in the probability of macro-mutations, i.e. the creation of children far away from parents. This can be a desirable feature, because the exploratory abilities of the strategy become enormous. On the other hand, there is a danger that the algorithm gets too chaotic. In the sequel we shall always take $\mu = \beta = 0$, hence using symmetric stable distribution $S_\alpha(\sigma, 0, 0)$ in the mutation operator.

Let us consider $\lambda$ realizations of the random variable $X$ with probability distribution $S_\alpha(\sigma, 0, 0)$ ordered in the sequence $X_{1:\lambda} < X_{2:\lambda} < \ldots < X_{\lambda:\lambda}$. The following condition is satisfied (see Theorem 2 in [23]):

$$X_{i:\lambda} \quad \text{has } k^{\text{th}} \text{ moment} \Leftrightarrow k - \alpha(\lambda - i + 1) < 0. \tag{7}$$

Condition (7) implies that the random variable $X_{1:\lambda}$ has the expected value if $\lambda > \frac{1}{\alpha}$. It means that the local convergence of an evolutionary algorithm endowed with $\alpha$-stable mutation can be quite effective provided the number of the best parent's descendants is large enough (i.e. greater than $\frac{1}{\alpha}$).

Another problem is that the most probable distance from the mutated point to the its offspring grows with the number of dimensions. This effect known as "dead surrounding" is limited for the isotropic stable mutation with lower $\alpha$ [24].

## 4    Benchmark Tests

First, we have compared the behavior of HGS with the stable mutation for different values of $\alpha$ and $\sigma$. That includes normal mutation cases for $\alpha = 2$. Both performed tests represent typical difficulties (multimodality, large plateaus) appearing in solving inverse parametric problems. In each test the computation was stopped when a given budget was reached. As far, as each fitness call has the same computational cost, we can accept the simplest budget definition as a number of benchmark function evaluations.

We have set the depth of the HGS tree to two levels. Leaves always use normal distribution with $\sigma = 0.1$ to perform mutation. The root applies different stable mutations with all combinations of $\alpha \in \{0.5, 1, 1.5, 2.0\}$ ($\alpha = 2$ means normal

**Table 1.** Parameters of HGS for all benchmark tests

|  | 3 dimensions | 10 dimensions |
|---|---|---|
| Root population | 30 | 100 |
| Leaf population | 6 | 20 |
| Budget (fitness evaluations no.) | 3000 | 10000 |
| Metaepoch length | 2 | 2 |
| Mutation rate | 0.5 | 0.5 |

mutation), and $\sigma \in \{0.4, 0.7, 1.4\}$. The HGS parameters collected in Table 1 were set according to our best experience (see e.g. [7,10–12,25]). In order to highlight the mutation impact we did not use the crossover.

We have compared the best fitness values obtained in tests for the three-dimensional Rastrigin function translated upwards by 1 in domain $[-5,5]^3$, with the global minimum value 1.0. Each test was performed 80 times, and the averages of best fitness found are presented in Table 2. The distributions of best fitness found for $\sigma = 0.4$ are presented in Fig. 2. The distributions for other values of $\sigma$ are similar.

**Table 2.** Average best fitness result in tests on Rastrigin function.

|  | $\sigma = 0.4$ | $\sigma = 0.7$ | $\sigma = 1.4$ |
|---|---|---|---|
| $\alpha = 2.0$ (normal mutation) | 1.179 | 1.225 | 1.254 |
| $\alpha = 1.5$ | 1.178 | 1.204 | 1.236 |
| $\alpha = 1.0$ | 1.197 | 1.220 | 1.250 |
| $\alpha = 0.5$ | 1.213 | 1.191 | 1.214 |

Another desired property of a global optimization search is the exploration ability, which can be measured as a number of global and local minimizers found by the strategy. A series of tests was performed for the following benchmark functions:

1. three-dimensional sum of three Gaussian functions,
2. three-dimensional sum of three Gaussian functions and the Rastrigin function,
3. as above, 10-dimensional case with ten Gaussian functions.

The search domain was set to $[-5,5]^N$. In the second and third benchmark of this group, each Gaussian function has minima much smaller than the Rastrigin component. The tests were executed 80 times for 3-dimensional cases and 40 times for 10-dimensional case. In every run we counted the number of Gaussians' extrema reached by HGS. The average results are presented in Table 3.

Results of both series of tests (see Tables 2 and 3) show that the stable mutation with $\alpha = 1.5$ or 1.0 applied to the HGS root delivers a good compromise between exploration and exploitation performance, and it is slightly better than the normal mutation ($\alpha = 2.0$). Applying stable mutation in HGS leaves does not improve its performance (results of such tests are not presented in this paper).

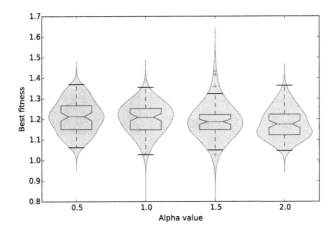

**Fig. 2.** Violin plot of best fitness obtained in Rastrigin test for $\sigma = 0.4$.

# 5  Applying *hp*-HGS with Stable Mutation for DC Logging Measurement Inversion

The hydrocarbon (oil and gas) exploration might be performed by the estimation of subsurface electrical properties. Logging instruments equipped with several transmitter electrodes move along a borehole axis emitting and receiving signals. We consider two types of problems: forward and inverse. The former consists of finding the voltage for a certain position of transmitter and receiver electrodes knowing resistivities of formation layers. A series of forward problems for consecutive positions of electrodes provides a vector of solutions called *logging curve*. The inverse problem consists in searching resistivities of formation layers for a

**Table 3.** Average number of extremes found in benchmark tests: A - sum of three Gaussian functions; B - as A with addition of Rastrigin function; C - as B, 10-dimensional case

| A | | | | B | | | |
|---|---|---|---|---|---|---|---|
| | $\sigma = 0.4$ | $\sigma = 0.7$ | $\sigma = 1.4$ | | $\sigma = 0.4$ | $\sigma = 0.7$ | $\sigma = 1.4$ |
| $\alpha = 2.0$ (normal) | 0.1375 | 0.2625 | 0.325 | $\alpha = 2.0$ (normal) | 0.1375 | 0.2625 | 0.325 |
| $\alpha = 1.5$ | 0.1 | 0.3 | 0.425 | $\alpha = 1.5$ | 0.1 | 0.3 | 0.425 |
| $\alpha = 1.0$ | 0.1375 | 0.3 | 0.4 | $\alpha = 1.0$ | 0.1375 | 0.3 | 0.4 |
| $\alpha = 0.5$ | 0.2 | 0.25 | 0.35 | $\alpha = 0.5$ | 0.2 | 0.25 | 0.35 |

| C | | | |
|---|---|---|---|
| | $\sigma = 0.4$ | $\sigma = 0.7$ | $\sigma = 1.4$ |
| $\alpha = 2.0$ (normal) | 0.65 | 1.8 | 3.075 |
| $\alpha = 1.5$ | 0.9 | 1.475 | 2.425 |
| $\alpha = 1.0$ | 0.95 | 1.2 | 1.825 |
| $\alpha = 0.5$ | 0.575 | 1.1 | 1.375 |

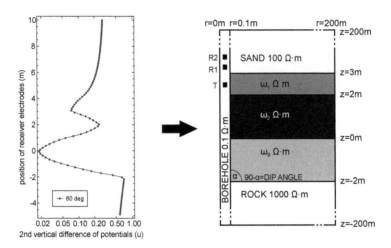

**Fig. 3.** Finding resistivities of formation layers from a given logging curve. T, R1 and R2 are the position of transmitter and two receivers respectively, $z$ - depth of a consecutive layers and $r$ - the radial coordinate.

given reference logging curve. It was formulated as a global optimization problem with the misfit computed as the square of the Euclidean distance between the computed logging curve and the reference one, usually obtained from the measurements. In our case, logging devices operate at very low frequencies (close to zero), which can be modeled as zero-frequency, direct current (DC).

We refer to [14] for details of direct and inverse DC problems, goal oriented $hp$-FEM application and proof of the dependency between the inverse error and the relative $hp$-FEM error, necessary for their economic scaling in the $hp$-HGS strategy.

We have searched for the values of three ground layer resistivities $\omega_0, \omega_1, \omega_2$ belonging to the cube $[0.1, 10^3]^3$ in our case study (see Fig. 3). The reference values are $\omega_0 = 1\ \Omega \cdot m$, $\omega_1 = 5\ \Omega \cdot m$ and $\omega_2 = 20\ \Omega \cdot m$. As in [14], to provide a more thorough search for the parameter values around 1 we transformed the original domain with the following mapping $\mathbb{R}^3 \ni x \longmapsto [\log_{10}(x_i) + 1]_{i=1,2,3} \in \mathbb{R}^3$, which resulted in the cube $[0, 6]^3$.

The parameters of HGS with the normal as well as with the $\alpha$-stable mutation are summarized in Table 4. These are the same values as in [14], except for $\alpha$ and $\sigma$ parameters for stable distribution. For the root population, the mutation with $\alpha = 0.5$ was used, because its heavy tail was supposed to enhance the exploration ability. For the intermediate level $\alpha = 1.5$ was chosen, which provided the best results in the benchmark tests. The leaves are focused on the exploitation, so the normal mutation with a small $\sigma$ was applied.

The HGS with the normal mutation found 5 well-fitted points with the misfit value below 0.1 (see Table 5), while the HGS with $\alpha$-stable mutation performed in the root deme found 16 points of the same quality (see Table 6).

**Table 4.** Parameters of HGS with the normal and stable mutation.

|  | Root | Intermediate level | Leaves |
|---|---|---|---|
| Population size | 12 | 6 | 4 |
| Mutation probability | 0.1 | 0.01 | 0.001 |
| Mutation $\sigma$ | Normal: 1.0, stable: 0.7 | 0.2 | 0.01 |
| Mutation $\alpha$ | Normal: 2.0, stable: 0.5 | Normal: 2.0, stable: 1.5 | 2.0 |
| Crossover probability | 0.5 | 0.5 | 0.5 |
| Crossover mean | 0.5 | 0.5 | 0.5 |
| Crossover std. dev. | 0.01 | 0.01 | 0.01 |
| Sprout std. dev. | 0.1 | 0.01 | |
| Sprout min. distance | 0.5 | 0.2 | |
| Sprout max. value | 2 | 0.5 | |
| Encoding scale ($\eta$) | 16384 | 128 | 1 |
| Ratio | 265 | 13557 | 694136 |

**Table 5.** Results of the HGS with the normal mutation.

|  | $\omega_0$ | $\omega_1$ | $\omega_2$ | $misfit$ |
|---|---|---|---|---|
| Point 1 | 1.436 | 5.081 | 64.404 | 0.0123941038654 |
| Point 2 | 0.955 | 7.895 | 33995.309 | 0.0155211450748 |
| Point 3 | 1.003 | 2.287 | 491.275 | 0.0309955725861 |
| Point 4 | 0.410 | 9.422 | 409.705 | 0.0788856673271 |
| Point 5 | 0.429 | 1.441 | 13317.938 | 0.0998952955352 |

The logging curves corresponding to the seven best found points with misfits below 0.03 are presented in Fig. 4. The curves have been also compared to the exact logging curve, drawn with the shade line.

By analyzing the log files we have estimated computational budget $T_b$ of $hp$-HGS with the normal and the stable mutation. Now fitness evaluation has a different computational cost at each $hp$-HGS level because the variable accuracy, so it is most convenient to define budget as the total serial execution time. For the normal mutation the budget is equal to 6206 min, while for stable mutation it is equal to 4597 min. It is the amount of time spent on solving the DC problem on a single workstation with quad cores, where all the calls of $hp$-FEM were serial, but the $hp$-FEM code itself utilized four cores for each computation. It can be estimated by means of the following formula: $T_b = t_0 * N_0 + t_1 * N_1 + t_2 * N_2$, where $t_0 = 2.2, t_1 = 2.7, t_2 = 10.0$ min are the average times of calling $hp$-FEM with the accuracy of the root, branch and leaf levels respectively, whereas $N_0, N_1, N_2$ are the numbers of such calls.

**Table 6.** Results of the HGS with the stable mutation.

|  | $\omega_0$ | $\omega_1$ | $\omega_2$ | $misfit$ |
|---|---|---|---|---|
| Point 1 | 0.762 | 3.045 | 23.769 | 0.013620991 |
| Point 2 | 0.714 | 6.552 | 34.347 | 0.013657428 |
| Point 3 | 1.118 | 8.149 | 37.615 | 0.016489642 |
| Point 4 | 0.912 | 4.092 | 215.083 | 0.025547867 |
| Point 5 | 0.748 | 4.181 | 715.807 | 0.029160002 |
| Point 6 | 0.624 | 2.360 | 21.728 | 0.032128412 |
| Point 7 | 0.654 | 4.141 | 6374.512 | 0.033704187 |
| Point 8 | 0.584 | 4.796 | 1454.993 | 0.037422516 |
| Point 9 | 1.199 | 5.640 | 14847.693 | 0.04148432 |
| Point 10 | 0.757 | 1.643 | 15.940 | 0.046510098 |
| Point 11 | 0.535 | 2.953 | 3348.759 | 0.0506232 |
| Point 12 | 1.734 | 6.780 | 68.596 | 0.057612481 |
| Point 13 | 1.144 | 2.998 | 3.476 | 0.085280937 |
| Point 14 | 0.788 | 15.403 | 306.036 | 0.09455748 |
| Point 15 | 0.417 | 1.625 | 2219.693 | 0.097377075 |
| Point 16 | 0.508 | 12.401 | 18735.271 | 0.09922374 |

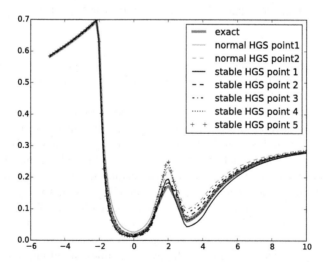

**Fig. 4.** The logging curves corresponding to the best solutions found. The labels of charts correspond to Tables 5 and 6. The bold green curve corresponds to the exact logging curve.

# 6    Conclusions

The selection of a global optimization strategy for solving parametric inverse problems should be performed very carefully, satisfying several contradictory criteria, such as good exploratory skills together with a relatively high accuracy, because of the usual ill conditioning, and the extremely tough economics, because of the huge computational cost of the forward problem computation.

The HGS with the stable mutation with $\alpha < 2$ applied in higher order demes (root demes and branches) significantly improves the exploratory skills of the composite strategy. In particular, the number of well-fitted individuals is more than three times greater in the case of DC logging measurements inversion. Moreover, this result was obtained within a smaller computational budget, about 2/3 of the budget spent in the normal mutation case.

The obtained computational experience makes an advantageous perspective of including the stable mutation in more advanced hierarchic stochastic searches combined with a convex, gradient-based optimization methods, such as the Hierarchic Memetic Search [25, 26].

# References

1. Tarantola, A.: Inverse Problem Theory. Society for Industrial and Applied Mathematics, Mathematics and its Applications. SIAM, Philadelphia (2005)
2. Garibaldi, L., Surace, C., Holford, K., Ostachowicz, W.M.: Damage Assessment of Structures. Trans Tech Publications, Zürich (1999)
3. Burczyński, T., Kuś, W., Długosz, A., Orantek, P.: Optimization and defect identification using distributed evolutionary algorithms. Eng. Appl. Artif. Intell. **17**(4), 337–344 (2004)
4. Barabasz, B., Gajda, E., Pardo, D., Paszyński, M., Schaefer, R., Szeliga, D.: *hp*-HGS twin adaptive strategy for inverse resistivity logging measurements. In: Borkowski, A., Lewiński, T., Dzierżanowski, G. (eds.) Proceedings of the 19th International Conference on Computational Methods in Mechanics CMM 2011, pp. 121–122. Warsaw University of Technology, Warsaw (2011)
5. Paruch, M., Majchrzak, E.: Identification of tumor region parameters using evolutionary algorithms and multiple reciprocity boundary element method. Eng. Appl. Artif. Intell. **20**(5), 647–655 (2007)
6. Engl, H., Hanke, M., Neubauer, A.: Regularization of Inverse Problems, Mathematics and its Applications. Springer, Heidelberg (1996)
7. Barabasz, B., Migórski, S., Schaefer, R., Paszyński, M.: Multi-deme, twin adaptive strategy hp-HGS. Inverse Prob. Sci. Eng. **19**(1), 3–16 (2011)
8. Pardalos, P., Romeijn, H.: Handbook of Global Optimization (Nonconvex Optimization and its Applications). Kluwer, Dordrecht (1995)
9. Marti, R.: Multi-start methods. In: Glover, F., Kochenberger, G. (eds.) Handbook of MetaHeuristics, pp. 355–368. Kluwer, Dordrecht (2003)
10. Schaefer, R.: Genetic search reinforced by the population hierarchy in Foundations of Genetic Algorithms 7, pp. 383–399. Morgan Kaufman, San Francisco (2003)
11. Wierzba, B., Semczuk, A., Kołodziej, J., Schaefer, R.: Hierarchical Genetic Strategy with real number encoding. In: Proceedings of the 6th Conference on Evolutionary Algorithms and Global Optimization, pp. 231–237 (2003)

12. Paszyński, M., Barabasz, B., Schaefer, R.: Efficient adaptive strategy for solving inverse problems. In: Shi, Y., van Albada, G.D., Dongarra, J., Sloot, P.M.A. (eds.) ICCS 2007, Part I. LNCS, vol. 4487, pp. 342–349. Springer, Heidelberg (2007)
13. Paszyński, M., Gajda-Zagórska, E., Schaefer, R., Pardo, D.: *hp*-hgs strategy for inverse ac/dc resistivity logging measurement simulations. Comput. Sci. **14**(4), 629–644 (2013)
14. Gajda-Zagórska, E., Schaefer, R., Smołka, M., Paszyński, M., Pardo, D.: A hybrid method for inversion of 3D DC logging measurements. Natural Computing. (2014). doi:10.1007/s11047-014-9440-y
15. Barabasz, B., Gajda-Zagórska, E., Migórski, S., Paszyński, M., Schaefer, R., Smołka, M.: A hybrid algorithm for solving inverse problems in elasticity. Int. J. Appl. Math. Comput. Sci. **24**(4), 865–886 (2014)
16. Demkowicz, L., Kurtz, J., Pardo, D., Paszyński, M., Rachowicz, W., Zdunek, A.: Computing with hp Finite Elements II. Frontiers: Three-Dimensional Elliptic and Maxwell Problems with Applications. Chapman & Hall/CRC, Boca Raton (2007)
17. Obuchowicz, A.: Multidimensional mutations in evolutionary algorithms based on real-valued representation. Int. J. Syst. Sci. **34**(7), 469–483 (2003)
18. Fang, K., Kotz, S., Ng, K.: Symmetric Multivariate and Related Distributions. Chapman and Hall, London (1990)
19. Rudolph, G.: Local convergence rates of simple evolutionary algorithms with cauchy mutations. IEEE Trans. Evol. Comput. **1**(4), 249–258 (1997)
20. Obuchowicz, A., Prętki, P.: Phenotypic evolution with mutation based on symmetric α-stable distributions. Int. J. Appl. Math. Comput. Sci. **14**(3), 289–316 (2004)
21. Schaefer, R., Barabasz, B.: Asymptotic behavior of hp–adaptive finite element method coupled with the hierarchic genetic strategy) by solving inverse problems. In: Bubak, M., van Albada, G.D., Dongarra, J., Sloot, P.M.A. (eds.) ICCS 2008. LNCS, vol. 5103, pp. 682–691. Springer, Heidelberg (2008)
22. Samorodnitsky, G., Taqqu, M.: Stable Non-Gaussian Random Processes. Chapman and Hall, New York (1994)
23. Obuchowicz, A., Prętki, P.: Isotropic symmetric α-stable mutations. In: IEEE Congress of Evolutionary Computation, pp. 404–410. IEEE Press (2005)
24. Obuchowicz, A.: Multidimensional mutations in evolutionary algorithms based on real-valued representation. Int. J. Syst. Serv. **34**, 469–483 (2003)
25. Smołka, M., Schaefer, R.: A memetic framework for solving difficult inverse problems. In: Esparcia-Alcázar, A.I., Mora, A.M. (eds.) Applications of Evolutionary Computation. LNCS, vol. 8602, pp. 137–148. Springer, Heidelberg (2014)
26. Smołka, M., Schaefer, R., Paszyński, M., Pardo, D., Álvarez-Aramberri, J.: Agent-oriented hierarchic strategy for solving inverse problems. Int. J. Appl. Math. Comput. Sci. (2015, accepted)

# Emergence of Cooperation in the Prisoner's Dilemma Driven by Conformity

Marco Alberto Javarone[1,2]($\boxtimes$), Antonio Emanuele Atzeni[3], and Serge Galam[4]

[1] Department of Mathematics and Computer Science,
University of Cagliari, Cagliari, Italy
[2] Department of Humanities and Social Science, University of Sassari, Sassari, Italy
marcojavarone@gmail.com
[3] Department of Physics, University of Cagliari, Cagliari, Italy
a.toni@hotmail.it
[4] CEVIPOF Centre for Political Research, CNRS and Sciences Po, Paris, France
serge.galam@sciencespo.fr

**Abstract.** We study the relations between strategies in game theory and the conformity. The latter is a behavior deemed relevant in social psychology and, as shown in several works, it strongly influences many social dynamics. We consider a population of agents that evolves in accordance with a payoff matrix which embodies two main strategies: cooperation and defection. In particular, agents play a game (e.g., the Prisoner's Dilemma) by choosing between these two strategies, in order to increase their payoff, i.e., their gain. During the evolution of the system, agents can change strategy according to an update rule, i.e., they can play sometimes as cooperators and sometimes as defectors. Usually, rules to update the strategy are driven by the payoffs of the neighbors of each agent. For instance, an agent imitates its best neighbor, i.e., the one having the highest payoff among the other neighbors. In this context, 'imitation' means to adopt the strategy of another agent. In order to study if and how the emergence of cooperation can be affected by a social influence, we provide agents with two different behaviors, i.e., conformity and nonconformity, they use to select their strategy. Numerical simulations show that conformity strongly affects these dynamics, as cooperation emerges in the population, even under conditions of the games that usually lead, almost all agents, to play as defectors.

**Keywords:** Game theory · Agent-based model · Conformity · Emergent phenomena

## 1 Introduction

Nowadays, the studying of the human behavior is of interest in several fields, as social psychology [1], physics and computer science [2–4]. In particular, the relatively modern field of social dynamics [3] represents the attempt to analyze human and social behaviors by using the framework of the statistical mechanics.

© Springer International Publishing Switzerland 2015
A.M. Mora and G. Squillero (Eds.): EvoApplications 2015, LNCS 9028, pp. 155–163, 2015.
DOI: 10.1007/978-3-319-16549-3_13

In this work, we focus our attention on conformity [1], a behavior deemed relevant in social psychology, in the context of game theory [5–8]. We consider two famous games, i.e., the Prisoner's Dilemma (PD hereinafter) and the Hack-Dove game (HD hereinafter). In particular, we study the evolution of a population of agents, embedded in a two dimensional space, that interact by playing the cited games. In both games, agents follow a strategy, i.e., cooperation or defection, that can be updated (by each agent) during the evolution of the system. Remarkably, in the proposed model, agents update their strategy according to their social behavior, i.e., conformist or nonconformist, in relation to the strategy followed by their neighbors, identified by the Euclidean distance. Previous works, as [9,10], found important relations between the emergence of cooperation [11] and agents' conditions, while they play different games. For instance, authors of [9] showed that a high level of cooperation can be reached when agents can randomly move in the space, when they play the PD. Instead, a defection strategy is followed by the whole population when agents are fixed (i.e., they cannot move). On the other hand, several studies in social dynamics showed that the human behavior can strongly affects dynamical processes in agent populations [4,12–15]. Therefore, we are interested in studying the relation between conformity and the emergence of cooperation in classical game theory. As result, we found that conformity strongly affects the cooperation among agents, in both considered games (i.e., the PD and HD). Notably, when agents select a strategy to play, driven by their behavior, a high level of cooperation can emerge even under conditions of games that usually lead agents to defect. The remainder of the paper is organized as follows: Sect. 2 introduces the proposed model, for investigating the relations between conformity and the emergence cooperation in two games: PD and HD. Section 3 shows results of numerical simulations. Finally, Sect. 4 ends the paper.

## 2   The Model

The proposed model considers a population of interacting agents embedded in a 2D space, i.e., a square of side $L = 1$ where, at the beginning, they are randomly spread with an uniform distribution. Furthermore, agents interact with their neighbors, identified by a distance rule. In particular, the set of neighbors $N_j(t)$ of the $j$th agent is computed by the Euclidean distance, by considering an interaction radius $r$ (equal for all agents). In so doing, all the agents that fall into the circle drawn around the $j$th agent are its neighbors, i.e., $N_j(t) = \{\forall z \in N \mid dist(j, z) < r\}$ with $dist(j, z)$ Euclidean distance between the $j$th agent and the $z$th one. Hence, it is possible to generate an agent network, where each agent is represented by a node and its interactions by edges. The average degree $\bar{k}$ of the agent network depends on the interaction radius $r$, used to define the social circle (i.e., the list of neighbors) of each agent. Notably, considering that $N$ agents are spread in a square of area $L^2 = 1$, we consider their density equal to $\rho = N$ and, since interactions are defined inside circles of area $\pi r^2$, the average degree can be computed as $\bar{k} = \rho \pi r^2$. Therefore, we can refer to this system both by the interaction radius $r$ and by the average degree $\bar{k}$. We focus our attention on two classical games, i.e., the Prisoner's Dilemma and the Hawk-Dove game. These games are described by the following payoff matrix

$$\begin{array}{cc} & \begin{array}{cc} C & D \end{array} \\ \begin{array}{c} C \\ D \end{array} & \begin{pmatrix} 1 & S \\ T & 0 \end{pmatrix} \end{array} \tag{1}$$

The set of strategies is $\Sigma = \{C, D\}$ where $C$ stands for "Cooperator" and $D$ for "Defector". Depending on the strategy chosen by opponent agents, they increase/decrease their payoff according to the cited payoff matrix, with $T$ representing the *Temptation*, i.e., the payoff that an agent gains if it defects while its opponent cooperates, that in turn gets the *Sucker's payoff S*. In accordance with a specific game, the parameters $T$ and $S$ have different values. In particular, the PD is characterized by $T$ and $S$ in the following ranges: $1 \leq T \leq 2$ and $-1 \leq S \leq 0$, whereas the following ranges hold for the HD: $1 \leq T \leq 2$ and $0 \leq S \leq 1$. It is worth to note that both games are played asynchronously, i.e., at every time step only one agent plays against its neighbors. In particular, the main steps of the proposed model are:

1. A randomly chosen agent, say the $j$th, computes the set of its neighbors in accordance with $r$;
2. The $j$th agent plays the game (i.e., the PD or the HD) with all its neighbors (recall that each single challenge involves only two agents at time);
3. All agents playing at this step compute their new payoff;
4. The selected agent updates its strategy according to a revision rule.

In so doing, each agent involved in the game accumulates its payoff according to its strategy (i.e., cooperation or defection) and to the payoff matrix. Let $\sigma_j(t)$ be a vector giving the strategy profile of the $j$th agent at time $t$, with $C = (1, 0)$ and $D = (0, 1)$, and let $M$ be the payoff matrix discussed above. Then, the payoff collected by the player $j$, at time $t$, can be computed as

$$\Pi_j(t) = \sum_{i \in N_j} \sigma_j(t) M \sigma_i^\top(t) \tag{2}$$

In the proposed model, the revision rule is based on the behavior of the considered agent (i.e., conformist or nonconformist). Therefore, the revision phase is performed by each agent without paying attention to its neighbors' payoffs. In so doing, conformist agents adopt the most popular strategy used in their social circle, whereas nonconformist agents do the opposite. Eventually, the considered agent randomly moves to another position inside the square, by performing a step of length $\epsilon$. The latter is constant and also equal for all the agents. Since at each time step one agent moves, the underlying random graph generated by agents' interactions varies over time, hence it can be considered as an adaptive network [16]. Therefore, every time an agent plays the game, it is very likely it faces with new opponents. Mapping strategies (i.e., cooperation and defection) to states (e.g., 0 and 1), the proposed model can be described in terms of opinion dynamics [2,3] where, at each time step, a sequence of strategy profiles (i.e., the agents' states) can be extracted: $\{\sigma_1, \ldots, \sigma_N\}_t$, with $N$ number of agents and $t$ considered time step. Finally, it is worth to note that, during each simulation, only one game is considered.

## 3    Results

We performed many numerical simulations of the proposed model in order to analyze how conformity affects the emergence of cooperation when agents play the PD and the HD. In particular, we study a population with $N = 100$ agents by varying the density of nonconformists $\rho_a$, and by considering two different scenarios: fixed agents $v = 0$ (i.e., agents that do not move) and moving agents $v = 0.01$ (i.e., agents that randomly move as described above). In so doing, the displacement of each agent is computed as $\epsilon = v \cdot \Delta t$; hence considering that the single action lasts for one time step (i.e., $\Delta t = 1$), $\epsilon = v \cdot 1$. The value of $\rho_a$ is in the set $[0.0, 0.25, 0.5, 0.75, 1.0]$, therefore we start with a configuration without nonconformist agents (i.e., $\rho_a = 0.0$) and we increase their amount until there are only nonconformists (i.e., $\rho_a = 1.0$). It is worth to recall that each simulation run, performed with a fixed value of $\rho_a$ and $v$, lasts for 50000 time steps.

### 3.1    Emergence of Cooperation

In order to analyze the evolution of the system, we show the TS-plane related to both games (i.e., PD and HD) — see Figs. 1 and 2. It is interesting to note that, although the PD and the HD are different games under several aspects, for instance the former is usually dominated by defector agents whereas in the latter a full cooperation can emerge for a wide parameters' range $T$ and $S$ (after a number of time step) [9], in the proposed model their evolutions are very similar. In particular, for $v = 0.01$, the cooperation emerges in several areas of the TS-plane in the event there are only conformist agents. Then, increasing $\rho_a$, both

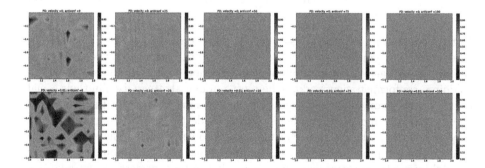

**Fig. 1.** Cooperation frequencies in the TS-plane of the PD game. On the top, results achieved by fixed agents. On the bottom, results achieved by moving agents. From left to right, results related to populations with increasing values of $\rho_a$ (from 0.0 to 1.0).

**Fig. 2.** Cooperation frequencies in the TS-plane of the HD game. On the top, results achieved by fixed agents. On the bottom, results achieved by moving agents. From left to right, results related to populations with increasing values of $\rho_a$ (from 0.0 to 1.0).

defection and cooperation disappear and mixed phases emerge. Mixed phases are characterized by a distribution of strategies almost uniform among agents over time. On the other hand, for $v = 0$, only small areas of high cooperation and high defection are present at $t = 0$; whereas, as $\rho_a$ increases, the evolution of the system is similar to those achieved by $v = 0.01$. As discussed before, the evolution of the system can be viewed also in terms of opinion dynamics, where the agents' strategy is mapped to a state (e.g., $\sigma = \pm 1$ or $\sigma \in [0, 1]$). In so doing, a relevant parameter is the magnetization of the system [17] defined as follows

$$< M >= \frac{|S_0 - S_1|}{N} \tag{3}$$

with $S_0$ and $S_1$ summations of agents having the state 0 and 1, respectively, considering that 0 represents the number of cooperators and 1 that of defectors. Since strategies are equally spread at the beginning of any simulation, at $t = 0$ the value of the magnetization is $< M(0) >\sim 0$; then during the evolution of system also $< M >$ varies over time. The initial scenario represents a disordered

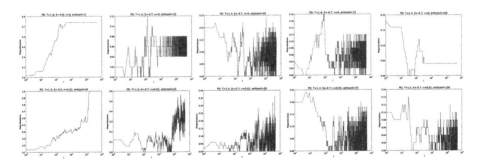

**Fig. 3.** Magnetization of the system, in random points of the TS-plane, as agents play the PD. On the top, results achieved by fixed agents. On the bottom, results achieved by moving agents. From left to right, results related to populations with increasing value of $\rho_a$, from 0.0 to 1.0.

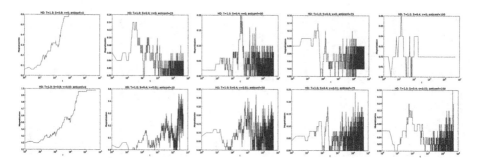

**Fig. 4.** Magnetization of the system, in random points of the TS-plane, when agents play the HD. On the top, results achieved by fixed agents. On the bottom, results achieved by moving agents. From left to right, results related to populations with increasing value of $\rho_a$, from 0.0 to 1.0.

phase of the system, so the evolution toward a full cooperation (or a full defection) corresponds to the evolution toward an ordered phase. Figure 3 illustrates the magnetization of the system when agents play the PD. As expected, it is possible to get $< M(t) > \sim 1$ if $\rho_a = 0$, as the system reaches several points (in the TS-plane) of full cooperation or full defection. Instead, increasing $\rho_a$ the system fluctuates around values far from the ordered phase. Figure 4 shows values of magnetization, in random points of the TS-plane, when agents play the HD. On a quality level, results are identical to those achieved by the PD game. Furthermore, it is interesting to observe that for $\rho_a = 1.0$, in both games when $v = 0$, the system seems to reach a steady-state in a disordered phase. Moreover, under these conditions the magnetization has few fluctuations before reaching its final value. Finally, although we performed 20 simulation runs under the same initial conditions, it is worth to highlight that results, shown in these figures, are related to single runs and not to average values (achieved by considering all simulations). This choice has been done because of the nature of results. In particular, we found that there are no relations between cooperation areas and defection areas with $(T, S)$ values. For instance, when $\rho_a = 0$, in different simulations the amount of cooperation areas is the same, but not their position in the TS-plane. Therefore, by averaging these results, a defection area can be overlapped to one of cooperation, giving as result meaningless interference patterns.

## 3.2   Conformists vs Nonconformists

As agents are provided with a social behavior, that drives the selection of their strategy, it is interesting to evaluate which behavior is more convenient. In particular, we compare the payoffs accumulated by conformist agents with those accumulated by nonconformist ones. Since simulations are performed with different values of $\rho_a$, summations of payoffs gained by the two categories of players are weighted, i.e., they are computed considering the amount of players of each

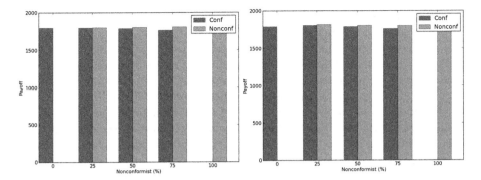

**Fig. 5.** Payoff accumulated by agents playing the PD in function of the density of non-conformist agents. On the left, results achieved by fixed agents. On the right, results achieved by moving agents. As indicated in the legend, blue bars are related to conformist agents, whereas red bars to nonconformist agents (Color figure online).

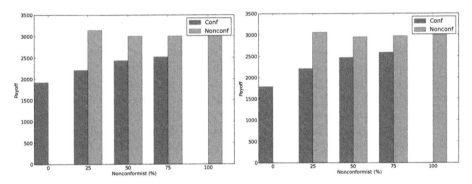

**Fig. 6.** Payoff accumulated by agents playing the HD in function of the density of non-conformist agents. On the left, results achieved by fixed agents. On the right, results achieved by moving agents. As indicated in the legend, blue bars are related to conformist agents, whereas red bars to nonconformist agents (Color figure online).

category. Figures 5 and 6 show results of this comparison in the PD and in the HD, respectively.

It is worth to note that in the PD we found a symmetrical scenario, i.e., playing as a conformist or as a nonconformist does not matter, because both categories of players gain overall the same amount of payoff. On the other hand, in the HD game we found that playing as a nonconformist allows to get higher payoffs. Finally, when comparing the accumulated payoffs between the two categories of agents, their velocity does not matter as results are identical for fixed and moving agents (considering the same game).

## 4    Discussion and Conclusions

In this work, we analyze the evolution of a population composed by agents that play a game, as the PD or the HD, and that are provided with a social behavior.

In particular, agents can be conformists or nonconformists, and their behavior drives the selection of their strategy (i.e., cooperation and defection). Conformity is a behavior deemed relevant in several contexts, spanning from social psychology to opinion dynamics and, in general, to social dynamics. Numerical simulations of the proposed model, performed considering both games (i.e., PD and HD), allow to achieve interesting results. Notably, although the PD and the HD are different games, in the proposed model their evolutions follow very similar paths. Both the TS-planes and the magnetization show the emergence of different phases in the population, i.e., from full cooperation (or full defection) to mixed phases characterized by the coexistence of cooperation and defection (i.e., steady-states). We highlight that, by using fixed agents, it is very difficult to achieve areas (in the TS-plane) of full cooperation, whereas it is more likely by using moving agents. This result has been achieved, by using a different strategy revision phase, by other authors (e.g., [9,10]). Moreover, it is worth to observe that in [18], authors found that cooperation can emerge by using fixed agents embedded in competitive environments. Therefore, we can state that both physical properties of agents (e.g., velocity and interaction radius) and social behaviors [19] are fundamental in these dynamics and can lead to cooperation. Finally, we compared performances achieved by conformists and nonconformists in both games. Remarkably, we did not find differences between the two social behaviors in the PD. On the other hand, in the HD, we observed that conformist agents gain higher payoffs than nonconformist ones. Furthermore, it seems that the agents' velocity does not matter to compare the two social behaviors (in both games). To summarize, we can state that conformity strongly affects the emergence of cooperation in populations playing the PD and the HD. In order to conclude, we deem relevant this result from different perspectives, as social dynamics, game theory and also social psychology. In particular, since games as the PD allow to model real scenarios where conformity may be present (e.g., financial markets and trader systems), further investigations, performed also by mapping other social behaviors, may shade some light to better understand the underlying mechanisms that lead to the achieved results.

# References

1. Aronson, E., Wilson, T.D., Akert, R.M.: Social Psychology. Pearson Ed, Saddle River (2006)
2. Galam, S.: Sociophysics: a review of Galam models. International Journal of Modern Physics C **19-3**, 409–440 (2008)
3. Castellano, C., Fortunato, S., Loreto, V.: Statistical physics of social dynamics. Rev. Mod. Phys. **81-2**, 591–646 (2009)
4. Gracia-Lazaro, C., Cuesta, J.A., Sanchez, A., Moreno, Y.: Human behavior in Prisoner's Dilemma experiments suppresses network reciprocity. Sci. Rep. **2**, 325 (2012)
5. Colman, A.M.: Game Theory and Its Applications Digital Printing (2008)
6. Galam, S., Walliser, B.: Ising model versus normal form game. Phys. A **389**, 481–489 (2010)

7. Pena, J., Volken, H., Pestelacci, E., Tomassini, M.: Conformity hinders the evolution of cooperation on scale-free networks. Phys. Rev. E **80**–1, 016110 (2009)
8. Pena, J., Volken, H., Pestelacci, E., Tomassini, M.: Conformity enhances network 20141299 in evolutionary social dilemmas. J. R. Soc. Interface **12**, 016110 (2015)
9. Antonioni, A., Tomassini, M., Buesser, P.: Random diffusion and cooperation in continuous two-dimensional space. J. Theor. Biol. **344**, 40–48 (2014)
10. Meloni, S., Buscarino, A., Fortuna, L., Frasca, M., Gomez-Gardenes, J., Latora, V., Moreno, Y.: Effects of mobility in a population of prisoner's dilemma players. Phys. Rev. E **79**–6, 067101 (2009)
11. Axelrod, R.: The Evolution of Cooperation. Basic Books, Inc., New York (1984)
12. Sznajd-Weron, K., Sznajd, J.: Opinion evolution in closed community. Int. J. Mod. Phys. C **11**–6, 1157 (2000)
13. Galam, S.: Contrarian deterministic effects on opinion dynamics: "the hung elections scenario". Phys. A: Stat. Mech. Appl. **333**, 453–460 (2004)
14. Javarone, M.A.: Social influences in opinion dynamics: the role of conformity. Phys. A: Stat. Mech. Appl. **414**, 19–30 (2014)
15. Javarone, M.A.: Network strategies in election campaigns. J. Stat. Mech. Theory Exp. **2014**, P08013 (2014)
16. Gross, T., Hiroki, S.: Adaptive Networks: Theory. Models and Applications. Springer, Heidelberg (2009)
17. Mobilia, M., Redner, S.: Majority versus minority dynamics: phase transition in an interacting two-state spin system. Phys. Rev. E **68**–4, 046106 (2003)
18. Javarone, M.A., Atzeni, A.E.: Emergence of cooperation in competitive environments. In: IEEE Computer Society - SITIS 2014 - Complex Networks (2014)
19. Javarone, M.A.: Models and framework for studying social behaviors. PhD Thesis (2013)

# An Experimental Evaluation of Multi-objective Evolutionary Algorithms for Detecting Critical Nodes in Complex Networks

Mario Ventresca[1]($^{\boxtimes}$), Kyle Robert Harrison[2],
and Beatrice M. Ombuki-Berman[2]

[1] School of Industrial Engineering, Purdue University, West Lafayette, IN, USA
mventresca@purdue.edu
[2] Department of Computer Science, Brock University,
St. Catharines, ON, Canada
{kh08uh,bombuki}@brocku.ca

**Abstract.** Identifying critical nodes in complex networks has become an important task across a variety of application domains. In this paper we propose a multi-objective version of the critical node detection problem, which aims to minimize pairwise connectivity in a graph by removing a subset of $K$ nodes. Interestingly, while it has been recognized that this problem is inherently multi-objective since it was formulated, until now only single-objective algorithms have been proposed. After explicitly stating the new multi-objective problem variant, we then give a brief comparison of six common multi-objective evolutionary algorithms using sixteen common benchmark problem instances. A comparison of the results attained by viewing the algorithm as a single versus multi-objective problem is also conducted. We find that of the examined algorithms, NSGAII generally produces the most desirable approximation fronts. We also demonstrate that while related, the best multi-objective solutions do not translate into the best single-objective solutions.

## 1 Introduction

The problem of identifying critical nodes in a network has recently attracted a significant amount of research attention. These critical nodes may be used to promote or mitigate a diffusive process spreading on the network, or to identify critical junctions through which the process spreads. A number of different definitions of a *critical node* have been proposed due to the variety of application domains where discovering such nodes is important. For instance, to define junctions in cell-signaling or protein-protein networks [6], to identify highly influential individuals [18], to determine smart grid vulnerability [23], to discover key points in brain functionality [17], and to determine individuals to target for vaccination or quarantine when mitigating disease spread [5,27,30].

In this paper we focus on the Critical Node Detection Problem (CNDP), as described in [4], where it was also proven to be $\mathcal{NP}$-hard. Given a network $G = (V, E)$ of $|V| = n$ nodes/vertices and $|E| = m$ links/edges, the goal of

© Springer International Publishing Switzerland 2015
A.M. Mora and G. Squillero (Eds.): EvoApplications 2015, LNCS 9028, pp. 164–176, 2015.
DOI: 10.1007/978-3-319-16549-3_14

the problem is to minimize pairwise connectivity in $G$ by removing no more than $K$ nodes. Several variants of the CNDP have been investigated. In [14], an integer linear programming model with a non-polynomial number of constraints is given and branch-and-cut algorithms are proposed. The particular case where $G$ is a tree structure was shown to be $\mathcal{NP}$-complete for non-unit edge costs [11]. A polynomial-time dynamic programming algorithm with worst-case complexity $\mathcal{O}(n^3 K^2)$ for solving the unit edge cost problem in graphs was proposed in [2]. Recently, s reformulation of the CNDP was proposed in [31,32] in order to reduce the number of constraints from $\Theta(n^3)$ to $\Theta(n^2)$. Approximation algorithms based on $\beta$-edge disruptors were given in [12,13] along with an alternative proof for the $\mathcal{NP}$-hardness of the CNDP. Bicriteria randomized rounding approaches based on an LP-relaxation have been proposed in [28,30]. Simulated annealing and population-based incremental learning algorithms without approximation bounds were given in [26]. A fast greedy algorithm has been recently presented for approximating solutions for large scale networks [29]. All of the aforementioned algorithms considered the CNDP as a single-objective problem.

The CNDP is also related to a variety of graph partitioning problems in the literature. For example, the minimum multi-cut problem [16], the $k$-cut problem [24], classical multi-way cut and multi-cut as well as $k$-cut problems [15], in addition to the sparsest cut problem [3]. Some problems having the most in common with the CNDP are the minimum contamination problem [21] and the sum-of-squares partitioning problem [5,7].

## 1.1 Our Contributions

In this work we propose a multi-objective approach to the critical node detection problem that we term the MOCNDP, and we provide experimental results that use a variety of standard evolutionary algorithms. Given the space limitations we are only able to show a subset of the results and limited analysis. Our contributions are more explicitly stated as:

1. *Propose MOCNDP:* Pairwise connectivity is composed of two separate objectives; maximizing the total number of connected components and minimizing the variance in the cardinality (number of nodes) among the connected components, after removing $K$ vertices from the original graph. Although it has been recognized since [4] that the goal of the CNDP is inherently multi-objective, to date there has not been any study that considers the multi-objectivity of the problem.
2. *Experimental comparison:* Six common multi-objective evolutionary algorithms are employed in order to discover solutions to the MOCNDP. We compare the ability of these algorithms to arrive at quality solutions against a set of benchmark CNDP problem instances described in [26].
3. *CNDP versus MOCNDP:* A solution to the MOCNDP will explicitly indicate the number of connected components and variance in their cardinality. It is then straightforward to calculate the corresponding objective evaluation for

the CNDP. We compare these results to determine the relationship between MOCNDP solutions and their CNDP counterparts.

The remainder of this paper is organized as follows. Section 2 describes the CNDP and the multi-objectivity of the problem, proposing the MOCNDP. In Sect. 3 the experimental setup and results are shown. Given space limitations only a subset of the results are indicated. Conclusions are giving in Sect. 4.

## 2    The Critical Node Detection Problem

The CNDP is an $\mathcal{NP}$-hard optimization problem, formulated in [4]. Given a network/graph $G = (V, E)$ of $|V| = n$ nodes and $|E| = m$ links, the goal of the CNDP is to remove $K$ nodes from $G$ such that the residual network $G \setminus R$ has minimum pairwise connectivity. Here, $R \subset V$ is a set of $K$ vertices, to be determined through the optimization process. The objective is thus to minimize:

$$\sum_{i=1}^{|D|} \binom{|C_i|}{2} \tag{1}$$

where $D$ is the set of connected components in $G \setminus R$ and $|D|$ is its cardinality. $C_i \in D$ is the $i^{th}$ component in $D$ and $|C_i|$ is the number of vertices it contains.

### 2.1    The Multi-objective CNDP

Since the introduction of the CNDP it has been recognized that (1) actually implies a multi-objective problem, as shown in [13]:

$$\sum_{i=1}^{|D|} \binom{|C_i|}{2} = \frac{1}{2} \left( \sum_{i=1}^{|D|} |C_i|^2 - |V| \right) = \frac{1}{2} \left( \frac{n^2}{|D|} - n \right) - \frac{1}{2} var(D) \tag{2}$$

where $var(D) = \sum_{i=1}^{|D|} \left( |C_i| - \frac{n}{|D|} \right)^2$ is the variance of the cardinality of the connected components. We identify this as being the basis for an alternative formulation. Notice that the single-objective formulation can be viewed as a weighted multi-objective problem. We propose to remove the weight factors and instead aim to maximize $|D|$ and minimize $var(D)$. Since $|V| = n$ is known, calculating (1) from a solution to the MOCNDP is straightforward.

## 3    Experimental Setup and Results

We evaluate a number of standard multi-objective evolutionary algorithms for the MOCNDP using standard benchmark problems from [26]. The experimental results highlight the performance of each algorithm in comparison to a random search, which is used as a control for the experiment. In addition, the MOCNDP solutions are evaluated using the traditional, single objective CNDP function to assess the relationship between the two formulations. We first provide an outline of the experimental setup and parameters.

**Table 1.** The sixteen benchmark problems and associated maximum $K$-critical nodes.

| Name | Vertices | Edges | $K$ | Name | Vertices | Edges | $K$ |
|------|----------|-------|-----|------|----------|-------|-----|
| ER_234 | 234 | 349 | 50 | BA_500 | 500 | 499 | 50 |
| ER_465 | 465 | 699 | 80 | BA_1000 | 1000 | 999 | 75 |
| ER_940 | 940 | 1399 | 140 | BA_2500 | 2500 | 2499 | 100 |
| ER_2343 | 2343 | 3499 | 200 | BA_5000 | 5000 | 4999 | 150 |
| WS_50 | 250 | 1249 | 70 | FF_250 | 250 | 400 | 13 |
| WS_500 | 500 | 1499 | 125 | FF_500 | 500 | 792 | 25 |
| WS_1000 | 1000 | 4999 | 200 | FF_1000 | 1000 | 1633 | 50 |
| WS_1500 | 1500 | 4499 | 265 | FF_2500 | 2500 | 4046 | 125 |

### 3.1 Setup

Here we describe the algorithms, their parameterization and the benchmark problem instances. All results were obtained using the MOEA 2.1 Java library [1], and ran on a Linux Mint Debian Edition operating system with an Intel i7-4930K 3.4 GHz CPU and 64 GB of RAM. Experiments were run for 20 trials.

**MO Algorithms:** We compare results attained by the MOCHC [22], PAES [19], eNSGAII [20], eMOEA [9], NSGAII [10], and PESA2 [8] algorithms. As a control, we also implement a random search. We use a bit string representation that indicates whether a particular node is present in a solution or not. The population size is equal to the size of the largest component in the benchmark instance and the mutation rate is inversely proportional to this size, both of which are common in the literature. Each algorithm is run to 3000 times the size of the largest network component. All algorithms utilize the HUX half uniform crossover and other default settings in the MOEA Framework.

**Data:** We utilize the benchmark data proposed in [26], and highlighted in Table 1. This data set contains sixteen undirected, unweighted networks created using common complex network generator algorithms: Barabasi-Albert, Watts-Strogatz, Forest Fire, and the Erdos-Renyi random graph. The first three of these models generate networks with a single component whereas the random graph algorithm may contain a number of connected components. Further information about the network structures can be found in [26].

### 3.2 Algorithm Performance

Our comparison is from two perspectives: (1) the quality of solutions with respect to the two objectives, and (2) the algorithms' ability to approximate the Pareto front. Concerning the latter perspective, the additive epsilon indicator [33], hypervolume [34], and spacing [25] measures are considered as they provide both an indication of the quality (i.e., proximity to the true front) and spread of solutions in the approximation front. The additive epsilon and hypervolume indicators are Pareto-compliant while the spacing measure is non-compliant.

**Additive Epsilon Indicator (AE):** is the minimum $\epsilon$ such that for every solution in the approximation front, there exists a solution in the reference front that is no more than $\epsilon$ better in all objectives.

**Hypervolume (H):** measures the volume of objective space dominated by an approximation front.

**Spacing (S):** quantifies the distribution of solutions in the approximation front.

We rank the algorithms performance using the following procedure. First, a Kruskal-Wallis test is performed to determine whether a performance difference exists between the algorithms. If so, then pairwise Mann-Whitney U-tests are conducted in order to determine where the differences occur and tabulate a "win" accordingly, based on a comparison of medians. Finally, a rank is assigned to each algorithm based on the difference in number of wins and losses. All statistical tests are performed at the 95 % confidence level. Due to space limitations, only summary results are given.

### 3.3    Final Solution Quality

In this section we compare the final results obtained for each objective by the six algorithms. Due to limited space a thorough examination is not possible, but we report the mean ($\mu$) and standard deviation ($\sigma$) of the results after 20 trials. Thus we report the expected behavior. Table 2 highlights these summary results, where bold entries denote the highest ranked objective values using the aforementioned statistical analysis procedure.

We observe that the NSGAII and eNSGAII algorithms produce solutions with the largest number of components, in general. Interestingly, while not particularly effective when considering any other measures, the MOCHC algorithm does produce solutions with the largest number of components on the ER_235, ER_465, and FF_500 problems. Another interesting result is that the PAES algorithm, while demonstrated to have the best hypervolume and additive epsilon values for the ER_465 and ER_940 problem, does not attain the highest number of components on these problems, nor any other of the problems.

Unlike the number of components, the variance objective was far more problem dependent. For the Barabasi-Albert problems, either NSGAII or eMOEA attain the smallest variance among component sizes. We see on the ER problems that PAES has the smallest variance among all algorithms. However, it does demonstrate a higher standard deviation on these problems. No real trend is observed for the Forest fire problems. We also note that on the Watts-Strogatz problems, the variance is unreliable and a number of invalid results were present.

### 3.4    Pareto Front Approximation

Tables 3, 4 and 5 show the results of the ranking procedure for the Barabasi-Albert, Erdos-Renyi, and Forest Fire networks. In most cases NSGAII attains the best values for the hypervolume and additive epsilon measures, but shows

**Table 2.** Summary results of the mean ($\mu$) and standard deviation ($\sigma$) for the two MOCNDP objectives across the benchmark instances.

| Problem | Algorithm | Components | | Variance | | Problem | Algorithm | Components | | Variance | |
|---|---|---|---|---|---|---|---|---|---|---|---|
| | | $\mu$ | $\sigma$ | $\mu$ | $\sigma$ | | | $\mu$ | $\sigma$ | $\mu$ | $\sigma$ |
| BA_500 | eMOEA | **312.6** | 0.5 | 0.62 | 0.00 | FF_250 | eMOEA | 88.3 | 2.1 | 1.86 | 0.18 |
| | eNSGAII | **312.9** | 0.3 | 0.62 | 0.01 | | eNSGAII | 89.0 | 2.1 | 1.77 | 0.18 |
| | MOCHC | 291.7 | 9.9 | 1.16 | 0.31 | | MOCHC | 88.1 | 2.4 | 1.82 | 0.20 |
| | NSGAII | **312.7** | 0.4 | **0.62** | 0.00 | | NSGAII | **89.4** | 1.8 | **1.72** | 0.16 |
| | PAES | 311.2 | 1.6 | 0.65 | 0.03 | | PAES | 87.9 | 2.7 | 1.77 | 0.20 |
| | PESA2 | 311.9 | 1.1 | 0.63 | 0.01 | | PESA2 | 88.5 | 2.2 | 1.75 | 0.18 |
| | Random | 239.5 | 4.6 | 4.66 | 0.89 | | Random | 46.7 | 7.2 | 454.93 | 2401.21 |
| BA_1000 | eMOEA | 589.9 | 0.3 | 1.01 | 0.00 | FF_500 | eMOEA | 210.3 | 2.1 | 0.97 | 0.04 |
| | eNSGAII | **590.0** | 0.0 | 1.01 | 0.00 | | eNSGAII | 209.9 | 2.5 | 0.94 | 0.04 |
| | MOCHC | 563.5 | 14.5 | 1.46 | 0.29 | | MOCHC | **211.0** | 2.4 | 0.96 | 0.05 |
| | NSGAII | 589.9 | 0.3 | **1.01** | 0.00 | | NSGAII | 209.7 | 3.1 | **0.93** | 0.03 |
| | PAES | 588.6 | 1.4 | 1.03 | 0.02 | | PAES | 208.1 | 2.7 | 0.95 | 0.05 |
| | PESA2 | 589.5 | 0.9 | 1.02 | 0.01 | | PESA2 | 208.1 | 3.1 | 0.95 | 0.04 |
| | Random | 413.1 | 9.8 | 12.79 | 3.55 | | Random | 122.7 | 5.2 | 47.44 | 33.09 |
| BA_2500 | eMOEA | **1119.0** | 5.7 | 4.39 | 0.15 | FF_1000 | eMOEA | 318.5 | 5.1 | **4.03** | 0.23 |
| | eNSGAII | **1119.9** | 5.6 | 4.39 | 0.16 | | eNSGAII | 321.0 | 5.2 | 4.17 | 0.33 |
| | MOCHC | 1105.6 | 11.4 | 4.76 | 0.36 | | MOCHC | 301.8 | 5.9 | 6.73 | 0.79 |
| | NSGAII | 1117.0 | 7.4 | **4.34** | 0.16 | | NSGAII | **326.9** | 7.0 | 4.55 | 0.85 |
| | PAES | 1106.2 | 6.2 | 4.70 | 0.21 | | PAES | 319.3 | 5.6 | 4.16 | 0.39 |
| | PESA2 | 1117.2 | 4.4 | 4.39 | 0.10 | | PESA2 | 319.3 | 4.8 | **4.03** | 0.26 |
| | Random | 623.8 | 16.6 | 91.69 | 16.10 | | Random | 143.2 | 6.7 | 1474.97 | 254.84 |
| BA_5000 | eMOEA | 1973.3 | 7.7 | **7.17** | 0.17 | FF_2500 | eMOEA | 476.4 | 5.6 | 10.52 | 0.73 |
| | eNSGAII | 1976.4 | 8.6 | 7.23 | 0.23 | | eNSGAII | 477.7 | 5.6 | 10.56 | 0.67 |
| | MOCHC | 1855.3 | 13.0 | 10.95 | 0.55 | | MOCHC | 385.0 | 8.4 | 45.16 | 6.10 |
| | NSGAII | **1978.5** | 11.5 | 7.36 | 0.46 | | NSGAII | **486.7** | 5.4 | 12.43 | 1.70 |
| | PAES | 1939.6 | 10.5 | 8.11 | 0.35 | | PAES | 473.7 | 7.0 | 10.62 | 0.89 |
| | PESA2 | 1971.5 | 5.3 | 7.40 | 0.14 | | PESA2 | 476.5 | 5.6 | **10.47** | 0.70 |
| | Random | 900.2 | 21.8 | 414.01 | 80.90 | | Random | 187.2 | 13.3 | 7078.06 | 963.17 |
| ER_234 | eMOEA | 61.2 | 2.3 | 12.01 | 13.48 | WS_250 | eMOEA | **7.2** | 1.4 | 3823.42 | 815.45 |
| | eNSGAII | 61.5 | 2.5 | 10.49 | 9.83 | | eNSGAII | 2.4 | 0.5 | 13087.30 | 2474.35 |
| | MOCHC | **62.5** | 2.7 | 16.23 | 12.67 | | MOCHC | **6.5** | 1.3 | 4460.09 | 1382.36 |
| | NSGAII | 62.2 | 2.9 | 15.28 | 13.89 | | NSGAII | 4.6 | 1.9 | 7551.23 | 3460.25 |
| | PAES | 59.5 | 2.4 | **5.11** | 1.88 | | PAES | 1.0 | 0.0 | NA | NA |
| | PESA2 | 60.5 | 2.1 | 10.12 | 12.61 | | PESA2 | 1.0 | 0.1 | NA | NA |
| | Random | 35.6 | 2.2 | 430.18 | 37.34 | | Random | 3.0 | 0.0 | 10416.60 | 64.48 |
| ER_465 | eMOEA | 101.1 | 3.2 | 304.82 | 34.84 | WS_500 | eMOEA | **41.5** | 2.5 | 1854.82 | 198.39 |
| | eNSGAII | 97.8 | 4.3 | 274.04 | 41.81 | | eNSGAII | 17.9 | 3.6 | 5967.07 | 1820.51 |
| | MOCHC | **102.1** | 3.6 | 286.56 | 33.43 | | MOCHC | 27.1 | 2.2 | 3777.43 | 379.39 |
| | NSGAII | 101.5 | 4.3 | 296.30 | 35.75 | | NSGAII | **42.4** | 2.1 | 1869.55 | 137.73 |
| | PAES | 90.2 | 5.9 | **215.90** | 78.52 | | PAES | 10.0 | 3.0 | 13226.46 | 4836.73 |
| | PESA2 | 95.2 | 4.5 | 250.48 | 59.13 | | PESA2 | 12.6 | 4.0 | 10696.66 | 5168.13 |
| | Random | 48.4 | 1.4 | 2009.30 | 83.49 | | Random | 7.1 | 0.3 | 17999.61 | 733.81 |

(Continued)

**Table 2.** (*Continued*)

| ER_940 | eMOEA | 190.5 | 3.4 | 1062.37 | 56.88 | WS_1000 | eMOEA | **4.6** | 1.4 | 149116.31 | 45420.14 |
|---|---|---|---|---|---|---|---|---|---|---|---|
| | eNSGAII | 184.5 | 3.8 | 1058.93 | 86.21 | | eNSGAII | 1.2 | 0.5 | NA | NA |
| | MOCHC | 179.6 | 2.2 | 1486.77 | 46.17 | | MOCHC | 3.4 | 1.0 | 204464.44 | 58524.47 |
| | NSGAII | **192.8** | 4.9 | 1011.98 | 52.69 | | NSGAII | **4.7** | 1.5 | 150344.05 | 54543.17 |
| | PAES | 183.2 | 6.3 | **961.36** | 127.76 | | PAES | 1.0 | 0.0 | NA | NA |
| | PESA2 | 182.3 | 4.3 | 1083.48 | 83.21 | | PESA2 | 1.0 | 0.0 | NA | NA |
| | Random | 86.1 | 1.6 | 5273.81 | 108.28 | | Random | 3.0 | 0.2 | 216277.22 | 21435.87 |
| ER_2343 | eMOEA | 319.3 | 3.2 | 8688.32 | 84.79 | WS_1500 | eMOEA | **32.2** | 2.7 | 41583.12 | 3863.97 |
| | eNSGAII | 297.2 | 4.1 | 9310.48 | 180.92 | | eNSGAII | 11.3 | 4.2 | 144741.13 | 58000.05 |
| | MOCHC | 276.5 | 1.8 | 11606.18 | 97.17 | | MOCHC | 15.0 | 1.7 | 95784.40 | 11325.50 |
| | NSGAII | **322.1** | 1.6 | **8626.23** | 48.92 | | NSGAII | **30.6** | 2.6 | 44283.78 | 3951.78 |
| | PAES | 298.0 | 4.6 | 9284.30 | 164.06 | | PAES | 1.9 | 2.6 | NA | NA |
| | PESA2 | 294.8 | 4.8 | 9488.07 | 242.53 | | PESA2 | 7.0 | 2.8 | 274558.48 | 187676.18 |
| | Random | 110.6 | 1.5 | 35930.06 | 575.20 | | Random | 6.5 | 0.7 | 226824.92 | 20049.19 |

**Table 3.** Ranking of algorithms on the Barabasi-Albert benchmark problems.

| Problem | Measure | Result | eMOEA | eNSGAII | MOCHC | NSGAII | PAES | PESA2 | Random |
|---|---|---|---|---|---|---|---|---|---|
| BA_500 | AE | Diff | 5 | 2 | −4 | 5 | −2 | 0 | −6 |
| | | Rank | 1 | 3 | 6 | 1 | 5 | 4 | 7 |
| | H | Diff | 0 | 0 | 0 | 0 | 0 | 0 | 0 |
| | | Rank | 1 | 1 | 1 | 1 | 1 | 1 | 1 |
| | S | Diff | 0 | 0 | −5 | 0 | 1 | 0 | 4 |
| | | Rank | 3 | 3 | 7 | 3 | 2 | 3 | 1 |
| BA_2500 | AE | Diff | 2 | 4 | −2 | 6 | −4 | 0 | −6 |
| | | Rank | 3 | 2 | 5 | 1 | 6 | 4 | 7 |
| | H | Diff | 2 | 5 | −3 | 5 | −3 | 0 | −6 |
| | | Rank | 3 | 1 | 5 | 1 | 5 | 4 | 7 |
| | S | Diff | 3 | 2 | −4 | 1 | −4 | 2 | 0 |
| | | Rank | 1 | 2 | 6 | 4 | 6 | 2 | 5 |

significantly poorer results for the spacing measure. That is, the performance of NSGAII versus the other techniques does not seem to be highly influenced by the network topology, or if so, all approaches are similarly influenced such that their relative performance remains. Comparison on two of the Barabasi-Albert networks and the Watts-Strogatz was not possible as the algorithms arrived at degenerate solutions. A more comprehensive analysis would consider different search operators and may alleviate this issue.

## 3.5   Correspondence Between Single and Multi-objective Solutions

In this section we evaluate the MOCNDP solutions using the single-objective formulation given by (1) in order to examine whether it may be fruitful to instead solve the MO formulation. Tables 6, 7, 8 and 9 present a summary of the results obtained for each of the benchmark problems. The mean ($\mu$), standard deviation ($\sigma$), minimum, and maximum values obtained by each algorithm are reported. Bold entries indicate algorithms which are assigned a rank of 1 using

**Table 4.** Ranking of algorithms on the Erdos-Renyi benchmark problems.

| Problem | Measure | Result | eMOEA | eNSGAII | MOCHC | NSGAII | PAES | PESA2 | Random |
|---------|---------|--------|-------|---------|-------|--------|------|-------|--------|
| ER_234 | AE | Diff | 0 | 3 | 4 | 4 | −3 | −2 | −6 |
| | | Rank | 4 | 3 | 1 | 1 | 6 | 5 | 7 |
| | H | Diff | 1 | 3 | 2 | 3 | −2 | −1 | −6 |
| | | Rank | 4 | 1 | 3 | 1 | 6 | 5 | 7 |
| | S | Diff | −1 | −1 | −1 | −2 | 4 | 1 | 0 |
| | | Rank | 4 | 4 | 4 | 7 | 1 | 2 | 3 |
| ER_465 | AE | Diff | −3 | 1 | 1 | 0 | 6 | 1 | −6 |
| | | Rank | 6 | 2 | 2 | 5 | 1 | 2 | 7 |
| | H | Diff | −1 | 1 | 2 | 0 | 3 | 1 | −6 |
| | | Rank | 6 | 3 | 2 | 5 | 1 | 3 | 7 |
| | S | Diff | 1 | 1 | −4 | 1 | −4 | −1 | 6 |
| | | Rank | 2 | 2 | 6 | 2 | 6 | 5 | 1 |
| ER_940 | AE | Diff | 1 | 1 | −4 | 2 | 5 | 1 | −6 |
| | | Rank | 3 | 3 | 6 | 2 | 1 | 3 | 7 |
| | H | Diff | 1 | −1 | −2 | 2 | 5 | −1 | −4 |
| | | Rank | 3 | 4 | 6 | 2 | 1 | 4 | 7 |
| | S | Diff | 0 | 0 | −1 | 0 | −5 | 0 | 6 |
| | | Rank | 2 | 2 | 6 | 2 | 7 | 2 | 1 |
| ER_2343 | AE | Diff | 4 | 1 | −4 | 6 | 1 | −2 | −6 |
| | | Rank | 2 | 3 | 6 | 1 | 3 | 5 | 7 |
| | H | Diff | 0 | 0 | 0 | 0 | 0 | 0 | 0 |
| | | Rank | 1 | 1 | 1 | 1 | 1 | 1 | 1 |
| | S | Diff | −3 | −1 | 1 | −1 | 0 | 1 | 3 |
| | | Rank | 7 | 5 | 2 | 5 | 4 | 2 | 1 |

the ranking procedure outlined in Sect. 3.2. These results demonstrate that the best MOCNDP solutions do not necessarily translate into best CNDP solutions.

For three of the four problems shown in Table 6 (BA_500, BA_1000, and BA_2500), the eNSGAII optimizer attains the lowest objective value. Along with eNSGAII and eMOEA, the highest rank for BA_500 is shared with the NSGAII algorithm. On the BA_5000 benchmark, the NSGAII performs best when considering the single-objective evaluation. In Table 7 we see that the PAES algorithm obtains the best CNDP scores, which is contradictory to the front analysis shown above, although PAES did yield a high ranking for the spacing objective.

When examining the single-objective results for the Forest Fire problems in Table 8, the NSGAII algorithm attains the best values for the 250 and 500 vertex instances, whereas the PESA2 algorithm shows the best single-objective values on the 1000 and 2000 vertex networks. Furthermore, the NSGAII algorithm ranks 5th on the larger two networks, 1000 and 2500 vertices, respectively, when the single-objective evaluation is considered, in contrast to having the best hypervolume and additive epsilon indicators on the same networks.

Table 9 presents the single-objective results when we consider the Watts-Strogatz benchmark problems. In general, we see that the eMOEA and NSGAII algorithms attain the lowest CNDP values. Interestingly, the WS_250 problem is the first, and only, benchmark in which MOCHC attains the best value when

**Table 5.** Ranking of algorithms on the Forest Fire benchmark problems.

| Problem | Measure | Result | eMOEA | eNSGAII | MOCHC | NSGAII | PAES | PESA2 | Random |
|---|---|---|---|---|---|---|---|---|---|
| FF_250 | AE | Diff | −1 | 2 | 0 | 4 | 0 | 1 | −6 |
| | | Rank | 6 | 2 | 4 | 1 | 4 | 3 | 7 |
| | H | Diff | −1 | 2 | 0 | 4 | 0 | 1 | −6 |
| | | Rank | 6 | 2 | 4 | 1 | 4 | 3 | 7 |
| | S | Diff | 0 | 0 | 0 | 0 | 0 | 0 | 0 |
| | | Rank | 1 | 1 | 1 | 1 | 1 | 1 | 1 |
| FF_500 | AE | Diff | −1 | 1 | 1 | 2 | 2 | 1 | −6 |
| | | Rank | 6 | 3 | 3 | 1 | 1 | 3 | 7 |
| | H | Diff | 0 | 1 | 1 | 2 | 1 | 1 | −6 |
| | | Rank | 6 | 2 | 2 | 1 | 2 | 2 | 7 |
| | S | Diff | 1 | 2 | −4 | 1 | −1 | 1 | 0 |
| | | Rank | 2 | 1 | 7 | 2 | 6 | 2 | 5 |
| FF_1000 | AE | Diff | 0 | 4 | −4 | 6 | 0 | 0 | −6 |
| | | Rank | 3 | 2 | 6 | 1 | 3 | 3 | 7 |
| | H | Diff | 0 | 4 | −4 | 6 | 0 | 0 | −6 |
| | | Rank | 3 | 2 | 6 | 1 | 3 | 3 | 7 |
| | S | Diff | 6 | 3 | −4 | −1 | −1 | 3 | −6 |
| | | Rank | 1 | 2 | 6 | 4 | 4 | 2 | 7 |
| FF_2500 | AE | Diff | 0 | 4 | −4 | 6 | 0 | 0 | −6 |
| | | Rank | 3 | 2 | 6 | 1 | 3 | 3 | 7 |
| | H | Diff | 1 | 2 | −5 | 6 | 0 | 1 | −5 |
| | | Rank | 3 | 2 | 6 | 1 | 5 | 3 | 6 |
| | S | Diff | 4 | 4 | −4 | −2 | 1 | 3 | −6 |
| | | Rank | 1 | 1 | 6 | 5 | 4 | 3 | 7 |

**Table 6.** Single-objective evaluation on the Barabasi-Albert benchmark instances.

| Algorithm | Problem | $\mu$ | $\sigma$ | Min | Max | Problem | $\mu$ | $\sigma$ | Min | Max |
|---|---|---|---|---|---|---|---|---|---|---|
| eMOEA | BA_500 | **312.6** | 0.5 | 312 | 313 | BA_2500 | **1119.0** | 5.7 | 1106 | 1129 |
| eNSGAII | | **312.9** | 0.3 | 312 | 313 | | **1119.9** | 5.6 | 1107 | 1129 |
| MOCHC | | 291.7 | 9.9 | 266 | 310 | | 1105.6 | 11.4 | 1070 | 1125 |
| NSGAII | | **312.7** | 0.4 | 312 | 313 | | 1117.0 | 7.4 | 1100 | 1129 |
| PAES | | 311.2 | 1.6 | 307 | 313 | | 1106.2 | 6.2 | 1087 | 1116 |
| PESA2 | | 311.9 | 1.1 | 309 | 313 | | 1117.2 | 4.4 | 1107 | 1128 |
| Random | | 239.5 | 4.6 | 230 | 248 | | 623.8 | 16.6 | 589 | 663 |
| eMOEA | BA_1000 | 589.9 | 0.3 | 589 | 590 | BA_5000 | 1973.3 | 7.7 | 1955 | 1989 |
| eNSGAII | | **590.0** | 0.0 | 590 | 590 | | 1976.4 | 8.6 | 1956 | 1992 |
| MOCHC | | 563.5 | 14.5 | 526 | 588 | | 1855.3 | 13.0 | 1818 | 1888 |
| NSGAII | | 589.9 | 0.3 | 589 | 590 | | **1978.5** | 11.5 | 1950 | 1999 |
| PAES | | 588.6 | 1.4 | 585 | 590 | | 1939.6 | 10.5 | 1905 | 1961 |
| PESA2 | | 589.5 | 0.9 | 586 | 590 | | 1971.5 | 5.3 | 1961 | 1984 |
| Random | | 413.1 | 9.8 | 390 | 435 | | 900.2 | 21.8 | 828 | 940 |

**Table 7.** Single-objective evaluation of solutions on the Erdos-Renyi instances.

| Algorithm | Problem | $\mu$ | $\sigma$ | Min | Max | Problem | $\mu$ | $\sigma$ | Min | Max |
|---|---|---|---|---|---|---|---|---|---|---|
| eMOEA | ER_234 | 650.2 | 427.5 | 405.5 | 2554.5 | ER_940 | 102315.2 | 4903.5 | 90915.5 | 112706.5 |
| eNSGAII | | 604.8 | 314.0 | 407.5 | 2291.5 | | 98881.1 | 8022.9 | 78863.5 | 117486.5 |
| MOCHC | | 784.7 | 410.9 | 429.5 | 1972.5 | | 134542.0 | 4943 7 | 125390.5 | 147126.5 |
| NSGAII | | 759.0 | 449.2 | 416.5 | 2231.5 | | 98770.8 | 6198.5 | 84469.5 | 113173.5 |
| PAES | | **438.3** | 55.1 | 400.5 | 940.5 | | **89427.0** | 12359.3 | 55505.5 | 116061.5 |
| PESA2 | | 590.4 | 391.0 | 401.5 | 2485.5 | | 99869.7 | 6582.4 | 88035.5 | 114152.5 |
| Random | | 7940.8 | 939.5 | 5981.5 | 10251.5 | | 228097.4 | 4062.3 | 219959.5 | 236072.5 |
| eMOEA | ER_468 | 16021.3 | 1977.1 | 11874 | 21249 | ER_2343 | 1389886.4 | 8443.7 | 1366721 | 1408267 |
| eNSGAII | | 14077.6 | 2380.8 | 9189 | 19456 | | 1386085.4 | 12809.8 | 1365073 | 1421740 |
| MOCHC | | 15253.7 | 2058.8 | 11876 | 22043 | | 1607117.5 | 10634.0 | 1584503 | 1638286 |
| NSGAII | | 15675.9 | 2277.1 | 10948 | 20825 | | 1391997.3 | 8117.4 | 1373322 | 1414975 |
| PAES | | **10649.1** | 4019.5 | 2950 | 20451 | | **1385986.0** | 11844.5 | 1363452 | 1418058 |
| PESA2 | | 12633.0 | 3004.3 | 6050 | 19112 | | 1401148.6 | 18253.3 | 1373333 | 1448817 |
| Random | | 49153.7 | 2246.3 | 45125 | 53508 | | 1988461.0 | 9923.2 | 1966310 | 2004116 |

**Table 8.** Single-objective evaluation on the Forest Fire benchmark instances.

| Algorithm | Problem | $\mu$ | $\sigma$ | Min | Max | Problem | $\mu$ | $\sigma$ | Min | Max |
|---|---|---|---|---|---|---|---|---|---|---|
| eMOEA | FF_250 | 308.0 | 7.2 | 294 | 325 | FF_1000 | **1774.1** | 33.6 | 1715 | 1894 |
| eNSGAII | | 302.9 | 6.7 | 294 | 321 | | 1793.8 | 48.5 | 1730 | 2098 |
| MOCHC | | 306.4 | 7.9 | 294 | 332 | | 2210.4 | 117.0 | 2031 | 2616 |
| NSGAII | | **300.0** | 4.9 | 294 | 311 | | 1849.8 | 135.4 | 1726 | 2377 |
| PAES | | 304.8 | 6.9 | 294 | 329 | | 1795.1 | 55.6 | 1711 | 2040 |
| PESA2 | | 302.8 | 6.4 | 294 | 321 | | **1774.1** | 36.2 | 1722 | 1961 |
| Random | | 4258.3 | 2333.0 | 1961 | 19604 | | 108002.7 | 21678.8 | 67482 | 166401 |
| eMOEA | FF_500 | 463.1 | 4.6 | 456 | 475 | FF_2500 | 5902.9 | 167.2 | 5645 | 6625 |
| eNSGAII | | 460.3 | 4.5 | 454 | 473 | | 5910.2 | 155.0 | 5676 | 6498 |
| MOCHC | | 461.2 | 4.1 | 455 | 475 | | 12893.7 | 1242.1 | 11163 | 19853 |
| NSGAII | | **459.8** | 3.6 | 452 | 470 | | 6350.0 | 413.9 | 5908 | 8425 |
| PAES | | 463.6 | 3.9 | 456 | 488 | | 5933.6 | 201.5 | 5662 | 7014 |
| PESA2 | | 464.2 | 4.5 | 455 | 473 | | **5891.1** | 160.1 | 5677 | 6645 |
| Random | | 3541.5 | 2111.9 | 1762 | 15960 | | 671881.6 | 123927.9 | 388336 | 895126 |

**Table 9.** Single-objective evaluation on the Watts-Strogatz benchmark instances.

| Algorithm | Problem | $\mu$ | $\sigma$ | Min | Max | Problem | $\mu$ | $\sigma$ | Min | Max |
|---|---|---|---|---|---|---|---|---|---|---|
| eMOEA | WS_250 | **13828.3** | 674.0 | 12089 | 14801 | WS_1000 | 315821.2 | 1624.9 | 313639 | 318403 |
| eNSGAII | | 16085.9 | 372.4 | 13497 | 16200 | | 319674.8 | 918.9 | 313664 | 320000 |
| MOCHC | | **14282.2** | 717.0 | 12543 | 15144 | | 316894.5 | 1644.9 | 312068 | 318403 |
| NSGAII | | 14582.8 | 1075.5 | 12209 | 15844 | | **315465.1** | 1873.9 | 312061 | 318403 |
| PAES | | 16200.0 | 0.0 | 16200 | 16200 | | 320000.0 | 0.0 | 320000 | 320000 |
| PESA2 | | 16198.2 | 33.0 | 15496 | 16200 | | 319999.6 | 18.3 | 319201 | 320000 |
| Random | | 15574.8 | 310.1 | 14661 | 15843 | | 317927.4 | 1100.1 | 313664 | 318403 |
| eMOEA | WS_500 | **39331.8** | 2895.0 | 32760.5 | 43915.5 | WS_1500 | **667698.1** | 12365.6 | 638709.5 | 686894.5 |
| eNSGAII | | 52097.1 | 4971.9 | 40270.5 | 61656.5 | | 710435.9 | 26741.9 | 654885.5 | 745438.5 |
| MOCHC | | 50202.4 | 2486.8 | 45565.5 | 54502.5 | | 710629.5 | 7702.1 | 695167.5 | 723662.5 |
| NSGAII | | **40709.4** | 2009.9 | 36725.5 | 43616.5 | | **676522.5** | 10401.4 | 652410.5 | 691581.5 |
| PAES | | 60377.6 | 4551.8 | 50404.5 | 68093.5 | | 758684.1 | 11017.4 | 710535.5 | 762612.5 |
| PESA2 | | 59109.0 | 4898.5 | 50798.5 | 66262.5 | | 738978.5 | 15037.5 | 712951.5 | 761378.5 |
| Random | | 64590.3 | 1516.4 | 60969.5 | 66984.5 | | 735761.5 | 11250.3 | 711901.5 | 752771.5 |

evaluated against the single objective. Another interesting observation is that the WS_250, WS_1000, and WS_2500 problems were the only 3 benchmarks in which the random sampling approach was not the worst performing algorithm, rather it attains ranks of 4, 4, and 5 on these problems, respectively. Due to degenerate multi-objective solutions, we cannot compare the single-objective results from the Watts-Strogatz problems to the multi-objective results.

## 4  Conclusions

In this paper we proposed a multi-objective critical node detection problem (MOCNDP). While it had been recognized previously that the critical node detection problem (CNDP) is inherently multi-objective, this is the first study which considered the problem using a multi-objective approach. The goals of the MOCNDP are to maximize the number of connected components and minimize the variance of their cardinalities. We compared the results using six common multi-objective evolutionary algorithms from three viewpoints: (1) on the attained values of the objectives, (2) on the ability to approximate the Pareto front, and (3) to determine the relationship between MOCNDP solutions and their CNDP counterparts. Three well-known multi-objective measures were used to analyze the quality of the MOCNDP solutions from the Pareto front perspective. This comparison demonstrated that the best solutions to the MOCNDP did not necessarily translate to the best solutions to the CNDP. This implies that high quality solutions are more difficult to obtain for the MOCNDP.

The multi-objective evolutionary optimizers were tested on a suite of recently proposed benchmark problems, representing a variety of different network properties and sizes. The results indicated that the NSGAII algorithm typically outperformed the other approaches when considering the hypervolume and additive epsilon measures. However, when the single-objective evaluation of the multi-objective solutions was considered, the best performance was more problem dependent and thus not directly related. Due to limited space, a more detailed comparison was not possible, including to results obtained in literature.

Future work includes expanding the number and types of networks, especially to incorporate real-world complex networks. To provide a more comprehensive analysis different search operators should also be considered, in addition to a larger set of multi-objective algorithms. Moreover, the multi-objective approach considered here removed the weighting on objectives that is directly implied by the single-objective CNDP formulation.

## References

1. MOEA Framework, version 2.1 (2014). http://www.moeaframework.org
2. Addis, B., Di Summa, M., Grosso, A.: Identifying critical nodes in undirected graphs: complexity results and polynomial algorithms for the case of bounded treewidth. Discret. Appl.Math. **161**(16–17), 2349–2360 (2013)

3. Arora, S., Rao, S., Vazirani, U.: Expander flows, geometric embeddings and graph partitioning. In: Proceedings of the 36th Annual ACM Symposium on Theory of Computing, pp. 222–231 (2004)
4. Arulselvan, A., Commander, C.W., Elefteriadou, L., Pardalos, P.M.: Detecting critical nodes in sparse graphs. Comput. Oper. Res. **36**(7), 2193–2200 (2009)
5. Aspnes, J., Chang, K., Yampolskiy, A.: Inoculation strategies for victims of viruses and the sum-of-squares partition problem. In: Proceedings of the 16th Annual ACM-SIAM Symposium on Discrete Algorithms, SODA 2005. Society for Industrial and Applied Mathematics, pp. 43–52 (2005)
6. Boginski, V., Commander, C.: Identifying critical nodes in protein-protein interaction networks. In: Benson, M. (ed.) Clustering Challenges in Biological Networks, pp. 153–166. Springer, Berlin (2009)
7. Chen, P., David, M., Kempe, D.: Better vaccination strategies for better people. In: Proceedings of the 11th ACM Conference on Electronic Commerce, pp. 179–188. ACM (2010)
8. Corne, D., Jerram, N., Knowles, J., Oates, M.: PESA-II: region-based selection in evolutionary multiobjective optimization. In: Proceedings of the Genetic and Evolutionary Computation Conference (2001)
9. Deb, K., Mohan, M., Mishra, S.: A fast multi-objective evolutionary algorithm for finding well-spread pareto-optimal solutions. Technical report, IIT-Kanpur (2003)
10. Deb, K., Pratap, A., Agarwal, S., Meyarivan, T.: A fast and elitist multiobjective genetic algorithm: NSGA-II. IEEE Trans. Evol. Comput. **6**(2), 182–197 (2002)
11. Di Summa, M., Grosso, A., Locatelli, M.: Complexity of the critical node problem over trees. Comput. Oper. Res. **38**(12), 1766–1774 (2011)
12. Dinh, T.N., Xuan, Y., Thai, M.T., Pardalos, P.M., Znati, T.: On new approaches of assessing network vulnerability: hardness and approximation. IEEE/ACM Trans. Netw. **20**(2), 609–619 (2012)
13. Dinh, T.N., Xuan, Y., Thai, M.T., Park, E.K., Znati, T.: On approximation of new optimization methods for assessing network vulnerability. In: INFOCOM, pp. 2678–2686 (2010)
14. DiSumma, M., Grosso, A., Locatelli, M.: Branch and cut algorithms for detecting critical nodes in undirected graphs. Comput. Optim. Appl. **53**(3), 649–680 (2012)
15. Engelberg, R., Könemann, J., Leonardi, S., (Seffi) Naor, J.: Cut problems in graphs with a budget constraint. In: Correa, J.R., Hevia, A., Kiwi, M. (eds.) LATIN 2006. LNCS, vol. 3887, pp. 435–446. Springer, Heidelberg (2006)
16. Garg, N., Vazirani, V., Yannakakis, M.: Primal-dual approximation algorithms for integral flow and multicut in trees. Algorithmica **18**, 3–20 (1997)
17. Joyce, K.E., Laurienti, P.J., Burdette, J.H., Hayasaka, S.: A new measure of centrality for brain networks. PLoS ONE **5**(8), e12200 (2010)
18. Kempe, D., Kleinberg, J., Tardos, E.: Maximizing the spread of influence in a social network. In: Proceedings of the 9th International Conference on Knowledge Discovery and Data Mining, pp. 137–146 (2003)
19. Knowles, J., Corne, D.: The pareto archived evolution strategy: a new baseline algorithm for pareto multiobjective optimisation. In: Proceedings of the 1999 Congress on Evolutionary Computation, vol. 1, pp. 98–105 (1999)
20. Kollat, J., Reed, P.: Comparing state-of-the-art evolutionary multi-objective algorithms for long-term groundwater monitoring design. Adv. Water Resour. **29**(6), 792–807 (2006)

21. Kumar, V.S.A., Rajaraman, R., Sun, Z., Sundaram, R.: Existence theorems and approximation algorithms for generalized network security games. In: Proceedings of the 2010 IEEE 30th International Conference on Distributed Computing Systems, pp. 348–357 (2010)

22. Nebro, A., Alba, E., Molina, G., Chicano, F., Luna, F., Durillo, J.: Optimal antenna placement using a new multi-objective CHC algorithm. In: 9th Annual Conference on Genetic and Evolutionary Computation, pp. 876–883 (2007)

23. Nguyen, D., Shen, Y., Thai, M.: Detecting critical nodes in interdependent power networks for vulnerability assessment. IEEE Trans. Smart Grid 4(1), 151–159 (2013)

24. Saran, H., Vazirani, V.: Finding k-cuts within twice the optimal. SIAM J. Comput. 24, 101–108 (1995)

25. Schott, J.: Fault tolerant design using single and multicriteria genetic algorithm optimization. Master's thesis, Massachusetts Institute of Technology (1995)

26. Ventresca, M.: Global search algorithms using a combinatorial unranking-based problem representation for the critical node detection problem. Comput. Oper. Res. 39(11), 2763–2775 (2012)

27. Ventresca, M., Aleman, D.: Evaluation of strategies to mitigate contagion spread using social network characteristics. Soc. Netw. 35(1), 75–88 (2013)

28. Ventresca, M., Aleman, D.: A derandomized approximation algorithm for the critical node detection problem. Comput. Oper. Res. 43, 261–270 (2014)

29. Ventresca, M., Aleman, D.: a fast greedy algorithm for the critical node detection problem. In: Zhang, Z., Wu, L., Xu, W., Du, D.-Z. (eds.) COCOA 2014. LNCS, vol. 8881, pp. 603–612. Springer, Heidelberg (2014)

30. Ventresca, M., Aleman, D.: A randomized algorithm with local search for containment of pandemic disease spread. Comput. Oper. Res. 48, 11–19 (2014)

31. Veremyev, A., Boginski, V., Pasiliao, E.L.: Exact identification of critical nodes in sparse networks via new compact formulations. Optim. Lett. 8(4), 1245–1259 (2014)

32. Veremyev, A., Prokopyev, O.A., Pasiliao, E.L.: An integer programming framework for critical elements detection in graphs. J. Comb. Optim. 28(1), 233–273 (2014)

33. Zitzler, E., Thiele, L., Laumanns, M., Fonseca, C., Da Fonseca, V.: Performance assessment of multiobjective optimizers: an analysis and review. IEEE Trans. Evol. Comput. 7(2), 117–132 (2003)

34. Zitzler, E., Thiele, L.: Multiobjective optimization using evolutionary algorithms - a comparative case study. In: Eiben, A.E., Bäck, T., Schoenauer, M., Schwefel, H.-P. (eds.) PPSN 1998. LNCS, vol. 1498, pp. 292–301. Springer, Heidelberg (1998)

# Self-Balancing Multimemetic Algorithms in Dynamic Scale-Free Networks

Rafael Nogueras and Carlos Cotta[✉]

Dept. Lenguajes y Ciencias de la Computación, Universidad de Málaga, ETSI Informática, Campus de Teatinos, 29071 Málaga, Spain
ccottap@lcc.uma.es

**Abstract.** We study the behavior and performance of island-based multimemetic algorithms, namely memetic algorithms which explicitly represent and evolve memes alongside solutions, in unstable computational environments whose topology is modeled as scale-free networks, a pattern of connectivity observed in real-world networks, such as peer-to-peer systems. We consider the utilization of self-balancing strategies in order to efficiently adjust population sizes to cope with the phenomenon of churn, as well as the dynamic re-wiring of connections in order to deal with connectivity losses caused by node failures. A broad experimental evaluation on different problems and computational scenarios featuring diverse volatility conditions shows that the combination of these two strategies leads to more robust performances, in particular in situations in which churn rates are large.

## 1 Introduction

The use of parallel and distributed models of population-based optimization algorithms is a well-known approach for improving the quality of the solutions obtained and for reducing the computational time required to obtain them [1]. While such parallel approaches have been known and in use since the late 80s, e.g., [6,20], it is only much more recently that the use of emerging computational environments such as peer-to-peer (P2P) networks [14] and volunteer computing networks [18] is being considered. These new computing platforms offer vast possibilities in terms of pervasiveness and computational power but also bring new challenges and difficulties: they are inherently dynamic systems whose resources are potentially enormous in a collective sense but are very volatile on an individual basis. As a consequence, algorithms running on these platforms must be fault tolerant and resilient to *churn* (a term coined to denote the collective effect of a plethora of peers entering or leaving the system independently along time).

Focusing on island-based metaheuristics deployed on this kind of unstable computational environments, it has been shown that churn can lead to the loss of the current incumbent solution [8] and will in general negatively affect the progress of the search. In order to cope with this, some fault-aware policy must be implemented, either for taking corrective measures (e.g., using redundant computation or restoration checkpoints) or for preventive purposes (having the

A.M. Mora and G. Squillero (Eds.): EvoApplications 2015, LNCS 9028, pp. 177–188, 2015.
DOI: 10.1007/978-3-319-16549-3_15

algorithm self-adapt on the fly to the presence of churn). The latter is the subject of this work, due to its intrinsic decentralized and emergent nature, better suited to computational scenarios lacking a global control center. More precisely, we consider the use of self-balancing strategies aimed to dynamically resize the population of islands, exchanging individuals among them to account for node failures or reactivations – see Sect. 2.2. These are applied to an island-based model of multimemetic algorithms (MMAs) [11], namely memetic algorithms that explicitly manipulate memes controlling the functioning of local search as a part of solutions [15,17]. We use a simulated computational environment that allows experimenting with different scenarios featuring diverse resource volatility as described in Sect. 2.1. One of the factors whose importance is being assessed here is the effect of dynamic rewiring of connections, that is, the on-line change of links among islands so as to keep rich connectivity patterns. This is described in Sect. 2.3. A broad empirical evaluation is used for this purpose in Sect. 3. We close the paper with conclusions and an outline of future work in Sect. 4.

## 2    Materials and Methods

### 2.1    Algorithmic Setting

As stated before, we consider the deployment of an island-based multimemetic algorithm on an unstable computational environment. We have $n_\iota$ panmictic islands, each of them running a multimemetic algorithm in which memes are attached to individuals and evolve alongside them. These memes are represented as pattern-based rewriting rules $A \to B$ following the model by Smith [19]. Therein $A, B$ are variable-length strings taken from $\Sigma \cup \{\#\}$, where $\Sigma$ is the same alphabet used to encode solutions and $\#$ represents a wildcard. The action of the meme is finding an occurrence of pattern $A$ in the solution and changing it by pattern $B$ if it leads to a fitness improvement (otherwise the solution is left unchanged). Memes are subject to mutation and are transferred from parent to offspring via local selection (offspring inherit the meme of the best parent). The use of memes aside, the MMA resembles a steady-state evolutionary algorithm using tournament selection, one-point crossover, bit-flip mutation, and replacement of the worst parent.

These islands are assumed to work in parallel, and are interconnected according to a certain topology $\mathcal{N}$. Migration is performed asynchronously: at the beginning of each cycle the island checks if migrants have been received from any neighboring nodes. If this is the case, they are accepted into the population according to the specific migrant replacement policy chosen. Later, at the end of each cycle, migration is stochastically performed much like the remaining evolutionary operators. If done, migrants are selected using a certain migrant selection policy and sent to neighboring islands. Following previous analysis of migration strategies in island-based MMAs [16], we use random selection of migrants and deterministic replacement of the worst individuals in the receiving island.

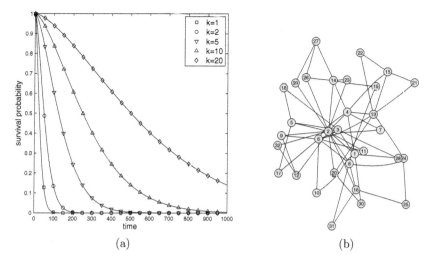

**Fig. 1.** (a) Failure probabilities under a Weibull distribution with the parameters used in Sect. 3. (b) Example of scale-free network generated with Barabási-Albert model ($n_\iota = 32$, $m = 2$).

This island-based model runs on a simulated distributed system composed of $n_\iota$ nodes. More precisely, these nodes are all initially available but can eventually abandon the system, only to reappear later, much like it is the case of P2P networks or volunteer computing platforms. In order to model the dynamics of the system, we consider that failures/recoveries are Weibull distributed. This distribution is commonly used in survival analysis and also fits computing environments such as, e.g., P2P networks – see [12]. In mathematical terms, the distribution is described by a shape parameter $\eta$ and a scale parameter $\beta$. The probability of a node being available up to time $t$ is $p(t, \eta, \beta) = \exp(-(t/\beta)^\eta)$. If the shape parameter is larger than 1 –as we set in the experiments, see Sect. 3– failure probabilities increase with time (i.e., the longer a node has been active the more likely it will go down and vice versa, the longer a node has been out of the system the more likely it will enter it again) – see Fig. 1a.

## 2.2 Self-Balancing Strategy

The volatility of computational resources implies that in the absence of any strategy to deal with the phenomenon of churn, the overall population size will fluctuate with the subsequent impact on genetic/memetic diversity. To cope with this, balancing strategies are required. These strategies must be decentralized, that is, decision making and information exchange has to be done locally among neighboring islands, since the underlying infrastructure is assumed to have no central control [13]. We consider here a variation of a direct-neighbor policy [22] based on the qualitative exchange of information among islands.

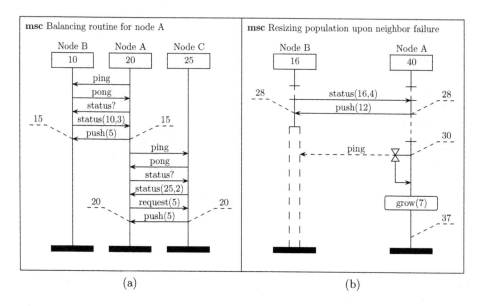

(a)                                    (b)

**Fig. 2.** (a) Standard balancing protocol. Node A communicates with its two neighbors and tries to balance its population with them. (b) Population resizing upon neighbor failure. Node A attempts to balance with node B and realizes it has gone down upon timeout of the ping message. Then it enlarges its own population using the information it gathered from B in their last exchange (i.e., by 7 = 28/4 in this case).

The basic balancing protocol is illustrated in the message sequence charts in Fig. 2a. This protocol is run by each island prior to entering each iteration of the main evolutionary cycle. Therein, a certain node A (whose population size is assumed to be $\mu_0$) communicates with its neighbors, pinging them to check they are active and if so, requesting information on their population size $\mu_i$ and number of active neighbors $\#n_i$. On the basis of this information (which is also stored in a local memory for later use) the population is enlarged or contracted in order to achieve local balance (that is, the mid-point between $\mu_i$ and $\mu_0$). This is done by transferring a certain number of individuals (selected at random from the corresponding population) from the larger peer to the smaller one to reach a local equilibrium (eventually attaining global equilibrium as well after a number of iterations [3]). In case some neighbor is detected to have just become inactive (i.e., it was active in the previous balancing attempt but not in the current one), the island enlarges its own population to compensate the loss of the neighboring island, as illustrated in Fig. 2b: using the information gathered in the last successful communication with the now-inactive island on its number of active neighbors $\#n_i$ and its last observed population size $\mu_i$, the node assumes the population lost is quantitatively distributed among these neighbors. Hence it increases its population (using random immigrants [7], that is, generating new random solutions and inserting them in the population) by the corresponding fraction $\mu_i/\#n_i$. Of course, it is possible that simultaneous

| **Algorithm 1.** Barabási-Albert Model |
|---|
| **function** BA-Model ($\downarrow m, n : \mathbb{N}$) : Network |
| // *net*: the network created |
| // *n*: number of nodes |
| // *m*: number of links for each node |
| $m_0 \leftarrow \min(n, m)$; |
| $net \leftarrow \text{CREATECLIQUE}(m_0)$; |
| $\delta[1 \ldots m_0] \leftarrow m_0$; |
| **for** $i \leftarrow m_0 + 1$ **to** $n$ **do** |
| $\quad net \leftarrow \text{ADDNODE}(net)$; |
| $\quad$ **for** $j \leftarrow 1$ **to** $m$ **do** |
| $\quad\quad k \leftarrow \text{PICK}(\delta)$ // Sampling w/o replacement proportional to $\delta$ |
| $\quad\quad \delta[k] \leftarrow \delta[k] + 1$; |
| $\quad\quad net \leftarrow \text{ADDLINK}(net, i, k)$; |
| $\quad$ **end** |
| $\quad \delta[i] \leftarrow m$; |
| **end** |
| **return** *net* |

failures of neighboring islands lead to the loss of a fraction of their populations. We have purposefully not dealt with this possibility for two reasons: on one hand, it is not a likely event in low-churn scenarios; on the other hand, its occurrence in high-churn scenarios can provide interesting information on the inherent resilience of these techniques/strategies. Finally, it must be also noted that the reciprocal situation of a failure, namely a node going up again is treated in pretty much the same way as in Fig. 2a, i.e., a standard balancing attempt in which one of the intervening parts has an empty population. Eventually, it may be the case that this process in not successful (because the reactivated island has no active neighbors or because these cannot donate a part of their populations if, e.g., they are empty as well). In this case the node resorts to self-reinitializing using a fixed population size $C_1$.

## 2.3 Network Topology and Dynamic Rewiring

The interconnection network is assumed to be scale-free, a complex topology commonly observed in many natural phenomena (and also in computational processes, such as P2P networks) in which node degrees exhibit a power-law distribution. To generate this kind of topology we use the Barabási-Albert (BA) model [2]: nodes are added one at a time, and linked to $m$ (a parameter) existing nodes. The attachment procedure is driven by preferential attachment, i.e., each new node is connected to $m$ existing nodes, selected with a probability proportional to their current degree. This is described in Algorithm 1.

An example of the application of this model is shown in Fig. 1b for $n = 32$ and $m = 2$. As can be seen, preferential attachment causes the network to feature a few nodes with many connections and increasingly more nodes with fewer

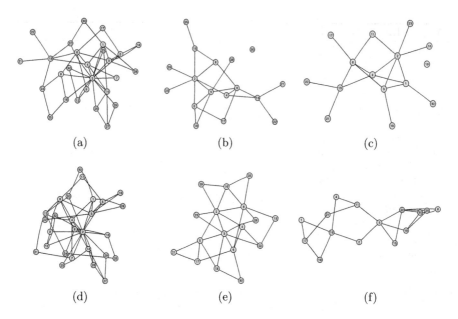

**Fig. 3.** Comparison of the evolution of the volatile network in Fig. 2b without rewiring (a)–(c) and with rewiring (d)–(f). These are three snapshots of the network state at $t = 100, 250, 500$ using $n_\iota = 32$ islands and volatility parameter $k = 10$ (see Sect. 3).

connections following the well-known scale-free pattern of connectivity. Notice now how the system evolves when node failures begin to take place (Fig. 3, upper row): the network becomes more sparse and even disconnected, exhibiting isolated nodes and pendant nodes. This can impair the functioning of the algorithm in different ways: firstly, it severely limits the flow of information via migration among islands, something essential in the island model; secondly, it disrupts the functioning of balancing algorithms resulting not just in quantitative losses of individuals but also in more frequent island reinitializations from scratch (due to the additional burden on effective balancing), hindering the progress of the search.

To alleviate these problems we consider the use of re-wiring strategies. These strategies proceed as follows: (1) neighbors determined to be inactive during the balancing stage are forgotten, and (2) whenever an island detects that its number of active neighbors has fallen below a predefined threshold (in our case, the value of parameter $m$ in the BA model used to create the network), it looks for additional neighbors to reach this minimum level. While this can be done in a purely decentralized way using the triad formation algorithm [9] or the newscast protocol [10], we have consider in this work a simpler alternative based on the use of the BA model. This serves as a proof of concept on the usefulness of the approach and paves the way for using eventually other rewiring approaches. The lower row of Fig. 3 shows the sate of the network in the very same scenario of activation/deactivation illustrated in the upper row when rewiring is used. Notice how the network maintains a rich connectivity and node isolation is avoided.

## 3    Experimental Analysis

We consider $n_\iota = 32$ islands whose initial size is $\mu = 16$ individuals and a total number of evaluations $maxevals = 50000$. Meme lengths evolve within $l_{min} = 3$ and $l_{max} = 9$, mutating their length with probability $p_r = 1/9$. We use crossover probability $p_X = 1.0$, and mutation probability $p_M = 1/\ell$, where $\ell$ is the genotype length. Parameter $m$ in the Barabási-Albert model is set to $m = 2$, and we let $p_{mig} = 1/80$. Regarding node deactivation/reactivation, we use the shape parameter $\eta = 1.5$ to have an increasing hazard rate, and scale parameters $\beta = -1/\log(p)$ for $p = 1 - (kn_\iota)^{-1}$, $k \in \{1, 2, 5, 10, 20, \infty\}$. Intuitively, these settings would correspond to an average of one island going down/up every $k$ cycles if the failure rate was constant (it is not since $\eta > 1$ but this creates a mental anchor to interpret these values). This provides different scenarios ranging from none ($k = \infty$) or low ($k = 20$) churn to extremely high ($k = 1$) churn. Parameter $C_1$ used during eventual island reinitialization from scratch is set to $2\mu = 32$ (this setting is motivated by the fact that the asymptotic number of active islands under the parameterization chosen is $n_\iota/2$). We perform 25 simulations for each algorithm and churn scenario. We denote by noB and LBQ the algorithmic variants without balancing and with balancing respectively. In addition we use the superscript $r$ to denote the use of rewiring (i.e., noB$^r$ and LBQ$^r$). We have considered three test functions, namely Deb's trap (TRAP) function [4] (concatenating 32 four-bit traps), Watson et al.'s Hierarchical-if-and-only-if (HIFF) function [21] (using 128 bits) and Goldberg et al.'s Massively Multimodal Deceptive Problem (MMDP) [5] (using 24 six-bit blocks) – see Appendix A.

Figure 4 shows the results obtained in terms of the deviation from the optimal solution in each of the problems for each algorithm as a function of the churn rate (the corresponding numerical data is provided in Table 1). It is clear that performance degrades with increasing churn rates, but the degradation trend is quite different for the different algorithms. Notice firstly that the variants that use balancing perform notably better than their unbalanced counterparts.

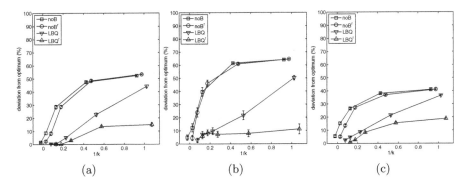

(a)                              (b)                              (c)

**Fig. 4.** Deviation from the optimal solution as a function of the churn rate. From left to right: TRAP, HIFF and MMDP

**Table 1.** Results (averaged for 25 runs) of the different MMAs on the three problems considered. The median ($\tilde{x}$), mean ($\bar{x}$) and standard error of the mean ($\sigma_{\bar{x}}$) are indicated.

| strategy | $k$ | TRAP $\tilde{x}$ | TRAP $\bar{x} \pm \sigma_{\bar{x}}$ | HIFF $\tilde{x}$ | HIFF $\bar{x} \pm \sigma_{\bar{x}}$ | MMDP $\tilde{x}$ | MMDP $\bar{x} \pm \sigma_{\bar{x}}$ |
|---|---|---|---|---|---|---|---|
| – | $\infty$ | 0.00 | 0.55 ± 0.18 | 0.00 | 1.00 ± 1.00 | 1.50 | 2.08 ± 0.33 |
| noB | 20 | 1.25 | 1.65 ± 0.39 | 0.00 | 4.88 ± 2.05 | 5.99 | 5.51 ± 0.77 |
| | 10 | 8.75 | 8.72 ± 1.09 | 0.00 | 12.30 ± 3.11 | 13.48 | 15.25 ± 1.03 |
| | 5 | 27.50 | 28.59 ± 1.49 | 44.44 | 39.61 ± 3.28 | 25.13 | 26.55 ± 0.69 |
| | 2 | 48.12 | 47.49 ± 0.71 | 61.98 | 61.51 ± 0.43 | 38.45 | 38.02 ± 0.51 |
| | 1 | 51.88 | 52.35 ± 0.57 | 64.76 | 64.17 ± 0.27 | 41.12 | 40.93 ± 0.54 |
| noB$^r$ | 20 | 1.25 | 2.32 ± 0.65 | 0.00 | 4.50 ± 1.88 | 4.49 | 5.11 ± 0.71 |
| | 10 | 9.38 | 8.43 ± 1.06 | 24.65 | 24.01 ± 3.49 | 13.48 | 13.62 ± 0.93 |
| | 5 | 29.37 | 28.73 ± 1.14 | 50.52 | 46.08 ± 2.51 | 28.30 | 27.30 ± 1.03 |
| | 2 | 48.75 | 48.40 ± 0.73 | 61.63 | 60.96 ± 0.64 | 37.29 | 36.91 ± 0.67 |
| | 1 | 53.13 | 53.28 ± 0.40 | 64.76 | 64.57 ± 0.25 | 41.12 | 41.05 ± 0.62 |
| LBQ | 20 | 0.00 | 0.50 ± 0.26 | 0.00 | 2.83 ± 1.64 | 3.00 | 2.56 ± 0.38 |
| | 10 | 0.00 | 0.45 ± 0.19 | 0.00 | 7.28 ± 2.32 | 4.49 | 4.71 ± 0.55 |
| | 5 | 5.00 | 5.22 ± 0.75 | 0.00 | 9.67 ± 2.55 | 8.99 | 8.72 ± 0.66 |
| | 2 | 21.88 | 22.83 ± 1.25 | 21.88 | 21.71 ± 3.39 | 21.80 | 21.48 ± 0.87 |
| | 1 | 44.38 | 44.15 ± 1.04 | 51.39 | 50.17 ± 1.79 | 36.78 | 36.38 ± 0.57 |
| LBQ$^r$ | 20 | 0.00 | 0.20 ± 0.16 | 0.00 | 6.06 ± 2.14 | 1.50 | 1.14 ± 0.22 |
| | 10 | 0.00 | 0.10 ± 0.07 | 0.00 | 8.44 ± 2.17 | 3.00 | 2.82 ± 0.40 |
| | 5 | 1.88 | 3.20 ± 0.60 | 0.00 | 7.27 ± 2.28 | 8.66 | 8.48 ± 0.65 |
| | 2 | 12.50 | 13.65 ± 0.90 | 0.00 | 7.92 ± 2.63 | 14.65 | 15.53 ± 0.87 |
| | 1 | 16.25 | 14.97 ± 1.36 | 0.00 | 11.20 ± 3.79 | 19.47 | 18.86 ± 0.73 |

This indicates that balancing is effectively contributing to maintaining the momentum of the search despite the volatility of the system. However, observe how as one moves toward the high end of churn rates (rightmost part of the figures) the performance of LBQ degrades at a fast pace, approaching the poor performance of noB variants. This is a clear signal that the increasing instability of the underlying network is negating the effectiveness of the balancing strategy. In fact, LBQ$^r$ has a much more gently degradation curve, being remarkably superior to the remaining algorithms on scenarios with high churn rates. This superiority is validated by a signrank test at $\alpha = 0.05$ level. Notice also that the use of rewiring has no effect on the performance of noB whose performance is virtually indistinguishable from noB$^r$. This confirms that none of the two strategy factors, namely balancing and rewiring, is capable on itself of ensuring resilient performance (although admittedly balancing has a higher impact in the low end of churn rates). On the contrary, they are synergistically interacting as supported by the consistently resilient behavior of LBQ$^r$. This is further illustrated in Fig. 5 in which the evolution of fitness on the TRAP function is shown for different churn rates: notice how the use of balancing allows attaining results analogous to those the unbalanced version yields in about twice as much more stable scenarios, but the search is not capable of progressing much for very high churn; rewiring allows overcoming this situation, favoring the sustained progress of the search even in the latter scenarios.

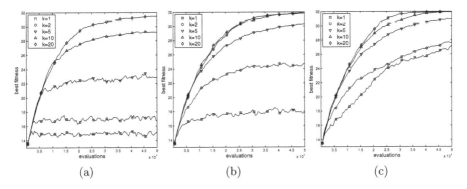

**Fig. 5.** Evolution of best fitness on the TRAP function for different churn rates. (a) noB (b) LBQ (c) LBQ$^r$. The results for noB$^r$ are very similar to noB.

A deeper look at the comparative effect of rewiring is obtained by performing a spectral analysis of the dynamics of island sizes. We have computed the power spectral density (PSD) of the evolution of island sizes in each run of LBQ and LBQ$^r$ and estimated the relationship between frequency and PSD via a power-law PSD $\sim f^\gamma$. Figure 6a shows the values of the so-obtained spectrum slopes ($\gamma$). For low churn rates $\gamma$ is closer to $-2$, indicating Brown noise. This can be interpreted by node volatility being low thus giving time to the algorithm to balance the island sizes in-between failures; the deactivation/reactivation of islands thus causes the mean island size to follow a rather random walk trajectory. As the churn rate increases, changes in node availability start to interact with the operation of the balancing process; the system does not settle into a stable state between deactivation/reactivation events causing new balancing flows which interfere with previous balancing waves. As a result the dynamics of island sizes starts to move to a regime close to pink noise ($\gamma = -1$) which is the signature of a self-organized system – see Fig. 6b and 6c for a depiction of mean-island-size trajectories for $k = 5$ (slope of the PSD of LBQ$^r$ close to $-1$) and $k = 2$ (idem for LBQ) respectively. We conjecture that differences between LBQ and LBQ$^r$ for the highest churn rates is due to the fact that the balancing process is seriously impaired in the former, causing many islands initializations from scratch, whereas balancing keeps working in the latter (albeit simultaneous node failures cause a net decrease of the total population size – cf. Sect. 2.2; notice at any rate that LBQ$^r$ is resilient enough to cope with this decrease as shown in Fig. 4).

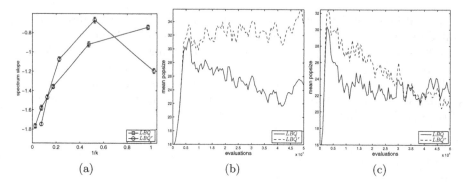

(a)                              (b)                              (c)

**Fig. 6.** (a) Slope of the power spectral density of the evolution of mean island sizes. (b) Mean island size with/without rewiring in LBQ for $k = 5$ (c) Idem for $k = 2$.


# 4   Conclusions

This work has focused on the study and analysis of island-based MMAs running on unstable computational environments, and how their performance is affected by the use of balancing strategies and rewiring policies. This kind of computational environments is typically found in emergent systems such as P2P networks or volunteer desktop grids and hence it is of the foremost interest to determine appropriate courses of action for the deployment of parallel metaheuristics on them. In this sense, it has been shown that the use of population balancing strategies is crucial in order to make the optimizer churn-aware and able to deal with resource volatility. However, these strategies are not enough to fully mitigate the degradation of performance in scenarios with very high rates of churn; they need the complement of other strategies such as rewiring policies aimed to keep the global network connectivity pattern, avoiding the disconnection of parts of the network or the apparition of bottlenecks disrupting the effective flow of information across the network.

The directions for future work are manifold. Further scalability analysis and study of the influence of network parameters is a line to be approached in the short term. Similarly so, we plan to analyze other rewiring strategies entirely based on local information [9,10] so as to confirm the behavioral patterns observed. As a longer-term objective, we believe it is worth designing more complex fault-aware policies based on a deeper understanding of the particular characteristics of the environment as perceived by the algorithm itself.

**Acknowledgements.** Thanks are due to the reviewers for useful suggestions. This work is partially supported by MICINN project ANYSELF (TIN2011-28627-C04-01), by Junta de Andalucía project P10-TIC-6083 (DNEMESIS) and by Universidad de Málaga, Campus de Excelencia Internacional Andalucía Tech.

# A   Test Suite

Deb's 4-bit fully deceptive function (TRAP) is defined as $f_{trap}(s) = 0.6 - 0.2 \cdot u(s)$ for $u(s) < 4$ and $f_{trap}(s) = 1$ for $u(s) = 4$, where $u(s_1 \cdots s_i) = \sum_j s_j$ is the number of 1 s in binary string $s$. A higher-order problem is built by concatenating $k$ such blocks.

The Hierarchical if-and-only-if (HIFF) function is a recursive epistatic function for binary strings of $2^k$ bits by means of two auxiliary functions $f$ and $t$ defined as

- $f(a, b) = 1$ for $a = b \neq \bullet$ and $f(a, b) = 0$ otherwise.
- $t(a, b) = a$ if $a = b$ and $t(a, b) = \bullet$ otherwise.

These two functions are used as follows:

$$\text{HIFF}_k(b_1 \cdots b_n) = \sum_{i=1}^{n/2} f(b_{2i-1}, b_{2i}) + 2 \cdot \text{HIFF}_{k-1}(b'_1, \cdots, b'_{n/2})$$

where $b'_i = t(b_{2i-1}, b_{2i})$ and $\text{HIFF}_0(\cdot) = 1$.

The basic MMDP block is defined for 6-bit strings as $f_{mmdp}(s) = 1$ for $u(s) \in \{0, 6\}$, $f_{mmdp}(s) = 0$ for $u(s) \in \{1, 5\}$, $f_{mmdp}(s) = 0.360384$ for $u(s) \in \{2, 4\}$ and $f_{mmdp}(s) = 0.640576$ for $u(s) = 3$. We concatenate $k$ copies of this basic block to create a harder problem.

# References

1. Alba, E.: Parallel Metaheuristics: A New Class of Algorithms. Wiley-Interscience, Hoboken (2005)
2. Albert, R., Barabási, A.L.: Statistical mechanics of complex networks. Rev. Mod. Phys. **74**(1), 47–97 (2002)
3. Bronevich, A.G., Meyer, W.: Load balancing algorithms based on gradient methods and their analysis through algebraic graph theory. J. Parallel Distrib. Comput. **68**(2), 209–220 (2008)
4. Deb, K., Goldberg, D.E.: Analyzing deception in trap functions. In: Whitley, L.D. (ed.) Second Workshop on Foundations of Genetic Algorithms, pp. 93–108. Morgan Kaufmann, Vail (1993)
5. Goldberg, D.E., Deb, K., Horn, J.: Massive multimodality, deception, and genetic algorithms. In: Männer, R., Manderick, B. (eds.) Parallel Problem Solving from Nature - PPSN II, pp. 37–48. Elsevier, Brussels (1992)
6. Gorges-Schleuter, M.: ASPARAGOS: an asynchronous parallel genetic optimization strategy. In: Schaffer, J.D. (ed.) Third International Conference on Genetic Algorithms, pp. 422–427. Morgan Kaufmann, San Francisco (1989)
7. Grefenstette, J.: Genetic algorithms for changing environments. In: Männer, R., Manderick, B. (eds.) Parallel Problem Solving from Nature II, pp. 137–144. Elsevier, Brussels (1992)
8. Hidalgo, J.I., Lanchares, J., Fernández de Vega, F., Lombraña, D.: Is the island model fault tolerant? In: Proceedings of the 9th Annual Conference Companion on Genetic and Evolutionary Computation, GECCO 2007, pp. 2737–2744. ACM, New York, NY, USA (2007)

9. Holme, P., Kim, B.J.: Growing scale-free networks with tunable clustering. Phys. Rev. E **65**, 026107 (2002)
10. Jelasity, M., van Steen, M.: Large-scale newscast computing on the Internet. Technical report IR-503. Vrije Universiteit Amsterdam, Department of Computer Science, Amsterdam, The Netherlands (October 2002)
11. Krasnogor, N., Blackburne, B.P., Burke, E.K., Hirst, J.D.: Multimeme algorithms for protein structure prediction. In: Guervós, J.J.M., Adamidis, P.A., Beyer, H.-G., Fernández-Villacañas, J.-L., Schwefel, H.-P. (eds.) PPSN 2002. LNCS, vol. 2439, pp. 769–778. Springer, Heidelberg (2002)
12. Liu, C., White, R.W., Dumais, S.: Understanding web browsing behaviors through weibull analysis of dwell time. In: Proceedings of the 33rd International ACM SIGIR Conference on Research and Development in Information Retrieval, SIGIR 2010, pp. 379–386. ACM, New York, NY, USA (2010)
13. Lüling, R., Monien, B., Ramme, F.: Load balancing in large networks: a comparative study. In: Third IEEE Symposium on Parallel and Distributed Processing, pp. 686–689. IEEE (December 1991)
14. Milojičić, D.S., Kalogeraki, V., Lukose, R., Nagaraja, K., Pruyne, J., Richard, B., Rollins, S., Xu, Z.: Peer-to-peer computing. Technical report. HPL-2002-57, Hewlett-Packard Labs (2002)
15. Neri, F., Cotta, C.: Memetic algorithms and memetic computing optimization: a literature review. Swarm Evol. Comput. **2**, 1–14 (2012)
16. Nogueras, R., Cotta, C.: An analysis of migration strategies in island-based multimemetic algorithms. In: Bartz-Beielstein, T., Branke, J., Filipič, B., Smith, J. (eds.) PPSN 2014. LNCS, vol. 8672, pp. 731–740. Springer, Heidelberg (2014)
17. Ong, Y.S., Lim, M.H., Chen, X.: Memetic computation-past, present and future. IEEE Comput. Intell. Mag. **5**(2), 24–31 (2010)
18. Sarmenta, L.F.: Bayanihan: web-based volunteer computing using java. In: Masunaga, Y., Katayama, T., Tsukamoto, M. (eds.) WWCA 1998. Lecture Notes in Computer Science, vol. 1368, pp. 444–461. Springer, Berlin Heidelberg (1998)
19. Smith, J.E.: Self-adaptation in evolutionary algorithms for combinatorial optimisation. In: Cotta, C., Sevaux, M., Sörensen, K. (eds.) Adaptive and Multilevel Metaheuristics, Studies in Computational Intelligence, vol. 136, pp. 31–57. Springer, Heidelberg (2008)
20. Tanese, R.: Distributed genetic algorithms. In: 3rd International Conference on Genetic Algorithms, pp. 434–439. Morgan Kaufmann Publishers Inc., San Francisco, CA, USA (1989)
21. Watson, R.A., Hornby, G.S., Pollack, J.B.: Modeling building-block interdependency. In: Eiben, A.E., Bäck, T., Schoenauer, M., Schwefel, H.-P. (eds.) PPSN 1998. LNCS, vol. 1498, pp. 97–106. Springer, Heidelberg (1998)
22. Zambonelli, F.: Exploiting biased load information in direct-neighbour load balancing policies. Parallel Comput. **25**(6), 745–766 (1999)

# Investigating Fitness Measures
# for the Automatic Construction
# of Graph Models

Kyle Robert Harrison[1], Mario Ventresca[2]($^{(\boxtimes)}$),
and Beatrice M. Ombuki-Berman[1]

[1] Department of Computer Science, Brock University,
St. Catharines, ON, Canada
{kh08uh,bombuki}@brocku.ca
[2] School of Industrial Engineering, Purdue University,
West Lafayette, IN, USA
mventresca@purdue.edu

**Abstract.** Graph models are often constructed as a tool to better understand the growth dynamics of complex networks. Traditionally, graph models have been constructed through a very time consuming and difficult manual process. Recently, there have been various methods proposed to alleviate the manual efforts required when constructing these models, using statistical and evolutionary strategies. A major difficulty associated with automated approaches lies in the evaluation of candidate models. To address this difficulty, this paper examines a number of well-known network properties using a proposed meta-analysis procedure. The meta-analysis demonstrated how these network measures interacted when used together as classifiers to determine network, and thus model, (dis)similarity. The analytical results formed the basis of a fitness evaluation scheme used in a genetic programming (GP) system to automatically construct graph models for complex networks. The GP-based automatic inference system was used to reproduce two well-known graph models, the results of which indicated that the evolved models exemplified striking similarity when compared to their respective targets on a number of structural network properties.

**Keywords:** Complex networks · Graph models · Centrality measures · Meta-analysis · Genetic programming

## 1 Introduction

A *complex network* is a collection of related elements in which the emergent patterns of connections hold significant meaning [23]. Complex networks are referred to as *complex* due to their intricate, tightly coupled structure and semantics, not their size alone [23], and arise in a wide variety of natural and artificial contexts. Examples of natural networks include social networks, which emerge from human

© Springer International Publishing Switzerland 2015
A.M. Mora and G. Squillero (Eds.): EvoApplications 2015, LNCS 9028, pp. 189–200, 2015.
DOI: 10.1007/978-3-319-16549-3_16

interaction, and biological networks, which aim to describe biological processes such as protein-protein interaction [5] and neural networks [24]. An example of artificial networks are technological networks, which describe artificially constructed systems such as the Internet and power-grid networks [1].

Devising algorithms that explain the growth patterns of networks has been a topic of interest for over 50 years [10]. These algorithms, known as *graph models*, are capable of generating networks of arbitrary size which replicate certain statistical and structural properties, such as proportions of transitive connections and path lengths. Graph models have a tremendous number of applications across many domains and allow both interpolation of previous network states and extrapolation of future states; see [16] for an overview of the many uses for graph models. While accurate graph models have many benefits, their applicability is governed by how easily they can be created and/or tailored for a specific network at hand. However, the task of constructing graph models from scratch has traditionally been done manually – a time-consuming and difficult process [23].

Automated approaches to graph model construction have the potential to significantly reduce the time and effort for their construction, especially in scenarios where the networks are large. A number of statistical methods to generate meta-models have been proposed to alleviate the manual effort required in building a graph model [8,17]. Similarly, genetic programming (GP) has also been recently proposed for the automated inference of graph models [2,3,22]. While the statistical methods are limited in the types of networks they can produce (e.g., Kronecker graphs produce log-normal distributions), GP provides a potential solution with less limitations. Furthermore, GP has the potential to reveal the underlying mechanisms that define the connections, whereas previous techniques do not. Although automated approaches alleviate prohibitive factors in graph model construction, they are by no means without their own difficulties. For example, verifying that a model accurately describes the target network is no trivial task, as the concept of similarity is loosely defined and dependent upon the network semantics. Furthermore, the process which created the target network is unknown, requiring the evaluation of the candidate graph model to be done through graph comparisons. It should be noted that graph comparison, in this context, is not an isomorphism problem, as the goal is not to reproduce the target network itself, but rather to infer a model which reasonably approximates the growth patterns that created the target network and, by extension, replicates its structural properties.

This paper first provides an analysis of network centrality measures of which the results are used as a basis for the fitness evaluation of a GP system to automate the construction of graph models. The remainder of this paper is structured as follows. Section 2 introduces the topic of graph models and network measures. Section 3 proposes a meta-analysis framework for the analysis of centrality measures. Section 4 describes the GP system used to automatically infer graph models, while the results of automatic inference are presented in Sect. 5. Finally, concluding remarks are given in Sect. 6.

## 2    Background

This section briefly introduces the network centrality measures and graph models used throughout the remainder of this study. For brevity, only limited, relevant information is provided.

### 2.1    Network Centrality Measures

Global network properties, such as the average geodesic path length which provides a sense of the information propagation time, are useful to quantify the overall structure of a network but are limited in that they generally disregard the emergent local behaviors of individual vertices. Fan *et al.* [11] point out that using only topological characteristics to evaluate complex network models can be misleading. As such, this study makes use of more localized, vertex-level properties to assess network similarity. *Centrality* refers to how central or "important" a vertex is within a network. The importance of a vertex is, however, subjectively based on the perception of "importance". As such, many definitions of importance, and corresponding measures of centrality, have been proposed. This work examined six well-known centrality measures, namely degree distribution (D), betweenness (B) [13], closeness (C) [14], local transitivity (LCC)[1], eigenvector centrality (EC) [6], and PageRank (PR) [7].

### 2.2    Graph Models

Graph models are typically stochastic or probabilistic algorithms which, through repeated execution, produce a set of graphs that depict commonalities with respect to certain properties, but are otherwise random [23]. The common properties among graphs generated by a model are dependent upon the model, but may include basic structural properties such as the degree distribution [4] and path lengths [25], or emergent properties such as community structure [18]. Note that a graph model is not expected to reproduce any specific graph, or to generate isomorphic graphs. Similarly, the automatic construction of graph models is not an isomorphism problem, thus producing isomorphic graphs is not the intention.

To perform the analysis of network measures, this work made use of six well-known graph models exhibiting a variety of different properties. The Growing Random (GR) model [4] demonstrated simple growth. The Barabasi-Albert (BA) [4] and Aging Preferential Attachment (APA) [9] models depicted scale-free degree distributions. The Erdos-Renyi (ER) [10] and Watts-Strogatz (WS) [25] models represented low and high clustering coefficients, respectively. Both the ER and WS models produced low average geodesic path lengths, which the latter was explicitly designed to achieve. Finally, the Forest Fire (FF) model [17] produced heavily-tailed degree distributions and community structure. Note that while all six aforementioned models were used to analyze the network measures, only the BA and ER models were used as targets for the GP system. A further discussion of graph models can be found in [15].

---

[1] Transitivity is also commonly referred to as the clustering coefficient.

# 3    Meta-Analysis of Network Properties

To determine the performance of a set of centrality measures, used to differentiate networks generated by different graph models, a method of combining single-measure results was devised as follows. For a given target graph $G$, graph model $M$, and set of measures $F$, $N$ instances of $M$ were generated. For each of the instances of $M$, each centrality measure was compared using a Kolmogorov-Smirnov (KS) test [19], at a 95 % confidence level, to that of the target graph, $G$. The power set (excluding the empty set) of $F$ was generated to examine all non-empty subsets of measures. For each subset of measures, the p-values corresponding to its members were combined using Fisher's method [12].

The procedure outlined above only compared a single target to a single model. To compare multiple models to a single target graph, a meta analysis procedure was used. A classification scheme was derived, allowing ROC curves to be used for analysis. To construct such a classifier, an assumption was made that if two graphs were generated by the same model, they would exhibit similar centralities and thus a high p-value would be obtained when compared. This assumption is reasonable in that a measure for which this doesn't hold must produce significantly different values for networks generated by the same model, and thus is not a good measure for determining network/model similarity. By extension of the above assumption, a good subset of measures should produce a high p-value when combined. If two graphs were produced by the same model, the combined p-value from each subset of measures was expected to be 1. Conversely, if the graphs were produced by different models, the combined p-value was expected to be 0. This reasoning was used to derive a classification system where the observed p-values from this procedure were taken as an approximation (i.e., the response) to the expected outcome.

The area under the curve (AUC) was calculated for each ROC curve as a measure of performance for the corresponding classifier. In the context of this work, the AUC represented the probability that $G$, originating from model $M$, will receive a higher p-value using Fisher's method when compared to graphs generated by $M$ than when compared to graphs not generated by $M$.

## 3.1    Meta-Analysis Results

This section presents the results obtained by repeating the meta-analysis procedure above using a target graph generated by each of the six models and aggregating the results. One might argue that using only a single target network may not be truly representative of the model family. However, in a real-world scenario, there is often only a single example of the network being modeled. Thus, using a single target network drew a closer parallel to a real-world scenario.

Figure 1 presents the ROC curves for 100 (smallest) and 1000 (largest) vertex networks. The higher AUC values observed for 1000 vertex networks demonstrated that larger networks were easier to distinguish due to their more pronounced and emergent structural differences. A key observation was that the highest AUC attained at each network size was produced by either the set containing the PageRank measure alone or both the PageRank and betweenness

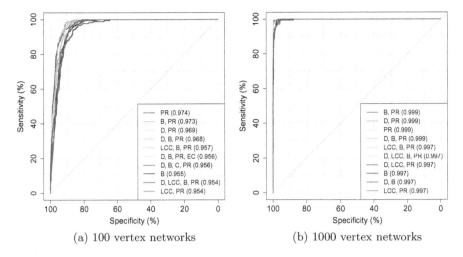

(a) 100 vertex networks          (b) 1000 vertex networks

**Fig. 1.** ROC curves depicting the ten measure sets with the highest area under the curve (AUC) values, shown in the legend, for various network sizes.

measures. At each of the four network sizes, the PageRank measure was included in each of the top five sets of measures. Furthermore, PageRank was present in nine of the top ten measure sets for the 100, 250, and 500 vertex networks and eight of the top ten sets when 1000 vertex networks were examined. Similarly, betweenness was present in at least five of the top ten fitness sets for each network size.

When two measures were combined, it was noted that combining the betweenness and PageRank measures would insignificantly change the AUC value relative to only using the PageRank measure, namely the AUC was different by at most 0.002. When three measures were considered, the subset which contained the degree, betweenness, and PageRank measures obtained the highest AUC. As the number of measures combined was increased beyond three, the subsets which attained the highest AUC became less intuitive. However, it was noted that the subsets which obtained the highest AUC always contained the degree, betweenness, and PageRank measures. Based on these observations, the degree, betweenness, and PageRank were chosen as measures of evolutionary fitness to be used by the GP system, detailed in the following section.

# 4 Automatic Construction of Graph Models

To demonstrate the effectiveness of the identified centrality measures as evolutionary fitness criteria, the LinkableGP system [20,21], a linear-object-oriented GP, was used to automatically construct graph models. An abstract class representing a generalized graph model, based on the model given in [20], was provided to the system to define the structure of the evolved models. This abstract model consisted of three unimplemented methods, namely *SelectVertices*, *CreateEdges*, and *SecondaryActions*, which were evolved by the GP system. The generalized model, beginning with an initially empty graph, constructed a network using a single loop, executed once for each vertex to be created. First, *SelectVertices* was executed, returning a collection of vertices, $C$, as potential candidates for the new vertex to attach to. For each vertex in $C$, *CreateEdges* was executed to produce a list of edges followed by *SecondaryActions*, which could add new vertices to $C$. Each of the evolved methods were provided their own language elements as detailed in the subsequent sections.

## 4.1   SelectVertices Method

For each of the methods listed below, a collection which prevented previously seen elements from being inserted was returned in either stack or queue form.

- **GetAll{Stack, Queue}(g)** – Select all vertices from $g$.
- **GetRandom{Stack, Queue}(g)** – Select a random vertex from $g$.
- **GetRandom{Stack, Queue}(g, n)** – Select $n$ random vertices from $g$.
- **GetRoulette{Stack, Queue}(g, f)** – Select a vertex from $g$ using roulette selection with probabilities assigned to vertices via the evaluator function $f$.
- **GetRoulette{Stack, Queue}(g, f, n)** – Select $n$ vertices from $g$ using roulette selection as above.

The vertex evaluator functions and composition operators below were made available to facilitate more robust selection procedures. In addition to these functions, integer and floating-point generators with (inclusive) ranges $(1, 10)$ and $(0.0, 1.0)$, respectively.

- **GetDegree( )** – Computes the degree of the vertex.
- **GetLocalTransitivity( )** – Computes the local transitivity of the vertex.
- **GetAge( )** – Computes the age of the vertex.
- **Add(f1, f2)** – Computes $f_1(v) + f_2(v)$.
- **Add(f, d)** – Computes $f(v) + d$.
- **Mult(f1, f2)** – Computes $f_1(v) \times f_2(v)$.
- **Mult(f, d)** – Computes $f(v) \times d$.
- **Pow(f, d)** – Computes $f(v)^d$.
- **InversePow(f, d)** – Computes $f(v)^{-d}$.

## 4.2   CreateEdges Method

Each of the functions made available to the *CreateEdges* method, shown below, returned a list of edges which were added to the graph after the secondary selection took place to prevent interference with the *SecondaryActions* procedure. A floating-point generator with an (inclusive) range $(0.0, 1.0)$ was also provided.

- **AddEdge(v1, v2)** – Return an edge between $v1$ and $v2$.
- **EmptyEdge( )** – Designates no edge was to be created.
- **AddEdgeWithProb(v1, v2, p)** – With probability $p$, return an edge between $v1$ and $v2$.
- **AddTriangle(v1, v2)** – Return two edges forming a triangle including $v1$, $v2$ and a randomly chosen neighbor of $v1$ or $v2$.

- **AddTriangleWithProb(v1, v2, p)** – Create an edge between *v1* and *v2*, and with probability *p*, create a triangle (as above).
- **Duplicate(v1, v2, p)** – Returns a list of edges between *v1* and each neighbor of *v2*. With probability *p*, an edge is also created between *v1* and *v2*.

### 4.3   SecondaryActions Method

The *SecondaryActions* method was responsible for performing actions as a direct result of adding a vertex and/or edge(s). Integer and floating-point constant generators with (inclusive) ranges $(0, 10)$ and $(0.0, 1.0)$, respectively, were also available.

- **AddNeighbours(c, n, v)** – Adds *n* randomly selected neighbors of vertex *v* to the taboo collection *c*.
- **GetRandomValue(a, b)** – Returns a uniformly random integer between *a* and *b*, inclusive, where *a* and *b* are integer arguments.
- **GetGeometricValue(p)** – Returns an integer generated according to a geometric distribution with probability *p*.

## 5   Results and Discussion

By evolving a graph model for a known algorithm, the evolved model can be easily validated against both the network used as a target, referred to as the *target graph*, as well as other networks generated by the model. Two well-known models, namely the BA and ER models were selected as target models. The BA model was selected as it produces scale-free, power-law degree distributions which are commonly found in real-world networks. While the BA model, as originally proposed, is limited in the degree distributions it can generate, the model nonetheless describes many real world networks such as actor affiliation networks and the World Wide Web [4]. The ER model was selected as it can exhibit non-zero clustering coefficients and does not produce a static number of edges each iteration. Furthermore, these two models have been used in previous works [2,3,22]. For this study, the BA model created a single edge per iteration and used linear preferential attachment while the connection probability of the ER model was set to 0.05 (5 %) to prevent excessive edge density.

For both models, a target graph was generated with 100 and 500 vertices. For each target graph, the GP system was run 30 times to produce a set of candidate models using empirically-determined parameters as follows. A population of 50 individuals was evolved over 50 generations and used an 80 % crossover rate and 20 % mutation rate. Tournament selection using 3 individuals was employed and elitism was set at 2 individuals per generation. Initial chromosome lengths were randomly assigned within the following ranges: 1–15 for the *SelectVertices* and *SecondaryActions* methods whereas the *CreateEdges* method had a smaller range of 1–5. A sum-of-ranks strategy was employed during evolution using three fitness measures, namely the KS test statistic comparing the degree distribution, betweenness centrality, and PageRank measures of a single network generated by the candidate model and the target network. The final model was selected as the highest ranked model from the 30 runs using sum-of-ranks. In addition to the centrality measures used during evolution, the number of edges, average geodesic path length (AGP), and global clustering coefficient (CC) were also compared between networks generated by the evolved model and the target model. Bold KS statistic entries denote the average test statistic was below the critical threshold.

## 5.1    Evolving the Barabasi-Albert Model

When a 100 vertex BA network was used as the target, both the mean and minimum observed AGP, shown in Table 1, were higher for the evolved model than the true model. Although the mean and minimum AGPs were 0.325 and 0.352 higher, respectively, both were within a single standard deviation of the true model. By definition, the transitivity of both the evolved and BA models was zero and the number of edges was constant. Examining the centrality measures, the average D statistic for the PageRank measure (0.159) was relatively high compared to the degree and betweenness measures (at 0.053 and 0.066 respectively), however, this value was still below the critical threshold of 0.192.

When a 500 vertex BA network was used as the target, the average AGP was 0.261 higher in graphs generated by the evolved model than the true model while the maximal difference was 0.776. However, examining the centrality measures demonstrated that the evolved and true models produced similar networks with respect to the employed fitness measures. With average KS statistics of 0.023, 0.026, and 0.073 for the degree, betweenness, and PageRank measures, respectively, the centrality measures were insignificantly different among networks generated by the evolved and true models. For comparison, Algorithm 2 presents the evolved $BA_{500}$ model, simplified to remove bloat, alongside the true BA model (Algorithm 1). Note that in the true model, the in-degree was used in a directed fashion which caused slightly different selection probabilities.

In summary, the BA model was effectively reproduced in both experiments, however, the evolved models demonstrated higher values for the AGP measure.

| **Algorithm 1.** $BA$ Model | **Algorithm 2.** Simplified $BA_{500}$ Model |
|---|---|
| **function** SELECTVERTICES($g$) | **function** SELECTVERTICES($g$) |
| $f \leftarrow$ GetInDegree( )  //Degree - 1 | $f \leftarrow$ GetDegree( ) |
| $S \leftarrow$ GetRouletteStack($g, f$) | $S \leftarrow$ GetRouletteStack($g, f$) |
| **return** $S$ | **return** $S$ |
| **end function** | **end function** |
| **function** CREATEEDGES($v, u$) | **function** CREATEEDGES($v, u$) |
| $E \leftarrow$ AddEdge($u, v$) | $E \leftarrow$ AddEdge($u, v$) |
| **return** $E$ | **return** $E$ |
| **end function** | **end function** |
| **function** SECONDARYACTIONS($v, S$) | **function** SECONDARYACTIONS($v, S$) |
| //No action | //No action |
| **end function** | **end function** |

**Table 1.** Comparison of networks generated by the evolved models and their respective true models.

| Vertices | | Measure | Min | $\mu$ | Max | $\sigma$ |
|---|---|---|---|---|---|---|
| 100 | $BA_{100}$ | Edges | 99 | 99 | 99 | 0 |
| | | AGP | 3.947 | 4.806 | 5.843 | 0.481 |
| | | CC | 0 | 0 | 0 | 0 |
| | Barabasi-Albert | Edges | 99 | 99 | 99 | 0 |
| | | AGP | 3.595 | 4.481 | 5.842 | 0.522 |
| | | CC | 0 | 0 | 0 | 0 |
| | Average D Statistic | Degree | **0.020** | **0.053** | **0.100** | 0.020 |
| | | Betweenness | **0.030** | **0.066** | **0.140** | 0.024 |
| | | PageRank | **0.090** | **0.159** | 0.300 | 0.043 |
| 500 | $BA_{500}$ | Edges | 499 | 499 | 499 | 0 |
| | | AGP | 5.497 | 6.353 | 7.640 | 0.560 |
| | | CC | 0 | 0 | 0 | 0 |
| | Barabasi-Albert | Edges | 499 | 499 | 499 | 0 |
| | | AGP | 5.261 | 6.092 | 6.864 | 0.434 |
| | | CC | 0 | 0 | 0 | 0 |
| | Average D Statistic | Degree | **0.010** | **0.023** | **0.050** | 0.011 |
| | | Betweenness | **0.012** | **0.026** | **0.050** | 0.009 |
| | | PageRank | **0.050** | **0.073** | 0.114 | 0.016 |
| 100 | $ER_{100}$ | Edges | 214 | 246.833 | 280 | 13.643 |
| | | AGP | 2.855 | 3.013 | 3.237 | 0.084 |
| | | CC | 0.026 | 0.048 | 0.070 | 0.012 |
| | Erdos-Renyi | Edges | 217 | 245.867 | 267 | 14.920 |
| | | AGP | 2.900 | 3.033 | 3.221 | 0.102 |
| | | CC | 0.024 | 0.051 | 0.067 | 0.010 |
| | Average D Statistic | Degree | **0.030** | **0.099** | 0.220 | 0.041 |
| | | Betweenness | **0.060** | **0.107** | **0.160** | 0.030 |
| | | PageRank | **0.060** | **0.106** | **0.140** | 0.024 |
| 500 | $ER_{500}$ | Edges | 6529 | 6660.767 | 6761 | 58.078 |
| | | AGP | 2.164 | 2.175 | 2.189 | 0.006 |
| | | CC | 0.051 | 0.053 | 0.054 | 0.001 |
| | Erdos-Renyi | Edges | 6094 | 6238.300 | 6366 | 62.745 |
| | | AGP | 2.209 | 2.223 | 2.240 | 0.007 |
| | | CC | 0.048 | 0.050 | 0.052 | 0.001 |
| | Average D Statistic | Degree | **0.080** | 0.145 | 0.224 | 0.033 |
| | | Betweenness | **0.044** | **0.069** | 0.090 | 0.013 |
| | | PageRank | **0.036** | **0.056** | 0.088 | 0.011 |

## 5.2  Evolving the Erdos-Renyi Model

When a 100 vertex ER network was used as a target, the evolved model showed a connection probability of 0.0507 – a difference of 0.0007 compared to the true model. The post-validation results, shown in Table 1, showed that the average number of edges, AGP, and CC measures were similar between the evolved model and the true model; the evolved model exemplified 0.0957 more edges, 0.020 lower AGP, and 0.003 lower CC, on average, than the true model. The average KS statistics at 0.099, 0.107, and 0.106 for the degree, betweenness, and PageRank measures, respectively, were all well below the critical threshold of 0.192 which further demonstrated the similarity among the evolved and true models.

| **Algorithm 3.** *ER* Model | **Algorithm 4.** Simplified $ER_{500}$ Model |
|---|---|
| **function** SELECTVERTICES($g$)<br>    $S \leftarrow$ GetAllStack($g$)<br>    **return** $S$<br>**end function** | **function** SELECTVERTICES($g$)<br>    $S \leftarrow$ GetAllStack($g$)<br>    **return** $S$<br>**end function** |
| **function** CREATEEDGES($v, u$)<br>    $E \leftarrow$ AddEdgeWithProb($v, u, 0.0500$)<br>    **return** $E$<br>**end function** | **function** CREATEEDGES($v, u$)<br>    $E \leftarrow$ AddEdgeWithProb($v, u, 0.0535$)<br>    **return** $E$<br>**end function** |
| **function** SECONDARYACTIONS($v, S$)<br>    //No action<br>**end function** | **function** SECONDARYACTIONS($v, S$)<br>    //No action<br>**end function** |

When a 500 vertex ER network was used as the target, the evolved model had a 0.0535 connection probability and exemplified roughly 422 more edges per graph, on average. As Table 1 demonstrated, networks produced by the evolved model had an AGP that was 0.048 higher than those produced by the true model, while the average transitivity was only 0.003 higher. The significantly different degree distributions (average KS statistic of 0.145) among networks generated by the true and evolved models were attributed to the increased connection probability, and therefore the increased expected degree, of the evolved model. Conversely, the average KS statistic for the betweenness and PageRank measures, 0.069 and 0.056, respectively, were both well below the critical threshold of 0.086. For comparison, Algorithm 4 presents the evolved $ER_{500}$ model, simplified to remove bloat, alongside the true ER model (Algorithm 3).

In summary, the GP system was able to reproduce the ER model with striking accuracy, however, slightly higher connection probabilities were evolved.

## 6  Conclusion

This paper proposed a meta-analysis framework to analyze the discriminatory power of centrality measures when comparing graph models of complex networks.

Six well-known graph models were used to evaluate six network centrality measures. Results indicated that of the examined centrality measures, the degree distribution, betweenness centrality, and PageRank were the most effective for quantifying the (dis)similarity of networks generated by different graph models. A genetic programming (GP) system for the automatic construction of graph models was proposed using the results of the meta-analysis to form the fitness evaluation. The GP system was used to automatically infer two well-known graph models, namely the Barabasi-Albert (BA) and Erdos-Renyi (ER) models. Target networks from these models were generated with 100 and 500 vertices, respectively, and used as the target networks within the GP system. Results indicated that these well-known graph models could be evolved with striking accuracy. Furthermore, the exceptional quality of the evolved models provided empirical evidence of the proposed meta-analysis' merit.

Many avenues of future study have become apparent throughout the course of this work. First and foremost, this paper only addresses undirected, unweighted networks and considers only centrality measures. Examining further, non-centrality network measures along with weighted and directed networks should be an immediate future study.

# References

1. Arianos, S., Bompard, E., Carbone, A., Xue, F.: Power grid vulnerability: a complex network approach. Chaos: an Interdisciplinary. J. Nonlinear Sci. **19**(1), 013119 (2009)
2. Bailey, A., Ventresca, M., Ombuki-Berman, B.: Genetic programming for the automatic inference of graph models for complex networks. IEEE Trans. Evol. Comput. **18**(3), 405–419 (2014)
3. Bailey, A., Ventresca, M., Ombuki-Berman, B.: Automatic generation of graph models for complex networks by genetic programming. In: Proceedings of the Fourteenth International Conference on Genetic and Evolutionary Computation Conference, GECCO 2012, pp. 711–718. ACM, New York, NY, USA (2012)
4. Barabási, A.L., Albert, R.: Emergence of scaling in random networks. Science **286**(5439), 509–512 (1999)
5. Berg, J., Lässig, M., Wagner, A.: Structure and evolution of protein interaction networks: a statistical model for link dynamics and gene duplications. BMC Evol. Biol. **4**(1), 51 (2004)
6. Bonacich, P.: Power and centrality: a family of measures. Am. J. Sociol. **92**, 1170–1182 (1987)
7. Brin, S., Page, L.: The anatomy of a large-scale hypertextual web search engine. Comput. Netw. ISDN Syst. **30**(1), 107–117 (1998)
8. Chung, F., Lu, L.: The average distance in a random graph with given expected degrees. Internet Math. **1**(1), 91–113 (2004)
9. Dorogovtsev, S.N., Mendes, J.F.F.: Evolution of networks with aging of sites. Phys. Rev. E **62**(2), 1842 (2000)
10. Erdös, P., Rényi, A.: On random graphs. Publicationes Mathematicae **6**, 290–297 (1959)
11. Fan, Z., Chen, G., Zhang, Y.: Using topological characteristics to evaluate complex network models can be misleading. arXiv preprint arXiv:1011.0126 (2010)

12. Fisher, R.: Statistical Methods for Research Workers. Oliver and Boyd, Edinburgh (1925)
13. Freeman, L.C.: A set of measures of centrality based on betweenness. Sociometry **40**, 35–41 (1977)
14. Freeman, L.C.: Centrality in social networks: conceptual clarification. Soc. Netw. **1**(3), 215–239 (1979)
15. Goldenberg, A., Zheng, A.X., Fienberg, S.E., Airoldi, E.M.: A survey of statistical network models. Found. Trends Mach. Learn. **2**(2), 129–233 (2010)
16. Leskovec, J., Chakrabarti, D., Kleinberg, J., Faloutsos, C., Ghahramani, Z.: Kronecker graphs: an approach to modeling networks. J. Mach. Learn. Res. **11**, 985–1042 (2010)
17. Leskovec, J., Faloutsos, C.: Scalable modeling of real graphs using Kronecker multiplication. In: Proceedings of the 24th International Conference on Machine Learning, pp. 497–504. ACM (2007)
18. Leskovec, J., Kleinberg, J., Faloutsos, C.: Graphs over time: densification laws, shrinking diameters and possible explanations. In: Proceedings of the eleventh ACM SIGKDD International Conference on Knowledge Discovery in Data Mining, pp. 177–187. ACM (2005)
19. Massey Jr., F.J.: The kolmogorov-smirnov test for goodness of fit. J. Am. Stat. Assoc. **46**(253), 68–78 (1951)
20. Medland, M.R., Harrison, K.R., Ombuki-Berman, B.: Demonstrating the power of object-oriented genetic programming via the inference of graph models for complex networks. In: 2014 Sixth World Congress on Nature and Biologically Inspired Computing (NaBIC), NaBIC 2014, pp. 305–311. IEEE (2014)
21. Medland, M.R., Harrison, K.R., Ombuki-Berman, B.: Incorporating expert knowledge in object-oriented genetic programming. In: Proceedings of the 2014 Conference on Genetic and Evolutionary Computation Companion, GECCO Comp 2014, pp. 145–146. ACM, New York, NY, USA (2014)
22. Menezes, T., Roth, C.: Symbolic regression of generative network models. Scientific reports 4 (2014)
23. Newman, M.: Networks: An Introduction. Oxford University Press, Oxford (2010)
24. Stam, C.J., Reijneveld, J.C.: Graph theoretical analysis of complex networks in the brain. Nonlinear Biomed. Phys. **1**(1), 3 (2007)
25. Watts, D.J., Strogatz, S.H.: Collective dynamics of small-world networks. Nature **393**(6684), 440–442 (1998)

# Object Detection in Natural Images Using the Brain Programming Paradigm with a Multi-objective Approach

Eddie Clemente, Gustavo Olague$^{(\boxtimes)}$, Daniel Hernández, José L. Briseño, and José Mercado

Proyecto EvoVisión, Departamento de Ciencias de la Computación, División de Física Aplicada, Centro de Investigación Científica y de Estudios Superiores de Ensenada, Carretera Ensenada-Tijuana No. 3918, Zona Playitas, 22860 Ensenada, BC, Mexico
{eclemen,dahernan,jmercado}@cicese.edu.mx,
{olague,briseno}@cicese.mx
http://cienciascomp.cicese.mx/evovision/

**Abstract.** In the last few decades the human vision system has been the focus of several researches, using it as a model for solving the object detection problem in digital images. In this work this approach is taken to define the algorithm called Artificial Visual Cortex (AVC) which is inspired in the information flow in the human visual cortex. Additionally, a new methodology for image description is proposed, which allows the detection and description of an object in the scene. Furthermore, this paper describes a new multi-objective learning technique called brain programming. This paradigm is implemented for the training stage of the proposed model in order to classify the *persons* set of the GRAZ-02 image database. The solutions found in this research outperform other techniques in the state-of-the-art.

**Keywords:** Artificial Visual Cortex · Object recognition · Object detection · Brain programming

## 1 Introduction

Sight is one of the most important senses for human beings, approximately 70 % of the information received by the brain comes from visual perception; this information helps in the process of making decisions and interacting with the environment. Hence, several scientific communities, such as computer vision, have focus their research in understanding the human vision system in order to emulate it. In this sense, there are several computational models, [1–10], inspired in the hierarchical structure of the human visual system, its neuropsychological theories and neurophysiological characteristics; some examples are: the feature integration theory [11], biased competition theory [12], Recognition-By-Components [13], simple and complex cells model [14], the two path cortical

© Springer International Publishing Switzerland 2015
A.M. Mora and G. Squillero (Eds.): EvoApplications 2015, LNCS 9028, pp. 201–213, 2015.
DOI: 10.1007/978-3-319-16549-3_17

model [15], to mention but a few. There is a model of particular interest for this paper, because it is inspired in the human visual cortex and it is implemented for object recognition; this model, proposed by Olague *et al.*, it is called Artificial Visual Cortex (AVC) [16], it shows great performance in establishing the absence or presence of an object in an image. In this way, we enhanced this model for the object detection task, in order to recognize and locate an object within a digital image.

The AVC model is based mainly on two models: a psychological model called feature integration theory and a neurophysiological model called the two pathway cortical model. The feature integration theory explains that visual attention in human beings is performed in two stages. The first one is called the pre-attentive stage, where the visual information is processed in parallel over the feature dimensions that compose a scene, which are: shape, color, orientation, spacial frequency, brightness and motion direction. The second stage is called focal attention, it integrates the features that were process independently on the previous stage, and focuses the attention on a region of the scene. Hence, visual attention is the capability of a creature, living or artificial, of focusing an object of interest on a visual environment [17]. Visual attention can be formally defined as "the process that establishes a relationship between the different properties in the scene, perceived through the visual system, and the objective of finding the best aspect for solving the task at hand" [18]. The second theory used for this work is the two pathway cortical model; this neurophysiological model states that the are two information pathways within the visual cortex, the dorsal and ventral streams; both subsystems receive the same visual information as input, but the difference between them is related to the information transformations performed in each of them [15]. The dorsal stream is mainly related to the spacial detection of objects and visual attention [19]. Thus, it is also known as the "where?" or "how?" pathway; the regions of the brain related to this task are: V1, V2, V3, V5, MST and PP, each region has a specific functionality and they are hierarchically organized. On the other hand, the ventral stream is linked to object recognition and shape representation; hence, it is also called the "what?" stream. The brain areas involved in this functionality are: V1, V2, V4, TEO and TE. Nevertheless, both information streams are interrelated in order to achieve their tasks [12, 19, 20].

The integration of these theories within a computational model as the AVC is based on the idea of defining an image as the graph of a function, which is then transformed by a series of operators within a hierarchical process; where each computational stage emulates the transformations that the visual information undergoes in the brain. In this way, the AVC model was designed for categorizing images regardless of the color, orientation, illumination conditions, scale or position of the object in the image, and one of its innovations is the way it selects prominent image features in order to build an abstract representation of the object. Hence, in images where the object of interest occupies a big portion of the image the classification rate achieved by the AVC model is 98 % or higher. Nevertheless, when the system is applied on natural images, like those present in the database proposed in [21], where the objects are smaller and immersed in a high content environment, the performances of the AVC is lower. This might occur because most of the features selected to build the image descriptor are selected from the environment, instead of the object of interest; on the other hand, it might occur due to the fact that the descriptor is built using scattered points from the last feature map, called mental map $(MM)$, where only the most prominent region is selected for the description of the image, but this might not correspond to the object of interest. Therefore, in this work we propose a new methodology for building the image descriptor, where the description is performed using an image region instead of sparse points; rendering the AVC model capable of selecting a region of the object of interest using class specific object attributes. Then, implicitly finding the object's location. Also, we propose a feedback operation using the first stages of the model for building the descriptor, since the first maps contain more information about the object. This new paradigm is called AVCMO due to the multi-objective approach taken for the training stage of the model in order to detect and describe the object of interest.

The remainder of this paper is organized as follows, Sect. 2 details the different stages of our approach, as well as the implementation of a multi-objective evolutionary system as the training paradigm for the AVCMO model. After, Sect. 3 describes the performance achieved by the AVCMO model for classifying the *persons* class of the GRAZ-02 database, and finally, the conclusion from this work are explained in Sect. 4.

## 2    Methodology

This section describes the AVCMO model, focusing on the new methodoly for building the image descriptor; also, the brain programming algorithm with a multi-objective approach is detailed here.

### 2.1    Description of the AVCMO

The AVCMO is divided in two main stages. In the first stage the system acquires and transforms the attributes that characterize the object; and in the second stage, the system locates the most prominent image region and extracts a description vector, which is later applied for classification purposes. These two stages are detailed next.

**Feature Acquisition and Transformation.** The input for the system is a digital color image in the RGB color model (red, green, blue); which is then transformed to the CMYK (cyan, magenta, yellow, black) and HSV (hue, saturation, value) color models, in order to build the set $I_{color} = \{I_r, I_g, I_b, I_c, I_m, I_y, I_k, I_h, I_s, I_v\}$, where each element corresponds to a component of the color models. The color bands in $I_{color}$ are then transformed by four evolved visual operators $(EVO)$ defined as $EVO_d : I_{color} \rightarrow VM_d$; where each operator is applied

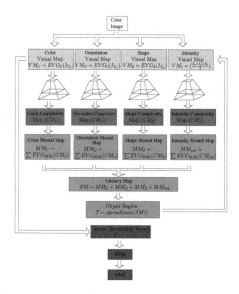

**Fig. 1.** Visual information flow.

independently aiming to highlight specific features of the object of interest, such as color $(C)$, orientation $(O)$, shape $(S)$ and intensity $(Int)$; these features are called dimension $(d)$ and follow an independent information flow, see Fig. 1. In this manner, $d$ is an element in the dimension set $d \in \{C, S, O, Int\}$; hence, each visual map $(VM_d)$ highlights promientent information from the object in the different features.

Then, once the visual maps are calculated they go through a center-surround process, this process is based on the functionality of the ganglion cells, where the activation of the cells corresponds to the difference between the stimulus on the central receptive field and the border one. From a computational point of view, the objective of this process is to generate a conspicuous map $(CM)$ per dimension, in accordance with the model in [3]. This subroutine is defined by two steps; first, starting from the $VM_d$ an eight level Gaussian Pyramid is created $P_d^{\sigma} = \{P_d^{\sigma=0}, P_d^{\sigma=1}, P_d^{\sigma=2}, ..., P_d^{\sigma=8}\}$, where $\sigma$ denotes the Gaussian blurring at each level and its size. The second step of this process uses this pyramid as input in order to generate six new maps as follows:

$$Q_d^j = P_d^{\sigma=\lfloor \frac{i+9}{2} \rfloor + 1} - P_d^{\sigma=\lfloor \frac{i+2}{2} \rfloor + 1},$$

where $j = 1, 2, ..., 6$. Since the levels in $P_d^{\sigma}$ have different size all the levels are scaled to the smaller size for calculating the differences. Then, each of these six maps is normalized and integrated through a summation operation, the resulting map is normalized and scaled to the size of the input $VM_d$; hence, this resulting map defines the $CM_d$.

**Object Detection and Description.** After building the conspicous maps, the next stage of the AVCMO aims to establish the image region with the most prominent information about the object of interest and create a description vector from it. This stage is analogous to the functionality of the V4 brain area, as well as the inferior temporal cortex (IT), since these two areas are related to the object classification task. Computationally speaking, in this stage of the process a set of visual operators are applied in order to create a mental map ($MM$) per dimension, see Fig. 1. In this way, a set of operator $EVO_{MM}$ is applied over each $CM_d$ seeking the most prominent features per dimension, this is: $MM_d = \sum_{i=1}^{k}(EVO_{MM_i}(CM_d))$, where $d$ is the feature dimension and $k$ representes the cardinality of the set $EVO_{MM}$. Thus, the sumatory integrates the output of all the operators in $EVO_{MM}$, creating the $MM_d$.

Once the mental maps are created, they are normalized between 0 and 1 using a lineal interpolation, see Eq. 1; then, they are integrated into a single saliency map $SM$, as shown in Eq. 2.

$$MM_d = \frac{MM_d - min(MM_d)}{max(MM_d) - min(MM_d)} \, . \tag{1}$$

$$SM = MM_C + MM_O + MM_F + MM_{Int} \, . \tag{2}$$

When the $SM$ is obtained, the coordinates of the highest value in the map are stored in a location vector $\boldsymbol{p}$. Then, a propagation operation is performed around this position, this requires a process of $n$ iterations, where we seek to add to the locations vector $\boldsymbol{p}(i)$ the position of the highest value located in the neighborhood around the points stored in $\boldsymbol{p}$. In this way, the $n$ elements of $\boldsymbol{p}(i)$ define a region $\varUpsilon$ on the saliency map, which establishes the area where the object is located. Even though $\varUpsilon$ defines the object location, the values used to describe the object will be extracted from previous stages of the process. This is, the region $\varUpsilon$ will be projected over the visual maps with the aim of obtaining the best features in each dimensions; then, the pixels with the highest values within each region in the $VM_d$ are selected. Again, a propagation operation is performed in order to obtain the $m$ highest values in each visual map. Finally, the $m$ values from each dimension are concatenated creating a description vector $\boldsymbol{\nu}$ of size $n$, which is then input into a support vector machine (SVM) for classification purposes. The construction of the description vector is detailed in the Algorithm 1 and it is depicted in Fig. 1.

## 2.2 Multi-objective Brain Programming

In the brain programming paradigm each solution has the same hierarchical structure defined by the AVCMO and what differentiates the solutions are the set of operators within them. This idea comes from analogy to the natural system, where evolution could modify the functionality of each brain area without altering the order in which they work. Brain programming follows the evolution cycle of genetic programming, but it proposes a new heterogeneous multi-tree representation for the individuals, as well as new crossover and mutation operator for this new representation.

```
Input:  SM, VM_d /*Saliency map and the array of visual maps */
Output:  p, ν /*Region coordinates for each visual map and the description vector */
p[1] ← coordMaxVal(SM)
SM[p[1].x, p[1].y] ← 0
for i ← 2 to n increase 1 do
    │  p[i] ← coordMaxValNeighbor(SM, p)
    │  SM[p[i].x, p[i].y] ← 0
end
foreach VM_d do
    │  p_d[1] ← coordMaxValReg(VM_d, p)
    │  v_d[1] ← getVal(VM_d, p_d[1])
    │  VM_d[p_d[i].x, p_d[i].y] ← 0
    │  for i ← 2 to n/4 increase 1 do
    │      │  p_d[i] ← coordMaxValNeighbor(VM_d, p_d)
    │      │  ν_d[i] ← getVal(VM_d, p_d[i])
    │      │  VM_d[p_d[i].x, p_d[i].y] ← 0
    │      │  ν ← concat(ν, ν_d)
    │  end
end
return p, ν
```

**Algorithm 1.** DESCRIPTOR

**Genotype.** One important aspect of the $EVOs$ is their independence, this facilitates their computational representation as an array. In this way, we can consider the next analogy with the biological system. The array of $EVOs$ is similar to a chromosome, and each operator can be considered as a gene, where each function or terminal used to build the $EVO$ as analogous to the nucleotides that form a gene. This means that the representation or genotype has three levels, the first one considers the whole chromosome as a unit, the second level are the genes and the third level are the functions that define the operators, see Fig. 2. Thus, the phenotype, defined as the physical manifestation of the genes, is the result of applying the within the structure of the Artificial Visual Cortex.

**Genetic Operators.** There are two types of crossover operations, one for chromosome level and the other for gene level operations, these are detailed next:

– *Chromosome level crossover:* the objective of this operator is the genetic combination and information exchange between chromosomes, this process is performed by exchanging array segments that constitute each of the parents. The method used is known as cut and splice. First, a crossover point is randomly selected on from the parent with the shortest string, then the same point is selected for the other parent; after, the new individual, offspring 1, is generated by joining the left size of the string from parent 1 and the right size from parent 2. In a similar way, the offspring 2 is built by using the left side of the string in parent 2 and the right size in parent 1. This process is depicted in Fig. 2a.
– *Gene level crossover:* this operator focuses on the operators that compose the gene. A crossover point is selected for each three using the smallest one. Then, parent 1 is selected to create offspring 1, where the sub-threes below the cross point are replaces by the sub-threes from below the cross point. Similarly, offspring 2 is created by taking parent 2 and replacing the sub-three from

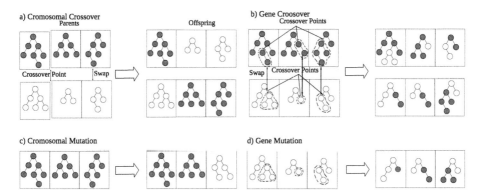

**Fig. 2.** The genetic operators are perform at two levels; Figure (a) shows the crossover operation at chromosome level, and (b) at gene level, while (c) and (d) depict the mutation operation at chromosome and gene level respectively.

parent 1. In this way, two new individuals are created. This process is shown in Fig. 2b.

**Mutation Operators.** Once the new individuals are created, they might be modified by one or two kinds of mutation operators: chromosome level mutation and gene level mutation. These operators work as follows:

- *Chromosome level mutation:* it consists on exchanging each of the operators that constitute the chromosome with a randomly generated operator, completely changing the genotype. This procedure can be seen in Fig. 2c.
- *Gene level mutation:* for each syntactic three a random mutation point is selected, then the sub-three below the mutation point is replaced by a new random sub-three. This kind of mutation only changes a portion of the each operator. This mutation operator is depicted in Fig. 2d.

**Functions and Terminals.** In the proposed model each $EVO$ is independent and is built using its own set of functions and terminals, see Table 1. Hence, we specially selected functions for each dimension, aiming to find the best features to characterize the object. Therefore, for the operator $EVO_O$ we use Gaussian smoothing filters with $\sigma = 1$ and $\sigma = 2$, as well as first and second order derivatives on the $x$ and $y$ directions. Meanwhile, for the color dimension, we selected functions like: color opponencies ($Op_{r-g}(I)$, $Op_{b-y}(I)$), complement function $((A)^c)$; for building the $EVO_C$ operator. In a similar way, aiming to find prominent shape features we propose to implement mathematical morphology functions such as: dilation ($A \oplus SE_x$), erosion ($A \ominus SE_x$), opening ($A \odot SE_s$), closing ($A \odot SE_s$), as well as other operations that result from combining these four; this set of functions is applied to construct the $EVO_S$ operator. In the case of the terminals, these are defined by the $I_{color}$ set, as well as the output from some functions applied over elements of the same set.

**Table 1.** Functions and terminals for the $EVO$.

| Functions for $EVO_O$ | Terminals for $EVO_O$ |
|---|---|
| $A + B,\ A - B,\ A \times B,\ A/B,\ |A|,\ |A + B|,$ $|A - B|,\ log(A),\ (A)^2,\ \sqrt{A},\ k + A,\ k - A,\ k \times A,$ $A/k,\ round(A),\ \lfloor A \rfloor,\ \lceil A \rceil,\ inf(A, B),\ sup(A, B),$ $G_{\sigma=1}(A),\ G_{\sigma=2}(A),\ D_x(A),\ D_y(A),\ thr(A)$ | $I_r,\ I_g,\ I_b,\ I_c,\ I_m,\ I_y,\ I_k,\ I_h,\ I_s,\ I_v,$ $D_x(I_x),\ D_{xx}(I_x),\ D_y(I_x),\ D_{yy}(I_x),$ $D_{xy}(I_x)$ |
| Functions for $EVO_C$ | Terminals for $EVO_C$ |
| $A+B,\ A-B,\ A\times B,\ A/B,\ log(A),\ exp(A),\ (A)^2,$ $\sqrt{A},\ (A)^c,\ thr(A)$ | $I_r,\ I_g,\ I_b,\ I_c,\ I_m,\ I_y,\ I_k,\ I_h,\ I_s,\ I_v,$ $Op_{r-g}(I), Op_{b-y}(I)$ |
| Functions for $EVO_S$ | Terminals for $EVO_F$ |
| $A+B,\ A-B,\ A\times B,\ A/B,\ k+A,\ k-A,\ k\times A,$ $A/k,\ round(A),\ \lfloor A \rfloor,\ \lceil A \rceil,\ A \oplus SE_d,\ A \oplus SE_s,$ $A \oplus SE_{dm},\ A \ominus SE_d,\ A \ominus SE_s,\ A \ominus SE_{dm},$ $Sk(A),\ Perim(A),\ A \circledast SE_d,\ A \circledast SE_s,\ A \circledast SE_{dm},$ $T_{hat}(A),\ B_{hat}(A),\ A \odot SE_s,\ A \odot SE_s,\ thr(A)$ | $I_r,\ I_g,\ I_b,\ I_c,\ I_m,\ I_y,\ I_k,\ I_h,\ I_s,\ I_v$ |
| Functions for $EVO_{MM}$ | Terminals for $EVO_{MM}$ |
| $A + B,\ A - B,\ A \times B,\ A/B,\ |A + B|,\ |A - B|,$ $log(A),\ (A)^2,\ \sqrt{A},\ G_{\sigma=1}(A),\ G_{\sigma=2}(A),\ D_x(A),$ $D_y(A)$ | $MC_d,\quad D_x(MC_d),\quad D_{xx}(MC_d),$ $D_y(MC_d),\ D_{yy}(MC_d),\ D_{xy}(MC_d)$ |

**Fitness Function.** The fitness function measures the performances of the solutions, which is related to the task at hand. In this case, we focus on the classification and localization of an object in an image. Thus, based on the characteristics of the model we propose two functions, one for measuring the classification performance and one for determining the quality of the solutions for localizing the object in the image. The first objective is the called Equal Error Rate (EER). This metric defines the probability of an algorithm for deciding if two instances correspond to the same class [22]. The EER is defined as the value that satisfies $fpr = fnr$; where $fnr$ is the false negative rate and $fpr$ is the false positive rate, fulfilling the following restriction: $fnr = 1 - tpr$; where, $tpr$ is the true positive rate. From a ROC (Receiver Operating Characteristic) curve, the EER can be calculated by extending a line from $(0,1)$ to $(1,0)$, the point where this line crosses the curve corresponds to the EER. In this way the first objective is defined as follows:

$$Objective_1 = EER. \tag{3}$$

The second objective is based on calculating the correspondance between a groundtruth of the object location in the image and the region $\Upsilon$ selected as the posible position. In this case, we use the F-measure defined by: $F_\alpha(\rho, \vartheta) = \dfrac{(1 + \alpha) \cdot (\rho \cdot \vartheta)}{(\alpha \cdot \rho) + \vartheta}$, where $\alpha$ controls the balance between precision $\rho$ and recall $\vartheta$, with $0 \leq \alpha \leq \infty$. If $\alpha < 1$ then $\rho$ is greater than $\vartheta$; on the contrary, if $\alpha > 1$ then $\vartheta$ is greater. Finally, when $\alpha = 1$, we say that the precision and coverage

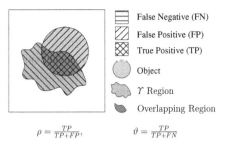

$$\rho = \frac{TP}{TP+FP}, \qquad \vartheta = \frac{TP}{TP+FN}$$

**Fig. 3.** Correspondence between the attended image region and the object region occupied by the object of interest applied for evaluating the precision $\rho$ and recall $\vartheta$ values.

are balanced. In this work we consider that $\alpha = 1$. The true positive elements correspond to the pixels that belong to the region $\Upsilon$ and the object region, the false positive are the pixels in $\Upsilon$ that are not part of the object of interest, while the false negative are the points in the object that are not included in the region $\Upsilon$, as seen in Fig. 3. In this way, after processing $n$ images that contain the object, the fitness function is defined by the average of the F-measure over the $\omega$ images, this is:

$$Objective_2 = \frac{1}{\omega} \sum_{i=1}^{\omega} \left( \frac{2 \cdot (\rho \cdot \vartheta)}{\rho + \vartheta} \right). \tag{4}$$

## 3    Experiments and Results

In this work, we approach the classification problem from a presence/absence perspective. We established a protocol composed of three steps; the first two define the training stage of the model, while the third one corresponds to the testing phase. Therefore we need three sets of images for the experiments, one per step. This protocol is described next:

1. *Training:* this step starts by evaluating each solution with an image set called training; one image descriptor is created per image. Then, these descriptors are used to generate a SVM model which labels of each descriptor linking the image to a class. In order to avoid over training we perform the second step.
2. *Validation:* in this step, we evaluate all the solutions using another image set, called validation; then, the descriptors found for this set are classified using the SVM model created in step 1. The classification results from this step are used as a fitness function and we continue the evolutionary process.
3. *Test:* once the brain programming optimization is finished, we take the solutions from the last generation along their corresponding SVM model in order to evaluate their classification performance on another image set, called test; this evaluation provides the performances of the solutions in order to compare them with other methods.

## 3.1  Image Data Base

The image data based used for this work is called GRAZ-02, it was proposed in [21]. This data base was constructed by using similar environments for all the classes. GRAZ-02 is composed of three classes, where 311 images belong to the persons class, 365 to the bikes class, 420 to the cars class and 380 images conform the background set. This last set does not contain persons, bikes or cars. For this work only the persons class was selected, using the same number of training and testing images as the experiments presented in [21]. Then, 150 images were selected for the training set, 75 images for validation and 75 images for the testing set. One of the advantages of this data base is that it provides segmented images for each of the classes, which was taken as reference for the F-measure evaluation. Figure 4 shows some image samples from the persons class in the GRAZ-02 data base.

**Fig. 4.** Sample images from the *persons* class.

## 3.2  Comparison with Other Methods

The evolutionary parameters for the experiments are: 30 generations, 400 individuals per generation, the initialization of the syntactic trees as done using the *half-and-half* method, using 9 levels as maximum tree depth, with a maximum of 15 genes per chromosome. These parameters were proposed after a tuning procedure. For the parent selection process we used the SPEA2 algorithm [23].

Figure 5 presents the solutions after evaluating the validation set. Note that the graphs show the inverse of the EER versus the average of the F-measure, since the optimization process is performed as a minimization task. One of the issues of an multi-objective approach is finding the best solution, in this case, it was selected according to its performance in classifying the test image set, in order to compare our solution with other methodologies. Nevertheless, due the multiobjective approach there are some solutions that achieve better results in locating the person within the image. Thus, the selected solution $AVCMO - S1$ is detailed in Fig. 5. The $AVCMO - S1$ model outperforms the methods in the

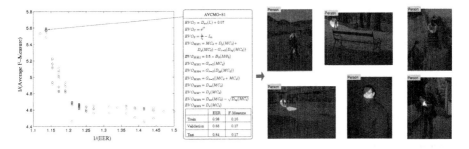

**Fig. 5.** The chart on the left side of the Figure shows the 400 solutions for the validation set. Note that after 30 generations there are some identical solutions due to the diversity loss, also there are several solutions with the same performances score. The $AVCMO-S1$ was selected since it achieves the best score in the testing process. Some test images where the solution is applied can be seen on the right side of the Figure.

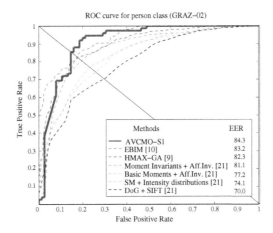

**Fig. 6.** Performance comparison of classification with other methods.

state-of-the-art, see Fig. 6, and it is also capable of finding the object location in the image; some examples of this process are shown in Fig. 5.

## 4    Conclusions and Future Work

This work shows a new methodology for building the description vector in the AVC model. This new strategy seeks to create the descriptor using the information of the image region where the object is located, implicitly finding its location. The training process for this model was performed using the evolutionary technique called brain programming, implemented from a multi-objective perspective. This new approach was applied for classifying the persons class of the GRAZ-02 data base, achieving better results than those in the state-of-the-art. Some future work would be to extend the experimentation to other classes in GRAZ-02 and GRAZ-01.

# References

1. Fukushima, K.: Neural network model for selective attention in visual pattern recognition and associative recall. Appl. Opt. **26**(23), 4985–4992 (1987)
2. Olshausen, B., Anderson, C., Van Essen, D.: A neurobiological model of visual attention and invariant pattern recognition based on dynamic routing of information. J. Neurosci. **13**(11), 4700–4719 (1993)
3. Walther, D., Itti, L., Riesenhuber, M., Poggio, T.A., Koch, C.: Attentional selection for object recognition - a gentle way. In: Bülthoff, H.H., Lee, S.-W., Poggio, T.A., Wallraven, C. (eds.) BMCV 2002. LNCS, vol. 2525, pp. 472–479. Springer, Heidelberg (2002)
4. Itti, L., Koch, C., Niebur, E.: A model of saliency-based visual attention for rapid scene analysis. IEEE Trans. Pattern Anal. Mach. Intell. **20**(11), 1254–1259 (1998)
5. Riesenhuber, M., Poggio, T.: Hierarchical models of object recognition in cortex. Nat. Neurosci. **11**(2), 1019–1025 (1999)
6. Serre, T., Kouh, C., Cadieu, M., Knoblich, G., Kreiman, U., Poggio, T.: Theory of object recognition: computations and circuits in the feedforward path of the ventral stream in primate visual cortex. Technical report. MIT-CSAIL (2005)
7. Mutch, J., Lowe, D.: Object class recognition and localization using sparse features with limited receptive fields. Int. J. Comput. Vis. **80**(1), 45–57 (2008)
8. Wersing, H., Körner, E.: Learning optimized features for hierarchical models of invariant object recognition. Neural Comput. **15**(7), 1559–1588 (2003)
9. Ghodrati, M., Khaligh-Razavi, S., Ebrahimpour, R., Rajaei, K., Pooyan, M.: How can selection of biologically inspired features improve the performance of a robust object recognition model? Plos One **7**(2), 1–15 (2012)
10. Huang, Y., Huang, K., Tao, D., Tan, T., Li, X.: Enhanced biologically inspired model for object recognition. IEEE Trans. Syst. Man Cybern. B Cybern. **41**(6), 1668–1680 (2011)
11. Treisman, A.M., Gelade, G.: A feature-integration theory of attention. Cogn. psychol. **12**(1), 97–136 (1980)
12. Desimone, R., Duncan, J.: Neural mechanisms of selective visual attention. Ann. Rev. **18**, 193–222 (1995)
13. Biederman, I.: Recognition-by-components a theory of human image understanding. Psychol. Rev. **94**(2), 115–147 (1987)
14. Hubel, D.: Exploration of the primary visual cortex, 1955–78. Nature **299**(5883), 515–524 (1982)
15. Mishkin, M., Ungerleider, L., Macko, K.: Object vision and spatial vision: two cortical pathways. TINS **6**, 414–417 (1983)
16. Olague, G., Clemente, E., Dozal, L., Hernández, D.E.: Evolving an artificial visual cortex for object recognition with brain programming. In: Schuetze, O., Coello Coello, C.A., Tantar, A.-A., Tantar, E., Bouvry, P., Del Moral, P., Legrand, P. (eds.) EVOLVE - A Bridge between Probability, Set Oriented Numerics, and Evolutionary Computation III, pp. 97–115. Springer, Heidelberg (2014)
17. Koch, C., Ullman, S.: Shifts in selective visual attention: towards the underlying neural circuitry. Hum. Neurobiol. **4**, 219–227 (1985)

18. Olague, G., Dozal, L., Clemente, E., Ocampo, A.: Optimizing an artificial dorsal stream on purpose for visual attention. In: Schuetze, O., Coello Coello, C.A., Tantar, A.-A., Tantar, E., Bouvry, P., Del Moral, P., Legrand, P. (eds.) EVOLVE - A Bridge between Probability, Set Oriented Numerics, and Evolutionary Computation III, pp. 141–166. Springer, Heidelberg (2014)
19. Milner, A., Goodale, M. (eds.): The Visual Brain in Action, 2nd edn. Oxford University Press, Oxford (2006)
20. Farivar, R.: Dorsal-ventral integration in object recognition. Brain Res. Rev. 61(2), 144–153 (2009)
21. Opelt, A., Pinz, A., Fussenegger, M., Auer, P.: Generic object recognition with boosting. IEEE Trans. Pattern Anal. Mach. Intell. 28(3), 416–431 (2006)
22. Reid, P.: Biometrics for Network Security. Prentice Hall Professional, Upper Saddle River (2004)
23. Bleuler, S., Laumanns, M., Thiele, L., Zitzler, E.: PISA – a platform and programming language independent interface for search algorithms. In: Fonseca, C.M., Fleming, P.J., Zitzler, E., Deb, K., Thiele, L. (eds.) EMO 2003. LNCS, vol. 2632, pp. 494–508. Springer, Heidelberg (2003)

# Fair Resource Allocation Using Multi-population Evolutionary Algorithm

Tohid Erfani[1][✉] and Rasool Erfani[2]

[1] Department of Civil, Environmental and Geomatic Engineering,
University College London, London, UK
t.erfani@ucl.ac.uk
[2] School of Engineering, Manchester Metropolitan University, Manchester, UK
r.erfani@mmu.ac.uk

**Abstract.** Resource allocation between selfish agents are performed under centralised and/or distributed mechanisms. However, there are issues in both cases. In centralised solution, although the resources are allocated in an efficient way, the allocation decisions may not be acceptable for some selfish agents making them reluctant to cooperation. In decentralised solution, although the problem is solved from each agent's perspective, the allocation leads to an inefficient usage of provided resources. For example, such an issue is evident in a water network distribution system where different agents share the river water and a central planner (CP) maximises the social welfare to the whole system. Issue arises when the CP solution is not acceptable by some agents. Therefore, a mechanism should be devised to encourage each agent to accept the CP decision. This paper introduces a mechanism in re-distributing the CP revenue value amongst the competing agents based on their contribution to the CP value. To find each user's contribution, this paper develops a parallel evolutionary search algorithm which enables the agents to autonomously solve their local optimisation problem whilst interacting with the other agents and the whole system. The search evolves towards a solution which is used as an incentive for calculating a fair revenue for each agent. The framework is applied to a river reach with five competitive users. Results show decentralised coupled centralised approaches has the potential to represent mechanisms for a fair resource allocation among competing self-interested agents.

**Keywords:** Resource allocation · Evolutionary algorithm · Parallel multi-population search · Mechanism design · Optimisation

## 1 Introduction and Background

Efficient resource allocation in a network structure is done from a central planner (CP) perspective through maximisation of the sum of all agents' utilities. However, the solutions derived from such an aggregated approach may not be acceptable by self-interested agents. The CP solution carries strong assumptions,

© Springer International Publishing Switzerland 2015
A.M. Mora and G. Squillero (Eds.): EvoApplications 2015, LNCS 9028, pp. 214–224, 2015.
DOI: 10.1007/978-3-319-16549-3_18

presupposing either central planning or perfectly accessibility to the resources for all agents. In CP models, the resources are allocated until marginal value of all users for the available resources remain the same. This leads to unsatisfactory results for some agents with better accessibility to the resources asking for a higher revenue distribution. As an example, consider a river reach where water should be allocated to each agent lying next to the river. The CP aggregated model

- does not recognize the asymmetric accessibility of the water to agents (e.g. from upstream to downstream),
- does not consider that each agent is selfish and acts in its own interests, and
- simulates the results which are only achievable with fully cooperative agents acting as if working under one agent authority.

The above motivations make the selfish agents reluctant to compromise on a CP solution if they envy other agents' benefit (revenue) value. Therefore, the key research question is to devise an encouraging revenue sharing system to guarantee both an efficient resource allocation and a fair revenue distribution.

Simulating resource allocation to overcome the above limitations has led to several attempts in mathematical programming, game theory and heuristic techniques. Amongst are a cascade-like sequential algorithm for upstream-downstream water allocation [1], distributed penalty based water allocation applied in the Yellow river basin [2,3] and multiple complementarity problem approach to simulate river basin allocation model [4]. Although these attempts satisfy the selfishness of each agent in maximising its utility function to achieve higher revenue, it leads to an inefficient solution from CP perspective. Therefore, it is desirable to keep the efficient CP solution but re-distribute the achieved revenue to the agents in a fair way; considering, of course, that the revenue is transferable between agents. To account for this, we define a notion of *fairness* based on each agent's contribution on achieving the CP solution. We calculate a unique solution with some favourable properties which guarantees the cooperation maintenance. To find the agent's impact on CP solution, as will be discussed in the next section, we need to know the best response of each agent on the action of the other group of agents and vice versa, simultaneously. To realize this, we develop an evolutionary algorithm solving interrelated optimisation problems in parallel guiding the search towards a feasible solution in a distributed manner. This will guarantee that the contribution's of each agent is properly captured for later fair revenue distribution. In the next section we start with some definitions and preliminaries. The rest of the Sect. 2 develops the algorithm and Sect. 3 applies it to a water network distribution problem. Section 4 discuss the results with some notes for further investigation and Sect. 5 concludes the paper with extra discussion for future work.

## 2 Proposed Approach

### 2.1 Preliminary and Definitions

Let $I = \{1 \ldots n\}$ denotes a set of agents. Further, assume that each agent $i$ controls vector $x_i \in \mathbb{R}^{n_i}$. Let $x_{-i}$ be a vector containing the strategies (allocation) of all agents excluding that of the agent $i$. Each agent by receiving allocation $x_i$ maximises his revenue via its utility function $u_i$. The utility $u_i$ of the strategy profile $\mathbf{x} = (x_1, \ldots, x_n) \in \mathbb{R}^n_+$ or in short $\mathbf{x} = (x_i, x_{-i})$ is $u_i(\mathbf{x}) = u_i(x_i, x_{-i})$. We define the followings.

***Definition (Central planner welfare maximisation (CP)):*** A solution is a social welfare maximisation or a central planner (CP) approach if it is derived by the following optimisation problem,

$$\mathbf{x}^* = \underset{\mathbf{x}}{argmax} \sum_{i \in I} u_i(\mathbf{x}), \qquad (CP)$$

where summation is over all the utilities of the agents. This leads to a solution from an outside observer as if he/she is responsible for the values of all agents.

***Definition (Contribution to cooperation):*** Define $U^* = \sum_{j \in I} u_j(\mathbf{x}^*)$. Further, assume that agent $i$ decides to leave the cooperation and act as a singleton (or in isolation) and let $U^*_{-i} = \sum_{j \neq i} u_j(x^*_{-i})$ be the summation of all other agent's revenue when $i$ leaves them. We define agent $i$'s impact on CP solution as,

$$\overline{u}_i = U^* - U^*_{-i},$$

which measures how much agent $i$ contributes to CP solution.

***Definition (Fairness):*** A revenue re-distribution mechanism is *fair* if the revenue for each agent $i$ follows the following equation:

$$u^r_i = \alpha_i \times U^*,$$

where,

$$\alpha_i = \frac{\overline{u}_i}{\sum_{j \in I} U^*_{-j}}.$$

This means that each agent gets an allocation based on his contribution to the CP solution. This definition makes sense and has two indirect properties; (a) it is *budget balanced*; that is, the sum of all $u^r_i$ equals the whole CP revenue value $U^*$, which in other words conveys that the mechanism collects and disburses the same amount of money from and to the agents; and, (b) it is *rational*; that is, no agent ever loses by participation (the revenue to each user is greater than zero). The above explains that the more contribution one agent has, the higher its revenue is. In this case, agents are encouraged to abide by the decision derived by CP problem ($\mathbf{x}^*$) if they are given a revenue following $u^r_i$ values.

$U^*_{-i}$ implies that agent $i$, which left the set of all agents, independently compete on the resources with agents $\{1, 2, \ldots, i-1, i+1, \ldots, n\}$. If agent $i$ knew the others' strategies, his strategic problem would become simple; he would be left with the single-agent problem of choosing a utility-maximising problem. However, the two problems formed by agent $i$ and agents $\{1, 2, \ldots, i-1, i+1, \ldots, n\}$ should be solved, simultaneously. This is because of the fact that agent $i$'s best

| **Algorithm 1.** Parallel multi-population search algorithm |
|---|

1   Randomly initialize $n$ populations of size $m$ $(pop_i)$;
2   Define $neighbours_i$ and set $ne_i = |neighbours_i|$;
3   Set $MaxGen$;
4   **while** $Not\ MaxGen$ **do**
5      **for** $i = 1$ **to** $n$ **do**
6         **for** $k = 1$ **to** $m$ **do**
7            Randomly pick $p_{s1} \neq p_{s2} \neq p_{s3} \neq p_k$ from $pop_i$;
8            $p_b \leftarrow$ reproduction $(p_{s1}, p_{s2}, p_{s3})$;
9            **if** $f_i(p_b) \geq f_i(p_k)$ **then**
10               $p_k \leftarrow p_b$
11         $pop_i^* \leftarrow$ The best individual in $pop_i$;
12      $\forall\ i, j = 1, ..., n,\ i \neq j,\ pop_i \leftarrow pop_j^* \wedge j \in neighbours_i$;

strategy depends on the interaction with the group he has left and which should not be ignored when finding $U_{-i}^*$ values. Therefore, $U_{-i}^*$ depends on the solution of two interrelated maximisation problems formed by agent $\{i\}$'s utility, $u_i$, and agents' $\{1, 2, \ldots, i-1, i+1, \ldots, n\}$ aggregated utilities, $\sum_{\substack{j \neq i \\ j \in I}} u_j(x_{-i})$ which should be solved at the same time. We will be using a parallel evolutionary technique defined next to deal with this two distributed problems.

## 2.2 Parallel Multi-population Search Algorithm

Here we formulate a general class of interrelated problems in which their optimisation problems are simultaneously solved in parallel while interacting with each other. In a most general case and where $n$ agents are solving their problems individually, each agent solves one optimisation problem and seeks its own optimal strategies while interacting with the others. More precisely, given $U : \mathbb{R}^n \to \mathbb{R}^n$ representing all $n$ agents' utilities, we find $\mathbf{x} = (x_1, \ldots, x_n) \in \mathbb{R}_+^n$ by simultaneously solving the following $n$ problems:

$$\underset{x_i}{\text{Max}} \qquad u_i(\mathbf{x}) \qquad\qquad\qquad\qquad (P_i)$$

$$\text{subject to} \qquad \mathbf{x} \in X_i.$$

where each agent $i$ controls vector $x_i \in \mathbb{R}^{n_i}$ to optimise the utility (objective) function $u_i$ subject to the constraints set $X_i$ containing $\mathbf{x} \in \mathbb{R}_+^n$. The interrelation is explained as the objective function and the constraints in $P_i$ depend on other agents' decisions.

To solve the $n$ agent problems $P_i$, $i = 1, ..., n$ simultaneously, we dedicate each problem $P_i$ to one agent $i$. Lets call $\mathbf{P}$ the problem formed by all $P_i$s. Since there is interconnection between each problem due to vector $\mathbf{x}$, we solve each problem whilst it communicates with the other problems by sharing information.

We use parallel genetic algorithm [5], concept of cellular evolutionary algorithm [6,7] and the idea of co-evolution with multi-population [8] to solve **P** with an extension that each (sub-)problem $P_i$ has its own objective function. This concept is used in [9] to gain faster convergence to Pareto solution in multiobjective optimisation problem. Let $x_{-i}$ be a vector containing the decision variables of all agents involved in problem $P_i$ excluding that of the agent $i$. The search algorithm is described by $n$ different search trajectories performing in parallel through the following mapping $H$:

$$x_i^{t+1} = H(\overline{x}_{-i}^t, x_i^t, P_i),$$

where $H$ shows the interconnection between the agents. $H$ acts as a synchronization map for agent $i$ to optimise problem $P_i$ given the decisions of other interacting agents in its neighborhood remain fixed shown by $\overline{x}_{-i}^t$. $H$ describes that $x_i$ value is updated by a search on problem $P_i$ at generation $t$ linking decisions $x_i$ and $\overline{x}_{-i}$. Due to problem $P_i$, each agent knows its own problem components and hence by communicating with other neighboring agents through $H$, it has local activity for exploring the search space. In what follows, we give details of the search algorithm to solve the agents problems in Algorithm 1.

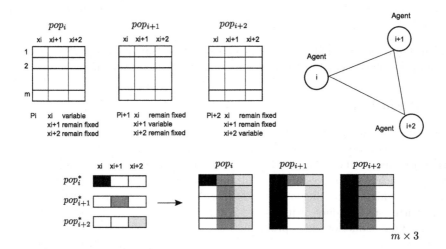

**Fig. 1.** Exchanging the best individual values within the the neighboring populations at the end of each generation for $ne_i = 3$. $x_i^*$ is fixed in $pop_{i+1}$ and $pop_{i+2}$, $x_{i+1}^*$ is fixed in $pop_i$ and $pop_{i+2}$, and finally $x_{i+2}^*$ is fixed in $pop_i$ and $pop_{i+1}$.

Each agent $i$ has a devoted search trajectory formed by a population of size $m$ (Line 1). $pop_i$ is a $m \times ne_i$ matrix and is populated randomly. $ne_i$ is the number of interacting agents given by the cardinal of the set $neighbours_i$ (Line 2). In other words $ne_i$ equals the number of neighboring agents affecting the decision of agent $i$ plus one. All individuals $p_k = (x_1, ..., x_{ne_i})$ in each population $i$ undergoes a reproduction in each generation $t$ of parallel searches (Line 8). At the end of each generation $t$, the neighboring agents ($j \in neighbours_i$) share their best

---

**Algorithm 2.** Steps to redistribute utilities amongst self-interested agents

---

1    Find $U^*$;
2    **for** $i = 1$ **to** $n$ **do**
3      Solve problem $P_1$ and $P_2$ using Algorithm 1;
4    For each agent $i$, calculate $\bar{u}_i$, $\alpha_i$;
5    $u_i^r \leftarrow \alpha_i \times U^*$;
6    Distribute to each agent $u_i^r$;

---

individuals to form the updated population for next generation $t + 1$ (Line 12). The population sharing scheme is illustrated in Fig. 1 where three populations are involved with $ne_i = 3$. As explained in the figure, each agent deals with problem $P_i$ optimising for $x_i$. At the end of each generation $t$, $pop_i^*$, the best individual in $pop_i$ based on its objective value, is obtained. $pop_i^*$ migrates to the population of the neighbors and remain fixed for the next generation $t + 1$. This makes each agent at the end of each generation to be informed of the decisions of the other neighboring agents involved in its own problem. Due to $n$ different search trajectories, the algorithm allows independent search for agents by relying only on locally available information. This procedure leads to the evolution of separate populations over successive generations, and the convergence is assumed when the agents cannot further improve their objective function values $f_i$.

### 2.3   Put It into Context

As stated earlier, to find the contribution $\bar{u}_i$ of each agent $i$ to the CP solution, we need to assure that the solution to agent $i$'s utility maximisation is the best response to the solution of sum of utilities of the other agents and vice versa. To do so, we split the set $I$ by removing one agent at a time from $I$ to form two problems $P_1$ and $P_2$ for each instances. Specifically, problem $P_1$ is the utility maximisation for agent $i$ ($u_i$) and problem $P_2$ is the aggregated utility maximisation for agents $1, 2, \ldots, i - 1, i + 1, \ldots, n$ ($\sum_{\substack{j \neq i \\ j \in I}} u_j(x_{-i})$). Problem $P_1$ and $P_2$ are then solved in parallel for each agent $i$ using Algorithm 1. The Algorithm 2 summarises the steps to obtain a fair resource allocation to different self-interested agents.

     The above shows that for a set of $n$ agents, it is required to solve $n + 1$ problems to find the $u_i^r$ values. In the next section, we look into the applicability of the algorithm to water allocation on a river reach with tributary.

## 3   Experimental Setup

### 3.1   Application of Parallel Algorithm

To demonstrate the proposed formulation, a water network is presented in Fig. 2. There are five different users situated from upstream to downstream named A to E. The users have simple quadratic economic functions

$$a_i x_i - b_i x_i^2,$$

as objective function and they intend to maximise their own benefit by abstracting water from the river. To make the comparisons easily interpretable, $\mathbf{a} = [2, 13, 13, 20, 21]$ is set for users A, B, C, D and E, respectively and $\mathbf{b}$ is a vector of $\mathbf{1}$ for all agents. The agents are interconnected using the mass balance equations and they all follow upstream-downstream relationship. It is assumed that $Q_1 = Q_2 = 10$ and the agents are competing for water abstraction. The independent optimisation formulations are given in Fig. 2 and the centralized formulation, CP, is given as follows.

maximise $\quad f_A(x_2) + f_B(x_4) + f_C(x_7) + f_D(x_{10}) + f_E(x_{12})$
subject to

$$Q_1 - x_1 = 0,$$
$$x_1 - x_2 - x_3 = 0,$$
$$x_3 - x_4 - x_5 = 0,$$
$$Q_2 - x_6 = 0,$$
$$x_6 - x_7 - x_8 = 0,$$
$$x_5 + x_8 - x_9 = 0,$$
$$x_9 - x_{10} - x_{11} = 0,$$
$$x_{11} - x_{12} - x_{13} = 0,$$
$$- x_{13} \leq 0.$$

The CP simulates a water market as if the water is sold from one agents to the others [10–12].

## 3.2   Search Algorithm Tuning

In this study, amongst different evolutionary operators, differential evolution (DE) [13] is adopted for reproduction stage in Line 7–8. Corresponding to each $p_k$, individuals $p_{s1}$, $p_{s2}$ and $p_{s3}$ are randomly chosen from population $pop_i$ and new vector $p_c$ is created by adding the weighted difference of $p_{s2}$ and $p_{s3}$ to the $p_{s1}$ given by,

$$p_c = p_{s1} + MF(p_{s2} - p_{s3}),$$

where $MR$ is the mutation rate. $p_c$ is accepted as a new vector, $p_b$, if the following is satisfied

$$p_b = \begin{cases} p_c & if \ \ rand(0,1) \leq CR \\ p_k & otherwise. \end{cases} \tag{1}$$

$CR$ is the probability of crossover and $rand$ is pseudo random number between 0 and 1. If vector $p_c$ violates the bound constraints, it gets the value half way between the $p_k$ and the bound violated. Since each instance has two interrelated

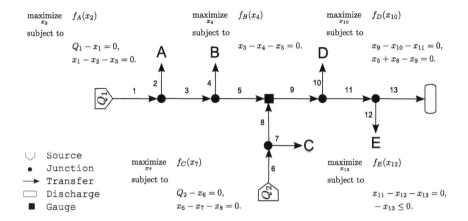

**Fig. 2.** Water distribution network and each agent's formulation

problem $P_1$ and $P_2$, therefore, $ne = 2$ in all cases. The population size for each agent is $m = 50$, the maximum number of generation is $MaxGen = 100$ and $MR$ and $CR$ values used within DE equal 0.7 and 0.5, respectively following [13]. The problems are solved 30 times to account for variability and the average value is reported. Since the problem is constrained to mass balance equations, different constraint-handling techniques such as a simple penalty function may be implemented. Since finding a penalty factor might be a challenge, we have used constraint domination following [14] which rank the feasible populations based on their objective values and infeasible ones only based on their extent of constraint violation. The CP instance uses DE with the same number of generations and population size. Matlab programming is used for coding and experiments.

## 4    Results and Discussions

Results of water distribution revenues are tabulated in Table 1. In centralized approach (CP), upstream users give up water to be abstracted by downstream user $E$ generating higher benefit to the whole system (summed to $249.32 = 0 + 30.89 + 30.89 + 88.64 + 98.89$). The water is allocated until each user's marginal value remains the same. In decentralized parallel approaches, five different problem instances are solved. The upstream agents benefit from their location in the river and intuitively downstream users have higher incentive to join the group of upstream agents. Specifically, results indicate that agent A enjoys from being upstream and hence fully satisfy himself and contribute 7.12 ($= 249.32 - (29.15 + 29.15 + 86.82 + 97.07)$) to the CP value. Agents B's problem situation is, however, different since agent A is now collaborating with B's downstream agents and is able to divert water to them leaving agent B without any water to abstract. This leads to $13.11$ ($= 249.32 - (0 + 36.82 + 94.57 + 104.82)$) contribution of agent B. The same kind of situation holds for problems of agent

D and E concluding 58.68 and 67.82 contribution. Agent C is on upstream tributary with independent water security contributing 57.57 ($= 249.32 - (0 + 22 + 79.75 + 90)$) to the CP solution. Table 1 summarises the contributions as well as the final revenue values $u_i^r$ for each agent. As can be seen, user A and C's final revenue has increased due to their location advantages while user D and E's final revenue is increased due to their high utility values they provide on CP solution. Although agent B and C have the same marginal values in their utility function (both are 13), agent B's contribution is not as important as agent C's which leads to $u_B^r < u_C^r$ (Note that, the revenue from CP solution is 30.89 for each agent B and C but their $u^r$ values are different). In other words, the analysis on this network shows that agent B is not as powerful as agent C, since, from CP perspective, its contribution worth less than that of user C's.

**Table 1.** Water allocation revenue distribution results

| Agent | Parallel Problems | Revenue | | | |
| | | Singleton ($P_1$) | Group ($P_2$) | Contribution ($\overline{u}_i$) | Final Value ($u_i^r$) |
|---|---|---|---|---|---|
| A | $\{A\}\{BCDE\}$ | 1.00 | 242.19 | 7.13 | 8.71 |
| B | $\{B\}\{ACDE\}$ | 0.00 | 236.21 | 13.11 | 16.00 |
| C | $\{C\}\{ABDE\}$ | 42.25 | 191.75 | 57.57 | 70.25 |
| D | $\{D\}\{ABCE\}$ | 0.00 | 190.64 | 58.68 | 71.60 |
| E | $\{E\}\{ABCD\}$ | 0.00 | 181.50 | 67.82 | 82.76 |
| CP | $\{ABCDE\}$ | n/a | 249.32 | n/a | n/a |

The results are averaged over 30 runs. The variance for all is less than 0.1.

### 4.1 Social Cost and Stability of Proposed Mechanism

The followings are two notes directly derived from the proposed solution concept.

*Social cost.* The contribution value $\overline{u}_i = U^* - U_{-i}^*$ can be differently interpreted. If for each agent $i$ we extend $\overline{u}_i$ equation, we get the following equation:

$$\overline{u}_i = U^* - U_{-i}^* = u_i^* - \left(U_{-i}^* - \sum_{j \neq i} u_j^*\right).$$

The value in the bracket is the *social cost* of agent $i$ since it measures the aggregated impact that agent $i$'s participation has on others' utilities. Therefore, $\overline{u}_i$ is derived in such a way that the social welfare value of agent $i$, $u_i^*$, is adjusted to the cost it has on society. The zero cost means that the existence of an agent in cooperation does not have any effect on the overall CP value, while the positive cost means that his existence in group makes the things worst for the others. The negative cost is also possible indicating how useful an agent's participation is on the cooperation. In our example, the social cost for users are $-7.14$, $22.17$, $-26.68$, $29.96$ and $31.07$ for A, B, C, D, and E, respectively. As can be seen, agents A and C have positive impact on society with negative social cost.

*Stability.* We note that the final $x_i^r$ values are unique. However, the solution might not be a *stable* one to be compromised on. Therefore, one might seek a solution for which each agent is guaranteed a value at least as the amount he could achieve by leaving the cooperation and act as a singleton (in isolation). As can be seen in Table 1, the final revenues $x_i^r$ are all greater than singleton values. Whether this is a coincidence or a properties of this solution concept, it should be discussed and analysed further.

## 5    Conclusion and Future Work

We consider how selfish agents are likely to consider cooperation with other inter-related agents to guarantee an efficient central planner (CP) solution. A fair revenue sharing redistribution mechanism is defined by measuring individual agent's contribution to the CP solution. Each agent's revenue is proportional to the impact he has on the CP solution. However, finding agent's contribution is a challenge. We have developed a parallel evolutionary approach to ensure that agent $i$'s utility maximisation solution is the best response to the sum of other agents' utility maximisation problem and vice versa. Each agent synchronises its best fitted individual in his population with the other competing agents. This maintains the agent's awareness of each others' decisions guiding the search to a feasible solution. The approach is tested on a water network distribution system where autonomous agents with individual economic objective functions situated within the river reach and are interconnected by water sharing relationship (upstream-downstream). The results show that the proposed approach is able to capture the true interrelation of the agents and to efficiently find their contribution to the CP value.

The revenue distribution is a fair and unique approach but its stability requires further investigation. This paper only proposed an evolutionary based framework to find the contribution of each agent to the CP solution. However, its algorithmic characteristics still needs to be explored. Future research can analyse the technique for feasibility assurance and possibly faster convergence by using different operators and heuristics. In addition, since $n$ instances of problems are independent from each other, a parallelization scheme can be implemented. This framework can also be extended to consider aerospace flow control problems, where the velocity profiles induced by dielectric barrier discharge plasma actuator are required to be represented by interrelated agents problems [15–17].

**Acknowledgements.** Four anonymous reviewers provided comments and suggestions that improved the content and presentation of the paper. All errors or omissions are the authors alone.

# References

1. Wang, L., Fang, L., Hipel, K.W.: Basin-wide cooperative water resources allocation. Eur. J. Oper. Res. **190**, 798–817 (2008)
2. Yang, Y.C.E., Cai, X., Stipanović, D.M.: A decentralized optimization algorithm for multiagent system-based watershed management. Water Resour. Res. **45**, W08430 (2009)
3. Yang, Y.C.E., Zhao, J., Cai, X.: Decentralized optimization method for water allocation management in the yellow river basin. J. Water Resour. Plan. Manag. **138**, 313–325 (2011)
4. Britz, W., Ferris, M., Kuhn, A.: Modeling water allocating institutions based on multiple optimization problems with equilibrium constraints. Environ. Model. Softw. **46**, 196–207 (2013)
5. Mühlenbein, H., Schomisch, M., Born, J.: The parallel genetic algorithm as function optimizer. Parallel Comput. **17**, 619–632 (1991)
6. Alba, E., Troya, J.M.: Cellular evolutionary algorithms: evaluating the influence. In: Deb, K., Rudolph, G., Lutton, E., Merelo, J.J., Schoenauer, M., Schwefel, H.-P., Yao, X. (eds.) PPSN 2000. LNCS, vol. 1917, pp. 29–38. Springer, Heidelberg (2000)
7. Tomassini, M.: Cellular evolutionary algorithms. In: Kroc, J., Sloot, P.M.A., Hoekstra, A.G. (eds.) Simulating Complex Systems by Cellular Automata. Understanding Complex Systems, vol. 2010, pp. 167–191. Springer, Heidelberg (2010)
8. Potter, M.A., De Jong, K.A.: Cooperative coevolution: an architecture for evolving coadapted subcomponents. Evol. Comput. **8**, 1–29 (2000)
9. Lee, D., Gonzalez, L.F., Periaux, J., Srinivas, K.: Efficient hybrid-game strategies coupled to evolutionary algorithms for robust multidisciplinary design optimization in aerospace engineering. IEEE Trans. Evol. Comput. **15**, 133–150 (2011)
10. Erfani, T., Huskova, I., Harou, J.J.: Tracking trade transactions in water resource systems: a node-arc optimization formulation. Water Resour. Res. **49**, 3038–3043 (2013)
11. Erfani, T., Binions, O., Harou, J.J.: Simulating water markets with transaction costs. Water Resour. Res. **50**, 4726–4745 (2014)
12. Erfani, T., Binions, O., Harou, J.: Protecting environmental flows through enhanced water licensing and water markets. Hydrol. Earth Syst. Sci. Discuss. **11**, 2967–3003 (2014)
13. Price, K.V., Lampinen, J.A., Storn, R.M.: Differential Evolution: A Practical Approach to Global Optimization. Springer, Heidelberg (2005)
14. Deb, K.: An efficient constraint handling method for genetic algorithms. Comput. Methods Appl. Mech. Eng. **186**, 311–338 (2000)
15. Erfani, R., Erfani, T., Utyuzhnikov, S.V., Kontis, K.: Optimisation of multiple encapsulated electrode plasma actuator. Aerosp. Sci. Technol. **26**, 120–127 (2013)
16. Erfani, R., Zare-Behtash, H., Kontis, K.: Influence of shock wave propagation on dielectric barrier discharge plasma actuator performance. J. Phys. D: Appl. Phys. **45**, 225201 (2012)
17. Erfani, R., Zare-Behtash, H., Kontis, K.: Plasma actuator: influence of dielectric surface temperature. Exp. Therm. Fluid Sci. **42**, 258–264 (2012)

EvoENERGY

# Multiobjective Methodology for Assessing the Location of Distributed Electric Energy Storage

José Gonçalves[1,2(✉)], Luís Neves[1,2,3], and António Gomes Martins[1,2]

[1] INESC – Institute for Systems Engineering and Computers at Coimbra, Coimbra, Portugal
jagoncalves@gmail.com, luis.neves@ipleiria.pt, agmartins@uc.pt
[2] Energy for Sustainability Initiative, University of Coimbra, Coimbra, Portugal
[3] Polytechnic Institute of Leiria, Leiria, Portugal

**Abstract.** The perception of the associated impacts among possible management schemes introduces a new way to assess energy storage systems. The ability to define a specific management scheme considering the different stakeholder objectives, both technical and economic, will increase the perception of available installation options. This paper presents a multiobjective feasibility assessment methodology using an improved version of the Non-dominated Sorting Genetic Algorithm II, to optimize the placement of electric energy storage units in order to improve the operation of distribution networks. The model is applied to a case study, using lithium-ion battery technology as an example. The results show the influence of different charging/discharging profiles on the choice of the best battery location, as well as the influence that these choices may have on the different network management objectives, e.g. increasing the integration of renewable generation. As an additional outcome, the authors propose a pricing scheme for filling the present regulatory gap regarding the pricing scheme to be applied to energy storage in order to allow the exploitation of viable business models.

**Keywords:** Genetic algorithms · Energy storage · Power distribution networks · Energy profiles · Energy service · NSGAII

## 1 Introduction

The new electricity network challenges presented by the integrating of integrate distributed generation can lead to a more complex and less secure power system operation.

In the context of a microgrid environment, distributed electric energy storage systems(DEESS) are presented as an option to enable the optimization of resources, by providing the capability of effectively balancing supply and demand [1]. However, a methodology is needed to evaluate the best allocation of DEESS to provide the needed energy services to the network.

The proposed methodology allows the perception of the associated impacts from possible ESS management schemes, considering a potential pricing scheme for the energy delivered within the current legal framework for the ESS exploitation, and different objectives for the operation of DEESS representing different stakeholders.

© Springer International Publishing Switzerland 2015
A.M. Mora and G. Squillero (Eds.): EvoApplications 2015, LNCS 9028, pp. 227–238, 2015.
DOI: 10.1007/978-3-319-16549-3_19

## 2    Electrical Energy Storage Systems

Previous research assessing the impact of energy storage systems (ESS) on the power system operation and economics has been focused on economic/optimal sizing.

As such, ESS has been modelled from the point of view of cost (economic models) or with a focus on the assessment of operational benefits, modelling the ESS response to power system disturbances at appropriate time scales (operational models) [2].

Some authors presented methodologies for evaluating the costs and benefits associated to energy storage [3, 4]. However none of those studies considered the ESS management scheme and its associated impacts.

Methodologies considering the use of electric vehicles (EV) may consider possible charging/discharging (C/D) schemes when providing specific energy service [5]. However this type of methodologies are more concerned with the unpredictability of the remaining energy available in the EVs than with their optimal grid distribution and associated impacts [6].

The storage management using intelligent C/D schemes is presented in [5] as a possible solution to release network capacity as well as to enable a more efficient operation. According to those authors, this approach may provide a basis to postpone grid reinforcements by investors, to decrease network losses, to avoid short interruptions and voltage quality problems, to shave power peaks and to smooth load curves.

A detailed literature review about the ESS operation, application, barriers and impact assessment was presented by the authors in Refs. [7, 8].

## 3    Definition of the Design Strategies

In order to fill the present regulatory gap regarding a possible pricing scheme to be applied to ESS the present methodology considers DEESS as special regime producers (SRP), thus benefiting from the same feed-in tariff used by renewable energy producers.

The pricing scheme proposed in this study considers that the electric ESS buys energy at the daily market price and sells it at SRP prices in high demand periods. This seems justifiable as the DEESS may play an important role to support the increased share of renewable energy (RE), avoiding the use of backup thermal generation. This study used an average SRP surplus tariff of 24.18€/MWh, corresponding to the available consumption data of 2008.

The strategy chosen for the current work was to optimize the location of each unit of the set of DEESS that would simultaneously maximize profits, minimize investment costs, network losses and voltage deviations. For that purpose, the authors chose to use an improved version of the Non-dominated Sorting Genetic Algorithm II (NSGAII).

The analysis was performed using daily profiles of demand, renewable generation and spot price obtained through clustering techniques applied to historical data. Network losses were determined by applying the demand and generation profiles as inputs to powerflow calculations, using Matpower and Matlab TM.

## 4 Methodology

To obtain the Pareto front representing the non-dominated solutions that represent the multiple optimization objectives, a previous characterization of the situation and a definition of the working objectives is needed, as presented in Fig. 1 for each scenario, using the iNSGAII in step 3. The algorithm was loaded with the network, technology characterization and service definition data block, defining this procedure as the first step of the methodology.

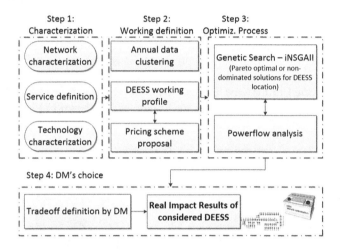

**Fig. 1.** Methodology definition for DEESS location assessment

The technology characterization block includes the technical characteristics of the considered ESS (battery plus power converter), since solutions depend on the technology and its working limits. This block provides information to define the working periods of the C/D profile in the DEESS working profile block and the capacity limits to be used in the optimization process and power flow analysis performed in the genetic search block INSGAII.

The network characterization block includes the daily demand diagram of the distribution substation and combines the active and passive elements of the studied electricity grid. Though the proposed methodology aims to study the best ESS location within a distribution network, considering different management schemes, it may be applied to any type of grid provided that the correct characterization is done.

The first step, the service definition is settled in this study with three main objectives, societal objectives, such as network power losses reductions and RE generation integration and private investor objectives, namely the maximization of income from buying and selling in different time periods.

The DEESS working profile block, within step 2, represents an intermediate stage for definition of the C/D schedule considering the ESS technology and the main proposed objectives. Therefore, it combines the objective of the DM with the technical limits of the considered ESS.

In order to define a C/D profile the storage elements and to evaluate the economical value of the operation, prototypes of daily load demand profiles (DLDp), as well as energy market rates profiles (EMRp) and renewable wind generation profiles (RWGp) were needed.

For solving this problem in step2: *Annual data clustering*, the authors developed a process to obtain such profiles using cluster analysis, namely through a competitive neural networks method, confirmed with a hierarchical clustering approach.

The output of this process was the definition of 5 clusters of daily diagrams for each data type from which a prototype could be derived as well as its representativeness in one year of data. The definition of the number of clusters was assessed by analyzing the tree dendogram and the distance between the centers of each cluster.

The step3 *iNSGAII* block uses the genetic algorithm to search for non-dominated solutions. The tool uses a "Binary Tournament Selection" based on the rank and crowding distance to choose the best individuals for the evolution process. Namely, an individual is selected in the rank is lesser than the other or if crowding distance is greater than the other for individuals in the same rank, as shown in Fig. 2.

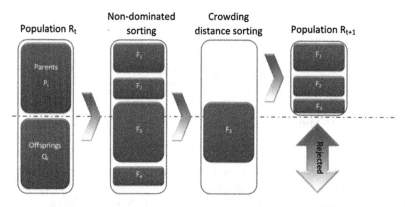

**Fig. 2.** Binary tournament selection in the improved NSGAII

For the considered case study, the iNSGAII population of possible solutions was assumed to be composed of 150 individuals while a maximum number of 100 generations was defined, both values that were consistently above those needed for convergence to be attained.

The tool evaluation functions were integrated in the algorithm using powerflow analysis to evaluate the impact of each individual solution on the network performance.

The final preferred solution must be chosen from the Pareto front resulting from step 3, by the DM, in step4: *DM's choice*, considering its own perception and assumed tradeoffs between the objectives. The resulting impact will finally be attained considering the DM's choice.

## 4.1  Improved NSGAII

As a tool to solve the multi-objective problem formulated in the current work, the authors chose an improved version of the NSGAII (iNSGAII) which has proven to be efficient, especially in power distribution operation and planning problems when compared with conventional algorithms and particle swarm optimization (PSO) [9, 10].

The iNSGAII draws on the work developed in [11], replacing the fixed genetic operators of conventional NSGAII with dynamic adaptation of crossover (pc) and mutation (pm) probabilities, according to the genetic diversity in the population.

This feature avoids premature convergence by maintaining the genetic diversity of the population ($G_{div}$) using the following heuristic updating principles:

1. Use large pc and small pm when $G_{div}$ in the current generation is large;
2. Use reduced pc and large pm when $G_{div}$ in the current generation is reduced.

The genetic diversity of one population is determined by the genetic variability of individuals being responsible for the dispersion of solutions in the feasible space. To measure the resemblance of individuals they must be regarded as a multidimensional vector using a distance vector.

If the distance is below a predefined threshold (Dth), we may assume the two individuals are similar; else, the two individuals are dissimilar [10].

$$d(i,j) = \sqrt{(g_i(1) - g_j(1))^2 + \cdots + (g_i(N) - g_j(N))^2} \qquad (1)$$

Where $g_i$ is the chromosome of individual "i" and $g_j$ the chromosome of individual "j".

To measure the genetic diversity (Gdiv), the following equation is used:

$$G_{div} = \left( \frac{\sum_{i=1}^{Nind} \sum_{j=i+1}^{Nind} 1_{\{d(i,j) > Dth\}}}{N_{ind} \times C_2} \right) \times 100 \qquad (2)$$

$G_{div}$ it is a variable in the range [0, 100] meaning that when the value is zero all individuals are similar and when it is 100 all individuals in the population are dissimilar.

For the optimization process, the authors used four multi criteria evaluation parameters presented in the following paragraphs as objective functions to be optimized simultaneously.

The first evaluation function to be minimized is the sum of the network power losses (PL) in all the n branches of the MV distribution network during the whole day. The elementary time interval is a quarter-hour (tj = 0.25 h) so the data set has 96 values (m = 96).

$$NEL = \sum_{i=1}^{n} \sum_{j=1}^{m} \frac{PL_{ij}}{t_j} \qquad (3)$$

The second evaluation function to be minimized is the network voltage quadratic mean deviation (*NVqmd*), for all individual voltage deviations (*VD*) in the *N* network buses compared with the voltage reference value $(V_{ref})$, during each elementary time interval.

$$NVqmd = \frac{\sqrt{\frac{\sum_{k=1}^{N}\left(VD_k^2 - V_{ref}^2\right)}{N}}}{\sum_{j=1}^{m} t_j} \tag{4}$$

The third evaluation function to be minimized is the network storage annualized cost $(NSAC)$ for installing $x$ units of DEESS, with an individual capital cost $(Cac)$. The $C_{ac}$ is calculated considering the global capital costs $(c_c)$ and the capital recovery factor $(CRF)$ as presented in Eq. 5, where $d$ is the dimensionless discount rate and $y$ the expected life of the equipment, measured in years;

$$\text{NSAC} = x \times C_{ac} = x \times c_c \times CRF = x \times c_c \times \frac{d(1+d)^y}{(1+d)^y - 1} \tag{5}$$

The fourth evaluation function is the network energy rate benefit $(NERB)$ considering the energy tariff $(C)$ and the required energy $(E)$ to charge $(ch)$ and discharge $(dch)$ in one day.

$$NERB = \sum_{j=1}^{m}(E_{dch} \times C_{dch} - E_{ch} \times C_{ch})_j \tag{6}$$

## 4.2 Network Characterization

The case study made use of the IEEE 69 bus three-phase balanced 12.66 kV RDS [12], a well-documented network, often used for research purposes.

The network was comprised by an 8 MVA substation and 69 nodes from which 48 are load-points (distribution transformers), with a total load of 3.8 MW and 2.69 MVAr (peak period). The network in its radial configuration had all the boundary tie-switches in the open position.

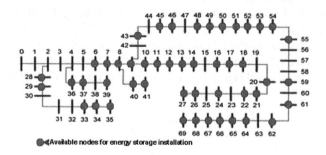

**Fig. 3.** 12.66 kV radial distribution systems

As shown in Fig. 3, the proposed RDS included 48 distribution transformers, which the DM considers as possible locations for the installation of the ESS units.

The decision maker can easily define the availability of a specific node for ESS installation using a binary number (1 or 0) (Table 1).

Table 1. Example of coding technique for identification of available buses

| Node number | 1 | 2 | 3 | 4 | ... | n − 1 | N |
|---|---|---|---|---|---|---|---|
| Availability Status | 0 | 1 | 1 | 0 | ... | 1 | 0 |

This information will be used to compose a reference vector in order to translate bus references into chromosomes and back. This technique will assure that all possible chromosomes correspond only to admissible solutions, also reducing their size to the maximum number of allowed storage sites (Table 2).

Table 2  Example of the reference chromosome

| Reference chromosome | Node number | 2 | 3 | ... | z |
|---|---|---|---|---|---|
| | Availability status for GA | 1 | 1 | ... | 1 |

## 4.3   Technology Characterization

The assessment of the DEESS evaluation impact is dependent of the considered technology. Therefore, the simulations were performed using data available from a manufacturer of nanophosphate lithium ion batteries.

The selected battery with the respective power converter were characterized according to the data available at the manufacturer website and technical publications [13, 14]. According to these data, a total energy of 64,35 Wh/cell was assumed to correspond to one hour of charging with 100 % of depth of discharge (DoD).

From the definitions of the battery manufacturer, the "1CA" (Cranking amperes) discharging profile was chosen, corresponding to a discharging current of 19.50 A, with 3.30 V per cell, or 64.35 W per cell. The proposed solution required roughly 0.1 m$^3$ for the battery systems (a battery pack of two Rows of 180 cells) without power converter (PC), a volume that could be easily integrated in any power transformer (PT) facility.

According to several manufacturers, a plausible 90 % PC efficiency [13] can be expected, with a nominal charging power of 23.17 kW and a discharging capacity of 20.85 kW per PT.

Considering the total of 360 cells and a unitary cell price of roughly 51.70 € [15], the capital cost is 18 612.00 €. Regarding the PC, an estimated cost of 6 949.80 € was obtained from [16]. The total cost of the storage system is estimated in 25 561.80 €.

Assuming an interest rate of 8 % and a lifetime of 15 years, the resulting annualized capital cost was 2 986.37 €.

### 4.4    Working Profile Definition

The proposed approach used three scenarios, regarding plausible objectives for the energy storage:

- Objective 1 – To maximize profit from daily energy spot market rates;
- Objective 2 – To minimize daily energy distribution network losses;
- Objective 3 – To maximize profit from renewable wind generation.

These objectives establish three possible C/D profiles to be evaluated under each defined prototype, during the optimization process, in terms of return on investment, grid losses, voltage deviation and net benefit of energy buying and selling operations in different time periods.

For objectives 1 and 2, the charging periods were established to use the periods of lowest rates and minimum network power losses, respectively, while the discharging periods were defined for the highest rates and maximum power losses, respectively.

Regarding scenario 3, the methodology intended to compare the average daily load diagram with each of the five wind energy production daily prototype diagrams, obtained during the data clustering stage.

In order to control the amount of RE supplied to the grid, a comparison was made between normalized profiles of wind generation and the average annual load demand (LD).

The C/D profiles were derived from the difference between the average LD profile and the five wind generation prototypes. Namely, a negative difference result represents a potential excessive wind generation and positive results represent the periods when stored energy should be delivered because demand is less likely to be supplied by RE generation.

For each objective, twenty-five simulations were performed as a result of combining the following prototypes:

- Set 1: The five EMRp combined with the five DLDp for Objective 1 and 2;
- Set 2: The five RWGp combined with the five EMRp for objective 3.

All the C/D profiles were gathered into an input binary matrix that defines the daily C/D periods to be used in the optimization process.

## 5    Results

The DEESS management scheme, which depends strongly on the fact that the DM has to balance his choices among three different objectives, has a marked influence on results. Different management schemes of wind integration lead, as depicted in Fig. 4, for a sub-set of input scenarios, to a variation of daily losses between 8416.87 kWh and 8473.22 kWh. For the sake of alleviating the computational burden, a single annual average LD profile was used, in the case of objective 3, instead of five different profiles. Nevertheless, five different profiles were preserved in the calculations, both for renewable (wind generation) production and for market energy rates.

The impact results for objectives 1 and 2 are similar, both presenting possible NEL reduction and NERB improvement among simulations, in which different management

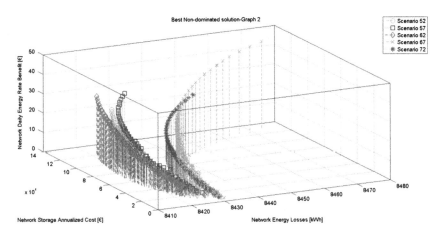

**Fig. 4.** Simulation results under objective 3

schemes influence the Pareto-fronts. However, depending on the considered LD prototype profile, different variations were obtained, showing that network operating conditions should be accounted for the DEESS assessment, as presented in Fig. 5.

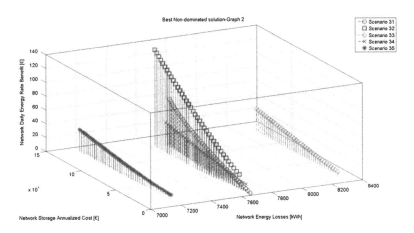

**Fig. 5.** Simulation results under objective 2

Figure 6 shows that the increase of investment in ESS units not necessarily contribute to the NEL reduction. It also shows that the management scheme may have an important influence in the final NEL. A possible future development that might prove useful consists on comparing the overall impacts of DEESS and of the conventional thermal backup to RE production.

Different evolution gradients are observable in Fig. 7, of NERB as regards to NSAC, pertaining to objective 3. This may prove useful to the decision maker when establishing tradeoffs between costs and revenues.

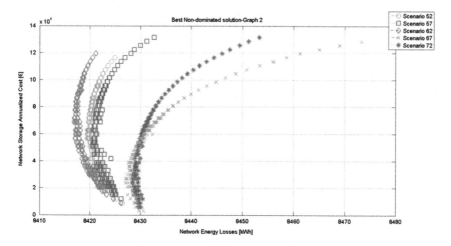

**Fig. 6.** NSAC vs NEL simulations under objective 3

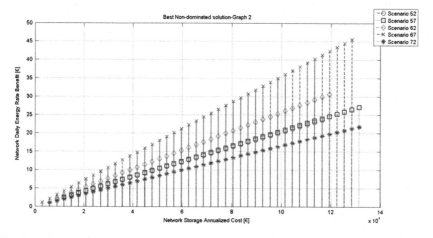

**Fig. 7.** Relation between NERB and NSAC among objective 3 performed simulation results

The methodological proposal presented in the paper, combining technical and economic evaluation parameters, is directed at facilitating the decision making process, especially when it aims to consider the combined preferences of societal and private stakeholders. In this context, the proposed tool can also play an assisting role in the definition of a regulating framework for deployment of DEESS and market integration.

## 6 Conclusions

The search for an optimal location of DEESS aiming the minimization of power losses, voltage deviation and investment, simultaneously maximizing the net income resulting from the difference between energy sale revenue and energy purchase cost in different time periods, required the use of a multiobjective optimization method. In this context, a genetic algorithm proved to be a suitable choice to assess non-correlated objectives.

The method chosen was an improved NSGAII algorithm as explained in [8], avoiding the need of a previous definition of fitness weight factors by the DM and using dynamic crossover and mutation probabilities, depending on the genetic diversity of the population of solutions. It becomes thus possible not to present an "optimal solution" to the DM but provide the opportunity to choose his/her preferred solution from the highest quality set of non-dominated solutions presented by the search tool, according to assumed tradeoffs between the objectives.

The present work also proposes a possible pricing scheme to be used for promoting DEESS exploitation since the existence of a regulatory framework may stimulate the existence of market players intending to invest on energy storage. As one of the main objectives is balancing the surplus/deficit periods of RE availability, the authors assumed that the energy recovered from energy storage should be rewarded on an equivalent basis to the energy that is displaced.

The stakeholders that can benefit from the developed methodology are the DSO and the SRP or any authority acting on behalf of societal interest.

Considering the different stakeholder interests the proposed methodology intends to provide a set of non-dominated solution instead of defining a single final solution. The definitive solution will depend of the DM final choice.

Increasing the flexibility of the C/D cycles of the storage medium could modify the economic results of the energy storage model. In fact, different algorithms used to determine the C/D cycle could lead to a different relation between the optimization objectives, being this a direction of study that the authors intend to pursue.

**Acknowledgments.** This work has been framed under the Energy for Sustainability Initiative of the University of Coimbra, and supported by the Energy and Mobility for Sustainable Regions Project CENTRO-07-0224-FEDER-002004, co-funded by the European Regional Development Fund (ERDF) through the «Programa Operacional Regional do Centro 2007–2013 (PORC)», in the framework of the «Sistema de Apoio a Entidades do Sistema Científico e Tecnológico Nacional». The work was also funded by the «Fundação para a Ciência e Tecnologia» under PEst-OE/EEI/UI0308/2014.

# References

1. EPRI: Electricity Energy Storage Technology Options., California (2010)
2. Divya, K.C., Østergaard, J.: Battery energy storage technology for power systems—an overview. Electr. Power Syst. Res. **79**, 511–520 (2009)
3. Schoenung, S.: Energy Storage Systems Cost Update A Study for the DOE Energy Storage Systems Program. Sandia National Laboratories, California (2011)
4. Kempton, W., Tomić, J.: Vehicle-to-grid power fundamentals: calculating capacity and net revenue. J. Power Sour. **144**, 268–279 (2005)
5. Lassila, J., Haakana, J., Tikka, V., Partanen, J.: Methodology to analyze the economic effects of electric cars as energy storages. IEEE Trans. Smart Grid. **3**, 506–516 (2012)

6. Battistelli, C., Baringo, L., Conejo, A.J.: Optimal energy management of small electric energy systems including V2G facilities and renewable energy sources. Electr. Power Syst. Res. **92**, 50–59 (2012)

7. Gonçalves, J.A.R., Martins, A.G., Neves, L.M.P.: Potential role of stationary urban distributed storage on the management of power systems. In: International Conference on Energy & Environment (ICEE 2013), Porto, p. 11 (2013)

8. Gonçalves, J.A.R., Vitorino, R.M., Neves, L.M.P., Martins, A.G.: Assessment of best location of distributed storage using improved genetic algorithms. Energy for Sustainability 2013, Sustainable Cities: Designing for People and the Planet, p. 7. Energy for Sustainability 2013, Coimbra (2013)

9. Vitorino, R.M., Jorge, H.M., Neves, L.P.: Loss and reliability optimization for power distribution system operation. Electr. Power Syst. Res. **96**, 177–184 (2013)

10. Vitorino, R.M., Neves, L.P., Jorge, H.M.: Network reconfiguration to improve reliability and efficiency in distribution systems. In: 2009 IEEE Bucharest PowerTech, pp. 1–7 (2009)

11. Vitorino, R.M., Jorge, H.M., Neves, L.P.: Multi-objective optimization using NSGA-II for power distribution system reconfiguration. Int. Trans. Electr. Energy Syst. (2013). doi:10.1002/etep.1819

12. Sahoo, N.C., Prasad, K.: A fuzzy genetic approach for network reconfiguration to enhance voltage stability in radial distribution systems. Energy Convers. Manag. **47**, 3288–3306 (2006)

13. Systems, A.: Nanophosphate Basics: An Overview of the Structure, Properties and Benefits of A123 Systems' Proprietary Lithium Ion Battery Technology (2013)

14. Systems, A.: Nanophosphate Lithium Ion Prismatic Pouch Cell (2012)

15. BuyA123baterries: buyA123batteries. http://www.buya123batteries.com/category_s/1825.htm

16. Vasconcelos, J., Ruester, S., He, X., Chong, E., Glachant, J.-M.: Seventh Framework Programme (European Commission): Electricity Storage: How to Facilitate its Deployment and Operation in the EU Final Report. European University Institute, European Union Centre in Taiwan, Firenze, Italy, Taipei, Taiwan (2012)

# Evolutionary Optimization of Smart Buildings with Interdependent Devices

Ingo Mauser[1]([⊠]), Julian Feder[2], Jan Müller[2], and Hartmut Schmeck[2]

[1] FZI Research Center for Information Technology, 76131 Karlsruhe, Germany
mauser@fzi.de
[2] Karlsruhe Institute of Technology – Institute AIFB, 76128 Karlsruhe, Germany
julian.feder@student.kit.edu, {jan.mueller,schmeck}@kit.edu

**Abstract.** To enable a more efficient utilization of energy carriers, energy management systems (EMS) are designed to optimize the usage of energy in future smart buildings. In this paper, we present an EMS for buildings that uses a novel approach towards optimization of energy flows. The system is capable of handling interdependencies between multiple devices consuming energy, while keeping a modular approach towards components of the EMS and their optimization. Evaluations of the EMS in a realistic scenario, which consists of a building with adsorption chiller, hot and cold water storage tanks as well as combined heat and power plant, show the ability to reduce energy consumption and costs by an improved scheduling of the generation of hot and chilled water for cooling purposes.

**Keywords:** Energy management · Smart building · Evolutionary Algorithm · Combined heat and power plant · Adsorption chiller

## 1 Introduction

The transition from fossil energy carriers towards renewable energy sources is one of today's most important challenges for society. To support this transition, the European Union has defined ambitious goals for the year 2030: A reduction of greenhouse gas emissions by at least $40\%$, an increase of the share of renewable energy to at least $27\%$, and an increase of energy efficiency by at least $27\%$ [1]. Apart from new technologies, a better usage of existing systems is a promising factor to achieve these goals. Considering the increasing usage of volatile renewable energy sources, an efficient utilization of energy carriers is getting increasingly complex [2]. Among other cases, this applies to energy usage in commercial and private buildings. To ensure efficient energy carrier utilization, sophisticated *energy management systems* (EMS) have been introduced [3].

In this paper we extend an EMS that is based on a modular approach for optimization. It uses a customizable, run-time based phrasing of the optimization problem, because the problem instance varies with respect to the devices that have to be optimized and the constraints to be considered from one building to another. The actual optimization utilizes a dynamically assembled and

© Springer International Publishing Switzerland 2015
A.M. Mora and G. Squillero (Eds.): EvoApplications 2015, LNCS 9028, pp. 239–251, 2015.
DOI: 10.1007/978-3-319-16549-3_20

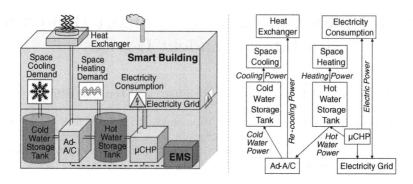

**Fig. 1.** Smart building scenario with EMS (left) and schema of power flows (right)

parametrized *Evolutionary Algorithm* (EA) [3,4], which can be adapted to the current optimization problem at run-time of the system.

The major contribution of this paper is the consideration of interdependencies between the devices. In particular, a flexible approach is presented for the optimization of interdependent devices with non-linear behavior. The term interdependency refers to the nature of energy consumption: The actual energy consumption of an interdependent device depends on the state of at least one other device and may also be non-linear in its energy consumption. The approach presented and evaluated in this paper is able to optimize diverse setups of buildings with different devices. Typical examples for interdependent devices in buildings can be found in the *heating, ventilating, and air conditioning system* (HVAC). To evaluate the EMS, a simulation of an EMS-controlled building has been carried out that is based on data of a real building.

Details about the energy management scenario and the EMS extended in this paper are given in Sect. 2. The major contribution of this paper—the *Energy Simulation Core* that enables the customizable optimization of interdependent energy-consuming devices—is presented in Sect. 3. In order to demonstrate the effectiveness of the presented approach, simulations with the setup shown in Sect. 4 have been conducted. The results are then discussed in Sect. 5. The paper is concluded with a summary and an outlook to further work.

## 2    Scenario and Energy Management System

### 2.1    Energy Management Scenario

This paper focuses on energy management and optimization of multiple energy carriers, such as electricity and hot water, in intelligent *smart buildings* (SB). The presented scenario (see Fig. 1) is based on a real SB environment and consists of a building with a *small combined heat and power plant* (μCHP), an *adsorption chiller* (Ad-A/C), as well as storage tanks for hot and chilled water. The chilled water, which is produced by the Ad-A/C, is used to cool a meeting room. The Ad-A/C is powered by the hot water that is generated by the μCHP. This hot

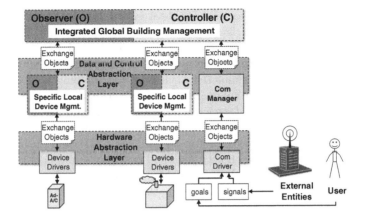

**Fig. 2.** Overview of Organic Smart Home

water is a secondary product of the $\mu$CHP in addition to electricity. Generation of electricity and production as well as consumption of chilled respective hot water are decoupled by the storage tanks. Such a system is called *trigeneration* or *combined cooling, heat and power* system.

## 2.2 Related Work

Similar systems with have been optimized using linear programming [5], non-linear programming [6], or Evolutionary Optimization [7–10]. However, these publications focus either only on optimization of the technical setup of the system [7,8], do not respect interdependencies or non-linearities [6,8,10,11], or perform only a scheduling that is exact to the hour [5,10,11]. In contrast, this paper schedules devices exact to the minute with respect to interdependencies and non-linearities of the devices, such as the non-linear interdependence of hot water input and cold water output of the Ad-A/C, using an EA.

## 2.3 Organic Smart Home

The *Organic Smart Home* (OSH) is an EMS that has been designed following the principles of *Organic Computing* [12] by using the generic *Observer/Controller Architecture*. This architecture constitutes one way to achieve controlled self-organization in technical systems utilizing a regulatory feedback mechanism [12]. An overview of the general system architecture is shown in Fig. 2. Major advantage of the OSH is its usability in both, real world energy management and simulations of buildings with different sets of devices in diverse scenarios [3].

The OSH utilizes different kinds of sensors and actuators to monitor and influence the *System under Observation and Control* (SuOC), in the present case a smart building. Every sensor and actor is assigned to a Local *Observer/Controller-unit* (O/C-unit). Every Local O/C-unit forms a closed control loop around the specific local device. To enable a global interaction between the devices, every Local O/C-unit is connected to a Global O/C-unit, responsible for the global building energy management. This hierarchical structure enables expedient responses to behavior, status, and interaction of different local agents, representing the physical or simulated devices in the building, as well as the global system, representing the smart building. Interaction with users or external entities is handled by a *Com Manager*, analogous to the handling of devices.

A *Hardware Abstraction Layer* (HAL) and device-specific drivers realize the abstraction from distinct devices, protocols, and communication media of components into generic exchange objects [3]. The Local O/C-units pass abstracted data to the Global O/C-unit, which aggregates the data of all Local O/C-units to the current state of the SuOC. Based upon this state, the energy management predicts the future global state and optimizes its control sequence in order to influence the SuOC with respect to given external and internal constraints as well as objectives defined by the user. The resulting schedule of planned actions and procedures, i.e., the control sequence, is then communicated back to the Local O/C-units, which apply it to the devices.

## 3    Energy Simulation Core

In the present paper, the OSH, which has a configurable, modular Optimization Algorithm [3], is enhanced by an additional component: the *Energy Simulation Core* (ESC). This component, which is depicted in Fig. 3, simulates the local electricity and thermal grids, i.e., the local electrical wiring and water pipes, as well as the energy consumption of interdependent devices while keeping a modular approach to the optimization. This modular approach is necessary, because the concrete operational scenarios in SBs with different setups of devices and characteristics of these devices, as well as the objectives of the users are widely unknown a priori to the installation of the EMS. Furthermore, these properties may change over time, when additional devices are being added to management and optimization. Moreover, the ESC enables the reuse of the abstracted models of the devices, which are already used for prediction purposes in the EMS.

### 3.1    ESC: General Architecture

The ESC is used in two parts of the EMS (see Fig. 3): the calculation of energy flows in every simulated time step, which in the present EMS is at every second, and the simulation of energy flows in the optimization process, which is done in time steps of 60 s. The calculation of energy flows is necessary to determine the actual electrical and thermal power consumption, when different producing and consuming devices are considered. For instance, active power generated by a photovoltaic system has usually a different payment scheme for feed-in than power generated by a $\mu$CHP.

Characteristics and control of thermal devices, such as water heaters and Ad-A/Cs, usually depend on the current state of the overall system, i.e., indoor and

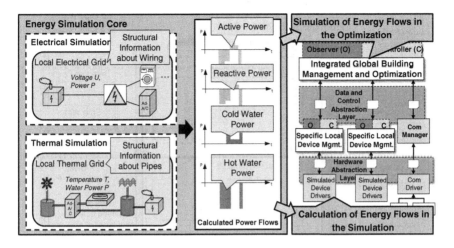

**Fig. 3.** Overview: Energy Simulation Core in the Organic Smart Home

outdoor temperature, as well as the water temperatures of hot and chilled water in the storage tanks. Additionally, these characteristics often include non-linear dependencies. For example, the required thermal energy in terms of hot water consumption of an Ad-A/C is non-linear with respect to the generated thermal energy in terms of chilled water. Therefore, the simulation of energy flows in the optimization requires a step-by-step approach when determining the future control sequence of the devices.

The ESC consists of two main components: the *Electrical Simulation* and the *Thermal Simulation*. Both sub-modules simulate their respective local grid with its different energy carriers. The local electricity grid consists of the wiring, i.e., the electrical connections between all devices consuming or producing electricity in a building. To be able to take their different payment schemes into account, active power produced by a photovoltaic system is regarded as a different *commodity* than active power produced by the μCHP.

Similarly, the local thermal grid contains all information about the physical interconnections, i.e., pipes, between devices consuming different thermal commodities, such as hot and chilled water. In addition to the power flows between the devices, the temperatures are communicated between the devices. Thus, devices can react on states of other devices: The μCHP starts producing hot water when the water temperature of the hot water storage tank falls below a certain threshold level. Furthermore, devices can determine their current power consumption or production based on the temperatures of other devices, such as water temperatures. For example, the hot water power consumption of an Ad-A/C depends on the hot water temperature in the storage tank.

The ESC handles the information exchange between all simulated devices, i.e., the actual power consumption and productions as well as the additional information, such as water temperatures or voltages. These simulated devices (see Fig. 3) are for one thing the simulation agents, i.e., simulation drivers, and

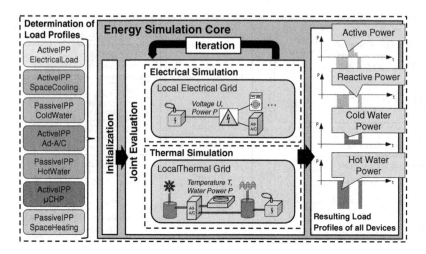

**Fig. 4.** Determination of load profiles using Interdependent Problem Parts

for another the *Interdependent Problem Parts* in the optimization, which are more closely described in the next subsection.

### 3.2    Interdependent Problem Parts

The modularity of the approach is further enabled by the introduction of *Interdependent Problem Parts* (IPP). These IPPs are an extended version of the *Problem Parts* presented in [3], which are provided by the Local O/C-units to handle the optimization of devices. Every device managed by the EMS provides an IPP that contains information about characteristics, behavior, predicted future states, such as the predicted power consumption, and possible control sequences of the device, as well as interdependencies with other devices. The IPPs are used in the ESC to determine load profiles of the devices with respect to their interdependencies (see Fig. 4).

There are two fundamentally different properties of an IPP: *controllability* and *activeness*. Controllability (see also [3,4]) refers to the the property whether a device offers the possibility of control, i.e., in the case of a *non-controllable* device the respective IPP has zero bits, whereas a *controllable* device has at least one bit in the optimization. Activeness refers to the property of whether the device is determining the power flow to other devices (*active*) or not (*passive*).

Depending on the optimization target, the same device may be handled alternatively with different IPPs. For instance, one IPP may be non-controllable and active, whereas another may be controllable and active. This means that in the first case the device controls itself, e.g., by using an on-off control, while in second case it receives an optimized control sequence by the global optimization. In both cases, the device determines actively its power flows.

### 3.3   Interdependent Problem Parts of the μCHP

The μCHP simulated in this paper is controllable, because it can be controlled using a signal that switches it on or off. In order to show the effect of optimization, it can also be run unoptimized using an IPP that is non-controllable by the optimization. Therefore, it uses two different types of IPPs: one IPP is non-controllable another is controllable.

Both IPPs implement an on-off control ensuring that the water temperature in the hot water storage tank remains within an upper and a lower temperature threshold. This thermal management ensures that every solution determined by the optimization leads to a valid solution: the μCHP is forced on or off in cases of violations of the threshold, even if the control sequence by the optimization would originally lead to a violation of the thresholds. In both cases, the μCHP is actively participating in the energy simulation, because its state, i.e., being switched on or off, and therefore its power generation of hot water and electricity, depends on at least one other device: the hot water storage tank. The encoding of the μCHP uses a sequence of bits that is interpreted as the control sequence, i.e., sequence of being switched on or off, and is more closely described in [4].

### 3.4   Interdependent Problem Parts of the Ad-A/C

The Ad-A/C uses IPPs that are similar to those of the μCHP. Other than that, it consumes hot water from the storage tank and produces chilled water that is stored in the chilled water storage tank. Additionally, it considers the outdoor temperature that determines the efficiency of the heat exchanger for the re-cooling process. Both IPPs, non- and controllable, implement an on-off control for ensuring that the chilled water temperature remains within its thresholds.

### 3.5   ESC and IPPs: Optimization Process

The optimization process in the OSH and its usage of the ESC are depicted in Fig. 5. Analogously to the optimization process in [3], the IPPs are constructed periodically and in case of certain special events in their relative Local O/C-units. Every IPP is initialized with information about the current device state and the current possibility of control.

In the scenario presented in this paper, the control sequences of an Ad-A/C and a μCHP have to be determined with respect to states of the storage tanks, predictions of future hot and chiller water power consumptions as well as outdoor temperature and price signals. The present example requires three bits for both, the Ad-A/C and the μCHP, for every five minutes in the optimization horizon. Among the IPPs for the controllable devices, the states of the storage tanks and the predicted power consumptions are handled as non-controllable IPPs.

All these IPPs are communicated to the Global O/C-unit and aggregated to represent the global optimization problem in the building for the current optimization period. They determine the length of individuals in the optimization

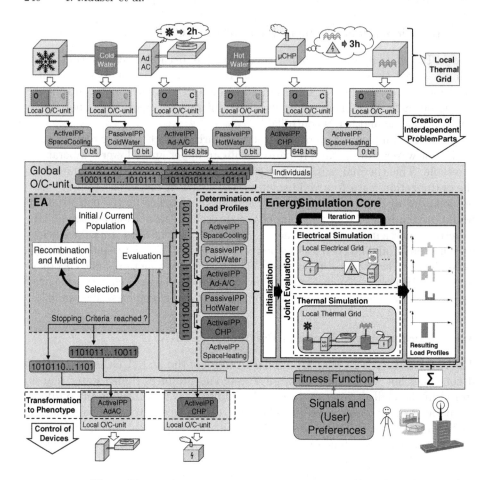

**Fig. 5.** Energy Simulation Core in the optimization process

process and its EA by defining an adequate number of bits required for the optimization of every device. Thus, every individual consists of sub-strings of bits, which have to be interpreted by their relative IPP in order to determine the load profile of the related device. This joint evaluation with the determination of load profiles is done using the ESC. The load profiles are combined to expected total future load profiles for the building, which are then evaluated to a fitness value using external signals, such as the costs of electricity and natural gas, or the feed-in tariff for electricity.

The EA runs until the stopping criterion, which in the present case is the maximum number of generations, has been reached. The sub-strings of the best individual are then transformed to their phenotypes, i.e., the control sequences for devices that can be controlled. In the scenario of this paper, these are the future periods when the Ad-A/C respective the μCHP are scheduled to be switched on or off.

**Table 1.** Experiments: combinations of Interdependent Problem Parts

| Experiment | IPP of Ad-A/C | IPP of $\mu$CHP | Appointments |
|---|---|---|---|
| A | Non-controllable | Non-controllable | Real, simulated |
| B | Non-controllable | Controllable | Real, simulated |
| C | Controllable | Non-controllable | Real, simulated |
| D | Controllable | Controllable | Real, simulated |

**Table 2.** Experiments: specifications of devices

| Device | Specification | Real device |
|---|---|---|
| Ad-A/C | Cooling power: 9 kW | *InvenSor LTC 09* |
| $\mu$CHP | Hot water power: 12.5 kW | *Senertec Dachs G 5.5* |
| | Electric active power: 5.5 kW | *standard* |
| | Natural gas power: 20.5 kW | |
| Hot water storage tank | 3250 liters | Custom-made tank |
| | Min. temperature: 57 °C | |
| | Max. temperature: 78 °C | |
| Chilled water storage tank | 3000 liters | Custom-made tank |
| | Min. temperature: 10 °C | |
| | Max. temperature: 15 °C | |

## 4    Experimental Setup

To evaluate the performance of the implemented ESC and to demonstrate its capability of handling interdependent devices, a simulated SB has been used. The specifications of the simulated SB and its devices are based on a real SB, the *FZI House of Living Labs*[1]. The EMS—the OSH—uses a sub-problem based EA for optimization purposes, which applies binary tournament selection, single-point-crossover with two offspring and bit-flip-mutation using an elitist $(\mu,\lambda)$-strategy with a rank based survivor selection [3]. Parameters of the operators have been calibrated manually (see Fig. 6) and set to a crossover probability of 0.7, a mutation probability of 0.005, and 200 generations with 100 individuals.

### 4.1    Simulated Devices

The simulated SB consists of a simulated Ad-A/C, a $\mu$CHP and simulated storage tanks for hot and chilled water. These have been modeled according to specifications of real devices (see Table 2). The efficiency of the Ad-A/C, which depends on the tank and outdoor temperatures, has been interpolated from the

---

[1] http://www.fzi.de/en/research/fzi-house-of-living-labs/.

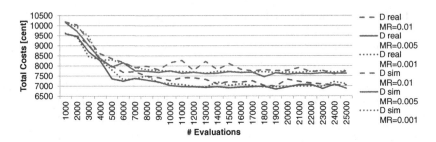

**Fig. 6.** Total Cost with different Numbers of Evaluations and Mutation Rates (MR)

technical specification. Standing loss $P_{\text{loss}}$ in kW of the storage tanks, depending on the current tank temperature $T_{\text{tank}}$ in °C and the ambient temperature $T_{\text{ambient}}$, which has been set to 20 °C, has been modeled based on measurements with $c = 0.040$ for the cold water and $c = 0.011$ for the hot water storage tank:

$$P_{\text{loss}}(T_{\text{tank}}) = -c \cdot (T_{\text{tank}} - T_{\text{ambient}}).$$

Optimization using the EA is triggered at least every four hours or when a temperature threshold of either the hot or the cold water storage tank has been violated. Optimization horizon is the next 18 h.

### 4.2    Test Scenarios and Experiments

In the simulations, eight different experiments with 30 random seeds each have been tested. All simulate four weeks in July 2013 with real outdoor temperatures. The experiments are presented in Table 1 and consist of the four combinations of controllable and non-controllable IPPs of the Ad-A/C and the μCHP as well as two different sets of appointments determining the cooling demand: *Simulated* cooling demand refers to simulated appointments in the meeting room, *real* cooling demand refers to real appointments in the meeting room pulled from the *Microsoft Exchange Calendar*. The simulated appointments are randomly generated using the following constraints based on the typical key data of appointments in the meeting room of the real building:

$$\#appointments\ per\ day \in \{1, 2\},$$
$$\#appointment\ duration\ in\ h \in \{2, 3, 4\},$$
$$pause\ between\ appointments\ in\ h \in \{2, 3, 4\}.$$

Cooling demand $P$ in kW as a function of the outdoor temperature $T$ in °C is calculated using the an empirical formula that is based on measurements in the real building. Above an outdoor temperature of about 21.9 °C, this model leads to a cooling demand that increases linearly with the outdoor temperature:

$$P(T) = \max(0;\ 0.4415 \cdot T - (0.4415 \cdot 21.8831)).$$

## 5    Results and Discussion

Simulation results (see Fig. 7 and Table 3) show an average improvement of the total monthly costs by up to 15.6 %. This improvement is realized in experiment D with real appointments in comparison to experiment A. The results of a t-test confirm the significance of improvements by the optimization with IPP in comparison to the non-optimized reference scenario.

Optimization of the Ad-A/C only (experiment C) leads to better results than the sole optimization of the $\mu$CHP (experiment B). Nevertheless, a higher volatility of the achieved total costs is observed. This can be explained by a surplus of hot and chilled water that remains in the storage tanks at the end of the simulation. In case of an optimized $\mu$CHP and Ad-A/C, the optimization ensures that the tank temperatures are kept at a low respective high temperature at any time without an appointment. Thus, the tank is not unnecessarily heated up respective cooled down to prevent standing loss. Especially when using real appointments, the volatility is higher. This is due to the nature of the real appointments, which are less often but longer than the simulated ones. Therefore,

**Table 3.** Simulation results: statistical values of the absolute total costs and the improvement over the non-optimized experiment A.

| | | Abs. Electricity Costs | | | | Improvement wrt. A [%] | | | | t-test |
|---|---|---|---|---|---|---|---|---|---|---|
| Experiment | Appointments | Min | Max | Avg | $s_n$ | Min | Max | Avg | $s_n$ | p-value |
| A | Real | 8224 | 8224 | 8224 | 0 | - | - | - | - | - |
| | Simulated | 8762 | 11555 | 9974 | 659 | - | - | - | - | - |
| B | Real | 7266 | 7504 | 7410 | 54 | 8.75 | 11.64 | 9.89 | 0.65 | 0.000 |
| | Simulated | 8078 | 10410 | 9100 | 578 | 3.76 | 14.24 | 8.70 | 2.90 | 0.000 |
| C | Real | 6969 | 7734 | 7304 | 213 | 5.94 | 15.25 | 11.18 | 2.59 | 0.000 |
| | Simulated | 7878 | 9984 | 8818 | 544 | 2.69 | 17.42 | 11.48 | 4.02 | 0.000 |
| D | Real | 6853 | 7046 | 6939 | 49 | 14.31 | 16.67 | 15.63 | 0.60 | 0.000 |
| | Simulated | 7631 | 9880 | 8589 | 551 | 7.87 | 19.90 | 13.82 | 3.12 | 0.000 |

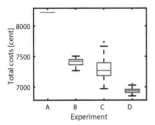
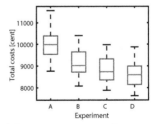

(a) Experiments with real appointments

(b) Experiments with simulated appointments

**Fig. 7.** Boxplot of the average costs in the experiments

on the last day of the simulation, the remaining hot water in the storage tank is not used to produce chilled water for an appointment in the meeting room.

# 6    Summary and Outlook

This paper presented an approach towards flexible and modular energy optimization in smart buildings using an EMS. The approach has been implemented as an additional module for an existing EMS that can be used in both, simulations and real-world control. The formulation of the problem instances at run-time of the EMS has been extended to cope with interdependent devices, such as trigeneration systems consisting of a combined-heat and power plant combined with an adsorption chiller as well as hot and chilled water storage tanks.

The implementation of the presented module has been tested in simulations of a scenario that is based on the characteristics of a real building. Results of the simulation show the ability of the system to manage and optimize such buildings. The energy costs of the building can be reduced by the optimization using the EA on average by up to 15 %. This improvement is mainly due to the better coordination of the adsorption chiller and the combined heat and power plant as well as the generation of chilled water in the morning, when the outdoor temperature allows for a better efficiency.

Future work shall verify the simulation results with additional data from real buildings. Furthermore, the approach presented in this paper will be extended to the optimization of a battery storage and hybrid household appliances that may use hot water from the storage tank, too, while substituting electricity.

# References

1. European Commission: A policy framework for climate and energy in the period from 2020 to 2030. Communication (2014)
2. Palensky, P., Dietrich, D.: Demand side management: Demand response, intelligent energy systems, and smart loads. IEEE Trans. Industr. Inf. **7**(3), 381–388 (2011)
3. Allerding, F., Mauser, I., Schmeck, H.: Customizable energy management in smart-buildings using evolutionary algorithms. In: Esparcia-Alcázar, A.I., Mora, A.M. (eds.) EvoApplications 2014. LNCS, vol. 8602, pp. 153–164. Springer, Heidelberg (2014)
4. Mauser, I., Dorscheid, M., Allerding, F., Schmeck, H.: Encodings for evolutionary algorithms in smart buildings with energy management systems. In: 2014 IEEE Congress on Evolutionary Computation (CEC), pp. 2361–2366. IEEE (2014)
5. Rong, A., Lahdelma, R.: An efficient linear programming model and optimization algorithm for trigeneration. Appl. Energy **82**(1), 40–63 (2005)
6. Geidl, M., Andersson, G.: Optimal power flow of multiple energy carriers. IEEE Trans. Power Syst. **22**(1), 145–155 (2007)
7. Ahmadi, P., Rosen, M.A., Dincer, I.: Multi-objective exergy-based optimization of a polygeneration energy system using an evolutionary algorithm. Energy **46**(1), 21–31 (2012)
8. Kavvadias, K., Maroulis, Z.: Multi-objective optimization of a trigeneration plant. Energy Policy **38**(2), 945–954 (2010)

9. Sakawa, M., Kato, K., Ushiro, S.: Operational planning of district heating and cooling plants through genetic algorithms for mixed 0–1 linear programming. Eur. J. Oper. Res. **137**(3), 677–687 (2002)
10. Wang, J.J., Jing, Y.Y., Zhang, C.F.: Optimization of capacity and operation for CCHP system by genetic algorithm. Appl. Energy **87**(4), 1325–1335 (2010)
11. Chicco, G., Mancarella, P.: Matrix modelling of small-scale trigeneration systems and application to operational optimization. Energy **34**(3), 261–273 (2009)
12. Müller-Schloer, C., Schmeck, H., Ungerer, T. (eds.): Organic Computing - A Paradigm Shift for Complex Systems, vol. 1. Springer, Heidelberg (2011)

# An Energy Management System Aggregator Based on an Integrated Evolutionary and Differential Evolution Approach

Andreia M. Carreiro[1](✉), Carlos Oliveira[1],
Carlos Henggeler Antunes[1,2], and Humberto M. Jorge[1,2]

[1] INESC Coimbra, Rua Antero de Quental nº 199, 3000-033 Coimbra, Portugal
{andreia.melo.carreiro,
carlosfilipeoliveira88}@gmail.com
[2] Department of Electrical Engineering and Computers,
Polo II – University of Coimbra, 3030-290 Coimbra, Portugal
{ch,hjorge}@deec.uc.pt

**Abstract.** The increasing penetration of renewable generation in the electric power system has been leading to a higher complexity of grid management due to its inherent intermittency, also with impact on the volatility of electricity prices. Setting the adequate operating reserve levels is one of the main concerns of the System Operator (SO), since the integration of a large share of intermittent generation requires an increased amount of reserve that is needed to balance generation and load. At the same time, the energy consumption in households has been steadily growing, representing a significant untapped savings potential due to consumption waste and load flexibility (i.e., the possibility of time deferring the use of some loads).

An aggregator has been designed to operate as an intermediary between individual energy management systems and the SO/Energy Market, capable of facilitating a load follows supply strategy in a Smart Grid context. The aggregator is aimed at using the flexibility provided by each end-user aggregated into clusters of demand-side resources to satisfy system service requirements, involving lowering or increasing the power requested in each time slot. This contributes to the balance between load and supply and coping with the intermittency of renewable sources, thus offering an attractive alternative to supply side investments in peak and reserve generation.

For this purpose, a multi-objective optimization model has been developed to maximize the aggregator profits, taking into account revenues from the SO/ Energy Market and payments to end-user clusters, and minimize the inequity between the amounts of load flexibility provided by the clusters to satisfy grid requests. An approach based on an evolutionary algorithm coupled with a differential evolution algorithm has been designed to deal with this model.

**Keywords:** Evolutionary algorithm · Differential evolution algorithm · Multi-objective · Energy management systems · Aggregator

© Springer International Publishing Switzerland 2015
A.M. Mora and G. Squillero (Eds.): EvoApplications 2015, LNCS 9028, pp. 252–264, 2015.
DOI: 10.1007/978-3-319-16549-3_21

# 1 Introduction

The efforts to reduce greenhouse gases (GHG) emissions, foreign energy dependence and the impacts of fossil fuel price volatility have been leading to a fast increase in the deployment of electricity generation based on renewable energy sources (RES), in particular photovoltaic and wind power. RES are being deployed not only as bulk generation facilities but also as distributed local generation connected to the electricity distribution grid or to private consumption infrastructures. The generation patterns associated with RES normally do not follow the typical end-user demand profile and cannot be predicted with great accuracy. The variability of wind electricity generation has to be managed in the short-term adjusting both generation and demand [1]. In electric power systems the end-users are nowadays subject to yearly fixed tariffs without knowing the entire market conditions. The System Operator (SO) should deal with the variability of electricity generation costs and the demand requests, in order to manage the electric power system securely and safely [1, 2].

The power output of RES is driven by environmental conditions, which are inherently variable and outside the control of generators and the SO. RES cannot be reliably dispatched or perfectly forecasted, and exhibit significant temporal variability. As a result, the proper integration of RES into the electric grid presents a major challenge and new tools are required to ensure the grid reliability. The adjustment is generally done using "fast-reacting" generation (as peaking power plants or spinning reserves) to safeguard the system against unexpected events such as generation deficit, speedy load variations or a combination of both [3, 4], which involve high costs. Therefore, other methods to compensate the imbalances in the electric power system should be envisaged. Electricity can be stored during periods in which supply exceeds demand and used during the peak hours. Demand can be reduced during peak hours, by interrupting, shifting or re-parameterizing the loads [5]. A better integration of intermittent RES in the electric power system needs to accommodate these issues, namely concerning the possibilities of managing demand in a perspective of integrated energy resource management to deal with the supply volatility.

The energy consumption in European Union (EU) households has been steadily growing during the last few years due to the widespread utilization of new types of loads and the requirement of higher levels of comfort and services [4]. The electricity consumption breakdown in EU households was characterized [6], and it was verified that some end-use loads present some kind of flexibility; therefore, if properly controlled these loads can be used as a demand side resource capable of offering a responsive behavior [7, 8]. As an example, washing and drying appliances can be rescheduled to other periods (in particular those with lower electricity prices) thus flattening the demand curve, or to periods of higher energy generation based on RES, also contributing to reduce GHG emissions. Thermal loads (cooling appliances, water heating, space heating/cooling and air conditioning systems) can be interrupted during shorts periods of time, without major reductions in service quality, to avoid the most unbalanced situations between generation and consumption, thus compensating the effects of the variability of RES availability.

The on-going transformations of the electric power system, namely concerning the exploitation of distributed generation and the evolution towards the smart grid, simultaneously require and facilitate a load follows supply strategy to cope with the penetration of RES and ensure an adequate level of power reserve [5]. Avoiding peak loads while maintaining the balance between the load and supply diagrams is increasingly important in order to reduce the need for additional generation capacity as a backup for volatile supply and face disturbances occurring in the network [5].

As far as security of supply is concerned, the most severe problems due to the power intermittence occur in peak load hours, since most system resources are already in use and a sudden reduction of power generation can have critical consequences on the system reliability. Thus, instead of acting on the supply side, Demand Response (DR)[1] programs and technologies have the potential to contribute to optimize consumption and reduce peak loads, in (near) real-time, allowing the participation of end-users in the electricity market. In this way, DR is an enabling strategy for the successful integration of RES in the electric system, in a perspective of integrated energy resource management, involving controlling flexible loads according to (price and/or emergency) signals from the grid and end-users' preferences. In addition, DR can become a new source of revenue for entities that "aggregate" this load flexibility.

In a smart grid context, it is expected that the traditional end-user will become a *prosumer* (i.e., simultaneously producer and consumer) and dynamic (time-differentiated) electricity tariffs will be offered [2]. In order to implement DR programs the household needs to have local energy management systems (EMS) based on fully interactive Information and Communication Technologies (ICT), to help the end-user optimizing the energy use without compromising comfort, achieving energy savings and satisfying constraints on the quality of the energy services provided, enabling the two-way communication between the house and the grid in order to improve the global performance of the electric power system [2, 3]. Otherwise, in a scenario of a low price signal from the grid, all EMS devices would attempt to achieve benefits for the end-user engaging in similar actions (e.g., by shedding the same type of loads), eventually taking no notice of the instability that could impair the operation of the system, since the true impact of household consumption arises when it is summed up over a large number of houses [4].

In this context, a few studies have addressed the combination of demand and supply sides to implement DR programs for the provision of system services, i.e. the balancing services that are provided by system operators for ensuring reliable system operations [7]. These services have been traditionally provided by generators, which are capable of adjusting their output rapidly in response to unanticipated imbalances between supply and demand. In the smart grid context, the provision of these services by aggregating electricity consumers using DR programs may become an attractive alternative [8].

This role can be performed by an aggregator energy management system (Energy Box Aggregator - EBAg), which is an intelligent decision-making mediator between the end-user (local energy box - LEB) and the grid (SO/Energy Market) allowing the

---

[1] According to the Federal Energy Regulatory Commission Demand Response may be defined as "changes in electric usage by end-use customers from their normal consumption patterns in response to changes in the price of electricity over time, or to incentive payments designed to induce lower electricity use at times of high wholesale market prices or when system reliability is jeopardized."

coordination of a large-scale dissemination of in-house DR devices (Fig. 1). The EBAg is aimed at using the demand-side flexibility provided by clusters of end-users to provide system service requirements, involving lowering or increasing the power requested in each time slot of a planning horizon. This contributes to balancing load and supply, avoiding peaks in the load diagram, and coping with the intermittency of RES, thus increasing the overall grid efficiency by offering an attractive alternative to supply side investments on peak and reserve generation [8].

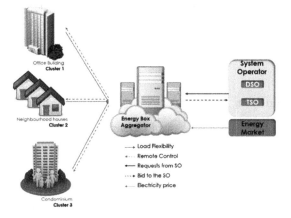

**Fig. 1.** EBAg global architecture

The purpose of this paper is to present an approach based on an evolutionary algorithm (EA) coupled with a differential evolution algorithm (DEA) to deal with a multi-objective optimization (MOO) model, as seen by the EBAg, considering the maximization of the EBAg profits, taking into account revenues from the SO/Energy Market, payments to end-user clusters and additional penalties, and the minimization of the inequity among clusters, i.e., the maximum relative difference between the load flexibility provided by the clusters and the one used by the EBAg, as a surrogate for fairness in the usage of end-user load flexibility.

This paper is structured as follows: Sect. 2 presents the MOO model formulation for the EBAg problem; Sect. 3 describes the algorithmic approach and the case study; Sect. 4 illustrates the results and discusses them, and Sect. 5 presents the main conclusions.

## 2 A MOO Model for the EBAg

The aim of this section is to define a framework for the EBAg role in the electric power system. This comprises the information that is transmitted from an LEB to the EBAg, and the relationships between the LEB and the grid (SO and energy market).

The large-scale deployment of LEB imposes an essential challenge concerning the coordination of grid and end-user objectives. I.e., requests from the grid should be weighed against end-user flexibility to shift or shed loads. In this way, the EBAg will gather flexibility from its end-users by means of each LEB, asking them to adjust their daily load profile, using a remuneration scheme specified in a contract with end-users associated in clusters. A critical issue is the incentive paid to the end-users to participate in these demand management programs and provide load operation in a cost effective way.

Thereby, the EBAg is able to sell the flexibility gathered, presenting offers to the grid, according to its requests, in the form of ancillary services, with the aim of offering benefits to all entities involved (increase retail profits, decrease consumption costs). The EBAg may receive signals from the SO, and take appropriate actions to avoid violation of network operational constraints. In case of abnormal operating conditions, the SO can request load increasing or decreasing, in each time slot, to the EBAg. The interaction with the SO may be also important for solving congestions in the distribution network.

## 2.1   Model Formulation

The MOO model as seen by the EBAg consists in: - maximizing its profits, taking into account the revenues of selling the load flexibility obtained from the end-user clusters to the grid and the rewards given to the clusters as well as the penalties paid to the grid for not meeting the flexibility requested and to the clusters for the amount of flexibility not used; - and minimizing inequity among clusters, i.e., minimizing the maximum relative difference between the load flexibility provided by the clusters and the one used by the EBAg, as a surrogate for fairness in the usage of end-user load flexibility.

Indices

$c$     1, 2, ...C - cluster, where C is the number of clusters associated with the EBAg. Each cluster gathers a set of end-users (LEB).

$t$     1, 2, ...T - time slot, considering a time resolution of 15 min (T = 96 time slots in one day).

Coefficients

$I_t^+$     Reward paid by the grid to the EBAg for the flexibility provided (load shedding, i.e. power decrease), in each time slot $t$.

$I_t^-$     Reward paid by the grid to the EBAg for the flexibility provided (load increase), in each time slot $t$.

$E_t^+$     Reward paid by the EBAg to the clusters (equal for all clusters) for the flexibility used (load shedding, i.e. power decrease), in each time slot $t$.

$E_t^-$     Reward paid by the EBAg to the clusters (equal for all clusters) for the flexibility used (load increase), in each time slot $t$.

$F_t^+$     Penalty paid by the EBAg to the grid for not complying with the contracted flexibility (load shedding, i.e. power decrease), in each time slot $t$.

$F_t^-$     Penalty paid by the EBAg to the grid for not complying with the contracted flexibility (load increase), in each time slot $t$.

$C_{ct}^+$     Penalty paid by the EBAg to the cluster $c$ for the amount of flexibility not used (load shedding, i.e. power decrease), in each time slot $t$.

$C_{ct}^-$  Penalty paid by the EBAg to the cluster $c$ for the amount of flexibility not used (load increase), in each time slot $t$.

$R_t^+$  Power reduction (load shedding) request by the grid to the EBAg in each time slot $t$.

$R_t^-$  Power increase request by the grid to the EBAg in each time slot $t$.

$Dmax_{ct}^+$  Maximum value of power the cluster $c$ can offer to the EBAg (decrease) in each time slot $t$.

$Dmax_{ct}^-$  Maximum value of power the cluster $c$ can offer to the EBAg (increase) in each time slot $t$.

$\partial_c^+$  Minimum fraction of $Dmax_{ct}^+$ that cluster $c$ may offer to decrease power (positive flexibility margin).

$\partial_c^-$  Minimum fraction of $Dmax_{ct}^-$ that cluster $c$ may offer to increase power (negative flexibility margin).

$D_{ct}^+$  Amount of power that cluster $c$ offers to decrease (load shedding) in time slot t, accounting for a range of variation in the cluster response.

$D_{ct}^-$  Amount of power that cluster $c$ offers to increase in time slot t, accounting for a range of variation in the cluster response.

$$D_{ct}^+ = rand\left(\partial_c^+, 1\right)Dmax_{ct}^+$$

$$D_{ct}^- = rand\left(\partial_c^-, 1\right)Dmax_{ct}^-$$

In this way $D_{ct}^+$ and $D_{ct}^-$ account for the uncertainty associated to the flexibility effectively provided by end-user clusters.

Decision variables

$P_t^+$  Amount of power (kW) that the EBAg is capable to offer to the grid, in each time slot $t$, corresponding to load shedding (power decrease).

$P_t^-$  Amount of power (kW) that the EBAg is capable to offer to the grid, in each time slot $t$, corresponding to power increase. $P_t^+ . P_t^- = 0$.

$L_{ct}^+$  Amount of power that the EBAg uses from cluster $c$ to decrease (load shedding) in time slot $t$.

$L_{ct}^-$  Amount of power that the EBAg uses from cluster $c$ to increase in time slot $t$. $L_{ct}^+ . L_{ct}^- = 0$.

Objective functions

Maximizing the EBAg profits, taking into account the revenues of selling the load flexibility obtained from the end-user clusters to the grid and the rewards given to the clusters as well as the penalties paid to the grid for not meeting the flexibility requested and to the clusters for the amount of flexibility made available and not used:

$$\max z_1 = \sum_t I_t^+ P_t^+ + \sum_t I_t^- P_t^- - \sum_t \sum_c E_t^+ L_{ct}^+ - \sum_t \sum_c E_t^- L_{ct}^- - \sum_t F_t^+ \left(R_t^+ - P_t^+\right)$$
$$- \sum_t F_t^- \left(R_t^- - P_t^-\right) - \sum_t \sum_c C_t^+ \left(D_{ct}^+ - L_{ct}^+\right) - \sum_t \sum_c C_t^- \left(D_{ct}^- - L_{ct}^-\right)$$

Minimizing inequity among clusters, i.e., minimizing the maximum relative difference between the load flexibility provided by the clusters and the one used by the EBAg:

$$\min z_2 = \max_c \sum_t (L_{ct} - D_{ct})/D_{ct}$$

Constraints

The amount of power that the EBAg uses from cluster $c$ to decrease/increase cannot be higher than the amount of power to decrease/increase offered by cluster $c$ in time slot $t$:

$$L_{ct}^+ \leq D_{ct}^+, \ for\ all\ c, t$$
$$L_{ct}^- \leq D_{ct}^-, \ for\ all\ c, t$$

The amount of power that the EBAg offers to the grid to decrease/increase cannot be higher than the amount of power required to decrease/increase in time slot $t$:

$$0 \leq P_t^+ \leq R_t^+, \ for\ all\ t$$
$$0 \leq P_t^- \leq R_t^-, \ for\ all\ t$$

The amount of power that the EBAg offers to the grid to decrease/increase cannot be higher than the total amount of power used to decrease/increase that is offered by the clusters in time slot $t$:

$$0 \leq P_t^+ \leq \sum_c L_{ct}^+, \ for\ all\ t$$

$$0 \leq P_t^- \leq \sum_c L_{ct}^-, \ for\ all\ t$$

## 3   Algorithmic Approach

The algorithmic approach should be able to deal with the main characteristics of the problem, specifically its combinatorial nature. According to the authors' previous experience on load scheduling in residential energy management systems and the problem characteristics, namely concerning the types of decision variables, EA and DEA were selected as the most adequate approaches. The aim herein is computing non-dominated fronts displaying a good spread along and expected convergence to the true Pareto-optimal front (which is unknown), which could enable to study the trade-offs between the two competing objective functions (maximizing the EBAg profits and minimizing the inequity among clusters).

The solution encoding in both approaches consists in an array of continuous variable, corresponding to decision variables $P_t^+$, $P_t^-$, $L_{ct}^+$, $L_{ct}^-$ in the model.

The EA is based on NSGA-II [9], presenting the following main features:

- Population size = 30 individuals.
- Random generation of initial population.
- Crossover operator: two algorithm versions have been developed with crossover (with probability of 0.2) and without crossover. The crossover operator "respects" the model decision variables expressed in the individual representation, in the sense that each variable (physical) information is never "broken".
- The mutation operator (with a probability of 0.2) works in each decision variable composing the individuals by randomly increasing/decreasing the amount of power within a given range.
- Stop condition: 10,000 generations.

The main features of the DEA are:

- Mutation variant of DE: DE/rand/2/bin, since it consistently presented the best performance in comparison with other permutation strategies of the base vector.

The parameters were tuned after extensive experimentation. Sets of 30 independent runs were carried out for each approach. The main features of the solutions then obtained were:

- The EA consistently provided good extreme (i.e., individual optima to each objective function) solutions but displaying only a few solutions in the non-dominated front. The EA was able to rapidly finding good solutions for both objective functions, namely regarding the profit objective function. The front then evolved in an intermittent manner with groups of (slightly) dominated solutions being outperformed by generally a single non-dominated solution. Then the final non-dominated front was well spread (in the sense of good individual optimal solutions) but irregularly covered (few solutions in the front).
- The DEA provided a well spread and covered non-dominated front in a significant number of runs, but with individual optimal solutions less good than in the EA case. The evolution of the front was quite regular. However, in a non-negligible number of runs the front was of low quality because no positive values of the profit objective function could be obtained.

The analysis of this behaviour of the algorithms in different instances of the problem led to the conclusion that once solutions with positive values for the profit objective function were attained, the DEA then smoothly evolved to a well-covered and well-spread front. Since this goal was easily achieved by the EA, which in turn computed better individual optimal values for the objective functions thus expanding the front, then both approaches were combined. The EA is used in a first phase to compute good extreme values and a few solutions scattered along the front with already satisfactory values for both objective functions, and in a second phase the DEA is used to further expand and fill up the front.

The hyper-volume indicator has been used throughout this algorithm refinement process to assess and compare the quality of the fronts obtained in the computational experiments.

### 3.1  Case Study

Experiments have been carried out based on real data gathered throughout one year, January 2013 to January 2014, of continuous (24/7) monitoring of electrical consumption with a time resolution of 15 min ($t$). These data provided a realistic basis for the specification of clusters, energy prices, baseline load profiles and load flexibility offered by each cluster. In the end-user side, 8 types of clients were defined based on their electricity consumption profile, which were aggregated into clusters according to their consumption average and load factor (ratio average load/peak load in a specified time period). For example, cluster 1 gathers the end-users with 0–5 % load factor and cluster 20 the clients with 95–100 % load factor.

The data for these experiments have been obtained from a sample of 9,000 daily load profiles of different Cloogy technology (www.cloogy.pt) users. Cloogy is an energy management solution that allows monitoring and controlling energy consumption in households, buildings and small industries.

The profile of the cluster in the absence of any flexibility request can be represented as a baseline load profile diagram (Fig. 2). The EBAg should know how each cluster responds to every admissible request signal sent to it.

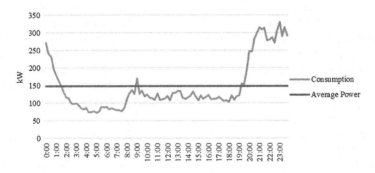

**Fig. 2.**  Load diagram of cluster 2: load factor between 5 % – 10 %, peak power 330 kW.

The flexibility margin indicated by each cluster reflects its availability to decrease/increase load in a given time slot, with respect to the baseline consumption. This "positive" and "negative" flexibility margins are displayed in Table 1.

To obtain the amount of flexibility for each cluster throughout the planning period this flexibility margin is applied to its load profile (Fig. 2). For instance, when the cluster load factor is 45 % and the consumption is higher than the average consumption it is possible to have load shedding (i.e., decrease in the load) up to 12.5 % (positive flexibility), and when the consumption is lower than the average consumption it is possible to have an increase of up to 10 % (negative flexibility). The load flexibility obtained based on the analysis previously elaborated is shown in Fig. 3.

**Table 1.** Positive and negative flexibility margins based on aggregate load factor

| Aggregate load factor | Positive flexibility | Negative flexibility |
|---|---|---|
| 0–10 % | 2.5 % | 0.0 % |
| 10–20 % | 5.0 % | 2.5 % |
| . . . . . . . . . . . . . . . | | |
| 40–50 % | 12.5 % | 10.0 % |
| . . . . . . . . . . . . . . . | | |
| 80–90 % | 2.5 % | 5.0 % |
| 90–100 % | 0.0 % | 2.5 % |

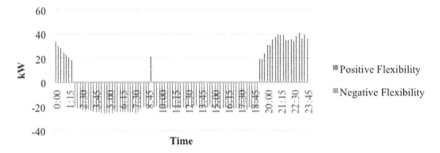

**Fig. 3.** Positive and negative flexibility of cluster 2

The revenues received by the EBAg from the grid and rewards given by the EBAg to the clusters are based on the electricity tariffs, considering significant variations in frequency and amplitude along the day in some way mimicking the wholesale electricity market.

## 4   Results and Discussion

The Pareto front is displayed in Fig. 4, which has been obtained coupling the EA with the DEA. The individual optimal solutions (maximizing EBAg profits and minimizing inequity) and three other compromise solutions are displayed in red. EA swiftly obtained very good solutions individually optimizing each objective function, thus extending the front, although with few solutions, and then DEA further improved those solutions and populated the front.

In the solution that maximizes the EBAg profits, 3127 kWh of flexibility were provided by load shedding with a remnant of 204 kWh that could not be offered due to cluster unavailability, leading to a profit of 654.3 € and 0.17 for the inequity indicator. In the solution that minimizes inequity among clusters, 2644 kWh of flexibility were provided by load shedding in clusters with a remnant not provided of 1357 kWh, leading to a profit of 557.9 € and 0.09 for the inequity indicator. The solution in the middle of the Pareto front could offer a flexibility of 2952 kWh, with a remnant 1357

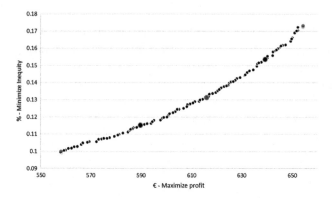

**Fig. 4.** Pareto front.

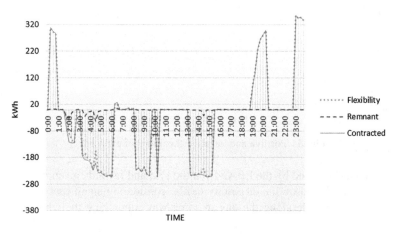

**Fig. 5.** Physical representation of the solution maximizing EBAg profits.

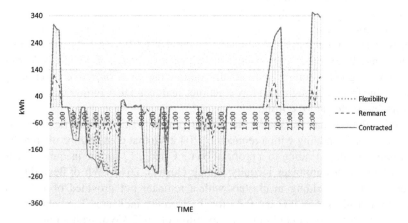

**Fig. 6.** Physical representation of the solution minimizing inequity.

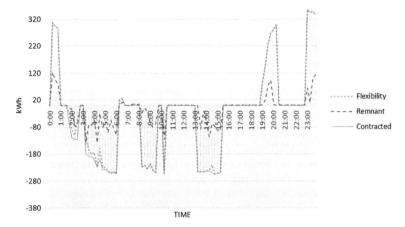

**Fig. 7.** Physical representation of the "middle" solution.

kWh not provided, achieving a profit of 615.9 € and 0.13 for the inequity indicator. Figures 5, 6, and 7 display the physical representation (load flexibility provided by the clusters to satisfy SO requests) of the solutions that maximize the EBAg profits, minimize the inequity among clusters, and the "middle" solution.

## 5 Conclusions

This paper presented a MOO model for an aggregator of local energy management systems, which uses the load flexibility provided by each end-user to respond to the grid requests and facilitate a load follows supply strategy in a Smart Grid setting, with potential benefits for all participants involved. The role of the EBAg is twofold: it makes the most of demand responsive loads according to in-house load flexibility and it provides system services contributing to improve the system operation.

The optimization model from the aggregator perspective presents multi-objective evaluation aspects (economic, quality of service, fairness) of the merits of potential solutions. An approach based on an evolutionary algorithm coupled with a differential evolution algorithm displayed an improved performance to obtain a well spread and populated Pareto front.

Future work will deal with the dynamic nature of the problem and uncertainty associated with input information of different nature.

**Acknowledgement.** This work has been developed under the Energy for Sustainability Initiative of the University of Coimbra and partially supported by the Energy and Mobility for Sustainable Regions Project (CENTRO-07-0224-FEDER-002004) and PEst-OE/EEI/UI308/2014.

# References

1. Kowli, A., Negrete-Pincetic, M., Gross, G.: A successful implementation with the smart grid: demand response resources. In: Power and Energy Society General Meeting 2010, Minneapolis, USA (2010)
2. Livengood, D., Larson, R.: The energy box: locally automated optimal control of residential electricity usage. Serv. Sci. **1**, 1–16 (2009)
3. Verschueren, T., Haerick, W., Mets, K., Develder, C., De Turck, F., Pollet, T.: Architectures for smart end-user services in the power grid. In: 2010 IEEE/IFIP Network Operations and Management Symposium Workshops, pp. 316–322 (2010)
4. EU Comission Task Force for Smart Grid (2010), Expert Group 1: Functionalities of smart grids and smart meters, Brussels, December 2010
5. Joo, J.Y., Ahn, S.H., Yoon, Y., Choi, J.W.: Option valuation applied to implementing demand response via critical peak pricing. In: IEEE Power Engineering Society General Meeting, 24–28 June 2007
6. Quinn, C., Zimmerle, D., Bradley, T.H.: The effect of communication architecture on the availability, reliability, and economics of plug-in hybrid electric vehicle-to-grid ancillary services. J. Power Sour. **195**, 1500–1509 (2010)
7. Fahrioglu, M., Alvarado, F.L.: Designing incentive compatible contracts for effective demand management. IEEE Trans. Power Syst. **15**(4), 1255–1260 (2000)
8. Agnetis, A., Dellino, G., Pascale, G., Innocenti, G., Pranzo, M., Vicino, A.: Optimization models for end-user flexibility aggregation in smart grids: the ADDRESS approach. In: 2011 IEEE 1st International Workshop on Smart Grid Modeling and Simulation (SGMS) (2011)
9. Deb, K., Pratap, A., Agarwal, S., Meyarivan, T.: A fast and elitist multiobjective genetic algorithm: NSGA-II. IEEE Trans. Evol. Comput. **6**(2), 182–197 (2002)

# EvoFIN

# Generating Directional Change Based Trading Strategies with Genetic Programming

Jeremie Gypteau, Fernando E.B. Otero, and Michael Kampouridis[✉]

School of Computing, University of Kent, Canterbury, UK
{jg431,F.E.B.Otero,M.Kampouridis}@kent.ac.uk

**Abstract.** The majority of forecasting tools use a physical time scale for studying price fluctuations of financial markets, making the flow of physical time discontinuous. Therefore, using a physical time scale may expose companies to risks, due to ignorance of some significant activities. In this paper, an alternative and novel approach is explored to capture important activities in the market. The main idea is to use an intrinsic time scale based on Directional Changes. Combined with Genetic Programming, the proposed approach aims to find an optimal trading strategy to forecast the future price moves of a financial market. In order to evaluate its efficiency and robustness as forecasting tool, a series of experiments was performed, where we were able to obtain valuable information about the forecasting performance. The results from the experiments indicate that this new framework is able to generate new and profitable trading strategies.

**Keywords:** Directional changes · Financial forecasting · Trading · Genetic programming

## 1 Introduction

The global financial system, recently rocked by the crisis, is open 24 h a day, 7 days a week and can be defined as a complex network of interacting agents (e.g., corporations, retail traders). With an average daily turnover of 3–4 trillion USD [1] and with price changes nearly every second, its activity varies at different times of a day and reacts on the announcement of political or economic news. As a consequence, financial time series are unevenly spaced and make the flow of physical time discontinuous [2]. The majority of traditional methods to observe price fluctuations in financial time series are based on physical time changes and, nowadays, it has become very difficult and challenging to observe price movements through this scale. For example, what researchers and practitioners tend to do is to use snapshots of the market, taken at fixed intervals. For instance, they first decide how often to sample the data, and then they take snapshots at the chosen frequency. Therefore, these snapshots create an interval-based summary, e.g. daily closing prices. However, this lacks realism. In everyday life, we record history by identifying key events.

© Springer International Publishing Switzerland 2015
A.M. Mora and G. Squillero (Eds.): EvoApplications 2015, LNCS 9028, pp. 267–278, 2015.
DOI: 10.1007/978-3-319-16549-3_22

To model the discontinuous fluctuations in term of volatility, new time scales were introduced in [3], called intrinsic time. Intrinsic time is an alternative approach that replaces the notion of physical time scale and looks beyond the constraints of the physical time within financial data and constitutes an event-driven approach. In the same paper, the concept of directional changes was introduced. A directional change event is characterized by a fixed threshold of different sizes and time in price time-series, eliminating any irrelevant details of price evolution. In this way, the price fluctuations are described by the frequency of directional change event over a sampling period, which provides an alternative measure of the risk.

While directional changes have already been used for summarising data in an event-based manner, they have not been used for forecasting purposes. Thus, in this paper our aim is to demonstrate that the new paradigm of DC leads to effective and profitable trading strategies, which can potentially outperform the traditional physical-time strategies that are currently widely used. In order to do this, we use a genetic programming algorithm to automatically generate trading strategies that make use of DC thresholds—strategies are created by combining the output of multiple thresholds in a single expression. The GP-generated trading strategies are compared against the use of fixed DC threshold to evaluate whether GP solutions explore the advantage of using multiple thresholds simultaneously or not.

The rest of this paper is organised as follows: Sect. 2 presents related work in the field of financial forecasting, and Sect. 3 gives an overview of the concept of directional changes. Section 4 then discusses how we used the genetic programming algorithm to generate trading strategies. Section 5 presents our experiments, and Sect. 6 concludes the paper and presents future work.

## 2   Related Work

There are numerous works that attempt to create trading strategies to be used in financial markets. Some recent examples include [4–7]. In [4], the authors studied the evolution of trading strategies for a hypothetical trader who chooses portfolios from foreign exchange technical rules that are derived from daily data. On the other hand, [5] presented evidence of time-of-day effects in foreign exchange returns, by using hourly data for the EUR/USD currency. Moreover, [6] used Genetic Network Programming to derive trading rules from the Tokyo stock market, by using daily closing prices. As we can observe, in all of the above works time has been taken in fixed intervals (daily, hourly). The same happens with other works in the literature. In fact, to the best of our knowledge, there are no forecasting/trading works that use non-fixed intervals. Lastly, [7] proposed the use of the so-called zig zag technical analysis indicator in two scenarios to predict trend reversals: using a fuzzy logic model and a neural network model. The zig zag indicator shares similarities with the concept of directional changes (i.e., both use a threshold to filter price movements), although directional changes includes the concepts of overshoots as well, as it will be discussed in Sect. 3.

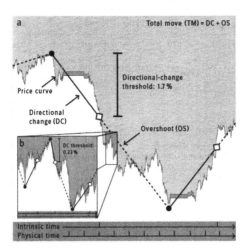

**Fig. 1.** Projection of a (a) two-week, (b) zoomed-in 36 h price sample onto a set of DC events defined by a threshold (a) $\theta = 1.7\%$, (b) $\theta = 0.23\%$. The DC events (diamonds) act as a natural dissection points, decomposing a total-price move between two extremal price levels (bullets) in to DC (solid lines) and OS (dashed lines) sections (source: [2]).

The first works to use the concept of directional changes were proposed in [2,3]. By doing so, new empirical scaling laws in foreign exchange data series were discovered. Then, [8] was the first work to formally present all definitions related to the paradigm of directional changes. Furthermore, [9] demonstrated the effectiveness of directional changes in capturing periodic market activities. To the best of our knowledge, the above are the only works that have used the concept of directional changes. However, none of these works have used DC for generating and evaluating trading strategies. Instead, they have only focused on theoretical aspects of directional changes—e.g. discovering new empirical scaling laws. This thus motivated us to use DC to derive new trading strategies. In the following section, we present in detail the concept of directional changes.

## 3   Directional Changes

A directional change (DC) event is identified by a change in the price of a given stock. This change is defined by a threshold value, which was in advance decided by the trader. Such an event can be either an upturn or a downturn event. After the confirmation of a DC event, an overshoot (OS) event follows. This OS event finishes once an opposite DC event takes place. The combination of a downturn event and a downward overshoot event represents a downward run and, the combination of an upturn event and an upturn overshoot event represents an upturn run. In other words, a downward run is a period between a downturn event and the next upturn event and an upturn run is a period between an upturn event and the next downturn event.

**Algorithm 1.** Pseudocode for generating directional changes events (source: [9]).

---

**Require:** Initialise variables (event is Upturn event, $p^h = p^l = p(t_0), \Delta x_{dc}(Fixed) \geq$
      $0, t_0^{dc} = t_1^{dc} = t_0^{os} = t_1^{os} = t_0$)

1: **if** event is Upturn Event **then**
2:     **if** $p(t) \leq p^h \times (1 - \Delta x_{dc})$ **then**
3:         $event \leftarrow DownturnEvent$
4:         $p^l \leftarrow p(t)$
5:         $t_1^{dc} \leftarrow t$ // End time for a Downturn Event
6:         $t_0^{os} \leftarrow t + 1$ // Start time for a Downward Overshoot Event
7:     **else**
8:         **if** $p^h < p(t)$ **then**
9:             $p^h \leftarrow p(t)$
10:            $t_0^{dc} \leftarrow t$ // Start time for Downturn Event
11:            $t_1^{os} \leftarrow t - 1$ // End time for an Upward Overshoot Event
12:        **end if**
13:    **end if**
14: **else**
15:    **if** $p(t) \leq p^l \times (1 + \Delta x_{dc})$ **then**
16:        $event \leftarrow UpturnEvent$
17:        $p^h \leftarrow p(t)$
18:        $t_1^{dc} \leftarrow t$ // End time for a Upturn Event
19:        $t_0^{os} \leftarrow t + 1$ // Start time for an Upward Overshoot Event
20:    **else**
21:        **if** $p^l > p(t)$ **then**
22:            $p^l \leftarrow p(t)$
23:            $t_0^{dc} \leftarrow t$ // Start time for Upnturn Event
24:            $t_1^{os} \leftarrow t - 1$ // End time for an Downward Overshoot Event
25:        **end if**
26:    **end if**
27: **end if**

---

Figure 1 presents an example of how a physical-time price curve is transformed to the so-called *intrinsic time* [2] and dissected into DC and OS events. Furthermore, Algorithm 1 presents the high-level pseudocode for generating directional changes events.

This new concept provides traders with new perspectives to price movements, and allows them to focus on those key points that an important event took place, blurring out other price details which could be considered irrelevant, or event noise. Furthermore, DC have enabled researchers to discover new regularities in markets, which cannot be captured by the interval-based summaries [2]. Therefore, these new regularities give rise to new opportunities for traders, and also open a whole new area for research.

One of the most interesting regularities that was discovered in [2] was the observation that a DC of threshold $\theta$ is on average followed by an OS event of the same threshold $\theta$. At the same time, it was observed that if on average a DC takes $t$ amount of physical time to complete, the OS event will take an amount of $2t$.

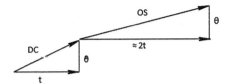

**Fig. 2.** An example of a scaling law presented in [2], which shows that (a) a DC event of threshold $\theta$ is followed by an OS event of also threshold $\theta$, and (b) the OS event lasts about the double amount of time that it took for the DC event to take place.

This observation is summarised in Fig. 2, and *was only made under DC-based summaries*. Furthermore, this astonishing observation was made on all of the 13 different currency exchange rates that the authors of [2] experimented with (findings were published in a prestigious financial journal). This thus leads us to hypothesise that such statistical properties could lead to profitable strategies, if appropriately exploited, mainly because such properties are not well-known to traders yet. Therefore, the DC area is a rich research area that could potentially lead to significant discoveries.

## 4    Generating DC-Based Trading Strategies

As we discussed in Sect. 3, a DC event is identified by a change in the price by a given threshold value. The use of different DC thresholds provides a different view of the data: smaller thresholds allow the detection of more events and, as a result, actions can be taken promptly; larger thresholds detect fewer events, but provide the opportunity of taking actions when bigger price variations are observed. In this section we present a trading strategy that combines the use of different threshold values using a GP algorithm. The aim is to automatically generate expressions that produce outputs based on multiple threshold values in an attempt to take advantage of the different characteristics of smaller/larger thresholds.

The proposed algorithm follows the standard tree-based GP configuration, summarised in Table 1. GP individuals' trees are created from nodes from a terminal and function sets. The function set is composed by boolean functions: binary functions {AND, OR, NOR, XOR} and the unary function {NOT}. The terminal set is composed by nodes representing the output of (randomly-generated) DC thresholds as boolean values: TRUE if the detected event is either an *Upward* or *UpwardOvershoot* event; FALSE if the detected event is either a *Downward* or *DownwardOvershoot* event. The values of the thresholds are randomly chosen at the start of the algorithm given user defined range. Figure 3 illustrates the structure of a GP individual tree. Note that an event is detected only after a confirmation point (end time of a downturn/upturn event); therefore, terminal values correspond to the current active event and this changes when a new event is detected.

**Table 1.** Configuration of the proposed GP algorithm.

| Configuration | Value |
|---|---|
| Individual structure | Tree |
| Function set | Boolean functions {AND, OR, NOR, XOR, NOT} |
| Terminal set | Randomly generated boolean terminals representing different DC threshold values |
| Tree initialisation | Ramped half-and-half |
| Genetic operators | Subtree mutation, one-point crossover and reproduction |
| Selection | Tournament selection |
| Termination criteria | Maximum number of generations |

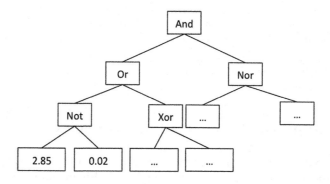

**Fig. 3.** A sample GP individual tree: internal nodes are represented by boolean functions, while leaf nodes correspond to different DC thresholds. Given a price value, terminal nodes output a boolean value according to the DC event detected.

In order to evaluate the output of an expression represented by the GP tree, the algorithm provides a price value to the terminal nodes, which enables the different threshold to detect a DC event. Based on the DC event detected, the terminal nodes output a boolean value.

### 4.1    Fitness Function

As each individual represents a trading strategy, the fitness function measures how good a candidate strategy is in terms of generating profit. The profit is determined by computing the amount of cash that each trading strategy could earn from the historic market activity (training data). In summary, the fitness function iterates over the training days and based on the output of the individual, takes the action of selling or buying a stock. Algorithm 2 presents the high-level pseudocode of the fitness function.

The evaluation of an individual is controlled by two parameters: the initial amount of money (cash) and number of stocks (stock balance). An individual can only buy a stock if it has available cash; similarly, it can only sell a stock if it has available stocks. The operation of buying a stock decreases the cash by the stock price and increases the stock balance by one; the operation of selling a stock decreases the stock balance by one and increases the cash by the selling price.

Recall that an individual potentially includes multiple DC thresholds—each threshold might represent different DC events given the same point in time—and its output is the result of the combination of the output of these thresholds. The rationale of using a combination of multiple thresholds is that it should help to buy or sell stocks at more favourable moments than using just a fixed threshold as an investment strategy.

According to Algorithm 2, the fitness function iteratively evaluates the output of an individual by iterating through the training data. At each iteration, the current price information (data point) is used as an input for each DC threshold node. Based on the detected event, the expression represented by an individual evaluates to a boolean value that indicated the action to be taken: buy one stock at the current price (TRUE); sell one stock at the current price (FALSE). From the sale and purchase of stocks, the fitness of an individual corresponds to the profit during the training period, calculated as

$$fitness = cash + (stockBalance \times last\ price), \tag{1}$$

where the *last price* is the value of a stock at the last data point. Therefore, the fitness function takes into consideration both buying and selling activities to calculate the profit of the trading strategy represented by the individual.

---

**Algorithm 2.** Pseudocode for the fitness function evaluation of a GP individual.

---

**Require:** : Initialise variables (index $= 0$, cash $= initial\ cash$, balanceStock $= 0$)
1: **for** $index < number\ of\ training\ days$ **do**
2:     $buy \leftarrow evaluate(individual)$
3:     **if** (buy is true **and** cash $\geq current\ price$) **then**
4:         $balanceStock \leftarrow balanceStock + 1$
5:         $cash \leftarrow cash - current\ price$
6:     **else if** (buy is false **and** balanceStock $\geq 0$) **then**
7:         $balaneStock \leftarrow balanceStock - 1$
8:         $cash \leftarrow cash + current\ price$
9:     **end if**
10:     $index \leftarrow index + 1$
11: **end for**
12: $fitness \leftarrow cash + (balanceStock \times last\ price)$

---

## 5   Computational Experiments

The goal of our experiments is twofold: (i) demonstrate that the paradigm of DC returns profitable strategies, and (ii) provide evidence that the strategies generated by the GP are more profitable than using a fixed threshold.

We run tests on 4 datasets, two stocks from the UK FTSE100 market (Barclays, Marks & Spencer), and two international indices (NASDAQ, and NYSE). Data consist of daily closing prices, where the training period is 1000 days long, and the testing period is 500 days. Given that stock prices are different across the datasets, the initial budget for each dataset is different—these will be presented in Subsect. 5.1. The rest of the experimental parameters are presented in Table 2. The GP algorithm is run 30 times on each dataset and the results presented correspond to the average value over the 30 executions; fixed thresholds are run just once per dataset, since they represent a deterministic strategy.

**Table 2.** Parameters of the GP algorithm used in the experiments.

| Parameter | Value |
|---|---|
| Max tree initial depth | 5 |
| Max tree depth | 8 |
| Generations | 300 |
| Population size | 300 |
| Tournament size | 2 |
| Reproduction probability | 0.01 |
| Crossover probability | 0.97 |
| Mutation probability | 0.01 |
| Elitism probability | 0.01 |
| Max DC threshold | 10 |
| Min DC threshold | 0 |

Finally, we mentioned above that we will be comparing our GP results with results generated by fixed thresholds. These fixed thresholds are: 0.02, 0.05, 0.10 0.20, 0.50, 1.0, 1.50, 2.00, 2.50, 3.00, 4.00, 4.50, and 5.00. The comparison will involve two steps: first, all fixed thresholds are evaluated in the training period; then, for each dataset, the best threshold (the one that provided the highest profit in the training data) is selected to be against the GP in the test period.

## 5.1   Results

The average of the training fitness over 30 runs with the GP algorithm are presented in Fig. 4 for the four following markets: Barclays (4A), Marks & Spencer (4B), NASDAQ (4C) and NYSE (4D). The individuals chosen for this observation were the ones that had the highest performance in the training period. We can observe that the GP search can produce more profitable solutions over the generations. Another interesting observation is that the best fitness value (profit) is considerably higher than the initial budget and also higher than the profit generated by the use of fixed threshold values, presented in Fig. 5.

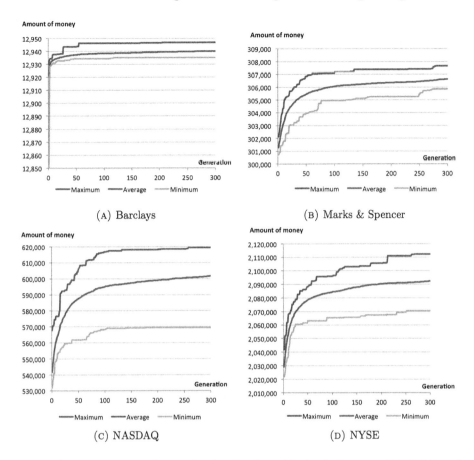

(A) Barclays                            (B) Marks & Spencer

(C) NASDAQ                              (D) NYSE

**Fig. 4.** Average training fitness for the Barclays, Marks & Spencer, NASDAQ and NYSE markets. The training period is 1000 days. Initial amount of cash for fitness evaluation for each dataset: (a) 7,000; (b) 300,000; (c) 500,000; and (d) 2,000,000 monetary units, respectively.

In order to evaluate the trading strategy evolved by the GP, we tested the solution on a separate set of data (test data), which was not used during training. The testing period correspond to 500 days. In the case of the GP, we report the average over the 30 runs of the solution created by the GP; in the case of fixed thresholds, we selected the threshold with the highest profit in the training data for each dataset (see Fig. 5)—therefore, different fixed thresholds are used for each dataset. Table 3 summarises the results obtained in the test set.

From Table 3 we can make several observations. First, the GP returns profit for all 4 datasets tested in this paper. For Barclays, there was an increase in profit by 163.47 monetary units (4.67 %), for Marks & Spencer an increase by 832.33 units (0.55 %), for NASDAQ an increase by 12,344.39 units (4.93 %), and for NYSE by 73,109.19 monetary units (7.31 %). The second observation we can

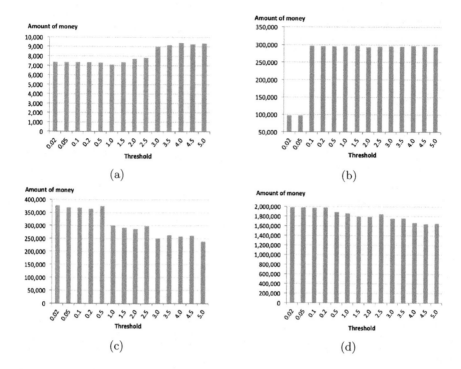

**Fig. 5.** Training fitness values for the different fixed thresholds for Barclays, Marks & Spencer, NASDAQ, and NYSE. The initial amount of budget for each dataset was (a) 500,000, (b) 250,000, (c) 2,000,000 and (d) 1,000,000 monetary units, respectively.

**Table 3.** Profit generated by the GP and fixed DC thresholds in the test data. The test period is 500 days. Initial amount of cash for fitness evaluation for each dataset: (a) 3,500; (b) 150,000; (c) 250,000; and (d) 1,000,000 monetary units, respectively. Fixed DC threshold used: Barclays (4 %), Marks & Spencer (0.1 %), NASDAQ (0.02 %) and NYSE (0.05 %).

| Dataset | GP | Fixed DC |
|---|---|---|
| Barclays | **3,663.47** | 3,007.55 |
| Marks & Spencer | **150,832.33** | 149,501.30 |
| NASDAQ | **262,344.39** | 254,450.72 |
| NYSE | **1,073,190.19** | 1,048,095.45 |

make is that this is not always the case with the fixed thresholds, where Barclays and Marks & Spencer returned losses. Finally, another observation we can make is that the GP results outperform the fixed threshold results under all 4 datasets tested in this work. Therefore, these results provide evidence that the GP evolved strategies are doing more than just using a fixed threshold. Overall, we consider these results promising: the GP successfully explored the use of multiple DC thresholds to evolve trading strategies that combine different thresholds to buy/sell stocks at more favourable moments.

## 6  Conclusion

In this paper we presented an approach to automatically generate trading strategies using a GP algorithm. Traditionally, financial forecasting tools are based on physical time to forecast the future price movement and probe the market activity at a fix interval of time. In the proposed approach, we argue that it is better to use an intrinsic time scale to forecast the market activity through the use of event based on Directional Changes (DC). To the best of our knowledge, DC has not been previously used to generate and evaluate trading strategies.

The proposed GP algorithm uses different DC threshold values as terminal nodes; the output of the DC nodes are combined into a single output using boolean functions. The rationale of allowing the combination of multiple thresholds is that it should help to create strategies that buy or sell stocks at more favourable moments. Computational experiments showed that the strategies evolved by the GP are more profitable than the use of a fixed threshold value, providing evidence that DC can be used for forecasting and that combining multiple thresholds is beneficial. On the one hand, the use of smaller DC thresholds detects more events, therefore actions can be taken promptly; on the other hand, the use of larger DC thresholds detects less events, but actions can be taken after observing bigger price variations.

There are several interesting research directions that can build on the approach presented in this paper. The first one is to explore different parameters settings of the algorithm with the aim of increasing the profit—e.g., at each buy/sell operation, currently only one stock is involved. There is an opportunity to identify situations where it will be better to buy/sell more stocks in the same operation. Second, we discussed that a DC event takes on average $t$ amount of physical time to complete, followed by an OS event that takes on average $2t$. The current GP does not explore the use of OS events—there is a clear opportunity to use OS events to further improve the evolved strategies, exploring the property that a DC event is followed by a OS event with twice its duration.

## References

1. International Monetary Fund: Global financial stability report (2009)
2. Glattfelder, J., Dupuis, A., Olsen, R.: Patterns in high-frequency FX data: discovery of 12 empirical scaling laws. Quant. Finance **11**(4), 599–614 (2011)
3. Olsen, R.B., Muller, U.A., Dacorogna, M.M., Pictet, O.V., Dave, R.R., Guillaume, D.M.: From the bird's eye to the microscope: a survey of new stylized facts of the intra-day foreign exchange markets. Finance Stochast. **1**(2), 95–129 (1997)
4. Neely, C.J., Weller, P.A.: Lessons from the evolution of foreign exchange trading strategies. J. Bank. Finance **37**(10), 3783–3798 (2013)
5. Breedon, F., Ranaldo, A.: Intraday patterns in FX returns and order flow. J. Money Credit Bank. **45**(5), 953–965 (2013)

6. Chen, Y., Mabu, S., Hirasawa, K., Hu, J.: Genetic network programming with sarsa learning and its application to creating stock trading rules. In: Proceedings of the IEEE Conference on Evolutionary Computation, Singapore, pp. 220–237 (2007)
7. Azzini, A., da Costa Pereira, C., Tettamanzi, A.G.B.: Modeling turning points in financial markets with soft computing techniques. In: Brabazon, A., O'Neill, M., Maringer, D.G. (eds.) Natural Computing in Computational Finance. SCI, vol. 293, pp. 147–167. Springer, Heidelberg (2010)
8. Tsang, E.: Directional changes, definitions. Working Paper WP050 2010, Centre for Computational Finance and Economic Agents (CCFEA). University of Essex (2010)
9. Aloud, M., Tsang, E., Olsen, R., Dupuis, A.: A directional-change event approach for studying financial time series. Economics: The Open-Access,Open-Assessment E-Journal 6(2012–36), 1–17 (2012)

# An Evolutionary Optimization Approach to Risk Parity Portfolio Selection

Ronald Hochreiter[(✉)]

Department of Finance, Accounting and Statistics,
WU Vienna University of Economics and Business, Vienna, Austria
ronald.hochreiter@wu.ac.at

**Abstract.** In this paper we present an evolutionary optimization approach to solve the risk parity portfolio selection problem. While there exist convex optimization approaches to solve this problem when long-only portfolios are considered, the optimization problem becomes non-trivial in the long-short case. To solve this problem, we propose a genetic algorithm as well as a local search heuristic. This algorithmic framework is able to compute solutions successfully. Numerical results using real-world data substantiate the practicability of the approach presented in this paper.

## 1 Introduction

The portfolio selection problem is concerned with finding an optimal portfolio $x$ of assets from a given set of $n$ risky assets out of a pre-specified asset universe such that the requirements of the respective investor are met. In general, investors seek to optimize their portfolio in regard of the trade-off between return and risk, such that the meta optimization problem can be formulated as shown in Eq. (1).

$$\begin{aligned} \text{minimize } &\texttt{Risk}(x) \\ \text{maximize } &\texttt{Return}(x) \end{aligned} \tag{1}$$

This bi-criteria optimization problem is commonly reduced to a single-criteria problem by just focusing on the risk and constraining the required mean, i.e. the investor sets a lower expected return target $\mu$, which is shown in Eq. (2).

$$\begin{aligned} \text{minimize } &\texttt{Risk}(x) \\ \text{subject to } &\texttt{Return}(x) \geq \mu \end{aligned} \tag{2}$$

Markowitz [1] pioneered the idea of risk-return optimal portfolios using the standard deviation of the portfolios profit and loss function as risk measure. In this case, the optimal portfolio $x$ is computed by solving the quadratic optimization problem shown in Eq. 3. The investor needs to estimate a vector of expected returns $r$ of the assets under consideration as well as the covariance matrix $\mathbb{C}$.

© Springer International Publishing Switzerland 2015
A.M. Mora and G. Squillero (Eds.): EvoApplications 2015, LNCS 9028, pp. 279–288, 2015.
DOI: 10.1007/978-3-319-16549-3_23

Finally the minimum return target $\mu$ has to be defined. Any standard quadratic programming solver can be used to solve this problem numerically.

$$\begin{aligned} \text{minimize} \quad & x^T \mathbb{C} x \\ \text{subject to } & r \times x \geq \mu \\ & \sum x = 1 \end{aligned} \tag{3}$$

While this formulation has been successfully applied for a long time, criticism has sparked recently. This is especially due to the problem of estimating the mean vector. To overcome this problem one seeks optimization model formulations that solely depend on the covariance matrix. Sometimes even simpler approaches are favored, e.g. the 1-over-N portfolio, which equally weights every asset under consideration. It has been shown that there are cases, where this simple strategy outperforms clever optimization strategies, see e.g. DeMiguel et al. [2].

Of course, the Markowitz problem can be simplified to a model without using returns easily by dropping the minimum return constraint. In this case one receives the Minimum Variance Portfolio (MVP), which is overly risk-averse.

One important technique used for practical portfolio purposes are risk-parity portfolios, where the assets are weighted such that they equally contribute risk to the overall risk of the portfolio. The properties of such portfolios are discussed by Maillard et al. [3] and alternative solution approaches are shown by Chaves et al., see [4,5], as well as Bai et al. [6].

In this paper, an evolutionary optimization approach to compute optimal risk parity portfolios will be presented. Evolutionary optimization approaches have been shown to be useful for solving a wide range of different portfolio optimization problems, see e.g. [7] or [8] and the references therein. See also the series of books on Natural Computing in Finance for more examples [9–11].

This paper is organized as follows. Section 2 describes the risk-parity problem in detail, Sect. 3 presents the evolutionary algorithm developed for solving the problem, and Sect. 4 presents numerical results. Finally, Sect. 5 concludes the paper.

## 2    Risk Parity Portfolio Selection

The type of risk-parity portfolios discussed in this paper are also called Equal Risk Contribution (ERC) portfolios. The idea is to find a portfolio where the assets are weighted such that they equally contribute risk to the overall risk of the portfolio.

We follow Maillard et al. [3] in their definition of risk contribution, i.e. reconsider the above mentioned portfolio $x = (x_1, x_2, \ldots, x_n)$ of $n$ risky assets. Let $\mathbb{C}$ be the covariance matrix, $\sigma_i^2$ the variance of asset $i$, and $\sigma_{ij}$ the covariance between asset $i$ and $j$. Let $\sigma(x)$ be the risk (i.e. standard deviation) of the portfolio as defined in Eq. (4).

$$\sigma(x) = \sqrt{x^T \mathbb{C} x} = \sum_i x_i^2 \sigma_i^2 + \sum_i \sum_{j \neq i} x_i x_j \sigma_{ij}. \tag{4}$$

Then the marginal risk contributions $\partial_{x_i}\sigma(x)$ of each asset $i$ are defined as follows

$$\partial_{x_i}\sigma(x) = \frac{\partial\sigma(x)}{\partial x_i} = \frac{x_i\sigma_i^2 + \sum_{j\neq i} x_j\sigma_{ij}}{\sigma(x)}.$$

If we are considering long-only portfolios then the optimal solution can be written as an optimization problem containing a logarithmic barrier term which is shown in Eq. (5) and where $c$ is an arbitrary positive constant. See e.g. also [12] for an alternative formulation. In this long-only case, a singular optimal solution can be computed.

$$\begin{array}{ll} \text{minimize} & x^T\mathbb{C}x - c\sum_{i=1}^n \ln x_i \\ \text{subject to } x_i > 0. \end{array} \tag{5}$$

However, if we want to include short positions then we need to find solutions in other orthants than in the non-negative orthant. See Bai et al. [6] for a log-barrier approach in this case, which is shown in Eq. (6).

$$\begin{array}{ll} \text{minimize} & x^T\mathbb{C}x - c\sum_{i=1}^n \ln\beta_i x_i \\ \text{subject to } \beta_i x_i > 0, \end{array} \tag{6}$$

where $\beta = (\beta_1, \beta_2, \ldots, \beta_n) \in \{-1,1\}^n$ defines the orthant where the solution should be computed. For each choice of $\beta$ the above optimization problem is convex and can be solved optimally. However, as shown in [6] there are $2^n$ different solutions. Investors may add additional constraints to specify their needs, however this cannot be modeled as one convex optimization problem, which is why an evolutionary approach is presented here. The general formulation of the long-short risk parity portfolio problem can be formulated as Eq. (7) as shown in [3].

$$\begin{array}{ll} \text{minimize} & \sum_{i=1,j=1}^n (x_i(\mathbb{C}x)_i - x_j(\mathbb{C}x)_j)^2 \\ \text{subject to } a_i \leq x_i \leq b_i, \\ \qquad\qquad \sum_{i=1}^n x_i = 1. \end{array} \tag{7}$$

## 3  Implementation

The solution is computed in two steps. First, a genetic algorithm will be employed and afterwards a local search algorithm will be applied.

### 3.1  Genetic Algorithm

We are using a standard genetic algorithm to compute risk-parity optimal portfolios. The algorithm was implemented using the statistical computing language R [13].

The fitness definition in the risk-parity setting is given by the deviance of each risk contribution from the mean of all risk contributions. Let us use the shorthand notation of $\Delta_i = \partial_{x_i}\sigma(x)$, so we compute the expectation $\Delta = \mathbb{E}(\Delta_i)$ and define the fitness $f$ as the sum of the quadratic distance of each risk contribution from the mean. This non-negative fitness value $f$ has to be minimized, where

$$f = \sum_i (\Delta_i - \Delta)^2$$

We use a genotype-phenotype equivalent formulation, i.e. we use chromosomes of length $n$ which contain the specific portfolio weights of the $n$ risky assets. Thus, an important operator is the repair operator, i.e. the sum of the portfolio is normalized to 1 after each operation.

The genetic operators used in the algorithm can be summarized as follows:

*Elitist selection:* The best $n_{ES}$ chromosomes of each population are kept in the population.

*Mutation:* A random selection of $n_M$ chromosomes of the parent population will be mutated. Up to a number of 15 % of the length of the respective chromosome will be changed to a random value between the portfolio bounds. Let $\ell$ be the length of the chromosome. First, a random number between 0 and 0.15 is drawn. This number is multiplied by $\ell$ and rounded up to the next integer value. This value represents the number of genes to be mutated. The mutation positions will be chosen randomly. Afterwards the randomly selected positions will be replaced with a random value between the upper and the lower investment limit of the respective asset.

*Random addition:* $n_R$ new and completely random chromosomes are added to each new population.

*Intermediate crossover:* Two chromosomes from the parent population will be randomly selected for an intermediate crossover. The mixing parameter between the two chromosomes will also be chosen randomly. $n_{IC}$ crossover children will be added to the next population. Let the mixing parameter be $\alpha$ and the two randomly chosen parent chromosomes $p_1$ and $p_2$ with genes $p_{1,1}, \ldots, p_{1,\ell}$ and $p_{2,1}, \ldots, p_{2,\ell}$ respectively, where $\ell$ is the length of the chromosome. An intermediate crossover will result in a child chromosome $c$ where the genes are set to

$$c_i = \alpha p_{1,i} + (1 - \alpha) p_{2,i} \quad \forall i = 1, \ldots, \ell.$$

## 3.2   Local Search

In a second step, a local search algorithm is applied to the best solution of the genetic algorithm. Thereby, within each iteration of the algorithm each asset weight of the $n$ assets of the portfolio is increased or decreased by a factor $\varepsilon$. Each of these $(2 \times n)$ new portfolios is normalized and if one exhibits a lower fitness value then this new portfolio will be used subsequently. The algorithm terminates if no local improvement is possible anymore or the maximum number of iterations has been reached.

# 4  Numerical Results

In this section the above described algorithm will be applied to real-world financial data to obtail numerical results, which can be used for practical portfolio optimization purposes. The first test using stock data from the DJIA index is described in Sect. 4.1 and both the long-only case (Sect. 4.2) as well as the long-short case (Sect. 4.3) is discussed. To check for scalability the algorithm is tested on all stocks of the S&P 100 index in Sect. 4.4 afterwards.

## 4.1  Financial Data and Setup

We use data from all stocks from the Dow Jones Industrial Average (DJIA) index using the composition of September 20, 2013, i.e. using the stocks with the ticker symbols AXP, BA, CAT, CSCO, CVX, DD, DIS, GE, GS, HD, IBM, INTC, JNJ, JPM, KO, MCD, MMM, MRK, MSFT, NKE, PFE, PG, T, TRV, UNH, UTX, V, VZ, WMT, XOM.

Using the R package `quantmod` [14] we obtain daily adjusted closing data from Yahoo! Finance. We use data from the beginning of 2010 until the beginning of November 2014 to compute the Variance-Covariance matrix, i.e. the matrix is entirely based on historical data. The data is solely used for comparison purposes such that a clever approximation algorithm for the Variance-Covariance matrix like those presented e.g. by [15,16] is not necessary for the purpose of this study. However it should be noted that the matrix is the important input parameter for the calculation.

The parameters used for the genetic algorithm are shown in Table 1. The local search algorithm was started twice, once with $\varepsilon = 0.01$ and subsequently with $\varepsilon = 0.001$. The number of maximum local search steps has been set to 500.

## 4.2  Computing DJIA Long-Only Portfolios

First, we compute a set if various long-only portfolios without using expected returns, i.e. the Minimum Variance Portfolio (MVP), the 1/N portfolio as well as the risk-parity portfolio using the algorithm developed in this paper and

**Table 1.** Parameters for the genetic algorithm.

| Parameter | Value |
| --- | --- |
| Initial population size | 200 |
| Maximum iterations | 300 |
| Elitist selection | 10 top chromosomes from parent population |
| Random addition | 50 new chromosomes |
| Mutation | 100 chromosomes from parent population |
| Intermediate crossover | 100 pairs of chromosomes from parent population |

**Table 2.** DJIA - long only - MVP, 1/N, and risk parity.

|      | x(MVP) | RCn(MVP) | x(1/N) | RCn(1/N) | x(RP) | RCn(RP) |
|------|--------|----------|--------|----------|-------|---------|
| AXP  | 0.0000 | 0.0408   | 0.0300 | 0.0444   | 0.0000 | 0.0404 |
| BA   | 0.0000 | 0.0374   | 0.0300 | 0.0411   | 0.0000 | 0.0366 |
| CAT  | 0.0000 | 0.0420   | 0.0300 | 0.0484   | 0.0000 | 0.0413 |
| CSCO | 0.0000 | 0.0338   | 0.0300 | 0.0382   | 0.0000 | 0.0329 |
| CVX  | 0.0000 | 0.0345   | 0.0300 | 0.0357   | 0.0000 | 0.0341 |
| DD   | 0.0000 | 0.0382   | 0.0300 | 0.0410   | 0.0000 | 0.0376 |
| DIS  | 0.0000 | 0.0383   | 0.0300 | 0.0394   | 0.0000 | 0.0384 |
| GE   | 0.0000 | 0.0395   | 0.0300 | 0.0416   | 0.0000 | 0.0395 |
| GS   | 0.0000 | 0.0370   | 0.0300 | 0.0451   | 0.0000 | 0.0356 |
| HD   | 0.0000 | 0.0323   | 0.0300 | 0.0319   | 0.0000 | 0.0328 |
| IBM  | 0.0207 | 0.0285   | 0.0300 | 0.0283   | 0.0000 | 0.0272 |
| INTC | 0.0000 | 0.0312   | 0.0300 | 0.0353   | 0.0000 | 0.0305 |
| JNJ  | 0.2015 | 0.0285   | 0.0300 | 0.0218   | 0.0376 | 0.0257 |
| JPM  | 0.0000 | 0.0424   | 0.0300 | 0.0502   | 0.0000 | 0.0417 |
| KO   | 0.0038 | 0.0285   | 0.0300 | 0.0255   | 0.0275 | 0.0334 |
| MCD  | 0.2421 | 0.0285   | 0.0300 | 0.0195   | 0.2333 | 0.0288 |
| MMM  | 0.0000 | 0.0345   | 0.0300 | 0.0359   | 0.0000 | 0.0340 |
| MRK  | 0.0000 | 0.0301   | 0.0300 | 0.0274   | 0.0000 | 0.0299 |
| MSFT | 0.0000 | 0.0308   | 0.0300 | 0.0327   | 0.0000 | 0.0307 |
| NKE  | 0.0000 | 0.0343   | 0.0300 | 0.0365   | 0.0000 | 0.0347 |
| PFE  | 0.0000 | 0.0306   | 0.0300 | 0.0289   | 0.0000 | 0.0300 |
| PG   | 0.1890 | 0.0285   | 0.0300 | 0.0187   | 0.3050 | 0.0322 |
| T    | 0.0745 | 0.0285   | 0.0300 | 0.0228   | 0.0330 | 0.0288 |
| TRV  | 0.0000 | 0.0317   | 0.0300 | 0.0308   | 0.0000 | 0.0322 |
| UNH  | 0.0000 | 0.0305   | 0.0300 | 0.0324   | 0.0000 | 0.0293 |
| UTX  | 0.0000 | 0.0364   | 0.0300 | 0.0382   | 0.0000 | 0.0361 |
| V    | 0.0000 | 0.0330   | 0.0300 | 0.0360   | 0.0000 | 0.0320 |
| VZ   | 0.0554 | 0.0285   | 0.0300 | 0.0222   | 0.1072 | 0.0304 |
| WMT  | 0.2130 | 0.0285   | 0.0300 | 0.0176   | 0.2565 | 0.0312 |
| XOM  | 0.0000 | 0.0325   | 0.0300 | 0.0326   | 0.0000 | 0.0323 |

described above. The results is shown in Table 2. Please note that the risk contribution has been normalized to 1. The fitness of the 1/N portfolio is 0.002253031, while the MVP exhibits a fitness of 0.00057129. The algorithm managed to find the Risk Parity portfolio with a fitness of 0.0005019655. A lower fitness is not possible due to the long-only constraint.

Furthermore, the convergence results in the long-only case can be seen in Fig. 1. The left picture shows the best fitness over 300 iterations, while the right picture shows the mean of the population fitness. The middle line depicts the mean of 100 instances while the upper and the lower line depict the 5 % as well as the 95 % quantile of the instances.

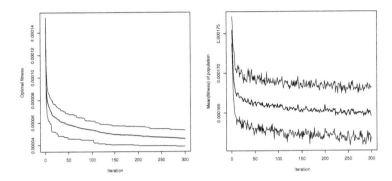

**Fig. 1.** Convergence of the genetic algorithm in the long-only case, i.e. the best (left) and the mean (right) fitness value of each iteration along with the 5 % as well as the 95 % quantile of 100 instances.

In the long-only case, a simple random multi-start local search algorithm like the one described in Sect. 3.2 above leads to the same result. We tested this by running it 100 times and figured out that both the GA+Local as well as the Random+Local approach led to the same optimal portfolio in all cases. However, the optimal solution of the genetic algorithm needed significantly less iterations compared to starting from random solutions. A statistical t-test returned $t = -60.5674$ ($df = 183.198$) and a p-value of 0 with respect to the number of local search iterations. However, this is different in the long-short case, which is described in the next section.

### 4.3   Computing DJIA Long-Short Portfolios

In the long-short case, a random multi-start local search heuristic does not return any useful result. However, the evolutionary approach works well. The long-short result with a lower bound of $-0.2$ is shown in Table 3. The convergence results in the long-short case can be seen in Fig. 2.

### 4.4   Scalability

To test for scalability of the algorithm, we used stocks from the S&P 100 index as of March 21, 2014. Again, we use historical data from the beginning of 2010 until the beginning of November 2014 to compute our Variance-Covariance matrix. Four stocks have been excluded due to data issues, i.e. ABBV, FB, GM, and

**Table 3.** DJIA - long-short - risk parity.

|     | AXP | BA | CAT | CSCO | CVX | DD | DIS | GE | GS | HD |
|-----|-----|-----|-----|------|-----|-----|-----|-----|-----|-----|
| x | −0.065 | −0.010 | −0.039 | 0.000 | −0.015 | −0.042 | −0.060 | −0.071 | 0.034 | 0.019 |
| RCn | 0.033 | 0.033 | 0.033 | 0.033 | 0.033 | 0.033 | 0.033 | 0.033 | 0.033 | 0.033 |

|     | IBM | INTC | JNJ | JPM | KO | MCD | MMM | MRK | MSFT | NKE |
|-----|-----|------|-----|-----|-----|-----|-----|-----|------|-----|
| x | 0.073 | 0.024 | 0.247 | −0.050 | 0.010 | 0.257 | 0.015 | 0.012 | 0.021 | −0.004 |
| RCn | 0.033 | 0.033 | 0.033 | 0.033 | 0.033 | 0.033 | 0.033 | 0.033 | 0.033 | 0.033 |

|     | PFE | PG | T | TRV | UNH | UTX | V | VZ | WMT | XOM |
|-----|-----|-----|-----|-----|-----|-----|-----|-----|-----|-----|
| x | 0.016 | 0.185 | 0.102 | 0.027 | 0.016 | −0.020 | 0.013 | 0.076 | 0.211 | 0.019 |
| RCn | 0.033 | 0.033 | 0.033 | 0.033 | 0.033 | 0.033 | 0.033 | 0.033 | 0.033 | 0.033 |

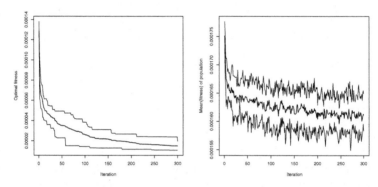

**Fig. 2.** Convergence of the genetic algorithm in the long-short case, i.e. the best (left) and the mean (right) fitness value of each iteration along with the 5 % as well as the 95 % quantile of 100 instances.

GOOG, such that the stocks with the following ticker symbols have been considered: AAPL, ABT, ACN, AIG, ALL, AMGN, AMZN, APA, APC, AXP, BA, BAC, BAX, BIIB, BK, BMY, BRK.B, C, CAT, CL, CMCSA, COF, COP, COST, CSCO, CVS, CVX, DD, DIS, DOW, DVN, EBAY, EMC, EMR, EXC, F, FCX, FDX, FOXA, GD, GE, GILD, GS, HAL, HD, HON, HPQ, IBM, INTC, JNJ, JPM, KO, LLY, LMT, LOW, MA, MCD, MDLZ, MDT, MET, MMM, MO, MON, MRK, MS, MSFT, NKE, NOV, NSC, ORCL, OXY, PEP, PFE, PG, PM, QCOM, RTN, SBUX, SLB, SO, SPG, T, TGT, TWX, TXN, UNH, UNP, UPS, USB, UTX, V, VZ, WAG, WFC, WMT, XOM.

The lower bound was set to −0.2. Figure 3 shows the resulting portfolio as well as the risk contribution of the assets. It can be seen that the algorithm arrives at a solution, which exhibits a rather exact risk parity solution with only slight differences from a perfect solution, which can be observed in the right plot of Fig. 3. To get a more detailed picture on the scalability, a clearer analysis of the proportion between the contribution of the evolutionary solution as well as the local search to the final solution would have to be accomplished, but this

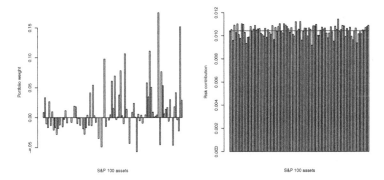

**Fig. 3.** S&P 100 - portfolio (left) and risk contribution (right).

will be left out for future research. From an investor's perspective the optimal portfolio solution exhibits quite a few number of assets, which would have to be shorted. To make the solution more realistic at least a net exposure constraint would have to be added. A cardinality constraint on the number of shorted assets would also be an option. Both constraints can be integrated rather easily in the evolutionary context, see e.g. [17–19]. However, such constraints would disable the possibility to obtain a perfect risk parity solution, which was the aim of the algorithm presented in this paper.

## 5   Conclusion

In this paper, we presented an evolutionary approach to compute optimal risk parity portfolios. This algorithm was designed to overcome the problem that only the long-only case can be solved conveniently using convex optimization models. A two-step approach using a genetic algorithm as well as a local search technique proved to be successful, especially in the long-short case. Another advantage is that further constraints can be integrated directly into the algorithm and this approach can be extended to other risk measures as well.

## References

1. Markowitz, H.: Portfolio selection. J. Finance **7**(1), 77–91 (1952)
2. DeMiguel, V., Garlappi, L., Uppal, R.: Optimal versus naive diversification: how inefficient is the 1/n portfolio strategy? Rev. Financ. Stud. **22**(5), 1915–1953 (2009)
3. Maillard, S., Roncalli, T., Teiletche, J.: The properties of equally weighted risk contribution portfolios. J. Portfolio Manage. **36**(4), 60–70 (2010)
4. Chaves, D., Hsu, J., Li, F., Shakernia, O.: Risk parity portfolio vs. other asset allocation heuristic portfolios. J. Investing **20**(1), 108–118 (2011)
5. Chaves, D., Hsu, J., Li, F., Shakernia, O.: Efficient algorithms for computing risk parity portfolio weights. J. Investing **21**(3), 150–163 (2012)

6. Bai, X., Scheinberg, K., Tutuncu, R.: Least-squares approach to risk parity in portfolio selection (2013). SSRN: http://dx.doi.org/10.2139/ssrn.2343406 23 October 2013
7. Sharma, B., Thulasiram, R.K., Thulasiraman, P.: Portfolio management using particle swarm optimization on GPU. In: 2012 IEEE 10th International Symposium on Parallel and Distributed Processing with Applications (ISPA), pp. 103–110. IEEE (2012)
8. Hochreiter, R.: Evolutionary stochastic portfolio optimization. In: Brabazon, A., O'Neill, M. (eds.) Natural Computing in Computational Finance. Studies in Computational Intelligence, vol. 100, pp. 67–87. Springer, Heidelberg (2008)
9. Brabazon, A., O'Neill, M.: Natural Computing in Computational Finance. Studies in Computational Intelligence, vol. 100. Springer, Heidelberg (2008)
10. Brabazon, A., O'Neill, M.: Natural Computing in Computational Finance, Volume 2. Studies in Computational Intelligence, vol. 185. Springer, Heidelberg (2009)
11. Brabazon, A., O'Neill, M., Maringer, D.: Natural Computing in Computational Finance, Volume 3. Studies in Computational Intelligence, vol. 293. Springer, Heidelberg (2010)
12. Spinu, F.: An algorithm for computing risk parity weights (2013). SSRN: http://dx.doi.org/10.2139/ssrn.2297383 30 July 2013
13. R Core Team: R: A Language and Environment for Statistical Computing. R Foundation for Statistical Computing, Vienna (2014)
14. Ryan, J.A.: Quantmod: Quantitative Financial Modelling Framework (2014). R package version 0.4-2
15. Ledoit, O., Wolf, M.: Improved estimation of the covariance matrix of stock returns with an application to portfolio selection. J. Empir. Finance 10(5), 603–621 (2003)
16. Ledoit, O., Wolf, M.: Honey, i shrunk the sample covariance matrix. J. Portfolio Manage. 30(4), 110–119 (2004)
17. Streichert, F., Ulmer, H., Zell, A.: Evolutionary algorithms and the cardinality constrained portfolio optimization problem. In: Dino Ahr, D.I., Fahrion, R., Oswald, M., Reinelt, G. (eds.) Operations Research Proceedings 2003, pp. 253–260. Springer, Heidelberg (2004)
18. Streichert, F., Ulmer, H., Zell, A.: Comparing discrete and continuous genotypes on the constrained portfolio selection problem. In: Deb, K., Tari, Z. (eds.) GECCO 2004. LNCS, vol. 3103, pp. 1239–1250. Springer, Heidelberg (2004)
19. Streichert, F., Ulmer, H., Zell, A.: Evaluating a hybrid encoding and three crossover operators on the constrained portfolio selection problem. In: Congress on Evolutionary Computation (CEC 2004), vol. 1, pp. 932–939. IEEE (2004)

# Training Financial Decision Support Systems with Thousands of Decision Rules Using Differential Evolution with Embedded Dimensionality Reduction

Piotr Lipinski[✉]

Institute of Computer Science, Computational Intelligence Research Group,
University of Wroclaw, Wroclaw, Poland
lipinski@ii.uni.wroc.pl

**Abstract.** This paper proposes an improvement of the training process of financial decision support systems, where evolutionary algorithms are used to integrate a large number of decision rules. It especially concerns the new computational intelligence approaches that try to replace the expert knowledge with their own artificial knowledge discovered using very large models from very large training datasets, where the large number of decision rules is crucial, because it defines the degree of freedom for the further learning algorithm. The proposed approach focuses on enhancing Differential Evolution by embedding dimensionality reduction to process objective functions with thousands of possibly correlated variables. Experiments performed on a financial decision support system with 5000 decision rules tested on 20 datasets from the Euronext Paris confirm that the proposed approach may significantly improve the training process.

## 1 Introduction

Recent trends in computational intelligence more and more often try to minimize the expert knowledge put in the learning system and replace it with their own artificial knowledge discovered using very large models from very large training datasets, usually with high performance, massive and parallel, computing. They require new computational approaches capable of processing very large datasets in reasonable time on reasonable hardware, such as deep machine learning [1] for learning advanced intelligent systems, deep neural networks [2] for solving large pattern recognition problems, or competitive evolutionary algorithms [3] for solving complex optimization problems.

This paper proposes an improvement of the training process of rule-based intelligent systems, such as decision support systems [4,5], classifier systems [6], multi-agent systems [7], and rule-selection systems [8,9], which are composed of a number of independent entities, agents or rules, integrated using evolutionary algorithms into one consistent system.

Since the number of decision rules included in the artificial knowledge acquired automatically from very large training datasets is usually very large (thousands of

© Springer International Publishing Switzerland 2015
A.M. Mora and G. Squillero (Eds.): EvoApplications 2015, LNCS 9028, pp. 289–301, 2015.
DOI: 10.1007/978-3-319-16549-3_24

rules), the search space of integration parameters has a very high dimension, which constitutes a bottleneck for many evolutionary algorithms. Although some feature selection mechanisms may be applied to reduce the number of decision rules [10], it is inappropriate, because many new computational intelligence approaches just aim at processing thousands of very naive and simple decision rules (often inefficient, when used separately) and combine them later in more efficient decision experts using advanced learning algorithms (the large number of rules is crucial, because it defines the degree of freedom for the learning algorithm).

However, instead of feature selection mechanisms, which focus on global dependencies between variables of the objective function, some techniques of detecting local correlations in the neighborhood of the local optimum during the runtime of the evolutionary algorithm lead to significant improvements. Such an approach is inspired by Estimation of Distribution Algorithms [3] that try to regard the population of candidate solutions as a data sample with a probability distribution approximating the probability distribution describing optimal solutions – similarly, the population of candidate solutions may be used to detect local correlations among variables, reduce the search space and simplify the optimization problem during runtime.

This paper focuses on enhancing the original Differential Evolution algorithm [11] by embedding dimensionality reduction based on Principal Component Analysis [12] and applying it to combine 5000 decision rules in a financial decision support system.

## 2 Embedded Dimensionality Reduction of the Search Space

In complex optimization problems with objective functions of a large number of variables, the main bottleneck is the dimensionality of the search space. In evolutionary algorithms, it leads to long chromosomes and consequently large populations as well as many iterations until convergence. However, in many practical applications, the objective function is often ill-conditioned, i.e. the variables of the function are not really independent, so the optimization problem may be reformulated and solved with a simpler objective function of a much smaller number of variables.

Although simplifying the objective function a priori may be a hard task, it may be simplified during the evolutionary algorithm run by the embedded dimensionality reduction of the search space. It may investigate the linear subspaces in the search space that contain the population. In the pessimistic case, the population would be chaotic and widespread across the entire search space without any significant dependencies, so the only one reasonable subspace to consider would be the entire search space itself. In the optimistic case, the population would be chaotic, but focused on a certain hyperplane, possibly of a lower dimensionality than the entire search space. It may happen when some variables of the objective function are correlated, so there are some dependencies between values of genes in the chromosome.

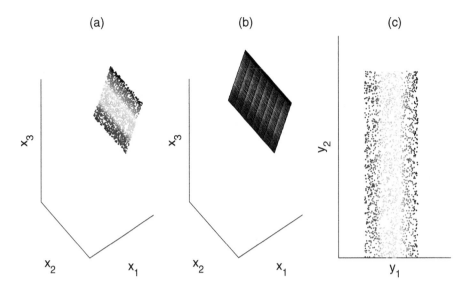

**Fig. 1.** An example of a 2-dimensional population embedded in the 3-dimensional search space: (a) the population in the original search space, (b) the plane defined by the population, (c) the population in the reduced search space.

It is worth noticing that such dependencies may be local, occurring only in a certain region of the search space, e.g. in the neighborhood of a local or global optimum of the objective function, where the current population focuses on, so they usually cannot be discovered by popular preprocessing methods before the evolution process starts [10].

Figure 1 presents a classic example illustrating the approach. The subplot (a) presents the population $\mathcal{P}$ in the original search space $\mathbb{R}^3$ with colors denoting the values of the objective function. It is easy to see that all the individuals lie in a certain plane in the search space presented in the subplot (b). Although the plane is embedded in the 3-dimensional search space, it is actually 2-dimensional, so the original population may be transformed from the original search space to a reduced search space $\mathbb{R}^2$, presented in the subplot (c). Finally, exploiting the original plane by the evolutionary algorithm is equivalent to exploiting the reduced search space.

## 3    Differential Evolution with Embedded Dimensionality Reduction

Algorithm 1 presents an overview of the Differential Evolution with Embedded Dimensionality Reduction (DEEDR) for an objective function $F : \mathbb{R}^n \to \mathbb{R}$ of correlated variables.

DEEDR begins with generating a random population $\mathcal{P}_0$ of $N$ individuals and evaluating it. In the main evolution loop, for each individual $\mathbf{x}$ from the current population $\mathcal{P}_t$, called the target vector, a new vector $\mathbf{v}$, called the donor vector, is created, then the donor vector is recombined with the target vector, using the binomial recombination [11], forming a new vector $\mathbf{u}$, called the trial vector, and finally, if the trial vector outperforms the target vector, it replaces it in the next population, as in classic DE [11]. In some main evolution iterations, DEEDR performs a subevolution, described in Algorithm 2, which analyses the current population, transforms it to a reduced search space, and performs the same routine as the main evolution, but on the selected subspace only.

---

**Algorithm 1.** Differential Evolution with Embedded Dimensionality Reduction (DEEDR) - Main Evolution

$\mathcal{P}_0 = $ Random-Population($N$)
Population-Evaluation($\mathcal{P}_0, F$)
$t = 0$
**while** not Termination-Condition($\mathcal{P}_t$) **do**
    **for all** $\mathbf{x} \in \mathcal{P}_t$ **do**
        pick randomly distinct $\mathbf{x}_1, \mathbf{x}_2, \mathbf{x}_3$ from $\mathcal{P}_t \setminus \{\mathbf{x}\}$
        $\mathbf{v} = \mathbf{x}_1 + \alpha \cdot (\mathbf{x}_2 - \mathbf{x}_3)$
        $\mathbf{u} = $ Binomial-Recombination($\mathbf{v}, \mathbf{x}$)
        **if** $F(\mathbf{x}) \leq F(\mathbf{u})$ **then**
            $\mathbf{u}$ will replace $\mathbf{x}$ in $\mathcal{P}_{t+1}$
        **end if**
    **end for**
    Population-Evaluation($\mathcal{P}_{t+1}, F$)
    $t = t + 1$
    **if** Subevolution-Starting-Condition() **then**
        Subevolution($\mathcal{P}_t$)
    **end if**
**end while**

---

The main evolution and the subevolution is run in such a way that first a number of main iterations is performed in the entire original search space to move the population to some promising regions of the search space, then a number of subevolution iterations is performed in a selected subspace and then the population is restored to the original search space in order to ensure whether the subspace corresponded to a neighborhood of the global optima or not. Few next main iterations may correct the population and move it to some other promising regions of the search space, and then a number of subevolution iterations exploit the new subspace.

### 3.1 Search Space and Population Reduction

Let $\mathcal{P} = \{\mathbf{x}_1, \mathbf{x}_2, \ldots, \mathbf{x}_N\} \subset \mathbb{R}^d$ be a population of $N$ individuals, where each individual $\mathbf{x}_i = (x_{i1}, x_{i2}, \ldots, x_{id})^T \in \mathbb{R}^d$, for $i = 1, 2, \ldots, N$, is a data point in the search space $\mathbb{R}^d$, where $d$ is the dimensionality of the original optimization problem.

**Algorithm 2.** Differential Evolution with Embedded Dimensionality Reduction (DEEDR) - Subevolution

---

Search-Space-Reduction()
$\mathcal{R}_0$ = Population-Reduction($\mathcal{P}_t$)
$s = 0$;
**while** not Subevolution-Termination-Condition($\mathcal{R}_s$) **do**
  **for all** $\mathbf{x} \in \mathcal{R}_s$ **do**
    pick randomly distinct $\mathbf{x}_1, \mathbf{x}_2, \mathbf{x}_3$ from $\mathcal{R}_s \setminus \{\mathbf{x}\}$
    $\mathbf{v} = \mathbf{x}_1 + \alpha \cdot (\mathbf{x}_2 - \mathbf{x}_3)$
    $\mathbf{u}$ = Binomial-Recombination($\mathbf{v}, \mathbf{x}$)
    **if** $F(\mathbf{x}) \leq F(\mathbf{u})$ **then**
      $\mathbf{u}$ will replace $\mathbf{x}$ in $\mathcal{R}_{s+1}$
    **end if**
  **end for**
  Reduced-Population-Evaluation($\mathcal{R}_{s+1}, F$)
  $s = s + 1$
**end while**
Search-Space-Restoring()
$\mathcal{P}_t$ = Population-Restoring($\mathcal{R}_{s-1}$)

---

The subevolution starts with determining the subspace of the search space $\mathbb{R}^d$ that contains the current population $\mathcal{P}_t$ and transforming it to a reduced population $\mathcal{R}_0$ based on Principal Component Analysis [12].

Each data point $\mathbf{x} \in \mathbb{R}^d$ may be represented, without loss of information, as a linear combination of any set of $d$ orthonormal vector $\mathbf{v}_1, \mathbf{v}_2, \ldots, \mathbf{v}_d \in \mathbb{R}^d$ by $\mathbf{x} = \sum_{i=1}^{d} \alpha_i \mathbf{v}_i$, where $\alpha_i = \mathbf{x}^T \mathbf{v}_i$ is a linear projection of the data point $\mathbf{x}$ onto the direction $\mathbf{v}_i$. Therefore, each data point $\mathbf{x}$ may be approximated by

$$\tilde{\mathbf{x}} = \sum_{i=1}^{K} \alpha_i \mathbf{v}_i + \sum_{i=K+1}^{d} \beta_i \mathbf{v}_i,$$

for certain $K$ denoting the dimensionality of the reduced search space and certain constants $\beta_{K+1}, \beta_{K+2}, \ldots, \beta_d \in \mathbb{R}$ (independent of $\mathbf{x}$).

Considering the entire population $\mathcal{P}$, the overall mean square approximation error is then

$$MSE(\mathbf{v}_1, \mathbf{v}_2, \ldots, \mathbf{v}_d, \beta_{K+1}, \beta_{K+2}, \ldots, \beta_d) = \sum_{k=1}^{N} |\mathbf{x}_k - \tilde{\mathbf{x}}_k|^2$$

$$= \sum_{k=1}^{N} \sum_{i=K+1}^{d} |(\mathbf{x}_k^T \mathbf{v}_i)\mathbf{v}_i - \beta_i \mathbf{v}_i|^2 = \sum_{k=1}^{N} \sum_{i=K+1}^{d} (\mathbf{x}_k^T \mathbf{v}_i - \beta_i)^2.$$

Comparing the derivative

$$\frac{\partial MSE(\mathbf{v}_1, \mathbf{v}_2, \ldots, \mathbf{v}_d, \beta_{K+1}, \beta_{K+2}, \ldots, \beta_d)}{\partial \beta_i} = 2\beta_i(N\beta_i - \sum_{k=1}^{N} \mathbf{x}_k^T \mathbf{v}_i)$$

to zero, for each $i = K + 1, K + 2, \ldots, d$, one may find that

$$\beta_i = \frac{1}{N} \sum_{k=1}^{N} \mathbf{x}_k^T \mathbf{v}_i = \bar{\mathbf{x}}^T \mathbf{v}_i,$$

where $\bar{\mathbf{x}}$ is the mean of the population $\mathcal{P}$.

Therefore,

$$MSE(\mathbf{v}_1, \mathbf{v}_2, \ldots, \mathbf{v}_d) = \sum_{k=1}^{N} \sum_{i=K+1}^{d} (\mathbf{x}_k^T \mathbf{v}_i - \bar{\mathbf{x}}^T \mathbf{v}_i)^2 = \sum_{i=K+1}^{d} \mathbf{v}_i^T \Sigma \mathbf{v}_i,$$

where $\Sigma$ is the covariance matrix of the population $\mathcal{P}$. It may be shown that the minimum of the above expression is equal to $\sum_{i=K+1}^{d} \lambda_i$, where $\lambda_{K+1}, \lambda_{K+2}, \ldots, \lambda_d$ denotes $(d-K)$ smallest eigenvalues of the covariance matrix $\Sigma$, and is obtained for corresponding eigenvectors. Therefore, the largest eigenvalues and the corresponding eigenvectors should be taken to construct the reduced search space.

Finally, the reduced population $\mathcal{R}_0$ consists of mappings $\mathbf{y} = \mathbf{D}^{-1/2}\mathbf{V}\mathbf{x}$ of individuals $\mathbf{x}$ from the original population $\mathcal{P}_t$, where $\mathbf{V}$ is the matrix of chosen eigenvectors, $\mathbf{D}$ is the diagonal matrix with eigenvalues on the main diagonal.

### 3.2   Reduced Population Evaluation

Although the evolutionary operators of the subevolution are derived from the main evolution without modifications, i.e. only the chromosome length changes, the problem occurs in evaluating the reduced population. It requires restoring a reduced individual $\mathbf{y} \in \mathbb{R}^K$ to the original search space and evaluating the objective function value for it. Since the reduction procedure consists in mappings on the orthonormal vectors, the restoring procedure is the same, i.e. $\mathbf{x} = \mathbf{D}^{1/2}\mathbf{V}^T\mathbf{y}$, where $\mathbf{V}$ is the matrix of chosen eigenvectors, $\mathbf{D}$ is the diagonal matrix with eigenvalues on the main diagonal.

### 3.3   Search Space and Population Restoring

After termination of the subevolution, the current reduced population is restored to the original search space by applying the same procedure as during the reduced population evaluation, described in the previous subsection.

## 4   Building Financial Decision Support System with Large Sets of Decision Rules

### 4.1   Decision Rules

Although there are a large number of popular decision rules for financial expertise, such as these based on the technical analysis [13], more and more approaches try to build their own decision rules from scratch. It corresponds to recent trends in computational intelligence that try to minimize the expert knowledge put in the intelligent system and replace it with their own artificial knowledge discovered using very large models from very large training datasets, usually with high performance, massive and parallel, computing.

The proposed approach aims at combining thousands of simple decision rules into one efficient decision expert. Such simple decision rules come from a simple Genetic Programming approach: It tries to construct binary decision trees, where internal nodes include conditions $I < \theta$ or $I > \theta$ ($I$ denotes an input variable, $\theta$ denotes a constant threshold) and terminal nodes include trading signals *buy*, *sell*, or *do nothing*. Input variables include stock price return rate, index return rate, macroeconomic indicators and some functions of them: moving averages, moving standard deviations and moving standard semi-deviation. Genetic Programming starts with a random set of decision trees and evolves them under the objective function defined by the profit of the decision tree over a certain training period obtained in a type of simulation (described in Sect. 4.3). It terminates after a small number of iterations to provide diversificated decision rules and avoid overfitting, even if decision rules are far from being optimal.

## 4.2 Decision Experts

Let $\mathcal{R} = \{R_1, R_2, \ldots, R_d\}$ be a set of decision rules. Each decision rules is a function $f : \mathcal{K} \mapsto s \in \mathbb{R}$ that maps a factual financial knowledge $\mathcal{K}$ (e.g. financial time series of recent stock price quotations) to a real number $s$ encoding a trading signal ($-1$ for a sell signal, 0 for a do-nothing signal, 1 for a buy signal). A decision expert $e : \mathcal{K} \mapsto s \in \mathbb{R}$ is a weighted average of decision rules with weights $w_1, w_2, \ldots, w_d \in \mathbb{R}$, i.e. $e(\mathcal{K}) = w_1 f_1(\mathcal{K}) + w_2 f_2(\mathcal{K}) + \ldots + w_d f_d(\mathcal{K})$.

## 4.3 Training Framework

Constructing decision experts may be formulated as an optimization problem over the search space $\mathbb{R}^d$ with an objective function $F : \mathbb{R}^d \to \mathbb{R}$ evaluating a financial relevance of the decision expert in a type of simulation over a certain training period. It starts with an initial capital: an initial amount of cash and an initial number of stocks. In successive days of the training period, the trading expert produces a trading signal. If it is a buy signal, a part of available cash is invested in stocks. If it is a sell signal, a part of available stocks is sold. Each transaction is charged with a transaction fee. Finally, the efficiency of the trading expert is defined by the Sharpe ratio [14] of daily return rates.

## 4.4 Solving the Optimization Problem

In the proposed approach, the main bottlenecks are the dimensionality of the search space, defined by the large number of decision rules, and the irregularity of the search space, due to many hidden correlations between decision rules. However, in such a large number of decision rules, many relations and redundancies may exist, so exploiting them may simplify the optimization problem. Embedded dimensionality reduction of the search space seems to be a reasonable idea.

## 5    Experimental Evaluation of the Proposed Approach

In order to evaluate the proposed approach, a number of computational experiments were performed on real-world data containing 20 datasets concerning 20 stocks chosen from the Euronext Paris. Performance of decision rules and decision experts was evaluated in the simulation, as described in Sect. 4.3, over the training period from January, 2, 2014 to August, 29, 2014 (168 trading days), with the initial capital of 2000 euro (a half of it in cash, a half of it in stocks), with the buy and sell thresholds of 25 % (i.e. on each buy decision, 25 % of current cash were invested; on each sell decision, 25 % of current stocks were sold) and with the transaction fee of 0.25 %. A set of 5000 decision rules was generated with the Genetic Programming approach, as described in Sect. 4.1.

Each dataset was processed twice: once with the original DE algorithm, and once with the improved DEEDR algorithm. In both cases, the population size was 500. The original algorithm run for 2500 iterations. The improved algorithm run for $500 + 10 * (100 + 100) = 2500$ iterations in total: after 500 iterations of the main evolution in the original search space, the embedded dimensionality reduction was turned on and the subevolution was run in the reduced search space for 100 iterations, then the main evolution was run in the original search space again for 100 iterations, and the last two steps were repeated 10 times. In order to avoid a premature convergence, the dimensionality reduction was limited to 125 dimensions (i.e. at least 125 of 5000 eigenvectors were used to

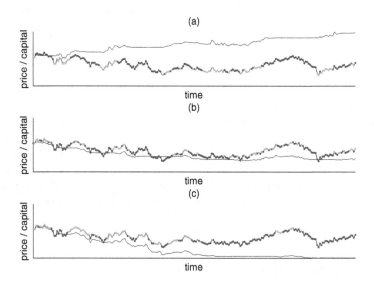

**Fig. 2.** Behavior of three selected decision rules, (a) the best one, (b) the average one, (c) the worst one, over the training period for the AXA dataset. The black line corresponds to the price of the stock. Trading decisions are marked with green (buy) or red (sell) points on the price line. The blue line corresponds to the capital obtained in the simulation by the decision rule (Color figure online).

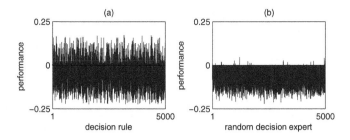

**Fig. 3.** Performance of (a) 5000 single decision rules and (b) 5000 random decision experts over the training period for the AXA dataset.

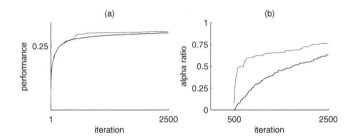

**Fig. 4.** Comparison of the DE and DEEDR algorithm on the AXA dataset: (a) the best objective value found in successive iterations (the mean of 10 runs) by DE (the black line) and DEEDR (the blue line), (b) the relative quality $\alpha$ of the best solution found (the mean of 10 runs) (Color figure online).

define the reduced search space, even if a less number of eigenvalues summed up to 0.95 % of variance). In both cases, the DE parameters was set to $\alpha = 0.5$ (the scale factor in the donor vector creation) and $Cr = 0.75$ (the crossover rate in the binomial recombination) [11].

Before studying the overall performance of the proposed approach, one typical case, concerning the AXA dataset, will be discussed in details. Figure 2 presents the behavior of three selected decision rules, (a) the best one, (b) the average one, (c) the worst one, over the training period. Figure 3(a) presents the performance of 5000 single decision rules. It is easy to see that decision rules are various, rather incidental, some of them are better, some of them are worse, because they were generated with the aim to collect numerous different decision rules and make them efficient later by combining them into decision experts using the DE and DEEDR algorithms. Figure 3(b) presents the performance of 5000 random decision experts. It is easy to see that although some single decision rules are efficient, their random combinations are not, i.e. combining decision rules into decision experts requires some effort.

Figure 4 compares the efficiency of the DE and DEEDR algorithm. Subplot (a) presents the best objective value found in successive iterations by both algorithms. Subplot (b) presents the relative quality of the best solution found,

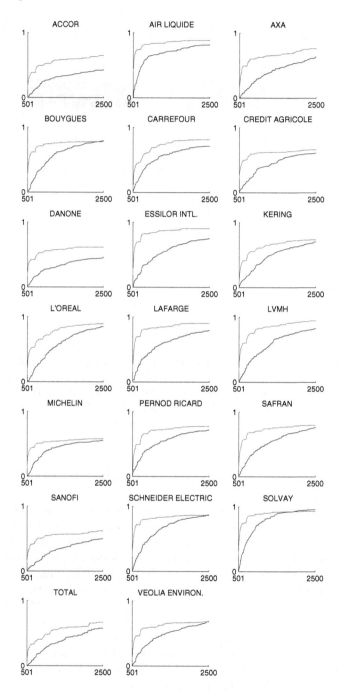

**Fig. 5.** Comparison of the DE and DEEDR algorithm on all the 20 dataset from the Euronext Paris: the relative quality $\alpha$ of the best solution found in successive iterations (the mean of 10 runs) by DE (the black line) and DEEDR (the blue line) (Color figure online).

**Table 1.** Comparison of the DE and DEEDR algorithm on all the 20 dataset from the Euronext Paris (means of 10 runs)

| Dataset | Performance | | | | Relative performance $\alpha$ | | | | $\alpha$ improvement (%) | |
| --- | --- | --- | --- | --- | --- | --- | --- | --- | --- | --- |
| | After 2500 iter. | | After 1000 iter. | | After 2500 iter. | | After 1000 iter. | | After 2500 iter. | After 1000 iter. |
| | DE | DEEDR | DE | DEEDR | DE | DEEDR | DE | DEEDR | | |
| ACCOR | 31.27 | 31.85 | 30.85 | 31.53 | 0.4244 | 0.6462 | 0.2650 | 0.5216 | 52.26 | 96.82 |
| AIR LIQUIDE | 22.61 | 22.71 | 22.36 | 22.64 | 0.8146 | 0.8844 | 0.6525 | 0.8375 | 8.57 | 28.36 |
| AXA | 27.86 | 28.13 | 27.17 | 27.85 | 0.6318 | 0.7598 | 0.3048 | 0.6256 | 20.26 | 105.25 |
| BOUYGUES | 51.42 | 51.33 | 49.13 | 51.08 | 0.7918 | 0.7788 | 0.4602 | 0.7429 | -1.64 | 61.43 |
| CARREFOUR | 21.52 | 21.69 | 21.08 | 21.47 | 0.7163 | 0.8118 | 0.4704 | 0.6896 | 13.33 | 46.60 |
| CREDIT AGRICOLE | 58.81 | 59.12 | 57.40 | 58.83 | 0.6106 | 0.6627 | 0.3803 | 0.6137 | 8.54 | 61.39 |
| DANONE | 19.54 | 20.01 | 18.98 | 19.84 | 0.4597 | 0.6157 | 0.2746 | 0.5585 | 33.91 | 103.34 |
| ESSILOR INTL | 30.05 | 30.33 | 29.46 | 30.21 | 0.7501 | 0.9066 | 0.4231 | 0.8399 | 20.86 | 98.49 |
| KERING | 29.38 | 29.59 | 27.06 | 28.73 | 0.7075 | 0.7393 | 0.3540 | 0.6093 | 4.49 | 72.12 |
| L'OREAL | 15.44 | 15.54 | 14.54 | 15.17 | 0.8465 | 0.8920 | 0.4109 | 0.7171 | 5.38 | 74.54 |
| LAFARGE | 48.95 | 49.47 | 47.41 | 49.11 | 0.7955 | 0.9015 | 0.4811 | 0.8281 | 13.33 | 72.13 |
| LVMH | 21.93 | 22.35 | 20.63 | 21.94 | 0.8228 | 0.9479 | 0.4315 | 0.8264 | 15.21 | 91.52 |
| MICHELIN | 35.05 | 35.13 | 34.59 | 34.99 | 0.5526 | 0.5801 | 0.3868 | 0.5303 | 4.98 | 37.10 |
| PERNOD RICARD | 24.00 | 24.12 | 23.32 | 23.97 | 0.7241 | 0.7735 | 0.4514 | 0.7128 | 6.82 | 57.89 |
| SAFRAN | 29.93 | 30.05 | 28.60 | 29.71 | 0.7669 | 0.7968 | 0.4220 | 0.7090 | 3.90 | 68.03 |
| SANOFI | 24.79 | 25.27 | 23.76 | 24.96 | 0.4989 | 0.6175 | 0.2486 | 0.5418 | 23.78 | 117.89 |
| SCHNEIDER ELECTRIC | 31.60 | 31.58 | 30.44 | 31.41 | 0.8710 | 0.8647 | 0.5375 | 0.8169 | -0.72 | 52.00 |
| SOLVAY | 32.71 | 32.62 | 31.99 | 32.49 | 0.9570 | 0.9300 | 0.7166 | 0.8845 | -2.82 | 23.42 |
| TOTAL | 30.23 | 30.42 | 29.64 | 30.04 | 0.5766 | 0.6685 | 0.2790 | 0.4815 | 15.94 | 72.61 |
| VEOLIA ENVIRON | 55.59 | 55.55 | 53.19 | 54.87 | 0.6873 | 0.6813 | 0.3773 | 0.5945 | -0.88 | 57.56 |

defined by the following linear transformation:

$$\alpha(\mathbf{x}) = \frac{F(\mathbf{x}) - F_0}{F_{max} - F_0},$$

where $F(\mathbf{x})$ is the objective value of the decision expert $\mathbf{x}$, $F_0$ is a baseline objective value (the value of the best solution found during initial 500 iterations of the original DE algorithm), and $F_{max}$ is the target objective value (the value of the best solution found by the original DE algorithm). It is easy to see that the improved DEEDR algorithm outperforms the original DE algorithm, not only in terms of the final solution, but also in terms of the computing time (the solution obtained after 1000 iterations is similar to the final solution of the original algorithm obtained after 2500 iterations).

Figure 5 presents a similar comparison concerning all the 20 datasets. In most cases, DEEDR outperformed DE. Table 1 presents a detailed summary of results. The second and the third column contain the best objective value found by the original and the improved algorithm, respectively. The forth and the fifth column contain the best objective value found in 1000 iterations. The next four columns presents the same information, but in terms of the relative quality $\alpha$ of the best solution. Finally, the last two columns contains the improvement factor – the ratio of $\alpha$ of DEEDR to the $\alpha$ of DE minus one. It is easy to see that DEEDR outperformed DE in 1000 iterations in all the cases, however, in 4 cases, DE was better in the final solution found (after 2500 iterations). It was caused by a premature convergence of DEEDR, avoidance of which may require individual parameter settings of the embedded dimensionality reduction. It is also worthy noticing that the difference in these 4 cases is rather small, which still makes DEEDR an interesting alternative for DE due to the much shorter computing time.

## 6    Conclusions

In this paper, an improvement of the original Differential Evolution algorithm was proposed for solving complex optimization problems with objective functions of a large number of possibly dependent variables, where the main bottleneck was the dimensionality of the search space, which led to long chromosomes and consequently large populations as well as many iterations until convergence.

A preliminary evaluation performed on a financial decision support system, where the proposed algorithm was used to discover the importance weights for 5000 trading rules, confirmed that the method may significantly improve the search process, especially in the case of complex objective functions with a large number of variables, which usually occur in many practical applications.

Moreover, the proposed approach enables to build decision support systems without using large expert knowledge, where the traditional decision rules usually coming from the expert knowledge may be replaced with a much larger number of simple decision rules acquired in an automatic manner (e.g. using Genetic Programming in the approach presented in this paper).

# References

1. Arel, I., Rose, D.C., Karnowski, T.P.: Deep machine learning - a new frontier in artificial intelligence research. IEEE Comput. Intell. Mag. **5**, 13–18 (2010)
2. Li, D., Hinton, G., Kingsbury, B.: New types of deep neural network learning for speech recognition and related applications: an overview. In: IEEE International Conference on Acoustics, Speech and Signal Processing, pp. 8599–8860 (2013)
3. Larranaga, P., Lozano, J.A.: Estimation of Distribution Algorithms. Kluwer Academic Publishers, Boston (2002)
4. Korczak, J., Lipinski, P.: Evolutionary building of stock trading experts in a real-time system. In: IEEE Congress on Evolutionary Computation, pp. 940–947 (2004)
5. Lipinski, P.: Parallel evolutionary algorithms for stock market trading rule selection on many-core graphics processors. Nat. Comput. Comput. Finance Stud. Comput. Intell. **380**, 79–92 (2012)
6. Sirlantzis, K., Fairhurst, M.C., Guest, R.M.: An evolutionary algorithm for classifier and combination rule selection in multiple classifier systems. In: International Conference on Pattern Recognition, pp. 771–774 (2002)
7. Hilletofth, P., Lattila, L.: Agent based decision support in the supply chain context. Ind. Manage. Data Syst. **112**, 1217–1235 (2012)
8. Ishibuchi, H., Yamamoto, T.: Fuzzy rule selection by multi-objective genetic local search algorithms and rule evaluation measures in data mining. Fuzzy Sets Syst. **141**, 59–88 (2004)
9. Nojima, Y., Ishibuchi, H.: Multiobjective genetic fuzzy rule selection with fuzzy relational rules. In: IEEE International Workshop on Genetic and Evolutionary Fuzzy Systems, pp. 60–67 (2013)
10. Webb, A.: Statistical Pattern Recognition. John Wiley, New York (2002)
11. Das, S., Suganthan, P.N.: Differential evolution: a survey of the state-of-the-art. IEEE Trans. Evol. Comput. **15**, 4–31 (2011)
12. Jolliffe, I.T.: Principal Component Analysis. Springer, New York (2002)
13. Murphy, J.: Technical Analysis of the Financial Markets. NUIF, New York (1998)
14. Sharpe, W.: Capital asset prices: a theory of market equilibrium under conditions of risk. J. Finance **19**, 425–442 (1964)

# EvoGAMES

# A Procedural Method for Automatic Generation of Spelunky Levels

Walaa Baghdadi[1], Fawzya Shams Eddin[1], Rawan Al-Omari[1],
Zeina Alhalawani[1], Mohammad Shaker[2], and Noor Shaker[3(✉)]

[1] Information Technology Engineering of Damascus, Damascus, Syria
{walaabaghdadi,fawziashamseddin91,
rawan.alomari91,zeina.helwani}@gmail.com
[2] Joseph Fourier University, Grenoble, France
mohammadshakergtr@gmail.com
[3] IT University of Copenhagen, Copenhagen, Denmark
nosh@itu.dk

**Abstract.** Spelunky is a game that combines characteristics from 2D platform and rogue-like genres. In this paper, we propose an evolutionary search-based approach for the automatic generation of levels for such games. A genetic algorithm is used to generate new levels according to aesthetic and design requirements. A graph is used as a genetic representation in the evolution process to describe the structure of the levels and the connections between the rooms while an agent-based method is employed to specify the interior design of the rooms. The results show that endless variations of playable content satisfying predefined difficulty requirements can be efficiently generated. The results obtained are investigated through an expressivity analysis framework defined to provide thorough insights of the generator's capabilities.

## 1 Introduction

Procedural Content Generation (PCG) is receiving increasing attention due to the advantages it provides in terms of speeding up the content generation process, enabling on-line generation, reducing the development budget and facilitating the creation of endless content variations [1]. Furthermore, since most PCG methods are based on extensive search in the content space [2], it is likely that utilising PCG approaches for generating content will yield novel solutions that can be directly used in the game [3,4] or employed as a form of inspiration for human designers.

Different techniques have been explored to automatically generate different aspects of content for different game genres [3–6] and some of them achieved remarkable results in commercial games [7–10]. *Rogue* is one of the early games where PCG is successfully employed to generate infinite variations of content as the game is being played. The game inspired many others and the automatic generation of dungeons is well investigated and used in several well-known games such as *Diablo* and *Dungeon Siege*. Most of the techniques used so far for dungeon generation however suffer from the lack of controllability as it is usually hard

© Springer International Publishing Switzerland 2015
A.M. Mora and G. Squillero (Eds.): EvoApplications 2015, LNCS 9028, pp. 305–317, 2015.
DOI: 10.1007/978-3-319-16549-3_25

to specify design constraints or requirements and they mostly tend to produce neat structures [1].

One of the recent well-known commercial game that combines characteristics from the dungeon and platform games is *Spelunky*. The game successfully employs PCG techniques to generate variations of structures that are unique with every replay. Such as most rough-like and dungeon generation methods, randomness forms the basis of diversity and hand crafted templates are used to control the level structures.

In this paper we present a procedural approach that allows the generation of variant content for a Spelunky-like game while permitting control over important content aspects. We analyse the game aspects and we employ the search-based approach of PCG [2] to generate game content. More specifically, a Genetic Algorithm (GA) is used to evolve game content where levels are represented using an indirect representation in the form of graphs that specify the navigation order of the rooms and the connections between them. A separated agent-based approach is then implemented to define the inner structure of each room. Rooms are then filled with different items according to a distribution scheme. We define a difficulty measure that scores levels according to their final structure and the presence of certain items and their placement. We show that infinite playable levels of varying difficulties can be generated and we present a thorough analysis of the results obtained.

## 2  Spelunky

Spelunky is an action adventure indie game that combines the characteristics of two genres: rogue-like and 2D platform games. The game was created by Derek Yu in 2008 as an open source game for PCs. An updated version of the game was released for Xbox Live Arcade which attracted millions of players.

The main game mechanic in Spelunky, similar to platformers, is jumping to collect items and to kill enemies. Much the same as in dungeon crawl games, the game is structured in rooms filled with collectable items and monsters. A common feature between Spelunky and most rough-like games is the presence of randomness which is the key element in generating the structure of the levels and placing enemies and decoration items (more details about the method used can be found in [1,11]).

The player controls *Spelunker*, the main character of the game. To win the game, the player should possess good playing skills as well as being able to efficiently manage different types of resources such as ropes, bumps and money.

Spelunky exhibits a number of properties that motivates exploration of the applicability of PCG and AI methods. It is a 2D game that combines properties from platform games in terms of gameplay with the graphical representation and layout of rogue-like games. Automatic generation of content for such a game is therefore an interesting problem as one should consider the characteristics of both genres. The game is also receiving an increasing interest in research as a benchmark for computational and artificial intelligence algorithms was recently proposed around this game [11].

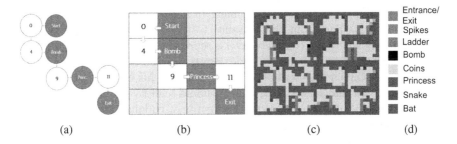

**Fig. 1.** (a) An example of an evolved graphical representation of a level and (c) the actual corresponding level map. The key rooms are presented in blue in (b) and the path is presented as direct links between the rooms. A gray room can contain anything. The different colours in the resultant level stands for different types of items as presented in the legend (Color figure online).

# 3   Modifications to the Original Game

We used the source code available for the first published version of the game as a base for our implementation. We made several modifications to the original code to allow complete automatic level generation with desired difficulty. Our modifications include adding an extra goal to the game, namely, Spelunker should save the princess; this requires finding and carrying her along while navigating safely to the exit. We also chose to lock the princess in a closed room to make the game more interesting since this necessitate searching for bombs to break the walls and enter the room. The bombs are placed in hidden places in one of the 16 rooms of the level.

In short, we are using the same art assets used in the original game but the gameplay in our version, called *InfiSpel*, consists of starting the journey in the entrance room, navigating through the level searching for the bomb, locating the princess and using the bomb to enter her room, carrying the princess and heading to the exit while overcoming challenges such as monsters and traps. These new requirements entailed heavily modifying the original source code.

# 4   Evolving Content in InfiSpel

In our level generation approach, a Genetic Algorithm (GA) method is employed to evolve content. When using GA, there are two main factors that are essential to the quality and performance: content representation and content quality.

## 4.1   Level Representation

The phenotype (level structure) is represented as an integer vector where each level consists of 16 rooms organised in a 4 × 4 matrix (such as in the original game). This representation is used to visualise the generated levels and to measure their quality.

Since we are interested in the placement of items and the presence of paths between the rooms and from the entrance to the exit, the genotype is represented indirectly where the complete level is represented as a graph in which each room is a node. The links between nodes are translated into direct connections between rooms while a missing link indicates a wall. This means that starting in the entrance room and following the links should lead to the exit in a playable level. More specifically, the genotype is a vector of codons carrying the following information: five integers identifying the start room, the bomb room, the S princess room, and the exit room, the length of the path from the entrance to the exit (measured as the number of rooms passed). These are followed by fields for storing the total number of monsters, the total number of collectable items and a list of connections. The total number of connections between the rooms is 28 (notice that we don't allow loops) and therefore the list of connections consists of 28 binary slots. Figure 1 presents an example level with its graph representation.

## 4.2   The Interior Design of Rooms

To construct the layout of each room, a digger algorithm is used and applied on each room separately. This method has been previously used to construct maps for First-Person Shooter games and showed fast performance and interesting results [12,13]. The method is used in a similar way in this paper. Initially, each room is filled with bricks (walls) with all cells having the value 1. The digger moves in the room switching the value of some of the cells from 1 to 0 hence generating walkable areas.

To dig one room, the digger performs the following steps:

1. The digger agent is placed in the center of a room.
2. The agent randomly choses one of the following directions for his next move: right, left, up and down. The agent moves in the direction chosen and change the value of the destination cell from 1 to 0.
3. The above process is repeated until a maximum number of moves is reached (35 moves is used in our implementation).
4. Walls are then digged, if necessary, to ensure a path between the start and the end rooms.

This method is repeated for each of the 16 rooms in each level resulting in rooms with various structures. Corridors between rooms are added later in the process according to the structure of the level evolved by GA.

## 4.3   Content Quality

Designing an interesting level that is fun to play is the ultimate goal when generating game content. Therefore, measuring the quality of the generated content is vitally important. This task is not obvious given that there is no universal agreement of what makes a good level or how to measure the "goodness" of a piece of content. Several attempts can be found in the literature on identifying the properties that should be present in a level to make it fun [14–16]. Several researches have employed these theory to generate content that is fun to play [5,17]. In our system, we based our definition of an interesting level design on two factors: the first contributes to a set of design requirements that we found to be important, while the second factor relates to the difficulty of a level which affects the challenge presented to the player which proven to be an important aspect for an optimal experience [16,18]. Generated levels are scored according to these two factors as follows:

$$fitness = 10\,\% * G_{score} + 90\,\% * D_{score}$$

where $G_{score}$ is a measure of the quality of the level design while $D_{score}$ assigns a fitness to the level according to its difficulty. The weights of these two factors are assigned experimentally after generating a number of levels, visualising them and tuning the values.

The following paragraphs explain how the $G_{score}$ and $D_{score}$ values are calculated.

**Design Constraints, $G_{score}$:** A score value is assigned to each level according to its final design. We identified a number of requirements, most of which contribute to playability and/or aesthetics, that should be satisfied in a level. These are the followings:

- Placement of the entrance room, $P_s$: in Spelunky, the entrance room should always be one of the rooms in the first or second row.
- Placement of the exit room, $P_e$: the exit room should be one of the rooms in the last two rows.
- Connections between mandatory rooms, $C$: a player in our game should be able to navigate to the exit going through the bomb room then the princess room. Therefore, for a level to be playable, there should be a path connecting these rooms directly or indirectly.
- Uniqueness of mandatory rooms, $U$: there shouldn't be more than one instance of each of the four mandatory rooms in each level. These include the start, exit, princess and bomb rooms. A level can not also contain any room that combines two of these features, for example, the princess can't be placed in the exit room.

The total design score of a level is calculated as follows:

$$G_{score} = 20 * P_s + 20 * P_e + 35 * C + 25 * U$$

If a level passes a certain predefined threshold ($G_{score}$ is higher than 90 %), the process continues to evaluating its difficulty. A high threshold is used since a level that breaks any of the above conditions is very likely to be either unplayable or uninteresting. The weights assigned to each of the above conditions are chosen experimentally.

**Spicing up the Level: Enemies and Items Distribution:** After generating the physical structure of a level and before calculating its difficulty, several auxiliary items are added to complete the level design. These include: enemies (including bats and snakes that are placed randomly or around gaps), traps such as spikes, resources such as bombs and ropes, ladders which are used to connect vertically adjacent rooms and coins and rubies.

In order to maintain a fair distribution of items over the whole map, the map is divided into $2 \times 2$ areas each containing $2 \times 2$ rooms. The items of each type are distributed in all areas equally. This is guaranteed by generating a list of possible positions in each region where an item of each type can be placed. An item is then placed at a randomly chosen position from this list.

**Level Difficulty:** The final phase after generating the level and adding different items is to assess its difficulty through evaluating the following conditions:

- Path length, $P_l$: the longer the path Spelunker should navigate to successfully reach the exit, the more difficult the level is since this requires facing more enemies and overcoming more obstacles. The length of a path should be at least 4 rooms (navigating only the four mandatory rooms).
- Vertical corridors, $V_c$: the presence of vertical corridors of a long length to connect two or more rooms makes the level harder to navigate since this necessitates the use of ropes or the existence of ladders. Otherwise, it is very likely that Speluker will lose a life due to falling a large distance.
- Number of Spikes, $N_{sp}$: spikes are special complication items that Spelunker can walk safely through but falling on them leads to a lose of life. The more the spikes the harder the level is.
- Number and type of enemies, $E$: as the number of enemies increases, the level becomes more difficult. Bats, $N_b$, are given the highest weight since they are the most dangerous as they move around and follow Spelunker when he is in a close distance. A lower weight is given to the placement of snakes around gaps, $N_{sg}$. The lowest weight is given to the presence of snakes, $N_s$.

The difficulty score is measured as a weighted sum of the normalised values (using min-max normalisation) of all of the above factors according to the equation:

$$D_{score} = 20 * P_l + 15 * V_c + 15 * N_{sp} + 20 * N_b + 20 * N_{sg} + 10 * N_s$$

The weights are chosen experimentally according to how the elements affect the difficulty of a level (the weight of the number of snake around gabs, $N_{sg}$, for instance, is higher than the weight assigned to the total number of snakes, $N_s$).

Three levels of increasing difficulty can be seen in Fig. 2. The figure clearly shows that the increase in difficulty is associated with the presence of more enemies, more vertical corridors, and paths of longer length.

## 5    Implementation Setup

The GA experimental parameters used are the following: 100 runs of 200 generations with a population size of 100 individuals. The mutation probability is

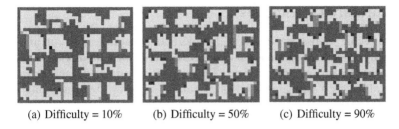

(a) Difficulty = 10%        (b) Difficulty = 50%        (c) Difficulty = 90%

**Fig. 2.** Three sample levels of increasing difficulty.

0.05, and we used two-point crossover with probability equals to 1. Tournament selection is used to reproduction. The stopping condition is to reach a predefined fitness, otherwise evolution continues for 200 generations.

## 6   Results and Evaluation

An experiment is conducted to evolve levels using the framework proposed. Evolution is repeated for 100 runs starting from a random population each time. Different levels of difficulty are specified and levels are evolved accordingly. This is done by scoring the evolved levels according to the equation:

$$fitness = 10\,\% * G_{score} + 90\,\% * (1 - Dis_{diffScore})$$

where $Dis_{diffScore}$ is the difference between the difficulty of the evolved levels and a target difficulty value.

The analysis showed that only 46 % of the total individuals passed the threshold specified on the design (having a $G_{score}$ higher than 90 %). Those levels were further evolved and evaluated for difficulty.

The amount of processing time and the number of generations required varies significantly when evolving levels of different predefined difficulty values. Table 1 presents the average time required and the total number of generation reached when evolving levels that are 10 %, 50 % and 90 % difficult. The results show that generating levels of medium difficulty ($diff = 50\,\%$) is the easiest. On the other hand, levels that are easy or hard ($diff = 10\,\%$ or $diff = 90\,\%$) require a longer evolution process and therefore significantly more time.

**Table 1.** The average time and the number of generations required to evolve levels of different difficulties.

| Difficulty | $Time(s)$ | $\#Generations$ |
| --- | --- | --- |
| 10 % | $16.3 \pm 5.32$ | $117.13 \pm 46.37$ |
| 50 % | $0.57 \pm 0.39$ | $6.76 \pm 4.49$ |
| 90 % | $18.45 \pm 1.62$ | $110.58 \pm 49.48$ |

# 7    Expressivity Analysis

To evaluate our content generator and explore its capabilities, we run an expressivity analysis that helps us better understand how our system works and elaborate on its strengths and weakness. The expressive range of a generator is the space of all levels it can generate [19]. It can be measured by generating a large number of representatives of the generator's output, defining expressive measures that capture the variations in the outputs along different dimensions, scoring the content according to the defined measures and visualising the results. In what follows, we describe several expressivity measures that we defined to analyse our generator. Some of the measures are inspired by previous work on expressivity analysis [19].

## 7.1    Frequency Analysis

The simplest and most compact method of showing the generator's characteristics is through calculating simple statistics about the components' frequency. Figure 3 presents a comparison between the average and the standard deviation normalised values (using min-max normalisation) of key items in 100 playable levels evolved for three difficulty scales. As can be seen, as the levels become more difficult an increasing number of enemies of different types with less ladders and coins are generated.

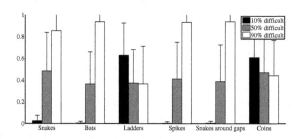

**Fig. 3.** The average values of generated items for 100 levels of different difficulties.

## 7.2    Color Map

To facilitate a more in-depth insight on the differences between the generated levels, we converted them into colour maps and projected them on one image. The resultant colour map is an image where the value of each pixel is the average colour value of all pixels at the same position in the full set of levels generated.

Analysis of the colour map can be done more clearly if they are generated for each item separately since this permits illustration of the distribution of the different items independently. Figure 4 presents three maps for the distribution of snakes in 100 levels of different difficulties. The two main interesting observations are the increase in the number of snakes as the difficulty increases and the fair distribution of snakes along all rooms.

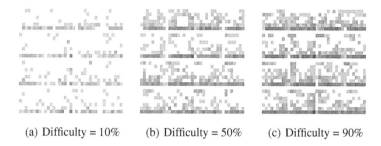

(a) Difficulty = 10%     (b) Difficulty = 50%     (c) Difficulty = 90%

**Fig. 4.** Colour maps for the distribution of snakes in 100 levels of increasing difficulties (Color figure online).

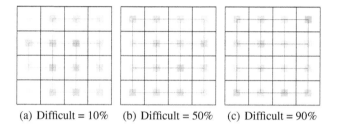

(a) Difficult = 10%     (b) Difficult = 50%     (c) Difficult = 90%

**Fig. 5.** The colour maps for the generated paths for 100 levels of different difficulties. The entrance room is presented in green, the exit room in red and the black lines corresponds to the connections between the rooms (Color figure online).

## 7.3 Visited Rooms and Generated Paths:

In order to plot the generate paths in a colour map, the entrance and exit rooms are given district colours (green and red, respectively) and the connections between the rooms are represented as solid lines.

The paths generated for multiple levels can be viewed in one image illustrating the variations in the designs according to the difficulty. Figure 5 presents the resultant path maps of 100 levels for various difficulty configurations. The figure shows that as the difficulty increases more rooms become part of the path as indicated by a higher frequency (darker colour) of visited rooms and darker links between the rooms. For further analysis, we calculated the average and standard deviation values of the lengths of the paths generated for different difficulty setups and the results are presented in Fig. 6. The figure clearly illustrates longer path lengths as the difficulty increases. Notice that a path of length 0 means that only the minimum number of rooms (in this case 4) should be traversed to reach the exit. Figure 7 presents the histogram for the number of rooms in the paths generated in 100 levels for three difficulty scale. The figure shows a clear bias towards generating longer paths as the difficulty increases.

## 7.4 Shortest Versus Winning Path Length

The shortest path is the number of rooms connecting the entrance to the exit (without necessarily passing through the bomb and princess rooms). Notice that

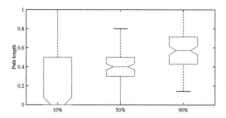

**Fig. 6.** The boxplot for generated path lengths for levels of increasing difficulty.

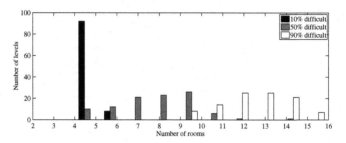

**Fig. 7.** The number of rooms in the paths generated in 100 levels for different difficulty scales.

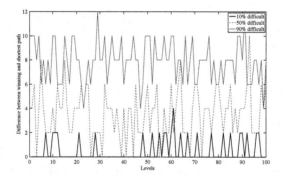

**Fig. 8.** The differences between the length of the winning paths generated and the corresponding shortest paths in 100 evolved levels of different difficulties.

following this path means reaching the end of the level but not winning the game. It is interesting to compare whether and by how much this path differs from the actual path the player has to follow to win the game, which we call the *winning path*, since this gives an indication of the efficiency of the evolution algorithm and its success in generating levels that deviate from being obvious.

Figure 8 presents the differences between the shortest and winning paths generated for 300 levels of increasing difficulty. The figure shows that for easy levels (10 % difficult), most of the generated winning paths are of the same length or slightly longer than the shortest possible paths. The difference however becomes larger as the levels become harder. The average observed differences between the shortest and the winning path lengths are 0.5, 3.56 and 7.88 rooms for levels that are 10 %, 50 % and 90 % difficult, respectively.

# 8 Conclusions

The paper presents a methodology for procedurally generating complete playable levels in games similar to Spelunky. A genetic algorithm is implemented to evolve game content. Level maps are represented as graphs where the nodes, the connections and the other design-specific properties are evolved. Rooms' inner structure is constructed by an agent-based approach and a distribution method is employed to place collectable items and enemies. Content quality is measured through a fitness function that scores levels according to how well they match predefined design and difficulty requirements. Finally, the evaluation of the system consists of defining and running a number of expressivity measures on 100 levels evolved for different settings. The results show that interesting playable content that satisfies our design requirements can be evolved and that using the proposed approach, levels of desired difficulty can be efficiently generated.

The suggested approach can easily scale to other games from the rouge-like and dungeon crawl genres that exhibit similar representation where levels are structured in rooms filled with monsters and rewarding items and connected via corridors.

An issue that we did not investigate in this paper, and is important in game design, is the amount of variations between the content evolved for the same setting. We focused in our expressivity analysis on the differences between the levels evolved for various experimental setups with minor analysis on the dissimilarity between the levels within each category. An interesting future work will be defining new measures that capture the diversity in the designs generated along more than one dimension to draw more robust conclusions and to improve the generator.

One way of taking this work one step further and rewarding content diversity is to explore the use of novelty search methods [20]. This approach has recently been used with promising results in many domains including computer games [21, 22]. An enhancement of this approach was recently suggested through combining it with a two-population feasible-infeasible [23]. The method can be employed in the framework proposed where individuals that satisfy a set of requirements are placed in the feasible population while the infeasible population contains those that break some of the constraints (in our case this might be invalidating the design constrains or being judge as unplayable). Evolution can then be performed on the two populations towards generating novel, yet playable solutions.

Another interesting future direction is to incorporate the player in the evolution process. In the current approach, players' preferences, how they perceive the evolved content and how the content affects their experience are not considered. Given that the ultimate goal of game design is to please players, indicators about the "goodness" of content to specific players are essential for generating high quality content. Therefore, future directions will also investigate ways of including the player in the content generation loop so that, for example, the difficulty of the next generated level is set according to its performance in a previous level or through an interactive approach where content are presented to players and evolved based on their reported, or measured, preferences.

**Acknowledgments.** The research was supported in part by the Danish Research Agency, Ministry of Science, Technology and Innovation; project "PlayGALe" (1337-00172).

# References

1. Shaker, N., Togelius, J., Nelson, M.J.: Procedural Content Generation in Games: A Textbook and an Overview of Current Research. Springer, New York (2014)
2. Togelius, J., Yannakakis, G.N., Stanley, K.O., Browne, C.: Search-based procedural content generation. In: Di Chio, C., et al. (eds.) EvoApplicatons 2010, Part I. LNCS, vol. 6024, pp. 141–150. Springer, Heidelberg (2010)
3. Hastings, E.J., Guha, R.K., Stanley, K.O.: Evolving content in the galactic arms race video game. In: Proceedings of the 5th International Conference on Computational Intelligence and Games, pp. 241–248. IEEE (2009)
4. Shaker, N., Nicolau, M., Yannakakis, G.N., Togelius, J., ONeill, M.: Evolving levels for super mario bros using grammatical evolution. In: IEEE Conference on Computational Intelligence and Games (CIG), pp. 304–311 (2012)
5. Togelius, J., Nardi, R.D., Lucas, S.M.: Making racing fun through player modeling and track evolution. In: Proceedings of the SAB 2006 Workshop on Adaptive Approaches for Optimizing Player Satisfaction in Computer and Physical Games (2006)
6. Shaker, M., Shaker, N., Togelius, J.: Evolving playable content for cut the rope through a simulation-based approach. In: Proceedings of the AAAI Conference on Artificial Intelligence and Interactive Digital Entertainment (2013)
7. Blizzard North: Diablo, Blizzard Entertainment, Ubisoft and Electronic Arts (1997)
8. Mojang: Minecraft, Mojang and Microsoft Studios (2011)
9. Maxis: Spore, Electronic Arts (2008)
10. Yu, D., Hull, A.: Spelunky, Independent (2009)
11. Scales, D., Thompson, T.: Spelunkbots api-an ai toolset for spelunky. In: 2014 IEEE Conference on Computational Intelligence and Games (CIG), pp. 1–8. IEEE (2014)
12. Cardamone, L., Yannakakis, G.N., Togelius, J., Lanzi, P.L.: Evolving interesting maps for a first person shooter. In: Di Chio, C., et al. (eds.) EvoApplications 2011, Part I. LNCS, vol. 6624, pp. 63–72. Springer, Heidelberg (2011)
13. Shaker, N., Shaker, M., Abuabdallah, I., Zonjy, M., Sarhan, M.H.: A quantitative approach for modeling and personalizing player experience in first-person shooter games (2013)
14. Koster, R.: A Theory of Fun for Game Design. Paraglyph Press, Phoenix (2004)
15. Malone, T.: What makes computer games fun? ACM (1981)
16. Chen, J.: Flow in games (and everything else). Commun. ACM **50**(4), 31–34 (2007)

17. Sorenson, N., Pasquier, P.: The evolution of fun: automatic level design through challenge modeling. In: Proceedings of the First International Conference on Computational Creativity (ICCCX), Lisbon, Portugal, pp. 258–267. ACM (2010)
18. Rani, P., Sarkar, N., Liu, C.: Maintaining optimal challenge in computer games through real-time physiological feedback. In: Proceedings of the 1st International Conference on Augmented Cognition, Las Vegas, NV, pp. 184–192 (2005)
19. Horn, B., Dahlskog, S., Shaker, N., Smith, G., Togelius, J.: A comparative evaluation of procedural level generators in the mario ai framework (2014)
20. Lehman, J., Stanley, K.O.: Abandoning objectives: evolution through the search for novelty alone. Evol. Comput. **19**(2), 180–223 (2011)
21. Mouret, J.-B., Doncieux, S.: Encouraging behavioral diversity in evolutionary robotics: an empirical study. Evol. Comput. **20**(1), 91–133 (2012)
22. Woolley, B.G., Stanley, K.O.: Exploring promising stepping stones by combining novelty search with interactive evolution. arXiv preprint arXiv:1207.6682 (2012)
23. Liapis, A., Yannakakis, G.N., Togelius, J.: Enhancements to constrained novelty search: two-population novelty search for generating game content. In: Proceeding of the Fifteenth Annual Conference on Genetic and Evolutionary Computation Conference, pp. 343–350. ACM (2013)

# Evolving Random Forest for Preference Learning

Mohamed Abou-Zleikha[1,2]([✉]) and Noor Shaker[1,2]

[1] Audio Analysis Lab, AD:MT, Aalborg University, Aalborg, Denmark
moa@create.aau.dk
[2] IT University of Copenhagen, Copenhagen, Denmark
nosh@itu.dk

**Abstract.** This paper introduces a novel approach for pairwise preference learning through a combination of an evolutionary method and random forest. Grammatical evolution is used to describe the structure of the trees in the Random Forest (RF) and to handle the process of evolution. Evolved random forests are evaluated based on their efficiency in predicting reported preferences. The combination of these two efficient methods for evolution and modelling yields a powerful technique for learning pairwise preferences. To test the proposed methodology and compare it to other methods in the literature, a dataset of 1560 sessions with detail information about user behaviour and their self-reported preferences while interacting with a game is used for training and evaluation. The method demonstrates ability to construct accurate models of user experience from preferences, behavioural and context data. The results obtained for predicting pairwise self-reports of users for the three emotional states *engagement*, *frustration* and *challenge* show very promising results that are comparable and in some cases superior to those obtained from state-of-the-art methods.

## 1 Introduction

Despite the recent advancement in methodologies for capturing users' affects, self-reporting is still widely used due to its reliability, directness and being less intrusive than other objective-based methods for collecting affects. Pairwise preferences is a popular method to collect self-reports [1,2]. Constructing user models from pairwise preferences is not an easy task due to the scarcity of machine learning and dataminig techniques that can be directly applied to preference data. Most of the methods employed deal with this problem as learning a global ranking function [3]. This, however, usually leads to less accurate models than those trained to learn pairwise preferences directly. This is mainly because of the nature of the problem which limits the possibility of accurately transforming preference data into rankings due to the relational structures of the data according to which ranking between subjects may not be commensurate (i.e. the existence of pairwise preference data points of the form: instance $A$ is preferred over $B$, instance $B$ is preferred over $C$ and $C$ is preferred over $A$).

Up until now, Neuroevolutionary Preference Learning (NPL) [4] has shown the best results in learning preference data for cognitive modelling. In a comparison study, this method gave more accurate results than those obtained by

A.M. Mora and G. Squillero (Eds.): EvoApplications 2015, LNCS 9028, pp. 318–330, 2015.
DOI: 10.1007/978-3-319-16549-3_26

other methods [4]. This method has therefore been extensively used in several studies where preference data is available [4–7]. These studies demonstrated that reported preferences can be predicted with high accuracies from information about the interaction between the user and the system as input and their reported affects as output using NPL.

In this paper, we propose a novel evolutionary-based method for learning pairwise preferences. Few other machine learning methods have been tested for this purpose, the results obtained by NPL, however, are mostly significantly better. The method proposed in this paper achieves higher results than those obtained by NLP in similar experimental setting. Furthermore, most of the proposed methods suffer from a limited expressive power in terms of the difficulty in interpreting the models and analysing the input-output relationship, a drawback that could be overcome using small RFs. Finally, constructing models of pairwise preferences through evolving random forest is an interesting problem that has not yet been explored yet.

The method we propose in this paper is novel (1) in terms of the technique used; we are not aware of any previous attempts for evolving random forest to learn a specific problem, and (2) in utilising the proposed approach for learning pairwise preferences. For comparison purposes, we are using the same dataset collected from players playing Super Mario Bros (SMB) that has already been used in several studies for modelling player experience from preference data using the NPL framework [7].

## 2  Preference Learning

Preference learning has received increasing attention in the machine learning literature in recent years [3]. The ranking problem has been categorised into three main types, namely label ranking, instance ranking and object ranking [3]. We focus on object ranking in this paper. Within object ranking, the goal is to learn a ranking function $f(.)$ that produces a ranking of a given subset of objects given their pairwise preferences. More formally, given a set of instances $Z$ and a finite set of pairwise preferences $x_i \succ x_j; (x_i, x_j) \in Z \times Z$, find a ranking function $f(.)$ that returns the ranking of this set $Z$. Here, $x_i \succ x_j$ means that the instance $x_i$ is preferred to $x_j$.

Various methods have been presented in the literature for the task of object ranking. Methods based on large-margin classifiers [8–10], Gaussian processes [11–13], and neuroevolution [4] have been investigated to learn the ranking function. Neuroevolutionary preference leaning proved to have a powerful approximation capability and to build efficient models of player experience in similar setups to the one at hand [4,5,14]. Other supervised learning methods such as standard backpropagation [15], rank support vector machine [16], Cohens method [17], linear preference learning [18] and pairwise preference leaning [3] have also been employed to learn pairwise preferences with various success. There exists a number of other attempts where the problem of pairwise preference learning is converted into learning a global classifier and therefore standard ranking method can not be applied [3]. This paper introduces a new paradigm for learning pairwise preferences and presents a test case where the suggested method demonstrated efficient learning capabilities.

## 3    Random Forest

A random forest is a tree-based non-parametric classification and regression approach [19]. The principle is to grow a number of trees on a random selection of samples in a training set. Each tree is a non-pruned decision tree. During the construction of each tree and when adding a new node, a randomly selected feature subset is chosen from the set of input features. The features in this subset are then investigated and the one with the best splitting results is chosen.

When the random forest is used for a classification task, the trees are treated individually and each of them is processed to predict the target class. The final classification result is then calculated as the majority vote of the predictions obtained by the individual trees. For a regression task, each tree predicts one target value and the forest prediction output is then calculated as the average of the predicted values of all its trees.

In this work, and since we are learning pairwise preferences, the random forest model is used as a regression model.

Compared to a single decision tree, the random forest assembles several trees that are trained on randomly selected subsets of the data. Because of the use of this method for training, random forest usually demonstrates better generalisation capabilities and higher degree of stability as well as achieving better performance than other classification and regression methods [20].

Formally, a random forest, $RF$, is a set of decision trees

$$RF = \{t_1, t_2, ..., t_T\} \tag{1}$$

where $t_i$ is the $i^{th}$ individual tree and $T$ is the total number of trees in a forest.

Each tree, $t_i$ in the forest is trained independently given a bagged version of the training data. Given a set of input features $F = f_1...f_n$, the $j^{th}$ node is split using the feature that maximises the information gain:

$$f_j = \arg\max_{f \in F_j} I(X_j, f) \tag{2}$$

where $F_j$ is a randomly selected feature subset of $F$ at node $j$, $X_j$ is the data at node $j$ and $I(X_j, f)$ is the information gain function.

One of the implementation used for the information gain is a function that aims at decreasing the impurity of the split data. For a regression task, impurity is defined as the mean squared prediction error between the predicted and the actual value.

Unlike a single decision tree, no pruning is applied, and as a result each tree grows until either a maximum depth is reached or the information gain becomes smaller than a predefined threshold.

# 4    Grammatical Evolution

Grammatical Evolution (GE) is an evolutionary algorithm based on Grammatical Programming (GP) [21]. The main difference between GE and GP is the genome representation; while a tree-based structure is used in GP, GE relies on a linear genome representation. Similar to general Genetic Algorithms (GAs), GE applies fitness calculations for every individual and it applies genetic operators to produce the next generation.

The population of the evolutionary algorithm is initialised randomly consisting of variable-length integer vectors; the syntax of possible solution is specified through a context-free grammar. GE uses the grammar to guide the construction of the phenotype output. The context-free grammar employed by GE is usually written in Backus Naur Form (BNF). Because of the use of a grammar, GE is capable of generating anything that can be described as a set of rules. GE is used previously to evolve single decision trees to solve a classification problem [22]. In this paper, we focus on the problem of preference learning and we evolve a random forest to learn this function.

Each chromosome in GE is a vector of codons. Each codon is an integer number used to select a production rule from the BNF grammar in the genotype-to-phenotype mapping. A complete program is generated by selecting production rules from the grammar until all non-terminal rules are mapped. The resultant string is evaluated according to a fitness function to give a score to the genome.

In this paper, a design grammar is defined to specify the structure of possible solutions to our problem (trees in our case). The grammar is then employed by GE to evolve a random forest according to a predefined fitness function. GE is employed because it combines the advantages of an evolutionary algorithm and due to the simple nature of the design grammar that allows and easy way of defining, interpreting and manipulating the structure of the solutions.

# 5    Evolving Random Forest

Standard implementations of RF are not applicable to solve the problem of preference learning since for any two given instances $A$ and $B$ in a pair, there is no specific target output to calculate the information gain at each node and to perform data splitting. This form of constrained-classification problems can only be solved using preference learning methods [3]. In contrast of the incremental approach that is usually used for building the trees, a holistic approach is proposed. In this approach, we build the whole trees randomly, then a set of modifications is performed on the forest trees targeting to improve the performance of the generated model. In our framework, we utilise grammatical evolution to evolve a forest so that for each pair in the pairwise dataset, the prediction value of a preferred sample is higher than that of the non-preferred one, i.e. $f(x_i) > f(x_j)$ if $x_i > x_j$ and $f(x_i) < f(x_j)$ if $x_i < x_j$. A Design Grammar (DG) is defined to describe the structure of possible solution (a tree) in the evolution process. The system is trained and tested using a dataset consisting of a set of pairs, each of which is associated with a preference value assigned by at least one user. Each of the evolved trees is evaluated using a fitness function that measures the number of correctly classified pairs, i.e. the number of pairs in which the output produced by the method matches the reported preference in the dataset.

## 5.1 Design Grammar

The DG is defined in a way that allows the construction of binary trees where each node is selected from one of the input features available. A simplified version of the DG is presented in Fig. 1. According to the grammar, the tree starts with an *internal node* which has a condition and two child nodes. Each of the child node can be either a leaf or another internal node. The condition in an internal node is a splitting condition based on one of the input features and a threshold. The leaves return a regression value between 0 and 100.

```
<Tree> := <Internal_Node>
<Internal_Node> :=  <Condition> <Child_Node>
                        <Child_Node>
<Child_Node> := <Leaf>   | <Internal_Node>
<Condition>:= <Feature> <Threshold>
<Feature> := feature1 |  feature2 | ...
<Leaf> := <Regression_value>
<Threshold> := [0,1]
<Regression_value> := [0,100]
```

**Fig. 1.** A simplified version of the grammar that specifies the structure of the trees in a forest.

## 5.2 The Evolution Process

GE is used to evolve RFs given the design grammar that defines the structure of the trees. The evolution process implemented can be described as follows: an population of $N$ tree is initialised randomly according to the grammar. During the evolution process and at each generation, the following process is repeated:

**Step 1.** Each member (a tree), $t$, of the population gets a bagged version of the dataset for evaluating its prediction accuracy.

The input data is organised in $d$-tuples (where $d$ is the number of input features). The data is then presented to each tree in the population in pairs: $A$ and $B$ for the preferred and non-preferred instances, respectively. Each tree outputs a real regression value for each instance presented, namely $y_{j.A}$ and $y_{j.B}$ for the pair $j$. If the output of the tree for the pair matches that in the dataset, i.e. there is a consistency between the sign of $y_{j.A} - y_{j.B}$ and the actual reported pairwise preference for the pair $j$, then we state that there is an 'agreement' between the output and the reported preferences. In the opposite case, we state that there is a 'disagreement'.

**Step 2.** Each tree $t$ in the population is evaluated via a fitness function $f_t$ that calculates the number of instances with an 'agreement' between the output and the reported preferences.

**Step 3.** The population is ranked and the best $n$ trees are chosen.

**Step 4.** A roulette-wheel selection scheme is used as the selection method.

**Step 5.** The Montana and Davis crossover is applied to selected parents for generating two offspring. Gaussian mutation occurs in each gene of each offspring's genome.

**Step 6.** The performance of the best $n$ trees is checked on a validation dataset. These trees replace the old forest if the performance obtained is better.

The algorithm terminates when a predefined total number of generations is reached. The best $n$ trees obtained in the final population are then evaluated on a testing set and the performance obtained is reported as the modelling performance.

# 6   Case Study: Player Data in Super Mario Bros

The dataset used for our experiments consists of rich information about game content, player behaviour, and self-reports of hundreds of players playing a modified version of an open source clone of the popular game *Super Mario Bros.*

We implemented a content generator for creating variations of levels. We further designed a post-experience game survey to collect subjective affective reports expressed as pairwise preferences of subjects playing two levels of the game following the 4-alternative forced choice experimental protocol proposed in [4]. Data from gameplay and questionnaires was collected from players over the Internet via a crowd-sourcing experiment. Complete games were logged enabling complete replays. The following three types of data were extracted from raw logs and replays: content, gameplay and annotated (self-reported) player experience of the three emotional states: *engagement*, *frustration* and *challenge*. For a complete detailed list of the different features extracted the reader may refer to [7].

One of the primary reasons for choosing the Mario dataset is because it offers rich information in terms of the features collected (30 different gameplay and content features). The other reason is that it contains information about players' pairwise self reports of three different emotional states permitting a thorough analysis of the capabilities of the modelling approach.

Evolutionary algorithms are well known for their efficiency in handling large input spaces and decision trees are popular as powerful classifiers and therefore evolving them for the task at hand promises models of high accuracies. However, due to the complex nature of self-reporting in general (being noisy because of their subjectivity) and the difficulties in accurately modelling pairwise preferences [4], the problem still introduces interesting challenges and constitutes an interesting direction for research.

## 7  Experimental Setup

A dataset of 1560 gameplay sessions (780 pairs) is used for training, validation and testing. The dataset was preprocessed to remove the instances where players show no clear preferences (the answers to the questionnaires were either that both games were equally liked or disliked). The sizes of the resultant datasets are 597, 531 and 629 pairs, for engagement, frustration and challenge, respectively. These datasets were split into 70 % for training and 15 % for validation and testing. Significance analysis is performed using t-test.

The existing GEVA software [23] was used as a core to implement the needed functionalities. The experimental parameters used are the following: 50 runs each ran for 100 generations with a population size of 3000 individuals, the ramped half-and-half initialisation method. Tournament selection of size 30, int-flip mutation with probability 0.3, one-point crossover with probability 0.5, and 0 maximum wraps were allowed. All parameters have been experimentally tuned.

## 8  Analysis

In the following sections we describe a number of analysis conducted to test the effect of different configurations on the modelling performance. We investigate factors such as the depth and the number of trees and we provide a preliminary analysis of the expressive power of the models.

### 8.1  Number of Trees

We ran several experiments to investigate the best number of trees to form a forest. Figure 2 presents the average accuracies obtained for predicting reported frustration from 50 runs of the algorithms with different number of trees ranging between 1 and 200. The results show that the accuracy increases as we add more trees to the forest up to the point where the forest consist of 100 trees after which a slight drop in the performance is observed. The significance test showed statistical better performance for the models with number of trees > 60

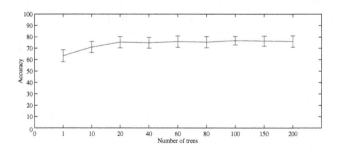

**Fig. 2.** The averages and standard deviations of the accuracies obtained from 50 forests of different number of trees for predicting frustration.

compared to those with a smaller number of trees (with no significant difference between the models' performance in each group). Given these results, the rest of this paper focuses only on analysis of models consisting of 100 trees as those yield the highest accuracies and provide a reasonable trade-off between the size and the performance of the models. Note that we accept with generalisation that this setup will also give good results for the other affective states while we acknowledge that it may not be the best configurations.

## 8.2   Depth of Trees

In order to investigate the effect of the depth of the evolved trees in a forest on the modelling performance, we run two experiments with forests of 100 trees where the maximum depth of trees is 10 or 20. The experiment is repeated for 50 times for each of the three emotional states and the average accuracies obtained are presented in Table 1. The statistical analysis showed no significant difference between the accuracies obtained by the two configurations for the three emotional states ($p - value > 0.05$). Therefore the analysis for the rest of the paper will focus on evolving models with tree depth equals to 10 as those are easier to analyse, faster to evolve, less complex and yield comparable accuracies to those of more sophisticated models.

**Table 1.** The averages and standard deviations of the accuracies obtained from 50 forests of different tree depths for predicting engagement, frustration and challenge.

| Tree depth | Engagement | Frustration | Challenge |
|---|---|---|---|
| 10 | 63.01 % ± 3.96 | 77.68 % ± 4.70 | 72.66 % ± 3.79 |
| 20 | 64.83 % ± 3.79 | 76.66 % ± 5.02 | 74.41 % ± 4.48 |

## 8.3   Expressive Power

One of the advantages of evolving decision trees is that they demonstrate powerful classification ability while preserving the expressive power being easy to interpret. In order to investigate the expressivity of the proposed approach, to emphasise the need for RF and for comparison purposes, we will discuss models of only one tree and compare them to more complex models of 100 trees. One-tree models are chosen since they are the easiest to interpret.

The results obtained from the comparison for predicting frustration can be seen in Fig. 2. The performance obtained for the best evolved tree, although relatively high (the average performance obtained is 63.34 %), is significantly lower than the one achieved by 100-tree forests ($p - value = 2.88 * 10^{-26}$). The results suggest that there is a trade-off between the models' expressivity and performance. In the next section, we present a methodology implemented to facilitate analysis of expressivity of forests of more than one tree thus preserving the performance while permitting high-level understanding.

## 9    Feature Importance

In order to understand the constructed models, we performed a preliminary analysis that helps shedding some light on the features important for predicting each emotional state. This is done by calculating the number of occurrences of each of the 30 input features in the forests constructed. The experiment is conducted with forests of 100 trees of depth 10 and repeated 50 times. Figure 3 presents the average number of times each feature is presented in each forest constructed. As can be seen, some features appear more often than others, and those are considered more important for predicting a particular affective state. It is interesting to note that the importance of features differs along the emotional state. For example, some features, such as 23 and 30 are more important for predicting frustration than engagement.

In general, it appears that the last eight features are the most important for predicting frustration. Most of these features (24–29) are related to content aspects while feature 30 stores the number of times the player died in the game and feature 23 stores the reason of the death (killed by an enemy or fell in a gap).

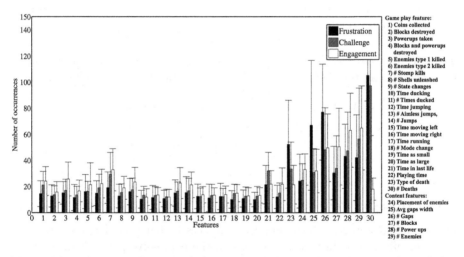

**Fig. 3.** The averages and standard deviations of the number of occurrences of the gameplay and content features in 50 forests evolved for the three emotional states.

The same set of features is also important for predicting reported preferences of challenge along with the two features 7 and 21 which stand for the number of enemies the player killed and the amount of time spent during the last trail (note that the player is given three lives to play), respectively.

The subset of features for predicting engagement consists of features with less number of occurrences than those of frustration and challenge. The set includes the feature 7 and features 24–29.

It is worth noting that most content features (24–29) are important for predicting the three states and that the number of player's death in the game is of significant importance for predicting frustration and challenge. This indicates that elicited affective states can be predicted up to a good degree from information about the design of the game and that there are key gameplay features that are of significant prediction power.

## 10    Comparison and Analysis

According to the results of our previous analysis, models with high accuracies can be evolved for predicting the three cognitive states using the proposed methodology. The averages and best accuracies obtained from 50 independent runs to evolve 50 forests of 100 trees of depth 10 for the three emotional states are presented in Table 2.

**Table 2.** Averages and best accuracies obtained from 50 runs of the experiments for evolving 50 random forests for the three emotional states.

|         | Engagement | Frustration | Challenge |
|---------|------------|-------------|-----------|
| Average | 63.01 %    | 77.68 %     | 72.66 %   |
| Maximum | 73.03 %    | 86.08 %     | 85.11 %   |

The best performance obtained is from the models for predicting frustration with accuracy up to 86 % that is significantly higher ($p - value = 3.60 * 10^{-32}$) than the one obtained from the models for predicting pairwise preferences of engagement, which have a best accuracy of 73.03 %. The frustration models also significantly out perform the models evolved to predict reported challenge preferences ($p - value = 8,05 * 10^{-6}$). The results indicate that reported pairwise preferences of engagement are the hardest to predict and that the evolved models for predicting reported frustration and challenge are of significant higher performance ($p - value = 4.78 * 10^{-19}$ between the performance of engagement and challenge models).

As discussed previously, one of the main reasons for choosing the Mario dataset is that it has been previously used to construct models of player experience primarily using NPL [7, 24]. In this paper, and to provide a fair comparison between NPL and the proposed approach, we compare the accuracies obtained by our evolved RF models and those obtained by NPL on the same Mario dataset using the same set of input features (a set of 30 statistical features capturing differences in content and players' behaviour as frequencies of events and actions). The averages and the best accuracies obtained in the earlier work by NPL are presented in Table 3 [7].

The comparison of the results obtained shows that reported frustration appears to be the easier to predict by the two approaches while engagement is the hardest. The analysis of the results (Tables 2 and 3) shows that our proposed method outperforms NPL for predicting frustration and challenge while comparable results are observed for predicting reported engagement.

**Table 3.** Averages and best accuracies obtained from 20 runs of the experiments for modelling player experience using neuroevoltionary preference learning for the three emotional states [7].

|            | Engagement | Frustration | Challenge |
|------------|------------|-------------|-----------|
| Average    | 67.18 %    | 76.50 %     | 74.03 %   |
| Maximum    | 73.50 %    | 83.00 %     | 79.10 %   |

The comparison presented confirms the efficiency of the proposed approach and demonstrates its ability to outperform NPL which has so far yield the most accurate results for predicting pairwise preferences in the same and similar problems [4, 5, 7].

## 11    Conclusions and Future Work

In this paper we present a novel approach for learning pairwise preferences through evolving a random forest. Grammatical evolution is used to evolve trees in a forest where each model is evaluated based on its efficiency when classifying preference data. The method proposed is tested on a big dataset of players' data where each instance of content and player behaviour is annotated with subjects' preferences. We investigated several setups and analysed the effect of the number of trees and their depth on the modelling accuracy. We further presented a preliminary analysis of the expressive power of our modelling approach. The comparison of the results with those obtained from a state-of-the-art method shows that comparable, and in some cases superior, accuracies can be achieved using the proposed approach.

The analysis of the expressivity of the models presented in this paper constitutes the first step towards more in-depth investigations. For example, in a dataset similar to the one used in this paper, the analysis the relationship between each input feature and reported emotional states is of utmost interest for game analyst and designers. Therefore, future work will include conducting more experiments to improve the readability of the models. One possibility is to use smaller number of trees which can be converted to a set of human-readable rules. Another essential factor when analysing the importance of features that we did not consider in this paper is their depth in the tree. Future direction will include accounting for this factor.

Another important direction, which is the ultimate goal of user experience modelling, is to utilise the constructed models as a ranking function of content given particular user behaviour. The best piece of content can then be used to generate user-adapted experience.

**Acknowledgement.** The research was supported in part by the Danish Research Agency, Ministry of Science, Technology and Innovation; project "PlayGALe" (1337-00172). This work also was supported in part by the Danish Council for Strategic Research of the Danish Agency for Science Technology and Innovation under the CoSound project, case number 11-115328. This publication only reflects the authors views. The authors would like to thank Prof. Georgios Yannakakis and Dr. Héctor P. Martinez for valuable discussions.

# References

1. Doyle, J.: Prospects for preferences. Comput. Intell. **20**(2), 111–136 (2004)
2. Joachims, T.: Optimizing search engines using clickthrough data. In: Proceedings of the Eighth ACM SIGKDD International Conference on Knowledge Discovery and Data Mining, pp. 133–142. ACM (2002)
3. Fürnkranz, J., Hüllermeier, E.: Preference Learning. Springer-Verlag New York Inc., New York (2010)
4. Yannakakis, G.N., Maragoudakis, M., Hallam, J.: Preference learning for cognitive modeling: a case study on entertainment preferences. IEEE Trans. Syst. Man, Cybern. Part A **39**, 1165–1175 (2009)
5. Martinez, H.P., Jhala, A., Yannakakis, G.N.: Analyzing the impact of camera viewpoint on player psychophysiology. In: International Conference on Affective Computing and Intelligent Interaction and Workshops, pp. 1–6. IEEE (2009)
6. Shaker, N., Shaker, M., Abu-Abdallah, I., Al-Zengi, M., Sarhan, M.H.: A quantitative approach for modelling and personalizing player experience in first-person shooter games. In: UMAP Workshops (2013)
7. Shaker, N., Yannakakis, G.N., Togelius, J.: Crowd-sourcing the aesthetics of platform games. IEEE Trans. Comput. Intell. Games, Special Issue on Computational Aesthetics in Games (2013)
8. Fiechter, C.N., Rogers, S.: Learning subjective functions with large margins. In: Proceedings of the Seventeenth International Conference on Machine Learning, Stanford University, pp. 287–294. Morgan Kaufmann Publishers (2000)
9. Herbrich, R., Graepel, T., Bollmann-Sdorra, P., Obermayer, K.: Learning preference relations for information retrieval. In: ICML 1998 Workshop: Text Categorization and Machine Learning, pp. 80–84 (1998)
10. Bahamonde, A., Bayón, G.F., Díez, J., Quevedo, J.R., Luaces, O., Del Coz, J.J., Alonso, J., Goyache, F.: Feature subset selection for learning preferences: a case study. In: Proceedings of the Twenty-First International Conference on Machine Learning, p. 7. ACM (2004)
11. Gervasio, M.T., Moffitt, M.D., Pollack, M.E., Taylor, J.M., Uribe, T.E.: Active preference learning for personalized calendar scheduling assistance. In: Proceedings of the 10th International Conference on Intelligent User Interfaces, vol. 5, pp. 90–97. Citeseer (2005)
12. Chu, W., Ghahramani, Z.: Preference learning with gaussian processes. In: Proceedings of the 22nd International Conference on Machine Learning, pp. 137–144. ACM (2005)
13. Madsen, J., Jensen, B.S., Larsen, J.: Predictive modeling of expressed emotions in music using pairwise comparisons. In: Aramaki, M., Barthet, M., Kronland-Martinet, R., Ystad, S. (eds.) CMMR 2012. LNCS, vol. 7900, pp. 253–277. Springer, Heidelberg (2013)

14. Pedersen, C., Togelius, J., Yannakakis, G.N.: Modeling player experience for content creation. IEEE Trans. Comput. Intell. AI Games **2**(1), 54–67 (2010)
15. Tesauro, G.: Connectionist learning of expert preferences by comparison training. In: Touretzky, D. (ed.) Advances in Neural Information Processing Systems 1, pp. 99–106. Morgan Kaufmann Publishers Inc., San Mateo (1989)
16. Herbrich, R., Graepel, T., Obermayer, K.: Support vector learning for ordinal regression. In: Ninth International Conference on Artificial Neural Networks, ICANN 1999 (Conf. Publ. No. 470), vol. 1, pp. 97–102. IET (1999)
17. Cohen, W.W., Schapire, R.E., Singer, Y., et al.: Learning to order things. J. Artif. Intell. Res. **10**, 243–270 (1999)
18. Runarsson, T.P., Lucas, S.M.: Imitating play from game trajectories: temporal difference learning versus preference learning. In: IEEE Conference on Computational Intelligence and Games (CIG), pp. 79–82 (2012)
19. Breiman, L.: Random forests. Mach. Learn. **45**(1), 5–32 (2001)
20. Criminisi, A., Shotton, J., Konukoglu, E.: Decision forests for classification, regression, density estimation, manifold learning and semi-supervised learning. Microsoft Research Cambridge, Technical report, MSRTR-2011-114, p. 12 (2011)
21. O'Neill, M., Ryan, C.: Grammatical evolution. IEEE Trans. Evol. Comput. **5**(4), 349–358 (2001)
22. Motsinger-Reif, A.A., Deodhar, S., Winham, S.J., Hardison, N.E.: Grammatical evolution decision trees for detecting gene-gene interactions. BioData Mining **3**(1), 1–15 (2010)
23. O'Neill, M., Hemberg, E., Gilligan, C., Bartley, E., McDermott, J., Brabazon, A.: Geva: grammatical evolution in java. ACM SIGEVOlution **3**(2), 17–22 (2008)
24. Shaker, N., Togelius, J., Yannakakis, G.N.: Towards automatic personalized content generation for platform games. In: Proceedings of the AAAI Conference on Artificial Intelligence and Interactive Digital Entertainment (AIIDE). AAAI Press (2010)

# Procedural Personas as Critics
# for Dungeon Generation

Antonios Liapis[1]([⊠]), Christoffer Holmgård[2], Georgios N. Yannakakis[1,2],
and Julian Togelius[2]

[1] Institute of Digital Games, University of Malta, Msida, Malta
{antonios.liapis,georgios.yannakakis}@um.edu.mt
[2] Center for Computer Games Research, IT University of Copenhagen,
Copenhagen, Denmark
{holmgard,juto}@itu.dk

**Abstract.** This paper introduces a constrained optimization method which uses procedural personas to evaluate the playability and quality of evolved dungeon levels. Procedural personas represent archetypical player behaviors, and their controllers have been evolved to maximize a specific utility which drives their decisions. A "baseline" persona evaluates whether a level is playable by testing if it can survive in a worst-case scenario of the playthrough. On the other hand, a Monster Killer persona or a Treasure Collector persona evaluates playable levels based on how many monsters it can kill or how many treasures it can collect, respectively. Results show that the implemented two-population genetic algorithm discovers playable levels quickly and reliably, while the different personas affect the layout, difficulty level and tactical depth of the generated dungeons.

## 1 Introduction

The generation of dungeons is one of the first instances of procedural content generation (PCG) with *Rogue* (Toy and Wichman 1980). Since then, many games have used algorithms to generate dungeons, e.g. *Diablo* (Blizzard 1996), *Daggerfall* (Bethesda 1996) and *Daylight* (Zombie Studios 2014). Generating dungeons has also been a fertile research topic as summarized by [1]; algorithmic approaches using constraints [2], grammars [3] and genetic algorithms [4] have been successfully applied to this task.

This paper introduces a method where procedural personas act as critics in a search-based procedural content generation (SBPCG) framework [5]. Procedural personas are artificial agents which represent archetypical player behaviors (e.g. rushing to the goal, killing monsters, collecting treasures). In this paper, the personas have been evolved on a set of authored dungeons, according to different fitnesses that match archetypical decisions-making priorities. The testbed game, named MiniDungeons, is a simple turn-based roguelike game; the game has been tested by human users and a close match between procedural persona playstyle and human playstyle was found [6].

© Springer International Publishing Switzerland 2015
A.M. Mora and G. Squillero (Eds.): EvoApplications 2015, LNCS 9028, pp. 331–343, 2015.
DOI: 10.1007/978-3-319-16549-3_27

Using procedural personas to test the evolving dungeons situates the proposed method as a type of simulation-based SBPCG. However, the persona-critics are used not only to evaluate how appropriate a dungeon is for a particular playstyle, but also whether the dungeon is actually playable. The requirement that a dungeon can be completed by a simple "baseline" persona — despite any stochasticity of the gameplay — adds another constraint to the generative process. This paper uses a two-population genetic algorithm for the purposes of constrained optimization, which evolves both feasible and infeasible dungeons [7]. Dungeons are tested by a "baseline" persona based on whether it can complete a worst-case scenario of the dungeon; this persona also evaluates infeasible dungeons' distance from feasibility. Playable levels are evaluated by a Monster Killer persona or a Treasure Collector persona based on how many monsters it can kill or how many treasures it can collect, respectively.

## 2   Previous Work

This Section covers the core background material (testbed game, procedural personas and evolutionary level design) on which the presented method is built.

### 2.1   MiniDungeons Game

MiniDungeons is a simple turn-based roguelike puzzle game, implemented as a benchmark problem for modeling decision making styles of human players [8]. MiniDungeons levels are laid out on a grid of $12 \times 12$ tiles: tiles can be walls (which obstruct movement), empty, or contain monsters, treasure, the level's entrance or exit. The player has full information of the level except for monsters' damage, as discussed below.

In MiniDungeons, a hero (controlled by the player) starts at the level's entrance and must proceed to the level exit: stepping on the exit tile concludes a level and loads the next one. A hero starts each level with 40 hit points (HP) and dies at 0 HP. The hero can collect treasure by stepping on treasure tiles: treasures have no in-game effect but a treasure counter is shown on the user interface. The hero can drink potions by stepping on potion tiles: potions heal 10 HP, up to the maximum of 40 HP. Finally, the hero can kill monsters by stepping on monster tiles: monsters do not move and only engage the hero if the hero moves onto their tile. Combat is stochastic: a monster deals a random number between 5 HP and 14 HP of damage to the hero and then dies.

For the purposes of collecting player data as well as for evolving procedural personas, ten MiniDungeons levels were created in advance (see Fig. 1). These levels were designed in a mixed-initiative fashion [9] and had several patterns which allowed different decision making styles to be exhibited. The authored levels have many branching points, but usually include an easy path (with minimal combat) between the entrance and the exit. Moreover, treasures and potions are often "guarded" by monsters, although some treasures are easily accessible and some monsters do not obstruct any paths. These patterns allow for different ways of traversing the level, as will be seen in Sect. 2.2.

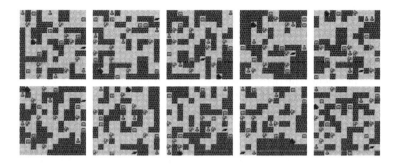

**Fig. 1.** The levels used for collecting player data and for evolving procedural personas.

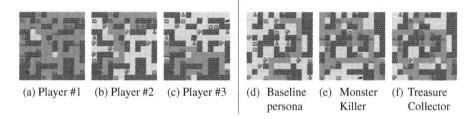

| (a) Player #1 | (b) Player #2 | (c) Player #3 | (d) Baseline persona | (e) Monster Killer | (f) Treasure Collector |

**Fig. 2.** Playtraces of human players and evolved procedural personas of MiniDungeons.

## 2.2   Procedural Personas

The MiniDungeons game was created for two purposes: (a) to investigate how human players enact decision making styles in a simple game, and (b) to construct artificial agents able to represent such decision making styles.

A core assumption of decision theory [10] is that human decision making under risk and uncertainty is shaped by *utility*. A utility function determines the decision maker's willingness to take risks for an expected reward, and is considered idiosyncratic. In digital games, the game's mechanics constitute affordances [11] which are likely to be of utility to the player. Using the MiniDungeons game as a testbed, 38 participants played all 10 levels of Fig. 1, as covered in detail in [6]: a few participants managed to collect all the treasures in every level (see Fig. 2a), while others rushed to the exit (see Fig. 2b) or miscalculated the risk of combat and died (see Fig. 2c). Such mechanics (treasure collection, death, reaching the exit) are thus likely sources of utility to players.

Procedural personas are artificial agents which represent archetypical decision making styles. In MiniDungeons, procedural personas consider several gameplay and level elements as sources of utility: killing monsters, collecting treasures, reaching the exit, performing as few actions as possible, or avoiding death. Previous work identified five procedural personas: a Monster Killer, a Treasure Collector, a "baseline" persona, a Speedrunner and a Survivalist, respectively. For the purposes of this paper, generated dungeons will be evaluated by personas evolved on all dungeons of Fig. 1 as per [6]. The controller for each persona is a combination of 7 linear perceptrons, with inputs being the hero's HP and distance to different elements (e.g. closest potion, closest "safe" treasure) and outputs being the desirability of a strategy (e.g. go to closest potion, go to closest treasure that does not involve combat). The strategy with the highest value is selected by the agent; the decision is re-evaluated in every step rather than upon completion of the strategy. The perceptrons' weights were evolved via an $(\mu + \lambda)$ evolutionary strategy without self-adaptation. The fitness of each agent was calculated from the utilities collected after all 10 levels were played. Focusing on the personas used in this paper, the baseline persona received a boost to its fitness for every exit it reached; the Treasure Collector received a fitness boost for every treasure collected and a smaller boost for every exit reached; the Monster Killer received a fitness boost for every monster killed and a smaller boost for every exit reached. Optimizing the controllers for these fitnesses resulted in personas exhibiting very different behaviors (see Fig. 2d–f).

The evolved procedural personas were compared to the human playtraces, in terms of persona-player agreement ratio. In every step a human took when playing, the persona was queried "what would be your next action given this game state?": if the persona's chosen action matched the human's, the agreement ratio increased. Summarizing the results of [6], most players had the highest agreement ratio with the Treasure Collector persona, while a smaller number of players matched the Monster Killer persona.

## 2.3   Constrained Optimization of Game Levels

Previous experiments on the constrained optimization of game levels focused on generating *map sketches*, i.e. low-resolution, high-level abstractions of complete levels [9]. Map sketches contain a small number of tiles which represent the most significant features of a level of a specific genre (e.g. weapon pickups in shooter games, player bases in strategy games). The simplicity of a map sketch allows it to be evolved in a straightforward and computationally lightweight manner. Map sketches of strategy games, roguelike dungeons and first-person shooters have been evolved according to a generic set of objectives which can be customized to the game genre at hand [12]. The constraints of such map sketches revolve around the connectedness between level features: for instance, in a map sketch for a strategy game all bases must be connected (via passable paths) with each other and with all of the map's resources. In order to ensure constraint satisfaction, evolution has been carried out via a FI-2pop GA [7] which can discover feasible individuals quickly and reliably even in highly constrained spaces [13].

MiniDungeons levels differ from map sketches in the fact that, despite a similarly small map size, they are directly playable. This introduces additional constraints on MiniDungeons levels in that they must be completable by procedural personas. Moreover, previous experiments optimized map sketches according to hard-coded objectives inspired by game design patterns [14], while MiniDungeons levels are evolved according to the play experience of the procedural personas that playtest them. In that regard, the procedural personas act as critics both on the playability and on the quality of the generated level: how this affects the evolutionary process will be explored in Sect. 4.

# 3   Methodology

This Section describes the two-population genetic algorithm used to evolve MiniDungeons levels, as well as the methods for assessing playability (the infeasible fitness function) and level quality (the feasible fitness function) via procedural personas.

## 3.1   Evolving Levels for MiniDungeons

A MiniDungeons level consists of 144 tiles, which can be empty or contain walls, monsters, treasures, potions, the level entrance or the level exit. In the genotype, a MiniDungeons level is represented directly as an array of integers: each integer describes the contents of a single tile in the level.

Due to the constraints on playability (discussed in Sect. 3.2), MiniDungeons levels are evolved via a feasible-infeasible two-population genetic algorithm (FI-2pop GA). The FI-2pop GA separates feasible individuals from infeasible ones (which do not satisfy one or more constraints), placing the former in a feasible population and the latter in an infeasible population [7]. The feasible population evolves to optimize the domain-specific measure of quality, while the infeasible population evolves to minimize its members' distance from the feasible border. As infeasible individuals approach the border of feasibility, the chances that their offspring will be feasible increase. Feasible offspring of infeasible parents migrate to the feasible population, and vice versa: this indirect form of interbreeding may increase the size and diversity of the feasible population. In order to ensure that the feasible population is sufficiently large for efficient optimization, the *offspring boost* mechanism is applied to the FI-2pop GA. The offspring boost is applied in cases where the feasible population is smaller than the infeasible population, and forces both feasible and infeasible populations to produce an equal number of offspring regardless of the number of parents in each population.

In the experiments described in this paper, evolution of MiniDungeons levels is driven by asexual mutation alone; preliminary experiments showed that recombination is slower to discover feasible individuals and can result in multiple entrances or exits in the same dungeon. Mutation may transform an empty tile to a wall tile and vice versa, a level feature (non-wall, non-empty tile) may swap places with another level feature chosen randomly, or any tile may swap places with an adjacent one. Every offspring has 5 % to 20 % of its tiles (chosen randomly) mutated in the above fashion. By evolving content solely via this mutation scheme, an offspring is ensured to contain the same number of monsters, treasures, potions, level entrances and level exits as its parent. Parents are chosen via fitness-proportionate roulette wheel selection; the same parent may be chosen multiple times to generate offspring. In each population (feasible and infeasible), the best individual is transferred to the next generation unchanged.

## 3.2   Assessing Playability with Personas

In order for a MiniDungeons level to be playable, a number of constraints need to be satisfied: (a) the level must contain a specific number of tiles of certain types, e.g. one entrance and one exit, (b) all features of the level (monsters, potions, treasures, exit) must be accessible via passable paths to the hero, and (c) the hero must be able to reach the exit without dying. Constraints of type (a) are automatically satisfied by seeding the initial population with levels containing the desired number of level features: since mutation does not add or remove features, the number of features in the initial population will remain constant throughout the evolutionary process. Constraints of type (b) require that a passable path exists between the level entrance and all other features in the level: levels that fail this constraint are evaluated based on how many features are inaccessible. Finally, constraints of type (c) require that an agent simulates a playthrough of the level. In order to ensure that the level can be completed regardless of the stochasticity of combat, a 'worst-case' scenario is constructed by assigning maximum damage (14 HP) to all monsters of the level. The agent chosen to perform the playthrough is the baseline persona, whose affordance is only to reach the exit: this persona does not get "distracted" by treasure or monsters, and is likely to finish the level quickly. If the baseline persona dies then this constraint is failed: however, an additional check for the number of tiles explored by the persona is performed. This additional constraint was added after preliminary experiments in order to ensure that the entrance and exit are not close to each other, so that even speedrunners face at least a minimal challenge. If a baseline persona completes the level having explored less than 12 tiles, the level fails to satisfy the constraint of type (c) and is evaluated based on how many tiles the baseline persona explored, or a worse score if the baseline persona died.

Combining constraints (b) and (c) into a fitness measure for infeasible content, the distance to feasibility is calculated via $d_{inf}$ of Eq. (1). The infeasible population evolves to minimize $d_{inf}$, which increases the chances of feasible content being discovered. Observing $d_{inf}$, there is a clear priority between constraints: levels that fail constraints of type (b) automatically fail constraint (c) and assume that the baseline persona died without even testing for it. Moreover, if a baseline persona dies then the level receives a much worse score than if it completes the level, even within a very small number of steps. This aims to guide infeasible content towards first becoming well-formed (with all features accessible to the hero), then minimally playable for the baseline persona.

$$
d_{inf} = \begin{cases} 1 + \frac{u_N}{N} & \text{if } u_N > 0 \\ 1 & \text{if baseline persona died} \\ \frac{1}{2}(1 - \frac{s_B}{C_s}) & \text{if baseline persona completed the level with } s_B < C_s \end{cases}
$$

(1)

where $N$ is the total number of level features (monsters, potions, treasures, exit) and $u_N$ is the number of features which are not accessible from the level entrance; $s_B$ is the number of tiles explored by the baseline persona in the worst-case scenario (all monsters dealing maximum damage) and $C_s$ is the minimum number of explored tiles for a level to be considered feasible ($C_s = 12$ in this study).

## 3.3   Assessing Level Quality with Personas

The main contribution of the procedural personas is towards the evaluation of feasible, playable game levels. However, it is not obvious what a persona (or indeed the human players it represents) looks for in a level. Granted that the decisions of procedural personas are shaped by their own utility functions, only events which affect their utility should be considered. This paper will consider the two most dominant (and distinct) procedural personas of past experiments: the Monster Killer (with a utility for killing monsters and reaching the exit) and the Treasure Collector (with a utility for collecting treasure and reaching the exit). Most playtraces of the 38 human players who tested MiniDungeons matched the Treasure Collector persona (86 %), while the Monster Killer was second (8 %). When evaluating a level it has just finished playing (either by reaching the exit or by dying), the Monster Killer assigns the score of Eq. (2) while the Treasure Collector assigns the score of Eq. (3). The values of $C_m$, $C_t$ and $C_r$ are taken directly from the fitness function which guided the evolution of each persona's controller[1]; the persona was evolved on 10 authored levels (see Fig. 1) and was evaluated on how it represents an archetypical decision making style (a Monster Killer that kills most monsters, a Treasure Collector that collects most treasure) [6]. Inversely, the scores of Eqs. (2) and (3) evaluate whether the level provides the desired utilities to personas that play optimally towards attaining them.

$$S_{MK} = \frac{(d_m C_m + C_r r)}{(N_m C_m + C_r)} \tag{2}$$

$$S_{TC} = \frac{(d_t C_t + C_r r)}{(N_t C_t + C_r)} \tag{3}$$

where $N_m$ and $N_t$ is the number of monsters and treasures in the level respectively; $d_m$ and $d_t$ is the number of dead monsters and collected treasures respectively; $r$ is 1 if the hero reached the exit and 0 if not; $C_m$, $C_t$ and $C_r$ are constants expressing the priority of monsters, treasures and level completion (respectively) in each persona's utility; for these personas $C_m = C_t = 1$ and $C_r = 0.5$. The denominator normalizes the score of Eqs. (2) and (3) between 0 (no affordances acquired) and 1 (all affordances acquired).

Intuitively, a persona prefers levels that allow it to maximize its utility function: i.e. a Monster Killer prefers levels that allow it to kill all monsters and a Treasure Collector prefers levels that allow it to collect all treasure. Due to the stochastic nature of combat, the same level is played by a persona multiple times ($R=10$ in this paper) with damage for each monster randomized in each playthrough. When maximizing the level's utility for a persona, the simulations' $S_{MK}$ and $S_{TC}$ scores are averaged in the fitness of Eq. (4) for a Monster Killer, and Eq. (5) for a Treasure Collector, respectively.

---

[1] The fitness function of all personas' controllers included a penalty for taking extraneous actions. Since this penalty was a control mechanism to avoid playthroughs taking too long rather than an explicit utility, it is omitted for the purposes of level evaluation.

$$F_{MK} = \frac{1}{R} \sum_{i=1}^{R} S_{MK}(i) \tag{4}$$

$$F_{TC} = \frac{1}{R} \sum_{i=1}^{R} S_{TC}(i) \tag{5}$$

Maximizing the utility function of a persona, however, may be somewhat naive considering the decisions taken within MiniDungeons. Maximizing the utility of a Treasure Collector, for instance, can be trivially solved by placing all the treasure in a straight path between the level entrance and the level exit. In such cases, the player does not take a decision at any point during play; there is no risk/reward where the idiosyncratic utility function would shape the decision. In order to provide an element of risk, and thus require that the persona makes *meaningful* decisions, the level can be evaluated on how different a playthrough is from the next. Due to the randomness of combat, different playthroughs by the same persona may result in a premature death, in more or fewer treasures collected or monsters killed. Using the standard deviation of $S_{MK}$ and $S_{TC}$ among the 10 simulations, Eq. (6) (for a Monster Killer) and Eq. (7) (for a Treasure Collector) aim to maximize the levels' risk involved in personas' decisions.

$$D_{MK} = \sqrt{\frac{1}{R-1} \sum_{i=1}^{R} (S_{MK}(i) - F_{MK})} \tag{6}$$

$$D_{TC} = \sqrt{\frac{1}{R-1} \sum_{i=1}^{R} (S_{TC}(i) - F_{TC})} \tag{7}$$

## 4    Experiments

The experiments described in this section test how the different procedural personas (Monster Killer and Treasure Collector) and different fitness functions of Eqs. (4)–(7) affect the evolutionary process and the final generated dungeons. Dungeons generated in this paper have the same properties as those of Fig. 1: a 12 × 12 tile grid containing one entrance, one exit, 8 monsters, 7 treasures and 4 potions (21 level features in total). All experiments in this paper were performed with a population size of 20 (including feasible and infeasible levels), and evolution runs for 100 generations; results were averaged from 20 independent evolutionary runs and each level is evaluated by a procedural persona via 10 playthroughs.

### 4.1    Discovery of Feasible Content

Despite the small map size of MiniDungeons, the constraints of connectivity of 21 level features and that of baseline persona survival were expected to make discovery of feasible individuals by random chance highly unlikely. Out of $10^6$ randomly initialized levels, 360 were feasible (for all constraints) and 958 satisfied the constraints of connectivity, i.e. $u_N = 0$ in Eq. (1). Evolving infeasible individuals allowed the FI-2pop GA to discover playable levels quickly despite the limited population size: the first feasible individual was discovered on average after 14.39 generations[2] (standard error: 1.40). This performance of the FI-2pop GA can be compared with a single population approach which handles infeasible individuals by applying the death penalty (i.e. fitness of 0). Using the same parameters as the FI-2pop GA and performing 20 evolutionary runs with each of Eqs. (4)–(7) (80 runs in total), the single population approach did not discover any feasible individuals in 21 of 80 runs (while all runs of the FI-2pop GA discovered playable levels). Moreover, among those runs where feasible individuals were found when using the death penalty, discovery of playable levels occurred after 35.42 generations (standard error: 0.84). As the difference in generation of discovery between FI-2pop GA and single-population GA is statistically significant ($p < 10^{-6}$ via two-tailed Student's $t$-test assuming unequal variances), it is clear that the FI-2pop GA can discover playable MiniDungeons levels faster and more reliably.

### 4.2   Quality of Feasible Content

Figure 3 displays the best final evolved levels of 20 evolutionary runs, for each fitness function of Eqs. (4)–(7). To better demonstrate the levels' gameplay, each level is accompanied by a visualization of different playthroughs of the persona that evaluates it. Levels evolved towards $F_{MK}$ tend to allow access from the entrance to the exit as well as to most potions (i.e. no monsters guard those level features); therefore it is the players' decision to pursue combat without it being forced upon them. Levels evolved towards $F_{TC}$ tend to leave most treasures

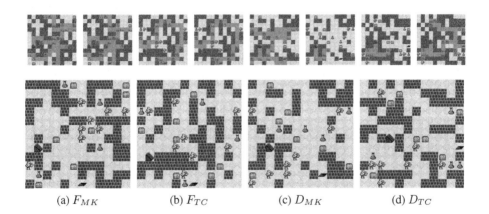

|          (a) $F_{MK}$          |          (b) $F_{TC}$          |          (c) $D_{MK}$          |          (d) $D_{TC}$          |

**Fig. 3.** Best evolved levels for the different fitness functions of Eqs. (4)–(7). The levels shown have the highest fitness among 20 independent runs. Above each level are two playthroughs of the persona for which the level is evolved (Monster Killer or Treasure Collector), with randomized damage values for each monster.

---

[2] Since the infeasible fitness ($d_{inf}$) is the same for all experiments, discovery of the first feasible individual is calculated based on all four sets of experiments ($F_{MK}$, $F_{TC}$, $D_{MK}$, $D_{TC}$).

unguarded (in Fig. 3b only one treasure, near the exit, is guarded by a monster) and therefore collecting all treasures is not a risky choice for the player. Levels evolved towards $D_{MK}$ tend to place more monsters at chokepoints, therefore guarding many of the level's features such as the exit, potions and treasure: in Fig. 3c the hero must face a minimum of two monsters in order to reach the exit, and a minimum of three monsters to reach the treasures in the middle of the map (the exit tile can not be crossed as it ends the level). Levels evolved towards $D_{TC}$ similarly place monsters at chokepoints: in Fig. 3d two monsters must be fought to reach the exit as well as the treasures in the middle of the map. While the Treasure Collector persona could theoretically have fought those two monsters and gained access to the 6 otherwise unguarded treasures, it opted to go for the bottom right treasure which often caused it to die. This odd decision demonstrates the bias introduced by the representation of the personas' controllers (the Treasure Collector went for the closest guarded treasure in this case) and by the levels they were evolved on (which rarely had so many monsters clustered in a map corner). This issue will be further discussed in Sect. 5.

To evaluate the quality of a generated level, the utility function of its persona-critic is a straightforward performance metric. Expanding on that, the quality of the persona's playthroughs in each level can be captured by other gameplay metrics, such as number of tiles explored, actions taken or times the persona died. Table 1 contains the gameplay metrics of the best final evolved levels as evaluated via 10 playthroughs of its persona-critic. Values in parentheses represent the deviation between playthroughs of the same level (rather than deviation between levels). For comparative purposes, Table 1 includes the gameplay metrics of the authored levels of Fig. 1, on which the personas were evolved. Observing Table 1, there is a clear difference between Monster Killer personas

**Table 1.** Metrics of the best final levels, derived from simulations with procedural personas. Each level is simulated 10 times, and the value in the table represents the average of those 10 simulations, averaged again across the 20 independent runs of the GA. The value in parentheses represents the standard deviation of that metric within the 10 simulations (on the same level), and is also averaged across the 20 runs of the GA. Included are the gameplay metrics of the authored levels of Fig. 1: the values are averaged from 10 simulations, with deviation between simulations (on the same level) in parentheses.

| | Monsters | Treasures | Potions | Explored | Actions | Death ratio | Damage |
|---|---|---|---|---|---|---|---|
| Monster Killer | | | | | | | |
| Auth. | 7.47 (0.47) | 0.95 (0.21) | 3.77 (0.15) | 45.19 (4.57) | 70.64 (10.34) | 0.68 (0.42) | 68.64 (5.25) |
| $F_{MK}$ | 7.91 (0.23) | 2.90 (0.28) | 3.99 (0.05) | 44.34 (2.32) | 78.81 (9.11) | 0.43 (0.47) | 72.63 (5.64) |
| $D_{MK}$ | 6.16 (1.15) | 2.39 (0.45) | 3.58 (0.51) | 35.66 (6.09) | 53.70 (12.75) | 0.92 (0.13) | 54.23 (6.16) |
| Treasure Collector | | | | | | | |
| Auth. | 5.93 (0.42) | 6.52 (0.61) | 2.47 (0.49) | 52.03 (6.12) | 84.25 (14.42) | 0.29 (0.42) | 55.72 (4.18) |
| $F_{TC}$ | 2.68 (0.03) | 7.00 (0.00) | 3.57 (0.02) | 43.57 (0.15) | 75.89 (0.68) | 0.00 (0.00) | 25.29 (4.97) |
| $D_{TC}$ | 3.30 (0.83) | 4.59 (2.07) | 2.34 (1.29) | 30.63 (12.39) | 41.97 (21.55) | 0.17 (0.19) | 30.84 (9.26) |

and Treasure Collector personas: Monster Killers kill far more monsters (unsurprisingly), drink more potions, die far more often and take much more damage than Treasure Collectors. Comparing between levels evolved towards $F_{MK}$ and $D_{MK}$, the former can be played by a Monster Killer persona more efficiently: more monsters are killed, more potions drunk and less deaths occur than with $D_{MK}$. The high death ratio of $D_{MK}$ is a direct result of the fitness computation: the most straightforward way to achieve a larger deviation in monster kills is by dying prematurely. This is achieved in the map design by "hiding" potions behind multiple monsters, whereas maps evolved towards $F_{MK}$ allow the hero to heal at any time (see Fig. 3). Comparing between levels evolved towards $F_{TC}$ and $D_{TC}$, it is obvious that the former present minimal challenge to the Treasure Collector persona: with $F_{TC}$, all 7 rewards are always collected — without the hero ever dying — in every simulation and in every best final level. In contrast, with $D_{TC}$ the hero collects less treasure with a high deviation in treasure collected between playthroughs, and has some chance of dying. Interestingly, the chance that the Treasure Collector dies is lower for maps evolved towards $D_{TC}$ than for authored maps on which it was evolved; this is different than with maps evolved towards $D_{MK}$, where the death ratio is higher than for authored maps. Observing the Treasure Collector's actions in maps evolved for $D_{TC}$, its cautious tactics (compared to the Monster Killer) led it to rush to the exit when at low HP, since unguarded treasures were rarely available.

## 5    Discussion

The experiments in Sect. 4 demonstrated the impact of the FI-2pop GA in the swift and reliable discovery of playable MiniDungeons levels. Moreover, the influence of the persona-critic was shown in the evolved dungeons' design patterns: levels evolved according to a Monster Killer had many unguarded potions while levels evolved according to a Treasure collector had many unguarded treasures. However, optimizing for most monsters killed or treasures collected resulted in MiniDungeons levels of limited interest, especially for $F_{TC}$ where there was no risk of dying when collecting all treasure. In contrast, maps evolved towards deviations between monsters killed ($D_{MK}$) or treasures collected ($D_{TC}$) featured a higher chance of dying for either persona, and therefore interesting risk/reward decisions. Maps evolved towards either $D_{MK}$ or $D_{TC}$ are superficially similar, as both fitnesses result in levels with more monsters guarding potions and treasure; the difference in gameplay metrics, therefore, is introduced by the different decisions and utility functions of the personas playtesting them. It may be worthwhile in future work to explore the potential of evolving maps based on how different the playthroughs between these two personas are.

However, the design patterns of evolved levels were biased by the personas' architecture as well as the levels that they were evolved on. Using two inputs for estimating the utility of treasure (closest treasure and closest unguarded treasure) works well for the authored levels the personas were evolved on (which had several unguarded treasures) but fell short when all treasures were guarded e.g. in Fig. 3d. Additionally, following a strategy such as "collect closest treasure" should avoid monsters when possible by using more sophisticated planning approaches than the ones currently in place. Finally, future work can explore how dungeons can be evolved according to personas with more elaborate utilities (e.g. a completionist persona targeting both monsters and treasure), or according to clones of human players, i.e. artificial agents evolved to match the decisions of a specific human player [15], thus providing personalized dungeons.

The algorithms covered in this paper can be applied to any problem that includes search in constrained spaces using simulations to evaluate content quality. Within games, procedurally generated content usually has to satisfy certain constraints; such constraints can be tested via planning [16], ensuring that a "perfect" or "worst-case" player can finish the game. However, in games with high stochasticity (e.g. roguelike games), with emerging tactics (e.g. multi-player strategy games) or where players don't always play optimally (e.g. sandbox games), simulations using one or more artificial agents to test the game can be useful both for playability checks (assuming more human-like perception, cognitive load and response times) and for evaluating the quality of completed playthroughs. Beyond games, constrained optimization is extensively applied in evolutionary industrial design [17] where simulations are often used to test robot locomotion or the performance of a machine part. The results of these simulations can act as constraints (e.g. minimal distance covered by a robot or lifetime of a machine part) in order to divide the search space into feasible and infeasible, allowing the FI-2pop GA to explore it using simulation-based fitnesses on the feasible and infeasible population.

## 6    Conclusion

This paper described a method for using procedural personas to evaluate the playability and quality of generated levels for the MiniDungeons game. Playability is determined by a "baseline" persona playing through a worst-case scenario of the level, with monsters dealing maximum damage. Using a two-population genetic algorithm to distinguish between feasible and infeasible content, discovery of playable levels is fast and reliable despite the highly constrained search space. To test the level's quality, a procedural persona simulates multiple playthroughs: a good level may require that the persona maximizes its utility or that the decisions taken by the persona affect its utility significantly. This paper tested two procedural personas, the Monster Killer and the Treasure Collector, and the final evolved levels demonstrated different map designs appropriate for each. Future work aims to improve the persona-critics, explore other simulation-based level evaluations, and increase the complexity of MiniDungeons.

**Acknowledgements.** The research was supported, in part, by the FP7 ICT project C2Learn (project no: 318480) and by the FP7 Marie Curie CIG project AutoGameDesign (project no: 630665).

# References

1. van der Linden, R., Lopes, R., Bidarra, R.: Procedural generation of dungeons. IEEE Trans. Comput. Intell. AI Games **6**(1), 78–89 (2013)
2. Roden, T., Parberry, I.: From artistry to automation: a structured methodology for procedural content creation. In: Rauterberg, M. (ed.) ICEC 2004. LNCS, vol. 3166, pp. 151–156. Springer, Heidelberg (2004)
3. Dormans, J.: Adventures in level design: generating missions and spaces for action adventure games. In: Workshop on Procedural Content Generation in Games (2010)
4. Hartsook, K., Zook, A., Das, S., Riedl, M.: Toward supporting stories with procedurally generated game worlds. In: Proceedings of the IEEE Conference on Computational Intelligence and Games, pp. 297–304 (2011)
5. Togelius, J., Yannakakis, G.N., Stanley, K.O., Browne, C.: Search-based procedural content generation: a taxonomy and survey. IEEE Trans. Comput. Intell. AI Games **3**(3), 172–186 (2011)
6. Holmgård, C., Liapis, A., Togelius, J., Yannakakis, G.N.: Evolving personas for player decision modeling. In: Proceedings of the IEEE Conference on Computational Intelligence and Games (2014)
7. Kimbrough, S.O., Koehler, G.J., Lu, M., Wood, D.H.: On a feasible-infeasible two-population (fi-2pop) genetic algorithm for constrained optimization: distance tracing and no free lunch. Eur. J. Oper. Res. **190**(2), 310–327 (2008)
8. Holmgård, C., Liapis, A., Togelius, J., Yannakakis, G.N.: Generative agents for player decision modeling in games. In: Poster Proceedings of the 9th Conference on the Foundations of Digital Games (2014)
9. Liapis, A., Yannakakis, G., Togelius, J.: Sentient sketchbook: computer-aided game level authoring. In: Proceedings of the ACM Conference on Foundations of Digital Games (2013)
10. Kahneman, D., Tversky, A.: Prospect theory: an analysis of decision under risk. Econometrica J. Econometric Soc. **47**, 263–291 (1979)
11. Gibson, J.J.: The theory of affordances. In: Shaw, R.E., Bransford, J. (eds.) Perceiving, Acting, and Knowing, pp. 67–82. Lawrence Erlbaum Associates, Hillsdale (1977)
12. Liapis, A., Yannakakis, G.N., Togelius, J.: Towards a generic method of evaluating game levels. In: Proceedings of the AAAI Artificial Intelligence for Interactive Digital Entertainment Conference (2013)
13. Liapis, A., Yannakakis, G.N., Togelius, J.: Generating map sketches for strategy games. In: Esparcia-Alcázar, A.I. (ed.) EvoApplications 2013. LNCS, vol. 7835, pp. 264–273. Springer, Heidelberg (2013)
14. Björk, S., Holopainen, J.: Patterns in Game Design. Charles River Media, Rockland (2004)
15. Holmgård, C., Liapis, A., Togelius, J., Yannakakis, G.N.: Personas versus clones for player decision modeling. In: Pisan, Y., Sgouros, N.M., Marsh, T. (eds.) ICEC 2014. LNCS, vol. 8770, pp. 159–166. Springer, Heidelberg (2014)
16. Horswill, I., Foged, L.: Fast procedural level population with playability constraints. In: Proceedings of the Artificial Intelligence and Interactive Digital Entertainment Conference (2012)
17. Michalewicz, Z., Dasgupta, D., Le Riche, R., Schoenauer, M.: Evolutionary algorithms for constrained engineering problems. Comput. Ind. Eng. J. **30**, 851–870 (1996)

# Evolving Diverse Strategies Through Combined Phenotypic Novelty and Objective Function Search

Davy Smith[✉], Laurissa Tokarchuk, and Chrisantha Fernando

Department of Computer Science and Electronic Engineering,
Queen Mary University of London, Mile End Road, London E1 4NS, UK
david.smith@qmul.ac.uk

**Abstract.** Novelty search is an algorithm which proposes open-ended exploration of the search space by maximising behavioural novelty, removing the need for an objective fitness function. However, we show that when applied to complex tasks, training through novelty alone is not sufficient to produce *useful* controllers. Alongside this, the definition of phenotypic behaviour significantly effects the strategies of the evolved solutions. Controller networks for the spaceship in the arcade game *Asteroids* were evolved with five different phenotypic distance measures. Each of these phenotypic measures are shown to produce controllers which adopt different strategies of play than controllers trained through standard objective fitness. Combined phenotypic novelty and objective fitness is also shown to produce differing strategies within the same evolutionary run. Our results demonstrate that for domains such as video games, where a diverse range of interesting behaviours are required, training agents through a combination of phenotypic novelty and objective fitness is a viable method.

## 1 Introduction

The training of agents through the promotion of diverse behavioural characteristics is a recent area within Evolutionary Robotics (ER) that suggests promising directions towards open-ended evolution [1–4]. In complex tasks, and when faced with uncertainty, a range of differing behavioural strategies emerge. The behavioural sciences observe in nature, not only a vast array of different species, but also a scale of behavioural differences within the same species [5].

Varying both the phenotypic definition and the distance metric used in the fitness assessment of an evolutionary task has been shown to produce widely different strategies amongst the population, suggesting the importance of domain specificity and the assessment metric in measuring phenotypic distance [2,3]. However, there has been little research which addresses a series of behavioural measures in order to highlight the effect that particular phenotypic definitions play on both objective fitness and the resulting useful behavioural strategies of the agents in the same domain. A series of experiments were undertaken

© Springer International Publishing Switzerland 2015
A.M. Mora and G. Squillero (Eds.): EvoApplications 2015, LNCS 9028, pp. 344–354, 2015.
DOI: 10.1007/978-3-319-16549-3_28

to assess the effect of varying phenotypic definitions on objective performance at an uncertain task. Agent controllers for the spaceship in the video game *Asteroids* were evolved on the same task, with fitness assessments based on a linear proportion of objective fitness and phenotypic novelty over five definitions of behaviour.

A linearly mixed fitness assessment is shown to produce controllers which adopt different strategies of play than controllers trained through standard objective fitness without significant effect on objective performance. A comparison of the complete state-action pairings of high scoring agents was undertaken to assess the diversity of the evolved solutions. Our results show that, dependant on an ideal mixing ratio, the linear combination of objective fitness and phenotypic novelty produces highly diverse solution populations.

## 2   Related Work

### 2.1   Novelty Search

Novelty search, as proposed by Lehman and Stanley [6,7], is an algorithm which removes the need for an objective fitness function through the assignment of high fitness values to novel behaviours in a population.

$$n(x) = \frac{1}{k} \sum_{i=0}^{k} dist(x, \mu_i) \tag{1}$$

The behavioural novelty $n(x)$ of an individual $x$ is defined as the mean behavioural distance between $x$ and its $k$ nearest neighbours, where $k$ is a user defined parameter and $\mu_i$ is the $i$th nearest neighbor of $x$ with respect to the distance $dist$. The value of $k$ includes both the behaviours of the current population and an archive of previous novel behaviours. Individuals with a value of $n(x)$ above a predefined novelty threshold are added to the archive, Eq. (1).

### 2.2   Phenotypic Diversity

It has been suggested that the success of ER to extend beyond simple tasks will be dependant upon adaptable and open-ended evolutionary procedures [8]. Current definitions exist within the literature which draw separations between *genotypic space* as the binary representation of genes in the population, *phenotypic space* as the topology of the networks produced by the genotype and *behaviour space* as the actions produced by the agent [2]. Here, however, we adopt a more biologically informed definition, in which the phenotype refers to any observable characteristics of an organism, which may include both network topology and the related behaviour of an agent [9].

The design of effective fitness functions in ER is a subjective process, therefore susceptible to human error and deception. If generalisable across domains, the promotion of phenotypic diversity may alleviate this limitation [6]. However, assessment methods based upon phenotypic diversity, which require a definition of the particular behaviour to encourage or diversify in a given domain, strictly translate rather than remove the human design process. Experiments which have shown novelty search to outperform objective fitness have concentrated on domain specific behavioural metrics, such as maximising the distance of the end navigation points of a robot within a maze [6]. Metrics have been proposed to generalise phenotypic novelty, for example through measuring the distance of output values from randomised input vectors given to the controller [10]. In a comparison of generic behaviour based on motor actions, Gomez suggested measuring the Normalised Compression Distance (NCD) of binary action vectors as yielding the most promising method for translation to different domains [10].

Although not strictly a diversity maintenance algorithm, novelty search receives increasing interest within ER research for its unique way in expanding the search space to multiple solutions in any given domain [6]. The introduction of novelty search uncovered many of the stepping stones towards open-ended evolution. Although novelty search may outperform objective fitness search in specific tasks, especially when the design of an objective fitness function may be difficult, it has been shown that the assessment of behavioural novelty alone is insufficient as a generalisable evolutionary technique in many domains [11,12]. Due to its divergent nature, novelty search continues to produce new solutions throughout the evolution, however these solutions may not be useful for the task at hand. The combination of novelty search and objective fitness, in which the diverse and expanding search space explored by novelty search is limited to *useful* solutions is a promising direction for the application of the algorithm.

Alongisde this, multiobjective optimisation of both novelty and objective fitness has shown to outperform purely objective fitness in biped locomotion tasks and maze navigation [4].

## 2.3   Neuro-Evolution Through Augmenting Topologies (NEAT)

Neuro-Evolution Through Augmenting Topologies (NEAT), developed by Stanley and Miikkulainen in 2002 [13], is an Evolutionary Algorithm (EA) for the evolution of Artifical Neural Networks (ANN). In addition to the mutation of weights between neurons, NEAT evolves the networks' topologies, creating phenotypically diverse populations. Increasing complexity is achieved by initialising a population of networks with minimal topologies and adding genes as the evolution progresses, leading to more diverse behaviour patterns. Neurons added to the network may be either feed-forward or recurrent, allowing for the emergence of a short term memory within networks. Additionally, in order to protect new innovations, historical markings are used to assign species to the population. Alongside evolutionary robotics tasks, NEAT has been widely applied to the evolution of video game agents in multiple domains [14–17].

## 2.4   Video Games for Evolutionary Research

Classic 2D video games are generally played within basic grid type worlds, with a limited number of agents and a small set of available actions. Although deceptively simple, the dynamics within these worlds are often complex and uncertain, requiring multiple diverse strategies and planning procedures for play. Unlike traditional maze navigation or pole balancing tasks, classic video games provide simulated worlds which require the acquisition of multiple skills, such as path finding, fights for survival, evasion, goals and sub-goals. Due to these rich worlds, there is a growing body of research in the application of EAs to classic video games, both for agents evolved for particular games, for example *Ms-Pacman* [18], and general games playing agents [16,19,20]. Typically within the literature, fitness assessment of the population is achieved through objective points scoring. However there are a number of games, including *Montezuma's Revenge* and *Pitfall* where points are not readily available. It has been recently suggested that an intrinsically motivated assessment of the diversity of agents' behaviours is a promising approach to allow evolution to continue in the absence of points [16].

# 3   Experimental Domain

A bespoke version of the classic arcade game *Asteroids* was used as an experimental domain (Fig. 1). The aim of *Asteroids* is to score as many points as possible

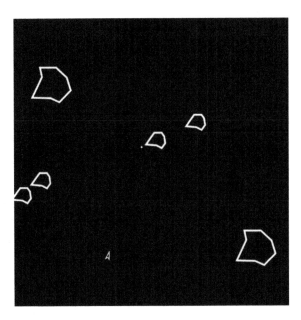

**Fig. 1.** Screenshot of the *Asteroids* video game

by shooting asteroids and avoiding collisions. The player controls a spaceship that has a left and right rotation, a forward thrust and the ability to shoot. Due to *Asteroids* being set in deep space, the spaceship is not effected by friction or gravity, therefore takes a long time to slow down after thrust is applied. As the name suggests, the enemies in the game are asteroids, which appear on the screen in waves, with random velocity and direction. Asteroids appear in three different sizes: starting off as large, and when hit splitting into two medium size asteroids, which in turn each split into a further two small asteroids. The first wave consists of three large asteroids. After the player has cleared all of the asteroids, the next wave begins, with one more large asteroid than the last. The playing field in *Asteroids* is constructed as a toroidal space, i.e. if asteroids or the ship move off the edge of the screen, they reappear on the opposite side.

## 4   Agent Model

### 4.1   Perceptual Field

The perceptual field for the agent was constructed as a dartboard-style map with binary inputs centred on its position and rotation, providing a discrete representation of polar coordinates relative to the agent (Fig. 2). Inputs to the map were assigned a value of zero if no asteroids were present within the related coordinate, and one if any number of asteroids appeared within the bounds. A series of trial experiments were conducted using a range of input maps with differing resolutions and sizes. The final perceptual field used consisted of 4 segments and 3 slices and a diameter of 0.8 of the world's length. In order to allow the agent the capacity to adapt to the toroidal nature of the playing space, it was also decided to allow the agents' perception to extend beyond the edges of the screen, overlapping to the opposite side (Fig. 2).

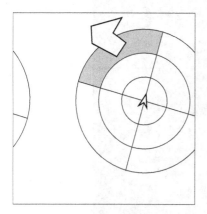

**Fig. 2.** Agent perceptual state map

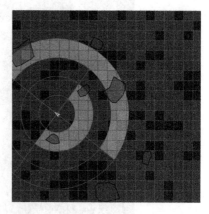

**Fig. 3. GC** phenotypic measurement

## 4.2   Controller Network

The NEAT algorithm was used to train the agents' controllers throughout this experiment. The dartboard state map was passed to the inputs of the network as a 12 dimensional binary array (with a value of one if at least one asteroid was detected in the position and zero otherwise) at each time step in the game. The networks were assigned three floating point outputs used to control left and right rotation and thrust, and one binary output for shooting. The NEAT algorithm's parameters were set to enable the evolution of recurrent nodes within the networks, allowing for the possibility of a short term memory to develop within the controllers.

# 5   Phenotypic Definitions

In the presented experiment, in order to determine the possibilities for a generalised method of evolution based on behavioural novelty, we apply a combination of both generic and domain specific behaviour measures. Although [10] suggests a metric using NCD as being optimal, due to the computational complexity of both NCD, which requires a compression to be calculated with each distance measurement, and novelty search, which introduces its own computational load due to the maintenance of an expanding archive, we forgo the NCD measurement, comparing instead the Hamming distance of action vectors, which has previously produced comparably similar results [2,10].

The following five differing phenotypic definitions were evaluated to establish the significance of a fitness based evolution based on behavioural distance.

1. **(AC) Action Count.** A set of one hundred states was randomly produced at the beginning of the evolutionary run and the set presented to the controllers before gameplay began in each generation. The euclidean distances between each of the resulting arrays of output vectors were then measured to establish the novelty value of the agents[1].
2. **(GC) Ground Covered.** The play area was divided into a $20 \times 20$ matrix and a counter was incremented the first time each time the agent was positioned within a square. The 1 dimensional euclidean distance was taken as the measurement between agents in the population (Fig. 3).
3. **(MAD) Mean Asteroid Distance.** The average distance from the agent to the asteroids in the playing field was taken at each time step during the game. The mean of these distances was then measured between agents.
4. **(MTR) Mean Thrust and Rotation.** The average thrust and rotation of the agent was taken throughout game play. The euclidean distance of the resulting two dimensional vector was measured.

---

[1] It may be noted that with this particular phenotypic definition, the behaviour is measured hypothetically, before the task has been performed. Therefore when evaluating through novelty search alone ($\lambda = 1.0$), the game does not need to even be played.

5. **(NA) N Actions.** Each game was initiated with the game state, i.e. identical asteroid positions and velocities. The first N actions was stored as a string (L for left, R for Right etc.) and the hamming distances between the strings taken (in this experiment $N = 100$).

# 6   Evolutionary Criteria

## 6.1   Experimental Parameters

Although relatively simple for a human player to grasp, *Asteroids* is a particularly difficult domain for evolutionary techniques. The agents' actions in the game directly effect the trajectory of the task, therefore introducing a high level of uncertainty. The same controller can receive a wide range of scores in different games, subsequently effecting fitness measures. In order to reduce this level of noise, 10 games were played by each controller in each generation of the evolutionary phase, and the objective fitness averaged. Due to the computationally exhaustive nature of novelty search over multiple assessments, the behavioural values were evaluated on one random game per generation.

Agents were allocated three lives in each round of the game. To remove the possibility of an agent discovering a linear trajectory which avoids collisions with all asteroids, therefore making the game last infinitely long, a timer was added to the task, requiring agents to hit an asteroid every 1000 update loops. Evolutionary runs were restricted to 1000 generations throughout, with the winning average scores over 40 evolutionary runs presented in Sect. 7.

## 6.2   Fitness Assessment

In each of the experiments the fitness of an individual $x$, where $x \in P$ was determined as a linear combination of behavioural novelty and points scored, with the ratio of each dependant upon a multiplier, $\lambda$ $[0, 1]$. The values assigned for behavioural novelty $x_b$ and points scored $x_s$ were normalised $n(x_i)$ against the maximum and minimum scoring individuals in $P$, to assign a final fitness value $f(x)[0, 1]$ (Eqs. 2 and 3).

$$n(x_i) = \frac{x_i - min(P_i)}{max(P_i) - min(P_i)} \tag{2}$$

$$f(x) = \lambda(n(x_b)) + (1 - \lambda)(n(x_s)) \tag{3}$$

# 7   Findings

## 7.1   Objective Performance

Figure 4 outlines the maximum points achieved by an agent for the average scores over 40 evolutionary runs of 1000 generations for varying mixing ratios of objective fitness and novelty search ($\lambda$ $[0 : 1]$). In each generation of the experiments, the average score over 10 games was assessed. Our results show that phenotypic definition directly effects the ability of the novelty search algorithm. Although outperforming random search, pure novelty search ($\lambda = 1$) performs significantly sub optimally over all tested behaviours compared to objective fitness search.

The linear combination of novelty search and objective fitness increases the performance of the agents compared with novelty search ($\lambda < 1$). The results show no significant improvement in objective fitness with the addition of novelty, however, of the five tested behaviours, AC, MAD, GC and MTR produced median fitnesses which outperformed the median objective fitness for $\lambda = \frac{1}{6}$, with only NA under performing. Of all tested behaviours, MTR with a mixing ratio of $\lambda = \frac{1}{6}$ produced the most successful results. The ideal mixing ratio of novelty search and objective fitness remained relatively consistent throughout the experiments. A small ratio of novelty search to objective fitness ($\lambda = \frac{1}{6}$) produced the highest results for GC, MTR, MAD and NA. AC, however, produced comparable results for both $\lambda = \frac{1}{6}$ and $\lambda = \frac{2}{6}$.

## 7.2    State-Action Distance Between Agents

Due to the tested domain being an interactive video game, good progress requires the agent to constantly alter the trajectory of play (i.e. by shooting asteroids). This makes the assessment of play strategies a difficult task. It was therefore decided to compare the full state-action parings for agent controllers to indicate the distance of actions between agents.

In order to assess the diversity of high performing strategies produced within a single evolutionary run, the four highest scoring individuals were stored over

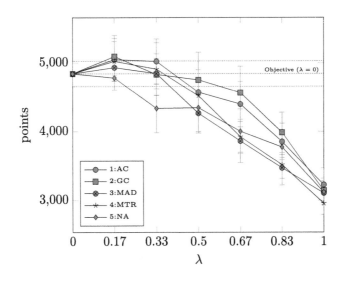

**Fig. 4.** Mean points scored using a linear combination of objective fitness and novelty search. (Error bars represent standard deviation)

the course of one training cycle of 1000 generations for each phenotypic type, using the optimally combined phenotypic-objective ratio ($\lambda = \frac{1}{6}$) alongside a separate, purely objective fitness run ($\lambda = 0$).

The actions performed for all combinations of the input state space were compared for these high scoring agents in order to establish the diversity of controller networks produced by the addition of phenotypic novelty. The state input map used in the trials consisted of a $5 \times 4$ two dimensional binary input matrix, giving $2^{20} = 1048576$ possible combinations. The resulting actions were converted into action strings (e.g. "ULS" = $\{up, left, shoot\}$) and the Hamming distances for each state-action pair between agents within the same phenotypic definitions were compared as a percentage (Table 1).

All Agents across all of the phenotypic definitions (Tables 1a to e), with the exception of agents one and three in the MTR phenotypic type (Table 1a), produce state-action parings with equal or higher distances than the objectively trained agents (Table 1f). This strongly indicates a more diverse set of actions for input states within singular evolutionary runs.

**Table 1.** Hamming distance of state-action mappings

(a) $\frac{1}{6}\lambda$ GC

|   | 1 | 2 | 3 | 4 |
|---|---|---|---|---|
| 1 | 0 | 80 | 73 | 55 |
| 2 | 80 | 0 | 68 | 80 |
| 3 | 73 | 68 | 0 | 77 |
| 4 | 55 | 80 | 77 | 0 |

(b) $\frac{1}{6}\lambda$ AC

|   | 1 | 2 | 3 | 4 |
|---|---|---|---|---|
| 1 | 0 | 75 | 66 | 76 |
| 2 | 75 | 0 | 75 | 59 |
| 3 | 66 | 75 | 0 | 76 |
| 4 | 76 | 59 | 76 | 0 |

(c) $\frac{1}{6}\lambda$ MAD

|   | 1 | 2 | 3 | 4 |
|---|---|---|---|---|
| 1 | 0 | 71 | 76 | 66 |
| 2 | 71 | 0 | 94 | 62 |
| 3 | 76 | 94 | 0 | 75 |
| 4 | 66 | 62 | 75 | 0 |

(d) $\frac{1}{6}\lambda$ MTR

|   | 1 | 2 | 3 | 4 |
|---|---|---|---|---|
| 1 | 0 | 100 | 9 | 61 |
| 2 | 100 | 0 | 99 | 84 |
| 3 | 9 | 99 | 0 | 61 |
| 4 | 61 | 84 | 61 | 0 |

(e) $\frac{1}{6}\lambda$ NA

|   | 1 | 2 | 3 | 4 |
|---|---|---|---|---|
| 1 | 0 | 84 | 78 | 95 |
| 2 | 84 | 0 | 79 | 94 |
| 3 | 78 | 79 | 0 | 69 |
| 4 | 95 | 94 | 69 | 0 |

(f) $\lambda = 0$

|   | 1 | 2 | 3 | 4 |
|---|---|---|---|---|
| 1 | 0 | 38 | 52 | 36 |
| 2 | 38 | 0 | 48 | 55 |
| 3 | 52 | 48 | 0 | 49 |
| 4 | 36 | 55 | 49 | 0 |

## 8   Limitations

Although a linear mixing of objective and novelty search was specifically chosen in order to assess the direct impact that novelty search has upon objective fitness, a comparison of our method with multimodal optimisation techniques would give further insight into the exact nature of this effect.

Also, due to the nature of the tested domain, in which agents have the ability to alter the environment and thus the trajectory of play, assessing the diversity of strategies produced by agents is a difficult task. In this experiment, we chose to highlight the distance between full state space to action mappings, however methods developed in the behavioural sciences may become more applicable to uncertain and changeable domains [5]. Assessment criteria could be established, for example, through the qualitative human assessment of videos of the agents playing the game.

## 9   Conclusion

As shown in Sect. 7, training through a combination of objective function and novelty search is a viable method to produce controllers which are not only high scoring, but also adopt multiple strategies. Alongside this, varying the particular phenotypic definition or metric used may further increase the diversity of strategies adopted. Our results indicate that training through a linear combination of objective fitness and novelty search with multiple phenotypic definitions is a viable methods to produce a range of useful controllers which adopt a diverse range of strategies.

Sandbox [21] and open-world games [22] are recent video game genres which promote exploratory and intrinsically motivated forms of play rather than fixed objectives. Investigations could be undertaken to assess the applicability of training non-player character (NPC) behaviours in such games, using combined objective and phenotypic novelty, where a diverse range of unpredictable and unique behavioural characteristics are required.

Although some of the possible sets of strategies which emerge through novelty search are not directly useful to the domain at hand, it does not follow that these strategies are without use for all domains. An interesting direction to further extend studies analysing the diversity of strategies produced through combined objective and phenotypic search, could assess the transferability of trained agents or agent populations into either different domains, or domains which alter over time.

**Acknowledgements.** We would like to thank the reviewers for their insightful comments and suggestions.

This work was funded by EPSRC through the Media and Arts Technology Programme, an RCUK Doctoral Training Centre EP/G03723X/1. Computational facilities were provided by the MidPlus Regional Centre of Excellence for Computational Science, Engineering and Mathematics, under EPSRC grant EP/K000128/1.

## References

1. Doncieux, S., Mouret, J.-B., Bredeche, N., Padois, V.: Evolutionary robotics: exploring new horizons. In: Doncieux, S., Bredèche, N., Mouret, J.-B. (eds.) New Horizons in Evolutionary Robotics. SCI, vol. 341, pp. 3–25. Springer, Heidelberg (2011)
2. Mouret, J.-B., Doncieux, S.: Encouraging behavioral diversity in evolutionary robotics: an empirical study. Evol. Comput. **20**(1), 91–133 (2012)

3. Cully, A., Mouret, J.-B.: Behavioral repertoire learning in robotics. In: Proceeding of the Fifteenth Annual Conference on Genetic and Evolutionary Computation Conference, pp. 175–182. ACM (2013)
4. Lehman, J., Stanley, K.O., Miikkulainen, R.: Effective diversity maintenance in deceptive domains (2013)
5. Martin, P.R.: Measuring Behaviour: An Introductory Guide. Cambridge University Press, Cambridge (1993)
6. Lehman, J., Stanley, K.O.: Exploiting open-endedness to solve problems through the search for novelty. In: ALIFE, pp. 329–336 (2008)
7. Lehman, J., Stanley, K.O.: Abandoning objectives: evolution through the search for novelty alone. Evol. Comput. **19**(2), 189–223 (2011)
8. Ruiz-Mirazo, K., Peretó, J., Moreno, A.: A universal definition of life: autonomy and open-ended evolution. Orig. Life Evol. Biosph. **34**(3), 323–346 (2004)
9. Johannsen, W.: The genotype conception of heredity. Am. Nat. **45**(531), 129–159 (1911)
10. Gomez, F.J.: Sustaining diversity using behavioral information distance. In: Proceedings of the 11th Annual Conference on Genetic and Evolutionary Computation, pp. 113–120. ACM (2009)
11. Cuccu, G., Gomez, F.: When novelty is not enough. In: Di Chio, C., et al. (eds.) EvoApplications 2011, Part I. LNCS, vol. 6624, pp. 234–243. Springer, Heidelberg (2011)
12. Mouret, J.-B.: Novelty-based multiobjectivization. In: Doncieux, S., Bredèche, N., Mouret, J.-B. (eds.) New Horizons in Evolutionary Robotics. SCI, vol. 341, pp. 139–154. Springer, Heidelberg (2011)
13. Stanley, K.O., Miikkulainen, R.: Evolving neural networks through augmenting topologies. Evol. Comput. **10**(2), 99–127 (2002)
14. Stanley, K.O., Bryant, B.D., Miikkulainen, R.: Real-time neuroevolution in the nero video game. IEEE Trans. Evol. Comput. **9**(6), 653–668 (2005)
15. Hastings, E.J., Guha, R.K., Stanley, K.O.: Evolving content in the galactic arms race video game. In: IEEE Symposium on Computational Intelligence and Games, CIG 2009, pp. 241–248. IEEE (2009)
16. Hausknecht, M., Lehman, J., Miikkulainen, R., Stone, P.: A neuroevolution approach to general atari game playing (2013)
17. Cardamone, L., Loiacono, D., Lanzi, P.L.: Evolving competitive car controllers for racing games with neuroevolution. In: Proceedings of the 11th Annual Conference on Genetic and Evolutionary Computation, pp. 1179–1186. ACM (2009)
18. Thawonmas, R., Ashida, T.: Evolution strategy for optimizing parameters in ms pac-man controller ice pambush 3. In: 2010 IEEE Symposium on Computational Intelligence and Games (CIG), pp. 235–240. IEEE (2010)
19. Hausknecht, M., Khandelwal, P., Miikkulainen, R., Stone, P.: Hyperneat-ggp: a hyperneat-based atari general game player. In: Proceedings of the Fourteenth International Conference on Genetic and Evolutionary Computation Conference, pp. 217–224. ACM (2012)
20. Mnih, V., Kavukcuoglu, K., Silver, D., Graves, A., Antonoglou, I., Wierstra, D., Riedmiller, M.: Playing atari with deep reinforcement learning. arXiv preprint arXiv:1312.5602 (2013)
21. Persson, M.: Minecraft (2009)
22. Murray, S., Ream, D., Doyle, R.: No man's sky (2015)

# It's Time to Stop: A Comparison of Termination Conditions in the Evolution of Game Bots

A. Fernández-Ares[✉], P. García-Sánchez, Antonio M. Mora,
Pedro A. Castillo, J.J. Merelo, María Isabel G. Arenas, and Gustavo Romero

Department of Computer Architecture and Technology,
University of Granada, Granada, Spain
antares@ugr.es

**Abstract.** Evolutionary Algorithms (EAs) are frequently used as a mechanism for the optimization of autonomous agents in games (bots), but knowing when to stop the evolution, when the bots are good enough, is not as easy as it would a priori seem. The first issue is that optimal bots are either unknown (and thus unusable as termination condition) or unreachable. In most EAs trying to find optimal bots fitness is evaluated through game playing. Many times it is found to be noisy, making its use as a termination condition also complicated. A fixed amount of evaluations or, in the case of games, a certain level of victories does not guarantee an optimal result. Thus the main objective of this paper is to test several termination conditions in order to find the one that yields optimal solutions within a restricted amount of time, and that allows researchers to compare different EAs as fairly as possible. To achieve this we will examine several ways of finishing an EA who is finding an optimal bot design process for a particular game, Planet Wars in this case, with the characteristics described above, determining the capabilities of every one of them and, eventually, selecting one for future designs.

**Keywords:** Videogames · RTS · Evolutionary algorithms · Termination criteria · Noisy fitness

## 1 Introduction

Evolutionary Algorithms (EAS) are one of the methods usually applied to find the best autonomous agent for playing a game, i.e. the best *bot* [1–4] through a process mimicking the natural evolution of the species. As in any other algorithm, the termination condition is a key factor as the rest of the experimental setup since it affects the algorithmic performance, with respect to the quality of the yielded solution, and also to the amount of resources devoted to the run. The usual stopping criterion in EAs [5] is reaching a constant number of generations (or evaluations), which is normally related to a fixed *computing power budget* for carrying out the run. Another usual approach is based in a number of generations in which the best solution is not improved or the distance to the optimum is not reduced [6]. However, neither of them might be useful in certain kind of problems such as games, mainly due to the noisy nature of the fitness function [2,7].

© Springer International Publishing Switzerland 2015
A.M. Mora and G. Squillero (Eds.): EvoApplications 2015, LNCS 9028, pp. 355–368, 2015.
DOI: 10.1007/978-3-319-16549-3_29

*Noise* is inherent in most games and even more fighting games, since the enemy behavior, the game environment, the bot itself, or all of them, may have an stochastic component which might make the result of a match vary from one run to the next. Thus, different values would be returned every time the fitness is measured by playing the game.

Independently of the chosen approach, it is usually impossible to reach a global optimum short of managing to obtain a bot that, as in Sun Tzu's "Art of war", is able to beat the opponent without fighting, as the opponents are usually not known before the EA is run. To face this problem, tournaments with previously-known opponents are used in the computation of the fitness function and an "optimum" is reached when a certain number of victories are achieved against them. However, using only one or a small number of opponents may lead to overfitted solutions that only beat the enemies that have been used during the 'training' phase (to compute the fitness) [8], while using more opponents might make evolution unwieldy consuming too many CPU cycles.

These two issues, noise and optimal fitness reachability, are normally not taken into account when choosing how to stop the evolution process. Usual approach is to use a fixed number of evaluations or a fixed amount of time, usually given by the game or challenge constraints. When this constraint is not imposed by a challenge or some other condition, this is not the right approach for finding the best game agent.

That is why finding the optimal termination condition is essential in the search for game bots that competes in a particular challenge. If there is not a fixed evaluation budget, the next usual solution is consume as much as possible, which is fair if you are designing a bot to participate in a competition [9]. However, from a methodological point of view, if you want to compare different approaches to design a bot it needs to be done in conditions that are as fair as possible, which might make *as much as you have got* a bit short on details: a independent stopping criterion is needed, since using any method for the same time or for the same number of evaluations can be misleading. The object of the process is to obtain an optimal bot and some methods might need more evaluations, or more time, than others. From a methodological point of view, it can be considered naive using a number of evaluations as the termination condition.

These three problems, noise, unknown optimum and fair comparison, are common to many games as well as for many other problems without a known (or reachable) set of optimal solutions. In this paper, we try to solve these issues by the introduction of novel stopping criteria for the EAs. They are compared against classical ones, and among themselves when trying to generate competitive bots for video games using Genetic Programming (GP) [10], as this method has proved to be quite flexible and has obtained good results in previous works [11].

*Planet Wars*[1] game has been chosen in our experiment, as it is a simple Real Time Strategy (RTS) combat-based game (only one type of resource, one type of attack and one type of unit), and also it has been widely used in the literature,

---

[1] http://planetwars.aichallenge.org/.

using different generation methods and fitness functions [8,9,12,13]. This game fulfills the two conditions mentioned above; initial position of bots is random and the decisions are stochastic, although the result of the combat is deterministic.

Summarizing, our objective in this study is to find a stopping criteria that converges to optimal solutions and that is independent of the method chosen. To measure the quality of every approach, we will consider time, or number of generations, needed to obtain the solution and the quality of that solution.

In general, it is possible that the conclusions could be extended to any problem solved via EAs with an unknown or unreachable optimum and noisy fitness, since the termination conditions chosen are independent of the game itself and just take into account evolutionary measures. In fact, they could be extended to any problem with the same characteristics.

## 2   State of the Art

Real world optimization problems often involve uncertain environment including noisy and/or dynamic environments [14,15]. Basic strategies to handle noisy fitness functions include using a larger population size, averaging to filter out the noise (re-sampling) [16,17], thresholding (employing a threshold value to be used in a selection operator for noisy fitness functions) [18] or changing the selection criteria. Other authors propose complex methods such as including the multipopulation approach, special operators or case-based memory [19].

In [7], Merelo et al. propose dealing with the problem of noisy fitness functions using two methods, the former based on re-evaluation of surviving individuals and the latter that uses a Wilcoxon test to compare a sample of individuals and partial-order them within the population.

As many EA depend on population diversity for its evolution, a termination condition given in terms of the rate of population diversity decrease would be useful. In this sense, Roche et al. [6] propose terminating the evolution process by analyzing the EA population diversity. Thus, they presents a numeric approximation to steady states that is used to detect the moment that the population has lost its diversity for algorithm termination.

Usually, the algorithm termination is decided based on a heuristic stopping criteria, such as the maximum number of evaluations or on reaching a performance level during the run. When the algorithm converges, it is terminated in order to avoid wasting computational resources. Although these criteria are suitable for well defined benchmark problems (the optimum is known), they are not applicable to real world problems. In these cases, more sophisticated heuristic stopping criteria have to be used [20,21].

In the last years some adaptive alternatives have been proposed as termination conditions. In this sense, Safe et al. [22] present a review of the state-of-the-art in the design of termination conditions and convergence analysis in GAs. The main problem is determining an accurate value for the number of generations, so that the GA convergence is guaranteed. Authors propose searching the minimum number of generations by means of a convergence analysis [23].

Finally, as stated in Hart et al. [24], when calculating metrics of parallel performance, it is incorrect to stop a parallel EA either after a fixed number of iterations or when the average fitness exhibits little variation. In this case, stopping rules based on the attainment of thresholds should be used, i.e. stopping the run when a solution that reaches this threshold is found [25]. Nevertheless, threshold definition requires a good estimation of the optimum of the problem under study, which is unavailable in many cases [22].

In this paper, several stopping criteria will be studied, considering the time needed to obtain the solution and the quality of that solution.

## 3   Methodology and Experimental Setup

As previously stated, in this paper we propose different termination criteria based on different EA features, such as the parameters of the algorithm (maximum number of generations) or the population (improvement, replacement or age).

The differences in performance obtained with each configuration will be analysed and compared. Although in this work we focus on a specific scenario (generation of competitive bots for the Planet Wars game), the results obtained could be applied to other similar problems. Therefore, we justify a general experimental and parameter setup, with the specific restrictions applied to the problem we are addressing.

### 3.1   Algorithm Features

Developed algorithm aim is to generate competitive bots from scratch (without human knowledge), so a GP algorithm has been used. These kind of algorithms have been previously used in the generation of bots in videogames [26–28].

A *generational* approach has been considered in the algorithm. In it, at least half of the population (the best chosen as parents) remains in the population from one generation to the next. This provides the algorithm with a higher exploration factor than a steady-state approach, which is very positive due to the huge search space of the problem we are solving.

A *Score Function* has been proposed in order to measure the quality of a generated bot (a solution or individual in the algorithm). This scoring method tries to reduce the effects of the noisy evaluation (following the guidelines of other works [8]) by computing fitness from the result of 30 different matches against an expert rival. Thus, the function considers the number of victories, turns to win and turns resisted before being defeated by the opponent (in the case of lose). The rival is *ExpGenebot*, introduced in [4], and based on the improvement of the heuristics proposed by a human player. This bot is, for this particular game, the state of the art available. ExpGenebot adapts its behaviour doing an initial analysis of the battle map and depending on the balance of forces between it and the enemy, i.e. location of the fleets and amount of ships. This rival has been chosen due to its potential variety of behaviours, so 30 different representative maps have been chosen for each evaluation (30 matches, 1 match per map), to ensure the bot behaves in a different way in every match. Thus, the fitness evaluation enhances the value of an individual.

Then, the fitness of each individual $i$ of the population is obtained using the next formula where $N$ is the number of simulations[2]:

$$Score_i = \alpha + \beta + \gamma \qquad (1)$$

$$\alpha = v, \alpha \in [0, NB] \qquad (2)$$

$$\beta = NB \times \frac{t_{win} + \frac{1}{N \times t_{MAX} + 1}}{\frac{t_{win}}{v+1} + 1}, \beta \in [0, NB], t_{win} \in [0, NB \times t_{MAX}] \qquad (3)$$

$$\gamma = \frac{t_{defeated}}{NB \times t_{MAX} + 1}, \gamma \in [0, 1], t_{defeated} \in [0, NB \times t_{MAX}] \qquad (4)$$

The terms used are: the number of battles $(NB)$ to test, the number of victories of the individual against ExpGenebot $(v)$, the sum of turns used to beat ExpGenebot $(t_{win})$ in winners simulations, the sum of turns when the individual has been defeated by ExpGenebot $(t_{defeated})$ in losing simulations and the maximum number of turns a battle lasts $(t_{MAX})$. This score aims to favour the victories against the turns to win and turns to be defeated, giving different ratios to each part of the equation. Therefore $\alpha$ has the highest ratio, the term $\beta$ adds an extra score taking into account the number of turns when the individual wins (lower numbers to win implies better bots), following a exponential curve; and finally, $\gamma$ adds a corresponding score from the turns to be beaten (higher number is better, as it is difficult to be beaten).

As previously said, each individual has been tested 30 times in different maps, therefore $NB = 30$, and the limit of turns is the default of the competition $(t_{MAX} = 1000)$.

GP algorithm evolves a binary tree formed by *decisions* (logical expressions that evaluate the current state of the game) and *actions* (the leafs of the tree: the amount of ships to send to a specific planet). This tree is evaluated in each player's planet, analysing the current state of the map/planet (decision), and how many ships send from that planet to an specific target planet (action). These target planets can be the wealthiest, the closest one, etc. owned by the player or the enemy, or neutral. The possible actions and decisions are listed in [11]. Table 1 summarizes the rest of the operators and parameters used in the algorithm. These parameters were also justified in that paper, obtaining competitive bots.

## 3.2 Termination Criteria

The traditional set of stopping criteria are either based on stagnation, checking for the existence of a solution in the set and a fixed budget. By combining them we have designed a set of five different algorithm stop criteria which are going to be checked in the paper, namely:

---

[2] The '1' in all denominators is used to avoid dividing by 0 and for the ratio calculation.

**Table 1.** GP parameters and operators used in the experiments. Details can be found in [11].

| Parameter name | Value |
| --- | --- |
| Population size ($N$) | 32 |
| Number of battles for scoring ($NB$) | 30 |
| Re-evaluation of individuals | Yes |
| Crossover type | Sub-tree crossover |
| Crossover rate | 0.5 |
| Mutation | 1-node mutation |
| Mutation step-size | 0.25 |
| Selection | 2-tournament |
| Replacement | Generational |
| Maximum tree depth | 7 |

- [NG] **Number of Generations**: it is the classical termination criteria in evolutionary algorithms. We will consider 30, 50, 100 and 200 generations since some papers [11] have mentioned the middle value. As indicated in the previous section, Hart [24] claims that this is not the right way to compare different approaches; however, we include it here as a baseline for comparison with the other approaches.
- [AO] **Age of Outliers**: if the age of individual is an outlier in the comparison with the rest of the population then it would be potentially an optimal solution and the algorithm can be stopped. The idea behind this criterion is that an individual surviving for several generations more than the rest of the population lead to be a very good player (much better than the rest), and thus, a potential optimal solution for the problem. The difference between the age of the outlier and the rest of the population is measured considering three factors: 1, 1.5, 2 and 2.5 times the interquartile range (IQR).
- [RT] **Replacement Rate**: when using an elitist strategy in which individuals are replaced only if the offspring is better, the fact that the population stops generating better individuals might be a sign of stagnation. Four different rates have been tested, namely $\frac{n}{2}$, $\frac{n}{4}$, $\frac{n}{8}$, and $\frac{n}{16}$. The values are based in the maximum number of replacements per generation. Our model defines a maximum of $n = N/2$ individuals to be potentially substituted by the offspring. Thus, the parameter values aim to test half of this probability, and half of the previous values, respectively.
- [FT] **Fitness Threshold**: a maximum value to obtain in the evolution could be set considering the top limit of the score function, 45. However, that value is a limit and never reachable unless the bot wins all the matches in just one turn (when the rival code makes a critical error and cannot be run). This, along with the toughness of ExpGenebot, makes the real fitness limit close to 40 instead. Thus, five thresholds have been defined taking this maximum value ($MAX_{SC}$) as a reference, namely: 20 (as half the maximum: $MAX_{SC}/2$), 30

(as half the maximum score plus half this value: $MAX_{SC}/2 + MAX_{SC}/4$), and the division in four parts of the interval these values compose: 22, 24, 26 and 28.

The justification of these values to check is related with the noisy nature of the fitness/score function, which leads us to think that the improvements of fitness will be very limited (very short steps will be attained in the evolution in the range of the high scores). In general, setting a fixed value that is a certain distance away to a known (and maybe unreachable) optimum is a compromise solution, since it is not known in advance whether this lower level will be even reached and, if it is, what would be the effort needed to go beyond that and whether a better solution (even including noise) could be found with a higher value.

- **[FI] Fitness Improvement:** in an ideal evolutionary process the fitness of the best individual must be improved every generation. However, the noisy nature of the problem (or the noisy fitness function) makes this difficult to be measured. Thus, the idea of this criterion is that if the best fitness is not improved during a number of generations, the algorithm must stop. As a difference with the traditional approach, the fitness to test every generation is the best overall, without regarding to which individual it corresponds. This is done because there is a re-evaluation process of all the individuals every generation so, due to the noise, the fitness of the best to date may vary in the following generation. Four possible values will be tested: 3, 7, 10 and 15 generations. These values have been set after a dedicated systematic experimentation phase, thus they are the minimum and maximum thresholds plus two intermediate values. These values would be strictly related with the problem difficulty so in order to set them in other cases an experimental process should be done to test the fitness variability or improvement rate per generation.

The first stop criterion is based in an algorithmic parameter, so the algorithm stops when this parameter reaches a value. For this criterion, the population status does not matter. Remaining criteria are population-based, i.e. they consider some of its features to test if the algorithm must stop. The feature of the population leads the stop criteria and so leads the end of the algorithm.

All these criteria will be tested in the following section. The objective of the experiments conducted is choosing the best stopping criterion among all the proposed, and even more, the best value to set on that criterion, depending on the problem to solve and on its features: noise, difficulty, computational limitations, or performance restrictions.

## 4   Experiments and Results

The experiments conducted have involved 36 runs[3], each of them configured including all the defined stop criteria, and also adding an extra termination one, i.e. getting to 500 generations, in order to avoid non-ending runs.

---

[3] This number has been used in order to leverage the computational power of a cluster with this number of nodes.

Thus, in every execution all the criteria are checked in every generation and, whenever one termination condition is met, the best individual to that moment (according to its score) is stored as the optimal solution for that criterion, because if that were the unique stop criterion, the algorithm would end. Once all the runs have finished or the extra termination has been met, we compute the average number of generations and the average score obtained for the same criterion in all different runs. There could happen that one criterion is never met in a run, then this will not be considered in the computation of that value but it decreases the completion rate of the criterion.

The first study concerns the fitness/score evolution in the runs, along with a study of the statistical differences between results. This has been carried out using a Kruskal-Wallis test, given that the Shapiro test concluded that the samples do not follow a Normal distribution. Thus, Fig. 1.a shows the scores obtained by the best individuals yielded for every stop criterion, and Fig. 1.b plots which stopping criteria are statistically different from others.

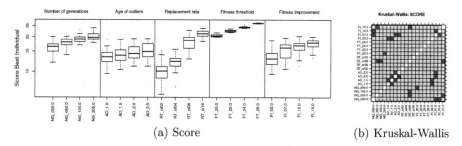

(a) Score                                              (b) Kruskal-Wallis

**Fig. 1.** (a) Scores of the best individuals (of all runs), grouped by criterion. (b) Kruskal-Wallis test of samples of each criterion by score (black means no statistically significant difference has been found). A logarithmic scale has been used in the plots.

The first detail to notice in the figure is the absence of some of the commented stop values for the *Fitness Threshold* criterion, namely 28 and 30, because they have not been reached in any of the runs. This is a problem derived from using a tough rival such as ExpGenebot. Thus, the maximum fitness/score obtained during the evolution is very limited, since it is very difficult that one bot could win against 30 specialised bots [29] (requirement for obtaining at least a score of 30). This is more evident if we take into account that the bots being evolved do not include any adaptive component that analyses the map, as ExpGenebot.

As it can also be seen in Fig. 1.a, all the criterion are well defined, since all the scores grow in every criterion block, so as more restrictive the criterion is (they are met with a lower probability), the higher the obtained score is. The score function is working as expected, even with the presence of noise, as the wide of the boxplots (score dispersion) demonstrates when the criteria become more restrictive. This is true in all the cases except in the *Age of Outliers* which is so far the criterion with the worse results, as it is also proved by the statistical test

(Fig. 1.b) which does not find significant differences between the scores obtained by every age-based criterion and the previous and next ones.

The *Replacement Rate* criterion yields the best distribution of results, with a clear fitness improvement tendency and a very good maximum score, close to that obtained by the *Fitness Thresholds*. However the latter is not as good as it seems, since the success/completion rate (times that the runs has reached that value) is the lowest among all for high threshold values. This will be shown in further results.

With respect to the number of generations reached by every criterion, Fig. 2.a shows their distribution in criterion blocks. It is complemented with the results of the Kruskal-Wallis test (Fig. 2.b), like in the score graphs.

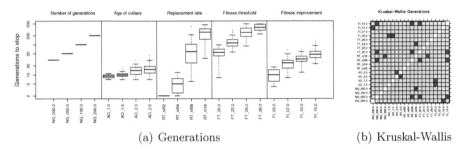

(a) Generations                           (b) Kruskal-Wallis

**Fig. 2.** (a) Generation attained (of all runs), grouped by criterion. (b) Kruskal-Wallis test of samples of each stop criterion by generations (black means no statistically significant difference has been found). A logarithmic scale has been used in the plots.

This figure proved again that the criteria are well defined, since everyone needs more generations to be reached when it is more restrictive (higher value or less probability to be met). *Age of Outliers* stop criterion is the fastest, reaching less generations, but, as previously stated, it is the worst regarding to the score. *Fitness Threshold* stop criterion needs more generations to finish, and even it never meets some of the conditions (as Table 2 shows in the completion rate column). The maximum score (around 27) is obtained in a number of generations close to the final limitation (500). This happens due to the difficulties for getting a high fitness/score value against the tough rival we have chosen for the evaluation. The *Fitness Improvement* criterion need just a few generations to stop. Finally the *Replacement Rate* shows quite variable results, going from a small amount of generations in the first values of the criterion, to a huge number in the most restrictive ones. Thus, sometimes it does not meet these conditions, as in *FT* case.

The Kruskal-Wallis test results (Fig. 2.b) are less conclusive this time, since they refer to the number of generations required for some criteria to be met. Thus, the test shows, for instance, that the most restrictive *FI* stop criteria do not present statistically significant differences with respect to the first *Number of Generations* values, so most of the runs have met the criteria in the same number of generations, which denotes a robustness factor for those criteria.

In addition to these two studies, a new measure factor has been computed by means of a benchmark based in battles against a different competitive bot available in the literature [4] in 100 maps (some of them used during the evolution). This test has been conducted for the best individual obtained when every criterion was met in every run, thus $20 \times 36$ bots have been tested.

The results of the benchmark (percentage of victories $\in [0, 1]$) are displayed in Fig. 3.a. Figure 3.b plots the linear regression analysis between the obtained score by the chosen bots, and the results in the benchmark. It has a value $R^2 = 0.9351$, which means an excellent correlation, and thus, the score function is quite well defined, since a high value corresponds to a very "good individual" indeed. Thus it can be considered the score or the number of victories interchangeably.

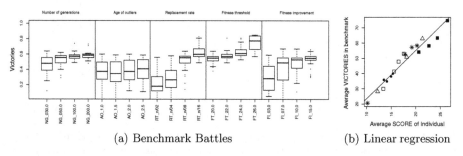

(a) Benchmark Battles                    (b) Linear regression

**Fig. 3.** (a) Percentage of victories in benchmark versus several opponents in 100 maps (training and not training). (b) Linear regression of the Score (fitness) with the results of the benchmark (Percentage of victories).

As it can be seen in Fig. 3.a, the best results are yielded by the most restrictive of each criterion, highlighting the *FT* results. This is also a reinforcement to the correctness of the score function.

Score and generations measures are compared in Fig. 4. As it can be seen, an improvement in the fitness/score means a higher number of generations are required. This happens in almost all the cases, with some exceptions such as some of *RT* criteria, which get a higher score value in less generations than other criteria. However, this happens due to the commented problem of noise.

Finally Table 2 presents all the results as a summary. It also shows the completion rate of every stop criterion (number of runs in which the criterion has been met). Moreover, a comparative set of values have been computed, considering the number of generations equal to 30 (usual in previous papers) as the standard value to relativize the rest.

Results show that the *AO* criterion is not a good one, as more restrictive values do not imply a significant score improvement. This can be taken as a proof that the oldest individuals in the population may not be the best solutions, so they are just the luckiest (win by chance).

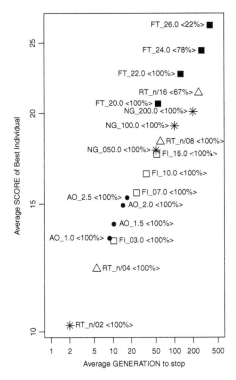

**Fig. 4.** Average score of the best individual and average reached generations per termination criteria.

**Table 2.** Average results of every criterion for the three measures: Number of generations (G), Score (S), and Victories in benchmark (V); plus the Completion rate in experiments (R). Relative values are computed with respect to *NG_30.0*.

| Stopping | Absolute | | | Relative | | | R |
|----------|-------|-------|-------|------|------|------|------|
| Criteria | G | S | V | G | S | V | |
| NC_030.0 | 30.00 | 16.31 | 45.02 | 1.00 | 1.00 | 1.00 | 1.00 |
| NG_050.0 | 50.00 | 17.80 | 52.72 | 1.70 | 1.09 | 1.15 | 1.00 |
| NG_100.0 | 100.00 | 19.21 | 57.25 | 3.37 | 1.18 | 1.25 | 1.00 |
| NG_200.0 | 200.00 | 20.25 | 58.39 | 6.70 | 1.24 | 1.27 | 1.00 |
| AO_1.0 | 8.83 | 13.46 | 35.89 | 0.29 | 0.83 | 0.78 | 1.00 |
| AO_1.5 | 10.33 | 14.07 | 34.83 | 0.34 | 0.86 | 0.76 | 1.00 |
| AO_2.0 | 14.61 | 14.93 | 38.08 | 0.49 | 0.92 | 0.83 | 1.00 |
| AO_2.5 | 17.17 | 15.30 | 39.92 | 0.57 | 0.94 | 0.87 | 1.00 |
| RT_n/02 | 2.00 | 10.20 | 20.58 | 0.07 | 0.63 | 0.45 | 1.00 |
| RT_n/04 | 5.47 | 12.21 | 28.17 | 0.18 | 0.75 | 0.61 | 1.00 |
| RT_n/08 | 78.64 | 18.16 | 50.94 | 2.62 | 1.11 | 1.11 | 1.00 |
| RT_n/16 | 248.21 | 21.34 | 62.92 | 8.27 | 1.31 | 1.37 | 0.66 |
| FT_20.0 | 55.08 | 20.62 | 54.22 | 1.84 | 1.26 | 1.18 | 1.00 |
| FT_22.0 | 127.56 | 22.65 | 58.25 | 4.25 | 1.39 | 1.27 | 1.00 |
| FT_24.0 | 276.71 | 24.39 | 63.39 | 9.22 | 1.50 | 1.38 | 0.77 |
| FT_26.0 | 378.88 | 26.45 | 74.75 | 12.63 | 1.62 | 1.63 | 0.22 |
| FI_03.0 | 10.31 | 13.34 | 30.00 | 0.34 | 0.82 | 0.65 | 1.00 |
| FI_07.0 | 24.56 | 15.54 | 41.39 | 0.82 | 0.95 | 0.90 | 1.00 |
| FI_10.0 | 35.47 | 16.50 | 47.94 | 1.18 | 1.01 | 1.04 | 1.00 |
| FI_15.0 | 52.22 | 17.56 | 53.00 | 1.74 | 1.08 | 1.15 | 1.00 |

Considering only the score, the best stop criterion is *FT*. However, this criterion has a very big disadvantage in this kind of problems: the optimum fitness might not be known, so defining it (setting the limits) would require a deep analysis in advance. Moreover, this criterion needs the highest amount of generations to be met and has the lowest completion rate, as the population may stagnate and do not reach the desired threshold.

The *FI* criterion is useful to 'detect' local optima. Increasing the restriction value of this method lets the EA more generations to escape from a local optimum, obtaining significantly better results. As the EA can quickly converge to a local optima, using this method could be equivalent to set a fixed (but unknown) number of generations, enough to detect a stagnation in the population (that can be useful in some evolutionary approaches). However, the results show that this criterion has stopped in local optima that other methods have surpassed.

Finally, *RT* provides the best results considering all metrics: generations, score and completion rate. It is based on replacement rate, so it indirectly measures how the whole population increases their abilities, without explicitly measure the average fitness. This is useful in this kind of problems, i.e. where there is a noisy fitness function and the optimal solution is unknown.

# 5   Conclusions

Using Evolutionary Algorithms (EAs) to generate bots for playing games have two main issues: the fitness is noisy and optimal bots are either not known or unreachable. This makes it difficult to find a good stopping criterion for the EA. In this paper four different stopping criteria, based in fitness and in the population, have been tested and compared with the classical approach of the fixed number of generations.

Several experiments have been conducted, using different metrics based in a score function, the number of generations reached for each criterion, and the number of victories that the best yielded bots per criterion have obtained against an external rival (not the same used in the fitness computation).

According to the results, initially, a stopping criterion based in *Fitness Threshold* would be the most desirable option, as it attains the best score. However, in this kind of problems, it is quite difficult to find an optimal fitness value to use (normally it is unknown). In addition, this method requires more computational budget, and it is possible that it never ends (the criterion is not met). Given this, and also according to the obtained results, the best option would be using a *Replacement Rate* as stopping criterion, since it is a compromise solution which relies in the population improvement without implicitly use the fitness.

Anyway, the presented results in the work could be used as a reference to choose the best criterion in every case, depending on the problem and on the restrictions. Thus, for instance, if we are facing a competition with a limited amount of computational time, we could select the best criterion considering score and victories taking into account the maximum number of generations that could be reached in that limit.

As future work, new problems (and algorithms) will be addressed to validate the proposed stopping criteria, using different environments and new score functions. In addition, mechanisms to improve the EA will be used in conjunction with the proposed methods, for example, increasing the search space when a stagnation of the population is detected.

**Acknowledgments.** This work has been supported in part by SIPESCA (Programa Operativo FEDER de Andalucía 2007–2013), TIN2011-28627-C04-02 (Spanish Ministry of Economy and Competitivity), SPIP2014-01437 (Dirección General de Tráfico), PRY142/14 (Fundación Pública Andaluza Centro de Estudios Andaluces en la IX Convocatoria de Proyectos de Investigación) and PYR-2014-17 GENIL project (CEI-BIOTIC Granada).

# References

1. Small, R., Bates-Congdon, C.: Agent Smith: Towards an evolutionary rule-based agent for interactive dynamic games. In: IEEE Congress on Evolutionary Computation, CEC 2009, pp. 660–666 (2009)

2. Mora, A.M., Montoya, R., Merelo, J.J., Sánchez, P.G., Castillo, P.A., Laredo, J.L.J., Martínez, A.I., Espacia, A.: Evolving bot AI in unreal$^{TM}$. In: Di Chio, C., et al. (eds.) EvoApplicatons 2010, Part I. LNCS, vol. 6024, pp. 171–180. Springer, Heidelberg (2010)
3. Esparcia-Alcazár, A.I., Martínez-García, A., Mora, A.M., Merelo, J.J., García-Sánchez, P.: Genetic evolution of fuzzy finite state machines to control bots in a first-person shooter game. In: GECCO 2010: Proceedings of the 12th Annual Conference on Genetic and Evolutionary Computation, pp. 829–830. ACM (2010)
4. Fernández-Ares, A., García-Sánchez, P., Mora, A.M., Guervós, J.J.M.: Adaptive bots for real-time strategy games via map characterization. In: CIG, pp. 417–721. IEEE (2012)
5. Bäck, T.: Evolutionary algorithms in theory and practice. Oxford University Press, New York (1996)
6. Roche, D., Gil, D., Giraldo, J.: Detecting loss of diversity for an efficient termination of eas. In: 15th International Symposium on Symbolic and Numeric Algorithms for Scientific Computing, SYNASC 2013, Timisoara, Romania, 23–26 September, pp. 561–566. IEEE (2013)
7. Merelo, J.J., Castillo, P.A., Mora, A., Fernández-Ares, A., Esparcia-Alcázar, A.I., Cotta, C., Rico, N.: Studying and tackling noisy fitness in evolutionary design of game characters. In: Rosa, A., Merelo, J.J., Filipe, J. (eds.) ECTA 2014 - Proceedings of the International Conference on Evolutionary Computation Theory and Applications, pp. 76–85 (2014)
8. Mora, A.M., Fernández-Ares, A., Guervós, J.J.M., García-Sánchez, P., Fernandes, C.M.: Effect of noisy fitness in real-time strategy games player behaviour optimisation using evolutionary algorithms. J. CST **27**(5), 1007–1023 (2012)
9. Fernández-Ares, A., Mora, A.M., Guervós, J.J.M., García-Sánchez, P., Fernandes, C.: Optimizing player behavior in a real-time strategy game using evolutionary algorithms. In: IEEE Conference on Evolutionary Computation, pp. 2017–2024. IEEE (2011)
10. Koza, J.R.: Genetic Programming: On the Programming of Computers by Means of Natural Selection. MIT Press, Cambridge (1992)
11. García-Sánchez, P., Fernández-Ares, A., Mora, A.M., Castillo, P.A., González, J., Guerv, J.J.M.: Tree depth influence in genetic programmingfor generation of competitive agentsfor RTS games. In: Esparcia-Alcázar, A.I., Mora, A.M. (eds.) EvoApplications 2014. LNCS, vol. 8602, pp. 409–419. Springer, Heidelberg (2014)
12. Lara-Cabrera, R., Cotta, C., Fernández-Leiva, A.: On balance and dynamism in procedural content generation with self-adaptive evolutionary algorithms. Nat. Comput. **13**(2), 157–168 (2014)
13. Nogueira-Collazo, M., Fernández-Leiva, A.: Virtual player design using self-learning via competitive coevolutionary algorithms. Nat. Comput. **13**(2), 131–144 (2014)
14. Jin, Y., Branke, J.: Evolutionary optimization in uncertain environments - a survey. IEEE Trans. Evol. Comput. **9**(3), 303–317 (2005)
15. Qian, C., Yu, Y., Zhou, Z.H.: Analyzing evolutionary optimization in noisy environments. CoRR: abs/1311.4987 (2013). http://arxiv.org/abs/1311.4987
16. Branke, J.: Creating robust solutions by means of evolutionary algorithms. In: Eiben, A.E., Bäck, T., Schoenauer, M., Schwefel, H.-P. (eds.) PPSN 1998. LNCS, vol. 1498, pp. 119–128. Springer, Heidelberg (1998)
17. Branke, J.: Evolutionary optimization in dynamic environments, pp. 125–172. Kluwer Academic Publisher (2001)

18. Markon, S., Arnold, D., Bäck, T., Beielstein, T., Beyer, H.: Thresholding - a selection operator for noisy ES. In: Kim, J.-H., Zhang, B.-T., Fogel, G., Kuscu, I. (eds.) Proceedings of 2001 Congress on Evolutionary Computation (CEC 2001), pp. 465–472. IEEE Press, Piscataway (2001)
19. Bhattacharya, M., Islam, R., Mahmood, A.: Uncertainty and evolutionary optimization: A novel approach. CoRR abs/1407.4000 (2014)
20. Goel, T., Stander, N.: A non-dominance-based online stopping criterion for multi-objective evolutionary algorithms. Int. J. Numer. Meth. Eng. **84**(6), 661–684 (2010)
21. Wagner, T., Trautmann, H.: Online convergence detection for evolutionary multi-objective algorithms revisited. In: Fogel, G., Ishibuchi, H. (eds.) Proceedings of International Congress on Evolutionary Computation (CEC 2010), pp. 3554–3561. IEEE press (2010)
22. Safe, M., Carballido, J.A., Ponzoni, I., Brignole, N.B.: On stopping criteria for genetic algorithms. In: Bazzan, A.L.C., Labidi, S. (eds.) SBIA 2004. LNCS (LNAI), vol. 3171, pp. 405–413. Springer, Heidelberg (2004)
23. Rudolph, G.: Convergence analysis of canonical genetic algorithms. IEEE Trans. Neural Netw. **5**, 96–101 (1994)
24. Hart, W., Baden, S., Belew, R., Kohn, S.: Analysis of the numerical effects of parallelism on a parallel genetic algorithm. In: Proceedings of the 10th International Parallel Processing Symposium, pp. 606–612. IEEE Computer Society (1996)
25. Sena, G., Megherbi, D., Isern, G.: Implementation of a parallel genetic algorithm on a cluster of workstations: travelling salesman problem, a case study. Future Gener. Comput. Syst. **17**, 477–488 (2001)
26. Esparcia-Alcázar, A.I., Moravec, J.: Fitness approximation for bot evolution in genetic programming. Soft Comput. **17**(8), 1479–1487 (2013)
27. Harper, R.: Evolving robocode tanks for Evo robocode. Genet. Programm. Evolvable Mach. **15**(4), 403–431 (2014)
28. Fernández Leiva, A.J., O'Valle Barragán, J.L.: Decision tree-based algorithms for implementing bot AI in UT2004. In: Ferrández, J.M., Álvarez Sánchez, J.R., de la Paz, F., Toledo, F.J. (eds.) IWINAC 2011, Part I. LNCS, vol. 6686, pp. 383–392. Springer, Heidelberg (2011)
29. Wolpert, D.H., Macready, W.G.: No free lunch theorems for optimization. IEEE Trans. Evol. Comput. **1**(1), 67–82 (1997)

# General Video Game Evaluation Using Relative Algorithm Performance Profiles

Thorbjørn S. Nielsen[1], Gabriella A.B. Barros[1], Julian Togelius[2],
and Mark J. Nelson[3]($\boxtimes$)

[1] Center for Computer Games Research, IT University of Copenhagen,
Copenhagen, Denmark
{thse,gbar}@itu.dk
[2] Department of Computer Science and Engineering, New York University,
New York, NY, USA
julian@togelius.com
[3] Anadrome Research, Copenhagen, Denmark
mjn@anadrome.org

**Abstract.** In order to generate complete games through evolution we need generic and reliably evaluation functions for games. It has been suggested that game quality could be characterised through playing a game with different controllers and comparing their performance. This paper explores that idea through investigating the relative performance of different general game-playing algorithms. Seven game-playing algorithms was used to play several hand-designed, mutated and randomly generated VGDL game descriptions. Results discussed appear to support the conjecture that well-designed games have, in average, a higher performance difference between better and worse game-playing algorithms.

## 1 Introduction

How well do knowledge-free algorithms play really bad video games? This might not be a question that has kept you awake at night, but as we shall show there are excellent reasons to consider it. Reasons having to do with understanding fundamental design characteristics of a broad class of simple video games, and laying the groundwork for automatically generating such games.

One way to generate complete games might be to search a space of games represented in a programming language like C or Java. However, the proportion of programs in such languages that can in any way be considered a game is quite small. Increasing the density of games in the search space can be achieved by searching programs defined in a game description language (GDL) designed to encode games.

Even searching a reasonably well defined space of games still supposes that we have a way of automatically telling good games from bad games (or not-quite-so-bad games from really bad games). In other words, we need a fitness function. Part of the fitness function could consist in inspecting the rules as expressed in the GDL, e.g. to make sure that there are winning conditions which could

A.M. Mora and G. Squillero (Eds.): EvoApplications 2015, LNCS 9028, pp. 369–380, 2015.
DOI: 10.1007/978-3-319-16549-3_30

in principle be fulfilled. But there are many bad games that fulfil such criteria. To really understand a game, you need to play it. It seems the fitness function therefore needs to incorporate a capacity to play the games it is evaluating.

This game-playing capacity needs to be *general*, because we know almost nothing about the games that will be evaluated. We can therefore not incorporate any domain knowledge about these games; we need algorithms that are as *knowledge-free* as possible. Examples of such algorithms are the various tree-search algorithms, such as Minimax and Monte Carlo tree search (MCTS), that have been widely used for playing various games. But online evolutionary algorithms might also be used as knowledge-free algorithms. In case a heuristic representing the quality of a particular in-game state is need, such a heuristic should be as neutral as possible, e.g. the score of the game.

Just being able to play a game does not in itself tell us how good the game is. Many boring games are perfectly playable by an algorithm. And because we don't know the game, we don't know what constitutes good or bad play, compared to how well or badly the game could be played. Instead we propose a measure of *relative* performance between algorithms, the Relative Algorithm Performance Profile (RAPP). The intuition is that good games are likely to have high skill differentiation: good players get better outcomes than bad players. A game that is *insensitive* to skill, by contrast, is not likely to be a good one. We therefore formulate the following hypothesis: the performance difference (measured as score and/or win-rate) between generally better game-playing algorithms and generally worse game-playing algorithms is on average higher for well-designed games than for poorly designed games. But there might very well be other interesting differences between classes of games that can be discerned by looking at the performance profiles of sets of game-playing algorithms; this study is intended as a preliminary investigation into the hypothesis that RAPP is a productive way of differentiating games.

We carry out this investigation using the General Video Game Playing platform (GVG-AI) and its associated Video Game Description Language (VGDL). This framework makes 20 hand-designed games available, mostly versions of well-known arcade games. We contrast those games with a large number of randomly generated games in the same language, and with a large number of "mutations" of the hand-designed games. A core assumption we make is that the hand-designed games are, on average, better designed than the randomly generated ones. We calculate a performance profile using several game-playing algorithms available in the GVG-AI framework and some new algorithms. The concrete contributions of this paper thus include two new variations on Monte Carlo-based game-playing, as well as a quantitative investigation of the performance profiles of these algorithms and the associated methodology for performing this study. However, we primarily see this work as groundwork for a reliable game fitness function, that will eventually allow us to generate good new sets of game rules.

## 2   Background

The idea of generating complete games through algorithms is not itself new. The problem in full generality is quite large, so usually a subset of the general problem is tackled. Videogames may be comprised of a large number of tangible and intangible components, including rules, graphical assets, genre conventions, cultural context, controllers, character design, story and dialog, screen-based information displays, and so on [2,7,8].

In this paper we look specifically at generating game rules; and more specifically the rules of arcade-style games based on graphical movement and local interaction between game elements, represented in VGDL. The two main approaches that have been explored in generating game rules are reasoning through constraint solving [11] and search through evolutionary computation or similar stochastic optimisation [1,4,13].

Generating a set of rules that makes for an interesting and fun game is a hard task. The arguably most successful attempt so far, Browne's Ludi system, produced a new board game of sufficient quality to be sold as a boxed product [1]. However, it succeeded partly due to restricting its generation domain to the rules of a rather tightly constrained space of board games. A key stumbling block for search-based approaches to game generation is the fitness/evaluation function. This function takes a complete game as input and outputs an estimate of its quality. Ludi uses a mixture of several measures based on automatic play of games, including balance, drawishness and outcome uncertainty. These measures are well-chosen for two-player board games, but may not transfer well to video games or single-player games, which have in a separate analysis been deemed to be good targets for game generation [12]. Other researchers have attempted evaluation functions based on the learnability of the game by an algorithm [13] or an earlier and more primitive version of the characteristic that is explored in this paper, performance profile of a set of algorithms [4].

### 2.1 Game Description Languages

Regardless of which approach to game generation is chosen, one needs a way to represent the games that are being created.[1] For a sufficiently general description of games, it stands to reason that the games are represented in a reasonably generic language, where every syntactically valid game description can be loaded into a specialised game engine and executed. There have been several attempts to design such GDLs. One of the more well-known is the Stanford GDL, which is used for the General Game Playing Competition [5]. That language is tailored to describing board games and similar discrete, turn-based games; it is also arguably too verbose and low-level to support search-based game generation. The various game generation attempts discussed above feature their own GDLs of different levels of sophistication; however, there has not until recently been a GDL for suitably large space of video games.

### 2.2 VGDL

The Video Game Description Language (VGDL) is a GDL designed to express 2D arcade-style video games of the type common on hardware such as the Atari

---

[1] See [9] for a discussion of game-rule representation choices.

2600 and Commodore 64. It can express a large variety of games in which the player controls a moving avatar (player character) and where the rules primarily define what happens when objects interact with each other in a two-dimensional space. VGDL was designed by a set of researchers [3,6] (and implemented by Schaul [10]) in order to support both general video game playing and video game generation. The language has an internal set of classes, properties and types that each object can defined by.

Objects have physical properties (i.e. position, direction) which can be altered either by the properties defined, or by interactions defined between specific objects. A VGDL description has four parts: the SpriteSet, which defines the ontology of the game – which sprites exist and what can they do; the LevelMapping, which maps from level description to game state; the InteractionSet, which defines what happens when sprites overlap, and the TerminationSet which defines how the game can be won or last.

## 2.3   The GVG-AI Framework

The GVG-AI framework is a testbed for testing general game playing controllers against games specified using VGDL. Controllers are called once at the beginning of each game for setup, and then once per clock tick to select an action. Controllers do not have access to the VGDL descriptions of the games. They receive only the game's current state, passed as a parameter when the controller is asked for a move. However these states can be forward-simulated to future states. Thus the game rules are not directly available, but a simulatable model of the game can be used.

```
BasicGame
   SpriteSet
      city > Immovable color=GREEN img=city
      explosion > Flicker limit=5 img=explosion
      movable >
         avatar > ShootAvatar stype=explosion
         incoming >
            incoming_slow > Chaser stype=city color=ORANGE speed=0.1
            incoming_fast > Chaser stype=city color=YELLOW speed=0.3

   LevelMapping
      c > city
      m > incoming_slow
      f > incoming_fast

   InteractionSet
      movable wall > stepBack
      incoming city > killSprite
      city incoming > killSprite scoreChange=-1
      incoming explosion > killSprite scoreChange=2

   TerminationSet
      SpriteCounter stype=city win=False
      SpriteCounter stype=incoming win=True
```

**Fig. 1.** Example of VGDL description - a simple implementation of the game Missile Command

The framework additionally contains 20 hand-designed games, which mostly consist of interpretations of classic video games. Figure 1 shows the VGDL description of the game *Missile Command.*

## 3   Method

There are three types of games tested: human-written VGDL games, mutated versions of those games, and randomly generated games.

### 3.1   Example Games

Two of the 20 games from the GVG-AI framework were deemed too monotonous after initial tests. In these two games the controllers all had similar scores for each run—or only one controller was able to increase its score. The remaining 18 hand-designed VGDL game descriptions are used as the baseline. Most are inspired

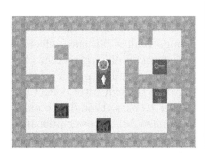
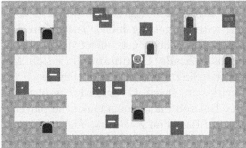
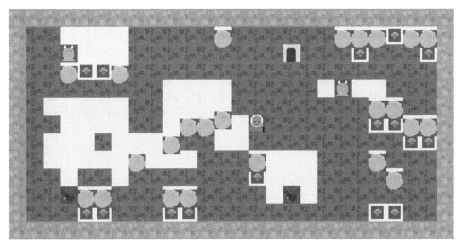

**Fig. 2.** A visual representation of a few of the VGDL example games. From top-left: *Zelda*, *Portals* and *Boulderdash*

by classic arcade (e.g. Boulderdash, Frogger, Missile Command and Pacman). The player controls a single avatar which must be moved quickly around in a 2D setting to win, or to get a high score. The player can increment a score counter in all of the games. A brief descriptions of each game (Fig. 2):

**Aliens** Based on *Space Invaders*. Aliens are spawned from the top of the screen; the player wins by shooting them all. **Boulderdash** Based on *Boulder Dash*. The avatar has to dig through a cave to collect diamonds while avoiding being smashed by falling rocks or killed by enemies. **Butterflies** The avatar has to capture all butterflies before all the cocoons are opened. Cocoons open when a butterfly touches them. **Chase** Chase and kill fleeing goats. However, if a fleeing goat encounters the corpse of another, it gets angry and starts chasing the player instead. **Digdug** Base on *Dig Dug*. The avatar collects gold coins and gems, digs through a cave, and avoids or shoots boulders at enemies. **Eggomania** Based on *Eggomania*. The avatar moves from left to right collecting eggs that fall from a chicken at the top of the screen, in order to use these eggs to shoot at the chicken, killing it. **Firecaster** The goal is to reach the exit by burning wood that is on the way. Ammunition is required to set things on fire. **Firestorms** The player must avoid flames from hell gates until reaching the exit of a maze. **Frogs** Based on *Frogger*. The player is a frog that has to cross a road and a river, without getting killed. **Infection** The objective is to infect all healthy animals. The player gets infected by touching a bug. Medics can cure infected animals. **Missile Command** Based on *Missile Command*. The player has to destroy falling missiles, before they reach their destinations. The player wins if any cities are saved. **Overload** The player must get to the exit after collecting coins. But too many coins make the player too heavy to pass through the exit. **Pacman** Based on *Pac-Man*. The goal is to clear a maze full of power pills and pellets, and avoid or destroy ghosts. **Portals** The objective is to get to a certain point using portals to go from one place to another, while at the same time avoiding lasers. **Seaquest** Based on *Seaquest*. The avatar is a submarine that rescue divers and avoids sea animals that can kill it. The goal is to maximise score. **Survive Zombies** The player has to flee zombies until time runs out, and can collect honey to kill the zombies. **Whackamole** Based on *Whac-a-Mole*. Must collect moles that appear from holes, and avoid a cat that mimics the moles. **Zelda** Based on *Legend of Zelda*. The objective is to find a key in a maze and leave the level. The player also has a sword to defend against enemies.

### 3.2   Controllers

Seven general videogame controllers were used to test the games. The controllers use different approaches, with a varying degree of intelligence. Three of the controllers are included in the GVG-AI framework, while the remaining were implemented for this work. Except for *OneStep-Heuristic*, the controllers only evaluate a given state according to its score and win/loss status.

**MCTS.** GVG-AI sample controller. "Vanilla" MCTS using UCT.

**GA.** GVG-AI sample controller. Uses a genetic algorithm to evolve a sequence of actions.

**OneStep-Heuristic.** GVG-AI sample controller. Heuristically evaluates the states reachable through one-step lookahead. The heuristic takes into account the locations of NPCs and certain other objects.

**OneStep-Score.** Similar to *OneStep-heuristic*, but only uses the score and win/loss status to evalue states.

**Random.** Chooses a random action from those available in the current state.

**DoNothing.** Returns a nil action. Literally does nothing.

**Explorer.** Design specifically to play the arcade-style games of the GVG-AI framework. Unlike the other controllers which utilise open-loop searches, it stores information about visited tiles and prefers visiting unvisited locations. Also addresses a common element of the VGDL example games, randomness. The controller gains an advantage by simulating the results of actions repeatedly, before deciding the best move.

### 3.3 Mutation of Example Games

A mutation process was repeatedly applied for each of the 20 example games mentioned in Sect. 3.1. The process consisted of changing the set of interaction rules (i.e. lines from the InteactionSet) defined in each game description. For each mutation, each interaction rule had a 25 % chance of being mutated, but with a requirement that at least one rule were changed. Mutation occurred by changing the objects in that interaction rule, the function on collision between said objects, and/or the function's parameters.

Several contrains were used during each mutation to avoid games with non-valid descriptions (which can cause crashes in the GVG-AI framework). Additionally, several constraints were used for the different function parameters, as to only allow "realistic" values. The range of these constraints were extrapolated (and slightly extended) from the example games. For instance, the parameter *limit* used by certain rules was limited to values between 0 and 10, as the same is true for the rules of the example games. This process was applied 10 times for each example game description, resulting in 200 generated game descriptions.

When testing the mutated games the same level descriptions as for their original counterparts were used (those mentioned in Sect. 3.1).

### 3.4 Random Game Generation

A set of 400 random VGDL game descriptions were generated by constructing the textual lines for different parts of a VGDL description: Generating an array of sprites (for the SpriteSet), interaction-rules (InteractionSet), termination-rules (TerminationSet) and level mappings (LevelMapping) (Fig. 3).

Before generating descriptions, we used similar constraints to those in Sect. 3.3, partly to avoid generating descriptions with invalid elements, and partly to increase the proportion of interesting outcomes. The number of sprites, interaction, and termination rules were randomly chosen, limited to 25, 25, and 2,

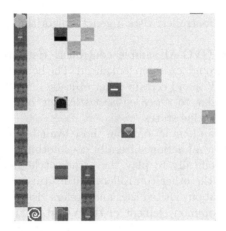

**Fig. 3.** Visual representation of one of the 400 randomly generated VGDL games

respectively. A simple level (only containing one of each sprite) was generated
for each of the generated games for test purposes.

## 4    Results

The seven controllers mentioned in Sect. 3.2 were used to play through a set
of example-, mutated and randomly generated games. Because of CPU budget
limitations, each game was played for a maximum of 800 clock ticks, and each
controller was restricted to use 50 ms on each tick. In the following sections,
we show results of these tests, analyse the average of all play-throughs for each
controller, and compare the results with each other.

To more accurately compare the score for the different controllers across the
range of different games, we normalise each score using a max-min normalisation.
Normalised averages and win rate averages are shown in Figs. 7 and 8, respectively. In Fig. 7, it is possible to see that the difference between the highest and
lowest scores is greater in the example and mutated games than in the generated
games. On the other hand, the average win rate of generated games surpasses
both examples and mutated games, as shown in Fig. 8.

In addition to the score and win-rate, the average entropy of actions chosen
for the player avatar is shown in the tables below.

### 4.1    Example Games

Averages and win-rates from the 18 human-designed example games are shown
in Fig. 4. The distributions of normalised scores show that more intelligent
controllers tend to have more success. It is worth noticing that the *score mean*
and *normalised score mean* have slightly different orderings. Notice also that distributions are slightly different when analysing the results of individual games.
For instance, in *Aliens*, Random has a higher average than Onestep.

| controller | score mean | std.dev. | normalised-mean | winrate | act-entropy |
|---|---|---|---|---|---|
| Explorer | 42.94 | 121.55 | 0.7966 | 0.4467 | 0.8860 |
| MCTS | 23.14 | 86.39 | 0.4935 | 0.2489 | 0.9006 |
| GA | 11.98 | 51.08 | 0.4010 | 0.1533 | 0.7052 |
| Onestep-S | 14.48 | 27.28 | 0.4149 | 0.0844 | 0.8848 |
| Onestep-H | 3.73 | 9.81 | 0.2350 | 0.1111 | 0.1943 |
| Random | 7.52 | 17.01 | 0.2493 | 0.0556 | 0.9016 |
| DoNothing | 0.39 | 4.02 | 0.1317 | 0.0556 | 0 |

**Fig. 4.** Results from the 20 example games

## 4.2 Mutated Example Games

When mutating games, two types of games are problematic: Games where the controllers never increase their score (and never win), and games where too many objects are created and each frame end up taking too long (>50 ms). We exclude both types of games in the following analysis.

Averages from playing the remaining 146 mutated games (of 200 total) are shown in Fig. 5. The scores have higher means and standard deviations, indicating outliers in the data. The ordering of the *normalised score mean*, however, shows a similar pattern as for the example games, with Explorer again excelling.

| controller | score mean | std.dev. | normalised-mean | win-rate | act-entropy |
|---|---|---|---|---|---|
| Explorer | 392.08 | 6441.77 | 0.8361 | 0.3055 | 0.8372 |
| MCTS | 140.49 | 1097.93 | 0.4799 | 0.1510 | 0.9012 |
| GA | 88.96 | 756.92 | 0.4254 | 0.1274 | 0.6693 |
| Onestep-S | 128.82 | 706.79 | 0.4418 | 0.1049 | 0.8444 |
| Onestep-H | 82.67 | 762.93 | 0.2580 | 0.1866 | 0.2033 |
| Random | 69.70 | 666.81 | 0.2581 | 0.1077 | 0.9030 |
| DoNothing | 81.55 | 945.71 | 0.1819 | 0.0959 | 0 |

**Fig. 5.** Results from mutated games

## 4.3 Randomly Generated Games

Figure 6 shows results for the 65 randomly generated games, with problematic games removed according to the same criteria as in the previous section.

First of all, *score std. deviations* are much higher than in the previous games, with the minimum being 199,406.58, over 1500 times larger than the highest in the set of example games (i.e. 121.55, by Explorer). Clearly, only the *normalised mean* can be on this set to compare scores across the different game types. The *normalised score means* and *win-rates* both have values that are more closely clustered together, than in the previous game sets.

| *controller* | *score mean* | *std.dev.* | *normalised-mean* | *win-rate* | *act-entropy* |
|---|---|---|---|---|---|
| Explorer | −18 207.91 | 227 282.72 | 0.6193 | 0.2566 | 0.7193 |
| MCTS | −4035.85 | 258 890.78 | 0.4395 | 0.2769 | 0.8392 |
| GA | −3501.65 | 262 508.97 | 0.4399 | 0.2480 | 0.5767 |
| Onestep-S | −16 680.67 | 231 600.95 | 0.3916 | 0.2191 | 0.8197 |
| Onestep-H | −25 728.97 | 195 365.78 | 0.3640 | 0.2025 | 0.4022 |
| Random | −23 348.24 | 199 405.58 | 0.3195 | 0.2105 | 0.8553 |
| DoNothing | −3051.34 | 259 562.33 | 0.3747 | 0.1846 | 0 |

**Fig. 6.** Results from randomly generated games

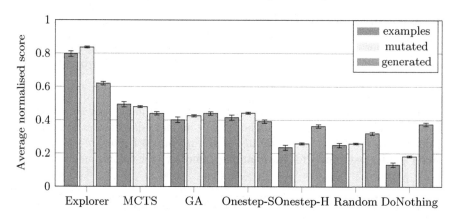

**Fig. 7.** Average normalised score

## 5    Discussion

The results in Sect. 4 display some interesting patterns. Win rates suggest a relationship between intelligent controllers' success and better game design; for better designed games, the relative performance of different types of algorithms differ more. This corroborates our hypothesis that RAPPs can be used to differentiate between games of different quality. In randomly generated games, which arguably tend to be less interesting than the others, smarter controllers (e.g. Explorer and MCTS) do only slightly better than the worse ones (i.e. Random and DoNothing). This is due to a general a lack of consistency between rules generated in this manner. Mutated games, however, derive from a designed game. Therefore, they maintain some characteristics of the original idea, which can improve the VGDL description's gameplay and playability. Furthermore, it is interesting that Random and DoNothing do well in some games, as seen in Fig. 8. While it is possible that random actions can result in good outcomes, this chance is very low, especially when compared to the chance of making informed decisions. In spite of that both Random and DoNothing do fairly well in randomly generated games. The performance of DoNothing emerges as a secondary

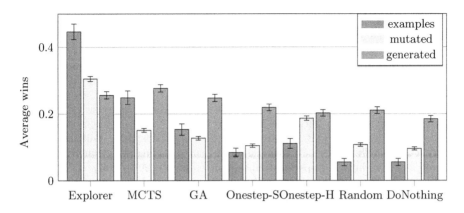

**Fig. 8.** Average wins

indicator of (good) design: in human-designed games, DoNothing very rarely wins or even scores.

## 6   Conclusion

Our intent has been to investigate evaluating video games via the performance of game-playing algorithms. We hypothesised that the performance difference between good and bad game-playing algorithms is higher on well-designed games, and therefore can be used as at least a partial proxy for game quality. To test this theory, we had seven controllers with varying levels of skill play 18 human-designed, 146 mutated, and 65 randomly generated VGDL games. The results seem to corroborate our initial conjecture, showing a clear distinction between results of more and less intelligent controllers for human-designed games but not for random games. We also suggest new controllers for GVG-AI: Explorer, OneStep-Score and DoNothing. The first one in particular shows strong overall performance compared to existing baselines such as "vanilla" MCTS.

**Acknowledgments.** Gabriella A.B. Barros acknowledges financial support from CAPES Scholarship and Science Without Borders program, Bex 1372713-3. Thanks to Diego Perez, Spyros Samothrakis, Tom Schaul, and Simon Lucas for useful discussions.

## References

1. Browne, C.: Automatic generation and evaluation of recombination games. Ph.D. thesis, Queensland University of Technology (2008)
2. Cook, M., Colton, S.: Ludus ex machina: building a 3d game designer that competes alongside humans. In: Proceedings of the 5th International Conference on Computational Creativity (2014)

3. Ebner, M., Levine, J., Lucas, S.M., Schaul, T., Thompson, T., Togelius, J.: Towards a video game description language. Dagstuhl Follow-Ups, vol. 6 (2013). http://drops.dagstuhl.de/opus/volltexte/2013/4338/

4. Font, J.M., Mahlmann, T., Manrique, D., Togelius, J.: Towards the automatic generation of card games through grammar-guided genetic programming. In: FDG, pp. 360–363 (2013)

5. Genesereth, M., Love, N., Pell, B.: General game playing: overview of the AAAI competition. AI Mag. **26**(2), 62–72 (2005)

6. Levine, J., Congdon, C.B., Ebner, M., Kendall, G., Lucas, S.M., Miikkulainen, R., Schaul, T., Thompson, T.: General video game playing. Dagstuhl Follow-Ups, vol. 6 (2013). http://drops.dagstuhl.de/opus/volltexte/2013/4337/

7. Liapis, A., Yannakakis, G.N., Togelius, J.: Computational game creativity. In: Proceedings of the 5th International Conference on Computational Creativity (2014)

8. Nelson, M.J., Mateas, M.: Towards automated game design. In: Basili, R., Pazienza, M.T. (eds.) AI*IA 2007. LNCS (LNAI), vol. 4733, pp. 626–637. Springer, Heidelberg (2007)

9. Nelson, M.J., Togelius, J., Browne, C., Cook, M.: Chapter 6: Rules and mechanics. In: Procedural Content Generation in Games: A Textbook and an Overview of Current Research. Springer (2015, to appear). http://www.pcgbook.com

10. Schaul, T.: A video game description language for model-based or interactive learning. In: Proceedings of the 2013 IEEE Conference on Computational Intelligence in Games, pp. 1–8 (2013)

11. Smith, A.M., Mateas, M.: Variations forever: flexibly generating rulesets from a sculptable design space of mini-games. In: Proceedings of the 2010 IEEE Symposium on Computational Intelligence and Games, pp. 273–280 (2010)

12. Togelius, J., Nelson, M.J., Liapis, A.: Characteristics of generatable games. In: Proceedings of the 5th Workshop on Procedural Content Generation in Games (2014)

13. Togelius, J., Schmidhuber, J.: An experiment in automatic game design. In: Proceedings of the 2008 IEEE Symposium on Computational Intelligence and Games, pp. 111–118 (2008)

# A Progressive Approach to Content Generation

Mohammad Shaker[1], Noor Shaker[2,(✉)], Julian Togelius[3],
and Mohamed Abou-Zleikha[4]

[1] Joseph Fourier University, Grenoble, France
mohammadshakergtr@gmail.com
[2] IT University of Copenhagen, Copenhagen, Denmark
nosh@itu.dk
[3] New York University, New York City, USA
julian@togelius.com
[4] Aalborg University, Aalborg, Denmark
moa@create.aau.dk

**Abstract.** PCG approaches are commonly categorised as constructive, generate-and-test or search-based. Each of these approaches has its distinctive advantages and drawbacks. In this paper, we propose an approach to Content Generation (CG) – in particular level generation – that combines the advantages of constructive and search-based approaches thus providing a fast, flexible and reliable way of generating diverse content of high quality. In our framework, CG is seen from a new perspective which differentiates between two main aspects of the gameplay experience, namely the order of the in-game interactions and the associated level design. The framework first generates timelines following the search-based paradigm. Timelines are game-independent and they reflect the rhythmic feel of the levels. A *progressive*, constructive-based approach is then implemented to evaluate timelines by mapping them into level designs. The framework is applied for the generation of puzzles for the *Cut the Rope* game and the results in terms of performance, expressivity and controllability are characterised and discussed.

## 1 Introduction

In procedural content generation for games (PCG), a commonly used distinction is that between constructive, generate-and-test and search-based approaches [1]. Constructive approaches work in a single pass and generate content in a predictable and typically short time. Several classic PCG algorithms are constructive in nature, e.g. Perlin noise, L-systems and variations on dungeon diggers, and constructive PCG is widely used in commercial games for "decorative" elements such as skyboxes and plants [2]. However, when generating content with playability constraints (also called "necessary" content), such as puzzles that need to have a solution, maps that need to be balanced or levels that need to be winnable, constructive approaches run into the problem that there is typically no way to guarantee such properties. To the extent that constructive methods are used for such content, the expressive range of the algorithms tend to

A.M. Mora and G. Squillero (Eds.): EvoApplications 2015, LNCS 9028, pp. 381–393, 2015.
DOI: 10.1007/978-3-319-16549-3_31

be severely curtailed in order to avoid the generation of unplayable content; see for example the unimaginative generated levels in many roguelikes and infinite runners.

One solution to this problem with constructive algorithms is to generate-and-test: apply some sort of test (is the map balanced? the puzzle solvable?) and keep regenerating until the content is good enough. However, depending on how strict the test is, it might take very long time until acceptable content is generated.

A more informed version of generate-and-test is search-based PCG. Here, an evolutionary algorithm or other stochastic global search algorithm is used to search content space for content that optimally satisfies some evaluation function – for example, map balance or level winnability. Evolutionary algorithms have excellent facilities for generating sets of diverse content artefacts, even while satisfying multiple fitness functions [3]. However, search-based approaches are still in general much slower than constructive approaches, often too slow to be used in real time. To make matters worse, the more sophisticated the playability demands are, the more computationally expensive the evaluation function becomes. In particular simulation-based evaluation functions which require an agent playing through part of the game are very time-demanding.

In this paper we present a new attempt at combining the diversity, flexibility and playability-preserving ability of search-based approaches with the speed of constructive approaches. We call this a *progressive* approach to the generation of playable content. The first step is to turn the CG problem on its head: instead of generating playable content directly, we first generate a timeline of in-game interactions that need to be performed in order to successfully play through the content artefact. This is done using a search-based approach, but as we can use a simple evaluation function based on lightweight simulation this part can be done quickly. Every time a timeline is evaluated, it is turned into level content. This is done using a constructive approach, where each point in the timeline is converted into a part of the level. As we shall see, this allows fast and reliable level generation with a considerable expressive range.

This paper presents the components of this approach in more detail. It then presents a case study of the application of the progressive method to generating puzzles for the physics-based puzzle game *Cut the Rope*. Finally, we report some observations on the performance and expressive range of this method in the given domain.

## 2   Evolving Game Content: A Progressive Approach

The framework we propose (presented in Fig. 1) consists of two layers: a Timeline Generator (TLG) and a Game Simulator (GS) where the generated timelines are evaluated and scored according to playability and/or other design constraints. The framework is search-based in the sense that the structures of the timelines are evolved by the TLG. Each individual is then simulated by the GS following a constructive approach (using a game specific software) and assigned a fitness according to predefined criteria. Evolution then continues to explore the generation of "better" timelines.

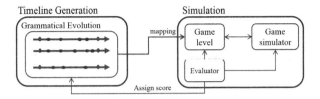

**Fig. 1.** The progressive content generation framework. Timelines are evolved by grammatical evolution and evaluated by the game simulator. The simulator progressively maps a timeline to a game design through simulating the game. A complete design is finally scored based on the result of the simulation and other design aspects.

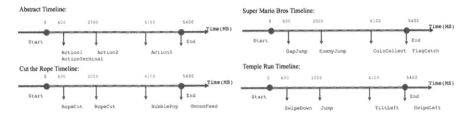

**Fig. 2.** An abstract timeline and its possible interpretations in different games.

## 2.1 Timeline Generation

We define a level timeline as a sequence of in-game interaction events that should occur at specific times throughout the game session. By taking all those actions at the specified times the level can be played through successfully (there might or might not be other equally successful timelines for a given level). For real-time games, the timeline is essential for meaningful gameplay experience as it reflects the rhythm of playing a level. The timelines in our framework are defined in a generic way that can be easily interpreted and applied in dissimilar games. Figure 2 shows different example timelines for different games. The first timeline contains abstract actions that can be instantiated into game-specific actions such as the instances presented for *Super Mario Bros* (SMB), *Cut the Rope* (CTR) and *Temple Run*.

The events in a timeline are presented given their temporal order (activation order). Some games are more order-sensitive than others. For instance, in games where the player can navigate in both directions, such as SMB, the order of placing the components is important from a design and aesthetics point of view, while in other games, such as CTR, the order in which the components are activated plays a key role in making the game playable (and in how difficult it is).

We use grammatical evolution [4] to define and evolve timelines since it provides a simple way of defining phenotype structure through the use of the design grammar. Grammatical evolution also facilitates adapting the framework to other games, as this requires only instantiating a new design grammar with the game-specific events.

```
<timeline>::=<IEs><TLE_terminal>
<IEs>::=<IE><TLEs_more>
<IEs_more>::=<IE>|<IE><IEs_more>
<IEs>::= <IE_1>|<IE_2>|<IE_3>
<IE_1>::=gameplayEvent1(<Time1>)
<IE_2>::=gameplayEvent2(<Time2>)
<IE_3>::=gameplayEvent3(<Time3>)
<IE_terminal>::=endOfLevelEvent(0)
<Time1>::=[500,3000]
```

**Fig. 3.** The design grammar employed to specify the levels' timeline.

**Grammatical Evolution.** Grammatical Evolution (GE) is the result of combining an evolutionary algorithm with a grammatical representation [4]. GE has been used extensively for automatic design with promising results [5–7] motivating the exploration of its applicability for automatic CG [8–10].

In our implementation of GE, the phenotype (a timeline) is a one-dimensional string of interaction events (IEs). IEs are the possible events that can happen during a game session; this can be a jump in SMB, a rope cut or an interaction between the candy and a bump in CTR or swipe in Temple Run. Each event in the timeline is associated with a timestamp that specifies the exact time during the game in which this event is activated. Instead of using an absolute timestamp for each IE, we assign a number that indicates the timespan elapsed since the previous event was activated. The use of elapsed time permits the incorporation of context (game specific) information. For instance, the frequency of doing an action and/or the waiting time required after performing a specific action is game-dependent. In fast-paced games, such as Temple Run, the player has to rapidly perform swipes and tilts to avoid losing, while in other games, such as SMB or Candy Crush, the amount of time available for the player to perform an action is relatively long. The use of elapsed time also allows for action dependent time variant as some actions are followed by a longer waiting time than others. (Pressing an air-cushion in CTR is usually followed by a relatively long waiting time allowing the candy to reach a specific position, but shooting a gun in a FPS game is mostly followed by rapid reactions from opponents.) Finally, the use of the elapsed time allows for more efficient search since it reduces the size of our search space by eliminating a high number of invalid individuals with the exact or an overlapping timestamps.

Figure 3 shows an abstract grammar employed by GE for timeline generation. The grammar is defined so that each level has at least two IEs and a terminal state (winning or losing the game). Each event can be one of the possible events in a game associated with an event-dependent timestamp.

The second part of the progressive approach is the use of a constructive method to evaluate the evolved timelines. Each timeline is passed on to a game simulator that progressively scans the timeline while building a compatible level design. A timeline is assigned a score by the simulator according to whether it could be matched with a playable design and to other heuristics that relate to aesthetics or design constrains.

## 2.2   Timeline Simulation

A timeline controls the order, the elapsed time and the type of the components that will be presented in a level. It does not however carry information about the components' specific properties such as their direction or their exact position in the game canvas. Moreover, the compatibility between the added components is not guaranteed (whether a specific action can actually be performed within a certain period of time from another). Thereafter, a generated timeline can not be guaranteed to be playable and therefore a timeline structure generated by the TLG needs to be evaluated. For this purpose, we use the game simulation layer. In this layer, each evolved timeline is mapped into its phenotype representation (a game level) while being simulated by an agent. Since we want our algorithm to be fast and reliable, and as the timelines contain missing information, our proposed approach to generate a matching design for a given timeline is to gradually construct the design as the timeline is being scanned, hence the word *progression*. More specifically, as the timeline is being simulated, components are added to the scene in a way that maximises the chance that the final design is playable according to the steps presented in Algorithm 1. Notice that we are aiming at generating playable designs but we consider playability as a minimal criterion and other factors might also be considered when assigning a score for a timeline.

---

**Algorithm 1.** The Progression Algorithm

---

**Data**: E : list of events in the timeline with their associated timestamps;
Set game timer T to 0;
Start simulation;
1 **while** *E contains more events, e* **do**
2     **if** *e is the End event* **then**
3        return the level design;
4     **if** $T = e.time$ **then**
5        create the associated component, c;
6        c.activate();
7     **if** $T > e.time$ *or lose* **then**
8        return invalid;

---

The algorithm starts by converting the genotype (timeline) into a list of interaction events with their associated timestamps. The simulator then resets the game timer and starts the simulation. This is done by scanning the list of events and activating the top event in the stack when the game timer becomes equal to the event's timestamp (lines 4–6). Activating an event means placing the associated component in the game canvas (more details about how to intelligently do this later) and simulating the event's action (jumping over a gap or popping a bubble). The simulation continues until the next event becomes activated (when the game timer reaches e.time) and this continues until the game termination event is reached (line 2) in which case the game is considered playable and the final design is returned.

Since the simulator can freely assign properties and positions to the components, it is likely that some of the configurations will fail to reach the termination event and consequently the timeline is considered invalid (line 7). Therefore, the simulator is optimised so that it places the components *intelligently*; i.e. whenever a component is to be added, it is placed in a way that its position intersects with the trajectory of an agent playing the part of the game constructed so far. This way we can guarantee the existence of a path between the components. The termination event is also placed along this path, if possible, ensuring a playable design.

The informative placement of components solves only part of the problem, there remains the part where the characteristics of the components also play a role in whether a timeline is playable (this could be for example placing a gap that is too wide for the player to jump over). In this case, a valid timeline might be misclassified as invalid (a false positive case). This issue can be easily solved by repeating the simulation a number of times to allow the exploration of different configurations (note however that there is still a slight chance of misclassification).

Finally, the simulation might fail because the structure of the events in the timeline is indeed invalid (too short or too long time between the events or incompatible sequence of components (for example, a gap followed by stairs in SMB)) (line 7).

### 2.3   Notes on the Progressive Approach

A core feature of our approach is that content is placed in a way that matches the timeline whilst guaranteeing playability (a timeline is always playable up to the point where the simulation fails). There is no need for any additional playability check afterwards. This is a main advantage over other CG methods proposed in the literature where two separated steps are usually employed to (1) generate complete designs and (2) performs a playability check [11,12] which results in a significantly slower performance than the one obtained by the proposed approach.

A vital contribution of the proposed framework is that it guarantees *usability*, i.e. all the components presented are necessary, and should be used, to complete the level, unlike previous attempts to generate content where this is not guaranteed [8,11,12]. This is an important issue in game design since the number of paths that could be followed to finish the game provides an estimate of difficulty. This issue, however, is more important in some games than others. The existence of extra components in SMB for example allows for level's segments with alternative paths, while in other games such as CTR that requires fine tuning of the components and their properties to preserve playability, the extra components are usually perceived as a design flaw.

Another important feature of the methodology followed is that the genotype-to-phenotype mapping is one-to-many, i.e. more than one playable design could be generated that match one evolved timeline (note that this could be the result of one or multiple runs of the algorithm). This is facilitated because of the imperfect information carried by the timeline which permits many successful interpretations. This is beneficial since it allows the designer to explore a number of alternatives or variants of the level that are structurally different but all share the exact in-game interactions.

Simulating a timeline indicates whether or not it could be mapped into a playable design. This forms the first step in evaluation. Other measures could also be considered in this step and depending on the designer preference, a fitness value will be returned indicating the "goodness" of the timeline.

In what follows, we demonstrate an application of our framework to a physics-based puzzle game to illustrate its applicability. We present the game and the modifications required to employ the method and we analyse the performance and the output obtained.

## 3 Customising the Framework for Cut the Rope

We use a clone of the game Cut the Rope as a testbed for our approach. The original CTR is a popular commercial physics-based puzzle video game released in 2010 by ZeptoLab for mobile devices. The game was a huge success and it has been downloaded more than 150 million times. The game has also many characteristics and challenges that motivate choosing it as a testbed; the physics constraints applied and generated by the different components of the game necessitate considering factors when evaluating the content generated other than the ones usually considered for other game genres, testing for playability is another issue that differentiates this type of games since this needs to be done based on a physics simulator, finally, the game defines a new genre that has slightly been researched.

The gameplay consists of performing certain actions on specific components to redirect the candy towards Om Nom, a frog-like creature. Timing is an essential property of the game as the player has to perform specific actions at certain times to successfully finish the game.

There are many different level components in the original game and we use the basic ones in our clone: ropes, air-cushions, bubbles, rockets and bumpers. The possible actions that could be performed thereafter are: a rope cut, an air-cushion press, a bubble pop, a rocket press or a void action (not taking any action, i.e., waiting for the candy to reach a certain position). More details about the different game components and the possible interactions can be found in [11].

### 3.1 Timeline Generation

Customising this layer for CTR implies instantiating a new design grammar with the possible events in CTR and assigning the appropriate timestamps. The final grammar can be seen in Fig. 4 where the timespan values are assigned for each IE experimentally based on several evaluations to reflect the components' specific properties. An example timeline evolved using this grammar is: *rope_cut(200) rope_cut(500) aircuh_press(700) rocket_press(600) omNom_feed(0)*. This timeline consists of four IEs (two rope cuts followed by pressing an air cushion and finally pressing a rocket) and a game-end event.

```
<timeline>::=<IEs><IE_terminal>

<IEs>::=<IE><IEs_more>
<IEs_more>::=<IE>|<IE><IEs_more>
<IE>::=<rope_cut>|<aircush_press>|<bubble_pop>|<bumper_inter>|<rocket_press>
<rope_cut>::=rope_cut(<default_ET>)
<aircush_press>::=aircush_press(<default_ET>)
<bubble_pop>::=bubble_pop(<short_ET>)
<rocket_press>::=rocket_press(<short_ET>)
<bumper_inter>::=bumper_inter(<long_ET>)
<IE_terminal>::=OmNom_feed(0)
<short_ET>::=[600,1600]
<default_ET>::=[800,1800]
<long_ET>::=[1200,2200]
```

**Fig. 4.** The design grammar employed to specify the levels' timeline in Cut the Rope.

### 3.2   Timeline Simulation and Evaluation

Since CTR is a physics-based game, simulating the game requires a physics simulator that can handle the different physical properties presented in the game. As there is no open source code available for the game, we had to implement our own clone using the original game assets. The simulator thus implemented is used to create designs that match given timelines following the algorithm presented in Algorithm 1. Figure 5(a) presents the different steps followed by the simulator when mapping the timeline: *rope_cut(200) rope_cut(500) aircuh_press(700) rocket_press(600) omNom_feed(0)* into a game design. As can be seen, as the simulator starts scanning the timeline, two ropes attached to the candy are added with a very short timespan in-between. The simulator then activates the associated IEs by cutting the ropes. This initiates a candy free movement and when the time for an interaction with an air cushion is reached, the simulator adds an air cushion in a position that intersects with the candy's trajectory. The air cushion is directly activated and this leads to a slight change in the candy's path as the result of blowing air. The candy keeps moving downwards affected by its gravity and it hits the rocket that is created after 700 ms from activating the air cushion. Finally, the simulator adds Om Nom in the rocket's path and this termination event successfully ends the simulation resulting in a playable level.

As discussed earlier, the characteristics of the added components have a great impact on whether or not the final design is playable. In our previous example, adding a rocket directed downwards will result in losing the game and thereafter misclassifying the timeline as invalid (see Fig. 5(b) for illustration). Several runs of the simulation while differentiating the properties of the components will lead to many design variants. Some of which are indeed playable designs proving the validity of a timeline. Examples of possible playable levels for the timeline discussed previously can be seen in Fig. 5(c).

The fitness function chosen to score the timelines is a weighted sum of several properties that capture different design, playability and aesthetic considerations. The list of features includes:

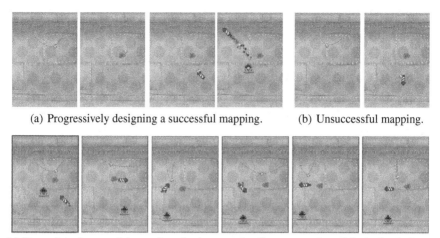

(a) Progressively designing a successful mapping.          (b) Unsuccessful mapping.

(c) Examples of successful mappings for the same timeline to a number of dissimilar designs.

**Fig. 5.** A successful, unsuccessful and some example possible designs for the timeline: *rope_cut(200) rope_cut(500) aircuh_press(700) rocket_press(700) omnom_feed(0)*.

- The total duration of gameplay calculated as the sum of all elapsed times.
- Trajectory loops: the arrangement of the components on the canvas might lead to situations where the same position will be revisited by the candy. This is considered an inferior design as some of the components become obsolete.
- Overlapping components which occurs when the elapsed time assigned for two adjacent events is too short.
- Playability: in some cases, the simulator will repeatedly fail to map the timeline to a playable design.

Notice that the first condition defines a design constraint since levels that are too long or too short are likely to be uninteresting. The second condition depends on how the simulator chooses to place the components in the canvas and repeating the simulation might lead to different results. The final two conditions are actual faults in the timeline and thereafter they are given the highest weights. The exact values assigned for the weights given to each of the above conditions are experimentally chosen.

## 4    Implementation and Experimental Setup

The existing GEVA software [13] was used to implement the TLG tier. The experimental parameters are the following: 100 runs were initialised with the ramped half-and-half method, each run lasted for 30 generations with a population size of 10 individuals. The maximum derivation tree depth was set at 100, tournament selection of size 2, int-flip mutation with probability 0.1, one-point crossover with probability 0.9, and 3 maximum wraps were allowed. The termination criterion is creating the first valid design[1].

# 5   Results and Analysis

As our framework constitutes two modules, we will focus our analysis on the timeline generation and the design generation separately.

## 5.1   Timeline Analysis

In order to assess the quality of the generated timelines, their variation and the generation efficiency, we ran the TLG for 100 timelines and analysed the results of the valid timeline evolved. The results show that in most cases two generations are required to get a valid timeline which can be achieved relatively quickly (within $7.23 \pm 9.19$ s) (note that this is mainly because of the efficiency of mapping the TL to a playable design). We also ran a simple analysis to investigate the difference in the length of the timeline evolved (the number of IEs). The results show that the average length is $4.83 \pm 0.82$. The analysis also showed that more than 85 % of the timelines are of length five or smaller. This tendency towards generating short timelines draws our attention to the design of our scoring scheme which does not account for the number of IEs. As a result, the system favours short timelines that could be easily mapped to valid designs.

To further investigate the generator's capabilities we calculated the number of occurrences of the different events in the timelines evolved. The results show that 48, 44, 47, 51 and 51 items are generated for *rope_cut, aircush_press, bubble_pop, bumper_inter and rocket_press*, respectively. The results approximate a uniform distribution demonstrating a good balancing capability.

As the order in which the events are presented in the timelines has a high impact on the gameplay experience, we ran an experiment to capture the temporal property of the timelines. For this purpose, the timelines are converted into sequences of strings where each event is given a unique identifier. We then calculated the distance between each pair of timelines using the Levenshtein distance measure. The average distance obtained is $2.29 \pm 0.91$. Given that the timelines length varies between 4 and 8, this means that an average of two operations (insertion, deletion or substitution) are required to change one sequence into the other and this indicates an adequate amount of structural variations.

## 5.2   Generator Expressivity Analysis

Visualising the distribution of the components helps us understand the simulator's capabilities and its expressive space. Colour maps is one of the methods used for this purpose [11]. This is done by generating a large amount of game

---

[1] A video showing the implementation of the framework in CTR is available online: http://noorshaker.com/CutTheRope.html.

**Fig. 6.** Om Nom's, blowers' and rockets' placement colour maps for 100 generated levels.

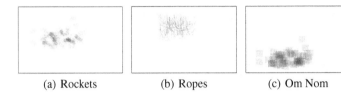

(a) Rockets          (b) Ropes          (c) Om Nom

**Fig. 7.** Colour maps for different components for 63 designs generated for the same timeline.

content, converting each instance into a pixelated image and projecting all instances on a single image. To analyse our generator, colour maps are applied on individual components to ease the analysis and to give a better visualisation. Figure 6 presents the colour maps obtained for Om Nom (assigned a green colour) in 100 levels generated from valid timelines. Note that Om Nom's placement corresponds to the position in the map where the end-game event takes place. The figure illustrates that a large portion of the canvas is explored.

The above visualisation helps use understand the diversity of levels generated from *different* timelines; given the two-step nature of the approach, it is also interesting to look at the diversity of levels generated from a *single* timeline. For this purpose, the game simulator is set to run 100 times while trying to map the timeline *rope_cut(700) rope_cut(1000) bubble_press(1000) rocket_press(1500) OmNom_feed(0)* into playable designs. As a result, the simulator was able to successfully generate 63 playable designs while failing the rest of the attempts. Figure 7 presents the distribution of rockets, ropes and Om Nom in the successful cases. The results illustrate a wide variety of structural differences for all items indicating that the same timeline can create numerous different levels, likely contributing to different types of player experience.

### 5.3   Comparison with Previous Attempts

In comparison with previous attempts to evolve playable content for the same testbed, our approach shows superiority in terms of speed, variety, control and usability of generated content. While it takes the simulation-based and the random agents 470 and 82 s to evolve a complete playable level [11, 12], the proposed methodology is able to evolve timelines with more than one associated design in 9.79 s while ensuring that all generated entities are used in all successful playthroughs.

# 6   Conclusions and Future Directions

In this paper we presented a framework for content generation in games. Our framework is built on the idea that by combining the advantages of search-based and constructive approaches for content generation, a fast and expressive generator can be built. The generator is composed of two main components: an evolutionary based timeline generator and a constructive-based game simulator. Each timeline is sequence of in-game events that can be mapped to a game design by the simulator. Timelines are evolved using grammatical evolution and evaluated by the simulator which progressively scans a timeline and adds components when necessary while preserving playability. A timeline can be mapped to more than one design, facilitating the exploration of multiple levels with the same rhythm. The framework is tested in a physics-based game where timelines are evolved and scored according to playability and aesthetic constraints.

There are a number of interesting future directions: (1) The method shows promising results in our testbed and it would be interesting to validate its generality by applying it to games from other genres such as first-person shooters or endless runners. (2) A measure of the game difficulty is somehow embedded in the definition of the timeline (the more the components and the shorter the time between the events the harder the level is). It would therefore be interesting to generate content of specified difficulty by modifying the calculation of the fitness. (3) One could also try to generate levels with multiple alternate timelines, that could be solved in different ways.

**Acknowledgments.** We thank ZeptoLab for giving us permission to use the original Cut The Rope graphical assets for research purposes. The research was supported in part by the Danish Research Agency, Ministry of Science, Technology and Innovation; project "PlayGALe" (1337-00172).

# References

1. Togelius, J., Yannakakis, G.N., Stanley, K.O., Browne, C.: Search-based procedural content generation. In: Di Chio, C., Cagnoni, S., Cotta, C., Ebner, M., Ekárt, A., Esparcia-Alcazar, A.I., Goh, C.-K., Merelo, J.J., Neri, F., Preuß, M., Togelius, J., Yannakakis, G.N. (eds.) EvoApplicatons 2010, Part I. LNCS, vol. 6024, pp. 141–150. Springer, Heidelberg (2010)
2. Shaker, N., Liapis, A., Togelius, J., Lopes, R., Bidarra, R.: Constructive generation methods for dungeons and levels. In: Shaker, N., Togelius, J., Nelson, M.J. (eds.) Procedural Content Generation in Games: A Textbook and an Overview of Current Research. Springer, Heidelberg (2015)
3. Preuss, M., Liapis, A., Togelius, J.: Searching for good and diverse game levels. In: 2014 IEEE Conference on Computational Intelligence and Games (CIG), pp. 1–8. IEEE (2014)
4. O'Neill, M., Ryan, C.: Grammatical evolution. IEEE Trans. Evol. Comput. 5(4), 349–358 (2001)

5. Hornby, G.S., Pollack, J.B.: The advantages of generative grammatical encodings for physical design. In: Proceedings of the 2001 Congress on Evolutionary Computation, vol. 1, pp. 600–607. IEEE (2001)
6. Byrne, J., Fenton, M., Hemberg, E., McDermott, J., O'Neill, M., Shotton, E., Nally, C.: Combining structural analysis and multi-objective criteria for evolutionary architectural design. In: Di Chio, C., Brabazon, A., Di Caro, G.A., Drechsler, R., Farooq, M., Grahl, J., Greenfield, G., Prins, C., Romero, J., Squillero, G., Tarantino, E., Tettamanzi, A.G.B., Urquhart, N., Uyar, A.Ş. (eds.) EvoApplications 2011, Part II. LNCS, vol. 6625, pp. 204–213. Springer, Heidelberg (2011)
7. O'Neill, M., Swafford, J.M., McDermott, J., Byrne, J., Brabazon, A., Shotton, E., McNally, C., Hemberg, M.: Shape grammars and grammatical evolution for evolutionary design. In: Proceedings of the 11th Annual Conference on Genetic and Evolutionary Computation, pp. 1035–1042. ACM (2009)
8. Shaker, N., Nicolau, M., Yannakakis, G., Togelius, J., O'Neill, M.: Evolving levels for super mario bros using grammatical evolution. In: IEEE Conference on Computational Intelligence and Games (CIG), pp. 304–311 (2012)
9. Shaker, N., Yannakakis, G.N., Togelius, J., Nicolau, M., ONeill, M: Evolving personalized content for super mario bros using grammatical evolution (2012)
10. Font, J., Mahlmann, T., Manrique, D., Togelius, J.: Towards the automatic generation of card games through grammar-guided genetic programming. In: FDG 2010, Proceedings of the Fifth International Conference on the Foundations of Digital Games (2013)
11. Shaker, M., Sarhan, M.H., Al Naameh, O., Shaker, N., Togelius, J.: Automatic generation and analysis of physics-based puzzle games. In: 2013 IEEE Conference on Computational Intelligence in Games (CIG), pp. 1–8. IEEE (2013)
12. Shaker, M., Shaker, N., Togelius, J.: Evolving playable content for cut the rope through a simulation-based approach. In: Proceedings of the AAAI Conference on Artificial Intelligence and Interactive Digital Entertainment (2013)
13. O'Neill, M., Hemberg, E., Gilligan, C., Bartley, E., McDermott, J., Brabazon, A.: Geva: grammatical evolution in java. ACM SIGEVOlution **3**(2), 17–22 (2008)

# The Role of Behavioral Diversity
# and Difficulty of Opponents in Coevolving
# Game-Playing Agents

Marcin Szubert[(✉)], Wojciech Jaśkowski, Paweł Liskowski,
and Krzysztof Krawiec

Institute of Computing Science, Poznan University of Technology, Poznań, Poland
{mszubert,wjaskowski,pliskowski,kkrawiec}@cs.put.poznan.pl

**Abstract.** Generalization performance of learning agents depends on
the training experience to which they have been exposed. In game-
playing domains, that experience is determined by the opponents faced
during learning. This analytical study investigates two characteristics of
opponents in competitive coevolutionary learning: behavioral diversity
and difficulty (performance against other players). To assess diversity, we
propose a generic intra-game behavioral distance measure, that could be
adopted to other sequential decision problems. We monitor both characteristics in two-population coevolutionary learning of Othello strategies,
attempting to explain their relationship with the generalization performance achieved by the evolved solutions. The main observation is the
existence of a non-obvious trade-off between difficulty and diversity, with
the latter being essential for obtaining high generalization performance.

**Keywords:** Behavioral diversity · Diversity maintenance · Test difficulty · Competitive coevolution · Generalization performance · Games ·
Othello

## 1    Introduction

Competitive coevolution has been regarded as an appealing alternative to
conventional evolutionary algorithms in domains where the objective function
is difficult to define or expensive to compute. Instead of relying on a static fitness function, in coevolution individuals are evaluated on the basis of interactions
with each other [1]. This approach is particularly suitable to games where it is
natural to assess the skills of a given game-playing agent by inspecting how it
performs against a set of opponents.

One of the main motivations behind using coevolution in games is the belief
that it is able to encourage *arms race* between competing individuals and thus
provide a pedagogical series of increasingly complex challenges [2]. However,
even if coevolution succeeds in providing progressively more difficult opponents,
it can still suffer from undesired phenomena known as coevolutionary pathologies
[3,4]. For instance, recent works on Othello demonstrate that in the long-term

© Springer International Publishing Switzerland 2015
A.M. Mora and G. Squillero (Eds.): EvoApplications 2015, LNCS 9028, pp. 394–405, 2015.
DOI: 10.1007/978-3-319-16549-3_32

perspective coevolution tends to overspecialize on beating the strong players while forgetting how to deal with the weaker ones, so that in the end the resulting strategies do not generalize well [5]. Consequently, in terms of generalization performance, coevolution has been found less effective than simple evolution with fitness evaluated against a set of random opponents [6].

In this paper, we attempt to improve the generalization performance of Othello-playing agents by promoting the diversity among the coevolving opponents. In contrast to many genotypic diversity maintenance techniques studied in the past [7–9], here we focus on the *behavioral* characteristics of individuals. For this purpose, we define a simple behavioral distance measure, applicable not only to Othello but to any sequential decision making problem. We hypothesize that by promoting both difficulty and behavioral diversity in the population of tests (opponents), coevolution can outperform the evolutionary algorithm with random sampling of opponents. To verify this thesis, we investigate the interplay between the behavioral diversity and difficulty of coevolving opponents as well as the relationships of these two issues with the generalization performance of evolved solutions.

## 2   Diversity Maintenance Techniques

In analogy to the key role played by diversity of living organisms in the theory of natural selection, maintaining diversity of candidate solutions in a population has been long perceived as crucial for the effectiveness of evolutionary algorithms [7]. Lack of diversity has been linked to major problems, including slow progress and premature convergence to suboptimal regions of the search space. In response, numerous diversity maintenance techniques have been proposed to sustain exploration of the search space.

The most popular approaches to diversity maintenance include *crowding* and *fitness sharing* [9], which both modify the selection process by promoting the individuals that are most different from the rest of population. For instance, fitness sharing consists in dividing fitness values by the *niche count* to demote the individuals which are similar to each other (i.e., occupy the same niche). Techniques like these do not directly manipulate genotypes and are thus often referred to as *implicit*; alternatively, diversity can be stimulated *explicitly* by simply increasing the strength of a mutation operator.

In the context of competitive coevolution, deficit of diversity can be linked with frequently reported pathologies such as overspecialization, mediocre stable states [3] or disengagement (loss of fitness gradient [4]). For instance, a population of opponents that has converged to a single difficult opponent may present a too demanding challenge for the candidate solutions and so disengage from them. Besides the conventional fitness sharing, a number of diversity maintenance techniques tailored for coevolution have been employed to remedy such situations. Examples include competitive fitness sharing [10] and reduced parasite virulence [11]. The impact of these techniques on the performance of a single-population coevolution was investigated by Chong *et al.* [12].

Most of diversity maintenance techniques rely on measuring some form of distance between the evolving individuals. Typically, the distance measure is defined in the original search space, i.e., at the level of genotypes. For instance, for solutions represented as vectors of real parameters, the Euclidean distance may be used to assess their similarity.

However, if the mapping between genotypes and phenotypes/behaviors is complex, which is often the case in nontrivial problems like games, individuals that are apart according to a genotypic distance measure can exhibit very similar behaviors. And vice versa: a minute modification of the genotype can fundamentally alter individual's behavior. For instance, consider the popular WPC strategy representation studied in this paper (cf. Sect. 4.1). Scaling of the entire genotype (weight matrix) has no effect on strategy behavior whatsoever, because it does not change the ordering of evaluations of board states (cf. Eq. 2). On the other hand, a small modification of a weight associated with, e.g., one of the central board locations, can change the way a strategy plays the opening of a game and so diametrically change its performance.

Promoting genotypic diversity does not guarantee thus diverse behaviors. Since it is the behavior that matters in the end, recent works [13,14] promote diversity by measuring distance directly in the space of behaviors. Although assessing behavioral distance typically requires defining a task-specific measure, generic measures for the entire class of sequential decision problems have been also proposed, based on, e.g., normalized compression distance [15].

In coevolutionary algorithms, competitive fitness sharing [10] can be seen as a step towards behavior-based diversity maintenance, as it measures the distance between individuals with respect to the results of their interactions with individuals in population. For instance, in the context of game-playing, it will promote the strategies winning with the opponents that few other strategies can beat.

In this paper, we consider two-population coevolutionary algorithm and, in contrast to most of the past works, focus on the behavioral diversity in the population of *tests* (opponents) and its relationship with the generalization performance in the population of solutions. To that aim, we devise a novel intra-game behavioral distance measure that compares players with respect to the decisions they make in particular game states. To the best of our knowledge, the only work that employs a comparable behavioral distance in competitive coevolution is the recent paper by Gomes *et al.* [16]. The authors define a task-specific distance measure for the predator-prey pursuit problem and apply it to promote behavioral novelty in both coevolving populations. In this context, the measure proposed in the next section has the advantage of being problem-independent.

## 3   Measuring Distance Between Game-Playing Agents

In order to maintain behavioral diversity, we propose a measure of behavioral distance between two game-playing agents. This measure relies on comparing actions the given agents would make in each of a predefined set of game states.

## 3.1 Behavior Characterization Vector

In sequential decision making problems [17], an agent can be identified with a policy $\pi$: $S \rightarrow A$ that, for each possible state of the environment $s \in S$ produces an action $a \in A$. Assuming that the environment has the Markov property, current state of the environment provides enough information to take an action, i.e., the history of previous states and actions is irrelevant. Therefore, the behavior of an agent can be fully characterized by independently considering the actions it would take in every possible state of the environment. Assuming a finite space of $m$ states, the behavior of an agent $t$ equipped with policy $\pi_t$ can be thus expressed as a vector:

$$\beta_t = \langle \pi_t(s_1), \pi_t(s_2), ..., \pi_t(s_m) \rangle,$$

which is referred to as *behavior characterization vector* [13,16]. We denote an agent by '$t$' to emphasize that in this paper we are ultimately interested in the behaviors of *tests* in a two-population coevolutionary algorithm.

$\beta$ captures the complete account of agent's behavioral characteristics: nothing more can be said about its behavior, because all possible states have been taken into account. In practice however, $m$ is often prohibitively large ($\approx 10^{28}$ for the game of Othello considered in this paper), so a technically realizable behavioral analysis needs to sacrifice the completeness by relying on a reasonably sized subset $S' \subseteq S$ of representative states. How informative a particular implementation of $\beta$ is, depends on the actual choice of $S'$. In board games like Othello, an interaction episode (game) between players always starts from the same initial state. Certain states are thus much more likely to be visited than others, and this observation will motivate the particular choice of $S'$ we describe in the experimental section.

## 3.2 Mean Behavioral Distance

We employ the behavior characterization vector as a means to measure the diversity in a population of agents – game strategies. Given the behavior characterization vectors $\beta_t$ and $\beta_{t'}$ of two game-playing agents (strategies) $t$ and $t'$, determined on the same subset of $m$ distinct states, we define the *behavioral distance* between them as:

$$d(t, t') = D_{Hamming}(\beta_t, \beta_{t'}) = \sum_{i=1}^{m} \delta \left( \beta_t[i], \beta_{t'}[i] \right), \tag{1}$$

where $\delta$ is the Kronecker delta. We resort to the Hamming distance, because definitions of actions depend on the problem of consideration. Without referring to problem-specific knowledge, it is impossible to judge how similar two actions are; the only statement that can be made for certain is whether they are identical or not. This is particularly true for Othello where actions are discrete and refer to different board positions. Obviously, in domains with continuous actions (e.g., $A = \mathbb{R}$), other ways of comparing individuals would apply (and, as a matter of fact, would be unavoidable, as two continuous actions are almost always distinct).

With $d$ as a means for pairwise comparison of agents' behaviors, we define the internal diversity of any nonempty set of agents $T$ as the average behavioral distance between a pair agents in $T$, i.e.,

$$d(T) = \frac{2}{|T|(|T| - 1)} \sum_{t,t' \in T,\, t \neq t'} d(t, t').$$

By definition, $d(T) \in [0, m]$.

## 4   Experimental Setup

In the following, we detail key elements which constitute the conceptual framework of this study: the definition of the game along with representation of its strategies, the algorithms that learn to play the game, and the performance measures used to assess quality and diversity of the obtained game-playing agents.

### 4.1   Othello and WPC Representation

**Othello.** Othello is a deterministic, perfect information, zero-sum board game played by two players on an $8 \times 8$ board. It involves black and white pieces. At the beginning of the game, each player has two pieces placed diagonally in the center of the board. The players take turns by placing one new piece on an empty board field. The black player moves first. A move is legal if the newly placed piece makes one or more of the opponent's pieces enclosed from both ends of a horizontal, vertical or diagonal segment. The enclosed pieces are then changed to the opposite colors. The game ends when neither player has a legal move. A player who has then more pieces on the board wins, or if both players have the same number of pieces, the game ends in a draw.

**Strategy Representation.** Our agents are represented by position-weighted piece counter (WPC), which is arguably the simplest state evaluation function for Othello [18]. WPC assigns a weight $w_i$ to board location $i$ and uses scalar product to calculate the utility $f$ of a board state $\mathbf{b}$:

$$f(\mathbf{b}) = \sum_{i=1}^{8 \times 8} w_i b_i, \tag{2}$$

where $b_i$ is 0, +1 or −1 for, respectively, an empty location, black piece, or white piece. The game-playing agents interpret $f(\mathbf{b})$ in a complementary manner: the black player prefers the moves leading towards the states with higher values, whereas the lower values are favored by the white player.

We employ WPC as a state evaluator in a 1-ply setup, i.e., given a board state, a game-playing agent generates all legal moves and applies $f$ to the resulting states. The state gauged as the most favorable determines the move to be made, while ties are resolved randomly.

## 4.2  Generalization Performance

Our objective is to find game-playing agents that maximize the *expected utility* [19]. We approximate the expected utility by playing a number of games against random opponents. A random opponent is a player drawn from the solution space, i.e., the space of all admissible WPCs, by which we mean WPCs with weights from the interval $[-10, 10]$.

The score awarded for a single game is either 0, 0.5 or 1 for lose, draw or win, respectively. For symmetry, we employ double games, where both agents play one game as black and the other as white. The performance measure is the average score in 25 000 double games against random opponents.

Since this measure tests how an individual generalizes over the space of all possible players, it is also referred to as *generalization performance* [6].

## 4.3  Learning Algorithms

Two evolutionary algorithms are employed to learn WPC weights. Both are driven by the interactions that take place between game-playing agents. Each evolutionary run consists of 500 generations, in each of them 5 000 games (2 500 double games) are played, which adds up to the total effort of 2 500 000 games per run.

**Coevolutionary Learning.** The first algorithm is a two-population competitive coevolutionary learning (CEL) [2], which maintains individuals separated into two populations: (i) candidate solutions, and (ii) tests. Tests act as opponents that challenge the candidate solutions. The fitness of a candidate solution is defined as the average result of interactions (i.e., double games) with all tests in the second population, while calculating the fitness of an opponent involves behavioral fitness sharing detailed in Sect. 4.4.

Both populations employ the $(\mu, \lambda)$-evolutionary strategy [20], where $\mu = 25$, $\lambda = 50$. Initially, they both contain $\lambda$ randomly generated individuals — real vectors of WPC weights drawn from $[-0.2, 0.2]$. The mutation operator perturbs all the weights using additive noise. The WPC weight $w_i'$ of an offspring is obtained by adding a small random value to the corresponding weight $w_i$ of the parent:

$$w_i' = w_i + \delta \cdot \mathcal{U}(-1, 1), \tag{3}$$

where $\mathcal{U}(-1, 1)$ is a real value drawn uniformly from the range $[-1, 1]$ and $\delta$ is the mutation strength. Weights resulting from mutation are clamped to the interval $[-10, 10]$ effectively making the value equal to the respective bound, e.g., if $|w_i'| > 10$, we set $w_i' := 10$. Consequently, the search space of strategies is a $[-10, 10]^{64}$ hypercube. For the population of candidate solutions we use $\delta_s = 0.1$, while for tests we consider multiple values $\delta_t = \{0.1, 1.0, 5.0, 10.0\}$.

**Random Sampling Evolutionary Learning.** We compare CEL with the random sampling evolutionary learning (RSEL) [6]. RSEL maintains a single population of candidate solutions bred in the same way as in CEL and differs from it only in fitness evaluation. In RSEL, the fitness of each candidate solution is computed as an average result of interactions with a sample $T$ of random opponents, which is drawn once per generation. For fair comparison with CEL, we set $|T| = \lambda = 50$.

Notice that the fitness employed in RSEL is an unbiased estimator of the generalization performance of the game-playing agent (cf. Sect. 4.2). RSEL has been found to surpass both one- and two-population coevolution on generalization performance for 1-ply Othello [5,6].

### 4.4 Diversity Maintenance Techniques

We equip CEL with two mechanisms that can promote diversity in the population of opponents: (1) increasing strength $\delta_t$ of the mutation operator, which can explicitly stimulate genotypic diversity, and (2) *Behavioral Fitness Sharing* (BFS) that implicitly promotes behavioral diversity (see Sect. 2).

BFS augments fitness sharing with behavioral distance between the opponents in the population of tests. The fitness $f_i'$ of an opponent $i$ is given by:

$$f_i' = \frac{f_i}{\sum_j max(0, 1 - \frac{d_{ij}}{\sigma})}, \tag{4}$$

where $f_i$ is the conventional fitness defined as an average interaction outcome between the opponent $i$ and the coevolving candidate solutions, $d_{ij}$ is the behavioral distance between opponent $i$ and opponent $j$ (Eq. 1), and $\sigma$ is the niche radius. Individuals whose distance to each other is lower than $\sigma$ share the fitness. We use $\sigma = \{0, 10, 20, 30, 40, 50, 60, 70\}$ and employ BFS in combination with the uniform mutation operator (Eq. 3) and mutation strength $\delta_t = \{0.1, 1.0, 5.0, 10.0\}$. Note that by setting $\sigma$ to 0 we completely turn off fitness sharing.

Computing $d_{ij}$ involves inspecting the behavior of both strategies on a number of states (cf. Sect. 3.1). For this purpose, we use a set of all $m = 71$ distinct Othello states reachable in the first 4 moves of the game.

### 4.5 Opponent Population Measures

Apart from the generalization performance of candidate solutions, we probe the populations of opponents in CEL with additional 'instruments'.

The first of them is the **behavioral diversity** in the population of opponents, expressed as the mean behavioral distance (Sect. 3.2). For two-population coevolution, this measure changes over time, since the population of opponents evolves. RSEL, in contrast, draws the opponent uniformly from the WPC space. Assuming that random WPCs are equally likely to make every admissible move in each of the 71 considered initial states, we can calculate the expected behavioral distance between any two opponents $t$ and $t'$ used by RSEL analytically:

$$\mathbb{E}\left[d(t,t')\right] = \mathbb{E}\left[\sum_{i=1}^{m} \delta\left(\beta_t[i], \beta_{t'}[i]\right)\right] = \sum_{i=1}^{m} \mathbb{E}\left[\delta\left(\beta_t[i], \beta_{t'}[i]\right)\right] = m\left(1 - \frac{1}{bf}\right) \approx 53.25,$$

where $m = 71$ and $bf$ is the branching factor (i.e., the average number of possible actions from each state), which at the early stages of the game of Othello is approximately equal to 4.

The second indicator of interest is **opponent difficulty**. In recent years, a significant amount of work has been devoted to study the population of opponents (a.k.a. tests or parasites), which play the role of *evaluation set* in two-population coevolution [5,6,21]. Noteworthy, it has been found that the effectiveness of the evaluation set (or population of tests) depends on its difficulty [22]. That is why, we employ it as another gauge in this study.

Since the game of Othello is symmetric, meaning that the roles of candidate solutions and tests are interchangeable, the difficulty of an opponent (test) boils down to its generalization performance (see Sect. 4.2). In other words, the better the opponent (generalization performance) the more difficult it is to beat (opponent difficulty). Technically, by opponents' difficulty we mean the average generalization performance of the players in the second co-evolving population.

## 5   Results

We performed 100 experimental runs of the CEL algorithm for each combination of $\delta_t$ and $\sigma$ parameters and 100 runs of the RSEL algorithm. For each generation, we measured the generalization performance of the individual with the highest fitness in the population of solutions. Additionally, in the case of CEL, we assessed also the behavioral diversity and difficulty in the population of opponents.

The averaged results of all experiments are illustrated in Fig. 1. The figure visualizes the impact of applying particular diversity maintenance techniques with different parameters on the generalization performance of solutions as well as on the behavioral diversity and difficulty of the coevolving opponents. The first observation is that both diversity preserving mechanisms result in improving the generalization performance. In particular, applying sufficiently strong mutation can lead to outperforming the RSEL algorithm (illustrated by the black curve in the plots). Fitness sharing alone does not attain that performance level, but it clearly benefits from moderate niche count (while low values of this parameter are clearly less advantageous).

Besides generalization performance, the figure confirms also that both considered diversity preservation methods succeed in increasing the behavioral diversity in the population of opponents. Finally, the last row of plots demonstrates the significant effect of diversity maintenance techniques on the difficulty of the coevolved opponents. One general observation is that the influence of behavioral fitness sharing technique and its niche radius parameter ($\sigma$) is much larger in the case of moderate mutation strength ($\delta_t$). If the mutation is strong, the population becomes explicitly diversified even without fitness sharing.

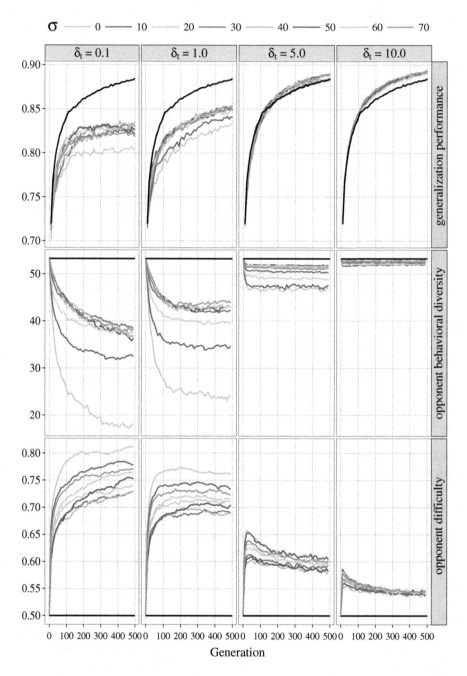

**Fig. 1.** The generalization performance of solutions vs. behavioral diversity and difficulty of opponents as a function of the number of generations, for different parameters
of diversity maintenance techniques. The black series correspond to the RSEL algorithm.

To better visualize the relationship between the behavioral diversity and the difficulty of opponents, we prepared a scatter plot shown in Fig. 2. Altogether, there are 3200 points in the plot, each of which corresponds to the final population of a single run of coevolutionary algorithm (each of 32 combinations of $(\sigma, \delta_t)$ parameters times 100 experimental runs). Additionally, an artificial point was added to the plot to illustrate the mean performance obtained with the RSEL algorithm. The coordinates of this point correspond to the expected values of difficulty and diversity in a random sample of opponents.

The figure evidences a trade-off between behavioral diversity and difficulty. The employed algorithms were unable to provide final populations of opponents that were both difficult and diverse at the same time (albeit it is not certain if such sets of opponents *exist* in the first place). Using small mutation strength lead to evolving populations of difficult opponents that behave very similarly to each other. Increasing the mutation strength allows to obtain richer repertoire of opponent behaviors but their mean difficulty simultaneously decreases. Importantly, the highest generalization performance was obtained by coevolutionary algorithms that maintained very diversified population of opponents that were on average slightly, albeit consistently, more difficult than the random ones.

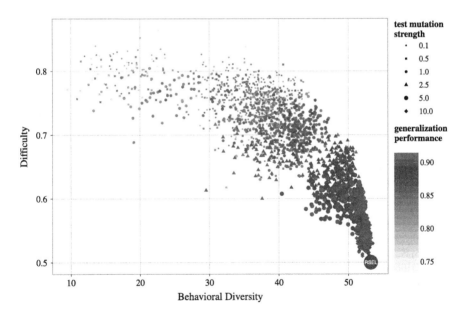

**Fig. 2.** The relationship between difficulty and diversity of the coevolving opponents and their impact on the generalization performance of solutions. Each point corresponds to the mean difficulty and diversity in the final generation of tests coevolved in a single evolutionary run. Shapes of points illustrate the strength of mutation operator operating in the population of tests. Colors reflect the generalization performance obtained by the corresponding population of solutions.

# 6  Conclusions

Encouraging the behavioral diversity, rather than the genotypic one, has been recently successfully applied to improve the performance of evolved robot controllers [13,14]. In this study we have adopted this idea to coevolution of Othello-playing agents, in order to verify whether learning against opponents that are both challenging (difficult) and behaviorally diverse can improve the generalization performance of developed strategies. We expected that the difficulty of opponents would arise naturally due to coevolutionary arms races. To maintain behavioral diversity, we have employed a novel measure of distance between game-playing agents which was integrated with the conventional fitness sharing method. Apart from that we also stimulated diversity explicitly by increasing the genotypic variation among opponents.

Although both methods of sustaining diversity in the population of opponents succeeded in improving behavioral diversity and resulted in higher generalization performance of solutions, they also lead to reduced difficulty of opponents. Due to this trade-off, diverse and simultaneously difficult opponent populations did not emerge, and we were not able to fully verify the initial hypothesis. While failing to provide such populations, behavioral diversity turns out to be a much stronger determinant of performance than difficulty. Though in part anticipated, the extent of this disproportion is rather striking: note that the populations of opponents that secure the best performance of host strategies are only slightly more difficult than the random ones (difficulty 0.6 or less). On the other hand, the high performance of RSEL is consistent with this observation.

**Acknowledgments.** This work has been supported by the Polish Ministry of Science and Higher Education, grant no. 09/91/DSMK/0568. W. Jaśkowski has been supported by the Polish National Science Centre grant no. DEC-2013/09/D/ST6/03932.

# References

1. Popovici, E., Bucci, A., Wiegand, R.P., de Jong, E.D.: Coevolutionary principles. In: Rozenberg, G., Bäck, T., Kok, J.N. (eds.) Handbook of Natural Computing, pp. 987–1033. Springer, Heidelberg (2012)
2. Nolfi, S., Floreano, D.: Coevolving predator and prey robots: do "arms races" arise in artificial evolution? Artif. Life **4**(4), 311–335 (1998)
3. Ficici, S.G., Pollack, J.B.: Challenges in coevolutionary learning: arms-race dynamics, open-endedness, and medicocre stable states. In: Proceedings of the Sixth International Conference on Artificial Life. ALIFE, pp. 238–247. MIT Press, Cambridge (1998)
4. Watson, R.A., Pollack, J.B.: Coevolutionary dynamics in a minimal substrate. In: Proceedings of the Genetic and Evolutionary Computation Conference (GECCO 2001), pp. 702–709. Morgan Kaufmann (2001)
5. Jaśkowski, W., Liskowski, P., Szubert, M.G., Krawiec, K.: Improving coevolution by random sampling. In: Proceeding of the Fifteenth Annual Conference on Genetic and Evolutionary Computation Conference. GECCO 2013, pp. 1141–1148. ACM, New York (2013)

6.  Chong, S.Y., Tino, P., Ku, D.C., Yao, X.: Improving generalization performance in co-evolutionary learning. IEEE Trans. Evol. Comput. **16**(1), 70–85 (2012)
7.  Goldberg, D.E., Richardson, J.: Genetic algorithms with sharing for multimodal function optimization. In: Proceedings of the Second International Conference on Genetic Algorithms and Their Application, pp. 41–49. L. Erlbaum Associates Inc., Hillsdale (1987)
8.  Mahfoud, S.W.: Niching methods for genetic algorithms. Ph.D. thesis, University of Illinois at Urbana-Champaign, Urbana, IL (1995)
9.  Sareni, B., Krahenbuhl, L.: Fitness sharing and niching methods revisited. IEEE Trans. Evol. Comput. **2**(3), 97–106 (1998)
10. Rosin, C.D., Belew, R.K.: New methods for competitive coevolution. Evol. Comput. **5**(1), 1–29 (1997)
11. Cartlidge, J., Bullock, S.: Combating coevolutionary disengagement by reducing parasite virulence. Evol. Comput. **12**(2), 193–222 (2004)
12. Chong, S.Y., Tino, P., Yao, X.: Relationship between generalization and diversity in coevolutionary learning. IEEE Trans. Comput. Intell. AI Game. **1**(3), 214–232 (2009)
13. Lehman, J., Stanley, K.O.: Abandoning objectives: evolution through the search for novelty alone. Evol. Comput. **19**(2), 189–223 (2011)
14. Mouret, J.B., Doncieux, S.: Encouraging behavioral diversity in evolutionary robotics: an empirical study. Evol. Comput. **20**(1), 91–133 (2012)
15. Gomez, F.J.: Sustaining diversity using behavioral information distance. In: Proceedings of the 11th Annual Conference on Genetic and Evolutionary Computation, GECCO 2009, pp. 113–120. ACM, New York (2009)
16. Gomes, J., Mariano, P., Christensen, A.L.: Novelty Search in competitive coevolution. In: Bartz-Beielstein, T., Branke, J., Filipič, B., Smith, J. (eds.) PPSN 2014. LNCS, vol. 8672, pp. 233–242. Springer, Heidelberg (2014)
17. Moriarty, D.E., Schultz, A.C., Grefenstette, J.J.: Evolutionary algorithms for reinforcement learning. J. Artif. Intell. Res. **11**, 241–276 (1999)
18. Lucas, S.M., Runarsson, T.P.: Temporal difference learning versus co-evolution for acquiring othello position evaluation. In: Louis, S.J., Kendall, G. (eds.) Proceedings of the 2006 IEEE Symposium on Computational Intelligence and Games, CIG 2006, IEEE, pp. 52–59 (2006)
19. de Jong, E.D.: The MaxSolve algorithm for coevolution. In: Proceedings of the 2005 Conference on Genetic and Evolutionary Computation. GECCO 2005, pp. 483–489. ACM, New York (2005)
20. Beyer, H.G., Schwefel, H.P.: Evolution strategies-a comprehensive introduction. Nat. Comput. **1**(1), 3–52 (2002)
21. de Jong, E.D., Pollack, J.B.: Ideal evaluation from coevolution. Evol. Comput. **12**(2), 159–192 (2004)
22. Szubert, M.G., Jaśkowski, W., Liskowski, P., Krawiec, K.: Shaping fitness function for evolutionary learning of game strategies. In: Proceedings of the 15th Annual Conference on Genetic and Evolutionary Computation. GECCO 2013, pp. 1149–1156. ACM, New York (2013)

# PowerSurge: A Serious Game on Power Transmission Networks

Sebastian von Mammen$^{(\boxtimes)}$, Fabian Hertwig, Patrick Lehner,
and Florian Obermayer

Organic Computing, University of Augsburg, Augsburg, Germany
{s.vonmammen,fabian.hertwig,florian.obermayer}@gmail.com,
lehner.patrick@gmx.de

**Abstract.** In this paper, we present an interactive serious game about power transmission systems. The system familiarizes novices with the basic design and behavior of such systems. Using simple drag and drop interactions, power plants and consumers are placed and connected in a virtual landscape that is presented from an isometric perspective. A series of tutorials fosters the user's mastery in building and controlling a complex system. The advanced user is challenged by tasks such as the redesign of an established power infrastructure to integrate a large percentage of regenerative power plants. Next to the interface, we detail the model that drives the simulation. The methodologies presented in this paper can be applied to a wide range of serious games about complex network designs.

**Keywords:** Interactive simulation · Serious games · Power grid · Power transmission · Complex systems

## 1 Introduction

Energy management is an important challenge that governments have to struggle with. The general trend to turn away from climate straining and unsafe technology such as nuclear power and fossil fuels to smaller but renewable energy sources requires a more decentralized energy distribution infrastructure [1]. The turn from all-time available power to regenerative but unsteady resources poses non-trivial challenges: Energy has to be efficiently stored locally to counteract the sporadic absence of wind and solar radiation, see for instance [2,3]. On the other hand, transportation of electricity from regions with high yield has to happen efficiently. Adapting the infrastructure is a difficult task, and it is useful to explore the existing capabilities and virtualize any changes before their implementation. A broad overview addressing the challenges of current Power Transmission Systems (PTS) is provided by [4].

In this paper, we present PowerSurge, an interactive simulator for PTS. We detail its user interface, gamification elements and the underlying model that drives the simulation. PowerSurge introduces users who are new to the field of

© Springer International Publishing Switzerland 2015
A.M. Mora and G. Squillero (Eds.): EvoApplications 2015, LNCS 9028, pp. 406–417, 2015.
DOI: 10.1007/978-3-319-16549-3_33

PTS to gain a high-level understanding of the challenges faced in their design and maintenance, and a feeling for complex behaviors in such networks. Due to the similarity to other complex science themes such as social or economic systems, see for instance [5], the methodologies presented in this paper can be transferred to a wide range of serious games.

In Sect. 2, we first survey existing power simulation systems, emphasizing their distinctive features. Next, in Sect. 3, we present our software, including its design principles, its user interface, and a detailed discussion of our domain model. We conclude with a short summary of our results and an outlook on future work and future use of the presented concept.

## 2   Related Work

Existing simulation and analysis software for power transmission and distribution systems is mainly aimed at industry professionals. Requirements for extensive knowledge in the field and access to data for a transmission network's components pose high barriers to entry for these programs.

*PowerWorld Simulator* [6], for instance, is a commercial product to interactively simulate large-scale power transmission systems in great detail. While there are educational and research licenses available to make it accessible for non-industry users, the project's source code and development are not open so its extensibility is rather limited.

Other projects like *OpenDSS* [7] and *GridLab-D* [8] are open source projects aimed at research and planning purposes. Both of these tools have extensive simulation and analysis capabilities and support a wide array of grid types and distribution elements, but they are not interactive simulators.

Additionally, all three of these systems require very detailed data about the elements of the transmission system to simulate, as they calculate all data of the network. While properties like reactive current and line frequency – both specific to AC power – are important in real systems, their meaning and impact is rather cryptic to the novice user. Beginners would have trouble finding, for example, the resistance and thermal properties of transmission lines, the efficiency of power plants and transformers, and many more data required to set up simulations in these existing systems.

## 3   PowerSurge Design

In this section, we detail the design concept of the PowerSurge software, including its user interface, gamification elements [9], and its underlying domain model.

### 3.1   Visualization of Simulated Units

To simplify the visual representation of the power transmission network, the system is based on the look and feel of a board game. Game pieces which can be placed on the playing field (a map of Germany) are *nodes* that represent power plants, consumers, distribution nodes and *transmission lines* which connect the nodes to form a network. The nodes are composed of a 3D model to represent the type of the node and a base plate on which additional data can be represented. The models are simplified but the optical characteristics of each node type allow for easy visual distinction by the user. The available node types are shown in Fig. 1.

**Fig. 1.** All node types available in our simulation. From left to right, these are: a distribution node, a consumer node, a nuclear power plant, a coal power plant, a hydro power plant, a wind park and a solar power plant.

The diameters of the transmission lines symbolize their power capacity. The magnitude and direction of the power flow is visualized by the movement speed and direction of the stripes on the connections' surfaces. An example network of the major power plants and cities near Augsburg and Munich is illustrated in Fig. 2.

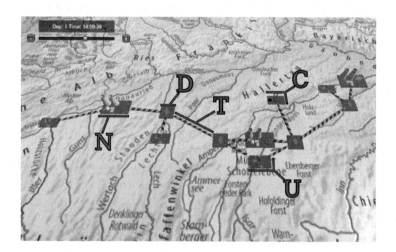

**Fig. 2.** An example network. The visible game elements are: nuclear power plants (N), a coal plant (C), cities (U) and distribution nodes (D), all of which are connected by transmission lines (T).

We used various techniques to represent the current state of the network. (1) A pie chart on the generator nodes' base plates fills according to the current load. The indicator also changes its color in a gradient from green to red the closer the load gets to the maximum output. (2) The maximum power output of a node is represented by its size. When a node is dropped onto the field, its size is scaled up or down according to its maximum output relative to the network's overall power generation. Whenever the distribution of power generation among all power plants on the field changes, the relative sizes are updated to reflect these changes. The same technique is used for the transmission lines. The more power it can transport, the thicker the line gets. (3) To show the direction of flow and the amount of electrical power transported by a line, the black lines on each transmission line's surface move in the direction of the power flow. The movement speed depends on the amount of power transferred on this line relative to the maximum power flow of all lines on the network. This way the user can quickly determine which lines transport a lot of power and which lines don't. An example of these relative sizes is shown in Fig. 3.

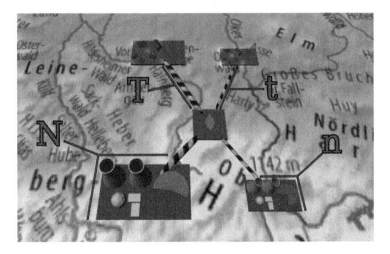

**Fig. 3.** Nodes and transmission lines are scaled according to their current load or power output. The thicker transmission line (T) currently transports more power than the thinner line (t). Analogously, the larger power plant (N) generates more power than the smaller one (n)

It is possible for a transmission line to be overloaded by a distinct percentage. While this should be avoided and is not a permanent solution for a stable network, it makes the network more resilient toward short bursts of power. In case a line is overloaded, the color of the white stripes on the line's surface turn red to alert the user to the problem.

Introspection of the various simulated units allows to access additional data such as the generator nodes' output (Fig. 4), the consumer nodes' power intake, maximum load, and daily load patterns, or the power lines' transported power, their maximal capacity, and their possible overload. For an overview of the date of the whole network, the sidebar presents various information like the total produced and consumed power, the amount of power lost due to resistance, the percentage of fossil or renewable energy production and further more information.

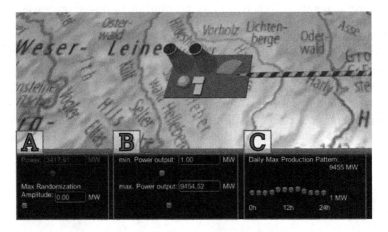

**Fig. 4.** The information bar for a generator node shows its current power output and the maximum output randomization amplitude (A), the minimum and maximum power output (B), and the daily maximum production pattern (C).

## 3.2   User Interaction

In our simulation, it is possible to change the parameters of all nodes and transmission lines while the simulation is running, and the user will experience a real time adaptation of the network to the new settings. To add nodes to the system, the user can select the desired type of node from the sidebar and then drop it anywhere on the field, though it is not possible to drop nodes on top of each other. Connections can be drawn between individual nodes, selecting them in *connection* mode. Yellow and red backdrops of the targeted nodes indicate whether or not a connection can be established. By clicking on a node or transmission line, that game piece gets selected, which is indicated by a green highlight around the object. While a game piece is selected, the user may remove it from the game – as long as this action is not forbidden by the game scenario the user is challenged with. This case may also keep the user from inspecting an object and changing all its parameters as seen exemplarily in Fig. 4.

## 3.3   Gamification

In order to encourage the user to explore the simulator the application offers three different stages of the game. We included a set of *tutorial levels* to introduce the user to the contents of the software, the meanings of the visualizations, the interaction mechanics, and the goals and challenges of the simulated domain.

The first tutorial level is exemplarily shown in Fig. 5. As soon as the user is familiar with the basic interaction mechanics and the relationships of the simulated units, he can prove himself in scenarios of increasing difficulty. In the according *scenario mode*, the user has to overcome some predefined constraints in order to achieve certain goals. One scenario asks, for instance, to provide at least 20 % of consumed power from renewable sources while using no more than 20 power plant and 30 transmission lines supplying a given set of consumers. The user is presented with a list of the subgoals for each scenario before it begins, and he can revisit this list at any time via the game menu. An example of this overview screen is shown in Fig. 6. After fulfilling all the subgoals of a scenario, the user is notified and he may advance to the next one. If subgoals are no longer satisfiable, for instance when a time-limit is exceeded, the user fails in that scenario. An appropriate *game over* screen is shown and the user may restart this scenario or switch to a different one.

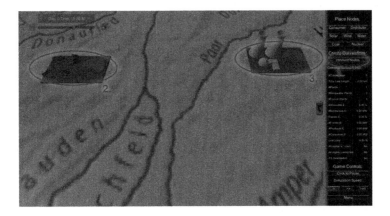

**Fig. 5.** The first tutorial level to guide the user step-by-step through the interaction mechanics and to familiarize him with the simulated domain. In red, we hint at a sequence of steps that establishes the required connection to move on to the next level (Color figure online).

PowerSurge also includes a *discovery mode*, a scenario free of any constraints, where users can try out various model configurations on their own agenda. When the simulation is running in discovery mode, the user may construct arbitrary power transmission networks with no restrictions on size of the network, resources spent or network composition. Even the otherwise imposed fixed time sequence is now softened: here, the user may go back and forward in time as desired. All produced data, i.e. time series of all the graph's variables, can be logged on disk as portable comma-separated lists for further analysis. Through this interface for scientific evaluation, one could, for instance, measure network properties, such as topology, robustness (in terms of redundancy and minimum supply) etc.

**Fig. 6.** Exemplary display of the goals of a scenario. These goals are presented to the user before diving into the simulation.

## 3.4   Scripting Game Contents

Especially in an educational setting it is important to have the flexibility of defining specific problem scenarios. PowerSurge is designed to be extended accordingly. Goals and constraints of new scenarios can be scripted based on a variety of possible subgoals provided by the engine. An overview of these subgoals is shown in Fig. 7. In the following, we describe some of these goals.

The first goal, i.e. *Max Time To Achieve Goals In Days*, sets a global time limit for all subgoals to be completed. Exceeding this limit, results in failing the scenario. The second one determines the minimum percentage of renewable energy produced in the Power Network. Additionally, a period can be set, how long the system has to supply that proportion continuously (using *AVGProduction Period Length*). Consider, for Instance, that at night there is less available renewable power available than on a bright sunny day, when solar radiation can also be harnessed. The goal, *Max Network Failure Time* denote the maximum limit of time a network failure is allowed to last. If *Network Failure Time Stacks* is set, that time will not be reset, if the system stabilizes again. A single-component graph is required, if the goal *Network Graph Must Be Complete* is set. This means that starting at any node, every other node on the playing field must be reachable. No disjoint network components are permitted. Each requirement is individually adjustable, being ignored if set to the default value (−1 or *disabled*). During the simulation, all of the subgoals are continuously tested to detect whether the overarching scenario goal is already met, or, in the worst case, cannot be reached any longer.

In PowerSurge, offering challenges to the user is synonymous with restricting his interaction possibilities, i.e. going from an all-flexible editor towards a concrete real-world problem perspective. Otherwise, the user could easily bypass the designed challenge by deleting lines or nodes, or by adjusting their production or throughput values. Therefore, we implemented a simple access rights management system for the simulated objects. As a result, user access can be individually adjusted for each object when setting up new scenarios. There are three access modes: (1) *Modify and delete* grants the user full rights to modify the object's properties or even remove it from the screen. (2) *Modify only* allows

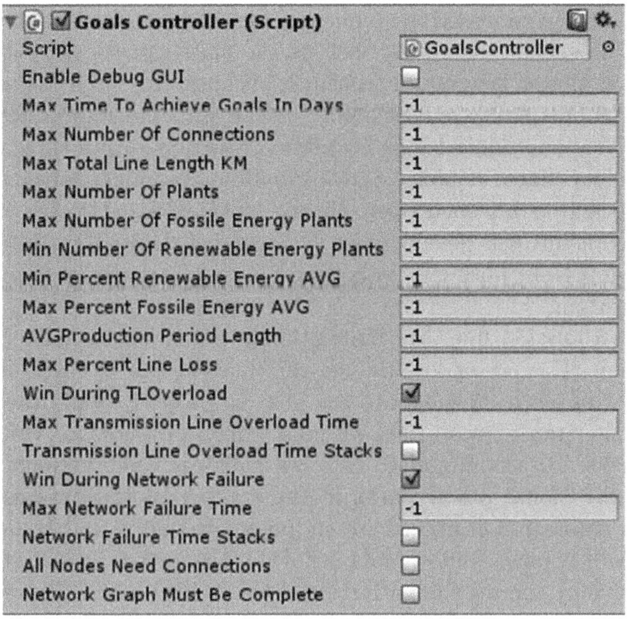

**Fig. 7.** Scriptable goals for new scenarios (entries with the default parameter $-1$ are not considered for the evaluation).

the user to modify all properties but not to remove the object itself. (3) *Sealed* means that the user can only view the placement's current properties to react to its behavior during play.

### 3.5   Domain Model

Formally, the power transmission network in our simulator is represented by an undirected graph. In this graph, the vertices or nodes are the consumers (e.g. cities), generators (power plants) and distributors (which neither produce nor consume power). All node types share one property, the power production/consumption $P_{self}$, which is positive/negative if the node generates/consumes power, or zero, if the node solely distributes power. In addition, the constant base consumption of a consumer node is captured by $P_{base}$. A load pattern defines the node's fluctuating power consumption over the course of a day. A generator node has both a minimum and a maximum power output value $P_{min}$ and $P_{max}$, respectively. Its output is further modified by a function of time (consider day/night cycle), and a randomized fluctuation with the amplitude of $P_{randAmp}$. The nodes are connected by means of transmission lines. The resulting graph is irreflexive, i.e. no node can be connected to itself. A transmission line is characterized by the two nodes $A$ and $B$ to which it is connected, its length $l$, its maximum power load $P_{max}$ and its maximum overload factor $f_{overload}$.

In addition to user-defined or scenario-dependent parameters, the simulation has to solve for specific variables, such as the actual power output of all generators and the power flow on all transmission lines. To derive these values, we set up a system of equality and inequality constraints modelling the behavior of the network. We then minimize an evaluation function within these constraints, using a boundary, linear equality and inequality constraints solver provided by the accessible and established open library ALGLIB [10,11]. We were able to directly embed it into our development environment, Unity3D[1]. In the following paragraphs we present both the evaluation function and all constraints imposed on its optimization.

As the transmission lines are bidirectional, power on each line can flow in either direction. The power loss due to the line's electrical resistance depends on the amount of power flowing into the line. To properly apply the power conservation to the transmission line, we must therefore know in which direction the power flows. To accommodate this, we split each bidirectional power line into two unidirectional power paths in the context of the optimization. This means that a transmission line whose endpoints we call A and B has four optimization variables, power inflow and outflow for the path from A to B ($P_{in}^{AB}$ and $P_{out}^{AB}$, respectively) and for the path from B to A ($P_{in}^{BA}$ and $P_{out}^{BA}$, respectively). The evaluation function h optimized by the solver is composed as follows:

$$h = \sum_{i \in lines} (L(i) + S(i) + O(i)) \tag{1}$$

where for a given transmission line $i$ the power loss $L(i)$, the squared power values $S(i)$ and the overload $O(i)$ are defined as:

$$L(i) = \lambda^{l(i)} * P_{in}^{AB}(i) + \lambda^{l(i)} * P_{in}^{BA}(i) \tag{2}$$

$$S(i) = P_{in}^{AB}(i)^2 + P_{out}^{AB}(i)^2 + P_{in}^{BA}(i)^2 + P_{out}^{AB}(i)^2 \tag{3}$$

$$O(i) = \begin{cases} E(i)^2 & \text{if } E(i) > P_{max}(i) \\ 0 & \text{otherwise} \end{cases} \tag{4}$$

$$E(i) = \max \left( |P_{in}^{AB} + P_{out}^{BA}|, |P_{in}^{BA} + P_{out}^{AB}| \right) \tag{5}$$

where $\lambda$ is the power retention factor per km of the transmission lines, $l(i)$ is the length of transmission line i, $P_{in}^{AB}(i)$, $P_{out}^{AB}(i)$, $P_{in}^{BA}(i)$ and $P_{out}^{BA}(i)$ are the power inflow and outflow of the two paths of transmission line i as explained above, and $P_{max}(i)$ is the maximum load of transmission line i. Power loss on the transmission lines (2) is the main criterion we want to minimize, so its inclusion is obvious. It should be noted here that the power loss is technically

$$P_{loss} = R \cdot I^2 = R \cdot \left( \frac{P_{flow}}{U} \right)^2 \sim P_{flow}^2$$

where $R$ is the line's electrical resistance, $U$ is the line voltage, $I$ is the current and $P_{flow} = U \cdot I$ is the total power flowing on the line. While the evaluation

---

[1] http://unity3d.com.

function could handle this quadratic function, the constraints for the optimizer must be linear in all variables. We therefore opted to use the linear relation $P_{loss} = R' \cdot P_{flow}$ (where $R' = \lambda^l$ is the power retention factor which acts as a stand-in for the line resistance) in both the constraints and the evaluation function in order to keep our system consistent. Including the sum of the squared endpoint power values (3) in the evaluation function minimizes the total power flow on the network. On the one hand, this serves to prevent power flow over detours – the more line endpoints need to be traversed by power flowing from generators to consumers, the more it factors into this summand. On the other hand, this prevents power from flowing in both directions at once on any transmission line, which would incur more power loss while reducing the net power transported over the respective line. Lastly, the overload summand (4) ensures that line overloading, while allowed, is discouraged. To achieve this, the overload summand is zero if the line is not overloaded. Once the line load enters the overload interval, this summand contributes the squared effective power flow of the line.

When searching for the equilibrium of a given power transmission network, the evaluation function discussed above is minimized with a set of constraints. This set is composed of two constraints for each node and eight constraints for each transmission line present in the network. A node $n$ of any type must meet the power balance constraint:

$$P_{self}(n) + \sum_{i \in cons(n)} (P_{in}(n, i) + P_{out}(n, i)) = 0 \qquad (6)$$

where $cons(n)$ is the set of all transmission lines connected to node $n$, $P_{in}(n, i) \leq 0$ is the power flowing from $n$ into the line $i$, and $P_{out}(n, i) \geq 0$ the power flowing from $i$ into $n$. This equality constraint (6) states that the total amount of power flowing into a node $n$ must equal the total amount of power flowing out of the node. In other words, taking the node's own power generation or consumption $P_{self}$ into account, no power may "magically" appear or disappear on the node. As previously mentioned, a distribution node $n_d$ neither generates nor consumes power, so its local power is constrained to 0:

$$P_{self}(n_d) = 0 \qquad (7)$$

The local power of a consumer node $n_c$ must exactly match the node's current consumption:

$$P_{self}(n_c) = P_{consume}(n_c, frac(t)) \leq 0 \qquad (8)$$

where the power consumption $P_{consume}(n_c, t)$ at simulation time $t$ (in days) is determined by the load pattern of the consumer node over the course of a day. As the simulation time $t$ is given in days, we extract its fractional part $frac(t)$ as the time of day. On a generator node $n_g$, the local power is constrained by the power output bounds:

$$0 \leq P_{min}(n_g) \leq P_{self}(n_g) \leq P_{max}(n_g, t) \qquad (9)$$

where the simulation time dependent maximum power output $P_{max}(n_g, t)$ is determined as:

$$P_{max}(n_g, t) = P_{pattern}(n_g, frac(t)) + uniform(-P_{randAmp}(n_g), P_{randAmp}(n_g))$$

The constant parameter $P_{min}(n_g)$ is the plant's minimum power output boundary. The plant's maximum power output is determined by a pattern $P_{pattern}(n_g, frac(t))$ analogously to the load pattern of consumer nodes. For renewable energy generation like wind and solar power, which are heavily subjected to natural fluctuations, an additional summand samples a uniformly random value within the given randomization amplitude $P_{randAmp}$. This fluctuation can be reduced or completely disabled for other plants, e.g. nuclear power plants, by setting $P_{randAmp} = 0$. For each transmission line $i$, these eight constraints apply:

$$\lambda^{l(i)} \cdot P_{in}^{AB}(i) + P_{out}^{AB}(i) = 0 \qquad \lambda^{l(i)} \cdot P_{in}^{BA}(i) + P_{out}^{BA}(i) = 0 \qquad (10)$$

$$P_{in}^{AB}(i) \leq 0 \qquad P_{in}^{BA}(i) \leq 0 \qquad P_{out}^{AB}(i) \geq 0 \qquad P_{out}^{BA}(i) \geq 0 \qquad (11)$$

$$|P_{in}^{AB}(i)| \leq f_{overload}(i) \cdot P_{max}(i) \qquad |P_{in}^{BA}(i)| \leq f_{overload}(i) \cdot P_{max}(i) \qquad (12)$$

The equality constraints (10) represent the power balance on the transmission line $i$. The amount of inflowing power $P_{in}^{AB}(i)$ or $P_{in}^{BA}(i)$, scaled by the line's power retention factor $\lambda^{l(i)}$, must equal the amount of outflowing power $P_{out}^{AB}(i)$ or $P_{out}^{BA}(i)$, respectively. The boundary constraints (11) state that the variables for power flowing into the line, $P_{in}^{AB}(i)$ and $P_{in}^{BA}(i)$, must have a negative sign, while those for power flowing out of the transmission line, $P_{out}^{AB}(i)$ and $P_{out}^{BA}(i)$, must have a positive one. Notice that it suffices to include only one of the inequality pairs (11) in the actual optimization. Together with the power conservation constraint (10), either of these boundary pairs implies the other one. Finally, the inequality constraints (12) ensures that power flow on no transmission line exceeds that line's effective maximum load, which is the product of the line's regular maximum load $P_{max}(i)$ and its maximum overload factor $f_{overload}(i)$.

## 4    Results and Future Work

We designed a system that allows the users to interactively learn about and explore the complexities inherent in power transmission systems. Several basic tutorials cover the basic relationships of producer and consumer nodes, introduce the intricacies of patching overloaded networks, and to minimize the utilization of resources such as the overall length of the power lines.

In a competition on interactive simulations, we presented PowerSurge to about 30 people, most of them students. They voted PowerSurge to be the best out of seven projects, including interactive simulations in domains as far apart as biology and traffic systems. Criteria in the competition comprised the complexity of the scientific model, the usability, and the visual appeal.

At this point, important aspects such as local energy storage systems are still missing, however, an understanding of the complex interplay between producers and consumers can already be gained. Apart from improving the functionalities of the simulator, we deem the following aspects as especially beneficial extensions: A highscore system could lead to a better grasp on the user performance and build social ties between the users, which is an important factor of motivation. Along these lines, multi-player modes could promote the collaborative (re-)design of power grids at moderate scales or increase the fun through one-on-one or team competitions. An extension of the time system could allow the user to go back in time and review the changes that were made to the system. Also it should be possible to create different branches of the timeline to tackle some of the problems with different ideas. New scenarios should allow for the definition of more constraints, for example the number of each type of node that can be planted. In addition to numerous other user-centered and technical improvements, we are planning to test our software as part of an educational curriculum.

# References

1. Steghöfer, J.P., Anders, G., Siefert, F., Reif, W.: A system of systems approach to the evolutionary transformation of power management systems. In: GI-Jahrestagung, pp. 1500–1515 (2013)
2. Herrmann, U., Kelly, B., Price, H.: Two-tank molten salt storage for parabolic trough solar power plants. Energy **29**(5), 883–893 (2004)
3. Paatero, J.V., Lund, P.D.: Effect of energy storage on variations in wind power. Wind Energy **8**(4), 421–441 (2005)
4. Masters, G.M.: Renewable and Efficient Electric Power Systems. Wiley, Hoboken (2013)
5. Colella, V.S., Klopfer, E., Resnick, M.: Adventures in Modeling: Exploring Complex, Dynamic Systems with StarLogo. Teachers College Press, Columbia University, New York (2001)
6. PowerWorld Corporation: PowerWorld Simulator, October 2014. http://www.powerworld.com/products/simulator/overview
7. Dugan, R.C.: Reference guide: the open distribution system simulator (opendss). Electric Power Research Institute, Inc. (2012)
8. Chassin, D., Schneider, K., Gerkensmeyer, C.: GridLAB-D: an open-source power systems modeling and simulation environment. In: 2008 Transmission and Distribution Conference and Exposition, T&D, IEEE/PES, IEEE, pp. 1–5 (2008). http://www.gridlabd.org/
9. Deterding, S., Sicart, M., Nacke, L., O'Hara, K., Dixon, D.: Gamification. using game-design elements in non-gaming contexts. In: CHI 2011 Extended Abstracts on Human Factors in Computing Systems, ACM, pp. 2425–2428 (2011)
10. Shearer, J., Wolfe, M.: Alglib, a simple symbol-manipulation package. Commun. ACM **28**(8), 820–825 (1985)
11. ALGLIB Project: ALGLIB: a cross-platform open source numerical analysis and data processing library, January 2014. http://www.alglib.net/

# Collaborative Diffusion on the GPU for Path-Finding in Games

Craig McMillan[✉], Emma Hart, and Kevin Chalmers

Institute for Informatics and Digital Innovation, Edinburgh Napier University,
Merchiston Campus, Edinburgh EH10 5DT, UK
{c.mcmillan,e.hart,k.chalmers}@napier.ac.uk

**Abstract.** Exploiting the powerful processing power available on the GPU in many machines, we investigate the performance of parallelised versions of pathfinding algorithms in typical game environments. We describe a parallel implementation of a collaborative diffusion algorithm that is shown to find short paths in real-time across a range of graph sizes and provide a comparison to the well known Dijkstra and A* algorithms. Although some trade-off of cost vs path-length is observed under specific environmental conditions, results show that it is a viable contender for pathfinding in typical real-time game scenarios, freeing up CPU computation for other aspects of game AI.

**Keywords:** GPU · Collaborative diffusion · Path-finding · Parallel · Games

## 1 Introduction

AI algorithms are one of the last areas within a typical game engine to exploit the computational power found in modern GPUs. With pathfinding algorithms being used within many games for navigation of computer controlled characters, developers could potentially exploit GPU hardware for this processing, hence freeing up the CPU for other more complex operations.

However developers need to carefully consider the types of algorithms that can be run on the GPU. Traditional pathfinding algorithms are often considered difficult to parallelize due to their highly divergent nature [1,2] which can have a significant impact on performance [3]. As a result it is necessary to consider algorithms with minimal divergence in which little or no effort is required to separate the problem into a number of parallel tasks. Such algorithms are described as *embarrassingly parallel* in order and are likely to result in the most effective use of the hardware.

We present a novel GPU implementation of the *collaborative diffusion* algorithm [4] which is embarrassingly parallel in its implementation and to the best of our knowledge has not been previously undertaken. We provide a comparison against two widely used pathfinding algorithms; A* [5] the most commonly used within games and parallel and sequential versions of Dijkstra [6] which is guaranteed to find the shortest path. The version of Dijkstra used exploits dynamic

© Springer International Publishing Switzerland 2015
A.M. Mora and G. Squillero (Eds.): EvoApplications 2015, LNCS 9028, pp. 418–429, 2015.
DOI: 10.1007/978-3-319-16549-3_34

parallelism, an efficient use of hardware that makes it possible to launch kernels from threads running on the device. We evaluate the performance of each of the algorithms in a general path search across a range of different map sizes before looking at scenarios and environments which would typically be found within a game. Results show that a GPU implementation of diffusion is able to find paths within 60 frames per second, often considered real-time within the games industry and scalable to large maps. We also show that the path length and cost of diffusion is comparable to A* and Dijkstra within game environments.

The remainder of this work is organised as follows. The next section reviews related work in the area of GPU pathfinding. Section 3 provides an overview of the A*, Dijkstra and collaborative diffusion algorithms while Sect. 4 outlines the CUDA API. Section 5 gives a detailed description of parallelising the algorithms. Section 6 discusses the results from the experiments carried out. Finally Sect. 7 presents the concluding remarks and future work to be carried out.

## 2    Related Work

Caggianese and Erra [7] describe a parallel version of A* which uses grid space decomposition to parallelise the algorithm such that it is suitable for the GPU using CUDA. They compared their approach to a GPU implementation of Real-Time Adaptive A* (P-RTAA*). Algorithms were tested on grids upto a size of $1024 \times 1024$ for multiple agents up to 262144. The approach proved faster than P-RTAA* for each group of agents tested achieving speed ups up to 45X. The algorithm found paths of similar length to A*, but showed a trade off in speed vs optimal path when using different sizes of planning blocks. However as speed is likely to be the hightest priority in real-time applications, longer sub-optimal paths may be an acceptable trade-off.

Ortega-Arranz *et al* [1] present a parallel implementation of Dijkstra's algorithm. Their implementation parallelizes the internal operations of the algorithm, exploiting the two internal loops within the algorithm. An *outer loop* is responsible for selecting a new current node while the *inner loop* checks each of the current nodes neighbours and calculates the new distance values. The *outer loop* is parallelized by simultaneously selecting multiple nodes that can be settled in parallel without affecting the algorithm correctness, and the *inner loop* by looking at each neighbour of a node in parallel. Ortega-Arranz *et al* compare their parallel implementation to an equivalent sequential implementation across a range of different graph sizes, achieving a 13X to 220x speed up with their GPU implementation compared to the CPU sequential implementation across the graph sizes tested.

## 3    Pathfinding Algorithms

We describe two potential but contrasting approaches for pathfinding in a game environment that lend themselves to parallelization on the GPU. For completeness, A* is also described given its frequent use in games.

### 3.1    Traditional Pathfinding Algorithms

Dijkstra's algorithm [6] solves the single-source shortest path problem for a non-negative weighted graph. Nodes in the graph can represent either a 2-dimensional grid or points in 3D space. For a given source node the algorithm finds the lowest cost path between that node and every other node in the graph. As Dijkstra will evaluate every node in the graph it can be computationally expensive. As a result it is rarely used within games.

A* [5] is an extension to Dijkstra's algorithm. Unlike Dijkstra, A* uses heuristics to determine which nodes in the graph to settle. A node is considered settled once the shortest path between that node and the source node has been found. This allows A* to search only a fraction of the nodes in a graph in order to find a low cost path between two nodes. This has led to A* becoming commonly used within many games due to its low computational overhead and ability to find low cost paths in real-time.

### 3.2    Collaborative Diffusion

Repenning [4] introduces Collaborative Diffusion, inspired by physical processes that spread matter over an N-dimensional physical or conceptual space over time. Repenning introduced the idea of using diffusion based techniques and the idea of antiobjects to find paths as a means to address some of the limitations of traditional path search algorithms [4]. *Collaborative diffusion* is based on the notion of programming concept of *antiobjects* — an object that appears to do the opposite of what might be expected [4]. For example, in the game Pac-Man it might be natural to assign path-finding computation to each of the ghost agents. However, by assigning this computation to the objects that define the background instead, opportunities for redistributing the computation in a manner that can be parallelized may improve performance. This results in a great deal of the computational intelligence being shifted into the environment; although the ghost agents appear to be intelligent, in reality the intelligence lies in the background which becomes a computational reflection of the game topology, including the player location and their state. This allows agents to collaborate and compete, resulting in sophisticated emergent behaviours. In addition to naturally emergent behaviours occurring, an added benefit is that the number of agents pathfinding within an environment also has no effect on the time taken by the algorithm to find a path as path searching is handled independently of the agents. As a result the use of antiobjects enables games with large numbers of agents to be built.

Collaborative Diffusion is typically used within a tile-based environment, each goal node is given an initially high diffusion value which is used as the starting node: over time this value is spread throughout the world according to Eq. 1 until each passable tile obtains its own value. $D$ refers to the diffusion value, $n$ the number of neighbouring nodes, $a$ the diffusion value of a neighbour, and $\kappa$ is the cost of the node. Neighbours are defined by a metric appropriate to the graph; in a typical 2-dimensional grid-world, the *Moore* neighbourhood comprising of the eight cells surrounding any given cells is typically used. Once values have diffused across the complete graph, a path can be backtracked to the goal from any node by simply moving to the neighbouring node with the largest value.

$$D = (\frac{1}{n} \sum_{i=0}^{n} a_i) \cdot \kappa \qquad (1)$$

To the best of our knowledge no research has been undertaken into a parallel GPGPU implementation of diffusion to perform searching. However, Sanders *et al.* [8] provide an example of a GPU implementation of simulating heat transfer via a similar diffusive process, and discuss performance considerations relating to how a grid is stored.

## 4  CUDA Overview

The Compute Unified Device Architecture (CUDA) platform [9] is a general purpose computing API that has been designed for performing tasks that would traditionally be executed on the CPU, on the GPU. CUDA was first released in 2007 by NVidia and is a proprietary platform for Nvidia hardware. CUDA applications consist of host code which is executed on the CPU and device code, also known as *kernel* code, which is executed on the GPU. The host system communicates with the device by copying over a set of data and then giving the device a task to perform on the data. This is typically done by splitting the work into multiple threads and each thread then performing the same operation on different parts of the dataset. While offering obvious opportunities for speed-up in comparison to the CPU, care must be taken in porting code. For example, branch divergence can lead to threads no longer being executed in parallel, with their computation becoming serialized. This can result in lower performance as the execution units on the GPU are not being fully utilized.

New with NVidia's Kepler GK110 architecture [10] is a *dynamic parallelism* feature that allows the GPU to launch threads directly and generate new work for itself without ever having to involve the CPU. This results in the ability to run more of an application on the GPU as kernels running on the device are able to adjust the number of threads being launched depending upon the needs of the application, improving both scalability and performance through support for more varied parallel workloads and freeing up the CPU for other operations.

## 5  Parallelising the Path-Finding Algorithms

### 5.1  Dijkstra

The Dijkstra algorithm partitions all nodes into two distinct sets, *unsettled* and *settled*. Initially all nodes are in the unsettled sets, e.g. they must be still evaluated. A node is moved to the settled set if a shortest path from the source to this node has been found. As outlined by Ortega-Arranz *et al* [1], Dijkstra can be thought of as operating around two loops: the *outer loop* selects the lowest cost node from the unsettled set while the unsettled set is not empty whilst the *inner loop* evaluates each of the current lowest cost nodes neighbours. Each node in the unsettled set must be checked one at a time with the fastest sequential implementations being based around an efficient implementation of a minimum priority queue to allow fast retrieval of the lowest cost node. Algorithm 1 shows the pseudo code for the *outer* and *inner* loops of the sequential Dijkstra implementation.

---

**Algorithm 1.** Sequential Dijkstra Outer and Inner Loops

---
```
 1: while unsettledSet != empty do
 2:       currentNode = node in unsettledSet with minimum distance[d]
 3:       remove currentNode from unsettledSet
 4:       for each neighbour n of currentNode do
 5:           //Calculate the cost of passing through the neighbour
 6:           cost = distance[currentNode] + length(currentNode, n)
 7:           if cost < distance[n] then
 8:               //Update the cost and parent of the neighbour
 9:               distance[n] = cost
10:               previous[n] = currentNode
11:               add n to unsettledSet
12:           end if
13:       end for
14: end while
```

---

The outer `while` loop can be parallelised by selecting multiple nodes from the unsettled set and settling them at the same time without effecting the algorithm's correctness. This set of nodes are known as the frontier set which is generated by selecting any node in the unsettled set which has a tentative distance of the current *minimum* +1.

Our parallel implementation makes use of CUDA *dynamic parallelism* allowing the entire Dijkstra process to be run directly on the GPU. Algorithm 2 outlines the parallel Dijkstra implementation.

## 5.2   Diffusion

The parallel diffusion algorithm is given in Algorithm 3. The sequential version differs in the manner in which the grids are stored in memory so that they can be accessed appropriately, with an additional process in the parallel version to pass the grids between host and device and vice versa. The speedup of the parallel version comes from the ability to process each node in the grid at the same time — this is easy to achieve as diffusion is embarrassingly parallel, meaning the problem can be split into a number of parallel tasks as each node has exactly the same calculation applied to it.

At the start of each iteration of the `while` loop, the value of the goal node is set so that it remains constant and spreads evenly throughout the grid. The goal value is then diffused over the grid according to Eq. 1. The diffusion value is multiplied by the node cost $\kappa$ in each calculation. Costs are set between 0 and 1 (where zero represents an impassable tile and 1 a fully passable tile). The diffusion value thus decays quickly in areas with a value closer to zero. Once the goal

---

**Algorithm 2.** Parallel Dijkstra Outer and Inner Loops

---

```
 1: while unsettledSetEmpty == FALSE do
 2:       //Get the minimum cost in the unsettled set
 3:       for all nodes in unsettled Set do                    ▷ Executed in parallel
 4:           getMinimumCost()
 5:       end for
 6:       //Create the frontier set
 7:       for all nodes in unsettled Set do                    ▷ Executed in parallel
 8:           if nodeCost[threadID] <= globalMin + 1 then
 9:               addToFrontier[threadID]
10:           end if
11:       end for
12:       //Evaluate frontier set
13:       for all nodes in frontier Set do                     ▷ Executed in parallel
14:           evaluateNode()
15:       end for
16:       //Check if the unsettled set is empty
17:       if unsettledSet == EMPTY then unsettledSetEmpty = TRUE
18:       end if
19: end while
```

---

**Algorithm 3.** Parallel Diffusion

---

```
1: while gridDiffused != TRUE do
2:       setGoals(inputGrid, goalGrid)           ▷ Executed in parallel for all nodes in map
3:       diffuseGrid(outputGrid, inputGrid)      ▷ Executed in parallel for all nodes in map
4:       if CheckGridDiffused(outputGrid) then
5:           gridDiffused == TRUE
6:       end if
7:       swapGrids(inputGrid, outputGrid)
8: end while
```

---

value has spread to every tile in the graph, it is possible to backtrack a path from any point in the graph.

# 6    Results

Sequential and parallel versions of Dijkstra and diffusion were implemented, alongside a sequential version of the A* algorithm. Sequential versions were written in C++, and parallel versions using the CUDA API.

Each algorithm was tested on 2D-grids ranging in size from $32 \times 32$ to $256 \times 256$. Two scenarios were tested; in the first each node had equal weight, while in the second each node was assigned a random weight between one and ten. For the diffusion algorithms this weight was normalized and inverted so that the weight is a value between zero and one. The source node was always in the top-left corner, and the goal in the bottom-right, giving paths with the maximum possible Euclidean distance. Sequential versions of the algorithms were run on a Intel(R) Core(TM) i7-2600K 3.4 GHz CPU while the parallel versions were run on an NVidia Tesla K40 GPU. All experiments were repeated 10 times and the time in milliseconds to obtain a path to the goal recorded. In each experiment the *cost* of a path was also noted.

## 6.1   Time to Find Goal Node

Figure 1 compares the results of all five algorithms, showing the average time taken to find a path across a range of graph sizes in which (a) all nodes had equal weight (b) nodes were assigned a random weight between one and ten.

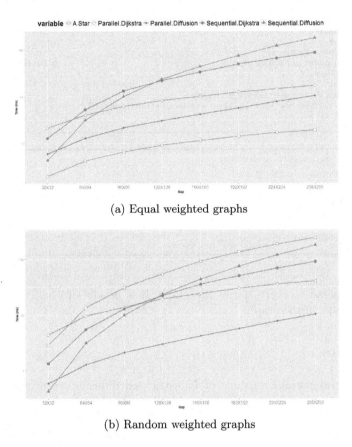

(a) Equal weighted graphs

(b) Random weighted graphs

**Fig. 1.** Time (ms) to find goal node for sequential and parallel algorithms across equal (a) and random (b) weighted graphs

In 1(a) we clearly see that A* outperforms both the sequential and parallel versions of Dijkstra and Diffusion. Collaborative Diffusion is faster than both the parallel and sequential versions of Dijkstra. In contrast, sequential diffusion fares worst of all the algorithms except in the single case of the smallest graph. The parallel version of Dijkstra scales better than its corresponding sequential version. This is due to the fact that when weights are equal sequentially Dijkstra requires $n^2$ iterations of the outer loop to find a path compared to only $n$ iterations in the parallel version for an $n \times n$ grid like those used in the tests. The situation is reversed however when using graphs with randomly weighted nodes.

In the weighted graphs 1(b), A* is the slowest algorithm in all but the smallest graph; upto 5× slower than parallel Dijkstra and upto 24× slower than the parallel diffusion implementation. Parallel diffusion is fastest in all cases except for the smallest graph. Parallel Dijkstra is slower than its sequential counterpart until a graph size of $160 \times 160$ is reached.

The poor performance of both A* and parallel Dijkstra in weighted graphs can be easily explained. A* is particularly successful in graphs with nodes of equal cost due to the use of a heuristic that enables it to search only a small fraction of the graph. However when node costs are random, the algorithm needs to search many more nodes. A* evaluated more than 90 % of the nodes in each of the weighted graphs compared to between 0.5 % and 4 % of nodes when the weights are equal. The performance of Dijkstra suffers when there is a large variation in weight between nodes due to the way in which the *outer loop* and *frontier set* works as when there is a large variation in weight between nodes, fewer can be settled simultaneously as they do not meet the criteria to be added to the frontier set, resulting in extra iterations of the *outer loop* required to process all the nodes in the graph. The performance of parallel diffusion remains relatively unchanged between the equal and randomly weighted graphs unlike that of A* and Dijkstra suggesting that while A* is faster in maps where all weights are equal, diffusion may be the better choice of algorithm in cases where weights are all random or where maps within a game are likely to change between areas of equal and random weight. Thus the performance of diffusion is not effected by the weights within a graph.

## 6.2   Path Length vs Path Cost

In many computer games, it is necessary to distinguish between paths of short length and paths of low cost. For example, the shortest path to a goal might involve crossing terrain such as water or a swamp that expends more energy than moving across grass. Therefore, it is of interest to compare the length of paths found by each of the algorithms to the cost. 20 random $128 \times 128$ grids were generated. In each instance, costs were randomly assigned to each node in the range one to ten. Figure 2 shows the path length (number of nodes in path) plotted against the path cost (summed cost of nodes in path) for each of the algorithms. As expected both A* and Dijkstra find low cost paths through each of the graphs. However, when compared to diffusion, the paths are of a greater length, with diffusion finding paths that are between 30 and 51 nodes shorter. This comes with the trade-off however of paths being between 90 and 195 units greater than those found by A* or Dijkstra. In games where the cost of the path is critical to the game play diffusion may not be the most suitable algorithm.

## 6.3   Obstacles

In addition to varying terrain types, the environment in a computer game is also likely to contain obstacles which are impassable such as walls or large buildings.

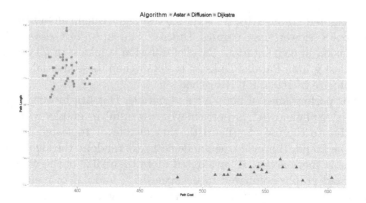

**Fig. 2.** Path Length vs Path Cost

Computer controlled characters must be able to find paths around these obstacles. To evaluate the performance of A*, parallel Dijkstra and parallel Diffusion in more realistic scenarios, we generate 4 maps with varying types of terrain and obstacles. For each of the maps we record the average time in milliseconds across 10 runs to find a path, along with the path length and the path cost. In each case the start node is the top left corner and the goal node is the bottom right corner. Figure 4 compares the paths found by both A* and Diffusion. Dijkstra has been omitted from this comparison as the paths found were near identical to A* and it took over 5× longer to find the paths than either of the other algorithms. Figure 3 records the time, length and cost of each experiment. In each case, t-tests show that the time difference is statistically significant at a 95 % confidence level.

| Algorithm | Time (ms) | Path Length | Path Cost |
|---|---|---|---|
| Diffusion | 0.61 | **32** | 50 |
| A* | **0.52** | 39 | **42** |
| Dijkstra | 2.87 | 39 | **42** |

(a) Map 1

| Algorithm | Time (ms) | Path Length | Path Cost |
|---|---|---|---|
| Diffusion | **0.59** | 49 | 113 |
| A* | 1.53 | 49 | 113 |
| Dijkstra | 6.08 | 49 | 113 |

(b) Map 2

| Algorithm | Time (ms) | Path Length | Path Cost |
|---|---|---|---|
| Diffusion | 0.75 | **39** | **39** |
| A* | **0.30** | 41 | 41 |
| Dijkstra | 2.34 | **39** | **39** |

(c) Map 3

| Algorithm | Time (ms) | Path Length | Path Cost |
|---|---|---|---|
| Diffusion | 1.27 | **75** | 147 |
| A* | **1.04** | 114 | **114** |
| Dijkstra | 8.07 | 114 | **114** |

(d) Map 4

**Fig. 3.** Time (ms), path length and path cost for the different algorithms across the different maps.

- **Map 1:** the path choice involves crossing a stream or using a lower cost bridge. A* opts for the lower cost moves, resulting in crossing the bridges (cost 42, path length 39), whereas diffusion 4(b) moves in a straight line (cost 50, path length 32), and is 1.17 times slower than A*.

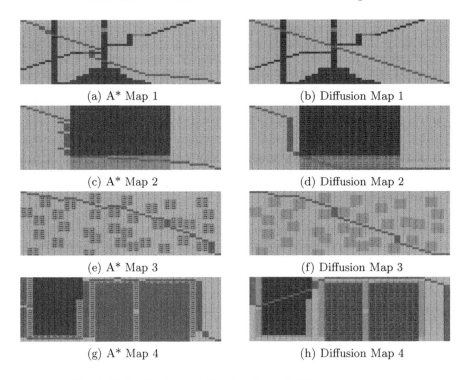

(a) A* Map 1                    (b) Diffusion Map 1

(c) A* Map 2                    (d) Diffusion Map 2

(e) A* Map 3                    (f) Diffusion Map 3

(g) A* Map 4                    (h) Diffusion Map 4

**Fig. 4.** Paths for A* and diffusion through different map types

- **Map 2:** approximately 50 % of the map is covered with high cost terrain. Both A* 4(c) and diffusion 4(d) found a path to the goal by moving through the area of lower cost terrain taking 49 nodes to reach the goal with a cost of 113. Although the paths are of equal length and cost, diffusion takes a straighter path with fewer turns, which is found 2.6 times faster than A*.
- **Map 3:** this contains a large number of impassable obstacles spread out across the map resulting in a large number of possible routes to the final goal. Diffusion 4(f) finds a shorter and cheaper path than A* 4(e) (cost, length = 39 vs 41 for A*). In this case A* was able to find a path 2.5 times faster than diffusion, albeit only with a difference of 0.45ms.
- **Map 4:** this contains a large number of nodes with high cost terrain separated by areas of impassable obstacles. This map provided the largest variation between the path length and path cost for each of the algorithms. A* 4(e) found a longer path taking 114 nodes to reach the goal compared to diffusions 4(h) 75 nodes. However the path found by A* is less costly than diffusion (114 vs 147). A* avoids all areas of terrain whereas diffusion takes short-cuts through the high cost areas. A* is 1.2 times faster in this case.

The results obtained in Sects. 6.1 and 6.2 show that in grids with nodes of equal weight, A* outperforms the parallel algorithm, with the converse being true on grids with randomly assigned weights. However, on maps 1–4 which attempt to reflect typical game scenarios, although diffusion performs fastest in only 1 out of 4 scenarios, all paths are found comfortably within 'real-time'. Figure 2 which analysed randomly weighted graphs suggests that diffusion finds paths of short-length at the expense of high-cost. Although this is the case in maps (1) and (4), in map (3) diffusion was able to find a path both shorter and less costly than A* and a path of equal length and cost in map 2. It appears that in an environment in which nodes are weighted in a structured rather than random manner, diffusion is a viable choice of method. Ultimately, the choice of algorithm will depend in the specific game in question, but the performance of diffusion in this respect may outweigh cost issues in many cases.

## 7   Conclusions

This paper has analysed the ability of three different path-finding algorithms to find paths through environments that are representative of those encountered in typical computer games, i.e. contain varied terrain or obstacles. In particular, we investigate whether path-finding algorithms such as Djikstra that traditionally might be thought of as too computationally expensive to be utilised within a game can be made tractable through exploiting the GPU. Additionally, we evaluated a path-finding algorithm called Collaborative Diffusion that has received little attention within the AI/Games literature.

A GPU implementation of diffusion performs particularly well in environments in which nodes do not have equal costs in terms of the time taken to find a path. This is particularly relevant for the majority of computer games in which environments consist of mixed terrain with variable energy costs for passing through. Timing results show that diffusion can be run on the GPU in real-time for graph sizes up to approximately $256 \times 256$ nodes: these sizes are well within the bounds of typical computer games — games such as Civilisation, StarCraft and SimCity all run in environments that are smaller than this. Diffusion typically finds shorter paths than either A* or Dijkstra, both of which favour paths with low cost — we note that from a game-playing perspective, the shortest path can often appear more realistic to an observer in taking a direct route. In environments containing obstacles, diffusion finds results comparable to A* in terms of cost and in a time-scale appropriate for real-time path finding. In addition, diffusion lends itself to use with multiple agents, opening up the possibility of emergent behaviours occurring, thus further enhancing the game-playing experience from a player perspective.

Currently, the evironments in which the algorithms have been evaluated are rather contrived. Future work will evaluate the performance of the parallelized algorithms within real game environments, using open-source APIs. Similarly it would be interesting to look at each of the algorithms in multi-agent scenarios, particularly diffusion as we have shown that the number of agents should have no effect on the time taken to find a path due to the nature of the algorithm yet the work carried out in [4] shows it can lead to a number of interesting emergent behaviours.

**Acknowledgement.** We gratefully acknowledge the support of NVIDIA Corporation with the donation of the Tesla K40 GPU used for this research.

# References

1. Ortega-Arranz, H., Torres, Y., Llanos, D.R., Gonzalez-Escribano, A.A.: new GPU-based approach to the shortest path problem. In: 2013 International Conference on High Performance Computing and Simulation (HPCS), pp. 505–511. IEEE (2013)
2. Johnson, T., Rankin, J.: Parallel agent systems on a GPU for use with simulations and games. Latest Advances in Information Science and Applications. In: Proceedings of the 1st International Conference on Computing, Information Systems and Communications (CISCO 2012), pp. 229–236. WSEAS Press (2012)
3. Han, T.D., Abdelrahman, T.S.: Reducing branch divergence in GPU programs. In: Proceedings of the Fourth Workshop on General Purpose Processing on Graphics Processing Units, GPGPU-4, pp. 3:1–3:8. ACM, New York, NY, USA (2011)
4. Repenning, A.: Collaborative diffusion: programming antiobjects. Technical report, University of Colorado (2006)
5. Hart, P., Nilsson, N., Raphael, B.: A formal basis for the heuristic determination of minimum cost paths. IEEE Trans. Syst. Sci. Cybern. **4**(2), 100–107 (1968)
6. Dijkstra, E.: A note on two problems in connexion with graphs. Numer. Math. **1**, 269–271 (1959)
7. Caggianese, G., Erra, U.: Exploiting GPUs for multi-agent path planning on grid maps. In: 2012 International Conference on High Performance Computing and Simulation (HPCS), pp. 482–488. IEEE (2012)
8. Sanders, J., Kandrot, E.: Cuda by Example. Addison Wesley, Reading (2010)
9. NVidia. Cuda toolkit 2013. https://developer.nvidia.com/cuda-toolkit. Accessed 17 October 2013
10. NVidia. Nvidia's next generation CUDA compute architecture Kepler gk110. Technical report, Nvidia (2013). http://www.nvidia.co.uk/object/nvidia-kepler-uk.html

# A Projection-Based Approach for Real-Time Assessment and Playability Check for Physics-Based Games

Mohammad Shaker[1], Noor Shaker[2]([✉]), Mohamed Abou-Zleikha[3], and Julian Togelius[4]

[1] Joseph Fourier University, Grenoble, France
mohammadshakergtr@gmail.com
[2] IT University of Copenhagen, Copenhagen, Denmark
nosh@itu.dk
[3] Aalborg University, Aalborg, Denmark
moa@create.aau.dk
[4] New York University, New York, USA
julian@togelius.com

**Abstract.** This paper introduces an authoring tool for physics-based puzzle games that supports game designers through providing visual feedback about the space of interactions. The underlying algorithm accounts for the type and physical properties of the different game components. An area of influence, which identifies the possible space of interaction, is identified for each component. The influence areas of all components in a given design are then merged considering the components' type and the context information. The tool can be used offline where complete designs are analyzed and the final interactive space is projected, and online where edits in the interactive space are projected on the canvas in realtime permitting continuous assistance for game designers and providing informative feedback about playability.

## 1 Introduction

Game design and content creation is complex and labour-intensive. Therefore, game developers have devoted large efforts to the development of reusable systems to facilitate game design and production. Third-party middleware companies also focus on reusability through providing essential game-independent functionalities such as path finding, animation and physics simulation [1, 2]. Most of these tools are designed for experts in game design and development.

Level design is an essential part of the game design process. Level designers put considerable time and effort into creating an interesting, playable level. This process is typically iterative where designers start with a simple sketch, check whether it is playable in its raw form and which parts work and don't work, and go back to the editing mode to change and embellish the level. This process is repeated until the designer is satisfied with the result.

© Springer International Publishing Switzerland 2015
A.M. Mora and G. Squillero (Eds.): EvoApplications 2015, LNCS 9028, pp. 430–442, 2015.
DOI: 10.1007/978-3-319-16549-3_35

Like for other labour-intensive processes, artificial intelligence techniques could be leveraged to assist and offload the designer. In particular, intelligent authoring tools could ease the design process and decrease time consumption, freeing the designer resource up for higher-level design tasks. Such tools should be easily accessible to game designers and provide comprehensible yet informative feedback [3,4]. There has recently also been much interest in developing tools that automatically check for playability, e.g. through the use of AI agents designed specifically to learn the rules of the game and explore the possible playable space afforded by the design [4].

One notable example of an industry-developed game-specific authoring tool is the one designed for the game *Rayman Legends* [5] which provides a user-friendly interface supported by automatic adjustment of basic features such as lighting, colour, and basic platform. The tool also allows real time editing and adjustment of the different game artefacts.

Recently, there has been increasing interest in academia in the creation of authoring and mixed-initiative tools. Some notable works include *SkectchaWorld* a tool for modelling 3D world through the use of a simple visual interface [6], *Tanagra* a mixed-initiative design tool for 2D platformer in which human and computer collaborate to design game levels [3], *Sentient Sketchbook* a tool that aids the design of game maps and automates playability check [7], *Ropossum* a mixed-initiative design tool that permits automatic generation and testing of physics-based puzzle games [8,9], and the assisted level design tool for the game *Treefrog Treasure* that enables visualisation of the reachability between the game components [10].

One of the core aspects when designing game levels and when implementing a designer-assistance tool is playability. Playability checking could be done in different ways. There are more or less direct approaches, based on e.g. verifying the existence of paths between different points [11], measuring gap widths and drop heights [3] or proving the existence of solutions when the game mechanics or some approximation thereof can be encoded as first-order logic [12]. However, in many cases you need to actually play the level in order to show that it is playable, and thus requires us to build an agent capable of playing the game [13]. Building an agent capable of proficiently playing a given game is rarely straightforward. The results obtained by most agents are usually the path followed to solve the level, if the level is playable [9] or simply a negative feedback indicating an unplayable design. Attention is rarely given to analysing or providing more informative feedback about the full interactive space afforded by the design artefacts. This can be highly beneficial for game designers since it provides information about the unused game components and the playable space in the level.

This paper introduces a new version of an authoring tool for physics-based game, and in particular a fast method for generating feedback to game level designers during the design process. We use the popular physics-based puzzle game *Cut the Rope* as a testbed for our approach. The AI inspects the current state of the game and projects possible future states; in contrast to the method used in a previous version of the tool, which was based on search in a

constrained space of game actions, the new method is based on search in a a
space of sequences of geometric operations. Part of the result of the method is
visualisation of the playable area, i.e. the proportion of the game level in which
actual interaction with the player can take place, on the game canvas. The area
is plotted on the canvas and updated with every edit by the designer. Thus, the
tool permits realtime visual feedback about the interaction space and whether
the game is solvable. This is achieved by defining an *influence area* for each
game component considering their physical properties and relative position. The
final interactive area is the combination of the influence areas of all components
presented in a design. Through accounting for the context information and the
physical properties, the agent is able to accurately infer the playable space without the need to simulate the game.

The current work builds on previous work by [14] on procedurally generating
content for the game using a search-based approach. This work was further
extended in [9] by implementing a simulation-based approach for playability
testing. The simulation used a Prolog-based agent that plays through the level
and considers only the most sensible moves at each state. Although the agent
is able to accurately detect a playable design, the method followed suffers from
a relatively high processing time (checking a single level takes an average of
$29.87 \pm 58.28\,\mathrm{s}$). Furthermore, the agent stops searching after finding the first
path that solves the level. Extracting all possible playable trajectories would
yield a substantial increase in the processing time.

The purpose of the work presented in this paper is not only to identify the
trajectory followed to solve the game, but also to provide an easy to interpret
visual illustration of all possible playable paths in real time. We believe that
this information is vitally important to game designers who are keen to easily
analyse their design and to rapidly realise the impact of their design choices on
player experience.

## 2   Cut the Rope: Play Forever

*Cut the Rope* is a popular commercial physics-based puzzle video game released
in 2010 by ZeptoLab for mobile devices. The game was a huge success and it
has been downloaded more than 100 million times. There is no open source code
available for the game so we had implemented our own clone using the CRUST
engine [15] and the original game art assets. Our clone, *Cut The Rope: Play
Forever*, does not implement all features of the original game, but includes all
the fundamental features and allows faithful reimplementation of a large portion
of the original levels.

## 3   The Influence Area

The fundamental concept in the method proposed here is the *Influence Area*
(IA) Each component in the game has its own physical properties that affect the
candy's trajectory, velocity and acceleration. The effect takes place when the

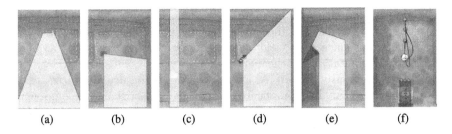

(a)          (b)          (c)          (d)          (e)          (f)

**Fig. 1.** Examples of the basic influence areas for the different game components. Inclu sion areas are presented in light colour while exclusion areas are in red.

candy falls within the IA of that component. A component's IA is is all possible trajectories the candy can follow when interacting with this component. An estimation of the IA is defined differently for each component according to its type as follows:

- Rope: The IA covers the candy's possible trajectories when detached from the rope. Since the physical properties of a rope resemble those of a spring, the rope's IA is defined as a trapezoid where its two legs are defined by the two lines passing through the rope's pin and one of its bases is the horizontal line passing through the candy (see Fig. 1(a) for an illustration).
- Air-cushion: Its IA is a trapezoid oriented in its blowing direction: one of its bases is the vertical line passing through the air-cushion, the distance to the other bases is defined based on the air blowing force; one of its legs is defined by a line passing through the air-cushion and angled slightly downwards due to the gravity force while the IA extends to the boundary of the canvas. An illustration is presented in Fig. 1(b).
- Bubble: The basic IA of a bubble is the simplest and is defined as a rectangle surrounding the bubble and extending upwards to the canvas boundaries. This covers the area of the bubble while floating and in the case of being pressed freeing the candy downwards as presented in Fig. 1(c).
- Rocket: Based on the rocket's direction, its IA is a trapezoid covering the candy's possible paths when set free. Consequently, the bases of the trapezoid are the vertical line passing through the rocket and the boundary of the canvas, its legs are the other canvas' boundary and a line starting at the rocket's position and angled according to its direction as can be seen in Fig. 1(d).
- Bumper: The IA of the bumper is the hardest to define due to its complex physical property and the dependency between its IA and the direction of the collision with the candy. The basic IA is defined as a six-point polygon covering all possible bouncing trajectories after the collision considering the effect of gravity. An example can be seen in Fig. 1(e).

The interactive space in a given design can then be identifying by combining the IAs of all components presented. We call this the *Projection Area* (PA). Note that the previously defined areas are carefully chosen approximations of the exact areas which could be more accurately determined by applying the laws of physics. We decided to consider these approximations instead of the exact calculations since they yield almost equally accurate results while being considerable computationally cheaper.

While the previously defined IAs are relatively easy to calculate, these are the most basic form of IAs. For complicated designs with more than one component, the IA of each component will typically be altered by the presence of another. Things get more complicated as the number of components increases and a more advanced solution becomes a necessity. The solution we propose differentiates between two types effects according to how the components' IAs interact: components of *inclusive* and *exclusive* effects. Components with inclusive effects are characterised by IAs that increases the PA already established either by expanding or by adding a new separated range. Exclusive effects, on the other hand, decrease the size of the PA through subtracting parts that became inaccessible as a result of adding a component with such property. Some of the components exhibit properties from the two types depending on their type and the other component of interaction. This applies for example to bumpers which expand the area in the direction that faces the candy and exclude the one in the other direction. Figure 1 presents some examples for both cases.

Given the components' characteristics and IAs, an agent can be implemented to provide an online visual feedback and playability check of complete designs or while the level is being designed through automatically expanding and/or reducing the final playable area as new components are being added or removed.

In the following sections, we describe the steps followed to identify the projection area using a projection agent.

## 4   The Projection Algorithm

The heart of the proposed method is the projection algorithm. This algorithm handles the interactions between the components and effectively and accurately defines the interactive area. The basic idea is that by starting with the ropes to which the candy is attached, and recursively expanding and/or subtracting fragments of the PA, we can ultimately deduce the area that is reachable by the candy. Eventually, we can assess whether a level is playable by examining the overlap between the resulting PA and Om Nom's position. If such an overlap exists, the level is playable. We considered a number of implementation choices when constructing the agent. In order to support these choices and clarify the reasoning behind them, we will start by explaining two scenarios where a naive implementation of the basic idea will not work.

**Scenario 1: Order Effect.** Combining the IAs of all components in one pass following Eq. 1 to build the final PA is not a feasible solution. This is mainly due to the nature of the game where the IA of a component depends primarily on the candy's current position, direction, and velocity and the order in which

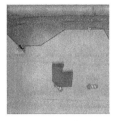

**Fig. 2.** Two different results of applying the IAs in different orders. The first image shows the IAs when applying: ropes, rockets and finally bumpers in order. The second image shows the IAs when applying: ropes, bumpers then rockets.

components are activated.

$$PA = \bigcup_{i=1}^{Components} IA_i \tag{1}$$

Consider an interaction between two ropes, two bumpers, two rockets and the candy as an example (Fig. 2). Applying the IAs of the components in a different order will lead to different results. For instance, if we apply the IAs in the order: ropes, rockets and finally bumpers, the result will be the PA presented in Fig. 2(a). As can be seen in this case, the IAs of the bumpers block the candy from reaching one of the rockets that lead to Om Nom and as a result, the level will be classified as unplayable. On the other hand, if we follow another order so that the IAs of the rockets are applied last, the resultant area will cover Om Nom and the level will be playable (Fig. 2(b)).

The order in which the components are handled is therefore essential since different order will lead to different PAs and consequently different judgement about playability. While it is vitally important to determine the sequence in which the components should be executed, this order is not obvious.

**Scenario 2: Solution Path.** One possible solution to the problem described in the previous section is to process the components according to the possible paths that could be followed to solve the game. This approach will also fail since it is highly likely that there will be more than one component that could be activated at any specific time during the game. The right order in which these components are handled can not be easily accurately defined (we will end up facing the same issue discussed in the first scenario). Furthermore, our goal is to define an area that constitutes all reachable positions and not only the ones that lead to the solution and this can not be achieved by relying solely on the solution path.

### 4.1 The Projection Algorithm

The above mentioned scenarios emphasise the need to a more intelligent strategy that considers rich context information and handles the ordering effect. This can

---

**Algorithm 1.** The Projection Algorithm

---

**Data**: List of components with their initial positions;
PA = ropes.applyIA();
coveredComps = PA.findCovered(allComps);
1 **while** *(not(empty(coveredComps))* **do**
2 |   coveredComps = PA.findCovered(allComps);
3 |   coveredComps = removeExcluded(coveredComps);
4 |   **for** *cc in coveredComps* **do**
5 |   |   PA += cc.applyIA();
6 |   |   projectionAlgorithm(PA);

---

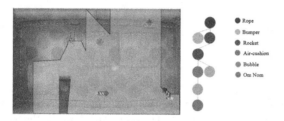

**Fig. 3.** Example level and the corresponding explored tree.

be achieved by constructing an agent that processes the components recursively one at time, analysing the game state and considering the possible interactions with other components in a depth-first approach until a stopping criteria is satisfied. The algorithm proposed is a search method that exhaustively traverses the full tree of possible paths. The resultant PA is the combination of all PAs for all paths explored. This permits extraction of the the full playable area (those interaction areas that lead to a solution and those that do not). We intentionally do not discard unsolvable paths since our goal is to help designers visualise the area that is used and in which players can take actions regardless of their outcome. The algorithm followed (Fig. 1) can be described as follows:

The algorithm handles two main data structures: a sorted list of components, *coveredComps*, and a PA (polygons represented as a list of points) that is constantly updated as new paths are explored. The algorithm starts by calculating the IAs of the ropes since the game always begins by cutting them to initiate the candy's movement. The components covered by the ropes are calculated and added to a set of covered components. The algorithm then iterates until the tree representing all possible paths is explored. In each iteration, a set containing the components covered by the IA of the currently processed component is calculated (line 2). The algorithm then checks if any of the covered components can be excluded (line 3) and removed from the set. A recursive call is then performed; the IA for each item in the set is calculated (line 5) followed by a recursive call to the algorithm with the newly formed PA (line 6).

Note that although the algorithm performs exhaustive search, the method takes on average $0.1 \pm 0.02$ s (over 100 runs) to process complete designs of

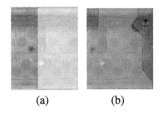

(a)             (b)

**Fig. 4.** The extended influence area of a bubble being covered by an air-cushion (a), and a bumper being covered by a bubble (b).

an average of $8.53 \pm 1.74$ components. This is because only few components become cover in every iterations and each level usually contains a small number of components. Figure 3 presents an example level and the full tree explored to calculate the PA. A step-by-step example of how the PA is calculated is presented in Sect. 6.1, however this example is presented to draw attention to the size of the tree and to clarify the very short amount of processing time required to traverse it.

The success of the projection algorithm depends on the following important details:

**Estimating the Interaction Direction.** An important factor that defines the IA of a component is the direction of interaction with the candy. For example, the IA of a bumper is reversible according to the direction of the collision. Simulating the game is one possible way to precisely set the direction. However this solution is too slow in many cases (an average of $29.87 \pm 58.28$ s is required to simulate one level [9] and the simulation has to be repeated for every edit). Moreover, we are not interested in the exact position but with a reliable estimation of the direction. For these reasons, the candy's direction is calculated according to the position of the last component with which the candy interacted. The algorithm proposed solves this issue by considering the order in which they become covered. Specifically, the direction of interaction with a component $n$ is the position of the component $n - 1$ in the recursive call.

**Handling Context.** We previously discussed the basic IA of each component and mentioned that the IA of one component is usually affected by the context. In the following, the IAs of some components are refined to account for their interaction (the IAs of the other components remain intact):

- Bubble: The presence of other components such as an air-cushion, a bumper or a rocket changes the IA of a bubble. When covered by a an air-cushion for example, the IA of the bubble extends so that the new area is a wider rectangle due to the effect of the air force.
- Bumper: The IA of a bumper is altered relative to the type of the other components placed nearby: the existence of a nearby bubble and an air-cushion,

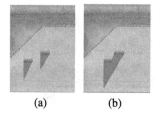

(a)               (b)

**Fig. 5.** Examples of the IA of two bumpers according to the distance between them. In (a), the bumpers are processed separately while in (b) their exclusion areas are combined since they are closer.

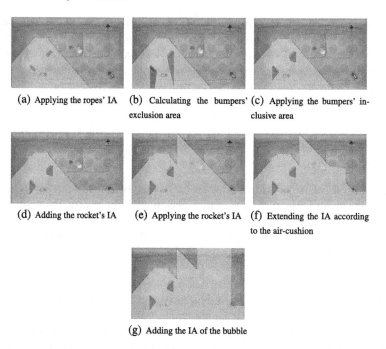

(a) Applying the ropes' IA    (b) Calculating the bumpers' (c) Applying the bumpers' in-
                              exclusion area             clusive area

(d) Adding the rocket's IA    (e) Applying the rocket's IA (f) Extending the IA according
                                                          to the air-cushion

(g) Adding the IA of the bubble

**Fig. 6.** The offline use of the algorithm. Projection area is presented in a light colour and excluded areas are presented in red (Colour figure online).

for instance, results in a new extended area as can be seen in Fig. 4. Also, the presence of another nearby bumper forms a new combined exclusive area as can be seen in Fig. 5.

When accounting for the above factors, the projection algorithm is capable of effectively constructing the PA and successfully detecting when the design is playable.

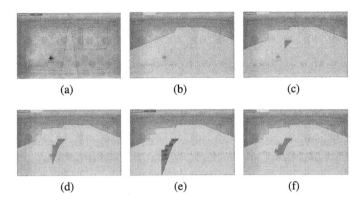

(a)                    (b)                    (c)

(d)                    (e)                    (f)

**Fig. 7.** The online use of the algorithm in Ropossum authoring tool. Projection area is presented in a light colour and excluded areas are presented in red (Colour figure online).

### 4.2 Implementation Details

The Clipper library [16] is used to preform polygon clipping. We used the C# version of the library and interface it with our physics engine (CRUST) to simulate the game[1].

## 5 Online and Offline Assessment

The projection algorithm presented and the scenarios discussed assume that the components and their positions are known and provided as input to the algorithm. In this case, the algorithm is used as a tool for post-design assessment of a level where the final interaction area is projected to give the designer a visual feedback. This information can be used to alter the initial design and changes to the PA can be visualised accordingly either in the offline mode (after all adjustments are made) or through the online mode.

In the online mode, the projection algorithm is activated while the scene is being edited. In this case, whenever a new component is placed in the canvas, the algorithm is called with the list of all components used so far. If the newly added component has an exclusive property, the PA is recalculated through a new run of the algorithm. Otherwise, the PA is expanded according to the type of the recently added component. This might result in covering other components in the scene and therefore the algorithm is called with the set of covered components only as input.

The IAs of the components were carefully tuned and the method has been tested on several cases and showed promising results in terms of accurately estimating the PA and identifying solvable designs. There is however no guarantee

---

[1] A video showing the method working is available online: http://noorshaker.com/CutTheRope.html.

that there are no levels on which the algorithm fails ((un)fortunately, we cannot report any). If such situations exist, we do not know whether the algorithm is biased towards false positives (cases where the method classifies unsolvable levels as solvable) or false negatives.

# 6    Showcases

Below we present two examples that showcase the algorithm's capabilities during both the offline and the online mode. Note that the algorithm works exactly the same in both cases and we differentiate between them to clarify and emphasise its capabilities.

## 6.1    Showcase 1: Offline Mode

In this example, a complete design is provided as input to the system to calculate and visualise the resulting playable area. Figure 6 presents an illustration of the steps followed by the algorithm. We start by calculating the ropes' IAs which in this case cover two bumpers and a rocket (Fig. 6(a)). Since the algorithm sorts the components so that bumpers are handled first, the areas excluded by the bumbers according to the candy's current position are then subtracted from the PA (Fig. 6(b)). Their coverage areas are then added to the PA, reincluding fragments of the area previously excluded (Fig. 6(c)). Continuing to handle the rest of the component, the IA of the covered rocket is then applied extending the PA to cover the other rocket (Fig.6(d)). The IA of the newly added rocket covers the air-cushion and the bubble (Fig. 6(e)). Recursively handling these two components results in first adding the IA of the air-cushion (Fig. 6(f)) then expanding the resultant area according to the IA of the bubble (Fig. 6(g)). At this stage, and since there are no more components to handle, the process is terminated and the level is considered playable. The visualisation of the PA in this case clearly illustrates that all components are accessible starting from the candy's initial position. It also reveals the active space of the canvas where actual interaction can take place.

## 6.2    Showcase2: Online Mode

The online use of the algorithm is illustrated in Fig. 7. We start by a simple level design of one rope and Om Nom (Fig. 7(a)). The player/designer can add, remove and/or reposition components using an authoring tool [8]. A green flag (top left) is used to indicate a playable design when adding a second rope (as in Fig. 7(b)). During the design process, the PA is continuously updated as the game state changes. Figure 7(c), (d) and (e) presents the updated PA after positioning three bumpers leading to the exclusion of Om Nom and as a consequence a detection of an unplayable level. This situation is overcame when the designer adds an air-cushion (Fig. 7(f)) which resets the flag.

**Table 1.** Comparison between the current approach and the previous ones. The table presents the time required to check if a design is playable (in seconds), the time required to evolve a playable design (in seconds) and the number of generations to reach the first valid solution.

| Agent | $Playability$ | $Evolution_{time}$ | $Generations$ |
|---|---|---|---|
| Pseudo-Random [14] | $0.98 \pm 0.64$ | $21.27 \pm 23.44$ | $2.63 \pm 1.82$ |
| Simulation-Based [9] | $29.87 \pm 58.28$ | $470.1 \pm 525.4$ | $2.48 \pm 1.58$ |
| Projection-Based | $0.1 \pm 0.02$ | - | - |

# 7  Ropossum Integration and Performance

The projection algorithm is incorporated as part of the authoring tool *Ropossum* [8]. Some of the functionalities previously provided are the automatic generation of playable content [14] and the automatic check for playability [9]. With projection areas as a newly added feature, designers can benefit from editing procedurally generated levels and visualising PAs of complete designs or during the level generation process. The method also supports playability check which can be done faster than the previous methods as presented in Table 1.

# 8  Conclusions

This paper presents a method for visualising and checking playability for physics-based puzzle games. The method proposed considers the physical properties of different game components and accordingly defines their space of influence. Informative combination of the influence areas of all components in a given design defines the playable space in which interaction with the player can take place. This was effectively achieved through a careful consideration of the context information. The algorithm executes in a short time and provides informative visual feedback both in the offline mode when the agent is set to work on a complete design and in the online mode while the level is being designed. While the method differs considerably from all previous methods for game level analysis that we know of in that it is based on the novel concept of Projection Areas and search in projection space, it is still at its core an artificial intelligence method that performs search in a problem- and domain-appropriate space.

There are a number of physics-based puzzle games where we see the proposed approach easily applicable. We are thinking of games such as Amazing Alex, Sprinkle, iBlast, Moki, Enigmo 2,Touch Physics 2, Chalk Ball, and Angry Birds; these games have similar properties to Cut the Rope in terms of in-game entities and their movement and interaction. Generalising the method to work for any game of this genre, perhaps by encoding mechanics in a description language for physical puzzle games, would be exciting future work.

**Acknowledgments.** We thank ZeptoLab for giving us permission to use the original Cut The Rope graphical assets for research purposes. The research was supported in part by the Danish Research Agency, Ministry of Science, Technology and Innovation; project "PlayGALe" (1337-00172).

# References

1. Havok (2011). www.havok.com
2. Interactive Data, 2011. SpeedTree
3. Smith, G., Whitehead, J., Mateas, M.: Tanagra: a mixed-initiative level design tool. In: Proceedings of the Fifth International Conference on the Foundations of Digital Games, pp. 209–216. ACM (2010)
4. Smith, A.M.: Open problem: Reusable gameplay trace samplers. In: Ninth Artificial Intelligence and Interactive Digital Entertainment Conference (2013)
5. Ubisoft, Ubisoft Montpellier, and Digital Eclipse, Rayman, Ubisoft (1995)
6. Smelik, R., Tutenel, T., de Kraker, K.J. Bidarra, R.: Integrating procedural generation and manual editing of virtual worlds. In: Proceedings of the 2010 Workshop on Procedural Content Generation in Games, p. 2. ACM (2010)
7. Liapis, A., Yannakakis, G., Togelius, J.: Sentient sketchbook: computer-aided game level authoring. In: Proceedings of ACM Conference on Foundations of Digital Games (2013)
8. Shaker, M., Shaker, N., Togelius, J.: Ropossum: an authoring tool for designing, optimizing and solving cut the rope levels. In: Proceedings of the AAAI Conference on Artificial Intelligence and Interactive Digital Entertainment (AIIDE). AAAI Press (2013)
9. Shaker, M., Shaker, N., Togelius, J.: Evolving playable content for cut the rope through a simulation-based approach. In: Proceedings of the AAAI Conference on Artificial Intelligence and Interactive Digital Entertainment (2013)
10. Bauer, A., Cooper, S., Popovic, Z.: Automated redesign of local playspace properties (2013)
11. Togelius, J., Preuss, M., Beume, N., Wessing, S., Hagelbäck, J., Yannakakis, G.N.: Multiobjective exploration of the starcraft map space. In: Proceedings of the IEEE Conference on Computational Intelligence and Games (CIG), pp. 265–272. Citeseer (2010)
12. Smith, A.M., Mateas, M.: Answer set programming for procedural content generation: a design space approach. IEEE Trans. Comput. Intell. AI Games **3**(3), 187–200 (2011)
13. Ortega, J., Shaker, N., Togelius, J., Yannakakis, G.N.: Imitating human playing styles in super mario bros. Entertain. Comput. **4**, 93–104 (2013)
14. Shaker, M., Sarhan, M.H., Al Naameh, O., Shaker, N., Togelius, J.: Automatic generation and analysis of physics-based puzzle games. In: 2013 IEEE Conference on Computational Intelligence in Games (CIG), pp. 1–8. IEEE (2013)
15. Millington, I.: Game Physics Engine Development. Morgan Kaufmann Pub, San Francisco (2007)
16. Johnson, A.: Clipper - an open source freeware library for clipping and offsetting lines and polygons (2014). http://www.angusj.com/delphi/clipper.php

# How the World Was MADE: Parametrization of Evolved Agent-Based Models for Backstory Generation

Rubén H. García-Ortega$^{(\boxtimes)}$, Pablo García-Sánchez, J.J. Merelo,
María Isabel G. Arenas, Pedro A. Castillo, and Antonio M. Mora

Department of Computer Architecture and Technology,
University of Granada, Granada, Spain
rhgarcia@ugr.es

**Abstract.** Generating fiction environments for a multi-agent system optimized by genetic algorithms (with some specific requirements related to the desirable plots), presents two main problems: first it is impossible to know in advance the optimal value for the particular designed fitness function, and at the same time, it creates a vast search space for the parameters that it needs. The purpose of this paper is to define a methodology to find the best parameter values for both, the evolutionary algorithm, and the own fictional world configuration. This design includes running, to completion, a world simulation represented as a chromosome, and assigning a fitness to it, thus composing a very complex fitness landscape.

In order to optimize the resources allocated to evolution and to have some guarantees that the final result will be close to the optimum, we systematically analyze a set of possible values of the most relevant parameters, obtaining a set of generic rules. These rules, when applied to the plot requisites, and thus, to the fitness function, will lead to a reduced range of parameter values that will help the storyteller to create optimal worlds with a reduced computation budget.

**Keywords:** Games · Plot · Content generation · Evolutionary algorithms · Agent based models

## 1 Introduction

In the very competitive cultural industry, that includes videogame creation, writers rack their minds in order to generate interesting fictional worlds.

In order to design these fictional worlds and the stories within them so that they are truly believable, efficient and massive, several automatic/autonomous methods have been proposed [1,2]. One of them, called MADE [1] finds 'interesting' character stories by running an evolutionary algorithm that optimizes a virtual world using a fitness function designed to better fit with the archetypes which the user desires they emerge in the world that he/she is designing.

MADE works as follows: every individual in the evolutionary algorithm is described by a chromosome that represents the parameters of one (or several

© Springer International Publishing Switzerland 2015
A.M. Mora and G. Squillero (Eds.): EvoApplications 2015, LNCS 9028, pp. 443–454, 2015.
DOI: 10.1007/978-3-319-16549-3_36

kinds of) finite state machine (FSM) [3] that is set to 'live' (interact) in a simulated environment. In [1] the evolutionary algorithm was run with a standard parameter configuration, meanwhile *sensible* non-evolutionary parameters (such as the size of the world or amount of food) were set as default values. There was no attempt to optimize these parameters, since the main intention seemed to be to have a prototype that allowed the authors to have an acid test of their proposed approach. That paper hinted at the fact that parameters such as the number of *profiles* (different types of finite state automaton present) had a big influence on the outcome, to the point of making it possible or not. However, other parameters, such as the number of simulated days the world is running, might also have influence, but the authors did not conclude to which level.

In this paper we will use the MADE open source simulator[1] and look at it from the evolutionary point of view so that we can check what kind of influence the configuration variables have in the outcome. We will do an experimental setup that will test different parameters (evolutionary and non-evolutionary), and eventually find a series of rules that will help the users of that framework to set the best values for their simulation (depending on their requirements or constraints). A discussion about the reasons to chose these parameters and values will be also presented.

The rest of the paper is organized as follows. Coming up next, we present the state of the art in parameter setting of simulated worlds. The next Sect. 3 will present the methodology, followed by the experimental setup in Sect. 4, whose results will be shown in Sect. 5. Finally, we will present our conclusions to finish the paper.

## 2    State of the Art

According to the taxonomy described by Togelius et al. [4] the problem of massively generating backstories for non-player characters (NPCs) can be considered *Procedural content generation (PCG)*, since it implies the generation of the characters and their relations in the game world. In this paper, we have used an *offline* approach since the computation is done in the phase of game design, also considered *search-based* due to the use of an evolutionary algorithm.

This paper is focused in the context of computational generation of massive plots without human interaction, and driven by goals proposed by the creator. Different approaches have been proposed in previous works (see the work of Arinbjarnar et al. [5] for a survey).

In 1976 the program called *Tale-Spin* [6] was able to produce purely text-based fairy tales where semi-autonomous characters showed emotions and relationships, with the shortcoming of creating very inconsistent plots. Then, different researches used the concept of *goals and pre-defined stories* to construct stories: In 1987, UNIVERSE [7] was used to create infinite soap opera style stories driven by goals provided by the author. It used fragments of stories

---

[1] Which can be downloaded from Github at https://github.com/raiben/made under a GNU/GPL V3 License.

to assign roles to stereotypical characters, relying on the reader the assumption of the characters' motivations. In 1994, Turner created Minstrel [8], a program which used case-based reasoning to generate stories about knights and ladies by replacing variables in existing stories and recombining them. It also used goals, in this case for the story and for every character. In 2008, Riedl and Leon used in [9] the same idea, conceptualizing a vignette as a small story assumed as 'interesting', thus they can compose complete stories when exposed sequentially.

The technique applied in this paper can be understood as the evolution of these researches adapted to massive worlds, where coherence is provided by the use of an Agent-Based Model (ABM for further references). Instead of using 'vignettes' to construct stories, our approach modifies the behavior of the agents and finds 'archetypes', i.e. behaviors and patterns universally accepted and present in the collective imaginary [10].

The idea of emerging plots from agents' interactions, that is, using agent-based models of the world to generate stories is not new. In 2007, Virtual storyteller [11], used agents that improvise using techniques from improvisational theater, a plot guide and a narrator. Our technique uses the same approach but there is no plot guide agent. Instead, a Genetic Algorithm (GA) guides the mood of the backstories created by finding 'archetypes' (selected by the user).

The search of a good plot can be addressed from the Evolutionary Computation (EC) point of view. To this aim in 2011, Nairat et al. proposed in [2] a generative drama approach that integrates human creativity by using an agent-based system where the characters are developed using interactive evolution. One year later, Cioffi-Revilla et al. [12] published a study that applies a combined EC-ABM approach to the challenge of understanding complex adaptive systems in social science. Their conclusions suggest further applications of EC to ABM in terms of multi-population models with heterogeneous agents, multi-objective optimization, dynamic environments, and evolving executable objects for modeling social change.

Our approach relies on this idea by using a GA to obtain the agents' life story that better fits the goals described by the user/author before the world is generated. It follows the methodology presented in [1]: systematize the generation of backstories in massive worlds, defining the elements of a complex world, and optimize the characters' behavior using GAs to extract information. Moreover, that work included a preliminary analysis of only one parameter: the number of profiles to use. Results in that paper shown that this parameter have a significant influence in the archetype-based fitness attained. The open-source simulator MADE used in the present work, was also introduced in that paper. However, the rest of parameters that conform the fictional setting (defined in [13]) were set as standard ad-hoc parameters.

In this research, we want to extend the previous study testing the rest of the parameters that model a story: the time, the world, the characters and the source of conflicts. These parameters might have a huge effect in the plot generation, where small variations could substantially alter the results, or on the other hand, some of them may be superfluous.

## 3   Methodology

As mentioned in Sect. 2, the proposed technique for generating fictional worlds relies in the use of a a combined EC-ABM approach (a GA in this case). The fitness function is configurable to fit the story needs. Then, some parameters have to be fixed: world constants, agents' constants and GA parameters. Finally, the GA has to search in a noisy space, due to the stochastic nature of the approach. The influence of each constant and parameter is, *a priori*, impossible to predict.

Our methodology systematizes the study of key parameters in the massive generation of backstories with an EC-ABM approach in order to optimize the resources allocated to evolution and to have some guarantees that the final result will be close to the optimum.

### 3.1   Problem Characterization

This methodology addresses to problems with the following characteristics:

1. Goal: The final goal is to generate stochastic virtual worlds massively inhabited by characters with backstories that are aligned with a mood defined by the writer.
2. Virtual world: The virtual world is modeled by the ABM.
3. Archetype: An archetype is a behavior pattern that can be present in a backstory.
4. Fitness: The evaluation of the virtual world can be based in the rates of archetypes (set by the writer) found in the characters that inhabit it.
5. Backstory: The backstory of a character is a set of actions and interpretations, coherent with the virtual world and the other agents.
6. Agent: The agent represents a character that performs actions in the virtual world depending on the neighborhood and its internal state.
7. Profile: The agents can be parametrized and their behavior (probabilities to perform actions) depends on these parameters. The profile (P) is the set of values for these parameters and is optimized by the GA.
8. Conflict: Every action is performed in a place and a time, affects to one or more agents and relates to the source of conflict.
9. Place: The agents occupy a location in a map, defined by its size (W).
10. Time: The world exists during a period of time (D). Every backstory is fed by actions as time goes by, in a bottom-up approach.
11. Source of conflict: The element that forces the agents to interact. For example, in this study, the food (F) can be considered as the source of conflicts between the agents; the element that the agents compete for.
12. Scenario: A set of archetypes that have to emerge.

### 3.2   Parameter Effects

As Morrell explains in [13], "fiction has three main elements: plotting, character, and place or setting", so, intuitively, these three elements can affect the backstories. In our problem, an agent is ruled by its profile, which defines its behavior.

Our technique uses the GA to evolve the profile(s) of the agents, so it will be part of the search space. Nevertheless, the use of different number of profiles (P) may also affect the behavior of the agents, since more profiles in the same world may imply new types of conflicts (as it was demonstrated in [1]).

The plotting is the result of the different conflicts, that are affected by the place, the time and the source of conflicts, which in this case is the food.

The place is defined by the size ($W$). Smaller maps usually imply more friction between the agents, thus different variations of $W$ may derive in different behaviors. The values that should be chosen are those that test a size smaller or equal to the neighborhood defined (letting all the agents access to all the resources and positions of the world), a size bigger than the neighborhood (forcing the agents to move to reach a new neighborhood) and much bigger (showing the effects of having a big inhabited world).

The time of the conflict is affected by the period of time that the world is given to run (D). In this sense, a longer period of time will usually imply more interactions, *ergo* more archetypes and better fitness, and eventually more agents in the world. In the other hand, the evaluation of an individual in the GA implies the execution of every agent and the evaluation of each backstory, thus more agents and bigger backstories may increment significantly the evaluation time. The values proposed for the study vary from a very short period of time to a bigger one, where the maximum is the agent's average lifetime. The food is modeled with the parameter (F). Changes in this parameter may increment or decrease the number of interactions.

Finally, exploration of the search space might be affected by the GA parameters. In this sense, the most significant parameter is the population size (S), since bigger populations will provide more accuracy but spend more execution time.

To sum up, our methodology will systematically combine more than two variants of five parameters and study how the fitness is affected. The parameters proposed for the problems characterized in Sect. 3.1 are the number of profiles (P), the world size (W), the virtual time (D), the food (F) and the population size of the GA (S).

### 3.3    Problem Specification

An agent in the MADE world is a representation of a brown rat modeled as a finite automaton that performs actions like move, eat, attack, defend, escape, find mate or breed.

The place where the conflicts appear is a square grid. A cell can only be occupied by one agent. Each agent can move and interact with other agents in a neighborhood of $7 \times 7$ cells around the rat. The time is a number of 'virtual days'. The rats are driven to survive and to have offspring, thus the source of conflicts is the food: agents attacks themselves to steal food before it is eaten by other agents. Systematically, a number of food rations appears in random positions on the map every virtual day. An agent may die of starvation, due to the damage inflicted by other agent or because its older.

MADE lets the writer select different archetypes that can be promoted in the world as described in [1]. In this paper we will study three different archetypes: An agent is considered a *villain* if it kills other agent as a result of a fight for the food, a *hero* if it attacks a *villain* and an *avenger* if it attacks other agent in revenge.

The fitness of the world is the sum of the value for each archetype rate, i.e. the number of characters that present the archetype divided by the total number of characters. To promote the appearance of all the archetypes, avoiding as much as possible the lack of any of them, the function presents a logarithmic curve where small rates get bigger values. As a consequence, the fitness of a world with a presence of two archetypes whose rate is 0.25 is bigger than the fitness of a world with one archetype whose rate is 0.5. The function used by MADE is described as:

$$F_A = \sum_{i=1}^{A} \frac{\log (1 + 10r_i)}{\log 11}, F_A \in [0, A] \tag{1}$$

where $A$ is the number of archetypes that takes part in the fitness and $r_i$ is the appearance rate of the archetype $i$ in the world, being $r_i \in [0, 1]$.

### 3.4   Converting Logs to Stories

Once the best values of the parameters have been found, the system can be run inside a game context to generate a whole set of secondary characters. For the simple reason of using agents in a bottom-up approach for the world generation, MADE provides a social network with family relationships, but also other related to the disputes and to possible archetypes, i.e. in our study, a 'hero' fights a 'villain' or an 'avenger' takes revenge on other character.

The storyteller will be able to tell a story about each character by accessing to its life-log. The life-log should have a pre-defined format understandable by the storyteller, with fields like the date, the action performed, the internal state, the direct object and the indirect object. Moreover, each agent should be tagged with the different archetypes it fulfills, the days that this archetype begins and ends, and the agents affected.

With this information within reach, the storyteller can create a story about the character by narrating its birthday, its name, the name and story of its parents, siblings and children (also using this technique for describing them), what the agent is (as archetype: 'villain', 'hero', 'avenger') and why (dates, characters related and supposed motivations).

## 4   Experimental Setup

As explained in Sect. 3.2, the parameters whose effect will be studied are the number of profiles (P), the world size (W), the virtual time (D), the food (F) and the population size of the GA (S). Different parameter values for each element will be studied to clarify their influence in the literary world generation, following the rules and recommendations presented in Sect. 3.2.

Since the size of the neighborhood is a square of $7 \times 7$ cells, the selected values for (W) are $5 \times 5$, $10 \times 10$ and $20 \times 20$ cells. Furthermore, these sizes would allow the existence of 25, 100 and 400 agents respectively at the same time.

Also, as the maximum lifetime of the agent is about 300 virtual days, the selected set of days (D) to study are 64, 128 and 256. More days would result in a huge amount of agents and backstories, harder to evaluate.

The set of values for the food (F), or source of conflicts, that conditions the actions (attack, share and defend, among others) are $1/2$, $1/4$ and $1/8$ of the number of cells of the map.

The set of values proposed for the population size (S) of the GA are 64, 128 and 256 individuals.

Finally, it is expected that the existence of different number of profiles (P) in the world will have a significant effect in the runs, specially in functions that require more than one archetype. We will compare the usage of 1, 2, 4 and 8 profiles for each scenario. As the usage of different number of profiles generate different individual sizes, and therefore different convergence times, the stop condition will be established depending of the best fitness (30 generations without improvement), to do a fair comparison.

For a more complete knowledge of the search space and the parameters effects, three different scenarios will be studied:

- $S_1$: Maximization of the 'villain' archetype ($A = 1$).
- $S_2$: Maximization of the 'villain' and the 'hero' archetypes ($A = 2$).
- $S_3$: Maximization of the 'villain', the 'hero' and the 'avenger' archetypes ($A = 3$).

Table 1 summarizes all the configuration parameters that will be compared (with their acronyms used in this paper), and the rest of the (fixed) parameters of the algorithm. The rest of the parameters of the MADE environment, such as the initial number of agents in the world, and the agent's parameters (such as the lifespan) are described in [1]. In this paper we will use their default values as, in principle, they are not related with the aspects that model a story.

## 5   Experiments and Results

In this paper, 9720 runs were carried out for each problem/scenario (30 times * 4 levels for $P$ * 3 levels for $D$ * 3 levels for $W$ * 3 levels for $S$ * 3 levels for $F$ that represent the possible combinations) to obtain the fitness for each combination.

Since the Kolmogorov-Smirnov test determines that the data we are using does not follow a normal distribution, a non-parametric test, the Kruskal-Wallis test, has been performed. The response variable used to perform the statistical analysis is the fitness at the end of each run.

The tables obtained by Kruskal-Wallis test show for each factor the degrees of freedom (FD), the experimental value of the statistical F (F value) and its

**Table 1.** Parameters used in the experiments.

| Parameter | Values |
|---|---|
| *Parameters under study* | |
| Number of profiles (P) | 1, 2, 4 and 8 |
| Number of virtual days (D) | 64, 128 and 256 |
| World dimension (W) | $5 \times 5$, $10 \times 10$ and $20 \times 20$ |
| Food (F) | 1/2, 1/4, 1/8 |
| GA population size | 64, 128 and 256 |
| *Fixed parameters* | |
| Mutation probability | 1/12 per gene |
| Parent pool size | Same as pool size |
| Selection method | Binary tournament |
| Elite | 10 % |
| Replacement method | Generational |
| Re-evaluation of individuals | yes |
| Stop condition | 30 generations without improving the best individual found |
| Runs per configuration | 30 |
| Initial world population | 15 |

associated p-value. If the output is smaller than 0.05, then the effect of this factor is statistically significant at 95 % confidence level (which indicates that different initial values of this parameter lead to significant differences on the fitness).

We have obtained values lower than 0.05 for all parameters in all scenarios (generated p-values tables have been omitted due to space constraints). These results show that all the parameters considered have a significant impact in the generation of the agents behavior. This confirm our hypothesis that the four elements that conform a story (time, characters, source of conflict and world) have a great repercussion in the generation of stories in the simulation environment.

Since a significant p-value only tells that the effects are not all equal (i.e., reject the null hypothesis), post-hoc tests might be used to determine which effects or outputs are significantly different from which other.

Therefore, a Kruskal-Wallis multi-comparison test has also been performed, showing significant differences among all parameter values, except for number of profiles (only using 1 profile has significant difference with respect to use 2, 4 and 8), and GA population size (64–128 and 128–256), both values (number of profiles and GA population size) in the scenarios $S_1$ and $S_2$. This can be explained because only one profile is necessary in these scenarios (as the hero and villain archetypes are based in attacking other rats, and therefore, can be shared by the same agent). Therefore, the fitness function $F_1$ and $F_2$ only differs in counting the archetype of an 'attacking' rat almost twice.

**Fig. 1.** Boxplots for parameter P (number of profiles)

All the results have also been plotted in order to better understand their differences (in Figs. 1, 2, 3, 4 and 5). At first glance, the median for D, W and F is 0 (or almost 0) for several values. This has several possible explanations: First, the number of profiles has quite an impact in the results (Fig. 1), as it was shown previously in [1].

Increasing the number of profiles means changing the search problem from finding a single finite state automaton whose behavior eventually results in a world compatible with our search to finding two or more compatible with it and among themselves. This also happens independently of the situation and including complex ones, like the Avenger scenario, so for the time being we should conclude that a single profile, that is, having the description of a single FSM that describes the behavior of the agents in the world, is the best option for any scenario.

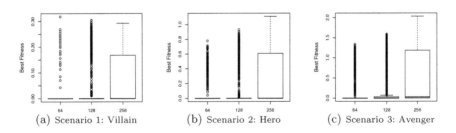

**Fig. 2.** Boxplots for the number of days (parameter D).

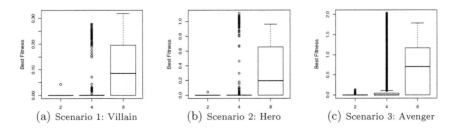

**Fig. 3.** Boxplots for food amount (parameter F)

A similar result is obtained for the number of days, whose results in the three scenarios can be seen in Fig. 2: A small amount of days (64) is not enough to allow the generation of any archetype, as there is no time to develop a story, or, in another words, for the events that we examine to compute fitness to occur, in most of the scenarios. This can also be said about the world dimension (Fig. 4): larger worlds are more sparsely populated and have less interaction events, so the chances of an encounter that can trig an event (for example, a fight) is more difficult.

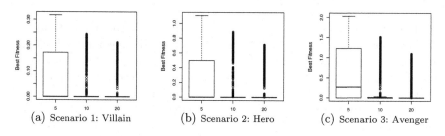

(a) Scenario 1: Villain     (b) Scenario 2: Hero     (c) Scenario 3: Avenger

**Fig. 4.** Boxplots for world size (parameter W)

From the study of these two parameters we can conclude that, at least for these scenarios and possibly for any scenario, the baseline number of days should be 256 and the world for this population should have a small size of 25 cells.

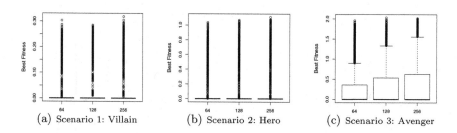

(a) Scenario 1: Villain     (b) Scenario 2: Hero     (c) Scenario 3: Avenger

**Fig. 5.** Boxplots for GA population size (parameter S)

Finally, the amount of food (Fig. 3), which is the main source of conflicts, also needs to be low enough so that it actually happens, in this case 1/8 of the world size.

With respect to the GA population size, Fig. 5 shows visually the confirmation of the tests: there are significant differences in the values for the Scenario 3. Because the large exploration space of this problem it is clear that larger sizes, in combination with a stop criterion based in changes of the best individual found, can obtain a higher range of possible solution values.

# 6   Conclusions

When using an hybrid EC-ABM approach to generate massive backstories in fiction environments its impossible to know in advance the optimal value of a fitness that models the appearance of different archetypes together and the search space may be enormous, so a previous study of the most important parameters is prescribed.

In this paper we define the problem addressed (in terms of goal, worlds, fitnesses, archetypes, backstories, agents, profiles, conflicts, places, time and scenario) and a problem specification with the MADE framework. Our methodology selects key parameters (size of population of the GA, size of the world, number of profiles, source of conflicts and virtual days) that affect the generation of conflicts and sets the values that are tested in the experiments, looking for significant differences in the fitness of the evolved worlds.

Our experiments prove that there are significant differences between the five parameters in three scenarios with different combinations of the archetype *villain*, *hero* and *avenger*. The best combination of parameters, that is, the one that gives on average the highest fitness, is the smallest map size ($5 \times 5$), the bigger number of virtual days (256), the fewer rate of food growth (1/8 of the number of cells), the lower number of profiles (1) and the bigger population size of the GA (256). This is due to the fact that the three possible archetypes emerge when a the fights occur, and that happens more probably when the world is small and there is little food. Anyway, the backstories size increase with the virtual days of execution, thus it is easier to find archetypes when more virtual days are executed, in other words, when all the agents have the opportunity to live their entire lives. This can be generalized to similar problems (and the rest of scenarios): the source of conflict should be forced to occur more times, and simultaneously, it is necessary to give enough time to these situations appear.

Another conclusion is that, even if the number of profiles (different behaviors in the world) could, *a priori*, allow for more complex archetypes to appear, the fact that they are codified in a chromosome changes the shape of the search space and increases its size and complexity, so that the number of generations the algorithm needs might be much more. It is never easy to establish termination conditions in these kind of evolutionary algorithms, so this is something that should be researched in the future.

Since it has been proved that conflicts, as in fiction, is what drives fitness up in the worlds we are designing, the actual number of conflicts happening in the world, its influence in the fitness and its relationship with world size and food growth will have to be assessed in future works. The influence of parameters such as the initial population could be tested, while different scenarios will be used with archetypes that not only rely in competition for food, like the affinity or the family relationships. To improve the accuracy of the parameter selection, human guided evaluation could be performed, but this is only one possible way of doing it. Finally, the results of the study could be applied to generate backstories in real game engines.

**Acknowledgements.** This work has been supported in part by SIPESCA (Programa Operativo FEDER de Andalucía 2007–2013), TIN2011-28627-C04-02 (Spanish Ministry of Economy and Competitivity), SPIP2014-01437 (Dirección General de Tráfico), PRY142/14 (Fundación Pública Andaluza Centro de Estudios Andaluces en la IX Convocatoria de Proyectos de Investigación) and PYR-2014-17 GENIL project (CEI-BIOTIC Granada).

# References

1. García-Ortega, R.H., García-Sánchez, P., Mora, A.M., Merelo, J.: My life as a sim: evolving unique and engaging life stories using virtual worlds. In: ALIFE 14: The Fourteenth Conference on the Synthesis and Simulation of Living Systems, vol. 14, pp. 580–587 (2014)
2. Nairat, M., Dahlstedt, P., Nordahl, M.G.: Character evolution approach to generative storytelling. In: Proceedings of the IEEE Congress on Evolutionary Computation, CEC 2011, pp. 1258–1263. IEEE, New Orleans, LA, USA, 5–8 June 2011
3. Booth, T.L.: Sequential Machines and Automata Theory, 1st edn. Wiley, New York (1967)
4. Togelius, J., Yannakakis, G.N., Stanley, K.O., Browne, C.: Search-based procedural content generation: a taxonomy and survey. IEEE Trans. Comput. Intell. AI Games **3**(3), 172–186 (2011)
5. Arinbjarnar, M., Barber, H., Kudenko, D.: A critical review of interactive drama systems. In: Abu-Shaaban, Y. (ed.) AISB 2009 Symposium, pp. 15–26. AI & Games, Edinburgh (2009)
6. Meehan, J.R.: The metanovel: writing stories by computer. Technical report, DTIC Document (1976). http://oai.dtic.mil/oai/oai?verb=getRecord& metadataPrefix=html&identifier=ADA031625
7. Lebowitz, M.: Story-telling as planning and learning. Poetics **14**(6), 483–502 (1985)
8. Turner, S.R.: The Creative Process: A computer Model of Storytelling and Creativity. Psychology Press, New York (2014)
9. Riedl, M.O., Leon, C.: Toward vignette-based story generation for drama management systems. In: Barber, H., Thue, D., eds.: Proceedings of the 2nd international conference on intelligent technologies for interactive entertainment (INTETAIN), workshop on integrating technologies for interactive stories, pp. 23–28 (2008)
10. Garry, J., El-Shamy, H.: Archetypes and Motifs in Folklore and Literature. M.E Sharpe, New York (2005)
11. Swartjes, I., Vromen, J.: Emergent story generation: Lessons from improvisational theater. In: Magerko, B.S., Riedl, M.O. (eds.) Intelligent Narrative Technologies: Papers from the AAAI Fall Symposium. Number FS-07-05 in AAAI Fall Symposium Series, pp. 146–149 (2007)
12. Cioffi-Revilla, C., De Jong, K., Bassett, J.K.: Evolutionary computation and agent-based modeling: biologically-inspired approaches for understanding complex social systems. Comput. Math. Organ. Theory **18**(3), 356–373 (2012)
13. Morrell, J.: Between the Lines: Master the Subtle Elements of Fiction Writing. Writer's Digest Books, Cincinnati (2006)

# A Benchmark for Virtual Camera Control

Paolo Burelli[1,2]($\boxtimes$) and Georgios N. Yannakakis[1,2]

[1] Department of Architecture, Design and Media Technology, Aalborg University
Copenhagen, Copenhagen, Denmark
[2] Institute of Digital Games, University of Malta, Msida, Malta
pabu@create.aau.dk, georgios.yannakakis@um.edu.mt

**Abstract.** Automatically animating and placing the virtual camera in a dynamic environment is a challenging task. The camera is expected to maximise and maintain a set of properties — i.e. visual composition — while smoothly moving through the environment and avoiding obstacles. A large number of different solutions to the problem have been proposed so far including, for instance, evolutionary techniques, swarm intelligence or ad hoc solutions. However, the large diversity of the solutions and the lack of a common benchmark, made any comparative analysis of the different solutions extremely difficult. For this reason, in this paper, we propose a benchmark for the problem of virtual camera control and we analyse a number of different problems in different virtual environments. Each of these scenarios is described through a set of complexity measures and, as a result of this analysis, a subset of scenarios is selected as the core of the benchmark.

## 1 Introduction

The virtual camera, in an interactive 3D environment, represents the point of view of the user and it deeply influences her way to perceive the environment and her ability to effectively accomplish any task. In applications such as 3D modellers and computer games, the virtual camera provides a mean for interacting with the virtual environment and has a large impact on the usability and the overall interactive experience [1]. Moreover, in 3D computer games the presentation of the game events largely depends on the camera position and movements; thus, virtual camera control has a significant impact on aspects such as gameplay and storytelling.

What is the optimal way of controlling the virtual camera is a an open research question: on one side of the control spectrum, direct control of the camera by the player increases the complexity of the interaction and eliminates the designer's control over game storytelling; on the other side, statically predesigned camera animations release the player from the burden of controlling the point of view, but they cannot guarantee a correct visualisation of all possible player actions. Furthermore, such approach is not applicable in multi-player games or in games where the content is procedurally generated as the designer has potentially no information a-priori to define the camera positions and movements.

A.M. Mora and G. Squillero (Eds.): EvoApplications 2015, LNCS 9028, pp. 455–467, 2015.
DOI: 10.1007/978-3-319-16549-3_37

Automatic virtual camera control aims at studying effective and efficient methods to control the camera behaviour through high-level and environment-independent requirements, such as the visibility of a particular object or the size of that object on the screen. Based on these requirements the method should dynamically and efficiently calculate a near optimal (or even optimal) path for the camera. Over the years a number of different approaches has been proposed, ranging from early ad hoc solutions [2] to more recent and flexible approaches [3], which tackle the task as an optimisation problem and apply different variations of search algorithms. However, while it is intuitively possible to detect a gradual improvement in the efficiency and effectiveness of the algorithms proposed, it is still not possible to precisely compare the algorithms and quantify the results achieved.

Contrarily to other fields, such as computer vision [4] or optimisation [5], in virtual camera control, there is a lack of a common well defined benchmark problem. As a result all researchers that proposed a contribution to the field had to design custom test problems in custom virtual environments, making a comparison between experiments and findings nearly impossible. For this reason, in this article, we present an analysis of the virtual camera control problem from an optimisation perspective and, based on this analysis, we introduce a set of test problems representing different challenges commonly met in virtual camera composition applications such as computer games. Each problem is evaluated according to a number of metrics about optimisation complexity and, from the results of this evaluation, a smaller subset of the most representative problems is selected to compose the benchmark. Finally, in an attempt to make the benchmark easily accessible and testable, we released it as an open source project on GitHub[1]. The project, along with the analysis presented in this paper, is intended as a starting point towards a normalisation of the evaluation practices in virtual camera control.

## 2   Background

With the introduction of three-dimensional computer graphics, virtual camera control immediately appeared as a challenging task. The first studies on virtual camera [6] focused primarily on designing interaction metaphors for manual camera control. However, direct control of the several degrees of freedom of the camera proved often to be problematic for the user [7], leading researchers to investigate the automation of camera control.

In 1988, Blinn [2] showcased one of the first examples of an automatic camera control system. Blinn designed a system to automatically generate views of planets in a space simulator of NASA. Although limited in its expressiveness and flexibility, Blinn's work inspired many other researchers trying to investigate efficient methods and more flexible mathematical models able to handle more complex aspects such as camera motion and frame composition [8]. More generic approaches model camera control as a constraint satisfaction problem.

---

[1] Available at: https://github.com/paoloburelli/VirtualCameraSandbox.

These approaches require the designer to define a set of desired frame properties, which are then modelled either as an objective function to be maximised by the solver or as a set of constraints that the camera configuration must satisfy. These constraints describe how the frame should look like in terms of object size, visibility and positioning. Bares et al. [9] presented a detailed definition of these constraints, which became the standard input of most automatic camera control methods.

Since Bares' definition, the problem of finding one or more camera configurations that satisfy a given set frame constraints has been tackled by a number of researchers [10]. A multitude of algorithms based, for instance, on genetic algorithms [11], particle swarm optimisation [12] or hill climbing [13] have been proposed and evaluated. However, while most of the articles composing the-state-of-the-art include an empirical evaluation of the algorithms, those evaluations have been carried out with different metrics and on different test problems. Furthermore, only few articles include a comparative analysis of the results of a new algorithm against other algorithms already introduced [3,14,15].

The work by Burelli et al. [12], for instance, includes an evaluation on three static camera control problems in an outdoor urban environment and lists convergence time and best solution quality as success criteria. Following a completely different approach, Lino et al. [13] use an animated scene from the film 1984 on which the test multiple shots. Their success criterion is based on the average frame-rate at which the system is able to calculate the camera solutions. In an attempt to create a uniform evaluation method, in this paper, we introduce a set of general problems for camera control and we suggest a series of metrics to evaluate the complexity of the problems and the performance of the algorithms.

## 3   Optimising the Virtual Camera

To describe virtual camera control as an optimisation problem we need to identify its basic characteristics, i.e. what is the solution space and what is the objective function that needs to be optimised.

The solution space contains all possible camera configurations and, according to the standard perspective camera model in OpenGL[2], a virtual camera is defined by six parameters: position, orientation, field of view, aspect ratio, near plane and far plane. Camera position is a three-dimensional vector of real values defining a Cartesian position. Camera orientation can be defined either using a quaternion, a set of three Euler angles or a combination of two three-dimensional vectors describing the front direction and the up direction. With the last four parameters, the domain of the virtual camera control objective function is at least 10-dimensional.

However, some parameters such as near and far planes are commonly constant, while other parameters are tightly related to the shot type. In particular, parameters such as field of view and aspect ratio are used dynamically and statically to express certain types of shots [8]. For this reason, we consider the field of

---

[2] Open Graphic Library - http://www.opengl.org.

view, the aspect ratio and the two planes as fixed parameters; the search space that composes the domain of our objective function is, therefore, six-dimensional and it contains all possible combinations of camera positions and orientations.

The objective function of the optimisation problem follows the concept of *frame constraints* introduced by Bares et al. [9] as properties that can be used to describe how the camera should behave. Through these constraints it is possible to define such behaviour in terms of how the frame generated by the camera should look like. Every frame constraint is converted into an objective function that, in a linear combination with all the constraints imposed, defines a camera composition objective function [16]. In this article, we consider three different constraints: *Vantage Angle, Object Projection Size* and *Object Visibility* that serve as representatives of all the constraints listed by Bares et al. [9].

### 3.1   Vantage Angle

The vantage angle constraint binds the camera position to the position and rotation of a target object. It requires the camera to be positioned so that the angle between the target object front vector and the front vector of the camera equals to a certain value. A vantage angle constraint is defined by three parameters: the target object, the horizontal angle and the vertical angle and its objective function is defined as follows:

$$f_\theta = f_\alpha \cdot f_\beta$$
$$f_\alpha = 1 - \frac{-\arctan(\frac{C_x}{C_z}) - \alpha}{180}$$
$$f_\beta = 1 - \frac{|\arcsin(C_y) - \beta|}{180} \tag{1}$$

where $\alpha$ is the desired horizontal angle between the camera and the target's front vector, $\beta$ is the desired vertical angle between the camera and the target's front vector and $C$ is the normalised camera position transformed in target relative space — i.e. the pace defined by the target's front, right and up vectors.

This frame constraint is equivalent to *OBJ VIEW ANGLE* constraint of the Bares et al. [9] list. However, from an optimisation perspective, it also equivalent to *CAM POS IN REGION*, since this constraint requires the camera to be positioned in a specific sub-space. Thus, both constraints limit the camera into a continuous region of space and affect only camera position.

### 3.2   Object Projection Size

The object projection size constraint binds the camera position and rotation to the position and size of a target object. It requires the area covered by the projection of a target object on the screen to have a specific size. The object projection size constraint is defined by two parameters: the target object and the fraction of the frame size that the projection should cover. The target object is approximated using a proxy geometry, e.g. an object aligned bounding box, and the satisfaction function is defined as follows:

$$f_\sigma = 1 - |\sigma_c - \sigma_d|$$

$$\sigma_c = \begin{cases} T_y/S_y & \text{if } T_y/S_y > T_x/S_x \\ T_x/S_x & \text{otherwise} \end{cases} \tag{2}$$

where $\sigma_d$ is the desired projection size, $S_x$ and $S_y$ are the width and height of the screen, and $T_x$ and $T_y$ are the projected width and height of the target object's proxy geometry. This frame constraint corresponds to the *OBJ PROJECTION SIZE* constraint of the Bares et al. [9] list.

### 3.3   Object Visibility

The object visibility constraint binds the camera position and rotation to the position and size of a target object. It requires the target object to be included in the frame and not hidden by any other object; both conditions are necessary to identify the target object as visible. In order to respect these two requirements the camera should be placed at a sufficient distance from the target and oriented in order to frame the target. Moreover, the volume between the camera and the target should not contain obstacles — i.e. any non-transparent object — that hide the target.

The objective function $f_\gamma$ of this frame constraint quantifies the ratio between the actual visible area of the projected image of the object and its total projected area and it is defined as:

$$f_\gamma = 1 - |\gamma_d - \gamma_c|$$

$$\gamma_c = \frac{\sum_{i=1}^{N} infov(v_i)}{N} \frac{\sum_{i=1}^{5}(1 - occ(e_i))}{5}$$

$$infov(x) = \begin{cases} 1 & \text{if } x \text{ is in the view frustum,} \\ 0 & \text{otherwise.} \end{cases} \tag{3}$$

$$occ(x) = \begin{cases} 1 & \text{if } x \text{ is occluded,} \\ 0 & \text{otherwise.} \end{cases}$$

where $\gamma_c$ is the current visibility value of the target object, $\gamma_d$ the desired visibility value, $v_i$ is the position of the $i^{th}$ vertex of the object's mesh, $N$ is the number of vertices of the mesh, function $infov(x)$ calculates whether a point is included in the field of view or not, $e$ is the list containing the positions of the four extreme vertices in field of view — i.e. the top, bottom, left and right vertices on screen — and the one closer to the center of the projected image. The $occ(x)$ function calculates whether the point $x$ is occluded by another object or not. The implemented version of the function is optimised not to calculate the second part of the function if the first part is equal to 0. The occlusion check is implemented by casting a ray towards the point defined by the vector $x$ and then checking whether the ray intersects any other object other than the target. The $infov(x)$ function is implemented by checking whether the point defined by $x$ is included within the six planes composing the view frustum.

The object visibility constraint includes the *OBJ IN FIELD OF VIEW, OBJ OCCLUSION MINIMISE, OBJ EXCLUDE OR HIDE* and *OBJ OCCLUSION PARTIAL* constraints of the list proposed by Bares et al. [9].

### 3.4  Objective Function

The complete virtual camera control objective function is a linear combination of the three aforementioned objective functions in which the objective function value of each constraint is defined within the interval [1,0]. The weights can be used by the designer of the composition task to prioritise the satisfaction of some frame constraints over others. This equation does not take into account the interplays between frame constraints; for instance, it might be argued that any constraint related to a subject should be deactivated if the subject is out of view. However, any consideration of this sort requires a semantic understanding of the shot description, which is out of the scope of this article.

## 4  The Benchmark

The starting point of the benchmark we propose in this article is a set of 36 virtual camera problems designed to represent virtual camera control tasks of different complexities. This initial set includes three different virtual environments which are used to test 12 different composition problems. The 12 composition problems include the optimisation of a Vantage Angle constraint, a Projection Size constraint, a Visibility Constraint and the combination of all three constraints. These four combinations are evaluated with one, two and three subjects (see Fig. 1d). In each test problem, the subjects are positioned and move around the environment in a random fashion. The subjects' speed is also randomised and varies from 0 to the average human walking speed (1.38 m/s). The subjects are shaped as stylized human beings, have human-like proportions and height (approx. 1.8 m tall) and are composed by 3800 triangles each.

The three test environments have been selected to provide a wide range of geometrical features commonly present in computer games and interactive virtual environments. Moreover, they have been designed to incorporate a wide variety of camera composition challenges with different levels of complexity. They include one indoor and two outdoor environments with different geometrical characteristics: a forest, a house and a rocky clearing. The *forest* environment is an outdoor virtual environment composed by a cluster of 42 plants of different sizes and shapes, made of approximately 244000 triangles; the subjects are placed between these trees that act as partial occluders and scattered obstacles. Such environments feature a highly multi-modal objective function landscape, due to the fact that the tree trunks, as other possible sparse-occluders, are thin obstacles that produce a slicing effect in the visibility objective function

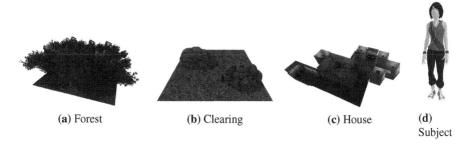

**(a)** Forest          **(b)** Clearing          **(c)** House          **(d)**
                                                                        Subject

**Fig. 1.** The three test environments and the human-like model used in the benchmark.

landscape. The second environment, the *house*, is an indoor environment with closed spaces separated by solid walls, open doors and transparent windows. The environment contains 182 objects and it is made of approximately 210000 triangles. As described in [17], walls act as large occluders inducing large areas of the objective function landscape to have little or no visibility gradient. The last environment, the *clearing*, is the simplest one from a geometrical perspective — i.e. it is made of approximately 10100 triangles. It contains two medium sized obstacles and the rest of the space is empty. This environment is expected to be the simplest in terms of optimisation complexity, as the lack of obstacles tends to produce objective function landscapes with smooth gradients and a small number of modalities.

The environments are composed only by static structures; however, the targets of the desired shots move along random paths, making the problem dynamic and unpredictable. Moreover, the test problems incorporating more than one subject at a time include a further challenge since each subject acts as a dynamic obstacle for the camera and the other subjects. The test problems include either one, two or three moving subjects. For each configuration of subjects, the three frame constraints defined in Sect. 3 are tested both independently and combined all together. We believe that the provided range of problems covers a large number of the possible virtual camera control tasks in terms of optimisation challenges. In each test problem, the objective function is a weighted sum of the objective functions of the different frame constraints included in the problem; all frame constraints have the same weight — i.e. no priority is given to any subject or particular property — and the overall objective function is bounded between 0 and 1.

### 4.1   Complexity

To fairly analyse and compare the performance of any algorithm, we need to define common complexity measures [18] within common test problems [19]. In turn, the choice of appropriate case studies is a key aspect of any comparative analysis since those affect both the validity and the extensibility of any findings. In our effort to measure the complexity of each scenario, we employ a set of complexity measures proposed by Törn et al. [18] and we extend them in order to tackle both dynamic and static cases.

Törn et al. classify global optimisation problems into four categories (unimodal, easy, moderate and difficult) based on three features of the objective function:

- The probability that the region of attraction of the global optimum — i.e. the area of the objective function that features a gradient converging towards the optimum — is missed during sampling.
- If and how embedded the global optima are — i.e. if there exist local optima near the global optima region of attraction, so that sampling around these leads to the detection of better solution and, eventually, of a global optimum.
- The number of local optima.

A global optimum in optimisation is the best solution to the problem, while a local optimum is a solution to the problem which maximises/minimises it locally but not globally. Based on the above criteria the first measure of complexity that corresponds to the *probability of missing the global optimum region*, $P$, is defined as follows:

$$P = (1 - p^*)^{N_f} \tag{4}$$

where $p^*$ is the percentage of the whole search space being a region of attraction of global optima and $N_f$ denotes the affordable number of objective function evaluations within one unit of time. In our analysis, we take 16.6 ms — the frame rendering duration at a 60 fps frame-rate — as a reference unit of time; this way, $P$ is roughly inversely proportional to the probability to find the optimal camera configuration within one frame. However, any unit of time could be adopted as long as it is coherent among the different problems and it is proportional to the time scale of the problem.

The *embeddedness* measure of complexity, $E$, is given by:

$$E = 1 - \frac{1}{n D_{max}} \sum_{i=1}^{n} D_{min}(x_i) \tag{5}$$

where $D_{min}(x)$ is the distance between solution $x$ and the closest global optima region of attraction and $D_{max}$ is the maximum distance between two points in the search space. In the experiment's search space, this distance equals to the length of the parallelepiped's diagonal.

The last complexity measure considered in this paper which corresponds to the *number of local optima*, $NoL$, is defined as follows:

$$NoL = \frac{A_{lo}}{A_{go}} \tag{6}$$

where $A_{lo}$ and $A_{go}$ are the search space sizes containing local and global optima, respectively.

Finally, to be able to capture the complexity of the problems also from a dynamic optimisation perspective, we need to extend these measures with an estimation of how the fitness landscape changes over time. Such a measure should capture the speed and the magnitude of the changes in the objective function and should give a comprehensive measure for the whole objective function landscape. For this purpose, we define a measure $D$ of the objective function dynamism calculated as follows:

$$D = \frac{1}{K}\frac{1}{T}\sum_{i=0}^{K}\sum_{j=0}^{N-1}|f(x_i, t_{j+1}) - f(x_i, t_j)| \tag{7}$$

where $K$ is the number of samples taken from the objective function at each sampling, $T$ is the duration of the animation, $N$ is the number of times the objective function is sampled during the animation, $f(x_i, t_j)$ is the objective function value of the sample $x_i$ at the $j^{th}$ time step and $f(x_i, t_j + 1)$ is the objective function value of the sample $x_i$ at time $j + 1$. The $D$ measure is a discrete approximation of the average absolute change in the objective function for all points in the solution space over time. High $D$ values correspond to highly dynamic problems, while a $D$ value that equals 0 corresponds to a static optimisation problem.

## 4.2   Categorisation and Selection

Table 1 presents the values of the aforementioned complexity measures for each test problem investigated. All the values have been calculated by discretising the solution space with a resolution of 0.5 m on the X and Z axis, 1 m on the Y axis and by sampling linearly 32 rotations per position. All the problems have been evaluated by sampling the objective function each half second for 10 s while the

**Table 1.** Complexity measures for each scenario. $P$ is the probability that the region of attraction is missed during random sampling, $E$ is the degree of how embedded the global optima are within local optimal solutions, $NoL$ is the ratio between local and global optima, and $D$ is the degree of dynamism. The most representative problems are highlighted.

| | Forest | | | | House | | | | Clearing | | | |
|---|---|---|---|---|---|---|---|---|---|---|---|---|
| | P | E | NoL | D | P | E | NoL | D | P | E | NoL | D |
| Angle 1 | 0.03 | 1.00 | 2.50 | 1.35 | 0.00 | 1.00 | 0.75 | 1.32 | 0.00 | 1.00 | 2.00 | 1.18 |
| Angle 2 | 0.04 | 1.00 | 2.00 | 1.27 | 0.18 | 1.00 | 2.25 | 1.21 | 0.33 | 0.88 | 2.25 | 1.09 |
| Angle 3 | 0.7 | 1.00 | 3.45 | 1.23 | 0.20 | 1.00 | 3.57 | 1.07 | 0.37 | 0.91 | 4.25 | 1.08 |
| Size 1 | 0.49 | 0.91 | 5.63 | 0.13 | 0.72 | 0.93 | 5.96 | 0.13 | 0.38 | 0.94 | 5.38 | 0.15 |
| Size 2 | 0.69 | 0.71 | 10.20 | 0.13 | 0.84 | 0.69 | 6.30 | 0.12 | 0.92 | 0.77 | 34.86 | 0.16 |
| Size 3 | 0.91 | 0.73 | 23.89 | 0.03 | 0.77 | 0.67 | 16.58 | 0.02 | 0.90 | 0.55 | 30.31 | 0.05 |
| Visib. 1 | 0.65 | 1.00 | 8.32 | 0.03 | 0.87 | 0.95 | 15.28 | 0.02 | 0.59 | 0.98 | 2.98 | 0.03 |
| Visib. 2 | 0.83 | 0.59 | 91.04 | 0.02 | 0.98 | 0.79 | 31.82 | 0.01 | 0.80 | 0.92 | 8.52 | 0.03 |
| Visib. 3 | 0.94 | 0.56 | 415.65 | 0.02 | 0.94 | 0.81 | 1305.63 | 0.01 | 0.78 | 0.88 | 8.18 | 0.02 |
| All 1 | 0.76 | 0.85 | 59.75 | 0.22 | 0.80 | 0.99 | 48.57 | 0.21 | 0.43 | 0.94 | 20.28 | 0.15 |
| All 2 | 0.64 | 1.00 | 68.35 | 0.16 | 0.76 | 0.99 | 54.00 | 0.19 | 0.78 | 0.89 | 26.56 | 0.15 |
| All 3 | 0.83 | 0.95 | 70.50 | 0.14 | 0.83 | 0.75 | 72.00 | 0.16 | 0.73 | 0.95 | 41.75 | 0.16 |

subjects move in the environment. This process has been repeated 20 times for each test problem to minimise the effects of the initial random placement of the subjects.

From a static optimisation perspective, the test problems are sorted into the four categories proposed by Törn et al. [18]: *unimodal, easy, moderate* and *hard*. Following this categorisation, the vantage angle test problems with one subject are categorised as *unimodal* or *easy*. These test problems have a smaller global optima attraction area and higher evaluation times resulting in $P$ values greater than 0. The projection size and visibility test problems with one subject fall as well in the *easy* category in all test environments, The projection size and visibility test problems with more than one subject are categorised as *moderate* in the rocky clearing virtual environment, while they are categorised as *difficult* in the other two environments. This is due to a higher $P$ value and the more embedded local optima.

When the problems are analysed with respect to their dynamism, a different picture emerges: the visibility and projection size problems have all a significantly lower $D$ value than the angle problems, revealing that the latter is the most complex set of problems from a dynamic optimisation perspective. The reason for such a difference in terms of dynamism is expected, as the angle objective function, depends on the subjects' orientation; therefore, even a little orientation change in terms of degrees, has an amplified effect on the objective function landscape proportional to the distance to the subject.

Due to the contradiction between static and dynamic complexity, we need to sort the problems in a two dimensional space, defined by $P$ and $D$. Sorting the problems in this manner allows us to reduce the number of test problems to be analysed by selecting a subset of non-dominated problems — i.e. the set of problems that are the most complex both in terms of dynamism and static optimisation complexity (See Fig. 2). To perform this selection, we can employ the concept of Pareto optimality: a solution is defined as Pareto optimal if it cannot be improved with respect to any aspect without worsening at least one other aspect. The subset having such characteristic is highlighted in Table 1 and it contains the following problems:

- Two visibility and one projection size problem categorised as *difficult* in terms of static optimisation complexity with extremely low dynamism. We name these problems as *difficult-slow*.
- Four problems with all frame constraints with moderate static optimisation complexity and moderate dynamism. We name these problems as *average*.
- Four vantage angle problems with low static optimisation complexity and very hight dynamism. We name these problems as *easy-fast*.

## 5   Performance Metrics

Another fundamental aspect of the benchmark is the definition of one or more success criteria and performance measures. For virtual camera optimisation in static environments, e.g. for the generation of a single shot, there are two well

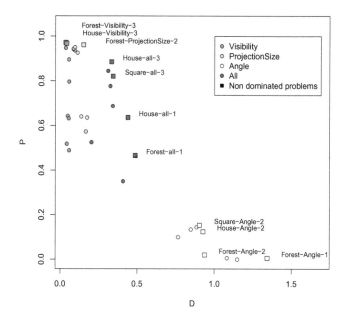

**Fig. 2.** Test problems sorted in a scatter plot according to their dynamism factor $D$ and their landscape complexity $P$. The Pareto front identified by the squares contains all the non dominated problems in terms of complexity and dynamism.

established performance measures, which have been already adopted in a number of previous studies: best solution quality and convergence time [3,12]. The first measure expresses how good the algorithm is in finding the right camera configuration and, thus, generate a good quality shot. The second one expresses how efficient the algorithm is in its process.

A different situation exists for camera optimisation in dynamic environments as there is no established performance measure for the algorithms. We suggest three different performance measures inspired from the literature in dynamic optimisation: accuracy, reliability and initial convergence time. The first measure describes how close the current best camera configuration found by the algorithm is to the best existing camera configuration at any given moment. To measure such aspect, we employ the average best function value measure suggested by Schönemann [20] to evaluate dynamic optimisation algorithms. The second measure, reliability, describes how often the algorithm succeeds to provide an acceptable solution during the optimisation. The measure employed to quantify this aspect is the percentage of time in which the algorithm is able to track accurately the moving optimum within a certain acceptance range. The value of such acceptance range is dependent on the perception of how the frame looks similar to the ideal frame so it can be any percentage of the optimum. The last measure describes how much time it takes the different algorithms to converge to an optimal camera configuration which is then tracked during the rest of the execution. The measure corresponds to the time taken initially by the algorithm to reach the point in which the solution found stops to improve; therefore, the algorithm stops to converge.

# 6    Conclusions and Future Work

The purpose of this article is to define a standard benchmark for future research in virtual camera control in games and beyond. For this reason, we have identified the building blocks of the camera control problem and we studied the complexity of each one of them. In particular, we isolated three principal objective functions, we made their associations to the state-of-the-art definition of frame constraints and we systematically analysed their complexity. Furthermore, we designed a suite of virtual environments and problems which have been analysed for their complexity both as dynamic and static optimisation problems. As a result of this analysis, we identified 11 test problems. These problems compose the core set of the benchmark and cover the most relevant issues identified in the analysis. Finally a number of possible performance measures has been proposed and described for different analysis scenarios.

The source code and the models composing the problems analysed in this article have been published as an open source project in the GitHub platform. This article and the open source project contribute towards the establishment of standard experimental practices in the field for virtual camera control. Based on the results presented, we envision a number of future research directions such as the identification of stereotypical animation patterns or the introduction of custom benchmarks for different applications such as storytelling or specific game genres. Furthermore, we believe that the thorough analysis of camera control complexity conducted in this paper can contribute to further development of more efficient virtual camera control algorithms.

# References

1. Pinelle, D., Wong, N.: Heuristic evaluation for games. In: CHI, CHI 2008, pp. 1453–1462. ACM Press, New York, USA (2008)
2. Blinn, J.: Where Am I? What Am I Looking At? IEEE Comput. Graph. Appl. **8**(4), 76–81 (1988)
3. Ranon, R., Urli, T.: Improving the efficiency of viewpoint composition. IEEE Trans. Vis. Comput. Graph. **2626**(c), 1–1 (2014)
4. Deng, J., Dong, W., Socher, R., Li, L.-J., Li, K., Fei-Fei, L.: ImageNet: a large-scale hierarchical image database. In: 2009 IEEE Conference on Computer Vision and Pattern Recognition (2009)
5. Mühlenbein, H., Schomisch, M., Born, J.: The parallel genetic algorithm as function optimizer. Parallel Comput. **17**, 619–632 (1991)
6. Ware, C., Osborne, S.: Exploration and virtual camera control in virtual three dimensional environments. ACM SIGGRAPH **24**(2), 175–183 (1990)
7. Drucker, S.M., Zeltzer, D.: Intelligent camera control in a virtual environment. In: Proceedings of Graphics Interface, pp. 190–199 (1994)

8. Arijon, D.: Grammar of the Film Language. Silman-James Press, Los Angeles (1991)

9. Bares, W.H., McDermott, S., Boudreaux, C., Thainimit, S.: Virtual 3D camera composition from frame constraints. In: ACM Multimedia, pp. 177–186. ACM Press, Marina del Rey, California, USA (2000)

10. Christie, M., Olivier, P., Normand, J.-M.: Camera Control in Computer Graphics. Computer Graphics Forum **27**, 2197–2218 (2008)

11. Halper, N., Olivier, P.: CamPlan: a camera planning agent. In: International Symposium on Smart Graphics, pp. 92–100. AAAI Press (2000)

12. Burelli, P., Di Gaspero, L., Ermetici, A., Ranon, R.: Virtual camera composition with particle swarm optimization. In: Butz, A., Fisher, B., Krüger, A., Olivier, P., Christie, M. (eds.) SG 2008. LNCS, vol. 5166, pp. 130–141. Springer, Heidelberg (2008)

13. Lino, C., Christie, M., Lamarche, F., Schofield, G., Olivier, P.: A real-time cinematography system for interactive 3D environments, pp. 139–148. In: Eurographics/ACM SIGGRAPH Symposium on Computer, Animation (2010)

14. Burelli, P., Yannakakis, G.N.: Combining local and global optimisation for virtual camera control. In: 2010 IEEE Symposium on Computational Intelligence and Games CIG, pp. 403–410 (2010)

15. Preuss, M., Burelli, P., Yannakakis, G.N.: Diversified Virtual Camera Composition. In: Di Chio, C., et al. (eds.) EvoApplications 2012. LNCS, vol. 7248, pp. 265–274. Springer, Heidelberg (2012)

16. Olivier, P., Halper, N., Pickering, J., Luna, P.: Visual composition as optimisation. In: Artificial Intelligence and Simulation of Behaviour (1999)

17. Burelli, P., Yannakakis, G.N., Global search for occlusion minimisation in virtual camera control. In: IEEE Congress on Evolutionary Computation, pp. 1–8. IEEE, Barcelona (2010)

18. Törn, A., Ali, M.M., Viitanen, S.: Stochastic global optimization: problem classes and solution techniques. J. Global Optim. **14**(4), 437–447 (1999)

19. Floudas, C.A., Pardalos, P.M.: A Collection of Test Problems for Constrained Global Optimization Algorithms. LNCS, vol. 455. Springer-Verlag, New York (1990)

20. Schönemann, L.: Evolution strategies in dynamic environments. In: Yang, S., Ong, Y.-S., Jin, Y. (eds.) Evolutionary Computation in Dynamic and Uncertain Environments. SCI, vol. 51, pp. 51–77. Springer, Heidelberg (2007)

# EvoIASP

# Alternating Optimization of Unsupervised Regression with Evolutionary Embeddings

Daniel Lückehe and Oliver Kramer[(✉)]

Computational Intelligence Group, Department of Computing Science,
University of Oldenburg, Oldenburg, Germany
{daniel.lueckehe,oliver.kramer}@uni-oldenburg.de

**Abstract.** Unsupervised regression is a dimensionality reduction method that allows embedding high-dimensional patterns in low-dimensional latent spaces. In the line of research on iterative unsupervised regression, numerous methodological variants have been proposed in the recent past. This works extends the set of methods by evolutionary embeddings. We propose to use a $(1 + \lambda)$-ES with Rechenberg mutation strength control to iteratively embed patterns and show that the learned manifolds are better with regard to the data space reconstruction error than the embeddings generated with naive Gaussian sampling. Further, we introduce a hybrid optimization approach of alternating gradient descent and the iterative evolutionary embeddings. Experimental comparisons on artificial test data sets confirm the expectation that a hybrid approach is superior or at least competitive to known methods like principal component analysis or Hessian local linear embedding.

**Keywords:** Dimensionality reduction · Unsupervised regression · Hybrid optimization

## 1 Introduction

Manifold learning and dimensionality reduction methods focus on the reduction of data space dimensionalities. Many approaches embed high-dimensional patterns by computing low-dimensional representations, which preserve important information like distances and neighborhoods. Dimensionality reduction methods can be employed for various tasks, e.g., visualization, preprocessing for pattern recognition methods and for symbolic algorithms. To allow human understanding and interpretation of high-dimensional data, the reduction to 2- and 3-dimensional spaces is an important task.

Iterative solution construction methods based on unsupervised regression (UR) [1,2] embed manifolds pattern by pattern, and use the data space reconstruction error (DSRE) to evaluate latent candidate solutions. The problem in optimizing UR models is that the optimization problem is difficult so solve. It suffers from a multimodal fitness landscape, the results often depend on the order the patterns are considered in the iterative process, and the optimization problem dimensionality scales linearly with the number of patterns. In this paper,

© Springer International Publishing Switzerland 2015
A.M. Mora and G. Squillero (Eds.): EvoApplications 2015, LNCS 9028, pp. 471–480, 2015.
DOI: 10.1007/978-3-319-16549-3_38

we propose two new strategies for the UR optimization problem. The first strategy is to improve the embedding process with evolution strategies (ES) with mutation strengths control that allow a more sophisticated search than repeated naive Gaussian sampling. Further, we propose to combine gradient descent in the DSRE fitness landscape with the evolutionary embedding process, i.e., with the evolutionary placement of low-dimensional representations. Although gradient descent is usually a powerful optimization approach, it easily gets stuck in local optima. Alternating evolutionary embeddings and gradient descent helps to overcome local optima.

This paper is structured as follows. In Sect. 2, we introduce the UR approach. Section 3 introduces the iterative solution construction process and proposes a novel approach based on $(1+\lambda)$-ES. This embedding strategy is combined with gradient descent to a novel hybrid alternating optimization approach in Sect. 4. Conclusions are drawn in Sect. 5.

## 2    Unsupervised Regression

The problem of dimensionality reduction is to find low-dimensional representations $\mathbf{x}_i \in \mathbb{R}^q$ of high-dimensional patterns $\mathbf{y}_i \in \mathbb{R}^d$ for $i = 1, \ldots, N$. The method we focus on in this paper is UR, where a regression model $f : \mathbb{R}^q \to \mathbb{R}^d$ with $q < d$ is used to map from the low-dimensional space to reconstruct the high-dimensional patterns. UR has first been applied to kernel density regression [3], and later to radial basis function networks (RBFs) [4], Gaussian processes [5], and neural networks [6]. In the past, nearest neighbor regression has been fitted to the UR framework [1] and extensions based on particle swarm optimization have been introduced [7]. Evolutionary approaches for dimensionality reduction focus on the evolutionary blackbox choice of attributes [8,9].

In the following, we introduce the UR optimization problem. In the optimal case, every pattern should be reconstructed with the regression model $f$, i.e., it should hold $f(\mathbf{x}_i) = \mathbf{y}_i$. With real-world data sets, this reconstruction is difficult to achieve and the optimization problem is difficult to solve. The difference between $f(\mathbf{x}_i)$ and $\mathbf{y}_i$ can be defined as error measure:

$$r(\mathbf{x}_i) = \|\mathbf{y}_i - f(\mathbf{x}_i)\|_2^2, \tag{1}$$

which is the DSRE mentioned in the introduction. For a matrix $\mathbf{Y} = [\mathbf{y}_i]_{i=1}^N$ of patterns and $\mathbf{X} = [\mathbf{x}_i]_{i=1}^N$ of latent positions, the DSRE of the complete manifold is defined as:

$$R(\mathbf{X}) = \frac{1}{N}\sum_{i=1}^N r(\mathbf{x}_i). \tag{2}$$

As regression model $f$, we use the Nadaraya-Watson estimator [10]:

$$f(\mathbf{x}_i, \mathbf{X}) = \sum_{j=1}^N \mathbf{y}_j \cdot \frac{\mathbf{K}_h(\mathbf{x}_i - \mathbf{x}_j)}{\sum_{k=1}^N \mathbf{K}_h(\mathbf{x}_i - \mathbf{x}_k)} \tag{3}$$

with kernel function $\mathbf{K}_h$ that usually employs a kernel parameter $h$, e.g., the bandwidth of the Gaussian kernel. In Nadaraya-Watson estimation, $\mathbf{x}_i$ itself affects the result of the model. Hence, leave-one-out cross-validation is employed for the DSRE computation to avoid overfitting. In the remainder of this paper, we use the Gaussian kernel:

$$\mathbf{K}(\mathbf{x}_i) = (2\pi)^{-1} \cdot e^{-\left(\mathbf{x}_i^2/2\right)} \tag{4}$$

# 3 Evolutionary Iterative Embeddings

In this section, we introduce an evolutionary iterative search in the space of latent positions and compare it to naive Gaussian sampling.

## 3.1 Iterative Search in Latent Space

An iterative solution construction scheme for UR manifolds has been proposed by Kramer [1,2] for k-nearest neighbors. It allows to compute UR based embeddings without initialization with other methods. The application of the iterative solution construction is also possible for further regression methods like the Nadaraya-Watson estimator, also often denoted as kernel regression in this context. Algorithm 1 shows the pseudocode of the approach.

---

**Algorithm 1.** Iterative UR approach

---

**Require:** $\mathbf{Y}$, $K$, $\kappa$
1: $\overline{\mathbf{X}} = [\mathbf{0}]$, $\overline{\mathbf{Y}} = [\mathbf{y}_1]$
2: **for** $i = 2$ to $N$ **do**
3:     choose $\mathbf{y}_i$ from $\mathbf{Y}$
4:     look for closest pattern $\mathbf{y}^*$ with latent position $\mathbf{x}^*$
5:     **for** $l = 1$ to $\kappa$ **do**
6:         $\mathbf{x}_i \sim \mathcal{N}\left(\mathbf{x}^*, \|\mathbf{y}_i - \mathbf{y}^*\|_2^2\right)$
7:     **end for**
8:     choose $\mathbf{x}_i$ that minimizes DSRE (see Eq. 2)
9:     $\overline{\mathbf{X}} = [\overline{\mathbf{X}}, \mathbf{x}_i]$, $\overline{\mathbf{Y}} = [\overline{\mathbf{Y}}, \mathbf{y}_i]$
10: **end for**

---

The first step of the pattern-wise solution construction process is to embed pattern $\mathbf{y}_1$ at an arbitrary position, e.g., at $\overline{\mathbf{X}} = [\mathbf{0}]$ and $\overline{\mathbf{Y}} = [\mathbf{y}_1]$. Let $\overline{\mathbf{Y}}$ be the matrix of embedded patterns in iteration $i$, i.e., $i - 1$ patterns have been embedded, and let $\overline{\mathbf{X}}$ be the corresponding matrix of latent positions. For each pattern $\mathbf{y}_i$ with $i > 1$, $\kappa$ latent candidate positions are sampled in latent space with Gaussian sampling:

$$\mathbf{x}_i \sim \mathcal{N}\left(\mathbf{x}^*, \|\mathbf{y}_i - \mathbf{y}^*\|_2^2\right) \tag{5}$$

with $\mathbf{x}^* = [\overline{\mathbf{X}}]_{j*}, \mathbf{y}^* = [\overline{\mathbf{Y}}]_{j*}$ and:

$$j^* = \arg \min_{j=1,\dots,i-1} \left\| \mathbf{y}_i - [\overline{\mathbf{Y}}]_j \right\|_2^2. \tag{6}$$

The candidate position that minimizes the DSRE is finally chosen for the new manifold $\overline{\mathbf{X}}$. We will refer to this approach as naive Gaussian sampling in the following.

## 3.2   Embeddings with $(1+1)$-ES

In this section, we employ a $(1+1)$-ES to find optimal latent positions instead of naive Gaussian sampling with Eq. 5. Naive Gaussian sampling is a one-step search that we now replace by evolutionary search with a generational scheme. In the new approach, latent candidate positions are generated with a $(1+1)$-ES and Gaussian mutation:

$$\mathbf{x}_i' = \mathbf{x}_i + \sigma \cdot \mathcal{N}(0,1). \tag{7}$$

We call the new method $(1+1)$-UKR and use the Nadaraya-Watson estimator with Gaussian kernel function. Step size $\sigma$ is initially set to $\sigma = \|\mathbf{y}_i - \mathbf{y}^*\|_2^2$. For adapting the mutation strengths $\sigma$, we used Rechenberg's 1/5th success rule [11]. After $T = 5$ generations, the success probability is determined via the number of successful generations $t$ with $p_s = t/T$, leading to a step size increase with $\sigma' = \sigma \cdot \tau$ with $\tau = 2.0$, if $p_s > 1/5$ and a decrease, if $p_s < 1/5$. We treat the latent position $\mathbf{x}^*$ of the closest embedded pattern $\mathbf{y}^*$ as infeasible point to prevent that multiple points are embedded at the same location.

The $(1+1)$-UKR embedding approach will be experimentally analyzed on the *Digits* data set with $N = 100$ patterns and uneven digits, the *Iris* data set with $N = 150$ and a data set called *Gaussian blobs* with $N = 60$ patterns with $d = 100$, randomly sampled around two centers with the Gaussian distribution. In all cases, pattern are embedded to a 2-dimensional latent space ($q = 2$), experiments are repeated 100 times, and mean values and standard deviations are shown. The bandwidth of the kernel function is set to $h = 0.675 \cdot \delta$ with the average distance between patterns in the training set:

$$\delta = \frac{1}{N-1} \cdot \sum_{i=1}^{N-1} \|\mathbf{y}_i - \mathbf{y}_{i+1}\|_2^2. \tag{8}$$

Figure 1 shows experimental comparisons of the $(1+1)$-UKR to the naive Gaussian sampling in latent space in terms of DSRE and corresponding standard deviation. On *Digits*, the ES achieves better results than naive Gaussian sampling with higher standard deviation. On *Iris*, the superiority of $(1+1)$-UKR is less significant due to a comparatively high standard deviation. Further, the plots show that naive Gaussian sampling is superior in the first steps. This is probably due to the fact that the ES may start with a solution, which is not the nearest neighbor and thus there is a positive probability of walking into the wrong direction. On the *Gaussian blobs* data set, a stable embedding is achieved in comparatively few steps. Also here, the ES generates better solutions, even if the advantage is marginal.

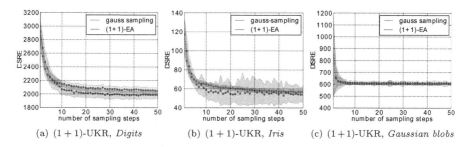

(a) $(1 + 1)$-UKR, *Digits*   (b) $(1 + 1)$-UKR, *Iris*   (c) $(1 + 1)$-UKR, *Gaussian blobs*

**Fig. 1.** Comparison of $(1 + 1)$-UKR to naive Gaussian sampling on *Digits*, *Iris*, and *Gaussian blobs*.

### 3.3 Embeddings with $(1 + \lambda)$-ES

In the following, we increase the offspring population and repeat a similar experimental setting. We employ a fix budget of 48 samplings, but increase the offspring population size $\lambda$. For example, a $(1 + 8)$-ES would run for six generations in this setting. Figure 2 shows the experimental results. The larger the population size $\lambda$, the lower is the achieved standard deviation of the DSRE. On *Digits*, $(1 + 1)$-UKR is the best approach. Here, the advantage of generations is obvious in comparison to larger population sizes. A $(1+12)$-UKR achieves the best results on *Iris*, in particular because of the small standard deviation. As the $(1 + 1)$-UKR shows the best results on average, we use this variant in the remainder of this work. On *Gaussian blobs*, also generational schemes are preferred to larger population sizes.

## 4 Hybrid Optimization

This section introduces a hybrid approach of evolutionary iterative search and gradient descent in the DSRE space.

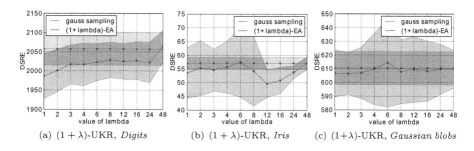

(a) $(1 + \lambda)$-UKR, *Digits*   (b) $(1 + \lambda)$-UKR, *Iris*   (c) $(1 + \lambda)$-UKR, *Gaussian blobs*

**Fig. 2.** Comparison of $(1 + \lambda)$-UKR on *Digits*, *Iris*, and *Gaussian blobs*.

## 4.1  Gradient Descent

Klanke and Ritter [12] have introduced an optimization framework based on gradient descent for the unsupervised kernel regression (UKR) model introduced in the previous section. UKR uses the Nadaraya-Watson estimator with kernel functions in the UR framework. By employing gradient descent:

$$\mathbf{X}' = \mathbf{X} - \alpha \cdot \nabla R(f(\mathbf{X}), \mathbf{Y}) \tag{9}$$

with learning rate $\alpha$, the DSRE, see Eq. 2, is minimized and an optimized latent space $\mathbf{X}'$ is obtained. We use the Broyden-Fletcher-Goldfarb-Shanno (BFGS) algorithm [13] to perform gradient descent. The gradient is defined as:

$$\nabla R(f(\mathbf{X}), \mathbf{Y}) = \begin{pmatrix} \frac{\partial R(f(\mathbf{X}),\mathbf{Y})}{\partial x_{11}} & \cdots & \frac{\partial R(f(\mathbf{X}),\mathbf{Y})}{\partial x_{n1}} \\ \cdots & \cdots & \cdots \\ \frac{\partial R(f(\mathbf{X}),\mathbf{Y})}{\partial x_{1m}} & \cdots & \frac{\partial R(f(\mathbf{X}),\mathbf{Y})}{\partial x_{nm}} \end{pmatrix} \tag{10}$$

The partial derivative of the DSRE is:

$$\frac{\partial R(\mathbf{Y}, f(\mathbf{X}))}{\partial x_{mn}} = \sum_{i=1}^{N} \left\| -2 \cdot (\mathbf{y}_i - f(\mathbf{x}_i, \mathbf{X})) \left( \frac{\partial f(\mathbf{x}_i, \mathbf{X})}{\partial x_{mn}} \right) \right\|_2 \tag{11}$$

The definition of the Nadaraya-Watson estimator gradient and the derivative of the Gaussian kernel function can be found in the appendix. Gradient descent is usually applied until the improvement of the DSRE falls under a defined threshold value. Figure 3 shows a visualization of three exemplary latent spaces with $q = 2$ colorized by DSRE w. r. t. a target pattern (white box) of the *Digits* data sets with $N = 100$ patterns for the two digits $'1'$ (green), $'3'$ (red). Dark red areas have the highest DSRE, while dark blue areas minimize the DSRE. The arrows show the gradient direction for all patterns in latent space.

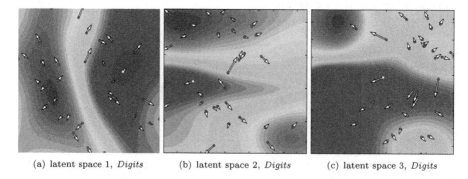

(a) latent space 1, *Digits*     (b) latent space 2, *Digits*     (c) latent space 3, *Digits*

**Fig. 3.** Visualization of DSRE of latent space w. r. t. to marked target pattern with gradient direction arrows on *Digits*.

## 4.2  Hybrid Optimization

The idea of the hybrid optimization approach is to combine the evolutionary iterative solution construction introduced in the previous section with the gradient descent approach. Algorithm 2 shows this hybridization as hybrid UKR (HybUKR) approach in pseudocode. Like in the case of iterative embeddings, the patterns are iteratively embedded with $(1+1)$-UKR. The candidate position $x_i$ with the minimal DSRE is finally chosen. After $\eta$ patterns have been embedded, gradient descent, see Sect. 4.1, is performed using BFGS. Special cases are $\eta = 1$, i.e., gradient descent is performed after each single embedding, or $\eta = N$, i.e., gradient descent is only called once after all patterns have been embedded. The case $\eta = N$ is the approach of UKR.

But the main advantage of this approach is that the gradient descent process can be performed multiple times during the iterative process, i.e. for $\eta \leq N/2$ to overcome local optima. Further, we suppose that choosing the same regression method for the iterative solution construction as for the gradient descent is beneficial, in particular in comparison to the initialization with other methods.

---

**Algorithm 2.** HybUKR approach

---

**Require: Y**, $\eta, \lambda$
1: $\overline{\mathbf{X}} = [\mathbf{0}]$, $\overline{\mathbf{Y}} = [\mathbf{y}_1]$
2: **for** $i = 2$ **to** $N$ **do**
3:     choose $\mathbf{y}_i$ from **Y**
4:     look for closest pattern $\mathbf{y}^*$ with latent position $\mathbf{x}^*$
5:     choose $\mathbf{x}_i$ that minimizes DSRE with $(1 + \lambda)$-ES
6:     $\overline{\mathbf{X}} = [\overline{\mathbf{X}}, \mathbf{x}_i]$, $\overline{\mathbf{Y}} = [\overline{\mathbf{Y}}, \mathbf{y}_i]$
7:     **if** $(i \mod \eta) = 0$ **then**
8:        **while** improvement of DSRE **do**
9:           gradient decent with BFGS
10:       **end while**
11:    **end if**
12: **end for**

---

## 4.3  Alternating Gradient Optimization

The interesting case of employing gradient descent multiple times during the iterative embedding process is analyzed in the following experiments. For embedding, we employ a $(1 + 1)$-UKR terminating after 48 generations.

Figure 4 shows the comparison of $(1 + 1)$-UKR (blue) and HybUKR (red) when embedding *Digits*, *Iris*, and *Gaussian blobs* in terms of the DSRE. The plots show that the DSRE is increasing with the number of patterns. HybUKR performs four gradient descent optimization processes with BFGS, i.e., after every iterative embedding of 1/4 of patterns has been completed. The results show that performing gradient descent leads to a significant performance increase. The gradient descent processes can be recognized as down-steps in the increasing DSRE curve. On *Iris*, areas of rapidly increasing DSRE at $i = 50$ and $i = 100$

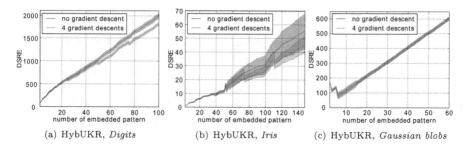

(a) HybUKR, *Digits*    (b) HybUKR, *Iris*    (c) HybUKR, *Gaussian blobs*

**Fig. 4.** Comparison of alternating gradient descent optimization to iterative embedding on *Digits*, *Iris*, and *Gaussian blobs*.

are situations, when patterns with new labels are added to the manifolds. Only marginal improvements can be achieved on the *Gaussian blobs* data set, while a small standard deviation is achieved. Interesting is the beginning of the *Gaussian blobs* embedding process, where single patterns result in large errors $r(\mathbf{x}_i)$. For an increasing number of patterns, more adequate positions can be found leading to a lower sum $R(\mathbf{X})$.

As last experiment, we compare HybUKR to other famous dimensionality reduction methods, i.e., principal component analysis (PCA) [14], isometric mapping (ISOMAP) [15], local linear embedding (LLE) [16], and the LLE variant called Hessian LLE. The implementations of PCA, ISOMAP, and the LLE variants are based on SCIKIT-LEARN [17]. Table 1 shows the DSRE results of HybUKR with gradient descent steps after $\eta = N, N/2, N/4$ patterns have been embedded, and without gradient descent. For methods that use a neighborhood graph (ISOMAP and LLE variants), the figures in parentheses state the optimal neighborhood size $k$ from the interval $[1, N]$. The DSRE results show that the alternating scheme with $\eta = N/4$ is the best HybUKR variant.

**Table 1.** Comparison of HybUKR variants, PCA, ISOMAP and LLE variants on the data sets *Digits*, *Iris* and *Gaussian blobs*

| method | opt. | $\eta$ | DSRE | | |
| | | | *Digits* | *Iris* | *Gaussian blobs* |
|---|---|---|---|---|---|
| HybUKR | none | - | $1985.4 \pm 55.7$ | $55.96 \pm 12.74$ | $604.75 \pm 11.24$ |
| | gradient | $N$ | $1786.2 \pm 44.9$ | $42.68 \pm 4.48$ | $603.21 \pm 8.52$ |
| | gradient | $N/2$ | $1771.9 \pm 38.0$ | $41.48 \pm 3.59$ | $\mathbf{602.31 \pm 2.36}$ |
| | gradient | $N/4$ | $\mathbf{1763.6 \pm 35.8}$ | $\mathbf{40.76 \pm 4.76}$ | $603.49 \pm 9.02$ |
| PCA | none | - | $2169.3$ | $59.109$ | $609.21$ |
| ISOMAP | none | - | $2042.6$ ($k = 12$) | $58.925$ ($k = 121$) | $609.04$ ($k = 40$) |
| LLE | none | - | $2068.9$ ($k = 32$) | $58.263$ ($k = 98$) | $616.87$ ($k = 58$) |
| Hessian LLE | none | - | $2069.4$ ($k = 29$) | $59.522$ ($k = 100$) | $609.34$ ($k = 20$) |

Another interesting observation is that the final gradient descent optimization process after all patterns have been embedded is quite important. For example on *Digits*, the DSRE when using gradient descent as post-optimization ($\eta = N, R = 1786.2 \pm 44.9$) is quite close to the DSRE of the alternating HybUKR variant ($N/4, R = 1763.6 \pm 35.8$), but is still significantly worse. The Wilcoxon rank-sum test confirms that the difference is statistically significant with a $p_{\text{value}} < 0.001$. Another important result is that HybUKR outperforms the standards methods, which may be due to the effect that HybUKR explicitly optimizes w.r.t. the DSRE. However, HybUKR generates significantly better DSRE values, which is an accepted measure for evaluating dimensionality reduction results. Also on *Gaussian blobs*, the HybUKR variants achieve better results than the standard methods and alternating scheme reduce the DSRE and the standard deviation with exception of the $\eta = N/4$ choice.

## 5   Conclusions

The unsupervised regression problem is difficult so solve. In this paper, we introduce two new algorithmic variants to overcome getting stuck in local optima of UR. The $(1 + \lambda)$-UKR is based on ES to improve the iterative optimization process. The evolutionary approach has been shown to be more flexible than naive Gaussian sampling in the iterative solution construction scheme. In particular, the $(1+1)$-UKR variant is a recommendable choice. Further, we employed the differentiable Nadaraya-Watson estimator with the differentiable Gaussian kernel function in an alternating optimization scheme with the $(1+1)$-UKR. The experiments have shown that the new HybUKR approach computes embeddings with better quality than related methods. Future prospective work will be to speedup HybUKR by parallelizing it on multi-core machines. In particular, the expensive computation of the UKR gradient will profit from a parallel implementation.

## A   Gradient Descent

HybUKR requires the gradient of the Nadaraya-Watson estimator, which is defined as:

$$\frac{\partial f(\mathbf{X})}{\partial x_{mn}} = \sum_{i=1}^{N} \mathbf{y}_i \cdot \left( \frac{1}{\sum_{j=1}^{N} \mathbf{K}_h(\mathbf{x} - \mathbf{x}_j)} \cdot \frac{\partial \mathbf{K}_h(\mathbf{x} - \mathbf{x}_i)}{\partial x_{mn}} \right.$$

$$\left. - \frac{\mathbf{K}(\mathbf{x} - \mathbf{x}_i)}{\left( \sum_{j=1}^{N} \mathbf{K}_h(\mathbf{x} - \mathbf{x}_j) \right)^2} \cdot \sum_{j=1}^{N} \frac{\partial \mathbf{K}_h(\mathbf{x} - \mathbf{x}_j)}{\partial x_{mn}} \right)$$

The derivative of the Gaussian kernel function is:

$$\mathbf{K}_h(\mathbf{x}_i - \mathbf{x}_j) = K_h(\|\mathbf{x}_i - \mathbf{x}_j\|_2^2) = \frac{1}{h} \cdot K\left( \frac{\|\mathbf{x}_i - \mathbf{x}_j\|_2^2}{h} \right)$$

# References

1. Kramer, O.: Dimensionalty reduction by unsupervised nearest neighbor regression. In: International Conference on Machine Learning and Applications (ICMLA), pp. 275–278. IEEE (2011)
2. Kramer, O.: Unsupervised nearest neighbors with kernels. In: Glimm, B., Krüger, A. (eds.) KI 2012: Advances in Artificial Intelligence. LNCS, vol. 7526, pp. 97–106. Springer, Heidelberg (2012)
3. Meinicke, P., Klanke, S., Memisevic, R., Ritter, H.: Principal surfaces from unsupervised kernel regression. IEEE Trans. Pattern Anal. Mach. Intell. **27**, 1379–1391 (2005)
4. Smola, A.J., Mika, S., Schölkopf, B., Williamson, R.C.: Regularized principal manifolds. J. Mach. Learn. Res. **1**, 179–209 (2001)
5. Lawrence, N.D.: Probabilistic non-linear principal component analysis with gaussian process latent variable models. J. Mach. Learn. Res. **6**, 1783–1816 (2005)
6. Tan, S., Mavrovouniotis, M.: Reducing data dimensionality through optimizing neural network inputs. AIChE J. **41**, 1471–1479 (1995)
7. Kramer, O.: A particle swarm embedding algorithm for nonlinear dimensionality reduction. In: Dorigo, M., Birattari, M., Blum, C., Christensen, A.L., Engelbrecht, A.P., Groß, R., Stützle, T. (eds.) ANTS 2012. LNCS, vol. 7461, pp. 1–12. Springer, Heidelberg (2012)
8. Nourashrafeddin, S., Arnold, D., Milios, E.E.: An evolutionary subspace clustering algorithm for high-dimensional data. In: Proceedings of the Annual Conference on Genetic and Evolutionary Computation (GECCO), pp. 1497–1498 (2012)
9. Vahdat, A., Heywood, M.I., Zincir-Heywood, A.N.: Bottom-up evolutionary subspace clustering. In: IEEE Congress on Evolutionary Computation, pp. 1–8 (2010)
10. Nadaraya, E.: On estimating regression. Theory Probab. Appl. **10**, 186–190 (1964)
11. Rechenberg, I.: Cybernetic solution path of an experimental problem. In: Ministry of Aviation, UK, Royal Aircraft Establishment (1965)
12. Klanke, S., Ritter, H.: Variants of unsupervised kernel regression: general cost functions. Neurocomputing **70**, 1289–1303 (2007)
13. Nocedal, J., Wright, S.J.: Numerical Optimization. Springer, New York (2000)
14. Jolliffe, I.T.: Principal Component Analysis. Springer Series in Statistics. Springer, New York (1986)
15. Tenenbaum, J.B., Silva, V.D., Langford, J.C.: A global geometric framework for nonlinear dimensionality reduction. Science **290**, 2319–2323 (2000)
16. Roweis, S.T., Saul, L.K.: Nonlinear dimensionality reduction by locally linear embedding. SCIENCE **290**, 2323–2326 (2000)
17. Pedregosa, F., Varoquaux, G., Gramfort, A., Michel, V., Thirion, B., Grisel, O., Blondel, M., Prettenhofer, P., Weiss, R., Dubourg, V., Vanderplas, J., Passos, A., Cournapeau, D., Brucher, M., Perrot, M., Duchesnay, E.: Scikit-learn: machine learning in Python. J. Mach. Learn. Res. **12**, 2825–2830 (2011)

# Hybrid Manifold Clustering with Evolutionary Tuning

Oliver Kramer[(✉)]

Computational Intelligence Group, Department of Computer Science,
University of Oldenburg, Oldenburg, Germany
`oliver.kramer@uni-oldenburg.de`

**Abstract.** Manifold clustering, also known as submanifold learning, is the task to embed patterns in submanifolds with different characteristics. This paper proposes a hybrid approach of clustering the data set, computing a global map of cluster centers, embedding each cluster, and then merging the scaled submanifolds with the global map. We introduce various instantiations of cluster and embedding algorithms based on hybridization of $k$-means, principal component analysis, isometric mapping, and locally linear embedding. A (1+1)-ES is employed to tune the submanifolds by rotation and scaling. The submanifold learning algorithms are compared w.r.t. the nearest neighbor classification performance on various experimental data sets.

**Keywords:** Manifold clustering · Dimensionality reduction · Evolutionary tuning

## 1 Introduction

In dimensionality reduction (DR), the task is to embed high-dimensional patterns $\mathbf{y}_1, \ldots, \mathbf{y}_N \in \mathbb{R}^d$ into low-dimensional latent spaces by learning an explicit mapping $\mathbf{F} : \mathbb{R}^d \to \mathbb{R}^q$ or by finding low-dimensional counterparts $\mathbf{x}_1, \ldots, \mathbf{x}_N \in \mathbb{R}^q$ with $q < d$ in latent spaces that conserve useful information of their high-dimensional pendants. The DR problem has intensively been studied in the past decade, but still turns out to be comparatively difficult to solve.

Methods like principal component analysis (PCA) [1], isometric mapping (ISOMAP) [2], and locally linear embedding (LLE) [3] learn a global map of all patterns. For some purposes, it might not be appropriate to embed all patterns within one manifold. This can have various reasons. For example in visualization, not a global map of data that puts all patterns into relation may be required, but a map that separates the groups of patterns and presents a reasonable embedding within each group. Patterns may lie in submanifolds with different characteristics that afford individual parameterizations for their optimal representation. Further, the runtime of many DR methods grows quadratically or cubically and does not scale well for large data sets. Embedding of smaller groups of patterns accelerates the learning process, and can additionally be parallelized on multicore machines.

A.M. Mora and G. Squillero (Eds.): EvoApplications 2015, LNCS 9028, pp. 481–490, 2015.
DOI: 10.1007/978-3-319-16549-3_39

In this paper, an easy-to-implement approach for manifold clustering is introduced. It first clusters the data to assign them to submanifolds. Then, the cluster centers are embedded with a DR approach to establish a global map structure. The patterns within each submanifold are separately embedded. This allows to employ different dimensionality reduction algorithms and different parameters within each submanifold. Finally, the separate embeddings are combined around each latent cluster center to one global map. To avoid overlaps and consider inter-cluster neighborhood relations, the submanifolds are rotated and scaled with evolution strategies (ES) [4].

This paper is structured as follows. In Sect. 2, we introduce the manifold clustering problem and present related work. The hybrid manifold clustering (HMC) algorithm is introduced in Sect. 3 and experimentally analyzed in Sect. 4 w.r.t. different submanifold measures. Conclusions are drawn in Sect. 5.

## 2    Manifold Clustering

In this section, we introduce the manifold clustering problem, present related work and introduce the DR method that will be basis of the HMC approach.

### 2.1    Problem Definition

Observed patterns $\mathbf{Y} = [\mathbf{y}_i]_{i=1}^N \in \mathbb{R}^d$ may lie in different submanifolds. Let $k$ be the number of potential submanifolds $\{\mathcal{M}_j\}_{j=1}^k$. Each submanifold may employ an own intrinsic dimension, i.e., the number of features that is necessary to represent the main characteristics of a subset of patterns. The manifold clustering problem is the task to simultaneously assign the patterns to clusters and to solve the DR problem within each submanifold. The DR problem is to find a low-dimensional representation $\mathbf{X} = [\mathbf{x}_i]_{i=1}^N \in \mathbb{R}^q$ of high-dimensional patterns with $q \ll d$ such that their most important characteristics like pattern distances and neighborhoods are maintained. Such characteristics can be measured with pattern similarities or classification accuracies, if labels are available.

The problem to simultaneously learn submanifolds and their embeddings is difficult to solve. Clusters have to be identified, and low-dimensional representations of the patterns have to be learned. Further, in each cluster different parameters can be chosen. Vidal [5] summarizes challenges of the manifold clustering problem. Essential characteristics of manifold clustering are the coupling between clustering of patterns and model estimation. A known distribution to clusters simplifies the model estimation process, as the model would allow the determination of the assignment to manifolds. But in general, the distribution to clusters is unknown. The problem in manifold clustering is the closeness of subspaces or their overlapping. Submanifolds may employ different characteristics with different intrinsic dimensionality.

## 2.2   Related Work

Manifold clustering algorithms based on algebraic methods employ matrix factorization e.g., by Costeira and Kanade [6] and by Gear [7], or employ polynomial algebra [8]. Kushnir *et al.* [9] introduce a submanifold learning variant based on density, shape, intrinsic dimensionality, and orientation. Iterative methods extend $k$-means, alternately fitting local PCA models to each submanifold and then assigning each pattern to its closest submanifold, e.g., k-planes [10] or k-subspaces [11]. Another iterative solution construction algorithm has been proposed by Kramer [12] based on unsupervised nearest neighbors [13] and an iterative $k$-means variant. For handling noise, statistical models like mixtures of probabilistic PCA [14] assume that data within submanifolds are generated with independent Gaussian distributions employing the maximum likelihood principle. Closely related to this work are the evolutionary submanifold learning algorithms that choose the employed attributes with evolutionary algorithms [15,16]. For example, Vahdat *et al.* [16] uses evolutionary multi-objective search to balance intra-cluster distance and connectedness of clusters. An further introduction to submanifold learning can be found in Vidal [5] and Luxburg [17].

## 3   Hybrid Manifold Clustering

In this section, we introduce the HMC approach based on six main steps. The idea of HMC is to cluster the data set, embed the clusters into submanifolds and then to combine the separate embeddings on a global map. The embedding task in submanifolds is easy to parallelize. Figure 1 shows the pseudocode of the proposed approach. The steps are explained in the following.

### 3.1   Clustering

The first step of the hybrid approach is the assignment of all patterns to clusters. Let $\mathbf{y}_1, \ldots, \mathbf{y}_N$ be the set of patterns. A clustering algorithm (e.g. $k$-means) assigns the patterns to clusters $\mathcal{M}_1, \ldots, \mathcal{M}_k$ that will be the basis of the submanifolds. The center of each submanifold is defined as $\mathbf{m}_j = \frac{1}{|\mathcal{M}_j|} \sum_{\mathbf{y} \in \mathcal{M}_j} \mathbf{y}$, where $|\mathcal{M}_j|$ is the cardinality of the set of patterns belonging to cluster $\mathcal{M}_j$. We employ $k$-means for clustering, which repeatedly assigns patterns to the closest intermediate center $\mathbf{m}_j$ and computes the new center based on this assignment. Other kinds of clustering algorithms can be applied. The success of the clustering approach is important for the assignment to submanifolds. For this sake, it is important to choose algorithms appropriate for the data set. This might be a problem, in particular in high-dimensional data spaces, where the distances can become less meaningful than in low-dimensional data spaces.

### 3.2   Global Map Embedding

After the clustering process, the cluster centers $\mathbf{m}_1, \ldots, \mathbf{m}_k \in \mathbb{R}^d$ are embedded in a $q$-dimensional space $\mathbb{R}^q$ with a DR algorithm to learn an appropriate global structure. This results in embeddings $\hat{\mathbf{m}}_1, \ldots, \hat{\mathbf{m}}_k \in \mathbb{R}^q$. In the experimental section, we will use neighborhood size $K = k$ for LLE and ISOMAP, i.e., we use the number $k$ of clusters as the largest possible value for $K$. A small number can be compensated by sampling more patterns from each cluster for the global map embedding process. The latent positions[1] $\hat{\mathbf{m}}_1, \ldots, \hat{\mathbf{m}}_k$ are the centers of the embeddings of the submanifolds that are computed in the next step.

---

**Algorithm 1.** HMC

---

**Require:** data set $\mathbf{Y}, \xi$
1: cluster $\mathbf{Y} \rightarrow$ clusters $\mathcal{M}_j$ with centers $\mathbf{m}_j$
2: embed global map $\rightarrow \hat{\mathbf{m}}_j$
3: embed clusters $\rightarrow \hat{\mathcal{M}}_j$
4: compute scaling factor $\xi$
5: map fusion (Eq. 3) $\rightarrow \mathbf{X}$
6: tuning with $(1+1)$-ES
7: **return** $\mathbf{X}$

---

**Fig. 1.** Pseudocode of HMC approach

### 3.3   Submanifold Embedding

For each cluster $\mathcal{M}_j$ with $j = 1, \ldots, k$, its patterns $\mathbf{y}_l$ with $l = 1, \ldots, |\mathcal{M}_j|$ are embedded with a DR method resulting in latent positions $\hat{\mathcal{M}}_j = \{\mathbf{x}_1, \ldots, \mathbf{x}_{|\mathcal{M}_j|}\}$ with $\mathbf{x}_i \in \mathbb{R}^q$. As most embedding methods scale at least quadratically or cubically with the number of patterns, the approach is faster than embedding all patterns at the same time, i.e., $O((N^2/k)\log(N/k)) < O(N^2\log(N))$.

### 3.4   Map Fusion

In the next step, the submanifold embeddings are merged on the global map. To avoid overlaps, the maximum extension

$$d_{\max} = \max_{j=1,\ldots,k} \left\{ \|\mathbf{x}_i - \mathbf{x}_l\|^2 | \mathbf{x}_i, \mathbf{x}_l \in \hat{\mathcal{M}}_j \wedge i \neq l \right\} \tag{1}$$

of all submanifolds is combined with the minimum distance

$$d_{\min} = \left\{ \|\hat{\mathbf{m}}_i - \hat{\mathbf{m}}_j\|^2 | i, j = 1, \ldots, k \wedge i \neq j \right\} \tag{2}$$

between the embeddings on the global map to a submanifold scaling factor $\xi = d_{\min}/d_{\max}$. With $\xi$, the final embedding is determined by placing the submanifolds at the positions of embeddings of the cluster centers

$$\mathbf{X} = \bigcup_{j=1,\ldots,k} \left\{ \hat{\mathbf{m}}_j + \xi \cdot \mathbf{x}_i | \mathbf{x}_i \in \hat{\mathcal{M}}_j \right\}. \tag{3}$$

---

[1] The notation $\mathcal{M}_j$ is used for cluster $j$ in data space with center $\mathbf{m}_j$, while $\hat{\mathcal{M}}_j$ is the corresponding submanifold in latent space with center $\hat{\mathbf{m}}_j$.

Befor the map fusion, the low-dimensional patterns in $\hat{\mathcal{M}}_j$ can also be normalized such that center $\hat{\mathbf{m}}_i$ is located at the origin $\hat{\mathbf{m}}_i = (0, \ldots, 0, )^T \in \mathbb{R}^q$. This HMC framework can be instantiated with various DR methods and separate settings for each submanifold. This will be investigated in more detail in the experimental section, where we concentrate on a comparison of PCA, ISOMAP, and LLE.

### 3.5   Evolutionary Tuning

The embedding processes in each submanifold are independent from each other. An adaptation of submanifolds on the level of the global map by scaling and rotation allows the improvement of the overall DR result. In the following, we propose to improve the submanifolds with an evolutionary post-optimization and tuning process. The objective is to minimize DR-oriented quality measures. For the labeled data sets, we demonstrate the tuning process with the $k$-nearest neighbor (kNN) classification error on the embeddings, i.e., the fitness function to be minimized is defined as the cross-validation (CV) error

$$E(\mathbf{X}) = \| f(\mathbf{x}_i) - \overline{y}_i \|^2 \tag{4}$$

with $i = 1, \ldots, N$, where $N$ is the number of patterns in the CV learning scheme employing the original labels $\overline{y}_i$. As this error measure is not differentiable, we employ ES as blackbox optimizer. A solution $\mathbf{z} = (r_1, \ldots, r_k, s_1, \ldots, s_k)$ is a vector of rotation angles $r_i \in [0, 360]$ and scaling factors $s_i \in \mathbb{R}^+$ for each submanifold $\hat{\mathcal{M}}_1, \ldots, \hat{\mathcal{M}}_k$. Hence, the optimization problem is a continuous $2k$-dimensional problem with bound constraints $0 \leq r_i \leq 360$ and $s_i > 0$. In the following, we employ a $(1+1)$-ES with Gaussian mutation $\mathbf{z}' = \mathbf{z} + \sigma \cdot \mathcal{N}(0, 1)$ and Rechenberg's 1/5th mutation strength control [18]. The fitness $E(\cdot)$ is computed for neighborhood size $k = 50$ of the kNN classification error. The step sizes start with initial values $\sigma_1^0$ for mutation of the rotation angels and $\sigma_2^0$ for mutation of the scaling factor. For the Rechenberg mutation rate control, we choose the generation window $G = 50$ and mutation parameter $\tau = 1.1$. The $(1 + 1)$-ES is based on death penalty for the bound constraints, i.e., candidate solutions are discarded, if they are infeasible. As termination condition, the ES stops after $T = 500$ generations.

## 4   Experimental Analysis

In the following, we evaluate various instantiations of HMC experimentally. Our HMC implementation is written in PYTHON, while the algorithms $k$-means, PCA, ISOMAP, and LLE built upon the SCIKIT-LEARN [19] machine learning framework. We compare the embeddings w.r.t. the kNN classification and regression error $E(\mathbf{X})$ using the latent representations $\mathbf{x}_1, \ldots, \mathbf{x}_N$ as training patterns and the original labels $\overline{y}_i$ of the labeled training data sets. The kNN error gives information about the neighborhood characteristics of the employed data set. Low errors show that the low-dimensional patterns preserve the most important characteristics of their high-dimensional counterparts and are therefore appropriate representations.

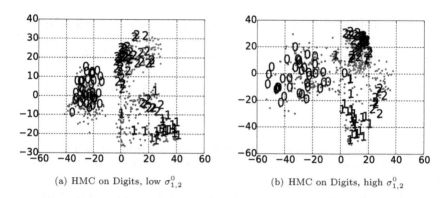

(a) HMC on Digits, low $\sigma_{1,2}^0$          (b) HMC on Digits, high $\sigma_{1,2}^0$

**Fig. 2.** Embeddings of Digits data with the HMC variant $k$-means-PCA and $(1+1)$-ES tuning. The colors correspond to the labels of the patterns, which are not used in the primary embedding process, but for the tuning optimization with the $(1+1)$-ES.

### 4.1   Exemplary Embeddings

Figure 2 shows exemplary embeddings of the Digits data set with HMC employing evolutionary tuning. Figure 2(a) shows an embedding of the HMC variant $k$-means-PCA with the $(1 + 1)$-ES on the 3-class Digits data set with $k = 50$. The submanifolds have been rotated slightly leading to a situation, where similar instances of different digits are located in a closer neighborhood. Figure 2(b) shows the result of a post-optimization with larger initial step sizes leading to a manifold with varying shape and higher kNN accuracies.

Figure 3 shows the embeddings of the Iris and the Photos data set with HMC and evolutionary tuning. Figure 3(a) shows the result of HMC and evolutionary post-optimization on the Iris data set. Figure 3(b) shows an embedding with HMC of Photos employing PCA. The three submanifolds are highlighted.

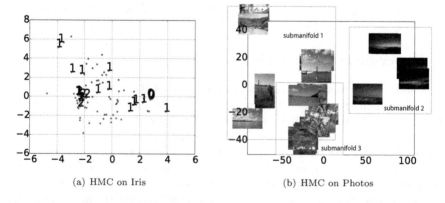

(a) HMC on Iris                              (b) HMC on Photos

**Fig. 3.** Embeddings of Iris with $k$-means-PCA HMC and embedding of Photo data set with LLE HMC and $(1 + 1)$-ES tuning.

**Table 1.** Comparison of evolutionary tuning by rotating and scaling of submanifolds on Digits, Iris, and Gauss.

|  | Digits 1 (5) | Digits 2 (10) | Iris | Gauss |
|---|---|---|---|---|
| HMC | 0.109 | 0.140 | 0.100 | 0.383 |
| $(1+1)$-EA | $0.056 \pm 0.05$ | $0.131 \pm 0.03$ | $0.067 \pm 0.06$ | $0.375 \pm 0.02$ |

Table 1 compares the kNN error of HMC with and without evolutionary tuning. For both Digits data sets, we choose $\sigma_1^0 = 50.0$ and $\sigma_2^0 = 0.001$. On the Iris data set, the setting $\sigma_1^0 = 5.0$ and $\sigma_2^0 = 0.001$ is chosen. The table shows that the $(1+1)$-ES improves the submanifold embeddings in all cases.

### 4.2   Benchmark Problems

Table 2 compares the classification and regression errors between native DR methods for preprocessing and HMC on the benchmark test set, see Appendix A. The target dimensionality is $q = 2$. The results show the kNN classification error with the MSE measure. The native embedding methods are compared to the HMC variants, which employ the corresponding DR method both for the global map and for the submanifolds. The evolutionary fine-tuning process runs with a $(1+1)$-EA for 500 generations. The evolutionary experiments are repeated 50 times and the mean with standard deviation is shown. The results on the MakeClass data set show that each native variant is significantly outperformed by the HMC approaches. The lowest error in mean has been achieved by the ISOMAP-HMC variant. Also on Digits the HMC variants outperform the native algorithms. Embedding in ten submanifolds results in a clear separation between the different classes and achieves significantly lower kNN classification errors. While the standard deviation is moderate in all cases, the PCA-HMC

**Table 2.** Comparison of basic DR for preprocessing to HMC on benchmark problem w.r.t kNN classification measure.

| Problem | PCA | | ISOMAP | | LLE | |
|---|---|---|---|---|---|---|
|  | Native | HMC | Native | HMC | Native | HMC |
| MakeClass | 0.296 | $0.211 \pm 0.009$ | 0.296 | $0.192 \pm 0.003$ | 0.297 | $0.224 \pm 0.004$ |
| Digits | 0.330 | $0.093 \pm 0.012$ | 0.330 | $0.094 \pm 0.015$ | 0.316 | $0.097 \pm 0.014$ |
| Faces | 0.542 | $0.616 \pm 0.001$ | 0.542 | $0.616 \pm 0.014$ | 0.543 | $0.630 \pm 0.003$ |
| Blobs | 0.048 | $0.063 \pm 0.009$ | 0.048 | $0.059 \pm 0.010$ | 0.047 | $0.060 \pm 0.013$ |
| Friedman 1 | 20.09 | $23.67 \pm 0.623$ | 20.09 | $24.35 \pm 0.613$ | 20.40 | $21.64 \pm 1.370$ |
| Friedman 2 | 20.48 | $22.12 \pm 0.764$ | 20.48 | $23.73 \pm 0.213$ | 20.66 | $23.05 \pm 1.309$ |
| Wind | 11.50 | $7.646 \pm 0.599$ | 11.50 | $7.271 \pm 0.714$ | 12.12 | $8.283 \pm 0.606$ |
| Fitness | 0.291 | $0.970 \pm 0.507$ | 0.291 | $1.106 \pm 0.382$ | 0.253 | $0.982 \pm 0.663$ |

variant is the best model in mean. On the Faces data set, all native and all HMC variants can only achieve a comparatively low accuracy. Here, the native variants even outperform the HMC variants. On Blobs, the mean results of HMC is slightly worse than the native variants. Also on the Friedmann regression problems, the native DR methods perform better in terms of kNN classification than the HMC approaches. On the Wind data set, HMC is superior, while it is again outperformed on the Fitness regression data set.

## 4.3 Runtime

Last, we analyze the runtime of HMC. With growing data set sizes the runtime increases. Figure 4(a) compares the runtime of ISOMAP and HMC on the MakeClass data set w.r.t. an increasing number of patterns, i.e., from $N = 500$ to $N = 5500$. HMC optimizes for $T = 100$ generations and employs $k = 2$ classes. Each experimental setting is repeated 30 times with new randomly generated data sets. The curves show the mean runtimes as well as the minimum and maximum values. The curves show that ISOMAP is slightly faster at the beginning, but is then the overhauled by HMC. HMC is slower at the beginning because of the evolutionary tuning process. As of $N = 1500$, ISOMAP is outperformed because its quadratic runtime complexity[2], while HMC works on a data set of size $N/k$. Interestingly, the runtime variance is comparatively low.

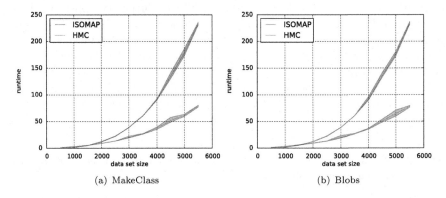

(a) MakeClass                           (b) Blobs

**Fig. 4.** Runtime comparison of native ISOMAP and HMC based on ISOMAP on (a) MakeClass and (b) Blobs data set

The corresponding results for ISOMAP on the Blobs data set are shown in Fig. 4(b), where a similar picture is drawn. ISOMAP is only slightly faster for the small data sets, i.e., until $N = 1500$. However, the choice of methods is a decision with tradeoff. The win in runtime might be a convincing argument for choosing HMC, also the accuracy in classification scenarios can be slightly worse. For visualization purposes, HMC might be a reasonable choice if submanifolds are present.

---

[2] The runtime of ISOMAP is $O(N^2 \log N)$.

## 5    Conclusions

The hybrid approach of clustering and subsequent embedding of patterns into submanifolds introduced in this paper can be instantiated with numerous clustering and DR algorithms. The embedding of cluster centers on a global map as well as scaling of the submanifolds before merging with the global centers leads to improved DR results in comparison to standard methods. We analyzed different combinations of DR methods for learning the global map and for embedding into submanifolds. The most important result is that the kNN classification and regression error based on submanifold embeddings is often lower than the accuracy based on standard methods. This indicates that HMC embeddings maintain more information of the data distribution in the submanifold latent spaces than classical approaches. In the future, we will analyze separate dimensionalities $q_j$ for each manifold $\hat{\mathcal{M}}_j$ optimized w.r.t. different DR measures.

## A    Benchmark Problems

MakeClass is a classification data set generated with the SCIKIT-LEARN [19] method `make_classification` with $d$ dimensions and two centers. The UCI Digits data set [20] comprises handwritten digits with $d = 64$. It is a frequent reference problem related to the recognition of handwritten characters and digits. The Faces data set is called *Labeled Faces in the Wild* [21] and has been introduced for studying the face recognition problem. The data set source is http:// vis-www.cs.umass.edu/lfw/. It contains JPEG images of famous people collected from the internet. The Gaussian blobs data set is generated with the SCIKIT-LEARN [19] method `make_blobs` and the following settings. Two centers, i.e., two classes are generated, each with a standard deviation of $\sigma = 10.0$ and variable $d$. Friedman 1 is a regression data set generated with the SCIKIT-LEARN [19] method `make_friedman1`. The regression problem has been introduced in [22], where Friedman introduces multivariate adaptive regression splines. Friedman 2 is also a regression data set of SCIKIT-LEARN [19] and can be generated with `make_friedman2`. The wind data set is based on spatio-temporal time series data from the National Renewable Energy Laboratory (NREL) western wind data set. The whole data set comprises time series of 32,043 wind turbines, each holding ten 3 MW turbines over a timespan of three years in a 10-minute resolution. The dimensionality is $d = 22$. Fitness is data set based on an optimization run of a $(15+100)$-ES [4] on the Sphere function $f(\mathbf{z}) = \mathbf{z}^T \mathbf{z}$ with $d = 20$ dimensions and 21000 fitness function evaluations. The patterns are the objective variable values of the best candidate solution in each generation, the labels are the fitness function values in each generation. The data set Photos contains thirty JPEG photos with resolution $320 \times 214$ taken with a SONY DSLR-A300. The Iris data sets consists of 150 4-dimensional patterns of three different types of irises.

# References

1. Jolliffe, I.: Principal Component Analysis. Springer Series in Statistics. Springer, New York (1986)
2. Tenenbaum, J.B., Silva, V.D., Langford, J.C.: A global geometric framework for nonlinear dimensionality reduction. Science **290**, 2319–2323 (2000)
3. Roweis, S.T., Saul, L.K.: Nonlinear dimensionality reduction by locally linear embedding. Science **290**, 2323–2326 (2000)
4. Beyer, H.G., Schwefel, H.P.: Evolution strategies - A comprehensive introduction. Natural Computing **1**, 3–52 (2002)
5. Vidal, R.: Subspace clustering. IEEE Signal Process Mag. **28**, 52–68 (2011)
6. Costeira, J.P., Kanade, T.: A multibody factorization method for independently moving objects. International Journal of Computer Vision **29**, 159–179 (1998)
7. Gear, C.W.: Multibody grouping from motion images. Int. J. Comput. Vis. **29**, 133–150 (1998)
8. Vidal, R., Ma, Y., Sastry, S.: Generalized principal component analysis (gpca). IEEE Trans. Pattern Anal. Mach. Intell. **27**, 1945–1959 (2005)
9. Kushnir, D., Galun, M., Brandt, A.: Fast multiscale clustering and manifold identification. Pattern Recognit. **39**, 1876–1891 (2006)
10. Bradley, P.S., Mangasarian, O.L.: k-plane clustering. J. Global Optim. **16**, 23–32 (2000)
11. Tseng, P.: Nearest $q$-flat to $m$ points. J. Optim. Theory Appl. **105**, 249–252 (2000)
12. Kramer, O.: Fast submanifold learning with unsupervised nearest neighbors. In: Tomassini, M., Antonioni, A., Daolio, F., Buesser, P. (eds.) ICANNGA 2013. LNCS, vol. 7824, pp. 317–325. Springer, Heidelberg (2013)
13. Kramer, O.: Dimensionalty reduction by unsupervised nearest neighbor regression. In: International Conference on Machine Learning and Applications (ICMLA), pp. 275–278. IEEE (2011)
14. Tipping, M.E., Bishop, C.M.: Mixtures of probabilistic principal component analysers. Neural Computation **11**, 443–482 (1999)
15. Nourashrafeddin, S., Arnold, D., Milios, E.E.: An evolutionary subspace clustering algorithm for high-dimensional data. In: Proceedings of the Annual Conference on Genetic and Evolutionary Computation (GECCO), pp. 1497–1498 (2012)
16. Vahdat, A., Heywood, M.I., Zincir-Heywood, A.N.: Bottom-up evolutionary subspace clustering. In: IEEE Congress on Evolutionary Computation, pp. 1–8 (2010)
17. von Luxburg, U.: A tutorial on spectral clustering. Stat. Comput. **17**, 1–24 (2007)
18. Rechenberg, I.: Cybernetic Solution Path of an Experimental Problem. Ministry of Aviation, Royal Aircraft Establishment, Farnborough (1965)
19. Pedregosa, F., Varoquaux, G., Gramfort, A., Michel, V., Thirion, B., Grisel, O., Blondel, M., Prettenhofer, P., Weiss, R., Dubourg, V., Vanderplas, J., Passos, A., Cournapeau, D., Brucher, M., Perrot, M., Duchesnay, E.: Scikit-learn: machine learning in Python. J. Mach. Learn. Res. **12**, 2825–2830 (2011)
20. Hull, J.: A database for handwritten text recognition research. IEEE PAMI **5**, 550–554 (1994)
21. Huang, G.B., Ramesh, M., Berg, T., Learned-Miller, E.: Labeled faces in the wild: a database for studying face recognition in unconstrained environments. Technical report, pp. 07–49. University of Massachusetts, Amherst (2007)
22. Friedman, J.H.: Multivariate adaptive regression splines. Ann. Stat. **19**, 1–67 (1991)

# A Supervised Figure-Ground Segmentation Method Using Genetic Programming

Yuyu Liang$^{(\boxtimes)}$, Mengjie Zhang, and Will N. Browne

School of Engineering and Computer Science, Victoria University of Wellington,
P.O. Box 600, Wellington 6140, New Zealand
{yuyu.liang,mengjie.zhang,will.browne}@ecs.vuw.ac.nz

**Abstract.** Figure-ground segmentation is an important preprocessing phase in many computer vision applications. As different classes of objects require specific segmentation rules, supervised (or top-down) methods, which learn from prior knowledge of objects, are suitable for figure-ground segmentation. However, existing top-down methods, such as model-based and fragment-based ones, involve a lot of human work. As genetic programming (GP) can evolve computer programs to solve problems automatically, it requires less human work. Moreover, since GP contains little human bias, it is possible for GP-evolved methods to obtain better results than human constructed approaches. This paper develops a supervised GP-based segmentation system. Three kinds of simple features, including raw pixel values, six dimension and eleven dimension grayscale statistics, are employed to evolve image segmentors. The evolved segmentors are tested on images from four databases with increasing difficulty, and results are compared with four conventional techniques including thresholding, region growing, clustering, and active contour models. The results show that GP-evolved segmentors perform better than the four traditional methods with consistently good results on both simple and complex images.

**Keywords:** Image segmentation · Genetic programming · Raw pixel values · Grayscale statistics

## 1 Introduction

Figure-ground segmentation is a basic computer vision task, which aims to separate foreground objects or regions of interest from their background. The results of figure-ground segmentations can be input to many higher-level tasks, such as object recognition, object tracking and image editing [1].

There are two ways to conduct figure-ground segmentation: bottom-up and top-down approaches [2]. Bottom-up approaches are unsupervised using image-based criteria, i.e. intensities or texture of image regions, or continuity and smoothness of boundaries [3]. Normally, they segment an image into regions and then recognize image regions that belong to one object. However, these methods are likely to segment an object to multiple parts, and some parts may

© Springer International Publishing Switzerland 2015
A.M. Mora and G. Squillero (Eds.): EvoApplications 2015, LNCS 9028, pp. 491–503, 2015.
DOI: 10.1007/978-3-319-16549-3_40

merge incorrectly. In contrast, the top-down (or class-based) methods are supervised, which learn from the prior knowledge about objects of interest, such as object classes and shape fragments, to direct the segmentation. As different types of images may contain different classes of objects, they require specific segmentation rules. Therefore, it is more suitable to apply top-down methods for figure-ground segmentation, which can learn segmentation rules from the object information [2].

Existing top-down methods include model-based methods [4,5] and fragment-based methods [2,3,6]. Deformable templates, active shape models and active contour models are commonly used models for image segmentation. Fragment-based methods utilize image fragments (or patches) to handle the variability of shape and appearance within a certain class [6]. There are two stages—the training and the segmentation stage. In the training stage, a fragment set is built from training images to capture possible shapes and appearance variances of the common object parts within a given class. Then the figure-ground segmentation of each fragment is generated manually or learned automatically. Based on this, test images are segmented. However, model-based methods involve a lot of human intervention, and the initial model must be located close to the target, otherwise it is difficult to obtain accurate results. Fragment-based methods require a lot of work to collect informative fragments.

Genetic programming (GP) is an evolutionary computation technique that can solve problems automatically. It can evolve algorithms driven by a fitness function, which is defined to evaluate each candidate solution's performance. Thus, GP does not require users to know or specify the solution's form or structure [7], which involves less human work compared with model and fragment based methods. In addition, as GP can produce algorithms automatically and uses less expertise bias, it is possible to evolve better methods than those determined by researchers.

GP has been introduced in image segmentation since 1990s, and only a limited number of works have been published. According to them, there are two ways to use GP for image segmentation. One is to employ GP directly to evolve segmentation methods [8–12]; the other is to use GP as an optimization technique [13]. The former one, using GP as an algorithm producer, is a top-down method and more widely used.

Papers [8–12], employing GP to evolve segmentation methods, regard segmentation tasks as an extension of classification problems and generate pixel-level classifiers. Poli [8] conducts pixel-classification-based segmentation, using GP to evolve filters from average intensity values of small cutouts of an image and arithmetic functions. Tested on several real medical images, the evolved algorithm is better than a neural network in sensitivity and specificity. Song et al. [9,10] employ GP to evolve texture classifiers from raw pixel values, arithmetic and logic operators to conduct texture segmentation. Results show that the methods can handle texture images with complex shapes and multiple textures. Singh et al. [11] utilizes GP to generate Matlab programs from raw pixel values and primitive image operators (e.g. filters, thresholding and histogram equalization). This technique is compared with a GA-based method on cell images, and consistently produces better results. Roberts [12] evolves segmentors from intensity values, arithmetic and image processing operators. Tested on mole images with skin lesions, the method achieves 92.3 % in sensitivity and 97.2 % in specificity.

Impressive results have been achieved by the existing GP-based segmentation papers [8–12], but these papers only choose simple images in a limited number of domains, including texture images in paper [9,10], cell images [11] and mole images [12]. Even though Poli [8] selects two real images, the images do not contain varying backgrounds and the shapes of the regions of interest are simple. Therefore, it is still not clear whether GP-based segmentation methods can handle a diverse range of images, especially complex images with cluttered backgrounds. Moreover, existing papers make few comparisons with traditional segmentation techniques, such as thresholding, clustering and region based methods.

This paper aims to develop a supervised image segmentation method using GP. Three sets of simple features will be used. We will investigate whether GP with these simple features can perform reasonably well on a diverse range of images, which are from four datasets with increasing difficulty on image segmentation. We will also investigate whether the GP-evolved segmentors can outperform conventional commonly used image segmentation methods on these datasets.

The rest of the paper is organized as follows. Section 2 describes our GP-based image segmentation system. Section 3 introduces four databases and three evaluation measures first, and then displays the performance of the evolved segmentation algorithms. Comparisons with traditional techniques are made in Sect. 4. In Sect. 5, conclusions are drawn.

## 2    GP-Based Image Segmentation System

This section describes how to utilize GP to evolve image segmentors in detail and the three kinds of features used in this paper. The three types of features are raw pixel values, histogram-based statistics and "histogram based statistics + first & second order moments + min & max & average gradient".

### 2.1    Construction of the Segmentation System

For GP-evolved image segmentation methods in the papers [8–12], image segmentation is handled as a supervised classification problem at the pixel level. In Song's papers [9,10], a pixel-classification-based segmentation framework is built, which is a common way to use GP in image-related tasks. Our paper follows this framework as described in Table 1.

Functions employed to evolve segmentors are listed in Table 2. There are only simple arithmetic and logic operators. The terminal set includes three kinds of simple features (described in Sect. 2.2). The settings of GP parameters are as follows. The population size is 500, and the crossover and mutation operators are selected, whose rates are 90 % and 10 % respectively. Other GP parameters

**Table 1.** The flow chart of pixel-classification based segmentation. (Adapted from [9])

| |
|---|
| Input:   test image (I); window size (n); step size (d) used to move the window |
| Output: segmented image |

1. Generate a classifier.
   a) Get cutouts (size: n*n ) of objects and non-objects with class labels.
   b) Extract features from the cutouts.
   c) Set up GP and evolve a classifier using the features.
2. Use the generated classifier to sweep I:
   a) Start from the top-left of I.
   b) Get a subimage (size: n*n); use the evolved operator to classify it.
   c) Label all pixels of the subimage with the result of b).
   d) Move the window to the right horizontally with d pixels and repeat b) and c), till the window reaches the right boundary.
   e) Move the window down vertically with d pixels and repeat b), c) and d), till the window reaches the down-right corner of I.

3. Generate the output with the labels of each pixel.
   a) Use the voting mechanism to decide the final label of each pixel.
   b) Assign pixels with the same label the same intensity, and output the result.

**Table 2.** Function set

| Function name | Definition | Function type |
|---|---|---|
| $Add(a_1, a_2)$ | $a_1 + a_2$ | Arithmetic |
| $Sub(a_1, a_2)$ | $a_1 - a_2$ | Arithmetic |
| $Mul(a_1, a_2)$ | $a_1 * a_2$ | Arithmetic |
| $Div(a_1, a_2)$ | $\begin{cases} a_1/a_2 & \text{if } a_2! = 0 \\ 0 & \text{if } a_2 == 0 \end{cases}$ | Arithmetic |
| $IF(a_1, a_2, a_3)$ | $\begin{cases} a_2 & \text{if } a_1 \text{ is true.} \\ a_3 & \text{if } a_1 \text{ is false.} \end{cases}$ | Logic |
| $<= (a_1, a_2)$ | $\begin{cases} true & \text{if } a_1 <= a_2 \\ false & \text{if otherwise} \end{cases}$ | Logic |
| $>= (a_1, a_2)$ | $\begin{cases} true & \text{if } a_1 >= a_2 \\ false & \text{if otherwise} \end{cases}$ | Logic |
| $= (a_1, a_2)$ | $\begin{cases} true & \text{if } a_1 == a_2 \\ false & \text{if otherwise} \end{cases}$ | Logic |
| $Between(a_1, a_2, a_3)$ | $\begin{cases} true & \text{if } a_1 >= a_2 \&\& a_1 <= a_3 \\ false & \text{if otherwise} \end{cases}$ | Logic |

follow the settings made by Koza [14], who popularizes GP. The fitness measure is the classification accuracy, which is $f = \frac{Number.of.correctly.classified.samples}{Number.of.total.training.samples}$ [9].

**Table 3.** Terminal sets

| Name | Description | Dimension |
|---|---|---|
| Terminal set 1 | Raw pixel values | $n * n$ (window size) |
| Terminal set 2 | Histogram based features | 6D |
| Terminal set 3 | Histogram based features + first & second order moments + Min & Max & Average gradient | 11D |

**Table 4.** Features

| Features | | Name | Description |
|---|---|---|---|
| 11D | 6D | Mean | Represent average intensity |
| | | Varince | Show intensity variation |
| | | Skewness | Measure histogram asymmetry |
| | | Kurtosis | Describe histogram flatness |
| | | Energy | - |
| | | Entropy | Measure histogram uniformity |
| | | First order moment | $M1 = \sum_{i=1}^{n} f(x_i, y_i) * d(x_i, y_i)/n$ |
| | | Second order moment | $M2 = \sum_{i=1}^{n} (f(x_i, y_i) * d(x_i, y_i) - M1)^2/n$ |
| | | Min, Max, Ave gradient | Encode edges and local contrast |

## 2.2   Features

Three types of features, including raw pixel values and grayscale statistics, are investigated to evolve image segmentors by GP in this paper, which are shown in Table 3. The histogram based approaches are first order measures and features extracted from image histograms can describe images' statistical properties [8]. In this paper, six histogram-based statistics, including mean, variance, skewness, kurtosis, energy, entropy, are used. Since histogram based features do not consider spatial relationships between pixels, we add spatial moments and gradient statistics to form the 11D features, combining histogram statistics, a first-order moment, a sencond-order moment and maximum (Max), minimum (Min), average (Ave) gradient.

Equations about two moments defined in Table 4 are based on the definitions: given a square region with size $n * n$, $f(x_i, y_i)$ is the pixel value; $d(x_i, y_i)$ is the distance of the pixel $(x_i, y_i)$ to the top left corner of the region. For min, max, average gradient: given an image $f(x, y)$, $\| \bigtriangledown f(x, y) \|$ is the magnitude of the image; $\frac{\partial f(x,y)}{\partial x} \approx \frac{f(x+1,y)-f(x-1,y)}{2}$; $\frac{\partial f(x,y)}{\partial y} \approx \frac{f(x,y+1)-f(x,y-1)}{2}$.

## 3   Experiments and Results

This section evaluates the evolved GP-based methods on four datasets in terms of the segmentation accuracy, $F_1$ measure and negative rate metric (NRM). Apart

**Table 5.** Images used in this paper

| Database | Images | | | |
|---|---|---|---|---|
| Bitmap | P14 | P24 | Rectangular | Butterfly |
| Brodatz | D24 | D34 | D24vs34 | |
| Weizmann | horse006 | horse010 | horse027 | horse110   horse119 |
| | horse121 | horse122 | horse159 | horse165   horse317 |
| PASCAL | 2007_000033   2007_000256 | 2007_000738 | 2007_001288 | |
| | 2007_001761   2007_002099 | 2007_002266 | 2007_002376 | |

from GP parameters, the window size and the shifting step are required by the system. As the cutouts or sub-images are captured by the window, it decides how big the sub-images are. The guideline for the selection of the window size is to guarantee each sub-image contains sufficient information to distinguish from those with different class labels. Moreover, it cannot be too large, which may cause that one sub-image contains parts belonging to different classes. The window size is set to 4 for bitmap images, and is set to 16 for other images. In addition, a big shifting step may lead to inaccurate results; while a small step causes too much calculation. In this paper, the shifting step is set to 2 for all test images.

## 3.1   Experimental Evaluation

This subsection gives an introduction to the four datasets and three evaluation methods that we select to access the proposed GP-based method.

**Databases.** Images from four databases are selected to test GP evolved systems. They are bitmap patterns [10], Brodatz texture database [15], Weizmann horse database [16] and PASCAL Visual Object Classes 2012 (PASCAL VOC2012) dataset [17]. Since one aim of this paper is to investigate whether the GP-evolved segmentors can deal with various types of images, images selected from these four datasets are increasingly difficult for the segmentation task. Table 5 displays some example images.

In Table 5, two images, named as P14vs24Rectangular and P14vs24Butterfly, are synthesized from two bitmap patterns, P14 and P24. These two images are binary images. The image, D24vs34Rectangular, is a grayscale texture image synthesized from two textures, D24 and D34. The ten gray horse images from the Weizmann database are real images and contain varying horse positions (e.g. running, standing and eating), but each image only contains one object. The eight passenger airplane images from the PASCAL dataset are also real images and are the largest test images. Moreover, they have varying background and some of them contain multiple objects. So they are considered the most difficult ones to segment.

**Evaluation Methods.** In this paper, three evaluation methods are employed to access the performance of the evolved methods. Firstly, a commonly used measure is segmentation accuracy.

$$Accuracy = (TP + TN)/Total.number.of.pixels.in.one.image \qquad (1)$$

Even though this measure is simple and commonly used, it is insufficient to tell whether the segmented results of an image are good or not. For example, if a test image, on which the object of interest takes up only a small proportion of the whole image, is segmented as non-object completely, the segmentation accuracy can still be high. Therefore, another two evaluation methods are selected. $F_1$ score (2) combines precision and recall together, and is a measure of test accuracies in the context of classification. However, it fails to take the true negative rate into account [18]. NRM (3) considers mismatches between a prediction and the ground truth [19]. It combines false negative rate and false positive rate into a single measure. $F_1$ reaches its best value at 1 and worst at 0, yet NRM is best at 0 and worst at 1.

$$F_1 = 2 * Precision * Recall/(Precision + Recall) \qquad (2)$$

$$NRM = (FNR + FPR)/2 \qquad (3)$$

where $Precision = TP/(TP + FP)$, $Recall = TP/(TP + FN)$, $FNR = FN/(TP + FN)$, $FPR = FP/(FP + TN)$. $TP$ (True Positive) and $FN$ (False Negative) mean points belonging to the objects of interest that are correctly and incorrectly detected by an evolved program respectively; $TN$ (True Negative) and $FP$ (False Positive) represent points belonging to the non-objects of interest that are correctly and incorrectly detected by the evolved program respectively. $FNR$ and $FPR$ stand for false negative rate and false positive rate respectively.

## 3.2 Results on Bitmap Patterns

There are 2000 training samples including 1000 P14 and 1000 P24 (Table 5) features. Table 6 lists result examples. The results of the intensity based segmentor

**Table 6.** Results of two synthetic bitmap images

| Feature | Result Examples |
|---------|-----------------|
| Intensity | |
| 6D Statistics | |
| 11D Statistics | |

are good, as regions of different patterns are located accurately. In contrast, segmentors evolved from grayscale statistics get unsatisfactory results, some of which are completely segmented as one pattern. Therefore, it is not sufficient to evolve segmentors using simple statistics to segment bitmap images.

### 3.3 Results on Brodatz Texture Images

For Brodatz texture images, two thousand training samples are generated equally from D24 and D34 texture images. Example results are shown in Table 7, which are also the first three out of 30 runs. In general, segmentors evolved from all the three kinds of low-level features show good achievements on texture images. According to these images, segmentors evolved from statistical features perform better due to more regular and clearer boundaries. However, in terms of statistical analyses (accuracy, $F_1$ and NMR), intensity and 6D statistics based segmentors have similar results, which are better than 11D statistics based one. The results indicate that the segmentation of texture images is sufficiently simple, so spatial features such as the moments are not needed.

### 3.4 Results on Weizmann Horse

In this part, ten horse images from Weizmann dataset are used to test the evolved methods. The leave-one-out (LOO) cross-validation, a model evaluation method [20], is used. Each training image provides 200 training samples, including 100 object and 100 background samples. Some result examples are listed in Table 8. It shows that horses have been located accurately and segmented horses have identifiable boundaries.

The statistical results are provided in Table 9. The best values in terms of the segmentation accuracy, F1 measure and NRM has been shown in bold. In general, the statistics-based segmentation is better than the intensity-based one. The GP (11D) segmentors produce an average accuracy of over 80 %, and the GP (6D) segmentors hold an average $F_1$ of 0.84.

**Table 7.** Result of D24vs34Rectangular

| Feature | Result Examples | Accuracy (%) | $F_1$ | NMR |
|---|---|---|---|---|
| Intensity | | $94.26 \pm 2.75$ | 0.94 | 0.15 |
| Statistics 6D | | $93.98 \pm 2.30$ | 0.94 | 0.07 |
| Statistics 11D | | $93.37 \pm 2.42$ | 0.93 | 0.07 |

**Table 8.** Result examples on Weizmann horse database (GT stands for ground truth; Inten. means intensity)

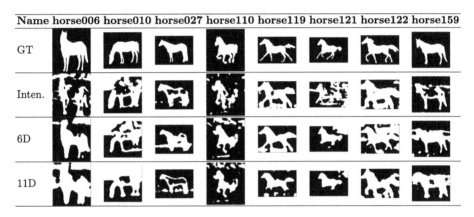

| Name | horse006 | horse010 | horse027 | horse110 | horse119 | horse121 | horse122 | horse159 |
|---|---|---|---|---|---|---|---|---|
| GT | | | | | | | | |
| Inten. | | | | | | | | |
| 6D | | | | | | | | |
| 11D | | | | | | | | |

Comparing 6D and 11D evolved segmentors, they have similar results on some images, including horse006, horse010, horse027, horse122, horse165 and horse317. On images horse110, horse119 and horse121, the 11D evolved segmentors are much better. Therefore, it can be concluded that the segmentors using 11D statistics outperforms those using raw pixel values and 6D statistics on Weizmann horse images. It shows that the segmentation task in this set of images is hard, so both histogram and spatial features are required, and raw pixel values alone cannot achieve good performance.

### 3.5 Results on PASCAL Database

The settings in this part are the same as those on the Weizmann database, except for the size of the training samples. Since the images of PASCAL database are much larger than those of Weizmann database, each training image provides 500 cutouts equally generated from objects and background of the image. According to Table 10, it is observed that GP-evolved segmentation methods can even handle real images with varying and complex backgrounds. Considering that there are only a limited number of training images, this is promising.

**Table 9.** Statistical results on Weizmann database using different features (Inten. means intensity)

| Name | Accuracy(%) | | | F1 | | | NMR | | |
|---|---|---|---|---|---|---|---|---|---|
| | Inten. | 6D | 11D | Inten. | 6D | 11D | Inten. | 6D | 11D |
| horse006 | $70.84 \pm 6.21$ | $\mathbf{80.98 \pm 2.57}$ | $79.97 \pm 4.56$ | 0.60 | **0.76** | 0.74 | 0.45 | 0.41 | **0.40** |
| horse010 | $61.93 \pm 3.68$ | $63.25 \pm 2.82$ | $\mathbf{65.20 \pm 3.63}$ | **0.55** | 0.54 | 0.54 | **0.51** | 0.52 | **0.51** |
| horse027 | $79.02 \pm 8.79$ | $\mathbf{82.26 \pm 3.50}$ | $81.48 \pm 8.01$ | 0.66 | 0.68 | **0.69** | 0.43 | **0.40** | **0.40** |
| horse110 | $78.85 \pm 10.02$ | $79.10 \pm 4.71$ | $\mathbf{85.28 \pm 5.18}$ | 0.61 | 0.61 | **0.70** | 0.47 | 0.48 | **0.41** |
| horse119 | $73.02 \pm 7.47$ | $78.64 \pm 7.89$ | $\mathbf{83.06 \pm 4.87}$ | 0.67 | 0.72 | **0.76** | 0.47 | 0.43 | **0.40** |
| horse121 | $68.91 \pm 7.08$ | $78.09 \pm 3.55$ | $\mathbf{82.93 \pm 4.12}$ | 0.52 | 0.63 | **0.69** | 0.53 | 0.49 | **0.45** |
| horse122 | $73.89 \pm 7.47$ | $\mathbf{76.71 \pm 9.81}$ | $75.72 \pm 9.68$ | 0.65 | **0.73** | 0.71 | 0.45 | **0.44** | 0.45 |
| horse159 | $\mathbf{80.66 \pm 3.70}$ | $76.11 \pm 14.07$ | $79.29 \pm 10.12$ | 0.65 | 0.68 | **0.71** | **0.45** | 0.47 | 0.47 |
| horse165 | $69.95 \pm 5.25$ | $79.99 \pm 4.39$ | $\mathbf{81.05 \pm 4.62}$ | 0.59 | **0.73** | **0.73** | 0.46 | 0.41 | **0.38** |
| horse317 | $70.30 \pm 6.46$ | $\mathbf{85.64 \pm 5.94}$ | $83.13 \pm 7.97$ | 0.70 | **0.87** | 0.84 | 0.44 | **0.41** | 0.42 |
| Average | $74.41 \pm 8.37$ | $77.37 \pm 9.09$ | $\mathbf{80.08 \pm 8.30}$ | 0.62 | **0.84** | 0.71 | 0.47 | 0.47 | **0.43** |

Statistical results are provided in Table 11. On image 2007_001288, the intensity based segmentor achieves similar results to the two statistics based ones. On the other seven images, statistics based segmentors are better. Comparing the segmentors evolved from 6D and 11D features, they have similar performance on these complex images with varying backgrounds generally. The 11D based segmetors provide slightly better results in average accuracy, $F_1$ and NRM.

## 4 Comparison with Other Methods

The proposed GP-based figure-ground segmentation method is compared with four common segmentation techniques, including thresholding, region growing, k-means clustering and active contour models (ACM). We follow the examples from the Matlab R2014b document to implement the thresholding [21] and ACM [22]. The region growing method is from Kroon [23], and the K-means method is Fonseca's work [24]. The best ones out of the intensity, 6D and 11D based segmentors are selected to compare with the four benchmark methods: segmentors evolved from raw pixel values are used for comparisons on bitmap and texture images; those evolved form 11D statistics on Weizmann and PASCAL datasets.

From Table 12, we can see that the four conventional segmentation methods can hardly conduct segmentation on bitmap and texture images; while our GP-based method produces more accurate results. Although our GP based method takes a much longer time to train/evolve the segmentors, it is fast when segmenting unseen images.

Figure 1 shows the performance of the five methods on Weizmann and PASCAL database in segmentation accuracy, $F_1$ and NRM. ACM achieves the highest accuracy, $F_1$ score and lowest NRM score. It is well known that ACM is sensitive to initial contours, and only those close to objects of interest can lead

**Table 10.** Result examples on PASCAL database (GT stands for ground truth; Inten. means intensity)

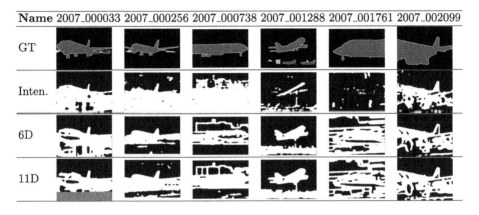

| Name | 2007_000033 | 2007_000256 | 2007_000738 | 2007_001288 | 2007_001761 | 2007_002099 |
|------|-------------|-------------|-------------|-------------|-------------|-------------|
| GT | | | | | | |
| Inten. | | | | | | |
| 6D | | | | | | |
| 11D | | | | | | |

**Table 11.** Statistical results on PASCAL database using different features (Ave. means average; Inten. means intensity)

| Name (2007_00) | Accuracy(%) | | | F1 | | | NMR | | |
|----------------|-------------|----|-----|--------|----|-----|--------|----|-----|
| | Inten. | 6D | 11D | Inten. | 6D | 11D | Inten. | 6D | 11D |
| 0033 | $71.33 \pm 5.01$ | $67.04 \pm 0.65$ | **$72.27 \pm 1.21$** | 0.50 | 0.53 | **0.58** | 0.52 | 0.52 | **0.51** |
| 0256 | $69.40 \pm 13.35$ | **$71.73 \pm 5.68$** | $70.39 \pm 5.20$ | 0.37 | **0.50** | 0.49 | 0.54 | **0.50** | **0.50** |
| 0738 | $59.71 \pm 12.25$ | $75.29 \pm 6.67$ | **$76.21 \pm 9.55$** | 0.47 | 0.65 | **0.67** | 0.51 | **0.48** | **0.48** |
| 1288 | **$82.49 \pm 2.85$** | $81.08 \pm 2.51$ | $80.76 \pm 2.75$ | 0.50 | **0.63** | **0.63** | 0.50 | 0.50 | 0.50 |
| 1761 | $61.99 \pm 3.89$ | **$65.92 \pm 2.45$** | $64.61 \pm 2.90$ | 0.42 | **0.61** | **0.61** | 0.51 | 0.49 | 0.50 |
| 2099 | $75.93 \pm 4.17$ | $75.05 \pm 2.51$ | **$77.03 \pm 3.39$** | 0.61 | 0.65 | **0.67** | **0.41** | 0.43 | 0.42 |
| 2266 | $76.47 \pm 2.70$ | **$81.32 \pm 2.03$** | $79.71 \pm 2.60$ | 0.53 | **0.68** | 0.67 | 0.50 | **0.49** | 0.50 |
| 2376 | $73.79 \pm 9.94$ | **$79.03 \pm 5.65$** | $76.19 \pm 5.24$ | 0.49 | **0.62** | 0.60 | 0.50 | **0.49** | 0.50 |
| Ave. | $71.39 \pm 10.63$ | $74.56 \pm 6.89$ | **$74.65 \pm 6.89$** | 0.49 | 0.61 | **0.62** | 0.50 | 0.5 | **0.49** |

**Table 12.** Comparison on bitmap and texture images

| Methods | Treshold | Kmeans | Region | ACM | GP(Intensity) |
|---------|----------|--------|--------|-----|---------------|
| BitmapRectangular | | | | | |
| BitmapButterfly | | | | | |
| TextureImage | | | | | |

to accurate segmentation results. GP(11D) and K-means clustering rank the second with slightly worse results.

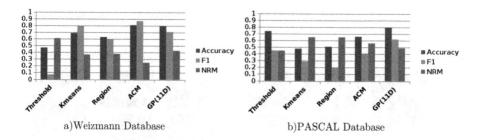

a)Weizmann Database          b)PASCAL Database

**Fig. 1.** Comparisons on Weizmann and PASCAL databases

When testing on images from the PASCAL database that containing varying backgrounds, ACM cannot compete with GP(11D) and thresholding. This may be because the objects' locations vary a lot, so it is difficult to get accurate initial placements for ACM. According to Fig. 1b, GP(11D) has the highest accuracy and $F_1$ score, and a relatively low NRM score. From the Weizmann to PASCAL database, it is obvious that the performance becomes worse for K-means, region growing and ACM; it becomes better for thresholding and GP(11D). Obviously, the GP(11D) method has consistently good results on the two complex datasets, while the other four traditional algorithms perform worse or cannot perform consistently well on different datasets.

## 5    Conclusions

This paper builds a supervised segmentation system, which utilizes GP to evolve segmentors automatically. Three kinds of simple features are investigated as the input of the system to evolve segmentors. The evolved methods are tested on four databases, including simple binary, synthetic texture images and complex real images. The results show that GP-evolved segmentors perform well consistently on all the four datasets. It indicates that GP-evolved segmentors can deal with various kinds of images. Compared with other traditional segmentation algorithms, the GP-based segmentation method achieves good results on both simple synthetic images and complex real images with variations. It means that the GP-based method can outperform conventional segmentation techniques.

In this paper, only simple features are employed to evolve segmentors. Our future work will investigate how well segmentation algorithms evolved from higher-level features (e.g. local binary patterns and Gabor features) can perform.

## References

1. Zou, W., Bai, C., Kpalma, K., Ronsin, J.: Online glocal transfer for automatic figure-ground segmentation. IEEE Trans. Image Process. **23**(5), 2109–2121 (2014)
2. Borenstein, E., Ullman, S.: Learning to segment. In: Pajdla, T., Matas, J.G. (eds.) ECCV 2004. LNCS, vol. 3023, pp. 315–328. Springer, Heidelberg (2004)

3. Borenstein, E., Ullman, S.: Class-specific, top-down segmentation. In: Heyden, A., Sparr, G., Nielsen, M., Johansen, P. (eds.) ECCV 2002, Part II. LNCS, vol. 2351, pp. 109–122. Springer, Heidelberg (2002)

4. Liu, J., Wang, J.: Application of snake model in medical image segmentation. J. Convergence Inf. Technol. **9**(1), 105–109 (2014)

5. Liu, C.Y., Iglesias, J.E., Tu, Z.: Deformable templates guided discriminative models for robust 3D brain MRI segmentation. Neuroinformatics **11**(4), 447–468 (2013)

6. Borenstein, E., Sharon, E., Ullman, S.: Combining top-down and bottom-up segmentation. In: Proceedings IEEE workshop on Perceptual Organization in Computer Vision, CVPR 2004 (2004)

7. Poli, R., Langdon, W.B., McPhee, N.F.: A Field Guide to Genetic Programming (2008). http://lulu.com

8. Poli, R.: Genetic Programming for feature detection and image segmentation. In: Fogarty, T.C. (ed.) AISB-WS 1996. LNCS, vol. 1143, pp. 110–125. Springer, Heidelberg (1996)

9. Song, A., Ciesielski, V.: Fast texture segmentation using genetic programming. In: The 2003 Congress on Evolutionary Computation, pp. 2126–2133. IEEE (2003)

10. Song, A., Ciesielski, V.: Texture segmentation by genetic programming. Evol. Comput. **16**(4), 461–481 (2008)

11. Singh, T., Nawwaf, K., Mohmmad, D., Rabab, W.: Genetic programming based image segmentation with applications to biomedical object detection. In: Proceedings of the 11th Annual Conference on Genetic and Evolutionary Computation, pp. 1123–1130. ACM (2009)

12. Roberts, M.E.: The effectiveness of cost based subtree caching mechanisms in typed genetic programming for image segmentation. In: Raidl, G.R., Cagnoni, S., Cardalda, J.J.R., Corne, D.W., Gottlieb, J., Guillot, A., Hart, E., Johnson, C.G., Marchiori, E., Meyer, J.-A., Middendorf, M. (eds.) EvoIASP 2003, EvoWorkshops 2003, EvoSTIM 2003, EvoROB/EvoRobot 2003, EvoCOP 2003, EvoBIO 2003, and EvoMUSART 2003. LNCS, vol. 2611, pp. 444–454. Springer, Heidelberg (2003)

13. Geng, J., Liu, J.: Image texture classification using a multiagent genetic clustering algorithm. In: Evolutionary Computation (CEC), pp. 504–508 (2011)

14. Luke, S.: The ECJ Owner's Manual (2014)

15. Picard, R.W., Kabir, T., Liu, F.: Real-time recognition with the entire Brodatz texture database. In: IEEE Conference on CVPR, pp. 638–639 (1993)

16. Weizmann Horses. http://avaminzhang.wordpress.com/2012/12/07/

17. The PASCAL Visual Object Classes Homepage. http://pascallin.ecs.soton.ac.uk/challenges/VOC/

18. Powers, D.M.: Evaluation: from precision, recall and F-factor to ROC, informedness, markedness correlation. Technical report SIE-07-001, School of Informatics and Engineering, Flinders University, Australia (2007)

19. Ashburner, J., Friston, K.J.: Unified segmentation. Neuroimage **26**(3), 839–851 (2005)

20. Validation. http://research.cs.tamu.edu/prism/lectures/iss/issl13.pdf

21. Thresholding Segmentation. http://au.mathworks.com/help/images/examples/correcting-nonuniform-illumination.html

22. Active Contour Based Segmentation. http://au.mathworks.com/help/images/ref/activecontour.htmlbtuep4x-7

23. Region Growing. http://www.mathworks.com/matlabcentral/fileexchange/19084-region-growing

24. K-means Image Segmentation. http://www.mathworks.com/matlabcentral/fileexchange/authors/129300

# A Multi-objective Evolutionary Algorithm for Interaction Systems Based on Laser Pointers

Francisco Chávez[1](✉), Eddie Clemente[2], Daniel E. Hernández[2],
Francisco Fernández de Vega[1], and Gustavo Olague[2]

[1] Department of Computer Science, University of Extremadura,
C/. Santa Teresa de Jornet, 38, 06800 Mérida, Spain
fchavez@unex.es
[2] Centro de Investigación Científica y de Educación Superior de Ensenada,
Carretera Ensenada-Tijuana 3918, Zona Playitas, 22860 Ensenada, BC, México

**Abstract.** In this paper we face the problem of accurate location of a laser spot that is used as interaction system in real environments. The work presented is compared with previous approaches where different algorithms work with a single objective, using images that has been previously simplified to reduce computing time. Instead, the new approach presented in this paper is capable of processing whole images. The results show that the inclusion of multi-objective methods allows us not only to detect the presence of the laser spot, the single objective in previous works, but also to obtain accurate information of the laser spot in the image, and thus provide the location of the device on which the user wants to act.

**Keywords:** Multi-objective evolutionary algorithm · Laser pointer · Interaction systems

## 1 Introduction

Smart homes allow users to easily control available devices, through efficient and simple domotic standards and techniques [1,13]. A home interaction system needs to be deployed to provide control capabilities to users. But, what is the most appropriate technique to provide such an interaction capability?

Our previous works were based on the use of laser pointer as an interaction element [5], thanks to its ease of use. This method had been previously used in different works [11,12] in other contexts: control events on a projection screen mainly. For interested readers, a wider literature review is available in [3]. Taking these works as our starting point, we expanded the concept of using the laser pointer as the tool used by the user to interact with a real home environment.

Laser pointers produce a laser-spot light that can be projected on different devices, those that the user wants to control. The correct location process becomes a complex image analysis problem of interest for the computer vision area. Thus, an interaction system that is based on the use of laser pointers, needs a robust set of algorithms capable of locating the laser spot, regardless of the lighting conditions, surface textures, etc.

© Springer International Publishing Switzerland 2015
A.M. Mora and G. Squillero (Eds.): EvoApplications 2015, LNCS 9028, pp. 504–516, 2015.
DOI: 10.1007/978-3-319-16549-3_41

In previous works we have presented different algorithms to detect the laser spot in a real environment. These algorithms were initially based on classic vision techniques such as Dynamic Thresholding (DT) or Template Matching (TM), and only tried to identify if a laser spot is present within the image section that has been previously defined by the user [2–7]. In order to improve results, those algorithms were later combined with automatic systems for decision making: the idea was to obtain an answer about the presence or absence of the laser spot. We used Fuzzy Rule-Based Systems (FRBS), which, through a set of image parameters are able to predict if the image analysed is a laser spot image. More recently, we added visual attention techniques, specifically Focus of Attention (FOA) [8–10,14–17] to even improve the accuracy of laser spots detection process. Good results were achieved when the problem was simplified: instead of working with a complete image obtained by the video camera, it was reduced to several small areas where the devices to control were located. Therefore, it was not necessary to know the location of the laser spot, only to detect whether the laser spot is present in every area of the image where home devices are located.

In this paper a new approach of the laser-spot detection process is presented. The idea is to analyse a whole home environment image, sent by the video camera, to detect the laser spot, and provide both, information about laser spot presence and its location if the laser spot is found. Once the location is determined, if this location corresponds to a home device, the domotic system will be in charge of sending a control order. We thus avoid previous configuration steps required by users to select specific image areas to be analysed by the specific computer vision algorithm.

The approach presented in this paper is based on the Artificial Visual Cortex (AVC), which is a bio-inspired model of the functionality of the human visual system. That is, there is a computational analogy of the transformations taking place in the two major pathways of information in the visual cortex, the dorsal route and the ventral route, where the goal of the first route is to locate the salient features of the objects in the scene, while the second route identifies the object from those characteristics. In this case, a multi-objective evolutionary algorithm is used to guide the AVC in the use of the features that correspond to the laser spot, and thus achieve their location and identification. The use of this kind of algorithms in computer vision problems [21–23] allowed us to foresee the interest for the problem we face. The results presented below demonstrate the usefulness of this new approach.

This paper is organized as follows: Sect. 2 describes the methodology based on the multiobjective algorithms for the location of the laser spot and its location. Section 3 describe the results obtained and finally, Sect. 4 presents our conclusions.

## 2  Methodology

The AVC model is based on neuropsychological feature integration theory proposed by Treisman and Gelade, [18] and the standard model proposed by Riesenhuber and Poggio, [19]. Both theories are synthesized in the computational AVC model, which is applied to object recognition, where the input to this model is a color image and its output is a label representing whether the object is present or not in the image. The use of this model consists of a learning phase, where the AVC is trained to recognize the object, in this case the laser spot. The proposal of this work is a multi-objective approach for obtaining the location and identification of the laser. The new AVC output is an image region and a label indicating whether this corresponds to the laser spot. Thus, the AVC can be divided into two stages, laser spot features acquisition and description, and its location.

The first stage consists of the extraction of features that help to identify the laser spot from well-defined characteristics, called dimensions, see [15]; which are: intensity $(I)$, orientation $(O)$, color $(C)$ and shape $(S)$. This is achieved after the application of specialized operators on each dimension, except for the intensity which is defined as the average of the red, green and blue bands of the input image. These operators are discovered by a process of artificial evolution, which are called evolved visual operators $(EVO)$, and they are applied in each dimension. That is, $EVO_d : I_{color} \rightarrow MV_d$; where $I_{color}$ is the set of the bands of different color models, that is, $I_{color} = \{I_r, I_g, I_b, I_c, I_m, I_y, I_k, I_h, I_s, I_v\}$, which corresponds to the color bands *red, green, blue, cyan, magenta, yellow, black, brightness, saturation and intensity.*

Each $EVO$ performs a mapping of the color bands in a visual map $MV_d$; and $d$, denotes an index on some dimension, $d \in \{I, O, C, S\}$ see Fig. 1. Each $MV_d$ is transformed into a conspicuity map $(MC_d)$ through a process called center-periphery, see [20]; which aims to select the salient information from each dimension. In a second step, the mind maps $(MM_d)$ are obtained over dimension by applying the following expression: $MM_d = \sum_{i=1}^{k}(EVO_{MM_i}(CM_d))$; where $EVO_{MM_i}$ belongs to a set of $k$ functions that have a purpose, to get areas of each $MC_d$ useful to describe and locate the laser spot. The information contained in each mind map is integrated into a saliency map, $MP$, result of an algebraic sum of each $MM_d$. Then, the point coordinates with the maximum value of $MP$ are obtained, $(u, v)$, and an expansion algorithm around this position is performed, where its output is a region $\Upsilon$, which is formed the $n$ points with the highest values surrounding $(u, v)$. Being $\Upsilon$, the possible region where is located the laser spot; however, the description of the laser spot is obtained from the $MV_d$, since these contain much information of the laser spot. Thus, around the coordinate $(u, v)$ for each $MV_d$ is applied an expansion algorithm; where the values of the resulting regions are concatenated to build the descriptor vector $\nu$ of the laser spot. Finally, this vector is interpreted as the presence or absence, $[0, 1]$, the laser spot through a support vector machine (SVM).

The main section of the implementation of the AVC method is the training. In this stage the $EVO$ operators are founded, being applied within the AVC structure, and in this way, to be capable to recognize and locate the laser spot. Thus, AVC training process is performed through an artificial evolution process, called brain programming, see the definition in [16]. Each $EVO$ is built by its own functions and terminals, see Table 1; thus, to obtain the feautres orientation it is applied the operator $EVO_O$, built some specialized functions such as

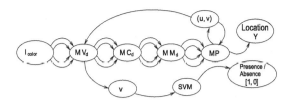

**Fig. 1.** AVC model.

Gaussian blurred with $\sigma = 1$ y $\sigma = 2$ ($G_{\sigma=1}(A)$, $G_{\sigma=2}(A)$), and derivatives of first and second order in different directions. To obtain the color features the operator $EVO_C$ is applied, which uses specialized functions and terminals as the complement of an image (($A)^c$), and color opponency ($Op_{r-g}(I)$, $Op_{b-y}(I)$). Similarly, to obtain the shape features, we propose to use morphological operators dilation ($A$ $oplusSE_x$), erosion ($A$ $ominusSe_x$), openness ($A$ $circledcircSE_s$) lock ($A$ $odotSE_s$), and compositions of these; with which you can define the operator $EVO_S$. Note that these functions are defined on the different color bands or in some cases on their derivatives.

**Table 1.** $EVO$ functions and terminals

| $EVO_O$ functions | $EVO_O$ terminals |
|---|---|
| $A+B$, $A-B$, $A \times B$, $A/B$, $A+B$, $A-B$, $A \times B$, $A/B$, $\|A\|$, $\|A+B\|$, $\|A-B\|$, $log(A)$, $(A)^2$, $\sqrt{A}$, $k+A$, $k-A$, $k \times A$, $A/k$, $round(A)$, $\lfloor A \rfloor$, $\lceil A \rceil$, $inf(A,B)$, $sup(A,B)$, $G_{\sigma=1}(A)$, $G_{\sigma=2}(A)$, $D_x(A)$, $D_y(A)$, $thr(A)$ | $I_r$, $I_g$, $I_b$, $I_c$, $I_m$, $I_y$, $I_k$, $I_h$, $I_s$, $I_v$, $D_x(I_x)$, $D_{xx}(I_x)$, $D_y(I_x)$, $D_{yy}(I_x)$, $D_{xy}(I_x)$ |
| $EVO_C$ functions | $EVO_C$ terminals |
| $A+B$, $A-B$, $A \times B$, $A/B$, $log(A)$, $exp(A)$, $(A)^2$, $\sqrt{A}$, $(A)^c$, $thr(A)$ | $I_r$, $I_g$, $I_b$, $I_c$, $I_m$, $I_y$, $I_k$, $I_h$, $I_s$, $I_v$, $Op_{r-g}(I)$, $Op_{b-y}(I)$ |
| $EVO_s$ functions | $EVO_s$ terminals |
| $A+B$, $A-B$, $A \times B$, $A/B$, $k+A$, $k-A$, $k \times A$, $A/k$, $round(A)$, $\lfloor A \rfloor$, $\lceil A \rceil$, $A \oplus SE_d$, $A \oplus SE_s$, $A \oplus SE_{dm}$, $A \ominus SE_d$, $A \ominus SE_s$, $A \ominus SE_{dm}$, $Sk(A)$, $Perim(A)$, $A \circledast SE_d$, $A \circledast SE_s$, $A \circledast SE_{dm}$, $T_{hat}(A)$, $B_{hat}(A)$, $A \odot SE_s$, $A \odot SE_s$, $thr(A)$ | $I_r$, $I_g$, $I_b$, $I_c$, $I_m$, $I_y$, $I_k$, $I_h$, $I_s$, $I_v$ |
| $EVO_{MM}$ functions | $EVO_{MM}$ terminals |
| $A+B$, $A-B$, $A \times B$, $A/B$, $\|A+B\|$, $\|A-B\|$, $log(A)$, $(A)^2$, $\sqrt{A}$, $G_{\sigma=1}(A)$, $G_{\sigma=2}(A)$, $D_x(A)$, $D_y(A)$ | $MC_d$, $D_x(MC_d)$, $D_{xx}(MC_d)$, $D_y(MC_d)$, $D_{yy}(MC_d)$, $D_{xy}(MC_d)$ |

Due to the independence between the operators $EVO$, the genotype is built as a chain of operators, where each operator is expressed as a syntax tree, see Fig. 2, this chain has been called chromosome and each operator is a gene. The first three correspond to genes $EVO_O$, $EVO_C$ and $EVO_S$; while the fourth to the *kth* gene represent the operators $EVO_{MM}$. This genotype construction involves a more complex life cycle with respect to the classical approach of genetic programming. That is, it is necessary to define new genetic operators to help explore the solution space. In this case, we have considered a crossover operator and mutation operator to the chromosome level; and a crossover operator and mutation to the gene level. A chromosome level, operators are similar to those used in the art of genetic algorithms; while for the mutation a chromosome position is selected and it is replaced by a syntax tree generated randomly. Furthermore, a gene level, the crossover and mutation operators are similar to those used in traditional genetic programming.

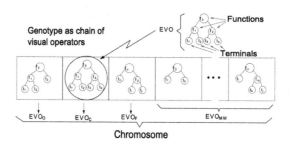

**Fig. 2.** Sample solution.

To select an appropriate objective function is crucial to solve the problem, in this case, during AVC training process is necessary to measure if the system is detecting correctly the laser spot also if it has been identified. To determine if the region $\Upsilon$ given by the AVC corresponding to the location of the laser, the measure F, which quantifies the overlapping area between the region and the laser spot is used $\Upsilon$, that is:

$$F - measure = \frac{2 \cdot VP}{2 \cdot VP + FN + FP}.$$

Where, $VP$ is the number of pixels in the overlap region; $FN$, is the number of pixels that belong to $\Upsilon$ minus pixels in the overlap region; and $FP$, are the pixels that belong to the region of the laser spot minus overlap region, see case 1 of the Fig. 3. Moreover, a measure that can account for the rights and wrongs in the laser spot identification process is the accuracy, which is calculated using the following expression:

$$Accuracy = \frac{\text{Images correctly classified}}{\text{Total images}}.$$

Considering the location and identification of the laser spot as independent outputs of AVC model, the following 6 cases can occur, see Fig. 3:

*Case 1:* The laser is identified as present, it really exists in the image, and the selected region corresponds to the laser spot location.

*Case 2:* The laser is identified as present, it exists in the image, and the selected region does not match the laser spot location.

*Case 3:* The laser is identified as present but this does not exist in the image, and the selected region does not correspond with any laser spot location.

*Case 4:* The laser is identified as absent but it is really present in the image, and the selected region corresponds with the laser spot location.

*Case 5:* The laser is identified as absent, it exists in the image, and the selected region does not match the laser spot location.

*Case 6:* The laser is identified as absent, it does not exist in the image, and the selected region does not match the laser spot location.

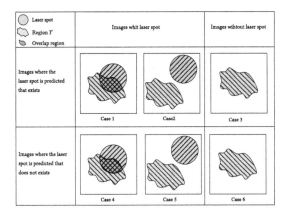

**Fig. 3.** Success and failure cases.

# 3   Experiments and Results

The experiments presented below were applied to a database consisting of 980 images, with two groups, 490 images each, with and without laser spot (see Fig. 4). All the images were acquired in an real home environment where complex situations were included: different light conditions, distances to surfaces were the laser spot is projected, different surface textures, object with shapes similar to laser spots, etc.

Experiments were designed in two stages. The first step consists of training AVC model, where we consider two sets of images taken randomly from the database, the first set is called training and the second is called validation. Each set is composed of 392 images, of which 196 contain the laser spot and the rest are background images. The second step consists on testing the best solutions (found during training) on a new set of 196 images selected randomly, called test; of which 98 contain the laser spot and the rest are background images. Thus, three different experiments were designed, where the minimization targets were different. However, the evolutionary optimization process have the same parameters for all experiments, these are: 40 generations, 256 individuals per generation, initializing syntax trees with the technique *half-and-half*, with a maximum depth of 9 levels for each tree and a maximum length of 15 genes per chromosome. SPEA2 algorithm was used for parent selection and individuals survival for each generation [24].

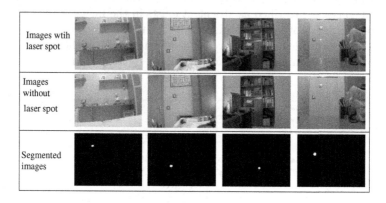

**Fig. 4.** Database.

It should be noted that during the first step a set of training images to generate the SVM model is used, and this SVM model generated is later used to classify the validation image set.

### 3.1 Experiment 1

In this experiment we try to minimize the error classification of the region $\Upsilon$ returned by the AVC. Thus, two objectives are considered:

- *Objective 1:* Obtaining those solutions that have selected the region with the laser spot and the image has been labelled correctly. In other words, minimizing the number of images that are not within the *Case 1*, see Fig. 3:

$$Objective1 = \frac{1}{\#\,Case\ 1\ \text{images}}.$$

- *Objective 2:* Minimizing the average number of pixels $\Upsilon$ that do not correspond to the laser-spot region, in the $k$ images that contains the laser spot, that is:

$$Objective2 = \frac{k}{\sum_{i=1}^{k}(F - measure_i)}.$$

Once the evolutionary process has been completed, the solutions obtained in the last generation are evaluated on the test set, which generates the Pareto-Front shown in Fig. 5. Some of these solutions are shown in Table 2. It should be noted that the success rate, percentages on the number of images on the Case 1, are greater than 90 %, however, this does not guarantee a correct images classification which do not contain the laser spot.

**Table 2.** Some solutions of experiment 1.

| Solution | Evaluation | |
|---|---|---|
| | 1/Objective1 | 1/Objective2 |
| | % Success rate Case 1 | Average F-measure |
| $S1_1$ | 96.4 % | 25.1 % |
| $S1_2$ | 93.8 % | 26.1 % |
| $S1_3$ | 92.8 % | 28.7 % |
| $S1_4$ | 91.8 % | 29.0 % |

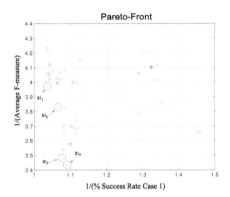

**Fig. 5.** Experiment #1, Pareto-Front.

## 3.2   Experiment 2

In this experiment an optimization with 3 objectives is proposed, which not only tries to have the highest number of success rate for Case 1, but also high accuracy.

– *Objective 1:* Minimize the number of misclassified images, that is:

$$Objective1 = \frac{1}{Accuracy}.$$

– *Objective 2:* Similar to the objective 2 in the experiment 1.
– *Objective 3:* Similar to the objective 1 in the experiment 1.

Again a Pareto-Front is obtained, see Fig. 6. Some of these solutions are shown in Table 3. It should be noted that in general, the classification accuracy decreases as the number of images that fall into Case 1 increases.

## 3.3   Experiment 3

The system priority is to eliminate the false positive, i.e., the laser spot is detected when this does not exist, or it is located in the wrong position. These are the objectives applied:

**Table 3.** Experiment 2 results.

| Solution | Evaluation | | |
|---|---|---|---|
| | 1/Objective1 | 1/Objective2 | 1/Objective3 |
| | Accuracy | Average F-measure | % Success rate Case 1 |
| $S2_1$ | 81.6% | 19.3% | 78.0% |
| $S2_2$ | 73.4% | 21.0% | 83.1% |
| $S2_3$ | 70.4% | 13.2% | 86.2% |
| $S2_4$ | 56.6% | 12.7% | 88.7% |

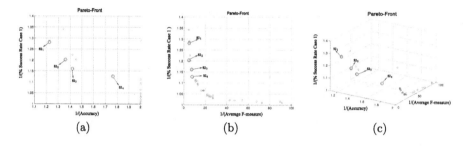

(a)                              (b)                              (c)

**Fig. 6.** Experiment #2, Pareto front.

– *Objective 1:* Similar to the objective 1 in the experiment 2.
– *Objective 2:* Similar to the objective 2 in the experiment 1.
– *Objective 3:* The percentage of images that fall into Case 2 and Case 3 is minimized, that is:

$$Objective3 = \frac{\#Case\ 2\ images}{Total\ images} + \frac{\#Case\ 3\ images}{Total\ images}$$

Some solutions are shown in Table 4, which correspond to those indicated in the Pareto-Front shown in Fig. 7. It should be noted that there is a solution on the Pareto-Front where the objective 3 is zero; but it is a case where all images

**Table 4.** Experiment 3 results

| Solution | Evaluation | | |
|---|---|---|---|
| | 1/Objective1 | 1/Objective2 | Objective3 |
| | Accuracy | Average F-measure | % Case 1 and 2 images |
| $S3_1$ | 83.6% | 22.1% | 24.4% |
| $S3_2$ | 80.6% | 24.4% | 10.2% |
| $S3_3$ | 77.5% | 24.5% | 10.7% |
| $S3_4$ | 77.0% | 25.5% | 21.9% |
| $S3_5$ | 75.5% | 23.8% | 6.1% |

have been classified as without laser spot, due to this, it is not included in the Table 4.

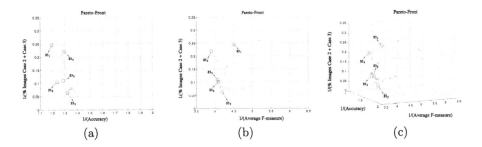

**Fig. 7.** Experiment #3, Pareto front.

In order to do a fair comparison between the solutions Table 5 shows the accuracy percentage of classification, the average F-measure and the number of images obtained in each case, using the complete test set of images. It should be noted that the solution $S3_1$ shows the best accuracy in the training process, while the solution $S1_1$ has minimized the false positive errors.

**Table 5.** Results comparative

| Solution | Accuracy | Average F-measure | Images per Case | | | | | |
|---|---|---|---|---|---|---|---|---|
| | | | C1 | C2 | C3 | C4 | C5 | C6 |
| **$S1_1$** | **73.4 %** | **25.1 %** | **45** | **1** | **0** | **6** | **46** | **98** |
| $S1_2$ | 70.4 % | 26.1 % | 42 | 0 | 2 | 10 | 46 | 96 |
| $S1_3$ | 71.9 % | 28.7 % | 44 | 1 | 2 | 11 | 42 | 96 |
| $S1_4$ | 73.4 % | 29.0 % | 46 | 3 | 3 | 10 | 39 | 95 |
| $S2_1$ | 81.6 % | 19.3 % | 46 | 29 | 13 | 1 | 22 | 85 |
| $S2_2$ | 73.4 % | 21.0 % | 40 | 15 | 9 | 9 | 34 | 89 |
| $S2_3$ | 70.4 % | 13.2 % | 31 | 18 | 9 | 0 | 49 | 89 |
| $S2_4$ | 56.6 % | 12.7 % | 25 | 4 | 16 | 2 | 67 | 82 |
| **$S3_1$** | **83.6 %** | **22.1 %** | **44** | **35** | **13** | **1** | **18** | **85** |
| $S3_2$ | 80.6 % | 24.4 % | 48 | 16 | 4 | 0 | 34 | 94 |
| $S3_3$ | 77.5 % | 24.5 % | 47 | 14 | 7 | 1 | 36 | 91 |
| $S3_4$ | 77.0 % | 25.5 % | 42 | 27 | 16 | 10 | 19 | 82 |
| $S3_5$ | 75.5 % | 23.8 % | 42 | 10 | 2 | 9 | 37 | 96 |

If we analyse the $S1_1$ solution, there are a big set of images that belong to the Case 1, 5 and 6 (see Fig. 4); that is, the classification system has been trained with a high accuracy, because the system obtains a correct decision about the region $\Upsilon$. We can observe that only one image was classified as false positive. However, there are errors when the laser-spot region is located, see Table 5.

Based on the presented results, we can say that the new multi-objective approach presented in this work allows to locate the laser spot with an accuracy larger than 70 % for the solutions that have been tested, and in some cases minimize near zero false positives. On the other hand, another objective of the algorithm was to locate exactly the laser-spot location within a complete image. In this case the solutions found in the above experiments show that it is possible to achieve a balance between these two objectives, but the path is still open to new improvement.

## 4   Conclusions

The work presented here shows a new method for accurate detection of a laser spot projected in a real environment. By using a multi-objective approach, the algorithm not only detects whether a laser dot is present, it also provides laser spots locations. Thanks to this new approach users do not need to crop images of the environment for the correct functioning of the system. The new algorithm can work with complete images.

The results presented in this work allow us to affirm that it is possible to detect the presence or absence of a laser spot while simultaneously providing precise location. Although the results can be improved, the methodology allows both objectives work properly together. This will allow us in the future to ensure new interaction systems using a laser pointer susceptible to incorporate path-tracking to detect gestures commands to control the devices.

**Acknowledgments.** This work was supported by the Seventh Framework Programme of the European Union through the International Research Staff Plan Marie Curie, FP7-PEOPLE-2013-IRSES, ACoBSEC 612,689 Grant, Ministerio de Educación, Cultura y Deporte of Spain under the project TIN2011-28627-C04-03, Gobierno de Extremadura, Consejería de Economía Comercio e Innovación and FEDER, GRU10029 project. This work has also been supported by CONACyT México through the project 155045–"Evolución de Cerebros Artificiales en Visión por Computador".

## References

1. Chan, M., Estève, D., Escriba, C., Campo, E.: A review of smart homes-present state and future challenges. Comput. Meth. Prog. Biomed. **91**(1), 55–81 (2008)
2. Chávez, F., Fernández, F., Alcalá, R., Alcalá-Fdez, J., Herrera, F.: Evolutionary learning of a laser pointer detection fuzzy system for an environment control system. In: 2011 IEEE International Conference on Fuzzy Systems (FUZZ), pp. 256–263 (2011)
3. Chávez, F., Fernández, F., Alcalá, R., Alcalá-Fdez, J., Olague, G., Herrera, F.: Hybrid laser pointer detection algorithm based on template matching and fuzzy rule-based systems for domotic control in real home environments. Appll. Intell., 1–17 (2010). doi:10.1007/s10489-010-0268-6

4. Chávez, F., Fernández, F., Alcalá-Fdez, J., Alcalá, R., Herrera, F., Olague, G.: Genetic tuning of a laser pointer environment control device system for handicapped people with fuzzy systems. In: IEEE International Conference on Fuzzy Systems (FUZZ IEEE 2010), pp. 1 8 (2010)
5. Chávez, F., Fernández, F., Gacto, M., Alcalá, R.: Automatic laser pointer detection algorithm for environment control device systems based on template matching and genetic tuning of fuzzy rule-based systems. Int. J. Comput. Intell. Syst. 5(2), 368–386 (2012)
6. Chávez, F., Clemente, E., Dozal, L., Fernández de Vega, F., Olague, G.: Auto-Ajuste del Foco de Atencion para la Mejora de un Sistema de Deteccion de Punto Laser. Congreso Espaol de Informtica., 713–722 (2013)
7. Clemente, E., Chávez, F., Dozal, L., Fernández de Vega, F., Olague, G.: Self-adjusting focus of attention by means of GP for improving a laser point detection system. In: Proceeding of the Fifteenth Annual Conference on Genetic and Evolutionary Computation Conference, pp. 1237–1244 (2013)
8. Clemente, E., Olague, G., Dozal, L., Mancilla, M.: Object recognition with an optimized ventral stream model using genetic programming. In: Di Chio, C., et al. (eds.) EvoApplications 2012. LNCS, vol. 7248, pp. 315–325. Springer, Heidelberg (2012)
9. Desimone, R., Duncan, J.: Neural mechanisms of selective visual attention. Ann. Rev. 18, 193–222 (1995)
10. Dozal, L., Olague, G., Clemente, E., Sánchez, M.: Evolving visual attention programs through EVO features. In: Di Chio, C., et al. (eds.) EvoApplications 2012. LNCS, vol. 7248, pp. 326–335. Springer, Heidelberg (2012)
11. Kemp, C., Anderson, C., Nguyen, H., Trevor, A., Xu, Z.: A point-and-click interface for the real world: laser designation of objects for mobile manipulation. In: 3rd ACM/IEEE International Conference on Human Robot Interaction (HRI 2008), pp. 241–248 (2008)
12. Kim, N.W., Lee, S.-J., Lee, B.-G., Lee, J.-J.: Vision based laser pointer interaction for flexible screens. In: Jacko, J.A. (ed.) HCI 2007. LNCS, vol. 4551, pp. 845–853. Springer, Heidelberg (2007)
13. Nakashima, H., Aghajan, H., Augusto, J.C.: Handbook of Ambient Intelligence and Smart Environments. Springer, New York (2010)
14. Olague, G.: Evolutionary Computer Vision - The First Footprints. Springer (to appear)
15. Olague, G., Clemente, E., Dozal, L., Hernández, D.E.: Evolving an artificial visual cortex for object recognition with brain programming. In: Schuetze, O., Coello, C.A., Tantar, A.-A., Tantar, E., Bouvry, P., Moral, P.D., Legrand, P. (eds.) EVOLVE - A Bridge between Probability, Set Oriented Numerics, and Evolutionary Computation III. SCI, vol. 500, pp. 97–119. Springer, Heidelberg (2014)
16. Olague, G., Dozal, L., Clemente, E., Ocampo, A.: Optimizing an artificial dorsal stream on purpose for visual attention. In: Schuetze, O., Coello, C.A., Tantar, A.-A., Tantar, E., Bouvry, P., Moral, P.D., Legrand, P. (eds.) EVOLVE - A Bridge between Probability, Set Oriented Numerics, and Evolutionary Computation III. SCI, vol. 500, pp. 141–166. Springer, Heidelberg (2014)
17. Pérez, C.B., Olague, G.: Evolutionary learning of local descriptor operators for object recognition. In: GECCO, pp. 1051–1058 (2009)
18. Treisman, A.M., Gelade, G.: A feature-integration theory of attention. Cogn. Psychol. 12(1), 97–136 (1980)
19. Riesenhuber, M., Poggio, T.: Hierarchical models of object recognition in cortex. Nature Neurosci. 11(2), 1019–1025 (1999)

20. Dozal, L., Olague, G., Clemente, E., Hernndez, D.E.: Brain programming for the evolution of an artificial dorsal stream. Cogn. Comput. **6**(3), 528–557 (2014)
21. Nakib, A., Oulhadj, H., Siarry, P.: Image histogram thresholding based on multi-objective optimization. Signal Process. **87**(11), 2516–2534 (2007)
22. Shirakawa, S., Nagao, T.: Evolutionary image segmentation based on multiobjective clustering. In: IEEE Congress on Evolutionary Computation, CEC 2009, pp. 2466–2473 (2009)
23. Nakib, A., Oulhadj, H., Siarry, P.: Non-supervised image segmentation based on multiobjective optimization. Pattern Recogn. Lett. **29**(2), 161–172 (2008)
24. Bleuler, S., Laumanns, M., Thiele, L., Zitzler, E.: PISA – a platform and programming language independent interface for search algorithms. In: Fonseca, C.M., Fleming, P.J., Zitzler, E., Deb, K., Thiele, L. (eds.) EMO 2003. LNCS, vol. 2632, pp. 494–508. Springer, Heidelberg (2003)

# Topology-Preserving Ordering of the RGB Space with an Evolutionary Algorithm

Francisco Flórez-Revuelta[(✉)]

Faculty of Science, Engineering and Computing, Kingston University,
Penrhyn Road, Kingston upon Thames KT1 2EE, UK
`F.Florez@kingston.ac.uk`

**Abstract.** Mathematical morphology (MM) is broadly used in image processing. MM operators require to establish an order between the values of a set of pixels. This is why MM is basically used with binary and grayscale images. Many works have been focused on extending MM to colour images by mapping a multi-dimensional colour space onto a linear ordered space. However, most of them are not validated in terms of topology preservation but in terms of the results once MM operations are applied. This work presents an evolutionary method to obtain total- and P-orderings of a colour space, i.e. RGB, maximising topology preservation. This approach can be used to order a whole colour space as well as to get a specific ordering for the subset of colours appearing in a particular image. These alternatives improve the results obtained with the orderings usually employed, in both topology preservation and noise reduction.

**Keywords:** Colour ordering · Topology preservation · Mathematical morphology · Evolutionary algorithm · RGB

## 1 Introduction

Mathematical morphology (MM) is used for image processing in different applications: noise filtering, shape simplification, edge detection, skeletonisation, shape analysis, segmentation... MM has two basic operators, erosion and dilation, from which many other morphological operations are derived. These operators rely on an ordering of the pixel values. MM is applied to a set provided with an order and with a supremum and an infimum pertaining to that order. This is the reason why MM has been mainly applied to binary or grayscale images. Extension to multi-variate data, as colour images, is not straightforward, because there is not an order relationship among vectors.

Several techniques have been developed to extend MM to colour images, getting partial or total orderings of different colour spaces (RGB, HSI, YIQ, Lab...). In marginal ordering MM operations are applied to each image channel independently, treating it as a grayscale image, combining the partial results to get the final image. This method is not generally accepted because new colours not present in the original image can appear due to this channel-wise filtering.

© Springer International Publishing Switzerland 2015
A.M. Mora and G. Squillero (Eds.): EvoApplications 2015, LNCS 9028, pp. 517–528, 2015.
DOI: 10.1007/978-3-319-16549-3_42

Another strategy is to treat the colour at each pixel as a vector. Order is then established by projecting the colour space onto a linear space. For instance, in the case of the RGB space, this projection can be defined as:

$$\psi : [0,1]^3 \to \mathbb{N}, \xi \in [0,1]^3 \to \psi(\xi) \in \mathbb{N} \qquad (1)$$

If this projection is an injective function, i.e. $\psi(\xi_1) \neq \psi(\xi_2), \forall \xi_1 \neq \xi_2$, then the ordering is total, otherwise it is partial. There is not a single projection to order the $n$ elements in a colour space, but $n!$ possibilities, i.e. all the possible permutations of the $n$ colours.

As stated in [1] some of the methods [2,3] aim to create a space-filling curve (SFC), i.e. a continuous curve whose range contains the entire colour space. Although [4] considers that total orderings created with SFC are rather artificial and often lack physical interpretation, [5] studied how different SFC, equivalent to some colour orderings, preserve the topology of colour spaces. Recent surveys on multivariate mathematical morphology can be found in [1,6].

The concept of topology preservation can be used to analyse how well a colour space is ordered. Topology preservation is a well-known problem in self-organising artificial neural networks as they are usually employed to map a high-dimensional input space into a lower dimensional space. Several measures of topology preservation have been proposed in [7–10]. This approach was used in [11] adapting a growing self-organising network to order the RGB space.

In this paper, a measure of topology preservation is used to determine the best total ordering of a colour space, i.e. RGB. Besides, as calculating a total order is computationally expensive, an evolutionary proposal to obtain a P-ordering is also presented. To the best of my knowledge there is not an evolutionary method that had been proposed for ordering a set of elements in terms of topology preservation. This problem is quite similar to other combinatorial optimisation problems, e.g. the Travelling Salesman Problem. Therefore, representation of individuals, and crossover and mutation operators already employed in those problems will be used in this work.

The remainder of this paper is organised as follows: Sect. 2 presents a measure of topology preservation and its application to different orderings. In Sect. 3, an evolutionary method to obtain a partial order of the RGB is presented based on the clustering of the RGB space and the ordering, maximising topology preservation, of the obtained cluster centres. Section 4 shows how these orderings are employed in MM operations. In Sect. 5 different orderings obtained with this method are shown and compared with state-of-the-art methods. Finally, Sect. 6 presents some conclusions and future work.

## 2   Topology Preservation of Colour Orders

The topographic product [7] is the most used topology-preservation measure in the area of self-organising neural networks where a low-dimensional network tries to adapt and represent a higher-dimensional input space. The topographic product compares the neighbourhood relationship between each pair of nodes in the network with respect to both their position in the network/graph/order and their reference vectors. The topological relationship between a node $j$ and its $k$ closer neighbours is obtained as:

$$P_3(j,k) = \left[ \prod_{l=1}^{k} \frac{d^V\left(w_j, w_{n_l^A(j)}\right)}{d^V\left(w_j, w_{n_l^V(j)}\right)} \cdot \frac{d^A\left(j, n_l^A(j)\right)}{d^A\left(j, n_l^V(j)\right)} \right]^{\frac{1}{2k}} \tag{2}$$

where $j$ is a node, $w_j$ is its reference vector, $n_l^V$ is the $l$-th closest neighbour to $j$ in the input space $V$ according to a distance $d^V$ and $n_l^A$ is the $l$-th nearest node to $j$ in the network according to a distance $d^A$.

This is extended to all the nodes and all the possible neighbourhood orders, obtaining the topographic product $P$:

$$P = \frac{1}{N(N-1)} \sum_{j=1}^{N} \sum_{k=1}^{N} \log\left(P_3(j,k)\right) \tag{3}$$

$P$ is equal to 0 if topology is preserved, deviating from 0 as topology is lost.

Then, the different colour orderings can be measured and compared in terms of their topology preservation of the colour space. Figure 1 shows several of these total orderings as well as their topology preservation value. For the sake of clarity, instead of ordering the entire 3D space, the results are shown for a reduced bidimensional space. The usually employed (a) lexicographical and (b) bit-interlacing orderings preserve worse the topology than other space-filling curves, for instance (c) a Hilbert-type curve with the origin in one corner and

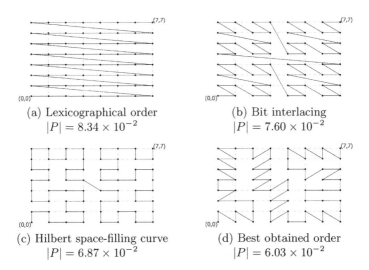

(a) Lexicographical order
$|P| = 8.34 \times 10^{-2}$

(b) Bit interlacing
$|P| = 7.60 \times 10^{-2}$

(c) Hilbert space-filling curve
$|P| = 6.87 \times 10^{-2}$

(d) Best obtained order
$|P| = 6.03 \times 10^{-2}$

**Fig. 1.** Different orderings of a bidimensional space. Lower $|P|$ values indicate better topology preservation.

the end at the opposite corner [12, Fig. 14]. However, all these orderings are far from (d) the best topology-preserving obtained ordering.

The advantage of the first two methods is that the position of one of the elements in the ordering is easy to estimate and, therefore, obtaining the extrema, i.e. supremum and infimum, in MM operations is fast. Estimating the extrema in orderings that do not follow a "simple" function can be very time consuming. Besides, obtaining the best ordering of a set of elements is an NP-complete problem. In fact, Fig. 1d has been obtained using the evolutionary algorithm presented in Sect. 3, so it cannot be ensured that it is the optimal ordering. Hence, obtaining the best total order for a colour space with a high number of elements, e.g. RGB, is currently infeasible.

# 3 Order of the RGB Space Maximising Topology Preservation

This infeasibility suggests that unless the search of the best ordering is reduced to "simple" functions, alternatives should be employed. A P-ordering, as defined in [1], can be obtained by clustering the colour space and ordering the cluster centres. This approach was considered in [11] where a linear growing neural gas was adapted to the RGB space. However, one of the drawbacks of this method is that both tasks, clustering and ordering, are carried out simultaneously; which affects the final result.

## 3.1 Ordering Method

In order to avoid this problem, this paper proposes a two-step process (Fig. 2). First, a clustering algorithm is employed to reduce the number of colours to be ordered. There is one constraint in this clustering process: two centres are fixed to $(0, 0, 0)$ and $(255, 255, 255)$ respectively. These two centres determine the extrema of the linear ordering. This work employs $k$-means, although any other clustering method can also be applied. Second, these clusters centres are ordered maximising topology preservation.

## 3.2 Evolutionary Ordering of the Cluster Centres

Obtaining the best ordering of a set of elements is an NP-Complete problem, similarly to the Travelling Salesman Problem (TSP). As the number of elements/clusters increases it is more computationally expensive to obtain their

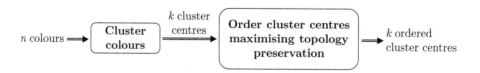

**Fig. 2.** Scheme of the ordering process.

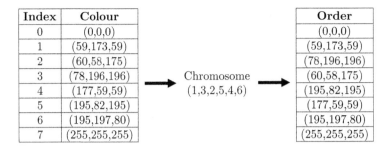

| Index | Colour |
|-------|--------|
| 0 | (0,0,0) |
| 1 | (59,173,59) |
| 2 | (60,58,175) |
| 3 | (78,196,196) |
| 4 | (177,59,59) |
| 5 | (195,82,195) |
| 6 | (195,197,80) |
| 7 | (255,255,255) |

| Order |
|-------|
| (0,0,0) |
| (59,173,59) |
| (78,196,196) |
| (60,58,175) |
| (195,82,195) |
| (177,59,59) |
| (195,197,80) |
| (255,255,255) |

Chromosome (1,3,2,5,4,6)

**Fig. 3.** Representation of the individual. The pre-established extrema are not considered in the chromosome.

best topology-preserving order. This is the reason why an evolutionary algorithm is proposed, in this paper, to obtain the ordering. The proposal employs a representation of the individuals, and crossover and mutation operators similar to those employed in other combinatorial optimisation problems.

**Representation of Individuals.** The proposed evolutionary algorithm employs the well-known path representation where the chromosome represents the sequence that establishes the order of the different colours or cluster centres. However, as the extrema of the ordering, typically $(0, 0, 0)$ and $(255, 255, 255)$, are fixed they are not included in the chromosome (Fig. 3).

**Crossover.** Many different crossover operators have been proposed for combinatorial optimisation. This work employs the Linear Order Crossover (LOX) proposed by Falkenauer and Bouffouix [13]. This operator follows four steps, namely:

1. Select at random a subsequence from one of the parents;
2. Start generating a new offspring by copying that subsequence into the corresponding positions of the new offspring;
3. Delete the elements that are already in the subsequence from the second parent; and
4. Place the elements in the unfilled positions of the offspring from left to right in the order that appear in the second parent.

An example of such a crossover operation is presented in Fig. 4.

**Mutation.** Different mutation operators have been proposed for combinatorial optimisation problems [14]. This work makes use of some of them:

- *Exchange mutation:* selects randomly two elements in the path and exchanges them;
- *Swap mutation:* selects randomly two consecutive elements and swaps them;

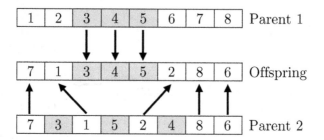

**Fig. 4.** Application of the linear crossover operator.

- *Insertion mutation:* selects randomly one element in the path, removes it from the current position, and inserts it in a randomly selected place;
- *Simple inversion mutation:* selects randomly two elements and it reverses the subsequence between those two cut points;
- *Scramble mutation:* selects a random subsequence and scrambles the elements in it; and
- *Displacement mutation:* selects a subsequence at random, removes it from the current position, and inserts it in a random place.

This work also includes a *Subsequence ordering mutation* that selects a random subsequence and orders it using the same evolutionary algorithm, following a recursive approach. This operator allows a faster convergence of the global evolution as it gets good solutions for a subsequence, with an associated lower computational cost.

### 3.3 Ordering of the Colours

Given a pair of colours $\xi_1, \xi_2 \in [0, 1]^3$, $\xi_1$ is lower than $\xi_2$ if $centre(\xi_1)$ is lower than $centre(\xi_2)$, according to the ordering obtained by the evolutionary process, where $centre(\xi_i)$ is the nearest cluster centre to colour $\xi_i$. However, both colours may be mapped onto the same cluster. In this case, different criteria can be considered to establish an order between them. For instance, ordering them according to their distance to the cluster centre or to their distance to the centre of the structuring element. However, after testing different alternatives, the best results have been obtained by comparing the relationship between the distances from each colour to the neighbouring cluster centres (Fig. 5). In that figure, $\xi_1 < \xi_2$ because $(d_{\xi_1}^{i-1}/d_{\xi_1}^{i+1}) < (d_{\xi_2}^{i-1}/d_{\xi_2}^{i+1})$. In case that both colours are mapped to the first cluster centre in the ordering then $d_{\xi_1}^{i-1} = d_{\xi_2}^{i-1} = 1$. Similarly, if they are mapped to the last centre, then $d_{\xi_1}^{i+1} = d_{\xi_2}^{i+1} = 1$.

## 4    Aplication to Mathematical Morphology

Once a colour order $\psi$ has been established, thereby allowing the calculation of the supremum ($sup^\psi$) and the infimum ($inf^\psi$) from a set of colours; the

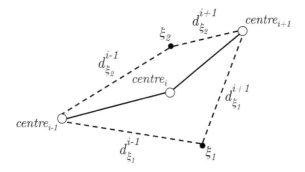

**Fig. 5.** Comparison between a pair of colours $\xi_1$ and $\xi_2$ when both are assigned to the same cluster centre $centre_i$. $centre_{i-1}$ and $centre_{i+1}$ are its neighbouring clusters centres according to the calculated ordering.

morphological operators for vectorial erosion ($\epsilon_B^\psi$) and dilation ($\delta_B^\psi$) of an RGB image $I$ using structuring element $B$ can be defined at every pixel $(x, y)$ as:

$$\epsilon_B^\psi(I)(x, y) = \inf_{\forall b \in B}{}^\psi I(x + b, y + b) \tag{4}$$

$$\delta_B^\psi(I)(x, y) = \sup_{\forall b \in B}{}^\psi I(x + b, y + b) \tag{5}$$

Structuring element $B$ defines the set of pixels that are considered in each morphological operation. They can have arbitrary shapes, but usually disks, squares, or crosses are employed.

All the other morphological operators using the colour order can be derived from these vectorial erosion and dilation definitions. For instance, the opening ($\gamma_B^\psi$) and the closing ($\phi_B^\psi$) are defined as:

$$\gamma_B^\psi(I)(x, y) = \delta_B^\psi(\epsilon_B^\psi(I))(x, y) \tag{6}$$

$$\phi_B^\psi(I)(x, y) = \epsilon_B^\psi(\delta_B^\psi(I))(x, y) \tag{7}$$

## 5   Experimentation

Comparing results with other works has been very difficult as there is not a public dataset that researchers in the field of colour mathematical morphology commonly employ. Most of the works compare the orderings based on the results obtained using them in mathematical morphology operations for specific applications, e.g. noise reduction. This paper follows a similar approach, choosing similar testbeds than the state-of-the-art methods.

The options and parameters of the evolutionary algorithm are:

- The size of the population has been set to 25 individuals;
- Parents are selected by fitness-ranking from the current population;

- All the mutations have the same probability to be selected;
- Next generation's population is selected by ranking with elitism for the best; and
- The evolution finishes if the best individual has not changed for 1,000 generations.

As stated above, the application of the *Subsequence ordering mutation* operator calls a new instance of the evolutionary algorithm with a subsequence chosen at random. In order to avoid a long duration in this recursive evolution the length of the subsequence is selected in the interval [8, 24]. These lengths have been empirically chosen as it has been observed that solutions for shorter subsequences are obtained almost immediately, and it is difficult to get a fast convergence for longer subsequences. Also for a fast convergence, the population has only 10 individuals and the number of generations without changes is limited to 100. Besides, in order to avoid further recursivity, the new EA does not use the *Subsequence ordering mutation* operator.

The following results and figures employ the best ordering obtained, out of 50 runs, for the set of colours considered in each case.

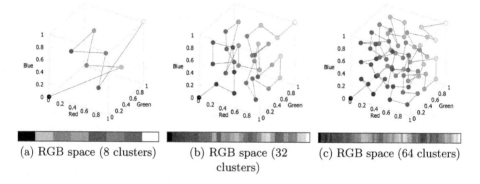

(a) RGB space (8 clusters)    (b) RGB space (32 clusters)    (c) RGB space (64 clusters)

**Fig. 6.** Evolutionary orderings of the RGB space for different number of cluster centres: (top) ordering in the 3D space, (bottom) ordered sequence of colours (color figure online).

Results for RGB orderings with different number of clusters are shown in Fig. 6. Table 1 shows the topographic preservation of those orderings and compares the results with the usually employed orderings. Using the topographic product for quality measurement, the evolutionary approach proposed in this paper obtains quite better quantitative results.

Recently, a new approach [15] considers the ordering of the colours that appear in a specific image or a set of them, not in the whole colour space. Then, orderings are specialised, leading to best results in MM operations. Adaptation of the evolutionary proposal to this specific ordering approach requires that the extrema of the ordering are set to the two colours in the image more similar to

**Table 1.** Absolute value of the topographic product $|P|$ for the different orderings of the colours shown in Fig. 6.

| Number of clusters | Lexicographical (RGB) | Bit interlacing | Evolutionary |
|---|---|---|---|
| 8 | 0.334 | 0.358 | **0.218** |
| 32 | 0.662 | 0.557 | **0.424** |
| 64 | 0.721 | 0.549 | **0.463** |

$(0,0,0)$ and $(255,255,255)$. As fewer colours have to be clustered, the quantisation error of the clustering decreases, obtaining an ordering that should improve the results of later operations (Fig. 7).

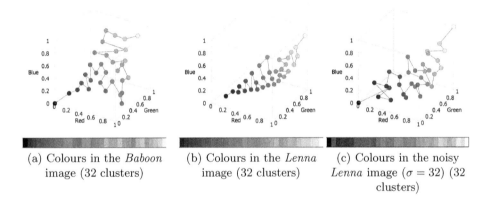

(a) Colours in the *Baboon* image (32 clusters)

(b) Colours in the *Lenna* image (32 clusters)

(c) Colours in the noisy *Lenna* image ($\sigma = 32$) (32 clusters)

**Fig. 7.** Specific orderings for the *Baboon* and *Lenna* images (see Fig. 8).

Following the approach in [1], the orderings proposed in this paper have also been examined in terms of noise reduction quality. The filter employed for smoothing is the open-close close-open (OCCO) operation defined for each pixel $(x, y)$ as:

$$OCCO_B^\psi(I)(x,y) = \frac{1}{2}(\gamma_B^\psi(\phi_B^\psi(I))(x,y) + \phi_B^\psi(\gamma_B^\psi(I))(x,y)) \tag{8}$$

where the structuring element $B$ is a cross of size $3 \times 3$. In all the MM operations the vectorial representation of each colour is mapped into its corresponding position in the ordering.

This operator has been applied to different images corrupted with uncorrelated gaussian noise (Fig. 8). The results in terms of normalised mean squared error ($NMSE$) are shown in Table 2. The best results are obtained when the specific orders for each one of the images are learned. They are quite stable, improving in almost all the cases the results obtained with the usually employed

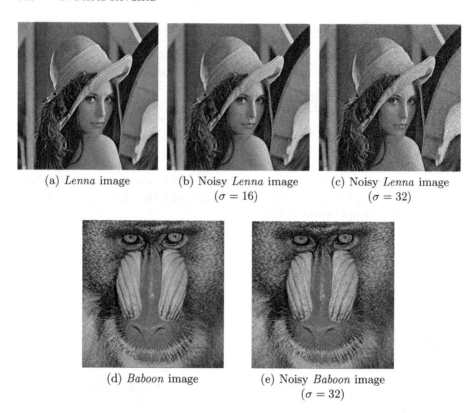

(a) *Lenna* image    (b) Noisy *Lenna* image    (c) Noisy *Lenna* image
                         ($\sigma = 16$)                ($\sigma = 32$)

(d) *Baboon* image       (e) Noisy *Baboon* image
                              ($\sigma = 32$)

**Fig. 8.** Images used in the experimentation.

lexicographical and bit-interlacing orders. They also improve the results presented in [1,11]. In the case of a general ordering for the whole RGB space the results are improved as the number of clusters is increased. This is what it should be expected, as in the limit where the number of clusters is equal to the number of colours in the RGB space the best topology-preserving total ordering would be obtained, and noise reduction should be improved. However, this is not the case for the *Lenna* image ($\sigma = 16$) where $NMSE$ increases with 64 clusters. The explanation to this is that the search space increases and the evolutionary algorithm used for calculating the ordering gets stuck in local minima. This is also the case when using specific orderings. Another cause for an increase in $NMSE$ incrementing the number of clusters in specific orderings is that noisy colours interfere in the calculation of the cluster centres (see in Fig. 7b and c the differences in the positions of the cluster centres because of the noise). Similar tests have been carried out to other images and noise levels, obtaining similar results.

**Table 2.** Normalised mean squared error obtained against images corrupted with Gaussian noise. In bold the results that improve the $NMSE$ obtained with the bit-interlacing order.

| Ordering | Number of clusters | $NMSE \times 100$ | | |
|---|---|---|---|---|
| | | Lenna ($\sigma = 16$) | Lenna ($\sigma = 32$) | Baboon ($\sigma = 32$) |
| General | 8 | 1.02 | 2.57 | 5.2 |
| | 32 | 0.81 | 2.16 | 4.46 |
| | 64 | 0.90 | **2.09** | **4.29** |
| Specific | 8 | **0.73** | **2.03** | 4.38 |
| | 32 | **0.74** | **2.08** | **4.32** |
| | 64 | **0.75** | **2.10** | **4.33** |
| Growing neural gas [11] | 8 | 0.84 | 2.23 | 4.50 |
| | 32 | 0.87 | 2.35 | 4.69 |
| | 64 | 0.89 | 2.28 | 4.62 |
| Lexicographical (RGB) | | 0.79 | 2.23 | 4.65 |
| Bit interlacing | | 0.75 | 2.16 | 4.35 |

# 6   Conclusions

This paper has presented a method to order the RGB space maximising topology preservation. As calculating topology preservation for the whole colour space is very expensive, a proposal based on clustering the colour space and ordering of the cluster centres has been proposed. This approach has been also employed to obtain specific orders for individual images. Extension to other colour spaces is straightforward modifying how the distances between colours are obtained, e.g. for the HSI space, in both the clustering and the calculation of the topographic product.

The main drawback of obtaining the best topology-preserving order is its computational cost. This paper has solved this issue proposing an evolutionary algorithm. However, further improvements need to be done in order to obtain better solutions and avoid local minima if the number of clusters is high, i.e. greater than 32.

Another future work will deal with finding the best "simple" topology-preserving total order for each colour space. Simple understood as easiness to estimate the extrema in MM operations.

Finally, a similar approach is going to be applied to other multivariate data to order higher-dimensional spaces, e.g. histograms, images... thereby allowing the application of mathematical morphology to other multivariate spaces.

# References

1. Aptoula, E., Lefèvre, S.: A comparative study on multivariate mathematical morphology. Pattern Recogn. **40**(11), 2914–2929 (2007)
2. Regazzoni, C., Teschioni, A.: A new approach to vector median filtering based on space filling curves. IEEE Trans. Image Process. **6**(7), 1025–1037 (1997)
3. Stringa, E., Teschioni, A., Regazzoni, C.S.: A classical morphological approach to color image filtering based on space filling curves. In: Proceedings of the IEEE-Eurasip Workshop on Nonlinear Signal and Image Processing, Antalya, Turkey, pp. 351–354 (1999)
4. Soille, P., Pesaresi, M.: Advances in mathematical morphology applied to geoscience and remote sensing. IEEE Trans. Geosci. Remote Sens. **40**(9), 2042–2055 (2002)
5. Chanussot, J., Lambert, P.: Total ordering based on space filling curves for multivalued morphology (1998)
6. Angulo, J.: Morphological colour operators in totally ordered lattices based on distances: Application to image filtering, enhancement and analysis. Comput. Vis. Image Underst. **107**(1–2), 56–73 (2007)
7. Bauer, H.U., Pawelzik, K.: Quantifying the neighborhood preservation of self-organizing feature maps. IEEE Trans. Neural Netw. **3**(4), 570–579 (1992)
8. Kaski, S., Lagus, K.: Comparing self-organizing maps. In: Vorbrüggen, J.C., von Seelen, W., Sendhoff, B. (eds.) ICANN 1996. LNCS, vol. 1112, pp. 809–814. Springer, Heidelberg (1996)
9. Villmann, T., Der, R., Herrmann, M., Martinetz, T.: Topology preservation in self-organizing feature maps: exact definition and measurement. IEEE Trans. Neural Netw. **8**(2), 256–266 (1997)
10. Bauer, H.U., Herrmann, M., Villmann, T.: Neural maps and topographic vector quantization. Neural Netw. **12**(45), 659–676 (1999)
11. Flórez-Revuelta, F.: Ordering of the RGB space with a growing self-organizing network. application to color mathematical morphology. In: Duch, W., Kacprzyk, J., Oja, E., Zadrożny, S. (eds.) ICANN 2005. LNCS, vol. 3696, pp. 385–390. Springer, Heidelberg (2005)
12. Rose, N.: Hilbert-type space-filling curves (2001). http://www4.ncsu.edu/njrose/pdfFiles/HilbertCurve.pdf
13. Falkenauer, E., Bouffouix, S.: A genetic algorithm for job shop. In: Proceedings of the IEEE International Conference on Robotics and Automation, vol. 1, pp. 824–829, April 1991
14. Larrañaga, P., Kuijpers, C.M.H., Murga, R.H., Inza, I., Dizdarevic, S.: Genetic algorithms for the travelling salesman problem: A review of representations and operators. Artif. Intell. Rev. **13**(2), 129–170 (1999)
15. Chevalier, E., Angulo, J.: Image adapted total ordering for mathematical morphology on multivariate images. In: Proceedings of the IEEE International Conference on Image Processing, pp. 2943–2947 (2014)

# Planar Surfaces Recognition
# in 3D Point Cloud Using a Real-Coded
# Multistage Genetic Algorithm

Mosab Bazargani[1]($\boxtimes$), Luís Mateus[2], and Maria Amélia R. Loja[1,3]

[1] LAETA, IDMEC, Instituto Superior Técnico,
Universidade de Lisboa, Lisbon, Portugal
mbazargani@gmail.com, amelialoja@tecnico.ulisboa.pt
[2] CIAUD, Faculdade de Arquitetura, Universidade de Lisboa, Lisbon, Portugal
lmmateus@fa.ulisboa.pt
[3] ISEL, IPL, Instituto Superior de Engenharia de Lisboa, Lisbon, Portugal

**Abstract.** Most frequent surface shapes of man-made constructions are planar surfaces. Discovering those surfaces is a big step toward extracting as-built/-is construction information from 3D point cloud. In this paper, a real-coded genetic algorithm (GA) formulation for planar surfaces recognition in 3D point clouds is presented. The algorithm developed based on a multistage approach; thereby, it finds one planar surface (part of solution) at each stage. In addition, the logarithmically proportional objective function that is used in this approach can adapt itself to scale and spatial density of the point cloud. We tested the proposed application on a synthetic point cloud containing several planar surfaces with different shapes, positions, and with a wide variety of sizes. The results obtained showed that the proposed method is capable to find all plane's configurations of flat surfaces with a minor distance to the actual configurations.

**Keywords:** Planar surface recognition · Multistage genetic algorithm · Logarithmic objective function · Point cloud

## 1 Introduction

Nowadays, 3D point clouds became a standard deliverable of recording and surveying methods. They can represent the geometry of built environments and objects almost in a continuous way. However, the current widely-used techniques for generating 3D models from 3D point clouds are mostly manual, and that causes results to be subjective, time-consuming, and error-prone [1]. In built environments, more surface types than planar surfaces are present. But since most of man-made constructions are built upon planar surfaces, recognition of those planar surfaces is often the first step toward extracting building information from 3D point clouds. Most methods for solving planar surface recognition in 3D point clouds use segmentation [2] and are heuristic.

© Springer International Publishing Switzerland 2015
A.M. Mora and G. Squillero (Eds.): EvoApplications 2015, LNCS 9028, pp. 529–540, 2015.
DOI: 10.1007/978-3-319-16549-3_43

This paper describes a novel Genetic Algorithm (GA) formulation for planar surface recognition without employing segmentation and without exploiting any prior knowledge about those surfaces. It uses a multistage approach, where it searches for one planar surface at each stage. It follows up the search process after finding one planar face and removing its relative points from the point cloud in order to find the next surface. It keeps doing this process until it fulfills a stopping condition. We tested the proposed application on a synthetic point cloud and results obtained show the method is capable to find all planar surfaces (with a wide variety of sizes) with a minor distance to the actual configurations.

The rest of the paper is organized as follows. Section 2 presents a brief review of related work that has been proposed to recognize planar faces in point clouds. Section 3 presents a real-coded multistage GA formulation for planar surface recognition in 3D point clouds and the logarithmically proportional objective function used in this work. Section 4 covers the experimental setup as well as the experimental results. Finally, Sect. 5 summarizes and concludes the paper.

## 2    Related Work

In most methods for solving this problem, first, a segmentation algorithm is being applied to the point cloud to identify invariant regions according to given criteria, such as curvature, orientation, and shape. Thereafter, each segment resulting from the segmentation procedure is checked by one of the three state-of-the-art approaches for planar surface recognition. Those methods can find more than one planar surface in a segment. Finally, the similar planar patches, that were found in each segment, are merged by using plane growing [3,4] or triangulated irregular network (TIN) meshes [5]. Those three state-of-the-art methods are region growing [6], Hough-transform [4], and RANSAC algorithms [7].

### 2.1    Applications of Planar Surface Recognition in 3D Modeling

Planar surface recognition is used in many applications of 3D modeling of constructions and environments [8–14]. Those applications mostly use one of the approaches that were mentioned previously or a variant of them. Some of those applications that are particularly applied for 3D modeling of constructions are discussed in the following of this subsection.

Chen and Chen [12] proposed a pipeline to reconstruct complete geometry of architectural buildings that are made of planar faces. They use region growing approach for detecting planar faces, and progressively merge points that are coplanar. The normal of a point $p$ is computed by least-squaredly fitting a plane to the set of points within its neighborhood, where the neighborhood is defined as a $7 \times 7$ pixels region centered at $p$. Although the method deals efficiently with architectural scenes comprising planar faces, it only produces a 3D model describing the exterior geometry of the building. Besides, it cannot be used for urban reconstruction problem.

Vosselman and Dijkman [13] dealt with reconstruction of urban environment. They use a 3D Hough-transform for extraction of planar-roof faces from irregularly distributed point clouds. In that work, authors assume that ground plans of buildings exist, and 3D building models are generated by combining the extracted roof faces and available buildings' ground plans. Peternell and Steiner [8] also employed Hough-transform approach for detecting planar patches in their work. Found planar patches are used to reconstruct building roofs, and the method can only be applied to objects that have been scanned from above.

RANSAC is the most widely used approach in application of planar surface recognition in 3D modeling because of its simplicity and efficiency. Jenke *et al.* [11] proposed a method to model an architectural scene as a collection of cuboids, that are built of planar facets. They applied RANSAC in the second stage of their application to automatically detect plane primitives in a point cloud. Their method is robust to noisy and sparse point clouds; however, it is restricted to modeling cuboids if at least five facets are detected as planar faces. Architectural structures with a limited number of facets, e.g., staircases or abandon walls, cannot be modeled in their application. Yousefzadeh *et al.* [14] also employed RANSAC for wall plane detection. Their application is restricted to the façade structure modeling and ground based laser data. Sanchez and Zakhor [9] proposed an application of planar 3D modeling of building interiors from point cloud with employing model-fitting and RANSAC. First, they discover planar faces in point clouds. Thereafter, they model building interior by using a set of planar primitives for modeling. Their method is restricted to interior geometry of the building.

## 3     A Real-Coded Multistage GA

This section introduces a real-coded multistage GA for planar surface recognition. The proposed algorithm for planar surface recognition in 3D point clouds is a parameter-based approach, since we are performing a direct search for parameters that define planes in the point cloud. According to implicit equation of a plane, i.e. $ax + by + cz + d = 0$, a plane is defined by four parameters, $a$, $b$, $c$, and $d$. A candidate solution for the GA is therefore represented by a chromosome vector with four genes, each a real number.

In the next subsections, first we describe the outline of the proposed algorithm; thereafter, the objective function that was used in this study will be elaborated.

### 3.1     Algorithm

The proposed algorithm for solving this problem is straightforward. It focuses on finding one planar surface at a time; thereafter finding one and removing its relative points from the point cloud, the search pivot of the algorithm turns toward another available planar surface in the point cloud. This formulation resembles sequential niching, which works by iterating a simple GA (sGA), and maintaining the best solution of each run off-line [15,16]. In contrast to the sequential niching, the best solution obtained by each run of sGA in the proposed algorithm is not a solution to the problem, but part of it. Algorithm 1 gives details of the steps involved in our approach to locate planar surfaces in a point cloud. It shows that there are two loops engaged in this process. The interior loop (lines 6 to 13 of Algorithm 1) is the iterative part of the sGA, and the exterior loop assures multistage behaviour of the algorithm.

The algorithm should be terminated after finding all required planar surfaces. That is achieved by appropriately setting up the stopping criteria for the exterior loop (line 3 of Algorithm 1). It can be when there is no point left in the point cloud—which only happens in a very ideal point cloud, or when the remaining points in the data set don't fulfill the conditions to be considered as planes. Since point clouds can contain a lot of noises as well as non-planar surfaces, we also apply another stopping criterion that avoids the algorithm to pursue further after finding all required planar surfaces. We device the new stopping criterion by utilizing a feature of the employed objective function (details about the objective function will be given in the next subsection). The employed objective function in this GA tends to find bigger planar surfaces (surfaces with more points) sooner than smaller ones. Thus, one, whomever is familiar with the targeted point cloud, should determine minimum size of the planar surface that is needed to be found in the point cloud. The size of that surface can be defined by the number of points located on it, $\delta$. However, despite the fact that the objective function tends to find bigger planar surfaces before smaller ones, finding a planar surface with $\delta$ number of points (or even less than that) does not mean that all bigger planar surfaces than $\delta$ have been already found. Because the objective function tends to do so, but does not guarantee so. Therefore, extra chance(s) to find planar surface(s) bigger than $\delta$ need to be given to the algorithm to examine that no planar surface with size bigger than $\delta$ is left in the point cloud. For the sake of simplicity, we assign the maximum number of fail attempts, $\beta$, to search for a bigger planar surface than $\delta$ in the point cloud. When we exceed $\beta$, the search operation will be extinguished.

Inside of the exterior loop of the algorithm, the sGA starts with initializing the population (line 4 of Algorithm 1). This procedure is performed once in each stage. In order to make the search process faster and avoid to search through sub-spaces of the 3D Euclidean space where there are no points present, we initialize the population with parameters of planes that pass through points in the point cloud. To accomplish this aim, each solution in the population is calculated based on three randomly-drawn points from the point cloud. And indeed, after finding a planar surface and removing its relative points from the point cloud, the initialization for the next stage will be done based on the remaining points in the point cloud.

After initialization and evaluation of population with a given objective function $f$ (see Subsect. 3.2), the iterative process of the sGA (interior loop) takes place (lines 6 to 13 of Algorithm 1). The considered stopping criterion for the sGA in our formulation is when the population is deemed as converged, and that happens when all solutions in the population represent parameters of the same plane. Since we use a real-coded GA representation, it is inadequate to inspect convergence based on genes' values. Instead we count number of points fitted in each solution (plane) in the population, and a population is considered as converged if and only if all solutions in the population have the same number of points fitted in them. Moreover, since we search for one plane at a time as well as to guarantee convergence in the population, we use an elitist strategy for the replacement (line 11 of Algorithm 1). To do so, we merge two populations, the current population and the newly generated solutions, and keep the best half of that to carry over to the next generation.

At this point (line 14 of Algorithm 1), after one population converged, number of points fitted in the discovered plane should be examined. If it is bigger than $\delta$, the discovered plane's parameters will be stored on a file and its relative points will be pulled out of the point cloud. Thereafter, if the stopping criteria of the exterior loop are not satisfied, we restart the population with the remaining points in the point cloud and repeat the sGA over again. We continue doing this until the stopping criteria become satisfied.

## 3.2    Objective Function

In order to guide the search for an appropriate set of parameters for a plane in 3D point cloud, we need to measure the proximity between a sampled plane (a solution in the population) and a hypothesized planar surface in the 3D point cloud. Since we want to move a sampled plane toward its closest hypothesized planar surface in the 3D point cloud, points far from the sampled plane should not play a part in the function evaluation of that sampled plane. In other words, only those points that are within a certain radius of a sampled plane must be considered for its objective function evaluation. This certain radius is called plane region, $r$, and is defined based on the scale and spatial density of the point cloud. The radius $r$ is inversely proportional to the spatial resolution of the point cloud. In other words, $r$ should be smaller for point clouds with a high density.

Since points in a point cloud don't define ideal geometric features, a plane threshold, $t$, which is the maximum acceptable distance between a geometrical plane and points that are considered as fitted in that plane needs to be defined. This parameter, alike $r$, is determined by whomever is familiar with the point cloud features.

The logarithmically proportional objective function [17] that we used in this study employs these two parameters. This function sums the logarithmic form of Euclidean distances of those points that are in the region of a sampled plane. Logarithmic function, $y = \log(x)$, has a higher growth rate in small values of $x$, rather than big values of $x$. This feature of logarithm gives the objective function the benefit of reducing effect of noises. In addition, in order to track small changes of a sampled plane, the plane region needs to be in the interval of the logarithmic function which has a significant growth rate. Since logarithmic growth is the inverse of exponential growth, $r$ is where these two functions intersect. To pose this issue to the objective function, the base of logarithm is derived from $r$, and $t$ (line 4 of Algorithm 2).

**Algorithm 1.** Outline of the real-coded multistage GA to planar surface recognition from 3D point cloud.

---

**Input**  : $\mu, \beta, \delta, C, f$
       /* $\mu$ is the population size */
       /* $\beta$ is maximum acceptable number of fail attempts */
       /* $\delta$ is minimum acceptable size of a plane (number of points) */
       /* $C$ is the point cloud */
       /* $f$ is the objective function */
**Output**: PLANES
       /* PLANES is a file with all discovered planes configurations */

1  $g \longleftarrow 0$;
2  $a \longleftarrow 0$;
3  **while** *C is not empty and* $a < \beta$ **do**
4     generate initial population $P(g)$ with using points in $C$;
5     evaluate the population $P(g)$ using the given objective function $f$;
6     **while** $P(g)$ *is not entirely converged* **do**
7        select population of promising solutions $S(g)$;
8        recombine $S(g)$;
9        mutate $S(g)$;
10      evaluate $S(g)$ using $f$;
11      apply elitist replacement on $P(g)$ and $S(g)$ to form a new population;
12      $g \leftarrow g + 1$;
13    **end**
14    **if** *number of fitted points in the discovered plane is bigger than* $\delta$ **then**
15      restore the discovered plane configuration in the PLANES;
16      remove fitted points in the discovered plane from the point cloud;
17    **else**
18      $a \leftarrow a + 1$;
19    **end**
20  **end**
21  **return** PLANES

---

The pseudocode that can be used to simulate the logarithmically proportional objective function described here is shown in Algorithm 2. This implementation is slightly different from the one described in [17]. This one lowers the logarithmic function under x-axis with subtracting the maximum value of the function, $\log_b r - \log_b t$, from logarithmic form of distances, in order to return values with a same sign (line 19 of Algorithm 2).

## 4  Experiments

This section describes both the experimental setup for the multistage GA and results from testing the proposed GA formulation. In order to measure accuracy of the proposed algorithm, a synthetic point cloud—which its genuine ground truth is available—is used.

The synthetic point cloud represents a cottage with two nested rooms and with a hip-roof (Fig. 1(a)). The cottage is settled in a plane of 16 by 12 m and

---

**Algorithm 2.** The pseudocode of the logarithmically proportional objective function.

---

**Input**  : $t, r, b, \varepsilon, C, p$
/* $t$ is the plane tolerance threshold */
/* $r$ is the plane region */
/* $\varepsilon$ is the smallest positive floating-point value */
/* $C$ is the point cloud */
/* $p$ is a chromosome, which contains a sampled-plane parameters */

**Output**: Objective function value

1  $v \longleftarrow 0$;
2  $l \longleftarrow 0$;
3  $fitness \longleftarrow 0$;
4  $b \longleftarrow \sqrt[r]{r/t}$;            // Calculate the base of logarithm
5  $max \longleftarrow \log_b r - \log_b t$;   // Maximum value of the logarithmic function
6  **foreach** $point, c, in C$ **do**
7      /* Euclidean distance between a point in the point cloud and $p$ */
8      $d \longleftarrow |c_x \times p_a + c_y \times p_b + c_z \times p_c + p_d|$;
9      $k \longleftarrow \sqrt{p_a^2 + p_b^2 + p_c^2}$;
10     /* Avoid divide by zero                                              */
11     **if** $k = 0.0$ **then**
12         $d \longleftarrow d/\varepsilon$;
13     **else**
14         $d \longleftarrow d/k$;
15     **end**
16     /* Fitness evaluation based on points within the plane region  */
17     **if** $0.0 < d \leq r$ **then**
18         $v \longleftarrow v + 1$;
19         $fitness \longleftarrow fitness + \log_b d - \log_b t - max$;
20     **end**
21     **if** $0.0 < d \leq t$ **then**    // Count number of fitted points
22         $l \longleftarrow l + 1$;
23     **end**
24     **if** $d = 0.0$ **then**    // Prevent fitness value to be $+\infty$
25         $v \longleftarrow v + 1$;
26     **end**
27 **end**
28 **if** $v = 0.0$ **then**
29     $fitness \longleftarrow -\infty$;   // An irrelevant plane to the point cloud
30 **else**
31     $fitness \longleftarrow -fitness/v \times l$;
32 **end**
33 **return** $fitness$

---

has an area about ∼80 square meters. The point cloud contains a total of 31657 points. Points are uniformly distributed on the surfaces with a density of almost 50 points per square meter. It is built over 37 planar surfaces with different sizes from ∼20 points to ∼10000 points. Although the proposed algorithm can find all planar surfaces in the point cloud, we only focused on finding planar faces sized above 200 points. This number was assumed as representing surfaces with architectural significance.

## 4.1    Operators and Experimental Setup

In the proposed multistage GA formulation (Subsect. 3.1), the initialization and replacement strategy are specified. The initialization in each stage is based on the remaining points from the previous stage. As for replacement, an elitist strategy which keeps the best solutions among the parent population and newly generated individuals is used. The following GA variation operators and setup are performed for testing the proposed algorithm.

We use Simulated Binary Crossover (SBX) which is proposed by Deb and Agrawal [18]. SBX uses a polynomial probability distribution to create the off-spring. It is a parent-centric recombination operator, because the offspring it produces are located around the parents. It has been shown that parent-centric operators have in general a better performance than mean-centric operators [19].

We employed a polynomial mutation operator which is introduced by Deb and Agrawal [20]. In this operator, a polynomial probability distribution is used to perturb a solution in a parent's vicinity, and it has a user-defined index parameter ($\eta_m$). A recent study from Deb and Deb [21] revealed that the polynomial mutation perform best in the distribution index $\eta_m \in [100, 150]$ and mutation probability $p_m \in [0.5, 1.5]/l$ (where $l$ is the number of variables in the chromosome).

With respect to the above mentioned GA variation operators, the GA setup for the experiment is as the following. We use tournament selection without replacement of size 5, SBX crossover with distribution index 2, and polynomial mutation with distribution index 100. The crossover probability was set to 0.5 and each gene undergoes SBX with probability 0.5. The mutation rate was set to $1/l$, i.e. 0.25. The experiments were performed with populations of size 50, 100, 200, 300, 400, 500, 600, and 700 individuals, and for each size, 100 independent runs were executed.

To see the proposed multistage GA in practice, besides the GA setup, point cloud related parameters (i.e., $t$, $r$, $\delta$, and $\beta$) also need to be tuned. As it was previously mentioned, these parameters are defined based on the features of the tackled point cloud. The plane tolerance threshold and the radius of plane region are set to 0.01 m and 0.50 m, respectively. In this paper, since we search for planar faces with an architectural meaning, $\delta$ is set to 200. Furthermore, the number of fail attempts, $\beta$, to find planar surfaces bigger than $\delta$ points is so initialized to three.

## 4.2    Results

In this subsection, we will examine the resulting planar surface recognition after running the multistage GA on the synthetic point cloud. As it was already mentioned, the algorithm is tuned to find planar faces that have at least 200 points fitted in them. There are 22 planar faces in the used synthetic point cloud with this feature. Figures 1(b–h) illustrate planes that were discovered from one run of the multistage GA in stages 1, 2, 3, 4, 20, 21, and 22, respectively. Discovered planes in each stage are shown by dots, and shadows are remaining planar surfaces in the point cloud to be found. Although the discovered plane in stage 3 (4319 points) has more points than the one discovered in stage 2 (1819 points), it can be easily observed in Figs. 1(b–h) that the algorithm generally tends to find bigger surfaces at the early stage of the run. Figure 1(i) represents remaining points in the point cloud after meeting the termination criteria.

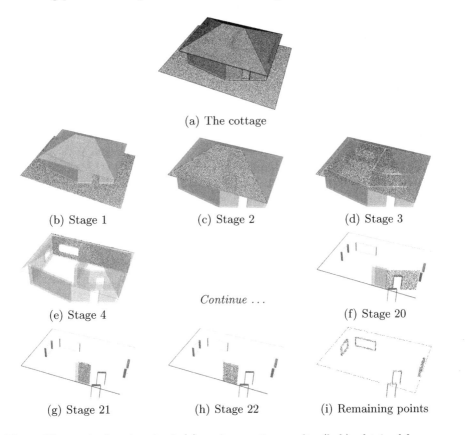

(a) The cottage

(b) Stage 1      (c) Stage 2      (d) Stage 3

(e) Stage 4      *Continue ...*      (f) Stage 20

(g) Stage 21      (h) Stage 22      (i) Remaining points

**Fig. 1.** The synthetic point cloud, (a), and respective results, (b–h), obtained from one run of the multistage GA using population size 400. In (b–h), discovered planar surface in each stage is shown by dots, and shadows present remaining planar surfaces in the point cloud. (i) remaining points in the point cloud after terminating the run.

In order to evaluate results obtained from executing 100 independent runs for seven different population sizes, the corresponding planar face in the point cloud for each discovered plane needs to be found. To accomplish this aim, the dihedral angle between each discovered plane and all the planar surfaces in the point cloud (the ground truth) were calculated. For each discovered plane, the planar surface in the point cloud that has the lowest dihedral angle with it and share at least one point with it was chosen as the correspondence. But a discovered plane was validated as correctly located if and only if it has the same number of points in its plane tolerance threshold as its corresponding planar surface in the point cloud. Thus, the success rate is the percentage of locating correctly all 22 planar surfaces over 100 independent runs for each population size (see Table 1). The discovered planar surfaces that do not have the same number of points in their planar tolerance threshold as their corresponding planar surfaces in the point cloud are considered as premature discovered planes; because, that happen when the population converges prematurely in one stage. The average of premature discovered planes over 100 runs for each population size are given in Table 1. In addition, the failed attempts rate in Table 1 shows the percentage of function evaluations that were wasted for three failed attempts in each population size over 100 independent runs, to find planar surfaces bigger than $\delta$ in the point cloud. The average of Euclidean distances between correctly discovered planes and points in their threshold over 100 runs for each population size is also depicted in Table 1.

Table 1 shows that increasing the population size does help the GA to obtain higher success rates. It reaches a 100% success rate in population sizes 400, 500, 600 and 700. In accordance to population sizing theory of GAs [22], larger populations sizes tend to produce a better solution quality, but also at the expense of more processing time. The improvement of solutions quality by increasing population size can be observed in the average of distances as well as average of premature discovered planes. From population size 400 on, when there is a 100% success rate, there is no any premature convergence in the population over 100 runs. It means all discovered planes have the same number of points in their tolerance threshold as their counterparts in the point clouds. The failed attempts rate—it shows the rate of function evaluations that were wasted for finding planar surfaces bigger than $\delta$ over 100 independent runs—is very small over average of function evaluations. Moreover, average of Euclidean distances of discovered planes to their relative points show a promising results.

**Table 1.** Results from testing the multistage GA on the synthetic point cloud. They are average over 100 independent runs.

| Pop size | Success rate (%) | Average of function evaluation | Average of distances (cm) | Failed attempts rate | Average of premature discovered planes |
|---|---|---|---|---|---|
| 50  | 51.7  | 23064  | 0.1055 | 4.3 | 2.72 |
| 100 | 93.5  | 53741  | 0.0541 | 2.7 | 1.17 |
| 200 | 99.0  | 81148  | 0.0240 | 3.1 | 0.17 |
| 300 | 99.9  | 105762 | 0.0142 | 3.3 | 0.06 |
| 400 | 100.0 | 131368 | 0.0117 | 3.6 | 0.00 |
| 500 | 100.0 | 153960 | 0.0101 | 3.8 | 0.00 |
| 600 | 100.0 | 183264 | 0.0093 | 4.0 | 0.00 |
| 700 | 100.0 | 212387 | 0.0089 | 4.0 | 0.00 |

# 5  Summary and Conclusions

This paper describes a real-coded multistage GA to planar surface recognition in 3D point clouds. The proposed algorithm focuses on finding one planar surface at each stage with using a sGA. Thereafter finding one planar surface and removing its relative points from the point cloud, it searches for another planar surface in the remaining points. We initialize the population in each stage based on the points in the point cloud, in order to avoid searching through sub-spaces of the 3D Euclidean space where there are no points. The results obtained from the proposed multistage GA formulation for this problem show that the multistage GA is capable of dealing with it quite well.

Note that the proposed multistage GA in this work resembles sequential niching. However, as opposed to the sequential niching, the best solution obtained by each run of sGA in the proposed algorithm is not a solution to the problem, but part of it. In addition, the use of the logarithmically proportional objective function decreases the impact of noises available in the point cloud. The results presented in this paper show that if the population is roughly sized for the expected planar surfaces in the point cloud, the multistage GA can reliably find all the planar surfaces with a very minor error to the actual configurations.

**Acknowledgments.** The authors would like to thank Fernando Lobo for his valuable comments and suggestions. This work was sponsored by the Portuguese Foundation for Science and Technology under grant PTDC/ATP-AQI/5355/2012.

# References

1. Tang, P., Anil, E., Akinci, B., Huber, D.: Efficient and effective quality assessment of as-is building information models and 3D laser-scanned data. In: Proceedings of ASCE International Workshop on Computing in Civil Engineering, pp. 486–493. McGraw-Hill (2011)
2. Tang, P., Huber, D., Akinci, B., Lipman, R., Lytle, A.: Automatic reconstruction of as-built building information models from laser-scanned point clouds: A review of related techniques. Autom. Constr. **19**, 829–843 (2010)
3. Jiang, X., Bunke, H.: Robust and fast edge detection and description in range images. In: Proceedings of IAPR Workshop on Machine Vision Applications, pp. 538–541 (1996)
4. Vosselman, G., Gorte, B., Sithole, G., Rabbani, T.: Recognising structure in laser-scanner point clouds. In: International Archives of the Photogrammetry, Remote Sensing and Spatial Information Sciences, vol. XXXVI-8/W2, pp. 33–38 (2004)
5. Gorte, B.: Segmentation of TIN-structured surface models. In: Proceedings Joint International Symposium on Geospatial Theory, Processing and Applications (2002)
6. He, Y., Zhang, C., Awrangjeb, M., Fraser, C.: Automated reconstruction of walls from airborne lidar data for complete 3D building modelling. In: International Archives of the Photogrammetry, Remote Sensing and Spatial Information Sciences, vol. XXXIX-B3, pp. 115–120 (2012)

7. Tarsha-Kurdi, F., Landes, T., Grussenmeyer, P.: Hough-transform and extended RANSAC algorithms for automatic detection of 3D building roof planes from lidar data. In: ISPRS Workshop on Laser Scanning, vol. XXXVI (2007)
8. Peternell, M., Steiner, T.: Reconstruction of piecewise planar objects from point clouds. Comput. Aided Des. **36**, 333–342 (2004)
9. Sanchez, V., Zakhor, A.: Planar 3D modeling of building interiors from point cloud data. In: 19th IEEE International Conference on Image Processing (ICIP), pp. 1777–1780 (2012)
10. Ozog, P., Eustice, R.M.: Real-time SLAM with piecewise-planar surface models and sparse 3D point clouds. In: Proceedings of the IEEE/RSJ International Conference on Intelligent RObots and Systems (IROS), pp. 1042–1049 (2013)
11. Jenke, P., Huhle, B., Straßer, W.: Statistical reconstruction of indoor scenes. In: International Conference in Central Europe on Computer Graphics, Visualization and Computer Vision (WSCG 2009), pp. 17–24 (2009)
12. Chen, J., Chen, B.: Architectural modeling from sparsely scanned range data. Int. J. Comput. Vis. **78**, 223–236 (2008)
13. Vosselman, G., Dijkman, S.: 3D building model reconstruction from point clouds and ground plans. In: International Archives of the Photogrammetry, Remote Sensing and Spatial Information Sciences, vol. XXXIV-3/W4, pp. 37–43 (2001)
14. Yousefzadeh, M., Leurink, F.H.M., Beheshti Jou, M.: A general data-driven algorithm for façade structure modeling using ground based laser data. In: International Archives of the Photogrammetry, Remote Sensing and Spatial Information Sciences, vol. XL-3, pp. 381–386 (2014)
15. Mahfoud, S.W.: A comparison of parallel and sequential niching methods. In: Eshelman, L.J. (ed.) Proceedings of the 6th International Conference on Genetic Algorithms, pp. 136–143. Morgan Kaufmann, Pittsburgh (1995)
16. Horn, J.: The nature of niching: Genetic algorithms and the evolution of optimal, cooperative populations. Technical report IlliGAL No. 97008, University of Illinois at Urbana-Champaign (1997)
17. Bazargani, M., Mateus, L., Loja, M.A.R.: Logarithmically proportional objective function for planar surfaces recognition in 3D point cloud. In: Sixth World Congress on Nature and Biologically Inspired Computing (NaBIC 2014). IEEE (2014)
18. Deb, K., Agrawal, R.B.: Simulated binary crossover for continuous search space. Complex Syst. **9**, 115–148 (1995)
19. Deb, K., Anand, A., Joshi, D.: A computationally efficient evolutionary algorithm for real-parameter optimization. Evol. Comput. **10**, 371–395 (2002)
20. Deb, K., Agrawal, S.: A niched-penalty approach for constraint handling in genetic algorithms. In: Artificial Neural Nets and Genetic Algorithms: Proceedings of the International Conference, pp. 235–243. Springer (1999)
21. Deb, K., Deb, D.: Analysing mutation schemes for real-parameter genetic algorithms. Int. J. Artif. Intell. Soft Comput. (IJAISC) **4**, 1–28 (2014)
22. Harik, G.R., Cantú-Paz, E., Goldberg, D.E., Miller, B.L.: The gambler's ruin problem, genetic algorithms, and the sizing of populations. Evol. Comput. **7**, 231–253 (1999)

# Gaussian Transformation Based Representation in Particle Swarm Optimisation for Feature Selection

Hoai Bach Nguyen[1], Bing Xue[1(✉)], Ivy Liu[2], Peter Andreae[1], and Mengjie Zhang[1]

[1] School of Engineering and Computer Science, Victoria University of Wellington, PO Box 600, Wellington 6140, New Zealand
{nguyenhoai2,Bing.Xue,Peter.Andreae,Mengjie.Zhang}@ecs.vuw.ac.nz
[2] School of Mathematics, Statistics and Operations Research, Victoria University of Wellington, PO Box 600, Wellington 6140, New Zealand
Ivy.Liu@msor.vuw.ac.nz

**Abstract.** In classification, feature selection is an important but challenging task, which requires a powerful search technique. Particle swarm optimisation (PSO) has recently gained much attention for solving feature selection problems, but the current representation typically forms a high-dimensional search space. A new representation based on feature clusters was recently proposed to reduce the dimensionality and improve the performance, but it does not form a smooth fitness landscape, which may limit the performance of PSO. This paper proposes a new Gaussian based transformation rule for interpreting a particle as a feature subset, which is combined with the feature cluster based representation to develop a new PSO-based feature selection algorithm. The proposed algorithm is examined and compared with two recent PSO-based algorithms, where the first uses a Gaussian based updating mechanism and the conventional representation, and the second uses the feature cluster representation without using Gaussian distribution. Experiments on commonly used datasets of varying difficulty show that the proposed algorithm achieves better performance than the other two algorithms in terms of the classification performance and the number of features in both the training sets and the test sets. Further analyses show that the Gaussian transformation rule improves the stability, i.e. selecting similar features in different independent runs and almost always selects the most important features.

**Keywords:** Particle swarm optimisation · Feature selection · Representation · Gaussian distribution · Classification

## 1 Introduction

In real-world classification problems, the dataset often has a large number of features, but not all features are relevant to the target concept. Irrelevant and

A.M. Mora and G. Squillero (Eds.): EvoApplications 2015, LNCS 9028, pp. 541–553, 2015.
DOI: 10.1007/978-3-319-16549-3_44

redundant features are not useful for classification, but may reduce the performance due to "the curse of dimensionality" [1]. Feature selection is the process of selecting a small subset of relevant features to reduce the dimensionality with the goal of increasing or at least maintaining the classification performance while speeding up the classification process [2].

Feature selection is a challenging task due mainly to two reasons: a large solution space and feature interaction. The space of possible feature subsets is the power set of the features, hence there are $2^n$ possible feature subsets for a dataset with $n$ features. If all features were completely independent, an efficient greedy algorithm could search this space fast by identifying and removing irrelevant features, leaving only the most useful features. However, feature interaction means that individually relevant features may become redundant and individually weakly relevant features may become highly relevant when combined with other features [1]. Therefore, finding an effective way to deal with feature interaction is critical in feature selection. Research in statistical data analysis also involves interaction between features. A newly developed statistical model [3,4] considers interaction between features to group similar features into clusters and dissimilar features into different clusters. Using this feature clustering information has shown to improve feature selection performance [5,6].

Even with such information, a powerful search algorithm is still needed to find the optimal feature subsets. Although different types of search techniques have been applied to features selection [1,2], existing approaches still suffer from the problem of being stagnation in local optima. Evolutionary computation (EC) techniques are well-known for their promising search ability, and have been applied to feature selection tasks with some success, such as genetic algorithms (GAs) [7], particle swarm optimisation (PSO) [8–11], and differential evolution (DE) [12]. However, many EC algorithms (including PSO, GAs, and DE) use a representation scheme with the same length/dimensionality as the number of features $n$, which forms a huge search space and limits the performance of these algorithms particularly when it is large.

Nguyen et al. [6] proposed a feature cluster based representation which significantly reduces the dimensionality of the search space. The proposed algorithm, named PSOR, [6] achieved better performance than a standard PSO-based algorithm, a PSO-based algorithm published in 2014 [8], and two typical conventional non-EC based feature selection algorithms. However, there is a potential limitation in that representation because the fitness landscape is not smooth (Details in Sect. 2.2). The performance of PSO can be significantly improved if the problem is encoded/represented in a search space with a smooth fitness landscape. This work aims to address this limitation and proposes a new algorithm to further improve the performance of PSO for feature selection.

## 1.1   Goals

The overall goal of this paper is to develop a new PSO algorithm for feature selection to reduce the dimensionality of the data and increase the classification performance. To achieve this goal, Gaussian distribution is introduced to the feature cluster based representation to smooth the fitness landscape, based on which a new PSO-based approach is proposed. The proposed algorithm involves the *feature cluster based representation* and the *Gaussian distribution*. It is examined and compared with two PSO-based algorithms: PSOR [6] that uses the feature cluster based representation without Gaussian distribution, and a PSO-based algorithm named GPSO [5] that uses a Gaussian distribution based updating mechanism but with the conventional representation. Specifically, we seek to show that

- the *feature cluster based representation* can improve feature selection performance by comparing the proposed algorithm with GPSO,
- the *Gaussian distribution* can improve the representation by comparing the proposed algorithm with PSOR, and
- the combination of the feature cluster based representation and the Gaussian distribution can further improve feature selection performance.

## 2   Background

### 2.1   Particle Swarm Optimisation (PSO)

Particle swarm optimisation (PSO) [13] is an EC method inspired by social behaviours, such as bird flocking and fish schooling. When using PSO to solve a problem, the solution is optimised by using a population, swarm, of candidate solutions, which are called particles. Each particle moves in the search space by updating its position as well as velocity. The current position of particle $i$ is represented by a vector $x_i = (x_{i1}, x_{i2}, \ldots, x_{iD})$, where $D$ is the dimensionality of the search space. These positions are updated by using another vector, called velocity $v_i = (v_{i1}, v_{i2}, \ldots, v_{iD})$, where each element is limited by a predefined maximum velocity: $v_{id} \in [-v_{max}, v_{max}]$. During the search process, each particle maintains a record of the position of its best performance as far, called *pbest*. It also records the best solution among the *pbest*s of its neighbours, called *gbest*. At the $t^{th}$ iteration in the search process, the velocity and position of each particle are updated according Eqs. (1) and (2):

$$v_{id}^{t+1} = w * v_{id}^t + c_1 * r_{i1} * (pbest_{id} - x_{id}^t) + c_2 * r_{i2} * (gbest_{id} - x_{id}^t) \quad (1)$$
$$x_{id}^{t+1} = x_{id}^t + v_{id}^{t+1} \quad (2)$$

where $d$ is the $d^{th}$ dimension, $w$ is inertia weight, $c_1$ and $c_2$ are acceleration constants, $r_{i1}$ and $r_{i2}$ are random values uniformly distributed in [0,1].

### 2.2   Representation in PSO for Feature Selection

In PSO for feature selection, each particle represents a subset of features and its position is typically specified by an $n-$dimensional vector, where each dimension corresponds to one feature in the dataset. Each element of the position vector is a real valued number between [0, 1], which represents a confidence level that the corresponding feature is selected. The feature subset is typically constructed by selecting each feature if the confidence level is above a predefined threshold $\theta$. Most EC techniques, such as GAs, DE, and artificial bee colony, use a similar representation. However, such a representation has a potential limitation in that it leads to a very high-dimensional search space when $n$ is large.

Although the representation is an important component in PSO (or EC), there has been little work on developing new representations in PSO for feature selection. One of the major challenges is that it is hard to develop a representation suitable for the updating mechanisms. Only small modifications have been made on the original representation. Some work has added further dimensions to the search space by including the parameters of the classifier in the position vector [9,11,14]. This cannot overcome the limitation of the original representation, but further increases the dimensionality and expands the search space even more.

Nguyen et al. [6] proposed a new feature cluster based representation with the dimensionality much smaller than $n$, where a statistical feature clustering model [3,4] was applied as a pre-processing step to partition the features into $c$ clusters. PSO was then used to select features from each cluster with a limit of at most $\sqrt{n_j}$ features from a cluster $j$ containing $n_j$ features. The size of the clusters were $n_1, n_2, \ldots, n_c$, then the maximum number of selected features was $\sum_{j=1}^{c} \sqrt{n_j}$, which was also the dimensionality of the particle position vectors. This is usually much smaller than $n$. The dimensions of the position vector were partitioned for the clusters so that the dimensions from $\sum_{k=1}^{j-1}(\sqrt{n_k}+1)$ to $\sum_{k=1}^{j}(\sqrt{n_k}+1)$ correspond to cluster $j$. To interpret a particle position vector as a feature subset, each element of the position vector specified a feature from its corresponding cluster. The interval $x_i \in [0,1]$ was segmented to $(n_j + 1)$ subranges, each corresponding to one feature in the $j$ cluster except the last subrange that corresponds to no feature. If a position value $x_{id}$ belongs to one of the first $n_j$ subranges, the corresponding feature will be selected. If $x_{id}$ belongs to the last subrange, no feature is selected from cluster $j$. More details about this representation can be found in [6].

The representation in [6] can successfully reduce the dimensionality of the search space and improve the performance, but has a limitation that it forms a unsmooth fitness landscape, which significantly influences the performance of PSO. In particular, as a position element changes within a subrange, there is no difference to the feature subset, but there will be sudden change to chose a different feature when the element crosses the boundary of the subrange. Suppose a feature $f$ corresponds to the range [0.4, 0.6]. For three position values, $p_1 = 0.42$, $p_2 = 0.58$ and $p_3 = 0.62$, $p_1$ and $p_2$ will select feature $f$ and $p_3$ will not. However, $p_3$ is closer to $p_2$ than $p_1$. This means during the search process of PSO, a relatively big change from $p_1$ to $p_2$ on a particle's position will not result in any change in its fitness value, but a relatively small change from $p_2$ to $p_3$ will suddenly change the fitness value. In other words, using the transformation rule, the fitness landscape of the feature selection problem is not smooth. Given that the proposed feature cluster based representation has achieved significantly better performance than PSO using the conventional representation [6], addressing this limitation is highly likely to further improve the performance.

# 3   Proposed Algorithm: GPSOR

This section proposes a new transformation rule for interpreting a position vector as a feature subset to address the limitation in the cluster based representation of PSOR. The new representation is expected to add more meaning to the movement of particles during the search process and form a smoother fitness landscape. In this work, the same statistical feature clustering model [3,4] is applied as a pre-processing step to partition features into different clusters.

The length of the representation in this paper is the same as in [6], which is $\sum_{j=1}^{c} \sqrt{n_j}$. The $n_j$ features in cluster $j$ are represented by $\sqrt{n_j}$ dimensions in the position vector. Each element of the vector specifies one of the features in the corresponding cluster to be included in the solution. The key difference is that the value of a position vector element is used to specify a feature in a probabilistic manner, using a Gaussian distribution to obtain a smoother search space. The interval $[0, 1]$ is also divided into $(n_j + 1)$ subrange and the length of each subrange is $s = 1/(n_j + 1)$. The first $n_j$ subranges correspond to the $n_j$ features in cluster $j$ and the last subrange corresponds to no feature being selected (in case all features in the cluster are irrelevant). A position value still has a corresponding feature depending on which subrange it belongs to. The difference here from [6] relies on developing a new transformation rule, which is a key factor in the representation to smooth the fitness landscape. To achieve this, Gaussian distribution (i.e. normal distribution, Eq. 3) is introduced here to interpret position values. Instead of directly determining which feature is selected, a position value is used to calculate the probabilities of features being selected through the Gaussian distribution.

$$f(x, \mu, \sigma) = \frac{1}{\sigma\sqrt{2\pi}} e^{-(x-\mu)^2/2\sigma^2} \tag{3}$$

## 3.1   Constructing Gaussian Transformation Rule

The PSOR algorithm interprets a value in the position vector of a particle as a feature to be included in the feature subset. Which feature to be included is determined by identifying which subrange of $[0,1]$ the position value lies in. The limitation of the PSOR algorithm is that small changes in a position value have no effect on the feature subset (and therefore the fitness value) until the value crosses the boundary of the subrange into the subrange corresponding to the next feature, at which point there is a sudden (non-smooth) change in the feature subset and the fitness value. GPSOR addresses this limitation by using the same representation as PSOR, but adding a small amount of Gaussian noise to each value in the position vector before identifying which subrange it is in, and therefore the feature it is specifying. This Gaussian noise means that as a value in the position vector approaches the boundary of a subrange, it has an increasing probability of specifying a neighbouring feature. The effect is to smooth the search space and provide an early indication of when the particle is moving towards a better (or worse) position in the search space.

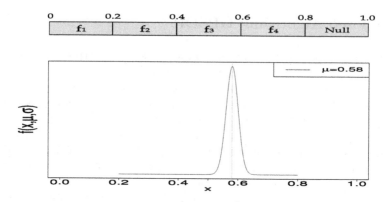

Fig. 1. Effect of applying the Gaussian distribution

The Gaussian noise for a value $x_{id}$ is currently generated from a Gaussian distribution with a standard deviation fixed at 1% of the width of subranges (i.e., $\frac{\sigma_d=1}{100*(1+\sqrt{(n_j)})}$, where $n_j$ is the size of the feature cluster corresponding to dimension $d$ ). This ensures that if a position vector $x_{id}$ is in the center of a subrange, the probability of selecting the feature corresponding to that subrange is about 99%, but as $x_{id}$ gets close to the boundary of the subrange, the probability decreases smoothly to around 50%. Figure 1 illustrates the distribution of $x_{id} = 0.58$ with the Gaussian noise for a feature cluster containing 4 features.

## 3.2 Selection of Features

The introduction of Gaussian distribution makes the position value and the move of particles more meaningful than directly using the position value to select a feature. This section discusses the details of how to use the Gaussian transformation rule to translate position values to features. For a position value corresponds to cluster $j$ with $n_j$ features, the selection of features from cluster $j$ is determined according to following three steps:

- build a Gaussian distribution function, $f(x, \mu, \sigma)$, using the position value as $\mu$ and $0.01 * s$, where $s = 1/(n_j + 1)$, as $\sigma$;
- use the inverse transform sampling method to generate a random number $r \in (0, 1)$ according to $f(x, \mu, \sigma)$;
- $r$ is used to determine which feature is selected from a certain cluster. A feature is selected if $r$ falls into its corresponding sub-interval.

Based on the built Gaussian distribution, the random number $r$ is likely to fall into the same sub-interval with the original position value, but has a chance with different probabilities to fall into other sub-intervals to select other features. For three position values, $p_1 = 0.5$, $p_2 = 0.58$ and $p_3 = 0.62$, their corresponding features are $f_3$, $f_3$ and $f_4$, respectively. If using the transformation rule in [6], $p_1$ and $p_2$ will select $f_3$, and $p_3$ will select $f_4$. This means a big move in the position from $p_1$ to $p_2$ does not change the solution, but a small move from $p_2$

to $p_3$ changes the solution. By using the proposed transformation rule, $p_1$ will be mostly likely to generate a random number to select $f_3$. $p_2$ will have a much lower probability than $p_1$ to select $f_3$, but $p_2$ has a similar probability to $p_3$ to select $f_3$ (or $f_4$). This means that solutions are gradually changed according to the position value, which makes the move of particles more meaningful and is expected to achieve better performance.

---

**Algorithm 1.** Pseudo-code of GPSOR

---

1: **begin**
2: randomly initialise the position and velocity of each particle;
3: initialise a feature subset $BFS$ with the empty feature set;
4: **while** $Maximum\ iteration$ is not reached **do**
5:     **for** each particle in the swarm **do**
6:         decode the position to a feature subset using the Gaussian distribution;
7:         evaluate the fitness based on the selected features;
8:         replace $BFS$ with the feature subset decoded from $gbest$ if it is better;
9:     **end for**
10:     update $pbest$ and $gbest$ of each particle;
11:     **for** $i = 1$ to $Population\ size$ **do**
12:         update $v_i$ of particle $i$ according to Eq. 1;
13:         update $x_i$ of particle $i$ according to Eq. 2;
14:     **end for**
15: **end while**
16: calculate the training and testing classification accuracy using $BFS$
17: return $BFS$, the training and testing classification accuracies;
18: **end**

---

### 3.3 Pseudo-code of the Algorithm

Based on the proposed Gaussian based transformation rule, a PSO-based feature selection algorithm named GPSOR is proposed here. The pseudo-code of GPSOR is shown in Algorithm 1. The fitness function of GPSOR is to minimise the classification error rate of the classifier built using the selected features, which is calculated by the Eq. (4).

$$Fitness = \frac{fp + fn}{tp + tn + fp + fn} \tag{4}$$

where tp, tn, fp, and fn denote true positives, true negatives, false positives, and false negatives, respectively.

## 4 Experimental Design

The proposed algorithm (GPSOR) is examined and compared with two PSO approaches, PSOR [6] using the cluster based representation without using Gaussian distribution, and GPSO [5] using the traditional representation and Gaussian distribution, where Gaussian distribution was used to determine how

**Table 1.** Datasets

| Dataset | #features | #clusters | #classes | #instances |
|---|---|---|---|---|
| Wine | 13 | 6 | 3 | 178 |
| Vehicle | 18 | 6 | 4 | 846 |
| Ionosphere | 34 | 11 | 2 | 351 |
| Sonar | 60 | 12 | 2 | 208 |
| Musk1 | 166 | 14 | 2 | 476 |
| Arrhythmia | 279 | 15 | 16 | 452 |
| Madelon | 500 | 11 | 2 | 4400 |
| Multiple Features | 649 | 15 | 10 | 2000 |

many features to be selected from a feature cluster. All the three methods use the statistical clustering model [3,4] as a pre-processing step to partition features into different clusters. The statistical model is not described here since it is not the focus of this paper and details can be seen from [3,4]. Since PSOR [6] has shown to be superior to two recent PSO algorithms without using statistical clustering and two conventional methods, GPSOR is also better than them if GPSOR can achieve better performance than PSOR. Therefore, the results of these algorithms are not listed here due to page limit.

Eight datasets (Table 1) chosen from the UCI machine learning repository [15] are used in the experiments. These datasets have different numbers of features, classes and instances. For each dataset, all instances are randomly divided into a training set and a test set, which contains 70 % and 30 % of the instances, respectively. In the experiments, the classification/learning algorithm is K-nearest neighbour (KNN) where K = 5. The parameters of PSO are set as follows [16]: $w = 0.7298, c_1 = c_2 = 1.49618, v_{max} = 6.0$, population size is 30, the maximum number of iterations is 100. The fully connected topology is used. All the three algorithms have been run for 30 independent times on each dataset. A statistical significance test, Wilcoxon test with significance level as 0.05, is performed to compare between the classification accuracies of different algorithms.

## 5  Experimental Results

Table 2 shows the experimental results, where "All" means that all the available features are used for classification. "Ave-size" shows the average number of selected features over the 30 runs. "Ave" and "Std" illustrate the average and standard deviation of the training or testing accuracies over the 30 independent runs. "Test" shows the results of the statistical significance tests between the accuracy of GPSOR and other algorithms. "+" or "−" means that the compared algorithm is significantly better or worse than GPSOR. "=" means there is no significant difference.

**Table 2.** Experimental results

| Dataset | Method | Ave-Size | Test set Ave±Std | Test | Training set Ave±Std | Test |
|---|---|---|---|---|---|---|
| Wine | All | 13 | 76.54 | - | 87.63 | - |
|  | GPSO | 5.4 | 96.59 ± 2.76 | - | 96.71 ± 7.77E-14 | - |
|  | PSOR | 4.75 | 96.70 ± 3.1 | - | 95.05 ± 0.58 | - |
|  | GPSOR | 4.60 | 97.70 ± 2.52 |  | 97.37 ± 0.42 |  |
| Vehicle | All | 18 | 83.86 | - | 88.17 | - |
|  | GPSO | 8.94 | 84.30 ± 0.62 | - | 86.11 ± 0.2 | - |
|  | PSOR | 5.87 | 84.72 ± 0.87 | = | 84.61 ± 0.56 | - |
|  | GPSOR | 7.30 | 84.74 ± 0.49 |  | 90.10 ± 0.4 |  |
| Ionosphere | All | 34 | 83.81 | - | 85.77 | - |
|  | GPSO | 7.66 | 89.5 ± 1.68 | + | 91.59 ± 0.47 | - |
|  | PSOR | 9.7 | 88.63 ± 1.68 | + | 90.04 ± 0.99 | - |
|  | GPSOR | 3.17 | 86.89 ± 1.8 |  | 93.90 ± 0.67 |  |
| Sonar | All | 60 | 76.19 | - | 83.44 | - |
|  | GPSO | 17.64 | 78.19 ± 4.14 | = | 86.74 ± 0.94 | - |
|  | PSOR | 14.33 | 78.94 ± 4.02 | = | 87.01 ± 2 | - |
|  | GPSOR | 10.17 | 78.25 ± 2.96 |  | 90.67 ± 1.6 |  |
| Musk1 | All | 166 | 83.92 | - | 92.19 | - |
|  | GPSO | 39.64 | 84.95 ± 2.73 | + | 90.02 ± 0.6 | - |
|  | PSOR | 35.03 | 83.12 ± 3.41 | = | 89.78 ± 1.25 | - |
|  | GPSOR | 38.93 | 83.29 ± 2.48 |  | 93.22 ± 1.37 |  |
| Arrhythmia | All | 279 | 94.46 | - | 94.79 | - |
|  | GPSO | 45.5 | 94.85 ± 0.34 | - | 94.87 ± 0.09 | - |
|  | PSOR | 44.17 | 94.96 ± 0.38 | - | 95.11 ± 0.2 | - |
|  | GPSOR | 42.03 | 95.12 ± 0.34 |  | 95.75 ± 0.18 |  |
| Madelon | All | 500 | 70.9 | - | 83.24 | - |
|  | GPSO | 36.08 | 85.68 ± 1.1 | + | 85.45 ± 0.73 | - |
|  | PSOR | 54.39 | 83.40 ± 2 | - | 83.73 ± 1.74 | - |
|  | GPSOR | 51.17 | 84.06 ± 1.65 |  | 89.20 ± 1.41 |  |
| Multiple Features | All | 649 | 98.63 | - | 99.35 | = |
|  | GPSO | 91.4 | 99.01 ± 0.13 | = | 99.38 ± 0.38 | = |
|  | PSOR | 51.07 | 98.84 ± 0.18 | = | 99.17 ± 0.09 | - |
|  | GPSOR | 51 | 98.86 ± 0.17 |  | 99.36 ± 0.07 |  |

## 5.1 Effectiveness of the GPSOR Search

To evaluate the effectiveness of the new representation in searching for an optimal fitness value, we need to look at the performance of GPSOR on the training set.

All the three PSO-based algorithms aim to minimise the training classification error rate (i.e. maximise the training accuracy). From Table 2, it can be observed that GPSOR achieved significantly better training performance than using all features, GPSO, and PSOR in almost all cases. Only on the Multiple Features dataset, there is no significant difference between the training accuracy of using all features, GPSO and GPSOR. The reason is that the training accuracy is already very high when using the original feature set, i.e. 99.35 %, which is hard to make significant improvement. The training results in Table 2 show that GPSOR using the representation with a lower dimensionality and the Gaussian distribution based transformation rule can better represent the problem and facilitate the search to significantly improve the performance of PSO for feature selection.

## 5.2   Comparison with PSO-Based Algorithms on the Test Set

According to Table 2, the number of features selected by GPSOR is much smaller than the total number of features, but using the selected features only, the KNN classification algorithm achieved significantly better classification accuracy than using all features in all cases. For example, on the Madelon dataset, GPSOR selected on average 51 features from the original 500 features, but achieved a significant increase in the classification accuracy of 13 %. The results suggest that the proposed GPSOR algorithm using Gaussian transformation rule based representation can successfully explore the search space to remove redundant and irrelevant features and increase the classification accuracy.

Comparing GPSOR with GPSO both of which used the statistical clustering information and Gaussian distribution, it can be observed that GPSOR selected fewer features than GPSO on seven out of the eight datasets, where the only exception is the Madelon dataset. GPSOR achieved significantly higher or similar classification accuracy than GPSO on five of the eight datasets. On the Ionosphere, Musk1 and Madelon datasets, GPSOR selected a smaller number of features than GPSO on the Ionosphere and Musk1 datasets, where GPSO achieved higher accuracy than GPSOR. On the Madelon dataset, GPSO outperformed GPSOR in terms of both the number of features and the test accuracy, but according the performance on the training set, an overfitting problem may happen since GPSOR achieved much better training classification accuracy than GPSO. On the Multiple Features datasets, since the accuracy of using all features is very high, both GPSO and GPSOR could not significantly increase the training performance. However, since GPSOR removed redundant and irrelevant features, the selected small features subsets have better generalisation on the unseen test set than the original large feature set and significantly improved the test accuracy. The results suggest that GPSOR using the representation with a lower dimensionality can make the problem to be better addressed by PSO to achieve higher classification performance. Meanwhile, the representation in GPSOR limits the maximum number of features selected from each cluster, which successfully helped it reduce the chance of selecting a large feature subset.

Comparing GPSOR with PSOR both of which using the statistical clustering information and the cluster based representation, GPSOR selected a smaller number of features than PSOR on six of the eight datasets, and achieved similar or significantly higher classification accuracy on seven of the eight datasets. The only excepted dataset where PSOR achieved better classification performance than GPSOR is the Ionosphere dataset, but the number of features selected by GPSOR is about three times smaller than that of PSOR. The results suggest that in most cases, by introducing Gaussian distribution to the representation to transform a position vector to a feature subset, GPSOR can further improve the performance in terms of the both the classification performance and the number of features.

### 5.3   Further Discussions

Figure 2 takes the Wine dataset as an example showing the features selected by PSOR and GPSOR in the 30 independent runs. The horizontal axis shows the index of the 13 features and the vertical axis shows the number of runs (numbers above the bars) that a feature is selected by PSOR or GPSOR in the 30 independent runs.

According to Fig. 2, the features selected by PSOR from the highest to the lowest frequency are Features 10, 7, 1, 3, 2, 6, 12, 11, 8, 4, 9, 5, and 13, while the order is Features 1, 10, 7, 6, 9, 12, 2, 4, 3, 11, 8, 5, and 13 for GPSOR. It can be observed that Features 10, 7 and 1 are important features since they were frequently selected by both PSOR and GPSOR. In contrast, Features 5 and 13 are most likely useless since they were not selected by the two algorithms at all. To further confirm this, a further comparison with an existing paper [17], where the importance of individual features in the Wine dataset were discussed through a single feature ranking method (not a PSO-based method). It shows that from the most important to the least important, the ranking is Features 7, 10, 12, 1, 9, 11, 6, 2, 13, 5, 4, 3, and 8. Therefore, it further suggests that both PSOR and GPSOR can select the important features (e.g. Features 7 and 10) to reduce the dimensionality of the dataset and improve the classification performance.

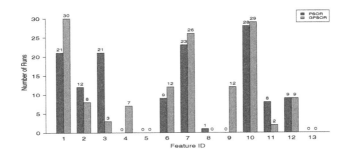

**Fig. 2.** NO. of runs that each feature was selected by PSOR and GPSOR.

According to Table 2, the average number of features selected by PSOR and GPSOR in the 30 runs are almost the same, which are 4.75 and 4.60. However, as can be seen from Fig. 2, the important features, Features 10, 7 and 1, were more frequently selected by GPSOR than by PSOR. This means that PSOR has a higher probability of selecting less important features than GPSOR in some runs. It also shows that the similarity (or consistency) between the 30 feature subsets selected by GPSOR in the 30 runs is higher than that of PSOR, which suggests GPSOR is more stable than PSOR. The high stability of GPSOR over PSOR was also reflected in Table 2 by the smaller standard deviation values. High stability is very important for a feature selection algorithm, which is key for users to identify and choose important features. The superior stability of GPSOR is mainly contributed by the introduction of the Gaussian distribution, which gives immediate and effective feedback to small movements of particles during the search process. In contrast, in PSOR, if a movement is not big enough to jump from one sub-interval to another, the fitness value of the particle will not change. Small movements toward a promising region in the search space might not be encouraged in PSOR. This limits the search ability and it is easy to be stuck into different local optima, which leads to more various feature subsets (i.e. lower stability) produced by PSOR than GPSOR.

# 6    Conclusions and Future Work

The goal of this paper was to develop a new PSO-based approach to feature selection with the expectation of reducing the number of features and increasing the classification performance. The goal has been successfully achieved by proposing a Gaussian distribution based transformation rule to interpret position vectors as feature subsets in a feature cluster based representation scheme, which smooths the fitness landscape and makes the movement of the particles more meaningful. The proposed algorithm, GPSOR, was compared with two recently developed algorithms, PSOR and GPSO, on commonly used classification tasks of varying difficulty. The experimental results show that the proposed algorithm was able to achieve better performance than these two algorithms in terms of the number of features and the classification performance. Further analyses showed that GPSOR using the Gaussian based transformation rule also increased the stability, i.e. selecting features more consistent than PSOR through different runs.

In many areas, such as gene analyses, the number of features often reaches to thousands or tens of thousands, which are referred to large scale problems. Feature selection is more important and more challenging than with hundreds of features. A novel representation to reduce the dimensionality is essential. Therefore, we intend to develop novel EC-based approaches to solving such large-scale feature selection problems by investigating novel representation schemes and search mechanisms in the future.

# References

1. Guyon, I., Elisseeff, A.: An introduction to variable and feature selection. J. Mach. Learn. Res. **3**, 1157–1182 (2003)
2. Liu, H., Motoda, H., Setiono, R., Zhao, Z.: Feature selection: an ever evolving frontier in data mining. In: FSDM. JMLR Proceedings, vol. 10, pp. 4–13 (2010)
3. Matechou, E., Liu, I., Pledger, S., Arnold, R.: Biclustering models for ordinal data. Presentation at the NZ Statistical Assn. Annual Conference, University of Auckland (2011)
4. Pledger, S., Arnold, R.. Multivariate methods using mixtures: correspondence analysis, scaling and pattern-detection. Comput. Stat. Data Anal. **71**, 241–261 (2014)
5. Lane, M.C., Xue, B., Liu, I., Zhang, M.: Gaussian based particle swarm optimisation and statistical clustering for feature selection. In: Blum, C., Ochoa, G. (eds.) EvoCOP 2014. LNCS, vol. 8600, pp. 133–144. Springer, Heidelberg (2014)
6. Nguyen, H.B., Xue, B., Liu, I., Zhang, M.: PSO and statistical clustering for feature selection: a new representation. In: Dick, G., et al. (eds.) SEAL 2014. LNCS, vol. 8886, pp. 569–581. Springer, Heidelberg (2014)
7. Zhu, Z., Ong, Y.S., Dash, M.: Markov blanket-embedded genetic algorithm for gene selection. Pattern Recogn. **40**(11), 3236–3248 (2007)
8. Xue, B., Zhang, M., Browne, W.N.: Novel initialisation and updating mechanisms in PSO for feature selection in classification. In: Esparcia-Alcázar, A.I. (ed.) EvoApplications 2013. LNCS, vol. 7835, pp. 428–438. Springer, Heidelberg (2013)
9. Boubezoul, A., Paris, S.: Application of global optimization methods to model and feature selection. Pattern Recogn. **45**(10), 3676–3686 (2012)
10. Xue, B., Zhang, M., Browne, W.N.: Particle swarm optimization for feature selection in classification: a multi-objective approach. IEEE Trans. Cybern. **43**(6), 1656–1671 (2013)
11. Vieira, S.M., Mendonça, L.F., Farinha, G.J., Sousa, J.M.: Modified binary PSO for feature selection using SVM applied to mortality prediction of septic patients. Appl. Soft Comput. **13**(5), 3494–3504 (2013)
12. Xue, B., Fu, W., Zhang, M.: Multi-objective feature selection in classification: a differential evolution approach. In: Dick, G., et al. (eds.) SEAL 2014. LNCS, vol. 8886, pp. 516–528. Springer, Heidelberg (2014)
13. Kennedy, J., Eberhart, R.: Particle swarm optimization. In: IEEE International Conference on Neural Networks, vol. 4, pp. 1942–1948 (1995)
14. Lin, S.W., Ying, K.C., Chen, S.C., Lee, Z.J.: Particle swarm optimization for parameter determination and feature selection of support vector machines. Expert Syst. Appl. **35**(4), 1817–1824 (2008)
15. Bache, K., Lichman, M.: Uci machine learning repository (2013)
16. Clerc, M., Kennedy, J.: The particle swarm- explosion, stability, and convergence in a multidimensional complex space. IEEE Trans. Evol. Comput. **6**(1), 58–73 (2002)
17. Xue, B., Zhang, M., Browne, W.N.: Single feature ranking and binary PSO based feature subset ranking for feature selection. In: Australasian Computer Science Conference (ACSC 2012), vol. 122, pp. 27–36 (2012)

# Genetic Programming with Alternative Search Drivers for Detection of Retinal Blood Vessels

Krzysztof Krawiec[1][✉] and Mikołaj Pawlak[2]

[1] Poznan University of Technology, Poznań, Poland
krawiec@cs.put.poznan.pl
[2] Poznan University of Medical Sciences, Poznań, Poland
mpawlak@ump.edu.pl

**Abstract.** A classification task is a test-based problem, with examples corresponding to tests. A correct classification is equivalent to passing a test, while incorrect to failing it. This applies also to classifying pixels in an image, viz. image segmentation. A natural performance indicator in such a setting is the accuracy of classification, i.e., the fraction of passed tests. When solving a classification tasks with genetic programming, it is thus common to employ this indicator as a fitness function. However, recent developments in GP as well as some earlier work suggest that the quality of evolved solutions may benefit from using other search drivers to guide the traversal of the space of programs. In this study, we systematically verify the usefulness of selected alternative search drivers in the problem of detection of blood vessels in ophthalmology imaging.

**Keywords:** Genetic programming · Search drivers · Binary classification · Image segmentation

## 1 Introduction

Genetic programming (GP) is a branch of evolutionary computation (EC) devoted to synthesis of programs and other executable structures. Programs are discrete, variable-length structures, and as such require specialized search operators. In this perspective, program synthesis tasks approached in GP are considered as a specific subclass of optimization problems.

There are however other aspects that make GP quite unique, one of them being the class of objective functions employed therein. Typically, they assess programs by running them on a set of *tests* (fitness cases). A test is a pair composed of program input and the corresponding desired output. If a program provided with the input returns an output that is close enough to the desired output, it is said to *pass* the test; otherwise, it *fails* it. The objective function aggregates the outcomes of program's application to particular tests, usually treating every test in the same way. For discrete domains, this may boil to simply counting the number of passed tests. For continuous outputs, the errors committed on particular tests are aggregated via mean square error or mean

© Springer International Publishing Switzerland 2015
A.M. Mora and G. Squillero (Eds.): EvoApplications 2015, LNCS 9028, pp. 554–566, 2015.
DOI: 10.1007/978-3-319-16549-3_45

absolute deviation, which corresponds to measuring the Euclidean or city-block distance between the vector of actual outputs and the vector of desired outputs.

This conventional formulation leads to a scalar objective function and so causes the program synthesis problem subscribe to the classical optimization paradigm, which is often considered as an asset. We argue however that there is also certain price to pay. The search algorithm has no access to program's performance on particular tests: it knows only its aggregated characteristics, averaged over the entire training set of tests. In effect, the outcomes of particular tests may compensate, so that two programs with completely different capabilities may receive the same fitness. Because in most of real-world problems some tests are easier than others, this entices evolution to focus on passing the easier tests, while neglecting the more difficult. Such overfocusing on a subset of tests is likely to lead to premature convergence. Also, postponing learning how to solve the harder tests may not be the best strategy for finding an optimal solution.

The risks incurred by relying on conventional scalar evaluation measures apply also to evolutionary image analysis. The problems solved in this domain are by definition test-based, with tests corresponding to entire images (image classification), objects in scenes (object recognition), and even single pixels (segmentation). By often engaging large numbers of information-rich tests, they particularly call for better ways of exploiting the outcomes of interactions between the evolving programs and tests.

Several approaches have been proposed in the past to address this issue. Typically, they boil down to replacing the conventional fitness with an alternative *search driver*. The objective of this study is to systematically assess the usefulness of selected search drivers on the real-world image analysis task, and so possibly arrive at certain recommendations concerning 'good practices' in this domain. More specifically, after shortly presenting the background in Sect. 2, we apply the methods reviewed in Sect. 3 to the task of segmentation of ophthalmological imagery (Sect. 4). In the experiment conducted in Sect. 5, we combine each alternative search driver with discrete and continuous feature definitions, and assess the generalization performance. Apart from this systematic analysis, the original contribution of this work is a new variant of implicit fitness sharing [1], capable of handling continuous program outputs.

## 2    Background

One of the most common applications of genetic programming in image analysis is image segmentation. In this study, we are interested in delineating a single type of anatomical structure in an image (blood vessels), viz. separating such structures from the background. In other words, the objective is to *segment out* a single category of objects (pixels in this case). Therefore, we will pose this task as follows: given an image, classify every pixel in that image to one of the two decision classes: positive or negative.

It is assumed that the decision on pixel's class can be made based on its neighborhood. A GP classifier will thus have access on an $m \times m$ square window (region of interest, ROI) for defining image features. By sliding a ROI over the entire image and applying a GP system to it, all pixels in an image can be classified.

The data gathered from different positions of the sliding window in a training image naturally forms a GP task. Each ROI position in a training image gives rise to a single test (fitness case). More formally, each test is a pair $(\mathbf{x}, y)$, where $\mathbf{x}$ is a vector of elementary features extracted from the ROI, and $y$ is the desired outcome of applying a GP classifier to $\mathbf{x}$. An interaction between a GP program and a test $(\mathbf{x}, y)$ boils down to feeding $\mathbf{x}$ into the program, running the program, and comparing its output $\hat{y}$ with the desired output $y$.

An important characteristics of applying GP to binary image segmentation in the above manner is that GP programs are supposed to operate as classifiers. Because the desired output $y$ may take on only two values, it may be tempting to pose this task in the Boolean domain. However, program input, by being gathered from a raster image, is by nature composed of continuous image features. To fully exploit the data available therein, it may be more appropriate to rely on instructions that operate in the continuous domain. In other words, posing this problem as a regression task is more natural given the nature of the input data.

The tension between the input characteristics that votes in favor of posing this problem as a regression task, and the desired output being a binary variable is the central topic of the study. It is not obvious what is the 'right' way of assessing the discrepancy between the desired output $y$ and the actual output $\hat{y}$, i.e., what is the right *search driver* to guide the GP search process.

## 3   The Methods

In this section, we review the search drivers used in the subsequent experiment and propose a novel variant of one of them. We limit our attention exclusively to scalar search drivers.

Let $y_i$ denote the desired output for the $i$th test, and $\hat{y}_i$ denote the actual program output. When approaching regression tasks, $y_i$'s can be arbitrary real values. In this study however, we are solving binary *classification* tasks, and we assume that $y_i \in \{-1, 1\}$, with $-1$ denoting the negative decision class and 1 corresponding to the positive class. Regardless of that, we will equip our GP systems with an instruction set typically used for regression, and interpret the continuous output of a GP tree as an indication of decision class. The interpretation of program output, i.e., how its divergence from the desired output impacts program's fitness, will vary depending on search driver. For clarity, we define all search drivers as measures that are to be minimized.

**L1.** Our first search driver is the total absolute error of $\hat{y}$ with respect to $y$:

$$f_{L1} = \sum_i |\hat{y}_i - y_i|.$$

Many selection methods common in GP, like tournament selection, interpret fitness as an ordinal (non-metric) variable, and are thus insensitive to the absolute values. Under this assumption, L1 is equivalent to the mean absolute deviation (MAD) and city-block distance.

**L2.** Analogously to L1, we define $f_{L2}$, which is the total *square* error of $\hat{y}$ with respect to $y$, i.e.,

$$f_{L2} = \sum_i (\hat{y}_i - y_i)^2.$$

Similarly to $f_{L1}$, $f_{L2}$ is equivalent, up to ordering, to the Euclidean distance and means square error (MSE).

L1 and L2 are designed for continuous spaces and as such penalize for *any* divergence from the desired values. Because we are interested here in solving binary classification tasks, and $-1$ and $1$ are the only desired output values possible, these search drivers seem overly restrictive. Intuitively, one should allow a program express its decision in a more general way, for instance by the sign of the output value. This observation leads to the next search driver.

**Hamming distance.** The next search driver counts the number of tests for which program output has the same sign as the desired value, i.e.,

$$f_H = \sum_i \begin{cases} 1 & if\ y_i \hat{y}_i > 0 \\ 0 & otherwise \end{cases}.$$

This search driver is equivalent to the Hamming distance between the vector of desired outputs and the binarized vector of program outputs. It is also equivalent to classification error (meant as the complement of classification accuracy used in machine learning).

Hamming distance is clearly less restrictive than L1 and L2 in expecting only the sign of program output to agree with the desired output. However, it assumes that the threshold between the negative and positive indications is zero, which, again, may seem quite arbitrary. An evolutionary process can hypothetically produce a program that perfectly classifies all training examples, but only when its output is thresholded on a different level. The subsequent search driver addresses this issue.

**Pearson correlation.** Another plausible search driver is the Pearson linear correlation coefficient of the vectors of actual and desired outputs:

$$f_P = 1 - \frac{cov(y, \hat{y})}{\sigma_y \sigma_{\hat{y}}}.$$

Compared to Hamming distance, $f_P$ is advantageous in not requiring the evaluated program to produce positive values for the positive class and vice versa. For that instance, a program that returns 3 for all the negative examples and 7 for all the positive ones will be (rightfully) considered as perfect by this measure ($f_P = 0$) In this sense, this search driver is adaptive.

On the other hand, the correlation coefficient is, similarly to L1 and L2, sensitive to any intra-class variance in the observed program outputs $\hat{y}_i$. For instance, a program that returns, as in the above example, the output value 3 for all negative examples, but 7 *or* 11 for the positive ones, will receive inferior fitness. This is unfortunate, as this program's predictive capability is supreme: it is enough to threshold its output at, say, 5, to arrive at perfect decision rule. Ideally, we would like to have a search driver that is both liberal about the location of the boundary between the negative and positive output indications, and on the other hand interprets program output as an ordinal, rather than metric, variable. The subsequent search driver fulfills these expectations.

**Area Under ROC curve (AUC).** AUC is the total area under the Receiver Operating Characteristics (ROC) curve, the parametric curve spanning the false positive (FP) rate and the true positive (TP) rate. In our case, the parameter that controls the traversal of ROC curve is simply the threshold $\tau$ imposed on program output: if $\hat{y}_i < \tau$, the example is classified as negative, otherwise it is assigned to the positive class. AUC summarizes the behavior of this decision rule of all values of $\tau$. By definition, AUC $\in [0, 1]$.

AUC is a natural way to characterize the trade-off between the FP rate and the TP rate. It can be cheaply calculated using the Mann-Whitney $U$ test:

$$f_{AUC} = \frac{n^- n^+ + n^- (n^- + 1)/2 - r}{n^- n^+},$$

where $n^-$ and $n^+$ are the sizes of the negative and the positive class, respectively, and $r$ is the sum of ranks of sorted program outputs for the positive examples, i.e., $\hat{y}_i$s. AUC thus does not impose any specific threshold on program output (like $f_H$), and also does not assume the outputs to linearly correlate with the desired outputs (like $f_P$). What matters is only the *ordering* of the outputs produced by a program.

All the search drivers reviewed so far share one common characteristics: they consider all tests equally important. In practice however, some tests are often more difficult than others. This is particularly evident in image segmentation and diagnostic problems like the one considered here, where for instance some pixels evidently belong to the background. The following search driver takes this aspect into account.

**Implicit fitness sharing.** The last search driver considered in this study is implicit fitness sharing (IFS), introduced by Smith *et al.* [2] and further explored for genetic programming by McKay [1,3]. IFS lets evolution assess the difficulty of particular tests and *weighs* the rewards granted for solving them. Given a set of tests $T$, the IFS fitness of a program $p$ in the context of a population $P$ is defined as:

$$f_{IFS}(p) = \sum_{t \in T(p)} \frac{1}{|P(t)|}, \tag{1}$$

where $T(p)$ is the subset of tests (pairs $(\mathbf{x}, y)$) solved by $p$, and $P(t)$ is the subset of programs in $P$ that solve test $t$. Thus, the $\frac{1}{|P(t)|}$ term serves here as an indicator of $t$'s difficulty. Note that the denominator in the above formula never zeroes, because if $p$ solves a given $t$, then $P(t)$ contains $p$.

IFS treats tests as limited resources: programs *share* the rewards for solving them, where a reward can vary from $\frac{1}{|P|}$ to 1 inclusive (the latter being the case when a program is the the only one in population that solves a test). Higher rewards are granted for solving tests that are rarely solved by population members (small $P(t)$), while importance of tests that are easy (large $P(t)$) is diminished. The assessed difficulties of tests change as $P$ evolves, which can help escaping local minima.

By assessing programs in the context of the current population, fitness sharing can be perceived as a simple form of coevolution, where individuals compete for tests and their fate depends on the performance of other individuals (though there are no direct, face-to-face interactions between them). From yet another perspective, fitness sharing is a diversity maintenance technique: an individual that solves a low number of tests can still survive if its competence is rare. In this way, IFS helps reducing crowding and premature convergence; it shares this characteristics with explicit fitness sharing proposed in [4], where population diversity is enforced by monitoring the distances between individuals.

IFS requires defining what does it mean that a program passes a test. The repertoire of search drivers presented above clearly demonstrates that there are may ways in which this can be done when a continuously-valued program has to be interpreted as a binary classifier.

We propose the following procedure to determine which tests in a given training set $T$ have been passed by which programs in the current population $P$. Assume there are $n$ tests in $T$, and let $T^- \subset T$ denote the negative examples in $T$, and let $T^+ \subset T$ denote the positive examples in $T$. Let $n^- = |T^-|$ and $n^+ = |T^+|$.

**1.** For every program $p \in P$:

**1.1.** Sort the outputs $\hat{y}_i$ produced by $p$ for tests $t_i \in T$ in an ascending order.
**1.2.** Let $T_p^- \subset T$ denote the subset of tests corresponding to the first $n^-$ elements of the sorted list, and let $T_p^+ \subset T$ the be the subset of the remaining $n^+$ tests. Define the subset of tests $T(p)$ solved by $p$ as

$$T(p) = T^- \cap T_p^- \ \cup \ T^+ \cap T_p^+ \tag{2}$$

**2.** For every test $t$, define the set of programs that pass $t$ as

$$P(t) = \{p \in P : t \in T(p)\}. \tag{3}$$

**3.** Use $T(p)$'s and $P(t)$'s to evaluate the individuals in $P$ according to Eq. (1).

Let us explain the rationale behind this algorithm. We assume that a perfect program would for all $n^-$ negative examples produce smaller output values than for any of the $n^+$ positive examples. By sorting the program outputs in step 1.1 and partitioning them into the subset of first $n^-$ elements and the remaining $n^+$ elements, we assess how close the program is to such behavior. The more negative examples end up in the former subset and the more positive examples in the latter, the better program's performance (cf. Eq. 2). On the other hand, how many programs fail a test in this sense is a natural measure of its difficulty (Eq. 3). Redefining $T(p)$ and $P(t)$ in this way allows us to retain the original formula of IFS (Eq. 1).

Similarly to AUC, by referring only to the ordering of outputs, the above algorithm will adapt to any boundary between the decision classes that a program comes up with.

Apart from IFS, other methods have been proposed that reward solutions for having rare characteristics. An example is co-solvability [5] that focuses on individual's ability to properly handle *pairs* of fitness cases, and as such can be considered a 'second-order' IFS. Such pairs are treated as elementary competences (skills) for which solutions can be awarded. Lasarczyk *et al.* [6] proposed a method for selection of fitness cases based on a concept similar to co-solvability. The method maintains a weighted graph that spans fitness cases, where the weight of an edge reflects the historical frequency of a pair of tests being solved simultaneously. Fitness cases are then selected based on a sophisticated analysis of that graph.

## 4   Clinical Problem and Image Segmentation Task

The condition of the human vascular system is an important diagnostic factor in a large number of medical conditions like atherosclerosis or diabetes, to mention the common ones. No wonder thus that almost every modality of medical imaging features an operation mode that visualizes veins and/or arteries, like X-ray/CT angiography or Doppler ultrasonography.

A body organ that is particularly sensitive to pathologies of the vascular system is the eye. A malfunctioning of blood vessels in the retina has severe impact on the quality of vision. Contemporary, the most common cause of such anomalies is diabetes, which in 2012 had 9.3 % incidence in the US[1] and continues to be on the rise. As a result, the diabetic retinopathy affects over a quarter of adults with diabetes, and is currently the most common cause of blindness in the Western world.

There are several medical imaging techniques that allow assessing the state of retinal vascular system, including fundus imaging, fluoresceine angiography, and optical coherence tomography (OCT, [7]). In this study, we consider the first of them, which is arguably technically most straightforward: fundus images are simply pictures of the back of the eye taken in visible band using a camera fitted with appropriate optics. Our source of data is the DRIVE database [8][2], the result of a screening study conducted in the Netherlands on 400 subjects aged 25–90. The database contains a sample of 40 subjects from that group, 7 of which show mild signs of early diabetic retinopathy, and the remaining ones represent the clinical norm. Each image is a color raster taken with a 3CCD camera, where the anatomical structures occupy the central circular area with a radius of approximately 540 pixels.

---

[1] http://www.diabetes.org/diabetes-basics/statistics/.
[2] http://www.isi.uu.nl/Research/Databases/DRIVE/.

The database is divided into a training set and a test set, both composed of 20 images taken from different patients. For every image, manual segmentation of retinal vessels is provided (the original database contains two segmentations for the test set, but only the 'gold standard' one is used in this experiment). Figure 1 presents an exemplary training image and the corresponding manual segmentation.

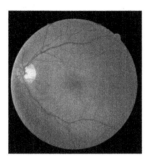 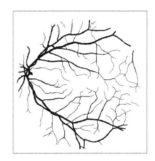

**Fig. 1.** An exemplary training image from the DRIVE database (left) and the corresponding manual segmentation (right).

## 5    Experimental Verification

In the experiment, we verify how useful are the particular GP search drivers presented in Sect. 3 for learning segmentation of blood vessels in the DRIVE database of fundus images (Sect. 4). In particular, we want to find out if the continuous variant of IFS proposed here brings any benefits. In parallel, we will determine whether the answers to these research questions depend to any extent on the characteristics of image features fed into programs.

**Methods.** The compared methods differ only in the search drivers presented in Sect. 3, which we employ as fitness function. Otherwise, all setups implement generational evolutionary algorithm and tree-based GP [9,10], with the initial population filled with the ramped half-and-half operator, subtree-replacing mutation engaged with probability 0.1, subtree-swapping crossover with probability 0.9, and tournament selection with tournament size 7.

Evolutionary runs last for 200 generations and work with population of 1000 programs. The instruction set comprises arithmetic ($+$, $-$, $*$ and protected division) and transcendental functions: $exp, sig(x) = 1/(1 + e^{-x})$, $lg|x|$, and normal distribution $n(x) = N_{(0,1)}(x)$. The terminals include the instructions that fetch image features, and constants drawn uniformly from the interval $[-1, 1]$. The incidence of constants in randomly generated trees is set to 0.1.

The final outcome of an evolutionary run is the best-of-run individual, i.e., the best individual found in any generation of the run.

**Training set.** We formulate the problem for GP as a classification task on the level of individual pixels. For a given pixel, the task for a GP classifier is to predict whether it represents a blood vessels or not. In this sense, each pixel forms a test (cf. Sect. 2).

Each of the 20 training images contains approximately 230 000 labeled pixels, far too many to be used for evolutionary training within a reasonable time-frame. Therefore, we select the training examples via sampling: from each training image, we draw at random 50 positive examples (pixels representing blood vessels) and 50 negative examples (pixels representing the background). Thus, the training set comprises $20 \times (50 + 50) = 2000$ fitness cases. The negative class is thus undersampled with respect to the positive one, and so GP works with balanced decision classes which should facilitate training. Originally, the decision classes are strongly imbalanced, with the positive class accounting for only about 12.7 percent of pixels [8].

**Image features.** As suggested earlier, this study focuses on the capability of different variants of GP to learn from the elementary image features, rather than on the features themselves. Therefore, we rely on relatively simple elementary image features inspired by BRIEF, Binary Robust Independent Elementary Features [11]. Originally, a single BRIEF feature is a binary indicator that tests the relationship between the values of two randomly chosen pixels $p_1$ and $p_2$ in the window $I$ (ROI), i.e., whether $I(p_1) > I(p_2)$. To this aim, the originally color images are first converted to the monochrome scale.

We hybridize the BRIEF features with GP in the following way. Firstly, we delegate the choice of pixels to be compared to the evolutionary process, rather than drawing a sample of such pairs (which was originally done in [11]). To that aim, we include in the instruction set a terminal $d(p_1, p_2)$ that compares the brightness values of the pixels $p_1$ and $p_2$, which leads to a **binary** outcome:

$$d_b(p_1, p_2) = \begin{cases} 1 & I(p_1) > I(p_2) \\ 0 & otherwise \end{cases}.$$

The locations of $p_1$ and $p_2$ are defined in the reference frame of the current ROI of the detector. Given a rectangular ROI $I$ of $m \times m$ pixels, there are $m^2(m^2 - 1)/2$ unique pairs of pixels. We use $m = 7$, which implies 1176 binary BRIEF features – input variables for a GP classifier.

Transforming two continuous pixel values into a binary indicator incurs substantial information loss. To preserve more information while still abstracting from the absolute pixel values, we consider also a **continuous** variant of BRIEF:

$$d_c(p_1, p_2) = I(p_1) - I(p_2).$$

**Objective performance indicator.** The compared methods use different fitness definitions as search drivers, which cannot be directly compared. To objectively compare the resulting classifiers, we employ the Area Under ROC curve indicator (AUC) detailed in Sect. 3. This performance indicator provides the full account (albeit aggregated to a single scalar) of the trade-off between the false positive rate and the true positive rate.

# 6   Results

Table 1 presents the average AUC of the best-of-run programs applied to the test set, averaged over 20 evolutionary runs. The estimation of AUC on the test set proceeds as for the training set, however this time 200 pixels are selected from each class for each of the 20 testing images, so the test set comprises $2 \times 200 \times 20 = 8000$ pixels.

**Table 1.** Test-set AUC of particular search drivers, aggregated over 20 evolutionary runs: average (left, with 0.95 confidence intervals) and median (right).

| | Average | | Median | |
| --- | --- | --- | --- | --- |
| | Binary ($d_b$) | Continuous ($d_c$) | Binary ($d_b$) | Continuous ($d_c$) |
| L1 | $0.389 \pm 0.008$ | $0.547 \pm 0.046$ | 0.381 | 0.511 |
| L2 | $0.717 \pm 0.014$ | $0.836 \pm 0.008$ | 0.720 | 0.836 |
| Hamming | $0.619 \pm 0.075$ | $0.811 \pm 0.011$ | 0.744 | 0.808 |
| Pearson | $0.799 \pm 0.006$ | $0.849 \pm 0.010$ | 0.802 | 0.853 |
| GP-AUC | $0.802 \pm 0.004$ | $0.902 \pm 0.007$ | 0.803 | 0.903 |
| IFS | $0.775 \pm 0.006$ | $0.904 \pm 0.006$ | 0.777 | 0.906 |

The superiority of the continuous features is unquestionable. For all search drivers, the AUC of the programs that access image by means of binary BRIEF features is substantially worse. For some methods (L1, Hamming) the gap on this performance indicator is dramatic. This applies to both training and testing set. Apparently, the instruction set used here does not interact well with the BRIEF features. When it comes to the usefulness of the particular search drivers, some observations are also evident. The worst performing search driver is L1: it does not perform well in any configuration. Compared to that, L2 achieves a much better level. The Hamming measure fares in between.

The top achievers are clearly the methods that abstract from the exact values of outputs produced by programs and take into account only their ordering, i.e. GP-AUC and IFS, followed by the Pearson correlation coefficient.

The similar performance of GP-AUC and IFS is not incidental. By comparing their descriptions in Sect. 3, it is easy to notice that they have much in common; in particular they both treat interpret output as an ordinal variable.

The differences between GP-AUC and IFS seem negligible, especially for the better performing continuous features. One cannot definitely claim any of them significantly better. Does it mean that the adaptation of IFS to the continuously-valued programs proposed in Sect. 3 does not bring any benefits?

It turns out it is not necessarily the case. In Table 2 we present the average sizes of the programs in the last populations of evolutionary runs and the best-of-run programs. The programs produced by IFS are substantially smaller than the ones evolved by GP-AUC, in spite of achieving roughly the same performance.

**Table 2.** Average size of the programs in the last populations of evolutionary runs (left) and of the best-of-run programs (right).

|         | Average size in population | | Average size of best-of-run | |
|---------|-----------------|-------------------|-----------------|-------------------|
|         | Binary ($d_b$)  | Continuous ($d_c$) | Binary ($d_b$)  | Continuous ($d_c$) |
| L1      | 1.0             | 12.0              | 1.0             | 14.6              |
| L2      | 12.6            | 52.5              | 16.1            | 57.3              |
| Hamming | 20.0            | 36.5              | 21.6            | 40.5              |
| Pearson | 56.0            | 30.7              | 60.5            | 35.1              |
| GP-AUC  | 46.2            | 31.9              | 50.7            | 34.0              |
| IFS     | 31.3            | 19.1              | 40.4            | 25.5              |

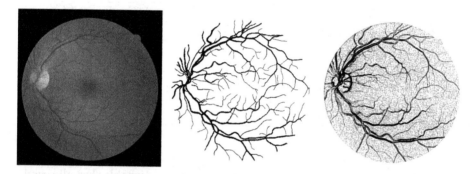

**Fig. 2.** A test image from the DRIVE database (test), the corresponding manual segmentation (middle), and the segmentation generated by the best program (GP-AUC, right). The rightmost image is not binary, because program output is not thresholded to visualize the continuous response of the detector.

The differences are observable in the averages taken over last populations, as well as in the average size of the best-of-run programs. The precise cause of this phenomenon is unclear; at this point we may only state that paying more attention to hard tests and less to the easy ones reduces code bloat.

Table 2 explains the surprising fact of L1 not surpassing 0.5 AUC in the binary configuration (Table 1): the average size of programs in that configuration is 1, which suggests that the specific way in which this search driver interprets the continuous program output precluded it from providing an effective search gradient, and search gets stuck with programs fetching single image features.

Figure 2 presents the segmentation obtained by applying the best detector from the GP-AUC runs and applying it an image from the testing set.

## 7   Conclusions

From the viewpoint of evolutionary image analysis, this work brings more evidence for the usefulness of BRIEF-like random features. Simplicity notwithstanding, they offer reasonably good performance at the low expense of testing a few pixels in the ROI. In absolute terms, the best test-set AUC obtained here is 0.925 (one of the runs of GP-AUC, followed by the best of GP-IFS runs with AUC of 0.923), not far from 0.952 reported by Staal *et al.* in [8].

The overall conclusion of this study is that the choice of search driver is essential for the performance of evolutionary program synthesis. Although, given enough time, evolutionary algorithm should in principle be able to produce a continuously-valued program that closely matches the discrete desired outputs, it may be more reasonable to rely on the alternative search drivers. The experimental outcomes clearly indicate the AUC or the extension of IFS proposed here when solving binary classification tasks. We anticipate analogous results for similar medical and non-medical detection tasks.

In a broader perspective, with this work we reveal the potential dwelling in the alternative search drivers, especially those like IFS, which scrutinize program behavior on every test and do not reward programs equally for passing them. Here, we proposed and examined only a very simple approach of this kind; there are no principle reasons for extending this to, e.g., semantic GP [12].

**Acknowledgments.** This study has been supported by the National Centre for Research and Development grant # PBS1/A9/20/2013 and National Science Centre grant NCN grant 2011/01/DNZ4/05801.

# References

1. McKay, R.I.B.: Fitness sharing in genetic programming. In: Whitley, D., Goldberg, D., Cantu-Paz, E., Spector, L., Parmee, I., Beyer, H.G. (eds) Proceedings of the Genetic and Evolutionary Computation Conference (GECCO-2000), Las Vegas, Nevada, USA, pp. 435–442. Morgan Kaufmann, 10–12 July 2000
2. Smith, R.E., Forrest, S., Perelson, A.S.: Searching for diverse, cooperative populations with genetic algorithms. Evol. Comput. **1**(2), 127–149 (1993)
3. McKay, R.I.B.: Committee learning of partial functions in fitness-shared genetic programming. In: Industrial Electronics Society, 2000. IECON 2000. 26th Annual Conference of the IEEE Third Asia-Pacific Conference on Simulated Evolution and Learning 2000, Nagoya, Japan, vol. 4, pp. 2861–2866. IEEE Press, 22–28 October 2000
4. Goldberg, D.E.: Genetic Algorithms in Search, Optimization, and Machine Learning. Addison-wesley, Reading (1989)
5. Krawiec, K., Lichocki, P.: Using co-solvability to model and exploit synergetic effects in evolution. In: Schaefer, R., Cotta, C., Kołodziej, J., Rudolph, G. (eds.) PPSN XI, Part II. LNCS, vol. 6239, pp. 492–501. Springer, Heidelberg (2010)
6. Lasarczyk, C.W.G., Dittrich, P., Banzhaf, W.: Dynamic subset selection based on a fitness case topology. Evol. Comput. **12**(2), 223–242 (2004). (Summer 2004)
7. Sikorski, B., Bukowska, D., Ruminski, D., Gorczynska, I., Szkulmowski, M., Krawiec, K., Malukiewicz, G., Wojtkowski, M.: Visualization of 3d retinal microcapillary network using oct. Acta Ophthalmol. **91** (2013)
8. Staal, J., Abrà moff, M.D., Niemeijer, M., Viergever, M.A., van Ginneken, B.: Ridge-based vessel segmentation in color images of the retina. IEEE Trans. Med. Imaging **23**(4), 501–509 (2004)

9. Koza, J.R.: Genetic Programming: On the Programming of Computers by Means of Natural Selection. MIT Press, Cambridge (1992)
10. Poli, R., Langdon, W.B., McPhee, N.F.: A field guide to genetic programming. http://lulu.com and http://www.gp-field-guide.org.uk (2008) (With contributions by J. R. Koza)
11. Calonder, M., Lepetit, V., Strecha, C., Fua, P.: BRIEF: binary robust independent elementary features. In: Daniilidis, K., Maragos, P., Paragios, N. (eds.) ECCV 2010, Part IV. LNCS, vol. 6314, pp. 778–792. Springer, Heidelberg (2010)
12. Moraglio, A., Krawiec, K., Johnson, C.G.: Geometric semantic genetic programming. In: Coello, C.A.C., Cutello, V., Deb, K., Forrest, S., Nicosia, G., Pavone, M. (eds.) PPSN 2012, Part I. LNCS, vol. 7491, pp. 21–31. Springer, Heidelberg (2012)

# Analysis of Diversity Methods for Evolutionary Multi-objective Ensemble Classifiers

Stefan Oehmcke[(⊠)], Justin Heinermann, and Oliver Kramer

Computational Intelligence Group, Department of Computing Science,
University of Oldenburg, Oldenburg, Germany
{stefan.oehmcke,justin.heinermann,oliver.kramer}@uni-oldenburg.de

**Abstract.** Ensemble classifiers are strong and robust methods for classification and regression tasks. Considering the balance between runtime and classifier accuracy the learning problem becomes a multi-objective optimization problem. In this work, we propose an evolutionary multi-objective algorithm based on non-dominated sorting that balances runtime and accuracy properties of nearest neighbor classifier ensembles and decision tree ensembles. We identify relevant ensemble parameters with a significant impact on the accuracy and runtime. In the experimental part of this paper, we analyze the behavior on typical classification benchmark problems.

**Keywords:** Ensemble classification · Multi-objective optimization

## 1 Introduction

To overcome algorithmic shortcomings and to achieve synergetic effects, the hybridization of various classifiers can be an effective strategy. This technique is known as ensemble learning and has developed to an outstandingly successful technique in machine learning. The key to good classification ensembles is to achieve diversity among the separate models. Two main types of ensembles are bagging ensembles [1] that consist of models that are trained independently, and boosting ensembles [2] that try to compensate the weakness of the ensemble by concentrating on the training of its components.

In ensemble learning two conflictive objectives have a significant impact on the machine learning model: accuracy and classifier runtime (training and testing time). Objective of this work is to balance accuracy and runtime to approximate a set of Pareto-optimal ensemble classifiers for two famous types of classifiers, i.e., k-nearest neighbor (kNN) classification and CART decision trees. As the problem turns out to be a difficult blackbox optimization problem with local optima, we employ evolutionary multi-objective optimization algorithms (EMOAs) to evolve the Pareto-optimal ensembles. In this paper, we aim at identifying relevant parameters to tune the ensembles, in particular concentrating on pattern and feature diversity. While not being interested in the most accurate classifier, we concentrate on finding a Pareto-optimal set of classifiers with evolutionary

© Springer International Publishing Switzerland 2015
A.M. Mora and G. Squillero (Eds.): EvoApplications 2015, LNCS 9028, pp. 567–578, 2015.
DOI: 10.1007/978-3-319-16549-3_46

multi-objective optimization. We analyze the balancing approach on a small yet relevant set of benchmark problems.

This paper is structured as follows. In Sect. 2, we introduce the new approach, which we call evolutionary selection of ensemble model (ESEM). In Sect. 3, pattern diversity methods are analyzed, while Sect. 4 concentrates on feature diversity. In Sect. 5 results are discussed and prospective future work is presented.

## 2    Evolutionary Selection of Ensemble Models

In this section, we first sketch the employed classification algorithms kNN and CART. We describe the idea of ensemble classification and repeat the concept of multi-objective evolutionary optimization and NSGA-ii. The depiction ends with the ESEM approach for optimization and balancing of ensemble classifiers.

### 2.1    Classifiers

ESEM employs two types of classifiers. The kNN-based variant uses nearest neighbor classification, which assigns the class label of the $k$-closest patterns in data space to an unknown pattern $\mathbf{x}'$. Let $\mathbf{X} = \{(\mathbf{x}_1, y_1), \ldots, (\mathbf{x}_N, y_N)\}$ be the set of observations of $d$-dimensional patterns $\mathbf{x}_i$ and class labels $y_i$ with $i = 1, \ldots, N$. For an unknown pattern $\mathbf{x}'$, kNN classification predicts the class label of the majority of the K-nearest patterns in data space. Further, a distance measure has to be defined in the space of patterns, e.g., the Euclidean distance in $\mathbb{R}^N$.

The classification and regression trees algorithm (CART) is a decision tree variant introduced by Breiman et al. [3]. CART uses a binary tree data structure and divides the data space $\mathbf{X}$ repeatedly into binary regions $R_m \subset \mathbf{X}$ with $m \in \{1, \ldots, n\}$ and $n \in [1, N]$. For every node of the tree, a threshold value $s_m$ for a chosen feature $\mathbf{x}_i$ exists. This threshold value specifies, which child path is taken and thus which region is chosen. The tree is generated with a greedy algorithm. At first, the root is created and the nodes are added successively. When a region $R_m$ is divided, two new Regions $R_{m1}(\mathbf{x}_i, s_m) = \{(\mathbf{x}_i, y) | \mathbf{x}_i \leq s_m\}$ and $R_{m2}(\mathbf{x}_i, s_m) = R_m \setminus R_{m1}$ emerge. To find the optimal feature and the threshold $(\mathbf{x}_i, s_m)^*$ for region $R_m$ the following applies:

$$(\mathbf{x}_i, s_m)^* = \arg \min_{(\mathbf{x}_i, s_m)} G(R_m, (\mathbf{x}_i, s_m)), \text{ with} \tag{1}$$

$$G(\cdot) = H(R_m) - \left(\frac{|R_{m1}|}{|R_m|} H(R_{m1}(\mathbf{x}_i, s_m))\right)^2 - \left(\frac{|R_{m2}|}{|R_m|} H(R_{m2}(\mathbf{x}_i, s_m))\right)^2$$

Here, $H(R_m)$ is the information gain of region $R_m$ and various functions can be used like the Gini index or the classification error. If the maximum recursion depth is reached, if only one pattern is in the region, or if a correct label assignment is certain, a leaf node with a label assignment is created. This label is determined with the majority of the patterns in this region. For an unknown pattern $\mathbf{x}'$, CART just follows the tree to one of the leaves for a label prediction.

## 2.2 Ensemble Classifiers

For supervised learning tasks, an ensemble model integrates several diverse models. The main idea is the improvement of accuracy compared to the single models while providing moderate computational cost. While numerous variants of ensemble algorithms exist, there is no free lunch when dealing with classification or regression tasks, i.e., there is no algorithm that can be used in every situation and for every data set.

In our work, we focus on the famous *bagging* (bootstrap aggregating) approach, which was introduced by Breiman [1] and is a relatively simple ensemble algorithm. The main idea is to build independent predictors using samples of the training set and average the output of these predictors. Breiman [1] shows that bagging ensembles of decision trees outperform single decision trees. This approach was extended with feature subsampling and is known as random forest algorithm [4]. Here, every decision tree is built with a subset sample from the training set and only uses a random subspace of the available features.

In contrast to bagging, *boosting* approaches like AdaBoost [2] train the ensemble members not independently but in an iterative kind of way. In every iteration, a new predictor is added to the ensemble and afterwards the prediction quality of the ensemble is tested on the training set instances. The wrong classified instances will be considered as more important in the next training iteration. While boosting may sometimes outperform bagging, it is more complex and can result in overfitting. Hence, we decide to focus on bagging ensembles in this work. Ensemble classifiers are well appropriate for be balanced by EMOAs with their important trade-off between runtime and accuracy and their crucial parameter-dependency.

## 2.3 Multi-objective Optimization

The idea of the ESEM approach is to treat the ensemble classifier tuning problem as unconstrained multi-objective optimization problem in $\mathbb{R}^N$ that minimizes two (in general $m$) conflictive objectives

$$\mathbf{f}(\mathbf{x}) = (f_1(\mathbf{x}), \dots, f_m(\mathbf{x}))^T \tag{2}$$

with

$$\min_{\mathbf{x} \in \mathbb{R}^N} \mathbf{f}(\mathbf{x}) = \min_{\mathbf{x} \in \mathbb{R}^N} (f_1(\mathbf{x}), f_2(\mathbf{x}), \dots, f_m(\mathbf{x}))^T \tag{3}$$

and $f_i(\mathbf{x}) : \mathbb{R}^N \to \mathbb{R}, i = 1, \dots, m$. Usually, the ensemble tuner is interested in a set of Pareto optimal solutions, which is the set of non-dominated solutions. If it holds $\forall i \in \{1, \dots, m\} : f_i(\mathbf{x}) \le f_i(\mathbf{x}')$, a solution $\mathbf{x}$ weakly dominates a solution $\mathbf{x}'$ ($\mathbf{x} \preceq \mathbf{x}'$). Solution $\mathbf{x}$ dominates solution $\mathbf{x}'$ ($\mathbf{x} \prec \mathbf{x}'$), if it holds $\mathbf{x} \preceq \mathbf{x}'$, and $\exists i \in \{1, \dots, m\} : f_i(\mathbf{x}) < f_i(\mathbf{x}')$. If $\mathbf{x} \not\preceq \mathbf{x}' \wedge \mathbf{x}' \not\preceq \mathbf{x}$, the solutions $\mathbf{x}, \mathbf{x}'$ are indifferent to each other ($\mathbf{x} \sim \mathbf{x}'$).

As evolutionary multi-objective optimization algorithm, we employ NSGA-ii [5], which is based on two steps. First, NSGA-ii applies non-dominated sorting, which assigns the domination level as ranks to its solutions. The lower the rank the less a solution is dominated. Second, NSGA-ii selects the candidate solutions that maximize the Manhattan metrics of its direct neighbors, which is called crowding distance.

## 2.4   ESEM Algorithm

The ESEM algorithm is an adaption of NSGA-ii to the application of ensemble classifier balancing. Algorithm 1 shows the pseudocode of the approach. At the beginning, $\mu$ ensembles are initialized and build population $P_0$. These candidate solutions are evaluated for all $m$ objectives and the results are stored for each one. Population $P_0$ is stored in set $\Theta$ for later use. The evolutionary process is iteratively repeated within the first loop until a termination condition is reached. In this paper, we terminate ESEM after $T$ generations.

A new generation starts with the creation of a new population. To that end, all parent ensemble solutions that survived are re-used. Then, $\lambda$ new ensembles are created by recombination and mutation. In our ESEM variant, we use $\rho$ parents and intermediate recombination. For more variation, the new solution is additionally mutated. The new ensemble solution is evaluated for all objectives. If the solution already exists in set $\Theta$, the computed objective values are used instead of performing new function evaluations. After $\lambda$ solution have been created for the new population, all are added to set $\Theta$. Next, the important steps from NSGA-ii that calculate domination rank and crowding distance are applied. At the end of a generation, only the $\mu$ ensembles are selected to survive that have maximum rank and minimum crowding distance. After the evolutionary process the non-dominated sorting is applied on set $\Theta$. Only solutions with rank one are returned as ESEM result.

We consider two objectives. The runtime objective

$$f_r = t_{train} + t_{pred} \qquad (4)$$

is the first one, considering average training time $t_{train}$ and prediction time $t_{pred}$ in terms of CPU-runtime. The second objective

$$f_{err} = e_{err} + \sigma \qquad (5)$$

combines the classification error $e_{err}$ and the corresponding standard deviation $\sigma$. This way only solutions with low classification error and standard deviation are considered as best ones, which favors stable over one-shot predictions. All measurements are based on stratified ten-fold cross-validation.

The employment of archive $\Theta$ offers two advantages. First, no fitness function evaluations of the same ensemble solution are performed and the runtime is decreased. Second, the archive can be stored and used for further ESEM runs.

## 2.5   Related Work

Evolutionary optimization has been employed for tuning parameters of machine learning algorithms. For example, for kernel methods like support vector machines

---

**Algorithm 1.** ESEM Algorithm

---

1  $P_0 \to$ init $\mu$ ensembles $\mathbf{x}_{1:\mu}$
2  **for** $i = 1$ **to** $m$ **do** $\mathbf{x}_{Fitness_i} = f_i(\mathbf{x}) \forall x \in P_0$;
3  $\Theta \to P_0$; $t = 0$
4  **repeat**
5  $\quad P_{t+1} \to P_t$
6  $\quad$ **for** $i=0$ **to** $\lambda$ **do**
7  $\qquad$ select $\rho$ parents from $P_t$
8  $\qquad \mathbf{x}^* \to$ recombination of parents
9  $\qquad$ mutate $\mathbf{x}^*$
10 $\qquad$ **if** $\mathbf{x}^* \neq \mathbf{x}^\theta \in \Theta$ **then**
11 $\qquad\quad | \quad \mathbf{x}^*_{Fitness_i} \to f_i(\mathbf{x}^*) \forall f_i \in \mathbf{f}$
12 $\qquad$ **else** $\mathbf{x}^*_{Fitness} \to \mathbf{x}^\theta_{Fitness}$ ;
13 $\qquad$ add $\mathbf{x}^*$ to $P_{t+1}$
14 $\quad \Theta \to \Theta + P_{t+1}$
15 $\quad \mathbf{x}_{rank} \forall \mathbf{x} \in P_{t+1} \to$ non-dominated sorting
16 $\quad$ crowding distance $\mathbf{x}_{\delta_c} \to \forall \mathbf{x} \in P_{t+1}$
17 $\quad P_{t+1} \to$ select $\mu$ ensembles $\mathbf{x} \in P_{t+1}$ with min. $\mathbf{x}_{rank}$ and max. $\mathbf{x}_{\delta_c}$
18 $\quad t \mathrel{+}= 1$
19 **until** *termination condition*;
20 $\mathbf{x}_{rank} \forall \mathbf{x} \in \Theta \to$ non-dominated sorting
21 $\Theta \to$ select $\mathbf{x} \in \Theta$, where $\mathbf{x}_{rank} = 1$

---

(SVMs), optimal models with a small generalization error could be found while providing a short runtime compared to exhaustive search, see [6]. Hu et al. [7] propose an evolutionary method for decision tree ensembles. The objective function is given by the accuracy.

A similar approach was proposed by Ishibuchi and Yamamoto [8] for ensemble selection of fuzzy models. Here, a multi-objective optimization is performed using NSGA-ii. Besides the classification accuracy, number and length of fuzzy-rules are considered as objective functions. In the field of neural network ensembles, Abbass [9] employs EMOAs combined with stratification of data sets. In contrast to EMOAs, Opitz und Shavlik [10] employ traditional multi-objective optimization for selecting neural networks for ensembles.

## 3  Pattern Diversity Analysis

With the following experiments, we want to determine, if a certain set of parameter settings **p** has an impact to the runtime $f_{runtime}$ and error $f_{err}$. Further, we study, which parameters in **p** have an impact on the objective function values. The expected impact is that if a parameter yields a positive effect on one objective, the other one is negatively affected. When both objectives can be satisfied with one particular setting, it does not need to be optimized with ESEM. Also, the difference between base algorithms is of interest, in particular, if the Pareto optimal fronts are significantly different.

In this section, we begin the analysis of parameters of ESEM concentrating on pattern diversity methods. In two series of experiments for pattern and feature diversity methods (see Sect. 4), we run the ESEM approach introduced in the previous section for 15 generations. The different methods are analyzed separately as they are orthogonal to each other, as remarked by Tumer and Oza [11].

A generation creates $\lambda = 60$ new offspring solutions and selects $\mu = 20$ parents that survive into the following generation. Half of the parents are selected with binary tournament selection [12] for self-adapting SBX-recombination [13]. The operator for mutation is the polynomial mutation [14], where the mutation strength is controlled with self-adaptation [15]. Solutions with an error larger than 0.25 or a runtime larger than 60 seconds will be penalized with a dynamic penalty [16]. The experiments are conducted on four datasets: MakeClass, Waveform2, ImageSegmentation, and BreastCancer. Every experiment is conducted twice, one with kNN and one with CART as base algorithm. The final ensemble classifier uses majority voting returning the most frequent label among all base classifiers. For statistical expressiveness, each experiment is repeated 20 times. When two samples are tested, the Wilcoxon signed-rank test is used. We use the Friedman-Test for comparisons with more than two samples. Significant p-values must have a critical Value $W$ less than 52 or a Friedman statistic under 7.8. Strongly significant values need a critical Value $W$ less than 37 or a Friedman statistic under 11.34. The base algorithm parameters are optimized beforehand with random optimization within 20 iterations.

Four points on the Pareto front are particularly interesting in our analysis. The first two are the minima $(T_{min})$ of classifier runtime and classification error. The second two are the runtime and the classification error of the first tercile $(T_{33})$. With this division of the solution set, uniformly distributed samples can be analyzed.

The first class of diversity methods we focus on are pattern diversity methods. These methods generate diversity among individual models through manipulation

**Table 1.** Analysis of diversity parameters $n_{part}, d_{part}, n_{est}, r_{train}, s_{feat}, r_{feat}$, and $l_{noise}$.

| Dataset | Alg. | significance | | | | | | |
|---------|------|:-----:|:-----:|:----:|:------:|:-----:|:-----:|:------:|
| | | $n_{part}$ | $d_{part}$ | $n_{est}$ | $r_{train}$ | $s_{feat}$ | $r_{feat}$ | $l_{noise}$ |
| MakeClass | CART | X | X | X | | | | X |
| | kNN | | | X | X | | | X |
| Waveform2 | CART | | | X | X | | | X |
| | kNN | | | X | X | | | X |
| ImageSeg. | CART | X | X | X | | | | X |
| | kNN | | | X | | X | X | |
| BreastC. | CART | | | X | | | | |
| | kNN | | X | X | X | X | X | |

of the patterns from the training set. The first parameter is the number of models $n_{est}$ used for an ensemble. This is not a diversity method, but the main drive of the ensemble method. Hence, it must be optimized along with the diversity methods. It is only reasonable to increase $n_{est}$, if the diversity is high enough [17]. The next parameters are the number of partitions $n_{part}$ and the amount of deletion $d_{part}$ from a partition like in "cross-validated committees"-method from Parmanto et al. [18]. In this method, first disjunct subsets $\{S_1, \ldots, S_{n_{part}}\}$ are created from the training set $S$. Now $n_{part}$ partitions $P$ are made applying $\forall i \in \{1, \ldots, n_{part}\}: P_i = S \setminus S_i$. Every model gets one of the partitions for training. If more models exist than partitions, multiple models get the same partition. Each model will remove $\lfloor \min(|P|, \max(1, d_{part} \cdot |P|)) \rfloor$ patterns from his new partition $P^*$. At last the bagging parameter $r_{train}$ defines that $\lfloor \max(1, r_{train} \cdot |P^*|) \rfloor$ pattern will be taken with replacement for the final training set.

Table 1 shows a study of all parameters. For the moment only the pattern parameter $n_{part}, d_{part}, n_{est}, r_{train}$ are considered. The parameter settings of one parameter on four different positions on the non-dominant front are compared. If the parameter settings differ in separate positions, it is useful to optimize this parameter with ESEM. The Friedman-Test is applied here. An 'X'-symbol marks significantly different values, while an underlined 'X'-symbol marks strongly

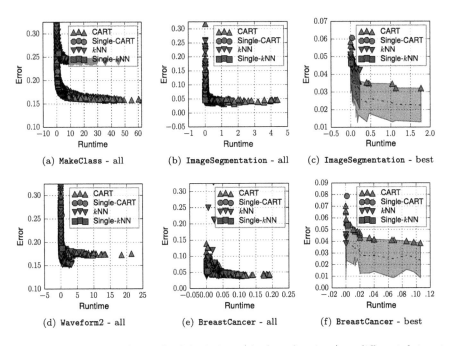

(a) `MakeClass - all`          (b) `ImageSegmentation - all`          (c) `ImageSegmentation - best`

(d) `Waveform2 - all`          (e) `BreastCancer - all`          (f) `BreastCancer - best`

**Fig. 1.** ESEM fronts with standard deviations (shadowed regions) on different data sets with optimized pattern diversity settings for `all` non-dominated ensemble solutions and the `best` solutions, respectively. Artificial datasets show a larger distance between classifier fronts, but are also less accurate and need more time.

**Table 2.** Pattern diversity results of ESEM with kNN and CART on the benchmark data sets. Bold values indicate a significant difference, underlined values indicate strong significance. The average number of non-dominated solutions is denoted as #ens., while the overall number of ensemble calls are denoted as #calls.

| Dataset | Alg. | $T_{min}$ inac. | | $T_{min}$ runt. | | $T_{33}$ inac. | | $T_{33}$ runt. | | #ens. | #calls |
|---|---|---|---|---|---|---|---|---|---|---|---|
| | | inac. | runt. | inac. | runt. | inac. | runt. | inac. | runt. | | |
| MakeClass | kNN | .240 | **<u>24.4</u>** | .419 | .006 | .250 | **2.99** | .277 | **<u>.459</u>** | 46.5 | 804 |
| | CART | **<u>.160</u>** | 40.2 | .441 | .009 | **<u>.176</u>** | 5.03 | **<u>.206</u>** | .931 | **<u>76.2</u>** | **770** |
| Waveform2 | kNN | **<u>.155</u>** | **2.45** | .357 | .008 | **<u>.165</u>** | .397 | **<u>.193</u>** | .083 | 27.7 | 725 |
| | CART | .174 | 8.04 | .417 | .013 | .187 | .655 | .214 | .084 | **35.6** | 757 |
| ImageSeg. | kNN | .043 | **<u>0.37</u>** | .227 | .003 | .048 | **<u>.084</u>** | .058 | **<u>.016</u>** | 22.2 | 681 |
| | CART | .041 | 1.96 | .391 | .008 | .051 | .337 | .067 | .072 | **34.8** | 721 |
| BreastC. | kNN | .042 | **<u>.037</u>** | .157 | .003 | .046 | **.020** | **<u>.057</u>** | .004 | 10.6 | **623** |
| | CART | .041 | .104 | .155 | .003 | .050 | .032 | .070 | .006 | **<u>20.4</u>** | 749 |

significantly different values. With exception of $n_{part}$, every pattern parameter differs in its settings at least three times.

Figure 1 shows a comparison of evolved kNN and CART fronts on the benchmark data sets with optimized pattern diversity methods. Dominant ensemble solutions of all experimental repetitions are marked with all, and the Pareto-optimal front of these solutions are marked with best. From the figures and the corresponding Table 2, we can make the following observations. In general, CART finds non-dominated solutions with a higher diversity, i.e., more different solutions, than kNN, probably because of the instability of CART. Further, the minimal runtime point is never significantly different for kNN and CART. On the MakeClass data set, we can observe that points are often indifferent. We conclude that kNN is faster but CART more accurate.[1] On Waveform2, we can observe that kNN dominates CART, in contrast to Fig. 1(d), where they appear to be close to each other. On the ImageSegmentation data set, we observe an indifferent quality of solutions. Only in the middle of the front, kNN performs better. The lowest error has been achieved by CART, see Fig. 1(c). On BreastCancer, kNN dominates, but only has few overall solutions, see Fig. 1(f). The evolved fronts for BreastCancer and ImageSegmentation appear to lie closely to each other, see Fig. 1(e) and (b). From this series of experiments, we conclude that the fronts differ significantly from each other and no "best" base algorithm has been found, as we might expect from the "no-free-lunch"-theorem.

# 4    Feature Diversity Analysis

In the following, we concentrate on feature diversity. The research objective and method are similar to Sect. 3, but now concern feature diversity rather than

---

[1] This observation could be confirmed in our experiments and is difficult to observe in Fig. 1(a) due to the limited plot resolution.

pattern diversity. Again, we consider $n_{est}$, but the results only confirm the pattern diversity experiment observations. With the first method we create a random subspace of features similar to the random forest method. This method needs two parameters $s_{feat}$, $r_{feat}$, which determine, how many features are used. Whereby $s_{feat}$ takes $n_{feat} = \lfloor \min(d, \max(1, d \cdot s_{feat})) \rfloor$ features from the original $d$ ones, without replacement. And $r_{feat}$ defines, that $\lfloor \max(1, n_{feat} \cdot s_{feat}) \rfloor$ features are taken with replacement from the $n_{feat}$ previously selected ones. Together, both parameters can control certainty of features appearing multiple times in the training set. Another method we apply is the noise injection with its parameter $l_{noise}$. The concept

$$\forall i \in \{1, \ldots, n_{feat-rep}\} : \mathbf{x}'_i = \mathbf{x}_i + \mathcal{N}(0, l^2_{noise}) \tag{6}$$

for manipulating features is similar to the approach by Raviv and Intrator [19], who use bagging and neural networks in their experiments. The approach is successful, because the diversity results in a robust and accurate ensemble, although the separate models perform worse. In the following experiment, we study the parameters $s_{feat}$, $r_{feat}$, and $l_{noise}$. Table 1 shows the experimental results comparing the parameter settings of one parameter on four different positions on the non-dominant front. If the parameter settings differ in separate positions, it is useful to optimize this parameter with ESEM. Again, bold p-values are significantly different and underlined values are strongly significantly different. The results show that every parameter needs dynamic optimization in at least one of the tested cases.

Figure 2(d) shows a comparison of kNN and CART fronts on `Waveform2` with optimized feature diversity methods. Dominant solutions of all experimental repetitions are shown on the left-hand side, while the Pareto-optimal front of these solutions are shown on the right hand side. The kNN front is more optimal, but on the other datasets the base algorithms are alternately better. Table 3 shows the corresponding experimental results with numerical values. In

**Table 3.** Feature diversity results of ESEM with kNN and CART on the benchmark data sets. Bold values indicate a significant difference, underlined values indicate strong significance. The average number of non-dominated solutions is denoted as #ens., while the overall number of ensemble calls are denoted as #calls.

| Dataset | Alg. | $T_{min}$ inac. | | $T_{min}$ runt. | | $T_{33}$ inac. | | $T_{33}$ runt. | | #ens. | #calls |
|---------|------|-------|-------|-------|-------|-------|-------|-------|-------|-------|--------|
|  |  | inac. | runt. | inac. | runt. | inac. | runt. | inac. | runt. |  |  |
| MakeClass | kNN | .239 | 150 | .286 | .648 | .250 | 17.2 | .264 | 3.38 | 39.6 | 851 |
|  | CART | <u>.177</u> | <u>60</u> | <u>.223</u> | .285 | **0.182** | **6.1** | <u>.193</u> | <u>1.89</u> | 42.1 | **776** |
| Waveform2 | kNN | <u>.154</u> | 55.9 | <u>.198</u> | .252 | **.163** | 7.36 | <u>.181</u> | 1.58 | 30.2 | 846 |
|  | CART | .185 | **32.1** | .253 | .352 | .196 | **5.42** | .214 | 1.12 | **34.9** | 801 |
| ImageSeg. | kNN | .041 | 4.11 | <u>.053</u> | 0.01 | **.044** | .558 | <u>.048</u> | <u>.044</u> | 19.7 | 774 |
|  | CART | .042 | 6.65 | .066 | 0.00 | .047 | .702 | .056 | .084 | **23.2** | **728** |
| BreastC. | kNN | <u>.041</u> | <u>.054</u> | <u>.049</u> | .007 | <u>.043</u> | <u>.019</u> | <u>.046</u> | .009 | 7.2 | 734 |
|  | CART | .046 | .381 | .071 | .005 | .052 | .063 | .061 | .018 | <u>**13.3**</u> | 715 |

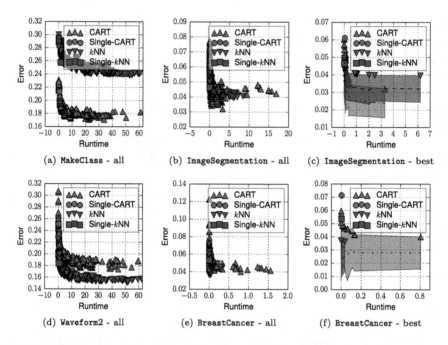

**Fig. 2.** ESEM fronts with standard deviations (shadowed regions) on different data sets with optimized pattern diversity settings for `all` non-dominated ensemble solutions and the `best` solutions, respectively. As with the pattern diversity method, the artificial datasets show a larger distance between classifier fronts, but are also less accurate and require a longer runtime.

general, we can observe that CART still finds more solutions in three of four cases. Further, CART dominates on the `MakeClass` data set, the fronts are not intersecting, see Fig. 2(a). On the `Waveform2` data set, we observe indifferent results: kNN achieves more accurate solutions, but CART is faster. On the `ImageSegmentation` data set, kNN weakly dominates, while the CART solutions show a high standard deviation. kNN dominates on `BreastCancer` with few solutions, see Fig. 2(f). The results confirm the pattern diversity observations. Fronts differ significantly from each other, and no "best" base algorithm can be found.

## 5   Conclusions

In this paper, we analyzed pattern and feature diversity methods for balancing ensemble classifiers. The main result is that balancing ensembles is worth the extra effort in comparison to single-objective tuning. The optimization process yields a broad front with significant diversity w.r.t. the criterions accuracy and runtime. In turn, we claim there exists the necessity to optimize with EMOAs to exploit the full diversity and allow the practitioner to choose from a Pareto-front with high diversity a posteriori. This result has practical implications for applications, where a compromise between runtime and accuracy is important. In our work, we could identify important parameters that are appropriate for optimization. The most important parameters were $r_{train}, r_{noise}, n_{est}$ with a significant influence on the learning result. The least important parameter was $n_{part}$, which we recommend to tune by hand. A further result is that different settings have been evolved for different problems and evolved parameters cannot be generalized to other problem classes.

An analysis that focuses on the question, if evolved parameters can be generalized *within* problem classes, will be subject to future work. Further experiments have shown that the multi-objective approach yields solutions that reach the level of single-objective optimization w.r.t. the accuracy criterion. In the future, we will concentrate on the combination of pattern and feature diversity methods. We plan to enhance the benchmark set and employ further ensemble classifier and EMOA types.

**Acknowledgements.** We thank the ministry of science and culture of Lower Saxony for supporting us with the graduate schools *Safe Automation of Maritime Systems (SAMS)* and *System Integration of Renewable Energies (SEE)*.

## A    Benchmark Problems

The experiments in this paper are based on the following benchmark problems. MakeClass is a classification data set generated with the SCIKIT-LEARN [20] method make_classification. MakeClass consists of $N = 13500$ patterns with three classes and $d = 20$ features, of which four are informative. In 0.002 % of the patterns, labels have been changed. Waveform2 by Breiman *et al.* [3] consists of $N = 5000$ patterns with $d = 59$ features. The data set is an artificial one consisting of waveform data with three waveforms BreastCancer from the UCI repository comprises $N = 699$ patterns with two labels (cancer and no cancer) and $d = 9$ features. ImageSegmentation from the UCI repository consists of $N = 2310$ with seven classes corresponding to seven images. Each pattern consists of an image region of size $3 \times 3$ pixels.

## References

1. Breiman, L.: Bagging predictors. Mach. Learn. **24**, 123–140 (1996)
2. Freund, Y., Schapire, R.E.: A decision-theoretic generalization of on-line learning and an application to boosting. In: Vitányi, P. (ed.) EuroCOLT 1995. LNCS, vol. 904, pp. 23–37. Springer, Heidelberg (1995)
3. Breiman, L., Friedman, J., Stone, C.J., Olshen, R.A.: Classification and Regression Trees. CRC Press, Boca Raton (1984)
4. Breiman, L.: Random forests. Mach. Learn. **45**, 5–32 (2001)
5. Deb, K., Pratap, A., Agarwal, S., Meyarivan, T.: A fast and elitist multiobjective genetic algorithm: NSGA-II. IEEE Trans. Evol. Comput. **6**, 182–197 (2002)
6. Huang, C.L., Wang, C.J.: A ga-based feature selection and parameters optimizationfor support vector machines. Expert Syst. Appl. **31**, 231–240 (2006)

7. Hu, Q.-H., Yu, D.-R., Wang, M.-Y.: Constructing rough decision forests. In: Ślzak, D., Yao, J.T., Peters, J.F., Ziarko, W.P., Hu, X. (eds.) RSFDGrC 2005. LNCS (LNAI), vol. 3642, pp. 147–156. Springer, Heidelberg (2005)

8. Ishibuchi, H., Yamamoto, T.: Evolutionary multiobjective optimization for generating an ensemble of fuzzy rule-based classifiers. In: Cantú-Paz, E., et al. (eds.) GECCO 2003. LNCS, vol. 2723, pp. 1077–1088. Springer, Heidelberg (2003)

9. Abbass, H.A.: Pareto neuro-evolution: Constructing ensemble of neural networks using multi-objective optimization. In: Proceedings of the IEEE Congress on Evolutionary Computation. vol. 3, pp. 2074–2080. IEEE (2003)

10. Opitz, D.W., Shavlik, J.W.: Actively searching for an effective neural network ensemble. Connect. Sci. **8**, 337–354 (1996)

11. Tumer, K., Oza, N.C.: Input decimated ensembles. Pattern Anal. Appl. **6**, 65–77 (2003)

12. Oei, C.K., Goldberg, D.E., Chang, S.J.: Tournament selection, niching, and the preservation of diversity. Urbana **51**, 61801 (1991)

13. Deb, K., Agrawal, R.B.: Simulated binary crossover for continuous search space. Complex Syst. **9**, 1–34 (1994)

14. Deb, L., et al.: Multi-objective Optimization Using Evolutionary Algorithms, vol. 2012. Wiley, Chichester (2001)

15. Schwefel, H.P.: Adaptive mechanismen in der biologischen evolution und ihr einfluß auf die evolutionsgeschwindigkeit. Interner Bericht der Arbeitsgruppe Bionik und Evolutionstechnik am Institut für Mess-und Regelungstechnik **215** (1974)

16. Joines, J.A., Houck, C.R.: On the use of non-stationary penalty functions to solve nonlinear constrained optimization problems with GA's. In: First IEEE Conference on Evolutionary Computation, pp. 579–584. IEEE (1994)

17. Fumera, G., Roli, F., Serrau, A.: A theoretical analysis of bagging as a linear combination of classifiers. IEEE Trans. Pattern Anal. Mach. Intel. **30**, 1293–1299 (2008)

18. Parmanto, B., Munro, P.W., Doyle, H.R.: Improving committee diagnosis with resampling techniques. In: Touretzky, D.S., Mozer, M.C., Hasselmo, M.E. (eds.) Advances in Neural Information Processing Systems, pp. 882–888. MIT Press, Cambridge (1995)

19. Raviv, Y., Intrator, N.: Bootstrapping with noise: an effective regularization technique. Connet. Sci. **8**, 355–372 (1996)

20. Pedregosa, F., Varoquaux, G., Gramfort, A., Michel, V., Thirion, B., Grisel, O., Blondel, M., Prettenhofer, P., Weiss, R., Dubourg, V., Vanderplas, J., Passos, A., Cournapeau, D., Brucher, M., Perrot, M., Duchesnay, E.: Scikit-learn: machine learning in python. J. Mach. Learn. Res. **12**, 2825–2830 (2011)

# Applying Non-dominated Sorting Genetic Algorithm II to Multi-objective Optimization of a Weighted Multi-metric Distance for Performing Data Mining Tasks

Muhammad Marwan Muhammad Fuad[(✉)]

Forskningsparken 3, Institutt for kjemi, NorStruct, The University
of Tromsø - The Arctic University of Norway, 9037 Tromsø, Norway
marwan.fuad@uit.no

**Abstract.** Multi-objective optimization (MOO) is a class of optimization problems where several objective functions must be simultaneously optimized. Traditional search methods are difficult to extend to MOO problems so many of these problems are solved using bio-inspired optimization algorithms. One of the famous optimization algorithms that have been applied to MOO is the non-dominated sorting genetic algorithm II (NSGA-II). NSGA-II algorithm has been successfully used to solve MOO problems owing to its lower computational complexity compared with the other optimization algorithms. In this paper we use NSGA-II to solve a MOO problem of time series data mining. The problem in question is determining the optimal weights of a multi-metric distance that is used to perform several data mining tasks. NSGA-II is particularly appropriate to optimize data mining problems where fitness functions evaluation usually involves intensive computing resources. Whereas several previous papers have proposed different methods to optimize time series data mining problems, this paper is, to our knowledge, the first paper to optimize several time series data mining tasks simultaneously. The experiments we conducted show that the performance of the optimized combination of multi-metric distances we propose in executing time series data mining tasks is superior to that of the distance metrics that constitute the combination when they are applied separately.

**Keywords:** Classification · Clustering · Data mining · Multi-metric · Multi-objective optimization · Time series

## 1 Introduction

A *time series* is an ordered collection of values measuring a certain phenomenon over a period of time. Formally, a time series $S$ of length $n$ is defined as; $S = \langle s_1 = \langle v_1, t_1 \rangle, s_2 = \langle v_2, t_2 \rangle, \ldots, s_n = \langle v_n, t_n \rangle \rangle$. These values can be real numbers or multi-dimensional vectors.

Time series data arise in many applications including medical, financial, and engineering ones. For this reason, time series data mining has received increasing attention over the last two decades.

© Springer International Publishing Switzerland 2015
A.M. Mora and G. Squillero (Eds.): EvoApplications 2015, LNCS 9028, pp. 579–589, 2015.
DOI: 10.1007/978-3-319-16549-3_47

Time series data mining handles several tasks such as *clustering, classification* and others. All these tasks are based on the concept of similarity which is measured using a *similarity measure* or a *distance metric*.

*Bio-inspired Optimization*, also called *Nature-inspired Optimization*, is a branch of optimization which, as the name indicates, is inspired by natural phenomena. It has diverse applications in engineering, finance, economics and other domains. In computer science bio-inspired optimization has been applied to networking, data mining, software engineering, and several other fields.

In this paper we apply a multi-objective algorithm called *Non-dominated Sorting Genetic Algorithm II* (NSGA-II) to determine the weights of a combination of distance metrics that gives optimal clustering and classification accuracy of time series data. The experiments we conducted show that the proposed combination outperforms the performance of the distance metrics that constitute it when they are used as stand-alone distances.

The rest of the paper is organized as follows; the related work is presented in Sect. 2, in Sect. 3 we introduce the new algorithm which we test in Sect. 4. We conclude in Sect. 5.

## 2  Background

Data mining is a fundamental branch of computer science that witnessed substantial progress in the last years. Data mining is defined as the process of discovering patterns in data. The process must be automatic or (more usually) semiautomatic. The patterns discovered must be meaningful in that they lead to some advantages. Data are invariably present in substantial quantities [1]. Data mining focuses mainly on finding hidden information in large amounts of data.

As with other domains in information technology, several papers have proposed applying bio-inspired algorithms to solve data mining problems [2, 3].

In the following we present a brief description of the most important data mining tasks.

**Classification:** The goal of classification is to assign an unknown object to one out of a given number of classes or categories [4].

Classification is based on four fundamental components [5]: 1- Class, which is a categorical variable representing the 'label' put on the object after its classification. 2- Predictors, which are represented by the attributes of the data to be classified. 3- Training dataset, which is the set of data containing values for the two previous components, and is used for 'training' the model to recognize the appropriate class based on available predictors. 4- Testing dataset, containing new data that will be classified by the model constructed in the previous steps.

One of the most popular classification techniques of time series is *Nearest-Neighbor Classification* (NNC). In NNC the query is classified according to the majority of its nearest neighbours [6]. Usually N is taken to be 1, thus applying a first nearest-neighbor (1-NN) rule using leaving-one-out cross validation. This means that every data object is compared to the other data objects in the dataset. If the 1-NN does not belong to the same class, the error counter is incremented by 1.

**Clustering:** It is the task of partitioning the data objects into groups, or clusters, so that the objects within a cluster are similar to one another and dissimilar to the objects in other clusters [7]. Clustering differs from classification in that there is no target variable for clustering. Instead, clustering algorithms seek to segment the entire data set into relatively homogeneous subgroups or clusters [8].

There are several basic clustering methods such as *Partitioning Methods, Hierarchical Methods, Density-Based Methods*, and *Grid-Based Methods. k-means*, is a centroid-based partitioning technique which uses the *centroid* (also called *center*), of a cluster; $c_i$, to represent that cluster. Conceptually, the centroid of a cluster is its center point. The centroid can be defined in various ways such as by the mean of the objects assigned to the cluster. *k*-means is one of the most widely used and studied clustering formulations [9].

In *k*-means clustering we have a set of *n* data points in *d*-dimensional space $R^d$ and an integer *k* and the problem is to determine a set of *k* points in $R^d$, the centroids, so as to minimize the mean distance from each data point to its nearest center [9].

More formally, the *k*-means clustering error can be measured by:

$$E = \sum_{i=1}^{k} \sum_{j=1}^{n_j} d(u_{ij}, c_i) \tag{1}$$

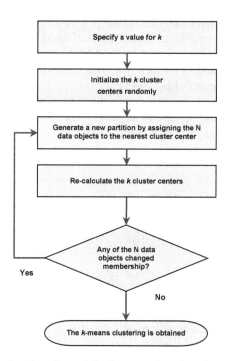

**Fig. 1.** Flow chart of the *k*-means clustering algorithm

Where $u_{ij}$ is the $j$th point in the $i$th cluster, and $n_j$ is the number of points in that cluster. The quality of the $k$-means clustering increases as the error given in Eq. (1) decreases. Figure 1 shows the flow chart of the $k$-means algorithm.

The number of clusters is decided by the user, or application-dependent, or given by some cluster validity measure.

$k$-means starts by selecting the centroids $c_i$, which are usually chosen randomly. In the second step the membership of each of the $n$ data points is determined by assigning it to the nearest cluster centroid. In the third step $c_i$ are re-calculated assuming the memberships obtained in step two are correct. If none of the $n$ data objects have changed their membership the algorithm stops otherwise it goes back to step two. Figure 2 shows an example of the different steps of the $k$-means clustering with $n = 30$ and $k = 3$. ☐

It is worth mentioning here that clustering has also been the subject of bio-inspired optimization. In [10] we presented a paper that applies differential evolution, a popular bio-inspired optimization algorithm, to the problem of $k$-means clustering.

**Similarity Search:** The concept of similarity on which classification, clustering, and other data mining tasks are based is a fundamental one in data mining. In the similarity search problem a pattern or a query is given and the similarity search algorithm aims to retrieve the data objects in the database that are "close" to that query according to some semantics that quantify this closeness. This closeness or similarity is quantified using a principal concept which is the *similarity measure* or its strongest form- the *distance metric*. Distance metrics satisfy the well-known metric axioms (non-negativity, symmetry, identity, triangle inequality). Metric spaces have many advantages, the most famous of which is that a single indexing structure can be applied to several kinds of queries and data types that are so different in nature. This is mainly important in establishing unifying models for the search problem that are independent of the data type. This makes metric spaces a solid structure that is able to deal with several data types [11].

There are many distance metrics used in the field of time series data mining. The most-widely known is the *Minkowski distance*. This is actually a whole family of distances, the most famous of which are:

**i- Euclidean Distance ($L_2$)-** defined between two time series $S$ and $T$ as:

$$L_2(S, T) = \sqrt{\sum_{i=1}^{n} (s_i - t_i)^2} \tag{2}$$

**ii- Manhattan Distance ($L_1$)-** defined as:

$$L_1(S, T) = \left| \sum_{i=1}^{n} (s_i - t_i) \right| \tag{3}$$

**iii- Maximum Distance ($L_\infty$)-** defined as:

$$L_\infty(S, T) = \max_i(|s_i - t_i|) \tag{4}$$

This distance is also called the *infinity distance* or the *chessboard distance*.

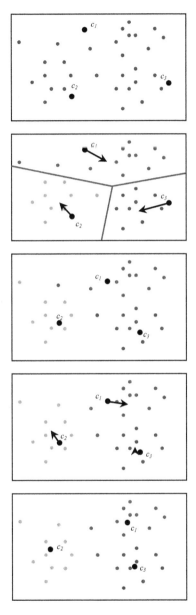

**Fig. 2.** The different steps of the $k$-means clustering algorithm

## 3   An Optimized Weighted Multi-metric Distance

Instead of using one distance metric to handle data mining tasks, we can use a combination of several distance metrics to get better results. This idea has been proposed by several researchers before. In [12] the authors propose utilizing a similarity function defined as a weighted combination of several metrics to handle the similarity search problem. A similar idea was proposed in [13] which presents a retrieval method based on a weighted combination of feature vectors. However, these two works do not suggest using any optimization algorithm to determine the weights.

In this paper we apply a combination $d$ of several distance metrics to handle classification and clustering tasks. This combination is defined as:

$$d(S, T) = \sum_{i=1}^{n} \omega_i d_i(S, T) \tag{5}$$

where $\omega_i \in [0,1]$.

## 3.1   Non-dominated Sorting Genetic Algorithm II (NSGA-II)

Our objective in this paper is to determine the values of $\omega_i$ in Eq. (5) that give a minimum $k$-means clustering error, and a minimum 1-NN classification error, simultaneously. We will obtain these weights through an optimization process.

Optimization is a ubiquitous problem that has a very broad range of applications. Optimization can be defined as the action of finding the best-suited solution of a problem within given constraints.

Formally, an optimization process can be defined as follows: Let $\vec{X} = [x_1, x_2, \ldots, x_{nbp}]$ (nbp is the number of parameters) be the candidate solution to the problem for which we are searching an optimal solution. Given a function $f : U \subseteq \mathbf{R}^{nbp} \to \mathbf{R}$, find the solution $\vec{X^*} = [x_1^*, x_2^*, \ldots, x_{nbp}^*]$ which satisfies $f\left(\vec{X^*}\right) \leq f(\vec{X}), \forall \vec{X} \in U$. The function $f$ is called *the fitness function* or the *objective function*. It is worth mentioning here that it is a convention for optimization problems to be expressed as minimization problems since any maximization optimization problem can be transformed into a minimization problem.

*Metaheuristics* are probabilistic optimization algorithms which are applicable to a large variety of optimization problems. Many of these metaheuristics are inspired by natural processes, natural phenomena, or by the collective intelligence of natural agents, hence the term bio-inspired optimization algorithms.

The largest family of bio-inspired optimization algorithms is *Evolutionary Algorithms* (EA). EA are population-based algorithms that use the mechanisms of Darwinian evolution such as selection, crossover, and mutation. Of this family we cite *Genetic Algorithms* (GA), *Genetic Programming* (GP), *Evolution Strategies* (ES), and *Differential Evolution* (DE).

GA is the main member of EA. In the following we present a description of the simple, classical GA. GA starts with a collection of individuals, also called *chromosomes*, each of which represents a possible solution to the problem at hand. This collection of randomly chosen chromosomes constitutes a population whose size *popSize* is chosen by the algorithm designer. This step is called *initialization*. In real-valued encoding GA a candidate solution is represented as a real-valued vector in which the dimension of the chromosomes is equal to the dimension of the solution vectors [14]. This dimension is denoted by *nbp*. The fitness function of each chromosome is evaluated. The next step is *selection* which determines the chromosomes that are fit enough to survive and possibly produce offspring. This is decided according to the fitness function of the chromosome. The percentage of chromosomes selected for mating is denoted by *sRate*. *Crossover* is the next step in which offspring of two parents are produced to enrich the population with fitter chromosomes. *Mutation*, which is a random alteration of a certain percentage *mRate* of chromosomes, is the other mechanism which enables the GA to examine unexplored regions in the search space. Now that a new generation is formed, the fitness function of the offspring is calculated and the above procedures repeat for a number of generations *nGen* or until a *stopping criterion* terminates the algorithm.                                                    □

Although single-objective optimization problems are widely-encountered, many practical optimization problems have to satisfy several criteria which are conflicting in many cases. This class of optimization problems is called *Multi-objective Optimization* (MOO). An *m*-dimensional MOO problem can be formulated as follows:

$$min\{f_1(\vec{X}), f_2(\vec{X}), \ldots, f_m(\vec{X})\}$$

Where $\vec{X} \in \mathrm{R}^{nbp}$

The optimal solution for MOO is not a single solution as for single-objective optimization problems, but a set of solutions defined as *Pareto optimal* solutions [15], also called a *non-dominated* solution. A solution is Pareto optimal if it is not possible to improve a given objective without deteriorating at least another objective.

The non-dominated sorting genetic algorithm (NSGA) [16] is one of the most popular algorithms to solve MOO. In NSGA, all non-dominated individuals are classified into one category, with a dummy fitness value proportional to the population size. This group is then removed and the remaining population is reclassified. The process is repeated until all the individuals in the entire population are classified. A stochastic remainder proportionate selection is used here [17].

NSGA, however, has been criticized for its high computational cost, its lack of elitism, and for its need to specify the sharing parameter. For these reasons, NSGA-II was proposed in [18]. NSGA-II can be summarized as follows [19]: a random parent population is initialized. The population is sorted based on non-domination in two fronts, the first front being completely a non-dominant set in the current population and the second being dominated by the individuals in the first front only. Each solution is assigned a rank equal to its non-domination level based on the front it belongs to. Individuals in the first front are assigned a fitness value of 1 and individuals in second are assigned a fitness value of 2 and so on. In NSGA-II the authors introduce a new parameter which is the *crowding distance*. This parameter measures how close every individual is to its neighbors. The crowding distance is calculated for each individual of the population. Parents are selected from the population by using a binary tournament selection based on the rank and the crowding distance. An individual is selected if its rank is less than that of the other or if its crowding distance is greater than that of the other. The selected population generates offspring from crossover and mutation operators. The population with the current population and current offspring is sorted again based on non-domination and only the best *popSize* individuals are selected, where *popSize* is the population size. The selection is based on the rank and on the crowding distance on the last front. The process repeats to generate the subsequent generations *nGen*.                                                □

In this paper we use NSGA-II to solve our multi-objective problem of determining the values of $\omega_i$ in Eq. (5) that give minimum *k*-means clustering error and minimum 1-NN classification error. Technically this is a bi-objective optimization problem, yet we think of it as a multi-objective problem since other distance-based data mining tasks can be added to the optimization problem at hand.

The reason for selecting NSGA-II is that most data mining tasks include a high-computational cost, so using an optimizer with a relatively low-computational cost such as NSGA-II is indispensable.

**Table 1.** The *k*-means clustering error of the combination and $L_2$, $L_1$, $L_\infty$ on the testing datasets datasets

| Dataset | *k*-means clustering error | | | |
|---|---|---|---|---|
| | $L_1$ | $L_2$ | $L_\infty$ | Combination |
| Synthetic_control | 0.43 | 0.29 | 0.36 | 0.27 |
| OSULeaf | 0.61 | 0.60 | 0.67 | 0.59 |
| Lighting2 | 0.44 | 0.37 | 0.37 | 0.35 |
| Lighting7 | 0.46 | 0.43 | 0.50 | 0.36 |
| SonyAIBORobotSurface | 0.13 | 0.34 | 0.31 | 0.08 |
| FaceFour | 0.39 | 0.46 | 0.45 | 0.33 |
| ECG200 | 0.31 | 0.31 | 0.38 | 0.28 |
| Yoga | 0.50 | 0.52 | 0.52 | 0.49 |
| OliveOil | 0.43 | 0.43 | 0.43 | 0.42 |
| CinC_ECG_torso | 0.51 | 0.53 | 0.54 | 0.48 |
| ChlorineConcentration | 0.60 | 0.60 | 0.60 | 0.59 |
| Haptics | 0.67 | 0.68 | 0.68 | 0.66 |
| MedicalImages | 0.67 | 0.66 | 0.70 | 0.63 |

## 4  Experiments

We conducted extensive experiments using time series datasets of different sizes and dimensions available at UCR [20]. This archive makes up between 90 % and 100 % of all publicly available, labeled time series data sets in the world, and it represents the interest of the data mining/database community, and not just one group [21].

The distances we are using in the combination in Eq. (6) are the Euclidean distance, the Manhattan distance, and the maximum distance (Eqs. (2), (3), (4)), so our combination is:

$$d(S, T) = \omega_1 L_1(S, T) + \omega_2 L_2(S, T) + \omega_3 L_\infty(S, T) \tag{6}$$

We tested our method on a variety of datasets. The length of the time series varied between 60 (Synthetic_control) and 1639 (CinC_ECG_torso). The size of the training sets varied between 20 (SonyAIBORobot Surface) and 467 (ChlorineConcentration). The size of the testing sets varied between 30 (OliveOil) and 3840 (ChlorineConcentration), so as we can see, we tested our method on a wide range of datasets of different lengths and sizes to avoid getting biased results.

For each dataset the experiment consists of two stages; the training stage and the testing stage.

In the training stage we perform an optimization process where the parameters of the optimization problem are the weights $\omega_i$; $i \in [1, 3]$. The outcome of this optimization problem is the weights $\omega_i$ which give the optimal $k$-means clustering and 1-NN classification.

In the testing stage, these optimal weights are used on the corresponding testing datasets to evaluate the error of the $k$-means clustering and 1-NN classification.

The weights that gave a minimum $k$-means clustering error and minimum 1-NN classification error on the testing datasets are shown in Tables 1, and 2, respectively.

Our final evaluation criterion on both classification and clustering was as follows: for each dataset, and for each task, we give the distance ($L_1$, $L_2$, $L_\infty$, or the combination) that gave the best results for that task 4 points, then 3 points for the second best and so on. In case where two distances gave the same result we give them the same points and we skip the following rank. So for the two tasks together each distance can obtain a maximum of 8 points, then we take the sum of all the points each distance/the combination obtained on all the datasets tested. The final rank on 1-NN classification error and for all the datasets is the following: 1-combination (48 points) 2- $L_2$ (36 points) 3- $L_1$ (30 points) 4- $L_\infty$ (25 points). The rank on $k$-means clustering error is the following: 1-combination (52 points) 2- $L_2$ (32 points) 2- $L_1$ (32 points) 4- $L_\infty$ (24 points).

**Table 2.** The 1-NN classification error of the combination and of $L_2$, $L_1$, $L_\infty$ on the testing datasets

| Dataset | 1-NN classification error | | | |
|---|---|---|---|---|
| | $L_1$ | $L_2$ | $L_\infty$ | Combination |
| Synthetic_control | 0.13 | 0.12 | 0.14 | 0.10 |
| OSULeaf | 0.29 | 0.27 | 0.29 | 0.26 |
| Lighting2 | 0.23 | 0.25 | 0.24 | 0.26 |
| Lighting7 | 0.41 | 0.43 | 0.49 | 0.42 |
| SonyAIBORobotSurface | 0.36 | 0.31 | 0.34 | 0.30 |
| FaceFour | 0.28 | 0.22 | 0.22 | 0.21 |
| ECG200 | 0.46 | 0.43 | 0.45 | 0.43 |
| Yoga | 0.15 | 0.17 | 0.19 | 0.15 |
| OliveOil | 0.16 | 0.13 | 0.15 | 0.11 |
| CinC_ECG_torso | 0.10 | 0.10 | 0.12 | 0.10 |
| ChlorineConcentration | 0.32 | 0.35 | 0.33 | 0.32 |
| Haptics | 0.66 | 0.63 | 0.63 | 0.61 |
| MedicalImages | 0.35 | 0.32 | 0.34 | 0.30 |

As we can see from these results, for the two tasks together, $k$-means clustering and 1-NN classification, the combination of distance-metrics gives the optimal results on the whole datasets, which validates our method.

## 5  Conclusion

In this paper we applied a multi-objective algorithm called NSGA-II to determine the weights of a combination of distance metrics used to perform two time series data mining tasks which are $k$-means clustering and 1-NN classification. In the experiments we conducted on different time series datasets we showed the superiority of the optimized weighted combination over the distance metrics that constitute it. The optimizer we used, NSGA-II, is particularly adapted to perform this optimization process as it is known for its relatively low computational cost.

When using bio-inspired optimization algorithms to solve data mining problems it is important to be careful that this may result in overfitting; a widely encountered phenomenon in data mining, as we showed in [22] and [23].

In the future we plan to generalize our work to handle different types of data. We also like to develop optimizing algorithms that are designed particularly to apply to data mining tasks.

## References

1. Witten, I.H., Frank, E.: Data Mining Practical Machine Learning Tools and Techniques, Second Edition edn. Elsevier, Amsterdam (2009)
2. Muhammad Fuad, M.M.: Differential evolution versus genetic algorithms: towards symbolic aggregate approximation of non-normalized time series. In: Sixteenth International Database Engineering & Applications Symposium– IDEAS 2012. BytePress/ACM, Prague, Czech Republic, 8–10 August 2012
3. Muhammad Fuad, M.M.: Using differential evolution to set weights to segments with different information content in the piecewise aggregate approximation. In: 16th International Conference on Knowledge-Based and Intelligent Information & Engineering Systems, KES 2012, Frontiers of Artificial Intelligence and Applications (FAIA). IOS Press, San Sebastian, Spain, 10–12 September 2012
4. Bunke, H., Kraetzl, M.: Classification and detection of abnormal events in time series of graphs. In: Last, M., Kandel, A., Bunke, H. (eds.) Data Mining in Time Series Databases. World Scientific, New Jersey (2003)
5. Gorunescu, F.: Data Mining: Concepts, Models and Techniques. Blue Publishing House, Cluj-Napoca (2006)
6. Vlachos, M., Gunopulos, D.: Indexing time-series under conditions of noise. In: Last, M., Kandel, A., Bunke, H. (eds.) Data Mining in Time Series Databases. World Scientific, New Jersey (2003)
7. Han, J., Kamber, M., Pei, J.: Data Mining: Concepts and Techniques, 3rd edn. Morgan Kaufmann, Burlington (2011)
8. Larose, D.T.: Discovering Knowledge in Data: An Introduction to Data Mining. Wiley, New York (2005)

9. Kanungo, T., Netanyahu, N.S., Wu, A.Y.: An efficient k-means clustering algorithm: analysis and implementation. IEEE Trans. Pattern Anal. Mach. Intell. **24**(7), 881–892 (2002)

10. Muhammad Fuad, M.M.: Differential evolution-based weighted combination of distance metrics for $k$-means clustering. In: Dediu, A.-H., Lozano, M., Martin-Vide, C. (eds.) TPNC 2014. LNCS, vol. 8890, pp. 193–204. Springer, Heidelberg (2014)

11. Zezula, P., et al.: Similarity Search - The Metric Space Approach. Springer, New York (2005)

12. Bustos, B., Skopal, T.: Dynamic Similarity Search in Multi-metric Spaces. Proceedings of the ACM Multimedia, MIR Workshop. ACM Press, New York (2006)

13. Bustos, B., Keim, D.A., Saupe, D., Schreck, T., Vranic, D.: Automatic selection and combination of descriptors for effective 3D similarity search. In: Proceedings of the IEEE International Workshop on Multimedia Content-based Analysis and Retrieval. IEEE Computer Society (2004)

14. Affenzeller, M., Winkler, S., Wagner, S., Beham, A.: Genetic Algorithms and Genetic Programming Modern Concepts and Practical Applications. Chapman and Hall/CRC, Boca Raton (2009)

15. El-Ghazali, T.: Metaheuristics: from Design to Implementation. John Wiley & Sons Inc, Hoboken (2009)

16. Srinivas, N., Deb, K.: Multi-objective function optimization using non-dominated sorting genetic algorithms. J. Evol. Comput. **2**(3), 221–248 (1995)

17. Maulik, U., Bandyopadhyay, S., Mukhopadhyay, A.: Multiobjective Genetic Algorithms for Clustering. Springer-Verlag GmbH, Heidelberg (2011)

18. Deb, K., Pratap, A., Agarwal, S., Meyarivan, T.: A fast and elitist multiobjective genetic algorithm: NSGA-II. In: IEEE Trans Evolutionary Computation (2002)

19. Ma, Q., Xu, D., Iv, P., Shi, Y.: Application of NSGA-II in parameter optimization of extended state observer. In: Challenges of Power Engineering and Environment (2007)

20. Keogh, E., Zhu, Q., Hu, B., Hao. Y., Xi, X., Wei, L., Ratanamahatana C.A.: The UCR time series classification/clustering homepage (2011). www.cs.ucr.edu/ ~ eamonn/time_series_data/

21. Ding, H., Trajcevski, G., Scheuermann, P., Wang, X., Keogh, E.: Querying and mining of time series data: experimental comparison of representations and distance measures. In: Proceedings of the 34th VLDB (2008)

22. Muhammad Fuad, M.M.: One-step or two-step optimization and the overfitting phenomenon: a case study on time series classification. In: The 6th International Conference on Agents and Artificial Intelligence- ICAART 2014. SCITEPRESS Digital Library, Angers, France, 6–8 March 2014

23. Muhammad Fuad, M.M.: On the application of bio-inspired optimization algorithms to fuzzy $c$-means clustering of time series. In: The 4th International Conference on Pattern Recognition Applications and Methods - ICPRAM 2015. SCITEPRESS Digital Library, Lisbon, Portugal, 10–12 January 2015

# EvoINDUSTRY

# Many-Objective Optimization of a Hybrid Car Controller

Tobias Rodemann[1](✉), Kaname Narukawa[1,3], Michael Fischer[2],
and Mohammed Awada[2]

[1] Honda Research Institute Europe, Carl-Legien-Straße 30,
63073 Offenbach, Germany
tobias.rodemann@honda-ri.de
[2] Honda R&D Europe, Carl-Legien-Straße 30, 63073 Offenbach, Germany
{michael_fischer,mohammed_awada}@honda.co.uk
[3] Honda R&D Ltd., Wako, Saitama, Japan
kaname_narukawa@n.f.rd.honda.co.jp

**Abstract.** Hybrid cars are a promising approach for providing individual mobility with lower $CO_2$-emissions and without compromising on affordability and driving range. In order to reach these targets a highly efficient control (energy management) is required. In mass production vehicles control is often organized using simple, quick, and easy to understand rule-based systems. Such a rule-base typically contains a moderate number of parameters which can be tuned using methods like evolutionary algorithms to improve performance. However, prior work basically targets a minimization of fuel consumption. In this work we present a many-objective evolutionary optimization that considers up to 7 objectives in parallel. We outline the additional optimization challenges that arise due to the large number of objectives and demonstrate that a substantial performance increase, over all objectives, can be achieved.

**Keywords:** Many-objective optimization · Hybrid cars · Data mining

## 1 Introduction

In order to optimally drive a certain, pre-defined driving cycle using a hybrid car a sophisticated controller is required. A hybrid powertrain allows to provide power partially or even completely using only the electric motor, employing the combustion engine only for some parts of the route or driving cycle. The controller has to decide if the current power demand is provided by combustion engine or electric motor, or, from a different perspective, using fuel or battery energy. This problem can not be solved statically since it depends on the current and future driving situations. Depending on the definition of optimality (e.g. minimum fuel consumption or $CO_2$-emission), the optimal power split might depend on the current speed of the car (and the resulting efficiency of the combustion engine) or the remaining state of charge (SOC) of the battery. A typical problem is that a locally (at the current point in time) good control might later

© Springer International Publishing Switzerland 2015
A.M. Mora and G. Squillero (Eds.): EvoApplications 2015, LNCS 9028, pp. 593–603, 2015.
DOI: 10.1007/978-3-319-16549-3_48

turn out to be bad, like for example when a car with an empty battery has to go uphill, leading to an unpleasant driving experience (low acceleration) and operation of the combustion engine in low efficiency regimes. A smarter (foresighted) strategy would have kept enough energy in the battery to master the climb, allowing a battery recharge in the subsequent down-hill phase.

A simple approach for a controller in a hybrid car is using a set of basic rules that decide on the current power split based on a few system inputs, like current speed and SOC. These controllers are easy to implement and validate. They are also simple enough to be computed at high frequencies even on very small on-board ECUs. Unfortunately, these controllers are often far away from an optimal control in terms of fuel consumption and drivability.

To reduce the gap to an optimal controller various optimization methods can be used to tune parameters in the rule-base, in order to provide a better performance on one or more relevant driving cycles.

A well-tested set of methods is provided through evolutionary algorithms. The computation of the fitness is typically done using a simulation model of the hybrid car with a defined driving cycle like the NEDC (New European Driving Cycle). Evolutionary algorithms (EAs) have a relatively high (offline) computation demand due to the semi-random search process, but are very flexible, i.e. they can quickly be adapted to handle new constraints and objectives, and require less domain knowledge on the optimization side. Their usefulness has been shown in several articles [1,5].

Prior work has mostly focused on a single objective, often fuel consumption, but the resulting operation strategies often lack in many other criteria. Some of the additional criteria are directly noticeable by the customer, like engine noise, others, like battery lifetime, are more important to the manufacturer.

In recent years several state-of-art MAny-Objective optimization (MAO) evolutionary algorithms have been proposed, which allow optimization for a larger number of objectives.

In this work we demonstrate the usage of a many-objective optimization algorithm, the SMS-EMOA [2], for tuning a rule-based controller for a hybrid car towards 7 different objectives. In a previous work [9] we have compared different optimization algorithms without giving too much detail about the specific application. In this paper our focus is more on the relation between many-objective optimization and the specific application of a hybrid car controller.

The following sections first give a brief outline of hybrid car technology as far as it concerns the optimization problem and the employed simulation system, then we describe in more detail the applied optimization algorithm. In the results section we show some of the found solutions and compare this to a manually tuned system. The summary and outlook section wraps up the work presented and sketches some of the remaining issues, especially the post-processing and visualization of the optimization results.

## 2   Hybrid Cars

A Hybrid Electric Vehicle (HEV) combines a standard internal combustion engine linked to a conventional fuel tank with an electric motor that can turn battery energy into wheel torque or act as a generator that recuperates energy. The higher cost and weight of hybrid vehicles through the additional motors, battery, and other parts is in theory compensated by a number of advantages:

- Higher mean operation efficiency of combustion engine resulting in lower fuel consumption
- Energy recuperation during braking and down-hill phases
- Better acceleration performance when using both engine and motor
- Reduced noise and emissions when engine is off

These advantages depend on the specific type of hybrid architecture and an efficient controller. Emission and noise benefits matter most in urban driving situations, and a wrong current SOC level (too high or too low) will reduce the benefits for engine operation, acceleration or recuperation. It is therefore essential to have a good energy management to make optimum use of the hybrid power supply.

In this work we will study a model car that is a plug-in serial hybrid with a battery capacity of 24.4 kWh (corresponding to approximately 150 km of pure electric driving range).

Typical driving cycles that are used to assess fuel consumption are rather short and could be managed fully without combustion engine. We are therefore using our own driving cycle, which is a combination of urban and extra-urban driving conditions. It is shown in Fig. 1. Its total length is 230 km, beyond the purely electric range. Note that in the following, remaining battery energy at the end of the driving cycle (above the 20 % minimum charge level) is translated into (reduced) fuel consumption for the final assessment of the driving strategy. For this we assumed that 1 kWh of remaining battery energy corresponds to 0.5 l of fuel.

### 2.1 Objectives

As outlined in the introduction there are several objectives besides fuel consumption that influence the perception of a car's performance by the customer.

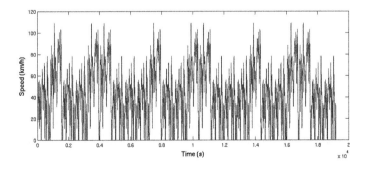

**Fig. 1.** Drive Cycle used for evaluating the performance of the hybrid energy management. Total cycle length is 230 km. We can see both urban and extra-urban (e.g. highway) parts.

Many of these criteria are difficult to define and there is rarely a hard constraint that can be set. In many cases, the different objectives are conflicting, so that a trade-off has to be found. It also turned out to be difficult to put relative weights to these objectives, since they are from rather different domains.

We have therefore decided not to integrate those objectives as fixed constraints nor to perform single-objective optimization using a weighted aggregation of objectives. Rather we include all separate objectives in a many objective optimization.

Since the focus in this article is not a detailed model of the car and the different objectives, we have decided to use simplified methods for computing objective values (also in order to keep computation times low). Specifically we are optimizing for the following objectives:

1. Fuel consumption (**FC**) (as l/100 km) over the full driving cycle. This measure directly correlates with the $CO_2$-emissions. This information is taken directly from the simulator using motor efficiency maps. The fuel consumed during the trip is reduced by the amount of fuel saved through the remaining battery energy at the end of the trip (see above).
2. Battery stress (**BS**): The battery as one of the most sensitive and expensive parts of the car has to be kept at a high State of Health (SOH) over the full lifetime of the car. The operation strategy therefore has to consider how the battery is affected by different control actions. Unfortunately, accurate battery aging models are very complex and difficult to calibrate. We therefore used a simplified model, by monitoring only (dis-)charging current to and from the battery and battery temperature. If currents or temperature leave a specified safety zone, battery stress is generated. The target of the optimization is to minimize these stress events.
3. Operation changes (**OPC**): A start and stop of the engine can often be heard and felt by the driver. It is therefore advisable to keep the frequency of on/off switches below a certain level. We therefore compute the number of on/off switches that happen within less than a given interval time (we chose 60 s) after the last on/off switch.
4. Emissions (**Emis**): While $CO_2$-emissions are directly proportional to the consumed fuel, other emissions like NOx are also linked to the operation of the combustion engine but only when the catalytic converter has not yet reached its operation temperature. We therefore compute emissions (excluding $CO_2$) considering the current temperature of the catalytic converter.
5. Urban operation (**U-Noise**): plugin-hybrid vehicles are a potential answer to pollution and noise problems in metropolitan areas, if the operation strategy manages to keep the combustion engine off while driving in the city. For this objective we count the number of simulation time steps when the engine is on while the car is driving slower than 50 km/h (urban speed limit).
6. Noise (**Noise**): A car generates noise from various sources, the two most important ones being tire and wind noise (resulting from car motion) on the one hand and engine noise on the other hand. While the former can't be avoided given a targeted speed of the car, the latter is influenced by the

operation strategy. We model wind and tire noise after [11] and engine noise using measured data. The noise objective will only consider instances when the engine noise exceeds tire and wind noise, because otherwise it will not be perceived by the driver. The objective is to minimize those instances.

7. Battery State-of-Charge (**SOC**): Since we translate the remaining state of charge into reduced fuel consumption, the operation strategy might decide to end the trip with a higher final state-of-charge. But there are several reasons to prefer a lower SOC: Firstly, for some battery types, lifetime is higher when the battery is kept at a lower state of charge. Secondly, when the car arrives with full batteries at a charging station, it can't use grid electricity to recharge. We therefore compute the accumulated SOC level (the area under the SOC curve) as our last objective.

We also add a penalty term to all objectives when the simulator reports an infeasible solution or does not finish due to some model inconsistency.

## 2.2 Rule-Based Controller

The core of the controller is a small set of rules, that are configured by a set of parameters (in *italics*):

- **Rule 1:** If speed is below $v_{off}$, turn off engine.
- **Rule 2:** If SOC is above $SOC_{max2}$, turn off engine. Note that $SOC_{max2}$ is not the maximum SOC of the battery but the SOC level below which the ICE will begin to recharge the battery.
- **Rule 3:** If SOC falls below $SOC_{min}$ turn on engine (overrides first rule)
- **Rule 4:** If engine is ON and speed is below $v_1$ use engine operation point 1 (revolutions per minute (rpm) $rev_1$ and torque $torque_1$)
- **Rule 5:** If engine is ON and speed is between $v_1$ and $v_2$ use operation point 2 ($rev_2$, $torque_2$)
- **Rule 6:** If engine is ON and speed is above $v_2$ use operation point 3 ($rev_3$, $torque_3$)

This simple rule base is associated with a set of 11 parameters. Initially the parameters were manually tuned by an engineer (a tedious task considering the large number of objectives). We will tune those parameters using our MAO method. The rules can be computed very quickly and are easy to understand, but their impact on different objectives is hard to predict.

Minimum and maximum values for parameters are given in Table 1. Parameter ranges are soft constrained by adding a penalty to all objectives proportional to the deviation of the parameters from the permitted range.

## 2.3 Simulation Environment

The behavior of the car is simulated using a model of a hybrid car implemented in Matlab/Simulink [8]. The runtime for a single simulated driving cycle is a couple of seconds (8 s on a standard desktop computer in Simulink Normal mode). This is sufficiently short for an extensive evolutionary optimization (using 10,000 iterations) that finishes in less than a day.

**Table 1.** Parameter ranges

| Parameter | Range | Parameter | Range |
|---|---|---|---|
| $SOC_{max2}$ (%) | [25,50] | $SOC_{min}$ (%) | [20,30] |
| $v_1$ (km/h) | [20,60] | $v_2$ (km/h) | [50,100] |
| $rev_1$ (/m) | [2500,3000] | $torque_1$ (N · m) | [5.23,12.56] |
| $rev_2$ (/m) | [3000,4000] | $torque_2$ (N · m) | [5.65,17.59] |
| $rev_3$ (/m) | [4000,5000] | $torque_3$ (N · m) | [7.77,23.03] |
| $v_{off}$ (km/h) | [20,50] | | |

# 3   Evolutionary Many Objective Optimization

In the literature the optimization for two or more objectives is often referred to as multi-objective optimization (MOO). For more than one objective there is for most applications not one single optimum solution. Rather, the target is to approximate the Pareto-front of non-dominated solutions. Therefore the target of MOO is to find a diverse set of non-dominated solutions that come as close to the Pareto-front as possible

For example, the *NSGA-II* algorithm proposed by Deb [4] is a standard multi-objective optimization algorithm that uses the distribution of solutions and their ranking regarding the Pareto-front as selection criteria. It has been successfully used in a number of applications [12] for two or three objectives.

In a recent paper [9] we have shown that for an optimization task with 6 or 7 objectives standard methods like NSGA-II [4] fail to improve the quality of the solution set over the course of generations.

Since methods which are commonly referred to as *multi*-objective optimization methods perform weakly for more than 3 objectives, the term *many*-objective optimization (MAO) has been introduced [6] to label a new class of algorithms that show better performance for a larger number of objectives.

## 3.1   SMS-EMOA

The SMS-EMOA (*S-M*atrix *S*election - *E*volutionary *M*ultiobjective *O*ptimization *A*lgorithm) [2] directly uses the hypervolume [14] of a population for the selection operator. The hypervolume is the volume in fitness space covered by a solution relative to a pre-defined reference point (e.g. the worst solution found). A population's hypervolume is the total hypervolume covered by all solutions of the population. It is maximized when the solutions approach the Pareto-front.

The SMS-EMOA is a steady-state optimization algorithm where the current candidate solution's hypervolume contribution is compared to those of solutions already in the population and the individual with the weakest contribution is removed. This method is conceptually very simple and as we have shown in [9] has a very good performance. The algorithm's drawback is the substantial computation effort for the hypervolume. For larger population sizes and number of objectives, hypervolume computation time can easily exceed fitness computation even for demanding applications. We encountered this effect when during the process of optimization we switched from 6 to 7 objectives and total optimization times increased substantially. Based on a comparison study of different methods for hypervolume computation [10] we decided that the method of While et al. [13] provides the best performance of all tested methods and drastically reduced computing times. With the new algorithm up to 10 objectives should be feasible on a typical computing budget. Table 2 shows the settings we used for the SMS EMOA.

**Table 2.** Settings used in the SMS-EMOA

| Parameter | Value |
|-----------|-------|
| Population size | 100 |
| Crossover probability | 1.0 |
| Mutation probability | 0.2 |
| Mutation distribution parameter $\eta_m$ | 20 |
| Crossover distribution parameter $\eta_c$ | 15 |
| Stopping condition | 10000 fitness evaluations |

# 4 Optimization Results

The result of the many-objective optimization is a population of (100) solutions (configurations) representing the set of trade-offs for all involved objectives. In the following we show a number of performance measures. To better compare with the baseline solution (parameters manually tuned by an engineer) all objective values are normalized by the values from the baseline solution, i.e. the baseline solution has a value of 1.0 for all objectives.

## 4.1 Summary of Optimization Results

First we show in Fig. 2 the development of the hypervolume of all solutions relative to the worst solution found (in all previous runs). We see that the hypervolume increases smoothly up to approximately 6000 iterations. The actual shown hypervolume in the plot might decrease due to either a wrongly specified reference point to calculate the hypervolume and the nature of SMS-EMOA [7].

We then show a plot of the pairwise correlations of objective values of all final solutions in Fig. 3. Diagonal elements show histograms of objective values, plots above the diagonal give pairwise correlations between two objectives each, while below diagonal elements show the correlation factor between the elements. Positive values are indicated as upward pointing arrows, zero correlation as right pointing and negative correlations as downward pointing arrows. We see that

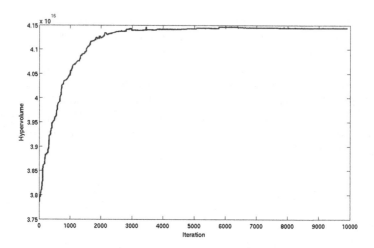

**Fig. 2.** Development of hypervolume over iterations for the SMS-EMOA optimization algorithm. Values were computed with unnormalized objective values.

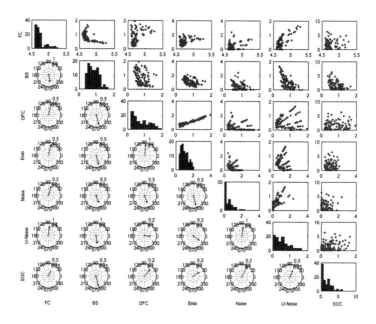

**Fig. 3.** Correlation plot of SMS-EMOA final solutions after optimization

some objectives (like Emission and operation point changes (OPC)) are highly correlated, others, like fuel consumption and battery stress, are anti-correlated. Especially the objective SOC seems to be rather uncorrelated to other objectives. Information like this can help the engineer to understand the basic compromises that need to be made, like between fuel consumption and battery lifetime in our

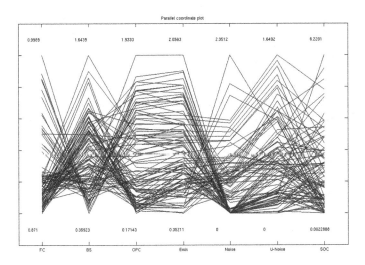

**Fig. 4.** Parallel coordinate plots in objective space of all 100 solutions in the final population of SMS-EMOA.

example. It also shows that either OPC or emissions might be removed as an objective with limited impact due to their strong correlation.

Figure 4 shows a parallel coordinate plot in objective space of the final 100 solutions from the SMS-EMOA. This plot again visualizes the relation between different objectives, the clustering of solutions in terms of objective values, and the resultant minimum and maximum values. Please note especially the very low (good) objective values for many solutions. The majority of objectives is below the baseline value (1.0) for a large share of the solutions. While fuel consumption was reduced only little, the other objectives can be improved by a large margin. The average reduction over all objectives was up to almost 50 % for the best solution. Among the solution set, there are also configurations that improve on all objectives (i.e. no deterioration compared to the baseline).

## 5    Discussion on Post-processing

Finding an optimal setting for a hybrid car controller is a challenging optimization task. However, due to recent advances in many-objective optimization algorithms and faster simulators, it is now possible to derive a larger set of solutions that provide a variety of parameter sets each being optimal in its own regard. We even found solutions that are better than a manually tuned one for all objectives. From a purely optimization point of view this is a very satisfying result, however, the engineer is stilled faced with the issue of deciding which strategy (solution) to implement. By design, many or even all solutions are non-dominated, that means that the majority of solutions is not clearly worse than any other solution. Some of the solutions might be sorted out by considering constraints that were not included in the optimization (e.g. because they are difficult to formalize). Also a clustering might reduce the number of candidates, if many solutions are rather similar. Another option might be to search for knee points [3] in objective space, these are solutions that strongly stand out (in terms of their objective values) relative to similar solutions. If the number of candidates has been reduced sufficiently, the remaining solutions could be implemented in a real car and validated directly (probably reducing the number of candidates further). Alternatively, using the insights gained during the optimization (distribution and correlation of objective values), the engineer might define weights for the different objectives and determine the best overall solution through weighted fitness aggregation.

Finally, the engineer might decide to implement several solutions (parameter sets) and shift the decision to a later stage, in an extreme case leaving the customer with the decision which solution to run currently in the car.

## 6  Summary and Outlook

In this work we have shown a many-objective optimization for the rule base of a hybrid car controller. Using 11 design parameters and 7 objectives, the well-known SMS-EMOA method finds solutions that provide a substantial improvement over the baseline solution, which was manually tuned by an engineer. While the main objective (fuel consumption) could be reduced only by a few percent, other objectives, which are often ignored, could be strongly improved. Total optimization time is less than a day without any technical speed-up, but can be brought down to far less than an hour using Simulink code export and parallelization. We also demonstrated how a visualization of optimization results can help the engineer to better understand the underlying optimization problem in terms of parameter and objective correlations and trade-offs. A challenge that remains is how to decide for one out of the set of final solutions from the optimizer. This decision will have to be made by the responsible engineer but could probably be supported by a clever visualization, analysis, and post processing of optimization results.

An important next step is to compare our optimization results to other methods like Dynamic Programming which promise a solution close the global optimum but only consider a single objective. It could be interesting to compare our solutions in terms of fuel consumption, but also the other objectives.

Another research direction we investigate is preference-based optimization. If the preference of a decision maker is available in optimization, the preference information can be used to focus the search on the preferred regions in the many-objective space by evolutionary algorithms.

## References

1. Bacher, C., Krenek, T., Raidl, G.: Reducing the number of simulationsin operation strategy optimization for hybrid electric vehicles. In: Esparcia-Alcázar, A.I., Mora, A.M. (eds.) EvoApplications 2014. LNCS, vol. 8602, pp. 553–564. Springer, Heidelberg (2014)

2. Beume, N., Naujoks, B., Emmerich, M.: SMS-EMOA: Multiobjective selection based on dominated hypervolume. Eur. J. Oper. Res. **181**(3), 1653–1669 (2007)
3. Branke, J., Deb, K.: Integrating user preferences into evolutionary multi-objective optimization. In: Jin, Y. (ed.) Knowledge Incorporation in Evolutionary Computation. STUDFUZZ, vol. 167, pp. 461–478. Springer, Heidelberg (2004)
4. Deb, K., Pratap, A., Agarwal, S., Meyarivan, T.: A fast and elitist multiobjective genetic algorithm: NSGA-II. IEEE Trans. Evol. Comput. **6**, 182–197 (2002)
5. Desai, C., Williamson, S.S.: Optimal design of a parallel hybrid electric vehicle using multi-objective genetic algorithms. In: IEEE Vehicle Power and Propulsion Conference, VPPC 2009, pp. 871 876. IEEE (2009)
6. Ishibuchi, H., Tsukamoto, N., Nojima, Y.: Evolutionary many-objective optimization: A short review. In: Proceedings of 2008 IEEE Congress on Evolutionary Computation (World Congress on Computational Intelligence), pp. 2419–2426. IEEE (2008)
7. Judt, L., Mersmann, O., Naujoks, B.: Do hypervolume regressions hinder EMOA performance? surprise and relief. In: Purshouse, R.C., Fleming, P.J., Fonseca, C.M., Greco, S., Shaw, J. (eds.) EMO 2013. LNCS, vol. 7811, pp. 96–110. Springer, Heidelberg (2013)
8. MATLAB: version 8.2 (R2013b). The MathWorks Inc., Natick, Massachusetts (2013)
9. Narukawa, K., Rodemann, T.: Examining the performance of evolutionary many-objective optimization algorithms on a real-world application. In: Proceedings of 2012 IEEE International Conference on Genetic and Evolutionary Computing, pp. 316–319. IEEE (2012)
10. Priester, C., Narukawa, K., Rodemann, T.: A comparison of different algorithms for the calculation of dominated hypervolumes. In: Proceedings of 2013 Genetic and Evolutionary Computation Conference, pp. 655–662. ACM (2013)
11. Sandberg, U.: Tyre/road noise: myths and realities. Technical report, Swedish National Road and Transport Research Institute (2001)
12. Wang, L., Ng, A.H.C., Deb, K. (eds.): Multi-objective Evolutionary Optimisation for Product Design and Manufacturing. Springer, London (2011)
13. While, L., Bradstreet, L., Barone, L.: A fast way of calculating exact hypervolumes. IEEE Trans. Evol. Comput. **16**, 86 (2012)
14. Zitzler, E., Thiele, L., Laumanns, M., Fonseca, C.M., Da Fonseca, V.G.: Performance assessment of multiobjective optimizers: An analysis and review. IEEE Trans. Evol. Comput. **7**(2), 117–132 (2003)

# Optimising the Scheduling and Planning of Urban Milk Deliveries

Neil Urquhart[(⊠)]

School of Computing, Edinburgh Napier University, Edinburgh, UK
n.urquart@napier.ac.uk

**Abstract.** This paper investigates the optimisation of the delivery of dairy products to households in three urban areas. The requirement for the optimisation to be part of the existing business process has determined the approach taken. The solution is maintained in an existing customer database, with manual amendments as customers are added and deleted. The optimisation challenge is to take this solution, reduce the distance travelled, and balance the load across rounds making the minimum number of changes to the delivery network. The approach taken utilises an Evolutionary Algorithm for ordering deliveries and a multi-agent approach to reassigning deliveries between rounds. The case study suggests that distance travelled may be reduced by up to 19 %, the deviation between round lengths may be considerably reduced, with only 10 % of customers being moved between rounds.

## 1 Introduction

### 1.1 Motivation

A food distribution company based in Central Scotland, deliver milk and associated dairy products to several thousand customer households each night. These deliveries form part of what is commonly referred to as the final mile, as they represent the final link in the supply chain to the consumer. There exists considerable scope for optimising deliveries to reduce costs and minimise environmental impact.

Deliveries are divided into rounds, each of which is operated by one van, starting and finishing from a central depot. The business has a high turnover of customers although the trend is towards the number of customers expanding over time, therefore updated schedules have to be produced every few days. The number of vans and drivers is determined by the business, but the allocation of deliveries to rounds and the route taken by each driver may be optimised. Drivers get to know the requirements of each customer, it is desirable, therefore to minimise the movement of customers between routes. A considerable challenge in this case is to ensure that the optimisation becomes part of the existing business process.

The remainder of this paper is organised as follows, firstly a review of relevant previous work (Sect. 1.2), a description of the problem and associated data

© Springer International Publishing Switzerland 2015
A.M. Mora and G. Squillero (Eds.): EvoApplications 2015, LNCS 9028, pp. 604–615, 2015.
DOI: 10.1007/978-3-319-16549-3_49

(Sect. 2), a description of the methodologies used (Sect. 3), results are then presented (Sect. 4) and conclusions (Sect. 5).

## 1.2   Previous Work

The problem as described in Sect. 1.1 may be considered to be a Vehicle Routing Problem (VRP) [1], a concise introduction to the field of vehicle routing problems may be found in [2] which charts the history of VRP solvers over the last 50 years. There is a wealth of existing literature on evolutionary approaches to solving VRP problems, using a variety of different approaches, an overview of earlier work may be found in [3] and the reader is referred to a recent survey by [4] for examples of the state-of-the art. Considerable success in solving VRPs has been achieved through the use of meta-heuristics, readers wishing to find out more about the range of meta-heuristics are referred to [5].

Within the problem under consideration, the ordering of customer visits within a single round is analogous to the Travelling Salesman Problem (TSP), which has been extensively investigated since the 1930s (for a brief history of TSP investigation see [6] which illustrates the breadth of approaches that have been used). The use of heuristic approaches to solve the TSP, such as Lin-Kernighan [7] are discussed in [8].

A similar problem to that described in Sect. 1.1 has been investigated in [9,10]. The authors used a framework, known as the Marketplace Framework, which combines software agents with Evolutionary Algorithms to design and optimise postal distribution networks. The approach taken uses a software agent to manage the optimisation of individual routes. Each agent incorporates an Evolutionary Algorithm which is used to optimise its route. If an agents route breaks local constraints (e.g. it is too long) then the agent may identify and return some deliveries to a coordinator which then reassigns the work to a more appropriate agent using an auction mechanism.

The requirement to only make minimal changes to an existing solution rules out many of the approaches suggested in literature as they involve constructing an entirely new solution. The Marketplace framework may prove more promising as it concentrates on optimising individual routes with minimal exchanges of deliveries between them.

## 2   Problem Description and Context

The company currently stores customers and their details within a Management Information System (MIS) used for accounting and general business purposes. Each customer is manually allocated to a round upon entry, and a sequence number allocated that specifies the order in which deliveries should be made. The planner is assisted in this task by a commercial online Geographical Information System. Drivers also feedback to the planners when they feel that the customer sequence is wrong. Given the level of customer turnover it is necessary to produce updated delivery lists every couple of days. The optimisation will use the manual solution from the customer database as a starting point and carry out two operations:

- Re-ordering deliveries within each round to reduce the distance travelled
- Re-allocating deliveries from one round to another to result in a reduction in overall distance travelled and reduce the difference in round lengths.

The search space size for a given round is $\frac{n!}{2n}$ (where $n$ is the number of customers), the delivery network bears many similarities to a vehicle routing problem (VRP). Most VRP solvers produce a single solution from a specific instance, starting from scratch each time. For this problem we must commence with the initial allocation of customers from the MIS and make a minimal number of changes to further optimise it, then subsequently update the MIS with the optimised solution. Many customers have specific requirements such as requiring the delivery to be left in a specific place, the company have found that allocating a regular driver to a delivery maximises the chances of that customer's delivery being made successfully and retaining the customer. We seek to minimise the transfer of customers between rounds unnecessarily, in order to ensure that customers have a regular driver.

Because of the real-world nature of this problem, a source of good quality geographical data, representing road networks is an essential requirement. The road network data used is derived from OpenStreetMap (OSM) [11]) and the calculation of distances between customers is carried out using GraphHopper [12]. GraphHopper is configured to use Dijkstra's Algorithm for path finding between customers, but according to requirements may be configured to use other algorithms such as A*. Within each run the results of requests to GraphHopper are cached to save repeated calls, however the cache is not maintained long-term as an urban street network can change due to temporary road closures. It should also be noted that a journey between two customers $A - B$ may have a differing length from $B - A$ due to one way streets and turn restrictions forcing differing routes to be used in different directions. Geocoding is a weak point of OSM, full address decoding is available using commercial GIS offerings, but no equivalent is supported by OSM. The solution adopted in this case allows us to use freely available UK postcode data that contains latitude and longitude points for each postcode within the UK. In practice for most urban areas, a geolocated postcode will provide a location at, or very close to, the actual location. The UK postcode data is Crown Copyright.

**Table 1.** The three test areas used.

| Area | Rounds | Deliveries |
|------|--------|-----------|
| Edinburgh | 8 | 2054 |
| Glasgow | 4 | 1070 |
| Warrington | 4 | 1126 |

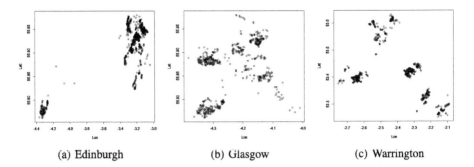

(a) Edinburgh    (b) Glasgow    (c) Warrington

**Fig. 1.** The three data sets used in this study.

Three problem instances, provided by the company, based on three depots are to be investigated, as outlined in Table 1, these represent typical delivery problems encountered by the company (see Fig. 1(a), (b) and (c)). At the time of writing the delivery rounds to the Edinburgh area were operated from the Glasgow depot, but the company was in the process of setting up a depot in the Edinburgh area from which to operate. Within the experiments undertaken a fourth problem instance was used, representing the Edinburgh customers operated from the proposed location of the Edinburgh depot.

In order to solve these problems, it is necessary to utilise a Geographical Information System (GIS), to find routes and distances between customers. GIS typically use techniques such as highway hierarchies [13] which can be expensive (in terms of computation time and cost when using commercial GIS services). An approach that could economise the number of calls made to such services would produce time savings and potentially financial savings.

# 3   Metholodology

## 3.1   The Marketplace Framework

In order to meet the requirement to optimise whilst minimising the perturbation between rounds we adopt the Marketplace framework [9,10] which is a Multi Agent System (MAS) based framework for optimising delivery networks. Within the framework each round is represented by a software agent, known as a Routing Agent, which is responsible for optimising its round and identifying if there is capacity for undertaking more deliveries or if there is a need to reduce the number of deliveries. Each routing agent incorporates an EA (as described in Sect. 3.2) to facilitate optimisation.

To allow the global optimisation of the delivery network, agents communicate via a co-ordinator agent to exchange work using an auction mechanism described below. The co-ordinator agent has a hierarchical relationship with the routing agents, in that its requests for objects and services from the routing agents cannot be refused. Internally the routing agents execute their EA without any direct control from the co-ordinator, geographical data (obtained using Open StreetMap and GraphHopper, see Sect. 2) is available to the routing agents as required.

The allocation of customers is initially based upon the data contained within MIS, this represents the previous solution and any manual additions or deletions of customers made since the optimiser was last executed. It is this initial allocation by the business that determines the number of delivery rounds and thus the number of agents within the framework. Each agent initially constructs a delivery round based on the deliveries allocated to it within the initial solution. Once each agent has constructed a round, the co-ordinator requests that the agent with the longest round identifies a group of customer deliveries to the coordinator for possible reallocation, after some empiricial investigation the group size was set to 5. This group of deliveries represents the 5 households that are furthest from their neighbour within the round. This is calculated for each customer by averaging the distance from each neighbour within the current round sequence (e.g. for customer $y$ in the sequence $x, y, z$ the distance would be $\frac{dist_{(x,y)}+dist_{(y,z)}}{2}$). Each of the routing agents are requested to submit bids for each of the surplus sections. The lowest bid identifies the delivery to be transferred and the agent who will take over the delivery. The role of the coordinator is summarised in the pseudo code in Algorithm 1. The identification of customers for potential reassignment using average distance as a metric identifies customers that contributing disproportionately to the length of the agent's route, but there is no guarantee that any customer identified will be able to be incorporated within another round giving a lower overall cost. By identifying a set of customers rather than a single customer we increase the chances of reassigning a customer that results in less distance travelled across the entire network.

This is a modification of the process described in [9] where only one delivery was identified. By identifying a group of deliveries for potential reassignment there is a greater chance that one of them will be adjacent to another round and therefore may be incorporated into that round at little cost.

The logic used to generate a bid is as follows:

$$bid = \frac{\sum_{w=0}^{n} dist_{(w,surplus)}}{n}$$
$$if(mydels > targetDels)bid = bid * 2$$
$$if(myDist > targetLen)bid = bid * 2$$
$$if(prevOwn == me)bid = MAX\_BID$$

where $surplus$ is an object representing the delivery to be bid upon, $dist_{(x,y)}$ returns the Euclidean distance from delivery $x$ to delivery $y$, $MAX\_BID$ is a constant representing the largest bid that may be returned, $myDels$ and $myDist$ are the current quantity of deliveries and length of round being managed by this agent and $targetDels$ and $targetLen$ are the average number of deliveries and average length of round within the network at present.

The bid is initially based on the average distance from the delivery under consideration to the other streets owned by that agent. Thus the closer the street to the other work owned by the agent, the lower the bid. Where the round managed by the agent has more deliveries than average or has a longer distance than average the bid is doubled in order to penalise it and reduce the chances of the item being allocated to it. The bidding mechanism is designed to obtain low bids when a delivery is close to existing deliveries being undertaken by that agent.

```
for each Agent a do
  | a.runEA();
end
for 1 to MAXTRANSACTIONS do
  | Agent worst = findLongestRound();
  | Custs[] worstCusts = worst.getWorstCusts();
  | lowestBid = ∞ ;
  | for each Customer c in worstCusts do
  |   | for each Agent a do
  |   |   | bid = a.bid(c);
  |   |   | if bid < lowestBid then
  |   |   |   | lowestBid=bid;
  |   |   |   | winner=a;
  |   |   |   | transferCust=c;
  |   |   | end
  |   | end
  | end
  | worst.remove(transferCust);
  | winner.add(transferCust);
  | worst.runEA();
  | winner.runEA();
end
```

**Algorithm 1.** The logic used within the coordinator agent.

## 3.2  Routing EA

Within each round, the ordering of customers is optimised using an Evolutionary Algorithm (EA). The EA uses a permutation of customers as a representation, a steady-state population of 300 individuals is maintained with 50 new child individuals being created each generation. Parents are selected using tournament selection, with a tournament size of two. Children are created using two-point crossover or by cloning with an equal probability. Each child has a single mutation operator applied to it. The mutation operator is selected randomly from the following operators:

– **Simple** Select a customer at random and move them to a randomly selected location
– **Swap** Select two customers at random from within the tour and swap them
– **Nearest Neighbour** - Select a customer at random, and move it to its nearest neighbour

- **Two-Opt** Apply a single 2-opt operation to the chromosome
- **AdjSwap** swap two adjacent customers.

The use of a set of 5 mutation operators allows the simplistic operators (such as Simple and Swap) to be use to explore the search space and discourage permature convergence, the more complex operators such as (Two-Opt and Nearest Neighbour) encourage the production of potentaily useful genetic material.

Fitness is calculated as the length of the resulting route. The EA parameters were determined through empirical experimentation and previous experience.

## 4    Results

### 4.1    Initial Results

The MarketPlace algorithm was executed using the coordinator as described in Algorithm 1. The algorithm is limited to 200 transactions, as each transaction potentially represents a single customer changing rounds, this results in 10 % of customers being assigned to a new round. The MarketPlace algorithm was executed 10 times for each dataset and the averaged results are presented in Table 2. Note that on average the algorithm reduces the total distance travelled by 10 %. The most significant improvement is in the average deviation in round distances within a solution, which reduces from 47 km to 4 km. We present the average result and the best, in practice the company will use the best result, however the number of runs undertaken will be dependant on the time available to the scheduler.

**Table 2.** Initial results (total distances) obtained, showing improvement after optimisation. All runs were carried out 10 times, both the best and average results are shown. Figures in brackets show the % improvement from the initial solution.

| Problem | Initial solution | Best after optimisation | Avg after optimisation |
|---|---|---|---|
| Glasgow | 850.75 | 676.28 (20.51 %) | 723.09 (15.01 %) |
| Warrington | 828.29 | 860.92 (−3.94 %) | 1009 (−21.82 %) |
| Edinburgh (from Glasgow) | 2471.94 | 1883.93 (23.79 %) | 2085.01 (15.65 %) |
| Edinburgh (from Edinburgh) | 1593.24 | 1448.54 (0.08 %) | 1647.59 (−3.41 %) |

### 4.2    The Effect of Selectively Cancelling Transactions

The original Marketplace framework [9] was found to stabilise to a situation where one item of work was exchanged continuously between two agents at that point the run was halted and the solution, in the form of a set of routes, was presented. In this study the authors were unable to consistently reproduce this behaviour, in cases where it did happen it was noted that the final transactions tended to be ones that increased the distances travelled. A slight trend was noted in that the transactions that caused the biggest increase in distance, also tended to have higher winning bids. In view of this a limit $maxBid$ was been set on winning bids, if the winning bid is greater than $maxBid$ then the transaction is cancelled. After some experimentation $maxBid$ was set to 10, this produced the results shown in Table 4 which are a partial improvement on the initial results presented in Table 2. Significant improvements are shown on the Warrington and Edinburgh from Edinburgh datasets. A slight increase in average round length was noted for the Edinburgh operated from Glasgow dataset. Performing a t-test on the raw results of the Edinburgh operated from Glasgow dataset produces a result of $p = 0.8559$ confirming that the slight increase in round length between Tables 2 and 4 is not statistically significant.

An example of a specific solution from the Edinburgh (operated from Glasgow) problem may be seen in Fig. 2 and Table 3 note that although the overall distance is reduced, the distance travelled by round 7 increases. In this case the MarketPlace framework has reallocated work to Round 8 in order to decrease

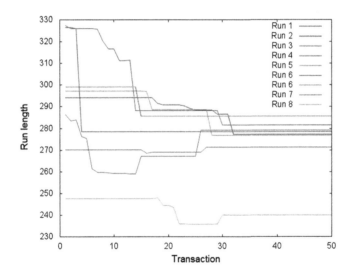

**Fig. 2.** A typical run of the Marketplace framework showing the decrease in round lengths over 50 transactions.

**Table 3.** Typical improvements in round distances

|  | Round 1 | Round 2 | Round 3 | Round 4 | Round 5 | Round 6 | Round 7 | Round 8 |
|---|---|---|---|---|---|---|---|---|
| Initial solution | 401.16 | 330.92 | 327.09 | 276.36 | 318.36 | 300.02 | 270.44 | 247.59 |
| Final solution | 277.33 | 278.39 | 281.56 | 279.19 | 276.77 | 285.68 | 271.43 | 239.97 |

the length of other rounds. Figure 2 shows the changes in round length on a typical executing of the Marketplace framework. Note that runs with lower initial distances increase whilst, the overall distance reduces. Note that runs 4 and 8 both increase their round lengths at points within the run, they accept more work as they have the capacity in order to reduce the workload of other agents.

## 4.3   The Effects of Clustering upon the Results

Performance on the Warrington dataset is significantly worse than the other datasets. A possible explanation is the grouping of the households as seen in Fig. 1(a), (b) and (c). The Warrington dataset appears to have far more distinct clusters, spread over a larger area, giving less scope to moving households between runs. K-Means analysis was carried out on each of the datasets, for a range of cluster quantities (Fig. 3(a), (b) and (c)). Note that the Glasgow dataset has probably has around 4 clusters, the Edinburgh dataset has 2 clusters and the Warrington data set has around 8 clusters. The sets with fewer clusters are more likely to have differing routes within the same cluster and potentially deliveries that are closer together and therefore the potential to exchange work between rounds.

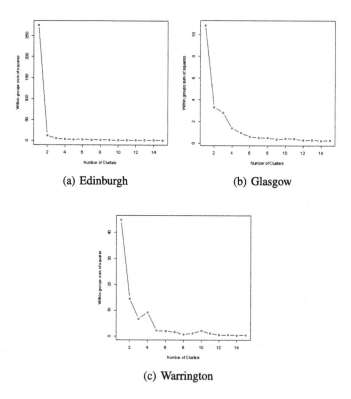

(a) Edinburgh          (b) Glasgow

(c) Warrington

**Fig. 3.** K-Means analysis on all three datasets.

**Table 4.** Initial results (total distances) obtained, showing improvement when $maxBid$=10. All runs were carried out 10 times, both the best and average results are shown. Figures in brackets show the % improvement from the initial solution.

| Problem | Initial solution | Best after optimisation | Avg. after optimisation |
|---|---|---|---|
| Glasgow | 850.75 | 643.27 (24.39 %) | 683.24 (19.69 %) |
| Warrington | 828.29 | 759.26 (8.33 %) | 806.56 (2.62 %) |
| Edinburgh (from Glasgow) | 2471.94 | 1900.92 (23.10 %) | 2091.48 (15.39 %) |
| Edinburgh (from Edinburgh) | 1593.24 | 1260.95 (20.86 %) | 1293.21 (18.83 %) |

### 4.4 The Relationship Between the GIS and the Marketplace Algorithm

The MarketPlace framework has the potential to reduce routing calls to the GIS in order to establish the route to be taken between customers. Consider a VRP solver that uses a grand tour representation [14] in which all customers are contained in one tour which is subsequently decoded into separate routes at the evaluation stage. In this case assuming a population based approach is taken the number of potential links required between customers would be $n^2 - n$. For example, in the case of the Edinburgh dataset, where $n = 2054$ the number of links potentially required would be 4,216,862. Because the Marketplace framework uses separate EAs within each agent, the search space is in effect, divided, in a typical run the MarketPlace algorithm will make an average 252,000 routing requests representing a reduction of up to 90 %.

## 5 Conclusions and Future Work

The objective of this research was to integrate an optimisation methodology into an existing business model. This has been achieved, by using the Market-place framework it has been possible to concentrate on minimising reassignments between routes, but having a significant effect on the global objectives of minimising distance travelled and the variation between rounds. If the business model had not required the solution to minimise reassignments a methodology based on creating a solution from scratch would have been adopted. It is acknowledged, that when only considering the distance objective, the solutions being found will be sub-optimal, yet these solutions which maintain the driver/customer relationship are those which are of most value to the business. The experiments outlined in Sect. 4 suggest that the EA incorporated within the Markeplace framework is a feasible method of making a significant optimisation to the manual solution. The Marketplace framework meets the requirement to optimise the existing solution as stored in the company database with minimal changes rather than creating a new solution from scratch. The results obtained suggest that by reordering the existing rounds and reallocating 10 % of customers a reduction in distance travelled of 10 % may be achieved.

The use of the Marketplace framework reduces the number of routing requests made, which when making calls to a GIS can represent a significant saving in time and possibly cost depending on the GIS adopted. It is acknowledged that when the algorithm is run repeatedly there the scope for optimisation will depend on the degree to which manual additions and deletions of customers have been made to the customer database.

Further research is required into the link between the natural clustering of customers (as determined by K-means analysis), delivery rounds and performance. In the Warrington example, there are more natural clusters than delivery rounds, which suggests that each delivery route will have to cover more than one cluster as well as minimising the chances that a cluster will be visited by two routes. In this case swapping a customer will most likely cause the accepting route to have to visit an additional cluster. The Edinburgh and Glasgow datasets have less clusters than rounds, therefore some/all clusters will be visited by more than one route, allowing exchanges between routes within a cluster. There may be implications for multiple vehicle routing problems using real-world data where the clustering of customers may prove to be significant when generating solutions.

**Acknowledgements.** This work was partially funded by the Scottish Funding Council Innovation Voucher scheme.

# References

1. Dantzig, G., Ramser, J.: The truck dispatching problem. Manag. Sci. **6**, 80–91 (1959)
2. Laporte, G., Toth, P.: Vehicle routing: historical perspective and recent contributions. EURO J. Transp. Logist. **2**, 1–2 (2013)
3. Fonseca, C.M., Fleming, P.J.: An overview of evolutionary algorithms in multiobjective optimization. Evol. Comput. **3**, 1–16 (1995)
4. Vidal, T., Crainic, T.G., Gendreau, M., Prins, C.: Heuristics for multi-attribute vehicle routing problems: a survey and synthesis. Eur. J. Oper. Res. (2013)
5. Gendreau, M., Potvin, J., Braysy, O., Lokketangen, A.: Metaheuristics for the vehicle routing problem and its extensions : a categorized bibliography. In: Golden, B., Raghaven, S., Wasil, E. (eds.) The Vehicle Routing Problem, pp. 143–169. Springer, New York (2008)
6. Cook, W.: Pursuit of the Traveling Salesman: Mathematics at the Limits of Computation. Princeton University Press, Princeton (2012)
7. Lin, S., Kernighan, B.W.: An effective heuristic algorithm for the traveling salesman. Oper. Res. **21**, 498–516 (1973)
8. Baraglia, R., Hidalgo, J.I., Perego, R.: A hybrid heuristic for the travelling salesman problem. IEEE Trans. Evol. Comput. **5**, 612–622 (2001)
9. Urquhart, N.: Building distribution networks using cooperative agents. In: Rennard, J. (ed.) Handbook of Research on Nature Inspired Computing for Economics and Management. Idea Group Reference, Hershey (2006)

10. Urquhart, N.B., Ross, P., Paechter, B., Chisholm, K.: Solving a real world routing problem using multiple evolutionary agents. In: Guervós, J.J.M., Adamidis, P.A., Beyer, H.-G., Fernández-Villacañas, J.-L., Schwefel, H.-P. (eds.) PPSN 2002. LNCS, vol. 2439, pp. 871–880. Springer, Heidelberg (2002)
11. Foundation, O.: (2014). http://www.openstreetmap.org
12. Karich, P.: Graphhopper (2014). https://graphhopper.com/
13. Sanders, P., Schultes, D.: Highway hierarchies hasten exact shortest path queries. In: Brodal, G.S., Leonardi, S. (eds.) ESA 2005. LNCS, vol. 3669, pp. 568–579. Springer, Heidelberg (2005)
14. Runka, A., Ombuki-Berman, M.D., Ventresca, M.. A search space analysis for the waste collection vehicle routing problem with time windows. In: Genetic and Evolutionary Computation Conference, GECCO 2009, pp. 1813–1814 (2009)

# Multi-Noisy-Hard-Objective Robust Design of Balanced Surface Acoustic Wave Filters Based on Prediction of Worst-Case Performance

Kiyoharu Tagawa[1(✉)] and Shoichi Harada[2]

[1] School of Science and Engineering, Kinki University,
Higashi-Osaka 577-8502, Japan
tagawa@info.kindai.ac.jp
[2] Graduate School of Science and Engineering Research, Kinki University,
Higashi-Osaka 577-8502, Japan

**Abstract.** This paper presents a novel computer-aided design method of Surface Acoustic Wave (SAW) filters which are widely used in the modern RF circuits of mobile communication systems. The performance of a SAW filter is specified by a number of criteria. Besides, the performance is deteriorated due to the uncertainties of physical coefficients and design parameters. In the multi-noisy-objective optimization problem of the SAW filter, the worst-case performance of a solution is considered based on the upper bounds of respective noisy-objective functions predicted statistically by multiple sampling. For finding various solutions for the problem effectively, a new evolutionary algorithm is proposed with three sample saving techniques. Finally, the influence of noise on the SAW filter is discussed through analysis of the obtained solutions.

**Keywords:** Robust optimal design · Multi-noisy-objective optimization

## 1 Introduction

Surface Acoustic Wave (SAW) is an acoustic wave traveling along the surface of a material exhibiting elasticity. SAW devices are mechanical and electrical devices that use the acoustic wave in electronic components to provide a number of different functions including delay lines, resonators, filters, and so on [9,12,13]. Recently, SAW filters are widely used in the modern Radio Frequency (RF) circuits of various mobile communication systems such as cellular phones. That is because SAW filters can provide small, thin, rugged, and cost competitive band-pass filters with outstanding frequency response characteristics.

The frequency response characteristics of a SAW filter is governed by its geometrical structure, namely the configuration of electrodes fabricated on a piezoelectric substrate. In order to avoid the trial and error design of SAW filters, computer-aided optimal design methods have been proposed [20]. In our previous paper [20], the structural design of a SAW filter was formulated as

© Springer International Publishing Switzerland 2015
A.M. Mora and G. Squillero (Eds.): EvoApplications 2015, LNCS 9028, pp. 616–628, 2015.
DOI: 10.1007/978-3-319-16549-3_50

Multi-objective Optimization Problem (MOP). In this paper, we also think about the influence of noise that is inevitable to produce practical SAW filters.

Many real-world MOPs have more than one objective function contaminated with noise. The presence of noise leads to different results for repeated evaluations of the same solution. Even though various Multi-Objective Evolutionary Algorithms (MOEAs) have been proposed for solving Multi-Noisy-objective Optimization Problems (MNOPs), most of them consider the robustness of solutions based on the average performance [15,16,21]. However, the worst-case performance is more important in real-world MNOPs [17]. The concept of min-max robustness is widely used to evaluate the worst-case performance for a solution [7]. The worst value of each objective function is found by the multiple sampling of the same solution [11]. However, it is hard to find the worst value of a stochastic objective function in a finite number of samples. Even though there is another interpretation of the uncertainty based on scenarios instead of noise, inversed MOPs have to be solved for evaluating the worst-case performance [2].

We formulate the structural design of a SAW filter as MNOP in which the predicted upper bounds of respective noisy objective functions are minimized simultaneously [18]. In order to reduce the number of expensive simulation-based function evaluations, we also propose a new MOEA adopting state-of-the-art techniques [5,8,18,19]. Finally, the influence of noise on the SAW filter is discussed through analysis of the solutions obtained by the proposed MOEA.

## 2    Balanced Surface Acoustic Wave Filter

### 2.1    Structure of Balanced SAW Filter

A balanced SAW filter consists of some electrodes fabricated on a piezoelectric substrate, namely Inter-Digital Transducers (IDTs) and Shorted Metal Strip Array (SMSA) reflectors. Figure 1 shows a symmetric structure of the balanced SAW filter consisting of one pitch-modulated transmitter IDT (IDT-T), two pitch-modulated receiver IDTs (IDT-Rs), and two SMSA reflectors.

In the balanced SAW filter shown in Fig. 1, port-1 connecting to IDT-T provides an input-port, while a pair of port-2 and port-3 connecting to respective IDT-Rs provides a balanced output-port. IDT-T converts electric input signals into acoustic signals. The acoustic signals are enhanced at the resonant frequency that depends on the geometrical structure of the balanced SAW filter. Then IDT-Rs reconvert the enhanced acoustic signals into electric output signals. As a result, the balanced SAW filter in Fig. 1 works as a band-pass filter.

### 2.2    Simulation Modeling of Balanced SAW Filter

The behavior of IDT can be simulated by using an equivalent circuit model in Fig. 2: port-a and port-b are acoustic signal ports, while port-c is an electric signal port [10]. The circuit model of SMSA reflector is derived from the circuit model of IDT by shorting the port-c. Circuit elements' values in Fig. 2, namely

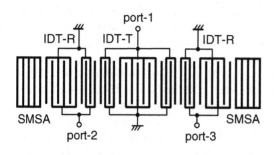

**Fig. 1.** Structure of balanced SAW filter

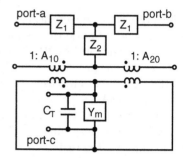

**Fig. 2.** Circuit model of IDT

transconductances $A_{10}$, $A_{20}$, admittance $Y_m$, and impedances $Z_1$, $Z_2$, depend on the structure of IDT and several physical coefficients. Especially, the velocity of SAW is a critical physical coefficient that takes a different value according to the quality of piezoelectric substrate and varies with the temperature [9].

An equivalent circuit model of the balanced SAW filter in Fig. 1 can be composed by linking circuit models of IDTs and SMSAs in their acoustic signal ports [20]. Thereafter, the equivalent circuit model of the balanced SAW filter is transformed in a network model represented by a scattering matrix $S$ as

$$\begin{bmatrix} b_1 \\ b_2 \\ b_3 \end{bmatrix} = S \begin{bmatrix} a_1 \\ a_2 \\ a_3 \end{bmatrix} = \begin{bmatrix} s_{11} & s_{12} & s_{13} \\ s_{21} & s_{22} & s_{23} \\ s_{31} & s_{32} & s_{33} \end{bmatrix} \begin{bmatrix} a_1 \\ a_2 \\ a_3 \end{bmatrix}, \tag{1}$$

where $a_p$, $p = 1, 2, 3$ denotes the electric input signal at port-$p$, while $b_p$ denotes the electric output signal at port-$p$. Scattering parameter ($s$-parameter) $s_{pq}$ provides the transition characteristic from the input port-$q$ to the output port-$p$, while $s$-parameter $s_{pp}$ provides the reflection characteristic at port-$p$.

According to the balanced network theory [1], differential mode input and output signals ($a_d$ and $b_d$) need to be segregated from common mode input and output signals ($a_c$ and $b_c$) at the balanced output-port in Fig. 1 as

$$\begin{cases} a_d = \dfrac{1}{\sqrt{2}}(a_2 - a_3), \\ b_d = \dfrac{1}{\sqrt{2}}(b_2 - b_3), \end{cases} \quad \begin{cases} a_c = \dfrac{1}{\sqrt{2}}(a_2 + a_3), \\ b_c = \dfrac{1}{\sqrt{2}}(b_2 + b_3). \end{cases} \tag{2}$$

From (2), the network model in (1) is revised as follows:

$$\begin{bmatrix} b_1 \\ b_d \\ b_c \end{bmatrix} = \begin{bmatrix} \sqrt{2} & 0 & 0 \\ 0 & 1 & -1 \\ 0 & 1 & 1 \end{bmatrix} S \begin{bmatrix} \sqrt{2} & 0 & 0 \\ 0 & 1 & -1 \\ 0 & 1 & 1 \end{bmatrix}^{-1} \begin{bmatrix} a_1 \\ a_d \\ a_l \end{bmatrix} = \begin{bmatrix} s_{11} & s_{1d} & s_{1c} \\ s_{d1} & s_{dd} & s_{dc} \\ s_{c1} & s_{cd} & s_{cc} \end{bmatrix} \begin{bmatrix} a_1 \\ a_d \\ a_c \end{bmatrix}. \tag{3}$$

# 3    Problem Formulation

## 3.1    Uncertain Design Parameters

In order to describe the structure of the balanced SAW filter in Fig. 1, we choose $D = 10$ design parameters $v_j$, $j = 1, \cdots, D$ as shown in Table 1. Each design parameter $v_j$ takes either a continuous value $v_j \in \Re$ or a discrete value spaced apart by $e_i \in \Re$. Furthermore, each $v_j$ is limited to the range $[v_j^L, v_j^U]$.

The width of IDT's fingers ($v_6 \in \Re$) and the width of SMSA's strips ($v_7 \in \Re$) are so fine that they are regarded as uncertain design parameters changed due to the processing error. Therefore, we assume that noisy values $\tilde{v}_j \in \Re$ of those design parameters are distributed normally as $\tilde{v}_j \sim \mathcal{N}(v_j, \sigma_j^2)$, $j = 6, 7$.

Table 1. Design parameters of balanced SAW filter

| $v_j$ | $[v_j^L, \quad v_j^U]$ | $e_j$ | Design parameter |
|---|---|---|---|
| $v_1$ | [200, 400] | – | Overlap between electrodes [$\mu m$] |
| $v_2$ | [12.0, 20.0] | 0.5 | Number of IDT-R's fingers |
| $v_3$ | [15.0, 25.0] | 1.0 | Number of IDT-T's fingers |
| $v_4$ | [1.0, 4.0] | 1.0 | Number of pitch-modulated IDT's fingers |
| $v_5$ | [50.0, 200.0] | 5.0 | Number of SMSA's strips |
| $v_6$ | [0.9, 1.1] | – | Width of IDT's fingers [$\mu m$] |
| $v_7$ | [0.9, 1.1] | – | Width of SMSA's strips [$\mu m$] |
| $v_8$ | [1.8, 2.0] | – | Pitch of pitch-modulated IDT's fingers [$\mu m$] |
| $v_9$ | [2.0, 2.2] | – | Pitch of SMSA's strips [$\mu m$] |
| $v_{10}$ | [1.95, 2.05] | – | Pitch of IDT's fingers [$\mu m$] |

## 3.2    Noisy Objective Functions

In order to evaluate the performance of the balanced SAW filter working as a band-pass filter, we define $M = 5$ objective functions from the $s$-parameters in (3). Let $\Omega$ be a set of 301 frequency points $\omega \in \Omega$ sampled from within the range: $850 \sim 1100$[MHz]. Subsets $\Omega_l$, $\Omega_p$, and $\Omega_h \subset \Omega$ have frequency points $\omega \in \Omega$ sampled respectively from the lower-frequency stop-band, the pass-band, and the higher-frequency stop-band of the balanced SAW filter. The values of $s$-parameters depend on the vector of design parameters $\boldsymbol{v} = (v_1, \cdots, v_D)$, physical coefficients, and the frequency point $\omega \in \Omega$. Because the vector of design parameters $\boldsymbol{v}$ includes two uncertain ones, namely $\tilde{v}_6$ and $\tilde{v}_7$, we denote the vector of noisy design parameters by $\tilde{\boldsymbol{v}}$. As stated above, the velocity of SAW $\theta \in \Re$ is also an uncertain physical coefficient. Let $\tilde{\theta} \in \Re$ be the noisy value of $\theta \in \Re$. Thereby, objective functions to be minimized are defined as

$$\begin{cases} f_1(v) = \max_{\omega \in \Omega_l} \{|s_{d1}(\tilde{v}, \omega, \tilde{\theta})|\}, \\[2mm] f_2(v) = 1 - \min_{\omega \in \Omega_p} \{|s_{d1}(\tilde{v}, \omega, \tilde{\theta})|\}, \\[2mm] f_3(v) = \max_{\omega \in \Omega_h} \{|s_{d1}(\tilde{v}, \omega, \tilde{\theta})|\}, \\[2mm] f_4(v) = \max_{\omega \in \Omega_p} \{|s_{11}(\tilde{v}, \omega, \tilde{\theta})|\}, \\[2mm] f_5(v) = \max_{\omega \in \Omega_p} \{|s_{dd}(\tilde{v}, \omega, \tilde{\theta})|\}, \end{cases} \tag{4}$$

where we assume that $\tilde{\theta}$ is also distributed normally as $\tilde{\theta} \sim \mathcal{N}(\theta, \sigma^2)$.

Because the absolute values of $s$-parameters in (3) are less than 1, the values of $f_m(v)$ are limited to the range: $0 \le f_m(v) \le 1$, $m \in \mathcal{I}_M = \{1, \cdots, M\}$.

## 3.3 Prediction of Worst-Case Performance

Each objective function $f_m(v)$ in (4) is contaminated with noise. Therefore, every time a solution $v$ is evaluated, a different objective function value may be returned. Let $f_m^n(v) \in \Re$, $n = 1, \cdots, N$ be observed values of $f_m(v)$. We assume that the observed values of $f_m(v)$ are distributed normally as

$$f_m^n(v) \sim \mathcal{N}(\mu_m(v), \sigma_m(v)^2) = \mathcal{N}(f_m(v), \sigma_m(v)^2), \tag{5}$$

where the mean $\mu_m(v) = f_m(v)$, $m \in \mathcal{I}_M$ and the variance $\sigma_m(v)^2$, $m \in \mathcal{I}_M$ are mutually independent functions that depend on the solution $v$.

Because the mean $\mu_m(v)$ and the variance $\sigma_m(v)^2$ in (5) are unknown, we will estimate those values, respectively, by the sample mean and the unbiased variance. Let $\{f_m^1(v), \cdots, f_m^n(v), \cdots, f_m^N(v)\}$ be a sample set of an objective function $f_m(v)$ for a solution $v$. From the sample set $\{f_m^n(v)\}$ of size $N$, we can calculate the sample mean $\overline{f}_m(v)$ and the unbiased variance $s_m(v)^2$ [18].

By using $\overline{f}_m(v)$ and $s_m(v)^2$ instead of $\mu_m(v)$ and $\sigma_m(v)^2$ respectively, the normal distribution in (5) is approximated by Student's t-distribution. We have already obtained the sample set $\{f_m^n(v)\}$ of size $N$. Let $f_m^{N+1}(v)$ be the $(N+1)$-th sample of $f_m(v)$, or the future observation of $f_m(v)$. Then the one-side prediction interval in which $f_m^{N+1}(v) \in \Re$ will fall can be derived as follows [18]:

$$-\infty < f_m^{N+1}(v) \le \overline{f}_m(v) + t(N-1, \alpha) s_m(v) \sqrt{1 + \frac{1}{N}} = f_m^U(v), \tag{6}$$

where $t(N-1, \alpha)$ is the $\alpha$-quantile of Student's t-distribution with $N-1$ degrees of freedom. The upper bound of the prediction interval is represented as $f_m^U(v)$. If the sample size is $N = 1$, the upper bound is defined as $f_m^U(v) = f_m^1(v)$.

## 3.4 Multi-Noisy-Hard-Objective Optimization Problem

Let $\boldsymbol{f}^n(v) = (f_1^n(v), \cdots, f_m^n(v), \cdots f_M^n(v))$, $n = 1, \cdots, N$ be observed values of an objective vector $\boldsymbol{f}(v) \in \Re^M$ depending on a solution $v$. From the sample set $\{f^n(v)\}$ of size $N$ and (6), we can predict the upper bound $f^U(v) \in \Re^M$ of the future observation $f^{N+1}(v) \in \Re^M$. Now, we restrict each of the predicted upper bounds $f_m^U(v) \in \Re$, $m \in \mathcal{I}_M$ to be less than a given $\gamma_m \in \Re$ because

1. in the design of SAW filter, every solution has to meet absolute standards,
2. a part of the Pareto-front is usually sufficient for decision making,
3. expensive evaluation may be omitted for unacceptable solutions.

Let $\gamma = \{\gamma_1, \cdots, \gamma_M\} \in \Re^M$ be a cut-off point specified by the designer. Multi-Noisy-Hard-objective Optimization Problem (MNHOP) is formulated as

$$\begin{cases} \text{minimize} & f^U(v) = (f_1^U(v), \cdots, f_m^U(v), \cdots, f_M^U(v)), \\ \text{subject to} & f_m^U(v) \leq \gamma_m, \; m \in \mathcal{I}_M = \{1, \cdots, M\}, \\ & v_j^L \leq v_j \leq v_j^U, \; j \in \mathcal{I}_D = \{1, \cdots, D\}, \end{cases} \quad (7)$$

where a solution $v$ is feasible if the solution $v$ satisfies all constraints.

**Definition 1.** *A objective vector $f^U(v) \in \Re^M$ is said to dominate the other $f^U(v') \in \Re^M$ and denoted as $f^U(v) \succ f^U(v')$, if the following condition is true:*

$$(\forall m \in \mathcal{I}_M : f_m^U(v) \leq f_m^U(v')) \; \wedge \; (\exists n \in \mathcal{I}_M : f_m^U(v) < f_m^U(v')). \quad (8)$$

**Definition 2.** *A objective vector $f^U(v)$ is said to weakly dominate the other $f^U(v')$ and denoted as $f^U(v) \succeq f^U(v')$, if the following condition is true:*

$$\forall m \in \mathcal{I}_M : f_m^U(v) \leq f_m^U(v') \quad (9)$$

Let $f^{N+1}(v)$ be the $(N+1)$-th sample, or the future observation of $f(v)$. Then the probability of $f^{N+1}(v)$ weakly dominating $f^U(v)$ is

$$\mathcal{P}(f^{N+1}(v) \succeq f^U(v)) = \prod_{m=1}^M \mathcal{P}(f_m^{N+1}(v) \leq f_m^U(v)) = (1-\alpha)^M, \quad (10)$$

where $\alpha$ $(0 < \alpha < 1)$ is the significance level specified in (6).

Contrarily, the probability of $f^U(v)$ weakly dominating $f^{N+1}(v)$ is

$$\mathcal{P}(f^U(v) \succeq f^{N+1}(v)) = \prod_{m=1}^M \mathcal{P}(f_m^U(v) \leq f_m^{N+1}(v)) = \alpha^M. \quad (11)$$

# 4   Proposed Evolutionary Algorithm

In order to obtain various non-dominated feasible solutions for MNHOP in (7) effectively, a new MOEA called DEUCR (Differential Evolution with U-cut, C-cut, and Resampling) is proposed. DEUCR is an extended variant of DEMHO [19]. Besides the way to evaluate solutions, DEUCR differs from DEMHO in three points. Firstly, DEUCR adopts three sample saving techniques [8,18] to reduce the number of function evaluations. Secondly, DEUCR uses a revised version of the reference-point based selection of NSGA-III [5] to keep the diversity of solutions. Thirdly, DEUCR utilizes the $D$-dimensional Halton sequence [14] for generating initial solutions as multiple real-vectors of low discrepancy.

## 4.1    Representation of Solution

Like DE [14], DEUCR has a set of solutions $x_i \in P$, $i = 1, \cdots, N_P$ which is called the population. Each solution $x_i \in P \subset [0, 1]^D$ is represented as

$$x_i = (x_{1,i}, \cdots, x_{j,i}, \cdots, x_{D,i}), \tag{12}$$

where $x_{j,i} \in \Re$ and $0 \leq x_{j,i} \leq 1$, $j = 1, \cdots, D$.

In order to apply a DEUCR to MNHOP in (7), each element $x_{j,i} \in [0, 1]$ of a solution $x_i$ is converted into a corresponding design parameters $v_j$ as

$$\begin{cases} v_j = (v_j^U - v_j^L) x_{j,i} + v_j^L, & \text{if } v_j \text{ is a continuous value,} \\ v_j = \text{round}\left(\dfrac{(v_j^U - v_j^L) x_{j,i}}{e_j}\right) e_j + v_j^L, & \text{if } v_j \text{ is a discrete value,} \end{cases} \tag{13}$$

where round$(r)$ rounds a real number $r \in \Re$ to the nearest integer.

We can get the vector of design parameters $v = (v_1, \cdots, v_D)$ uniquely from the corresponding solution $x_i$. Therefore, to simplify the notation, we sometimes represent an objective vector as $f(x_i) \in \Re^M$ instead of $f(v) \in \Re^M$.

## 4.2    Reproduction

In order to generate a candidate for a solution, which is called the trial vector $u \in [0, 1]^D$, we use a basic strategy of DE named "DE/rand/1/bin" [14]. The ability of the strategy depends on the control parameters, namely the scale factor $F$ and the crossover rate $CR$. Therefore, we introduce a self-adaptive setting of them [3] into DEUCR. According to the self-adaptive setting, every solution $x_i \in P$, $i = 1, \cdots, N_P$ has its own control parameters $F_i$ and $CR_i$.

Each solution $x_i \in P$ is assigned to the target vector in turn. By using $F$ and $CR$ derived from $F_i$ and $CR_i$, the strategy generates the trial vector $u$ from the target vector $x_i \in P$. Then the trial vector $u$ is compared to the target vector $x_i \in P$. If $f^U(u)$ weakly dominates $f^U(x_i)$, $u$ replaces $x_i$. On the other hand, when they are non-dominated each other, $u$ is added to $P$. Otherwise, $u$ is discarded. As a result, if the trial vector $u$ survives, the control parameters $F$ and $CR$ used for generating $u$ are assigned to the new solution $u \in P$.

## 4.3    Sample Saving Techniques

Each solution $x_i \in P$ has its own sample size to evaluate the upper bound. By using three sample saving techniques, namely U-cut, C-cut [18], and resampling [8], DEUCR decides the sample sizes of respective solutions adaptively.

Two pruning techniques called C-cut and U-cut can judge hopeless solutions only by a few sampling and skip their evaluations. We choose a relatively small initial sample size $N$. However, if a sample $f^{n_i}(x_i) \in \Re^M$, $n_i < N$ does not dominate the cut-off point $\gamma \in \Re^M$, $x_i$ is probably infeasible. Therefore, C-cut skips the remaining sampling of $x_i \in P$. Then $f^U(x_i)$ is evaluated from the

**Algorithm 1.** DEUCR APPLIED TO MNHOP

1: $\boldsymbol{P}$ := GENERATE_INITIAL_POPULATION($N_P$);  /* the Halton sequence */
2: **for** $i$ := 1 to $N_P$ **do**
3:     $\boldsymbol{S}_i$ := $\emptyset$;  $n$ := 1;
4:     **do** /* C-cut */
5:         $\boldsymbol{S}_i$ := $\boldsymbol{S}_i \cup \{\boldsymbol{f}^n(\boldsymbol{x}_i)\}$;  $n$ := $n + 1$;
6:     **while** $(\boldsymbol{f}^n(\boldsymbol{x}_i) \succeq \boldsymbol{\gamma}) \wedge (n < N)$
7:     $\boldsymbol{f}^U(\boldsymbol{x}_i)$ := PREDICT_UPPER_BOUND($\boldsymbol{S}_i$);
8: **end for**
9: **repeat**
10:     **for** $i$ := 1 to $N_P$ **do**
11:         $\boldsymbol{u}$ := STRATEGY($\boldsymbol{x}_i \in \boldsymbol{P}$);  /* Generate the trial vector $\boldsymbol{u} \in [0, 1]^D$ */
12:         $\boldsymbol{S}_u$ := $\emptyset$;  $n$ := 1;
13:         **do** /* C-cut &U-cut */
14:             $\boldsymbol{S}_u$ := $\boldsymbol{S}_u \cup \{\boldsymbol{f}^n(\boldsymbol{u})\}$;  $n$ := $n + 1$;
15:         **while** $(\boldsymbol{f}^U(\boldsymbol{x}_i) \not\succ \boldsymbol{f}^n(\boldsymbol{u})) \wedge (\boldsymbol{f}^n(\boldsymbol{u}) \succeq \boldsymbol{\gamma}) \wedge (n < N)$
16:         $\boldsymbol{f}^U(\boldsymbol{u})$ := PREDICT_UPPER_BOUND($\boldsymbol{S}_u$);
17:         **if** $\boldsymbol{f}^U(\boldsymbol{u}) \succeq \boldsymbol{f}^U(\boldsymbol{x}_i)$ **then**
18:             $\boldsymbol{x}_i$ := $\boldsymbol{u}$;  /* Replace $\boldsymbol{x}_i \in \boldsymbol{P}$ by $\boldsymbol{u}$ */
19:         **else**
20:             **if** $\boldsymbol{f}^U(\boldsymbol{x}_i) \not\succ \boldsymbol{f}^U(\boldsymbol{u})$ **then**
21:                 $\boldsymbol{P}$ := $\boldsymbol{P} \cup \{\boldsymbol{u}\}$;  /* $|\boldsymbol{P}| > N_P$ */
22:             **end if**
23:         **end if**
24:     **end for**
25:     $\boldsymbol{P}$ := TRUNCATION_METHOD($\boldsymbol{P}, N_P, \eta$);  /* $|\boldsymbol{P}| = N_P$ */
26:     **for** $i$ := 1 to $N_P$ **do**
27:         **if** $\boldsymbol{x}_i \in \boldsymbol{Q} = \{\boldsymbol{x}_i \in \boldsymbol{P} \mid \boldsymbol{f}^U(\boldsymbol{x}_i) \succeq \boldsymbol{\gamma}\}$ **then**
28:             $\boldsymbol{f}^U(\boldsymbol{x}_i)$ := PREDICT_UPPER_BOUND($\boldsymbol{S}_i$ := $\boldsymbol{S}_i \cup \{\boldsymbol{f}^{n_i+1}(\boldsymbol{x}_i)\}$);
29:         **end if**
30:     **end for**
31:     $\boldsymbol{P}$ := CHANGE_ORDER($\boldsymbol{P}$);  /* Change the order of $\boldsymbol{x}_i \in \boldsymbol{P}$ randomly */
32: **until** a termination condition is satisfied;
33: Output all non-dominated feasible solutions in $\boldsymbol{Q} \subseteq \boldsymbol{P}$;

---

sample set $\boldsymbol{S}_i = \{\boldsymbol{f}^n(\boldsymbol{x}_i) \mid n = 1, \cdots, n_i\}$. In a comparison between the trial vector $\boldsymbol{u}$ and the target vector $\boldsymbol{x}_i \in \boldsymbol{P}$, U-cut is used in addition to C-cut. If $\boldsymbol{f}^U(\boldsymbol{x}_i) \in \Re^M$ dominates $\boldsymbol{f}^{n'}(\boldsymbol{u}) \in \Re^M$, $n' < N$, then $\boldsymbol{f}^U(\boldsymbol{x}_i)$ dominates $\boldsymbol{f}^U(\boldsymbol{u})$ in short odds. Therefore, U-cut skips the remaining sampling of $\boldsymbol{u}$, too.

After the survival selection described later, resampling takes another sample $\boldsymbol{f}^{n_i+1}(\boldsymbol{x}_i)$ of each feasible solution $\boldsymbol{x}_i \in \boldsymbol{P}$ and reevaluates its upper bound $\boldsymbol{f}^U(\boldsymbol{x}_i)$ from the sample set $\boldsymbol{S}_i \cup \{\boldsymbol{f}^{n_i+1}(\boldsymbol{x}_i)\}$, $n_i = |\boldsymbol{S}_i|$. By using the resampling, the sample sizes $n_i$ of some excellent solutions $\boldsymbol{x}_i \in \boldsymbol{P}$ may exceed the initial sample size $N$ as $n_i > N$. Consequently, we can raise the precision of them.

Algorithm 1 provides the pseudo-code of DEUCR. First of all, C-cut is used to generate a sample set $\boldsymbol{S}_i = \{\boldsymbol{f}^n(\boldsymbol{x}_i)\}$ for each initial solution $\boldsymbol{x}_i \in \boldsymbol{P}$.

## 4.4   Survival Selection

Because some trial vectors are added to the population $P$, the number of solutions in $P$ becomes $N_P \leq |P| \leq 2\,N_P$ at the end of each generation. In order to return the population size to $N_P$, a two-stage selection method is applied to $P$. The framework of the two-stage selection method has been devised for Multi-Hard-objective Optimization Problem (MHOP) [19]. Hard-objective differs from constrained objective because the former has no conflict with its constraint. If an objective function $f_m^U(v)$ is minimized in MNHOP, its constraint $f_m^U(v) \leq \gamma_m$ will be satisfied sooner or later. Let $Q = \{x_i \in P \mid f^U(x_i) \succeq \gamma\}$ be a set of feasible solutions. Feasible solutions $x_i \in Q \subseteq P$ have priority over infeasible ones. For selecting infeasible solutions, the following selection method chooses either Step 2.1 or Step 2.2 based on a control parameter $\eta$ ($0 \leq \eta \leq 1$). Sub-selection method in Step 2.1 is used to keep the diversity of infeasible solutions.

[Selection Method]

**Step 1.** If $|Q| \geq N_P$ then apply the sub-selection method to $Q \subseteq P$.
**Step 2.** If $|Q| < N_P$ then select all feasible solutions $x_i \in Q$. Thereafter, the shortage is selected from the set of infeasible solutions $Q^c = P \setminus Q$ as
**Step 2.1.** If $|Q| \leq \eta\,N_P$ then apply the sub-selection method to $Q^c \subseteq P$.
**Step 2.2.** Otherwise, select the necessary number of solutions $x_i \in Q^c \subseteq P$ in the ascending order on the violation distance $d(x_i) \in \Re$ defined as

$$d(x_i) = \sum_{m=1}^{M} \max\{0,\ (f_m^U(x_i) - \gamma_m)\}. \tag{14}$$

In order to sort the solutions assigned the same non-domination rank [6], the following sub-selection method creates a number of reference points $w_t \in \Re^M$, $t \in \mathcal{I}_H = \{1, \cdots, H\}$ systematically on the hyper-plane that intercepts each of $M$ axes at the cut-off point $\gamma_m$, $m \in \mathcal{I}_M$ [4]. Like NSGA-III [5], the niche count $\rho_t$, $t \in \mathcal{I}_H$ is also calculated for every reference point $w_t \in \Re^M$ based on the perpendicular distance $\pi(w_t, x_i)$ between $w_t$ and $x_i \in P$. However, unlike NSGA-III, $\pi(w_t, x_i)$ is evaluated repeatedly to select isolated solutions.

[Sub-selection Method]

**Step 1.** Decide the non-domination rank [6] for each solution $x_i \in P$ and then select $N_P$ solutions from $P$ in the ascending order on the rank.
**Step 2.** If some solutions need to be selected from $P_r \subseteq P$ with the same rank, repeat the following procedure until the shortage of solutions is selected.
    1. Calculate niche count $\rho_t$ for every reference point $w_t$, $t \in \mathcal{I}_H$.
    2. Select a reference point $w_{t'}$, $t' \in \mathcal{I}_H$ with the minimum $\rho_{t'}$.
    3. Evaluate $\pi(w_{t'}, x_i)$ for every solution $x_i \in P_r$.
    4. Select a solution $x_{i'} \in P_r$ with the minimum $\pi(w_{t'}, x_{i'})$.
    5. Update the niche count $\rho_{t'}$ of $w_{t'}$ such as $\rho_{t'} = \rho_{t'} + 1$.

## 5    Numerical Experiments

DEUCR was coded by the Java language. The simulator of the balanced SAW filter was coded by MATLAB and transformed into the library that could be used in the Java program. Control parameters of DEUCR were chosen as $N_P = 100$, $N = 5$, $H = 70$ and $\eta = 0.2$. The termination condition was given by a maximum of $10^5$ function evaluations. The simulation-based evaluation of $\boldsymbol{f}^n(\boldsymbol{v})$ was so time consuming that DEUCR was applied to MNHOP in (7) only 6 times.

Through $10^5$ function evaluations, DEUCR examined $16,829$ solutions in the average. Actually, DEUCR could skip the evaluations of hopeless solutions much more than DEUC [18]. However, decision makers have interest in the solutions of MNHOP rather than the performance of DEUCR. Therefore, we took a union of the solutions obtained by six runs of DEUCR and assessed them.

Figure 3 plots $100 \times 6 = 600$ solutions obtained by DEUCR after 500 and $10^5$ function evaluations in the objective space: $(f_3^U, f_4^U)$. Symbol "•" denotes feasible solutions, while "×" denotes infeasible ones. Comparing Fig. 3(b) to Fig. 3(a), we can confirm the convergence of solutions achieved by DEUCR. The diversity of solutions is still kept in Fig. 3(b). After $10^5$ function evaluations, we could find 93 non-dominated feasible solutions in the 600 final solutions.

In order to assess the influence of noise on the performance of SAW filter, we obtained 468 non-dominated feasible solutions for MHOP in which $\boldsymbol{f}(\boldsymbol{v}) \in \Re^M$ was minimized instead of $\boldsymbol{f}^U(\boldsymbol{v}) \in \Re^M$. Figure 4 compares the solutions of MNHOP with the solutions of MHOP (no noise) in the minimum values (solid line) and the maximum values (broken line) of respective objective functions. The cut-off points $\gamma_m$, $m \in \mathcal{I}_M$ are also described in Fig. 4. From the comparison of the minimum values of $f_m^U(\boldsymbol{v})$ and $f_m(\boldsymbol{v})$, the objective functions $f_4^U(\boldsymbol{v})$ and $f_5^U(\boldsymbol{v})$, namely the reflection characteristics at input and output ports, become worse drastically. Furthermore, the diversity of solutions has been lost in $f_1^U(\boldsymbol{v})$ and $f_3^U(\boldsymbol{v})$, namely the transition characteristics, due to the existence of noise.

Table 2(a) shows correlation coefficients $\lambda$ between two objective function values calculated from the above 468 solutions of MHOP. Table 2(a) also shows

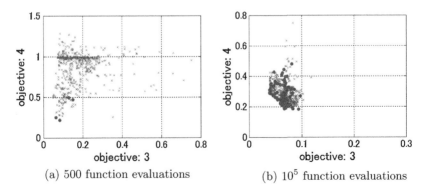

(a) 500 function evaluations          (b) $10^5$ function evaluations

**Fig. 3.** Solutions of MNHOP in the objective space: $(f_3^U, f_4^U)$

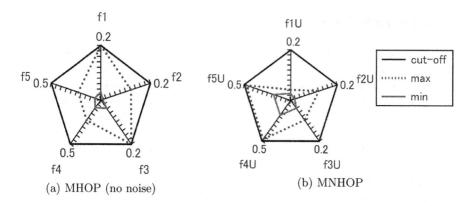

**Fig. 4.** Objective function values of non-dominated feasible solutions

**Table 2.** Correlation between two objective functions

(a) MHOP (no noise)

| $\lambda$ | $f_1$ | $f_2$ | $f_3$ | $f_4$ | $f_5$ |
|---|---|---|---|---|---|
| $f_1$ | 1 | ▽ | — | — | ▽ |
| $f_2$ | −0.28 | 1 | ▽ | △ | △ |
| $f_3$ | −0.06 | −0.24 | 1 | — | — |
| $f_4$ | 0.15 | 0.50 | −0.19 | 1 | △ |
| $f_5$ | −0.26 | 0.22 | −0.07 | 0.47 | 1 |

(b) MNHOP

| $\lambda$ | $f_1^U$ | $f_2^U$ | $f_3^U$ | $f_4^U$ | $f_5^U$ |
|---|---|---|---|---|---|
| $f_1^U$ | 1 | ▽ | ▽ | ▽ | ▽ |
| $f_2^U$ | −0.61 | 1 | — | △ | △ |
| $f_3^U$ | −0.33 | −0.16 | 1 | — | — |
| $f_4^U$ | −0.62 | 0.98 | −0.21 | 1 | △ |
| $f_5^U$ | −0.62 | 0.98 | −0.21 | 0.99 | 1 |

the result of statistical test about $\lambda$. The null hypothesis is $\lambda = 0$, while the alternative hypothesis is $\lambda \neq 0$. Symbol △ (▽) means that the null hypothesis is rejected with a significance level: 0.05. As a result, we accept the alternative hypothesis and expect $\lambda > 0$ ($\lambda < 0$). On the other hand, "—" means that the null hypothesis can't be rejected. Even though the values of $\lambda$ are not so large, we can confirm $\lambda \neq 0$ in many cases. Similarly, Table 2(b) shows correlation coefficients $\lambda$ calculated from the above 93 solutions of MNHOP. We can observe the similarity between Table 2(a) and (b). Therefore, the fundamental characteristics of SAW filter are maintained despite the existence of noise.

## 6 Conclusion

The performances of SAW filters are deteriorated due to the uncertainties of physical coefficients and design parameters. Therefore, a computer-aided design method of SAW filters based on the prediction of the worst-case performance was proposed. The proposed DEUCR is applicable to various real-world problems formulated as MNHOP. Even though DEUCR requires new control parameters, namely a cut-off point and reference points, appropriate values of them should be decided easily for real-world MNHOPs from their specifications.

Future work will include an in-depth evaluation of DEUCR on a broad range of instances of MNHOP. Furthermore, handling the objective function values contaminated with non-Gaussian noise remains as an active area of research.

# References

1. Bockelman, D.E., Eisenstadt, W.R.: Combined differential and common-mode scattering parameters: theory and simulation. IEEE Trans. Microw. Theory Tech. **43**(7), 1530–1539 (1995)
2. Branke, J., Avigad, G., Moshaiov, A.: Multi-objective worst case optimization by means of evolutionary algorithms. Working Paper. WBS, University of Warwick, Coventry (2013). http://dx.doi.org/10.1016/j.ejor.2014.03.013
3. Brest, J., Greiner, S., Bošković, B., Merink, M., Žumer, V.: Self-adapting control parameters in differential evolution. a comparative study on numerical benchmark problems. IEEE Trans. Evol. Comput. **10**(6), 646–657 (2006)
4. Das, I., Dennis, J.: Normal-boundary intersection: a new method for generating the pareto surface in nonlinear multicriteria optimization problems. SIAM J. Optim. **8**(3), 631–657 (1998)
5. Deb, K., Jain, H.: An evolutionary many-objective optimization algorithm using reference-point-based nondominated sorting approach, part I: solving problems with box constraints. IEEE Trans. Evol. Comput. **18**(4), 577–601 (2014)
6. Deb, K., Pratap, A., Agarwal, S., Meyarivan, T.: A fast and elitist multiobjective genetic algorithm: NSGA-II. IEEE Trans. Evol. Comput. **6**(2), 182–197 (2002)
7. Ehrgott, M., Ide, J., Schöbel, A.: Minmax robustness for multi-objective optimization problems. Eur. J. Oper. Res. (2014). http://dx.doi.org/10.1016/j.ejor.2014.03.013
8. Fieldsend, J.E., Everson, R.M.: The rolling tide evolutionary algorithm: a multi-objective optimizer for noisy optimization problems. IEEE Trans. Evol. Comput. **19**, 103–117 (2014)
9. Hashimoto, K.: Surface Acoustic Wave Devices in Telecommunications - Modeling and Simulation. Springer, Heidelberg (2000)
10. Kojima, T., Suzuki, T.: Fundamental equations of electro-acoustic conversion for an interdigital surface-acoustic-wave transducer by using force factors. Jpn. J. Appl. Phys. Suppl. **13**, 194–197 (1992)
11. Kuroiwa, D., Lee, G.M.: On robust multiobjective optimization. Vietnam J. Math. **40**(2&3), 305–317 (2012)
12. Lu, X., Mouthaan, K., Soon, Y.T.: Wideband bandpass filters with SAW-filter-like selectivity using chip SAW resonators. IEEE Trans. Microw. Theory Tech. **62**(1), 28–36 (2014)
13. Nakamura, H., Komatsu, T., Nakanishi, H., Tsurunari, T., Fujiwara, J.: Reduction of transverse leakage for SAW resonators on $LiTaO_3$ substrate. In: Proceedings of the IEEE International Ultrasonics Symposium, pp. 1248–1251 (2012)
14. Price, K.V., Storn, R.M., Lampinen, J.A.: Differential Evolution - A Practical Approach to Global Optimization. Springer, Heidelberg (2005)
15. Rakshit, P., Konar, A., Das, S., Jain, L.C., Nagar, A.K.: Uncertainty management in differential evolution induced multiobjective optimization in presence of measurement noise. IEEE Trans. Syst. Man Cybern. Syst. **44**(7), 922–937 (2013)
16. Shim, V.A., Tan, K.C., Chia, J.Y., Mamun, A.A.: Multi-objective optimization with estimation of distribution algorithm in a noisy environment. Evol. Comput. **21**(1), 149–177 (2013)
17. Soares, G.L., Adriano, R.L.S., Maia, C.A., Jaulin, L., Vasconcelos, J.A.: Robust multi-objective TEAM22 problem: a case study of uncertainties in design optimization. IEEE Trans. Magn. **45**(3), 1028–1031 (2009)

18. Tagawa, K., Harada, S.: Multi-noisy-objective optimization based on prediction of worst-case performance. In: Dediu, A.-H., Lozano, M., Martín-Vide, C. (eds.) TPNC 2014. LNCS, vol. 8890, pp. 23–34. Springer, Heidelberg (2014)
19. Tagawa, K., Imamura, A.: Many-hard-objective optimization using differential evolution based on two-stage constraint-handling. In: Proceedings of the GECCO 2013, pp. 671–678 (2013)
20. Tagawa, K., Sasaki, Y., Nakamura, H.: Optimum design of balanced SAW filters using multi-objective differential evolution. In: Deb, K., et al. (eds.) SEAL 2010. LNCS, vol. 6457, pp. 466–475. Springer, Heidelberg (2010)
21. Voß, T., Trautmann, H., Igel, C.: New uncertainty handling strategies in multi-objective evolutionary optimization. In: Schaefer, R., Cotta, C., Kołodziej, J., Rudolph, G. (eds.) PPSN XI. LNCS, vol. 6239, pp. 260–269. Springer, Heidelberg (2010)

# Clustering Local Tourism Systems
# by Threshold Acceptance

Joseph Andria[1][(✉)] and Giacomo di Tollo[2]

[1] Dipartimento di Scienze Economiche, Aziendali e Statistiche,
University of Palermo, Palermo, Italy
joseph.andria@unipa.it
[2] Dipartimento di Management, Universitá Ca' Foscari, Venice, Italy
giacomo.ditollo@unive.it

**Abstract.** Despite the importance of tourism as a leading industry
in the development of a country's economy, there is a lack of criteria
and methodologies for the detection, promotion and governance of local
tourism systems. We propose a quantitative approach for the detection of
local tourism systems that are optimal with respect to geographical, economic, and demographic criteria. To this end, we formulate the issue as
an optimization problem, and we solve it by means of Threshold Acceptance, a meta-heuristic algorithm which does not require us to predefine
the number of clusters and also does not require all geographic areas to
belong to a cluster.

## 1 Introduction

For many countries, tourism represents a consistent part of the gross domestic
product, and is a key activity to develop employment in related service industries
as accommodation, transportation, hospitality, and catering. The importance
and multidimensionality of tourism has led to an increased attention by both
academics and governments [1–5]. A particular focus has been given to modelling
local government systems in order to foster tourism development and to evaluate public policies [6,7]. Recently, there have been studies aimed in grouping
together tourist attractions in order to define systems whose entities contribute
to create added value [8,9]. To this aim, the notion of *clustering* can be successfully applied to tourism, since tourist attractions may be grouped together
into clusters to optimize a combination of factors in order to produce added
value. Porter [10] has defined clusters as geographical concentrations of interconnected companies whose joint activity leads to a competitive advantage to
its members. Clusters have a long-term impact on the local economy, and they
remain active until the reason of its existence holds [11]. In the traditional analysis, clusters are either composed of businesses that produce substitute goods
(horizontal clusters) or businesses that produce intermediate goods which are
then assembled together (vertical clusters). In tourism instead, businesses operate in a context in which cooperation and competition co-exist, leading to the
definition of *diagonal clusters* [12,13] where businesses produce complementary

© Springer International Publishing Switzerland 2015
A.M. Mora and G. Squillero (Eds.): EvoApplications 2015, LNCS 9028, pp. 629–640, 2015.
DOI: 10.1007/978-3-319-16549-3_51

goods or services and benefit from externalities specific to the tourism industry [14]. It has been shown that geographical areas with the strongest presence of clusters are the most successful in tourism [6]. The reason of identifying tourist clusters is twofold: fist, it is related to administrative rules that have imposed the definition of tourist clusters for regulation purposes; then, there exists some kind of tourism that implicitly define clusters, hence a definition of clusters w.r.t. constraints imposed by the nature of tourism itself may be used to foster that particular type of tourism in a given region. In our work, we are focusing on the first reason, in order to comply with some administrative rules introduced by the Italian legislation, since the Sicilian Regional Actuative Decree n. 4 - 2010 has defined a series of requirements to recognise a geographical entity as a local tourism system. A framework imposed in view of the second goal is left for future work. In this paper we introduce a method that is able to define clusters in a given geographical area without any assumption nor constraints with respect to the administrative aggregate or the number of clusters: we define the problem as an optimisation problem and we solve it by means of a meta-heuristic approach referred to as *Threshold Accepting* (TA). We want to stress out that our focus is on the application of a metaheuristic to the problem at hand: an exhaustive experimental comparison about several metaheuristics is out of the scope of this paper, and will be left for further works. Please notice that we do not predefine the number of clusters and also allow areas not to belong to any cluster. Our goal is to show that our procedure produces clusters that are able to explain the tourist features of a region. The resulting geographical regions (clusters) have to have the following features [15,16]:

1. clusters have to represent a tourist destination network in a well-defined area, where a small number of tourism sites are located and visitors can access them by a one-day trip;
2. clusters have to be a tourism complex, which includes various multiple tourism attractions (accommodations, restaurants, amusement parks etc.).

The rest of the paper is organised as follows: Sect. 2 gives us an overview about the related literature on the topic. Section 3 describes our formulation of the problem. Section 4 outlines our experimental analysis, before concluding and stressing out possible future research on Sect. 5.

## 2    Related Works

An area's tourist development cycle can be divided into diverse phases [17]: in a first phase, referred to as *discovery* phase, a small number of tourists discover the area, making their own travel arrangements, following irregular journey patterns; then, when the number of visitors increases, the local communities (i.e., the economic actors belonging to the cluster) start to provide services for the tourists mass (*local initiative* phase). In the following phase (referred to as *institution-alisation*), the area's specific features are recognized by the tourist potential visitors, and the area gains popularity. Finally the area may enter in either a *consolidation* or a *stagnation* phase, due to changes in the visitor preferences, emergence of new tourism districts etc. The public sector plays a crucial role in this cycle (above all in the last phases) by promoting sustainable development, thus hindering a possible decline [18]; hence there are more and more laws and guidelines concerning the definition of tourist districts and measures to promote them. In Italy the legislator has defined the role of local tourism systems in the Legislative Decree n. 79 - 2011, which entitles the Italian regions to recognise and promote these systems as part of their policies and management tasks. Hence, a method to identify local systems have to be developped. Identifying clusters is relevant not only for regulatory purposes. Indeed the need of clustering a given geographical area is inherent to some kinds of tourism itself. For instance, when taking into account drive tourism, it has been shown that the distance of 320 miles (roundtrip) can be identified as a transition point between a single destination and a multidestination travel [19]. A local authority willing to promote drive tourism, needs to consider this information in order to create clusters in which the pairwise distance between municipalities in a cluster does not exceed this distance. On the other hand, the distance between municipalities belonging to different clusters should always be bigger than this threshold. Some work on partitioning a region in tourist districts exists in the literature. Sim [9] defined a standard for tourist zones, and used it to divide a Korean region into five zones; [8] use network analysis to understand which municipalities are apt to be part of a rural tourism districts in Jangheung-gun and Jeollanam-do (Korea). Most work is based upon the granularity of a region [20,21], but some authors have shown that it is not suitable to work at this level of granularity [22] since it imposes binding constraints over the cluster composition. We end this section by noticing that the idea of applying intelligent algorithms to tourism clustering problems is still not exploited: the few existing approaches [23,24] aim to find attractive areas rather than clustering or partitioning; they are more focused on web and social-network based content, and use data which cannot be reconducted to the ones at hand, hence a comparison is not possible.

## 3   Problem Formulation

A geographical area consists of territorial units (municipalities), and can be represented by a non oriented graph whose vertices are the territorial units. The graph is denoted

$$G = (V, E)$$

where $V = \{1, \ldots, n_U\}$ is the set of vertices corresponding to the $n_U$ territorial units and $E = \{1, \ldots, n_E\}$ is the set of edges representing the pairwise distance between territorial units. To each vertex $i$ is associated a value $w_i$ representing the attractiveness of the territorial unit (see what follows). To each edge $k$ connecting vertices $h_k$ and $t_k$ is associated a value $e_k$ corresponding to the inverse distance between $h_k$ and $t_k$. In our work we aim at identifying clusters of vertices forming tourism systems. To this goal, we have to introduce the concept of attractiveness: The attractiveness of a geographical entity can be defined as its capacity to contribute to the tourist well-being (see for instance [20, 25, 26]). Following [25], we translate this concept into a measure for the aggregate attractiveness as perceived by tourists. A geographical area can offer a number of features such as hotels, outdoor accommodations and bed and breakfast, restaurants, night clubs, travel agencies, tourist guides, cultural life, transportation infrastructure etc. The potential of a given unit to attract tourism is a function of these features. Features taken into account in our work are detailed in Table 1 (see what follows). Each feature is assessed by the quantity of homogeneous elements offered by all operators working in a given territorial unit (i.e. beds assess the receptiveness, number of private and public transportation companies assessing the local access and mobility, and so on). Let $P_i$ be the tourist presence (i.e., the quantity of nights spent by tourists in accomodation facilities belonging to territorial unit $i$) and $p_i = P_i / \sum_{l \in V} P_l$ indicate the relative tourist presence of geographical entity $i$ w.r.t. the whole region taken into account. To measure the potential of a feature $j$ in a territorial unit $i$ we introduce $S_{ji}$ as the value of feature $j$ in a given territorial unit $i$. The ratio $S_{ji} / \sum_{l \in V} S_{jl}$ represents the relative frequency of feature $j$ in the territorial unit $i$. Let $n_F$ be the number of features considered. The attractiveness $w$ of the territorial unit $i$ is measured by

$$w_i = \sum_{k=1}^{n_F} \frac{S_{ki}}{p_i \sum_{\ell=1}^{n_U} S_{k\ell}} \qquad i = 1, \ldots, n_U. \tag{1}$$

By aggregating territorial units in clusters, we want to create aggregates whose attractiveness is bigger than the sum of attractiveness of its components. The attractiveness of cluster $p$ can be computed as

$$v_p = \sum_{i \in V_p} w_i + \sum_{c \in E_p} (w_{h_c} + w_{t_c}) e_c \tag{2}$$

where $V_p$ and $E_p$ are respectively the sets of vertices and edges forming cluster (local system) $p$, with $h_c$ and $t_c$ being endpoints of edge $c$. The second term represents the gain obtained by aggregating territorial units. The overall value associated to a given clustering can be written as:

$$\Phi(y) = \sum_{\substack{i=1 \\ y(i) \neq 0}}^{n_U} w_i + \sum_{k=1}^{n_E} \delta_{y(h_k), y(t_k)} \left( w_{h_k} + w_{t_k} \right) e_k \tag{3}$$

where $y$ is an array of length $n_U$ with values $y(i) \in \{0, 1, \ldots, K\}$ indicating the local system (cluster) to which the vertex $i$ belongs. The municipalities with same value $y(i)$ belong to the same cluster. The symbol $\delta$ is the Kronecker delta. Since $G$ is symmetric, we assume $n_E = \frac{(n_U)(n_U - 1)}{2}$. By maximising Eq. (3) we solve the *Unconstrained Tourism Cluster Problem*.

### The Optimization Problem

Our goal is to identify a clustering which maximizes the value of $\Phi(y)$ in Eq. (3). As a benchmark we have chosen the region *Sicily*, and our goal is to cluster its

390 municipalities. For the purpose of the application, the attractiveness weights of the municipalities are estimated based on the features given in Table 1 by using Eq. (1) where $S_{ki}$ represents, in turn, for the $i - th$ territorial unit, the "cultural heritage goods", the "number of companies operating in transport", the "number of beds of all the receptive structures", etc. Data refers to the period 1998–2002. The constraints to be taken into account are specific to the geographical region under consideration. To comply with the guidelines provided by the Sicilian Regional *Actuative Decree n.4 - 2010* [27] and in order to be officially recognised, a tourist district has to satisfy the following constraints:

1. Its population has to be no smaller than 150.000 residents;
2. Its receptive capacity must be no lower than 7.500 beds;
3. It has to show commercial activity by having at least one commercial shop per 350 residents.

Moreover we introduce an upper bound $n_K$ for the number of local systems. Adding these constraints to Eq. (3) leads to the *Constrained tourism clustering problem*, whose formulation is the following:

$$\max \; \Phi(y) \tag{4}$$

$$\sum_{k \in V_p} S_{2,k} \geq 150.000 \qquad p = 1, \ldots, K \tag{4'}$$

$$\sum_{k \in V_p} S_{5,k} \geq 7.500 \qquad p = 1, \ldots, K \tag{4''}$$

Table 1. Overall features statistics. Data refer to the whole region Sicilia, over the period 1998–2002.

| | Mean | Median | Std | Skewness | Kurtosis |
|---|---|---|---|---|---|
| Municipalities area *(km²)* | 66.01 | 37 | 79.82 | 2.64 | 9.03 |
| Population | 12,914 | 4,713 | 40,537 | 12.15 | 178.83 |
| Cultural heritage goods | 0.98 | 0 | 3.50 | 11.16 | 161.38 |
| Transport | 41.98 | 15 | 139.40 | 10.22 | 119.31 |
| Beds in Hotels, B&B..., | 461.15 | 47 | 1215.74 | 4.47 | 23.44 |
| Beds in Hospitals | 48.78 | 0 | 312.29 | 11.32 | 137.54 |
| Sport, Cultural activity | 47.19 | 17 | 162.97 | 11.22 | 148.03 |
| Financial intermediaries | 25.85 | 6 | 107.27 | 11.15 | 144.36 |
| Commercial Businesses | 435.88 | 135 | 1603.42 | 11.59 | 155.82 |
| Distance from airport *(km)* | 81.69 | 75.90 | 44.45 | 0.22 | −0.72 |

$$\frac{\sum_{k \in V_p} S_{2,k}}{\sum_{k \in V_p} S_{9,k}} \geq 350 \qquad p = 1, \dots, K \tag{4'''}$$

$$K \leq n_K \tag{4''''}$$

We are solving this optimization problem by using a particular local search technique, Threshold Accepting [28,29], which is a trajectory method whose pseudo-code is given in Algorithm 1.

---

**Algorithm 1.** Pseudocode for Threshold Accepting

---
1: Initialize rounds and steps $n_R$, $n_S$
2: Compute threshold sequence $\tau_r$, $r = 1, 2, \dots, n_R$
3: Generate starting solution $y^c$
4: **for** $r = 1$ to $n_R$ **do**
5:    **for** $i = 1$ to $n_S$ **do**
6:       Generate $y^n \in \mathcal{N}(y^c)$ (neighbor of $y^c$)
7:       **if** $f(y^c) < f(y^n) + \tau_r$ **then** $y^c = y^n$
8:    **end for**
9: **end for**

---

Statement 7 allows the algorithm to escape local maxima by accepting solutions which are worse than the current one, in which the worsening is not bigger than a given threshold ($\tau_r$) whose value decreases to zero over execution. The values sequence is estimated by means of the empirical distribution of distances between objective values of neighboring positions. The starting solution is a $n_U$-sized randomly generated vector $y$ whose values represents the cluster a municipality belongs to ($y_i \in \{0, 1, \dots, n_K\}, \forall i$). A neighboring solution is obtained by randomly picking an element of the vector (i.e., choosing a municipality) and changing its associated value (cluster) to a randomly chosen integer between 0 and $n_K$. Constraints are taken into account by adding a penalty term to the objective function in case of violation. Due to the non deterministic nature of the solution, the algorithm is restarted, and the best result represents the solution to the problem. A discussion about the quality of such solutions can be found in [30]. A more detailed description of the implementation of Threshold Accepting can be found in [31,32].

## 4   Empirical Results

The aforementioned Sicilian Regional Actuative Decree n. 4 - 2010 has defined a series of requirements to recognise a geographical entity as a local tourism system. According to these requirements, a number of geographical entities have been classified as local tourism systems. These local systems (referred to as tourist districts) have been determined by administrative and political procedures. This section aims to compute the clusters with our model, and compare their behaviour to the *tourist districts*. The goal is to understand whether our approach could lead to results that are better than just considering districts and verifying some administrative rules. Hence, we solve the *Constrained Tourism Clustering Problem* by threshold accepting, and we compare the results with the tourist districts defined by the Regione Sicilia. The optimisation algorithm is implemented in Matlab R2007a and is available upon request. Figure 1 shows the Tourist Districts (a) along with clusters that have been obtained with TA by solving the *Constrained Tourism Clustering Problem* (b) and the *Unconstrained Tourism Clustering Problem* (c).

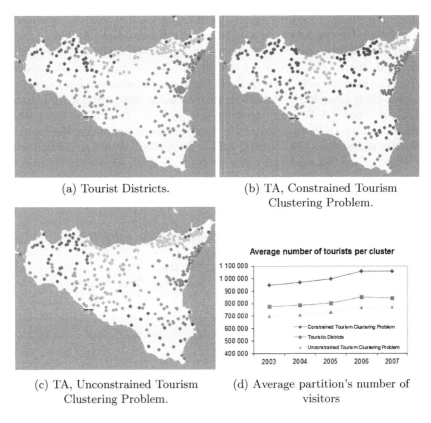

(a) Tourist Districts.

(b) TA, Constrained Tourism Clustering Problem.

(c) TA, Unconstrained Tourism Clustering Problem.

(d) Average partition's number of visitors

**Fig. 1.** Comparison between existing tourist districts (a) and clusters obtained by TA (b)(c), with corresponding out-of-sample number of tourists per year

The algorithm has been executed over data stemming from the period 1998–2002. In order to assess the performances of the obtained clusters, we are computing the number of tourists that have visited these clusters during the years

**Table 2.** Tourist overnight stays. Data refers to the whole Sicily over years 2003–2007.

|          | 2003   | 2004   | 2005   | 2006   | 2007   |
|----------|--------|--------|--------|--------|--------|
| Mean     | 33,724 | 34,233 | 35,183 | 37,371 | 37,441 |
| Median   | 1,153  | 1,210  | 1,524  | 1,631  | 1,641  |
| Std      | 116694 | 119396 | 120711 | 126798 | 125559 |
| Skewness | 6.25   | 6.27   | 6.11   | 6.08   | 6.06   |
| Kurtosis | 47.10  | 47.03  | 44.04  | 43.35  | 43.23  |

2003–2007 [33], so this assessment is a true out-of-sample analysis. Statistics about the tourist stays are reported on Table 2.

Since Threshold Accepting is not deterministic, a first analysis is aimed to know whether the algorithm is robust w.r.t. different runs. To this goal, we have implemented the *partition-distance* defined by [34]: applying two different clustering methods on the same set of elements $N$, we obtain two partitions $P_0$ and $P_1$. The partition-distance $D(P_0, P_1)$ is the minimum number of elements that must be deleted from $N$ so that the two induced partitions are identical. We have run our TA 30 times to solve our problem, computing the pairwise partition distance $D(P_i, P_j)$, $1 \leq i \leq j \leq 30$, and then computing the mean and standard variation over the obtained values. Results are shown on Table 3, along with statistics for the cardinality of clusters, execution time and the objective function. Values show us that the algorithm's results are rather robust, so we will continue our analysis by using the results of a randomly chosen run, without loss of generalisation.

**Table 3.** Statistics about the results obtained by TA, 30 runs

|                                      | Cardinality | | Distance | | Time (s) | | OF | |
|--------------------------------------|------|-----|-------|------|--------|-------|--------|--------|
|                                      | Mean | Var | Mean  | Var  | Mean   | Var   | Mean   | Var    |
| Tourist districts (no TA)            | 16   | -   | -     | -    | -      | -     | 135.82 | -      |
| Constrained Tourism Clustering       | 12   | 2.18| 14.82 | 3.48 | 106.03 | 12.01 | 192.98 | 377.86 |
| Unconstrained Tourism Clustering     | 16   | 1.03| 12.51 | 3.02 | 98.16  | 9.38  | 195.83 | 239.38 |

We remark that the value of the objective function we want to maximise is higher when using our approaches (for both constrained and unconstrained formulations) than the one computed on the original Tourist Districts. We remark also that in the problem formulation we impose an inequality constraint $(4'''')$ in order to limit the maximum number of clusters. This constraint is not required neither by legislative texts nor by theoretical grounds. We have taken into account the possibility of imposing it just in order to make a comparison w.r.t. the Tourist District: since there are 16 Tourist District in Sicily, we are imposing that the number of clusters to be found for the *Constrained Tourism Clustering Problem* shall be no greater than 16: the user just has to set an upper bound $n_K$ in $(4'''')$, and this constraint is not binding for arbitrarily large values of $n_K$. Another remark is that the cardinality of clusters found by the *Unconstrained Tourism Clustering Problem* is similar to the number of Tourist Districts. When considering the *Constrained Tourism Clustering Problem*, the cardinality decreases to 12 for the effect of the population constraint which forbids us to have small clusters. We can also remark the implications of this difference over the out-of-sample number of visitors: by observing panel (d) in Fig. 1 we note that the yearly average number of visitors in the clusters obtained with the constrained tourism clustering is bigger than the one computed for the unconstrained case as well as for the tourist districts. This comes with no surprise w.r.t. unconstrained case, but it represents a good feature w.r.t. the tourist districts: it means that the tourist districts recognised by the legislative authority have a smaller number of visitors w.r.t. the ones that could be obtained by using our model based approach. Furthermore we can remark that there are tourist districts that fulfil all constraints imposed by the regulations, but whose activity related to the tourism is poor since their tourist presences are negligible and close to zero. We can see it in Fig. 2, where we have plotted, for every year, all values of tourist presences for every single cluster found by the three clusters identification methods taken into account (Constrained Tourism Clustering Problems, Unconstrained Tourism Clustering Problem, and original Tourist District). We can notice that clusters having the smallest number of visitors are always the ones belonging to the Tourist Districts. This does not happen when defining the tourist districts by means of TA (Constrained Tourism Clustering): all clusters have a satisfactory number of visitors over time.

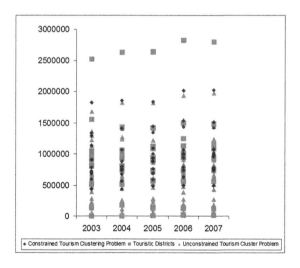

**Fig. 2.** Yearly presences for clusters obtained by TA and tourist districts.

We finish this section by pointing out that the clusters obtained via our TA approach are good instruments to understand the tourist behaviour of geographical regions: TA does not rely in any assumptions nor parameters to create the clusters, whose composition offers a good partitioning that takes into account the specific features of the geographic entity. Furthermore, the obtained clusters show a better tourist flow than existing tourist districts. We want to stress out the fact that the data taken into account for creating the partitions are the same taken into account by the legislative authority to recognise a territorial unit as a tourist district.

## 5    Conclusions

In this paper we have emphasized the role of clustering to identify local tourism systems compliant with the guidelines provided by the regulation: this issue has been modeled as an optimization problem and solved by Threshold Accepting. The optimisation problem has been solved for both the constrained tourism clustering problem and the unconstrained tourism clustering problem and the solutions have been compared with the regional tourist districts. Our approach has shown that tourist districts recognised by the local legislative authority have a smaller number of visitors than the ones obtained by using our approach. This result highlights the importance of introducing a quantitative model of competitiveness of a tourism cluster for regional development and demonstrates the importance of using real-world variables and indicators for an optimal tourist governance. Our future research will take into account different benchmarks in order to study how the algorithm behaves with respect to different geographical patterns; then, we will analyze the dynamic of clusters over time to understanding how this might affect tourist demand. Last, we will take into account the clustering problem induced by the nature of some tourist attitudes itself, such as drive turism, in order to investigate how the guidelines imposed by administrative rules may hinder or foster specific tourist flows.

## References

1. Gormsen, E.: The impact of tourism on coastal areas. GeoJournal **42**(1), 39–54 (1997)
2. Ritchie, J., Crouch, G.: The Competitive Destination: A Sustainable Tourism Perspective. CABI Publishing Series, CABI Pub, Cambridge (2003)
3. Butler, R.: The Tourism Area Life Cycle. Aspects of Tourism, vol. 1. Channel View Publications, Clevedon (2006)
4. Hawkins, D., Mann, S.: The world bank's role in tourism development. Ann. Tourism Res. **34**(2), 348–363 (2007)
5. Macbeth, J.: Towards an ethics platform for tourism. Ann. Tourism Res. **32**(4), 962–984 (2005)
6. Jackson, J., Murphy, P.: Clusters in regional tourism an Australian case. Ann. Tourism Res. **33**(4), 1018–1035 (2006)
7. Leask, A.: Progress in visitor attraction research: towards more effective management. Tourism Manage. **31**(2), 155–166 (2010)
8. Lee, S., Choi, J., Yoo, S., Oh, Y.: Evaluating spatial centrality for integrated tourism management in rural areas using GIS and network analysis. Tourism Manage. **34**, 14–24 (2013)

9. Sim, I.: A study on the establishment of tourism zone and development strategic. Korean Acad. Soc. Cult. Tourism **4**, 199–223 (2002)

10. Porter, M.: On Competition. Harvard Business School Publishing, Boston (1998)

11. Brenner, T., Gildner, A.: The long-term implications of local industrial clusters. Eur. Plann. Stud. **14**(9), 1315–1328 (2006)

12. Di Tollo, G., Tanev, S., De March, D., Ma, Z.: Neural networks to model the innovativeness perception of co-creative firms. Expert Syst. Appl. **39**(16), 12719–12726 (2012)

13. Brandenburger, A.: Co-opetition/Adam M. Brandenburger and Barry J. Nalebuff, 1st edn. Doubleday, New York (1996)

14. Yang, Y.: Agglomeration density and tourism development in China: an empirical research based on dynamic panel data model. Tourism Manage. **33**(6), 1347–1359 (2012)

15. Yabuta, M., Scott, N.: Dynamic properties of a tourism destination network. Tourism Anal. **16**(4), 493–498 (2011)

16. Yabuta, M., Scott, N.: A theoretical framework of the dynamic property of the tourism destination network. Technical report, the University of Queensland (2010)

17. Stansfield, C.: Atlantic city and the resort cycle background to the legalization of gambling. Ann. Tourism Res. **5**(2), 238–251 (1978)

18. Butler, R.: The concept of a tourist area cycle of evolution: implications for management of resources. Can. Geogr. Le Gographe Can. **24**(1), 5–12 (1980)

19. Hwang, Y., Fesenmaier, D.: Multidestination pleasure travel patterns: empirical evidence from the American travel survey. J. Travel Res. **42**(2), 166–171 (2003)

20. Jin, X., Weber, K., Bauer, T.: Impact of clusters on exhibition destination attractiveness: evidence from mainland China. Tourism Manage. **33**(6), 1429–1439 (2012)

21. Enright, M.: Regional clusters: what we know and what we should know. In: Brcker, J., Dohse, D., Soltwedel, R. (eds.) Innovation Clusters and Interregional Competition. Advances in Spatial Science, pp. 99–129. Springer, Heidelberg (2003)

22. Pearce, D., Tan, R., Schott, C.: Distribution channels in international markets: a comparative analysis of the distribution of new Zealand tourism in Australia, great Britain and the USA. Curr. Issues Tourism **10**(1), 33–60 (2007)

23. Sakai, T., Tamura, K., Kitakami, H.: Density-based adaptive spatial clustering algorithm for identifying local high-density areas in georeferenced documents. In: 2014 IEEE International Conference on Systems, Man and Cybernetics (SMC), pp. 513–518, October 2014

24. Sakai, T., Tamura, K., Kitakami, H.: A new density-based spatial clustering algorithm for extracting attractive local regions in georeferenced documents. In: 2014 Proceedings of the International MultiConference of Engineers and Computer Scientists, pp. 360–365 (2014)

25. Cracolici, M., Nijkamp, P.: The attractiveness and competitiveness of tourist destinations: a study of southern italian regions. Tourism Manage. **30**(3), 336–344 (2009)

26. Ryan, C.: The Tourist Experience. Continuum (2002)

27. Regione Siciliana: Criteri e modalità per il riconoscimento dei distretti turistici. Gazzetta Ufficiale della Regione Siciliana (2010)

28. Dueck, G., Scheuer, T.: Threshold accepting: a general purpose optimization algorithm appearing superior to simulated annealing. J. Comput. Phys. **90**(1), 161–175 (1990)

29. Moscato, P., Fontanari, J.: Stochastic versus deterministic update in simulated annealing. Phys. Lett. A **146**(4), 204–208 (1990)

30. Gilli, M., Schumann, E.: Optimal enough? J. Heuristics **17**(4), 373–387 (2011)
31. Gilli, M., Winker, P.: Heuristic optimization methods in econometrics. In: Belsley, D.A., Kontoghiorghes, E. (eds.) Handbook of Computational Econometrics. Wiley, Chichester (2009)
32. Gilli, M., Maringer, D., Schumann, E.: Numerical Methods and Optimization in Finance. Academic Press, London (2011). ISBN 978-0-12-375662-6
33. Istat: Primo Repertorio Statistico dei Comuni della Sicilia. Sistema Statistico Nazionale (2008)
34. Gusfield, D.: Partition-distance: a problem and class of perfect graphs arising in clustering. Inf. Process. Lett. **82**(3), 159–164 (2002)

# EvoNUM

# Seed Disperser Ant Algorithm:
# An Evolutionary Approach for Optimization

Wen Liang Chang[1], Jeevan Kanesan[1($\boxtimes$)],
and Anand Jayant Kulkarni[2]

[1] Nature Inspired Meta-heuristic Group, Department of Electrical Engineering,
Faculty of Engineering, University Malaya, Kuala Lumpur, Malaysia
wen_liang@siswa.um.edu.my, jievan@um.edu.my
[2] Department of Mechanical Engineering, Symbiosis Institute of Technology,
Symbiosis International University, Lavale, Pune, Maharastra, India
anand.kulkarni@sitpune.edu.in

**Abstract.** The Seed Disperser Ant Algorithm (SDAA) is inspired from
the evolution of Seed Disperser Ant (*Aphaenogaster senilis*) colony. The ants
in the colony are highly related siblings sharing average 75 % similarity in
genotype. Hence, the genotype of every ant represents variables in binary form
that are used to locally search for optimum solution. Once the colony matures, in
other words a local optimum solution reached, nuptial flights take place where
female genotype copies the male genotype originating from another colony. Once
all colonies saturate new young queen emerges to establish new colonies. This
diversifies the search for global optimum. The SDAA is validated by solving four
30 dimensional classical benchmark problems and six composite benchmark
functions from CEC 2005 special session. The optimal results are found to be
better than the selected state-of-the-art swarm intelligence based optimization.

**Keywords:** Seed disperser ant algorithm · Evolutionary computation ·
Optimization

## 1 Introduction

In the field of optimization, many evolutionary computation (EC) techniques have been
proposed in recent years. This includes Swarm Intelligence (SI) inspired from social
behavior of insects and animals as well as Evolutionary Algorithms (EAs) based on
survival of the fittest individual. Some of the SI techniques include particle swarm
optimization (PSO) [1], Cuckoo Search (CS) [2] and Grey Wolf Optimizer (GWO) [3].
PSO developed by Kennedy and Eberhart [1] simulates the movement of animals as in
a flock of birds or a school of fish. The working principle of this algorithm is based on
collision-proof birds' movement. Later several variations of PSO were developed such
as Evolutionary Particle Swarm Optimization (EPSO) [4], Iteration particle swarm
optimization (IPSO) [5], Global Particle Swarm Optimization (GPSO) [6] and Chaos-
Particle Swarm Optimization (CPSO) [7]. EPSO is a general-purpose algorithm whose
roots are in Evolution Strategies. IPSO is developed by sizing the distributed generation unit and applying new velocity of each particle before updating the position.
Similarly, GPSO improved and enhanced the convergence speed of classical PSO by

© Springer International Publishing Switzerland 2015
A.M. Mora and G. Squillero (Eds.): EvoApplications 2015, LNCS 9028, pp. 643–654, 2015.
DOI: 10.1007/978-3-319-16549-3_52

sharing information of particle position between the dimensions at any iteration. CPSO is a combination of PSO with chaos search strategy. CS is based on cuckoo bird's behavior. Studies show that it could outperform existing algorithms such as PSO. Recently, GWO was inspired from grey wolves' (*Canis lupus*) leadership hierarchy and hunting mechanism. To the best of authors' knowledge, GWO is one of the few works that used composite benchmark functions from CEC 2005 special session. Their results outperformed other meta-heuristics such as PSO, GSA, DE and CMA-ES in 50 % of the composite benchmark functions. Rashedi proposed Gravitational Search Algorithm (GSA) [8] which is based on the law of gravity, where the agents/particles' performance is measured by their masses. The gravitational forces of these particles attracted each other to accelerate and directing these particles towards the optimum solution. Self-supervised learning behavior in cohort was developed by Kulkarni [9]. The optimization is carried out as every candidate tries to improve its own behavior by observing the behavior of other candidate in that cohort.

In EAs, Genetic Algorithms (GA) [10, 11], Memetic Algorithms (MA) [12, 13] and Differential Evolution (DE) [14, 15] exploit population evolution using genetic operators to search for global optimum. MA is a variant of genetic algorithm (GA) that embeds individual learning procedure capable of performing local refinements through genetic operators. Similarly, DE efficiently explores the search space for global optimum solutions by emphasizing on mutation. There is also Covariance Matrix Adaptation Evolution Strategy (CMA-ES) [16] which is an evolution strategy that adapts the full covariance matrix of a normal search (mutation) distribution. Compared to many other evolutionary algorithms, an important property of the CMA-ES is its invariance against linear transformations of the search space.

In this paper, a new nature inspired meta-heuristic is proposed. It is based on evolution process of seed disperser ant (*Aphaenogaster senilis*) [17] referred to as Seed Disperser Ant Algorithm (SDAA). SDAA mimics Seed Disperser Ants' evolutionary strategy to improve its fitness for continuous survival. Unlike conventional evolutionary techniques that involves genetic processes, ants' haploid-diploid genetic make-up uses Kin Altruism [18, 19] for its colony survival. This haploid-diploid genetic code is the chromosome that represents the possible solution of the problem. The colony is populated by sterile female workers and queen ant/s which have diploid genes. On contrary, male ants are haploids. Male ants have wings to perform nuptial flight [20] where they will fly out and mate with the queen from other than its own colony. This avoids inbreeding and encourages diversification. The mated queens will start laying eggs in their respective colony. The search for optimum or near optimum is constructed in two ways, both locally and globally. In local search, each egg or offspring is produced when existing haploid gene copies alleles from the adjacent haploid gene that forms the diploid. This allows the offspring to be highly related to each other. In fact, the genotype similarity [21] between ants from the same colony remains as high as 75 % for search exploitation. Once local search saturates, the colony develops fit young queen that forms new colony. This explores the search for global optimum. The young queen/s will start new colony and the process of local search starts again. The process is repeated until the problem converges to optimal solutions. The organization of this paper is as follows; the SDAA is described in Sect. 2, followed by results and discussion in Sect. 3 and conclusions are provided in Sect. 4.

## 2    Seed Disperser Ant Algorithm for Optimization

Seed Disperser Ant Algorithm (SDAA) exploits the haploid-diploid gene structure to locally search for fitter genes followed by gene exchange during mating process. Haploid cell $h$ contains only one complete set of chromosomes. In this algorithm, we represent variables in the form of the binary haploid. Diploid consists of two sets of chromosomes: usually, one set from the queen and another set from the male. In a diploid state, the haploid number is doubled. Thus, this condition is also known as $2h$.

### 2.1    Seed Disperser Ant Algorithm

Consider a general minimization of unconstrained problem as follows:

$$\text{Minimize} f(L_h) = f(x_1, \ldots x_i, \ldots x_N)$$
$$\text{Subject to } \Psi_i^{lower} \leq x_i \leq \Psi_i^{upper}, \, i = 1, \ldots N \tag{1}$$

As a general case, assume the objective function $f(L_h)$ as the fitness of haploid male ant in the colony which naturally improves by improving its haploid gene code of male ant $L_h = (x_1, \ldots x_i, \ldots x_N)$. Assuming every colony produce many virgin queens for mating with the refer gene haploid $[R_h]_{C_i}$ as the identity gene of the colony. The mated queens $[Q_d]_{C_i}$ are represented by Eq. (2). The mated queen is represented by pairing binary gene code of male ant and its complement $[R_h]_{C_i}$.

$$[Q_d]_{C_i} = [L_h]_{C_i} [R_h]_{C_i} \tag{2}$$

where,

$$C_i = i^{th} \text{ colony}$$

Initially, male ant haploid gene $(L_h)$ is generated randomly represented in binary form. The virgin queens are unable to fly. The male ants have wings and perform nuptial flight by flying out to find another colony to mate with the virgin queen inside or near the colony. New male ants are generated from the mated queens. The new male ants are formed when haploid gene $(L_h)$ copies binary bits from haploid refer gene $(R_h)$ commencing from least significant bit (LSB) to most significant bit (MSB) and vice versa. Then, best male ants are selected to perform nuptial flight with next virgin queens of other colonies. After few nuptial flight cycles, the fitness of male haploid gene $(L_h)$ in the present generation becomes saturated. Also, after few nuptial flights, the colony will produce new virgin queen. New virgin queens are produced when the saturated fittest male mates with the queen. The best haploid gene from haploid gene $(L_h)$ in the mother queen is brought forward to new generation queens' haploid refer gene $(R_h)$. This new queen is assumed to be leading a new fitter colony. The new colony is considered fitter as the boundary size to generate offspring males is limited by shrinking towards the fittest haploid gene $(L_h)$. The optimization process continues with nuptial flight and new queen generation until saturation. The optimization flowchart based on AA is shown in Fig. 1.

The procedure begins with the initialization of control parameters such as number of colony $C$, shrinking factor $r$, and saturation number $S$. Initially, upper boundary $UB_i$ and lower boundary $LB_i$ are fixed as given in equations below.

$$UB_i = \Psi_i^{upper} \tag{3}$$

$$LB_i = \Psi_i^{lower} \tag{4}$$

**Step 1:** Male ant haploid $L_h$ is generated randomly as shown in Eq. (5) below:

$$[L_h]_{C_i} = [x_1, \ldots x_i, \ldots x_N]_{C_i} \tag{5}$$

where

$$x_i = LB_i + rand \times (UB_i - LB_i)$$
$$rand \in [0, 1]$$
$$N = \text{number of dimension}$$

**Step 2:** $N$ number of $x_i$ is represented in binary form for the male haploid gene $[L_h]_{C_i}$ in every colony. The binary code gene is complemented to form colonies' identity haploid refer gene $[R_h]_{C_i}$ as shown as Eq. (6) below:

$$[R_h]_{C_i} = \overline{[L_h]_{C_i}} \tag{6}$$

Then, every mated queen $[Q_d]_{C_i}$ is formed as given in Eq. (2).

**Step 3:** The new male ants with haploid gene is generated for next mating process. The new male ants haploid gene $[O_{h,p}]_{C_i}$, $(p = 1, 2, \ldots P)$ is formed when the haploid gene $[L_h]_{C_i}$ copies binary bits from haploid refer gene $[R_h]_{C_i}$ from least significant bit (LSB) to most significant bit (MSB) and vice versa. $P$ number of new male ants is formed depending on the number of bits in $[L_h]_{C_i}$. The Eq. (7) generates new male ants' haploid in decimal number form as shown below:

$$[x_i]_{C_i, O_{h,p+1}} = [x_i]_{C_i, O_{h,p}} + m(i, n) \times (2^{n-1}) \tag{7}$$

Where

$$m(i, n) = [x_{i,n}]_{C_i, R_h} - [x_{i,n}]_{C_i, L_h},$$
$$m(i, n) = 1, 0 \text{ or } -1$$
$$p = 1, 2, \ldots P$$
$$i = i^{th} \text{ dimension}$$
$$n = n^{th} \text{ of bit}$$
$$k = \text{number of bits, (LSB} = 1, \text{ MSB} = k)$$

For LSB to MSB,

$$n = 1, 2, \ldots, k;$$

For MSB to LSB,

$$n = k, (k-1), (k-2), \ldots, 1;$$

**Step 4 (Nuptial Flight):** All the new male ant haploid gene $[O_{h,p}]_{C_i}$ is evaluated by the objective function. The best $[O_{h,p}]_{C_i}$ from each colony is chosen to be the male haploid gene $[L_{h(fit)}]_{C_i}$ that will perform nuptial flight to mate with next colony virgin queen. Best haploid gene $L_{h(best)}$ is selected from the new male haploid genes $[L_{h(fit)}]_{C_i}$ of all colonies. The fitness/solution of the best haploid gene $L_{h(best)}$ is recorded as current best solution.

**Step 5 (Mating):** Mating process produces fitter male ant where the new $[L_{h(fit)}]_{C_i}$ will combine with haploid refer gene of the subsequent colony, $C_{i+1}$. The fittest male mated queen of the colony is represented in the Eq. (8) as shown below:

$$\text{In colony } C_{i+1}, \ [L_h]_{C_{i+1}} [R_h]_{C_{i+1}} = [L_{h(fit)}]_{C_i} [R_h]_{C_{i+1}} \tag{8}$$

and for the $1^{st}$ colony $C_1$:

$$\text{In colony } C_1, \ [L_h]_{C_1} [R_h]_{C_1} = [L_{h(fit)}]_{C_N} [R_h]_{C_1}$$

This process will continue with Step 3 to 5 until saturation. If saturated, go to Step 6.

**Step 6:** Shrink the search boundary by the shrinking factor $r$ based on the $L_{h(best)}$ as the center of the boundary if the search boundary still converging for better solution and go to Step 7. The shrinking process is shown as equations below:

$$\text{Boundary size, } B_i = r \times (UB_i - LB_i) \tag{9}$$

Then $UB_i$ and $LB_i$ are generated as shown below:

$$UB_i = [x_i]_{L_{h(best)}} + \frac{1}{2} B_i \tag{10}$$

$$LB_i = [x_i]_{L_{h(best)}} - \frac{1}{2} B_i \tag{11}$$

**Step 7 (Generate New Queen):** In this new generation, all the $[L_h]_{C_i}$ and $[R_h]_{C_i}$ is regenerated similar to Step 1. However, one of the queen's haploid refer gene $[R_h]_{C_i}$ is replaced with current generation's best haploid gene $L_{h(best)}$. This is to bring forward the best haploid gene found on current generation queen to the next generation queen's diploid gene. This is show as the equation below:

$$[R_h]_{C_{random}} = L_{h(best)} \tag{12}$$

The algorithm continues from Step 1 to 7 until convergences to minimum solution. The best haploid gene $L_{h(best)}$ is accepted as the minimum solution of the optimization problem.

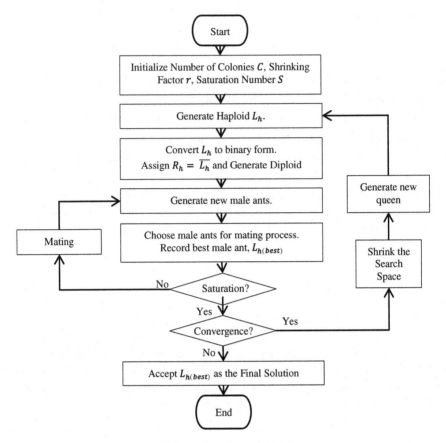

**Fig. 1.** A flowchart of SDAA

## 3   Numerical Experiments and Results

The Seed Disperser Ant Algorithm (SDAA)was validated by optimizing 30 dimensional test problems of Ackley function [22], Rastrigin function [23], Rosenbrock function [24] and Sphere function [23].The optimum of the Rosenbrock function is located in a deep and narrow parabolic valley with a flat bottom. The gradient based methods may need a large number of iterations to reach the global minimum [24]. The sphere function is unimodal and strongly convex function and the Ackley function is highly multimodal with unique global minimum [25].The Rastrigin function has several local minima. It is highly multimodal, but locations of the minima are regularly distributed [26]. All these functions are difficult to be optimized and are widely used as benchmarks in literature to evaluate the performance of optimization techniques. The theoretical global optimum for all the benchmarks is zero. The simulations were carried out 30 times in MATLAB 8.1 (R2012a) using computer run on Windows 7 platform with Intel i7-4770, 3.40 GHz processor and 12 GB RAM.

**Table 1.** Simulation Result of 30 dimensional test problems.

|        |        | Sphere | Rosenbrock | Rastrigin | Ackley |
|--------|--------|--------|------------|-----------|--------|
| PSO    | Best   | N/A    | N/A        | N/A       | N/A    |
| [27]   | Mean   | 0.0000 | 131.5866   | 24.0864   | N/A    |
|        | Std.   | N/A    | N/A        | N/A       | N/A    |
| PSO    | Best   | 1.22E + 03 | 1.79E + 03 | 9.38E + 01 | 9.48E + 00 |
|        | Mean   | 3.70E + 03 | 1.17E + 04 | 1.48E + 02 | 1.27E + 01 |
|        | Std.   | 1.53E + 03 | 7.31E + 03 | 2.63E + 01 | 1.45E + 00 |
| IPSO   | Best   | 8.71E + 02 | 7.16E + 02 | 6.06E + 01 | 7.48E + 00 |
|        | Mean   | 2.25E + 03 | 5.47E + 03 | 1.19E + 02 | 1.00E + 01 |
|        | Std.   | 8.05E + 02 | 5.08E + 03 | 2.41E + 01 | 1.16E + 00 |
| EPSO   | Best   | 5.40E + 03 | 1.62E + 04 | 1.36E + 02 | 1.30E + 01 |
|        | Mean   | 1.14E + 04 | 9.36E + 04 | 2.35E + 02 | 1.63E + 01 |
|        | Std.   | 3.85E + 03 | 7.21E + 04 | 3.69E + 01 | 1.14E + 00 |
| GPSO   | Best   | 1.47E-10 | 5.36E-07 | 4.47E-07 | 5.59E-05 |
|        | Mean   | 4.51E-06 | 3.26E-05 | 2.96E-05 | 4.23E-04 |
|        | Std.   | 6.10E-06 | 5.57E-05 | 4.28E-05 | 2.83E-04 |
| CPSO   | Best   | 1.4356E-81 | 1.3465E-05 | 0.0000E + 00 | 6.3330E-07 |
|        | Mean   | 3.0421E-12 | 4.8167E-02 | 2.5235E-03 | 1.3865E-04 |
|        | Std.   | N/A    | N/A        | N/A       | N/A    |
| CS     | Best   | 4.29E-15 | N/A      | 1.77E-15  | 1.65E-07 |
|        | Mean   | 6.04E-13 | N/A      | 4.72E-09  | 1.10E-06 |
|        | Std.   | N/A    | N/A        | N/A       | N/A    |
| SDAA   | Best   | 0.0000E + 00 | 1.7472E-07 | 0.0000E + 00 | 8.88178E-16 |
|        | Mean   | 0.0000E + 00 | 4.1264E-05 | 0.0000E + 00 | 8.88178E-16 |
|        | Std.   | 0.0000E + 00 | 7.7075E-05 | 0.0000E + 00 | 0.0000E + 00 |
|        | F.E. (Avg.) | 11625 | 54934  | 22270     | 16375  |
|        | Time (s) | 13.29 | 160.08   | 19.67     | 16.64  |

**Table 2.** Result of selected Composite benchmark functions.

|        |      | CF1 | CF2 | CF3 | CF4 | CF5 | CF6 |
|--------|------|-----|-----|-----|-----|-----|-----|
| SDAA   | Mean | 2.8800E-17 | 16.4943 | 179.3623 | 335.8192 | 6.4585 | 457.4799 |
|        | Std. | 1.0973E-17 | 6.43434 | 40.6356 | 77.7292 | 2.5709 | 43.3633 |
| GWO    | Mean | 43.83544 | 91.80086 | 61.43776 | 123.1235 | 102.1429 | 43.14261 |
|        | Std. | 69.86146 | 95.5518 | 68.68816 | 163.9937 | 81.25536 | 84.48573 |
| PSO    | Mean | 100 | 155.91 | 155.91 | 314.3 | 83.45 | 861.42 |
|        | Std. | 81.65 | 13.176 | 13.176 | 20.066 | 101.11 | 125.81 |
| GSA    | Mean | 6.63E-17 | 200.6202 | 180 | 170 | 200 | 142.0906 |
|        | Std. | 2.78E-17 | 67.72087 | 91.89366 | 82.32726 | 47.14045 | 88.87141 |
| DE     | Mean | 6.75E-02 | 28.759 | 144.41 | 324.86 | 10.789 | 490.94 |
|        | Std. | 1.11E-01 | 8.6277 | 19.401 | 14.784 | 2.604 | 39.461 |
| CMA-ES | Mean | 100 | 161.99 | 214.06 | 616.4 | 358.3 | 900.26 |
|        | Std. | 188.56 | 151 | 74.181 | 671.92 | 168.26 | 8.32E-02 |

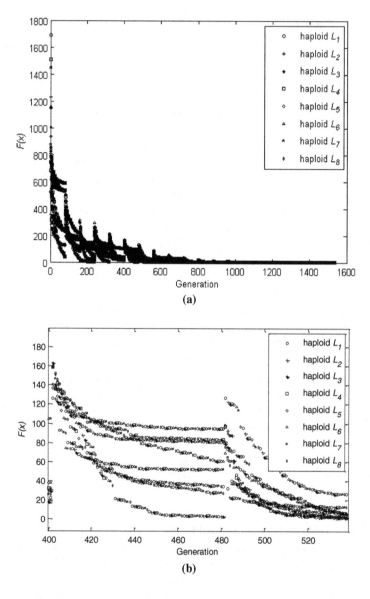

**Fig. 2.** (a) Plot for Composite benchmark functions CF1. (b) Enlarged plot of Composite benchmark functions CF1

Table 1 shows the comparative results between PSO, IPSO, EPSO, GPSO, CPSO, CS and SDAA. The results show SDAA is able to obtain better result compared to other algorithms. The average function evaluations (F.E.) of obtaining the results are shown in Table 1. In most of the result, SDAA is able to achieve close to theoretical global minimum.

SDAA is also validated by optimizing 10 dimensional Composite benchmark functions from CEC 2005special session [28] as shown in Appendix A. These are complex optimization problems that are difficult to solve as they are shifted, rotated, expanded, and combined variants of the classical functions which offer the greatest complexity among the others benchmark functions. Moreover there are huge numbers of local optima in these benchmark functions. Table 2 shows the result of Composite benchmark functions from CEC 2005 special session. SDAA solves the Composite benchmark functions of CF1, CF2 and CF5 with improved result and lower standard deviation compared to GWO, PSO, GSA, DE and CMA-ES. Figure 2(a) shows the plot for Composite benchmark functions CF1 using SDAA. Figure 2(b) shows the enlarged version of Fig. 2(a) between $400^{th}$ to $540^{th}$generation. Figure 2(b) shows the nuptial flight between the male and queen generates fitter male in every new generation. Subsequently, new queen emerges from the fittest male that is highlighted by the peak. The peak is due to random queen and male produced within shrunken boundary with the fittest gene as centroid. The random queens and males cause marginal drop in fitness, nevertheless exploring for better solutions.

In SDAA, the search shrinks within certain fixed range based on the fittest haploid value. SDAA uses local search expansion to help reduce the burden of shrinking factor that is responsible to localize the search. The shrinking factor is maintained at 0.75 for all test benchmarks for SDAA. The colony size is fixed at eight for all benchmark tests carried out in this work. By exhibiting altruistic behavior, the best haploid is allowed to be used by other haploids as reference to improve their respective fitness. This is carried out when other haploids locate global fitness via robust local search on altruistic haploid. In this way, SDAA achieves global optimum.

## 4   Conclusion

The SDAA technique is successfully introduced by exploiting the kin altruism characteristics of seed disperser ant. The high relatedness measured by genotype similarity between the ants in a colony is useful to exploit and explore the search for global optimum. SDAA is validated by solving several benchmark problems. The result showed that SDAA is competitive in obtaining the best global optimum in all test problems compared to PSO, IPSO, EPSO, GPSO, CPSO, CS, GWO, GSA, DE and CMA-ES. Shrinking factor is used to tune the search for global optimum where the value is fixed at 0.75 for all the test benchmarks evaluated by SDAA. In future, the authors would like to expand this work to solve real world problems such as engineering constrained problems.

**Acknowledgement.** This work is supported by ER011-2013A, Ministry of Science, Technology and Innovation, Malaysia (MOSTI).

# Appendix A

Composite benchmark functions

| Functions | Dim. | Range | $f_{min}$ |
|---|---|---|---|
| **CF1** | | | |
| $f_1, f_2, f_3, \dots, f_{10}$ = Sphere Function | 10 | [-5, 5] | 0 |
| $[\delta_1, \delta_2, \delta_2, \dots, \delta_{10}] = [1,1,1,\dots,1]$ | | | |
| $[\lambda_1, \lambda_2, \lambda_2, \dots, \lambda_{10}] = \left[\frac{5}{100}, \frac{5}{100}, \frac{5}{100}, \dots, \frac{5}{100}\right]$ | | | |
| **CF2** | | | |
| $f_1, f_2, f_3, \dots, f_{10}$ = Griewank's Function | 10 | [-5, 5] | 0 |
| $[\delta_1, \delta_2, \delta_2, \dots, \delta_{10}] = [1,1,1,\dots,1]$ | | | |
| $[\lambda_1, \lambda_2, \lambda_2, \dots, \lambda_{10}] = \left[\frac{5}{100}, \frac{5}{100}, \frac{5}{100}, \dots, \frac{5}{100}\right]$ | | | |
| **CF3** | | | |
| $f_1, f_2, f_3, \dots, f_{10}$ = Griewank's Function | 10 | [-5, 5] | 0 |
| $[\delta_1, \delta_2, \delta_2, \dots, \delta_{10}] = [1,1,1,\dots,1]$ | | | |
| $[\lambda_1, \lambda_2, \lambda_2, \dots, \lambda_{10}] = [1,1,1,\dots,1]$ | | | |
| **CF4** | | | |
| $f_1, f_2$ = Ackley's Function | | | |
| $f_3, f_4$ = Rastrigin's Function | | | |
| $f_5, f_6$ = Weierstras's Function | 10 | [-5, 5] | 0 |
| $f_7, f_8$ = Griewank's Function | | | |
| $f_9, f_{10}$ = Sphere Function | | | |
| $[\delta_1, \delta_2, \delta_2, \dots, \delta_{10}] = [1,1,1,\dots,1]$ | | | |
| $[\lambda_1, \lambda_2, \lambda_2, \dots, \lambda_{10}] = \left[\frac{5}{32}, \frac{5}{32}, 1,1, \frac{5}{0.5}, \frac{5}{0.5}, \frac{5}{100}, \frac{5}{100}, \frac{5}{100}, \frac{5}{100}\right]$ | | | |
| **CF5** | | | |
| $f_1, f_2$ = Rastrigin's Function | | | |
| $f_3, f_4$ = Weierstras's Function | | | |
| $f_5, f_6$ = Griewank's Function | 10 | [-5, 5] | 0 |
| $f_7, f_8$ = Ackley's Function | | | |
| $f_9, f_{10}$ = Sphere Function | | | |
| $[\delta_1, \delta_2, \delta_2, \dots, \delta_{10}] = [1,1,1,\dots,1]$ | | | |
| $[\lambda_1, \lambda_2, \lambda_2, \dots, \lambda_{10}] = \left[\frac{1}{5}, \frac{1}{5}, \frac{5}{0.5}, \frac{5}{0.5}, \frac{5}{100}, \frac{5}{100}, \frac{5}{32}, \frac{5}{32}, \frac{5}{100}, \frac{5}{100}\right]$ | | | |
| **CF6** | | | |
| $f_1, f_2$ = Rastrigin's Function | | | |
| $f_3, f_4$ = Weierstras's Function | | | |
| $f_5, f_6$ = Griewank's Function | 10 | [-5, 5] | 0 |
| $f_7, f_8$ = Ackley's Function | | | |
| $f_9, f_{10}$ = Sphere Function | | | |
| $[\delta_1, \delta_2, \delta_2, \dots, \delta_{10}] = [0.1, 0.2, 0.3, 0.4, 0.5, 0.6, 0.7, 0.8, 0.9, 1]$ | | | |
| $[\lambda_1, \lambda_2, \lambda_2, \dots, \lambda_{10}] = \left[0.1 \times \frac{1}{5}, 0.2 \times \frac{1}{5}, 0.3 \times \frac{5}{0.5}, 0.4 \times \frac{5}{0.5}, 0.5 \times \frac{5}{100}, 0.6 \times \frac{5}{100}, 0.7 \times \frac{5}{32}, 0.8 \times \frac{5}{32}, 0.9 \times \frac{5}{100}, 1 \times \frac{5}{100}\right]$ | | | |

* Dim. = dimension

* $f_{min}$ = Global minimum point

# References

1. Eberhart, R.C., Kennedy, J.: A new optimizer using particle swarm theory. In: Proceedings of the sixth international symposium on micro machine and human science, New York, NY (1995)
2. Yang, X.-S., Deb, S.: Cuckoo search via Lévy flights. In: World Congress on Nature & Biologically Inspired Computing, 2009, NaBIC 2009. IEEE (2009)
3. Mirjalili, S., Mirjalili, S.M., Lewis, A.: Grey wolf optimizer. Adv. Eng. Softw. **69**, 46–61 (2014)
4. Miranda, V., Fonseca, N.: EPSO-evolutionary particle swarm optimization, a new algorithm with applications in power systems. In: Proceedings of the Asia Pacific IEEE/PES Transmission and Distribution Conference and Exhibition. Citeseer (2002)
5. Lee, T.-Y., Chen, C.-L.: Unit commitment with probabilistic reserve: An IPSO approach. Energy Convers. Manag. **48**(2), 486–493 (2007)
6. Jamian, J.J., et al.: Global particle swarm optimization for high dimension numerical functions analysis. J. Appl. Math. **2014**, 14 (2014)
7. Liu, L., Zhong, W.-M., Qian, F.: An improved chaos-particle swarm optimization algorithm. J. East China Univ. Sci. Technol. **36**(2), 267–272 (2010)
8. Rashedi, E., Nezamabadi-Pour, H., Saryazdi, S.: GSA: a gravitational search algorithm. Inf. Sci. **179**(13), 2232–2248 (2009)
9. Kulkarni, A.J., Durugkar, I.P., Kumar, M.: Cohort intelligence: A self supervised learning behavior. In: Systems, 2013 IEEE International Conference on Man, and Cybernetics (SMC). IEEE (2013)
10. Mitchell, M.: An Introduction to Genetic Algorithms. MIT press, Cambridge (1998)
11. Goldberg, D.E., et al.: Genetic algorithms: A bibliography. Urbana **51**, 61801 (1997)
12. Moscato, P.: On evolution, search, optimization, genetic algorithms and martial arts: Towards memetic algorithms. Caltech concurrent computation program, C3P Report, Vol. 826, p. 1989 (1989)
13. Moscato, P., Cotta, C., Mendes, A.: Memetic algorithms. In: New Optimization Techniques in Engineering, pp. 53–85. Springer, New York (2004)
14. Storn, R., Price, K.: Differential evolution–a simple and efficient heuristic for global optimization over continuous spaces. J. Global Optim. **11**(4), 341–359 (1997)
15. Qin, A.K., Huang, V.L., Suganthan, P.N.: Differential evolution algorithm with strategy adaptation for global numerical optimization. IEEE Trans. Evol. Comput. **13**(2), 398–417 (2009)
16. Auger, A., Hansen, N.: A restart CMA evolution strategy with increasing population size. In: The 2005 IEEE Congress on Evolutionary Computation, 2005. IEEE (2005)
17. Cheron, B., et al.: Queen replacement in the monogynous ant Aphaenogaster senilis: supernumerary queens as life insurance. Anim. Behav. **78**(6), 1317–1325 (2009)
18. Ashton, M.C., et al.: Kin altruism, reciprocal altruism, and the Big Five personality factors. Evol. Hum. Behav. **19**(4), 243–255 (1998)
19. Osiński, J.: Kin altruism, reciprocal altruism and social discounting. Personality Individ. Differ. **47**(4), 374–378 (2009)
20. Kenne, M., Dejean, A.: Nuptial flight of myrmicaria opaciventris. Sociobiology **31**(1), 41–50 (1998)
21. Queller, D.C., Strassmann, J.E.: Kin selection and social insects. Bioscience **48**, 165–175 (1998)
22. Adorio, E.P., Diliman, U.: Mvf-multivariate test functions library in c for unconstrained global optimization. Technical report, Department of Mathematics, UP Diliman (2005)

23. Molga, M., Smutnicki, C.: Test functions for optimization needs (2005). http://eccsia013. googlecode.com/svn/trunk/Ecc1/functions_benchmark.pdf
24. Shang, Y.-W., Qiu, Y.-H.: A note on the extended Rosenbrock function. Evol. Comput. **14**(1), 119–126 (2006)
25. Kulkarni, A.J., Tai, K.: Probability collectives: a decentralized, distributed optimization for multi-agent systems. In: Mehnen, J., Köppen, M., Saad, A., Tiwari, A. (eds.) Applications of Soft Computing. ASC, vol. 58, pp. 441–450. Springer, Heidelberg (2009)
26. Xu, W., et al.: A piecewise linear chaotic map and sequential quadratic programming based robust hybrid particle swarm optimization. Inf. Sci. **218**, 85–102 (2013)
27. Shi, Y., Eberhart, R.C.: Empirical study of particle swarm optimization. In: Proceedings of the 1999 Congress on Evolutionary Computation, 1999, CEC 1999. IEEE (1999)
28. Liang, J., Suganthan, P., Deb, K.: Novel composition test functions for numerical global optimization. In: Swarm Intelligence Symposium, 2005, SIS 2005, Proceedings 2005 IEEE. IEEE (2005)

# Neuro-evolutionary Topology Optimization with Adaptive Improvement Threshold

Nikola Aulig$^{(\boxtimes)}$ and Markus Olhofer

Honda Research Institute Europe GmbH,
Carl-Legien-Straße 30, 63073 Offenbach/Main, Germany
{nikola.aulig,markus.olhofer}@honda-ri.de

**Abstract.** Recently a hybrid combination of neuro-evolution with a gradient-based topology optimization method was proposed, facilitating topology optimization of structures subject to objective functions for which gradient information is difficult to obtain. The approach substitutes analytical sensitivity information by an update signal represented by a neural network approximation model. Topology optimization is performed by optimizing the network parameters by an evolutionary algorithm in order to devise an update signal for each design step. However, the typically very large number of required evaluations renders the method difficult to apply in practice. In this paper, we aim at a more efficient use of computational resources by augmenting the original approach by an adaptive improvement threshold as stopping criterion for the neuro-evolution. The original and augmented methods are studied on the minimum compliance problem for different feature types and different number of hidden neurons. It is demonstrated that the number of evaluations can be reduced by up to 80 % with very little change of the resulting objective values and structures.

**Keywords:** Neuro-evolution · Topology optimization · Hybrid algorithm · Covariance matrix adaptation · Adaptive improvement threshold

## 1 Introduction

The field of topology optimization considers the task of providing engineers with concepts of mechanical structures early in the design process. Topology optimization algorithms address this by targeting to find the optimal distribution of material and void regions within a predefined design space. Various mathematical gradient based-algorithms and population-based stochastic search algorithms have been proposed.

An overview mainly on the mathematical approaches can be found in [1] or [2]. Widely applied are the density-based methods [3] in which each cell of the discretized design space is assigned a continuous design variable. Figure 1 shows an example of a topology optimization design space with boundary conditions and the solution obtained with a state of the art density-based topology optimization algorithm [4].

© Springer International Publishing Switzerland 2015
A.M. Mora and G. Squillero (Eds.): EvoApplications 2015, LNCS 9028, pp. 655–666, 2015.
DOI: 10.1007/978-3-319-16549-3_53

Alternatively, numerous evolutionary methods with varying representations can be found in literature, for
example solid geometry modeling [5],
bit-array encoding [6], a two-phase
approach based on skeleton convergence [7], tree encoding [8], or compact unstructured representations [9].
Other approaches perform topology
optimization based on modeling a cellular growth process as in [10] or
[11]. Recently also topology optimization applications have been proposed
based on neuro-evolution by augmenting topologies [12,13]. On one hand
stochastic methods for topology optimization can be applied even to complex objective functions in engineering
optimization or problems with black-

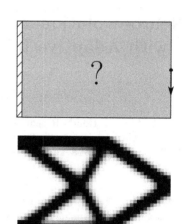

**Fig. 1.** Top: design space with applied
force and supports; bottom: result of topology optimization from [4] for compliance
minimization.

box solvers, for which gradient information is difficult to obtain. However, usually
these methods struggle with the very high dimensional search spaces of typical
topology optimization problems [14] or introduce assumptions on the solutions
in order to reduce the search space dimensionality. On the other hand, mathematical algorithms are effective and deal well with a very high number of design
variables but always require predefined analytical gradient information specific
to the objective function.

Recently, a hybrid approach for topology optimization based on a gradient-
based method and a neuro-evolution has been proposed: neuro-evolutionary
topology optimization (NETO) [15,16]. The approach aims at bridging the gap
between stochastic methods and gradient-based methods and enables the usage
of problem specific state information such as displacements and energies. These
local state features are mapped to an update signal by an artificial neural network
approximation model, which replaces the analytical sensitivities in a density-
based topology optimization. The model parameters and thus the update signal
are optimized by an evolutionary search. This maintains the flexibility of a high
dimensional representation of the structure itself, yet the evolutionary search
is only confronted with the lower dimensional model representation. The approach aims for enhancing the gradient-based topology optimization methods for
objective functions for which gradients cannot be easily obtained, e.g. due to
black-box, noisy or highly complex problems.

In this paper, we increase the efficiency of the NETO approach by augmenting
it with an improvement threshold. When applied, the neuro-evolution duration
depends on the actual improvement of the design. As soon as the improvement of
the design is sufficient, the neuro-evolution is stopped and the next iteration can
start, thus reducing the number of evaluations. In Sect. 2, we briefly review the

topology optimization problem and the neuro-evolutionary approach. In Sect. 3 the proposed extension is described. The setup of the experiments and results are presented in Sect. 4 and the paper is concluded in Sect. 5.

# 2   Neuro-evolutionary Topology Optimization

In this section we will briefly review the neuro-evolutionary topology optimization (NETO) method from [16]. Foremost, this includes details on the mathematical density-based topology optimization methods, due to the hybrid nature of the approach.

## 2.1   Topology Optimization

Density-based topology optimization methods [3] operate on the cells of a finite element model of the discretized design space. Originally each cell is assigned a binary variable which can either represent material or void. The binary problem is relaxed by using a material interpolation scheme like solid isotropic material with penalization (SIMP) [17]. Each element $i$ of the mesh, with $i = 1, \ldots, N$, is assigned a continuous material density variable $\rho_i \in [\rho_{\min}, 1]$, with a minimum density $\rho_{\min}$ for avoiding numerical difficulties. Using SIMP, the Young's modulus of the material within an element is interpolated according to $E_i(\rho_i) = \rho_i^p E_0$, with the Young's modulus of the material $E_0$ and a penalization $p$, which renders the usage of intermediate densities inefficient.

Generally a topology optimization problem can be stated as:

$$
\begin{aligned}
\min_{\boldsymbol{\rho}} \; & f(\boldsymbol{\rho}, \mathbf{u}(\boldsymbol{\rho})) \\
\text{s.t.} : \; & \mathbf{r}(\boldsymbol{\rho}, \mathbf{u}) = \mathbf{0}, \\
& V(\boldsymbol{\rho}) = V_f, \\
& 0 < \rho_{\min} \leq \rho_i \leq 1, \; i = 1, \ldots, N,
\end{aligned}
\tag{1}
$$

with the vector of design variables $\boldsymbol{\rho}$ (respectively densities), the objective function $f$, the residual $\mathbf{r}$ of solving the state equation and the structural state $\mathbf{u}$. A constraint $V_f$ is imposed on the volume of the design $V(\boldsymbol{\rho})$, specifying the proportion of design space which is to be filled with material.

Topology optimization problems can be solved iteratively by an optimality criteria method (OC-update) [3]. The OC rule is an update scheme that redistributes material among the design variables and maintains the volume constraint. Commonly it is used in conjunction with analytical sensitivity information $\frac{\partial f}{\partial \rho_i}$. However, gradient information is not available in the general case and therefore NETO substitutes it by a heuristic update signal $S_{\boldsymbol{\theta}}(\mathbf{s}_i)$. The update signal depends on the model parameters $\boldsymbol{\theta} \in \mathbb{R}^D$ and features $\mathbf{s}_i \in \mathbb{R}^J$ obtained mainly from the state $\mathbf{u}$, with the number of features $J$ and the number of model parameters $D$. Determining the model parameters $\boldsymbol{\theta}$ is described in the next section. The OC-update can compactly be formulated as:

$$\rho_i^{\text{new}} = \max\left(\rho_{\min}, \max\left(\rho_i - m, \min\left(1, \min\left(\rho_i + m, \rho_i \cdot (S_{\boldsymbol{\theta}}(\mathbf{s}_i)/\Lambda)^{\frac{1}{2}}\right)\right)\right)\right), \tag{2}$$

with the move-limit $m$ and the Lagrange multiplier $\Lambda$, which can be determined by a bi-sectioning algorithm. For simplicity we assume in (2) that every element has unit volume.

Commonly topology optimization requires a regularization method in order to ensure existence of solutions and avoid numerical instabilities like checkerboard patterns. In our framework filtering of sensitivities is utilized. It can be applied to the vector of update signals exactly as for analytical sensitivities. For a detailed description of the filtering method the reader is referred to the literature [18].

In NETO, the topology optimization can be considered as an outer optimization loop, consisting of the evaluation of the design, evolutionary optimization of the model parameters, determination of the model prediction, filtering of the predictions, and updating the design with the optimality criteria update. The step addressing the network optimization is described in the next section.

## 2.2   Neuro-evolution

In [16] a multi-layer perceptron with sigmoidal activation functions $g$ and a single hidden layer with $h$ hidden neurons is proposed as model for the update signal:

$$S_{\boldsymbol{\theta}}(\mathbf{s}_i) = g(\boldsymbol{\theta}_2^T \cdot g(\boldsymbol{\theta}_1^T \cdot \mathbf{s}_i)), \tag{3}$$

with the weights $\boldsymbol{\theta}_1$ connecting input neurons with hidden neurons and the weights $\boldsymbol{\theta}_2$ connecting the hidden neurons with the single output neuron, with $\boldsymbol{\theta}^T = [\boldsymbol{\theta}_1^T \; \boldsymbol{\theta}_2^T]$. No bias is applied in the output neuron. For $h$ hidden neurons the number of weights is $D = (J + 2) \cdot h$.

In order to devise a suitable update signal $S_{\boldsymbol{\theta}}(\mathbf{s}_i)$ its parameters $\boldsymbol{\theta}$ are tuned by evolutionary optimization in each iteration of the topology optimization. The model parameters are optimized such that the objective value of the design after one update step is minimal, i.e. the objective value of a candidate $\boldsymbol{\theta}$ is evaluated by emulating an update of the design:

$$\min_{\boldsymbol{\theta}} f(\boldsymbol{\rho}^{\text{new}}(\boldsymbol{\theta})). \tag{4}$$

Concretely, the update signal $S_{\boldsymbol{\theta}}(\mathbf{s}_i)$ for all design variables is computed with (3), an OC update (2) is performed, and the objective value of the new resulting design vector $f(\boldsymbol{\rho}^{\text{new}})$ is evaluated using finite element analysis. Note that the feature vector depends on the current design: $\mathbf{s}_i = \mathbf{s}_i(\boldsymbol{\rho})$.

An evolutionary strategy with covariance matrix adaptation (CMA-ES) [19] is applied for the task of tuning the model parameters, since it has been shown effective in neuro-evolution [20]. The evolutionary optimization loop is embedded as a step in each iteration of the topology optimization. After the CMA-ES is completed the evolved model is provided to the topology optimization and used for an actual design update. In the following iteration of the topology optimization the model is optimized based on the new design. Since we expect the optimal model to change continuously with the design, the model from the previous optimization is used as starting point for the CMA-ES.

## 3   Augmenting NETO with Adaptive Improvement Threshold

In the original NETO approach [16] the stopping criteria for the CMA-ES optimization of the model parameters is to reach a fixed number of iterations. Then, the design is updated and accepted without further restrictions. It suggests itself, that a large number of the evaluations spend in the neuro-evolution are not required in case a sufficiently good model is found early in the optimization. Furthermore it is expected that the model may generalize, i.e. it can be reused for the next update of the design without additional optimization. The difficulty that resides is how to judge that a model is sufficiently optimized to stop, respectively skip, the neuro-evolution. We propose to tackle this by an $\underline{A}$daptive $\underline{I}$mprovement $\underline{T}$hreshold (AIT). The computational flow of the NETO-AIT algorithm is shown in Fig. 2, and the modification of NETO is expressed by the possibility to reject designs in a "check design improvement"-step and using the rejection as trigger for the neuro-evolution.

We define an improvement threshold $\Delta f_{\text{th}}$ and a minimum threshold $\Delta f_{\text{th}}^{\min}$. Furthermore, a number of evaluations $N_{\text{Eval}}$ and a limit on the evaluations taken during one topology optimization iteration $N_{\text{iter}}^{\max}$ are defined. Initially, following the flow in Fig. 2 the neuro-evolution is started and runs for $N_{\text{Eval}}$ evaluations. Then it is interrupted, the design is updated and the design improvement is checked against the threshold. The design improvement is measured as $\Delta f = a \cdot |f^{\text{new}} - f^{\text{old}}|/f^{\text{old}}$, with $a = +1$ if $f^{\text{new}} - f^{\text{old}} < 0$ and $a = -1$ otherwise. A counter variable $N_{\text{iter}} = 0$ is initialized.

1. **If $\Delta f >= \Delta f_{\text{th}}$**: The design is improved sufficiently and thus the model does not need further optimization. The design is accepted, the topology optimization continues and $N_{\text{iter}}$ is set to zero. The current model is reused again for the next update of the design. **Otherwise**: $N_{\text{iter}}$ is increased by $N_{\text{Eval}}$ and it is continued at 2.
2. **If $N_{\text{iter}} < N_{\text{iter}}^{\max}$**: The neuro-evolution is continued for another $N_{\text{Eval}}$ evaluations and it is continued at 1. **Otherwise**: $\Delta f_{\text{th}}$ is adapted and set to $\max(\Delta f_{\text{th}}/2, \Delta f_{\text{th}}^{\min})$ and it is continued at 3.
3. **If $\Delta f >= \Delta f_{\text{th}}$**: The design is improved sufficiently, with respect to the adapted (reduced) improvement threshold. The topology optimization continues and $N_{\text{iter}}$ is set to zero. The current model is reused again for the next update of the design. **Otherwise**: The overall optimization process is stopped.

The advantage of this convergence scheme is that the model is optimized until it at least achieves the specified improvement of the design, avoiding a creeping behavior that might be caused by low quality models. Furthermore, the number of evaluations can be reduced, since the model is reused as long as its quality is sufficient. Note that in steps one and three the same condition is checked, however with different consequences in the false case. The computational flow of the AIT augmentation is shown in Fig. 3. The figure corresponds to a detailed description of the check design improvement step in Fig. 2.

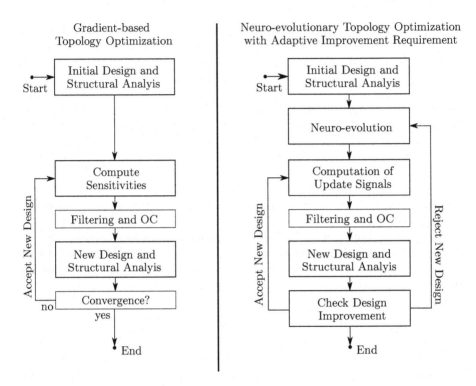

**Fig. 2.** Comparison of the computational flow for density-based topology optimization with analytical gradients (left) and neuro-evolutionary topology optimization using adaptive improvement threshold (right).

## 4    Experiments

### 4.1    Setup

The NETO algorithm is intended for engineering optimization problems for which gradients are difficult to obtain. However, for empirical evaluation, the standard problem of minimizing compliance problem (i.e. maximizing stiffness) is chosen, in order to evaluate the novel optimization approach on a test problem for which a well established baseline exists. The minimum compliance problem can be stated as in (1) with $f(\boldsymbol{\rho}, \mathbf{u}(\boldsymbol{\rho})) = c(\boldsymbol{\rho}) = \mathbf{u}^T \mathbf{f}$ and $\mathbf{r}(\boldsymbol{\rho}, \mathbf{u}) = \mathbf{K}(\boldsymbol{\rho})\mathbf{u} - \mathbf{f}$,

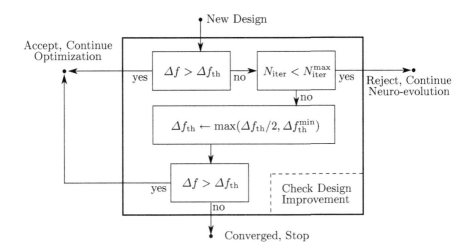

**Fig. 3.** Flowchart of the adaptive improvement threshold augmentation for the NETO algorithm.

with the structural compliance $c$, the global displacements vector $\mathbf{u}$, the forces vector $\mathbf{f}$ and the global stiffness matrix $\mathbf{K}$.

A vector of basic local state features (LSF) associated with design variable $i$, is defined in [16]: $\mathbf{s}_i^{\mathrm{I}} = \begin{bmatrix} \mathbf{u}_i^T & \rho_i \end{bmatrix}^T$, with the elemental displacement vector $\mathbf{u}_i$. This set of features is considered, since it represents the important case of little previous knowledge on the problem and is referred to as LSF Group I. In case of the minimum compliance problem, the elemental displacements are naturally the most basic features available for the problem since the state equation is solved using a finite element solver, which provides the state of the structure in form of the displacement vector $\mathbf{u}$. A second group of features, LSF Group II, is defined as $\mathbf{s}_i^{\mathrm{II}} = \begin{bmatrix} \mathrm{SED}_i & \rho_i \end{bmatrix}^T$, with the strain energy density $\mathrm{SED}_i$ in element $i$, representing the case of a problem for which a strong feature is available or can be constructed from the basic features.

The NETO algorithm without and with the adaptive improvement threshold (NETO-AIT) are compared by application to the topology optimization of a cantilever structure within a two-dimensional rectangular design space as depicted in the top of Fig. 1. The design space is discretized into $N = 45 \times 28 = 1260$ elements with an element size of $1\,\mathrm{mm} \times 1\,\mathrm{mm}$. The applied load is $F = 1\,\mathrm{N}$. A volume constraint with $V_f = 0.4$ is chosen, Young's modulus and Poisson's ratio of the material are set to $E_0 = 1\,\mathrm{N/mm^2}$ and $\nu = 0.3$ respectively. The radius of the sensitivity filter is set to $r_{\min} = 2\,\mathrm{mm}$. A homogenous distribution of material ($\rho_i = V_f, i = 1, \ldots, N$) is used as initial design guess. The baseline for compliance value and visual comparisons is depicted in the bottom of Fig. 1. The compliance value of the baseline is $c_{\mathrm{base}} = 54.6\,\mathrm{Nmm}$. It is important to emphasize again that the proposed algorithm should not be compared in number of evaluations to an algorithm that uses the analytical gradient, as it is intended for problems where analytical gradients are not available. However in order to

**Table 1.** Median results obtained by NETO and NETO-AIT of 5 runs with different random seeds.

| | NETO | | NETO, AIT | | Change | |
|---|---|---|---|---|---|---|
| | $c$/Nmm | $N/10^3$ | $c^{\text{AIT}}$/Nmm | $N^{\text{AIT}}/10^3$ | $\Delta c_{/\%}$ | $\Delta N_{/\%}$ |
| LSF Group I | | | | | | |
| $h = 5$ | 75.2 | 420.1 | 75.0 | 130.2 | 0.2 | 69.0 |
| $h = 15$ | 54.0 | 480.7 | 54.1 | 253.4 | −0.1 | 47.3 |
| LSF Group II | | | | | | |
| $h = 5$ | 52.6 | 37.8 | 52.4 | 9.8 | 0.4 | 74.2 |
| $h = 15$ | 51.9 | 43.4 | 52.0 | 8.1 | −0.1 | 81.5 |

evaluate the algorithm, the result by using analytical gradients can be used as a baseline.

Since the NETO algorithm is a hybrid algorithm it requires choosing the hyper parameters of both, the CMA-ES and the topology optimization. Based on the experience from experiments not documented within this study a rather large value of 10 for the global step size of the CMA-ES was found to yield good results. Populations sizes are determined as recommended for the CMA-ES. A rather small move limit $m = 0.01$ is chosen for the OC-update, ensuring a stable convergence of the design.

For NETO-AIT the initial improvement threshold is chosen $\Delta f_{\text{th}} = 4\,\%$, with $\Delta f_{\text{th}}^{\min} = 0.1\,\%$. For LSF Group I, $N_{\text{iter}}^{\max} = 10 \cdot 10^3$ and $N_{\text{Eval}} = 2000$ are chosen. For LSF Group II, $N_{\text{iter}}^{\max} = 1 \cdot 10^3$ and $N_{\text{s}} = 200$ are chosen. The conventional NETO is converged when the change of the objective is lower than $f_{\text{req}}^{\min}$.

Generally in neuro-evolution the optimal number of hidden neurons which provides the best performance is unkown. Therefore we study resulting compliance and evaluations of NETO and NETO-AIT for $h = 5, 15$ neurons in the hidden layer, capturing the case of a rather simple and a more complex network. With $J^I = 9$ this results in search spaces of $D = 55$ and $D = 165$ in the case of LSF Group I and with $J^{II} = 2$ this results in $D = 20$ and $D = 60$ in case of LSF Group II, respectively. Accordingly, the model search space dimensionality is much lower than that of the topology design with $N = 1260$ elements. Each optimization is run for 5 different seeds and the median run in terms of compliance is further analyzed.

The implementation uses Matlab code from [4] and the CMA-ES Matlab implementation by Hansen following [19].

## 4.2 Results

The median results of running NETO and NETO-AIT depending on network sizes and feature choices are shown in Table 1.

$h = 5$     $h = 5$ (AIT)     $h = 15$     $h = 15$ (AIT)

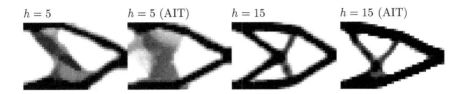

**Fig. 4.** Optimized structures obtained using LSF Group II, for 5 and 15 hidden neurons and NETO with and without AIT.

For evaluating the effects of using NETO-AIT the percentual improvement of the objective function and the percentual reduction of evaluations are considered. These are defined as:

$$\Delta c^{\mathrm{AIT}} = (c - c^{\mathrm{AIT}})/c, \tag{5}$$

$$\Delta N^{\mathrm{AIT}} = (N - N^{\mathrm{AIT}})/N. \tag{6}$$

Accordingly the larger a value the more favorable is NETO-AIT over NETO.

**LSF Group I.** From Table 1 it can be seen that the best solution in LSF Group I is obtained for 15 hidden neurons, both for NETO and NETO-AIT. In this case the number of required evaluations for NETO-AIT has been reduced by almost half, while the loss of the obtained objective value is only about one per mill.

For 5 hidden neurons the complexity of the model is most likely not sufficient to model the necessary update signal in contrast to the case of 15 hidden neurons. For this reason, the obtained compliance value is far of that of the baseline. Still the compliance of the structures for 5 hidden neurons is even slightly improved by NETO-AIT although the number of evaluations has been reduced by to almost 70 %.

The structural results are depicted in Fig. 4. Visually comparing to the baseline solution, for 15 hidden neurons, the structure obtained by NETO is similar. The structures of NETO-AIT for 15 hidden neurons show a downwards shift of material in the center resulting in a different topological design. The solution by NETO-AIT is an alternative structure which is almost equivalent in terms of compliance. It is obvious that the algorithm did not provide good solutions for 5 hidden neurons.

The baseline design would result from the optimization if the model is exactly modeling the analytical sensitivities, which are given as [3]:

$$\frac{\partial c}{\partial \rho_i} = -p\rho_i^{p-1}\mathbf{u}_i^{\mathrm{T}}\mathbf{k_0}\mathbf{u}_i, \tag{7}$$

with the elemental stiffness matrix $\mathbf{k_0}$. For the considered case this is a multivariate polynomial function in the features, i.e. it contains notable nonlinearity. It can therefore be expected that the results depend on the capability of the

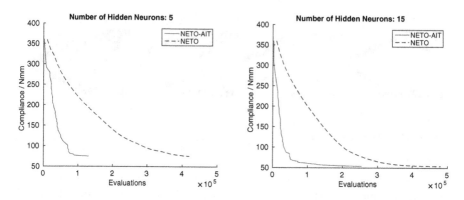

**Fig. 5.** Compliance during the optimization plotted versus the number of evaluations, for NETO and NETO-AIT with LSF Group I.

$h = 5$ $\qquad\qquad$ $h = 5$ (AIT) $\qquad\qquad$ $h = 15$ $\qquad\qquad$ $h = 15$ (AIT)

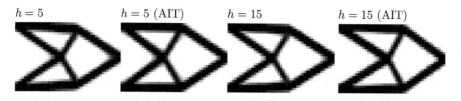

**Fig. 6.** Optimized Structures obtained using LSF Group II, for 5 and 15 hidden neurons and NETO with and without AIT.

model to represent those nonlinear properties. In the case of $h = 5$ the model complexity is not large enough to model the nonlinearity between features and sensitivity.

The plots of the objective versus number of evaluations is plotted in Fig. 5. For both $h = 5$ and $h = 15$ NETO-AIT converges much faster to similar values of the objective function than NETO.

**LSF Group II.** From Table 1 it can be seen that the number of evaluations has been reduced substantially, by applying NETO-AIT, up to over 80 % in the case of $h = 15$ and almost 75 % in the case of $h = 5$, while the objective values are not changing significantly. A slight improvement is observed for $h = 5$ while the objective value is increased slightly for $h = 15$.

Compared to LSF Group I there is no large difference between the small and the large network size results, and objective values are improved while the number of evaluations is much lower. This is related to using the strain energy density as feature which is proportionally related to the analytical sensitivities and facilitates the learning task, such that $h = 5$ is sufficient.

The structural results from NETO and NETO-AIT are depicted in Fig. 6 When visually comparing these results to the baseline structure in Fig. 1 it can be seen that essentially the same structure is obtained for all runs. The slight improvement of the objective values compared to the baseline can be explained

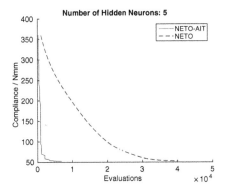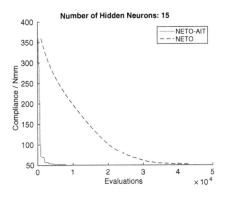

**Fig. 7.** Compliance during the optimization plotted versus the number of evaluations, for NETO and NETO-AIT with LSF Group II.

by considering that the evolutionary optimization can exploit random variations, ending up with a design that contains less penalized intermediate densities and thus an improved objective value.

Objective function values versus number of evaluations is plotted in Fig. 7. Just as for LSF Group I, NETO-AIT converges much faster than NETO to similar values of the objective function.

## 5   Conclusions

We presented an adaptive improvement threshold to reduce the number of evaluations required by the recently proposed hybrid neuro-evolutionary topology optimization approach. In experiments in which model features and model sizes were varied, it was observed that NETO-AIT consistently converged much faster, i.e. the number of evaluations could be reduced by up to 80 % in the best case. This advantage is traded-off against a slight change in the objective values of the resulting structures, which can be considered insignificant since the main target of topology optimization is to provide a conceptual idea for a structure, which is post-processed in a subsequent step. We therefore conclude that the adaptive improvement threshold, based on which a sufficient optimization of the network model is detected, is a valuable extension to the original approach and facilitates applications of the algorithm to different objective functions.

## References

1. Deaton, J., Grandhi, R.: A survey of structural and multidisciplinary continuum topology optimization: post 2000. Struct. Multi. Optim. **49**(1), 1–38 (2014)
2. Sigmund, O., Maute, K.: Topology optimization approaches. Struct. Multi. Optim. **48**(6), 1031–1055 (2013)
3. Bendsøe, M., Sigmund, O.: Topology Optimization Theory, Methods and Applications, 2nd edn. Springer, Berlin (2004)

4. Andreassen, E., Clausen, A., Schevenels, M., Lazarov, B., Sigmund, O.: Efficient topology optimization in matlab using 88 lines of code. Struct. Multi. Optim. **43**(1), 1–16 (2011)
5. Ahmed, F., Bhattacharya, B., Deb, K.: Constructive solid geometry based topology optimization using evolutionary algorithm. In: Bansal, J.C., Singh, P.K., Deep, K., Pant, M., Nagar, A.K. (eds.) Proceedings of Seventh International Conference on Bio-Inspired Computing: Theories and Applications (BIC-TA 2012). AISC, vol. 201, pp. 227–238. Springer, India (2013)
6. Wu, C.-Y., Tseng, K.-Y.: Topology optimization of structures using modified binary differential evolution. Struct. Multi. Optim. **42**(6), 939–953 (2010)
7. Balamurugan, R., Ramakrishnan, C., Swaminathan, N.: A two phase approach based on skeleton convergence and geometric variables for topology optimization using genetic algorithm. Struct. Multi. Optim. **43**(3), 381–404 (2011)
8. Madeira, J., Pina, H., Rodrigues, H.: GA topology optimization using random keys for tree encoding of structures. Struct. Multi. Optim. **40**(1–6), 227–240 (2010)
9. Hamda, H., Jouve, F., Lutton, E., Schoenauer, M., Sebag, M.: Compact unstructured representations for evolutionary design. Appl. Intell. **16**(2), 139–155 (2002)
10. Pedro, H.-T.C., Kobayashi, M.H.: On a cellular division method for topology optimization. Int. J. Numer. Methods Eng. **88**(11), 1175–1197 (2011)
11. Steiner, T., Trommler, J., Brenn, M., Jin, Y., Sendhoff, B.: Global shape with morphogen gradients and motile polarized cells. In: Proceedings of the 2009 IEEE Congress on Evolutionary Computation. IEEE, Trondheim (2009)
12. Evins, R., Vaidyanathan, R., Burgess, S.: Multi-material compositional pattern-producing networks for form optimisation. In: Esparcia-Alcázar, A.I., Mora, A.M. (eds.) EvoApplications 2014. LNCS, vol. 8602, pp. 189–200. Springer, Heidelberg (2014)
13. Cheney, N., Ritz, E., Lipson, H.: Automated vibrational design and natural frequency tuning of multi-material structures. In: Proceedings of the 2014 Conference on Genetic and Evolutionary Computation, GECCO 2014, Vancouver, BC, Canada, pp. 1079–1086. ACM, New York (2014)
14. Sigmund, O.: On the usefulness of non-gradient approaches in topology optimization. Struct. Multi. Optim. **43**(5), 589–596 (2011)
15. Aulig, N., Olhofer, M.: Evolutionary generation of neural network update signals for the topology optimization of structures. In: Proceeding of the Fifteenth Annual Conference Companion on Genetic and Evolutionary Computation Conference Companion, GECCO 2013 Companion, Amsterdam, Netherlands, pp. 213–214. ACM, New York (2013)
16. Aulig, N., Olhofer, M.: Neuro-evolutionary topology optimization of structures by utilizing local state features. In: Proceedings of the 2014 Conference on Genetic and Evolutionary Computation, GECCO 2014, Vancouver, BC, Canada, pp. 967–974. ACM, New York (2014)
17. Bendsøe, M.: Optimal shape design as a material distribution problem. Struct. Optim. **1**, 193–202 (1989)
18. Sigmund, O.: Morphology-based black and white filters for topology optimization. Struct. Multi. Optim. **33**(4–5), 401–424 (2007)
19. Hansen, N., Kern, S.: The CMA evolution strategy: A comparing review. In: Lozano, J.A., Larrañaga, P., Inza, I., Bengoetxea, E. (eds.) Towards a New Evolutionary Computation. Studies in Fuzziness and Soft Computing, vol. 192, pp. 75–102. Springer, Heidelberg (2006)
20. Heidrich-Meisner, V., Igel, C.: Neuroevolution strategies for episodic reinforcement learning. J. Algorithms **64**(4), 152–168 (2009)

# Evaluating Reward Definitions
# for Parameter Control

Giorgos Karafotias$^{(\boxtimes)}$, Mark Hoogendoorn, and A.E. Eiben

Vrije Universiteit Amsterdam, Amsterdam, The Netherlands
g.karafotias@vu.nl

**Abstract.** Parameter controllers for Evolutionary Algorithms (EAs) deal with adjusting parameter values during an evolutionary run. Many ad hoc approaches have been presented for parameter control, but few generic parameter controllers exist. Recently, successful parameter control methods based on Reinforcement Learning (RL) have been suggested for one-off applications, i.e. relatively long runs with controllers used out-of-the-box with no tailoring to the problem at hand. However, the reward function used was not investigated in depth, though it is a non-trivial factor with an important impact on the performance of a RL mechanism. In this paper, we address this issue by defining and comparing four alternative reward functions for such generic and RL-based EA parameter controllers. We conducted experiments with different EAs, test problems and controllers and results showed that the simplest reward function performs at least as well as the others, making it an ideal choice for generic out-of-the-box parameter control.

## 1 Introduction

This paper is concerned with the automated setting of evolutionary algorithm (EA) parameters. In this regard, there are two major approaches, parameter tuning (before the run) and parameter control (during the run) [4]. These do not only differ in technical detail, but also their niche of application. Tuning is the appropriate approach for repetitive problems where the tuning costs are compensated by the number of EA runs, while control is more suited for one-off design problems [5]. Here we are concerned with parameter control. Our long term objective is to develop generic, parameter independent methods for controlling the values of EA parameters on the fly. This will be a significant improvement with respect to current practice, where most parameter control mechanisms are designed for one particular parameter [11].

To this end, we have studied Reinforcement Learning (RL) as a generic parameter control mechanism and have shown that RL controllers are successful: adding an RL-based parameter control mechanism to an EA can make it significantly better than using static default parameter values [10,12]. In this paper we extend this investigation by looking more closely at a pivotal component in RL, the reward definition.

© Springer International Publishing Switzerland 2015
A.M. Mora and G. Squillero (Eds.): EvoApplications 2015, LNCS 9028, pp. 667–680, 2015.
DOI: 10.1007/978-3-319-16549-3_54

The main research question we address here is whether there is a generally good reward function that outperforms others and makes a given EA better than its 'standard' version (with default parameter values). Furthermore, we want to see the differences between various reward functions in terms of simplicity and effectivity. For an experimental comparison we consider three different RL mechanisms and four reward functions that lead to twelve combinations for the parameter control mechanism. These are compared using four different EAs, each applied to several problems. We run all RL and reward function combinations with each EA and problem combination and compare them in terms of performance, sensitivity, and simplicity.

## 2  Related Work

The related work discussed here focuses on the reward function for RL control of EAs. For an extensive review on parameter control we refer the reader to [11].

Reinforcement learning has been employed for EA parameter control in several cases with various reward definitions. Muller et al. [14] used temporal difference learning to control the mutation step size for real valued Evolution Strategies (a $(1 + 1)$-ES) using success rate (from the 1/5 rule [17]) to define state. They tested four reward types: (i) 1, 0 or $-1$ if the success rate increased, remained the same or decreased respectively, (ii) the difference of the current fitness minus the fitness of the previous step, (iii) 1, 0 or $-1$ if the fitness improved, remained the same or deteriorated respectively and (iv) the realised step length in the search space multiplied by the reward as defined in (iii). They reported better results with the latter (iv) and hypothesised that it is because it best approximated the theoretical progress rate for a $(1 + 1)$-ES.

Pettinger and Everson [15] suggested the RL-GA, a Genetic Algorithm (GA) with an RL agent to control the selection of mutation and crossover operators. Actions are taken per offspring creation, thus rewards are calculated per operator application. They defined reward as the difference of the fitness of the best parent minus the fitness of the best offspring. This difference is normalised by the fitness of the best parent. They report that experiments with alternative reward functions showed that this reward type was the most suitable and stress that penalisation of actions that decrease fitness is important. However, neither the alternative reward definitions nor the relevant results are shown in the paper. Chen et al. [2] presented a modified RL-GA, the SCGA that replaces Q-Learning with SARSA but retains the same reward definition. A modification of this same reward definition was also used by Sakurai et al. [16]. They suggested dividing the reward with the computation time needed by the operator and, also, provided a definition for an aggregated reward on population level that is either the average or the maximum of the rewards received for individual applications of an operator.

Considering variation operator control, a reduced version of RL (the multi-armed bandit framework) has been extensively used for adaptive operator selection (see [11] for a list). Since the selection of a variation operator takes place on the basis of each new offspring produced, reward is often calculated as the improvement in the fitness of the child(ren) as compared to the parent(s) or a reference fitness of the whole population, for example [7] and [8].

The approaches described so far were defined for parameter specific controllers and use parameter specific calculations, thus are not directly applicable to our test case in this paper. However, generalised versions, when possible[1], are considered here. These are a fixed reward and a measure of fitness improvement (using a reference or not).

Finally, in the area of generic (parameter independent) control, Eiben et al. [3] proposed a generic RL controller using temporal difference learning; they defined reward as the improvement of the best fitness values (following [14]). Karafotias et al. [10,12] have presented generic RL parameter controllers based on SARSA learning using as a reward the improvement (or decline) of the current best fitness. Improvement is calculated as a ratio (current fitness to the previous) to alleviate the problem of having very high rewards at the beginning of an evolutionary run as compared to the rewards towards the end. The improvement ratio was scaled with the number of evaluations used (in cases where the population size or the number of offspring are among the parameters controlled). This reward definition is also considered in this paper.

# 3 Reinforcement Learning Parameter Control and Reward Definitions

In this paper we investigate different reward definitions for a RL-based parameter controller for EAs. In specific, we are focusing on the context of a generic parameter controller that is used out of the box for one-off applications, since this is the case where the reward definition can be challenging (this will be made clear below).

According to Sutton and Barto [18], the reward function for a RL agent should indicate the final goal to be achieved without any biased knowledge about "how" injected by the designer. In the case of controlling the parameters of an EA, the final goal is of course to yield a final fitness as good as possible[2]. However, that information is not available before the end of the run and, in the case of an one-off problem, the controller has only one single run to learn and apply a good parameter control policy[3].

Therefore, we require a reward that is calculated after each parameter change (e.g. iteration of the EA) from the beginning and throughout the run but, at the same time, is able to approximate the goal of an optimal solution achieved

---

[1] Notice that, for example, as discussed above, the reward definition that Muller et al. [14] found most efficient cannot be generalised.

[2] Any other other information (e.g. diversity) would introduce a bias on the controller's strategy.

[3] If, on the contrary, we consider a controller for a repetitive application, we could train the controller off-line using multiple training runs, thus being able to take the final best fitness of each run as the reward.

by the end of the run. We define the following four reward functions (assuming a minimisation problem):

- *Improvement of current best fitness* $\Delta_f$: The most straightforward idea is to use the improvement in fitness since the last action (parameter change). To make rewards more proportionate (EAs make big improvements in the beginning of a run as compared to the end) a ratio is used, though the result is still scale sensitive (the scale of the reward depends on the scale of the improvement). Scale sensitivity can be seen as a potential problem considering how easy huge improvements in fitness are in the beginning of a run and how hard are tiny advances near the end. The improvement ratio is divided by the number of evaluations spent during the last generation (for cases where the population size or number of offspring are among the parameters controlled). The reward is calculated as

$$R(s_t, a_t) = \Delta_f = C \cdot \frac{\frac{f_B^t}{f_B^{t+1}} - 1}{Evals_{t+1} - Evals_t} \qquad (1)$$

  where $f_B^t$ is the best fitness in the population at time $t$, $Evals_t$ is the total number of evaluations spent up to time $t$ and $C$ is a scaling constant.
- *Binary 0/1*: A very simple reward function that gives 1 when any improvement is made and 0 otherwise.

$$R(s_t, a_t) = \begin{cases} 1, if f_B^{t+1} < f_B^t \\ 0, otherwise \end{cases} \qquad (2)$$

  where $f_B^t$ is the best fitness in the population at time $t$. This function is completely scale insensitive since the reward is constant and independent from any fitness values. However, because positive rewards are constant, it cannot distinguish between optimal and suboptimal actions.
- *Weighted improvement of current best fitness* $W(\Delta_f)$: This reward is inspired by reinforcement comparison [18], $\Delta_f$ from Eq. 1 is trimmed by a reference reward.

$$R(s_t, a_t) = W(\Delta_f) = \Delta_f - Ref(N) \qquad (3)$$

  where $\Delta_f$ is defined in Eq. 1 and $Ref$ is the average of the $N$ last non-zero $\Delta_f$[4]. This reward is a middle solution between the previous two. It is less scale sensitive than the simple $\Delta_f$, thanks to the reference reward, but, unlike the binary, it is also able to discriminate between an optimal and a suboptimal action.
- *Raw current best fitness* $f_B$: Finally, a very straightforward option is to define reward as the best fitness found in the population.

$$R(s_t, a_t) = -f_B^{t+1} \qquad (4)$$

---

[4] We did not use the more intuitive ratio $\frac{\Delta_f}{Ref(n)}$ because preliminary experiments showed the difference $\Delta_f - Ref(N)$ to perform better.

This reward has the good property of monotonously increasing (if the EA is elitist and non-restarting), thus giving higher rewards to most recently successful actions. Since it relies on absolute fitness and not relative improvements, the issue of scale sensitivity is not applicable here.

These four reward functions differ, as explained, in scale sensitivity while some also introduce meta-parameters. We can also assign a level of simplicity to each (as a concept, implementation and applicability). The $0/1$ reward is the simplest concept with the widest applicability (it is the only one usable when EA individuals cannot be directly evaluated but only compared). The raw best fitness is also quite simple as a concept and implementation. On the other hand, the $\Delta_f$ and $W(\Delta_f)$ rewards are deemed less simple as concepts and implementations. A summary is given in Table 1.

**Table 1.** The defined reward functions along with certain characteristics.

|                | Scale sensitivity | Simplicity | Meta-parameters |
| -------------- | ----------------- | ---------- | ------------------------------- |
| $\Delta_f$     | High              | Less       | Scaling factor $C$              |
| $0/1$          | None              | Good       | None                            |
| $W(\Delta_f)$  | Moderate          | Less       | Scaling factor $C$, window size $N$ |
| $f_B$          | None              | Good       | None                            |

## 4    Experimental Setup

We run experiments with four different EAs from the literature, each solving four different problems. When selecting the problems for the EAs there are two options. We could use the same problems for all EAs or specify a different set for each of them separately. In our opinion, the second option is preferable because the EAs have been designed for and validated on different type of problems. Using targeted problems makes the task for the RL controllers more challenging, thus, the study more interesting. Three RL controllers are applied to each of the EA/problem combinations and for each controller/EA/problem setting all the different reward functions defined in Sect. 3 are tried. Below, more details are provided on each part of the setup.

First, the EA/problem combinations are described. Here, the algorithms and problems are chosen from the numeric optimisation domain because they are well understood and studied within the EA community. Note that these problems often originate from real world applications. In specific, the following combinations have been used:

1. A simple self-coded real valued Evolution Strategy (ES) with Gaussian mutation with one $\sigma$, uniform crossover and tournament selection for parents and survivors. The parameters controlled are the population size $\mu$, the generation gap $g$ (the ratio of offspring to parents), the mutation step size $\sigma$ and the

survivor tournament size $k_s$ (the parent tournament size is fixed to two). The Simple ES was tested with four standard test functions: Rastrigin, Schwefel, Schaffer and Fletcher & Powell.

2. The Cellular GA [1] implemented for the BBOB2013[5] competition by Holtschulte and Moses [9][6]. The parameters controlled are the crossover operator (two-point or arithmetic), the crossover probability $p_c$, the mutation operator (Gaussian, uniform, decreasing Gaussian or alternating uniform and Gaussian), the mutation rate $p_m$ and the mutation variance $m_{var}$. The selection operators are fixed (ranking and select best). The Cellular GA was tested with BBOB functions 21–24.

3. The GA MPC (GA with Multi-Parent Crossover) by Elsayed et al. [6], winner of the CEC2011 competition on real world applications[7]. The parameters controlled are the population size $\mu$, the maximum size of the parent tournament $k_{max}$, the randomisation probability $p_r$, the relative size of the archive $f_a$ and the mean $\beta_m$ and standard deviation $\beta_{std}$ of the normal distribution used for $\beta$ (used in crossover). The survivor selection is fixed ("select best"). The GA MPC was tested with four real world problems from the CEC2011 competition (7, 11.8, 12 and 13).

4. The IPOP-10DDr CMA-ES by Liao and Stützle [13] from the BBOB 2013 competition[8]. The parameters controlled are the backward time horizon for distribution cumulation $c_c$, the step size cumulation $c_s$, the step size damping parameter $d$, the mixing between rank-one and rank-mu update $\mu_{cov}$ and the recombination type (equal, linearly decreasing or super-linearly decreasing). The population and offspring sizes are set by the IPOP-DDr mechanism. The restart conditions were kept to defaults. The CMA ES was tested with BBOB functions 21 to 24.

To evaluate the different reward functions, we apply three parameter controllers based on RL to all the EAs described above. These controllers have been introduced in [10] and [12]. They are based on Temporal Difference learning and a dynamic segmentation of the state space based on work by Uther and Veloso [19]. They differ mostly in the way they treat the action (i.e. EA parameter) space.

1. The discrete RL (D-RL) controller that discretises parameters into fixed intervals as was introduced in [10]. The parameters of the RL controller were set to the values shown in Table 2 for all experiments. The number of discretisation bins was chosen for each EA separately to yield a reasonable number of control actions. The precise settings per experiment are shown in Table 3.

---

[5] http://coco.gforge.inria.fr/doku.php?id=bbob-2013.

[6] The source code was acquired directly from the authors.

[7] http://www3.ntu.edu.sg/home/epnsugan/index_files/CEC11-RWP/CEC11-RWP. htm. The source code of GA MPC is available at the same competition page.

[8] The source code for the (IPOP) CMA-ES was acquired from https://www.lri.fr/ hansen/cmaes_inmatlab.html. The 10DDr variation was added by us.

2. The RL-IP controller that uses interpolation of fixed points in the parameter space and was described in [12]. The parameters of the RL-IP are the same as the discrete RL controller. The number of points per parameter (resolution) was set for each EA separately for the same reasons as setting the bins for D-RL.
3. The RL-SMC controller that uses a sample of points and was introduced in [12]. The SMC mechanism has three additional settings (see Table 2) compared to the other two RL controllers. For all RL-SMC experiments, the sample size was 40.

**Table 2.** RL Controllers' Parameters. The TD, state tree and traces parameters are used by all three versions while the SMC column is specific to the RL-SMC controller only.

| TD | | State tree | | Traces | | SMC | |
|---|---|---|---|---|---|---|---|
| Param | Value | Param | Value | Param | Value | Param | Value |
| $\epsilon$ | 0.1 | $A_m$ | 60 | $\lambda$ | 0.8 | $\tau_i$ | 1 |
| $\gamma$ | 0.8 | $A_f$ | 0.2 | $e_{min}$ | 0.001 | $\tau_\delta$ | 0.005 |
| $\alpha$ | 0.9 | $D_{max}$ | 0.05 | | | $\sigma$ | 0.95 |
| $\alpha_0$ | 0.2 | $p_s$ | 0.1 | | | | |

The four reward functions described in Sect. 3 were tested with all controller and EA/problem combinations. Furthermore, since the focus of the controllers and rewards in this paper is one-off applications, we are interested in how the performance of a controller/reward combination compares to the performance yielded when the EA is run without any parameter control. Thus, we also run every EA/problem combination with the EA's parameters static and set to their default values (as provided in the original code)[9]. In this setting (one-off design problems) we are interested in achieving maximal performance given a certain amount of effort, thus, the termination criterion of all runs was reaching the maximum number of evaluations ($15 \cdot 10^4$ for all runs with the GA-MPC and $10^6$ for all other runs).

Each algorithm/problem/controller/reward combination was run 30 times. The setup is summarised in Table 3[10] showing the EAs, their parameters with ranges and default values, their corresponding test problems and the settings of the controllers whose meta-parameters vary according to the controlled EA. Since the reward functions do not vary over the different combinations they are not mentioned in the table.

---

[9] For a comparison of the controllers used in this paper to other benchmarks we refer the reader to [10] and [12].

[10] The source code for this experiment is available for download at http://www.few.vu.nl/~gks290/resources/evostar2015.tar.gz.

**Table 3.** Experimental setup

| EA | Parameters, ranges, default values | Problems | D-RL | RL-IP |
|---|---|---|---|---|
| Simple ES | $\mu \in [10, 80]$, $\mu = 20$ <br> $g \in (0, 7]$, $g = 2$ <br> $\sigma \in (0, 2]$, $\sigma = 0.8$ <br> $k_s \in [2, 80]$, $k_s = 2$ | Rastrigin Fletcher&Powell, Schaffer, Schwefel in 10 dimensions | Action bins: 5 | Resolution: 5 |
| Cellular GA | $xover \in \{2p, Ar\}$, <br>    $xover = 2p$ <br> $p_c \in [0.6, 1]$, $p_c = 0.9$ <br> $mut \in \{G, U, G_d, C\}$, <br>    $mut = G$ <br> $p_m \in (0, 0.4]$, $p_m = 0.1$ <br> $m_{var} \in (0, 0.4]$, <br>    $m_{var} = 0.2$ | BBOB2013 $f_{21}$, $f_{22}$, $f_{23}$, $f_{24}$ in 40 dimensions | Action bins: 4 | Resolution: 4 |
| GA MPC | $\mu \in [50, 130]$, $\mu = 90$ <br> $k_{max} \in [3, 15]$, $k_{max} = 3$ <br> $\beta_m \in [0.3, 1.1]$, $\beta_m = 0.7$ <br> $\beta_{std} \in (0, 0.5]$, <br>    $\beta_{std} = 0.1$ <br> $p_r \in (0, 0.4]$, $p_r = 0.1$ <br> $f_a \in [0.3, 0.7]$, $f_a = 0.5$ | CEC2011 $f_7$, $f_{11.8}$, $f_{21}$, $f_{22}$ | Action bins: 4 | Resolution: 4 |
| IPOP-10DDr CMA ES | $c_c \in [0, 1]$, $c_c = 0.0909$ <br> $c_s \in [0, 1]$, $c_s = 0.1375$ <br> $d \in [1, 5]$, $d = 1.1375$ <br> $\mu_{cov} \in [1, 20]$, <br>    $\mu_{cov} = 4.5409$ <br> $xover \in \{E, D_l, D_{sl}\}$, <br>    $xover = D_{sl}$ | BBOB2013 $f_{21}$, $f_{22}$, $f_{23}$, $f_{24}$ in 40 dimensions | Action bins: 4 | Resolution: 4 |

# 5    Results and Discussion

In this section we discuss the results of our experiments. Table 5 shows all results in terms of final best fitness averaged over all repeats. For every EA/problem combination there are two more variable dimensions: the controller and the reward function used. Subsequently, there is one (independent) section in the table for each of the controllers while each row of every subtable shows the results for a specific reward function. In previous work [12], we have performed a comparison between the controllers; here we focus on the results from the perspective of reward functions, and attempt a general comparison of the four rewards across different controllers, EAs and problem settings.

For each EA/problem/controller setting in Table 5, the best performing reward function(s) are denoted as well as those that perform significantly better than default static values (the performance of the latter is also shown for comparison). As we have shown previously, the RL controllers are successful (i.e. significantly better than using static default parameter values) when the algorithm is not very refined or particularly tailored to the problem [12]. The results of Table 5 extend this (in general) to the new reward definitions as well. However, they do not show a clear winner among reward definitions or, at least, a pattern of which reward would be better for specific problems or algorithms or controllers (with the the exception of the $W(\Delta_f)$ being particularly suitable to the Simple ES when controlled by the RL-IP).

**Table 4.** Summary of all results from the perspective of reward functions. The table is separated into three sections, one for each controller tested. The two rows denote how many times the result (best final fitness averaged over 30 runs) with each reward is the best (or not significantly worse than the best) and how many times it is significantly better than the performance using default static parameter values.

| | D-RL | | | | RL-IP | | | | RL-SMC | | | |
|---|---|---|---|---|---|---|---|---|---|---|---|---|
| | $\Delta_f$ | $f_i$ | 0/1 | $H(\Delta_f)$ | $\Delta_f$ | $f_i$ | 0/1 | $H(\Delta_f)$ | $\Delta_f$ | $f_i$ | 0/1 | $H(\Delta_f)$ |
| *Best* | 12 | 11 | 16 | 9 | 8 | 9 | 11 | 13 | 14 | 16 | 15 | 14 |
| *Better than static* | 8 | 8 | 9 | 7 | 8 | 7 | 9 | 8 | 7 | 6 | 6 | 6 |

A better overview of the results is given in Table 4 showing the success count of each reward (i.e. how many times it is significantly better than default static parameter values) and the winning count (i.e. how many times it is the best or not significantly worse than the best reward) for each controller. We are mostly interested in the former count since the target application of the controllers is one-off problems where control aims at improving the performance of a single run that would otherwise use default static parameter values. The winning count can be seen as a secondary measure. We see that the binary reward definition is slightly better for the D-RL and RL-IP controllers, while for RL-SMC $\Delta_f$ seems to be better. However, these performance differences are marginal; we can say that $\Delta_f$ and 0/1 are generally equivalent in performance.

Subsequently, we compare the two best performing reward functions ($\Delta_f$ and 0/1) and try to understand why they perform equally well. We would assume that scale sensitivity would impact performance but $\Delta_f$ and 0/1 lie on opposite extremes in terms of scale sensitivity - see Sect. 3. To better understand these two effects, we examined the Q values over time since this is the part of the RL mechanism that is affected by the reward definition. In specific, every state-action pair has a Q value that estimates the long-term return expected if this specific action is taken when in this specific state. Whenever a state-action pair occurs, its Q value is updated using the immediate reward received (the exact formulas for these updates are given in [12]). We would expect a scale sensitive function to create higher Q values and, especially, very high peaks at the beginning of a run as large fitness improvements are typically made in the beginning of the run. Figures 1 and 2 show examples of the normalised maximum Q value (both over all states and only for the current state) over time for two problems of the Simple ES using the D-RL controller. The 0/1 reward does indeed keep the maximum Q value lower then the $\Delta_f$ and that is a consistent observation across settings. However, this impact of the scale (in)sensitivity of the function cannot be correlated to performance: the differences between the different reward types shown in Figs. 1 and 2 are similar but in the former the two reward functions yielded similar performance while in the latter the binary

**Table 5.** Results of all experiments. There are three sections, one for each controller. Every section includes four subtables with the results for each algorithm. Subtables show the performance of the algorithm with four problems and the four reward types tested in this experiment. Performance is shown in terms of final fitness averaged over all repeats. Underlined values are significantly better than static default (in grey) and bold values denote the winner(s) (not significantly worse than the best). Significant difference was decided when a two-sided Kolmogorov-Smirnov test with $\alpha = 0.05$ rejected the null hypothesis that two samples came from the same distribution. All problems are minimisation. Cases where quite distant mean values are deemed not significantly different and, subsequently, cases where higher mean values are among the winners while lower mean values are not are due to extreme outliers.

**D-RL**

| | Simple ES | | | | Cellular GA | | | |
|---|---|---|---|---|---|---|---|---|
| | Rastrigin | FP | Schaffer | Schwefel | BBOB $f_{21}$ | BBOB $f_{22}$ | BBOB $f_{23}$ | BBOB $f_{24}$ |
| static | 27.50 | 733.6 | 19.80 | 8168.6 | 40.89 | -998.80 | 9.06 | **471.8** |
| $\Delta_f$ | 0.67 | 166.2 | 9.85 | 779.2 | 40.80 | -999.18 | **8.48** | 484.6 |
| $f_i$ | 1.93 | 168.6 | 1.80 | 7.8 | 41.07 | -998.90 | 8.67 | 490.3 |
| 0/1 | 0.45 | 294.8 | 4.72 | 113.1 | 40.78 | -999.27 | 8.39 | 505.2 |
| $W(\Delta_f)$ | 2.93 | 257.0 | 2.16 | 11.2 | 40.98 | -998.49 | 8.80 | 490.9 |

| | GAMPC | | | | IP-10DDr | | | |
|---|---|---|---|---|---|---|---|---|
| | CEC $f_7$ | CEC $f_{18}$ | CEC $f_{21}$ | CEC $f_{22}$ | BBOB $f_{21}$ | BBOB $f_{22}$ | BBOB $f_{23}$ | BBOB $f_{24}$ |
| static | 1.68 | 1945573 | 16.20 | 15.2 | **41.3** | **-997.60** | 6.889 | **131.54** |
| $\Delta_f$ | 0.95 | 947905 | 16.41 | 19.3 | 41.6 | -997.75 | 6.902 | 128.90 |
| $f_i$ | 0.91 | 980303 | 16.01 | 18.3 | 41.8 | -998.29 | 6.904 | 126.92 |
| 0/1 | 0.98 | 948013 | 16.74 | 19.9 | 41.4 | -997.20 | 6.908 | 125.38 |
| $W(\Delta_f)$ | 0.88 | 947568 | 16.75 | 18.6 | 41.5 | -997.27 | 6.914 | 125.43 |

**RL-IP**

| | Simple ES | | | | Cellular GA | | | |
|---|---|---|---|---|---|---|---|---|
| | Rastrigin | FP | Schaffer | Schwefel | BBOB $f_{21}$ | BBOB $f_{22}$ | BBOB $f_{23}$ | BBOB $f_{24}$ |
| static | 27.5 | 733.6 | 19.8 | 8168.6 | 40.89 | -998.8 | 9.06 | **471.8** |
| $\Delta_f$ | 2.2 | 529.6 | 4.4 | 708.2 | 40.80 | -999.0 | **8.60** | 510.2 |
| $f_i$ | 4.2 | 79.7 | 2.2 | 800.3 | 40.82 | -997.9 | 8.74 | 469.7 |
| 0/1 | 4.1 | 444.4 | 5.0 | 70.4 | 40.78 | -999.2 | 8.62 | 476.6 |
| $W(\Delta_f)$ | 0.2 | 46.6 | 1.1 | 34.87 | 40.86 | -998.7 | 8.48 | 481.8 |

| | GAMPC | | | | IP-10DDr | | | |
|---|---|---|---|---|---|---|---|---|
| | CEC $f_7$ | CEC $f_{18}$ | CEC $f_{21}$ | CEC $f_{22}$ | BBOB $f_{21}$ | BBOB $f_{22}$ | BBOB $f_{23}$ | BBOB $f_{24}$ |
| static | 1.68 | 1945573 | 16.2 | 15.2 | **41.30** | **-997.6** | 6.8890 | **131.5** |
| $\Delta_f$ | 0.92 | 997692 | 17.6 | 18.7 | 41.45 | -998.1 | 6.9326 | 126.8 |
| $f_i$ | 0.99 | 1039461 | 16.9 | 19.0 | 41.42 | -998.3 | 6.8954 | 127.4 |
| 0/1 | 0.98 | 982950 | 17.2 | 18.5 | 41.61 | -996.9 | 6.9344 | 127.6 |
| $W(\Delta_f)$ | 0.91 | 949211 | 17.1 | 19.6 | 41.65 | -998.4 | 6.9321 | 127.3 |

**RL-SMC**

| | Simple ES | | | | Cellular GA | | | |
|---|---|---|---|---|---|---|---|---|
| | Rastrigin | FP | Schaffer | Schwefel | BBOB $f_{21}$ | BBOB $f_{22}$ | BBOB $f_{23}$ | BBOB $f_{24}$ |
| static | 27.5 | 733.6 | 19.8 | 8168.6 | 40.8 | -998.8 | 9.06 | **471.8** |
| $\Delta_f$ | 8.0 | 1027.2 | 7.1 | 488.3 | 41.6 | -998.6 | 8.82 | 498.9 |
| $f_i$ | 11.0 | 1833.4 | 3.5 | 7.9 | 41.4 | -998.0 | 9.01 | 525.8 |
| 0/1 | 9.3 | 1334.4 | 3.1 | 59.8 | 41.5 | -998.4 | 8.89 | 514.0 |
| $W(\Delta_f)$ | 9.8 | 1324.9 | 3.7 | 30.9 | 42.2 | -997.2 | 9.10 | 533.9 |

| | GAMPC | | | | IP-10DDr | | | |
|---|---|---|---|---|---|---|---|---|
| | CEC $f_7$ | CEC $f_{18}$ | CEC $f_{21}$ | CEC $f_{22}$ | BBOB $f_{21}$ | BBOB $f_{22}$ | BBOB $f_{23}$ | BBOB $f_{24}$ |
| static | 1.680 | 1945573 | 16.20 | 15.2 | **41.3** | **-997.6** | 6.889 | **131.5** |
| $\Delta_f$ | 0.902 | 1009638 | 16.94 | 17.8 | 41.4 | -998.1 | 6.904 | 126.8 |
| $f_i$ | 0.908 | 1156982 | 16.75 | 15.8 | 41.7 | -997.7 | 6.935 | 127.6 |
| 0/1 | 0.882 | 1056653 | 16.99 | 16.7 | 41.5 | -997.4 | 6.921 | 129.7 |
| $W(\Delta_f)$ | 0.937 | 1129855 | 16.13 | 17.1 | 41.6 | -996.9 | 6.930 | 130.8 |

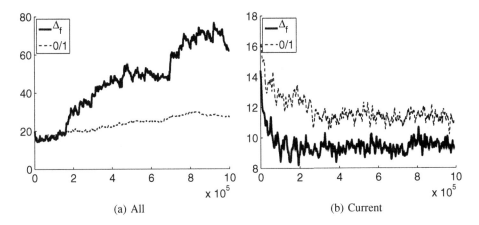

**Fig. 1.** The (normalised) maximum Q value taken at each time step as (a) an average of the maximums of all states and (b) the maximum of the current state only. This is the setting of Simple ES, Fletcher & Powell, D-RL. Lines are averages over the 30 runs. The lines for the current state are smoothed with a rolling average of window size 10000.

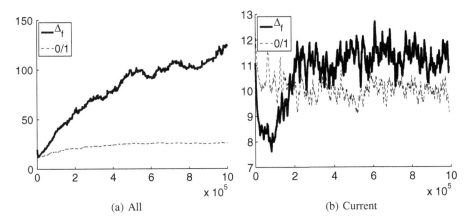

**Fig. 2.** The (normalised) maximum Q value taken at each time step as (a) an average of the maximums of all states and (b) the maximum of the current state only. This is the setting of Simple ES, Schwefel, D-RL. Lines are averages over the 30 runs. The lines for the current state are smoothed with a rolling average of window size 10000.

reward was significantly better. Furthermore, the assumption that scale sensitivity would result in too high rewards early in the run that could have a long lasting misleading effect, does not occur. There is indeed a slight peak of the global maximum Q (Figs. 1-a and 2-a) when using the $\Delta_f$ but values quickly decay, while the current maximum Q (Figs. 1-b and 2-b) is not affected.

From a different perspective, it is interesting why the 0/1 performs equally well as the $\Delta_f$ when it foregoes certain information (the magnitude of improvement). One explanation could be that, in the context of an EA, making any improvement is more important than its magnitude since such an event will give new direction to the search process (escaping a local optimum). Another influencing factor could be the selection mechanism of the controller, i.e. whether it is greedy or probabilistic; in the latter case we would expect that the magnitude of rewards would influence the selection of actions. However, this does not seem to affect the balance between the $\Delta_f$ and 0/1 rewards: the D-RL uses a greedy selection while the RL-SMC a probabilistic but our results on reward performance were similar for these two. Additionally, we run a control experiment with D-RL using a softmax (i.e. probabilistic) selection instead of a greedy but the results did not show a difference in terms of the comparison between the $\Delta_f$ and 0/1 rewards.

Regarding simplicity and meta-parameters, the 0/1 reward has an obvious advantage over $\Delta_f$. It is much simpler as an approach (and applicable also to EA cases where individuals cannot be evaluated by a direct fitness value but only comparisons between individuals are possible) and it does not introduce any new meta-parameters. Overall, the 0/1 reward is the most preferable among the ones tested: it performs equally well or better while being the simplest and without introducing meta-parameters.

## 6  Conclusion

Parameter control approaches can significantly improve the performance of EAs in particular settings. Though several control schemes have been proposed, the vast majority are ad hoc extensions for a particular type of EA. Our aim is a generic parameter controller that works with any EA and parameter. In this direction, we have previously shown that RL is an effective method. We did not, however, investigate the effect of the reward function though RL mechanisms are highly dependent on it.

In this paper we introduced various reward functions and evaluated them in different settings. Four reward function were compared: (i) the improvement of the current best fitness; (ii) a binary reward expressing whether an improvement was made; (iii) a weighted improvement function of the current best fitness, and (iv) the raw fitness. Experiments showed that the most simple (i.e. binary) reward function performed slightly better for two controllers and slightly worse for the third. This is surprising as the binary function is unable to distinguish between marginal and good improvements. It can however be considered good news, as a simple parameter-free reward scheme can easily be adopted for generic parameter control, thereby ideally suiting our vision for an out-of-the-box controller that can be applied without any need for tailoring.

For future work, it is necessary that further experiments with more EAs, problems (and maybe RL controllers) are conducted to provide a perhaps more conclusive performance comparison. Additionally, further analysis of the effect of the reward function on the RL mechanisms (e.g. time series analysis of Q values) could reveal interesting patterns, explain why certain rewards work better for certain controllers and/or EAs and, ideally, lead to a decision mechanism that can on-the-fly choose the most appropriate reward function for the controller, EA and problem combination being solved.

# References

1. Alba, E., Dorronsoro, B.: Cellular Genetic Algorithms, 1st edn. Springer, Heidelberg (2008)
2. Chen, F., Gao, Y., Chen, Z., Chen, S.: SCGA: controlling genetic algorithms with Sarsa(0). In: International Conference on Computational Intelligence for Modelling, Control and Automation, 2005 and International Conference on Intelligent Agents, Web Technologies and Internet Commerce, vol. 1, pp. 1177–1183 (2005)
3. Eiben, A.E., Horvath, M., Kowalczyk, W., Schut, M.C.: Reinforcement learning for online control of evolutionary algorithms. In: Brueckner, S.A., Hassas, S., Jelasity, M., Yamins, D. (eds.) ESOA 2006. LNCS (LNAI), vol. 4335, pp. 151–160. Springer, Heidelberg (2007)
4. Eiben, A.E., Hinterding, R., Michalewicz, Z.: Parameter control in evolutionary algorithms. IEEE Trans. Evol. Comput. **3**(2), 124–141 (1999)
5. Eiben, A.E., Smith, J.: Introduction to Evolutionary Computing. Springer, Heidelberg (2003)
6. Elsayed, S., Sarker, R., Essam, D.: GA with a new multi-parent crossover for solving IEEE-CEC2011 competition problems. In: Proceedings of the 2011 IEEE Congress on Evolutionary Computation, pp. 1034–1040. IEEE Press, New Orleans, USA (2011)
7. Fialho, Á., Da Costa, L., Schoenauer, M., Sebag, M.: Extreme value based adaptive operator selection. In: Rudolph, G., Jansen, T., Lucas, S., Poloni, C., Beume, N. (eds.) PPSN 2008. LNCS, vol. 5199, pp. 175–184. Springer, Heidelberg (2008)
8. Gong, W., Fialho, A., Cai, Z.: Adaptive strategy selection in differential evolution. In: Pelikan, M., Branke, J. (eds.) Proceedings of the Genetic and Evolutionary Computation Conference (GECCO-2010), pp. 409–416. ACM, Portland (2010)
9. Holtschulte, N.J., Moses, M.: Benchmarking cellular genetic algorithms on the BBOB noiseless testbed. In: Proceeding of the Fifteenth Annual Conference Companion on Genetic and Evolutionary Computation Conference Companion, GECCO 2013 Companion, pp. 1201–1208. ACM (2013)
10. Karafotias, G., Eiben, A.E., Hoogendoorn, M.: Generic parameter control with reinforcement learning. In: Arnold, D.V. (ed.) GECCO 2014: Proceedings of the 16th annual conference on Genetic and evolutionary computation, pp. 1319–1326. ACM, New York (2014)
11. Karafotias, G., Hoogendoorn, M., Eiben, A.E.: Parameter control in evolutionary algorithms: trends and challenges. IEEE Transactions on Evolutionary Computation (2014, to appear). doi:10.1109/TEVC.2014.2308294
12. Karafotias, G., Hoogendoorn, M., Weel, B.: Comparing generic parameter controllers for EAs. In: 2014 IEEE Symposium on Foundations of Computational Intelligence (FOCI), pp. 46–53, December 2014
13. Liao, T., Stützle, T.:. Bounding the population size of IPOP-CMA-ES on the noiseless BBOB testbed. In: Proceeding of the Fifteenth Annual Conference Companion on Genetic and Evolutionary Computation Conference Companion, pp. 1161–1168. ACM (2013)

14. Muller, S., Schraudolph, N., Koumoutsakos, P.: Step size adaptation in evolution strategies using reinforcement learning. In: 2002 Congress on Evolutionary Computation (CEC 2002), pp. 151–156. IEEE Press, Piscataway, NJ, Honolulu, USA 12–17 May 2002

15. Pettinger, J., Everson, R.: Controlling genetic algorithms with reinforcement learning. In: Langdon, W., et al. (eds.) Proceedings of the Genetic and Evolutionary Computation Conference (GECCO-2002), page 692, pp. 9–13. Morgan Kaufmann, San Francisco (2002)

16. Sakurai, Y., Takada, K., Kawabe, T., Tsuruta, S.: A method to control parameters of evolutionary algorithms by using reinforcement learning. In: 2010 Sixth International Conference on Signal-Image Technology and Internet-Based Systems (SITIS), pp. 74–79 (2010)

17. Schwefel, H.-P.: Evolution and Optimum Seeking. Wiley, New York (1995)

18. Sutton, R.S., Barto, A.G.: Introduction to Reinforcement Learning. MIT Press, Cambridge (1998)

19. Uther, W.B., Veloso, M.: Tree based discretization for continuous state space reinforcement learning. In: Proceedings of the Fifteenth National/tenth Conference on Artificial Intelligence/innovative Applications of Artificial Intelligence, AAAI 1998/IAAI 1998, pp. 769–774. American Association for Artificial Intelligence (1998)

# Chromatic Selection – An Oversimplified Approach to Multi-objective Optimization

Giovanni Squillero[✉]

Politecnico di Torino, Corso Duca Degli Abruzzi 24, 10129 Torino, Italy
giovanni.squillero@polito.it

**Abstract.** This short paper introduces the *chromatic selection*, a simple technique implementable with few tens of lines of code, that enable handling multi-value fitness functions with a single-objective evolutionary optimizer. The chromatic selection is problem independent, requires no parameter tuning, and can be used as a drop-in replacement for both parent and survival selections. The resulting tool will not be a full-fledged multi-objective optimizer, lacking the ability to manage Pareto fronts, but it will efficiently seek a single, reasonable, compromise solution. In several practical problems, the time saved, both in computation and development, could represent a substantial advantage.

**Keywords:** Multi-objective evolutionary algorithm · Evolutionary optimization · Selection scheme

## 1 Introduction

Over the years, evolutionary computation (EC) has shown the capability to tackle quite difficult problems with very complex fitness landscapes. Evolutionary optimizers were demonstrated able to identify both single optima and whole Pareto sets in multi-objective problems [2,3]. Several practical situations lie between these two extremes. Practitioners often face problems involving more than one objective function to be optimized simultaneously, but these goals are not conflicting. Indeed, a full-fledged multi-objective evolutionary algorithm (MOEA) would be perfectly suited to solve them, but implementing it from scratch, or modifying an existing single-objective evolutionary algorithm (EA), would definitely be a time-consuming and error-prone activity. Moreover, the overhead involved in finding a full Pareto front could be inappropriate when a single solution can simultaneously optimizes *almost all* objectives.

A multi-objective optimization problem where a single solution optimizes all objectives is considered "trivial", however it may not be trivial to solve it efficiently with limited resources. For instance, it is not uncommon to discover the need to include an additional objective to the fitness function during the deployment or maintenance of an optimizer. Such additional objective may be an aspect of the problem that needs to be considered that does not conflict with the previous goals. Here, the main challenge is to be able to adapt the optimizer, taking into consideration the new specification, as swiftly as possible.

© Springer International Publishing Switzerland 2015
A.M. Mora and G. Squillero (Eds.): EvoApplications 2015, LNCS 9028, pp. 681–689, 2015.
DOI: 10.1007/978-3-319-16549-3_55

To transform a working single-objective EA to a simplified MOEA able to solve trivial problems requires changing the fitness of the new problem from a vector $\mathbf{f} = (f_0, f_1, ..., f_n)$ to a scalar number $\overline{f}$ that can be handled by the old tool. The straightforward approach is to add together all $n + 1$ components of the fitness vector, possibly scaling each one with a coefficient $c_i$ according to its relative importance or other considerations. That is:

$$\overline{f} = \sum_{i=0}^{n} c_i \cdot f_i \tag{1}$$

Another common situation in practice is seeking an acceptable compromise between mildly conflicting goals. This is not true multi-objective optimization, because the user is looking for a single solution and not a Pareto front. If a clear priority can be assigned to the different objectives, then the problem can be easily tackled setting a lexicographic ordering for the components of the fitness vector: the fitness $\mathbf{f} = (f_0, f_1, ..., f_n)$ is greater than the fitness $\mathbf{g} = (g_0, g_1, ..., g_n)$ if, and only if, $\forall i < j, f_i = g_i \wedge f_j > g_j$. However not all objectives can be prioritize. Here, the main challenge is to devise an appropriate method for combining goals. Indeed, creating an aggregate function is, again, the most common solution, and defining coefficients the most common problem.

As said before, the simplistic approach shown in Eq. (1) is frequently acceptable in both scenarios, although it is known not to work correctly if the Pareto front is concave. Apart for the sum itself, it requires no modification whatsoever to the original evolutionary optimizer, and it is quite efficient. However, the choice of the scale factors $c_i$ is critical: the different fitness components may have different ranges, or their relationship might not be linear. Thus, the ease in implementing it, is often repaid with the need of extensive, problem-dependent fine tuning.

This short paper presents the new *chromatic selection*, a very simple selection scheme based on tournament selection that can be used to handle almost effortlessly multiple-value fitness functions with a single-objective evolutionary optimizer. The chromatic selection is problem independent, requires no parameters related to the fitness values, and can be used as a simple drop-in replacement of the original code. It handles both *parent selection* and *survival selection*; both the selective pressure in the former, and the amount of determinism in the latter can be easily adjusted whether the user feels that need. Preliminary experimental results show its efficacy in a standard test bench.

The rest of the is organized as follows: Sect. 2 introduces the isea of chromatic selections; Sect. 3 shows the experimental evaluation; and Sect. 4 concludes the paper.

## 2    Chromatic Selection

The chromatic selection is based on the *chromatic comparison operator*. Its functioning is fairly simple: each time two multi-objective fitness values are compared, only one component of their vectors is considered and the remaining are ignored. The component used for the comparison is chosen randomly with probability biased by the difference between the values in the two vectors. The rationale is to favor comparisons in the components where the fitness differ most.

$$\forall i \in [0, n], \quad \mathcal{C}_i = \frac{\max(f_i, g_i) - \min(f_i, g_i)}{\max(f_i, g_i)} \tag{2}$$

Operatively, when two fitness vector $\mathbf{f} = (f_0, f_1, ..., f_n)$ and $\mathbf{g} = (g_0, g_1, ..., g_n)$ are compared, a *chroma* value is assigned to each component. Assuming that all components in fitness values are strictly positive, it simply measures the normalized difference between the respective components in the two vectors (see Eq. 2). The target component used for the actual comparison is selected using a standard roulette wheel on the chroma values. The pseudo-code of the function is shown in Algorithm 1.

The chromatic comparison is not deterministic: confronting the same individuals repeatedly may yield different results. As it consider only two fitness values at a time, it is always used to compare individuals inside the same generation. Thus, it should be less prone to bias and not suffer from non-linearity in the fitness function.

---

**Algorithm 1.** Chromatic comparison operator

---

**Require:** $\forall i : f_i \geq 0 \wedge g_i \geq 0$
  **function** CCOMPARE($\mathbf{f}, \mathbf{g}$)
    **for** $i = 0$ to $n$ **do**
      **if** $f_i = 0$ and $g_i = 0$ **then**
        $C_i \leftarrow 0$
      **else**
        $C_i \leftarrow \frac{\max(f_i, g_i) - \min(f_i, g_i)}{\max(f_i, g_i)}$
      **end if**
      $i \leftarrow i + 1$
    **end for**
    $c \leftarrow$ ROULETTEWHEEL($C_0, C_1, ..., C_n$)
    **if** $f_c > g_c$ **then**                         ▷ Actual comparison
      $s \leftarrow 1$
    **else if** $f_c < g_c$ **then**
      $s \leftarrow -1$
    **else**
      $s \leftarrow 0$
    **end if**
    **return** $s$
  **end function**

---

Given a standard single-objective EA, with a population of $\mu$ individuals and offspring size of $\lambda$, few modification are required to transform parent and survival selections.

## 2.1   Parent Selection

Parent selection is performed using a tournament of size $\tau$: $\tau$ individuals are randomly chosen from the population, they are compared using the chromatic comparison operator, and eventually the fittest is selected (Algorithm 2).

---

**Algorithm 2.** Chromatic parent selection

---

**function** PARENTSELECTION( )
   $c \leftarrow$ RANDOMINDIVIDUAL( )                            ▷ Current champion
   **for** $i = 1$ to $\lfloor \tau \rfloor$ **do**
      $o \leftarrow$ RANDOMINDIVIDUAL( )
      **if** CCOMPARE$(c, o) < 0$ **then**
         $c \leftarrow o$
      **end if**
   **end for**
   **if** RAND$(0,1) < \tau - \lfloor \tau \rfloor$ **then**      ▷ Add extra individual to the tournament
      $o \leftarrow$ RANDOMINDIVIDUAL( )
      **if** CCOMPARE$(c, o) < 0$ **then**
         $c \leftarrow o$
      **end if**
   **end if**
   **return** $c$
**end function**

---

The parameter $\tau$ represents the selective pressure. The default is $\tau = 2$, the standard in several EAs. It roughly correspond to the selective pressure experienced in a single-objective algorithm where parent selection is performed through a roulette wheel on linearized fitness. To enable a smooth adjustment of the pressure, a floating point $\tau$ can be used: $\lfloor \tau \rfloor$ individuals always take part in the tournament, then, there is a probability $p = \tau - \lfloor \tau \rfloor$ to pick an additional one [5].

## 2.2   Survival Selection

As in real multi-objective problems, individuals cannot be directly ranked on their fitness. MOEAs adopt the concept of *levels*, however one of the goal of chromatic selection is avoiding the Pareto-dominance calculations.

A technique similar to the one used in early evolutionary programming [4] is adopted: each individual plays $\gamma$ games against random opponents taken from the population, and the outcome of such games is defined by the chromatic comparison operator. Individuals score 3 points for each victory and 1 point for each draw. Eventually, the population is ranked according to this score, and individuals at the bottom of the list are discarded (Algorithm 3).

By default, the number of game $\gamma$ played by each individuals is set to $\gamma = 10 \cdot (\mu + \lambda)$, but this value can be used to further increase or decrease randomness, favoring exploration ($\gamma < 10\mu + 10\lambda$) or exploitation ($\gamma > 10\mu + 10\lambda$).

**Algorithm 3.** Chromatic survival selection

---

**function** SLAUGHTERING( )
    **for** $i = 1$ to $\mu + \lambda$ **do**                          ▷ Run tournament
        $c \leftarrow$ **individual**$[i]$
        $s_i = 0$
        **for** $j = 1$ to $\gamma$ **do**
            $o \leftarrow$ RANDOMINDIVIDUAL( )
            $r \leftarrow$ CCOMPARE$(c, o)$
            **if** $r > 0$ **then**
                $s_i \leftarrow s_i + 3$
            **else if** $r = 0$ **then**
                $s_i \leftarrow s_i + 1$
            **end if**
        **end for**
    **end for**
    **individual** $\leftarrow$ SORT(**individual**, **s**)        ▷ Sort individuals using $s_i$
    **individual** $\leftarrow$ **individual**$[0 : \mu]$       ▷ Discard *less fit* individuals
**end function**

---

## 3   Experimental Evaluation

Experiments compare the performance of a simple GA tackling multi-objective problems when using the simplest aggregated fitness function (i.e., the sum of terms of Eq. (1) with $\forall i : c_i = 1$), and when using chromatic selection.

A very simple evolutionary algorithm is used: a steady-state genetic algorithm (GA) with a *one-cut crossover* and a *random mutation* operators. The GA evolves for a fixed number of $G$ generations with no other stopping condition. Experiments were performed using the standard selection algorithms and the chromatic selections. Both the GA and the chromatic selection have been implemented in Go and can be downloaded from Bitbucket[1].

The first test problem considered is the *multi-objective knapsack problem* (MOKP), a variant of the more popular *knapsack problem* [1]. Unlike the standard version, MOKP consider $k$ knapsacks $(0, 1, ..., k - 1)$. If the object $b$ is taken (i.e., $x_b = 1$), it brings a different value $V_{b,i}$ in each knapsack $i$. Objective functions correspond to the values of the different knapsacks. See Eq. (3).

$$f_i = \sum_{b=0}^{N-1} x_b \cdot V_{b,i} \tag{3}$$

Indeed, MOKP is often used to empathize the necessity to consider the full Pareto front instead of just summing up contributions. However, trying to solve it with a single-objective EA may be regarded as a paradigmatic example of seeking a single, compromise solution for a complex problem.

The second test is the *partitioned one-max problem* (P1M), a test-problem derived from the well known one-max. The original version is a single-objective

---

[1] https://bitbucket.org/squillero/chromatic.

**Table 1.** Experiment settings.

| Parameter | | Symbol | Value |
|---|---|---|---|
| GA | Population size | $\mu$ | 30 |
| | Offspring size | $\lambda$ | 20 |
| | Max generation | G | 1,000 |
| Chromatic Selection | Selective pressure | $\tau$ | 2 |
| | Games before slaughtering | $\gamma$ | 500 |
| Test function | P1M bits | B | 1,000 |
| | MOKP objects | N | 1,000 |

problem, the fitness of a candidate solution is the number of 1's found in its genome; in the modified version bits are partitioned into $p$ sets $S_i$ of equal size, the fitness of each set is, again, of 1's. To differentiate the sub-goals, each set is further scaled by a power of ten. See Eq. (4).

$$f_i = 10^i \sum_{b \in S_i} b \qquad (4)$$

The problem exemplifies a typical scenario: the fitness is not a scalar value, but a vector; the problem is trivial from the point of view of multi-objective optimization because there exists a solution that can maximize all the objectives (i.e., a solution composed of all 1's); the user is seeking a single solution, not a Pareto-front; due to the relative scale of the fitness values, combining the different sub-objectives is not straightforward.

Settings used in the experiments are reported in Table 1: GA parameters are almost irrelevant; chromatic selection's are defaults; the number of MOKP's objects and P1M's bits define the complexity of the test problems. The *performance* of the algorithm are measured as, respectively, the aggregate fitness in the MOKP, and the number of 1's in the P1M, for every new individual.

Figure 1 shows the performances of the GA on MOKP with one knapsack and on P1M with one partition, i.e., the standard problems. It can be noted that chromatic selection does not introduce any degradation in the performance.

The first experiments compare the performance of solving the MOKP with 2, 5, 10, 20, 50, and 100 knapsacks. For each 10 experiments have been run. Results are reported in Fig. 2, and clearly shows that the chromatic selection does not damage a simple EA seeking a compromise solution for a multi-objective problem. With the MOKP, using the aggregate fitness is probably one of the best thing that can be done without a real multi-objective methodology.

The second set of experiments is more interesting and compare the performance when solving the P1M. Six partitioning are used $p \in (2, 5, 10, 20, 50, 100)$, and for each 10 experiments have been run. Results are reported in Fig. 3. While when the GA is driven by the the simple aggregate fitness performances degrade as partitions increase, they are almost stable with chromatic selection.

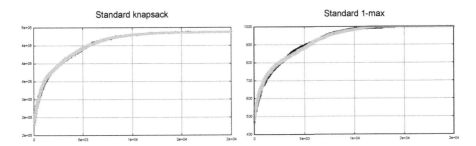

**Fig. 1.** Performance of a simple GA trying to solve the "knapsack" and the "1-max" test problems. Graphs show the fitness against the number of evaluated individuals: when using standard selection (black); and when using the chromatic selection (gray). Results almost completely overlap.

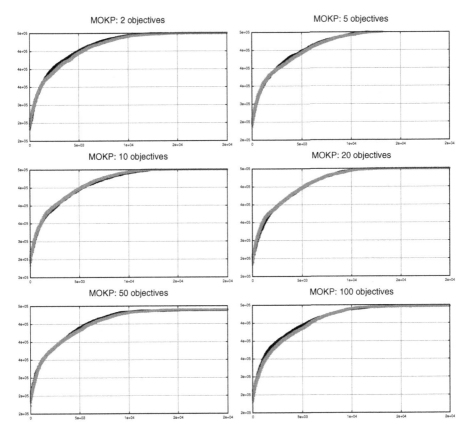

**Fig. 2.** Performance of a simple GA trying to solve the multi-objective knapsack problem with 2, 5, 10, 20, 50, and 100 knapsacks. Graphs show the aggregated fitness against the number of evaluated individuals: when using the aggregated fitness to drive the search (gray); and then using the chromatic selection (black). The same random seed and initial state are used. Results almost completely overlap.

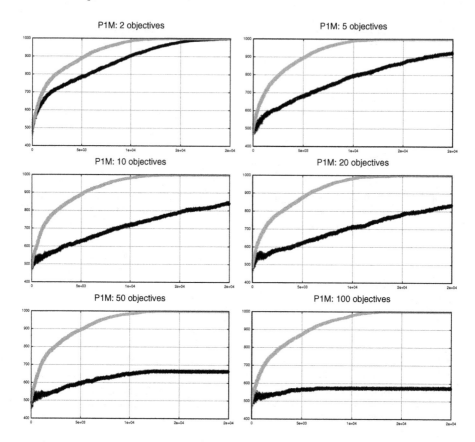

**Fig. 3.** Performance of a simple GA trying to solve the partitioned one-max for different number of partitions: $p \in (2, 5, 10, 20, 50, 100)$. Graphs show the the number of **1**'s against the number of evaluated individuals: when using the aggregated fitness (lower stripe, black); and when using the chromatic selection (upper stripe, gray). In the former case, the performances clearly degrade with the number of partitions; differently, for the latter, performances are almost independent from the number of partitions.

The low performances may be explained considering the presence of *hitch-hikers*, like **0**'s in partition $S_0$ that are propagated through generations because they are located close to some **1**'s in partition $S_{p-1}$. Moreover, the use of the aggregated fitness is likely to impair the variability in the gene pool, favoring only individuals with **1**'s in high valued $S_i$'s.

The simple sum of the fitness's terms cannot be used if such terms have different magnitudes. In the specific example, the problem could have been solved by tweaking coefficients $c_i$ in Eq. (1), because the different magnitude was constant. However, in real problem this is not always the case.

Differently, when the chromatic selection is used, increasing $p$ does not cause an immediate reduction of the performances. The stripes are almost overlapped, except around the first quarter of the plot. It should be also noted that the performance with $p = 1$, corresponding to the original one-max, are indistinguishable in the two tools. The chromatic parent selection behaves exactly like a tournament selection if the fitness vector contains only one component; and the chromatic survival selection does not worsen the performance.

## 4 Conclusions

This paper propose the chromatic selection, a simple technique that can be implemented with few tens of lines and used as a drop-in replacement for both parent selection and survival selection. Chromatic selection allows to handle multi-objective problems with a standard EA, originally created for single-objective problems. The result is not a true MOEA, and lacks the ability to find Pareto fronts. However, in practical problems, the time saved, both in computation and development, could possibly represent a significant advantage.

The experimental results shows that the chromatic selection is problem independent, removes the need to set different parameters and to tweak constants. When used for single-objective problem the chromatic parent selection is equivalent to the normal tournament selection, and experiments suggest that it is at least *as good as* a simple aggregate fitness. Results also demonstrates that performances do not degrade when pursuing different non-conflicting goals, and, unlike other approaches, are independent from the scale of the terms. In particular, experiments on parallel one-max show that components may differ up to 100 orders of magnitude.

Future works include a more through comparison with alternative methodologies, such as using chroma values directly as weights in the aggregated fitness (Eq. 1). Moreover, mechanisms to handle abrupt changes in the magnitude of the fitness components are currently under examination; for instance, the use of rolling averages to normalize chroma values in Eq. 2.

## References

1. Bazgan, C., Hugot, H., Vanderpooten, D.: Solving efficiently the 0–1 multi-objective knapsack problem. Comput. Oper. Res. **36**(1), 260–279 (2009)
2. Coello Coello, C.A., Lamont, G.B., Van Veldhuisen, D.A.: Evolutionary Algorithms for Solving Multi-objective Problems. Springer, Heidelberg (2007)
3. Eiben, A.E.: Introduction to Evolutionary Computing, vol. 2, pp. 3–48. Springer, Berlin (2010)
4. Fogel, L.J.: Autonomous automata. Ind. Res. **4**, 14–19 (1962)
5. Sanchez, E., Schillaci, M., Squillero, G.: Evolutionary Optimization: the $\mu$GP Toolkit, 1st edn. Springer, New York (2011)

# EvoPAR

# Parallel Cooperation for Large-Scale Multiobjective Optimization on Feature Selection Problems

Dragi Kimovski[1], Julio Ortega[2(✉)], Andrés Ortiz[3], and Raúl Baños[4]

[1] University of Information Science and Technology, Ohrid, Macedonia
dragi.kimovski@uist.edu.mk
[2] Department of Computer Architecture and Technology,
CITIC, University of Granada, Granada, Spain
jortega@ugr.es
[3] Department of Communications Engineering, University of Málaga,
Málaga, Spain
aortiz@ic.uma.es
[4] Department of Business Administration and Management,
Catholic University of Murcia, Murcia, Spain
rbanos@ucam.edu

**Abstract.** Recently, the interest on multiobjective optimization problems with a large number of decision variables has grown since many significant real problems, for example on machine learning and pattern recognition, imply to process patterns with a high number of components (features). This paper deals with parallel multiobjective optimization on high-dimensional feature selection problems. Thus, several parallel multiobjective evolutionary alternatives based on the cooperation of subpopulations are proposed and experimentally evaluated by using some synthetic and BCI (Brain-Computer Interface) benchmarks. The results obtained show different improvements achieved in the solution quality and speedups, depending on the parallel alternative and benchmark profile. Some alternatives even provide superlinear speedups with only small reductions in the solution quality.

**Keywords:** Cooperative coevolution · Feature selection · Multiobjective clustering · Parallel evolutionary algorithms

## 1 Introduction

Recently, interest on multiobjective problems with many decision variables has grown up [1, 2] motivated by both, the relevance of applications involving such kind of large-scale optimization problems, and the current availability of multi-core microprocessors (with either homogeneous or heterogeneous architectures) and high bandwidth networks that allow an easy access to parallel computers.

Many of these large-scale applications imply high-dimensional pattern classification or modeling tasks where feature selection techniques should be applied for dimensionality reduction to remove redundant, noisy-dominated, or irrelevant features.

© Springer International Publishing Switzerland 2015
A.M. Mora and G. Squillero (Eds.): EvoApplications 2015, LNCS 9028, pp. 693–705, 2015.
DOI: 10.1007/978-3-319-16549-3_56

In particular, dimensionality reduction is a very important issue for increasing learning accuracy and result comprehensibility, and even more important whenever the number of features in the input pattern is higher than the number of available patterns (the *curse of dimensionality* problem) [3]. A review on feature selection techniques used in bioinformatics is provided in [4] along with analyses and references of feature selection in bioinformatics applications such as sequence analysis, microarray analysis, and mass spectra analysis. Dimension reduction in the input patterns has been also applied to EEG (Electroencephalogram) classification for recognizing epileptiform patterns [5]. Precisely, EEG classification has to cope with problems that usually imply to use patterns with a large number of features to describe EEG signals. For example, BCI pattern recognition tasks have to be accomplished from relatively few feature vectors of very high dimensionality.

As the size of the search space depends exponentially on the number of possible features, an exhaustive search of the best set is not feasible, even for a modest number of features. Thus, procedures based on branch-and-bound, simulated annealing, or evolutionary algorithms have been proposed, and parallel processing could be also considered as an interesting approach to take advantage of high performance computer architectures for feature selection. Nevertheless, previous approaches for parallel feature selection [6–8] have neither considered feature selection from a parallel multiobjective approach nor from a cooperative coevolutionary implementation as we propose here. Recent works [9] have approached feature selection for either supervised or unsupervised classification problems as multiobjective problems.

This way, our contributions in this paper deal with feature selection in applications with a large number of decision variables, formulated as a multiobjective optimization problem, and implemented by parallel cooperative coevolutionary procedures. In Sect. 2, some issues on parallel coevolutionary multiobjective optimization are reviewed including references to previous works on the subject. Section 3 provides a classification of cooperation alternatives and describes the parallel cooperation alternatives here proposed. The corresponding results obtained from experiments on benchmarks corresponding to a feature selection application implemented as a multiobjective optimization problem on different benchmarks are presented and discussed in Sect. 4. Finally, the conclusions are given in Sect. 5.

## 2 Coevolutionary Multiobjective Optimization

In a multiobjective optimization problem, a vector of decision variables, $\mathbf{x} = [x_1, x_2, \ldots, x_n]$ ($\mathbf{x} \in R^n$), that satisfies a restriction set, $g(\mathbf{x}) \leq 0$, $h(\mathbf{x}) = 0$, and optimizes a vector of objectives, $\mathbf{f}(\mathbf{x}) = [f_1(\mathbf{x}), f_2(\mathbf{x}), \ldots, f_m(\mathbf{x})]$, is searched. The objectives are usually in conflict, and the concept of optimum must be redefined in this context. Thus, instead of providing only one optimal solution, the procedures applied to these multiobjective optimization problems should obtain a set of non-dominated solutions, known as Pareto optimal solutions, from which a decision agent will choose the most convenient solution in the current circumstances. These Pareto optimal solutions are optimal in the sense that in the corresponding hyper-area known as *Pareto front*, there is not any solution worse than any of the other ones when all the objectives are taken into account. Thus, they are *non-dominated* solutions.

To tackle multi-objective optimization problems, we will consider the use of evolutionary algorithms, which have been widely applied to multi-objective optimization. Indeed, the multiobjective evolutionary algorithms (MOEA) have brought a different point of view on the resolution of these problems with respect to the classic methods previously proposed, as they can obtain very good approximations to the corresponding Pareto sets.

The solution of large scale multiobjective problems including many decision variables has not been widely studied, and only some recent papers describe approaches to cope with them. One of the approaches considered in these works is *coevolution*. In a coevolutionary approach, several subpopulations, including individuals representing different parts of the solutions, explore different zones of the searching space and use their results to compose the final solution to the problem by competition or cooperation. In this paper we have considered cooperative coevolution, which is the usual approach in optimization problems.

Figure 1 illustrates a population of N individuals with F decision variables. The population has been divided into p subpopulations of N/p individuals, which evolve independently along a given number of iterations by only changing a subset of F/p decision variables (the ones in the white chunks in Fig. 1). After some generations of concurrent evolution, the subpopulations combine their solutions (block Combine_&_Distribute in Fig. 1) and continue their evolution along some new independent generations. Selection of individuals and diversity maintenance operations in a MOEA require comparisons that imply the whole population or a big part of it. This means that

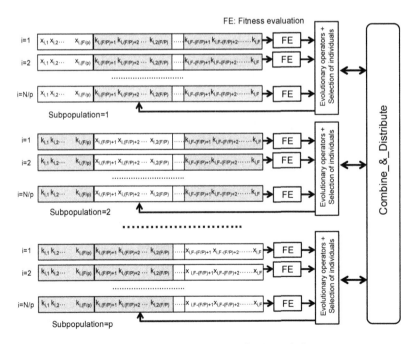

**Fig. 1.** Concurrent evolution of subpopulations

the described concurrent evolution of subpopulations modifies the behavior of the algorithm with regard to the sequential version. Most times, it is difficult to predict the behavior of this kind of parallelization, which is why it must be evaluated for each particular implementation.

A pseudo-code corresponding to a parallel master-worker version for the coevolutionary approach of Fig. 1, is shown in Algorithm 1. In row 03 of the Worker[i] process, the i-th worker independently executes *genpar* iterations of the implemented MOEA by using one of the subpopulations initialized by the Master process in its sentence 01. Then, in the following do-while loop, the *Combine_&_Distribute* function is applied by the Master process, in sentence 10, to take advantage of the work done by other subpopulations (the corresponding Worker[i] processes) in their previous *genpar* independent iterations. Besides defining different alternatives for the cooperation/ competition among processes in the search of the best feature selection for the application at hand, the *Combine_&_Distribute* function also distributes the new subpopulations that will evolve in parallel (sentence 03 in the Worker[i] process).

| **Master process** | | |
|---|---|---|
| 01 | | Initialize a **Population** composed of P subpopulations, SP[i] (i=1,..,P), of N/P individuals |
| 02 | | **for** i=1 to P workers |
| 03 | | Send the i-th subpopulation SP[i] to **Worker[i]**; |
| 04 | | **end**; |
| 05 | | t=1; |
| 06 | | **do** |
| 07 | | **for** i=1 to P workers |
| 08 | | Receive subpopulation SP[i] from **Worker[i]**; |
| 09 | | **end**; |
| 10 | | **Combine_&_Distribute** (SP[1], SP[2],...,SP[P]); |
| 11 | | **for** i=1 to P workers |
| 12 | | Send the i-th subpopulation SP[i] to **Worker[i]**; |
| 13 | | **end**; |
| 14 | | t=t+1; |
| 15 | | **while** stop criterion is not reached; |
| **Worker[i]** | | |
| 01 | | **while** true |
| 02 | | Receive subpopulation SP[i] from **Master** process |
| 03 | | Execute **MOEA** on SP[i] for *genpar* iterations |
| 04 | | Send subpopulation SP[i] to **Master** process |
| 05 | | **end**; |

**Algorithm 1.** Pseudo-code for parallel coevolution of subpopulations

An expression to estimate the speedup, $S = T_1/T_p$, in a parallel MOEA implemented according to Algorithm 1 can be obtained from Eq. (1), corresponding to the processing time for *gen* iterations of a sequential MOEA:

$$T_1 = gen\left(kNt_{fitness} + kN^2t_{non-dom} + Nt_{evolution} + N^r t_{niching}\right) \tag{1}$$

and Eq. (2), that corresponds to the parallel computing time with P processors:

$$T_p = \left(\frac{gen}{genpar}\right)\left(\left(genpar\left(\left(\frac{N}{P}\right)(kt_{fitness} + t_{evolution}) + \left(\frac{N}{P}\right)^2 kt_{non-dom} + \left(\frac{N}{P}\right)^r kt_{niching}\right)\right) + t_{comb}(N, P)\right) \tag{2}$$

The terms in parenthesis in Eq. (1) respectively correspond to the evaluation of the fitness for a population of *N* individuals in a problem with *k* objectives; the determination of the non-dominated individuals (it requires to compare the individuals of the population by using their $k$ objectives); the application of the evolutionary operators (mutation, crossover, etc.) to the $N$ individuals of the population or a subset of individuals in the population; and the application of a procedure to maintain the distribution of individuals along the present Pareto front (the complexity of these operations is taken into account through the parameter $r$). Parameters $t_{fitness}$, $t_{non\text{-}dom}$, $t_{evolution}$ and $t_{niching}$ determine the relative weights of these different terms. In expression (2), *genpar* in $T_p$ corresponds to the number of generations executed in parallel by each worker processor onto a subpopulation of $N/P$ individuals. The amount of time corresponding to the communication and *Combine_&_Distribute* function is $t_{comb}(N, P)$, and depends on the number of individuals to be exchanged between processors, and the number of processors that have to communicate themselves and on the interconnection topology. This speedup model allows us to explain different observed speedup behaviors, including super-linear speedups, considered as a possibility in the taxonomy for speedups of parallel evolutionary algorithms provided in [10].

# 3   Alternatives for Parallel Cooperation in MOEA

Cooperative coevolution was firstly introduced for evolutionary mono-objective optimization in [11], where each subpopulation of individuals explores a subset of decision variables through an evolutionary algorithm and solutions are built and evaluated through cooperative exchange of solutions between subpopulations. Cooperative coevolution has been extended to multiobjective optimization problems [12], and several other approaches to this research area have been proposed [2, 13–20]. These proposals are analysed in [20] according to the MOEA they use, the mechanism they apply to select the solutions to cooperate, whether they use an archive (centralized or not centralized), and whether a parallel implementation is available or not.

In what follows, we detail the cooperation alternatives we have defined to implement our proposed procedures. To describe them, a given a population $\{\Sigma_1,$ $\Sigma_2, \ldots, \Sigma_N\}$ of N individuals is considered, where each individual i is codified by $\Sigma_i = (x_{i,1}, x_{i,2}, x_{i,3}, \ldots, x_{i,F})$ being F the number of decision variables. The space explored by a given subpopulation is defined by the subset of components that can be modified by the operators of the evolutionary algorithm applied to this subpopulation (Fig. 1). Without loss of generality, it will be supposed that the decision variables assigned to a given subpopulation are adjacent in the codification of the individuals (otherwise, a permutation can be applied to sort the variables). After each generation, a subpopulation j provides a set of non-dominated solutions, $ND_j$.

A cooperation procedure for multiobjective optimization is defined for a given subpopulation $s$ by composing a subset of individuals in this subpopulation with individuals selected from other subpopulation $cs$ (from cooperating subpopulation). A cooperative coevolutionary approach can be characterized according to three dimensions: (1) the selection of solutions in a subpopulation to be used to cooperate (selection operator for cooperation); (2) the way new solutions are built from the selected solutions (composition operator); and (3) the dynamic behavior of the selection and composition operators (static/dynamic characteristics of the selection/composition operators). Of course, there are many other classification possibilities that arise whenever implementation details related with the considered computing platform or the MOEA characteristics are considered but they will not be considered in this paper.

With respect to the selection operators, the alternatives to select individuals from the subpopulation $cs$ that cooperate with the given subpopulation $s$, are the following ones: (1) *random selection* of p non-dominated individuals in subpopulation $cs$ (set $ND_{cs}$); and (2) *algorithmic selection* of p non-dominated individuals in subpopulation $cs$ (set $ND_{cs}$), according to additional properties of the individuals. For example, it is possible to use crowding distances, or other defined properties of the solutions different from the cost functions to be optimized that have been already considered to determine the non-dominance relation among solutions.

The alternatives for obtaining a composed population of individuals from the population $s$ with selected individuals of the population $cs$, are the following ones: (1) *union* of solutions; and (2) *crossing* of solutions. Figure 2a and b illustrate the effect of these alternatives, in the simple case of two processes, P1 and P2, and two decision variables, X1 and X2, such that each process explores one variable (P1 explores X1, and P2 explores X2). In the case of *composition by union* of Fig. 2a, the selected solution (K1, K2*) in the subpopulation explored by P2, allows the process P1 to explore X1 in the hyperplane X2 = K2*. This way, this type of cooperation includes new hyperplanes in the subpopulation that can be explored by a given process. The *composition by crossing* inserts new solutions, obtained by the cooperating processes, in the hyperplane explored by the process that receives these solutions. Thus in Fig. 2b a solution (the one marked with the squared point) is included in the hyperplane with X2 = K2 constant that is been explored by P1.

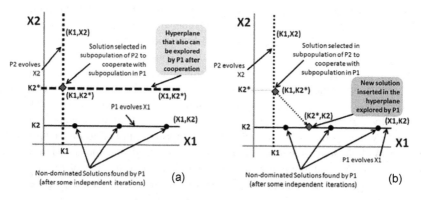

**Fig. 2.** Composition by union (a) and by crossing (b) with two decision variables X1 and X2 explored by P1 and P2 respectively

The alternatives for selection and composition can be maintained along the whole execution of the algorithm or be changed according to some given criteria (third dimension in the cooperation alternatives). Of course, many other alternatives to hybridize selection and composition operators can be designed and implemented. Thus, it is possible to change the number of solutions selected to cooperate, to alternate composition by union or crossing, etc.

In this paper we propose and evaluate three different definitions for the *Compose_&_Distribute* function of Algorithm 1 according to the cooperative options previously described. ALT1 uses composition by union (Fig. 2a). The non-dominated solutions obtained by different subpopulations define a set where a new set of non-dominated solutions is built by choosing solutions which are non-dominated and uniformly distributed in the front. The subpopulations again execute independent generations starting from the same set of solutions in the population although they explore different subsets of decision variables (features). ALT2 and ALT3 implement composition by crossing (Fig. 2b). While ALT2 uses all the non dominated solutions in the subpopulation to cooperate with other subpopulations, ALT3 only choose a subset of non-dominated solutions. In both cases, the set of solutions from which the subpopulations continue their independent generations is randomly defined among the non-dominated solutions and the solutions received from other subpopulations. We have also implemented a master-worker parallel procedure that exclusively distributes the fitness evaluation of the individuals of the population. This procedure (called MWE) only reduces the term $kNt_{fitness}$ of expression (1) by a factor equal to the number of workers (P) and, as it presents the same behaviour than the sequential procedure, constitutes a good reference to compare with the parallel cooperative coevolutionary procedures ALT1, ALT2 and ALT3.

# 4 Experimental Results

The proposed parallel procedures have been evaluated in a cluster with nodes based on two Intel Xeon E5520 processors (4 cores and 2 threads per core) at 2.7 GHz, 16 GB RAM per node, and connected by Infiniband.

A multiobjective approach for feature selection [9] in an unsupervised classifier based on the self-organized map (SOM) [21] is the application used to evaluate the procedures. The two cost functions take into account the distances from each pattern to classify to its nearest one: the smaller the distances per individual in close individuals and the larger the distances per individual in far ones, the better is the clustering. More details about this application can be found in [22]. The experiments have been accomplished by using several synthetic benchmarks, and other benchmarks generated from the dataset 2D motion provided at [23] for a BCI motor imagery classification problem (they can be obtained upon request to the authors). They correspond to classification problems with a high number of features, 152 in b152, 384 in b384, 480 in b480a and b480b, and 512 features in the benchmarks b512a and b512b, and a lower number of patterns (from 160 to 200).

In all cases, we have used NSGA-II [24], as it can be considered as one of the most referenced and implemented state-of-the-art MOEA. The population includes N = 240 individuals distributed among subpopulations with N/P individuals (P = number of processors) that independently evolve along 5 generations. Then, the Combine_&_ Distribute function is executed and the process is repeated 10 times (each one once the independent 5 generations). After some experiments to select the parameter values that provide competitive classification performances (shown below, in Table 1), we have used simulated binary crossover with a crossover probability of 0.9, a mutation probability equal to 1/n (n is the number of decision variables), and distribution indices for crossover and mutation operators equal to 20.

As this paper mainly deals with the parallel cooperative multiobjective alternatives for large-scale applications, we do not provide an exhaustive comparison among our sequential multiobjective approach and other previous feature selection procedures. Nevertheless, Table 1 shows, by using the benchmarks b512a and b480a, that the procedure here proposed (Unsupervised MO, in bold characters in Table 1), is comparable or even better that other approaches [25] such as Backward FS, ReliefF filter, and PCA, with SOM and SVM [26] for clustering/classification.

**Table 1.** Comparison of different feature selection and classification methods (for benchmarks b480a and b512a)

| Bench. | Procedure | T (s) | Accuracy | | | | Kappa Index |
|---|---|---|---|---|---|---|---|
| | | | C1 | C2 | C3 | C4 | |
| b512a | Backward FS/ Multic. SVM | 9945.10 | **1.00** | **1.00** | **1.00** | **1.00** | **1.00** |
| | ReliefF, k=20 / SOM | 0.92 | 0.75 | 0.85 | 0.85 | 0.85 | 0.91 |
| | ReliefF, k=20 / SVM | 0.92 | 0.75 | 0.85 | 0.85 | 0.75 | 0.51 |
| | PCA, 10 PCs/ SOM | 0.36 | 0.80 | 0.50 | 0.70 | **1.00** | 0.37 |
| | PCA, 10 PCs / Multic. SVM | 0.36 | 0.80 | 0.90 | 1.00 | 0.90 | 0.72 |
| | **Unsupervised MO/ SOM** | 1293.10 | **1.00** | **1.00** | **1.00** | **1.00** | **1.00** |
| b480a | Backward FS/ Multic. SVM | 25632.10 | **0.88** | **0.71** | 0.82 | | **0.54** |
| | ReliefF, k=12 / SOM | 7.92 | 0.18 | 0.47 | 0.64 | | 0.28 |
| | ReliefF, k=12 / SVM | 7.92 | 0.76 | 0.58 | 0.47 | | 0.30 |
| | PCA, 10 PCs/ SOM | 0.46 | 0.58 | 0.70 | 0.52 | | 0.16 |
| | PCA, 10 PCs / Multic. SVM | 0.46 | 0.76 | 0.56 | 0.35 | | 0.23 |
| | **Unsupervised MO/ SOM** | 5376.50 | 0.58 | 0.70 | **0.88** | | 0.46 |

The comparison has been done by using accuracy measures for each class of the corresponding benchmark (C1 to C4 in b512a and C1 to C3 in b480a), and the kappa coefficient value [27]. As higher values for these measures means better performances, it is clear from Table 1 that our proposed multi-objective feature selection procedures are competitive with other state-of-the-art procedures. Although the benchmark b512a correspond to a problem with many features (512) and a low number of patterns (200), it is not a very difficult classification problem as our purpose is to check whether our methods are able to find the features that provide the best classification results. A more difficult classification problem is the b480a benchmark that corresponds to a BCI application with three classes, 480 features and 170 patterns. The unsupervised multiobjective approaches provide values of the Kappa index only overcome by the backward FS procedure with SVM that provides a value of 0.54, but consumes much more runtime.

Table 2 provides the averages of the hypervolume metric (hyperv.) for 2, 4, 6, and 8 processors, obtained after the experiments with the unsupervised classification alternative by using the different benchmarks. It also provides the standard deviation in percentage of the average hypervolume (std%), and the percentage of variation of the average hypervolume obtained by a parallel alternative with respect to the value obtained by the sequential algorithm (%dev). Values in bold in Table 2 correspond to cases where better qualities are obtained in the parallel implementation than in the sequential one. Any experiment with different parallelization alternative, benchmark, and number of processors has been repeated 15 times. As it can be seen, all the alternatives reach quality measures having less than 10 % of difference with respect to the average quality obtained by the sequential alternative, except in the case of b152 and ALT3, with 2 processors (12.8 % worse than the sequential alternative). Nevertheless, ALT1 allows better average qualities than sequential executions in case of 2 processors for all the benchmarks evaluated and in case of 4 processors for b152 and b512a, and MWE with 2, 4, 6 and 8 processors for b480a and with 2, 4, and 6 processors for b384.

**Table 2.** Performance comparison of MWE (master-worker evaluation), ALT1, ALT2 and ALT3 (parallel subpopulation evolution): % deviation with respect to sequential performance (% dev); average hypervolume achieved (hyperv); and ± percentage of standard deviation with respect to average hyperv.

| Bench. | N. Proc | MWE %dev | MWE hyperv | MWE ±std(%) | ALT1 %dev | ALT1 hyperv | ALT1 ±std(%) | ALT2 %dev | ALT2 hyperv | ALT2 ±std(%) | ALT3 %dev | ALT3 hyperv | ALT3 ±std(%) |
|---|---|---|---|---|---|---|---|---|---|---|---|---|---|
| b152 | 2 | -4.8 | 149.93 | 4.20 | **4.0** | **163.64** | 4.20 | -8.8 | 144.41 | 2.78 | -12.8 | 139.25 | 1.39 |
|  | 4 | -2.1 | 153.92 | 2.87 | **5.0** | **165.40** | 3.79 | -7.4 | 146.23 | 2.07 | -6.7 | 147.30 | 2.12 |
|  | 6 | -3.2 | 152.29 | 5.36 | -1.6 | 154.73 | 5.38 | -8.3 | 145.07 | 1.92 | -7.9 | 145.65 | 1.93 |
|  | 8 | -4.4 | 150.50 | 2.07 | -2.1 | 153.96 | 9.50 | -6.5 | 147.47 | 2.00 | -5.9 | 148.31 | 2.40 |
| b384 | 2 | **2.2** | **35.44** | 3.51 | **3.6** | **35.71** | 2.09 | -3.3 | 33.35 | 2.70 | -3.9 | 33.12 | 2.89 |
|  | 4 | **0.7** | **34.68** | 3.63 | -1.3 | 34.00 | 4.55 | -3.3 | 33.35 | 3.83 | -2.6 | 33.58 | 4.07 |
|  | 6 | **0.1** | **34.46** | 2.25 | -5.7 | 32.59 | 1.67 | -5.1 | 32.76 | 1.78 | -5.8 | 32.54 | 2.97 |
|  | 8 | -0.9 | 34.11 | 1.51 | -4.0 | 33.10 | 3.00 | -6.3 | 32.38 | 1.15 | -8.1 | 31.85 | 2.34 |
| b480a | 2 | **0.4** | **70.70** | 2.89 | **8.8** | **77.19** | 2.68 | -0.2 | 70.26 | 3.05 | -0.4 | 70.16 | 2.90 |
|  | 4 | **0.7** | **70.94** | 2.05 | -2.4 | 68.75 | 3.24 | -1.4 | 69.69 | 3.97 | -4.0 | 67.71 | 2.12 |
|  | 6 | **1.0** | **71.12** | 3.57 | -4.6 | 67.31 | 2.49 | -7.8 | 65.30 | 2.82 | -8.4 | 64.96 | 2.15 |
|  | 8 | **1.5** | **71.49** | 1.94 | -3.3 | 68.01 | 2.74 | -5.8 | 66.58 | 1.35 | -5.5 | 66.73 | 5.93 |
| b480b | 2 | -3.2 | 68.94 | 0.58 | **4.5** | **74.46** | 4.23 | -4.5 | 68.10 | 2.66 | -2.1 | 69.68 | 2.30 |
|  | 4 | -2.5 | 69.42 | 3.08 | -6.5 | 66.81 | 2.79 | -6.9 | 66.54 | 0.91 | -6.6 | 66.74 | 1.28 |
|  | 6 | -2.6 | 69.29 | 1.47 | -7.3 | 66.31 | 0.72 | -8.2 | 65.87 | 2.41 | -8.2 | 65.77 | 1.89 |
|  | 8 | -0.9 | 70.52 | 1.19 | -7.9 | 65.89 | 1.68 | -6.9 | 66.58 | 4.51 | -8.4 | 65.61 | 1.90 |
| b512a | 2 | -0.9 | 74.55 | 1.77 | **11.2** | **84.80** | 1.37 | -1.3 | 74.31 | 2.38 | -0.4 | 75.00 | 2.03 |
|  | 4 | -0.1 | 75.19 | 2.45 | **4.7** | **78.98** | 2.97 | **1.3** | **76.24** | 2.19 | **1.1** | **76.08** | 2.20 |
|  | 6 | -3.1 | 73.06 | 1.11 | -0.2 | 75.12 | 1.26 | -0.8 | 74.65 | 2.30 | **1.4** | **76.34** | 3.88 |
|  | 8 | -1.8 | 73.92 | 0.77 | -2.2 | 73.63 | 2.59 | **1.5** | **76.40** | 2.43 | -0.7 | 74.75 | 2.21 |
| b512b | 2 | -2.4 | 79.13 | 1.07 | **5.0** | **85.31** | 1.79 | -4.3 | 77.65 | 2.37 | -4.1 | 77.79 | 1.46 |
|  | 4 | -2.6 | 78.93 | 1.48 | -2.7 | 78.87 | 3.49 | -3.6 | 78.17 | 1.18 | -3.7 | 78.14 | 2.38 |
|  | 6 | -1.0 | 80.18 | 2.57 | -6.3 | 76.21 | 2.32 | -4.8 | 77.26 | 1.94 | -4.4 | 77.58 | 3.93 |
|  | 8 | -0.0 | 80.97 | 1.39 | -9.7 | 73.84 | 2.20 | -3.4 | 78.34 | 1.94 | -3.7 | 78.12 | 3.40 |

The statistical significance of the results has been analyzed by applying a Kolmogorov-Smirnoff test. The results of this test indicate that the quality measures do not follow normal distributions. Thus, we have applied a Kruskal-Wallis analysis instead of an ANOVA test. The results indicate that the differences on solution qualities between the sequential and the parallel alternatives MWE and ALT1 are not statistically significant (this was expected for MWE). Otherwise, the differences on solution qualities between the sequential procedure and ALT2 and ALT3 are statistically significant.

Figure 3 provides the curves that fit the results of efficiency (speedup divided by number of processors) obtained by the different parallel alternatives, MWE, ALT1, ALT2, and ALT3 for the six datasets (b152, b384, b480a, b480b, b512a and b512b. The models used to fit the data for each parallel alternative have been obtained from Eqs. (1) and (2). Figure 3 also includes the averages of the experimental efficiencies obtained with their corresponding error bars.

The specific values of the parameters in the models obtained from Eqs. (1) and (2) for the different parallel alternatives make it possible to explain the speedup and efficiency behaviors observed in each case. In MWE, the parallelization only contributes to divide, by the number of processors P, the time required to evaluate the fitness of the individuals in the population, and determines the linear behavior of the curve in this case. Nevertheless, the larger the number of processors, higher is the communication cost, and the speedup deviates from its linear behavior. In ALT1, ALT2 and ALT3, besides the term on $1/P$ in Eq. (2), the terms on $1/P^2$ and $1/P^r$ would imply a superlinear behavior. Nevertheless, in ALT1, these terms are lower than the term on $1/P$, and the combination/communication term proportional to P also determines efficiencies below one and a speedup that grows at a rate lower than P.

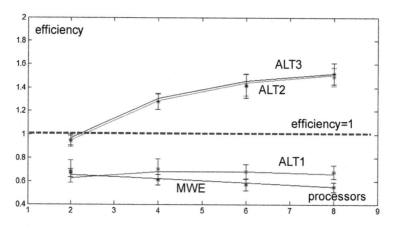

**Fig. 3.** Efficiency curves for MWE, ALT1, ALT2, and ALT3 that fit the experimental values.

Figure 3 also shows that ALT2 and ALT3 present similar behavior for the efficiency. In both cases, the terms on $1/P^2$ and $1/P^r$ of Eq. (2) are the highest ones, and determine a super-linear increase with P in the speedup. Moreover, the combination-communication costs in ALT2 and ALT3 are lower than the communication cost in MWE and the combination-communication cost in ALT1 as the amount of bits to communicate is lower in ALT2 and ALT3. Thus, the decrease in the speedup rate as the number of processors increases is slower. Despite a faster decrease in the speedups as the number of processor increases could be possible, the behaviors of ALT2 and ALT3 shown in Fig. 3 are sufficiently different to that of MWE and ALT1. It is worth mentioning that, as in the implementations of the parallel evolution of subpopulations corresponding to ALT1, ALT2, and ALT3, the worker processors communicate synchronously through the master processor, the questions related with the topology of communications and migration policies do not apply here. Precisely, to adapt the *Combine_&_Distribute* function to be implemented under island approaches could open interesting opportunities to take advantage of multicomputer architectures with a higher number of processors.

## 5 Conclusions

Several parallel implementations (ALT1, ALT2, and ALT3) of cooperative coevolutionary algorithms for multiobjective optimization based on NSGA-II have been proposed for problems with a large number of decision variables. These procedures have been applied to feature selection in unsupervised classification, where they have been evaluated by using both, synthetic benchmarks, and real benchmarks for EEG classification in BCI applications.

Some relevant conclusions regarding to cooperation among subpopulations can be drawn from the obtained experimental results. Parallel alternative ALT1, where the subpopulations cooperate through the option of union of solutions (Fig. 2a in Sect. 3) provides statistically similar results than the sequential procedure for all the benchmarks analyzed, although achieving lower speedups than alternatives ALT2 and ALT3. These two alternatives are based on the cooperation by crossing of solutions from different subpopulations (Fig. 2b). They reach superlinear speedups although, on average, the quality of the solutions they find are statistically worse than those obtained by the sequential procedure (a worsening of 10 %, at most). This way, it seems to be a trade-off among speedups and quality of the solutions found. The differences in the speedups and efficiencies observed in the parallel alternatives here presented can be explained by a simple model, described through Eqs. (1) and (2), that has been fitted to the experimental results obtained.

New definitions for the *Combine_&_Distribute* function, including new hybrid alternatives for cooperation and its implementation through an island model, and further experimentation with a bigger set of high-dimensional feature selection benchmarks on EEG classification and bioinformatics, are important issues for our future work. The comparison of the proposed parallel alternatives when they are implemented inside other multi-objective optimization algorithms (such as SPEA2, NSGA, SFGA2, etc.), and a deep study about the influence of the evolutionary parameters in the performance of the different parallel alternatives, also constitute important topics to consider.

**Aknowledgements.** This work has been funded by projects TIN2012-32039 (Spanish "Ministerio de Economía y Competitividad" and FEDER funds) and P11-TIC-7983 ("Junta de Andalucía").

## References

1. Durillo, J., Nebro, A., Coello Coello, C.A., García-Nieto, J., Luna, F., Alba, E.: A study of multiobjective metaheuristics when solving parameter scalable problems. IEEE Trans. Evol. Comput. **14**(4), 618–635 (2010)

2. Antonio, L.M., Coello Coello, C.A.: Use of cooperative coevolution for solving large scale multiobjective optimization problems. In: IEEE Congress on Ecolutionary Computation, pp. 2758–2765, 20–23 June 2013, Cancún, Mexico, vol. 43, no. 2, pp. 445–463 (2013)
3. Raudys, S.J., Jain, A.K.: Small sample size effects in statistical pattern recognition: recommendations for practitioners. IEEE Trans. Pattern Anal. Mach. Intell. 13(3), 252–264 (1991)
4. Saeys, Y., Inza, I., Larrañaga, P.: A review of feature selection techniques in bioinformatics. Bioinformatics 23(19), 2507–2517 (2007)
5. Acir, N., Güzeliş, C.: An application of support vector machine in bioinformatics: automated recognition of epileptiform patterns in EEG using SVM classifier designed by a perturbation method. In: Yakhno, T. (ed.) ADVIS 2004. LNCS, vol. 3261, pp. 462–471. Springer, Heidelberg (2004)
6. Sun, Z.: Parallel feature selection based on MapReduce. In: Wong, W.E., Zhu, T. (eds.) Computer Engineering and Networking. LNEE, vol. 277, pp. 299–306. Springer, Heidelberg (2012)
7. Zao, Z., Zhang, R., Cox, J., Duling, D., Sarle, W.: Massively parallel feature selection: an approach based on variance preservation. Mach. Learn. 92, 195–220 (2013)
8. de Souza, J.T., Matwin, S., Japkowitz, N.: Parallelizing feature selection. Algoritmica 45, 433–456 (2006)
9. Handl, J., Knowles, J.: Feature selection in unsupervised learning via multi-objective optimization. Int. J. Comput. Intell. Res. 2(3), 217–238 (2006)
10. Alba, E.: Parallel evolutionary algorithms can achieve super-linear performance. Inf. Process. Lett. 82(1), 7–13 (2002)
11. Potter, M., De Jong, K.A.: A cooperative coevolutionary approach to function optimization. In: Davidor, Y., Männer, R., Schwefel, H.-P. (eds.) PPSN 1994. LNCS, vol. 866, pp. 249–257. Springer, Heidelberg (1994)
12. Coello Coello, C.A., Lamont, G.B., Veldhuizen, D.A.: Evolutionary Algorithms for Solving Multi-objective Problems (Chapter 3), 2nd edn. Springer, New York (2007)
13. Mao, J., Hirasawa, K., Murata, J.: Genetic symbiosis algorithm for multi-objective optimization problem. In: Proceedings of the 2000 IEEE International Workshop on Robot and Human Interactive Communication, pp. 137–142 (2000)
14. Keerativuttitumrong, N., Chaiyaratana, N., Varavithya, V.: Multi-objective co-operative co-evolutionary genetic algorithm. In: Guervós, J.J.M., Adamidis, P.A., Beyer, H.-G., Fernández-Villacañas, J.-L., Schwefel, H.-P. (eds.) PPSN 2002. LNCS, vol. 2439, pp. 288–297. Springer, Heidelberg (2002)
15. Coello Coello, C.A., Sierra, M.R.: A coevolutionary multi-objective evolutionary algorithm. In: IEEE Congress on Evolutionary Computation, vol. 1, pp. 482–489 (2003)
16. Maneeratana, K., Boonlong, K., Chaiyaratana, N.: Multi-objective optimisation by co-operative co-evolution. In: Yao, X., Burke, E.K., Lozano, J.A., Smith, J., Merelo-Guervós, J. J., Bullinaria, J.A., Rowe, J.E., Tiňo, P., Kabán, A., Schwefel, H.-P. (eds.) PPSN 2004. LNCS, vol. 3242, pp. 772–781. Springer, Heidelberg (2004)
17. Iorio, A.W., Li, X.: A cooperative coevolutionary multiobjective algorithm using non-dominated sorting. In: Deb, K., Tari, Z. (eds.) GECCO 2004. LNCS, vol. 3102, pp. 537–548. Springer, Heidelberg (2004)
18. Tan, K.C., Yang, Y.J., Goh, C.K.: A distributed cooperative coevolutionary algorithm for multiobjective optimization. IEEE Trans. Evol. Comput. 10(5), 527–549 (2006)
19. Goh, C.-K., Tan, K.C.: A coevolutionary paradigm for dynamic multi-objective optimization. In: Goh, C.-K., Tan, K.C. (eds.) Evolutionary Multi-objective Optimization in Uncertain Environments. SCI, vol. 186, pp. 153–185. Springer, Heidelberg (2009)

20. Dorronsoro, B., Danoy, G., Nebro, A.J., Boubry, P.: Achieving super-linear performance in parallel multi-objective evolutionary algorithms by means of cooperative coevolution. Comput. Oper. Res. **40**, 1552–1563 (2013)
21. Kohonen, T.: Self-organizing Maps. Springer, Heidelberg (2001)
22. Kimovski, D., Ortega, J., Ortiz, A., Baños, R.: Feature selection in high-dimensional EEG data by parallel multi-objective optimization. In: Proceedings of the IEEE Cluster, Madrid, pp. 314–322 (2014)
23. https://sites.google.com/site/projectbci/
24. Deb, K., Agrawal, S., Pratab, A., Meyarivan, T.: A fast elitist non-dominated sorting genetic algorithms for multi-objective optimisation: NSGA-II. In: Deb, K., Rudolph, G., Lutton, E., Merelo, J.J., Schoenauer, M., Schwefel, H.-P., Yao, X. (eds.) PPSN 2000. LNCS, vol. 1917, pp. 849–858. Springer, Heidelberg (2000)
25. Theodoridis, S., Koutroumbas, K.: Pattern Recognition. Academic Press, New York (2009)
26. Vapnik, V.N.: Statistical Learning Theory. Wiley-Interscience, New York (1998)
27. Cohen, J.: A coefficient of agreement for nominal scales. Educ. Psychol. Meas. **20**, 37–46 (1960)

# Automatic Evolution of Parallel Sorting Programs on Multi-cores

Gopinath Chennupati$^{(\boxtimes)}$, R. Muhammad Atif Azad, and Conor Ryan

Bio-Computing and Developmental Systems Group,
Computer Science and Information Systems Department,
University of Limerick, Limerick, Ireland
{gopinath.chennupati,atif.azad,conor.ryan}@ul.ie

**Abstract.** Sorting algorithms that offer the potential for data-parallel execution on parallel architectures are an excellent tool for the current generation of multi-core processors that often require skilled parallelization knowledge to fully realize the potential of the hardware.

We propose to automate the evolution of *natively* parallel programs using the Grammatical Evolution (GE) approach to utilise the computational potential of multi-cores. The proposed system, *Multi-core Grammatical Evolution for Parallel Sorting* (MCGE-PS), applies GE mapping along with explicit OpenMP `#pragma` compiler directives to automatically evolve data-level parallel iterative sorting algorithms. MCGE-PS is assessed on the generation of four non-recursive sorting programs in C. We show that it generated programs that can solve the problem that are also parallel. On a high performance Intel processor, MCGE-PS significantly reduced the execution time of the evolved programs for all the benchmark problems.

**Keywords:** Grammatical evolution · Automatic parallelization · Recursion · Program synthesis · OpenMP · Evolutionary parallelization

## 1 Introduction

Moore's law has remained true with the doubling of number of processing elements on integrated chips for every eighteen months. Especially in the industrial terms, the addition of more transistors means enabling more processing power, more importantly, an increase in the number of cores. As a result, the availability of dual and quad cores has been common while the advent of eight and, sixteen (or even more) cores on personal computers (PCs) is inevitable. However, high performance machines such as Intel Polaris, picoChip PC200 contain 80 and 200+ cores, respectively. While they offer great performance scale up, it depends on how the programs that are scheduled to execute are implemented.

The difficulty of delivering on this has been described as the *third software crisis* [4], that is, the actual realised speed of the processors is limited by the software running on them. This is caused by many factors, including in difficulty for serially trained programmers to think and write in a parallel way, barriers

© Springer International Publishing Switzerland 2015
A.M. Mora and G. Squillero (Eds.): EvoApplications 2015, LNCS 9028, pp. 706–717, 2015.
DOI: 10.1007/978-3-319-16549-3_57

in code restructuring, and the difficulty in obtaining and proving functional equivalence of serial and parallel programs. Potentially successful attempts to address these concerns include the invention of automatic data parallelizers, parallel compilers, and novel programming languages such as Go, Cilk, IPython, etc. However, most of these attempts are limited by their complexity and the difficulty for programmers to adequately adopt a parallel mind set.

Evolutionary Computation is a natural tool to combat these issues, as it can automate much of the processes. In this paper, we offer an evolutionary technique in order to produce natively parallel programs that can exploit the computational power of multi-core machines along with the production of a qualitative solution for a problem at hand.

We do this by combining Grammatical Evolution (GE) and OpenMP (open multi-processing) API [15] to automatically evolve complete parallel programs. We manifest this as *GE + Multi-Cores = Automatic Parallel Programming*, a step towards automatic generation of natively parallel programs, the spiritual successor to *Genetic Programming (GP) + Data Structures = Automatic Programming!* [10].

Our approach avoids the need to think in parallel by using standard GE techniques to evolve parallel code. We evaluate it on 4 iterative sorting algorithms, to the best of our knowledge, it is the first attempt to automatically generate a natively parallel sort.

The rest of the paper is managed as follows: Sect. 2 introduces the background knowledge on sorting and parallel code generation; Sect. 3 details the proposed approach; Sect. 4 presents the experimental results; and finally, Sect. 5 concludes and outlines future directions.

## 2    Background

Sorting reorganizes a sequence in a logical (ascending/descending) order. It is crucial in scientific and commercial applications that include weather prediction, finance, internet, etc. It must be quick, and is suitable for parallelization.

For example, the *Quicksort* algorithm operates on different parts of a sequence by partitioning and fixing a *pivot* element that orders the sequence. To that end, the challenge then in this paper is to automatically exploit that parallelism using an artificial intelligence technique, GE. However, first we review the evolution of sorting algorithms in Sect. 2.1 then, the generation of parallel programs in Sect. 2.2.

### 2.1    Evolutionary Techniques for Sorting

Although we aim to generate parallel code for non-recursive sorting, in this section, we review both recursive and non-recursive attempts regardless of parallelization. Hillis [7] applied simulated evolution on sorting networks through the co-evolution of test sequences. It effectively improved the performance and evolved a minimal 16-input network.

O'Reilly and Oppacher [16] attempted to evolve an iterative sorting using GP and failed. They used variable decrementing, element indexing, loops as primitive functions while the array size, constant 1 and, loop variables as terminals. However, they [17] succeeded with the use of a swapping primitive function.

In conjunction with [16], Kinnear [8,9] also generated a bubble sort except with a minor change in swap, where the disordered adjacent elements were swapped, similar to the compare operator [7] used in sorting networks. The fitness measure was sequence disorder that also discouraged code growth. Spector et al., [21], evolved recursive sorting with PushGP system that also used swapping, indexed comparisons and the list size.

Abbott [1] studied application of Object Oriented Genetic Programming (OOGP) for an integer sorting in Java. It included both the Java's built-in and the user defined methods that were able to generate both insertion and bubble sort. However, it was unclear on the evolution of bubble sort.

Agapitos and Lucas [2,3] also applied OOGP to evolve recursive sorting in Java. List processing methods and a higher order primitive function (*filter*) were used in [2], where different variations in the fitness function were analysed. Later, evolution of modular recursive sorting [3] showed that the evolutionary method generated better programs when compared against undirected random search.

A recent attempt by O'Neil et al., [14] presented an application of GE for program synthesis through the evolution of bubble sort in Python, where a series of loops, nested loops with swapping succeeded to solve integer sorting.

## 2.2 Evolutionary Parallel Code Generation

Automatic parallel code generation can broadly be classified into two classes: *auto-parallelization of serial code* and *generation of natively parallel code*. The former relies highly on the existence of a *working program* to identify the parallelizable parts, while the latter addresses two problems, that of generating a working program which is also parallel.

Evolutionary computation has a limited repertoire of attempts in both these categories. In *auto-parallelization*, Walsh and Ryan used GP in *PARAGEN-I* [19, Chapter-5] to automatically map the serial programs onto multiprocessors by neglecting the dependency analysis, however, it was challenged by complex loop structures. Later, *PARAGEN-II* [19, Chapter-7] evolved transformations in two modes: *ATOM* and *LOOP*, where, the former dealt with simple instructions while, the latter evolved loop sequences. Thereafter, Ryan and Ivan [20] extended *PARAGEN-II* to merge independent tasks of multiple loops into one loop.

Genetic algorithms (GA) were also used for auto-parallelization, where, Nisbet [13] presented Genetic Algorithm Parallelization System (GAPS) to choose optimal order of transformations. Then, Williams in *REVOLVER* [23] applied GAs using two representations (*gene-transformation, gene-statement*) for the evolution of both the program structures and transformations.

On the other hand, in native parallel code generation, a relatively relevant attempt by Trenaman [22] achieved concurrent execution of autonomous agents in the design of controllers in virtual world using a multi-tree GP. In an other attempt, Poli [18] evolved higher degree parallel programs using parallel distributed GP and simulated in virtual environment.

With the abundance of multi-core machines, evolution of parallel code is crucial for improving the performance. In relation to that Chennupati et al., [5] introduced *Multi-Core Grammatical Evolution* (MCGE) by evolving data parallel regression programs. To that end, the proposed work in this paper, multi-core grammatical evolution for parallel sorting, *MCGE-PS* elaborates on MCGE (termed as MCGE-I) in advancing multi-core computing.

# 3    Multi-core Grammatical Evolution (MCGE)

A multi-core processors share the memory among the available cores. A simple *fork/join* parallelization helps to exploit the parallelism. For that, we use OpenMP in this paper, described in next section.

## 3.1    OpenMP

The OpenMP API [15] is a shared memory parallel programming paradigm. It offers compiler directives, run time library routines and, environment variables in Fortran and C/C++ that implicitly schedules the multi-threaded execution on multi-cores, where each core is a process. It consists of *pragmatic information (pragma)* that directs the compiler to perform parallelization.

In C/C++, an OpenMP pragma syntax is written as follows:

*#pragma omp directive_name [clause[[,]clause]...] {< statement block >}*

where, a *directive_name* contains one of the constructs: *parallel, parallel sections* and, *parallel for* that is followed by a clause *private(variable), shared(variable)* that makes a variable private and/or shared to the thread. As the pragmas are uncharacteristic to basic C, the compiler ignores a pragma when it fails to recognize and runs in serial. A complete description of OpenMP is in [15].

## 3.2    MCGE-PS

MCGE-PS is an extension to MCGE-I and similarly employs data parallelism to improve performance. The key difference is the use of richer grammars with MCGE-PS that include multiple OpenMP pragmas as well as iterative functions (include nested loops, similar to [14]); these additions dramatically improve the generalizability of the system, and, although the search space increases as a result, we show that the system is capable of producing high quality results.

Note that the MCGE-PS evolution follows that of the standard GE, except for the fact that the grammars are designed to include the pragmatic information. As with PARAGEN-I [19], MCGE-PS also omits the dependency analysis, alternatively, it resolves dependencies through the selection of pragmas that suite the program correctness. Along with the parallelism and correctness, it is important to solve the problem, for that, the design of the MCGE-PS grammars is non-trivial, hence, we describe it on an example problem, *Quicksort.*

**Design of Quicksort Grammar:** We discuss the design of grammars in terms of parallelism exploitation that is followed by the problem specific knowledge. To achieve explicit parallelism pragmas are included in the following manner.

$\langle program \rangle$        ::= $\langle omppragma \rangle$ $\langle private \rangle$ $\langle shared \rangle$ $\langle code \rangle$

$\langle omppragma \rangle$        ::= #pragma omp parallel for
             |   #pragma omp parallel
             |   #pragma omp parallel sections

$\langle shared \rangle$        ::= shared($\langle var \rangle$) '{' $\langle newline \rangle$

$\langle private \rangle$        ::= private($\langle index \rangle$)

$\langle var \rangle$        ::= A | S

$\langle index \rangle$        ::= i | j | top | start | last | pivot

In the above grammar segment, the non-terminal symbol $< omppragma >$ contains different alternatives of pragmas, of which GE selects an appropriate choice that executes the code it encircles in parallel. The pragmas *parallel for* and *parallel* offer efficient parallelism, but, the selection of the directive is up to the evolution. The selected pragmas offer different variants of parallelism, by the manner in which they operate the threads on shared and private variables, where the non-terminals $< shared >$ and $< private >$ choose them respectively.

In this case, the shared variables: input array ($A$) contains the sequence of elements, the auxiliary stack ($S$) is used to fix the order of the elements. Similarly, the non-terminal $< index >$ represents the thread-private variable, an index of $A$ or $S$. For example, the input array ($A$) is shared among the OpenMP processes to allow simultaneous execution while its indices are kept private to ensure correctness in computations. That way, the same program operates on multiple data items producing an SPMD characteristic parallel sorting.

Thereafter, the *Quicksort* problem specific grammars include nested loops. The following grammar segment presents the nested loops.

$\langle code \rangle$        ::= $\langle forstack \rangle$ $\langle omppragma \rangle$ $\langle private \rangle$ $\langle shared \rangle$ $\langle partition \rangle$

$\langle forstack \rangle$        ::= for (; top >= 0; ) '{' $\langle newline \rangle$ $\langle forline \rangle$ $\langle newline \rangle$

$\langle forline \rangle$        ::= $\langle forsassign \rangle$; $\langle newline \rangle$ $\langle forsassign \rangle$; $\langle newline \rangle$ $\langle index \rangle$
             = abs($\langle index \rangle$ $\langle bop \rangle$ $\langle const \rangle$));

$\langle forsassign \rangle$        ::= $\langle index \rangle$ = $\langle var \rangle$[$\langle index \rangle$ $\langle pushpop \rangle$]

$\langle partition \rangle$        ::= for(j = start; j <= last-1; j++) '{' $\langle newline \rangle$ $\langle part \rangle$

We keep the loop structures and initializations systematic so as to prevent both infinite loops and loop entry failures. The non-terminal $< forstack >$ is the outer loop that pops the stack till it becomes empty while the non-terminal $< partition >$ represents the inner loop that partitions the array of elements.

The non-terminal $< code >$ represents the parallelization pragmas on inner loop. Note that in *Quick sort*, partition $(< partition >)$ fixes a pivotal element so that the elements to the left are smaller and to the right are bigger than the pivot.

The following grammar segment represents the partition functionality.

⟨*part*⟩ ::= ⟨*partcond*⟩ ⟨*newline*⟩ '}' ⟨*swap*⟩ ⟨*pivotele*⟩

⟨*partcond*⟩ ::= if( ⟨*var*⟩[⟨*index*⟩] ⟨*lop*⟩ ⟨*var*⟩[⟨*index*⟩] ) '{' ⟨*newline*⟩ ⟨*index*⟩++; ⟨*newline*⟩ ⟨*swap*⟩'}'

⟨*pivotele*⟩ ::= ⟨*index*⟩ = ⟨*absval*⟩; ⟨*newline*⟩ ⟨*stackcond*⟩ ⟨*newline*⟩ ⟨*stackcond*⟩ '}'

⟨*stackcond*⟩ ::= if(⟨*pivotcond*⟩) '{' ⟨*newline*⟩ ⟨*stackpush*⟩; ⟨*newline*⟩ ⟨*stackpush*⟩; ⟨*newline*⟩ '}'

⟨*pivotcond*⟩ ::= ⟨*absval*⟩ ⟨*lop*⟩ ⟨*index*⟩

⟨*stackpush*⟩ ::= ⟨*var*⟩[⟨*pushpop*⟩⟨*index*⟩] = ⟨*absval*⟩

⟨*absval*⟩ ::= abs(⟨*index*⟩ ⟨*bop*⟩ ⟨*const*⟩)

The non-terminals $< partcond >$ and $< partitionele >$ show the partition functionality and, fixing the pivot element respectively. The prime reasons to include such a problem specific information is due to the lessons learnt from literature. That is, for example, evolution of a simple bubble sort included the adjacent element *swap* [9] (a problem specific information) observing the failed attempts in [16]. Similarly, the attempts in [14] with the evolution of both sequential and nested loops also failed before the inclusion of *swap*, again a problem specific information. Our preliminary investigations (not reported here because of space restrictions) also showed a similar behaviour without partitioning. Moreover, in this paper the focus is to evolve a *parallel sort* that solves the problem rather than exploring the search space of the problem hence, the consideration of such a problem specific knowledge.

Similarly, we include the swap operation in the following manner.

⟨*swap*⟩ ::= temp = ⟨*aelement*⟩; ⟨*newline*⟩ ⟨*aelement*⟩ = ⟨*aelement*⟩; ⟨*newline*⟩ ⟨*aelement*⟩=temp; ⟨*newline*⟩

⟨*aelement*⟩ ::= A[abs(⟨*index*⟩ ⟨*bop*⟩ ⟨*const*⟩)]

⟨*bop*⟩ ::= + | -

⟨*lop*⟩ ::= >= | <= | < | >

⟨*const*⟩ ::= 0 | 1 | 2 | 3 | 4 | 5 | 6 | 7 | 8 | 9

⟨*pushpop*⟩ ::= ++ | −−

⟨*newline*⟩ ::= \n

The non-terminal $< swap >$ performs the exchange of elements similar to [9]. The non-terminal $< alement >$ refers to an absolute index of an array that is to prevent accessing the out of index locations. The grammars also include the search space of constants ($< const >$) in the range 0 ... 9, the logical and binary operations are shown in $< lop >$ and, $< bop >$ respectively. The non-terminal $< pushpop >$[1] represents the push and pop operations over the auxiliary stack.

Note that an inappropriate choice of the pragma and/or the OpenMP variables produces a badly fit individual. Also note that to transform the genotypes to *natively parallel programs* the GE mapping needs no alterations in its basic functionality.

**Generality of the Grammars:** Converting the outer loop (iterate over a stack) to iterate over the input array and excluding the partition functionality from *Quicksort* grammars makes it general enough for other sorting programs. In fact, the grammars then resemble the program synthesis grammars in [14], except that the grammars in this paper are in C as opposed to those written in Python. Also note that, in contrast to [14], we restrict the grammars from the use of an output array, however, we use an auxiliary stack ($S$) only for *Quicksort*.

MCGE-PS expresses programs in C and, it is possible to generalize to other programming environments that support the OpenMP like fork/join parallelism.

### 3.3   Other MCGE Evaluated Grammars

A total of four grammars were used (including Quicksort), which are summarized in Table 1. In terms of overlap, the grammars are relatively similar to each other, with approximately 90 % code except for Quicksort. It uses slightly more local variables (7) compared to that of the other problems as it contains a stack and partition that use 4 extra local variables (top, start, last, pivot) specified in the non-terminal $< index >$.

The grammars contain a mixture of structures that include: loops, nesting, loops over arrays, branching, use of temporary variables, arrays, shared and/or private (OpenMP specific) variables that prescribe an interesting context for data parallelism. It is also important to measure the scalability of our approach on industrial-scale problems. That in turn answers the scalability of the fundamental search engine, GE, a matter of future investigation.

## 4   Experiments

The experimental settings of GE include a population of 500 individuals that are initialized using Sensible Initialization (similar to ramped half-and-half technique in GP) with a grow probability of 0.5 where, the minimum derivation tree depth

---

[1] Note that the same non-terminal is used for increment/decrement of a Rank in Rank sort algorithm.

**Table 1.** The problem set considered, input type and the local variables (LV).

| # | Problem | Description | Input | LV |
|---|---------|-------------|-------|-----|
| 1 | Bubble sort | Loops through an array of elements compares the adjacent elements and orders (swaps) it in ascending order | int [ ], int | 3 |
| 2 | Quick sort | Partitions an array over a pivot then, rearranges in the order of the smaller to the left and the bigger to right | int [ ], int, int | 7 |
| 3 | Odd-Even sort | Operates in two phases, Odd numbered processes exchange with their right, even numbered processes with the right | int[ ], int | 2 |
| 4 | Rank sort | Orders the array with the rank (number of elements less than the selected) of an element | int [ ], int | 2 |

is 9, and the maximum[2] is 25. We employ one-point crossover (0.9 probability), a point mutation (0.01 probability per gene) with a steady state replacement strategy and, wrapping is disabled. An evolutionary cycle of 100 generations is repeated for 50 runs with the same set of random number generating seeds in each setup. The input array to the problem is randomly generated with 100 integers in the range $(0, 100)$.

We investigate two different approaches that compare in terms of fitness of the evolved programs. To this end, the fitness is maximized by first computing the disordered pairs of the evolved sort sequence and then normalized it in between 0 and 1.

Of the two approaches, the former evolves the programs using the grammars described in Sect. 3.2 and referred to as *const-10* hereafter, while the latter reduces the constants $(< const >)$ search space from $(0, \ldots, 9)$ to just $(0, 1)$ and referred to as *const-limit* hereafter.

We use an Intel (R) Xeon (R) CPU E7-4820 (16 cores) that has 2 GHz processor speed with 18 MB of L3 shared cache and a 64-bit Debian Linux operating system. We use libGE [12], a C++ implementation of GE. The evolved parallel programs are compiled using GNU GCC (– version 4.4.5) with *-fopenmp* option and are executed on multiple cores of the CPU.

### 4.1 Experimental Results

In the results, we report two key statistics: the mean best fitness and the mean best execution time of the MCGE-PS evolved parallel programs.

**Fitness:** The mean best fitness is the average fitness over 50 runs of the best evolved programs at the respective generation for 100 generations.

---

[2] Note that leaving the maximum depth to the default value (10) results in an error as the derivation tree depth of the grammars include a larger value than the default.

Figure 1 presents a comparative analysis of the mean best fitness results of both the variations on all the 4 experimental problems. On all the four problems, a Student's *t-test* shows significant difference in the mean best fitness at a significance level of $\alpha = 0.05$, where the *const-limit* variation exhibits an improvement in the performance.

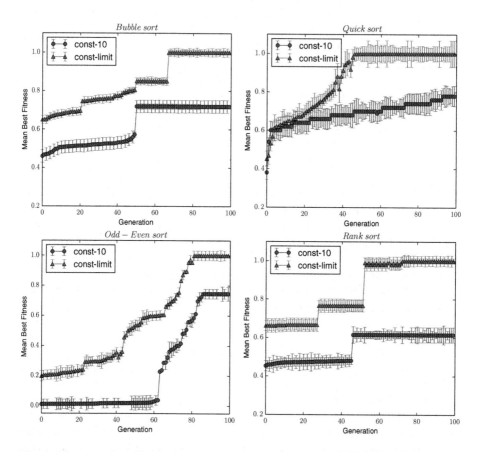

**Fig. 1.** The mean best fitness (with standard deviation) of MCGE-PS evolved parallel programs averaged across 50 runs of 100 generations, where the graphs represent the results of *const-10, const-limit* on the 4 experimental problems.

However, the *const-10* case has failed to sort the sequence in all the four problems. Alternatively, the reduction of constant space (*const-limit*) has successfully solved all the problems in all the runs. An obvious reason for this is because of the limited $< const >$ search space, which with the reduction in *const-limit* helped to generate a successful solution. The results indicate that the problems are not easy to solve. For example, *Quicksort* problem even with *const-limit* requires 47 generations to produce optimal solution. Although syntactically ideal solution is generated early, finding an optimal solution takes longer.

**Execution Time:** The purpose of the evolved parallel programs is to exploit the performance boost offered by multi-core architectures. Therefore we report the *mean best execution time* of the evolved programs. It is the total execution time taken by the best of generation programs within a run; the mean (average across 50 runs) of this time is reported in this paper. In general, measuring the exact execution time of a program is difficult as system performance is impacted by many factors, such as the nature of the shared resources (i.e. the manner in which they are scheduled, whether or not they are parallel, etc.) as well as on the number of users sharing them, the parallelism offered by the processors. We neglect all the factors except the parallelism exerted. Fortunately, the OpenMP timer utility (*omp_get_wtime()*) can be used to abstract virtually all that information away, and thus report only on the actual execution time.

**Table 2.** Mean best execution time (in secs) (mean [standard deviation]) of four problems averaged across 50 runs of MCGE-PS for 100 generations each.

| Problem | Cores | | | | |
|---|---|---|---|---|---|
| | 1 | 2 | 4 | 8 | 16 |
| 1 | 3483.12 [11.45] | 3334.08 [11.51] | 985.88[14.24] | 568.22 [13.18] | 297.01 [9.33] |
| 2 | 4366.24 [21.17] | 4543.43 [18.12] | 1333.52 [19.17] | 668.99 [20.37] | 389.64 [15.21] |
| 3 | 3197.36 [24.31] | 2396.46 [22.11] | 1146.21 [26.43] | 435.23 [26.29] | 257.25 [23.25] |
| 4 | 3193.12 [25.47] | 2058.35 [21.33] | 960.97 [27.35] | 481.91 [31.11] | 245.08 [29.42] |

Table 2 shows the mean best execution time of the evolved parallel programs of MCGE-PS that are compared with a varying number of cores from 2 to 16 on an Intel Xeon multi-core processor. The results demonstrate that the execution time has been reduced significantly with an increase in the number of processor cores that is proved with a t-test at a significance level of $\alpha = 0.05$. However, the evolved programs that contain *parallel sections* directive reported an incorrect solution while the programs that contain *parallel* or *parallel for* produce correct results. It is due to the fact that the programs with the former pragma creates a parallel region with multiple threads where, the work sharing construct (*sections*) tries to identify independently executable functions as is applicable only to achieve functional parallelism. Hence, the programs with this choice are treated as the worst fit individuals. While the programs with the latter pragmas create multiple threads (*parallel*) and identifies an iterative work-sharing construct (*for*) that executes the assigned task in parallel. In this case, the work in the *for* loop is scheduled across all the available cores that ensures optimization in performance.

Also note that an insignificant result was recorded when the programs were scheduled to execute on 2 cores (Table 2). It is due the extra overhead added through grammars [6] as well as the OpenMP scheduling issues, and code growth. With this it is important to analyse these effects on the efficiency of the evolved programs so does the computational complexity and, from that different performance tuning alternatives, a matter of future research.

## 5   Conclusions

This paper presented a novel technique for the evolution of natively parallel iterative sorting algorithms on multi-core architectures that obviates the need for the dependency analysis in native parallel code generation. The results demonstrated a comparative analysis of two different variations that measured the quality of the evolved solutions. While we also presented a scale-up in the performance of evolved programs on a high performance multi-core (Intel Xeon) machine.

The third software crisis is a massive opportunity for Evolutionary Computation. The complexity of modern software requires the use of these tools, and this work is an important step in that direction. This work has a rich prospectus for extension in many directions: We propose to analyse the impact of parallel program generation on code growth that depict the computational overhead of threads (similar to [6]). Thereafter, we plan to analyse the computational complexity of the evolved parallel programs (similar to [2]). Furthermore, we aim to extend it to interpreted languages (similar to [11]) so as to alleviate the hindrance of compilation in order to reduce the evolutionary simulations that rely on external system calls. Finally, we recommend to further optimize by promoting maximum parallelism in the evolved programs.

## References

1. Abbott, R., Parviz, J.G.B.: Guided genetic programming. In: Arabnia, H.R., Kozerenko, E.B. (eds.) Proceedings of the International Conference on Machine Learning; Models, Technologies and Applications, pp. 28–34. CSREA Press (2003)
2. Agapitos, A., Lucas, S.M.: Evolving efficient recursive sorting algorithms. In: IEEE Congress on Evolutionary Computation, pp. 2677–2684. IEEE (2006)
3. Agapitos, A., Lucas, S.: Evolving modular recursive sorting algorithms. In: Ebner, M., O'Neill, M., Ekárt, A., Vanneschi, L., Esparcia-Alcázar, A.I. (eds.) EuroGP 2007. LNCS, vol. 4445, pp. 301–310. Springer, Heidelberg (2007)
4. Amarasinghe, S.: (How) can programmers conquer the multicore menace? In: Proceedings of the International Conference on Parallel Architectures and Compilation Techniques, pp. 133–133. ACM (2008)
5. Chennupati, G., Azad, R.M.A., Ryan, C.: Multi-core GE: automatic evolution of CPU based multi-core parallel programs. In: Proceedings of the Genetic and Evolutionary Computation Conference Companion, pp. 1041–1044. ACM (2014)
6. Chennupati, G., Fitzgerald, J., Ryan, C.: On the efficiency of multi-core grammatical evolution (MCGE) evolving multi-core parallel programs. In: Proceedings of the Sixth World Congress on Nature and Biologically Inspired Computing (NaBIC), pp. 238–243. IEEE (2014)
7. Hillis, W.D.: Co-evolving parasites improve simulated evolution as an optimization procedure. Physica D: Nonlinear Phenom. **42**(1), 228–234 (1990)

8. Kinnear Jr., K.E.: Evolving a sort: lessons in genetic programming. In: IEEE International Conference on Neural Networks, pp. 881–888. IEEE (1993)
9. Kinnear Jr., K.E.: Generality and difficulty in genetic programming: evolving a sort. In: Forrest, S. (ed.) Proceedings of the 5th International Conference on Genetic Algorithms, pp. 287–294. Morgan Kaufmann, Urbana-Champaign, IL, USA (1993)
10. Langdon, W.B.: Genetic Programming and Data Structures: Genetic Programming + Data Structures = Automatic Programming! Kluwer Academic Publishers. Norwell, MA, USA (1998)
11. Langdon, W.B., Banzhaf, W.: A SIMD interpreter for genetic programming on GPU graphics cards. In: O'Neill, M., Vanneschi, L., Gustafson, S., Esparcia Alcázar, A.I., De Falco, I., Della Cioppa, A., Tarantino, E. (eds.) EuroGP 2008. LNCS, vol. 4971, pp. 73–85. Springer, Heidelberg (2008)
12. Nicolau, M., Slattery, D.: libge - grammatical evolution library (2006). http://bds.ul.ie/libGE/index.html
13. Nisbet, A.: GAPS: a compiler framework for genetic algorithm (GA) optimised parallelisation. In: Sloot, P., Bubak, M., Hertzberger, B. (eds.) High-Performance Computing and Networking. LNCS, vol. 1401, pp. 987–989. Springer, Heidelberg (1998)
14. O'Neill, M., Nicolau, M., Agapitos, A.: Experiments in program synthesis with grammatical evolution: a focus on integer sorting. In: IEEE Congress on Evolutionary Computation, pp. 1504–1511. IEEE (2014)
15. OpenMP Architecture Review Board: OpenMP application program interface version 3.0 (2008). http://www.openmp.org/mp-documents/spec30.pdf
16. O'Reilly, U.M., Oppacher, F.: An experimental perspective on genetic programming. In: Manner, R., Manderick, B. (eds.) Parallel Problem Solving From Nature 2, pp. 331–340. Elsevier Science, Brussels (1992)
17. O'Reilly, U.M., Oppacher, F.: A comparative analysis of genetic programming. In: Angeline, P.J., Kinnear Jr., K.E. (eds.) Advances in Genetic Programming, vol. 2. MIT Press, Cambridge (1996)
18. Poli, R.: Evolution of graph-like programs with parallel distributed genetic programming. In: Proceedings of the International Conference on Genetic Algorithms, pp. 346–353 (1997)
19. Ryan, C.: Automatic Re-engineering of Software Using Genetic Programming. Genetic Programming. Springer, Heidelberg (1999)
20. Ryan, C., Ivan, L.: Automatic parallelization of arbitrary programs. In: Langdon, W.B., Fogarty, T.C., Nordin, P., Poli, R. (eds.) EuroGP 1999. LNCS, vol. 1598, pp. 244–254. Springer, Heidelberg (1999)
21. Spector, L., Klein, J., Keijzer, M.: The push3 execution stack and the evolution of control. In: Proceedings of the Genetic and Evolutionary Computation Conference, pp. 1689–1696. ACM, New York (2005)
22. Trenaman, A.: Concurrent genetic programming, tartarus and dancing agents. In: Langdon, W.B., Fogarty, T.C., Nordin, P., Poli, R. (eds.) EuroGP 1999. LNCS, vol. 1598, pp. 270–282. Springer, Heidelberg (1999)
23. Williams, K.P.: Evolutionary algorithms for automatic parallelization. Ph.D. thesis, University of Reading (1998)

# EvoRISK

# Heuristics for the Design of Safe Humanitarian Aid Distribution Itineraries

José M. Ferrer[1]([⊠]), M. Teresa Ortuño[2], Gregorio Tirado[2],
and Begoña Vitoriano[2]

[1] Sección Departamental de Estadística e Investigación Operativa,
Facultad de Medicina, Universidad Complutense de Madrid,
Plaza de Ramón y Cajal, 28040 Madrid, Spain
jmferrer@pdi.ucm.es
[2] Departamento de Estadística e Investigación Operativa,
Facultad de Matemáticas, Universidad Complutense de Madrid,
Plaza de Ramón y Cajal, 28040 Madrid, Spain
{tortuno,gregoriotd,bvitoriano}@mat.ucm.es

**Abstract.** After a disaster strikes, one of the main activities to be developed from a logistics point of view is the design of humanitarian aid distribution plans. In this work the problem of designing safe feasible itineraries for last-mile distribution under the risk of being assaulted, as well as assuring the equity of the distribution, is addressed. The task of simply finding feasible solutions for this problem is highly complex. In this paper we present a constructive randomized heuristic to generate a variety of solutions within a small computational time, and we also provide some ideas of how to modify this constructive algorithm in order to use it within a metaheuristic framework.

**Keywords:** Humanitarian logistics · Heuristics · Distribution planning

## 1 Introduction

Nowadays, disasters are often seen as the consequence of inappropriately managed risk, being these risks the product of hazards and vulnerability. In this way, developing countries, due to their greater vulnerability, suffer the greatest costs when a disaster occurs.

Once a disaster strikes a country, the distribution of humanitarian aid to a population affected is one of the most fundamental operations in what is nowadays called "Humanitarian Logistics", defined as the process of planning, implementing and controlling the efficient, cost-effective flow and storage of goods and materials as well as related information, from the point of origin to the point of consumption, for the purpose of meeting the end beneficiaries requirements and alleviate the suffering of vulnerable people, [the Humanitarian Logistics Conference, 2004 (Fritz Institute)]. In the last decade it has been an increasing interest in the study of this field, pointing out the similarities and differences between

© Springer International Publishing Switzerland 2015
A.M. Mora and G. Squillero (Eds.): EvoApplications 2015, LNCS 9028, pp. 721–731, 2015.
DOI: 10.1007/978-3-319-16549-3_58

humanitarian and business logistics [1] and developing new models valid for the special characteristics of this kind of problems. See [7] for a survey on Decision Aid Models and Systems for Humanitarian Logistics, which can give an idea of the last developments in the field.

As stated by several authors (see [5,6,8], among others), traditional logistic objectives, such as minimizing operation cost, are not the most relevant ones in humanitarian operations. Other factors, such as time of operation, or the design of safe and equitable distribution plans, come to the front, and new models and algorithms are needed to cope with these special features.

## 2   Problem Description

The problem addressed in this work concerns last-mile distribution in disaster relief operations, which is the final stage of a humanitarian relief chain. It refers to delivery of goods from local distribution centers to the people in need. In particular, the problem addressed consists of designing routes for vehicles among nodes that have an available quantity of goods or have a demand of those goods, choosing the most suitable types of vehicles and determining the flow of the aid. More specifically, the problem addressed is described through the following elements:

1. Transportation Network. Nodes representing the locations of pick-up, delivery or connection, and main links characterized by distance and average velocity.
2. Goods. Information about the amount of aid available or required at each node.
3. Vehicles. Several types are considered, characterized by capacity, average velocity, variable and fixed costs and availability in each node of the network. Fixed costs represent the cost of moving the vehicle one unit of length, while variable costs represent the cost of transporting one unit of aid through one unit of length, for each type of vehicle.
4. Operation elements. They include the global quantity to be distributed in the operation and the budget available, as well as the knowledge about the state of the roads or the safety of each zone.

The problem consists of designing the vehicle routes so that a fixed quantity of humanitarian aid is distributed, meeting the following set of conditions:

1. All nodes can be used for transshipment of goods among vehicles.
2. Availability of connections can be unknown when planning. The disaster may have blocked or destroyed some roads, but that information is usually not fully available. The design of routes will take this fact into account by trying to choose connections with greater probability of being available.
3. Under extreme conditions, as the ones arising after a disaster in highly vulnerable places, the vehicles could be assaulted during the mission. Assuming that a single vehicle has greater probability of being assaulted than a convoy, and that the greater the number of vehicles traveling together the lesser the probability of being robbed, all vehicles traveling through a link will be forced to travel together forming a convoy.

4. Each vehicle can pass several times through a node, but only once through an arc.
5. As usual in this type of situations, the available goods are not enough to cover the demand. Then, equity in the distribution will be sought, by trying to attend similar percentages of demand in all demand nodes.
6. In some situations help can be more urgently needed in some places than in others. A graduation on the priority of the nodes can be considered.
7. Reducing operation costs is not the main objective, but this must be taken into account by ensuring that the available budget is not exceeded.
8. After the delivery, vehicles return to their origin nodes following the cheapest possible path. No risk of being assaulted will be considered for empty vehicles.

In [9] a goal programming static flow model to deal with a variant of this problem is presented, providing an approximation to the best distribution plan using up to six conflicting criteria. The model presented does not consider the individual movement of vehicles through the network, but gives an idea of the flow of the vehicles and load. In this work the model is extended to allow a more detailed planning, which explicitly considers the movement of vehicles along time, and a heuristic procedure is proposed.

To illustrate the functioning of the constructive algorithm introduced in the following section, we will use a small instance whose logistic network is described in Fig. 1. There are 2 depots with 15 + 15 tons of humanitarian aid available, 3 demand nodes needing 10, 15 and 15 tons and 2 connection nodes. We will have two types of vehicles, with different capacities and velocities as stated in Fig. 1, and 2 vehicles of each type available at each depot and at one connection node. Finally, the planned amount of humanitarian aid to be distributed in the operation is 25 tons.

# 3   Constructive Algorithm

The requirement of vehicles having to travel together forming a convoy on every trip of the plan in order to increase the safety of the itineraries, together with the combination of other limitations such as the vehicle and humanitarian aid availability, make it very hard to build not only optimal, but even just feasible solutions for the problem. For this reason, the development of heuristics for this problem is especially difficult. This section introduces a constructive algorithm we have developed for the design of feasible distribution itineraries for aid distribution in the context described before. It generates feasible solutions from scratch, adding new elements to the partial solution constructed at each iteration until a final feasible plan is constructed. However, differently as it happens in many other combinatorial optimization problems, in which generating feasible solutions can be done in a very fast and simple way, this constructive algorithm is far from trivial. Ensuring the feasibility of the solution at each iteration is highly complex, especially due to the precedence constraints induced on the vehicle and humanitarian aid flow by the requirement of vehicles traveling together. Besides,

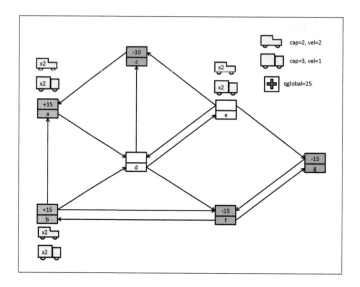

**Fig. 1.** Instance data

the algorithm makes use of some randomization mechanisms when choosing the new elements to be added to the current partial solution, with the aim of being able to provide a variety of feasible solutions when run several times. In what follows the constructive algorithm will be described.

**Preprocess.** First of all, a preprocess is performed in order to facilitate the resolution of the problem. It comprises several tasks, such as checking some simple conditions that may indicate that the problem is infeasible or simplifying the logistic network by removing unnecessary links. Besides, the cheapest return path from each demand node back to the depots is calculated before the construction of the solution is initiated.

**Vehicle Itineraries.** The itineraries to be followed by the vehicles are designed iteratively. At each iteration, the vehicle to be moved and the next link to be traversed by that vehicle are selected randomly, repeating this process until all itineraries are complete. However, the candidate links that can be traversed by each vehicle may change at each iteration, due to the precedence relations induced by the requirement of vehicles traveling together forming a convoy and thus having to depart and arrive at the same time. This precedence relations must be updated at each iteration based on the new link added to the itineraries. When all itineraries are completed, the convoys traversing each link are determined, together with their departure and arrival times at the nodes. Note that the speed of a convoy is determined by the slowest vehicle, and for that reason the final schedules of the vehicles cannot be calculated until all itineraries are fully determined.

Figure 2 shows the flow of vehicles obtained after the itinerary design phase of the constructive algorithm is executed on the small instance considered. For example, initially there are two small vehicles following the itinerary $r_1 = a - d - e - d - f - g$ and two other ones doing $r_2 = e - c - a$. However, these itineraries will be improved later, as we will show.

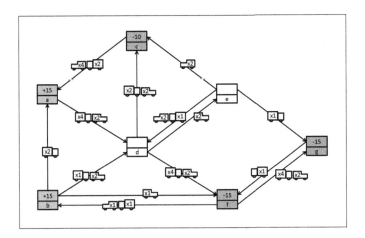

**Fig. 2.** Partial solution after designing the vehicle itineraries

**Flow of Aid.** Once the schedules of the vehicles are determined, a flow of humanitarian aid compatible with these schedules and the other data from the logistic map must be found. To facilitate this task, an auxiliary transportation network containing only the links used by the vehicles is built, so that the flow of aid can only be sent by links traversed by vehicles. A dummy source node, connected by dummy edges to all depots with humanitarian aid available, and a dummy sink node, with dummy edges arriving from each demand node, are also added to the auxiliary network so that it is a transportation network. The capacity of each dummy edge leaving the source equals the amount of aid available at the arriving depot, and analogously, the capacity of each dummy edge arriving at the sink equals the demand of the leaving node. The capacity of the real edges belonging to the original network is equal to the sum of the capacities of all vehicles traversing them according to the itineraries determined.

A compatible flow of aid is thus calculated by applying an adapted version of the Ford-Fulkerson algorithm [4] to this modified transportation network based on the schedules of the vehicles. There are several modifications, mainly caused by the requirements of vehicles traveling together forming convoys, that need to be introduced in the standard version of the algorithm so that it works with our modified transportation network and the constraints of the problem are respected. As a result, only forward moves meeting the precedence constraints induced by the schedules of the vehicles are allowed, and backward moves are not permitted because they may produce precedence violations. At each iteration, the following node to be labeled is thus chosen randomly among the available candidates according to the precedence relations. Furthermore, since backward moves are not allowed and thus existing flow cannot be diverted, but the nodes to be labeled are chosen randomly, the algorithm is allowed to make several tries at each iteration to try to find an increasing flow path. Finally, the main stopping criterion of the algorithm is based on whether the total planned amount of humanitarian aid is distributed or not, but it also stops if a predetermined number of unsuccessful tries to find increasing flow paths is reached. If the latter happens, it indicates that finding an aid flow compatible with the existing vehicle schedule was not possible. In that case, the current itineraries are discarded and the itinerary design phase is restarted.

Following the vehicle itineraries, Fig. 3 shows how the flow of aid, represented by a red cross, is sent through the network in the example instance. At this point, the amount of aid transported through each link is ensured not to exceed the total capacity of the vehicles traversing it, but each vehicle has not been assigned a particular amount to be transported yet. Note also how the amount of aid available or demanded at each node changes, so that now only $1 + 4$ tons are available at the depots, the demand of node $c$ is completely fulfilled and nodes $f$ and $g$ still require 2 and 13 additional tons, respectively.

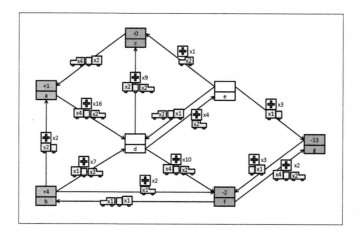

**Fig. 3.** Partial solution after generating the flow of aid

**Transshipment of Aid.** If the adapted Ford-Fulkerson algorithm is executed successfully, a flow of aid compatible with the precedence relations induced by the schedules of the vehicles is obtained. At this point, the departure and arrival times of all convoys can be fully calculated. Since the precedence relations are verified, the departure and arrival times should be consistent, meaning that the departure of a convoy from a node cannot happen before the arrival of all vehicles belonging to that convoy. However, even though the construction process enforces this through the precedence constraints, the solution may still be infeasible if there is load transshipment between vehicles. The problem is that, if one vehicle $v_1$ arrives empty to a given node $a$ and must depart with load carried to $a$ by another vehicle $v_2$, the arrival time of vehicle $v_2$ at $a$ could be later than the scheduled departure time of $v_1$ from $a$. This is clearly not feasible. However, it may happen even though all precedence constraints related to the formation of convoys are verified, because this cannot be checked until the flow of aid is fully determined.

To identify this situation, the amount of humanitarian aid available at each node, which will be called stock, after each departure or arrival event, is calculated. If at some point one convoy departs carrying load that has not arrived yet, a negative stock is created, indicating that the current solution is actually not feasible. Every time a negative stock is found at a node, the subsequent convoy arrivals bringing humanitarian aid to that node are searched and additional precedence constraints enforcing the arrival of aid to be performed before the departure causing the negative stock are added. These additional constraints, together with the already existing ones, will force the negative stock to be eliminated. Then, the new departure and arrival times of the convoys and the partial stocks at each node are calculated according to the extended precedence constraints, and the process is iterated until no negative stocks are left. If at some point the algorithm fails to find a compatible aid flow, it means that the current negative stock cannot be eliminated and thus the itinerary generation phase is also restarted.

When both the itinerary and flow generation phases are completed successfully and there are no negative stocks left, the solution is guaranteed to be feasible. However, once feasibility is achieved, the solution can be further improved by applying a final post-processing phase. Figure 4 shows the final solution of the example instance obtained after applying this postprocessing phase.

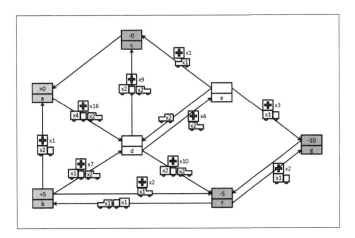

**Fig. 4.** Final solution after the postprocessing phase

A description of the different parts of the post processing phase appended to the basic constructive algorithm will be given in what follows, together with an illustration of how each part modifies the solution shown in Fig. 3 to obtain the final solution shown in Fig. 4.

**Postprocessing: Improving Equity.** A solution is fully equitable if the same proportion of demand is fulfilled at each demand node. Furthermore, for a fixed amount of humanitarian aid to be distributed in the planned operation, this ideal proportion can be easily calculated and is independent of how the distribution is performed. As a result, if in a given solution one node receives more humanitarian aid than the ideal proportion, this means necessarily that another node receives less, and thus the solution is not equitable. In fact, the solution will be less equitable the larger the difference between both proportions is. With this criterion, if the solution built by the constructive algorithm does not distribute the ideal demand proportion to all nodes, we will try to redistribute the load to find a more equitable solution. In order to do this, we search for demand nodes which did not reach the ideal demand level but received some more aid that was diverted to some other nodes, and we try to keep some of that aid in those nodes in need. However, doing this requires rescheduling the rest of the flow leaving those selected nodes, which is not trivial at all. This is done by solving another max flow problem over a new auxiliary graph.

In the solution shown in Fig. 3 there were 3 tons of humanitarian aid sent directly from demand node $g$ to demand node $f$. However, since $f$ was receiving 12 out of a total of 15 tons demanded, while $g$ was only receiving 2 out of 15, during this postprocessing phase the solution was modified at this point, keeping those 3 tons at $g$ and thus obtaining a more equitable solution.

**Postprocessing: Improving Utilization of Depots.** Since the algorithm is a heuristic, humanitarian aid may be sent to depots in which there is unused aid after completing the distribution operation, even though this is clearly suboptimal. In this situation, what we try to do is to eliminate as much incoming flow of aid as possible at the depots with unused aid, so that the aid available there is actually used. This is done by solving another max flow problem on a new auxiliary network containing all nodes and only the arcs traversed by vehicles.

In the solution shown in Fig. 3, 2 tons of aid were sent from depot $b$ to depot $a$. However, at the end of the operation, there were still 1 ton available at depot $a$, meaning that 1 of the 2 units sent from $b$ to $a$ was not necessary. This situation was thus identified when postprocessing the solution and as a result the amount of aid sent from $b$ to $a$ is reduced to only 1 ton, obtaining a solution with a smaller cost in which the aid available at depot $a$ is fully distributed.

**Postprocessing: Removing Unnecessary Vehicles.** In the first phase of the algorithm, the itineraries of the vehicles are extended as much as possible in order to allow for the distribution of as much aid as possible in the second phase. However, once the flow of aid is determined, the last part of some of those itineraries and some intermediate circuits may not be necessary. Then, the itinerary of each vehicle is checked and the paths that are not necessary for the transportation of aid are removed.

In the original solution shown in Fig. 3, but also caused by the modifications described above to improve the equity and the utilization of the depots in the solution, there were a few vehicle paths that were not strictly needed to perform the operation. These unnecessary paths were removed, as it was the case, for example, of the paths of all vehicles traveling from $c$ to $a$ and from $g$ to $f$, and also of some of the vehicles traveling from $e$ to $c$, from $e$ to $d$, from $d$ to $f$ and from $f$ to $g$. As a result, the route $r_1 = a - d - e - d - f - g$ followed by the two vehicles commented earlier is reduced to $r_1' = a - d - e - d - f$ and the one $r_2 = e - c - a$ is reduced to $r_2' = e - c$, which are shorter and thus cheaper.

**Postprocessing: Route Crossing.** This last postprocessing phase is focused on interchanging parts of two routes with the aim of eliminating additional unnecessary paths or decreasing the length of the return routes back to the depot. This is also illustrated in the final solution depicted in Fig. 4. The routes $r_1' = a - d - e - d - f$ and $r_2' = e - c$, already improved in the previous postprocessing phase by eliminating unnecessary arcs and vehicles, can be further improved by breaking them into two parts, $r_1' : [a-d-e] + [d-f]$, $r_2' : [e] + [c]$, and reconnecting the solution by swapping those parts, obtaining new improved routes $r_1'' = a - d - e - c$ and $r_2'' = e - d - f$. These routes deliver the same amount of aid to the same locations but the total length of the routes back to the depot is smaller.

## 4   Metaheuristics

The generation of feasible solutions for the problem approached in this paper is especially difficult, and thus the constructive algorithm introduced in the previous section is focused on producing solutions verifying all constraints of the problem with a small computational effort. It uses randomization in order to be able to provide a variety of solutions, but it also considers implicitly some of the attributes that must be optimized: the cost or the duration of the distribution operation, by making the most of the vehicles and building routes as short as possible; the equity of the distribution, by spreading the flow of aid among all demand nodes; and the security of the itineraries, by forcing the vehicles to travel together forming convoys in order to decrease the probability of an assault. This is done implicitly, with no need to measure those attributes through the construction process. However, to further improve the solutions provided by the constructive algorithm by applying more sophisticated solution methods such as metaheuristics, it is necessary to measure the attributes of interest, so that they can guide the search process.

Furthermore, the constructive algorithm proposed before can be used to feed improving heuristics with a variety of initial solutions, but also as a basis for more sophisticated metaheuristics in which the construction process is modified to incorporate relevant information obtained from previously obtained solutions. This information can be exploited to guide the construction process through different memory mechanisms. In particular, the proposed constructive algorithm could be extended to a Greedy Randomized Adaptive Search Procedure (GRASP) [3] and an Ant Colony Optimization (ACO) algorithm [2] by following some of the ideas explained in what follows.

The GRASP algorithm would consist of two phases. In the first phase, the constructive algorithm would be used to build an initial elite set with selected different solutions with a reasonably good quality, and in the second phase a modified version of the constructive algorithm would be executed to obtain better solutions. The construction of the solutions in this modified version would be guided by some greedy functions representing the contribution of the elements to be added to the solutions according to the attributes to be optimized (Greedy part of GRASP), and by the intensity functions representing the frequency with which those elements are used in the elite set taken as a reference (Adaptive part of GRASP). Then, the candidate elements that could be added to the solution at each iteration would be evaluated according to both functions, and probabilities are assigned to all candidates so that those with a better evaluation (higher greedy contribution and more similar to the elite solutions) are more likely to be chosen. Finally, the next element to be added to the solution would be selected randomly according to those probabilities (Randomized part of GRASP), iterating this construction process until a feasible solution is obtained. This solution would be improved using local search (Search part of GRASP) and considered as a potential member of the elite set: if its overall diversity and quality is improved, one former elite solution would be replaced by the new solution found and the elite set would be updated accordingly. By iterating this construction process we should be able to improve the elite set at each iteration, and this memory mechanism should help building better final solutions.

On the other hand, the ACO algorithm would be based on several multi-ant procedures to be applied at the different construction phases of the algorithm. For example, in the itinerary design phase each vehicle would be represented by one ant, and in the aid flow phase the ants would be associated to aid batches to be delivered. In both cases, the next element of the solution would be chosen randomly according to its attractiveness and the pheromone trail left by previous ants, combining the available local information with the information provided by the ants and adding a randomization element to introduce diversification. This construction process would also be iterated to allow the ants learn from one iteration to another and thus improve the quality of the solutions.

Both metaheuristics are intended to use a priori information, represented by the greedy functions in GRASP and the attractiveness in ACO, and a posteriori information, updated at each iteration and stored through a memory mechanism, represented by the elite set in GRASP and the ant pheromone trails in ACO. The former is mostly used to guide the search at the beginning of the execution of the algorithm when no more information is available. However, the latter is based on learning from previous solutions and thus the amount of that information increases iteratively, improving the guiding process and leading to better final solutions at the end of the execution of the algorithm.

**Acknowledgments.** This research was carried out with financial support from the Government of Spain, grant TIN2012-32482, and from the local Government of Madrid, grant S2013/ICE-2845 (CASI-CAM).

# References

1. Balcik, B., Beamon, B.M.: Facility location in humanitarian relief. Int. J. Logist. Res. Appl. **11**(2), 101–121 (2008)
2. Dorigo, M., Birattari, M.: Ant colony optimization. In: Encyclopedia of Machine Learning, pp. 36–39. Springer, US (2010)
3. Feo, T.A., Resende, M.G.: Greedy randomized adaptive search procedures. J. Glob. Optim. **6**, 109–113 (1995)
4. Ford, L.R., Fulkerson, D.R.: Maximal flow through a network. Can. J. Math. **8**(3), 399–404 (1956)
5. Huang, M., Smilowitz, K., Balcik, B.: Models for relief routing: equity, efficiency and efficacy. Transp. Res. Part E **48**(1), 2–18 (2012)
6. Nolz, P.C., Doerner, K.F., Gutjahr, W.J., Hartl, R.F.: A Bi-objective metaheuristic for disaster relief operation planning. In: Coello Coello, C.A., Dhaenens, C., Jourdan, L. (eds.) Advances in Multi-Objective Nature Inspired Computing. SCI, vol. 272, pp. 167–187. Springer, Heidelberg (2010)
7. Ortuño, M.T., Cristobal, P., Ferrer, J.M., Martin-Campo, F.J., Muñoz, S., Tirado, G., Vitoriano, B.: Decision aid models and systems for humanitarian logistics. a survey. In: Montero, J., Ruan, D., Vitoriano, B. (eds.) Decision Aid Models for Disaster Management and Emergencies. ACIS, vol. 7, pp. 17–44. Atlantis Press, Amsterdam (2012)
8. Ortuño, M.T., Tirado, G., Vitoriano, B.: A lexicographical goal programming based decision support system for logistics of humanitarian aid. TOP **19**, 464–479 (2011)
9. Vitoriano, B., Ortuño, M.T., Tirado, G., Montero, J.: A multi-criteria optimization model for humanitarian aid distribution. J. Glob. Optim. **51**(2), 189–208 (2011)

# Improving Maritime Awareness with Semantic Genetic Programming and Linear Scaling: Prediction of Vessels Position Based on AIS Data

Leonardo Vanneschi[1]([✉]), Mauro Castelli[1], Ernesto Costa[2], Alessandro Re[1], Henrique Vaz[3], Victor Lobo[1,4], and Paulo Urbano[3]

[1] NOVA IMS, Universidade Nova de Lisboa, 1070-312 Lisbon, Portugal
`lvanneschi@novaims.unl.pt`
[2] CISUC, Department of Informatics Engineering, University of Coimbra, 3030-290 Coimbra, Portugal
[3] LabMAg, Faculdade de Cincias, Universidade de Lisboa, 1749-016 Lisbon, Portugal
[4] Portuguese Naval Academy, Alfeite, 2810-001 Almada, Portugal

**Abstract.** Maritime domain awareness deals with the situational understanding of maritime activities that could impact the security, safety, economy or environment. It enables quick threat identification, informed decision making, effective action support, knowledge sharing and more accurate situational awareness. In this paper, we propose a novel computational intelligence framework, based on genetic programming, to predict the position of vessels, based on information related to the vessels past positions in a specific time interval. Given the complexity of the task, two well known improvements of genetic programming, namely geometric semantic operators and linear scaling, are integrated in a new and sophisticated genetic programming system. The work has many objectives, for instance assisting more quickly and effectively a vessel when an emergency arises or being able to chase more efficiently a vessel that is accomplishing illegal actions. The proposed system has been compared to two different versions of genetic programming and three non-evolutionary machine learning methods, outperforming all of them on all the studied test cases.

## 1 Introduction

Given the rapidly changing and increasingly complex nature of global security, interest for novel techniques to pledge protection and safeguard of persons and goods has been growing in the last few years. This is especially visible in the maritime domain, where chances of emergencies and/or violations are particularly frequent. Maritime domain awareness deals with the situational understanding of maritime activities that could impact the security, safety, economy or environment. As discussed in the 2014 *International Maritime Security Conference* (http://www.mscconference.com.), "maritime security is not an end in itself but it is vital to other forms of security". Maritime security is crucial to national as

© Springer International Publishing Switzerland 2015
A.M. Mora and G. Squillero (Eds.): EvoApplications 2015, LNCS 9028, pp. 732–744, 2015.
DOI: 10.1007/978-3-319-16549-3_59

well as human security: drug traffickers, gun-runners and terrorists often use the established sea-routes of vulnerable illegal migrants on the journey to their destination to circumvent border controls. Furthermore, the sea provides a livelihood for fishermen and seafarers, and maritime crime and exploitation can represent a serious threat for those persons. While all these reasons highlight the importance of having a constant surveillance of the sea, it is clear that it is not possible to ensure a complete coverage of maritime areas with coast guard vessels. In this context, computational intelligence systems can represent an important tool for improving maritime awareness at a reasonable cost.

While the use of intelligent systems is a hot topic in the field of maritime awareness, many possibilities remain to be explored. In this paper, we present a system based on Genetic Programming (GP) [1] that integrates two different well known GP advances, joining them for the first time in s single framework: geometric semantic genetic operators (introduced by Moraglio et al. in 2012 [2] and efficiently implemented by Vanneschi et al. in 2013 [3,4]) and linear scaling (introduced by Keijzer in 2003 [5]). This new GP system will be used for addressing a particular task related to one aspect of maritime awareness. The objective is to build models that can be used, in case of emergence, to predict the position of a vessel by only using information related to its previous positions in a given time interval. An accurate prediction will facilitate the work of coast guards in organizing a rescue operation, maximizing the chances of success and also reducing the cost associated to the exploration of a maritime area. The proposed system is compared to two other versions of GP (a standard version of GP, as originally defined by Koza in [1] and a recently proposed variant of GP, called Geometric Semantic GP [2], that uses geometric semantic operators but no linear scaling) and three non-evolutionary machine learning methods (Linear Regression [6], Multi-layered Artificial Neural Networks, trained with the Back-propagation learning rule [7], and Support Vector Machines with second degree polynomial kernel [8]). The idea behind this work is that, given the complexity of the problem and the large amount of available data, standard GP is not enough sophisticated for finding good solutions. For this reason, we integrate it with two well known and successful improvements, that have shown excellent results in isolation on several different applicative domains so far, but that have never been used together in a single system before. Geometric semantic genetic operators have been chosen for their extremely promising property of inducing unimodal error surfaces for any problem that consists in matching sets of predicted values into known targets (like supervised learning problems, such as classification or regression). Moreover, as discussed in [3,9,10], geometric semantic genetic operators are often able to produce better performance with respect to standard genetic operators for several complex real-life applications and, thanks to a recently proposed efficient implementation [4], when compared to the latter ones, they require a significantly smaller computational time for reaching a good quality solution. This is an important aspect considering the large amount of data that characterizes the problem studied here. At the same time, linear scaling has been chosen for its recognized ability of improving GP performance.

More in particular, as shown in [5], linear scaling is often able to better optimize training data (compared to standard GP), without a corresponding overfitting.

The paper is organized as follows: Sect. 2 briefly reviews some previous works related to the use of computational intelligence techniques in the area of maritime awareness. Section 3 describes the data used in this work, presenting also the system used by vessels for sending navigation information. Section 4 presents the two GP improvements that are integrated in the proposed system: geometric semantic genetic operators and linear scaling. Section 5 presents the experimental settings and discusses the obtained results. Finally, Sect. 6 concludes the paper, summarizing the main results achieved and suggesting ideas for possible future research.

## 2    Related Work

The use of computational intelligence methods for improving maritime awareness has been investigated in the last decade. In particular, a large part of the existing works has focused on the definition of systems to perform anomaly detection. For instance, in [11] a Collaborative Knowledge Exploitation Framework (CKEF) is proposed to support the analysts in efficiently managing and exploiting relevant knowledge assets to achieve maritime domain awareness in joint operations centres of the Canadian Forces. In particular, an effort has been dedicated to implement, within the CKEF, a proof-of-concept prototype of a rule-based expert system to support the analysts regarding anomaly detection. This expert system performed automated reasoning and generated recommendations (or alerts) about maritime anomalies, thereby supporting the identification of vessels of interest and threat analysis. The system has been designed to reduce the false alarm rate, and it also provides explanations as to why a vessel may be of interest. In the same vein, in [12], a prototype of an automated reasoning capability was proposed, exploiting ontologies expressed in description logic to support the maritime staff in detecting anomalies, in classifying vessels of interest, and in identifying and categorizing maritime threats. The work discusses the development of a maritime domain ontology of a significant size and proposes an automated reasoning service for the exploitation of this ontology. Practical exploitation examples are also presented, making use of a description logic inference engine to detect anomalies and classify vessels of interest.

As another example of a rule-based expert system, in [13] an unsupervised clustering of normal vessel traffic patterns was proposed and implemented. Patterns were represented as the momentary location, speed and course of tracked vessels. The learnt cluster models were then used for anomaly detection in sea traffic. A qualitative analysis revealed that the most distinguishing anomalies found in the traffic are vessels crossing sea lanes and vessels traveling close to and in the opposite direction of sea lanes.

As reported in [14], a different approach to perform anomaly detection is based on the use of classification algorithms via a data-driven approach. The main difficulty, in this case, is related to the fact that conventional classification algorithms generally cannot be directly applied to the maritime security domain, due to the lack of adequate samples and known cases that should be classified as anomalous [15]. An alternate data-driven approach is to build normal models via discovering knowledge from historical data [16]. Besides this, many other approaches have been proposed to perform anomaly detection, and for an extensive literature review the reader is referred to [17].

Lobo, in [18], proposes the use of Self-Organizing Maps (SOMs) (or Kohonen networks) to address different problems in the maritime domain. In particular, the paper discusses the use of SOMs for clustering satellite images (as in [19,20]) and it describes an application of SOM that concerns reflectance spectra of ocean waters [21].

We conclude the section by citing the work proposed in [14], where genetic algorithms (GAs) have been used to enhance maritime situational awareness. In particular, authors proposed a knowledge discovery system based on GAs, named GeMASS. In the development of GeMASS, a machine learning approach was applied to discover knowledge that is applicable in characterizing maritime security threats. One feature of the system is its ability of learning from streaming data and to generate up-to-date knowledge in a dynamic way. Based on the knowledge discovered, the system functions to screen vessels for anomalies in real-time. Results obtained using a prototype of GeMASS have demonstrated the appropriateness of GAs in addressing maritime awareness problems.

## 3    Employed Data and Datasets Construction

Data used in this work have been collected using the Automatic Identification System (AIS). As explained in [22], AIS is an international standard for ship-to-ship, ship-to-shore, and shore-to-ship communication of information, including vessel identity, position, speed, course, destination and other data of critical interest for navigation safety and maritime security. As explained in [23], information transmitted by AIS equipment consists in dynamic, static and voyage related information. Dynamic information, such as vessel heading, course, speed, position, etc., is broadcast in near real-time, dictated by the vessels speed and heading change. In this work, as a case study, we considered AIS data related to vessels that transit near Atlantic and Mediterranean coasts of the Iberian Peninsula. Several types of vessels have been considered, including passenger ships, cargoes, tankers, tugboats, fishing ships, navigation aid vessels and military ships. The presence of several types of vessels makes the problem of predicting their positions even more challenging: in fact, different types of boats generally present different behaviors. For instance, while passenger boats present a common behavior that is quite easy to predict, fishing ships are usually characterized by particular trajectories, several periods where the boat stops in particular areas and a high variance in terms of cruise speed. In other terms, it is not possible to build a unique model that is able to accurately predict the position of all the considered types of boat.

While data of different types of boats have been collected, the first step of our experimental study has consisted in building regression datasets for each vessel. In details, for each vessel we built two different datasets: one containing the information about the longitude and the second with information related to the latitude of the vessel in different instances. Following the suggestion by domain experts involved in this study, we have considered latitude and longitude independently. Hence, the different algorithms have been used to build two different predictive models: one for the latitude and the other for the longitude. The datasets used have the following form: each row in a dataset consists in a series of variables that represent the position (latitude or longitude) of a vessel in different consecutive measured instants (usually there is an interval of 10 min between two consecutive observations), while the dependent variable (or target) represents the position of the vessel after 4 h from the last available observation. In each dataset, we used 20 observations related to 20 consecutive measured positions for creating the window between input data and target in the regression datasets. For some vessels, there are missing data in the dataset: in this case, we used a simple linear interpolation in order to infer the missing data from the available ones. If on the one hand we are aware that linear interpolation is not always realistic in the context of trajectory reconstructions of vessels, on the other hand linear interpolation is simple and in many cases allows us to reconstruct rather faithfully the missing information between two consecutive missing points. For this reason, we decided to adopt linear interpolation as a first attempt. Efforts will be made in the future to improve this step, by using more sophisticated interpolation methods. The number of instances in each dataset depends on the route traveled by vessels: longer routes are associated with a larger amount of observations (AIS information) than shorter ones. In this work, three different regression datasets were constructed and used in our experimental study, collecting data of a cargo vessel, of a fishing boat and of a military vessel respectively. The time series that allowed us to generate the regression dataset of the cargo vessel (CARGO from now on) contained 1478 measured positions (expressed in latitude and longitude pairs); the time series of the fishing boat (FISHING from now on) contained 8542 measured positions and the time series of the military vessel (MILITARY from now on) contained 3795 measured positions.

## 4    Genetic Programming Advances Integrated in the System

**Geometric Semantic Genetic Programming.** Even though the term semantics can have several different interpretations, it is a common trend in the GP community (and this is what we do also here) to identify the semantics of a solution with the vector of its output values on the training data [24,25]. Under this perspective, a GP individual can be identified with a point (its semantics) in a multidimensional space that we call semantic space. The term Geometric Semantic Genetic Programming (GSGP) indicates a recently introduced variant of GP in which traditional crossover and mutation operators are replaced by so called geometric semantic operators, which exploit semantic awareness and induce precise geometric properties on the semantic space.

Geometric semantic operators, introduced by Moraglio et al. [2], are becoming more and more popular in the GP community [24] because of their property of inducing a unimodal fitness landscape on any problem consisting in matching sets of input data into known targets (like for instance supervised learning problems such as regression and classification). To have an intuition of this property (whose proof can be found in [2]), let us first consider a Genetic Algorithms (GAs) problem in which the unique global optimum is known and the fitness of each individual (to be minimized) corresponds to its distance to the global optimum (our reasoning holds for any employed distance). In this problem, if we use, for instance, ball mutation[1] [26] (i.e. a variation operator that slightly perturbs some of the coordinates of a solution), then any possible individual different from the global optimum has at least one fitter neighbor (individual resulting from its mutation). So, there are no local optima. In other words, the fitness landscape is unimodal, and consequently the problem is characterized by a good evolvability.

Now, let us consider the typical GP problem of finding a function that maps sets of input data into known target values (as we said, regression and classification are particular cases). The fitness of an individual for this problem is typically a distance between its predicted output values and the target ones (error measure). Geometric semantic operators simply define transformations on the syntax of the individuals that correspond to geometric crossover and ball mutation in the semantic space, thus allowing us to map the considered GP problem into the previously discussed GA problem. In particular[2], *geometric semantic crossover* generates, as the unique offspring of parents $T_1, T_2 : \mathbb{R}^n \to \mathbb{R}$, the expression:

$$T_{XO} = (T_1 \cdot T_R) + ((1 - T_R) \cdot T_2)$$

where $T_R$ is a random real function whose output values range in the interval $[0, 1]$. Analogously, *geometric semantic mutation* returns, as the result of the mutation of an individual $T : \mathbb{R}^n \to \mathbb{R}$, the expression:

$$T_M = T + ms \cdot (T_{R1} - T_{R2})$$

where $T_{R1}$ and $T_{R2}$ are random real functions with codomain in $[0, 1]$ and $ms$ is a parameter called mutation step.

As Moraglio et al. point out, these operators create much larger offspring than their parents and the fast growth of the individuals in the population rapidly makes fitness evaluation unbearably slow, making the system unusable. This phenomenon clearly depends also on population size [27], but is generally present even when using small populations. In [3,4], a possible workaround to this problem was proposed, consisting in an implementation of Moraglio's operators

---

[1] Similar considerations hold for many types of crossover, including various kinds of geometric crossover [26].

[2] Here we report the definition of the geometric semantic operators as given by Moraglio et al. for real functions domains, since these are the operators we will use in the experimental phase. For applications that consider other types of data, the reader is referred to [2].

that makes them not only usable in practice, but also very efficient. Basically, this implementation is based on the idea that, besides storing the initial trees, at every generation it is enough to maintain in memory, for each individual, its semantics and a reference to its parents. As shown in [3], the computational cost of evolving a population of $n$ individuals for $g$ generations is $O(ng)$, while the cost of evaluating a new, unseen, instance is $O(g)$.

Geometric semantic operators have a known limitation [4,24]: the reconstruction of the best individual at the end of a run can be a hard (and sometimes even impossible) task, due to its large size. This basically turns GP into a black-box system.

**Linear Scaling.** Linear scaling, first introduced for improving GP in symbolic regression in [5], consists in modifying the fitness function by calculating the slope and intercept of the formula coded by a GP individual. Given that $y_i = T(H_i)$ is the output of the GP individual $T$ on the input data $H_i$, a linear regression on the target values $t$ can be performed using the equations:

$$b = \frac{\sum_{i=1}^{m}[(y_i - \overline{y})(t_i - \overline{t})]}{\sum_{i=1}^{m}(t_i - \overline{t})}$$

$$a = \overline{t} - b\overline{y}$$

where $m$ is the number of fitness cases (i.e. the number of instances in the training set) and $\overline{y}$ and $\overline{t}$ denote the average output and the average target value respectively. These expressions respectively calculate the slope and intercept of a set of outputs $y$, such that the sum of the squared errors between $t$ and $a + by$ is minimized. After this, any error measure can be calculated on the scaled formula $a + by$, for instance the Root Mean Square Error ($RMSE$):

$$RMSE(t, a + by) = \sqrt{\frac{\sum_{i=1}^{m}(a + by_i - t_i)^2}{m}}$$

If $a$ is different from 0 and $b$ is different from 1, the procedure outlined above is guaranteed to reduce the $RMSE$ for any formula $y = T(H_i)$ [5]. The cost of calculating the slope and intercept is linear in the size of the training set, and it could eventually be further reduced by applying statistical methods to reduce the number of needed fitness cases [28]. By efficiently calculating the slope and intercept for each individual, the need to search for these two constants is removed from the GP run. GP is then free to search for that expression whose shape is most similar to that of the target function. The efficacy of linear scaling in GP for many symbolic regression problems has been widely demonstrated in [5].

## 5   Experimental Study

**Experimental Settings.** The proposed GP system (called GSGP-LIN from now on) uses geometric semantic crossover and mutation and applies linear scaling to each individual in the population. It will be compared to standard GP (STGP), i.e. the canonic version of GP as introduced by Koza in [1], and Geometric Semantic GP (GSGP), i.e. a version of GP that uses geometric semantic genetic operators, but without linear scaling. Moreover, GSGP-LIN was also compared to three non-evolutionary state-of-the-art machine learning techniques, namely: Linear Regression [6], Multi-layered Feed-Forward Artificial Neural Networks, trained with the Backpropagation learning rule (also called Multilayer Perceptron) [7], and Support Vector Machines with second degree polynomial kernel [8].

For all the studied computational techniques, a total of 30 runs have been performed. In each run, a different partition between training and test data has been considered. In particular, 70 % of the instances, selected at random with uniform distribution, have been used as training data, while the remaining 30 % have been used as test data. For the studied GP systems, at each generation the training fitness of the best individual, as well as its fitness on the test set (that we call test fitness) were recorded. In our experimental results we report the median of these values for the 30 runs. The median was preferred over the mean because of its higher robustness to outliers. Also, to ensure a good population diversity [29], all the runs used populations of 200 individuals allowed to evolve for 1000 generations. Trees initialization was performed using the Ramped Half-and-Half method [1] with a maximum initial depth equal to 6. The function set contained the arithmetic operators, including division protected as in [1]. The terminal set contained a number of variables that corresponds to the number of observations in a given time window. Crossover rate was equal to 0.7, while mutation rate was 0.3. Survival from one generation to the other was always guaranteed to the best individual of the population (elitism). For GSGP and for GSGP-LIN, a random mutation step extracted with uniform distribution from the [0, 1] range has been considered in each mutation event, as suggested in [9]. The results discussed in the next section have been obtained using the GSGP implementation freely available at http://gsgp.sourceforge.net and documented in [4], enriched with the implementation of linear scaling in the case of GSGP-LIN. Regarding the considered non-evolutionary machine learning techniques, we have used the implementation provided in the Weka public domain software [30] with the default Weka parameter settings.

**Experimental Results.** Median errors calculated over 30 independent runs are reported for the three different boats (CARGO, FISHING and MILITARY) and for all the studied computational systems in Table 1. To analyze the statistical significance of these results, a set of tests has been performed on the median errors. As a first step, the Kolmogorov-Smirnov test has shown that the data are not normally distributed and hence a rank-based statistic has been used. Successively, the Wilcoxon rank-sum test for pairwise data comparison has been used (with Bonferroni correction) under the alternative hypothesis that the samples do not have equal medians. In Table 1, **bold font** is used to indicate results that are statistically better than the ones achieved with the other considered techniques, employing the usual significance level $\alpha = 0.05$. As it is possible to

**Table 1.** Comparison between the six different computational methods studied in this work. Median error calculated over 30 independent runs (each one with a different training-test partition) are reported.

| Vessel | Method | Longitude | | Latitude | |
|--------|--------|-----------|-----------|----------|----------|
| | | Train | Test | Train | Test |
| CARGO | Multilayer Perceptron | 1.90E-02 | 1.85E-02 | 1.49E-02 | 1.47E-02 |
| | Linear Regression | 3.90E-02 | 3.92E-02 | 4.37E-02 | 4.39E-02 |
| | SMO Regression | 3.32E-02 | 3.26E-02 | 2.19E-02 | 2.23E-02 |
| | STGP | 8.98E-02 | 8.94E-02 | 7.04E-02 | 7.05E-02 |
| | GSGP | 8.18E-02 | 8.27E-02 | 7.1E-02 | 7.37E-02 |
| | GSGP-LIN | **4.74E-03** | **4.9E-03** | **5.36E-03** | **5.43E-03** |
| FISHING | Multilayer Perceptron | 1.81E-02 | 1.80E-02 | 3.32E-02 | 3.32E-02 |
| | Linear Regression | 7.42E-02 | 7.43E-02 | 5.91E-02 | 5.90E-02 |
| | SMO Regression | 3.75E-02 | 3.75E-02 | 2.34E-02 | 2.34E-02 |
| | STGP | 1.12E-02 | 1.13E-02 | 1.27E-02 | 1.27E-02 |
| | GSGP | 1.12E-02 | 1.12E-02 | 1.26E-02 | 1.27E-02 |
| | GSGP-LIN | **1.14E-03** | **1.17E-03** | **1.53E-03** | **1.54E-03** |
| MILITARY | Multilayer Perceptron | 1.82E-02 | 1.82E-02 | 2.57E-02 | 2.56E-02 |
| | Linear Regression | 2.27E-02 | 2.27E-02 | 1.38E-02 | 1.35E-02 |
| | SMO Regression | 5.43E-03 | 5.38E-03 | 6.76E-03 | 6.79E-03 |
| | STGP | 8.97E-02 | 8.97E-02 | 6.25E-02 | 6.24E-02 |
| | GSGP | 8.74E-02 | 8.97E-02 | 5.83E-02 | 5.84E-02 |
| | GSGP-LIN | **6.12E-04** | **6.63E-04** | **2.97E-04** | **3.1E-04** |

see, results produced by GSGP-LIN are statistically better (i.e. lower error) than the ones produced by all the other methods for all the studied test cases, both on training and on test data.

Besides this, for pairwise comparisons, we have also calculated the $Z$-scores and, using them, we have computed the effect size (or $r$-values), obtained by dividing the $Z$-scores by the squared root of the size of the sample (in our case $2 * 30 = 60$, given that we have performed 30 runs). The effect size can be used to understand if the magnitude of the effect we observed is *high* ($r >= 0.5$), *medium* ($0.3 \leq r < 0.5$) or *low* ($r < 0.3$). Effect size pairwise results obtained on the test set for the same experiments as in Table 1 are reported in Table 2. All the other results (effect size on the training set, and $p$-values and $Z$-scores on both training and test set) are not reported here because of the page limit imposed to this publication.

As Table 2 shows, whenever GSGP-LIN is compared to any other method, the effect size is high. This means that GSGP-LIN clearly outperforms all the other studied methods. On the other hand, when we compare GSGP with the other studied methods, we can see that the effect size is not always high, and in

**Table 2.** Effect size ($r$-values) for the same experiments as in Table 1. The effect size is high when $r >= 0.5$ (**bold font**), medium when $0.3 \leq r < 0.5$ (*italics* font) and low when $r < 0.3$ (plain text font). Only results on the test set are reported here. In this table, MP stand for Multilayer Perceptron and Lin stands for Linear Regression.

| | | LONGITUDE | | | | | LATITUDE | | | | |
|---|---|---|---|---|---|---|---|---|---|---|---|
| | | Lin | SMO | STGP | GSGP | GSGP-LIN | Lin | SMO | STGP | GSGP | GSGP-LIN |
| CARGO | MP | low | low | low | low | **high** | low | low | low | low | **high** |
| | Lin | | **high** | low | low | **high** | | **high** | low | low | **high** |
| | SMO | | | low | low | **high** | | | low | low | **high** |
| | STGP | | | | low | **high** | | | | low | **high** |
| | GSGP | | | | | **high** | | | | | **high** |
| FISHING | MP | low | low | **high** | **high** | **high** | low | **high** | **high** | **high** | **high** |
| | Lin | | **high** | **high** | **high** | **high** | | **high** | **high** | **high** | **high** |
| | SMO | | | **high** | **high** | **high** | | | **high** | **high** | **high** |
| | STGP | | | | low | **high** | | | | low | **high** |
| | GSGP | | | | | **high** | | | | | **high** |
| MILITARY | MP | low | **high** | low | low | **high** | **high** | **high** | low | low | **high** |
| | Lin | | **high** | low | low | **high** | | **high** | low | low | **high** |
| | SMO | | | low | low | **high** | | | low | low | **high** |
| | STGP | | | | low | **high** | | | | *medium* | **high** |
| | GSGP | | | | | **high** | | | | | **high** |

particular, it is low when GSGP is compared to STGP. Anyway, it is important to highlight the difference in terms of execution time between GSGP and STGP: GSGP is approximately 100 times faster than STGP and this is an important feature in this particular domain, where a large amount of data is available and thus computation can be particularly costly. Furthermore, it is also interesting to point out that the performance of GSGP and the one of STGP are comparable to the ones achieved with the studied non-evolutionary machine learning techniques. As a conclusion, we can state that the use of linear scaling in integration with geometric semantic operators is crucial for achieving better results with respect to the other considered techniques.

To conclude this section, we report in Fig. 1 the target routes of the three studied different vessels, together with the trajectory reconstructed using GSGP-LIN. From the figure, it is possible to appreciate the accuracy of the prediction that is possible to achieve using GSGP-LIN. The behaviors of the considered vessels are clearly very different between each other. In particular, the fishing boat has the most irregular behavior, while the military vessel follows a very regular route. Finally, the cargo vessel has a behavior that can be considered half-a-way between the complexity of the fishing boat trajectory and the simplicity of the military one. In all the three cases, GSGP-LIN is able to generate a predicted trajectory that very faithfully approximates the real one. To summarize, the obtained results hint that GSGP-LIN may be a suitable tool for predicting the position of vessels and that the quality of the prediction is independent from the particular type of vessel under exam and the complexity of the trajectory of that vessel.

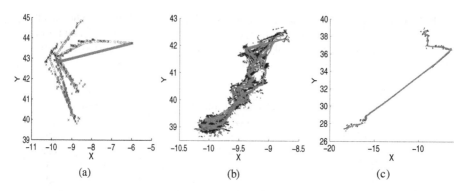

**Fig. 1.** Predicted routes of the three studied different vessels compared to real routes, reported in a latitude-longitude space. Results obtained with GSGP-LIN. Gray points represent the route, while black points are used to represent the predicted trajectory. Plot (a) shows the trajectory of the CARGO vessel; plot (b) reports the trajectory of the FISHING boat; and plot (c) shows the trajectory of the MILITARY vessel.

## 6  Conclusion

Maritime domain awareness deals with the situational understanding of maritime activities that could impact the security, safety, economy or environment. Computational intelligence methods have emerged as an effective tool for improving maritime awareness. In this study, a new Genetic Programming (GP) system has been proposed in order to address one important task related to the maritime safety: the prediction of vessels position based on AIS information. AIS is one of the systems that vessels use for sending information about their position and navigation data. The momentary or prolonged lack of AIS related information can be interpreted as an anomalous behavior or can indicate a state of emergence. In such situations, coast guards need to known the most probable position of the vessel for starting a rescue task. The GP system we proposed integrates two well known methods to improve GP performance: geometric semantic genetic operators and linear scaling. This system was compared to two other versions of GP and three non-evolutionary machine learning methods, outperforming all of them for all the studied test cases. Also, from the decision maker perspective, the models obtained with the proposed system are able to describe the behavior (i.e., the trajectory) of the vessels in a rather reliable way. Future work involves the extension of the proposed system to address other maritime awareness related problems like, for instance, the identification of illicit activities.

**Acknowledgments.** The authors acknowledge project MassGP (PTDC/EEI-CTP/ 2975/2012), FCT, Portugal.

## References

1. Koza, J.R.: Genetic Programming: On the Programming of Computers by Means of Natural Selection. MIT Press, Cambridge (1992)

2. Moraglio, A., Krawiec, K., Johnson, C.G.: Geometric semantic genetic programming. In: Coello, C.A.C., Cutello, V., Deb, K., Forrest, S., Nicosia, G., Pavone, M. (eds.) PPSN 2012, Part I. LNCS, vol. 7491, pp. 21–31. Springer, Heidelberg (2012)

3. Vanneschi, L., Castelli, M., Manzoni, L., Silva, S.: A new implementation of geometric semantic GP and its application to problems in pharmacokinetics. In: Krawiec, K., Moraglio, A., Hu, T., Etaner-Uyar, A.Ş., Hu, B. (eds.) EuroGP 2013. LNCS, vol. 7831, pp. 205–216. Springer, Heidelberg (2013)

4. Castelli, M., Silva, S., Vanneschi, L.: A C++ framework for geometric semantic genetic programming. Genet. Programm. Evolvable Mach. 16(1), 73–81 (2015)

5. Keijzer, M.: Improving symbolic regression with interval arithmetic and linear scaling. In: Ryan, C., Soule, T., Keijzer, M., Tsang, E.P.K., Poli, R., Costa, E. (eds.) EuroGP 2003. LNCS, vol. 2610, pp. 70–82. Springer, Heidelberg (2003)

6. Weisberg, S.: Applied Linear Regression. Wiley Series in Prob. and Stat. Wiley, Hoboken (2005)

7. Haykin, S.: Neural Networks: A Comprehensive Foundation. Prentice Hall, Upper Saddle River (1999)

8. Scholkopf, B., Smola, A.: Learning With Kernels: Support Vector Machines, Regularization, Optimization and Beyond. Adaptative computation and machine learning series. The MIT Press, Cambridge (2002)

9. Vanneschi, L., Silva, S., Castelli, M., Manzoni, L.: Geometric semantic genetic programming for real life applications. Genet. Program. Theory Pract. 14, 3–29 (2013). Springer

10. Vanneschi, L.: Improving genetic programming for the prediction of pharmacokinetic parameters. Memetic Comput. 6(4), 255–262 (2014)

11. Roy, J.: Anomaly detection in the maritime domain. In: Proceedings of SPIE, vol. 6945, pp. 69414–69450 (2008)

12. Roy, J., Davenport, M.: Exploitation of maritime domain ontologies for anomaly detection and threat analysis. In: Waterside Security Conference (WSS), pp. 1–8 (2010)

13. Laxhammar, R.: Anomaly detection for sea surveillance. In: 2008 11th International Conference on Information Fusion, pp. 1–8, June 2008

14. Chen, C.H., Khoo, L.P., Chong, Y.T., Yin, X.F.: Knowledge discovery using genetic algorithm for maritime situational awareness. Expert Syst. Appl. 41(6), 2742–2753 (2014)

15. Riveiro, M., Falkman, G., Ziemke, T.: Visual analytics for the detection of anomalous maritime behavior. In: 12th International Conference on Information Visualisation, IV 2008, pp. 273–279, July 2008

16. Brax, C., Niklasson, L.: Enhanced situational awareness in the maritime domain: an agent-based approach for situation management. In: SPIE 7352, Intelligent Sensing, Situation Management, Impact Assessment, and Cyber-Sensing, pp. 1–10 (2009)

17. Kazemi, S., Abghari, S., Lavesson, N., Johnson, H., Ryman, P.: Open data for anomaly detection in maritime surveillance. Expert Syst. Appl. 40(14), 5719–5729 (2013)

18. Lobo, V.: Application of self-organizing maps to the maritime environment. In: Popovich, V., Claramunt, C., Schrenk, M., Korolenko, K. (eds.) Information Fusion and Geographic Information Systems. Lecture Notes in Geoinformation and Cartography, pp. 19–36. Springer, Heidelberg (2009)

19. Villmann, T., Mernyi, E., Hammer, B.: Neural maps in remote sensing image analysis. Neural Netw. 16(34), 389–403 (2003)

20. Hardman-Mountford, N., Richardson, A., Boyer, D., Kreiner, A., Boyer, H.: Relating sardine recruitment in the northern benguela to satellite-derived sea surface height using a neural network pattern recognition approach. Prog. Oceanogr. **59**(23), 241–255 (2003)

21. Niang, A., Gross, L., Thiria, S., Badran, F., Moulin, C.: Automatic neural classification of ocean colour reflectance spectra at the top of the atmosphere with introduction of expert knowledge. Remote Sens. Environ. **86**(2), 257–271 (2003)

22. Tetreault, B.: Use of the automatic identification system (AIS) for maritime domain awareness (MDA). In: Proceedings of MTS/IEEE OCEANS, vol. 2, pp. 1590–1594 (2005)

23. International Association of Maritime Aids to Navigation and Lighthouse Authorities (IALA): IALA guidelines on the universal automatic identification system (AIS) (2002)

24. Vanneschi, L., Castelli, M., Silva, S.: A survey of semantic methods in genetic programming. Genet. Program Evolvable Mach. **15**(2), 195–214 (2014)

25. Castelli, M., Vanneschi, L., Silva, S.: Semantic search based genetic programming and the effect of introns deletion. IEEE Trans. Cybern. **44**(1), 103–113 (2013). doi:10.1109/TSMCC.2013.2247754. ISSN: 2168-2267

26. Krawiec, K., Lichocki, P.: Approximating geometric crossover in semantic space. In: Raid, G. et al. (ed.) GECCO 2009, 8–12 July, pp. 987–994. ACM (2009)

27. Poli, R., McPhee, N.F., Vanneschi, L.: The impact of population size on code growth in gp: Analysis and empirical validation. In: Proceedings of the 10th Annual Conference on Genetic and Evolutionary Computation. GECCO 2008, pp. 1275–1282. ACM (2008)

28. Giacobini, M., Tomassini, M., Vanneschi, L.: Limiting the number of fitness cases in genetic programming using statistics. In: Guervós, J.J.M., Adamidis, P.A., Beyer, H.-G., Fernández-Villacañas, J.-L., Schwefel, H.-P. (eds.) PPSN 2002. LNCS, vol. 2439, pp. 371–380. Springer, Heidelberg (2002)

29. Tomassini, M., Vanneschi, L., Fernández, F., Galeano, G.: A study of diversity in multipopulation genetic programming. In: Liardet, P., Collet, P., Fonlupt, C., Lutton, E., Schoenauer, M. (eds.) EA 2003. LNCS, vol. 2936, pp. 243–255. Springer, Heidelberg (2004)

30. Weka Machine Learning Project: Weka. http://www.cs.waikato.ac.nz/~ml/weka

# Automatic Generation of Mobile Malwares Using Genetic Programming

Emre Aydogan[(⊠)] and Sevil Sen

Department of Computer Engineering, Hacettepe University, Ankara, Turkey
{emreaydogan,ssen}@cs.hacettepe.edu.tr

**Abstract.** The number of mobile devices has increased dramatically in the past few years. These smart devices provide many useful functionalities accessible from anywhere at anytime, such as reading and writing e-mails, surfing on the Internet, showing facilities nearby, and the like. Hence, they become an inevitable part of our daily lives. However the popularity and adoption of mobile devices also attract virus writers in order to harm our devices. So, many security companies have already proposed new solutions in order to protect our mobile devices from such malicious attempts. However developing methodologies that detect unknown malwares is a research challenge, especially on devices with limited resources. This study presents a method that evolves automatically variants of malwares from the ones in the wild by using genetic programming (GP). We aim to evaluate the efficacy of current anti-virus products, using static analysis techniques, in the market. The experimental results show the weaknesses of the static analysis tools available in the market, and the need of new detection techniques suitable for mobile devices.

**Keywords:** Mobile malware · Static analysis · Obfuscation · Evolutionary computation · Genetic programming

## 1 Introduction

Mobile devices have become an inevitable part of our lives. They provide us many useful functionalities such as reading and writing e-mails, surfing on the Internet, showing facilities nearby, video conferencing, voice recognition, and the like. However the popularity and adoption of mobile devices also attract virus writers in order to harm our devices. According to Kaspersky security report [1], nearly 145.000 new malicious programs are appeared in 2013 and 98.1 % of these programs target Android platform. Hence, in order to protect our devices from such threats, researchers and security companies have been working on developing effective and efficient anti-virus systems recently.

There are some techniques available for malware analysis and detection with varying strengths and weaknesses. Two common types of malware detection techniques according to how code is analyzed are static and dynamic analysis. Since dynamic analysis might not be affordable on some mobile devices due to their strong limitations in terms of power consumption, most of the proposed

© Springer International Publishing Switzerland 2015
A.M. Mora and G. Squillero (Eds.): EvoApplications 2015, LNCS 9028, pp. 745–756, 2015.
DOI: 10.1007/978-3-319-16549-3_60

approaches in the literature rely on static analysis up to date. However, these tools are known to be vulnerable to some obfuscation techniques and new attacks. How they are effective against known attacks, variants of known attacks, and unknown attacks needs investigation. This is the main aim in this study. In order to be able to assess the security solutions proposed for mobile devices, we automatically generate new attacks from existing ones.

In this study, we evolve new malwares, variants of known malwares, by using genetic programming (GP) in order to evaluate the performance of existing static analysis tools. The aim here is to generate new malwares automatically that we could strengthen our static analysis tools automatically as well. Because most of the existing static tools update their signature databases when they experience new/unknown malwares, automating this process will make our detection systems more robust against attacks. While the proposed approach here only automates the generation of new/unknown attacks here, the framework is planned to be extended with developing existing solutions automatically in the future.

GP has already been applied in some approaches in the literature [2–5] in order to evolve new attacks and new malwares. However most of these approaches are not fully automatic and only proposed for a specific type of attacks. A security expert is generally needed to analyse the code and to extract parameters that changes in different variants of viruses' codes, so a representation of the problem could be constructed for GP. Here, we aim to create a fully automatic system by employing some obfuscation techniques on source codes of existing malwares by using GP. The results show that GP could generate effective attacks which are able to evade from existing eight anti-virus systems which are among the most successful mobile security solutions [6]. Furthermore, it is shown that GP shows [7,8] better performance than solely applying obfuscation techniques as usually proposed in the literature. It is also shown that the approach could produce more evasive malwares than Zelix Klassmaster [9], which is a well-known Java bytecode obfuscator.

The rest of the paper is organized as follows: Sect. 2 summarizes the related approaches in the literature. In Sect. 3, we give some background information such as the details of Android system and the GP. In Sect. 4, we describe the proposed method for generating new malwares. The performance of the model is discussed in Sect. 5. Finally Sect. 6 is devoted to concluding remarks and future works.

## 2    Related Work

Researchers have been working on suitable security solutions for mobile devices in the last few years. Many security companies have already brought their mobile solutions out. Most of these solutions are based on static analysis due to their suitability to power-constrained mobile devices. Since many mobile anti-virus solutions are out now, how they are effective against known and unknown malwares needs investigation.

There are two main studies in order to evaluate commercial anti-virus products against obfuscation techniques on Android platform in the literature. In [7], they proposed a system called ADAM that evaluates the effectiveness of anti-virus systems against malware samples which are generated by employing some obfuscation techniques automatically while preserving the original malicious function. Rastogi et al. [8] has developed a system called DroidChameleon that evaluates Android anti-malware products against obfuscation attacks that are extended form of the attacks in [7]. They automatically mutate Android applications by using polymorphic and metamorphic techniques.

Christodorescu and Jha [10] proposed a technique based on a transformation of a source code for creating test samples for desktop malware detection systems. Their technique aims to evaluate the resilience of anti-virus systems to various obfuscation techniques. Morales et al. [11] evaluate and test how anti-virus systems protect hand-held devices against known malwares. Their results indicate that all four anti-virus systems produce high false negative rates. They also state that high false positive rates are the results of simple signature detection algorithms employed by the products. Moser et al. [12] proposed a malware detectors rely on semantic signatures and employed a model checking for detection. They showed that static analysis alone is not efficient to detect malware, it should be complemented with dynamic analysis techniques.

Wu L. et al. [13] proposed a computer virus evolution model. Their work based on Immune Genetic Algorithm. Noreen et al. [14] applied genetic operators to Beagle virus in order to create new variants of it. They also apply this approach to Silvio virus threatening the ARM-Linux based smart phones and generate new variants of Silvio viruses using Markov models [15]. In [16], they proposed a methodology that aims to generate new malwares by changing the semantic of malwares. They extract abstract representation of an malware, then use GP to evolve a new malware from this representation.

Ilsun et al. [17] analyze the obfuscation techniques commonly used by virus writers. They aim to understand how to use these techniques. Christodorescu et al. [18] propose a malware normalizer that reverts obfuscated malwares to original one by undoing the obfuscations. Their goal is to increase the detection rate of virus detectors.

Kayacık et al. [2] use GP to evolve buffer overflow attacks in order to obfuscate the true intent of the attacker. In [3], they also use GP to generate mimicry buffer overflow attacks with the objective of finding possible vulnerabilities before attackers exploit them. Their goal is to generate attacks that seem like benign, hence they could evade detection. They extend their work in [4] by increasing the number of detectors (5) and adding delay parameter in order to build evasion attacks. In [5], they compare two approaches, "white-box" and "black-box", while the former uses the internal knowledge of the detectors to generate evasion attacks, the latter uses only the output of the detectors.

As far as we know, there are only two approaches proposed for mobile anti-virus evaluation against new attacks [7,8]. They clearly present how ineffective anti-virus systems is against code obfuscation techniques. The target of our study is also to test existing anti-virus solutions. However we investigate the use of GP to achieve that. It is shown that automatically evolved malwares could be more evasive than malwares generated by solely employing obfuscation techniques as in [7,8]. GP automatically employs the best evasion strategies by reducing the size of the search space.

## 3   Android Platform

Android is an operating system based on the Linux kernel and runs dalvik byte-code which is a similar form of Java bytecode. There are normally multiple *.class* files in a Java application, however an Android application has a single *.dex* file consists of all the classes. The java source codes are compiled and packaged into an *.apk* file. *.apk* file is the file format to run on a device or on an emulator for Android and contains all of the elements like *.dex* file, manifest file, source codes, resource files, and the like.

```
.method public A (Landroid/widget/AdapterView;Landroid/view/View;IJ)V
invoke-direct (p0), Lcom/keepwired/utility/controls/FileChooser;->B()V
invoke-direct (p0), Lcom/keepwired/utility/controls/FileChooser;->C()V
invoke-virtual (p0, p0, v3), Lcom/keepwired/utility/controls/FileChooser;->D(Landroid/content/Context;Ljava/lang/
        String;)V
.end method

.method private B()V
invoke-direct (v3, p0), Lcom/keepwired/utility/controls/FileChooser$2;->E(Lcom/keepwired/utility/controls/
        FileChooser;)V
.end method

.method private C()V
invoke-direct (v4, p0), Lcom/keepwired/utility/controls/FileChooser$3;->F(Lcom/keepwired/utility/controls/
        FileChooser;)V
invoke-direct (v3, p0), Lcom/keepwired/utility/controls/FileChooser$4;->G(Lcom/keepwired/utility/controls/
        FileChooser;)V
.end method

.method public D(Landroid/content/Context;Ljava/lang/String;)V
.end method
```

**Fig. 1.** Code fragment

Since we aim to use source codes of existing malwares in order to evaluate anti-virus products by using GP, we should be able do reverse engineering on these malwares. Although we could get Java source codes from an Android application easily by using some existing tools [19,20], we cannot convert them back to the *.apk* file due to some errors encountered during the transformation process. These errors could not be resolved automatically. Therefore, we use *.smali* codes that are sequences of assembly-like dalvik bytecode instruction sets [21]. We can access *.smali* codes by extracting them from *.dex* file inside the *.apk* file. *.smali* files extracted using apktool [22] and Smali/BakSmali [23]. Then the converted *.smali* files could be used to construct an *.apk* file. A sample smali class file is shown in Fig. 1.

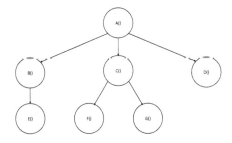

**Fig. 2.** CFG for code fragment in Fig. 1

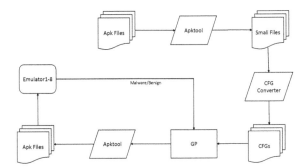

**Fig. 3.** Simplified schema of experiments

## 4    The Model

The conceptual schema of our experiments is shown in Fig. 3. Firstly, we extract smali codes from malicious application in order to obtain CFGs (Control Flow Graph). As stated before, we use smali codes instead of Java codes which enable us to repack the application. After obtaining smali codes, we create CFGs of each malicious application in order to represent them in GP. GP is an evolutionary computation technique inspired from natural evolution. It has been one of the most employed evolutionary computation (EC) technique, since it is introduced by Koza [24]. We use the toolkit ECJ [25] for the GP implementation in the experiments. In this study, malicious applications, is represented by control flow graphs (CFG) which are given as inputs to GP.

As we mentioned, to represent an *.apk* file in GP, we extract control flow graph of each functions in the application. Applications considered here do not consist of recursive functions. An example CFG is shown in Fig. 2. Each CFG corresponds to a tree, each method is represented by nodes, and the edges indicate the flow between methods. Each program is represented by an individual in GP and each individuals have different sizes of trees (CFGs) because of the fact that each *.apk* file has variable number of functions. In GP, crossover or mutation operators are applied to these CFGs. Crossover operation exchanges sub-trees of individuals. To be able to obtain executable programs, only methods with the same declarations having the same return type, the equal number of parameters with the same types are allowed to exchange. This allows us to create new malwares from existing malwares. However since the high value of crossover rate increase the number of non-executable individuals, the crossover operation is assigned to a low rate (0.1) in the experiments. And when we use crossover operator, we have to check whether newly generated programs execute properly and perform malicious activities. In order to check this, we developed a dynamic analysis tool [26]. This tool runs applications and extract some features in runtime from Android apps. The machine learning approaches are applied on these features in order to decide whether the application is malicious or not. If the application cannot be executed properly, the dynamic analysis tool does not return any value in a time interval.

Mutation operator is also applied on sub-trees which are randomly chose. It uses the five obfuscation techniques. These techniques aim to generate different variants of the malwares while preserving the original malicious function. To perform these transformations, respectively, we take .*apk* file as an input, unpack smali codes using apktool, apply obfuscation techniques on smali codes, repack smali codes into .*apk* file and finally sign it before being installed on the emulator. Rename Local Identifier (RI) changes one of the local identifiers of a method with a string generated by a random string. Two-fold Code Reordering (CR2) is based on reordering the codes of a method in the program. We reorder the codes of a method by inserting *goto* statement at the top and bottom parts of the method. Three-fold Code Reordering (CR3) has the same logic with the two-fold code reordering. The only difference is to insert 3 *goto* statement instead of 2 in this obfuscation strategy. So we change the order of the codes, however, we preserve the execution sequences of the codes at runtime. In Junk Code Insertion (JK), three instructions are inserted. Firstly, we add a local variable to the method. Primitive types such as string, int, double are used to identify the local variable. Then, PrintStream object is inserted to print out the local variable, defined one step before. Finally, the code calls the *println* function of the PrintStream object. Data Encryption (DE) encrypts all the strings that have been used in the method. Firstly, the encryption is done by using a randomly generated key. Then the string is replaced with its encrypted version ciphered with the key. The key is defined in the method as well. Finally, *decrypt* function of the SimpleCrypto class is called. If Crypto package is not already included in the code, it will be added. In every mutation operation, one obfuscation technique is selected and applied to the node namely source codes of the function that selected randomly by GP. In order to generate more evasive attacks, we set the mutation rate to a high value, 0.9. The other GP parameters are selected as follows: 10 for population size, 100 for generation, 7 for tournament selection. The parameters not mentioned here are the default parameters of the ECJ toolkit.

We also sign each generated programs with a random key not to cause any errors while trying to install the application on the emulator. We generate random key with keytool [27]. To sign the generated programs, we use jarsigner [28] that is used to signs and verifies Java Archive (.*jar*) files.

Since the fitness function defines how the individuals solves the problem or come close to the solution, defining a well-representative fitness function is very important in any GP application. In our fitness function here, we use the output of 8 anti-virus systems which are among the most successful mobile security solutions. The anti-virus systems are selected according to their protection score given in AV-TEST [6]. Our second criteria to choose the anti-virus systems, we explore if we could get the output of the anti-virus run on a emulator. Hence we use the solutions which produce log files. Table 1 lists the anti-virus systems employed in our experiments. Each anti-virus is executed on different emulators (official Android emulator) to simulate the execution of evolved malwares and the response of anti-virus against them. The fitness function takes values between 0 and 1. It is aimed to be minimized and defined as follows:

$$fitness = \frac{\text{number of antivirus systems detecting the individual}}{\text{total number of anti-virus systems}} \qquad (1)$$

Table 1. Anti-virus products used.

| Vendor | Product | Version |
|--------|---------|---------|
| Eset | Eset Mobile Security | 3.0.882.0-16 |
| GData | Gdata Internet Security | 25.0.0 |
| Ikarus | Ikarus mobile.security | 1.7.20 |
| Kaspersky | Kaspersky Internet Security | 11.1.3.10 |
| Avast | Avast Mobile Security | 3.0.7550 |
| Trend Micro | Trend Micro Mobile Security | 5.0.0.1225 |
| BitDefender | BitDefender Mobile Security | 2.18.119 |
| Norton | Norton Mobile Security | 3.8.6.1533 |

## 5   Results

### 5.1   Dataset

We use the dataset given in [29]. It is the first malware dataset introduced in the literature. Many studies have already used this dataset in order to compare their result with other approaches. The dataset include 1,260 Android malwares in 49 malware families collected within more than a year, between August 2010 and October 2011. We randomly select malwares from the dataset and their produced CFGs are given to the GP algorithm. The only criteria we used to select malwares is to be detectable by the anti-virus systems. The number of anti-virus systems detecting malwares is not taken into account. The GP algorithm is run many times with different inputs. In some runs, GP produces non-executable or non-compilable individuals due to difficulties faced with while modifying the smali files. These outputs are not discussed in the results.

**Table 2.** The detection ratio of obfuscated/evolved malwares employing just one obfuscation technique by the 8 anti-virus systems

| | OR | JK | DE | CR2 | CR3 | RI | MU | XO + MU |
|---|---|---|---|---|---|---|---|---|
| NickySpy_1ce27fa92a313da39f1e31e97d3ac05a8d6ffe78 | 8 | 7 | 8 | 7 | 7 | 8 | 5 | 7 |
| NickySpy_63e642f0d859e096342321c9e03baca7cd1210fa | 8 | 8 | 8 | 7 | 7 | 8 | 6 | 6 |
| Asroot_0c059ad62b9dbccf8943fe4697f2a6b0cb917548 | 7 | 7 | 6 | 7 | 7 | 7 | 6 | 6 |
| GPSSMSSpy_0eb4b7737df1b8b52213599e405d71c9be8a68ac | 6 | 5 | 5 | 6 | 6 | 6 | 5 | 5 |
| GPSSMSSpy_4d43d7771e480de34dbf748867152406b91a0de8 | 6 | 5 | 5 | 6 | 6 | 6 | 5 | 5 |
| HippoSMS_bd7e85f5a0c39a9aeecc05dbc99a9e5c52150ba6 | 8 | 7 | 5 | 8 | 7 | 7 | 4 | 7 |
| FakeNetflix_0936b366cbc39a9a60e254a05671088c84bd847e | 6 | 6 | 4 | 6 | 6 | 6 | 3 | 3 |
| DroidKungFu2_8bb6106b7c1160e8812788bbd16b563f5a00080a | 7 | 7 | 7 | 7 | 7 | 7 | 6 | 6 |
| GPSSMSSpy_af727f5e23e69bfe2321f5d556c63f741dae8283 | 6 | 5 | 5 | 6 | 6 | 6 | 4 | 5 |
| GPSSMSSpy_73c1657ddf52cc82b57c2db80554c59927e7970a | 6 | 5 | 5 | 6 | 6 | 6 | 4 | 5 |
| GPSSMSSpy_94b56252ff610126135c568b1cc7b92405b9e608 | 6 | 5 | 5 | 6 | 6 | 6 | 4 | 5 |
| GPSSMSSpy_5900250af412b7147764706847cf1dbc54cd6e0e | 6 | 5 | 5 | 6 | 6 | 6 | 4 | 5 |
| DroidKungFu1_02d2e109d16d160f77a645f44314fedcdbcd6e18 | 8 | 8 | 8 | 8 | 8 | 8 | 7 | 7 |
| RogueLemon_08a21de6b70f584ceddbe803ae12d79a33d33b50 | 6 | 5 | 4 | 6 | 6 | 6 | 4 | 5 |

## 5.2   Comparison with One-Level Obfuscation

Table 2 demonstrates the results by employing just one obfuscation technique to malwares. The column MU shows the performance of malwares generated by GP using only mutation operator and the column MU+XO shows the performance of malwares generated by GP using mutation and crossover operators together. For example, the original version of the malware given in the first row (OR) is detected by all anti-virus systems. If we apply different obfuscation techniques solely to the malware as many approaches in the literature, it could avoid being identified from some anti-virus systems. However, if we apply GP to the malware, it shows the lowest detection rate. Table 2 shows that if we use GP using mutation and crossover operator together, the detection results increase comparing to GP using only mutation operator due to that crossover operator is very error prone because of exchanging codes between apps are very hard to deal with. There are also some results that GP is not able to outperform some obfuscation techniques. However it never produces worse results than them as expected. We obtain more malwares producing the same result with the output of GP. Since we want to emphasize the best results, we do not list all malwares evolved in the table.

As shown in Table 2, Rename local identifier transformation (RI) is not very effective against anti-virus systems. It is only effective against HippoSMS malware. Because RI just changes the name of the constant strings with an arbitrary string. Two-fold code reordering (CR2) does also only affect the NickySpy malware and able to evade from only one anti-virus. The best improvement on results is performed by data encryption (DE). Data Encryption hides the value of the constant strings so that if attacker wants to send message to premium-rate service, attack the websites or read secret information from mobile devices, he could easily hide their intent. The junk code insertion transformation (JK) also produces good results, even though it only adds a simple function which display a random value on the screen. Finally three-fold code reordering (CR3) leads to better results than RI and CR2, but not as good as DE and JK.

**Table 3.** The detection ratio of obfuscated/evolved malwares employing two obfuscation techniques by the 8 anti-virus systems

| | JK-DE | CR2-DE | DE-RI | CR3-DE | JK-CR3 | JK-RI | CR2-RI | JK-CR2 | CR3-RI | MU | XO + MU | ZEL |
|---|---|---|---|---|---|---|---|---|---|---|---|---|
| NickySpy_1ce27fa92a219da29f1e91e97d2ac05a9d6ffe79 | 7 | 7 | 9 | 7 | 7 | 7 | 7 | 7 | 7 | 5 | 7 | 6 |
| NickySpy_63e642f0d859e096342321c9e03baca7cd1210fa | 7 | 7 | 8 | 7 | 8 | 7 | 7 | 8 | 7 | 6 | 6 | 6 |
| Asroot_0c059ad62b9dbccf8943fe4697f2a6b0cb917548 | 6 | 6 | 6 | 6 | 6 | 7 | 7 | 7 | 6 | 6 | 6 | 6 |
| GPSSMSSpy_0eb4b7737df1b8b52213599e405d71c9be8a68ac | 5 | 5 | 5 | 5 | 5 | 6 | 6 | 6 | 6 | 5 | 5 | 4 |
| GPSSMSSpy_4d43d7771e480de34dbf748867152406b91a0de8 | 5 | 5 | 5 | 5 | 5 | 6 | 5 | 5 | 5 | 5 | 5 | 4 |
| HippoSMS_bd7e85f5a0c39a9aeecc05dbc99a9e5c52150ba6 | 5 | 5 | 5 | 5 | 6 | 7 | 7 | 7 | 6 | 4 | 7 | 5 |
| FakeNetflix_0936b366cbc39a9a60e254a05671088c84bd847e | 4 | 4 | 4 | 4 | 6 | 6 | 6 | 6 | 6 | 3 | 3 | 5 |
| DroidKungFu2_8bb6106b7c1160e8812788bbd16b563f5a00080a | 7 | 7 | 7 | - | - | 7 | 7 | 7 | - | 6 | 6 | 6 |
| GPSSMSSpy_af727f5e23e69bfe2321f5d556c63f741dae8283 | 5 | 5 | 5 | 5 | 5 | 5 | 6 | 5 | 5 | 4 | 5 | 4 |
| GPSSMSSpy_73c1657ddf52cc82b57c2db80554c59927e7970a | 5 | 5 | 5 | 5 | 5 | 5 | 6 | 5 | 5 | 4 | 5 | 4 |
| GPSSMSSpy_94b56252ff610126135c568b1cc7b92405b9e608 | 5 | 5 | 5 | 5 | 5 | 6 | 6 | 6 | 6 | 4 | 5 | 4 |
| GPSSMSSpy_5900250af412b7147764706847cf1dbc54cd6e0e | 5 | 5 | 5 | 5 | 6 | 5 | 6 | 6 | 5 | 4 | 5 | 4 |
| DroidKungFu1_02d2a10a116f160f77e6d56f4314fedcdbcd6e18 | 9 | 9 | 9 | - | - | 9 | 9 | 9 | - | 7 | 7 | 9 |
| RogueLemon_08a21de6b70f584ceddbe803ae12d79a33d33b50 | 4 | 4 | 4 | - | - | 6 | 6 | 6 | - | 4 | 5 | 4 |

## 5.3   Comparison with Two-Level Obfuscation

There are several studies that employing obfuscation techniques to malwares one by one [7] or two obfuscation techniques together [8]. GP could apply multiple obfuscation techniques over nodes. Therefore, we compare our GP with technique that applies two obfuscation techniques together over malwares. The results can be shown in Table 3. When we apply Two-fold and Three-fold code reordering together, we fail to produce compiled apps so that we exclude their results in Table 3. We also apply obfuscation techniques in groups of triple and four, but due to that obfuscation techniques affect each other, the rate of the compiled apps has been very low and results not shown in Table 3. Evolutionary computation can prevent such problems, with respect to its nature ability that eliminate non-compiled and non-executable malwares. "-" in Table 3 denotes malwares that can be compiled but cannot be installed on emulators properly. Table 3 shows that when we apply obfuscation techniques in groups of two, there is no further improvement comparing to one by one.

We also evaluate the resilience of the anti-virus systems by using a well-known obfuscator, Zelik KlassMaster [9]. The column ZEL in Table 3 shows the detection rate of the anti-virus systems against malwares obfuscated by the obfuscator. The results show that GP (MU) produces comparable results with the obfuscator. It produces more evasive malwares for 4 applications. Only two malwares obfuscated by Zelix KlassMaster [9] produces better results than our approach. In the future, we aim to compare our approach with more obfuscators in the literature.

## 5.4   Evelution of Static Analysis Tools

To sum up, we could say that our approach produces many malwares in one run, and it generally evolves more evasive attacks than five obfuscation techniques automatically. It allow us to test the anti-virus systems against unknown attacks as shown in Table 4. As shown, Avast Mobile Security is the most robust system against new attacks. It detects all obfuscated malwares in this study except one if we apply mutation and crossover operators together. BitDefender only misses one malware evolved by GP. Kaspersky and TrendMicro are also successful enough to be able to detect all obfuscation techniques. But three evolved

**Table 4.** The performance of anti-virus systems against obfuscated and evolved malwares

|              | OR | JK | DE | CR2 | CR3 | RI | MU | MU + XO |
|--------------|----|----|----|-----|-----|----|----|---------|
| Eset         | 8  | 8  | 6  | 8   | 8   | 8  | 4  | 6       |
| GData        | 6  | 6  | 6  | 6   | 6   | 6  | 5  | 5       |
| Ikarus       | 13 | 8  | 6  | 12  | 11  | 13 | 7  | 12      |
| Kaspersky    | 13 | 12 | 12 | 13  | 13  | 13 | 10 | 10      |
| Avast        | 14 | 14 | 14 | 14  | 14  | 14 | 14 | 13      |
| TrendMicro   | 13 | 12 | 11 | 12  | 12  | 12 | 9  | 12      |
| BitDefender  | 14 | 14 | 14 | 14  | 14  | 14 | 13 | 13      |
| Norton       | 13 | 11 | 11 | 13  | 13  | 13 | 5  | 11      |
| Total        | 94 | 85 | 80 | 92  | 91  | 93 | 67 | 82      |

malwares achieve to be undetected by Kaspersky and TrendMicro. Although the detection performance of GData is very low (6/14), it is very effective against all obfuscation techniques, except one evolved malware by GP. Norton Mobile Security is the most ineffective solution against evolved malwares. Although it detects 13 malwares out of 14 per obfuscation techniques, we achieve to evolve 8 malwares that could avoid being recognized by Norton using GP (MU) and to evolve 2 evasive malwares by using GP (MU+XO). Our evolved malwares are also very effective against Eset. We also manage to escape from Ikarus Mobile Security. However, DE outperforms our method on one malware.

There are three main important advantages of using GP to create new, unseen malwares. Firstly, GP reduces the search space and helps to find the best effective obfuscation techniques upon malwares rapidly. It eliminates non-compilable or non-executable solutions naturally. More evasive malwares could be evolved by increasing the number of obfuscation techniques employed in GP. Secondly, GP could allow to co-evolve both malwares and anti-malware systems automatically. We aim to automatically improve anti-malware systems in the future. The last advantage of using GP is bloating. Generally bloating is not desired in GP applications. However bloating has a positive effect in our method that causes to generate more complex programs, hence more evasive malwares.

## 6    Conclusion

We propose a method that evaluates current anti-virus systems for Android platform. We apply GP to Android malwares in order to generate the variants of malwares with the objective of evading from anti-virus systems. We compare our results with the obfuscation techniques and the Zelix KlassMaster obfuscator [9]. We employ obfuscation techniques either one by one or in groups of two on malwares. Our results show that all the anti-virus systems have a weakness against obfuscation techniques and we can further decrease their detection ratio against evolved malwares by using GP.

To the best of our knowledge, this is the first work that generates evolved mobile malwares using GP in mobile platforms. One of the main characteristics of the proposed system is being fully automatic. In the future, more obfuscation techniques are planned to be added to the algorithm. Moreover, it is aimed to be compared with more obfuscators in the literature. We also aim to evolve both malwares and anti-malwares simultaneously in the future.

**Acknowledgement.** This study is supported by the Scientific and Technological Research Council of Turkey (TUBITAK-112E354). We would like to thank TUBITAK for its support.

# References

1. Kaspersky Lab.: Mobile malware evolution: 3 infection attempts per user in 2013. http://www.kaspersky.com/about/news/virus/2014/Mobile-malware-evolution-3-infection-attempts-per-user-in-2013
2. Kayacık, H.G., Heywood, M.I., Zincir-Heywood, A.N.: On evolving buffer overflow attacks using genetic programming. In: Proceedings of the 8th Annual Conference on Genetic and Evolutionary Computation, pp. 1667–1674. ACM (2006)
3. Kayacık, H.G., Zincir-Heywood, A.N., Heywood, M.I., Burschka, S.: Generating mimicry attacks using genetic programming: a benchmarking study. In: Proceedings of IEEE Symposium on Computational Intelligence in Cyber Security, pp. 136–143 (2009)
4. Kayacık, H.G., Zincir-Heywood, A.N., Heywood, M.I.: Can a good offense be a good defense? Vulnerability testing of anomaly detectors through an artificial arms race. Appl. Soft Comput. 11(7), 4366–4383 (2011)
5. Kayacık, H.G., Zincir-Heywood, A.N., Heywood, M.I.: Evolutionary computation as an artificial attacker: generating evasion attacks for detector vulnerability testing. Evol. Intel. 4(4), 243–266 (2011)
6. AV-TEST: The independent it-security institute. http://www.av-test.org/en/home/
7. Zheng, M., Lee, P.P.C., Lui, J.C.S.: ADAM: an automatic and extensible platform to stress test android anti-virus systems. In: Flegel, U., Markatos, E., Robertson, W. (eds.) DIMVA 2012. LNCS, vol. 7591, pp. 82–101. Springer, Heidelberg (2013)
8. Rastogi, V., Chen, Y., Jiang, X.: DroidChameleon: evaluating android anti-malware against transformation attacks. In: Proceedings of the 8th ACM SIGSAC Symposium on Information, Computer and Communications Security, pp. 329–334. ACM (2013)
9. Zelix KlassMaster: Java obfuscator - zelix klassmaster. http://www.zelix.com/
10. Christodorescu, M., Jha, S.: Testing malware detectors. In: Proceedings of the 2004 ACM SIGSOFT International Symposium on Software Testing and Analysis, pp. 34–44 (2004)
11. Morales, J., Clarke, P., Deng, Y., Golam Kibria, B.: Testing and evaluating virus detectors for handheld devices. J. Comput. Virol. 2(2), 135–147 (2006)
12. Moser, A., Kruegel, C., Kirda, E.: Limits of static analysis for malware detection. In: Proceedings of Computer Security Applications Conference, pp. 421–430 (2007)
13. Wu, L., Zhang, Y.: Research of the computer virus evolution model based on immune genetic algorithm. In: Proceedings of the 10th IEEE/ACIS International

Conference on Computer and Information Science, pp. 9–13. IEEE Computer Society (2011)

14. Sadia, N., Shafaq, M., Zubair, S.M., Muddassar, F.: Evolvable malware. In: Proceedings of the 11th Annual Conference on Genetic and Evolutionary Computation, pp. 1569–1576. ACM (2009)

15. Shahzad, F., Saleem, M., Farooq, M.: A hybrid framework for malware detection on smartphones using ELF structural & PCB runtime traces. Technical report, TR-58 FAST-National University, Pakistan (2012)

16. Noreen, S., Murtaza, S., Shafiq, M.Z., Farooq, M.: Using formal grammar and genetic operators to evolve malware. In: Kirda, E., Jha, S., Balzarotti, D. (eds.) RAID 2009. LNCS, vol. 5758, pp. 375–377. Springer, Heidelberg (2009)

17. You, I., Yim, K.: Malware obfuscation techniques: a brief survey. In: Proceedings of the International Conference on Broadband, Wireless Computing, Communication and Applications, pp. 297–300 (2010)

18. Christodorescu, M., Kinder, J., Jha, S., Katzenbeisser, S., Veith, H., Munchen, T.U.: Malware normalization. Technical report, 1539, University of Wisconsin (2005)

19. JAD: Java decompiler download mirror. http://varaneckas.com/jad/

20. JEB: The interactive android decompiler. http://www.android-decompiler.com/

21. Android: Bytecode for the dalvik VM. https://source.android.com/devices/tech/dalvik/dalvik-bytecode.html

22. Apktool: A tool for reverse engineering android apk files. https://code.google.com/p/android-apktool/

23. Smali: An assembler/disassembler for androids dex format. https://code.google.com/p/smali/

24. Koza, J.R.: Genetic Programming: On the Programming of Computers by Means of Natural Selection. MIT Press, Cambridge (1992)

25. ECJ: A java-based evolutionary computation research system. http://cs.gmu.edu/eclab/projects/ecj/

26. Ozkan, H.B., Aydogan, E., Sen, S.: An ensemble learning approach to mobile malware detection. Technical report, Department of Computer Engineering, Hacettepe University (2014)

27. Oracle: keytool - key and certificate management tool. http://docs.oracle.com/javase/7/docs/technotes/tools/solaris/keytool.html

28. Oracle: jarsigner.http://docs.oracle.com/javase/7/docs/technotes/tools/windows/jarsigner.html

29. Zhou, Y., Jiang, X.: Dissecting android malware: characterization and evolution. In: Proceedings of the 2012 IEEE Symposium on Security and Privacy, pp. 95–109. IEEE Computer Society (2012)

# EvoROBOT

# On the Tradeoff Between Hardware Protection and Optimization Success: A Case Study in Onboard Evolutionary Robotics for Autonomous Parallel Parking

Mostafa Wahby and Heiko Hamann[(⊠)]

Department of Computer Science, University of Paderborn, Paderborn, Germany
mostafaw@mail.uni-paderborn.de, heiko.hamann@uni-paderborn.de

**Abstract.** Making the transition from simulation to reality in evolutionary robotics is known to be challenging. What is known as the reality gap, summarizes the set of problems that arises when robot controllers have been evolved in simulation and then are transferred to the real robot. In this paper we study an additional problem that is beyond the reality gap. In simulations, the robot needs no protection against damage, while on the real robot that is essential to stay cost-effective. We investigate how the probability of collisions can be minimized by introducing appropriate penalties to the fitness function. A change to the fitness function, however, changes the evolutionary dynamics and can influence the optimization success negatively. Therefore, we detect a tradeoff between a required hardware protection and a reduced efficiency of the evolutionary optimization process. We study this tradeoff on the basis of a robotics case study in autonomous parallel parking.

## 1 Introduction

In evolutionary robotics [1,2], simulations are a key tool due to limited resources and costly robot experiments. However, if simulations are overused, key challenges of evolutionary robotics might be either overlooked or difficult to resolve [3]. For example, "some subtleties of control are contained within the robot–world interface and are easily overlooked" [3]. It is also well-known that the transition from simulation to the real robot is challenging which is refereed to by the term 'reality gap' problem [2,4,5]. Both, pushing evolutionary robotics to higher degrees of autonomy, for example by online, onboard evolution [6–9], and getting closer to solving real-world problems, require to cover the robotics-related challenges of evolutionary robotics completely. Complex interactions between hardware features of the robot and the evolutionary dynamics should be expected. Especially dynamic robot behaviors that rely heavily on physical features, such as friction and inertia, are difficult to simulate and inherently complex [5]. However, even tasks that are easily simulated can be problematic when hardware protection is an issue as discussed in the following.

© Springer International Publishing Switzerland 2015
A.M. Mora and G. Squillero (Eds.): EvoApplications 2015, LNCS 9028, pp. 759–770, 2015.
DOI: 10.1007/978-3-319-16549-3_61

The transition from simulation to the real robot creates problems that go beyond what is summarized as reality gap problem. Not only the optimal controllers differ between simulation and reality, also elements of the evolutionary algorithm might require adaptations. It is crucial to protect the real robot from damages to allow for a rapid and cost-effective synthesis of robot controllers (collision avoidance has been investigated in evolutionary robotics from the very beginning [10]). For example, the robot might fall over, get stuck, or might be exposed to high accelerations due to collisions.

One option is to limit the robot's accelerations to decrease the impact of collisions. However, that way we deliberately exclude potentially efficient solutions to the problem. Another option is to implement a hardware protection layer that is interlaced between the application layer (here the evolutionary algorithm and the currently evaluated controller) and the hardware layer [11]. The hardware protection layer constantly monitors actuator control values and the sensor input, possibly supported by a world model, while trying to classify whether a certain control value is too risky, that is, detecting critical situations. Accordingly the robot would be stopped in dangerous situations. Such an approach might be quite complex and requires a high reliability of sensors and good sensor coverage which might be difficult to achieve especially for simple robots. The sensor configuration of the robot might not allow to prevent collisions at all times. Hence, a more efficient approach could be to solve the problem within the framework of evolutionary computation and adapt the fitness function such that controllers are favored that generally tend to prevent critical situations. This way hardware protection is easier to achieve because most of the controllers in the population at later generations will generally tend to stay away from walls. Hence, we face lower requirements for sensor reliability and sensor coverage because the robot would generally spent less time in dangerous situations. For some tasks, however, the task might actually require the robot to put itself intro critical situations. An example is parking a car, which is a simple but suitable task for our following study (a simulation study of parallel parking using evolutionary algorithms was reported in [12]). As part of the task the robot has to get close to walls (obstacles) and hence has to risk collisions. When evolving the controllers on the robot directly, the robot's hardware needs to be protected. This can be done by penalizing collisions or close approaches to walls explicitly in the fitness function. However, then we impose additional constraints which might increase the difficulty to evolve efficient behaviors. More conservative behaviors might be favored (i.e., collision risk minimized) which might be more difficult to evolve. Therefore, we face a tradeoff between preventing damage to the robot and achieving an efficient evolutionary optimization process.

This hardware-protection-vs.-efficiency tradeoff is a general challenge of evolutionary robotics with far-reaching impact. As we seek to increase the autonomy of evolutionary robotic systems, it is getting more important that the robot stays fully functional (i.e., no damages and no deadlock situations) at all times without human interaction. In particular, it is a challenge to the new concept of embodied online onboard evolution [6–9] which follows the idea of a fully autonomous evolutionary process on the robot hardware. In the following, we investigate the above mentioned tradeoff in simulation and report robot experiments of onboard evolution as showcase. We present the robot and the robot arena that were used in the robot experiments as well as the simulation that was used for preliminary tests. In Sect. 3 we give implementation details of the evolutionary algorithm and the designed fitness function, followed by a section reporting the results.

## 2   Robot and Robot Arena

In this work, we report robot experiments of embodied onboard evolution in a parallel parking scenario. Our robot called 'LegoBot' (see Fig. 1(a)) was built using the following components: Lego$^{TM}$ bricks, which were used to build the car chassis and allow for a high degree of customization; a DC motor, which drives the back wheels; a servo motor, for the front wheel steering; four HC-SR04 ultrasonic ranging modules ($S_r$, $S_l$, $S_f$ and $S_b$), each sensor is placed on one side of the robot, see Fig. 1(b), they provide distance readings of up to four meters with a measuring angle of 15°; and a Raspberry Pi Linux board which collects the data from the ultrasonic sensors and instructs the motors according to the Artificial Neural Network (ANN) controller.

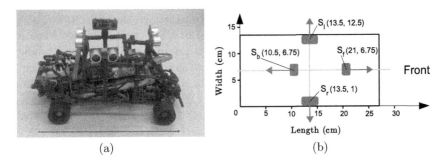

(a)                                    (b)

**Fig. 1.** (a) our car-like robot 'LegoBot' (arrowhead indicates front); (b) its dimensions and sensor setting (left sensor $S_l$, right sensor $S_r$, front sensor $S_f$, and back sensor $S_b$).

In addition, a rectangular arena of dimensions 120 cm×80 cm was built. Two rectangular objects of dimensions 40 cm×23.5 cm and 20 cm×23.5 cm are placed in the arena to represent a parking slot. The parallel parking slot length equals twice the length of the robot as seen in Fig. 2(a). By replacing the 20 cm×23.5 cm rectangular object on the right by another object of dimensions 35 cm×23.5 cm, we obtain a narrower parking slot which equals about one and a half the length of the robot[1] as shown in Fig. 2(b). Note that the LegoBot has limited agility

---

[1] For example in North America, parallel parking slots are standardized to a width of about 2.76 m and a length of about 6.1 m. While the average dimensions of a mid-size car are 4.1 m in length and 1.85 m in width. Approximately, a parallel parking slot length and width are equal to one and a half of an average mid-size car.

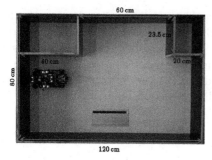
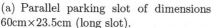

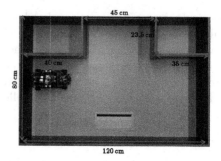

(a) Parallel parking slot of dimensions 60cm×23.5cm (long slot).

(b) Parallel parking slot of dimensions 45cm×23.5cm (short slot).

**Fig. 2.** Real world parallel parking arena scenarios.

compared to typical cars, because the maximum steering angle of the LegoBot is 31° only. In the following, we use both available parking slot lengths to define parking tasks of different difficulty.

In simulation, we have a 120 cm×80 cm arena in a simulated environment using Player/Stage[2] [13] as shown in Fig. 3. The parking slot has dimensions 60 cm×23.5 cm. The actual simulated arena and parking slot dimensions match those of the real world parking slot mentioned above, see Fig. 2(a). The red cuboid in Fig. 3 represents a simulated LegoBot and is placed in the arena in a ready to reverse position. The simulated robot settings were configured to match the properties of the robot in reality as follows: simulated robot velocity 20 cm/s, front wheel steering velocity 137.7 °/s, steering angles in seven discrete positions: −31°, −21°, −11°, 0°, 11°, 21° and 31°.

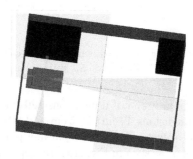

**Fig. 3.** Simulated robot and arena.

---

[2] Player/Stage is a popular open source software for research in robotics and sensor systems, see http://playerstage.sourceforge.net.

## 3    NEAT and Fitness Functions

Our implementation is based on MultiNEAT[3] [14] which is a portable software library implementing NEAT that uses the complexification method [15]. Multi-NEAT includes many external libraries which allow the user to connect the NEAT functions and methods with other algorithms easily. In this work, the MultiNEAT software library is used in the simulations and it is also run on the robot in our experiments, in order to evolve ANN controllers which are able to perform the parallel parking task efficiently in both simulation and real world environments. NEAT relies on many parameters to define the evolution process. Table 1 specifies the NEAT parameters used in our experiments. These parameters were fine-tuned to the parallel parking task. We evolve ANN with four input neurons, a variable number of neurons on the hidden layer based on NEAT, two output neurons (*DCMotorControl* and *ServoMotorControl*), and an unsigned sigmoid activation function (see Fig. 4). This simple controller approach was chosen because our focus is on the hardware-protection-vs.-efficiency tradeoff.

**Table 1.** Used NEAT parameters.

| Parameter | Value | Parameter | Value |
|---|---|---|---|
| *PopulationSize* | 30 | *CrossoverRate* | 0.5 |
| *DynamicCompatibility* | True | *MutateWeightsProb* | 0.9 |
| *CompatTreshold* | 2.0 | *WeightMutationMaxPower* | 5.0 |
| *YoungAgeTreshold* | 15 | *YoungAgeFitnessBoost* | 1.0 |
| *OverallMutationRate* | 0.5 | *WeightReplacementMaxPower* | 5.0 |
| *OldAgeTreshold* | 35 | *MutateWeightsSevereProb* | 0.5 |
| *MinSpecies* | 5 | *WeightMutationRate* | 0.75 |
| *MaxSpecies* | 25 | *MaxWeight* | 20 |
| *SurvivalRate* | 0.6 | *MutateAddNeuronProb* | 0.04 |
| *RouletteWheelSelection* | False | *MutateAddLinkProb* | 0.03 |
| *RecurrentProb* | 0 | *MutateRemoveLinkProb* | 0.03 |

The sensor input is provided by the four ultrasonic sensors mounted on the LegoBot. The output *ServoMotorControl* controls the angles of the front steering wheels. The primary output of the network is limited to $[0, 1]$ and then mapped to seven intervals. Each interval is associated with a steering angle (as mentioned above, seven possible steering positions between $-31°$ and $+31°$). The output *DCMotorControl* controls the movement state of the back wheels (i.e., drive axle). The primary output is also limited to $[0, 1]$ but then mapped to three intervals. Each interval is associated with a movement state: forward, backward, and stopped.

---

[3] It was developed by Peter Chervenski and Shane Ryan around 2008 at NEAT Sciences Ltd.

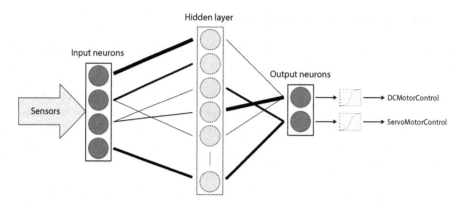

**Fig. 4.** An example of an ANN with four input neurons and two output neurons. The connection weights are represented by the thickness of the connection lines.

**Table 2.** Used fitness function parameters for each experiment: simulation long slot (simulation experiment with 60 cm parking slot), robot long slot (robot experiment with 60 cm parking slot), robot short slot (robot experiment with 45 cm parking slot), and robot forward parking short slot (robot experiment with 45 cm parking slot and robot enters parking slot forwards).

| Parameter | Simulation long slot | Robot long slot | Robot short slot | Robot forward parking |
|---|---|---|---|---|
| Crashing penalty $P_{crash}$ | Varied | 0.4 | 0.4 | 1 |
| Stopping penalty $P_{stop}$ | 0.2 | 0.2 | 0.2 | 0.2 |
| Alignment penalty threshold $\theta_{align}$ | 0.07 | 0.07 | 0.07 | 0.07 |
| Alignment penalty weight $w_{align}$ | 0.1 | 0.15 | 0.15 | 0.1 |
| Balancing penalty threshold $\theta_{bal}$ | 0.6 | 0.6 | 0.45 | 0.45 |
| Balancing penalty weight $w_{bal}$ | 0.5 | 0.5 | 0.5 | 1.0 |
| Sensor weight front $w_f$ | 2.0 | 2.0 | 2.0 | 2.0 |
| Sensor weight right $w_r$ | 2.0 | 2.0 | 2.0 | 2.0 |
| Sensor weight back $w_b$ | 2.0 | 2.0 | 4.0 | 4.0 |
| Transposition penalty $P_{trans}$ | 0 | 0 | 0.1 | 0.15 |
| Transposition threshold $\theta_{trans}$ | 0 | 0 | 1 | 5 |
| Sensor error threshold $\theta_{sensor}$ | – | – | 0.4 | 0.4 |
| Max. error $E_{max}$ | 6.0 | 6.0 | 6.0 | 7.0 |
| Evaluation time steps $T$ | 75 | 75 | 58 | 66 |
| Total evaluation time | 4.5 s | 4.5 s | 3.5 s | 4.0 s |

We have put an effort into the design of the fitness function to minimize the number of required evaluations and allow for an evolutionary approach onboard the robot. The evaluation of a controller begins with placing the robot at the starting position manually (human interaction). Then the currently evaluated

controller steers the robot for a period of time (see Table 2 for the used parameters). During the evaluation the robot acquires sensor data to calculate an
accumulated fitness autonomously. The LegoBot requires 0.06 s to receive the
readings from all four sensors (based on the technical specification of the used
ultrasonic sensors). Consequently, the time frame is divided into a number of
discrete steps with an interval of 0.06 s each.

We consider the following behavioral features for the design of the fitness function: reaching the parking slot, positioning the robot at the center of the parking
slot (balancing), avoiding to hit the walls, continuous movement, and the required
time. The first aspect (reaching the parking slot) is the main objective that considers how close the robot is positioned to the parking slot. The second aspect
(balancing) penalizes controllers that position the robot not correctly at the center of the parking slot. The third aspect is to avoid hitting any walls during the
parking process. The fourth aspect is to keep the robot moving continuously during the simulation run. Therefore, occasional temporary stops during the evaluation are penalized even if the respective controller parks the robot successfully in
the end. The fifth aspect is minimizing the number of transpositions (i.e., transposition maneuvers in terms of changing the robot's direction) performed by the
robot during the parking process, therefore, unnecessary transpositions are penalized. The robot is considered to have performed a transposition, if it changes its
steering angle of the front wheels or the direction of rotation of its back wheels.
The last aspect is to enforce a reasonable time frame, that is, the controller should
be able to perform an efficient and successful parking process within short time.
We define the fitness function $F$ to evaluate all these behavioral aspects via the
deviation, error $E$, from a theoretical best behavior

$$E = \left( \sum_{t=1}^{T} P_{\text{align}}(t) + P_{\text{stop}}(t) \right)$$
$$+ w_f S_f(T) + w_r S_r(T) + w_b S_b(T) + P_{\text{bal}} + P_{\text{crash}}, \tag{1}$$
$$F = (E_{\text{max}} - E)^2, \tag{2}$$

for the number of evaluation time steps $T$. Features $P_{\text{align}}$ and $P_{\text{stop}}$ are accumulated over time, whereas $P_{\text{align}}$ depends on the sensor reading of the current time
step $t$. In contrast, the three sensor readings $S(T)$ only take the sensor reading of
the last time step $T$. In total, Eq. 1 introduces five different types of penalties. At
time step $t$, if the distance between the robot and the obstacles on the right side
of the robot exceeds a certain limit ($\theta_{\text{align}}$), the controller receives the alignment
penalty $P_{\text{align}}(t) = S_r(t) w_{\text{align}}$. The idea is to minimize the distance between
the robot and the wall on its right side, which favors the behavior of staying
parallel and close to the wall. The controller receives a stopping penalty $P_{\text{stop}}(t)$
at time steps $t$ for which the robot stops its motor (otherwise $P_{\text{stop}}(t) = 0$). If
the robot hits any obstacle at any time step $i$, the controller is considered to
be unsuccessful. Therefore, it receives a crashing penalty $P_{\text{crash}}$ and the evaluation is immediately stopped. Hence, the controller cannot collect additional,
accumulated penalties: $\forall t > i, P_{\text{align}}(t) + P_{\text{stop}}(t) = 0$. The robot is stopped at

the end of each evaluation. Then the sum of the front and back sensor is tested $S_f + S_b < \theta_{\text{bal}}$, which indicates whether the robot is placed correctly within the parking slot. Therefore, the balancing penalty $P_{\text{bal}} = |S_b(T) - 0.04 - S_f(T)|w_{\text{bal}}$ is added to the total error with the aim of balancing the robot in the parking slot. The robot is perfectly balanced for $|S_b(T) - S_f(T)| = 0.04$ because the sensors are positioned asymmetrically on the robot, see Fig. 1(b). Moreover, the final weighted sensor readings $w_f S_f(T) + w_r S_r(T) + w_b S_b(T)$ are added to the total error value $E$. To specify the optimization problem as a maximization problem, we define fitness $F$ as the squared difference between a theoretical maximal error $E_{\text{max}}$ and the calculated error value $E$. Table 2 specifies the fitness function parameters that were used in each experiment. In the following we report results of four experiments. For the two last experiments (robot short slot and robot forward parking, see Sec. 4), the transposition penalty is introduced. If the total number of transpositions $m$ (i.e., moving back and forth) exceeds a certain limit $m > \theta_{\text{trans}}$ the controller receives a transposition penalty ($P_{trans}$) at each additional transposition.

Finally, we have to take care of sensor errors. The robot is evaluating its performance autonomously onboard, which means that the fitness function is sensitive to sensor errors. The ultrasonic sensors work best when facing walls perpendicular to the sensors. Highly inaccurate readings (typically largely overestimated) can occur when the sensors face a smooth surfaces at flat angles because then the reflection of the sound waves is disadvantageous. In our setup that is a relatively frequent situation and during the evaluation process some distance measurements might be wrong. To prevent the assignment of wrong fitness due to sensor errors, we implement the following simple error correction method. A current sensor reading is dropped and replaced by its predecessor if the difference between them exceeds the threshold $\theta_{\text{sensor}}$.

## 4   Experiments

We report results of four experiments: simulation long slot (simulation experiment with 60 cm parking slot, forward drive turned off), robot long slot (robot experiment with 60 cm parking slot, forward drive turned off), robot short slot (robot experiment with 45 cm parking slot, forward drive turned on), and robot short slot forward parking (robot experiment with 45 cm parking slot, forward drive turned on, and robot enters parking slot forwards).

Our first result is from simulations (simulation long slot). With this experiment we investigate the above mentioned tradeoff between hardware protection and optimization success. The crashing penalty $P_{\text{crash}}$ is the feature in the fitness function that influences the tendency to approach walls closely in the evolved behaviors. A high crashing penalty $P_{\text{crash}}$ favors the emergence of conservative behaviors that stay far away from walls if possible. A low crashing penalty favors the emergence of risk-taking behaviors that might approach walls closely. Our hypothesis is that setting the crashing penalty to high values is effective in minimizing the number of collisions but it also decreases the efficiency of the optimization process. In contrast, setting the crashing penalty to low values has a minor

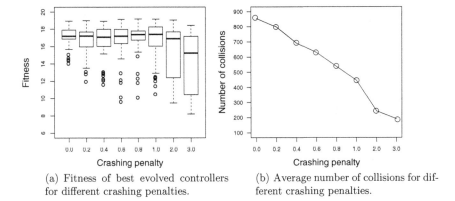

(a) Fitness of best evolved controllers for different crashing penalties.

(b) Average number of collisions for different crashing penalties.

**Fig. 5.** Simulation results for the analysis of the tradeoff between hardware protection and optimization success (varied crashing penalty $P_{\mathrm{crash}}$, simulation long slot).

effect on the optimization success but is also ineffective in limiting the number of collisions. Hence, we face a tradeoff which needs to be balanced between preserving the robot's intactness while enabling an efficient evolutionary search. We test eight different crashing penalties $P_{\mathrm{crash}} \in \{0, 0.2, 0.4, 0.6, 0.8, 1, 2, 3\}$. For each penalty value, 50 evolutionary runs of 60 generations each with a population size of 30 were done. In total that are 400 evolutionary runs, which required about 37.5 days of computation time. The results are shown in Fig. 5. There is a clear trend of decreasing fitness with increasing crashing penalty in Fig. 5(a) which shows the fitness of the best controllers of the last generation from each evolutionary run. The total number of collisions per evolutionary run averaged over 50 runs and depending on the crashing penalty is shown in Fig. 5(b). Clearly, an increasing crashing penalty effectively limits the number of collisions. However, crashing penalties of high values ($P_{\mathrm{crash}} > 1$) decrease the fitness of the best evolved controllers, that is, the evolved behaviors are of reduced quality. Crashing penalties of low values ($P_{\mathrm{crash}} \leq 1$) allow to evolve high quality behaviors while decreasing the number of collisions linearly with increasing penalty. However, a number of over 400 collisions is possibly still unsatisfying (depending on the robustness of the robot hardware). This finding supports our hypothesis. In the following robot experiments, the crashing penalty $P_{\mathrm{crash}}$ was set to intermediate values (see Table 2).

Three robot experiments with different configurations were performed as onboard evolution on the robot to show the effectivity of our approach. This required running the evolutionary process directly on the Linux board on the LegoBot (based on MultiNEAT, robot determines fitness autonomously based on sensor measurements, human interaction for replacing the robot between evaluations). For each of the first two experiments (robot long slot and robot short slot), 10 independent evolutionary runs were done, each with five generations and a population size of 30 (i.e., in total 1500 evaluations). Each evolutionary run required about 19 min (for a quick experimenter replacing the robot to the starting position with an average of only three seconds). In total, about three hours were required to accomplish each of these two experiments. The robot was initially placed at the left side of the arena, in a ready to reverse starting position. The setup for the robot-short-slot experiment is seen in Fig. 6(a). In the third robot experiment (robot short slot forward parking), the task difficulty is increased further. The robot's initial position is changed to the right side of the arena as seen in Fig. 6(b). Hence, the robot has to use the forward drive to get into the parking slot. In this setting, the parking slot is too short to allow for forward parallel parking with only one forward movement. The robot needs to switch to reverse and drive backwards while steering to reach a balanced final position. As a result, the parallel parking task of this last experiment is the most challenging. Again 10 evolutionary runs were done but with 10 generations each. Each evolutionary run required about 35 min which totals to about six hours for all runs. A video is available online[4] that shows a complete evolutionary run.

(a) robot experiment, short slot.

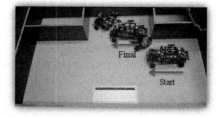
(b) robot, short slot, forward parking.

**Fig. 6.** Illustration of the evolved behaviors for the onboard evolution robot experiments with short parking slot, (a) backward and (b) forward parking (arrowhead indicates robot's front).

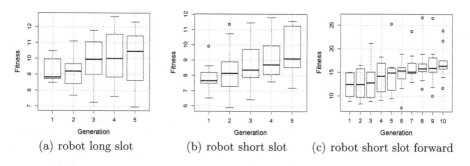

(a) robot long slot     (b) robot short slot     (c) robot short slot forward

**Fig. 7.** Onboard evolution robot experiments, fitness of the best controllers per generation of the 10 evolutionary runs for (a) long parking slot, backward; (b) short parking slot, backward; (c) short parking slot, forward parking.

---

[4] http://youtu.be/L4mnuVJmepk.

The best fitness over generations for the robot long slot experiment is shown in Fig. 7(a). The evolutionary approach is effective as indicated by an increase of fitness. However, the optimization process has not yet converged as indicated by a missing saturation effect. Given the high cost of these experiments we allocated most of our resources to the last and most complex experiment. The best fitness over generations for the robot short slot experiment is shown in Fig. 7(b). Again, the evolutionary approach is effective as indicated by an increase of fitness but the experiment was stopped early to save resources. The parking behavior of the evolved best controllers is similar for both of these experiments. For the robot short slot experiment, it is illustrated in Fig. 6(a). From the starting position, the robot starts to reverse into the parking slot with an appropriate steering angle. As soon as the robot starts entering the parking slot, the steering angle is reversed to the other direction ending up in the final position. A video is available online[5] that shows the whole parking process. The best fitness over generations for the third robot experiment, the robot short slot forward parking experiment, is shown in Fig. 7(c). An increase in fitness is clearly seen as well as a saturation effect during the last three generations. The best evolved parking behavior is shown in Fig. 6(b). From the starting position the robot uses the forward drive with an appropriate steering angle to place itself inside the parking slot facing the front wall. Next, it changes its steering angle to face the corner of the parking slot, giving itself enough room to steer back and to place itself in the final position (video online[6]).

Finally, we determine the number of collisions per evolutionary run averaged over all runs in each robot experiment. For the robot long slot experiment we get in average 81 collisions, for robot short slot an average of 88 collisions, and for robot short slot forward parking we have 144 collisions in average. For all three experiments about half of the evaluations were ended with a collision and the robot's motor was turned off for protection. This ratio is considered to be good because we influence the robot behavior only via the fitness function. The effect of the crashing penalty is established slowly over several generations starting from a population of random controllers that typically generate many collisions.

## 5   Conclusion

We have reported the concept of the tradeoff between hardware protection and the optimization success in onboard evolution. In robot experiments there is a requirement to minimize the number of events that expose the robot to high accelerations. This is particularly relevant for addressing the autonomy challenge of evolutionary robotics, that is, we want to create autonomous evolutionary processes that form highly adaptive systems [6–9]. We have to prevent damage to the robot but at the same time we do not want to overly constrain explorations of the search space by the evolutionary algorithm. Awareness of this tradeoff helps to define an appropriate fitness function. In our simulation experiments

---

[5] http://youtu.be/9pz_rezn_3Q.
[6] http://youtu.be/n-KSrIwp87k.

we have shown the impact of different crashing penalties and in our onboard evolution robot experiments we have shown the effectivity of our approach.

In future work we will compare the approach of introducing changes to the fitness function to minimize the number of collisions with the implementation of a hardware protection layer. Furthermore, we plan to investigate the impact of this study on the concept of embodied online onboard evolution.

# References

1. Nolfi, S., Floreano, D.: Evolutionary Robotics: The Biology, Intelligence, and Technology of Self-Organizing Machines. MIT Press, Cambridge (2000)
2. Bongard, J.C.: Evolutionary robotics. Commun. ACM **56**(8), 74–83 (2013)
3. Nelson, A.L., Barlow, G.J., Doitsidis, L.: Fitness functions in evolutionary robotics: a survey and analysis. Robot. Auton. Syst. **57**, 345–370 (2009)
4. Jakobi, N., Husbands, P., Harvey, I.: Noise and the reality gap: the use of simulation in evolutionary robotics. In: Morán, F., Merelo, J.J., Moreno, A., Chacon, P. (eds.) ECAL 1995. LNCS, vol. 929. Springer, Heidelberg (1995)
5. Koos, S., Mouret, J.B., Doncieux, S.: The transferability approach: crossing the reality gap in evolutionary robotics. IEEE Trans. Evol. Comput. **17**(1), 122–145 (2013)
6. Eiben, Á.E., Haasdijk, E., Bredeche, N.: Embodied, on-line, on-board evolution for autonomous robotics. In: Levi, P., Kernbach, S. (eds.) Symbiotic Multi-Robot Organisms: Reliability, Adaptability, Evolution, pp. 362–384. Springer, Heidelberg (2010)
7. Haasdijk, E., Bredeche, N., Eiben, Á.E.: Combining environment-driven adaptation and task-driven optimisation in evolutionary robotics. PLoS ONE **9**(6), e98466 (2014)
8. Haasdijk, E., Bredeche, N.: Controlling task distribution in MONEE. In: Liò, P., Miglino, O., Nicosia, G., Nolfi, S., Pavone, M. (eds.) Advances In Artificial Life (ECAL 2013), pp. 671–678 (2013)
9. Stradner, J., Hamann, H., Zahadat, P., Schmickl, T., Crailsheim, K.: On-line, on-board evolution of reaction-diffusion control for self-adaptation. In: Adami, C., Bryson, D.M., Ofria, C., Pennock, R.T. (eds.) Alife XIII, pp. 597–598. MIT Press, Cambridge (2012)
10. Floreano, D., Mondada, F.: Automatic creation of an autonomous agent: genetic evolution of a neural-network driven robot. In: Proceedings of the 3rd International Conference on Simulation of Adaptive Behavior (SAB 1994), pp. 421–430. MIT Press (1994)
11. Levi, P., Kernbach, S. (eds.): Symbiotic Multi-Robot Organisms: Reliability, Adaptability, Evolution. Springer, Heidelberg (2010)
12. Ronchetti, F., Lanzarini, L.C.: Automatic vehicle parking using an evolution-obtained neural controller. In: Presentado en el XII Workshop Agentes y Sistemas Inteligentes (WASI), pp. 71–80 (2011)
13. Vaughan, R.: Massively multi-robot simulation in stage. Swarm Intell. **2**(2–4), 189–208 (2008)
14. Chervenski, P., Ryan, S.: MultiNEAT. http://www.multineat.com/
15. Stanley, K., Miikkulainen, R.: Evolving neural networks through augmenting topologies. Evol. Comput. **10**(2), 99–127 (2002)

# Real-World Reproduction of Evolved Robot Morphologies: Automated Categorization and Evaluation

Eivind Samuelsen and Kyrre Glette[✉]

Department of Informatics, University of Oslo, Oslo, Norway
{eivinsam,kyrrehg}@ifi.uio.no

**Abstract.** This paper describes the real-world reproduction of a handful of robots selected from a larger sample of simulated models previously generated by an evolutionary algorithm. The five robots, which are selected by automatic clustering to be representative of different morphological niches present in the sample, are constructed in the real world using off-the-shelf motor components, combined with 3D printed structural parts that were automatically generated based on the simulator models. A lab setup, involving evolution of turning gaits for each robot, is used to automate the experiments. The forward walking speeds of the constructed robots are measured, and compared with the simulated speeds. While some of the robots achieve near-identical results, some show a large performance loss compared to their simulated prototypes, underlining the reality gap issue seen in similar previous works.

## 1 Introduction

There is a high need for autonomously operating robotic systems in remote, hostile, or otherwise isolated environments, such as remote planets, disaster areas, deep mines, or subsea installations. At the same time, human intervention is difficult, time-consuming, costly, or at worst impossible, and thus robots which are able to automatically repair or adapt themselves to new situations would be a great advantage. With the recent and frequent advances in 3D printing technology, such as an increasing number of materials, higher speeds, and portability, new possibilities open up for the design or repair of robotic systems. For example, one could imagine a team of robots, including a mobile 3D printer, capable of repairing or producing new robot morphologies in situ [1].

Evolutionary robotics (ER) approaches the challenge of automatic design and adaptation of robotic systems through the use of evolutionary algorithms. While ER research has mainly concentrated on optimization of robotic control systems, e.g. for legged robots [2], using software simulations it is also possible to address the challenge of simultaneously optimizing robot morphology and control [3].

Automated robot design without a fixed topology introduces an encoding challenge, as more complex data structures are needed to describe the space of possible solutions. Thus, ER research has produced a wide variety of coding

© Springer International Publishing Switzerland 2015
A.M. Mora and G. Squillero (Eds.): EvoApplications 2015, LNCS 9028, pp. 771–782, 2015.
DOI: 10.1007/978-3-319-16549-3_62

schemes for describing morphology. Examples include directly encoded module-based [4] or graph-based [3] approaches, and an approach using LEGO bricks and servo motors as modular building blocks [5]. Generative and developmental methods, where complex phenotypes are generated from simpler genotypes through some sort of indirect encoding, have been successfully applied to evolve morphology, for example by using cyclic graphs [6], gene regulatory network-inspired encodings [7], and scalar-field generating methods based on compositional pattern producing networks both with rigid [8] and soft [9] bodies. These generative methods can produce highly complex and structured results from very terse information [10] and are known to outperform direct encoding in simple morphology optimization tasks [11]. Robots designed by some of these methods have also been reproduced in real life [3,10].

ER in general faces a reality gap challenge, that is, controllers evolved in simulation often perform much worse on the real robot [12]. This is due to inaccuracies in simulation combined with evolution's tendency to produce overfit solutions. Thus, one may end up with solutions which exploit features nonexistent in the real world. While this is already a significant challenge for controllers transferred to robust engineer-designed robots, the additional freedom in the morphological dimension only increases the potential size of a reality gap. There are only a few examples of evolved robot morphologies and control systems resulting in physical, actuated robots [3,5,10], and the main challenges for these have been a lack of complexity or regularity in the structures, or low real life performance due to reality gap issues. In order for morphology-based ER to be a convincing approach, there is a need for demonstration of robust, high-performing approaches and more thorough performance evaluations.

In this paper we pursue this goal by building on our previously proposed generative encoding scheme for evolution of robot morphology and control [13] to present a full construction process for physical robots from the simulation results. The approach represents a flexible way to create relatively lightweight and regular robots of controllable complexity, and thus should have a potential of resulting in well-performing robots. With the help of a clustering algorithm working on morphological distance, we pick 5 different robots representative of the different morphologies evolved in simulation, construct them, and demonstrate a thorough way of evaluating their real-world performance. The evaluation setup is able to automatically perform a high number of evaluations and is thus suitable for future real-world learning experiments and investigations into transferability from simulation to the real world.

The remainder of this paper is organized as follows: In Sect. 2, the methods used to evolve, select, construct, and test the robots are presented. Section 3 presents the resulting robots and their performance. Section 4 discusses the results, before a conclusion and pointers for future work are given in Sect. 5.

## 2   Methods

This section describes the methods used to perform the experiments in this paper. First, we describe the previous results these experiments are based on, before we present the selection method used to pick representative robots, and details about the hardware reproduction. Then we describe the hardware testing methods and performance evaluation procedures.

## 2.1 Evolving Robots Through Simulation

A large number of robots were evolved in a simulated environment in [14]. The evolutionary algorithm uses a genotype inspired by the high-level genetic coding used in nature to specify the shape of different body segments to encode robots with a various number of symmetric limbs around a central spine structure. All sets of limbs are coded with the same program, but variation based on a number of evolved parameters that are specific to each section along the spine.

The robots were evaluated with three objective functions: maximizing forward movement in a simulated environment, minimizing the estimated weight of the robot, and maximizing diversity. The weight of the simulation robot model was used as the weight estimate. Diversity was measured as the mean morphological distance to all other robots in both parent and offspring generations.

The simulation was done using the PhysX simulation engine. The robot was first simulated for 1 s in order to let it settle on the ground, before the robot's position was reset. The evaluation was then done by letting the robot move freely in the environment for 7 s and then measuring the displacement of the "head" of the robot in a predefined forward direction, so that the robots most proficient in moving in that direction would survive. A custom set of joint constraints were used to simulate the motors in the robot joints. Additionally, the control system was designed with a torque limit limiting the actual applied torque to 1 Nm. The environment itself consisted of an infinite ground plane and long, low obstacles at regular intervals in the forward direction. Parameters for the simulation and environment are summarized in Table 1.

**Table 1.** Simulation parameters

| General | PhysX version | 3.3 beta-2 | | |
|---|---|---|---|---|
| | Timestep | $1/128$ s | | |
| Friction | Env. static | 0.20 | Robot static | 0.30 |
| | Env. dynamic | 0.15 | Robot dynamic | 0.30 |
| | Env. restitution | 0.40 | Robot restitution | 0.30 |
| Motor | Static friction | 0.15 Nm | Dynamic friction | $\frac{1.65\,\text{Nm}}{97\,\text{rpm}}$ |
| | Appliable torque | 1.8 Nm | | |
| Obstacle | Width | 0.02 m | Height | 0.02 m |
| | Length | 0.02 m | Spacing | 0.5 m |

## 2.2    Selecting Representative Robots

The experiments in [14] produced 42000 solutions across 210 runs, most of which had differing morphologies to some extent. Only five of these could be printed given the available time and resources; selecting these five purely at random would most likely give a poor sample of the different morphologies, so a method was used in order to select robots who are each representative of a larger group of robots:

Evolutionary runs with the same control system and diversity measure were selected, so that they differed only in the random seed used. The distance measure was an approximation of the graph edit distance (GED) introduced in the same article. From these runs, 12 were arbitrarily selected, maintaining some of the variety between runs while reducing the number of candidates further to 2400. Candidates with a forward movement performance lower than a certain threshold value were then filtered out, reducing the number of candidates further down to 949.

The remaining candidates were then grouped into six clusters using hierarchical clustering. The distance measure used for clustering was the same as the one used in the diversity measure they were evolved with. The additional sixth cluster was a "trap cluster" intended to collect a specific kind of robot that was known to appear in the runs, with only one set of limbs and no tail, which moved by rolling around. Although very interesting, this locomotion method was impossible to reconcile with the laboratory setup described in Sect. 2.5.

## 2.3    Constructing the Robots

From the beginning, the genetic encoding used in [14] was designed to produce robots that are possible to construct in the real world. The scale of the robots and the joint simulation parameters were designed to fit the modular servo motors Dynamixel AX series produced by Robotis. Specifically, the simulated joint parameters, as well as the actual servo motors used on the constructed robots were of the AX-18 model.

Each link in the produced robots consists of one variable-length capsule combined with sockets to attach the servo motors for each joint. In order to minimize weight the capsules were made hollow, with a thickness of 1.5 mm, and evenly spaced holes throughout in order to keep wires inside the capsule and also to make it easier to clean away the support material used by the printer.

The sockets are hand-designed in a CAD program to fit the servos correctly, including matching holes for easy assembly. In order to attach the sockets to the central capsule, which must be custom-generated for each link, the fact that intersecting meshes will be merged into one solid object implicitly by the 3D printer was exploited. Thus one only needs to have the capsule and socket meshes positioned correctly and contained in the same data file. To attach side sockets, which can have an arbitrary rotation relative to the capsule, an additional set of four supporting bars were generated that each aligned with one end of a socket in each end and with the surface of the capsule in the middle.

The parts were printed in an Objet Connex 500 multi-material 3D printer, using the DurusIvory digital material, a predefined mixture of VeroWhitePlus (a rigid but somewhat brittle) and DurusWhite (a softer, polypropylene-like material). It was soon discovered that this material, and in fact, most plastic materials, had significantly lower friction against the floor carpet in the leg than the friction values modeled in simulation. In order to increase the friction between robot and floor, hockey tape was added to the endpoints of each limb on the robots.

## 2.4 Hardware Testing Setup

In order to perform measurements with the hardware efficiently, the experiments were automated by programming the robots to turn back when they go out of bounds; when the robot reaches a certain distance from the center of the floor, the control system is replaced with one that makes the robot turn either left or right until it is approximately headed for the center of the floor. When the robot has finished turning, it is then switched back to its original control system and the evaluation resumes by restarting the unfinished period. In order to avoid the measurements being affected by the turning motion, the first period after resuming evaluation is discarded.

For these experiments, turning control systems were generated by running an evolutionary algorithm with two objective functions: maximizing turning velocity and minimizing positional displacement. The population was seeded with 60 mutations of the original forward movement control system and run for 60 generations. The evolution used uniform Gaussian mutation and whole arithmetic recombination. All the evolved turning systems worked satisfactory in real hardware, except for those for robot 2, who had too large positional displacement. This was remedied by further parameter tuning on the real robot.

The robots contain no power source, so they need to be wired to a power source and controller located elsewhere. In order to let the robot move freely without tripping in the wire, the wire was put through a pulley in the center of the ceiling to a winch that is programmed to let out approximately enough wire to let the robot move freely based on the robots position relative to the center of the floor.

The position and orientation measurements were done using a motion capture system. This enables very accurate measurements with minimal modification of the robots. Three reflex balls were attached to one of the central parts of the robot, enabling the motion capture system to identify the robot as a rigid body with a position and orientation. The motion capture system used was a NaturalPoint OptiTrack with 8 infrared Flex 3 cameras. The cameras were positioned in the lab ceiling, at the corners and midpoints of the walls.

## 2.5 Performance Evaluation

In order to provide a fair comparison of the simulated performance of the robots and the performance in hardware, the same evaluation procedure is used in both cases. Since the robots were originally evolved to maximize forward movement, this has been used as the performance metric in these experiments as well.

At the end of each period the displacement of the robot during the period, in the direction it was heading at the start of the period, is measured. The period length was set to 1 s to align with the control system cycle length. After every fourth period the mean displacement per second over the last four periods is stored as a single evaluation. 50 evaluations were done on each robot both in simulation and in hardware in order to get a good statistical sample of the performance.

## 3    Results

This section will present the results of the experiments described in the section above. First, a description of the selected robots is given in the subsection below, before the performance measurements are reported in Sect. 3.2.

### 3.1    The Selected Robots

The twelve runs selected had a total of 2400 candidate robots. After removing the robots that did not meet the performance criteria, this was reduced to 949 robots. The distribution of these in the six clusters are shown in Table 2. As expected, one cluster contained only robots with rolling behavior. One other cluster (number 1) contained mainly rolling robots as well, but this cluster contained two distinct sub-groups, where a second, smaller group of around 19 robots had a tail one or two sections long that hindered the rolling motion, and which had developed a dragging gait instead.

The distribution of the clusters in objective space is shown in Fig. 1, showing that the clusters roughly match up with different trade-offs between forward movement ability, weight and diversity. It can be seen that cluster 5, while largest in number of individuals, consists mostly of robots that survived due to having distinct morphologies rather than being light or efficient.

**Table 2.** The morphological clusters.

| Cluster | Robots | Description |
|---------|--------|-------------|
| 1 | 138 | Two limbs with two joints each, mostly rolling behavior |
| 2 | 86 | Two active limbs with one joint each, midsection either limbless or with nonfunctional limbs |
| 3 | 254 | Four limbs with two joints each |
| 4 | 4 | Four limbs with two joints each plus limbless waist section |
| 5 | 458 | Six limbs with two joints each |
| (6) | 9 | Two limbs with one joint each, no tail, typically with rolling behavior |

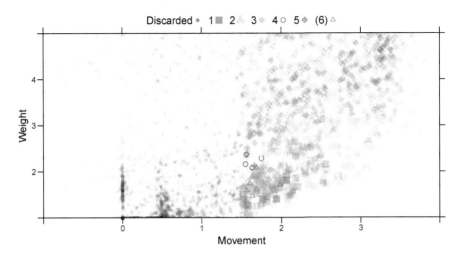

**Fig. 1.** Objective-space distribution of the clusters. The diversity dimension is omitted, but generally speaking solutions far from the movement-weight pareto front will have a higher diversity score. The small dots are the individuals that were discarded before clustering because of low fitness. (In grayscale, cluster 2 is difficult to see, but occupies most of the area in between clusters 4 and 6.)

In three of the five clusters (clusters 2, 4 and 5) the centroid robot was picked as its representative. In cluster number 1 a representative of the dragging sub-group was selected by hand. In cluster 3 a representative with a more interesting gait than the centroid, but close to it (rank 13 in closeness to the centroid), was chosen to improve the gait variation between the representatives. Body schematics for the five selected robots and photographs of the finished robots are shown in Fig. 3.

Robot 1 has two limbs and a tail, each with two joints, and drags itself forward with the limbs. Robot 2 had four limbs and two joints in the waist, but only one joint in each limb. It achieves a trotting gait (neighboring limbs are in opposite phase) by having a large synchronized swing in the waist joints. Robots 3 and 4 both have four limbs with two joints per limb. Robot 3, which has one waist joint, exhibits a bounding gait (front and rear limbs are out of phase and the robot makes a small leap each time the back limbs pushes the robot forward). Robot 4 has two waist joints and a pronk-like gait (all limbs are approximately in sync).

Robot 5 has six limbs, with two joints in each limb. The two rear limbs are considerably larger than the other two pairs. This robot has a bounding-like gait, where each limb pair is in sync; the front and middle limbs have a small phase difference between them, and the rear limbs are approximately in opposite phase of the other pairs. The limbs touch the ground in order from front to back. As the middle limbs move backwards the rear limbs lift above the middle limbs,

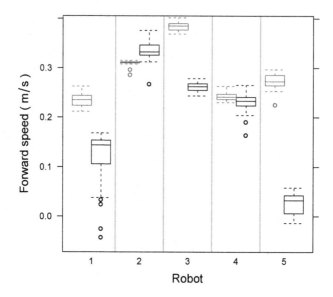

**Fig. 2.** Performance box plot of the five robots. The left column of each robot is the simulated measurements and the right box is the measurements in hardware. Each of the boxes represents 50 measurements.

touching them near the knee joints during maximum forward extension of the rear limbs.

## 3.2   Performance

The distribution of the performance measurements is shown in Fig. 2. Table 3 show a summary of the mean performance for each robot. Robots 2 and 4 have overlapping performance ranges between simulation and hardware and mean performance ratio close to one, while the other three robots have significantly lower performance in hardware. Robot 5 has the largest performance loss: the mean performance in hardware is only 9.4 % of the mean simulated performance. Second worst is robot 1 with a 49 % performance loss, while robot 3 has 31.8 % lower performance in hardware.

**Table 3.** Mean performance summary.

| Robot | 1 | 2 | 3 | 4 | 5 |
|---|---|---|---|---|---|
| Simulation (m/s) | 0.235 | 0.311 | 0.384 | 0.242 | 0.274 |
| Hardware (m/s) | 0.120 | 0.335 | 0.262 | 0.231 | 0.026 |
| Ratio | 0.510 | 1.079 | 0.682 | 0.955 | 0.094 |

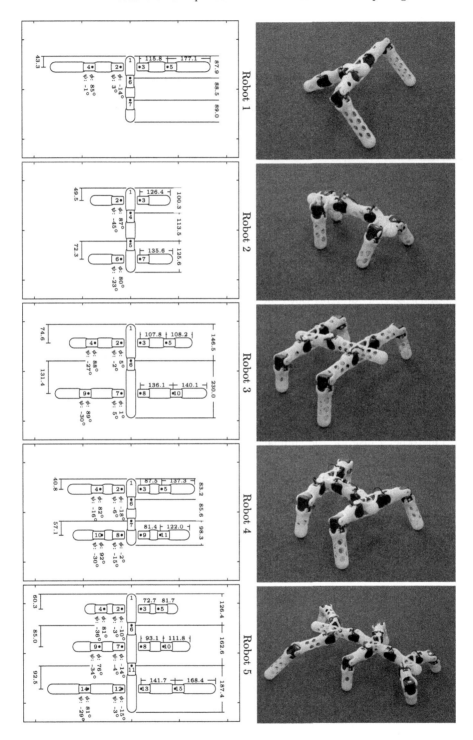

**Fig. 3.** Schematic view and photographs of the robots. All lengths are in millimeters.

# 4 Discussion

The hierarchical clustering produced clusters that seemed to match up reasonably well with what was expected, based on randomly sampling the populations by hand. It also managed to find a rare but interesting robot class, represented by robot 4, with a double-jointed waist, of which there were only four in the entire set of 949 robots that met the performance criteria.

While the structural strength of the printed parts generally proved to be sufficient for these experiments, in one instance (robot 4), one of the spine parts broke at the intersection between the capsule shape and the bars attaching the limbs. A new, stronger design was created and printed in order to complete the experiments.

The performance in hardware relative to simulation varies from robot to robot, with some robots having about the same performance, while others perform considerably worse in hardware. These results are in agreement with similar experiments such as [3,5].

The robots that had the lowest loss of performance in this experiment were also the least risky designs. Both the dragging motion of robot 1 and the bounding motion of robots 3 and 5 are dependent on friction being simulated correctly, and in this case they were evolved in an environment with larger friction than in the real-world lab. Robots 2 and 4, on the other hand, employed gaits that are less sensitive to changes in friction since they do not rely on pushing forward against the ground, but rather on alternating between having parts resting on the ground and moving them forward. One simple measure to avoid friction problems might be to underestimate friction in simulation, in order to give a conservative estimate of the performance of friction-dependent gaits.

One other cause for the simulation-hardware performance loss is limb collisions. Some of the robot gaits caused limbs to collide, which might not be modeled well enough in simulation. Robot 5 in particular had a gait that caused collision or at least near collision once every period. From a performance perspective, there seems to be little reason for gaits to cause self-collisions, so one could perhaps introduce some form of collision discouragement in evolution to mitigate this. Using a closed-loop control system might also help, because the control system would be better able to correct itself post-collision.

# 5 Conclusion and Future Work

This paper has documented the transferral of robots, that were automatically designed in simulation, into real hardware. From a large pool of robot designs drawn from previous experiments, five robots were constructed, each acting as a representative for a larger group of robots with similar morphologies. The representatives were found using a clustering algorithm, and then a functioning mechanical body was created from the design using modular servo motors combined with a combination of hand-designed and automatically generated plastic parts manufactured using a 3D-printer.

A lab setup was created that enabled thorough performance measurements both in simulation and hardware using the same measure. Measurements in the lab were compared to similar measurements in simulation, demonstrating that, at least for some of the robots, forward walking speeds in the same range as the well-studied hand-designed AIBO robot (see for example [2,15]), were achieved. However, there was large variation in how well the real-life reproduction performed compared to the simulated model.

This confirms that some sort of measure is needed in order to make the products of simulated evolution correlate better with real hardware in terms of performance. On the simulation side, noise may be added to model external effects. Forces such as friction, where the conditions are expected to vary between environments in the real world anyway, should perhaps be underestimated in order to avoid having robots exploit effects that are not certain to appear in reality. On the hardware side, it might be possible to implement some sort of adaption technique on the control system in order to regain some of the performance seen in simulation.

The transferability approach [16] is a promising method for dealing with the reality gap in the evolution of controllers for fixed-morphology robots, by building a transferability model based on real-world samples. For such a method to work also with evolved morphologies, there would be a need for selecting a limited but representable set of morphologies for real-world sampling. As such, the methods presented in this paper could be a possible approach, and this application should be investigated in future work.

## References

1. Revzen, S., Bhoite, M., Macasieb, A., Yim, M.: Structure synthesis on-the-fly in a modular robot. In: 2011 IEEE/RSJ International Conference on Intelligent Robots and Systems (IROS), pp. 4797–4802 (2011)
2. Hornby, G., Takamura, S., Yokono, J., Hanagata, O., Yamamoto, T., Fujita, M.: Evolving robust gaits with AIBO. In: Proceedings IEEE International Conference on Robotics and Automation ICRA 2000, vol. 3, pp. 3040–3045 (2000)
3. Lipson, H., Pollack, J.: Automatic design and manufacture of robotic lifeforms. Nature **406**, 974–978 (2000)
4. Leger, C.: Automated synthesis and optimization of robot configurations: an evolutionary approach. Ph.D. thesis, Carnegie Mellon University (1999)
5. Macinnes, I., Di Paolo, E.: Crawling out of the simulation: evolving real robot morphologies using cheap reusable modules. In: Pollack, J., Bedau, M., Husbands, P., Ikegami, T., Watson, R. (eds.) Artificial Life IX: Proceedings of the Ninth International Conference on the Simulation and Synthesis of Life, pp. 94–99. MIT Press, Cambridge (2004)
6. Sims, K.: Evolving virtual creatures. In: Proceedings of the 21st Annual Conference on Computer Graphics and Interactive Techniques, SIGGRAPH 1994, pp. 15–22 (1994)
7. Bongard, J.: Evolving modular genetic regulatory networks. In: Proceedings of the 2002 Congress on Evolutionary Computation, CEC 2002, vol. 2, pp. 1872–1877. IEEE (2002)

8. Auerbach, J.E., Bongard, J.C.: Environmental influence on the evolution of morphological complexity in machines. PLoS Comput. Biol. **10**(1), e1003399 (2014)
9. Hiller, J., Lipson, H.: Automatic design and manufacture of soft robots. IEEE Trans. Robot. **28**(2), 457–466 (2012)
10. Hornby, G.S., Lipson, H., Pollack, J.B.: Generative representations for the automated design of modular physical robots. IEEE Trans. Robot. Autom. **19**(4), 703–719 (2003)
11. Komosinski, M., Rotaru-Varga, A.: Comparison of different genotype encodings for simulated three-dimensional agents. Artif. Life **7**(4), 395–418 (2001)
12. Jakobi, N., Husbands, P., Harvey, I.: Noise and the reality gap: the use of simulation in evolutionary robotics. Advances in Artificial Life. LNCS, vol. 929, pp. 704–720. Springer, Heidelberg (1995)
13. Samuelsen, E., Glette, K., Torresen, J.: A hox gene inspired generative approach to evolving robot morphology. In: Proceedings of the 15th Annual Conference on Genetic and Evolutionary Computation, pp. 751–758. ACM (2013)
14. Samuelsen, E., Glette, K.: Some distance measures for morphological diversification in generative evolutionary robotics. In: Proceedings of the 16th Annual Conference on Genetic and Evolutionary Computation, pp. 721–728. ACM (2014)
15. Röfer, T.: Evolutionary gait-optimization using a fitness function based on proprioception. In: Nardi, D., Riedmiller, M., Sammut, C., Santos-Victor, J. (eds.) RoboCup 2004. LNCS (LNAI), vol. 3276, pp. 310–322. Springer, Heidelberg (2005)
16. Koos, S., Mouret, J.B., Doncieux, S.: The transferability approach: crossing the reality gap in evolutionary robotics. IEEE Trans. Evol.Comput. **17**(1), 122–145 (2013)

# Evolving Generalised Maze Solvers

David Shorten[(✉)] and Geoff Nitschke

Department of Computer Science, University of Cape Town, Rondebosch,
Cape Town 7700, South Africa
{dshorten,gnitschke}@uct.ac.za
http://cs.uct.ac.za

**Abstract.** This paper presents a study of the efficacy of comparative controller design methods that aim to produce generalised problem solving behaviours. In this case study, the goal was to use neuro-evolution to evolve generalised maze solving behaviours. That is, evolved robot controllers that solve a broad range of mazes. To address this goal, this study compares *objective, non-objective* and *hybrid* approaches to direct the search of a neuro-evolution controller design method. The objective based approach was a fitness function, the non-objective based approach was novelty search, and the hybrid approach was a combination of both. Results indicate that, compared to the fitness function, the hybrid and novelty search evolve significantly more maze solving behaviours that generalise to larger and more difficult maze sets. Thus this research provides empirical evidence supporting novelty and hybrid novelty-objective search as approaches for potentially evolving generalised problem solvers.

**Keywords:** Neuro-Evolution · Evolutionary robotics · Novelty search · Maze solving

## 1 Introduction

A long time goal of *Artificial Intelligence* (AI) is to produce artificial brains capable of eliciting generalised problem solving behaviours equivalent to those observed in nature [1]. Some research has focused on controller design methods which specifically aim to be general problem solvers across a broad range of task domains [2–6]. However, an alternate approach is to demonstrate the efficacy of existing controller design methods as a generalised problem solvers in a given task, and then extract the method's underlying principles in order that the method is applicable to a broad range of task domains.

Given that *Neuro-Evolution* (NE) [7] aims to emulate the evolutionary process that has produced generalised problem solvers in nature, NE is one such promising approach. That is, biological neural networks have evolved to be capable of learning a vast range of behaviors to potentially solve any task an organism may encounter in its natural environment [8]. Although the methods used in NE are vast simplifications of the processes which occurred in nature, a resemblance does exist.

© Springer International Publishing Switzerland 2015
A.M. Mora and G. Squillero (Eds.): EvoApplications 2015, LNCS 9028, pp. 783–794, 2015.
DOI: 10.1007/978-3-319-16549-3_63

This study's research objective is to test if NE is an appropriate controller design method for evolving generalised problem solving behaviours, and to elucidate the necessary defining features of such controller design methods. As an initial step towards addressing this general objective, this study tests the efficacy of an NE controller design method with a *fitness function* [9], *novelty search* [10], and a *novelty-fitness* hybrid for evolving generalised maze solvers. That is, evolved maze solving behaviours that can solve any given maze.

Even though various NE controller design methods are frequently only tested on *specific* tasks, we hypothesize that only small changes are required in order that such methods evolve *general* problem solving behaviours. That is, evolved behaviours that are applicable across a range of task domains. In related NE research, a *specific* task can be viewed as one in which an NE method evolves a controller that solves a single instance of a fully deterministic task. Thus, if a given *Artificial Neural Network* (ANN) controller is evaluated multiple times on this task it will always follow an identical trajectory through the task's state space. This implies that such tasks are solvable by a controller that *memorizes* a specific sequence of sensory-motor couplings, rather than meaningfully interpreting sensory inputs and appropriately mapping them to motor outputs. Examples of such specific tasks are pole-balancing [11,12], navigation of a single maze [10,13,14] and biped [10] and quadruped [15] gait evolution.

A highly specific task can be made *general* either by making the environment stochastic or requiring that a controller is solve multiple instances of the task, each of which differ in some manner. Examples of stochastic environments in the NE literature are abstracted *Markov Decision Processes* [16] and GO playing against a non-deterministic opponent [17]. An example task domain with multiple instances is the multi-agent pursuit-evasion task with variable agent starting positions [18,19]. A particularly relevant study was the evolution of ANN controllers for generalised helicopter control [20] using both stochastic environments and multiple task instances. However, with the exception of notable research such as that of Rajagopalan *et al.* [21], finding the evolution of generalised problem solvers was positively correlated with connection density in ANNs, there is a lack of research on how NE can be scaled to more general tasks.

Recent research established the evolutionary robotics task of evolving maze solving controllers as a useful controller evolution benchmark [10,13,14]. However, all previous work has focused on controller evolution to solve a single maze. In this research, the task was made general via requiring that evolved controllers be able to solve *any* given maze. Such generalised maze solving controllers are evolvable using novelty search or a hybrid fitness-novelty search to direct controller evolution. In comparison, fitness function directed controller evolution performed significantly worse in evolving generalised maze solvers.

## 2   Methods

### 2.1   Novelty Search

Traditionally, evolutionary algorithms have been driven by a fitness function [9]. This function usually indicates how far a phenotype (solution) is from a user defined objective. The closer the phenotype is to the objective, the more likely it is that the associated genotype will be selected for reproduction. *Novelty search* (NS) [10] represents a radical departure from this paradigm, given that NS does not explicitly define an objective but rather rewards evolved phenotypes based purely on their novelty. That is, a genotype is more likely to be selected for reproduction given that the genotype's encoded behaviour (phenotype) is sufficiently different from all the other phenotypes produced thus far in the evolutionary run. A criticism of NS is that it is equivalent to random search [13]. However, recent experimental results indicated that controllers evolved with a NS metric attained some degree of generality. That is, controllers evolved to solve one maze could be successfully transferred to solve different mazes [13]. However, the most convincing proof of NS efficacy is that in comparison to objective driven NE, it produces significant performance improvements in a range of tasks that include maze-solving, evolving bipedal robotic gaits [10], evolving programs with genetic programming [22] and grammatical evolution [23].

To elicit further performance gains in these tasks, various research has tested hybrid NS and fitness metrics. These include using a fitness function combining traditional fitness and a novelty metric [24], restarting converged evolutionary runs using novelty [24], a minimal criteria (for survival and reproduction of controller behaviours) novelty search [25], a progressive minimal criteria (incrementing the requirements for reproduction throughout the evolutionary process) [26], and novelty search combined with speciation techniques [27]. Inden *et al.* [27] found that NS was outperformed by a hybrid objective-novelty metric in pole-balancing, maze solving and quadruped gait evolution tasks. Similarly, Lehman and Stanley [25] found that their minimal criteria novelty search evolved solutions more consistently than objective base search. Gomes *et al.* [26] found that their progressive minimal criteria novelty metric outperformed pure NS in a swarm robotics task. However, it has also been found that an objective based search can outperform NS on the deceptive *tartarus* task [24] as well as pole balancing and a visual discrimination task [27].

This raises the question as to what the defining features of a task, controller design method, and environment are such that NS, or a hybrid novelty-objective metric is able to out-perform objective based search. Lehman and Stanley [10] have argued that if a task's fitness landscape is characterized by low fitness regions being necessary stepping stones for evolution to reach desired high fitness regions, then NS will perform well. Lehman and Stanley [10] also propose that if a domain is *deceptive* then NS will perform particularly well. However, aside from the *hard maze* example [10] the exact defining features of a deceptive task remains unclear. Alternatively, Kistemaker and Whiteson [28] propose that the success of NS is dependant on whether differences in evolved controller behaviours are reflected in differences in the fitness of the controllers' descendants.

A key question is how NS performs in tasks with huge solution spaces, where there is a high degree of probability that the continued discovery of novel solutions will not produce a desired solution within a reasonable amount of time. This research question was tested via applying NS to maze solving with some of the outer walls of a maze removed [10]. Results indicated that the performance of NS degraded to be comparable to objective based search. However, the performance of NS in this version of the task could likely be increased via imposing heuristic constraints that bias evolved behaviours.

Thus, this research investigates the performance of NS in the maze solving domain for a range of large and structurally diverse mazes. In this work, the maze solving behaviours of a simulated robot was evolved for 100 different mazes. This allowed for the evolution of a diverse range of novel maze solving behaviours. The behavioural diversity metric used in this research was such that a robot $A$, can behave identically to another robot $B$, on ninety-nine mazes, but by differing on only one maze enables it to distinguish itself as being different from $B$. This is different to the concept of *increasing the dimensionality of the behaviour representation* [10], where a robot's behaviour is frequently sampled during a given task evaluation. This is due to the fact that, during a single task trial, a robot's behaviour at a given simulation iteration is dependant upon its behaviour at an earlier iteration, and a robot's movements early on will affect the probability of it solving the task (finding a path through the maze) at a later point. However, behaving in a certain manner in one maze does not affect the robot's behaviour in another maze.

Any implementation of NS requires that genotypes have a novelty representation, which is typically a vector of floating-point values. In addition to this, a behavioural diversity metric is required which will assign a novelty value, which is analogous to a fitness value, to any given genotype and its corresponding phenotype. An often used metric, also used in this research, is that of *sparseness*, shown in Eq. 1 [10].

$$\rho(x) = \frac{1}{k} \sum_{i=0}^{k} \text{dist}(\mu_i, x) \tag{1}$$

Here, $\mu_i$ is in the $k$ nearest neighbours of $x$ in both the population and an archive of previously seen genotypes and *dist* is a distance measure.

## 2.2 Neuro-Evolution of Augmenting Topologies (NEAT)

This study uses the *Neuro-Evolution of Augmenting Topologies* (NEAT) method [29]. NEAT is an established NE method that was selected since it has been previously employed in similar studies [10,13,14]. NEAT evolves both the topology and the weights of ANNs via a process of complexification. That is, at the start of artificial evolution, ANNs in the population are functionally simple, with minimal numbers of nodes and connections. During the course of evolution, further nodes and connections are added to ANNs, where increasing the number of nodes and connections in an ANN increases the search space dimensionality. An advantage of NEAT is that this complexifying process is likely to find a solution in a lower dimension search space than the large network which would have to be specified *a priori* if a fixed topology method were to be able to solve a variety of problem types [29]. Other distinguishing features of NEAT are speciation, which

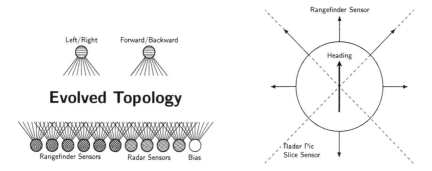

**Fig. 1.** (Left) ANN controller used in the experiments. (Right) Sensory configuration of robots in the simulated maze task. Both figures adapted from [10].

protects innovation, and historical markings, which aid in the crossover of structurally different ANNs. In this study, the real-time version of NEAT, rtNEAT [30] was used as it has been demonstrated as effective in related task domains.

Robot ANN controllers were evolved with the goal of being able to solve any perfect maze generated on a grid structure [31], where each grid cell was of a pre-set size. Although evolved on a 13 × 13 grid, the goal was to produce generalised maze solvers. Hence, evolved controllers were tested on *harder* mazes in a validation set. Figures 2 and 3 present examples of the mazes used for the evolution and validation of maze solving behaviours.

### 2.3   Maze Generation

The evolution and validation of maze solving behaviours required large maze sets. These sets were produced automatically using the *Daedalus* software written by Walter Pullen [32]. All mazes were perfect mazes generated on a grid structure [31]. Large quantities of mazes were generated using this software's implementation of the randomized Prim's algorithm [33] and then scripts were run to remove the duplicates.

### 2.4   Generalised Maze-Solvers

The methods are similar to those used by Lehman and Stanley [10], the key difference being the inclusion of a hybrid novelty-objective metric, and evaluating controllers over a set of mazes, rather than a single maze. The parameters for NEAT and NS were also similar to those used by Lehman and Stanley [10].

Experiments were implemented as an extension of *Novelty Search C++* used by Lehman and Stanley [10]. The large number of maze navigation simulations which had to be conducted per robot controller (that is, for each genotype in the population) necessitated that we parallelize the genotype evaluation process. This was done using the Boost MPI library [34] to facilitate parallel processing on clusters. Robots were equipped with six rangefinder sensors and four radar sensors in the configuration presented in Fig. 1. The rangefinder sensors indicated the distance to the nearest wall along a line radiating out from the centre of the robot at a specific angle. The radar sensors divided the space around the robot into four equally sized quadrants and indicated whether or not the goal was in the quadrant. The main difference between the approach presented here and other investigations of NS in the maze domain was that instead of each genotype evaluation equating to one task trial, that is, one attempt to navigate a single maze, each controller was required to navigate every maze in a set of 100. The purpose of making a task trial consist of a set of 100 mazes, was to gauge a controller's general maze solving behaviour.

Robots were given 8000 time steps to navigate any given maze, where as 800 were used in the work of Lehman and Stanley [10]. This increase is due to the larger size of mazes used in this study and also generalised maze solving requires sufficient exploration of the maze, as opposed to simply finding the shortest path. A robot's behaviour representation was a vector of floating point numbers which consisted of the $x$ and $y$ coordinates of the robot every 2000 time steps in each of its 100 maze solving simulations. Thus, each robot's behavioural representation was a vector of 800 floating point numbers. The novelty metric used was that of sparseness, as shown in Eq. 1. The distance metric between vectors was simply the average difference between corresponding elements.

Also, the simulated robot was changed from a wheeled robot with momentum to a tracked one without any momentum. That is, every time step, a robot's speed and angular velocity were specified by Eqs. 2 and 3, respectively.

$$s = (o_1) * 0.5 \tag{2}$$

$$\omega = (o_2 - 0.5) * 10.0 \tag{3}$$

Here $s$ represents the speed of the robot, $\omega$ represents its angular velocity and $o_1$ and $o_2$ represent the ANN outputs, in the range $[0, 1]$. The robot can only move forwards, since a wall following behaviour (a typical maze solving behaviour [32]) requires that the robot be able to move in only one direction. However, exploratory experimentation (results not presented here), showed that allowing the robot to move in reverse had a minimal impact on task performance.

The collision radius of the robot with the walls was reduced from four to 0.5 units. The purpose of these changes in the robot's movement and its collision radius was the result of preliminary experiments finding that the maze environment of Lehman and Stanley [10] did not allow for the evolution of generalised solvers. Exploratory experiments attempted to elucidate the exact relationship between these parameters, the defining maze features, and successful evolution of maze solving behaviours. However, due to the large computational and time expense of evolving maze solving behaviours across a vast range of mazes for various task and method parameters, this is still the subject of ongoing research.

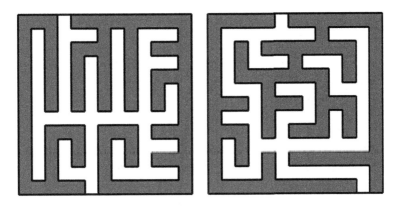

**Fig. 2.** Examples of the mazes used in the training set. (Left) Less difficult and deceptive. (Right) More difficult and deceptive.

**Fig. 3.** Examples of the mazes used in the validation set. (Left) Less difficult and deceptive. (Right) More difficult and deceptive.

## 3    Experiments

### 3.1    Objective Versus Non-objective Search

Experiments compared the task performance of non-objective (NS) versus objective versus a hybrid NS-Objective search approach. Thus the three test cases were NE directed by novelty, NE directed by fitness, where robot behaviour fitness was the number of mazes it was able to solve, and finally NE directed by a hybrid fitness-novelty function. This hybrid fitness-novelty function was $f = n + \frac{m}{2}$. Here $n$ is the robot's novelty score and $m$ is the number of mazes that it solved. Exploratory experiments indicated that using this hybrid fitness function, the behaviour of NE was distinct from NE directed by NS and NE directed by fitness. More specifically, the populations converged on solving behaviours, unlike NS, yet evolution performed better than fitness.

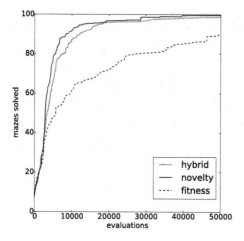

**Fig. 4.** Number of mazes solved by the best evolved controller, averaged over 20 runs, against the number of evaluations.

**Table 1.** (Top) Average number of training mazes solved by best evolved robot controller after 50000 evaluations, over 20 runs as well as the number of runs which produced a controller capable of solving all 100 mazes. Also shown is the average number of mazes solved in the generalisation test as well as the number of tested agents capable of solving all 10000 mazes. Standard deviations are in parentheses. (Bottom) $p$ values for the differences in the means shown in the upper table (Mann-Whitney-U test [35]).

|  | training | | generalisation | |
|---|---|---|---|---|
|  | Mazes Solved | Successful Runs | Mazes Solved | Successful Agents |
| Hybrid | 98.7 (4.1) | 18 | 9911 (267) | 10 |
| Novelty | 99.6 (1.2) | 17 | 9954 (88) | 9 |
| Fitness | 89.8 (17.6) | 10 | 9735 (419) | 1 |

| training | | | | generalisation | | | |
|---|---|---|---|---|---|---|---|
|  | Hybrid | Novelty | Fitness |  | Hybrid | Novelty | Fitness |
| Hybrid | - | 0.4 | 0.009 | Hybrid | - | 0.5 | 0.02 |
| Novelty | 0.4 | - | 0.007 | Novelty | 0.5 | - | 0.03 |
| Fitness | 0.009 | 0.007 | - | Fitness | 0.02 | 0.03 | - |

Each experiment tested one of these three approaches, and each experiment was run 20 times. Each run was ended after 50000 new individuals had been added to the population. That is, given that rtNEAT was used [30], there was continuous replacement of genotypes. Also, each genotype (robot) was tested on all 100 mazes in the training set, where each run consisted of over five million maze navigation simulations. Results are presented in Fig. 4 and Table 1. It was found that the NS and hybrid NS-objective schemes yielded statistically comparable task performance, where as both approaches out-performed the fitness function directed NE (Sect. 4).

## 3.2 Validation of General Maze Solving

One test of behavioural generality, is to place evolved controllers (behaviours) in new environments in which they were not evolved and to measure their task performance in these new environments. The 100 mazes used for maze solving behavioural evolution were a sample of the space of all mazes for the given maze size and structural criteria.

To test the general nature of evolved behaviours, the first behaviour (genotype) capable of solving all 100 mazes in the evolution set for each of the 20 runs, under each of the different incentives, was saved.

Since some evolutionary runs did not evolve maze solving behaviours, 17 saved genotypes from NS directed NE, 18 from NS-Objective and 10 from fitness were tested. A set of 10000 mazes was constructed using the same methods as for the evolution set except that these mazes were *harder*, constructed on a $21 \times 21$ grid instead of a $13 \times 13$ grid. Figures 2 and 3 present examples of some harder mazes. An agent which is a perfect wall-follower will not find these larger mazes more difficult. However, the larger distance which an agent is required to cover in one of these mazes means that there are more opportunities for mistakes to be made.

Nine of the behaviours evolved under NS were able to solve all 10000 mazes. The mean number solved was 9954, with a standard deviation of 88 and a minimum of 9662. Ten of the behaviours evolved under the NS-Objective hybrid were able to solve all 10000 mazes. The mean number solved was 9911, with a standard deviation of 264 and a minimum of 8815. Only one of the behaviours evolved under pure fitness were able to solve all 10000 mazes. The mean number solved was 9735, with a standard deviation of 419 and a minimum of 8799.

## 4   Discussion

Experimental results (Fig. 4) indicate that given the three schemes for directing the evolution of maze solving behaviours, NS, NS-Objective hybrid and a fitness function, there was no statistically significant difference between the average task performance of NS and NS-Objective directed NE. However, there was a statistically significant difference between these approaches and fitness function directed NE (Table 1). This result contributes to increasing empirical evidence on the value of NS or an an NS-Objective hybrid in tasks with varying degrees of deception versus a purely objective function based search [10,13,25–27]. For example, related work has similarly yielded comparable task performances for evolved maze solving behaviors between a range of hybrid NS-Objective functions and NS search [27]. Moreover, the results presented here show that NS and NS-Objective hybrids can be successful in very large behaviour spaces.

This experimental comparison was not explicitly designed to support the efficacy of NS or an NS hybrid search in contrast to objective based approaches, but rather to elucidate what constitutes an effective NE method capable of evolving generalised problem solvers (in this case study, specifically, maze solving behaviours). Further to this research goal, an analysis of evolved behaviours indicates that multiplicative factors converting controller outputs to robot speed and angular velocity, are important contributors to the functionality of the best evolved maze solving behaviours. However, the impact of controller parameters and task environment features on the evolution of behaviours able to generalise to harder task versions, is the subject of ongoing research.

In terms of the functionality of all evolved behaviours, emergent wall following behaviours were observed in all general maze solving behaviours evolved using NS, NS-Objective and fitness function directed NE, supporting the notion that a well established general maze solving behaviour [32] is attainable by NE. Also, the capability of many of the highest performing behaviours (those that solved all 100 mazes in the initial set), to solve all 10000 of a set of *harder* validation mazes, further supports the efficacy of NE for producing generalised maze solvers. These results support the study's research objective of using NE to evolve generalised problem solvers. The evolution of generalised maze solvers is an initial step towards this objective, where comparatively testing NS, NS-Objective hybrid, and objective based search was necessary to help elucidate the defining features of an NE controller design method able to evolve generalised problem solving behaviours.

The generality test was to validate evolved behaviours in a *harder* maze set. A majority of the best behaviours evolved by NS, NS-Objective and fitness function directed NE were able to solve all 10000 mazes in the validation set. However, the NS and NS-Objective approaches evolved more maze-solving behaviours that generalised to the validation set (Table 1).

A key result is the higher (statistically significant) task performance of NS and NS-Objective hybrid search, compared to objective based search. This suggests that the task environment contains features making it amenable to the evolution of effective maze solvers by NS or an NS-Objective hybrid. Previous work [10,13] indicates that NS performs well in deceptive tasks. Assuming that the high performance of NS in a domain indicates that it is deceptive, then we can conclude that generalised maze-solving is such a domain. However, the notion of deception remains ill defined, and it is difficult to tell *a priori* if a task is deceptive. In mazes, deceptiveness is intuitively gauged by observation, but it is unclear whether tasks such as generalised maze-solving, pole-balancing, quadruped robotic locomotion, and visual discrimination tasks also have elements of deception. In such tasks, the efficacy of NS or a NS-Objective hybrid search approach is yet to be satisfactorily demonstrated [27].

## 5    Conclusion

As a step towards addressing the research goal of defining controller design methods that elicit generalised problem solving behaviour, this paper presented a comparison of NE methods for generating generalised maze solving behaviours. The experimental comparison used objective (fitness function) versus non-objective (NS) versus a hybrid NS-Objective search as a means of guiding the NE controller design method. This study's specific aim was to elucidate if NE is appropriate for generating generalised maze solvers, and tested the three search metrics as the NE method's salient feature. Results indicated that the NS and NS-Objective approaches yielded comparable task performances, but out-performed a fitness function directed NE. These results support previous work that indicate that NS directed NE is appropriate for solving deceptive tasks. However, the efficacy of controller evolution driven by fitness, NS and NS-Objective hybrid search for eliciting problem solving behaviours in a broader range of tasks, especially those that do not include deception, is the subject of future research.

# References

1. Goertzel, B., Pennachin, C.: Artificial General Intelligence. Springer, Heidelberg (2007)
2. Schmidhuber, J.: Ultimate cognition à la gödel. Cogn. Comput. **1**(2), 177–193 (2009)
3. Hutter, M.: Universal Artificial Intelligence. Springer, Heidlberg (2005)
4. Looks, M., Goertzel, B., Pennachin, C.: Novamente: an integrative architecture for general intelligence. In: AAAI Fall Symposium, Achieving Human-Level Intelligence (2004)
5. Genesereth, M., Love, N., Pell, B.: General game playing: overview of the AAAI competition. AI Mag. **26**(2), 62–72 (2005)
6. Finnsson, H., Björnsson, Y.: Simulation-based approach to general game playing. In: AAAI, vol. 8, pp. 259–264 (2008)
7. Floreano, D., Dürr, P., Mattiussi, C.: Neuroevolution: from architectures to learning. Evol. Intel. **1**(1), 47–62 (2008)
8. Rozin, P.: The evolution of intelligence and access to the cognitive unconscious. In: Sprague, J.M., Epstein, A.N. (eds.) Progress in Psychology, pp. 245–280. Academic Press, New York (1976)
9. Eiben, A., Smith, J.: Introduction to Evolutionary Computing. Springer, Heidelberg (2003)
10. Lehman, J., Stanley, K.: Abandoning objectives: evolution through the search for novelty alone. Evol. Comput. **19**(2), 189–223 (2011)
11. Gomez, F., Miikkulainen, R.: Solving non-markovian control tasks with neuroevolution. In: IJCAI, vol. 99, pp. 1356–1361 (1999)
12. Gomez, F.J., Schmidhuber, J., Miikkulainen, R.: Efficient non-linear control through neuroevolution. In: Fürnkranz, J., Scheffer, T., Spiliopoulou, M. (eds.) ECML 2006. LNCS (LNAI), vol. 4212, pp. 654–662. Springer, Heidelberg (2006)
13. Velez, R., Clune, J.: Novelty search creates robots with general skills for exploration. In: Proceedings of the 2014 Conference on Genetic and Evolutionary Computation, pp. 737–744. ACM (2014)
14. Shorten, D., Nitschke, G.: How evolvable is novelty search? (2014)
15. Clune, J., Beckmann, B., Ofria, C., Pennock, R.: Evolving coordinated quadruped gaits with the hyperneat generative encoding. In: IEEE Congress on Evolutionary Computation, CEC 2009, pp. 2764–2771. IEEE (2009)

16. Coleman, O., Blair, A., Clune, J.: Automated generation of environments to test the general learning capabilities of AI agents
17. Richards, N., Moriarty, D., Miikkulainen, R.: Evolving neural networks to play go. Appl. Intell. **8**(1), 85–96 (1998)
18. Yong, C., Miikkulainen, R.: Coevolution of role-based cooperation in multiagent systems. IEEE Trans. Auton. Mental Dev. **1**(3), 170–186 (2009)
19. Shorten, D., Nitschke, G.: Generational neuro-evolution: restart and retry for improvement. In: Proceedings of the 2014 Conference on Genetic and Evolutionary Computation, pp. 225–232. ACM (2014)
20. Koppejan, R., Whiteson, S.: Neuroevolutionary reinforcement learning for generalized helicopter control. In: Proceedings of the 11th Annual Conference on Genetic and Evolutionary Computation, pp. 145–152. ACM (2009)
21. Rajagopalan, P., Rawal, A., Holekamp, K., Miikkulainen, R.: General intelligence through prolonged evolution of densely connected neural networks. In: Proceedings of the 2014 Conference Companion on Genetic and Evolutionary Computation Companion, pp. 35–36. ACM (2014)
22. Lehman, J., Stanley, K.: Efficiently evolving programs through the search for novelty. In: Proceedings of the 12th Annual Conference on Genetic and Evolutionary Computation, pp. 837–844. ACM (2010)
23. Urbano, P., Georgiou, L.: Improving grammatical evolution in santa fe trail using novelty search. In: Advances in Artificial Life, ECAL, vol. 12, pp. 917–924 (2013)
24. Cuccu, G., Gomez, F., Glasmachers, T.: Novelty-based restarts for evolution strategies. In: 2011 IEEE Congress on Evolutionary Computation (CEC), pp. 158–163. IEEE (2011)
25. Lehman, J., Stanley, K.: Revising the evolutionary computation abstraction: minimal criteria novelty search. In: Proceedings of the 12th Annual Conference on Genetic and Evolutionary Computation, pp. 103–110. ACM (2010)
26. Gomes, J., Urbano, P., Christensen, A.L.: Progressive minimal criteria novelty search. In: Pavón, J., Duque-Méndez, N.D., Fuentes-Fernández, R. (eds.) IBERAMIA 2012. LNCS, vol. 7637, pp. 281–290. Springer, Heidelberg (2012)
27. Inden, B., Jin, Y., Haschke, R., Ritter, H., Sendhoff, B.: An examination of different fitness and novelty based selection methods for the evolution of neural networks. Soft Comput. **17**(5), 753–767 (2013)
28. Kistemaker, S., Whiteson, S.: Critical factors in the performance of novelty search. In: Proceedings of the 13th Annual Conference on Genetic and Evolutionary Computation, pp. 965–972. ACM (2011)
29. Stanley, K., Miikkulainen, R.: Evolving neural networks through augmenting topologies. Evol. Comput. **10**(2), 99–127 (2002)
30. Stanley, K., Bryant, B., Miikkulainen, R.: Real-time neuroevolution in the nero video game. IEEE Trans. Evol. Comput. **9**(6), 653–668 (2005)
31. Xu, J., Kaplan, C.: Image-guided maze construction. ACM Trans. Graph. (TOG) **26**, 29 (2007)
32. Pullen, W.: Think labyrinth: Daedalus (2014)
33. Osmankovic, D., Konjicija, S.: Implementation of q learning algorithm for solving maze problem. In: MIPRO, 2011 Proceedings of the 34th International Convention, pp. 1619–1622. IEEE (2011)
34. Gregor, D., Troyer, M.: Boost. mpi (2006)
35. Flannery, B., Teukolsky, S., Vetterling, W.: Numerical Recipes. Cambridge University Press, Cambridge (1986)

# Evolving Robot Controllers for Structured Environments Through Environment Decomposition

Rodrigo Moreno[1]([✉]), Andres Faiña[2], and Kasper Støy[2]

[1] Universidad Nacional de Colombia, Bogota, Colombia
rmorenoga@unal.edu.co
[2] IT University of Copenhagen, Copenhagen, Denmark
{anfv,ksty}@itu.dk

**Abstract.** In this paper we aim to develop a controller that allows a robot to traverse an structured environment. The approach we use is to decompose the environment into simple sub-environments that we use as basis for evolving the controller. Specifically, we decompose a narrow corridor environment into four different sub-environments and evolve controllers that generalize to traverse two larger environments composed of the sub-environments. We also study two strategies for presenting the sub-environments to the evolutionary algorithm: all sub-environments at the same time and in sequence. Results show that by using a sequence the evolutionary algorithm can find a controller that performs well in all sub-environments more consistently than when presenting all sub-environments together. We conclude that environment decomposition is an useful approach for evolving controllers for structured environments and that the order in which the decomposed sub-environments are presented in sequence impacts the performance of the evolutionary algorithm.

**Keywords:** Evolutionary robotics · Environment decomposition · Sequential evolution

## 1 Introduction

In this paper we demonstrate how to evolve one robot controller that is able to traverse a structured environment. The approach consists of decomposing a structured environment, such as an office building or a pipe system, into simpler ones, like turns or doorways, and evolve the robot to traverse these sub-environments. A robot that can perform well in these sub-environments can generalize its behavior to any larger environment composed of the simpler ones.

The robot used is a sensor-less snake-like robot built using a simple 1 degree of freedom modular robot. There are two general controller types a robot can use, hierarchical controllers, and monolithic controllers. Using a hierarchical controller different individual controllers could be used for different sub-environments

© Springer International Publishing Switzerland 2015
A.M. Mora and G. Squillero (Eds.): EvoApplications 2015, LNCS 9028, pp. 795–806, 2015.
DOI: 10.1007/978-3-319-16549-3_64

requiring a decision mechanism to decide between all of them. A decision mechanism cannot be implemented in our current robot due to the lack of sensors, so we make use of a monolithic controller instead. The controller used is based on central pattern generators. Central pattern generators are commonly used to control the locomotion of complex robots that have limited computational capabilities [1].

Using a monolithic controller we have to ensure that it works in all sub-environments. Two methods can be used for this purpose: One is to evaluate the fitness of all individuals in all sub-environments at the same time. In this case performance in all sub-environments should be a compound measure of the fitness. Another approach is to introduce the sub-environments in sequence to the evolutionary algorithm. One individual is evaluated in the next sub-environment only if it performs well in the last one.

In our work a narrow corridor environment is decomposed into turns and bumps. Using the approaches of evaluating individuals in all sub-environments at the same time and in sequence we evolve controllers for these sub-environments and compare how fast and consistently a solution can be found. The best controller obtained by the evolutionary process is tested in two environments composed of the sub-environments and it is shown that it can successfully traverse through both of them. Results also show that presenting the sub-environments in a sequence improves how consistently the evolutionary process can find a solution compared to when there is no sequence present and that the order of the sequence impacts how fast a controller can be found. Overall, environment decomposition is shown to be an an useful approach for evolving controllers for structured environments.

## 2   Related Work

Previous task decomposition work focuses on generating behaviors for specific tasks that are combined to solve a main task [2–7]. In [2] Lee et al. use task decomposition to evolve controllers for pushing a box to a goal with a Khepera robot by evolving controllers for the sub tasks of getting to the box, circling the box and pushing the box in a certain direction. Controllers are evolved independently for each task and a decision mechanism is needed for all the different evolved controllers to work as one [3,4]. Alternatively to task decomposition, in our work instead of decomposing a given task we are given an environment that we decompose into sub-environments that could also be seen as sub-tasks.

Also, in task decomposition, it has been shown that introducing a sequence when learning multiple tasks improves the speed and reliability of the evolutionary algorithm [5,8–10]. Layered learning and incremental learning introduce the idea of a sequence in how the robot controllers are evolved for different tasks. In layered learning decomposed tasks are solved by evolving the simplest tasks separately first and then stopping the process, freezing the found solutions and using them to start new evolution processes to solve the next more complex ones. The sequence continues until the goal task has been solved. In [6] Stone et al.

evolve a controller for three tasks in a robot soccer environment: ball interception, pass evaluation and pass selection. Co-evolution is also used along layered learning to generate controllers for subtasks, in [3] Whiteson et al. co-evolve different layers at the same time as well as the decision mechanism. As it uses decision mechanisms, layered learning is a case of evolving hierarchical controllers. Here we focus on a sensor-less robot due to the ease of hardware implementation so any sensor-based decision mechanism is not possible to implement. Instead we are using a monolithic controller for it to be good in all sub-environments at the same time, something similar to what is done in incremental evolution.

In incremental evolution [7] the same task is presented to the evolutionary algorithm with various levels of difficulty starting by the easiest one. As the robot is able to solve the task the difficulty is risen gradually until the robot learns the behaviors needed to solve a desired level of complexity in the given task. The same controller is expected to include the new found behaviors without using extra parts or modules. The changes involve gradually moving the position of a goal to force the appearance of different behaviors [8], changing the height of a wall that a robot has to go over, as in [11,12], or increasing the sharpness of a curve in a maze for a mobile robot to learn how to turn [13]. Although incremental evolution involves changing the environment it remains relatively similar through the changes. Bongard et al. [8–10] show that the order in which different behaviors are incrementally learned is important for the success rate of the evolutionary process. In their work a quadruped robot with grasping capabilities is more successful in learning how to manipulate an object first and then move towards it than the other way around. Similarly, one could specify the ordering of the sub-environments in the sequence presented to the evolutionary algorithm to also change the performance of an environment decomposition learning process. Multi-objective optimization has also been used in incremental evolution to evolve behaviors without specifying a sequence [14].

The main contributions of this paper are: the idea of evolving a monolithic controller for structured environments by using environment decomposition as an alternative to task decomposition. Additionally we investigate whether introducing a sequence in how the sub-environments are presented could make the evolutionary process find a solution faster and more consistently and if the order of the sequence impacts the performance of the algorithm.

## 3 Experimental Setup

### 3.1 Simulated Modular Robot and Environments

We have modeled a snake-like robot in the V-REP simulator. V-REP is an open source robot simulator that can work with different physics engines [15]. We create a chain of 8 modules using the simple cubic modular robot shown in Fig. 1 that has only one rotational degree of freedom. Modular reconfigurable robots are a special class of robots that are built from basic units, called modules, with or without autonomy, that can reconfigure themselves to perform different

**Table 1.** Parameters of the simulation

| Parameter | Value |
|---|---|
| Physics Engine | Bullet |
| Module mass | 0.14 (Kg) |
| Max. Joint Torque | 2.5 (Nm) |
| Dimensions | 10 × 10 × 15 (cm) |
| Physics Time Step | 0.0135 (s) |

**Table 2.** Parameters of the controller

| Parameter | Value | Range |
|---|---|---|
| $a_r$ | 50 | - |
| $a_x$ | 30 | - |
| $\omega$ | $2\pi \times 0.65$ | - |
| $w_{ij}$ | 7 | - |
| $R$ | - | $[-1; 1]$ |
| $X$ | - | $[-1; 1]$ |
| $\Delta\phi$ | - | $[-\pi/2; \pi/2]$ |

tasks [16]. The module model used here is designed to be easily implemented and a first prototype has already been designed and built [17].

Each module can be connected to other modules using two connection surfaces. The module can be oriented in two ways: with it's rotational axis parallel to the horizontal plane or with the rotational axis parallel to the vertical plane. Using modules in each orientation different types of chains can be generated. In this paper a fixed chain was built with alternating orientation. The physical parameters used for the simulation can be seen in Table 1.

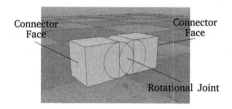

**Fig. 1.** The basic module is made of two cubic parts linked by a rotational joint. Each part has only one connector face.

Each module is controlled using an internal central pattern generator(CPG). Central pattern generators are neural structures that can be found in the spine of animals and that can generate complex movements from basic input. The CPGs inside the modules are modeled as phase coupled nonlinear oscillators as in [1] which provide a sinusoidal output that can be controlled by using three main parameters: Amplitude $R$, offset $X$ and phase difference with neighbors $\Delta\phi$, providing a simple way of achieving coordinated movement from distributed controllers.

Equation (1) shows the coupling between different oscillator phases as a weighted sum, Eqs. (2) and (3) describe control laws that make the amplitude $r$ and offset $x$ in the output (4) converge to the desired values $R$ and $X$. The parameters $a_x$, $a_r$ and $w_i$ are weights used to control the speed of convergence of the amplitude and offset to their respective set points and the coupling strength of the phase difference, their values can be seen on Table 2. The output $\theta$ in Eq. (4) controls the movement of the rotational joint in each module. For this experiment the same value of amplitude, offset and phase difference is used for all modules and will be changed by the evolutionary algorithm. The values each parameter can take can be seen in Table 2.

$$\dot{\phi}_i = \omega_i + \sum_j (w_{ij} Sin(\phi_j - \phi_i - \Delta\phi_{ij})) \tag{1}$$

$$\ddot{r}_i = a_r(\frac{a_r}{4}(R_i - r_i) - \dot{r}_i) \tag{2}$$

$$\ddot{x}_i = a_x(\frac{a_x}{4}(X_i - x_i) - \dot{x}_i) \tag{3}$$

$$\theta_i = x_i + r_i Cos(\phi_i) \tag{4}$$

The narrow corridor environment shown in Fig. 2, in which the robot can find turns and obstacles as well as long empty segments is decomposed into four sub-environments (Fig. 3): *Straight*, *Turnleft*, *TurnRight* and *Bump*. By being good in all four sub-environments the robot should be able to move through any narrow corridor composed of these parts. The environments have been built using walls and obstacles available in the simulator.

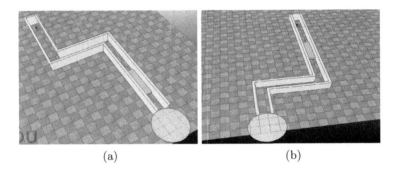

(a)                              (b)

**Fig. 2.** Two narrow corridors with turns and obstacles. The light blue rectangle is a small bump. The circle represents the goal area (Colour figure online).

The starting position of the last module of the chain in all four sub-environments can be seen in Fig. 3d. Sub-environment *Straight* (Fig. 3a) is a straight corridor in front of the starting position, *TurnLeft* (Fig. 3c) its a left turn after a shorter straight corridor, *Bump* (Fig. 3b) has a step that doubles the robot's height after some distance from the start of the same straight corridor as in *Straight*, and *TurnRight* (Fig. 3d) is a turn in the opposite direction of *TurnLeft*. The robot should move from its starting position to the end of each corridor in a limited amount of time $T$, and all sub-environments have a similar distance from the initial position of the robot to the goal position (circle at the end of the corridor).

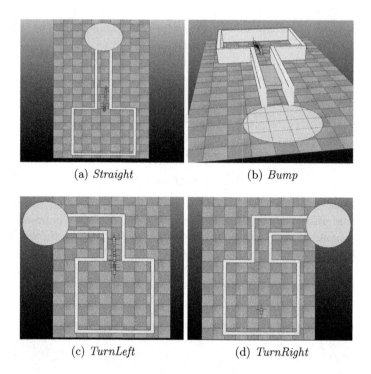

(a) *Straight*                    (b) *Bump*

(c) *TurnLeft*                    (d) *TurnRight*

**Fig. 3.** The four sub-environments in which the robot is evaluated. The circle represents the goal area, fitness is measured as the distance to the goal along the corridor in each case. The initial position of the last module of the robot is shown in (d).

### 3.2    Evolutionary Algorithm

To evolve the 3 controller parameters of the CPG, namely amplitude $R$, offset $X$ and phase difference with neighbors $\Delta\phi$, for the robot to get out of different sub-environments we used the Differential Evolution Algorithm [18], the specific parameters used for the algorithm are displayed in Table 3. The algorithm was implemented using the JEAF [19] framework on a 32 core AMD Opteron Linux machine. The fitness function for each sub-environment is defined in two stages: first, if the robot is not able to get out of the corridor under the maximum amount of time the fitness will be the distance to the goal $D$ plus the maximum time allowed for the trial $T$ in simulation time. Once the robot gets to the goal circle (Fig. 3) its fitness will be the time it takes to complete the maze $t$, so the fitness for each sub-environment looks like this:

$$F = \begin{cases} D + T & \text{if goal not reached} \\ t & \text{if goal reached} \end{cases} \tag{5}$$

In this way the robot can reach the goal and continue to improve its fitness by being quicker. The robot controller is evolved in two ways:

**Table 3.** Differential Evolution Parameters

| Parameter | Value |
|---|---|
| Population Size | 32 |
| Number of Generations | 300 |
| F | 0.9 |
| CR | 0.9 |
| Max. Evaluation time $T$ | 40 (s) |

**Learning All Sub-environments at once.** For this scenario the controller is evaluated in all four sub-environments and the total fitness is measured using two methods: the average fitness and the worst fitness of all four. In the case of the worst fitness the robot has to have a good performance in all sub-environments in order to have a good fitness. An individual has reached the goal in all sub-environments if its fitness is less than $T$, which is the same for all four sub-environments.

**Learning All Sub-environments in Sequence.** The robot is evaluated in all four sub-environments in a sequential fashion. Only if the individual being evaluated is able to get to the goal of one sub-environment under the maximum allowed time it is evaluated in the next sub-environment until an individual is capable of getting out of all four sub-environments. Sub-environments are shown to the robot in three different experiments: *Straight - TurnLeft - Bump - TurnRight* (S1), *Straight - Bump - TurnLeft - TurnRight* (S2) and *Straight - TurnRight - TurnLeft - Bump* (S3). These first three sequences cover all permutations of the sub-environments *TurnLeft, TurnRight* and *Bump* that are no mirrors of each other, that is turning left and then turning right is considered to be the same as turning right and then turning left. The *Straight* sub-environment is always shown to the robot at the beginning of these three initial sequences as it is the simplest and all the others include a straight element in the beginning.

The last sequence considered (*Bump - TurnRight - TurnLeft - Straight*, S4) changes this as it puts the *Straight* sub-environment at the end. Each individual receives a bonus fitness corresponding to a value that is designed to be at least greater than the maximum observed fitness a robot can get in an individual sub-environment (this parameter is based in the observed fitness of several runs of the evolution process) so the total fitness is:

$$F = \begin{cases} 1000/f_1 & \text{if goal not reached in env 1} \\ 1000/f_2 + 100 & \text{if goal reached in env 1} \\ 1000/f_3 + 200 & \text{if goal reached in env 1 and env 2} \\ 1000/f_4 + 300 & \text{if goal reached in env 1 and env 2 and env 3} \end{cases} \quad (6)$$

Being $f_i$ the fitness obtained on sub-environment $i$ using (5). In this case an individual has reached the goal on all sub-environments if its fitness is above

$1000/T + 300$, in this case 325. In all cases the evolution process is given a maximum of 300 generations to find a suitable controller for all four sub-environments.

## 4  Results

Figure 4a shows the average of the best individual fitness per generation for 10 runs of the evolutionary process using the average fitness with no sequence. Figure 4b shows the fitness for each sub-environment in one run in the case of using the average fitness. It should be noted that using the average fitness can be deceiving in that a solution can perform really well in some sub-environments while performing poorly in the others. Using the average fitness doesn't ensure that a controller is good in all sub-environments at the same time, however in this case all runs generate controllers that are successful in all sub-environments.

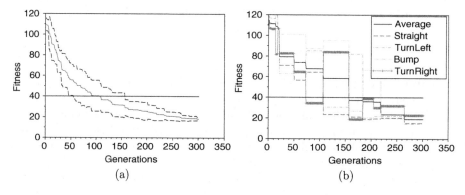

(a)                                          (b)

**Fig. 4.** Average and standard deviation of the best individual fitness per generation (a) for 10 runs evaluating all four sub-environments at the same time with the average fitness. Also, fitness in each sub-environment for 1 run (b). A fitness under 40 (*bottom line*) means an individual is successful in a sub-environment.

Figure 5 shows the best individual fitness per generation and the average of the best individual fitness per generation for 11 evolution runs using the worst fitness with no sequence. It can be seen that by using the worst fitness the evolutionary process cannot find a solution in 2 of the 11 runs for the allowed number of generations.

In Fig. 6 the average best fitness per generation for all the sequences used in the sequence learning scenario is shown. It can be seen that in all the cases where a sequence is introduced the evolutionary process is able to find a solution for all four sub-environments every time. An analysis of variance to compare the number of generations it takes for all strategies to generate a controller that is successful in all environments showed a significant difference, $F(5, 53) = 3.73$, $p = 0.0057$. The means and standard deviations are presented in Table 4. Post-hoc comparisons using a Tukey HSD test showed that sequences S1 and S2 are significantly faster than S4 in generating controllers.

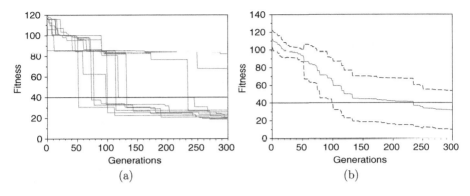

**Fig. 5.** Best individual fitness per generation (a) and average of best individual fitness per generation with standard deviation (b) for 11 runs of evolution evaluating all four sub-environments at the same time with the worst fitness. A fitness under 40 (*bottom line*) means an individual is successful in all sub-environments.

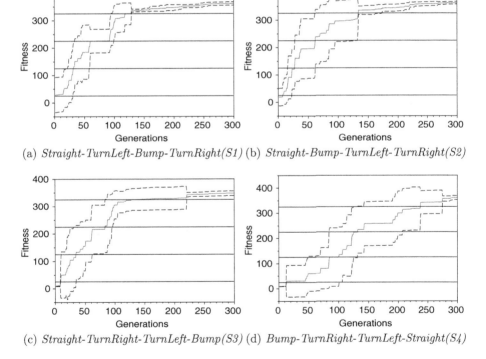

(a) *Straight-TurnLeft-Bump-TurnRight(S1)* (b) *Straight-Bump-TurnLeft-TurnRight(S2)*

(c) *Straight-TurnRight-TurnLeft-Bump(S3)* (d) *Bump-TurnRight-TurnLeft-Straight(S4)*

**Fig. 6.** Average best individual fitness per generation, with standard deviation, for 10 runs of evolution evaluating sub-environments in sequence. (*Black lines*) indicate environment transitions when a controller has successfully reached the goal in each one (Colour figure online).

**Table 4.** Average number of generations with standard deviation to find a controller that solves all sub-environments for all runs for all strategies.

|         | Worst | Average | S1 | S2 | S3 | S4 |
|---------|-------|---------|------|------|-------|-------|
| **Average** | 111.1 | 108.4 | 99.8 | 94.7 | 103.9 | 175.8 |
| **SD** | 52.26 | 51.89 | 22.35 | 48.71 | 52.02 | 59.65 |

When presented with the two environments from Fig. 2 the sequence S1 produces controllers that are able to traverse both corridors under 300 seconds in 18 out of 20 runs. Controllers obtained using the Average fitness are able to traverse both corridors in 14 of 20 runs and using the worst fitness in 17 of 20 runs. In contrast the sequence S4 produces controllers successful in 11 of 20 runs. Unsuccessful controllers in the larger environments can be attributed to the controllers exploiting features of the simulation to get a good fitness [20].

## 5    Discussion

Results show that controllers evolved by using environment decomposition were able to generalize for the larger environments even when no assumptions were made on how the robot could go from one sub-environment to another.

It can be seen that, when presenting the evolutionary algorithm with all sub-environments at the same time, although the average fitness can be a deceiving measure in this case it performs better than the worst fitness measure in evolving controllers for all sub-environments in all runs. This may be due to the worst measure giving bad fitness to controllers that perform well in almost all sub-environments but perform poorly in one. This condition is relaxed with the average fitness measure by which this kind of controllers get a better fitness.

When the sub-environments are presented in sequence it is shown that the evolutionary algorithm finds solutions for all runs, again in contrast with the worst measure case. Also, introducing a sequence ensures that a controller is good in all environments as opposed to using the average measure. The S1 sequence (Fig. 6a) performs specially well as is not only able to find solutions quickly for all four sub-environments but also in a consistent way when compared to the other strategies.

The significant difference between sequences S1,S2 and S4 indicates that the order of the sub-environments influences the result. Changing the place of the *Straight* sub-environment in the sequence (S4) makes the overall process take on average more generations to find a solution that satisfies all four sub-environments (Table 4). This indicates the idea that some environments are more or less complex to learn after learning others.

## 6    Conclusions and Future Work

It can be concluded that environment decomposition is an useful approach for evolving controllers for structured environments as controllers evolved in the decomposed sub-environments generalize their behavior to more complex environments composed of the simpler ones. Introducing a sequence when presenting an evolutionary algorithm with the different sub-environments helps generate controllers more reliably and the specific sequence has an impact in the performance of the process. Future work includes investigating how the approach scales to structured, but more complex environments, using sensors for implementing a decision mechanism in the controller and considering the problem of how a robot can go from one sub-environment to another. We also aim to verify our results on the physical system once it is completed.

**Acknowledgments.** This project is supported in part by grant 23418 of the program "Programa nacional de proyectos para el fortalecimiento de la investigación, la creación y la innovación en posgrados en la Universidad Nacional de Colombia 2013" of Universidad Nacional de Colombia.

# References

1. Crespi, A., Lachat, D., Pasquier, A., Ijspeert, A.J.: Controlling swimming and crawling in a fish robot using a central pattern generator. Auton. Robots **25**(1–2), 3–13 (2008)
2. Lee, W.P., Hallam, J., Lund, H.H.: Learning complex robot behaviours by evolutionary computing with task decomposition. In: Birk, A., Demiris, J. (eds.) Learning Robots. LNCS, vol. 1545, pp. 155–172. Springer, Heidelberg (1998)
3. Whiteson, S., Kohl, N., Miikkulainen, R., Stone, P.: Evolving soccer keepaway players through task decomposition. Mach. Learn. **59**(1–2), 5–30 (2005)
4. Lessin, D., Fussell, D., Miikkulainen, R.: Open-ended behavioral complexity for evolved virtual creatures. In: Proceedings of the GECCO 2013, p. 335. ACM Press, New York, USA (2013)
5. Rossi, C., Eiben, A.E.: Simultaneous versus incremental learning of multiple skills by modular robots. Evol. Intell. **7**(2), 119–131 (2014)
6. Stone, P., Veloso, M.M.: Layered learning. In: de Mantaras, R.L., Plaza, E. (eds.) ECML 2000. LNCS (LNAI), vol. 1810, pp. 369–381. Springer, Heidelberg (2000)
7. Gomez, F., Miikkulainen, R.: Incremental evolution of complex general behavior. Adapt. Behav. **5**(3–4), 317–342 (1997)
8. Bongard, J.: Behavior chaining: incremental behavioral integration for evolutionary robotics. Artif. Life XI Number **1976**, 64–71 (2008)
9. Auerbach, J., Bongard, J.C.: How robot morphology and training order affect the learning of multiple behaviors. In: IEEE Congress on CEC 2009, pp. 39–46, Trondheim, May 2009
10. Bongard, J.C.: Morphological and environmental scaffolding synergize when evolving robot controllers. In: GECCO 2011 1st workshop on evolutionary computation for designing generic algorithms, p. 179. ACM Press, Dublin, Ireland (2011)
11. Mukosaka, N., Tanev, I., Shimohara, K.: Performance of incremental genetic programming on adaptability of snake-like Robot. IES2013 **24**, 152–157 (2013)
12. Kuyucu, T., Tanev, I., Shimohara, K.: Genetic transposition inspired incremental genetic programming for efficient coevolution of locomotion and sensing of simulated snake-like robot. In: Proceedings of the Eleventh European Conference on the Synthesis and Simulation of Living Systems ECAL-2011, pp. 439–446. MIT Press, Paris (2011)

13. Song, G.B., Cho, S.B.: Combining incrementally evolved neural networks based on cellular automata for complex adaptive behaviors. In: First IEEE Symposium on Combinations of Evolutionary Computation and Neural Networks, pp. 121–129. IEEE, San Antonio, TX (2000)

14. Mouret, J.-B., Doncieux, S.: Incremental Evolution of animats' behaviors as a multi-objective optimization. In: Asada, M., Hallam, J.C.T., Meyer, J.-A., Tani, J. (eds.) SAB 2008. LNCS (LNAI), vol. 5040, pp. 210–219. Springer, Heidelberg (2008)

15. Rohmer, E., Singh, S.P.N., Freese, M.: V-REP: A versatile and scalable robot simulation framework. In: 26th IEEE/RSJ International Conference on Intelligent Robots and Systems (IROS 2013), pp. 1321–1326. IEEE, Tokyo, November 2013

16. Jantapremjit, P., Austin, D.: Design of a modular self-reconfigurable robot. In: Australian Conference on Robotics and Automation. Citeseer, Sydney, Australia (2001)

17. Moreno, R., Gomez, J.: Simple chain type modular robot hardware (2011). https://www.youtube.com/watch?v=x6UQfC4KALA

18. Storn, R., Price, K.: Differential evolutiona simple and efficient heuristic for global optimization over continuous spaces. J. Global Optim. **11**(4), 341–359 (1997)

19. Caamano, P., Tedin, R., Paz-Lopez, A., Becerra, J.A.: JEAF: A Java Evolutionary Algorithm Framework. In: IEEE Congress on Evolutionary Computation, CEC 2010, pp. 1–8, December 2007. IEEE, Barcelona, July 2010

20. Jakobi, N.: Evolutionary robotics and the radical envelope-of-noise hypothesis. Adapt. Behav. **6**(2), 325–368 (1997)

# Autonomous Learning of Procedural Knowledge in an Evolutionary Cognitive Architecture for Robots

Rodrigo Salgado, Francisco Bellas[(✉)], and Richard J. Duro

Integrated Group for Engineering Research, Universidade da Coruña,
A Coruña, Spain
{rodrigo.salgado,francisco.bellas,richard}@udc.es
http://www.gii.udc.es

**Abstract.** This paper describes a procedure to provide a way for the Multilevel Darwinist Brain evolutionary cognitive architecture to be able to learn and preserve procedural knowledge while operating on-line. This procedural knowledge is acquired in the form of ANNs that implement behaviors in the sense of traditional evolutionary robotics. The behaviors are produced in real time as the robot is interacting with the world. It is interesting to see in the results presented that this approach of learning procedural representations instead of exhaustively selecting the appropriate action every instant of time provides better generalization results and more efficient action sequences.

## 1 Introduction

Researchers in autonomous robotics have tried to computationally reproduce the complex processes occurring within the brain with the aim of obtaining robots that are more autonomous [1, 2]. This area of research has been termed cognitive robotics because these robots are characterized by their cognition. Thus, a cognitive robot is capable of acquiring knowledge in an autonomous and adaptive way and, as a consequence, its behavior can be really autonomous.

Cognitive architectures are the computational implementation of cognition in robots. Most traditional cognitive architectures, such as SOAR [3], LIDA [4], Micro-PSI [5], OpenCogPrime [6] or IMA [7], include memory systems based on theoretical concepts from neuroscience and cognitive psychology. Two main types of memory systems in terms of the length of time things are retained are usually considered, Short-Term Memory (STM) and Long-Term Memory (LTM). Even though different models of memory organization have been proposed [8–11], there is a certain consensus on the fact that STM contains, among other elements, a sensory memory (SM) that stores the information perceived by the perceptual system and a working memory (WM). This WM can be taken as a cache that actively preserves information relevant to the current task for a short period of time. This information in the STM usually undergoes a process of consolidation until it is permanently stored in the LTM.

LTM preserves a large amount of information for a long time [11]. In terms of the elements that are kept in it, it is generally divided in two types. First, the *procedural* or

© Springer International Publishing Switzerland 2015
A.M. Mora and G. Squillero (Eds.): EvoApplications 2015, LNCS 9028, pp. 807–818, 2015.
DOI: 10.1007/978-3-319-16549-3_65

*implicit* memory is related with implicit knowledge and non-conscious processes like acquired skills. This memory is involved with remembering how to do things without an explicit declaration of it, that is, "without having to think", and it is populated through a process of repetition of procedures that become automatic. These memory items are strongly linked to the perceptions or states that trigger them and, therefore, can be directly activated by these perceptions or states.

On the other hand, the *declarative* or *explicit* memory stores conscious knowledge and it can be subdivided in two types again. The *semantic* memory stores general knowledge about the world including facts and properties of objects, and the *episodic* memory stores events or episodes that occurred during a lifetime contextualized in time and space, namely, life experiences. These explicit memories do not really trigger events; they are used by cognitive processes to decide. To state it simply, they are used within "thinking" processes.

Thus, two main types of knowledge need to be acquired and preserved in the LTM of a cognitive architecture to be used by the robot. On one hand, one needs to have declarative knowledge, which is usually presented in the form of models of the external and internal world of the robot, or explicit data related to specific occurrences of things. In other words, modules within a cognitive structure are required that permit the robot to infer how the world or itself are going to behave. They allow it to answer questions about this and thus carry out internal simulation or "thought processes" in order to be able to make decisions on what to do or on what procedural knowledge to apply. On the other, a robot needs to acquire and, if possible preserve, procedural knowledge, that is, knowledge on how to do things (skills). In fact, this knowledge is crucial, and the faster it can be applied when the correct circumstances arise, the better the chance of survival.

In this paper, we are going to study how the autonomous acquisition of procedural knowledge can be implemented in a specific cognitive architecture that has been under development by the authors since [12], the Multilevel Darwinist Brain (MDB). The main capabilities of this architecture have already been tested in terms of on-line modeling through autonomous interaction with the environment [12–21] based on Darwinian principles, since learning processes are performed using evolutionary algorithms. However, in most of the experiments carried out in previous work, a simple action generation mechanism was applied, without considering the acquisition of procedural knowledge. Basically, using the models the MDB learns, a series of possible actions were internally tested and evaluated (in a sort of "thought" process), and the one that would lead to the highest predicted satisfaction was chosen. Obviously, even though this approach has been quite successful in simple tasks [16], it is rather limited, as the system is only considering the next instant of time and there is no memory of sequences of actions performed that were successful. Additionally, the whole "thought" process needs to be run every time an action is required. Obviously, this does not allow for immediate or reflex responses related to assimilated previous experience.

The basic idea to include procedural knowledge in the MDB is that whenever a "thought" process takes place, instead of selecting an action, the MDB selects a *behavior* (selection structure whose inputs are perception or sensor values and directly provide as outputs motor commands) to control the robot. Thus, the selected behavior is the one in charge of providing actions or motor commands for as long as it remains the current behavior. This approach decouples the "thought" process from the action or motor command selection process. A behavior module can be almost instantaneous in its response to perceptions, it is able to provide actions or motor commands for unlimited lengths of time, it can be stored for future cases in which this behavior may become useful again, and it can be improved over time with local adaptation processes. In other words this approach opens up a wealth of possibilities that simple actions could not fulfill and introduces real procedural knowledge within the MDB.

The remaining of the paper is structured as follows: Sect. 2 contains a summary of the main elements of the MDB in its current version. Section 3 is devoted to the formal description of procedural knowledge acquisition within the MDB. Section 4 contains a practical example of application of this new learning system and its comparison to exhaustive action selection. Finally, in Sect. 5 the main conclusions that can be extracted from this work are presented.

## 2  The Multilevel Darwinist Brain

The Multilevel Darwinist Brain (MDB) is an evolutionary cognitive architecture that allows an artificial agent to learn from its experience in a dynamic and unknown environment in order to fulfill its motivations or objectives [12–21]. This architecture is based in 4 basic elements:

- *Models*: prediction structures that conform the *declarative knowledge* an agent has. Three types of basic models are considered: world, internal and satisfaction models. In a cognitive developmental architecture like the MDB, these models are not predefined and must be acquired through interaction with the world. The MDB relies on the use of evolutionary algorithms for model learning [16] and the typical prediction structures used for models have been Artificial Neural Networks.
- *Behaviors*: a behavior is a decision structure that provides the action to be applied in time $t$ from the sensorial input in $t$. They make up the *procedural knowledge* the agent has because they can be assimilated as learned skills. As in the case of models, the behaviors should not be predefined in a cognitive mechanism like the MDB, and they must be learned on line. How to perform this learning process is the main topic of this paper.
- *Episodes*: real world samples that are obtained from the robot sensors and actuators after applying an action. Within the MDB these episodes are made up of the sensorial information plus the applied action in time $t$ and the sensorial information derived from the execution of the action in time $t + 1$.
- *Memories*: two main kind of memory elements are considered: Long-Term (LTM) and Short-Term (STM) [20]. The STM is made up of a *model memory*, which contains models and behaviors that are relevant to the current task, and an *episodic buffer (EB)* that stores the last episodes experienced by the robot. The EB has a very limited capacity according to the temporal nature of the STM. The LTM is made up of a *declarative memory (DM)*, which contains the models that have been consolidated due to their significance and reliability, and a *procedural memory (PM)* that stores the consolidated behaviors. It is important to highlight that both DM and PM are filled during the robot lifetime in a completely autonomous fashion, that is, no predefined library of models or behaviors are considered.

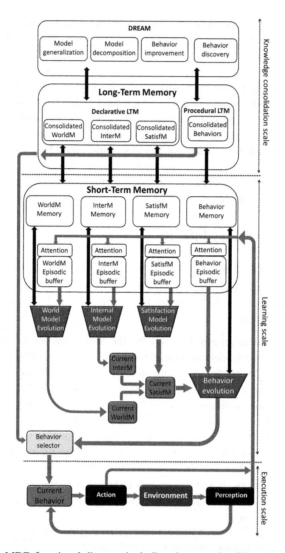

**Fig. 1.** MDB functional diagram including the procedural learning system

Figure 1 displays a functional diagram of the MDB presented here, including the behavior learning process, which is the main topic of this work. As we can see, the MDB is structured into three asynchronous time scales, one devoted to the execution of actions in the environment in real time (execution scale), the second that deals with the learning of models (learning scale) and the third one dealing with the processes of knowledge consolidation, which we are associating to sleeping [21]. The elements present in the execution scale necessarily run in the robot's physical hardware while the elements present in the learning and knowledge consolidation scales can run on it if the computational power allows it, but they can also run in distributed computers. The operation of the MDB can be described in terms of these scales.

In the learning scale, all the learning processes are executed in parallel, both for the models (World Model Evolution, Internal Model Evolution and Satisfaction Model Evolution in Fig. 1) and behaviors (Behavior Evolution in Fig. 1). Each time the robot executes an action in the environment, a new MDB *iteration* starts with a new episode that is stored in the EB of each type of model (WorldM EB, InterM EB, SatisfM EB). At this moment, the model evolution starts using as population the models stored in the model memory (WorldM Memory, InterM Memory, SatisfM Memory). This evolution is carried out during a small number of generations to avoid a premature convergence of the model towards a specific EB [16] and the model memories are preserved through iterations. After each evolutionary process finishes, the best model is selected as the current model for each type (Current InterM, Current WorldM and Current SatisfM).

The set of current models in a given iteration make up the best internal representation the robot has in that instant of time, and they are applied in the behavior learning process that will be explained in detail in the following section. Behaviors are also evolved in order to have a population of behavior candidates (Behavior Memory in Fig. 1) that can be quickly adapted in the case of changes in the environment. As in the case of models, the population of behaviors is stored and preserved through iterations. The evolution of behaviors starts each iteration and is carried out for a small number of generations too. Once the behavior evolution process finishes, the best individual is selected as the current behavior and, if it is predictably better that the current behavior, it is transferred to the execution scale to be used to select the action with the aim of having the most updated behavior in use.

In the execution time scale, the robot has a behavior selector onboard that chooses the behavior that will be applied in real time as demanded by the task. By default, it uses the behavior obtained in the learning scale, which is continuously updated if a better one is obtained. If the satisfaction value decreases continuously, other behaviors imported from the procedural LTM can be selected.

The knowledge consolidation scale operates mainly over the Long Term Memory (LTM) and the processes involved in the consolidation of declarative and procedural knowledge, that is, models and behaviors. These processes have been called the DREAM (Deferred Restructuring of Experience for Autonomous Machines) and they have been recently added to the MDB [21].

## 3   Procedural Knowledge Learning in the MDB

To explain the learning process of procedural knowledge within the MDB in a formal way, some concepts about the underlying cognitive model must be introduced first.

The external perception $e(t)$ of an agent is made up of the sensory information it is capable of acquiring through its sensors from the environment in which it operates. Consequently, the external perception can be expressed as a function of the last action $A(t-1)$ performed by the agent and the sensory perception it had of the external world in the previous time instant $e(t-1)$ through a function $W$ *(World Model)*:

$$e(t) = W[e(t-1), A(t-1)]$$

The internal perception $i(t)$ of an agent is made up of the sensory information provided by its internal sensors, its proprioception. Internal perception can be written in terms of the last action $A(t-1)$ performed by the agent and the sensory perception it had from the internal sensors in the previous time instant $i(t-1)$ through a function $I$ (*Internal Model*):

$$i(t) = I[i(t-1), A(t-1)]$$

The satisfaction $s(t)$ of the agent may be defined as a magnitude or vector that represents the degree of fulfilment of the motivation or motivations of the agent and it can be related to its internal and external perceptions through a function $S$ (*Satisfaction Model*). Thus, generalizing:

$$s(t) = S[e(t), i(t)] = S[W[e(t-1), A(t-1)], I[i(t-1), A(t-1)]]$$

The main objective of the MDB cognitive architecture is the satisfaction of the motivation of the agent, which, without any loss of generality, may be expressed as the maximization of the value of the satisfaction $s(t)$ in each instant of time. The action selection process of the MDB must explore the possible action space in order to maximize the resulting satisfaction. This exploration is carried out using the models $W$, $I$ and $S$, which must be learned during the robot interaction with the environment. These models make up the declarative knowledge of the MDB, and they are crucial in the procedural learning process.

As commented in the previous section, behaviors ($B$) are decision structures that provide the action to be applied in time $t$ from the sensorial input in $t$. Formally:

$$A(t) = B[e(t), i(t)]$$

In the current version of the MDB, as in the case of models, behaviors have been represented by means of Artificial Neural Networks (ANN). Thus, behavior learning consists in adjusting the parameters of the ANN by means of an evolutionary algorithm. Each iteration of the MDB, a new episode is obtained, and the evolution of behaviors starts using the individuals stored in the Behavior Memory. This memory includes a population of behaviors that are initially random and that are evolved using the models as "simulators of the current reality". Thus, to evaluate an individual $i$ of this population ($B_i$), the following procedure is applied over all the episodes of the Behavior Episodic Buffer:

1. An episode $j$ of the Behavior EB is taken: $[e_j(t), i_j(t)]$
2. It is the input to the behavior $B_i$ under evaluation, obtaining an action $A_{ij}$:

$$A_{ji}(t) = B_i[e_j(t), i_j(t)]$$

3. This action is used as an input in the current world and internal models ($W_c$ and $I_c$) together with the episode $j$, providing the predicted external and internal sensing values:

$$e_j(t+1) = W_c[e_j(t), A_{ji}(t)]$$

$$i_j(t+1) = I_c[i_j(t), A_{ji}(t)]$$

4. From these predicted sensorial information, the current satisfaction model ($S_c$) provides the predicted satisfaction for the action:

$$s_j(t+1) = S_c[e_j(t+1), i_j(t+1)]$$

This process is repeated for all the episodes and the predicted satisfaction obtained is averaged, making up the fitness for behavior $B_j$. The remaining behaviors in the Behavior Memory are evaluated using the same episodes and the same current models. When evolution finishes, the behavior with the highest fitness (out of all those evolved and the current behavior) is selected as the current behavior and it is transferred to the execution scale. The behaviors that are successful in this execution scale can be incorporated to the procedural LTM after passing a consolidation process in the knowledge consolidation scale [21]. Consequently, with this new learning system, the MDB is now capable of creating and preserving procedural knowledge in an autonomous fashion.

It must be pointed out that this behavior learning process is carried out on line using models that are being learned on line too. Consequently, in the first stages of learning, the behaviors will be wrongly evaluated because the models are still under development. Anyway, as will be shown in the next section, this coupled evolution converges for both models and behaviors.

## 4   Operation Example

The previous procedure for autonomous learning of procedural knowledge within the MDB has been tested in a simulated robotic experiment (see Fig. 2 for a snapshot). Specifically, we have used the Webots simulator with a modified AIBO model [17] in a simple learning example of reaching an object. We place the AIBO robot in an empty scenario that only contains a pink ball. Each iteration, the robot moves its neck in order to find the ball and estimates a distance and an angle from the camera information. This sensorial data is provided to the MDB, which must calculate the most appropriate action in order to reach the ball. The AIBO movement has been simplified in a single action that represents the turning angle of the robot with a fixed linear speed. Thus, this single action was encoded in the range [1:21], being 1 a left turn of 180° and 21 a right turn of 180°, with intermediate turns in the rest of the range. The experiment is conceptually very simple but it implies the autonomous acquisition of four models and one behavior.

In particular, three world models have been set up. The first one predicts the distance to the ball from the previous distance, angle and the applied action. The second one predicts the angle to the ball from the previous angle, distance and the applied action. The third one provides the visibility or non-visibility of the ball from the distance, angle and applied action and it is required to avoid learning when the robot does not perceive the ball [17] (absence of stimulus). Moreover, one satisfaction model

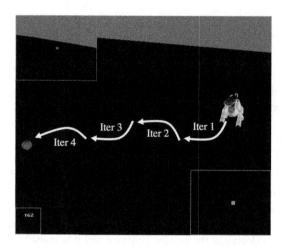

**Fig. 2.** Snapshot of the simulated experiment

has been defined, which has three inputs, the distance, the angle and the visibility predicted by the three world models, and provides the predicted satisfaction. This satisfaction is higher as the robot is nearer to the ball in a frontal direction and it is zero if the robot does not see the ball. Finally, one behavior has been defined. It has two inputs, the distance and angle, and one output, the angular speed, and it takes control of the robot in real time.

As usual in the MDB, models and behaviors have been represented by ANNs, in this case, multilayer perceptrons. The parameters of these networks have been evolved using the Differential Evolution (DE) algorithm with the implementation *DE/1/rand/ bin* extracted from the JEAF library [22]. Table 1 displays the main parameters of the MDB and DE used in this experiment. The DREAM processes have not been considered in this experiment.

To test the behavior learning procedure, we have executed the same experiment described above using an exhaustive action selection strategy, so that we can compare

**Table 1.** MDB parameterization in the AIBO experiment

|  | World models | Satisfaction model | Behavior |
|---|---|---|---|
| EB size ($C_{eb}$) | 40 | 40 | 40 |
| ANN size | 3-6-3-1 | 3-6-1 | 2-5-1 |
| Generations per iteration | 2 | 2 | 2 |
| Population size (Model and Behavior Memories) | 40 | 40 | 40 |
| Generations per iteration | 2 | 2 | 2 |
| F (Differential Evolution) | rand(0.3,0.6) | rand(0.3,0.6) | rand(0.3,0.6) |
| CR (Differential Evolution) | rand(0.7,0.9) | rand(0.7,0.9) | rand(0.7,0.9) |

the results obtained to a reference procedure that provides always the best possible action. Specifically, each iteration, all the actions in a predefined set of 20 discrete actions (from 1 to 21) are used as inputs to the three current world models obtaining predicted sensing values that are used as inputs in the current satisfaction model. This way, we have a predicted satisfaction for each action, and the best one is selected and executed by the robot. These actions make up the robot response over time and can be compared to those provided by the learned behaviors. It must be highlighted that, in addition all the advantages of behaviors commented in the introduction, they are computationally much less costly to execute than the exhaustive action selection. It implies executing just one ANN while the other implies executing, in this case, four ANNs for the whole set of predefined actions.

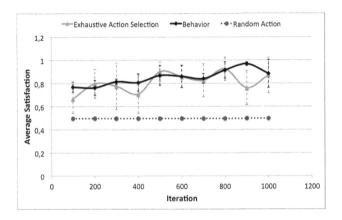

**Fig. 3.** Evolution of the average satisfaction in ten independent runs using the behavior learning procedure (black), the exhaustive action selection (grey), and a random one (dotted)

Figure 3 shows the evolution of the average satisfaction of ten independent runs using the behavior learning procedure (black), the exhaustive action selection (grey) and a random action selection (dotted) to use as a reference. To obtain these data for the behavior learning case, the current behavior was taken from the MDB every 100 iterations until iteration 1000, and applied to 188 different combinations of initial robot and ball position (uniformly distributed over the environment), thus creating a sort of testing procedure. In these 188 cases, the selected action was executed in the robot and a real satisfaction value was computed and averaged. For the exhaustive action selection, the current models of the same iterations were taken and used to select the action in the 188 cases, obtaining a comparable satisfaction measure. The random action selection is a straight line because the same average satisfaction has been represented for each iteration. As shown in the figure, the behaviors provided a very similar satisfaction to that obtained with the exhaustive procedure, which is a highly successful result taking into account all the advantages of behaviors in terms of computational cost, reusability and generalization.

To confirm this general response from a practical point of view, Table 2 contains the number of actions required to reach the ball in 6 different configurations of robot-ball initial position (specific distance and angle to the ball are displayed in the table), both for the behaviors and the exhaustive action-selection procedure. As in the previous case, the data have been calculated in different iterations of the learning process, extracting from the MDB the current behavior and models in each case and testing them under the same conditions. It can be observed that, in general, the behaviors required a lower number of actions to reach the ball in the same configurations (grey cells), confirming its successful learning.

**Table 2.** Number of actions required to reach the ball in different iterations for the behavior (B) and the exhaustive action selection (E) in 6 simulated configurations

| | Conf 1 d=3,9m a=-39'71° | | Conf 2 d=3m a=0° | | Conf 3 d=3,9m a=39'71° | | Conf 4 d=2,9m a=-58'85° | | Conf 5 d=1,5m a=0° | | Conf 6 d=2,9m a=58'85° | |
|---|---|---|---|---|---|---|---|---|---|---|---|---|
| Iteration | B | E | B | E | B | E | B | E | B | E | B | E |
| 50 | - | - | - | - | - | - | - | - | - | 7 | - | - |
| 150 | - | 20 | - | 15 | - | 22 | - | 15 | 5 | 7 | - | 16 |
| 250 | 22 | 29 | 16 | 18 | 23 | 28 | 16 | 20 | 6 | 7 | 16 | 16 |
| 350 | 21 | 29 | 15 | 14 | 21 | 29 | 15 | 24 | 6 | 16 | 15 | 23 |
| 450 | 20 | 20 | 15 | 16 | 20 | 21 | 15 | 17 | 6 | 8 | 15 | 17 |
| 550 | 21 | 32 | 17 | 40 | 22 | 30 | 17 | 20 | 8 | 22 | 17 | 21 |
| 650 | 24 | 19 | 17 | 15 | 26 | 20 | 16 | 15 | 6 | 7 | 17 | 15 |
| 750 | 19 | 38 | 15 | 28 | 20 | 38 | 15 | 30 | 6 | 8 | 15 | 29 |
| 850 | 19 | 19 | 14 | 15 | 20 | 21 | 14 | 15 | 6 | 6 | 14 | 15 |
| 950 | 19 | 27 | 14 | - | 20 | - | 15 | 24 | 6 | 14 | 15 | - |

A very relevant aspect in the MDB is how the action selection affects model learning. That is, models are learned from the episodes obtained by the robot and the variability of these episodes is crucial if one seeks models that are as general as possible. It must be taken into account that all the evolutionary processes start at the same time in the MDB from random ANNs. In the exhaustive action selection, only the models must be learned, so once they improve, the selection improves accordingly. With the behavior learning system, the behavior is learnt concurrently with the models, and the effect of this coupled learning must be analyzed.

In this sense, we have represented in Fig. 4 the evolution of the absolute error in a testing set of configurations for the distance (black) and the angle (grey) model using the exhaustive action selection (dotted line) and the learned behaviors (continuous line). Specifically, each iteration, the distance and angle models were executed over a set of 2000 random perceptions and actions extracted from the simulator, and the predicted distance and angle were compared to the real ones obtained by the robot. The absolute error averaged over these 2000 configurations is represented in the figure. As it can be clearly observed, the models obtained in both cases provide basically the same error level in this testing set, so we can conclude that the behavior learning does not affect the correct model learning.

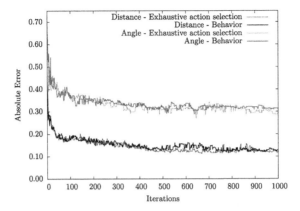

**Fig. 4.** Evolution of the absolute error in a testing set for the distance (black) and angle (grey) models using the exhaustive action selection (dotted) and the behaviors (continuous)

## 5 Conclusions

Procedural knowledge corresponds to implicit knowledge in human brains, that is, unconscious knowledge like skills or reflexes that are executed without "thinking". It is a key aspect in human development and it is also a key aspect in cognitive architectures for robots, mainly because it avoids inefficient action selection procedures and allows facing higher level cognitive processes that make use of it. In this paper, a specific implementation of a procedural knowledge learning system has been developed for the Multilevel Darwinist Brain and tested in a simple but illustrative experiment. It is based on the classical concept of behavior, a decision structure that provides the action to be applied from the sensorial inputs. These behaviors are learned on-line using the world, internal and satisfaction models that make up the declarative knowledge in the MDB as "simulators" of the real world. In this learning system, both models and behaviors are learned concurrently. The results using this approach in a simulated experiment are comparable (or even outperform) an exhaustive action selection procedure, which is very relevant taking into account the generality of this new approach. It has also been confirmed that model learning is not deteriorated as a consequence of this coupled learning. This opens up a wealth of very interesting possibilities as, now, there is a formal representation of behaviors that can be stored and recalled, slightly modified to adapt to new situations, or they could even be composed through modulation strategies in order to achieve complex behavioral patterns that can be elicited almost instantaneously.

**Acknowledgements.** Funding for this work was related to the preparation of the DREAM project in the EU's H2020 R&I programme under grant agreement No 640891.

## References

1. Asada, M., MacDorman, K.F., Ishiguro, H., Kuniyoshi, Y.: Cognitive developmental robotics as a new paradigm for the design of humanoid robots. Robot. Auton. Syst. **37**, 185–193 (2001)

2. Krichmar, J.L., Edelman, G.M.: Principles underlying the construction of brain-based devices. In: Proceedings of AISB 2006, vol. 2, pp. 37–42 (2006)
3. Laird, J.E.: Extending the soar cognitive architecture. In: Proceeding of the 2008 Conference on Artificial General Intelligence, pp. 224–235. IOS Press, Amsterdam (2008)
4. Franklin, S.: Cognitive robots: perceptual associative memory and learning. In: IEEE International Workshop on Robot and Human Interactive Communication, pp. 427–433 (2005)
5. Bach, J.: Principles of synthetic intelligence PSI: an architecture of motivated cognition, 1st edn. Oxford University Press Inc., New York (2009)
6. Goertzel, B., de Garis, H.: XIA-MAN: an extensible, integrative architecture for intelligent humanoid robotics. In: Proceedings of the BICA 2008, pp. 86–90 (2008)
7. Kawamura, K., Gordon, S., Ratanaswasd, P., Erdemir, E., Hall, J.: Implementation of cognitive control for a humanoid robot. Int. J. Humanoid Rob. 5(4), 547–586 (2008)
8. Atkinson, R., Shiffrin, R.: Human memory: A proposed system and its control processes. Psychol. Learn. Motivation 2, 89–195 (1968)
9. Baddeley, A.D., Hitch, G.: Working memory. In: Bower, G.H. (ed.) The Psychology of Learning and Motivation: Advances in Research and Theory, vol. 8, pp. 47–89 (1974)
10. Solms, M., Turnbull, O.: The Brain and the Inner World. Karnac/Other Press, Cathy Miller Foreign Rights Agency, London (2002)
11. Cowan, N.: What are the differences between long-term, short-term, and working memory? Prog. Brain Res. 169, 323–338 (2008)
12. Duro, R.J., Santos, J., Bellas, F., Lamas, A.: On line darwinist cognitive mechanism for an artificial organism. In: Proceedings Supplement Book SAB2000, pp. 215–224 (2000)
13. Bellas, F., Duro, R.J.: Multilevel darwinist brain in robots, initial implementation. In: Proceedings IROS 2004, pp. 25–32 (2004)
14. Bellas, F., Becerra, J.A., Duro, R.J.: Induced behavior in a real agent using the multilevel darwinist brain. In: Mira, J., Álvarez, J.R. (eds.) IWINAC 2005. LNCS, vol. 3562, pp. 425–434. Springer, Heidelberg (2005)
15. Bellas, F., Becerra, J.A., Duro, R.J.: Internal and external memory in neuroevolution for learning in non-stationary problems. In: Asada, M., Hallam, J.C., Meyer, J.-A., Tani, J. (eds.) SAB 2008. LNCS (LNAI), vol. 5040, pp. 62–72. Springer, Heidelberg (2008)
16. Bellas, F., Duro, R.J., Faiña, A., Souto, D.: Multilevel Darwinist Brain (MDB): Artificial evolution in a cognitive architecture for real robots. IEEE Trans. Auton. Ment. Dev. 2(4), 340–354 (2010)
17. Santos-Diez, B., Bellas, F., Faiña, A., Duro, R.J.: Lifelong learning by evolution in robotics: Bridging the gap from theory to reality. In: Proceedings EIS 2010, pp. 48–53 (2010)
18. Duro, R.J., Bellas, F., Caamaño, P., Varela, G.: Automatic model decomposition and reuse in an evolutionary cognitive mechanism. Evol. Syst. 1(2), 129–141 (2010)
19. Duro, R.J., Bellas, F., Becerra, J.A.: Evolutionary architecture for lifelong learning and real-time operation in autonomous robots. In: Angelov, P., Filev, D.P., Kasabov, N. (eds.) Evolving Intelligent Systems: Methodology and Applications. Wiley, Hoboken (2010)
20. Bellas, F., Caamaño, P., Faiña, A., Duro, R.J.: Dynamic learning in cognitive robotics through a procedural long term memory. Evol. Syst. 5(1), 49–63 (2014)
21. Duro, R.J., Bellas, F., Becerra, J.A., Salgado, R.: A role for sleep in artificial cognition through deferred restructuring of experience in autonomous machines. In: del Pobil, A.P., Chinellato, E., Martinez-Martin, E., Hallam, J., Cervera, E., Morales, A. (eds.) SAB 2014. LNCS, vol. 8575, pp. 1–10. Springer, Heidelberg (2014)
22. Caamaño, P., Tedín, R., Paz-López, A., Becerra, J.A.: JEAF: A java evolutionary algorithm framework. In: Proceedings WCCI 2010, pp. 3081–3088 (2010)

# Evolutionary Training of Robotised Architectural Elements

Claudio Rossi[1][✉], Pablo Gil[2,3], and William Coral[1]

[1] Centre for Automation and Robotics UPM-CSIC,
Universidad Politécnica de Madrid, Madrid, Spain
claudio.rossi@upm.es
[2] The Barlett School of Architecture, London, UK
[3] Universidad Europea de Madrid, Madrid, Spain

**Abstract.** We present our work on the training of robotised architectural components of intelligent buildings, focusing on main architectural components and features such as façades, roofs and partitions. The parameters governing such components may be either quantitative (such as temperature, humidity, configuration of the elements) or qualitative (such as ergonomics and aesthetics), which cannot easily be described by mathematical parameters. Due to their complexity,it is often impossible -or at least impractical, to hardcode suitable controllers for such robotised structures. Thus, we propose the use of Artificial Intelligence learning techniques, concretely Evolutionary Algorithms, so that the user can teach the robotised components how to behave in response to changing environmental conditions or user preferences. This idea is tested on an intelligent rooftop with variable geometry, that learns optimal configurations with respect to ambient light during training sessions.

**Keywords:** Evolutionary robotics · Embodied evolution · Intelligent buildings

## 1 Introduction

A recent research topic in Architecture deals with buildings that have the capability of changing the morphology or geometrical configuration of some of their main components[1] such as façades, rooftops and partitions.

This feature allows them to perform accordingly to dynamic eventualities such as the activities that take place in the buildings and environmental conditions. This can potentially improve the comfort, empathy and wellbeing of the users but also the optimisation of resources employed, i.e. energy efficiency. This is also related to other characteristics that are associated to architecture such as symbolic, artistic and expressive values, which depend also on the variable understanding of these values in time.

---

[1] Here we focus on reconfigurable moving elements, but reconfiguration may also be applied to other fixed inmotics elements such as intelligent lighting systems etc.

© Springer International Publishing Switzerland 2015
A.M. Mora and G. Squillero (Eds.): EvoApplications 2015, LNCS 9028, pp. 819–830, 2015.
DOI: 10.1007/978-3-319-16549-3_66

For the purpose of changing their geometrical configuration, morphing elements are equipped with a set of sensors and actuating elements, that shall be moved according to some perception-control-action loop. Thus, they can be considered *robotic systems* at all effects.

Our aim is to provide such robotic systems with suitable intelligent controllers, not hardcoded at design time, but rather learned by an adaptive mechanism such as Evolution, according to user-defined evaluation criteria. Providing the structures with some sort of artificial intelligence allows them to be *instructed* and also easily allows human-in-the-loop learning strategies to be adopted. Furthermore, an intelligent system is more suited to provide the level of interactivity needed to respond intelligently to real-time user needs[2].

The use of artificial intelligence and machine learning techniques for teaching the structure how to behave appears to be a natural choice. In our current work, we are investigating the use of Evolutionary Robotics concepts.

Evolutionary Robotics (ER) is commonly associated to *mobile* robots, i.e. physical or simulated mobile agents, whose controllers and/or morphologies are designed or optimised by an evolutionary process[3]. But more in general, the general purpose of ER is the "creation of autonomous robots" [1], or the "construction and deployment of autonomous and adaptive machines" [2].

The work presented here fully complies with such general definitions. However, the particularity of our "robots" and of their applications makes them unique within the field of ER. In the case at hand, two main issues must be dealt with. First, from the mechatronics point of view, the high geometrical complexity of the structures, as well as the number of sensors and actuators involved. Second, in architectural design, we shall take into account factors which cannot be easily described by mathematical parameters, since they are related to social and/or aesthetic models, to ergonomic factors (e.g. "comfort") and even to psychological states of the users.

Having a human instructor in the loop allow non-quantitative and subjective parameters to be assessed and easily incorporated in the training. We consider that human-driven evolution is a key paradigm for dealing with intelligent structures, since it allows an interaction that brings closer the functioning of the machine to the necessities expressed by the user.

To illustrate our line of work, we take into consideration the *Armadillo Skyvent* concept (Fig. 1, see also Sect. 2).

---

[2] From the Architectural point of view, our work focuses on complex dynamic systems that can go beyond an action-reaction working scheme, and that follow user centred behaviour instead. Thus, structures should be coupled with a level of real-time interactivity so that the system can respond intelligently, by which we mean "anticipating the needs of the user in respect to the quality of his environment or in respect of the interaction with a building component in particular".

[3] Works can also be found in robotic manipulators, especially for trajectory planning and optimisation, controller optimisation and for solving inverse kinematics of complex robots.

**Fig. 1.** Rendering of the *Armadillo Skyvent*, a robotised rooftop.

## 1.1 Related Work

The field of Evolutionary Robotics began developing in the early '90s, with pioneer work first in simulation [3] and then with the first experiments on the evolution of neurocontrollers for real robots [4–7]. Currently, ER is a very active field of research, ranging from evolution of gait controllers, of complex behaviours (either individual or collective), learning and adaptation, and even evolution of robot morphology. A recent state of the art of Evolutionary Robotics can be found in [1], and an overview of current trends has been recently published by Bongard [2]. Three *Grand Challenges* in ER are presented in [8].

In our current work, we are applying concepts borrowed from classic Evolutionary Robotics, namely Neural Networks-based controllers for encoding perception/action patterns, and Evolutionary Algorithms as a training technique for generating such patterns. A variety of techniques have been adopted for generating and training neural network-based robotic controllers. We refer the reader to [9] for a recent review of the literature on neuro-evolution. Here, we adopt fixed topology feed forward Neural Networks, trained using a (1+1)-Evolutionary Strategy (see Sect. 2.1).

As far as Evolutionary Algorithms (EAs) applied to Architecture is concerned, pioneer works can be dated back to 1995, when J. Frazer published his book *An Evolutionary Architecture* [10] where the use of "modern" computer-based technologies and artificial-life computing paradigms for generating architectural artefacts is proposed. Examples of using Genetic Algorithms -among other techniques- are described, for example in the optimisation of a yacht hull or in the evolution of "well proportioned" Tuscan columns. These examples introduce the two main application classes of *optimisation* and *synthesis* of structures.

Nowadays, the body of literature on Evolutionary Algorithms applied to Architecture is fairly big. Yet, existing works in the literature can still be grouped into two main application classes:

- evolutionary algorithms for optimisation of structures, layout or components
- evolutionary algorithms for automated or assisted design of structures

Examples of the first class can be found e.g. in optimising the layouts of floor plans [11], site plans [12], optimising building façades [13] and systems [14],

**Fig. 2.** The diaphragm facade system designed by Ateliers Jean Nouvel (1987) for the Institut du Monde Arabe, Paris

although the main body of application of EAs is the optimisation of geometrical structures [15–17].

Automated design of structures is proposed e.g. in [18], while EA-based generative techniques for designing buildings are proposed in [19–22]. A recent review can be found in [23]. A subclass of the generative techniques is related to the *embryogenetics* of structures, i.e. their "growing" (see, e.g., [24]).

Besides of the use of EAs as optimisation and (semi-)automated design tools, the use of EAs a as *learning* technique is -to the best of our knowledge- new in Architecture. Learning comes into play when dealing with intelligent buildings.

### 1.2   Intelligent Buildings

The concept of *intelligent building* has been introduced since the eighties to refer to any quality of intelligence that might be attributable to a building, although there are many definitions that have been proposed for it. It is notorious the early attention given to the role of electronics and computing, with the idea of an intelligent building as a building that incorporates single-purpose dedicated electronic systems. This line of work is mostly focused on the services of the building such as heating, ventilation and air conditioning (HVAC), electricity, data and security. This idea develops later towards a more integrated approach in which a computer controls the different systems to provide an integral response to environmental shifts or changes in necessities of use or users conditions (see the Intelligent Building Pyramid [25,26]). In general terms, the concept of intelligence applied to a building is commonly associated to *domotics* or *inmotics*, which are established disciplines within the field of architecture studies and that are commonly found in contemporary buildings.

Here, we focus on a different aspect: main architectural components.

### 1.3   Morphing Architectural Elements

In many cases, morphing architectural elements are meant as artistic creations (see, e.g., the façade system proposed by *WHITEvoid*[4], consisting of a number of tiltable metal flake bodies that can change the way they reflect the sunlight).

---

[4] http://www.whitevoid.com.

**Fig. 3.** The Al Bahar Towers Responsive Facade designed by AEDAS (2013)

However, there is a growing interest in providing them with functional purposes, in order to react to changing environmental, psychological or social conditions. Examples of work dedicated to morphing architectural components such as walls, roofs, floors or other main architectural components are still uncommon. Representative examples can be found in the Diaphragm Façade Dystem of the Institut du Monde Arabe in Paris (Fig. 2), designed by Ateliers Jean Nouvel and built in 1987, and the Al Bahar Towers Responsive Façade (Fig. 3) designed by AEDAS and built in 2013. In both cases the control system of the façade responds to the insolation conditions through a network of light sensors which signal the activation of the dynamic façades when needed. The Homeostatic Façade System by Martina Decker and Peter Yeadon[5] is composed by "ribbons" that open and close to control solar heat gain through it, and adopts low power consumption dielectric elastomers wrapped over a flexible polymer core. As a last example, the *kinetic media façade* designed by SOMA Architecture [27], fulfils a climatic function. It consists of a series of flexible glass fibre reinforced polymer louvers, driven by servomotors, whose bending allows regulating the amount of light that enters into the building (Fig. 4). In all such examples, the control logic is hardcoded in the system. For a review of recent works in this field we refer the interested reader to [28].

**Fig. 4.** Kinetic façade, Thematic Pavilion of the Expo 2012, Yeosu, South-Korea, designed by SOMA Architecture, Vienna.

---

[5] http://www.deckeryeadon.com.

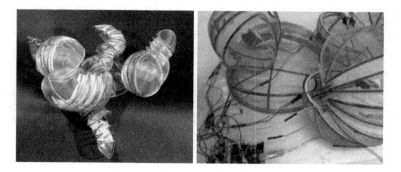

**Fig. 5.** Left: Mock-ups of the concepts considered; right: detail of the setup of the electronic components of the prototypes.

## 2    Evolutionary training of the *Armadillo Skyvent*

The *Armadillo Skyvent* prototype (Fig. 1) is a concept that takes its inspiration from the spherically segmented foldable shell of the armadillo. It consists of a series of intersecting segmented spheres that can open and close. The different kinetic segmented structures can open and close in such a way to provide a level of desired light and ventilation, but also allowing the entrance of rain if desired. The intelligence of the system relies on learning the configurations that the user prefers according to different environmental factors.

A mock-up of such concept has been prototyped and robotised (Fig. 5). The prototype is built with plywood and aluminum for the rigid parts and latex for the joints. Three of the spheres have been provided with servo-motors that allow them to fold/unfold. Three light sensors are located at fixed points to detect the direction of the source of light, and a fourth light sensor is located in the center at the base of the structure, to detect the amount of light received according to the configuration of the spheres. A human instructor is required for the training in order to provide different light conditions. The training process is thus interactive.

The prototype adopts an Arduino Uno$^{TM}$ micro controller to drive the actuators and to receive the sensors' readings. Figure 5 shows the mechatronics in place.

The intelligent controller of the prototype adopts a three layered feed forward neural network, whose connection weights are adjusted during the training process. The network has three inputs, corresponding to the three external light sensors, and three outputs (three servos for the actuated spheres). The number of neurones of the middle layer has been empirically set to five. A sigmoid transfer functions are used for the middle layer neurones, and linear transfer functions are used for the output layer neurones.

### 2.1    Evolutionary Training

In the cases at hand, no well pre-defined input-output training patterns are available. The only feedback the structures can be provided during training is

**Table 1.** Parameters of the Evolutionary Algorithm. (Note that weights from the bias units are also accounted for in the chromosome length.)

| Parameter | Value |
|---|---|
| Algorithm type | Evolution Strategy |
| Selection strategy | $(\mu + \lambda)$ (best of parent and offspring) |
| Population size | $\mu = 1$ |
| No. of offrspring | $\lambda = 1$ |
| Chromosome length $n$: | $(3+1) \times 5 + (5+1) \times 3 + 1 = 39$ |
| Gene type | Floating-point, range $[0,1]$ |
| Mutation | Gaussian perturbation $N(0, \sigma), \sigma$ encoded in the chromosome |
| Learning rate | $\tau = \sqrt{n}$ |

their improvement with respect to the previous behaviour. Thus, supervised training techniques (e.g. backpropagation and its variants) cannot be used. For this reason, we adopted a reinforced learning scheme, implemented as a (1+1)-Evolutionary Strategy. Note that here we face a major constraint since we deal with real, physical artefacts of which one unique prototype exists. Other classes of population-based EAs commonly used to train neural networks are therefore ruled out.

As customary in evolutionary strategies, phenotypic traits (neural network's weights) are encoded in a $n + 1-$dimensional array of floating-point values, and a Gaussian perturbation mutation operator is employed. Gene $n + 1$ encodes a common mutation rate.

Table 1 summarises the main features of the algorithm, and Fig. 6 illustrates the training scheme we adopted. A training epoch consists of a series of *stimuli* to which the system reacts, taking a certain configuration according to its logic. The reaction of the structure to each of the stimuli is evaluated. At the end of

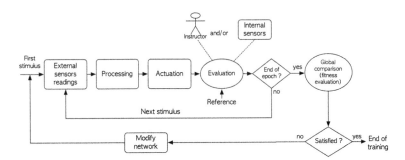

**Fig. 6.** Training process. The external loop corresponds to one loop (generation) of the evolutionary algorithm.

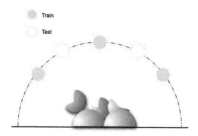

**Fig. 7.** Training and testing configurations.

the training epoch, the global behaviour of the robotised structure is evaluated, and if the instructor is satisfied with the behaviour of the structure the training ends. Otherwise, the network is modified according to the (1+1)-ES logic.

Note that the "partial evaluation" step (cf. Fig. 6) is performed against a reference value, which, depending on the application, can be performed either by a human instructor (e.g. for qualitative assessment) or automatically for quantitative parameters. Here, such evaluations are performed automatically by computing the difference between desired and actual light perceived by the internal sensor.

## 3   Experimental Results

Using the prototype described in the previous section, we have performed pilot trials to test the system and the learning process.

Five stimuli (sunlight directions) were used, three for training (45 degrees left, zenit and 45 degrees right) and two for testing (see Fig. 7).

The structure should learn to configure itself in such a way to maintain an average illumination at the central sensor in a given range of $[500–700]^6$, regardless the position of the sun. The fitness of an individual was the difference between the obtained value (average over the set of stimuli) and the closest limit of the desired range.

In these training sessions the prototype was able to learn the desired behaviour, on average, in 14.6 generations, with a standard deviation of 3.84 over ten trials (see Table 2). Figure 8 reports the results of the first tests with the prototype. Notice that due to the stopping criteria adopted, each experiment can terminate in a different number of generations. Thus, each point of the plot is

**Table 2.** Number of generations (training steps).

| Experiment # | 1 | 2 | 3 | 4 | 5 | 6 | 7 | 8 | 9 | 10 | Avg | Stdev |
|---|---|---|---|---|---|---|---|---|---|---|---|---|
| No. of generations | 22 | 11 | 10 | 10 | 13 | 17 | 16 | 18 | 15 | 14 | 14.6 | 3.84 |

---

[6] This is an a-dimensional value corresponding to the range of the sensor, where 0 corresponds to total darkness and 1024 correspond to direct sunlight.

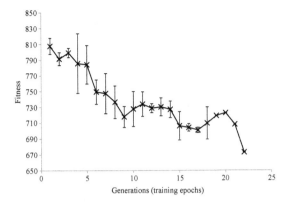

**Fig. 8.** Results of the training of the prototype.

the average fitness over all the runs that has reached at least the corresponding number of generations.

The assessment performed on the two test positions showed that the average illumination at the central sensor were in the target range of [500–700] in all but two cases (80 % success rate).

### 3.1 Discussion

The experiments reported above have demonstrated that controllers for intelligent buildings, or at least intelligent architectural elements, can successfully be generated applying Evolutionary Robotics techniques.

It must be pointed out that given the size prototype taken into account (number of inputs and outputs), from the point of view of artificial intelligence the learning task was expected to be "easy" to be learnt by the neural controller. Indeed, in these early trials the prototype was able to learn the task in few training sessions. Nevertheless, we are confident that our approach can be successfully applied to more complex structures, as Evolutionary Robotics have already demonstrated its power in many other applications (see, e.g., [29]).

The experiments performed were not completely satisfactory as far as the generalization capability shown by the controller, which may depend either on the simple network architecture adopted or on the evolutionary strategy adopted This leads us to think that for more complex structure this may not be suited, and more advanced EAs shall be employed, such as the CMA-ES (see, e.g., [30]), or more advanced neuroevolution techniques such as NEAT, that was used successfully in feedback-based learning in the NERO game [31], or its evolution, the Hyper-NEAT [32].

## 4    Conclusion and Future Work

Robotised architectural components of intelligent buildings are elements provided with the capability of changing their morphology or geometrical configuration in order to dynamically adapt to environmental conditions, to the use of the building in a particular moment and to the preferences of the users. This has the purpose of improving comfort, empathy and wellbeing of the users, as well ass the optimisation of resources employed during its functioning.

Such components are equipped with a set of sensors actuating elements, that are moved according to some perception-control-action loop, and can be therefore considered *robotic systems*. In our current work, we aim at providing such systems with some degree of autonomy, adaptivity and learning capabilities.

From the Architectural point of view, considering intelligent buildings as autonomous embodied agents, allows us to apply the full arsenal of Evolutionary Robotics techniques (amongst others), exploiting the potential of artificial evolution beyond structural design and optimisation. At the same time, behavioural learning in intelligent structures adds a completely new dimension to Evolutionary Robotics, and is a promising field of research.

Current work is being devoted to extensive experimentation with the concept described earlier, as well as with other different prototypes, with the purpose of assessing their real-time behaviour and exploring interaction with the user, either by direct communication through a user interface, or by a more sophisticated cognitive system capable of detecting automatically the user's state and anticipate his/her needs and preferences.

We envision intelligent buildings as complex dynamic systems whose behaviour will go beyond simple action-reaction functioning, where architectural components seemingly acquires a "life" of their own, where certain characteristics that were not programmed or considered at design time *emerge* as a property from the point of view of human perception (see [33]). For example, a certain rhythmic elimination of foul air ("breathing"), or a "beautiful" cadence in the movements.

In conclusion, considering the building as an intelligent robotic system at all effects opens a new way of interaction between Architecture, Robotics and Artificial Intelligence which is full of potential both from the point of view of research and impact in people's life. The work we have presented here represents one of the first examples of such a fruitful interaction.

**Acknowledgements.** The prototype used in this work have been designed by Marta Medina, student of the course on "Digital Fabrication" held by the second author. We also acknowledge the valuable discussions with the students of the course on "Intelligent Control" held by the first author, and in particular Alejandro Maroto micro-controllers programming and experimentation.

# References

1. Floreano, D., Husbands, P., Nolfi, S.: Evolutionary robotics. In: Siciliano, B., Khatib, O. (eds.) Springer Handbook of Robotics, pp. 1423–1451. Springer, Heidelberg (2008)
2. Bongard, J.C.: Evolutionary robotics. Commun. ACM **56**(8), 74–83 (2013)

3. Sims, K.: Evolving virtual creatures. In: Annual Conference Series, pp. 15–22, July 1994
4. Floreano, D., Mondada, F.: Automatic Creation of an Autonomous Agent: Genetic Evolution of a Neural-network Driven Robot, pp. 421–430. MIT Press, Cambridge (1994)
5. Harvey, I., Husbands, P., Cliff, D.: Seeing the light: artificial evolution, real vision. In: Proceedings of the Third International Conference on Simulation of Adaptive Behavior: From Animals to Animats. SAB94, pp. 392–401. MIT Press, Cambridge (1994)
6. Cliff, D., Husbands, P., Harvey, I.: Explorations in evolutionary robotics. Adapt. Behav. **2**(1), 73–110 (1993)
7. Husbands, P., Harvey, I.: Evolution versus design: controlling autonomous robots. In: Proceedings of the Third Annual Conference of AI, Simulation and Planning in High Autonomy Systems, 1992. Integrating Perception, Planning and Action, pp. 139–146, Jul 1992
8. Eiben, A.: Grand challenges for evolutionary robotics. Front. Robot. AI **1**(4) (2014)
9. Kowaliw, T., Bredeche, N., Chevallier, S., Doursat, R.: Artificial neurogenesis: An introduction and selective review. In: Kowaliw, T., Bredeche, N., Doursat, R. (eds.) Growing Adaptive Machines. SCI, vol. 557, pp. 1–60. Springer, Heidelberg (2014)
10. Frazer, J.: An Evolutionary Architecture. Architectural Association Publications, London (1995)
11. Michaleka, J.J., Choudhary, R., Papalambros, P.Y.: Architectural layout design optimization. Eng. Opt. **34**(5), 461–484 (2002)
12. Finucane, E., Derix, C.: Evolving urban structures using computer optimisation techniques. In: Proceedings of Generative Art International Conference, pp. 195–196 (2006)
13. Caldas, L.G., Norford, L.K.: A genetic algorithm tool for design optimization. Proc. ACADIA **99**, 260–271 (1999)
14. Angelov, P., Zhang, Y., Wright, J., Hanby, V., Buswell, R.: Automatic design synthesis and optimization of component-based systems by evolutionary algorithms. In: Cantu-Paz, E., et al. (eds.) GECCO 2003. LNCS, vol. 2724, pp. 1938–1950. Springer, Heidelberg (2003)
15. Li, L.: The optimization of architectural shape based on genetic algorithm. Front. Archit. Res. **1**(4), 392–399 (2012)
16. Papapavlou, A., Turner, A.: Structural evolution: a genetic algorithm method to generate structurally optimal delaunay triangulated space frames for dynamic load. In: 27th eCAADe Conference (2009)
17. von Buelow, P., Falk, A., Turrin, M.: Optimization of structural form using a genetic algorithm to search associative parametric geometry. In: Proceedings of First International Conference on Structures and Architecture (ICSA 2010), pp. 195–196 (2010)
18. von Buelow, P.: Using evolutionary algorithms to aid designers of architectural structures. In: Bentley, P.J., Corne, D.W. (eds.) Creative Evolutionary Systems, pp. 315–336. Morgan Kaufmann Publishers Inc., San Francisco (2002)
19. Bentley, P.J.C.E.: Evolutionary Design by Computers. Morgan Kaufmann Publishers Inc., San Francisco (1999)
20. De Landa, M.: Deleuze and the use of the genetic algorithm in architecture. In: Leach, N. (ed.) Designing for a Digital World, pp. 383–406. Wiley, New York (2002)

21. Hemberg, M., O-Reilly, U.M., Menges, A., Jonas, K., da Costa Goncalves, M., Fuchs, S.R.: Genr8: architects experience with an emergent design tool. In: Romero, J., Machado, P. (eds.) The Art of Artificial Evolution: A Handbook on Evolutionary Art and Music. Natural Computing Series, pp. 167–188. Springer, Heidelberg (2008)
22. Marin, P., Bignon, J.C., Lequay, H.: A genetic algorithm for use in creative design processes. In: Proceedings of the Association for Computer-Aided Design in Architecture (ACADIA) (2008)
23. Kicinger, R., Arciszewski, T., Jong, K.D.: Evolutionary computation and structural design: a survey of the state-of-the-art. comput. struct. **83**(23–24), 1943–1978 (2005)
24. Kowaliw, T., Grogono, P., Kharma, N.: Environment as a spatial constraint on the growth of structural form. In: GECCO '07: Proceedings of the 9th Annual Conference on Genetic and Evolutionary Computation, pp. 1037–1044. ACM, New York (2007)
25. Harrison, A.: The optimization of architectural shape based on genetic algorithm. Facilities **10**(8), 14–19 (1992)
26. Harrison, A.: Towards the intelligent city. In: Klepfisch, G. (ed.) 1st International Congress on Intelligent and Responsive Buildings. CIB Working Commission WO98, pp. 175–183. Technologisch Instituut vzw (1999)
27. Knippers, J., Scheible, F., Jungjohann, H., Oppe, M.: Kinetic media façade consisting of GFRP louvers. In: Proceedings of the 6th International Conference on FRP Composites in Civil Engineering (CICE 2012) (2012)
28. Loonen, R., Trka, M., Cstola, D., Hensen, J.: Climate adaptive building shells: state-of-the-art and future challenges. Renew. Sustain. Energy Rev. **25**, 483–493 (2013)
29. Floreano, D., Dürr, P., Mattiussi, C.: Neuroevolution: from architectures to learning. Evol. Intel. **1**, 47–62 (2008)
30. Igel, C., Suttorp, T., Hansen, N.: A computational efficient covariance matrix update and a (1+1)-cma for evolution strategies. In: Proceedings of the 8th Annual Conference on Genetic and Evolutionary Computation. GECCO '06, pp. 453–460. ACM, New York (2006)
31. Stanley, K.O., Bryant, B.D., Miikkulainen, R.: Real-time neuroevolution in the nero video game. IEEE Trans. Evol. Comput. **6**(9), 653–668 (2005)
32. Gauci, J., Stanley, K.O.: Autonomous evolution of topographic regularities in artificial neural networks. Neural Comput. **22**(7), 1860–1898 (2010)
33. Gil, P.: Numen Architecture. An architecture influenced by the numinous attributes of animals. Ph.D. thesis, The Bartlett School of Architecture, UCL, London (2015)

# Evolving Controllers for Programmable Robots to Influence Non-programmable Lifeforms: A Casy Study

Payam Zahadat$^{(\boxtimes)}$ and Thomas Schmickl

Artificial Life Lab of the Department of Zoology, Karl-Franzens University Graz, Universitaetsplatz 2, 8010 Graz, Austria
{payam.zahadat,thomas.schmickl}@uni-graz.at

**Abstract.** In this paper, a decentralized reaction-diffusion-based controller is evolved for a set of robots in an arena interacting with two simulated juvenile bees as non-programmable agents. The bees react to the stimuli that are emitted by the robots. The evolutionary process successfully finds controllers that produce proper patterns which guide the bees towards a number of given targets. The results show a preference of heat as the dominant stimulus causing movement of the bees.

**Keywords:** Evolutionary computation · Decentralized control · Robotics · Reaction-diffusion based controllers · Interactive agents

## 1 Introduction

In many cases in Evolutionary Robotics (ER) [1,2], we deal with robots that move and make changes in their environment by manipulating passive objects. Some times, on the other hand, we aim to influence the behaviour of active agents that contain their own autonomous control mechanisms and interact with their environment independently. In this case, our robots need to act properly as a part of the agent's environment to maintain appropriate interaction with the agent. Animals are such autonomous agents. Groups of animals show complex patterns and behaviours arising from self-organization in the society based on local interactions [3,4]. Some animals have been studied regarding the stimuli they generate and react to. The stimuli that are perceived by an animals can be initiated from the environment or generated by other animals. In the case of honey bees, such stimuli include heat, vibration, and light [5].

In the context of an ongoing project ASSISI$_{bf}$ [6,7], we work towards guiding juvenile (still non-flying) bees to exhibit target behaviours. Young bees prepare brood cells for the honeybee queen, thus play an important role in the age demography and colony size dynamics of honeybees. They locate themselves and perform their colony work preferentially in the so called "broodnest" region of the hive which shows a complex field of temperature and other stimuli. Therefore, they are a central group of bees predicted to allow manipulating the development

© Springer International Publishing Switzerland 2015
A.M. Mora and G. Squillero (Eds.): EvoApplications 2015, LNCS 9028, pp. 831–841, 2015.
DOI: 10.1007/978-3-319-16549-3_67

of the whole colony through a group of artificial (robotic) agents. This way, honeybees, important pollinators in ecology and agriculture which are currently affected by various threats, e.g. colony collapse disorder, can be monitored and probably also supported by such a novel bio-hybrid honeybee-robotic system.

In order to manipulate the behavior of the bees, a set of homogeneous autonomous stationary robots, called CASUs (Combined Actuator Sensor Units), are placed in an environment that is shared with bees. The robots can emit a number of stimuli that, based on knowledge from literature [5,8,9] we believe bees react to them (e.g., heat, vibration, light). The different stimuli are of different physical nature and stimulate various reactions of the bees. Specific combinations of such stimuli emitted in certain spatiotemporal patterns can lead to specific behaviours of the bees. In this work we aim to evolve decentralized controllers for the CASUs to generate the appropriate stimuli patterns that will guide a group of bees to a desired movement. Feedbacks from the behaviour of the bees is used for evaluating the controllers during evolution.

In biological systems, pattern formation and symmetry breaking that leads to formation of various patterns, start from early phases in an organism's development. In embryos, e.g. fruit fly Drosophila melanogaster [10,11], polarization of an organism is induced by some maternal cue in the form of morphogen gradients. This was also suggested by [12]. By using these gradients in the environment of the organism, some information is provided that is used for localization of the organism's units (cells) and participates in the process of development. The same concept has been used by many researchers in the field of artificial evolution and developmental systems by applying different representations (e.g., [13–15]). For example, by using Boolean logic circuits [13], gene regulatory networks [16], or neural networks [17,18]. In this work, we used an instance of reaction-diffusion systems as the decentralized controllers for the robots.

Reaction-diffusion models are inspired by intracellular signalling in biological organisms. The models involve a process of local reaction between substances and diffusion of substances across the organism. Artificial Homeostatic Hormone System (AHHS) is an example of Reaction-diffusion models which is used to control the CASU robots. It has been originally introduced in [19] and successfully implemented for controlling locomotion in robots and generating complex patterns [20–22].

Here, we present the results of evolving AHHS controllers for simulated CASU robots that emit stimuli influencing the behaviour of simulated bees. The evolved solutions and the effectivity of the different stimuli in the evolved controllers are investigated demonstrating the preference of some stimuli over the others resulted from the evolutionary paradigm.

## 2    System Description

The idea of this work is to evolve decentralized controllers for a system consisting of two types of autonomous agents: one type of agents are unprogrammable but predictable (bees), and the other type are programmable and evolvable (robots).

The system consists of a bounded arena with a number of CASU robots mounted on it, forming a grid and a number of juvenile bees moving in the arena. Juvenile bees are not able to fly. The robots emit several stimuli of different physical nature. Based on their physical properties, the stimuli emitted by a robot or by a user operator may diffuse in the arena and reach other robots. The bees may perceive the stimuli and change their behaviours accordingly. The CASU robots only perceive the light intensity. The robots are controlled by reaction-diffusion-based controllers containing virtual substances, called hormones. The dynamics of the virtual hormones are based on a number of rules and the diffusion rate of each hormone to the neighbouring robots (see Sect. 3 for description of the applied controller). Figure 1 illustrates a conceptual example of the system consisting of two CASU robots and two bees.

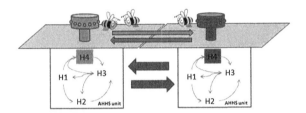

**Fig. 1.** The main concept of the experiment illustrated by an example consisting of two robots: The AHHS controller units with identical genomes run independently in different cells (robots). The units interact with each other via diffusion of hormones. There are four hormones represented in this example ($H1$ to $H4$). Some hormones ($H4$) are associated with production of some stimuli in the CASU robots. Stimuli can flow (diffuse) over the arena and reach the other CASU robot. Bees can sense the stimuli and react to them by standing still or moving to the neighbouring cell.

## 3    Short Summary of AHHS

An Artificial Homeostatic Hormone System (AHHS) [19] is a reaction-diffusion-based system inspired by Turing process [23] that describes processes of natural growth and pattern formation. An AHHS is defined by a set of artificial hormones and a set of rules. The *hormones* are the state variables of the system. The *rules* define interactions between the hormones. Each rule defines the influence of a hormone on the concentration level of another hormone within an AHHS unit[1]. A diffusion process is defined as a means of communication between neighbouring units by transferring hormones from a unit to the neighbours in the direction of the gradient. The dynamics of the hormones are regulated by a set of associated parameters. These parameters include the rate of diffusion, the production rate, and the decay rate of each hormone. The sensory inputs influence the system by changing the hormone levels of an AHHS unit directly or via special rules.

---

[1] In this regard, AHHS is similar to Gene Regulatory Networks (GRNs).

In the same way, particular hormones determine the output of each unit (for more details please see [19, 22]). An AHHS genome consists of all the parameters associated to different hormones and rules. The genomes are identical for all the AHHS units (e.g. robots) in a multi-unit organism and are adaptable to a given task by an evolutionary process.

In a formal representation, the dynamics of hormone concentration $H$ at time $t$ for hormone $h$ is represented as follows:

$$\frac{\Delta H_h}{\Delta t} = \alpha_h + D_h \nabla^2 H_h(t) - \mu_h H_h(t)$$
$$+ \sum_i \mathcal{L}_i(t), \tag{1}$$

where $\alpha_h$, $D_h$, and $\mu_h$ are base production rate, diffusion rate, and decay rate of hormone $h$, respectively. $\mathcal{L}_i(t)$ is the influence of a rule $i$.

A rule is defined as:

$$\mathcal{L}_i(t) = \theta(H_k(t))(H_k(t)\lambda_i + \kappa_i), \tag{2}$$

The output of the rule is applied to hormone concentration $H_h(t)$ and the input is $H_k(t)$ ($h = k$ is allowed). $\lambda_i$ and $\kappa_i$ are two parameters of the rule called dependent dose and fixed dose. These values are allowed to be negative. Trigger function $\theta$ determines whether or not the rule is executed:

$$\theta(x) = \begin{cases} 1 & \text{if } min_i < x < max_i \\ 0 & \text{else} \end{cases}, \tag{3}$$

where $min_i$ and $max_i$ are parameters of the rule (0.0 and 1.0 in this implementation).

## 3.1   Stimuli

Every CASU robot acts as a source of three different types of stimuli, say types A, B, C. Stimuli types are different in terms of their physical properties and the reaction of the bees to them (see Table 1). A stimulus of type A is attractive (e.g. heat and chemicals) and a stimulus of type B is repulsive (e.g. light and magnetic field). A bee tends to move away towards a neighbouring cell if the intensity of stimulus type A is higher or the intensity of stimulus type B is lower in the neighbouring cell. A stimulus type C is stopper (e.g. vibration), meaning that if the level of the stimulus is above a threshold value, the bee stops in the cell ignoring the attractive or repulsive stimuli.

The behaviour of a bee positioning in a cell, say *newcell*, is formulated by the following equation:

$$attr_i = (A_i - A_{curr}) + (B_{curr} - B_i)$$
$$newcell = \begin{cases} \text{arg max}_i \, attr_i, & \text{if } attr_i > 0 \text{ and } C_i < th \\ curr & \text{otherwise} \end{cases} \tag{4}$$

**Table 1.** Characteristics of stimuli

| Stimulus | TypeA/Heat | TypeB/Light | TypeC/Vibration |
|---|---|---|---|
| Effect | Attractive | Repulsive | Stopper |
| Diffusion rate | 0.2 | 0 | 0.01 |
| Decay rate | 0.1 | 1 | 0.9 |
| Instantly reachable | no | yes | no |
| Directional/Blockable by bees | no | yes | no |

where $curr$ is the current cell and $A_i$, $B_i$, and $C_i$ are respectively the intensities of stimuli type A, B, and C in cell $i$.

In this experiment we use an abstract simulation of heat, light, and vibration as examples of stimuli of types A, B, C respectively. The intensity of the stimuli and the increase amount of the stimuli in each time-step are both limited between 0 and 1.

In the simulation, every time-step assumes to correspond to 1 s in reality. The threshold value for the reaction of the bees to the vibration is set to 0.05 and other parameters are represented in Table 1. The effects of stimuli on the bees are assumed to be linear for simplification of the simulation.

## 4    Experiment

In the following experiments, a 2-dimensional grid arena of size $5 \times 5$ is simulated. Every cell of the grid contains a CASU robot that is controlled by an AHHS unit. The AHHS units can communicate with the units in their von Neumann neighbourhood via diffusion of virtual hormones. The AHHS genomes are identical in all the units and evolve by using the Wolfpack-inspired Evolutionary Algorithm (WEA) [24]. The evolutionary algorithm is chosen due to its capability of maintaining diversity in the population along with its simplicity of implementation.

Each CASU can emit three different types of stimuli. The bees are simulated based on their natural reactions to the stimuli. The goal is to guide the bees to reach a number of given target positions in the arena.

A virtual hormone of every AHHS unit is associated to each of the stimuli-emitters of the CASUs. The concentration level of the associated hormone in every time-step is used to determine the additional amount of intensity of the stimulus. AHHS genomes with 8 hormones and 15 rules are evolved to adapt the decentralized controller for the desired behaviour of the bees.

The reproduction operator of the evolutionary algorithm is mutation (no crossover). Proportional selection (based on fitness) operating on the upper half of the population is used to generate offspring. The population size is 30. The experiment is repeated for 25 independent evolutionary runs.

## 4.1   Task

At the beginning, two simulated bees are placed in (0,2) and (4,2) positions. The simulation runs for 20 time-steps. In the first time-step, the light is turned on manually with maximum intensity in the top-right corner of the arena in order to break the symmetry of the arena. The manually added light is removed after the first time-step.

The task of the controllers is to lead the bees to reach a number of targets (Fig. 2a) in 10 time-steps and stay there until the end of the simulation. The fitness function is calculated based on the number of targets reached by the bees and the distance to the next target as follows:

$$Fitness = N_{reahed} + 1 - R$$
$$R = \frac{distancToTarget}{W + H} \qquad (5)$$

where $N_{reahed}$ is the number of targets that are already reached, and $R$ is the relative distance to the next target. $W$ and $H$ are respectively the width and the height of the arena (equal to 5).

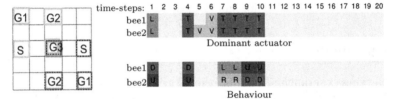

a) Arena configuration          b) Sequence of dominant (effective) stimuli and behaviours

**Fig. 2.** (a) The arena, starting points and target positions of the bees. Yellow (solid) and orange (dashed) squares indicate the targets for two different bees. The bees start at their S positions and they have to reach G1, G2, and G3 in maximum 10 time-steps and stay in G3 until the end of the experiment (until 20th time-step). (b) Sequence of dominant stimuli (top two rows), and actions of the bees (bottom two rows). L, T, and V respectively indicate light, heat, and vibration as dominant stimuli for the particular bee in the particular time-step. D, U, L, R, indicate a movement to toward the bottom, top, left, and right respectively. The empty squares (very light gray coloured) indicate no movement of the bee in that time-step (Color online figure).

## 4.2   Results

Figure 4 represents the fitness trajectory over the number of evaluations. As it is represented in the figure, maximum fitness is reached for the median of the evolved solutions of all runs after 30,000 evaluations while the maximum fitness was reached by some runs already after 5,000 evaluations.

In order to have a better understanding of the solutions we looked at the stimuli emitted by the evolved controllers. Figure 5a considers only the steps

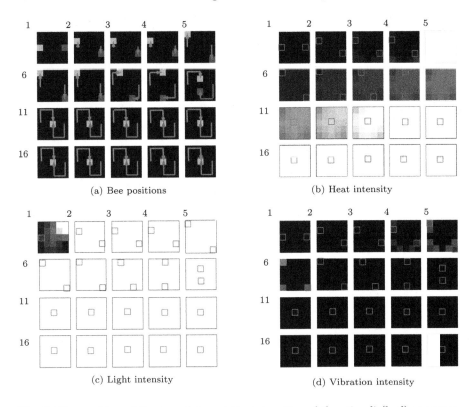

(a) Bee positions

(b) Heat intensity

(c) Light intensity

(d) Vibration intensity

**Fig. 3.** The position of the bees (a), and the intensities of the stimuli (b–d) are represented for every time-step (numbers indicate time-steps).

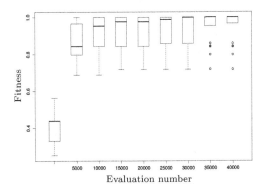

**Fig. 4.** Fitness progression for 25 runs. The fitness values are scaled between 0 and 1. Box-plots indicate median and quartiles, whiskers indicate the most extreme data points which are no more than 1.5 times the length of the box away from the box, circles indicate outliers.

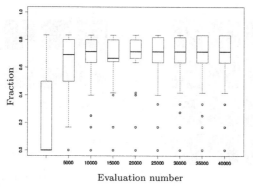

(a) Fraction of movements with dominance of heat

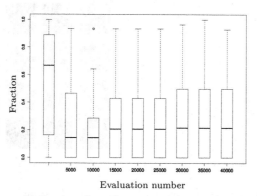

(b) Fraction of standing steps with dominance of vibration

**Fig. 5.** Proportion of dominant stimulus in movement (a) and standing still steps (b). Each data point represents the proportion achieved by the fittest controller over time. Data is pulled from 25 independent repetitions of the experiment. Box-plots indicate median and quartiles, whiskers indicate the most extreme data points which are no more than 1.5 times the length of the box away from the box, circles indicate outliers.

where bees are moving. Recall that movement is caused by light and/or heat stimuli. Figure 5a represents the proportion of the movements of the bees where heat is the dominant stimulus. As the figure shows, heat is the most dominant stimulus that is responsible for moving the bees from their places. It is the case in most of the runs. In one of the runs the movement is caused only by light. There is no run where heat is the stimulus for triggering movement for the whole duration of the run. It is because at the beginning, when heat is uniformly low over the arena, light is manually emitted for a short time. The low proportion for the heat in the early steps of evolution is due to the dominance of the vibration stimulus in the early evaluations that prevents the movement of the bees. The number of the movements during the early evaluations is very low and its usually only limited to one movement that is initiated by the manual light. The number of steps where both light and heat agree on one direction for moving a bee are negligible during the whole evolution (data not shown).

For a bee to stay in a cell, either vibration is more than the threshold value or there is no preferable cell in the immediate neighbour in terms of light and heat stimuli. Figure 5b represents the proportion of standing steps where vibration is dominant (over the no-preference status). The figure does not show a high median for the proportion of vibration stimulus in the evolved solutions.

Figure 2b shows the behaviour of the bees against an example evolved controller for the robots. The dominant stimuli and the action that the bee takes is represented over the 20 steps of the experiment. The figure shows that the bees do not move in many steps due to no preference for the neighbouring cells. The status of the arena over the 20 steps, and the intensity of each stimuli are represented in Fig. 3. As it is represented in the figure, heat starts to emit in the corners at the beginning and the emission goes towards the centre of the arena. after some time the whole arena gets a uniform heat. Light is only effective at the first step which is emitted due to the manual turn on. Vibration is generated around the corners of the arena and for a short time is the effective stimulus keeping the bees at their places.

## 5    Conclusion

A reaction-diffusion based controller called AHHS (Artificial Homeostatic Hormone System) is evolved as a decentralized controller for a simulated system consisting of controllable agents and non-controllable agents. The controllable agents are stationary-robots that their controllers are under evolution. The robots emit three different stimuli which cause reactions in the non-controllable agents. The non-controllable agents are bees that, based on the relevant literature [5,8,9] are sensitive to a number of stimuli including light, heat, and vibration, which are emitted by the robots in the experiment investigated in this work. Due to the interaction between the robots and the bees, the bees are successfully guided to locate themselves in a number of pre-defined targets. The influence and the dominance of the different stimuli are then investigated and it is shown that evolution prefers to use heat over light for causing movements.

**Acknowledgments.** This work is supported by: EU-ICT project 'ASSISI_bf', no. 601074; Austrian Federal Ministry of Science and Research (BM.W F).

## References

1. Nolfi, S., Floreano, D.: Evolutionary Robotics: The Biology, Intelligence, and Technology of Self-Organizing Machines. MIT Press, Cambridge (2000)
2. Bongard, J.: Evolutionary robotics. Commun. ACM **56**, 74–83 (2013)
3. Camazine, S., Deneubourg, J.L., Franks, N.R., Sneyd, J., Theraulaz, G., Bonabeau, E.: Self-Organizing Biological Systems. Princeton University Press, Princeton (2001)

4. Saverino, C., Gerlai, R.: The social zebrafish: behavioral responses to conspecific, heterospecific, and computer animated fish. Behav. Brain Res. **191**, 77–87 (2008)

5. Szopek, M., Schmickl, T., Thenius, R., Radspieler, G., Crailsheim, K.: Dynamics of collective decision making of honeybees in complex temperature fields. PLoS ONE **8**, e76250 (2013)

6. Schmickl, T., et al.: ASSISI: mixing animals with robots in a hybrid society. In: Lepora, N.F., Mura, A., Krapp, H.G., Verschure, P.F.M.J., Prescott, T.J. (eds.) Living Machines 2013. LNCS, vol. 8064, pp. 441–443. Springer, Heidelberg (2013)

7. Zahadat, P., Bodi, M., Salem, Z., Bonnet, F., de Oliveira, M.E., Mondada, F., Griparic, K., Haus, T., Bogdan, S., Mills, R., Mariano, P., Correia, L., Kernbach, O., Kernbach, S., Schmickl, T.: Social adaptation of robots for modulating self-organization in animal societies. In: Proceedings of the 2nd FoCAS Workshop on Fundamentals of Collective Systems (2014)

8. Berthold, R., Benton, A.W.: Honey bee photoresponse as influenced by age. Part I. workers. Ann. Entomol. Soc. Am. **63**, 136–139(4) (1969)

9. Nieh, J.C.: The stop signal of honey bees: reconsidering its message. Behav. Ecol. Sociobiol. **33**, 51–56 (1993)

10. Driever, W., Nusslein-Volhard, C.: The bicoid protein determines position in the drosophila embryo in a concentration-dependent manner. Cell **54**, 95–104 (1988)

11. Ephrussi, A., Johnston, D.S.: Seeing is believing - the bicoid morphogen gradient matures. Cell **116**, 143–152 (2004)

12. Wolpert, L.: The French Flag problem: a contribution to the discussion on pattern development and regulation. In: Waddington, C.H. (ed.) The Origin of Life: Toward a Theoretical Biology, pp. 125–133. Aldine Publishing Company, Chicago (1968)

13. Miller, J.F.: Evolving developmental programs for adaptation, morphogenesis, and self-repair. In: Banzhaf, W., Ziegler, J., Christaller, T., Dittrich, P., Kim, J.T. (eds.) ECAL 2003. LNCS (LNAI), vol. 2801, pp. 256–265. Springer, Heidelberg (2003)

14. Bowers, C.P.: Simulating evolution with a computational model of embryogeny: obtaining robustness from evolved individuals. In: Capcarrère, M.S., Freitas, A.A., Bentley, P.J., Johnson, C.G., Timmis, J. (eds.) ECAL 2005. LNCS (LNAI), vol. 3630, pp. 149–158. Springer, Heidelberg (2005)

15. Gordon, T.G.W., Bentley, P.J.: Bias and scalability in evolutionary development. In: Proceedings of the 7th Annual Conference on Genetic and Evolutionary Computation, GECCO 2005, pp. 83–90. ACM, New York (2005)

16. Chavoya, A., Duthen, Y.: Use of a genetic algorithm to evolve an extended artificial regulatory network for cell pattern generation. In: Proceedings of the 9th Annual Conference on Genetic and Evolutionary Computation, GECCO 2007, pp. 1062–1062. ACM, New York (2007)

17. Federici, D.: Using embryonic stages to increase the evolvability of development. In: GECCO 2004 Workshop Proceedings, Seattle, Washington, USA (2004)

18. Devert, A., Bredeche, N., Schoenauer, M.: Robustness and the halting problem for multicellular artificial ontogeny. IEEE Trans. Evol. Comput. **15**, 387–404 (2011)

19. Schmickl, T., Crailsheim, K.: Modelling a hormone-based robot controller. In: MATHMOD 2009–6th Vienna International Conference on Mathematical Modelling (2009)

20. Stradner, J., Hamann, H., Schmickl, T., Crailsheim, K.: Analysis and implementation of an artificial homeostatic hormone system: a first case study in robotic hardware. In: The 2009 IEEE/RSJ International Conference on Intelligent Robots and Systems (IROS 2009), pp. 595–600. IEEE Press (2009)

21. Zahadat, P., Schmickl, T.: Generation of diversity in a reaction-diffusion-based controller. Artif. Life **20**, 319342 (2014)
22. Zahadat, P., Crailsheim, K., Schmickl, T.: Evolution of spatial pattern formation by autonomous bio-inspired cellular controllers. In: Lio, P., Miglino, O., Nicosia, G., Nolfi, S., Pavone, M. (eds.) 12th European Conference on Artificial Life (ECAL 2013), pp. 721–728. MIT Press (2013)
23. Turing, A.M.: The chemical basis of morphogenesis. Philos. Trans. R. Soc. London. B Biol. Sci. **B237**, 37–72 (1952)
24. Zahadat, P., Schmickl, T.: Wolfpack-inspired evolutionary algorithm and a reaction-diffusion-based controller are used for pattern formation. In: Proceedings of the 2014 Conference on Genetic and Evolutionary Computation, GECCO 2014, pp. 241–248. ACM, New York (2014)

# EvoSTOC

# Applying Ant Colony Optimization to Dynamic Binary-Encoded Problems

Michalis Mavrovouniotis[(✉)] and Shengxiang Yang

School of Computer Science and Informatics,
Centre for Computational Intelligence (CCI), De Montfort University,
The Gateway, Leicester LE1 9BH, UK
{mmavrovouniotis,syang}@dmu.ac.uk

**Abstract.** Ant colony optimization (ACO) algorithms have proved to be able to adapt to dynamic optimization problems (DOPs) when stagnation behaviour is addressed. Usually, permutation-encoded DOPs, e.g., dynamic travelling salesman problems, are addressed using ACO algorithms whereas binary-encoded DOPs, e.g., dynamic knapsack problems, are tackled by evolutionary algorithms (EAs). This is because of the initial developments of the introduced to address binary-encoded DOPs and compared with existing EAs. The experimental results show that ACO with an appropriate pheromone evaporation rate outperforms EAs in most dynamic test cases.

## 1 Introduction

Ant colony optimization (ACO) algorithms have shown good performance when applied to difficult optimization problems under static environments [1]. In general, ACO has been initially developed to tackle permutation-encoded problems [1]. There are also a few applications for binary-encoded problems, such as the multidimensional knapsack problem [2–6]. Most of the existing ACO applications assume stationary environments. However, in many real-world applications we have to deal with dynamic environments, where the optimum changes and needs re-optimization.

Similarly to other nature-inspired algorithms [7,8], ACO algorithms can adapt to dynamic changes since they are also inspired from nature, which is a continuous adaptation process. Practically, ACO can adapt to dynamic changes by transferring knowledge from past environments, using the pheromone trails, to speed up re-optimization [9]. The challenge to such algorithms when addressing dynamic optimization problems (DOPs) is that they suffer from the stagnation behaviour, where all ants construct the same solution from early stages of the algorithm execution. The adaptation capabilities of ACO rely on the pheromone evaporation where a constant amount of pheromone is deducted to eliminate pheromone trails that represent bad solutions that may bias ants to search to the non-promising areas of the search space. ACO algorithms have been successfully applied to dynamic extensions of the aforementioned permutation-encoded problems, e.g., dynamic travelling salesman problems (TSPs) [10,11] and dynamic vehicle routing problems (VRPs) [12,13].

© Springer International Publishing Switzerland 2015
A.M. Mora and G. Squillero (Eds.): EvoApplications 2015, LNCS 9028, pp. 845–856, 2015.
DOI: 10.1007/978-3-319-16549-3_68

In this paper, we investigate the performance of ACO for solving dynamic binary-encoded optimization problems. Such problems have been successfully tackled by evolutionary algorithms (EAs) [14,15], but not by ACO. Therefore, the original ACO framework is modified to construct binary-encoded solutions rather than permutation-encoded solutions (e.g., for the TSP) [4,16]. In addition, we study the effect of introducing different pheromone evaporation rates and pheromone update policies into ACO for DOPs. As a result, a binary ACO framework, denoted $ACO_\mathbb{B}$, is established and integrated to the exclusive-or (XOR) DOP generator which can generate different dynamic test cases from given stationary binary-encoded problems [17]. Using this generator, an experimental study of comparing the proposed $ACO_\mathbb{B}$ with an existing genetic algorithm (GA) [14] and a population-based incremental learning (PBIL) algorithm [15].

The rest of the paper is organized as follows. Section 2 describes in detail the proposed $ACO_\mathbb{B}$. Section 3 describes the dynamic test environment for this study, including the details for the integration of $ACO_\mathbb{B}$ with the XOR DOP. Section 4 describes the experiments carried out on a series of different DOPs including relevant analysis. Finally, Sect. 5 concludes this paper with directions for future work.

## 2    Binary Ant Colony Optimization

The ACO metaheuristic consists of a population of $\mu$ ants that construct solutions and share information among each other via their pheromone trails. ACO was initially developed for the TSP [18] and later on applied for other optimization problems [1]. Only a few applications exist where the ants construct solutions with binary representation [16], mainly for the multidimensional knapsack problem [2–6]. In most existing applications only stationary environments were considered.

The proposed binary-version of ACO (i.e., $ACO_\mathbb{B}$) closely follows the original ACO framework (see more details in [1]). Hence, in this section, we describe in detail only the $ACO_\mathbb{B}$. The main differences of the $ACO_\mathbb{B}$ from most existing binary-versions of ACO is that: it is designed to generally address binary-encoded problems rather than being dependent on the characteristics of the multidimensional knapsack problem, with the exception of the binary ant algorithm (BAA) [16]. This algorithm was also applied to dynamic problems but was not evaluated on the XOR DOP which is the most acceptable test suite for dynamic environments. The main difference of the proposed $ACO_\mathbb{B}$ from BAA relies on the way pheromone trails are updated.

### 2.1    Initialization

Typically, the pheromone table $\mathbf{P}$ of an ACO algorithm for the TSP, is defined as $\mathbf{P} = (\tau_{ij})_{n \times n}$, where $n$ is the size of the problem instance (i.e., the number of cities for the TSP) and $\tau_{ij}$ is the amount of pheromone between cities $i$ to $j$. In contrast, the pheromone table of the binary framework of ACO (i.e., $ACO_\mathbb{B}$) is defined as

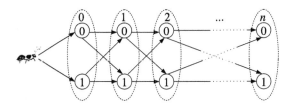

**Fig. 1.** Construction graph of ants for binary-encoded optimization problems of $n$ size

$\mathbf{P} = (\tau_{ij})_{n \times 2}$. This is because the ants can only reach two possible values. The construction graph for optimization problems with a binary space is presented in Fig. 1, where the pheromone trails are associated to the corresponding directed arcs.

Let $(i, j)$ denote the associated pheromone trail of state $i$ (i.e., $i = 0, \ldots, n$) to value $j$ (i.e., $j \in \{0, 1\}$). Initially, all the pheromone trails are set with an equal amount $\tau_0 \leftarrow \mu C^*, \forall(i, j)$ where $C^*$ and $\mu$ are the optimal solution (or approximation) and the population size, respectively.

## 2.2    Constructing Solutions

Each ant $k$ performs $n$ construction steps and uses a probabilistic rule to select the next state to visit, where each state is associated with only two possible values as presented in Fig. 1. More precisely, the probability an ant $k$ uses to select a value $j$ for state $i$ is defined as follows:

$$p_{ij}^k = \frac{\tau_{ij}}{\sum_{l \in \{0,1\}} \tau_{il}}, j \in \{0, 1\}, \tag{1}$$

where $\tau_{ij}$ is the associated pheromone trail of state $i$ to value $j$. Typically, heuristic information is considered together with the existing pheromone trails on the conventional ACO. For example, when ACO is applied on the TSP, the inverse of the distance between cities is used as the heuristic information [18]. For the problems tackled in this paper, there is no available heuristic information and, thus, only the pheromone information is considered. In fact, the construction of solutions based on probabilities (e.g., the pheromone trails table) is similar with the probability vector used in PBIL [15]. However, the "probability vector" in $ACO_{\mathbb{B}}$ is maintained differently from the PBIL.

## 2.3    Pheromone Update Policy

The pheromone trails in $ACO_{\mathbb{B}}$ are updated by applying evaporation as follows:

$$\tau_{ij} \leftarrow (1 - \rho)\,\tau_{ij}, \forall(i, j), \tag{2}$$

where $\rho \in (0, 1]$ is the evaporation rate and $\tau_{ij}$ is the existing pheromone value. After evaporation, the best-so-far ant deposits pheromone as follows:

$$\tau_{ij} \leftarrow \tau_{ij} + \Delta\tau_{ij}^{bs}, \forall(i, j) \in \boldsymbol{x}^{bs}, \tag{3}$$

where $\Delta\tau_{ij}^{bs} = C^{bs}$ and $\boldsymbol{x}^{bs} \in \{0,1\}^n$ are the amount of pheromone that the best ant deposits and the best ant's solution, respectively, and $C^{bs}$ is the fitness of the best-so-far ant. In contrast, the existing BAA algorithm allows all ants to deposit pheromone [16]. Since only the best ant deposits pheromone, the algorithm will quickly converge towards the best solution of the first iteration. Therefore, pheromone trail limits are imposed in order to avoid this behaviour such that $\tau_{min} \leq \tau_{ij} \leq \tau_{max}, \forall(i,j)$, where $\tau_{min}$ and $\tau_{max}$ are the lower and upper pheromone trail values [3,19]. The upper pheromone trail value is modified whenever a new best solution is found such that $\tau_{max} = \mu C^{bs}$ (where initially $\tau_{max} = \tau_0$). The lower pheromone trail value is set to $\tau_{min} = \tau_{max}/2\mu$. In this way, the lower pheromone trail value is also modified whenever a new best solution is found.

## 2.4   Response to Dynamic Change

ACO algorithms are able to use knowledge from previous environments using the pheromone trails generated in the previous iterations. For example, when the changing environments are similar, the pheromone trails of the previous environment may provide knowledge to speed up the optimization process to the new environment. However, the algorithm needs to be flexible enough to accept the knowledge transferred from the pheromone trails, or eliminate the pheromone trails, in order to adapt well to the new environment.

ACO algorithms can be applied directly to DOPs without any modifications due to the pheromone evaporation. Lowering the pheromone values enables the algorithm to forget bad decisions made in previous iterations. When a dynamic change occurs, evaporation eliminates the pheromone trails of the previous environment from areas that are not visited frequently and may bias ants not to adapt well to the new environment. The adaptation via pheromone evaporation may be a sufficient choice when the changing environments are similar; otherwise, the pheromone trails may misguide ants towards non-promising areas in the search space.

# 3   Dynamic Test Environments

## 3.1   Generating Dynamic Environments

The XOR DOP generator [15,17] can construct dynamic environments from any binary-encoded stationary function $f(\boldsymbol{x})(\boldsymbol{x} \in \{0,1\}^n)$ by a bitwise XOR operator. Suppose the environment changes in every $f$ algorithmic iterations, the dynamics can be formulated as follows:

$$f(\boldsymbol{x},t) = f(\boldsymbol{x} \oplus \boldsymbol{M}(k)), \tag{4}$$

where "$\oplus$" is the XOR operator (i.e., $1\oplus1 = 0$, $1\oplus0 = 1$, $0\oplus0 = 0$), $k = \lceil t/f \rceil$ is the index of the period and $\boldsymbol{M}(k)$ is the XORing mask that occurs incrementally and is defined as follows:

$$\boldsymbol{M}(k) = \boldsymbol{M}(k-1) \oplus \boldsymbol{T}(k), \tag{5}$$

where $\boldsymbol{T}(k)$ is an intermediate binary template randomly created with $m \times n$ ones. Parameters $m \in [0,1]$ and $f$ control the magnitude and frequency of change of a DOP, respectively. A higher value of $m$ means severer dynamic changes, whereas a lower value of $f$ means faster dynamic changes.

In this paper, four 100-bit binary-encoded problems are selected as the stationary problems to generate DOPs. Each problem consists of 25 copies of 4-bit building blocks and has an optimum of 100. The first one is the *OneMax* function, which aims to maximize the number of ones in a solution. The second one is the *Plateau* function, where each building block contributes four (or two) to the total fitness if its unitation (i.e., the number of ones inside the building block) is four (or three); otherwise, it contributes zero. The third one is the *RoyalRoad* function where each building block contributes four to the total fitness if its unitation is four; otherwise, it contributes zero. The fourth one is the *Deceptive* function, where the building block is a fully deceptive sub-function. Generally, the difficulty of the four functions for optimization algorithms is increasing in the order from OneMax to Plateau to RoyalRoad to Deceptive.

### 3.2   Integration of ACO with the XOR DOP Generator

EAs are typically integrated with the XOR DOP generator [14]. The binary template is applied to each individual within the population of an EA. In this way, the XOR DOP generator shifts the population to a different area in the fitness landscape. Similarly, the binary template can be applied to the solutions constructed by the ants within the $\text{ACO}_\mathbb{B}$.

Since the population in ACO is re-constructed on every iteration, the binary template is applied before the population is cleared for the new iteration. Hence, the fitness of the solutions constructed using the same pheromone trails before and after a dynamic change (whenever the binary template is applied) will differ depending on the magnitude of change.

## 4   Experimental Study

### 4.1   Experimental Setup

For each algorithm on a DOP, $R = 30$ independent runs were executed on the same environmental changes. The algorithms were executed for $E = 1000$ iterations and the overall offline performance is calculated as follows:

$$\bar{P}_{offline} = \frac{1}{E} \sum_{i=1}^{E} \left( \frac{1}{R} \sum_{j=1}^{R} P_{ij}^* \right), \tag{6}$$

where $P_{ij}^*$ defines the fitness of the best-so-far ant since the last dynamic change of iteration $i$ of run $j$ [7].

Dynamic test environments are generated from the four aforementioned binary-encoded function, described in Sect. 3, using the XOR DOP generator with $f$ set to 10 and 50, indicating quickly and slowly changing environments, respectively, and $m$ set to 0.1, 0.2, 0.5, 0.8 and 1.0, indicating slightly, to medium, to severely changing environments, respectively. As a result, ten dynamic environments (i.e., 2 values of $f \times 5$ values of $m$) from each stationary function are generated to systematically analyze the algorithms on the DOPs.

## 4.2   Analysis of the Pheromone Evaporation Rate

To investigate the effect of the pheromone evaporation in $ACO_\mathbb{B}$, different evaporation rates, i.e., $\rho \in \{0.0, 0.02, 0.05, 0.1, 0.2, 0.3, 0.4, 0.5, 0.6, 0.7, 0.8, 0.9\}$, are selected. In Fig. 2, the offline performance of $ACO_\mathbb{B}$ with the different evaporation rates is presented and the following observations can be drawn.

First, the performance of $ACO_\mathbb{B}$ is degraded when $\rho = 0.0$ (i.e., pheromone evaporation is not used) in comparison with the performance of $ACO_\mathbb{B}$ when $\rho > 0.0$ (i.e., pheromone evaporation is used) in most DOPs. This is natural because the evaporation rate is the adaptation mechanism within $ACO_\mathbb{B}$. More precisely, pheromone trails distributed to the optimum of the previous environment are eliminated by pheromone evaporation to help ants generate new pheromone trails for the optimum of the current environment.

Second, when the evaporation rate is set to $\rho \in [0.1, 0.4]$, the performance of $ACO_\mathbb{B}$ is usually superior than when it is set to other values. This is because a higher value of $\rho$ may destroy the knowledge gained from previous iterations, whereas a lower value of $\rho$ may not help the adaptation process on the new environment. Usually, when the magnitude of change increases; a higher evaporation rate performs better. For example, on *OneMax*, *Plateau* and *RoyalRoad* with $f = 50$, an evaporation rate of 0.1, 0.2, 0.3 and 0.4 performs the best when the magnitude of change is 0.1, 0.2 and 0.5, 0.8 and 1.0, respectively.

## 4.3   Analysis of the Pheromone Update Policy

In this section, we investigate four pheromone update policies for $ACO_\mathbb{B}$ (with $\rho = 0.2$): (1) only the best ant deposits pheromone; (2) all ants deposit pheromone[1]; (3) only the best ant deposits pheromone and limits are imposed[2]; and (4) all the ants deposit pheromone and limits are imposed. In Fig. 3, the offline performance for the different pheromone update policies are presented and several observations can be drawn.

First, the performance is degraded when only the best ant deposits pheromone in most DOPs. This is because high concentration of pheromone trails are quickly generated to the solution of the best ant. Hence, stagnation behaviour occurs and the algorithm cannot adapt well to the changes. In contrast, the performance is better when all ants deposit pheromone because the pheromone trails are distributed among several solutions rather than to one solution.

---

[1] Similar update policy with the existing BAA [16].
[2] This pheromone update policy is the one described in Sect. 2 and finally associated with $ACO_\mathbb{B}$.

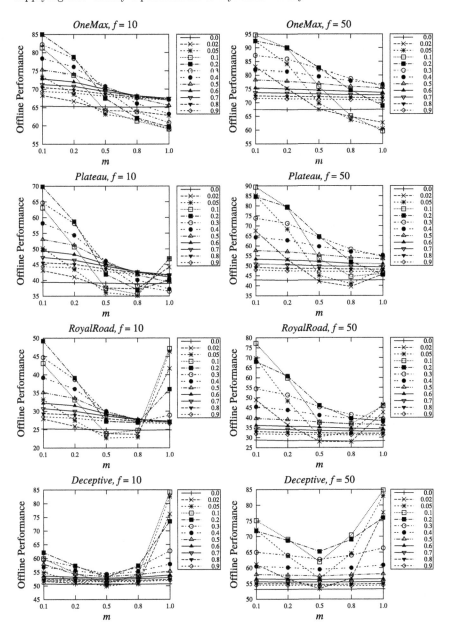

**Fig. 2.** Offline performance of ACO$_\mathbb{B}$ with different pheromone evaporation rates for different DOPs

Second, the performance is improved when trails limits are imposed when only the best ant deposits pheromone in most DOPs. This is because the stagnation behaviour described previously is addressed. The difference between the

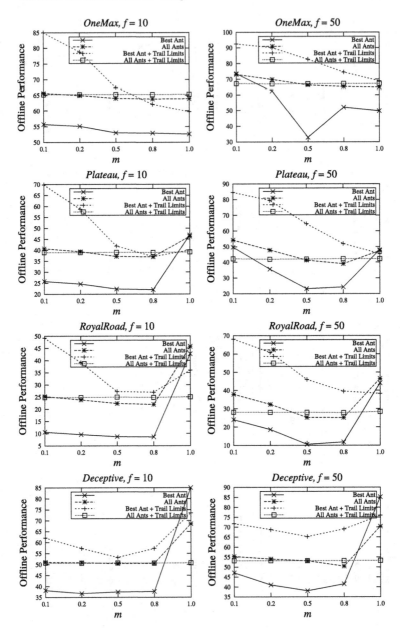

**Fig. 3.** Offline performance of $ACO_B$ with different pheromone update policies for different DOPs

maximum and minimum pheromone trails is not significantly different, and thus, more chances are given to the less attractive areas (in terms of pheromone) to be explored. In contrast, the performance is similar when trail limits are imposed when all the ants deposit pheromone.

Third, when trails limits are not imposed in general, the performance of $ACO_\mathbb{B}$ is often improved when $m = 1.0$. When a DOP changes with $m = 1.0$ using the XOP DOP generator, it basically switches between two environments consecutively. Hence, memory enhanced algorithms may be more suitable in such special cases since the environments re-appear [14]. In fact, the pheromone table within $ACO_\mathbb{B}$ can be considered as an adaptive memory scheme. However, the pheromone trails cannot store exactly the solutions when trail limits are imposed.

## 4.4   Analysis of Algorithm Comparisons

In the experiments, we compare the proposed $ACO_\mathbb{B}$ with GA [14] and PBIL [15] used in DOPs. Since $ACO_\mathbb{B}$ is not enhanced with additional components to address DOPs, only the standard versions of GA and PBIL algorithms are used. The population size for all algorithms was set to $\mu = 120$ for a fair comparison. For GA the parameters were set to typical values as follows: generational, uniform crossover with $p_c = 0.6$, flip mutation with $p_m = 0.01$, and fitness proportionate selection with elitism of size 1. For PBIL the parameters were also set to typical values as follows: the learning rate $\alpha = 0.25$, mutation probability

**Table 1.** Experimental results of the algorithms regarding the offline performance. Bold value or values indicate(s) that the algorithms are significantly better or insignificantly different than the other algorithms, respectively

| DOPs, $m \Rightarrow$ | $f = 10$ | | | | | $f = 50$ | | | | |
|---|---|---|---|---|---|---|---|---|---|---|
| | 0.1 | 0.2 | 0.5 | 0.8 | 1.0 | 0.1 | 0.2 | 0.5 | 0.8 | 1.0 |
| Algorithms | *OneMax* | | | | | | | | | |
| GA | 73.4 | 69.6 | 64.4 | **62.8** | **62.0** | 82.7 | 79.2 | 72.3 | 68.0 | 65.6 |
| PBIL | 74.8 | 66.8 | 57.7 | 55.1 | 54.2 | **92.6** | 86.0 | 69.6 | 60.0 | 55.6 |
| $ACO_\mathbb{B}$ | **85.0** | **78.8** | **67.5** | 62.1 | 59.7 | **92.5** | **90.1** | **82.7** | **74.5** | **68.9** |
| Algorithms | *Plateau* | | | | | | | | | |
| GA | 57.6 | 49.9 | 39.5 | 36.8 | 41.3 | 75.6 | 69.0 | 56.4 | 49.0 | 45.8 |
| PBIL | 50.5 | 39.6 | 29.1 | 29.1 | **49.4** | **84.0** | 69.5 | 43.9 | 40.3 | **48.0** |
| $ACO_\mathbb{B}$ | **69.8** | **58.7** | **41.9** | **37.0** | 40.0 | **84.6** | **79.5** | **64.6** | **51.9** | 45.4 |
| Algorithms | *RoyalRoad* | | | | | | | | | |
| GA | 44.1 | 36.3 | **27.1** | **27.1** | 39.8 | 66.6 | 57.9 | 44.8 | **40.3** | 41.6 |
| PBIL | 25.1 | 19.7 | 14.5 | 15.5 | **48.3** | 56.5 | 39.6 | 23.6 | 25.9 | **45.2** |
| $ACO_\mathbb{B}$ | **49.2** | **39.1** | **27.2** | 26.9 | 36.0 | **68.1** | **60.8** | **46.0** | 39.5 | 38.3 |
| Algorithms | *Deceptive* | | | | | | | | | |
| GA | 55.1 | 52.9 | 51.2 | 52.8 | 67.1 | 64.2 | 61.5 | 58.7 | 62.2 | 72.5 |
| PBIL | 55.0 | 49.4 | 44.9 | 47.5 | **86.8** | 69.7 | 64.3 | 57.0 | 65.5 | **86.9** |
| $ACO_\mathbb{B}$ | **62.1** | **57.5** | **53.2** | **57.3** | 73.5 | **71.8** | **68.7** | 65.2 | 69.0 | 76.0 |

$p_m = 0.02$, mutation shift $\delta_m = 0.05$ and elitism of size 1. For ACO$_\mathbb{B}$, the parameters were set as follows: the evaporation rate $\rho = 0.2$.

The offline performance of ACO$_\mathbb{B}$ compared with the other algorithms is presented in Table 1. Kruskal–Wallis tests were applied followed by posthoc paired comparisons using Mann–Whitney tests with the Bonferroni correction. Moreover, the dynamic behaviour of the algorithms on different DOPs is presented in Fig. 4. From the experimental results, several observations can be made by comparing the behaviour of the algorithms.

First, ACO$_\mathbb{B}$ outperforms both PBIL and GA in most DOPs with $m = 0.1$, $m = 0.2$, $m = 0.5$ and $m = 0.8$. It can be clearly observed from Fig. 4 that ACO$_\mathbb{B}$ maintains higher fitness than the competing algorithms during almost all the environmental changes. The mutation operator applied directly to the evolving population of GA may help the population to adapt to dynamic changes but slows down the optimization process. PBIL maintains the highest fitness on the initial environment (between iterations $0 - 100$) but then it is unable to maintain it. In contrast to the GA's case, the mutation operator applied to the probabilistic vector of PBIL may not be sufficient to move the population from the previously converged optimum (except when $f = 50$ with $m = 0.1$ and $m = 0.25$).

Second, PBIL outperforms both GA and ACO$_\mathbb{B}$ in most DOPs with $m = 1.0$. We have previously described the cyclic characteristic of this specific dynamic

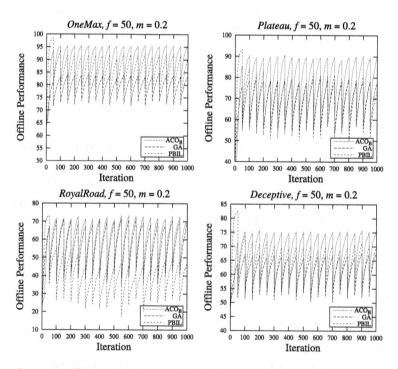

**Fig. 4.** Dynamic offline performance of algorithms on DOPs with $f = 50$ and $m = 0.2$

case and that the pheromone table of $ACO_{\mathbb{B}}$ can be viewed as an adaptive memory scheme. Similarly, the probabilistic vector in PBIL can be also viewed as an adaptive memory scheme. Hence, the probabilistic vector of PBIL may be able to store and maintain information for the two environments that can be reused when they re-appear. In contrast, the information may be destroyed from the pheromone table of $ACO_{\mathbb{B}}$ by the pheromone evaporation.

## 5    Conclusions

In this paper, the application of ACO to binary-encoded optimization problems in dynamic environments is investigated. The proposed $ACO_{\mathbb{B}}$ is designed to construct binary-encoded solution biased by pheromone trails. The effect of using different pheromone update policies and pheromone evaporation rates is studied for $ACO_{\mathbb{B}}$ in DOPs.

The $ACO_{\mathbb{B}}$ is integrated with the XOR DOP generator and a series of dynamic test cases are systematically constructed from several benchmark stationary problems. From the experiments, several concluding remarks can be drawn. First, pheromone evaporation enhances the adaptation capabilities of $ACO_{\mathbb{B}}$. An evaporation rate between $\rho \in [0.1, 0.4]$ achieves the best performance in DOPs but it is dependent on the magnitude of change of the DOP: the higher the magnitude the higher the rate. Second, the use of pheromone trail limits address the stagnation behaviour of $ACO_{\mathbb{B}}$. Third, $ACO_{\mathbb{B}}$ adapts faster than GA and PBIL. Hence, better overall performance is achieved during the dynamic changes.

For future work, $ACO_{\mathbb{B}}$ can be applied to the dynamic knapsack problem, which is closer to a real-world application. In fact, the performance of $ACO_{\mathbb{B}}$ can be furthermore improved since heuristic information is available to the knapsack problem using the weights and profits [20]. Another interesting future work is to further investigate the performance of $ACO_{\mathbb{B}}$ in DOPs that re-appear.

**Acknowledgement.** This work was supported by the Engineering and Physical Sciences Research Council (EPSRC) of U.K. under Grant EP/K001310/1.

## References

1. Dorigo, M., Stützle, T. (eds.): Ant Colony Optimization. MIT Press, London (2004)
2. Alaya, I., Solnon, C., Ghédira, K.: Ant algorithm for the multi-dimensional knapsack problem. In: International Conference on Bioinspired Optimization Methods and their Applications, pp. 63–72 (2004)
3. Ke, L., Feng, Z., Ren, Z., Wei, X.: An ant colony optimization approach for the multidimensional knapsack problem. J. Heuristics **16**(1), 65–83 (2010)
4. Kong, M., Tian, P.: Introducing a binary ant colony optimization. In: Dorigo, M., Gambardella, L.M., Birattari, M., Martinoli, A., Poli, R., Stützle, T. (eds.) ANTS 2006. LNCS, vol. 4150, pp. 444–451. Springer, Heidelberg (2006)
5. Kong, M., Tian, P., Kao, Y.: A new ant colony optimization algorithm for the multidimensional knapsack problem. Comput. Oper. Res. **35**(8), 2672–2683 (2008)

6. Leguizamon, G., Michalewicz, Z.: A new version of ant system for subset problems. In: Proceedings of the 1999 Congress on Evolutionary Computation, CEC 1999, vol. 2, pp. 1459–1464 (1999)

7. Jin, Y., Branke, J.: Evolutionary optimization in uncertain environments - a survey. IEEE Trans. Evol. Comput. **9**(3), 303 317 (2005)

8. Nguyen, T.T., Yang, S., Branke, J.: Evolutionary dynamic optimization: A survey of the state of the art. Swarm Evol. Comput. **6**, 1–24 (2012)

9. Angus, D., Hendtlass, T.: Ant colony optimisation applied to a dynamically changing problem. In: Hendtlass, T., Ali, M. (eds.) IEA/AIE 2002. LNCS (LNAI), vol. 2358, pp. 618–627. Springer, Heidelberg (2002)

10. Mavrovouniotis, M., Yang, S.: Ant colony optimization with immigrants schemes for the dynamic travelling salesman problem with traffic factors. Appl. Soft Comput. **13**(10), 4023–4037 (2013)

11. Guntsch, M., Middendorf, M., Schmeck, H.: An ant colony optimization approach to dynamic tsp. In: Proceedings of the 2001 Genetic and Evolutionary Computation Conference, pp. 860–867 (2001)

12. Mavrovouniotis, M., Yang, S.: Ant colony optimization with immigrants schemes for the dynamic vehicle routing problem. In: Di Chio, C., Agapitos, A., Cagnoni, S., Cotta, C., de Vega, F.F., Di Caro, G.A., Drechsler, R., Ekárt, A., Esparcia-Alcázar, A.I., Farooq, M., Langdon, W.B., Merelo-Guervós, J.J., Preuss, M., Richter, H., Silva, S., Simões, A., Squillero, G., Tarantino, E., Tettamanzi, A.G.B., Togelius, J., Urquhart, N., Uyar, A.Ş., Yannakakis, G.N. (eds.) EvoApplications 2012. LNCS, vol. 7248, pp. 519–528. Springer, Heidelberg (2012)

13. Montemanni, R., Gambardella, L.M., Rizzoli, A.E., Donati, A.V.: Ant colony system for a dynamic vehicle routing problem. Comb. Optim. **10**, 327–343 (2005)

14. Yang, S.: Genetic algorithms with memory- and elitism-based immigrants in dynamic environments. Evol. Comput. **16**(3), 385–416 (2008)

15. Yang, S., Yao, X.: Population-based incremental learning with associative memory for dynamic environments. IEEE Trans. Evol. Comput. **12**(5), 542–561 (2008)

16. Fernandes, C.M., Rosa, A.C., Ramos, V.: Binary ant algorithm. In: Proceedings of the 9th Annual Conference on Genetic and Evolutionary Computation, GECCO 2007, pp. 41–48. ACM, New York (2007)

17. Yang, S.: Non-stationary problem optimization using the primal-dual genetic algorithm. In: Proceedings of the 2003 IEEE Congress on Evolutionary Computation, pp. 2246–2253 (2003)

18. Colorni, A., Dorigo, M., Maniezzo, V.: Distributed optimization by ant colonies. In: Proceedings of the European Conference on Artificial Life, pp. 134–142. Elsevier (1991)

19. Stützle, T., Hoos, H.: The max-min ant system and local search for the traveling salesman problem. In: Proceedings of the 1997 IEEE International Conference on Evolutionary Computation, pp. 309–314 (1997)

20. Fidanova, S.: Aco algorithm for MKP using various heuristic information. In: Dimov, I., Lirkov, I., Margenov, S., Zlatev, Z. (eds.) NMA 2002. LNCS 2542, pp. 438–444. Springer, Berlin Heidelberg (2003)

# An Experimental Study of Combining Evolutionary Algorithms with KD-Tree to Solving Dynamic Optimisation Problems

Trung Thanh Nguyen[✉], Ian Jenkinson, and Zaili Yang

School of Engineering, Technology and Maritime Operations,
Liverpool John Moores University, Liverpool L3 3AF, UK
T.T.Nguyen@ljmu.ac.uk

**Abstract.** This paper studies the idea of separating the explored and unexplored regions in the search space to improve change detection and optima tracking. When an optimum is found, a simple sampling technique is used to estimate the basin of attraction of that optimum. This estimated basin is marked as an area already explored. Using a special tree-based data structure named KD-Tree to divide the search space, all explored areas can be separated from unexplored areas. Given such a division, the algorithm can focus more on searching for unexplored areas, spending only minimal resource on monitoring explored areas to detect changes in explored regions. The experiments show that the proposed algorithm has competitive performance, especially when change detection is taken into account in the optimisation process. The new algorithm was proved to have less computational complexity in term of identifying the appropriate sub-population/region for each individual. We also carry out investigations to find out why the algorithm performs well. These investigations reveal a positive impact of using the KD-Tree.

## 1 Introduction and Research Questions

### 1.1 Dynamic Problems and Evolutionary Dynamic Optimisation

Real-world applications are naturally dynamic. Customer demands change, internet bandwidth fluctuates, policies are being revised, and a changing climate are some examples of real-world dynamic problems. To deal with the inherent time-dependence of the real-world, finding effective ways to solve dynamic problems is very important. If a dynamic problem is solved online when time goes by, it is called dynamic optimisation problem (DOP) [1]. Among many different approaches to solving DOPs, evolutionary algorithms (EAs), is a common approach. The field of applying EAs to solving DOPs is called evolutionary dynamic optimisation (EDO).

### 1.2 Detecting Changes in DOPs

In addition to the need of finding the optimum as quickly as possible (as in static problems), in DOPs the solver also has to react to changes to track the changing

© Springer International Publishing Switzerland 2015
A.M. Mora and G. Squillero (Eds.): EvoApplications 2015, LNCS 9028, pp. 857–868, 2015.
DOI: 10.1007/978-3-319-16549-3_69

optimum [2]. There are two approaches: the algorithm either react to changes implicitly by some form of self-adaptation, or the algorithm need to react to changes explicitly. This paper focuses on the second approach. For most EAs following this approach, reacting to changes requires the knowledge of when a change occurs [2]. How to know when a change occurs is an important factor and it needs to be taken into consideration when an algorithm is designed.

Regarding the knowledge of the moments of changes, there are two schools of thought. The first school of thought considers that algorithms are well informed of changes or changes can be detected easily by just using one/a few detectors [3–7]. This approach makes sense for solving the current continuous academic benchmark problems, where the whole search space changes at once.

However, in many real-world applications, especially in constrained problems, only a part of the space changes and knowledge of environmental change might not be accessible [1,8,9]. In such situations, using just a few detectors to detect changes might not be sufficient because the detectors might not be in the changing region in the search space [2]. The second school of thought considers change detection an important part of the optimisation process rather than just a few detectors. To incorporate change detection in algorithms, some research tried to maintain enough diversity to cover the whole search space [10] or to distribute specific detectors in different search regions [11]. Some studies tried to detect changes by finding the statistical difference between the populations from two consecutive generations [9]. Some detected changes by monitoring the previous best found solutions [12]. The main disadvantages of methods following this school of thought is the additional computational cost spent on detecting/adapting changes in the whole search space. This cause methods following this approach perform generally worse than methods following the first school of thought in solving current benchmark problems.

This difference in performance between the two schools of thoughts raise an important research question of how to improve the efficiency of change detection.

### 1.3    Tracking Multiple Peaks in DOPs

One of the most commonly used approaches for EDO is to cover multiple regions of the search space, and separately monitor the movement of optima at each region. This way, multiple optima can be tracked at the same time, and if any of those optima become the global optimum after a change, they would likely be found more quickly. A natural way to track multiple regions is to use multiple populations, one for each region. Multi-population is the most used approach to solve some standard benchmark problems in the field of EDO.

In multi-population/multi-region approach, it is essential that the sub populations/regions are not overlapped so that one area is not searched by two or more sub-populations and an area is not being re-searched multiple times if there is no change. To avoid overlapped sub-populations/regions, existing methods either define each sub-population/region as a hypercube or sphere, then prevent individuals from other sub-populations to enter the cube/sphere [13,14], or use distance calculations to estimate the basins of attractions of peaks and use these basins as the separate regions for each sub-population [15].

The above techniques, however, are computationally expensive due to the distance calculations (analysed in Sect. 3). Finding a more efficient method to separate tracking regions, hence, is an important research question.

This paper describes an attempt to answer the two questions above.

# 2 Avoiding Revisiting Explored Areas and Improving Change Detection

## 2.1 Distributing Detectors Effectively

After having explored a certain part of the search space, if an algorithm remembers the structure of the explored search space, it might be able to use that knowledge to better distribute detectors, e.g. sending more detectors to rugged areas (having more optima) and fewer detectors to smooth areas (having fewer optima). In addition, if it can be assumed that changes in the basin of an optimum might likely change the value and position of the optimum itself, each basin may just need a detector right at the previously found optimum.

Placing detectors at the optima, however, can only detect changes that alter basin's height/position. For other basin changes, it might be necessary to frequently send detectors to the explored basin to check for any newly appearing solution. Such new solutions should only be accepted if they are shown to be promising. Otherwise, they should be discarded and the detectors should be sent to other areas. To implement this idea, it is essential to estimate the basin sizes. Estimating basin sizes also helps maintain just one sub-population per one peak/basin. Although estimating the basin size is a common goal of multi-population approaches, existing methods may not be able to achieve it. Their pre-determined fixed-size search area may not correctly cover the exact basin.

The next subsection proposes a method to estimate basins of attraction.

## 2.2 Estimating Optima's Basins of Attraction

As mentioned earlier, the problem with many existing methods to estimate optima's basins of attraction is that these methods are both computationally expensive and inaccurate. The procedure below (Algorithm 1) proposes a simple and computationally cheap estimation by taking a number of consecutive samples along each dimensional axis until a slump in fitness is found. This procedure can be applied to all dimensional axes to create a hyper-rectangle, which approximately covers the basin of attraction of a found optimum.

## 2.3 Separating Explored Areas from Unexplored Areas

To separate sub-populations/regions, for every individual many existing algorithms has to calculate individual distances to all sub-populations, then assign

---

**Algorithm 1.** BasinEstimation(d)

---

Note:     It is assumed that the problem is maximisation
$d$        The chosen dimensional axis along which samples are made
$\mathbf{x}^*(d)$    The $d^{th}$ coordination of optimum $\mathbf{x}^*$
$d_{\min}, d_{\max}$ Min and max range of search space in dimension $d$
$\delta$        Sample step size, $\delta = (d_{\max} - d_{\min})/50$
$(l, u)$     Range of the basin in dimension $d$

1. Initialisation: $u = l = x^*(d)$
2. Identifying the upper range $u$ of the basin:
   - **while** $(f(u) < f(u + \delta))$ $u = u + \delta$ //continue to go right until out of the basin
   - **else** $u = u + \delta/2$ //approximated upper boundary
3. Identifying the lower range $l$ of the basin:
   - **while** $(f(l) > f(l - \delta))$ $l = l - \delta$ //continue to go left until out of the basin
   - **else** $l = l - \delta/2$ //approximated lower boundary
4. Return $(l, u)$

---

each individual to its closest sub-population. This is a computationally expensive task, as mentioned in Sect. 1.3. Another downside is that each sub-population/ region has to maintain its own regional information and this information needs to be re-calculated at every generation.

In the previous subsection, an idea has been proposed to estimate the basins of attraction for found optima. This way of estimating basin can be used as a basis for a new idea to separate the sub-regions/populations with low compu-tational cost. The idea is to make use of a special data structure named the K-dimensional tree (KD-tree) [16]. KD-Tree is a special kind of binary tree spe-cialised for representing multi-dimensional spaces into hyper-rectangles. Each non-leaf node of the tree represents a cutting hyperplane perpendicular to one of the k dimensions. This cutting hyperplane will divide the space into two parts, represented by the two subtrees of the node. Figure 1 shows how a KD-Tree can be used to divide a two-dimensional space.

This special property inspires the authors to develop a modified version of the KD-Tree to represent the areas covered by sub-regions/populations and to distinguish explored and unexplored areas (Fig. 1). The modified tree still split the space in the same way as that of the original version: at each step the space will be splitted at a chosen plane. However, the newly modified KD-tree has a major structural difference. In the original KD-tree, each node represents (i) a chosen dimension axis that is perpendicular to the splitting hyperplane, and (ii) one point in the space that the splitting hyperplane must go through. On the contrary, in the modified version *there is no point in each node although the nodes still represent the chosen dimensions and cutting splits to divide the space.* In addition, *each leaf of the modified tree represents a hyper-rectangle bounded by the cutting hyperplanes rather than the point the cutting hyperplane goes through.*

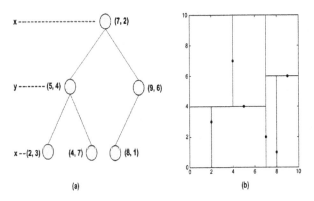

(a)                              (b)

**Fig. 1.** These figures, reproduced from [17], show how a two-dimensional space is decomposed using a KD-tree. (a): the tree, and (b): the decomposed space.

---

**Algorithm 2.** TreeConstruction(x, B(x))

---

x      A newly found optimum
$B(\mathbf{x})$ Estimated basin of $\mathbf{x}$
$N_d$    A hyper-rectangle represented by the tree node at depth $d$

1. Identify the leaf node (hyper-rectangle) $N_d$ containing optimum $\mathbf{x}$
2. **If** $B(\mathbf{x}) \subset N_d$ //check if the basin of $\mathbf{x}$ is within the hyper-rectangle $N_d$
   (a) **If** another optimum $\mathbf{x}'$ is in $N_d$: split $N_d$ in the middle between $B(\mathbf{x})$ and $B(\mathbf{x}')$, at a dimension $i$ where distance($B(\mathbf{x}), B(\mathbf{x}')$) is largest.
   (b) **Else:** Consider $N_d$ the search area of the sub-region/population that tracks $\mathbf{x}$
3. **Else** //go up the tree to find a hyper-rectangle large enough to contain $B(\mathbf{x})$
   (a) $N_d = N_{d-1}$ //Because $N_d$ is not large enough for $B(\mathbf{x})$, we have to resize $N_d$. We do so by going up to the parent node $N_{d-1}$ and redo its split.
   (b) Merge $N_d$ //Merge $N_d$ for resplitting later.
   (c) Repeat step 2

---

In this modified KD-Tree, each estimated basin of the found optima is represented as a hyper-rectangle in the tree. This hyper-rectangle also indicates the cover area of the corresponding sub-population. Algorithm 2 shows the process of using a modified KD-Tree for separating regions in EDO:

This tree construction procedure help separating the regions covering different peaks automatically. In addition, it takes only $O(\log M)$ (where $M$ is the number of sub-regions/populations) for each individual to identify which sub-region/population the individual belongs to. The procedure also allows the tree to adaptively adjust its structure in response to changes. For example, if a new optimum appears or an existing optimum has moved and the current hyper-rectangle is no longer able to cover the optimum's basin, the size of the hyper-rectangle will be adjusted accordingly. Another benefit is that, since we need only one KD-tree to memorise all regions/populations in the space, sub-regions/populations no longer have to manage their own regional information.

## 2.4    Local Search

EAs are considered relatively slow to converge. To speed up convergence speed, once a population starts to converge, a local search is applied to the best found solution to find the optimum more quickly and accurately. A population is considered starting to converge when the standard deviation of fitness values in the population becomes smaller than a threshold $\beta$. We choose the Brent local search, first used for EA research in [18,19]. This local search does not require any derivative information, hence can function as a black-box local search. The disadvantage is that it is generally much slower than local searches requiring derivative information such as conjugate gradient or quasi-Newton.

## 2.5    Tracking the Optima Movements

Although some existing methods maintain a full sub-population around an optimum to track its potential movement, it might not be necessary. Within the basin of a found optimum, tracking should only be triggered if there is a change that alters the basin. Following this idea, we propose the followings:

1. For changes that alter the existing optimum: simply re-evaluate the value of the optimum at every generation. If the values in two generations are different, a change has occurred and we track the moving optimum by applying the Brent local search to identify its new location.
2. For changes that lead to a new optimum without changing the existing ones, re-evaluating existing optima does not work. To deal with this, we allow individuals to venture into any explored basin, but prevent them from converging to existing optima. To do so, for each found optimum we define a hypercube, which has the optimum at its centre and has a length of $0.8 * l_{min}$ where $l_{min}$ is the smallest edge of the hyper-rectangle covering the optimum's basin. Any individual within this hypercube, but with worse value than the optimum's value, will be randomly re-initialised to the unexplored areas.

## 2.6    The EA-KDTree Algorithm

We integrate all the above ideas into a simple Genetic Algorithm (GA). The new EA is called EA-KDTree. The algorithm works as follows. First, a KD-Tree is created with one root node representing the whole search space. Then, whenever a new optimum is found, the algorithm estimates the optimum's basin using BasinEstimation() (Algorithm 1). The hyper-rectangle representing this estimated basin is added as a leaf to the KD-Tree, and the space is divided accordingly. This basin is recorded in the tree as an explored area. In addition, its optimum is monitored for changes and the algorithm will be prevented from re-converging to this optimum. A pseudo code is given in Algorithm 3.

---

**Algorithm 3.** Pseudo code of EA-KDTree

---

1. Initialisation:
   - Unexplored area = the whole search space
   - Explored area = null
2. For each generation, in the unexplored area:
   (a) Simple GA to search for good basins
   (b) Once GA starts converging (stdDev of population fitness $< \beta$), use Brent local search to find the optimum $\mathbf{x}^*$.
   (c) $B(\mathbf{x}^*)$ =BasinEstimation($\mathbf{x}^*$) (Algorithm 1)
   (d) TreeConstruction($\mathbf{x}^*, B(\mathbf{x}^*)$) //Add the estimated basin to explored area list
3. For each generation, in the explored area:
   (a) Search for any newly appearing optimum
       i. Allow GA'sindividuals to enter explored basin
       ii. If individuals converge to a hypercube length $0.8 * l_{\min}$ around the optimum but with worse values, reinitialise them in unexplored areas
       iii. Else go to step 2a
   (b) For each gen., re-evaluate fitness of found optima
       i. If changes detected, go to 2b //local search to track the moving optimum
4. Return to step 2

---

## 3   Complexity Analysis

Many existing multi-population methods that track multiple peaks are computationally expensive since they have to do distance calculations. For example, for each generation, methods in [13,14] and similar studies require distance calculations with a complexity of $O(MNn^2)$ where $M$ is the number of sub-populations, $N$ is the number of individuals and $n$ is the number of variables. The method in [15] requires at least $O(mN^2)$ where $m$ is the number of samples needed to detect the basin of attraction. In comparison, EA-DKTree complexity is significantly less: for each generation it only requires $O(N \log M)$ to identify the correct search region for all individuals (in EA-KDTree $M$ is the number of regions monitored by the algorithm). If we need to restructure the KD-Tree, the cost to restructure is $O(M \log M)$, which is not computationally expensive.

## 4   Experimental Results

### 4.1   Experimental Settings

For this experiment, we choose the classic MovPeaks [20] benchmark problem. This is arguably most tested dynamic academic problem to date. The MovPeaks has multiple peaks whose locations, widths, and heights can change over time. To facilitate cross-comparison among different algorithms, three standard scenarios were proposed, of which scenario 2 was most commonly used. Due to that, in this experiment the algorithms will be tested on Scenario 2 (Table 1).

**Table 1.** Parameter settings for EA-KDTree and MovPeaks

| EA-KDTree | Pop size | 25 |
|---|---|---|
| | Elitism | Yes |
| | Selection method | Roullette wheel |
| | Mutation method | Gaussian, $P = 0.15$ |
| | Crossover method | Arithmetic, $P = 0.8$ |
| MovPeaks Problem Settings | Number of runs | 30 |
| | Number of peaks | 10 |
| | Number of dimensions | 5 |
| | Change frequency | 5000 evaluations |
| | Peak heights | $[30, 70]$ |
| | Peak widths | $[1, 12]$ |
| | Change severity $s$ | 1.0 |

Parameter tuning was not done for EA-KDTree because the purpose is to provide a proof of principle. All parameters of the EA are the default values (Table 1) as used in recent research in the field (see justifications in [8]).

The chosen performance measure is the common *modified offline error* [21].

## 4.2 Experimental Results - Comparing with Current State-of-the-arts

EA-KDTree is compared with current state-of-the-art population-based methods that follows the aforementioned school of thoughts in change detection to judge the potential of the proposed ideas. The peer algorithms were chosen from: Group 1 include algorithms with complete or semi-complete change detection methods, and Group 2 include algorithms with no change detection or with just one detector, as seen in Tables 2 and 3. EA-KDTree belongs to Group 1. Note that in Group 1, some algorithms offer a full change detection/adaptation mechanism (including EA-KDTree) while some others rely on re-evaluating the current best solution in each sub-population/region only (Cellular DE, mQSO and Sa multi-swarm). The latter are supposed to have better performance than the earlier in the MovPeaks but might not be as robust in detecting changes in some real-world problems.

As seen in Tables 2 and 3, EA-KDTree has the best performance among all Group 1 algorithms (algorithms with (semi) complete change detection). The results in the tables also indicate that due to not having to detect changes comprehensively, most algorithms in Group 1 have worse performance than most in Group 2. EA-KDTree is, however, an exception. It is still better than most algorithms in Group 2 except CDE and CPSO. Overall, EA-KDTree is the second best EA and the third best meta-heuristics of all algorithms. The few better methods are those with no complete change detection. As previously discussed, these methods might become less effective in problems where changes occur in only a part of the search space. Note that here we do not consider methods that react to changes implicitly (e.g. [22]) or methods that are not population-based.

It is worth noting that EA-KDTree performance, however, has a quite large standard deviation. This suggests that the algorithm might not always be completely reliable. We hypothesize that this might be due to the Brent local search, which is stochastic and hence may needs a large number of evaluations in certain situations. This causes a larger standard deviation. This limitation, however, can easily be alleviated by using a more powerful local search.

**Table 2.** Methods with (semi)-complete change-detection (Group 1).

| Algorithm | Offline errors |
|---|---|
| **EA-KDTree** | **1.50 ± 0.47** |
| Cellular DE [5] | 1.64 ± 0.02 |
| mQSO [12] | 1.75 ± 0.06 |
| Sa multi-swarm [23] | 1.77 ± 0.05 |
| Self-Organizing Scouts [21] | 4.01 |
| MOEA DCN [24] | 4.60 ± 0.085 |
| Random-immigrant [24] | 5.82 ± 0.109 |
| Hyper-mutation [24] | 5.88 ± 0.082 |

## 4.3   Experimental Results - Studying Algorithmic Components

In this section we investigate why and which algorithmic component helps EA-KDTree to have a good performance. We will investigate if the proposed ideas make it possible to (i) correctly approximate the basins of attraction, (ii) divide the space using KD-Tree, (iii) track the moving basins, and (iv) prevent the population from converging to an existing optimum again unless it has changed.

**Table 3.** Methods with no complete change-detection (Group 2).

| Algorithm | Offline errors |
|---|---|
| CDE [25] | 0.92 ± 0.07 |
| CPSO [3] | 1.06 ± 0.07 |
| MSO [26] | 1.51 ± 0.04 |
| ESCA [4] | 1.53 ± 0.02 |
| Cellular DE [5] | 1.64 ± 0.02 |
| DynDE [6] | 1.75 ± 0.03 |
| MEPSO [7] (5 detectors) | 4.02 ± 0.56 |
| jDE ([27], implemented by [25]) | 5.88 ± 0.31 |

**Approximating the basins and dividing the space using KD-Tree:** We investigate the ability of the algorithm in approxmating the basin and dividing the space by comparing Simple GA + KD-Tree with Simple GA. The only difference between the two algorithms is the implementation of the KD-Tree and along with it the procedure BasinEstimation (Algorithm 1). To compare, we plot the position of individuals over different generations (for both algorithms) and also plot the division of the space by the KD-Tree (for GA+KD-Tree) to see if the proposed idea can help estimate the basins and divide the space correctly.

Figure 2 shows that after 11 generations GA+KDTree can find all optima, while the original GA is unable to do so after 50 generations. Furthermore the simple GA converges to just one optimum and hence fails to track multiple optima simultaneously. Another interesting observation is that the hyper-rectangles divided by the KD-Tree fits well with optima's basins. This illustrates the clear advantage of estimating the basin and dividing the search space using KDTree. Figure 2c also shows that in the hyper-rectangle on the right half (the explored area), there is almost no individual because they have already been re-initialised to the unexplored area (the left half). This demonstrates that EA-KDTree is able to distinguish between explored and unexplored areas, as well as to prevent individuals from reconverging to an existing optimum.

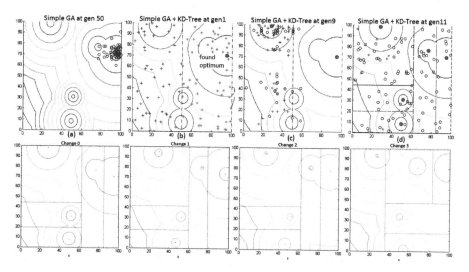

**Fig. 2.** Top: Simple GA vs Simple GA+KDTree; Bottom: EAKD-Tree adjusts its tree to track the moving optima's basins

**Using KD-Tree to track moving optima:** We investigate if TreeConstruction (Algorithm 2) can help EA-KDTree to adaptively adjust its tree structure to track the moving optima by plotting the structure of the KDTree against the search landscape at different moments when changes occur (Fig. 2).

Figure 2 shows EAKD-Tree has clearly adjusted the size of its hyper-rectangles to adapt with changes. At change 3, due to the radical level of changes, the

KD-Tree even completely changes its structure to better cover the changing basins and optima. The figure confirms that the algorithm is able to resize/relocate its hyper-rectangles to better fit with the changes in both basin sizes and locations of the optima. This ensures that moving optima are tracked successfully.

## 5    Conclusion and Future Work

This paper presented a new method to adaptively separate the unexplored and explored areas in search spaces. This method helps improve tracking the moving optima and detecting changes. The resulting algorithm performs competitively against current state-of-the-art, while having the benefits of offering less computational complexity and better change detection, even when being applied to even a not-usually-effective simple GA.

The paper has the following contributions: (a) a novel use of KD-Tree to separate and track explored regions, with low computational cost; (b) a simple method to correctly estimate basins of attraction of optima; (c) a new competitive algorithm; and (d) detailed analyses to provide more insights of the behaviours of the new algorithm.

There are a number of areas for future research. First, we will use a more powerful EA, for example DE or PSO instead of simple GA. Second, we plan to tune the parameters to have better results. Third, we will investigate replacing the current Brent local search with a different local search that is more reliable.

**Acknowledgment.** This work is supported by a Seed-corn grant award by the Chartered Institute of Logistics and Transport, an EU-funded project named Intelligent Transportation in Dynamic Environments (InTraDE), a research grant from RCUK NEMODE, and a British Council's UK-ASEAN Knowledge Partnership grant.

## References

1. Nguyen, T.T.: Continuous Dynamic Optimisation Using Evolutionary Algorithms, Ph.D. thesis, Birmingham (2011). http://etheses.bham.ac.uk/1296
2. Nguyen, T.T., Yang, S., Branke, J.: Evolutionary dynamic optimization: a survey of the state of the art. Swarm Evol. Comput. **6**, 1–24 (2012)
3. Yang, S., Li, C.: A clustering particle swarm optimizer for locating and tracking multiple optima in dynamic environments. IEEE Trans. Evol. Comput. **14**(6), 959–974 (2010)
4. Lung, R., Dumitrescu, D.: Evolutionary swarm cooperative optimization in dynamic environments. Natural Comput. **9**(1), 83–94 (2010)
5. Noroozi, V., Hashemi, A.B., Meybodi, M.R.: CellularDE: a cellular based differential evolution for dynamic optimization problems. In: Dobnikar, A., Lotrič, U., Šter, B. (eds.) ICANNGA 2011, Part I. LNCS, vol. 6593, pp. 340–349. Springer, Heidelberg (2011)
6. Mendes, R., Mohais, A.: Dynde: a differential evolution for dynamic optimization problems. In: CEC, pp. 2808–2815 (2005)

7. Du, W., Li, B.: Multi-strategy ensemble particle swarm optimization for dynamic optimization. Inf. Sci. **178**(15), 3096–3109 (2008)
8. Nguyen, T.T., Yao, X.: Continuous dynamic constrained optimisation - the challenges. IEEE Trans. Evol. Comput. **16**(6), 769–786 (2012)
9. Richter, H.: Detecting change in dynamic fitness landscapes. In: Congress on Evolutionary Computation, pp. 1613–1620 (2009)
10. Grefenstette, J.J.: Genetic algorithms for changing environments. In: Parallel Problem Solving from Nature 2, pp. 137–144 (1992)
11. Morrison, R.W.: Designing Evolutionary Algorithms for Dynamic Environments. Springer, Berlin (2004). ISBN 3-540-21231-0
12. Blackwell, T., Branke, J.: Multiswarms, exclusion, and anti-convergence in dynamic environments. IEEE Trans. Evol. Comput. **10**(4), 459–472 (2006)
13. Oppacher, F., Wineberg, M.: The shifting balance genetic algorithm: improving the ga in a dynamic environment. In: GECCO, pp. 504–510 (1999)
14. Branke, J., Kaußler, T., Schmidt, C., Schmeck, H.: A multi-population approach to dynamic optimization problems. In: Adaptive Computing in Design and Manufacturing (2000)
15. Ursem, R.K.: Multinational GA optimization techniques in dynamic environments. In: Genetic and Evolutionary Computation Conference, pp. 19–26 (2000)
16. Bentley, J.L., Friedman, J.H.: Data structures for range searching. ACM Comput. Surv. **11**(4), 397–409 (1979)
17. Wikipedia, KD-tree. Accessed on 07 April 2014
18. Nguyen, T.T., Yao, X.: An experimental study of hybridizing cultural algorithms and local search. Int. J. Neural Syst. **18**(1), 1–18 (2008)
19. Nguyen, T.T., Yao, X.: Hybridizing cultural algorithms and local search. In: Corchado, E., Yin, H., Botti, V., Fyfe, C. (eds.) IDEAL 2006. LNCS, vol. 4224, pp. 586–594. Springer, Heidelberg (2006)
20. Branke, J.: Evolutionary Optimization in Dynamic Environments. Kluwer, Dordrecht (2001)
21. Branke, J., Schmeck, H.: Designing evolutionary algorithms for dynamic optimization problems. In: Tsutsui, S., Ghosh, A. (eds.) Theory and Application of Evolutionary Computation: Recent Trends, pp. 239–262. Springer, Berlin (2003)
22. Li, C., Yang, S.: A general framework of multipopulation methods with clustering in undetectable dynamic environments. IEEE Trans. Evol. Comput. **16**(4), 556–577 (2012)
23. Blackwell, T.: Particle swarm optimization in dynamic environment. In: Yang, S., Ong, Y.-S., Jin, Y. (eds.) Evolutionary Computation in Dynamic and Uncertain Environments. SCI, pp. 29–49. Springer, Heidelberg (2007)
24. Bui, L., Nguyen, M.-H., Branke, J., Abbass, H.: Tackling dynamic problems with multiobjective evolutionary algorithms. In: Knowles, J., Corne, D., Deb, K., Chair, D.R. (eds.) Multiobjective Problem Solving from Nature, pp. 77–91. Springer, Heidelberg (2008)
25. du Plessis, M.C., Engelbrecht, A.P.: Using competitive population evaluation in a differential evolution algorithm for dynamic environments. Eur. J. Oper. Res. **218**(1), 7–20 (2012)
26. Kamosi, M., Hashemi, A.B., Meybodi, M.R.: A new particle swarm optimization algorithm for dynamic environments. In: Panigrahi, B.K., Das, S., Suganthan, P.N., Dash, S.S. (eds.) SEMCCO 2010. LNCS, vol. 6466, pp. 129–138. Springer, Heidelberg (2010)
27. Brest, J., Zamuda, A., Boskovic, B., Maucec, M., Zumer, V.: Dynamic optimization using self-adaptive differential evolution. In: CEC, pp. 415–422 (2009)

# Coevolutionary Intransitivity in Games: A Landscape Analysis

Hendrik Richter[✉]

Faculty of Electrical Engineering and Information Technology,
HTWK Leipzig University of Applied Sciences, Postfach 30 11 66,
04251 Leipzig, Germany
richter@eit.htwk-leipzig.de

**Abstract.** Intransitivity is supposed to be a main reason for deficits in coevolutionary progress and inheritable superiority. Besides, coevolutionary dynamics is characterized by interactions yielding subjective fitness, but aiming at solutions that are superior with respect to an objective measurement. Such an approximation of objective fitness may be, for instance, generalization performance. In the paper a link between rating– and ranking–based measures of intransitivity and fitness landscapes that can address the dichotomy between subjective and objective fitness is explored. The approach is illustrated by numerical experiments involving a simple random game with continuously tunable degree of randomness.

## 1 Introduction

Despite earlier promises and optimism, using coevolutionary algorithms (CEAs) for evolving candidate solutions towards an optimum remains a complicated and almost arcane matter with generally unclear prospects of success [13,15,20]. This is prominently caused by a defining feature of coevolution. CEAs are driven by fitness that originates from interaction of candidate solutions with other candidate solutions. In other words, the fitness obtained from these interactions is subjective as it depends on which candidate solutions are actually interacting and when in coevolutionary run–time the interactions take place. The interactions can be understood as to constitute tests, which leads to labeling such kinds of coevolutionary problems as test–based problems [15,17]. Test–based problems particularly occur in game playing or game–like contexts, for instance in situations where the players' strategies are subject to (competitive) coevolutionary optimum finding [15,19]. It has been argued that in games with players and strategies the player space can be understood a phenotypic according to the framework of fitness landscapes [10,16], while the strategy space is genotypic [1,14]. This view is adopted in the following discussion.

Notwithstanding that coevolutionary dynamics is induced by subjective fitness, the aim of using a CEA is identifying candidate solutions that are superior in a more general sense. Hence, in coevolution next to the fitness resulting from

© Springer International Publishing Switzerland 2015
A.M. Mora and G. Squillero (Eds.): EvoApplications 2015, LNCS 9028, pp. 869–881, 2015.
DOI: 10.1007/978-3-319-16549-3_70

(a limited number of) tests, a second notion of fitness is helpful. Such a fitness generalizing subjective fitness occurs in test–based problems in different forms. For games with players and strategies, there is usually no absolute quality measurement, or an absolute quality measurement would require to evaluate all possible test cases, which is computationally infeasible [4,5,19]. To circumvent this problem and enable experimental studies of the relationships between subjective fitness and absolute quality measurements, number games have been proposed, for instance minimal substrates [18,21]. These artificial problem settings postulate an absolute quality, called objective fitness [7]. In this line of reasoning, coevolutionary dynamics can be understood as aiming at progress in objective fitness by proxy of subjective fitness. Consequently, a main difficulty in designing CEAs stems from the question of how well subjective fitness represents objective fitness. In analogy to the (postulated) objective fitness of number games, for games with players and strategies all general quality measurements of subjective fitness are interpretable as objective fitness. This implies that for game playing there may only be an approximation of objective fitness and different approximations are possible, for instance different instances of generalization performance [4,5]. Put another way, this interpretation suggests that in game playing there are different degrees of objective fitness.

Application examples of CEAs have frequently reported experiments showing mediocre performance, mostly attributed to coevolutionary intransitivity [3,9,21]. Generally speaking, intransitivity occurs when superiority relations are cyclic. Such cyclic superiority relations have consequences for coevolutionary dynamics as intransitivity may occurs across subsequent generations. In such a case, it may be that all solutions at generation $k + 1$ are better than at $k$, and that the same applies for $k + 2$ with respect to $k + 1$. This, however, does not imply that the solutions at $k + 2$ are strictly better than at $k$. Cyclic superiority relations that occur across generations are connoted as coevolutionary (dynamic) intransitivity. In this paper, the problem of coevolutionary intransitivity is linked to the dichotomy between subjective and objective fitness. This is done by combining a rating– and ranking–based measuring approach of intransitivity proposed by Samothrakis et al. [19] with a framework of codynamic fitness landscapes recently suggested [18]. Codynamic fitness landscapes enable to analyse the relationship between objective and subjective fitness for all possible solutions of the coevolutionary search process. The landscape approach proposed particularly explores how coevolutionary intransitivity is related to the objective–versus–subjective–fitness issue. The remainder of the paper is structured as follows. In the next section, the concept of codynamic landscapes composed of objective and subjective fitness is briefly recalled. In Sect. 3, intransitivity is discussed. For the discussion, a simple random game is introduced, where the degree of randomness can be continuously tuned. It is shown that intransitivity can be characterized by different types of intransitivity measures. Numerical experiments with the simple random game are presented in Sect. 4, and Sect. 5 concludes the paper with a summary.

# 2 Coevolution, Codynamic Landscapes and Number Games

This section focuses attention on an approach recently suggested [18] that is useful for understanding coevolutionary dynamics through codynamic fitness landscapes. Such landscapes allow studying the relationship between objective and subjective fitness which, in turn, mainly determines coevolutionary dynamics.

We define objective fitness as the triple of search space $S$ with search space points $s \in S$, neighborhood structure $n(s)$ and fitness function $f_{obj}(s)$. The objective fitness landscape can be considered as to describe the optimization problem to be solved by the CEA. This problem solving is based on coevolutionary interactions between potential solutions which yields subjective fitness. Hence, subjective fitness can be viewed as the way the CEA perceives the problem posed by the objective fitness. From this, it appears to be sensible to assume that the subjective landscape possesses the same search space and neighborhood structure, but has a fitness function $f_{sub}$ that more or less strongly deviates from the objective fitness $f_{obj}$. This can be seen as the subjective fitness usually overestimating or underestimating objective fitness. Moreover, for a coevolutionary run, the deviation between objective and subjective fitness is dynamic. In other word, the coevolutionary dynamics dynamically deforms the subjective fitness landscape. In the following, the link between subjective and objective fitness is exemplified for a number game, which is also called a coevolutionary minimal substrate [18,21].

In this number game a population $P$ of players is considered that inhabits the search spaces $S$. The search space is one–dimensional and real–valued. At each instance of the game $k = 0, 1, 2, \ldots$, the players of $P(k)$ may have possible values $s \in S$. An objective fitness function is defined over the search space, that is $f_{obj}(s)$, which consequently casts an objective fitness landscape. The subjective fitness of $P(k)$ is the result of an interactive number game. Therefore, for each calculation of the subjective fitness $f_{sub}(s)$ for a player from $P$, a sample $\sigma(E)$ of evaluators from $E \subseteq P$ is randomly selected. This sample is statistically independent from the sample for the next calculation. Denote $\mu$ the size of the sample $\sigma(E)$ out of $\lambda$ evaluators, with $\mu \leq \lambda$. The number game further defines that the fitness $f_{sub}(s)$ with respect to the sample $\sigma(E)$ is calculated by counting the (averaged) number of members in $\sigma(E)$ that have a smaller objective fitness $f_{obj}(\sigma_i(E))$, $i = 1, 2, \ldots, \mu$, than the objective fitness $f_{obj}(s)$ [18]:

$$f_{sub}(s) = \frac{1}{\mu} \sum_{i=1}^{\mu} \text{eval}(s, \sigma_i(E)) \quad \text{with} \quad \text{eval}(s, \sigma_i) = \begin{cases} 1 & \text{if } f_{obj}(s) > f_{obj}(\sigma_i) \\ 0 & \text{otherwise} \end{cases}.$$

(1)

Note that the number game considered postulates objective fitness and defines by Eq. (1) how subjective fitness is obtained by a coevolutionary interaction. In the next section, this perspective of subjective and objective fitness is applied to games with players and strategies. A population of players is engaged to evaluate their subjective fitness by interaction with other players.

# 3   Static and Coevolutionary Intransitivity in Games

A relation $R$ is called intransitive over a set $S$ if for three elements $\{s_1, s_2, s_3\} \in S$ the relation $(s_1 R s_2) \wedge (s_2 R s_3)$ does not always imply $s_1 R s_3$. An instance of intransitivity is superiority relations that are cyclic, which in its most obvious and purest form appears in game playing. Cyclic superiority relations here mean that for three players and three strategies $s_1$, $s_2$ and $s_3$, the player using $s_1$ wins against $s_2$, and $s_2$ wins against $s_3$, but $s_1$ loses against $s_3$. A simple example is a rock–paper–scissor game, where "paper" wins over "rock", "scissor" wins over "paper", but "scissor" loses against "rock". Thus, "paper", "rock" and "scissor" are possible strategies a player can adopt in this game. Note that this kind of intransitivity is a feature of the preference in a single round of the game. Hence, such an intransitivity is static (and actually game–induced) and has no immediate link to (co-)evolutionary dynamics. Consequently, the next question is how these superiority relations resemble situations with coevolutionary intransitivity and can be understood by the dichotomy between subjective and objective fitness. To obtain (co-)evolutionary dynamics, the players need to adjust their strategies, and the game needs to be played for more than one round. In other words, studying iterated games is also interesting as it serves to juxtapose static (game–induced) intransitivity with coevolutionary (dynamic and search–induced) intransitivity.

One way to build a relationship between game results and fitness is to apply a rating system. Examples of rating systems are the Elo system to evaluate chess players [8,11], or the Bradley–Terry–Luce model of paired comparison [2,12]. Recently, it has been shown that this methodology is also useful for analyzing coevolutionary intransitivity [19]. A rating system creates a probabilistic model based on past game results that can be seen as a predictor of future results. Most significantly, the rating system also imposes a (temporal) ranking of the players. In the following, these ideas are applied to a simple random game where the degree of randomness can be tuned. The game consists of players using a strategy to perform against all other players once, called a round robin tournament. The game outcome, which can be interpreted as payoff, is subject to the players' ratings and random. Given that the game has $N$ players, there are $\frac{N(N-1)}{2}$ games in a single round robin. Define a percentage $p_{rand}$ of games that have a random result to obtain $p_{rand} \cdot \frac{N(N-1)}{2}$ games whose outcome is chance with a predefined distribution. The remaining games end deterministically according to the rating difference between the players. Thus, such a game falls into the category of perfect and incomplete information. Viewed over a series of round robin tournaments, this interaction between rating–based determinism and random chance creates temporal "rating triangles", where a player scores high results (and has a high rating) over a certain time, but may also lose against a nominal weaker (low–rating) player, which over time may or may not show the same characteristics towards a third player. Such a behavior complies with coevolutionary (dynamic and actually search–induced) intransitivity. In addition, the game can also reproduce rock–paper–scissor–like intransitivities. For $N$ players the

**Table 1.** Results of the simple random game for three instance of the game

| # | rt(0) | #1 | #2 | #3 | #4 | #5 | sc(0) | rt(1) | #1 | #2 | #3 | #4 | #5 | sc(1) | rt(2) | gp | rank | sc(2) |
|---|-------|----|----|----|----|----|-------|-------|----|----|----|----|----|-------|-------|-----|------|-------|
| 1 | 1600 | x | 1 | 1 | 1 | 1 | 4 | 1630 | x | 0 | 1 | 1 | 1 | 3 | 1642 | 3.5 | 1 | 1 |
| 2 | 1600 | 0 | x | 1 | 0 | 1 | 2 | 1600 | 1 | x | 1 | 1 | 0 | 3 | 1615 | 2.5 | 2 | 4 |
| 3 | 1600 | 0 | 0 | x | 1 | 1 | 2 | 1600 | 0 | 0 | x | 0 | 0 | 0 | 1570 | 1 | 4.5 | 0 |
| 4 | 1600 | 0 | 1 | 0 | x | 1 | 2 | 1600 | 0 | 0 | 1 | x | 1 | 2 | 1600 | 2 | 3 | 2 |
| 5 | 1600 | 0 | 0 | 0 | 0 | x | 0 | 1570 | 0 | 1 | 1 | 0 | x | 2 | 1573 | 1 | 4.5 | 3 |

maximal number of static intransitivities is

$$\#_{intra\ max} = \binom{N}{3} = \frac{(N-2)(N-1)N}{6}, \tag{2}$$

see [6,19]. Any three players form a triangle of cyclic superiority relations if they each win one game against the other two. Thus, for $N$ not very large, the (average) number of actual static intransitivities can be determined by enumeration and gives a static intransitivity measure called the intransitivity index (itx) [6,19]. As an alternative, Samothrakis et al. [19] suggested to use a difference measure based on Kullback–Leibler divergence (kld) between the prediction made by the rating system and the actual outcome to measure static intransitivity. Both quantities itx and kld are subjects of the numerical experiments reported in the next section.

A game in a coevolutionary setting involves finding the strategy a player should adopt to score best according to a given understanding of performance. This clearly implies that the performance measurement should generalize a single round robin tournament. Thus, if there are several instances of round robin tournaments, the overall results can also be accounted for by generalization performance [4,5]. Each instance of a round robin can be scaled to a generation of coevolutionary run–time. Generalization performance is defined as mean score of a solution in all possible test cases. Because considering all possible test cases may be computationally infeasible, Chong et al. [4,5] used a statistical approach involving confidence bounds to estimate the amount of needed test cases for a given error margin. Given this understanding, and assuming that all strategies are equally likely to be selected as test strategies, the generalization performance of strategy $i$ is:

$$\mathrm{gp}_i = \frac{1}{\mathcal{K}} \sum_{k=1}^{\mathcal{K}} \mathrm{sc}_i(k), \tag{3}$$

where $\mathrm{sc}_i(k)$ is the score the $i$-th strategy yields in the $k$-th instance of a round robin tournament. The needed number of instances $\mathcal{K}$ depends on the bounds given by Chong et al. [4,5]. Generalization performance also builds a relationship between actual game results and fitness and therefore can be seen as an alternative to a rating system.

As an example of the simple random game assume that there are five players ($N = 5$), denoted as #1 to #5, which each act upon a unknown, but internally adjusting strategy. Further assume that as an a–priori evaluation all players are considered equal and have the same rating, say rt(0) = 1600. These players are now engaged in a round robin tournament, where a win scores 1 and a loss counts 0. The results achieved depend on the pre–game rating and random. Assume that these results were scored, see Table 1, column 3–7. While player #1 wins all games and #5 loses all games, the players #2–#4 build a rock–paper–scissor triangle of cyclic superiority relations. These results somehow violate the expectations established by the initial (pre–game) rating, which could have been met by all players winning 2 out of 4 games. Furthermore, the results show clearly that the game cannot be completely deterministic with respect to the a–priori evaluation. In other words, a rating and ranking approach subsumes the game history and can only be a predictor of future game results. The quality of prediction depends on the percentage of random game results. Also, from the results of the round robin, it is not evident whether player #1 was as successful as it was because its strategy was (objectively) good, or because the strategies of the other players were (objectively) poor. All, the round robin gives is a comparison.

The a–priori rating were indicating that all players have the same rank (and hence there is no ranking difference between them), but the results were showing otherwise. Hence, the round robin tournament updates the rating, producing an after–game rating. According to the Elo system [8,11], which is adopted here, this is done via first calculating the expected outcome.

$$ex_i(k) = \sum_j \frac{1}{1 + 10^{(rt_j(k) - rt_i(k))/400}}. \tag{4}$$

The quantity $ex_i(k)$ summarizes winning probabilities of player #$i$ with respect to all other players in round $k$. For a single game, that is $j = 1$, the quantity $ex_i$ is the expected winning probability for the player #$i$ winning against player #$j$. For the example with all players having the same rating, the expected outcome is also the same, namely $ex_i = 2$. The rating of the players is updated according to the difference between expectation and actual score:

$$rt_i(k + 1) = rt_i(k) + K(sc_i(k) - ex_i(k)). \tag{5}$$

The $K$ is called the $K$–factor, which tunes the sensitivity between the rating and the results of a single round robin tournament. Using $K = 15$, the new rating rt(1) gives differences between the players, see Table 1, column 9. The best player #1 is now ranked highest, the poorest player #5 is ranked lowest. Also note that the players #2–#4 engaged in the game–induced intransitivity triangle still share the same rating as before. Now assume the next round of the game. The strategies of the players have been adjusted, supposedly by a (competitive) coevolutionary search process. See the results in Table 1, column 10–14. The outcome generally confirms the impression of the first round with player #1 still being strong. Violating the expectations are the good scores of the players #2 and #5, and the poor score of player #3. Note that in this round the players #1, #2, and #5 as well as the players #2, #4, and #5 form a

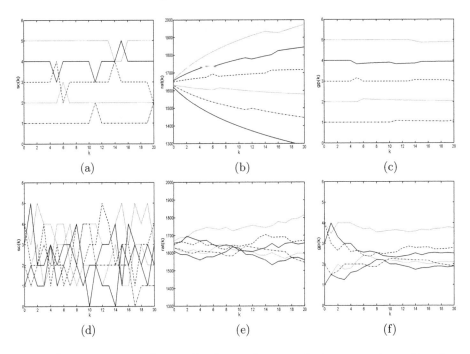

**Fig. 1.** Scores, ratings, and generalization performance for two percentages of random games: (a)–(c), $p_{rand} = 0.01$; (d)–(f), $p_{rand} = 0.75$.

rock–paper–scissor triangle of game–induced intransitivity. Contrary to the first round, these players now neither have the same score, nor the same pre–game or after–game rating. This after–game rating rt(2) is calculated according to Eq. (5) and given in Table 1, column 16.

As there are now two instances of the round robin tournament, an first estimation of the generalized performance gp can be obtained by averaging the scores according to Eq. (3). The results are given in Table 1, column 17. Conforming with this account of quality evaluation, player #1 is best, and can be ranked first, followed by players #2 and #4. The ranking with respect to generalization performance is given in Table 1, column 18. Note that the ranking gives average ranks for tied ranks as for player #3 and #5 (gp = 1 leads to rank = 4.5), which preserves the sum over all ranks. Further note that this ranking is almost equal to the ranking according to ratings, with the exception of players #3 and #5 which have a very similar but not equal rating.

Now, the simple random game is interpreted according to the landscape view of subjective and objective fitness. Recall that subjective fitness is associated with fitness gained by individuals through interaction with others. According to this view, a round robin tournament yields subjective fitness: $f_{sub} = sc(k)$. Objective fitness, in turn, generalizes subjective fitness in terms of an absolute quality measurement. Possible candidates are the rating $f_{obj} = rt(k)$ or generalization performance $f_{obj} = gp(k)$. Defining subjective and objective fitness in such a way also gives raise to reformulating coevolutionary intransitivity. Generally speaking, coevolutionary intransitivity involves cycling of (objective) solution quality. This cycling may be caused by subjective fitness not adequately representing objective fitness. Hence, subjective fitness may drive evolution into search space regions visited before but evaluated differently, or generally into directions not favorable. Hence, coevolutionary (dynamic) intransitivity can be understood as temporal mismatches in order between subjective and objective fitness. Consider again the example of the game whose results are given in Table 1. Suppose another instance of the round robin is played, and (omitting the specific results) the scores are in Table 1, column 19. The rating $rt(k)$ is considered to be objective, while $sc(k)$ is subjective. For player #1, the rating is $rt_1 = 1600 \le 1630 \le 1642$, while its score is $sc_1 = 4 > 3 > 1$, which is a temporal mismatch between objective and subjective fitness. If we were to suppose for a moment that the rating declared as objective fitness is indeed the quantity to achieve in coevolutionary search, and if a CEA were to use score for guiding this search, then player #1 would likely be misguided. On the other hand, for player #2, the rating $rt_2 = 1600 \le 1630 \le 1642$, and the score $sc_2 = 2 < 3 < 4$ show a match between subjective and objective fitness. These conditions can be reformulated employing a ranking function with tied ranks and gives a measure of coevolutionary intransitivity. Hence, the player–wise temporal mismatch (ptm) can be defined as the average number of rank mismatches: $rank(f_{obj}(k), f_{obj}(k+1)), f_{obj}(k+2)) \ne rank(f_{sub}(k), f_{sub}(k+1)), f_{sub}(k+2))$ for each player for a given number of instances of round robins.

An alternative measure of coevolutionary intransitivity that is related to the ptm just discussed stems from the fact that coevolutionary selection is based on comparing subjective fitness values. Hence, the fitness ranking within one instance of the game (or one generation) gives indication as to what direction is preferred. If difficulties in the search process are caused by how well subjective fitness represents objective fitness, then the difference in the ranking according to subjective fitness and the ranking according to objective fitness for each instance is also a suitable measure of coevolutionary intransitivity. Therefore, the quantity $|rank(f_{sub}(k)) - rank(f_{obj}(k))|$ over all players for each instance $k$ is another measure of coevolutionary intransitivity and is called collective ranking difference (crd). The observations discussed so far suggest some relationships, namely that game–induced, static intransitivity has ambiguous effect on coevolutionary progress, and that coevolutionary, dynamic intransitivity can be expressed as ranking differences between objective and subjective fitness. In other words, the quantities ptm and crd may be useful as measures of coevolutionary intransitivity. All these relationships can be studied by numerical experiments, which are the topic of next section.

## 4   Numerical Experiments

The report of experimental results starts with the time evolution of the simple random game introduced in the last section. Figure 1 shows the scores, ratings

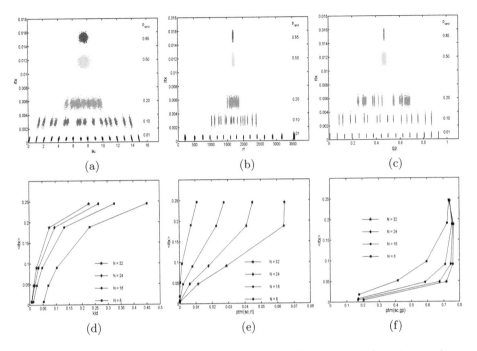

**Fig. 2.** Intransitivity measure itx versus score = sc(k), rating rt(k) and generalization performance gp(k) (a–c) as scatter plots; relationships between the intransitivity measure itx, kld, and ptm (d–f)

and generalization performances for two different percentages of random results ($p_{rand} = 0.01$ and $p_{rand} = 0.75$) and $N = 6$ players and 20 instances of a round robin. The experiments are initialized with ratings rt(0) being slightly spread around the value rt(0) = 1600. The randomly determined chance to win or to lose is evenly distributed. The figures show curves for a single instance of the randomly determined part of the game outcomes. Hence, the curves are not meant to be statistically significant, but for illustrating typical behaviour only. It can be seen that for a low number of random outcome (Fig. 1a–c) the scores each player achieves are mainly defined by the initial rating. Small differences in the initial rating are amplified and lead to well–sorted long–term rankings of both the rating and generalization performance. For a large number of random game results (Fig. 1d–f) the scores are almost purely chance which is evenly distributed. Consistently, ratings and generalization performances tend to approach the expected value implied by the underlying distribution for all players alike. The next experiments address the relationships between static (game–induced) intransitivity expressed by the measure itx and quantities representing subjective as well as objective fitness. The scatter plots given in Fig. 2a–c are for $N = 16$ players and five levels of $p_{rand}$. The experimental setup includes a repetition of each run for 100 times for 1000 instances of the round robin, where the first 200 instances are discarded to omit transients. Note that this gives a sufficient

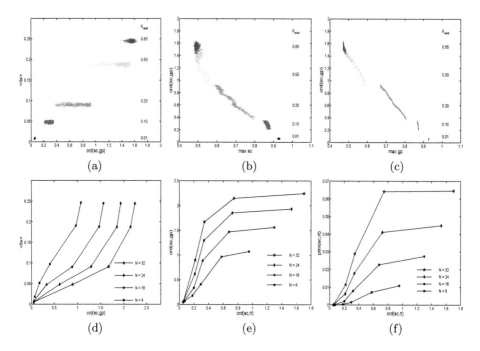

**Fig. 3.** Intransitivity measure crd versus time average itx, max sc, and max pg (a–c) as scatter plots; relationships between the intransitivity measure crd, itx, and ptm (d–f)

number of instance according to the bounds of generalization performance [4,5]. Hence, the results can be seen as statistically significant. In fact, the 99 % confidence intervals are so small that they are not depicted in the figures. It can be seen that for each level of randomness in the game, we obtain a distinct level of static intransitiviy measured by itx, where rising $p_{rand}$ also increases itx. What is interesting is that there is almost no variation in score, rating or generalization performance for a given level of intransitivity itx. This indicates that static intransitivity seems to have little influence on neither subjective nor objective fitness. This is particularly visible for low levels of $p_{rand}$ where these is a clear sorting according to the range of fitness a given player achieved but this is not connected to differences in the itx. A next experiment explores the relations between the index based measure itx and the probabilistically motivated measure kld, see Fig. 2d. Here as well as in the following figure the results are for four different number of players $N$ ($N = 8, 16, 24, 32$) and five levels of random results $p_{rand}$; the time–average itx, denoted $\langle$itx$\rangle$, is given, the quantities are normalized according to the number of players. It can be seen that between both quantities there is a proportional relationship, which on the one hand generally confirms the result in [19], but does not show that itx is more brittle that kld. For the studied game it can be concluded that both quantities are interchangeable. Next, the relationship between the static intransitivity and the dynamic intransitivity measure player–wise temporal mismatch (ptm) is studied, Fig. 2e,f. For the mismatch ptm based on rating as objective fitness (Fig. 2e) there is a linear relationship, at least for small values of $p_{rand}$, for the mismatch ptm based on generalization performance (Fig. 2f), no sensible conclusions about relations can be drawn. Finally, we focus on the rank–based dynamic intransitivity measure collective ranking difference (crd), see Fig. 3. The Fig. 3a–c again shows scatter plots, now for the crd based on score as subjective fitness and generalization performance as objective fitness for $N = 16$ players and five levels of $p_{rand}$. It can be seen that although different $p_{rand}$ give different itx, there is no differ- ence in the crd, Fig. 3a. However, there is a almost linear relation between the measure crd and max sc and max gp, at least for lower levels of $p_{rand}$. This can be interpreted as the crd scaling with the time evolution of the subjective and objective fitness, but not with the time evolution of static intansitivity, compare to Fig. 2a–c, which does not show such a characteristics. For the time–averages, there is a scaling for different number of players and different levels of random- ness $p_{rand}$, see Fig. 3d. In Fig. 3e, the relation between the crd based on rating as objective fitness (crd(sc,rt)) and the crd based on generalization performance as objective fitness (crd(sc,gp)) is shown. It can be seen that both quantities scale piece-wise linear for $p_{rand}$ not very large, which allows to conclude that both quantities account for the same intransitivity properties. Finally, the relation between the crd and ptm is shown, Fig. 3f. It can be seen that the ptm scales weaker than the crd, particularly for a small number of players and high random- ness, and it can be conjectured that the crd is a more meaningful coevolutionary intransitivity measure than the ptm.

## 5   Conclusions

This paper is a contribution to the ongoing discussion about the effect of intran- sitivities on coevolutionary progress. An approach was presented that allowed to link a rating– and ranking–based measuring approach of intransitivity [19] with a framework of fitness landscapes to enable analyzing the relationship between objective and subjective fitness. For experimentally illustrating the approach a simple random game with continuously tunable degree of randomness was pro- posed. Apart from the random, the game results depend on the ratings of the players, which reflect the past success of each player. Thus, the game proposed characterizes many real–world games as their outcome is also a function of chance as well as of predictions based on game history.

For studying the effect of intransitivity, measures were explored. In extension of existing static intransitivity measures, dynamic measures that can account for coevolutionary intransitivity were proposed. These measure are based on rank- ings between subjective and objective fitness and it was shown that coevolu- tionary intransitivity can be understood as a ranking problem, and hence be accounted for by ranking statistics. To enlarge the scope of the presented app- roach, as a next step the intransitivity measures could be studied for other types of game for instance social games as the iterated prisoner's dilemma or board game such as Othello.

# References

1. Antal, T., Ohtsuki, H., Wakeley, J., Taylor, P., Nowak, M.A.: Evolutionary game dynamics in phenotype space. Proc. Nat. Acad. Sci. **106**, 8597–8600 (2009)
2. Bradley, R.A., Terry, M.E.: Rank analysis of incomplete block designs, I. The method of paired comparisons. Biometrika **39**, 324–345 (1952)
3. de Jong, E.D.: Intransitivity in coevolution. In: Yao, X., et al. (eds.) PPSN 2004. LNCS, vol. 3242, pp. 843–851. Springer, Heidelberg (2004)
4. Chong, S.Y., Tino, P., Yao, X.: Measuring generalization performance in coevolutionary learning. IEEE Trans. Evolut. Comp. **12**, 479–505 (2008)
5. Chong, S.Y., Tino, P., Ku, D.C., Yao, X.: Improving generalization performance in coevolutionary learning. IEEE Trans. Evolut. Comp. **16**, 70–85 (2012)
6. Frank, O., Harary, F.: Cluster inference by using transitivity indices in empirical graphs. Jour. Am. Statist. Assoc. **77**, 835–840 (1982)
7. de Jong, E.D.: Objective fitness correlation. In: Lipson, H. (ed.) Proceedings of the Genetic and Evolutionary Computation Conference, GECCO 2007, pp. 440–447. ACM, New York (2007)
8. Elo, A.E.: The Rating of Chess Players, Past and Present. Batsford, London (1978)
9. Funes, P., Pujals, E.: Intransitivity revisited coevolutionary dynamics of numbers games. In: Beyer, H.G., O'Reilly, U.M. (eds.) Proceedings of the Genetic and Evolutionary Computation Conference, GECCO 2005, pp. 515–521. Morgan Kaufmann, San Francisco (2005)
10. Kallel, L., Naudts, B., Reeves, C.R.: Properties of fitness functions and search landscapes. In: Kallel, L., Naudts, B., Rogers, A. (eds.) Theoretical Aspects of Evolutionary Computing, pp. 177–208. Springer, Heidelberg (2001)
11. Langville, A.N., Meyer, C.D.: Who's #1? The Science of Rating and Ranking. Princeton University Press, Princeton (2012)
12. Luce, R.D.: Individual Choice Behaviours: A Theoretical Analysis. Wiley, New York (1959)
13. Miconi, T.: Why coevolution doesn't "work": superiority and progress in coevolution. In: Vanneschi, L., Gustafson, S., Moraglio, A., De Falco, I., Ebner, M. (eds.) EuroGP 2009. LNCS, vol. 5481, pp. 49–60. Springer, Heidelberg (2009)
14. Nowak, M.A., Tarnita, C.E., Antal, T.: Evolutionary dynamics in structured populations. Phil. Trans. R. Soc. B **365**, 19–30 (2010)
15. Popovici, E., Bucci, A., Wiegand, R.P., de Jong, E.D.: Coevolutionary principles. In: Rozenberg, G., Bäck, T., Kok, J.N. (eds.) Handbook of Natural Computing, pp. 987–1033. Springer, Heidelberg (2010)
16. Richter, H., Engelbrecht, A. (eds.): Recent Advances in the Theory and Application of Fitness Landscapes. ECC, vol. 6. Springer, Heidelberg (2014)
17. Richter, H.: Fitness landscapes that depend on time. In: Richter, H., Engelbrecht, A. (eds.) Recent Advances in the Theory and Application of Fitness Landscapes. ECC, vol. 6, pp. 279–314. Springer, Heidelberg (2014)
18. Richter, H.: Codynamic fitness landscapes of coevolutionary minimal substrates. In: Coello Coello, C.A. (ed.) Proceedings of the IEEE Congress on Evolutionary Computation, IEEE CEC 2014, pp. 2692–2699. IEEE Press, Piscataway (2014)
19. Samothrakis, S., Lucas, S.M., Runarsson, T.P., Robles, D.: Coevolving game-playing agents: measuring performance and intransitivities. IEEE Trans. Evolut. Comp. **17**, 213–226 (2013)

20. van Wijngaarden, R.P.T., de Jong, E.D.: Evaluation and diversity in co-evolution. In: Rudolph, G., Jansen, T., Lucas, S., Poloni, C., Beume, N. (eds.) PPSN 2008. LNCS, vol. 5199, pp. 631–640. Springer, Heidelberg (2008)
21. Watson, R.A., Pollack, J.B.: Coevolutionary dynamics in a minimal substrate. In: Spector, L., et al. (eds.) Proceedings of the Genetic and Evolutionary Computation Conference, GECCO 2001, pp. 702–709. Morgan Kaufmann, San Francisco (2001)

# Making IDEA-ARIMA Efficient in Dynamic Constrained Optimization Problems

Patryk Filipiak$^{(\boxtimes)}$ and Piotr Lipinski

Computational Intelligence Research Group, Institute of Computer Science,
University of Wroclaw, Wroclaw, Poland
{patryk.filipiak,lipinski}@ii.uni.wroc.pl

**Abstract.** A commonly used approach in Evolutionary Algorithms for Dynamic Constrained Optimization Problems forces re-evaluation of a population of individuals whenever the landscape changes. On the contrary, there are algorithms like IDEA-ARIMA that can effectively anticipate certain types of landscapes rather than react to changes which already happened and thus be one step ahead with the dynamic environment. However, the computational cost of IDEA-ARIMA and its memory consumption are barely acceptable in practical applications. This paper proposes a set of modifications aimed at making this algorithm an efficient and competitive tool by reducing the use of memory and proposing the new anticipation mechanism.

## 1 Introduction

Dynamic Optimization Problems (DOPs) and Dynamic Constrained Optimization Problems (DCOPs) have drown the attention of many scientists during the last decade since these two models, unlike their stationary counterparts, assume a more realistic point of view that either an objective function or a set of feasible solutions or both of them may change in time [1–4].

For the scope of this paper let us assume that $F^{(t)} : D \longrightarrow \mathbb{R}$ is the dynamic objective function with $D \subseteq \mathbb{R}^d$, $d > 0$, $t \in \mathbb{N}_+$ and $G_i^{(t)} : D \longrightarrow \mathbb{R}$ for all $i = 1, \ldots, m$ are the dynamic constraint functions. The aim is then as follows: For all $t \in \{t_1, t_2, \ldots, t_n\} \subset N_+$ find $x^{(t)} \in D$ such that

$$x^{(t)} = \arg\min\{F^{(t)}(x) : x \in D \ \wedge \ \forall_{i=1,\ldots,m} \ G_i^{(t)}(x) \geqslant 0\}. \tag{1}$$

A commonly used approach in Evolutionary Algorithms (EAs) dedicated to the above-defined D(C)OPs implements the so called *reactive* behaviour which forces them to re-evaluate the population of individuals whenever a change of the landscape is detected. Although such mechanism often guarantees at least fairly good level of tracing the moving optima and localizing the newly appearing ones as it was shown in [5–8], it is tempting to utilize the knowledge gained during the run of an EA in order to predict the future landscape and act one step ahead of the changes. This alternative approach is usually referred to as *proactive* behaviour. One of the first proactive EAs was introduced by Hatzakis and

© Springer International Publishing Switzerland 2015
A.M. Mora and G. Squillero (Eds.): EvoApplications 2015, LNCS 9028, pp. 882–893, 2015.
DOI: 10.1007/978-3-319-16549-3_71

Wallace who used an Auto-Regressive model for anticipating the future shape of Pareto optimal front in [9]. Bosman presented his learning and anticipation mechanism in [10]. Later on, Simões and Costa proposed an EA equipped with a Markov chain predictor to forecast the future states of the environment [11].

IDEA-ARIMA is a proactive EA that uses the Auto-Regressive Integrated Moving Average [12] model for anticipating the future evaluations of a fitness function. It was demonstrated in [13] that this algorithm can accurately anticipate some periodically changing environments and simultaneously guarantee a good constraint handling. However, the computational cost of running IDEA-ARIMA and its demand for a huge amounts of memory are barely acceptable in practical applications. A critical analysis of IDEA-ARIMA including a detailed description of an algorithm followed by an identification of its weakest parts is discussed further in Sect. 2.

A contribution of this paper includes a number of modifications aimed at making IDEA-ARIMA an efficient and competitive tool by reducing the use of memory and proposing the new anticipation mechanism which no longer requires maintaining a separate population of individuals yet directly injects the candidate solutions in the most probable future promising regions. It also addresses the problem of possibly inaccurate forecasts by introducing a small fraction of random immigrants spread evenly across the search space. All the proposed modifications of IDEA-ARIMA are elaborated in Sect. 3.

The suggested modifications were evaluated using the set of popular benchmark functions. The experimental results are summarized in Sect. 4, then some conclusions are given in Sect. 5.

## 2   Critical Analysis of IDEA-ARIMA

IDEA-ARIMA was first introduced in [13] as an extension of Infeasibility Driven Evolutionary Algorithm (IDEA) which is known for its robustness in solving constrained optimization problems [14]. The original IDEA deals with constraints by incorporating an additional optimization criterion called *violation measure* that indicates "how far" from a nearest feasible region a given individual is. By using a multi-objective optimization mechanism similar to NSGA-II [15], IDEA simultaneously maximizes the fitness function and minimizes the violation measure which allows it to find the optima located on the boundaries of feasible regions. Moreover, IDEA is able to approach these optima from both sides, i.e. from a feasible and an infeasible one, which typically speeds up the convergence [14]. Note that even though IDEA was initially dedicated to Stationary Optimization Problems (SOPs) it also has a potential of handling some DCOPs as it was indicated in [8].

Taking into account the above-mentioned pros of IDEA, the IDEA-ARIMA was meant to be a proactive EA that would hybridize the robust constraint handling mechanism guaranteed by IDEA with a commonly used linear prediction model called Auto-Regressive Integrated Moving Average (ARIMA) [12] applied for anticipating the most probable future fitness values. This conglomerate was believed to form a powerful tool able to solve DCOPs effectively. Despite the fact that some experimental results presented in [13] were very promising, they also revealed the two weakest points of IDEA-ARIMA which are the considerable computational cost and the huge memory demands.

Let us now shed some light on the anticipation strategy used in IDEA-ARIMA in order to indicate the sources of the two main drawbacks of this EA. First of all, in this approach a dynamism of the environment is perceived through the recurrent evaluations of a set of samples $S \subset \mathbb{R}^d$ $(d > 0)$. Every sample $s \in S$ is associated with the time series of its past evaluations $(X_t^s)_{t \in T}$, i.e.

$$\forall_{t \leq t_{now}} \quad X_t^s = F^{(t)}(s). \tag{2}$$

In other words, all the historical values of the objective function $F$ for all the samples $s \in S$ up to the present moment $t_{now} \in T$ are collected and made available at any time. On the top of it, the ARIMA model is applied for predicting the future values of the objective function $\widetilde{X}_{t_{now}+1}^s = \widetilde{F}^{(t_{now}+1)}(s)$ based on the past observations $(X_t^s)_{t \leq t_{now}}$. As a result, the whole future landscape $\widetilde{F}^{(t_{now}+1)}$ can be anticipated by extrapolating the set

$$\{\widetilde{F}^{(t_{now}+1)}(s) ; \; s \in S\}, \tag{3}$$

using the $k > 0$ nearest neighbours method. The point is that the size of $S$ tends to grow extremely fast from one iteration of IDEA-ARIMA to another (cf. Algorithm 1) thus consuming more and more memory and additionally it requires an increasing number of invocations of the evaluation function for keeping all the samples up-to-date with the environment.

---

**Algorithm 1.** Pseudo-code of IDEA-ARIMA.

---

$S_1 = \emptyset$
$P_1 = \text{RandomPopulation}()$
$\text{Evaluate}(P_1)$
**for** $t = 1 \rightarrow N_{gen}$ **do**
  **if** the function $F$ has changed **then**
    $\text{Re-evaluate}(P_t)$
    $S_t = S_t \cup P_t$
    $\text{Re-evaluate}(S_t \setminus P_t)$
    **if** $t - 1 > N_{train}$ **then**
      $P_t = \text{ReducePopulation}(P_t \cup \widetilde{P}_t)$
    **end if**
  **end if**
  $P_{t+1} = \text{IDEA}(P_t, F^{(t)}, N_{sub})$
  **if** $t > N_{train}$ **then**
    $\widetilde{P}_{t+1} = \text{RandomPopulation}()$
    $\widetilde{P}_{t+1} = \text{IDEA}(\widetilde{P}_{t+1}, \widetilde{F}^{(t+1)}, N_{sub})$
  **end if**
  $S_{t+1} = S_t$
**end for**

---

Secondly, a proper use of the information concerning the anticipated future landscape gathered by IDEA-ARIMA is assured by introducing a *predictive* population $\widetilde{P}_{t+1}$ which comprises of $M > 0$ individuals being evolved separately from a *regular* population $P_t$ and evaluated with the anticipated future fitness function $\widetilde{F}^{(t+1)}$ instead of $F^{(t)}$. Later on, when the next time interval begins (i.e. $t \leftarrow t + 1$), the individuals from the predictive population are immediately transferred to $P_t$ so that the EA could begin to explore the newest promising regions straight away. Nevertheless, the anticipation mechanism firstly requires some historical data in order to provide accurate forecasts about $\widetilde{F}^{(t+1)}$ thus for the initial $N_{train} > 0$ generations it is only fed with data $(X_t^s)_{t \leq N_{train}}$ for $s \in S$ and produces no outputs. Although, from the efficacy perspective, after this presumably short period, an emergence of the predictive population appears to be a yet another source of increase in the computational cost since these individuals also require evaluations (although without essentially invoking the evaluation function $F^{(t)}$) and an application of some evolutionary operators.

The entire pseudo-code of IDEA-ARIMA is given in Algorithm 1. It begins with generating the population $P_1$ by picking up randomly $M > 0$ individuals and taking the empty set of samples $S_1$. Then the main loop of the EA is run for $N_{gen} > 0$ generations. Whenever a change of the objective function $F^{(t)}$ is detected (i.e. the evaluation of at least one of the randomly chosen individuals has just changed), the whole population $P_t$ is re-evaluated and then added to the set of samples $S_t$. Providing that the training period of the anticipation mechanism $t = 1, 2, \ldots, N_{train}$ is over, and thus the population $\widetilde{P}_t$ is ready, the individuals from $P_t$ and $\widetilde{P}_t$ are grouped together and immediately reduced to the fixed population size $M > 0$. Eventually, regardless the changes of $F^{(t)}$, the original IDEA is run for $0 < N_{sub} \ll N_{gen}$ iterations (those will be referred to as *subiterations*). Later on, the predictive population $\widetilde{P}_{t+1}$ is initialized randomly and evolved within the same number of $N_{sub}$ subiterations of IDEA however the anticipated objective function $\widetilde{F}^{(t+1)}$ is used here instead of $F^{(t)}$.

# 3   Proposed Modifications of IDEA-ARIMA

The two drawbacks of IDEA-ARIMA emphasised in the previous section can be overcome in a number of ways. A rather straightforward one would be to simply bound the set of samples $S$ and suggest a strategy for keeping it up-to-date with the environment. Some ideas concerning that approach will be discussed at first. A further modification proposed in this paper is a bit more complex. The idea behind it is to modify the model of spreading the information about the anticipated future objective function. Instead of introducing a whole predictive population $\widetilde{P}$ and evolving it separately, a single sample that currently has the highest anticipated fitness $\widetilde{F}$ can be selected out of the finite set $S$ in order to deliver that information into the population $P$. However, this scenario can only succeed providing that the forecast is accurate. Otherwise it could significantly deteriorate the performance of the EA. This risk can be minimized by introducing a *small* fraction of individuals located near the estimated future optimum and additionally another *small* fraction of random immigrants spread uniformly across the search space. In this case, though, the proper sizes of *small* fractions would remain an open issue. That is why the mechanism for auto-adaptation of these fraction sizes will be introduced further in this section.

### 3.1  Bounded Set of Samples

IDEA-ARIMA assumes that the set of samples $S$ grows from generation to generation by 0 up to $M$ new elements, where $M > 0$ is the size of a population $P$. It is the consequence of the operation presented in the 7th line of Algorithm 1 that reads $S_t = S_t \cup P_t$. It is tempting to get rid of this operation and instead select randomly $M$ samples during the initialization step and stick to them throughout the whole run. Unfortunately, this leads to rather mediocre results. However, the set $S$ can still be bounded to $M$ elements providing that the least contributing samples are removed any time $S$ exceeds its maximum size. In terms of time series analysis, the least contributing samples can be those with the longest history trail (i.e. the oldest ones) since they are most likely to become over-learnt. For the scope of this paper let us refer to this slightly modified IDEA-ARIMA with a set of samples $S$ permanently bounded to $M$ as IDEA-ARIMA $M$.

### 3.2  Small Fractions Instead of Predictive Population

After the training period (i.e. for $t > N_{train}$) IDEA-ARIMA essentially maintains two populations, namely $P_t$ and $\widetilde{P}_{t+1}$, each of which needs to be evolved and evaluated separately. As a result, the computational time is doubled. Now, that we have bounded the set of samples, it can be more efficient to simply compare all of the anticipated fitness values and select a sample $s^* \in S$ such that $s^* = \arg\min\{\widetilde{F}^{(t+1)}(s)\,;\ s \in S\}$. Of course, introducing a single sample into $P_t$ may be not enough in order to move the population towards it, especially that the foreseen fitness value $\widetilde{F}^{t+1}(s^*)$ is likely to be slightly distorted. To alleviate that, a whole fraction of individuals concentrated around $s^*$ can be introduced instead. Let us call it the *anticipating fraction*. Probably the most appropriate way of generating the anticipating fraction is by using Gaussian distribution $\mathcal{N}(s_i^*, \varepsilon)$ where $i = 1, \ldots, d$ and $\varepsilon > 0$. Although, it is worth noticing that since a prediction population $\widetilde{P}_{t+1}$ in IDEA-ARIMA is always created from scratch hence it is evenly distributed across the search space. This in turn guarantees a safety buffer in case of the erroneous anticipation because there are dozens of randomly placed candidate solutions in $\widetilde{P}_{t+1}$ that may potentially attract the attention of individuals from $P_t$ while the two populations would be eventually grouped together. Fortunately, the same behaviour can be assured by introducing a fraction of random immigrants (let us call them the *exploring fraction*) into $P_t$ apart from the anticipating fraction described above. The point is that the proper sizes of these fractions, name them $0 < size_{anticip} < M$ for the anticipating fraction and $0 < size_{explore} < M$ for the exploring one, are strictly problem-dependent thus cannot be estimated once for all the possible cases. Finally, it has to be stated that the condition $size_{anticip} + size_{explore} < M$ must be satisfied for all time.

## 3.3  Auto-adaptation of Fraction Sizes

After introducing the two fractions defined above a population $P_t$ can be thought of as a mixture of the three subsets, namely $P_t^{anticip} \subset P_t$ built up of the anticipating fraction of $size_{anticip}$ individuals, $P_t^{explore} \subset P_t$ built up of the exploring fraction of $size_{explore}$ individuals, and the remaining $P_t^{exploit} = P_t \backslash (P_t^{anticip} \cup P_t^{explore})$ fraction of $size_{exploit} = M - size_{anticip} - size_{explore}$ individuals responsible for exploiting the promising regions identified so far.

---

**Algorithm 2.** Pseudo-code of UpdateFractionSizes($P_t$) procedure where $P_t = P_t^{explore} \cup P_t^{exploit} \cup P_t^{anticip}$ and $M =$ population size.

---

$(P_t^{best}, P_t^{medium}, P_t^{worst}) = \text{RankFractions}(P_t^{explore}, P_t^{exploit}, P_t^{anticip})$
$dist_{medium} = |\text{BestEvaluation}(P_t^{best}) - \text{BestEvaluation}(P_t^{medium})|$
$dist_{worst} = |\text{BestEvaluation}(P_t^{best}) - \text{BestEvaluation}(P_t^{worst})|$
$size_{best} = \min \{size_{max}, size_{best} + \delta\}$
$size_{medium} = \max \left\{ size_{min}, (M - size_{best}) \cdot \frac{dist_{worst}}{dist_{worst} + dist_{medium}} \right\}$
$size_{worst} = M - size_{best} - size_{medium}$

---

**Algorithm 3.** Pseudo-code of mIDEA-ARIMA.

---

$S_1 = \text{RandomSamples}()$
$P_1 = \text{RandomPopulation}()$
$\text{Evaluate}(P_1)$
**for** $t = 1 \rightarrow N_{gen}$ **do**
  **if** the function $F$ has changed **then**
    $\text{Re-evaluate}(P_t)$
    $S_t = \text{ReduceSamples}(S_t \cup P_t, M)$
    $\text{Re-evaluate}(S_t \backslash P_t)$
    **if** $t - 1 > N_{train}$ **then**
      $P_t^{exploit} = \text{ReducePopulation}(P_t, size_{exploit})$
      $P_t = P_t^{explore} \cup P_t^{exploit} \cup P_t^{anticip}$
      $(size_{explore}, size_{exploit}, size_{anticip}) = \text{UpdateFractionSizes}(P_t)$
    **end if**
  **end if**
  $P_{t+1} = \text{IDEA}(P_t, F^{(t)}, N_{sub})$
  **if** $t > N_{train}$ **then**
    $s_t^* = \text{BestSample}(S_t, \widetilde{F}^{(t+1)})$
    $P_{t+1}^{anticip} = \text{AnticipatingFraction}(s_t^*, size_{anticip})$
    $P_{t+1}^{explore} = \text{ExploringFraction}(size_{explore})$
  **end if**
  $S_{t+1} = S_t$
**end for**

---

At first, all the fraction sizes are assumed equal $size_{explore} = size_{exploit} = size_{anticip} = M/3$ yet after the training period of $N_{train}$ generations those can be adapted automatically. The updating rule is presented in Algorithm 2. It begins with finding a single best individual per fraction as its representative. Then, all the three fractions are given labels adequate to the fitness of their respective representatives. The fraction containing the best representative is labeled *best*, the second best is labeled *medium* and the last one—*worst*. Next, the size of the *best* fraction is increased by $0 < \delta \ll M$. The remaining $M - size_{best}$ "vacant slots" are disposed between the *medium* and *worst* fractions proportionally to the differences in fitness of their representatives and the representative of the *best* fraction. Clearly, all the three sizes must sum up to $M$. They are also restricted to the range $[size_{min}, size_{max}]$ where $0 < size_{min} < size_{max} < M$ in order to prevent from the excessive domination of a certain fraction causing the exclusion of the others. The suggested values of parameters used in UpdateFractionSizes procedure are $\delta = 10\% \times M$, $size_{min} = \delta$ and $size_{max} = M - \delta$.

### 3.4   mIDEA-ARIMA

A pseudo-code of the modified IDEA-ARIMA algorithm (abbreviated to mIDEA-ARIMA) is given in Algorithm 3. It differs from the original IDEA-ARIMA in few places. First of all, it begins with a non-empty set $S_1$ containing of $M$ randomly selected samples. Secondly, after the training period is over, it picks up a best sample $s_t^*$ out of $S_t$ in each generation by taking into account the anticipated fitness values $\widetilde{F}^{(t+1)}$. Then, it prepares the anticipating fraction $P_{t+1}^{anticip}$ concentrated around $s_t^*$ and the exploring fraction $P_{t+1}^{explore}$ uniformly distributed across the search space. Finally, during the next time step (providing that the landscape has changed since the last iteration) it reduces the set of samples $S_t \cup P_t$ to the maximum number of $M$ elements and also reduces the population $P_t$ into $size_{anticip}$ individuals. Later on, it composes the new population out of the three fractions $P_{explore}$, $P_{exploit}$, $P_{anticip}$ and updates their respective sizes for the next generation.

## 4   Experiments

The experiments were performed on the following benchmark problems.

*Benchmarks G24* [2] Minimize the function

(a) *G24_1, G24_6c*

$$F^{(t)}(x) = -\left[\sin\left(k\pi t + \frac{\pi}{2}\right) \cdot x_1 + x_2\right],$$

(b) *G24_2*

$$F^{(t)}(x) = -\left[p_1(t) \cdot x_1 + p_2(t) \cdot x_2\right],$$

$$p_1(t) = \begin{cases} \sin\left(\frac{k\pi t}{2} + \frac{\pi}{2}\right), t \mid 2 \\ p_1(t-1), \quad t \nmid 2 \end{cases}, \quad p_2(t) = \begin{cases} p_2(\max\{0, t-1\}), t \mid 2 \\ \sin\left(\frac{k\pi(t-1)}{2} + \frac{\pi}{2}\right), t \nmid 2 \end{cases}$$

(c) *G24_8b*

$$F^{(t)}(x) = -3\exp\left\{-\left[(p_1(t) - x_1)^2 + (p_2(t) - x_2)^2\right]^{\frac{1}{4}}\right\},$$

$$p_1(t) = 1.4706 + 0.8590 \cdot \cos(k\pi t), \quad p_2(t) = 3.4420 + 0.8590 \cdot \sin(k\pi t)$$

subject to

(a) *G24_1, G24_2, G24_8b*

$$G_1(x) = 2x_1^4 - 8x_1^3 + 8x_1^2 - x_2 + 2 \geq 0,$$
$$G_2(x) = 4x_1^4 - 32x_1^3 + 88x_1^2 - 96x_1 - x_2 + 36 \geq 0,$$

(b) *G24_6c*

$$G_1(x) = 2x_1 + 3x_2 - 9$$
$$G_2(x) = \begin{cases} -1 \text{ if } x_1 \in [0, 1] \cup [2, 3] \\ 1 \text{ otherwise} \end{cases}$$

where $x = (x_1, x_2) \in [0, 3] \times [0, 4]$, $t \in \mathbb{N}_+$ and $0 \leq k \leq 2$.

*Benchmark mFDA1* [13] Minimize the function

$$F^{(t)}(x) = 1 - \sqrt{\frac{x_1}{1 + \sum_{i=2}^{n} \left(x_i - \sin\left(\frac{\pi t}{4}\right)\right)^2}}$$

subject to

$$G_j(x) = \frac{3[x_2 - \frac{1}{2}(\alpha_j + \beta_j)]^2}{2(\alpha_j - \beta_j)^2} - x_1 + \frac{1}{4} \geq 0,$$

$$\alpha_j = \sin\left(\frac{\pi(j+1)}{4}\right), \quad \beta_j = \sin\left(\frac{\pi(j+1)}{4}\right), \quad j \in \{1, 2, 3, 4\}.$$

where $x = (x_1, x_2) \in [0, 1] \times [-1, 1]$ and $t \in \mathbb{N}_+$.

Each of the above benchmarks was run in the three severity variants $k \in \{0.1, 0.25, 0.5\}$ and four frequency variants expressed as a number of subiterations between consecutive environmental changes $N_{sub} \in \{1, 2, 5, 10\}$.

The compared algorithms were split into the three groups.

1. IDEA with:
   - re-initialization of a population each time a change of the landscape is detected (further referred to as *IDEA reset*),
   - introduction of a fixed-sized exploring fraction (*IDEA explore*),
   - introduction of an exploring fraction of the size adapted online according to the UpdateFractionSizes procedure yet without the anticipating fraction (*IDEA adapt*).

2. IDEA-ARIMA with:
   - the set of samples bounded to $M$ (*IDEA-ARIMA M*),
   - the set of samples bounded to $2M$ (*IDEA-ARIMA 2M*),
   - the unbounded set of samples (*IDEA-ARIMA $\infty$*).
3. mIDEA-ARIMA with:
   - non-empty anticipation fraction and empty exploring fraction (*mIDEA-ARIMA anticip*),
   - non-empty anticipation fraction and non-empty exploring fraction (*mIDEA-ARIMA anticip/explore*),
   - non-empty anticipation fraction and non-empty exploring fraction of the sizes adapted online according to the UpdateFractionSizes procedure (*mIDEA-ARIMA adapt*).

Tables 1, 2 and 3 summarize the offline performances obtained for all the analyzed benchmark functions with severity regulator $k$ set to 0.1, 0.25 and 0.5 respectively. The results are averaged over 50 independent runs each of which lasted for $N_{gen} = 100$ generations. In the cases with fixed-sized fractions, the optimal sizes are given in brackets, e.g. (0.7) means $size_{explore} = 0.7 \times M$ while (0.1/0.6) stands for $size_{anticip} = 0.1 \times M$ and $size_{explore} = 0.6 \times M$.

It is clearly seen that *mIDEA-ARIMA anticip/explore* outperformed the other algorithms in nearly all the cases. Particularly, it gave better results than *IDEA-ARIMA $\infty$* even though the latter required more evaluations and memory. It also turned out that even the simplest modification including only a bounding of $S$ resulted in fairly good offline performances. A comparison with *IDEA-ARIMA 2M* revealed that doubling the maximum size of $S$ gave satisfactory results only in cases with greater $N_{sub}$ values.

**Table 1.** Offline performances averaged over 50 independent runs with $k = 0.1$.

| Bench | $N_{sub}$ | IDEA | | | IDEA-ARIMA | | | mIDEA-ARIMA | | |
|---|---|---|---|---|---|---|---|---|---|---|
| | | Reset | Explore | Adapt | M | 2M | $\infty$ | Anticip | Anticip/explore | Adapt |
| G24_1 | 1 | −3.34 | −3.66 (0.7) | −3.47 | −3.62 | −3.33 | −3.67 | −3.73 (0.4) | **−3.80** (0.1/0.6) | −3.70 |
| | 2 | −3.42 | −3.71 (0.7) | −3.60 | −3.60 | −3.42 | −3.70 | −3.74 (0.3) | **−3.81** (0.1/0.6) | −3.77 |
| | 5 | −3.56 | −3.75 (0.7) | −3.72 | −3.37 | −3.58 | −3.73 | −3.75 (0.3) | **−3.83** (0.1/0.6) | −3.81 |
| | 10 | −3.69 | −3.80 (0.9) | −3.80 | −3.39 | −3.66 | −3.74 | −3.76 (0.4) | **−3.84** (0.3/0.7) | −3.83 |
| G24_2 | 1 | −1.45 | −1.69 (0.7) | −1.54 | −1.69 | −1.62 | −1.68 | −1.68 (0.7) | **−1.73** (0.1/0.5) | −1.70 |
| | 2 | −1.50 | −1.71 (0.7) | −1.61 | −1.69 | −1.66 | −1.69 | −1.68 (0.2) | **−1.73** (0.2/0.4) | −1.71 |
| | 5 | −1.62 | −1.74 (0.7) | −1.71 | −1.66 | −1.69 | −1.70 | −1.69 (0.4) | **−1.75** (0.1/0.4) | −1.72 |
| | 10 | −1.70 | **−1.76** (0.7) | −1.75 | −1.69 | −1.71 | −1.72 | −1.70 (0.3) | **−1.76** (0.2/0.3) | −1.73 |
| G24_6c | 1 | −2.86 | −3.07 (0.6) | −2.93 | −3.05 | −2.97 | −3.11 | −3.10 (0.1) | **−3.13** (0.2/0.2) | −3.09 |
| | 2 | −2.92 | −3.13 (0.6) | −3.02 | −2.94 | −2.92 | −3.14 | −3.02 (0.6) | **−3.15** (0.1/0.5) | −3.12 |
| | 5 | −3.04 | −3.15 (0.7) | −3.12 | −2.66 | −2.94 | −3.06 | −2.98 (1.0) | **−3.16** (0.1/0.6) | −3.15 |
| | 10 | −3.13 | **−3.17** (0.7) | −3.16 | −2.74 | −2.98 | −3.07 | −2.99 (0.8) | **−3.17** (0.1/0.7) | **−3.17** |
| G24_8b | 1 | −1.30 | −1.52 (0.7) | −1.37 | −1.52 | −1.33 | −1.58 | −1.57 (0.4) | **−1.63** (0.1/0.6) | −1.58 |
| | 2 | −1.37 | −1.56 (0.7) | −1.47 | −1.54 | −1.41 | −1.62 | −1.59 (0.5) | **−1.65** (0.1/0.7) | −1.62 |
| | 5 | −1.50 | −1.62 (0.7) | −1.59 | −1.53 | −1.53 | −1.68 | −1.63 (0.5) | **−1.68** (0.1/0.7) | −1.67 |
| | 10 | −1.61 | −1.68 (0.7) | −1.68 | −1.58 | −1.62 | **−1.71** | −1.66 (0.5) | **−1.71** (0.2/0.6) | −1.70 |
| mFDA1 | 1 | 0.12 | 0.06 (0.7) | 0.10 | 0.05 | 0.05 | 0.05 | 0.04 (0.4) | **0.03** (0.3/0.4) | 0.05 |
| | 2 | 0.09 | 0.05 (0.7) | 0.08 | 0.04 | 0.04 | 0.04 | 0.03 (0.6) | **0.02** (0.4/0.4) | 0.03 |
| | 5 | 0.05 | 0.04 (0.7) | 0.04 | 0.04 | 0.04 | 0.02 | 0.02 (0.7) | **0.01** (0.3/0.5) | 0.02 |
| | 10 | 0.03 | 0.02 (0.7) | 0.03 | 0.04 | 0.03 | **0.01** | **0.01** (1.0) | **0.01** (0.2/0.6) | **0.01** |

**Table 2.** Offline performances averaged over 50 independent runs with $k = 0.25$.

| Bench | $N_{sub}$ | IDEA | | | IDEA-ARIMA | | | mIDEA-ARIMA | | |
|---|---|---|---|---|---|---|---|---|---|---|
| | | Reset | Explore | Adapt | M | 2M | ∞ | Anticip | Anticip/explore | Adapt |
| G24_1 | 1 | −3.33 | −3.58 (0.4) | −3.41 | −3.52 | −3.31 | −3.59 | −3.72 (0.8) | **−3.76** (0.1/0.5) | −3.70 |
| | 2 | −3.40 | −3.62 (0.7) | −3.53 | −3.49 | −3.35 | −3.67 | −3.73 (0.8) | **−3.77** (0.1/0.6) | −3.74 |
| | 5 | −3.54 | −3.65 (0.7) | −3.64 | −3.37 | −3.45 | −3.76 | −3.72 (0.7) | **−3.78** (0.2/0.6) | −3.77 |
| | 10 | −3.67 | −3.75 (0.9) | −3.74 | −3.38 | −3.60 | −3.79 | −3.74 (0.8) | **−3.80** (0.2/0.8) | −3.79 |
| G24_2 | 1 | −1.57 | −1.71 (0.7) | −1.59 | −1.62 | −1.47 | −1.53 | -1.63 (0.5) | **−1.81** (0.1/0.6) | −1.78 |
| | 2 | −1.60 | −1.74 (0.7) | −1.65 | −1.61 | −1.49 | −1.55 | −1.59 (0.6) | **−1.82** (0.3/0.7) | −1.78 |
| | 5 | −1.72 | −1.80 (0.7) | −1.76 | −1.49 | −1.61 | −1.60 | −1.61 (0.6) | **−1.84** (0.1/0.7) | −1.77 |
| | 10 | −1.80 | −1.83 (0.7) | −1.83 | 1.64 | 1.75 | −1.68 | −1.68 (0.6) | **−1.85** (0.7/0.3) | −1.77 |
| G24_6c | 1 | −2.84 | **−3.06** (0.5) | −2.87 | −3.04 | −3.00 | −3.03 | −2.95 (0.1) | **−3.06** (0.1/0.5) | −3.02 |
| | 2 | −2.90 | −3.07 (0.5) | −2.96 | −3.01 | −3.03 | −3.09 | −2.94 (1.0) | **−3.10** (0.1/0.6) | −3.06 |
| | 5 | −3.02 | −3.09 (0.7) | −3.07 | −2.62 | −2.95 | **−3.13** | −2.94 (0.8) | −3.11 (0.1/0.7) | −3.10 |
| | 10 | −3.11 | −3.13 (0.9) | −3.13 | −2.60 | −2.92 | −3.13 | −2.88 (1.0) | **−3.14** (0.1/0.9) | −3.13 |
| G24_8b | 1 | −1.31 | −1.44 (0.7) | −1.35 | −1.41 | −1.24 | −1.51 | −1.43 (0.6) | **−1.55** (0.1/0.6) | −1.48 |
| | 2 | −1.37 | −1.46 (0.7) | −1.42 | −1.39 | −1.27 | −1.57 | −1.47 (0.6) | **−1.60** (0.1/0.7) | −1.55 |
| | 5 | −1.50 | −1.54 (0.9) | −1.54 | −1.33 | −1.35 | −1.57 | −1.50 (0.5) | **−1.64** (0.3/0.7) | −1.62 |
| | 10 | −1.61 | −1.64 (0.9) | −1.65 | −1.41 | −1.46 | −1.61 | −1.55 (0.4) | **−1.70** (0.1/0.7) | −1.69 |
| mFDA1 | 1 | 0.12 | 0.08 (0.7) | 0.11 | 0.08 | 0.08 | 0.07 | 0.09 (0.8) | **0.06** (0.1/0.7) | 0.08 |
| | 2 | 0.09 | 0.07 (0.7) | 0.09 | 0.08 | 0.06 | **0.05** | 0.08 (0.6) | **0.05** (0.1/0.7) | 0.07 |
| | 5 | 0.05 | 0.04 (0.7) | 0.05 | 0.09 | 0.06 | **0.03** | 0.07 (0.4) | 0.04 (0.1/0.7) | 0.05 |
| | 10 | 0.02 | 0.02 (0.7) | 0.02 | 0.09 | 0.06 | **0.01** | 0.07 (0.9) | 0.02 (0.1/0.9) | 0.04 |

**Table 3.** Offline performances averaged over 50 independent runs with $k = 0.5$.

| Bench | $N_{sub}$ | IDEA | | | IDEA-ARIMA | | | mIDEA-ARIMA | | |
|---|---|---|---|---|---|---|---|---|---|---|
| | | Reset | Explore | Adapt | M | 2M | ∞ | Anticip | Anticip/explore | Adapt |
| G24_1 | 1 | −3.30 | **−3.64** (0.6) | −3.41 | −3.49 | −3.43 | **−3.64** | −3.40 (0.3) | **−3.64** (0.1/0.6) | −3.54 |
| | 2 | −3.37 | −3.64 (0.6) | −3.49 | −3.45 | −3.43 | −3.65 | −3.42 (0.3) | **−3.66** (0.1/0.6) | −3.60 |
| | 5 | −3.51 | −3.59 (0.7) | −3.56 | −3.43 | −3.41 | **−3.68** | −3.44 (0.1) | −3.65 (0.1/0.7) | −3.62 |
| | 10 | −3.63 | −3.68 (0.8) | −3.67 | −3.40 | −3.45 | −3.64 | −3.44 (0.5) | **−3.70** (0.1/0.7) | −3.67 |
| G24_2 | 1 | −1.55 | −1.63 (0.7) | −1.56 | −1.51 | −1.40 | −1.28 | −1.43 (0.7) | **−1.72** (0.1/0.7) | −1.69 |
| | 2 | −1.59 | −1.64 (0.7) | −1.61 | −1.49 | −1.45 | −1.30 | −1.40 (0.2) | **−1.74** (0.2/0.7) | −1.70 |
| | 5 | −1.69 | −1.71 (0.7) | −1.71 | −1.37 | −1.51 | −1.32 | −1.28 (0.9) | **−1.77** (0.3/0.7) | −1.70 |
| | 10 | −1.76 | −1.77 (0.9) | −1.77 | −1.47 | −1.62 | −1.34 | −1.40 (0.9) | **−1.79** (0.3/0.7) | −1.71 |
| G24_6c | 1 | −2.92 | −3.12 (0.6) | −2.93 | −2.95 | −2.88 | −3.10 | −2.98 (0.3) | **−3.13** (0.1/0.5) | −3.10 |
| | 2 | −2.97 | −3.16 (0.6) | −3.02 | −2.99 | −2.99 | −3.12 | −2.99 (0.4) | **−3.17** (0.1/0.6) | −3.14 |
| | 5 | −3.10 | −3.17 (0.7) | −3.13 | −3.00 | −3.00 | −3.04 | −3.00 (0.2) | **−3.18** (0.1/0.7) | −3.16 |
| | 10 | −3.20 | **−3.22** (0.7) | −3.21 | −3.01 | −3.01 | −3.04 | −3.01 (0.1) | **−3.22** (0.1/0.7) | −3.21 |
| G24_8b | 1 | −1.33 | −1.48 (0.7) | −1.38 | −1.42 | −1.29 | −1.51 | −1.30 (0.2) | **−1.59** (0.1/0.7) | −1.48 |
| | 2 | −1.41 | −1.50 (0.7) | −1.47 | −1.38 | −1.30 | **−1.63** | −1.33 (0.1) | −1.56 (0.1/0.7) | −1.52 |
| | 5 | −1.59 | −1.59 (0.9) | −1.59 | −1.34 | −1.34 | **−1.72** | −1.37 (0.4) | −1.62 (0.1/0.8) | −1.59 |
| | 10 | −1.74 | −1.74 (0.9) | −1.74 | −1.37 | −1.45 | **−1.77** | −1.41 (0.3) | −1.74 (0.1/0.9) | −1.70 |
| mFDA1 | 1 | 0.12 | **0.07** (0.7) | 0.13 | 0.08 | 0.08 | **0.07** | 0.15 (0.2) | **0.07** (0.1/0.7) | 0.10 |
| | 2 | 0.10 | 0.07 (0.7) | 0.10 | 0.07 | **0.06** | **0.06** | 0.15 (0.5) | 0.07 (0.1/0.7) | 0.09 |
| | 5 | 0.05 | 0.05 (1.0) | 0.05 | 0.07 | 0.07 | **0.04** | 0.16 (0.3) | 0.05 (0.1/0.9) | 0.09 |
| | 10 | **0.01** | **0.01** (1.0) | **0.01** | 0.09 | 0.09 | 0.02 | 0.15 (0.5) | **0.01** (0.1/0.9) | 0.08 |

Figure 1 presents the results of 50 runs of those algorithms that do not require a prior estimation of proper fraction sizes. After each run the winning algorithm scored +3 points, the second best +2 points and the third best +1 point. It can be seen that *mIDEA-ARIMA adapt* performed best in many cases, especially in rapidly changing environments. It also has to be mentioned that in this comparison *IDEA-ARIMA M* again proved its surprising effectiveness.

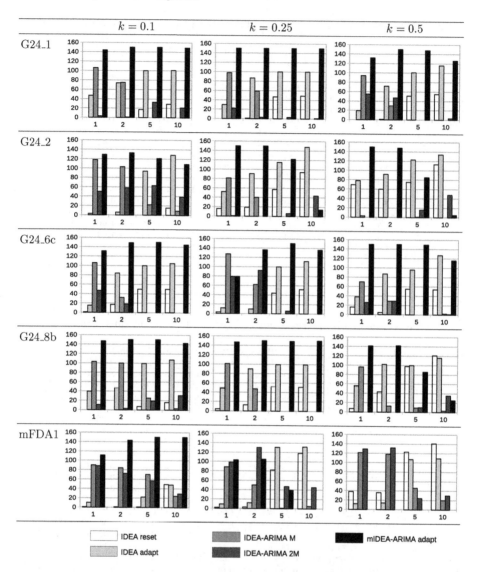

**Fig. 1.** Results of 50 runs of algorithms not requiring a prior estimation of proper fraction sizes. Each winning algorithm scored +3 points, the second best +2 points and the third best +1 point.

## 5 Conclusions

In this paper a number of modifications of IDEA-ARIMA were proposed. The introduced mIDEA-ARIMA proved its potential in solving DCOPs although it increased the space of possible input parameters of the EA. To alleviate that issue the online auto-adaptation mechanism was suggested.

The experiments performed on the popular benchmark problems revealed the superiority of mIDEA-ARIMA over the original IDEA-ARIMA in terms of the offline performance, a number of evaluations and a memory consumption.

# References

1. Branke, J.: Evolutionary Optimization in Dynamic Environments. Kluwer, Norwell (2002)
2. Nguyen, T., Yao, X.: Benchmarking and solving dynamic constrained problems. In: Proceedings of the IEEE Congress on Evolutionary Computation (CEC 2009), pp. 690–697 (2009)
3. Nguyen, T., Yao, X.: Continuous dynamic constrained optimisation - the challenges. IEEE Trans. Evol. Comput. **16**, 769–786 (2012)
4. Yang, S., Yao, X.: Evolutionary Computation for Dynamic Optimization Problems. SCI, vol. 490. Springer, Heidelberg (2013)
5. Aragón, V.S., Esquivel, S.C.: An evolutionary algorithm to track changes of optimum value locations in dynamic environments. J. Comput. Sci. Technol. **4**(3), 127–134 (2004)
6. Liu, X., Wu, Y., Ye, J.: An improved estimation of distribution algorithm in dynamic environments. In: Proceedings of the 4th International Conference on Natural Computing (ICNC 2008), pp. 269–272 (2008)
7. Tinós, R., Yang, S.: A self-organizing random immigrants genetic algorithm for dynamic optimization problems. Genet. Program. Evolvable Mach. **8**(3), 255–286 (2007)
8. Singh, H.K., Isaacs, A., Nguyen, T.T., Ray, T., Yao, X.: Performance of infeasibility driven evolutionary algorithm (IDEA) on constrained dynamic single objective optimization problems. In: Proceedings of the IEEE Congress on Evolutionary Computation (CEC 2009), pp. 3127–3134 (2009)
9. Hatzakis, I., Wallace, D., Dynamic multi-objective optimization with evolutionary algorithms: a forward-looking approach. In: Proceedings of the 8th Annual Conference on Genetic and Evolutionary Computation (GECCO 2006), pp. 1201–1208 (2006)
10. Bosman, P.A.N.: Learning and anticipation in online dynamic optimization. In: Yang, S., Ong, Y.-S., Jin, Y. (eds.) Evolutionary Computation in Dynamic and Uncertain Environments. SCI, vol. 51, pp. 129–152. Springer, Heidelberg (2007)
11. Simões, A., Costa, E.: Evolutionary algorithms for dynamic environments: prediction using linear regression and Markov chains. In: Rudolph, G., Jansen, T., Lucas, S., Poloni, C., Beume, N. (eds.) PPSN 2008. LNCS, vol. 5199, pp. 306–315. Springer, Heidelberg (2008)
12. Box, G.E.P., Jenkins, G.M., Reinsel, G.C.: Time Series Analysis: Forecasting and Control. Wiley, New York (2013). Wiley.com
13. Filipiak, P., Michalak, K., Lipinski, P.: Infeasibility driven evolutionary algorithm with ARIMA-based prediction mechanism. In: Yin, H., Wang, W., Rayward-Smith, V. (eds.) IDEAL 2011. LNCS, vol. 6936, pp. 345–352. Springer, Heidelberg (2011)
14. Singh, H.K., Isaacs, A., Ray, T., Smith, W.: Infeasibility driven evolutionary algorithm for constrained optimization. In: Mezura-Montes, E. (ed.) Constraint Handling in Evolutionary Optimization. SCI, vol. 198, pp. 145–165. Springer, Heidelberg (2009)
15. Deb, K., Pratap, A., Agarwal, A., Meyarivan, T.: A fast and elitist multiobjective genetic algorithm: NSGA-II. IEEE Trans. Evol. Comput. **6**, 182–197 (2002)

# General

# A Concept for Real-Valued Multi-objective Landscape Analysis Characterizing Two Biochemical Optimization Problems

Susanne Rosenthal and Markus Borschbach[(⊠)]

Chair of Optimized Systems, Faculty of Computer Science,
University of Applied Sciences, FHDW,
Hauptstr. 2, 51465 Bergisch Gladbach, Germany
{Susanne.Rosenthal,Markus.Borschbach}@fhdw.de

**Abstract.** Landscape analysis is an established method to provide an insight into the characteristic properties of an optimization problem with the aim of designing a suitable evolutionary algorithm for a given problem. However, these conventional landscape structures require sophisticated notions for multi-objective optimization problems. This work presents a real-valued multi-objective landscape analysis concept that allows the investigation of multi-objective molecular optimization problems. Sophisticated definitions for ruggedness, correlation and plateaus on multi-objective real-valued landscapes are introduced and indicators are proposed for this purpose. This landscape concept is realized on a generic three- and four-dimensional biochemical minimization problem and the results of this analysis are discussed regarding the design principles of a multi-objective evolutionary algorithm.

**Keywords:** Real-valued multi-objective landscape · Molecular landscape · Analysis concept · MOEA design

## 1 Introduction

The design of a Multi-Objective Evolutionary Algorithm (MOEA) for a specific class of optimization problems requires the knowledge of the landscape characteristics [1] to tune the algorithm for an increased search performance. The use of MOEAs for molecule optimization has increased significantly, but the general understanding of the molecular landscape properties with the aim of designing an appropriate MOEA to search the molecular space is missing [2]. The analysis of the landscape structure provides information about the landscape characteristics and difficulties of molecular optimization problems. This information provides a better insight into the composition of a search performance optimized MOEA regarding a particular type of algorithm, the types of variation operators and the selection pressure for a suitable balance of global and local search behavior. Nevertheless, it is known that the fitness landscape structure influences the EA performance and various techniques for statistical analysis as qualitative technique and information analysis as quantitative technique are proposed

© Springer International Publishing Switzerland 2015
A.M. Mora and G. Squillero (Eds.): EvoApplications 2015, LNCS 9028, pp. 897–909, 2015.
DOI: 10.1007/978-3-319-16549-3_72

(see [3] for an overview) to analyze single-objective fitness landscapes. In the case of multi-objective landscapes, the important landscape structures modality, ruggedness, correlation and plateaus have to be generalized or defined in a more sophisticated manner. A respectable amount of work has been done in the area of multi-objective landscape analysis for combinatorial optimization problems, e.g. assignment problems [1,4,5]. In [4], potentially useful indicators are discussed characterizing multi-objective landscapes: the modality is characterized by the number and distribution of global optima. From the multi-objective point of view, these global optima are a set of non-dominated or Pareto optimal solutions. The fitness distance correlation (FDC) in the case of single-objective landscapes is a correlation coefficient that indicates the distance between a set of local optima to the nearest global optima. Due to the generalization to multi-objective landscapes, non-dominated solutions (NDS) are considered as global optima. The critical point of this notion is that each of the NDS is the optimum of one single-objective function and therefore, the correlation between the NDS is not necessarily resembling to the correlation between different local optima of a single-objective function. However, the correlation between NDS provides useful information referring to a search process of MOEA moving along the Pareto front. Additionally, concepts are introduced by Garrett, which define other distance indicators: the Euclidean distance between the solutions or mathematically spoken between the fitness vectors or the angle between these fitness values as an alternative distance indicator. These proposed metrics have not been investigated empirically or theoretically so far. An intuitive definition for landscape ruggedness is also given by Garrett. The autocorrelation of the random walks between known Pareto optimal solutions is used to investigate the path ruggedness between the Pareto optima. A further elaboration of these concepts or empirical investigations are missing by today. [4]

A traditional and systematical molecular landscape analysis is presented in [2,8]. Herein, the purpose of the molecular landscape analysis is defined by the examination of the common principle -molecular structure similarity is often related to similar molecule properties- for the underlying optimization problem. Four molecular functions are analyzed separately according to the landscape properties modality, ruggedness, neutrality, local optima and basins. This landscape analysis is based on random walks of length 100 and 500 over a search space with a complexity of $23^5$ feasible peptides (5-mer peptides consisting of 23 amino acids). Feasible solutions are character strings of length 5, neighboring solutions differs in exactly one amino acids and one-point mutation is used as moving operator to explore the neighborhood.

In this work, a concept for multi-objective landscape analysis is proposed with the aim of analyzing a multi-objective molecular landscape (MOML), which involves the ideas of Garrett. The analysis results are used for design considerations of a MOEA with optimized search performance for the purpose of multi-objective biochemical optimization. This concept is based on the considerations of important properties modality, correlation, ruggedness and plateaus on real-valued multi-objective landscape. Sophisticated definitions of these landscape properties are presented and discussed. Furthermore, indicators are proposed for this purpose. These techniques are simple to calculate and most important - independent of the optimization problem dimension. This concept is applied on a generic three- and four-dimensional biochemical optimization problem and the results are interpreted according to the guidance of the search process of a MOEA.

## 2    A Concept for MOML Analysis

The evolution of a landscape analysis concept in general requires the determination of the fitness landscape components: the components of a fitness landscape are a set of genotypes (configuration of the solutions), the fitness functions which evaluate the genotypes and the genetic operators, which represent the move operator to explore the neighborhood. Stadler presented the formal description of the landscape composition [6]:

**Definition 1.** *A landscape consists of three ingredients: a set $X$ of configurations; a notation $X$ of the neighborhood, the nearness, distances or accessibility on $X$; and a fitness function $f : X \to \mathbb{R}$.*

A landscape analysis starts by specifying metrics that characterize the geometric properties. The selection of suitable metrics depends on the organization of the configuration space $X$ and has to take account of the optimization problem. Reidys and Stadler [7] stated three distinct approaches for the organization of $X$:

1. transition probabilities are used to describe the movement from one configuration to another. The process is describable by Markov chains and is especially applied in the case of combinatorial optimization problems.
2. in the field of computer sciences, genetic operators (mutation or recombination) are usually used as move operators to create new configurations.
3. rigorous mathematical analysis is performed by specified metrics or topologies on $X$.

The set $X$ comprises all feasible peptides and is given by a character string. According to [8,9], the neighborhood of a configuration is explored by one-point mutation as move operator and neighbored configurations are differing by exactly one amino acid or a character in the MOEA terminology. The one-point mutation is used as move operator for an insight into the mutation potential of a MOEA and to avoid highly differing consecutive configurations, which are potentially produced by a recombination operator. Small changes in the configurations provide information about the effectiveness of the local search of a MOEA. The organization of the configuration set refers to the second approach of Reidys and Stadler as the other approaches are unsuitable: The use of Markov chains is not advisable because of the general difficulty to efficiently design high complex spaces [10], which usually occurs in molecular spaces. Furthermore, $X$ allows no mathematical definitions of metrics of topologies.

**Modality.** The modality or the investigation of the optima density is examined based on measurements of the random walk part consisting only of the NDS or the individuals of the first front. The modality requests information about the number of NDS, a potential clustering of these or otherwise a large distribution over the MOML. For this purpose, the individuals of the random walk are ranked into fronts. For an Optima Distribution Analysis (ODA), the average Euclidean distance $d_{ODA}$ between all possible combinations of non-dominated fitness values $\boldsymbol{x}_i$ is determined:

$$d_{ODA} = \frac{1}{K} \sum_{i,j} d_{ij} \text{ with } d_{ij} = |\boldsymbol{x}_i - \boldsymbol{x}_j| \text{ for } i,j = 1, ..., M \text{ and } i < j, \quad (1)$$

where $M$ is the number of fitness vectors in the first front and $K = \binom{M}{2}$ the number of all possible combinations of differences $d_{ij}$. The value of $d_{ODA}$ is a measure for the central tendency of the non-dominated solution diversity. Otherwise, $d_{ODA}$ globally seen as mean value has its limitation in the case of extremal boundary values. Therefore, the diversity of the NDS is quantified via the average distance of all distances $d_{ij}$:

$$d_{MAD} = \frac{1}{K} \sum_{i,j} |d_{ij} - \bar{d}| \text{ with } i,j = 1, ..., M \text{ and } i < j. \quad (2)$$

with $\bar{d} = d_{ODA}$. The higher the diversity values, the wider is the spread of the NDS over the search space. In the case that the range of the objective function values are differing drastically, the use of the normalized Euclidean distance is advisable. Another indicator for the distribution of NDS is the measurement of the so-called 'beeline' between two consecutive NDS along the random walk path. Therefore, the magnitude of the beeline between two consecutive fitness vectors $\boldsymbol{x}_{i+1}$ and $\boldsymbol{x}_i$ is determined and is set in relation to $\bar{c} = \sum_{i=1,...,N-1} |\boldsymbol{y}_{i+1} - \boldsymbol{y}_i|$, the average Euclidean distance between two consecutive fitness vectors $\boldsymbol{y}_{i+1}$ and $\boldsymbol{y}_i$ of the random walk with $N$ as the number of random walk steps to classify the distribution tendency:

$$b_i = \frac{|\boldsymbol{x}_{i+1} - \boldsymbol{x}_i|}{\bar{c}} \text{ with } i,j = 1, ..., M - 1, \quad (3)$$

where $x_i$ are ordered according to their occurring in the random walk. A low number of $b_i$ indicates that the corresponding distance between the two consecutive NDS is relatively small compared to the average distance of all consecutive distances of the random walk.

**Correlation.** The correlation is a measure for the relationship between two configurations in the landscape. A correlation analysis of the single fitness functions provides some information about the correlation tendency of the corresponding fitness values. In the case of MOMLs, the correlation between the single molecular fitness functions is of great interest as the high correlation between two time series of different fitness functions theoretically reduces the optimization problem dimension and therefore the problem difficulty. The correlation matrix is a suitable analysis technique for this purpose:

$$M_{corr} = \begin{pmatrix} 1 & corr(f_1, f_2) & ... & corr(f_1, f_k) \\ corr(f_2, f_1) & 1 & ... & corr(f_2, f_k) \\ \vdots & \vdots & \ddots & \vdots \\ corr(f_k, f_1) & corr(f_k, f_2) & ... & 1 \end{pmatrix}, \tag{4}$$

where $M_{corr}$ is symmetrical and consists of the Pearson correlation coefficients of the fitness function $f_i$ and $f_j$:

$$corr(f_i, f_j) = \frac{\sum_{i=0}^{n}(f_i - \bar{f}) \cdot (f_j - \bar{f})}{\sigma_{f_i} \cdot \sigma_{f_j}} \tag{5}$$

In this context, the correlation coefficients lie in a range of $[-1; 1]$, where negative value symbolize a potential anti-proportional linear relationship and a positive value a possible proportional linear relationship. Furthermore, no or at least a low correlation is given by $|corr(x, y)| < 0.3$. A weak correlation is given by $0.3 \le |corr(x, y)| \le 0.8$ and $|corr(x, y)| > 0.8$ indicates a high linear correlation.

**Ruggedness.** The ruggedness refers to the relationship between each configuration and its neighbors. A landscape is said to be rugged if it reveals high varying fitness values, the greater the fitness differences the more rugged is the landscape. From this point of view, the analysis technique for MOML ruggedness is based on the difference vectors determined between each two consecutive fitness vectors of the random walk. A measure for the variation of the fitness vector values is the magnitude of the absolute value calculated of the difference vectors. The absolute value of the difference vectors provides an insight in the magnitude of differences between the single molecular fitness functions. A closer consideration of the absolute values as a measure for fitness difference leads to the insight that this value does not take account of the fitness variation of the single molecular fitness functions in the sense that potentially only a few of these fitness functions are responsible for a high absolute value. Furthermore, another view on the absolute value reveals that it is no indicator for the direction of the single molecular function moving and therefore no indicator for the increase, decrease or stagnation of the different fitness functions. These considerations lead in conclusion to a definition of ruggedness: a real-valued multi-objective fitness landscape is regarded as rugged if the single fitness functions are moving differently with high fitness differences. As a consequence, this landscape is regarded as smooth if all fitness functions are moving equally or only a very few of these functions are directed differently and with small fitness differences.

The information about the single fitness function directions are provided by the difference vectors between the consecutive fitness vectors. A suitable indicator for the direction of the difference vectors is the angle between the difference vectors as - in general - an angle between vectors is an indicator for similarity [9]:

$$similarity(\boldsymbol{x}, \boldsymbol{y}) = cos(\theta) = \frac{\boldsymbol{x} \cdot \boldsymbol{y}}{|\boldsymbol{x}| \cdot |\boldsymbol{y}|} \tag{6}$$

For the angle between two consecutive difference vectors, which provide information about the relative position of three consecutive fitness vectors and therefore of the fitness variance direction of a configuration and its neighbors along the random walk, the following geometrically interpretation is stated: an angle of 0 refers to two vectors pointing in the same direction. This implies, that the single fitness values of the consecutive random walk steps, which define these two difference vectors, are all positioned in the same direction. Otherwise, an angle of more than 90 indicates a moving to a large part of single fitness function in different directions. In the case of stagnating objective function values, the difference vector is the zero vector and the angle is not defined. In that case, the angle is set to 0.

Hence, to gain an insight into the potential ruggedness and structure of a MOML, the angle between every two consecutive difference vectors is calculated. Furthermore, the length of the random walk path consisting of the difference vectors, of which two forming an particular angle $\angle(x_{i+1}, x_i) = a$ with $a \in [0; 180]$ is determined to gain information about the magnitude of fitness differences. This path length allows no statistically reasonable interpretation as these values depend on the subspace dimension of the search space covered by the random walk steps. Therefore, this path length is set in relation to the number of random walk steps. The fitness vectors have been normalized to ensure comparative values.

$$p_{length} = \frac{\sum |x_{i+1}| + |x_i|}{2 \cdot (N - 1)}. \tag{7}$$

**Plateaus.** Another important structure of a landscape are the plateaus. The number and size distribution of plateaus are investigated by neutrality measures [2]. In MOML, plateaus are characterized in two different aspects: firstly, plateaus are characterized according to the stagnation of all objective functions values over several steps of the time series and secondly - in a more global view - according to the number of consecutive time series steps in the same Pareto front. The plateau characterization in the sense of objective function stagnation is determined via:

$$|x_{i+1} - x_i| \leq 1 \text{ for } i = 1, ..., N - 1. \tag{8}$$

## 3    Computational Landscape Analysis and Discussion

**Simulation Onsets.** Short peptide sequences of a length of 20 consisting of 20 canonical amino acids constitute the search space. Therefore, the search space has a complexity of $20^{20}$ feasible solutions and is further discrete for the proposed physiochemical fitness functions as there are real-valued solution vectors which have no corresponding configurations in the search space. The MOML analysis is performed via random walks with one-point mutation to investigate the neighbored molecular landscape. The mutation of the same amino acid is excluded to avoid a stagnation of the random walk. The start configuration of

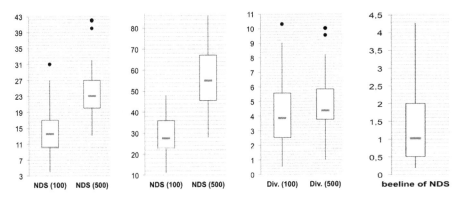

**Fig. 1.** No. of NDS (3D-MOML).    **Fig. 2.** No. of NDS (4D-MOML).    **Fig. 3.** Diversity of NDS (3D-MOML).    **Fig. 4.** Beeline of NDS (3D-MOML).

the random walk is initialized randomly. The phenotypes of the MOML are real-valued vectors of length $k$ according to the number of objectives. Random walks of length 100 and 500 are performed and the consecutive real-valued vectors of each random walk are termed time series. For statistic reason, these random walks are repeated at least 30 times.

**Physiochemical Properties.** Three of the four physiochemical fitness functions are provided by the BioJava library [11]. BioJava is a Java tool that provides different physiochemical property data as well as a module for sequence alignment for peptides and proteins composed of the 20 canonical amino acids. The Needleman Wunsch algorithm (NMW) provided by BioJava is used as global sequence alignment to a pre-defined reference peptide. The optimal alignment is found in a quantitative way by assigning scores for matches, mismatches and gaps. NMW uses different scoring models. Here, the BLOcks SUbstitution Matrix (BLOSUM 100) is used with the percentage identity of 100 [12]. Two further physio-chemical functions are utilized of BioJava: the Molecular Weight (MW) is computed by the sum of the mass of each amino acid plus a water molecule. The Instability Index (InstInd) of a peptide is calculated by the summation of the Dipeptide Instability Weight Values (DIWV) of each two consecutive amino acids in the peptide sequence. The summarized value is normalized then by the peptide length. The fourth physio-chemical function is the Hydrophilicity (Hydro), which is calculated by the method of Hopp and Woods [13]: hydrophilic parts of a peptide are determined by a sliding window of a fixed size over the sequence and averaging the corresponding amino acid scales. Here, the window size is the entire peptide length. All this fitness functions act comparatively to a pre-defined reference peptide and have to be minimization for optimization. The fitness function NMW, MW and Hydro constitute the 3D-MOP. The 4D-MOP has to optimize NMW, MW, Hydro and InstInd.

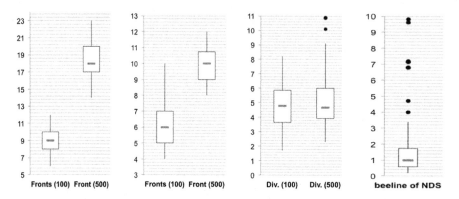

**Fig. 5.** Number of fronts (3D-MOML).    **Fig. 6.** Number of fronts (4D-MOML).    **Fig. 7.** Diversity of NDS (4D-MOML).    **Fig. 8.** Beeline of NDS (4D-MOML).

**Experiments.** In a first step, the modality is investigated for the 3D- and 4D-MOP. Therefore, the number of individuals in the first front, the total number of detected fronts, the diversity of the individuals and the relational beeline is determined by random walks of length 100 or 500 respectively. Figures 1 and 2 depict the number of NDS (NDS) detected in the time series of length 100 and 500. Figure 1 reveals that 50 % of the NDS are in a inter-quartile range determined by 10 % to 17 % of the Random Walk Length (RWL). An increase of the RWL (right boxplot of Fig. 1) results in an increase of the NDS round about 83.9 %. The number of NDS in the time series of the 4D-MOML is on average significantly higher than for the 3D-MOML (Fig. 2). The inter-quartile range of the time series of length 100 (Fig. 2) is determined by 23 % to 36 % of the RWL. A comparison of the time series of length 100 in Figs. 1 and 2 reveals an increase of the NDS round about 53 % in the case of 4D-MOML. An increase of the RWL from 100 to 500 (right boxplot of Fig. 2) results in an increase of NDS round about 84, 2 %, this value is comparable to the results of the 3D-MOML. Concluding, the investigation of larger times series reveals a larger number of NDS, but this increase is of a lower level than the increase of the RWL. Further, the 4D-MOML provides a significantly higher number of NDS than the 3D-MOML. This effect is due to the lower front diversity in the case of 4D-MOML. Figures 5 and 6 depict the front diversity of the 3D- and 4D-MOML in the time series of length 100 and 500. Figure 5 reveals that 50 % of the front numbers in the time series of length 100 are in the inter-quartile range determined by 8 and 10 fronts. An increase of the RWL to 500 results in an increase of the detected front number round about 104 % referring to the results of the time series of a length of 100. The front diversity is significantly lower in the case of the 4D-MOML (Fig. 6).The increase of the RWL from 100 to 500 (right boxplot in Fig. 6) results in an front diversity increase of round about 52,3 %. This percentage increase is only a half of the average increase observed in the 3D-MOML. This is a consequence of the fact that the average number

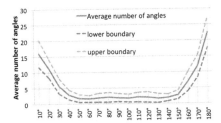

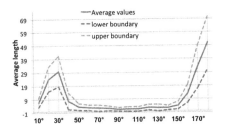

**Fig. 9.** Average number of angles between two consecutive difference vectors (3D-MOML).

**Fig. 10.** Average length of the two consecutive difference vectors enclosing a particular angle (3D-MOML).

of NDS in the random walks of a length of 100 is significantly higher than in the case of the 3D-MOML, but the increase of the NDS number by an increase of the RWL is comparable. Therefore, the increase of the front diversity by an increase of the RWL is significantly lower.

Figures 3 and 7 present the spread of the NDS diversity in the time series of length 100 and 500. In general, the diversity $d_{MAD}$ of the NDS - computed by Eq. (2) - is of the same level for the 3D- as well as 4D-MOML. Only, the diversity of the NDS in the 3D-time series of length 100 reveals a tendency for lower diversity values. Figures 4 and 8 depict the average rational beeline (Eq. (3)) between each consecutive NDS in time series of length 100. The boxplots reveal that some of the NDS are clustered and others are positioned in a wide range of distance: 50 % of the relational beeline values are between $0, 5$ and 2 in the case of the 3D-MOML (Fig. 4), which indicates that the distance between the corresponding consecutive NDS is more than half $(0, 5)$ or twice $(2)$ of the average distance between all consecutive solutions time series. The relational beeline values of the 4D-MOML are between $0, 6$ and $1, 7$, which indicate that the distance between the consecutive NDS is more than a half $(0, 6)$ or more than one and a half $(1, 7)$ of the average distance between all consecutive solutions (Fig. 8). However, Fig. 8 reveals some outliers up to a value of 10. This indicates that some distances between the NDS are significantly higher.

The correlation matrix of the physio-chemical functions is given by (Eq. (4)):

$$M_{corr} = \begin{pmatrix} 1 & 0.047 & 0.252 & 0.09 \\ \cdots & 1 & -0.014 & -0.032 \\ \cdots & \cdots & 1 & -0.266 \\ \cdots & \cdots & \cdots & 1 \end{pmatrix}. \tag{9}$$

The matrix entries reveal no linear relationship between the time series of each two molecular fitness functions: there is a weak relationship between NMW and MW (Eq. (9): $corr(f_1, f_3) = 0.252$) as well as InstInd and Hydro (Eq. (9)): $corr(f_3, f_4) = -0.266$ and no correlation between the other combinations. As a consequence, the dimension of a MOML constituted of these four molecular functions is equal to the number of participating objective functions.

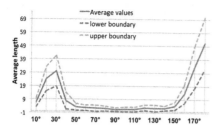

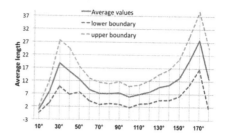

**Fig. 11.** Average number of angles between two consecutive difference vectors (4D-MOML).

**Fig. 12.** Average length of the consecutive difference vectors enclosing a particular angle (4D-MOML).

Figures 9 and 10 depict the average number of angles and the average path length with a particular bending of the 3D- time series - categorized in intervals of ten degree on the x-axis. The depicted upper and lower boundaries mark the one-sigma interval. The highest number of angles are detected in the interval of $[170; 180)$ (Fig. 9). This indicates that the difference vectors are oppositely directed and the single objective functions are increasing, decreasing or stagnating over three steps of the time series in very different manners. Exemplary spoken: one objective function increases from one time series step to the next one and decreases afterwards. The second function is exactly moving the other way around and the third function is stagnating from the first to the second solution and increasing or decreasing afterwards. This reveals that the landscape is very rugged along a large number of random walk steps. The second highest number of angles is in the interval of $[0; 10)$. This indicates that the difference vectors are similarly directed and the single objective functions are increasing, decreasing or stagnating in a similar manner. Exemplary spoken: one of the objective functions is stagnating over three time series steps and the other two functions are increasing or decreasing over these three steps. The number of angles in the interval of $[40; 150)$ is almost stable. In general, the larger the angle the larger the number of objective functions revealing oscillating moving behavior in a different manner over three time series steps.

A similar pattern is achieved by calculating the average path length with a particular bending provided by the difference vectors which enclose particular angles (Fig. 10). The highest length is achieved in the interval $[170; 180)$ indicating large differences between the single molecular function values with mainly oscillating behavior. The second highest length is achieved in the intervals $[10; 30)$ indicating large differences between the solutions of the time series mostly positioned in the same direction. The length of the difference vectors enclosing angles in the interval $[40; 150)$ are small and reveal slight changes of the single objective function values. Figures 11 and 12 depict the corresponding results for the 4D-MOML. Compared to the results of the 3D-MOML, the maxima of average number of angles and the average path length are in the intervals $[20; 30)$ and $[160; 170)$ and the values of the interval $[40; 160)$ are higher in the

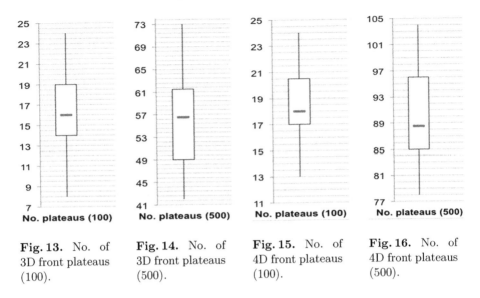

**Fig. 13.** No. of 3D front plateaus (100).

**Fig. 14.** No. of 3D front plateaus (500).

**Fig. 15.** No. of 4D front plateaus (100).

**Fig. 16.** No. of 4D front plateaus (500).

case of the 4D-MOML. This is a consequence of the fact that the probability of the four objective functions moving similarly or oscillating simultaneously is lower than for a lower number of objective functions. Plateaus are a structural property that provides some information about clustered similar qualified solutions. Firstly, plateaus are identified in MOML by consecutive equal or nearly equal fitness values for each molecular function (see Eq. (8)). In the 30 random walks of length 100 on the 3D-MOML, 20 plateaus have been identified totally: two plateaus of each two consecutive equal fitness values have been identified in five random walks, a plateau of three consecutive equal fitness values have been found in one random walk and the remaining 9 plateaus have been identified in different random walks each consisting of two consecutive equal fitness values. Only 8 plateaus have been detected in the corresponding random walks, each of length 2. Figures 13, 14 and 15, 16 depict the number of front-plateaus in the 3D- and 4D-MOML detected in 30 random walks of length 100 and 500. Front-plateaus are more globally characterized by consecutive time series steps in the same Pareto front. In general, an increase of the time series length results in an increase of the plateaus for the 3D- and 4D-MOML. The number of plateaus is always higher in the case of the 4D-MOML, a consequence of the lower front diversity. Thus, the increase of the plateau number is significantly slower than the increase of the time series length. This is once more a consequence of the higher front diversity in larger time series. In the case of 3D-MOML: 14, 5 % and 7 % of the plateaus detected in the time series of length 100 and 500 are first front plateaus. The average plateau sizes are 2, 31 and 2, 18. The average plateaus size of the first front plateaus are on average larger with 2, 7 and 2, 3 in the time series of length 100 and 500. In the case of 4D-MOML: 36, 5 % and 12, 9 % are first front plateaus in the time series of length 100 and 500. Compared to the 3D-MOML, these percentage increases are a consequence of the lower front diversity of the 4D-MOML. The average plateau sizes are $3,04$ and $2,42$. The average plateaus size of the first front plateaus are $3,08$ and $2,75$ in the time series of length $100$ and $500$.

## 4    Conclusions and Future Work

The results of the 3D- and 4D-MOML analysis provide some important hints regarding the design of a MOEA: the 3D- and 4D-MOML are very rugged and no significant structure is discernible according to the distribution of the NDS over the landscapes. The 3D-MOML reveals a higher front diversity and therefore fewer solutions are in the optimal front compared to the 4D-MOML. Further, the average first-front-based plateau size is accordingly smaller. These facts make the 3D-MOML more rugged and therefore more challenging for a MOEA than the 4D-MOML. In general, the significant number of front plateaus in both MOMLs require a specific balance of global and local search behavior of the MOEA: the variation operators of the MOEA have to support a global search in the first generations of the MOEA to tap potential high quality solutions widely spread over the landscape. In the later generations, a more local search behavior of the MOML supports the search process in the neighborhood of the previously detected high quality solutions. The 4D-MOML reveals a higher number of NDS caused by the lower front diversity which requires far-reaching differentiation of the NDS. The most intuitive way to perform this differentiation is by assistance of the selection procedure. A strategy providing a good differentiation is an indicator-based selection strategy. The increase of the RWL and therefore of the investigated MOML does not result in a corresponding increase of NDS in both MOMLs. Further, the NDS are unevenly distributed over the search space. These facts indicate that an increase of the population size does not result in highly improved MOEA performance from a statistical point of view.

The optimization results verifying the 3D-MOP difficulties compared to the 4D-MOP are the topic of future work. Apart from these two biochemical MOP, the generality of this concept is validated on classical MOP as another topic of future work.

## References

1. Merz, P., Freisleben, B.: Fitness landscape analysis and memetic algorithms for the quadratic assignment problem. IEEE Trans. Evol. Comput. **4**(4), 337–352 (2000)
2. Emmerich, M., Lee, B.V.Y., Render, A., Faddiev, E., Kruisselbrink, J., Deutz, A.H.: Analyzing molecular landscapes using random walks and information theory. Chem. Cent. J. **3**(1), 20 (2009)
3. Merkuryeva, G., Bolshakovs, V.: Benchmark fitness landscape analysis. Int. J. Simul. Syst. Sci. Technol. **12**(2), 38–45 (2011)
4. Garrett, D., Dasgupta, D.: Multi-objective landscape analysis and the generalized assignment problem. In: Maniezzo, V., Battiti, R., Watson, J.-P. (eds.) Learning and Intelligent Optimization. LNCS, vol. 5313, pp. 110–124. Springer, Heidelberg (2007)

5. Knowles, J.D., Corne, D.W.: Towards landscape analysis to inform the design of a hybrid local search for the multi-objective quadratic assignment problem. In: HIS, pp. 271–279 (2002)
6. Stadler, P.M.: Fitness Landscape. Lecture Notes in Physics, vol. 585. Springer, Heidelberg (2002)
7. Reidys, C.M., Stadler, P.F.: Combinatorial landscape. SIAM Rev. **44**, 3–54 (2002)
8. Lee, B.V.Y.: Analyzing Molecular Landscapes using Random Walk and Information Theory. LIACS, University of Leiden, Masterthesis (2009)
9. Tan, P.N., Steinbach, M., Kumar, V.: Introduction to Data Mining. Pearson Addison Wesley, Boston (2006)
10. Ceperly, D., Chen, Y., Crain, R.V., Meng, X., Mira, A., Rosenthal, J.: Challenges and advances in high dimensional and high complexity monte carlo computation and theory. In: Proceedings of the Workshop at the Banff International Research Station for Mathematical Innovation Discovery (2012)
11. BioJava, version 3.0.8. http://biojava.org/wiki/Main_Page
12. Henikoff, S., Henikoff, J.G.: Amino acid substitution matrices from protein blocks. Proc. Natl. Acad. Sci. USA **89**(22), 10915–10919 (1992)
13. Hopp, T.P., Woods, K.R.: A computer programm for predicting protein antigenic determinants. Mol. Immunol. **20**(4), 483–489 (1983)

# Author Index

Abou-Zleikha, Mohamed 318, 381, 430
Alhalawani, Zeina 305
Al-Omari, Rawan 305
Andreae, Peter 541
Andria, Joseph 629
Antunes, Carlos Henggeler 252
Arenas, María Isabel G. 355, 443
Atzeni, Antonio Emanuele 155
Aulig, Nikola 655
Awada, Mohammed 593
Aydogan, Emre 745
Azad, R. Muhammad Atif 706

Baghdadi, Walaa 305
Baños, Raúl 693
Barros, Gabriella A.B. 369
Bazargani, Mosab 529
Bellas, Francisco 807
Berrocal-Plaza, Víctor 103
Borschbach, Markus 897
Bouvry, Pascal 14
Browne, Will N. 491
Bucur, Doina 29
Burelli, Paolo 455

Carnicer, A.D. 42
Carreiro, Andreia M. 252
Castelli, Mauro 732
Castillo, Pedro A. 355, 443
Chalmers, Kevin 418
Chang, Wen Liang 643
Chávez, Francisco 504
Chennupati, Gopinath 706
Clemente, Eddie 201, 504
Coral, William 819
Costa, Ernesto 732
Cotta, Carlos 177
Cuadra, L. 42

Danoy, Grégoire 14
De Falco, Ivanoe 79, 115
de Vega, Francisco Fernández 504
Del Arco, M.A. 42
di Tollo, Giacomo 629
Duro, Richard J. 807

Eddin, Fawzya Shams 305
Eiben, A.E. 667
Erfani, Rasool 214
Erfani, Tohid 214

Faiña, Andres 795
Feder, Julian 239
Fernández-Ares, A. 355
Fernando, Chrisantha 344
Ferrari, Gianluigi 91
Ferreira, M. 128
Ferrer, José M. 721
Filipiak, Patryk 882
Fischer, Michael 593
Flórez-Revuelta, Francisco 517
Folino, Gianluigi 54

Galam, Serge 155
García-Ortega, Rubén H. 443
García-Sánchez, Pablo 355, 443
Gil, Pablo 819
Glette, Kyrre 771
Gomez-Pulido, Juan A. 128
Gonçalves, José 227
Grochol, David 67
Gypteau, Jeremie 267

Hamann, Heiko 759
Harada, Shoichi 616
Harrison, Kyle Robert 164, 189
Hart, Emma 418
Heinermann, Justin 567
Hernández, Daniel E. 504
Hernández, Daniel 201
Hertwig, Fabian 406
Hochreiter, Ronald 279
Holmgård, Christoffer 331
Hoogendoorn, Mark 667
Huertas, Carlos 3

Iacca, Giovanni 29

Jaśkowski, Wojciech 394
Javarone, Marco Alberto 155
Jenkinson, Ian 857
Jorge, Humberto M. 252

Juárez-Ramírez, Reyes   3
Jurkowski, Wiktor   14

Kampouridis, Michael   267
Kanesan, Jeevan   643
Karafotias, Giorgos   667
Kimovski, Dragi   693
Korenek, Jan   67
Kramer, Oliver   471, 481, 567
Krawiec, Krzysztof   394, 554
Kulkarni, Anand Jayant   643

L. Briseño, José   201
Lanza-Gutierrez, Jose M.   128
Laredo, Juan Luis Jiménez   14
Laskowski, Eryk   79
Lehner, Patrick   406
Liang, Yuyu   491
Liapis, Antonios   331
Lipinski, Piotr   289, 882
Liskowski, Paweł   394
Liu, Ivy   541
Lobo, Victor   732
Loja, Maria Amélia R.   529
Lückehe, Daniel   471

Martins, António Gomes   227
Mateus, Luís   529
Mauser, Ingo   239
Mavrovouniotis, Michalis   845
McMillan, Craig   418
Mercado, José   201
Merelo, J.J.   355, 443
Monica, Stefania   91
Mora, Antonio M.   355, 443
Moreno, Rodrigo   795
Muhammad Fuad, Muhammad Marwan   579
Müller, Jan   239

Narukawa, Kaname   593
Nelson, Mark J.   369
Neves, Luís   227
Nguyen, Hoai Bach   541
Nguyen, Trung Thanh   857
Nielsen, Sune S.   14
Nielsen, Thorbjørn S.   369
Nitschke, Geoff   783
Nogueras, Rafael   177

Obermayer, Florian   406
Obuchowicz, Adam K.   143

Oehmcke, Stefan   567
Olague, Gustavo   201, 504
Olejnik, Richard   79
Olhofer, Markus   655
Oliveira, Carlos   252
Ombuki-Berman, Beatrice M.   164, 189
Ortega, Julio   693
Ortiz, Andrés   693
Ortuño, M. Teresa   721
Otero, Fernando E.B.   267

Pawlak, Mikołaj   554
Pereira, J.S.   128
Pisani, Francesco Sergio   54
Portilla-Figueras, J.A.   42
Priem-Mendes, S.   128

Re, Alessandro   732
Richter, Hendrik   869
Rodemann, Tobias   593
Romero, Gustavo   355
Rosenthal, Susanne   897
Rossi, Claudio   819
Ryan, Conor   706

Salcedo-Sanz, S.   42
Salgado, Rodrigo   807
Samuelsen, Eivind   771
Sánchez-Pérez, Juan M.   103
Scafuri, Umberto   79, 115
Schaefer, Robert   143
Schmeck, Hartmut   239
Schmickl, Thomas   831
Schneider, Reinhard   14
Sekanina, Lukas   67
Sen, Sevil   745
Shaker, Mohammad   305, 381, 430
Shaker, Noor   305, 318, 381, 430
Shorten, David   783
Smith, Davy   344
Smołka, Maciej   143
Squillero, Giovanni   29, 681
Støy, Kasper   795
Szubert, Marcin   394

Tagawa, Kiyoharu   616
Talbi, El-Ghazali   14
Tarantino, Ernesto   79, 115
Tirado, Gregorio   721

Togelius, Julian   331, 369, 381, 430
Tokarchuk, Laurissa   344
Tonda, Alberto   29
Tudruj, Marek   79

Urbano, Paulo   732
Urquhart, Neil   604

Vanneschi, Leonardo   732
Vaz, Henrique   732
Vega-Rodríguez, Miguel A.   103
Ventresca, Mario   164, 189

Vitoriano, Begoña   721
von Mammen, Sebastian   406

Wahby, Mostafa   759

Xue, Bing   541

Yang, Shengxiang   845
Yang, Zaili   857
Yannakakis, Georgios N.   331, 455

Zadnik, Martin   67
Zahadat, Payam   831
Zhang, Mengjie   491, 541

Printed in the United States
By Bookmasters